Collins
LATIN
DICTIONARY
& GRAMMAR

Published by Collins
An imprint of HarperCollins Publishers
Westerhill Road
Bishopbriggs
Glasgow G64 2QT

Second Edition 2016

10 9 8 7 6 5 4 3 2 1

© HarperCollins Publishers 2016

ISBN 978-0-00-816767-7

Collins® is a registered trademark of
HarperCollins Publishers Limited

collins.co.uk/languagesupport

Typeset by Sharon McTeir

Printed and bound in Great Britain by
Clays Ltd, St Ives plc

A catalogue record for this book is available
from the British Library.

If you would like to comment on any aspect
of this book, please contact us at the given
address or online.
E-mail: dictionaries@harpercollins.co.uk
 facebook.com/collinsdictionary
 @collinsdict

Acknowledgements
We would like to thank those authors and
publishers who kindly gave permission for
copyright material to be used in the Collins
Corpus. We would also like to thank Times
Newspapers Ltd for providing valuable
data.

Dictionary based on the Collins Latin Gem
© 1957 by Professor D. A. Kidd, Canterbury
University

GRAMMAR TEXT AND DICTIONARY
SUPPLEMENTS BY
Mary Wade

FOR THE PUBLISHER
Susie Beattie
Gerry Breslin
Dave White
Sarah Woods

LATIN CONSULTANTS
Ian Brookes
Denis Bruce
Michael D. Igoe

CONTENTS

ABBREVIATIONS

adj	adjective	MED	medicine
abl	ablative	MIL	military
acc	accusative	*mod*	modern
adv	adverb	*n*	noun
AGR	agriculture	NAUT	nautical
ARCH	architecture	*neg*	negative
art	article	*nom*	nominative
ASTR	astronomy	*nt*	neuter
AUG	augury	*num*	numeral
COMM	business	*occ*	occasionally
CIRCS	circumstances	*p*	participle
compar	comparative	*pass*	passive
conj	conjunction	*perf*	perfect
cpd	compound	*perh*	perhaps
dat	dative	*pers*	person
defec	defective	PHILOS	philosophy
ECCL	ecclesiastical	*pl*	plural
esp	especially	POL	politics
excl	exclamatory	*ppa*	perfect participle active
f	feminine	*ppp*	perfect participle passive
fig	figurative	*prep*	preposition
fut	future	*pres*	present
gen	genitive	*pron*	pronoun
GEOG	geography	*prop*	properly
GRAM	grammar	PROV	proverb
impers	impersonal	*relat*	relative
imperf	imperfect	RHET	rhetoric
impv	imperative	*sg*	singular
indecl	indeclinable	*sim*	similarly
indic	indicative	*subj*	subjunctive
inf	informal	*superl*	superlative
infin	infinitive	THEAT	theatre
interj	interjection	UNIV	university
interrog	interrogative	*usu*	usually
LIT	literature	*vi*	intransitive verb
loc	locative	*voc*	vocative
m	masculine	*vt*	transitive verb
MATH	mathematics		

INTRODUCTION

Whether you are learning Latin for the first time or wish to "brush up" what you learned some time ago, this dictionary is designed to help you understand Latin and to express yourself in Latin, if you so wish.

HOW TO USE THE DICTIONARY

Entries are laid out as follows:

Headword

This is shown in **bold type**. On the Latin-English side all long vowels are shown by placing a ⁻ above them. Latin nouns show the genitive singular form in bold. Latin verbs show the first person singular of the present indicative as the headword, followed by the infinitive, the first person singular of the perfect indicative and usually the past participle, all in bold type:

> **elegīa, -ae**
> **elementum, -ī**
> **ēlevō, -āre**
> **ēmātūrēscō, -ēscere, -uī**

Part of Speech

Next comes the part of speech (noun, verb, adjective etc), shown in *italics*. Part of speech abbreviations used in the dictionary are shown in the abbreviations list (p iv). Where a word has more than one part of speech, each new part of speech is preceded by a black lozenge (♦). If a Latin headword is a preposition, the case taken by the preposition comes immediately after the part of speech, in *italics* and in brackets.

> **era, -ae** *f*
> **ticklish** *adj*
> **thunder** *n* tonitrus *m* ♦ *vi* tonare, intonare.
> **ērgā** *prep (with acc)* towards; against.

Meanings

Where a word or a part of speech has only one meaning, the translation comes immediately after the part of speech. However, many words have more than one meaning. Where the context is likely to show which translation is correct, variations in meaning are simply separated by a semicolon. But usually there will also be an "indicator" in italics and in brackets. Some meanings relate to specific subject areas, for example religion, politics, military matters etc – these indicators are in small italic capitals.

ēnsiger, -ī *adj* with his sword.
toy *n* crepundia *ntpl* ♦ *vi* ludere.
toll collector *n* exactor *m*; portitor *m*.
eō, īre, īvī *and* **iī, itum** *vi* to go; (MIL) to march; (*time*) to pass; (*event*) to proceed, turn out.

v

Translations

Most words can be translated directly. On the English-Latin side, translations of nouns include the gender of the Latin noun in *italics*. However, sometimes a phrase is needed to show how a word is used, but in some cases a direct translation of a phrase would be meaningless - in these cases, an explanation in *italics* is given instead. In other cases, the user will need more information than simply the translation; in these cases, "indicators" are included in the translation(s), giving, for instance, the case required by a Latin verb or preposition or further details about a place or person.

> **thumb** *n* pollex *m*; **have under one's** ~ in potestate sua habere.
> **elephantomacha, -ae** *m fighter mounted on an elephant.*
> **Erymanthus, -i** *m mountain range in Arcadia (where Hercules killed the boar).*
> **thwart** *vt* obstare (*dat*), officere (*dat*).

Pronunciation

Since Latin pronunciation is regular, once the basic rules have been learned (see pp *viii, ix*), the dictionary does not show phonetic transcriptions against each headword, but does show all long vowels.

Other Information

The dictionary also includes:

- basic grammar section
- information about life in Roman times:
  — how government and the army were organized — how numbers and dates were calculated and expressed — family relationships — geographical names — major Roman authors — key events in Roman history — (*important historical and mythological characters and events are listed within the body of the main text*).
- a section on Latin poetry and scansion
- a list of Latin expressions commonly used in English today

LATIN ALPHABET

The Latin alphabet is the one which has been almost universally adopted by the modern languages of Europe and America. In the Classical period it had 23 letters, namely the English alphabet without letters **j**, **v** and **w**.

Letter v
The symbol **v** was the capital form of the letter **u**, but in a later age the small **v** came into use to represent the consonantal **u**, and as it is commonly so employed in modern editions of Latin authors, it has been retained as a distinct letter in this dictionary for convenience.

Letter j
The symbol **j** came to be used as the consonantal **i**, and is found in older editions of the Classics, but as it has been almost entirely discarded in modern texts, it is not used in this dictionary, and words found spelt with a **j** must therefore be looked up under **i**.

Letters w, y, z
The letter **w** may be seen in the Latinized forms of some modern names, e.g. **Westmonasterium**, Westminster. The letters **y** and **z** occur only in words of Greek origin.

ORTHOGRAPHY

Many Latin words which begin with a prefix can be spelled in two ways. The prefix can retain its original spelling, or it can be assimilated, changing a letter depending on the letter which follows it. Compare the following:

ad before **g**, **l**, **r** and **p**:

adpropinquare	appropinquare
adgredi	aggredi
adloquor	alloquor
adrogans	arrogans

ad is also often assimilated before **f** and **n**:

adfectus	affectus
adnexus	annexus

and **ad** is often shortened to a before **sc**:

adscendere	ascendere

in changes to **il** before **l**, to **im** before **m** or **p** and to **ir** before **r**.

con becomes **cor** when followed by another **r** and **col** when followed by **l**.

We have provided cross-references in the text to draw your attention to the alternative forms of words. Thus, although **arrogantia** does not appear in the Latin-English section, the cross-reference at **arr-** will point you to the entry for **adrogantia**, where the translation is given.

PRONUNCIATION

The ancient pronunciation of Latin has been established with a fair degree of certainty from the evidence of ancient authorities and inscriptions and inferences from the modern Romance languages. It is not possible, of course, to recapture the precise nuances of Classical Latin speech, but what follows is now generally accepted and generally understood as a reasonably accurate guide to the sounds of Latin as spoken by educated Romans during the two centuries from Cicero to Quintilian.

ACCENT

The Latin accent in the Classical period was a weak stress, perhaps with an element of pitch in it. It falls, as in English, on the second last syllable of the word, if that syllable is long, and on the third last syllable if the second last is short. Disyllabic words take the accent on the first syllable, unless they have already lost a final syllable, e.g. **illīc(e)**.

Inflected words are commonly learned with the accent wrongly placed on the last syllable, for convenience in memorizing the inflexions. But it is advisable to get the accent as well as the ending right.

The correct accent of other words can easily be found by noting carefully the quantity of the second last syllable and then accenting the word as in English, according to the rule given above. Thus **fuērunt** is accented on the second last syllable because the **e** is long, whereas **fuerant** is accented on the third last, because the **e** is short.

VOWELS

Vowels are pure and should not be diphthongized as in certain sounds of Southern English. They may be long or short. Throughout this Dictionary all vowels known or believed by the best authorities to be long are marked with a line above them; those unmarked are either known to be short or of uncertain quantity.

	Short		Long
agricola	rat	rāmus	rather
hedera	pen	avē	pay
itaque	kin	cīvis	keen
favor	rob	ampliō	robe
nebula	full	lūna	fool

y is a Greek sound and is pronounced (both short and long) as **u** in French ie **rue**.

DIPHTHONGS

*ae*stas	tr*y*
*au*dio	t*ow*n
h*ei*	p*ayee*
m*eu*s	*ay-oo* *with the accent on first sound*
mo*ec*ha	t*oy*
t*ui*tus	L*ou*is

CONSONANTS

*b*alneae		*b*a*b*y	
a*bs*temius		a*ps*e	
su*bt*ractus		a*pt*	
*c*astra		*c*ar	
*ch*orda		sepul*ch*re	
inter*d*o		*d*og	
cōn*fl*ō		*f*ortune	
in*g*redior		*g*o	
*h*abeō		*h*and	*(but faintly)*
*i*aceo		*y*es	*(consonantal i = j)*
*K*alendae		oa*k*	
conge*l*ō		*l*et	
co*m*es		*m*an	*(final m was hardly sounded and may have simply nasalized the preceding vowel)*
pā*n*is		*n*o	
pa*ng*o		fi*ng*er	
stu*p*eō		a*p*t	
ra*ph*anus		*p*ill	
exse*qu*or		*qu*ite	
sup*r*emus		b*r*ae	*(Scottish)*
magnu*s*		*s*i*s*ter	*(never as in rose)*
lae*t*us		*s*top	
*th*eātrum		*t*ake	
*v*apor	*(and consonantal u)*	*w*in	
de*x*tra		si*x*	*(ks, not gs)*
*z*ona		*z*ero	

Double consonants lengthen the sound of the consonant.

QUICK REFERENCE
GRAMMAR

DECLENSIONS OF NOUNS

1st Declension

	mainly f		*m*	
SING				
Nom.	terra	crambē	Aenēās	Anchīsēs
Voc.	terra	crambē	Aenēā	Anchīsā,-ē
Acc.	terram	crambēn	Aenēam,-ān	Anchīsam,-ēn
Gen.	terrae	crambes	Aenēae	Anchīsae
Dat.	terrae	crambae	Aenēae	Anchīsae
Abl.	terra	cramba	Aenēā	Anchīsā

PLURAL		
Nom.	terrae	crambae
Voc.	terrae	crambae
Acc.	terrās	crambās
Gen.	terrārium	crambārum
Dat.	terrīs	crambīs
Abl.	terrīs	crambīs

2nd Declension

	mainly m				
SING					
Nom.	modus	Lūcius	Dēlos (f)	puer	liber
Voc.	mode	Lūcī	Dēle	puer	liber
Acc.	modum	Lūcium	Dēlon	puerum	librum
Gen.	modī	Lūcī	Dēlī	puerī	librī
Dat.	modō	Lūciō	Dēlō	puerō	librō
Abl.	modō	Lūciō	Dēlō	puerō	librō
PLURAL					
Nom.	modī			puerī	librī
Voc.	modī			puerī	librī
Acc.	modōs			puerōs	librōs
Gen.	modōrum			puerōrum	librōrum
Dat.	modīs			puerīs	librīs
Abl.	modīs			puerīs	librīs

	nt
SING	
Nom.	dōnum
Voc.	dōnum
Acc.	dōnum
Gen.	dōnī
Dat.	dōnō
Abl.	dōnō
PLURAL	
Nom.	dōna
Voc.	dōna
Acc.	dōna
Gen.	dōnōrum
Dat.	dōnīs
Abl.	dōnīs

3rd Declension

Group I: *Vowel stems, with gen pl in* **-ium**

	m and f		*nt*	
SING				
Nom.	clādēs	nāvis	rēte	animal
Voc.	clādēs	nāvis	rēte	animal
Acc.	clādem	nāvem,-im	rēte	animal
Gen.	clādis	nāvis	rētis	animālīs
Dat.	clādī	nāvī	rētī	animālī
Abl.	clāde	nāve,-ī	rētī	animālī
PLURAL				
Nom.	clādēs	nāvēs	rētia	animālia
Voc.	clādēs	nāvēs	rētia	animālia
Acc.	clādēs, -īs	nāvēs, -īs	rētia	animālia
Gen.	clādium	nāvium	rētium	animālium
Dat.	clādibus	nāvibus	rētibus	animālibus
Abl.	clādibus	nāvibus	rētibus	animālibus

Group II: *Consonant stems, some with gen pl in* **-ium**, *some in* **-um** *and some in either. Monosyllabic nouns ending in two consonants (e.g.* **urbs** *below) regularly have* **-ium**.

	m and f			*f*	*nt*
SING					
Nom.	urbs	amāns	laus	aetās	os
Voc.	urbs	amāns	laus	aetās	os
Acc.	urbem	amantem	laudem	aetātem	os
Gen.	urbis	amantis	laudis	aetātis	ossis
Dat.	urbī	amantī	laudī	aetātī	ossī
Abl.	urbe	amante	laude	aetāte	osse

PLURAL					
Nom.	urbēs	amantēs	laudēs	aetātēs	ossa
Voc.	urbēs	amantēs	laudēs	aetātēs	ossa
Acc.	urbēs	amantēs	laudēs	aetātēs	ossa
Gen.	urbium	amantium, -um	laudum, -ium	aetātum, -ium	ossium
Dat.	urbibus	amantibus	laudibus	aetātibus	ossibus
Abl.	urbibus	amantibus	laudibus	aetātibus	ossibus

Group III: *Consonant stems, with gen pl in* **-um**

	m and f			*nt*	
SING					
Nom.	mōs	ratiō	pater	nōmen	opu
Voc.	mōs	ratiō	pater	nōmen	opus
Acc.	mōrem	ratiōnem	patrem	nōmen	opus
Gen.	mōris	ratiōnis	patris	nōminis	operis
Dat.	mōrī	ratiōnī	patrī	nōminī	operī
Abl.	mōre	ratiōne	patre	nōmine	opere

PLURAL					
Nom.	mōrēs	ratiōnēs	patrēs	nōmina	opera
Voc.	mōrēs	ratiōnēs	patrēs	nōmina	opera
Acc.	mōrēs	ratiōnēs	patrēs	nōmina	opera
Gen.	mōrum	ratiōnum	patrum	nōminum	operum
Dat.	mōribus	ratiōnibus	patribus	nōminibus	operibus
Abl.	mōribus	ratiōnibus	patribus	nōminibus	operibus

Group IV: *Greek nouns*

	m		*f*		*nt*
SING					
Nom.	āēr	hērōs	Periclēs	Naias	poēma
Voc.	āēr	hērōs	Periclē	Naias	poēma
Acc.	āera	hērōa	{ Periclem, Periclea	Naiada	poēma
Gen.	āeris	hērōis	Periclis, -i	Naiadis, -os	poēmatis
Dat.	āerī	hērōī	Periclī	Naiadī	poēmatī
Abl.	aere	hērōe	Pericle	Naiade	poēmate

PLURAL					
Nom.	āeres	hērōes		Naiades	poēmata
Voc.	āeres	hērōes		Naiades	poēmata
Acc.	āeras	hērōas		Naiadas	poēmata
Gen.	āerum	hērōum		Naiadum	poēmatōrum
Dat.	āeribus	hērōibus		Naiadibus	poēmatīs
Abl.	āeribus	hērōibus		Naiadibus	poēmatīs

DECLENSIONS OF NOUNS

	4th Declension		**5th Declension**	
	mainly m	*nt*	*mainly f*	
SING				
Nom.	portus	genū	diēs	rēs
Voc.	portus	genū	diēs	rēs
Acc.	portum	genū	diem	rem
Gen.	portūs	genūs	diēī	reī
Dat.	portuī	genū	diēī	reī
Abl.	portū	genū	diē	rē
PLURAL				
Nom.	portūs	genua	diēs	rēs
Voc.	portūs	genua	diēs	rēs
Acc.	portūs	genua	diēs	rēs
Gen.	portuum	genuum	diērum	rērum
Dat.	portibus, -ubus	genibus, -ubus	diēbus	rēbus
Abl.	portibus, -ubus	genibus, -ubus	diēbus	rēbus

CONJUGATIONS OF VERBS

ACTIVE

PRESENT TENSE

	First parāre *prepare*	Second habēre *have*	Third sūmere *take*	Fourth audīre *hear*

Indicative

SING				
1st *pers*	parō	habeō	sūmō	audiō
2nd *pers*	parās	habēs	sūmis	audīs
3rd *pers*	parat	habet	sūmit	audit
PLURAL				
1st *pers*	parāmus	habēmus	sūmimus	audīmus
2nd *pers*	parātis	habētis	sūmitis	audītis
3rd *pers*	parant	habent	sūmunt	audiunt

Subjunctive

SING				
1st *pers*	parem	habeam	sūmam	audiam
2nd *pers*	parēs	habeās	sūmās	audiās
3rd *pers*	paret	habeat	sūmat	audiat
PLURAL				
1st *pers*	parēmus	habeāmus	sūmāmus	audiāmus
2nd *pers*	parētis	habeātis	sūmātis	audiātis
3rd *pers*	parent	habeant	sūmant	audiant

IMPERFECT TENSE
Indicative

SING

1st pers	parābam	habēbam	sūmēbam	audiēbam
2nd pers	parābās	habēbās	sūmēbās	audiēbās
3rd pers	parābat	habēbat	sūmēbat	audiēbat

PLURAL

1st pers	parābāmus	habēbāmus	sūmēbāmus	audiēbāmus
2nd pers	parābātis	habēbātis	sūmēbātis	audiēbātis
3rd pers	parābant	habēbant	sūmēbant	audiēbant

Subjunctive

SING

1st pers	parārem	habērem	sūmerem	audīrem
2nd pers	parārēs	habērēs	sūmerēs	audīrēs
3rd pers	parāret	habēret	sūmeret	audīret

PLURAL

1st pers	parārēmus	habērēmus	sūmerēmus	audīrēmus
2nd pers	parārētis	habērētis	sūmerētis	audīrētis
3rd pers	parārent	habērent	sūmerent	audīrent

FUTURE TENSE
Indicative

SING

1st pers	parābō	habēbō	sūmam	audiam
2nd pers	parābis	habēbis	sūmēs	audiēs
3rd pers	parābit	habēbit	sūmet	audiet

PLURAL

1st pers	parābimus	habēbimus	sūmēmus	audiēmus
2nd pers	parābitis	habēbitis	sūmetis	audiētis
3rd pers	parābunt	habēbunt	sūment	audient

Subjunctive

SING

parātūrus, -a, -um	sim	*or*	essem
habitūrus, -a, -um	sis		essēs
sūmptūrus, -a, -um	sit		esset
audītūrus, -a, -um			

PLURAL

paratūrī, -ae, -a	simus	*or*	essēmus
habitūrī, -ae, -a	sitis		essētis
sūmptūrī, -ae, -a	sint		essent
audītūrī, -ae, -a			

PERFECT TENSE
Indicative

SING
1st *pers*	parāvī	habuī	sūmpsī	audīvī
2nd *pers*	parāvistī	habuistī	sūmpsistī	audīvistī
3rd *pers*	parāvit	habuit	sūmpsit	audīvit

PLURAL
1st *pers*	parāvimus	habuimus	sūmpsimus	audīvimus
2nd *pers*	parāvistis	habuistis	sūmpsistis	audīvistis
3rd *pers*	parāvērunt, -e	habuērunt, -e	sūmpsērunt, -e	audīvērunt, -e

Subjunctive

SING
1st *pers*	parāverim	habuerim	sūmpserim	audīverim
2nd *pers*	parāveris	habueris	sūmpseris	audīveris
3rd *pers*	parāverit	habuerit	sūmpserit	audīverit

PLURAL
1st *pers*	parāverimus	habuerimus	sūmpserimus	audīverimus
2nd *pers*	parāveritis	habueritis	sūmpseritis	audīveritis
3rd *pers*	parāverint	habuerint	sūmpserint	audīverint

PLUPERFECT TENSE
Indicative

SING
1st *pers*	parāveram	habueram	sūmpseram	audīveram
2nd *pers*	parāverās	habuerās	sūmpseras	audīveras
3rd *pers*	parāverat	habuerat	sūmpserat	audīverat

PLURAL
1st *pers*	parāverāmus	habuerāmus	sūmpserāmus	audīveramus
2nd *pers*	parāverātis	habuerātis	sūmpserātis	audīverātis
3rd *pers*	parāverant	habuerant	sūmpserant	audīverant

Subjunctive

SING
1st *pers*	parāvissem	habuissem	sūmpsissem	audīvissem
2nd *pers*	parāvissēs	habuissēs	sūmpsissēs	audīvissēs
3rd *pers*	parāvisset	habuisset	sūmpsisset	audīvisset

PLURAL
1st *pers*	parāvissēmus	habuissēmus	sūmpsissēmus	audīvissēmus
2nd *pers*	parāvissētis	habuissētis	sūmpsissētis	audīvissētis
3rd *pers*	parāvissent	habuissent	sūmpsissent	audīvissent

FUTURE PERFECT TENSE
Indicative

SING				
1*st* pers	parāverō	habuerō	sūmpserō	audīverō
2*nd* pers	parāveris	habueris	sūmpseris	audīveris
3*rd* pers	parāverit	habuerit	sūmpserit	audīverit
PLURAL				
1*st* pers	parāverimus	habuerimus	sūmpserimus	audīverimus
2*nd* pers	parāveritis	habueritis	sūmpseritis	audīveritis
3*rd* pers	parāverint	habuerint	sūmpserint	audīverint

IMPERATIVE
Present

SING	parā	habē	sūme	audī
PLURAL	parāte	habēte	sūmite	audīte

Future

SING				
2nd pers	parātō	habētō	sūmitō	audītō
3rd pers	parātō	habētō	sūmitō	audītō
PLURAL				
2nd pers	parātōte	habētōte	sūmitōte	audītōte
3rd pers	parantō	habentō	sūmuntō	audiuntō

INFINITIVE
Present

parāre	habēre	sūmere	audīre

Perfect

parāvisse	habuisse	sūmpsisse	audīvisse

Future

parātūrus,	-a, -um, esse	
habitūrus,	-a, -um, esse	
sūmptūrus,	-a, -um, esse	
audītūrus,	-a, -um, esse	

PASSIVE

PRESENT TENSE

Indicative

SING

1st pers	paror	habeor	sūmor	audior
2nd pers	parāris	habēris	sūmeris	audīris
3rd pers	parātur	habētur	sūmitur	audītur

PLURAL

1st pers	parāmur	habēmur	sūmimur	audīmur
2nd pers	parāminī	habēminī	sūmiminī	audīminī
3rd pers	parantur	habentur	sūmuntur	audiuntur

Subjunctive

SING

1st pers	parer	habear	sūmar	audiar
2nd pers	parēris	habeāris	sūmāris	audiāris
3rd pers	parētur	habeātur	sūmātur	audiātur

PLURAL

1st pers	parēmur	habeāmur	sūmāmur	audiāmur
2nd pers	parēminī	habeāminī	sūmāminī	audiāminī
3rd pers	parentur	habeantur	sūmantur	audiantur

IMPERFECT TENSE

Indicative

SING

1st pers	parābar	habēbar	sūmēbar	audiēbar
2nd pers	parābāris	habēbāris	sūmēbāris	audiēbāris
3rd pers	parābātur	habēbātur	sūmēbātur	audiēbātur

PLURAL

1st pers	parābāmur	habēbāmur	sūmēbāmur	audiēbāmur
2nd pers	parābāmini	habēbāmini	sūmēbāminī	audiēbāminī
3rd pers	parābāntur	habēbantur	sūmēbantur	audiēbantur

Subjunctive

SING

1st pers	parārer	habērer	sūmerer	audīrer
2nd pers	parārēris	habērēris	sūmerēris	audīrēris
3rd pers	parārētur	habērētur	sūmerētur	audīrētur

PLURAL

1st pers	parārēmur	habērēmur	sūmerēmur	audīrēmur
2nd pers	parārēminī	habērēminī	sūmerēminī	audīrēminī
3rd pers	parārentur	habērentur	sūmerentur	audīrentur

FUTURE TENSE
Indicative

SING

1st pers	parābor	habēbor	sūmar	audiar
2nd pers	parāberis	habēberis	sūmēris	audiēris
3rd pers	parābitur	habēbitur	sūmētur	audiētur

PLURAL

1st pers	parābimur	habēbimur	sūmēmur	audiēmur
2nd pers	parābimini	habēbimini	sūmēminī	audiēminī
3rd pers	parābuntur	habēbuntur	sūmentur	audientur

PERFECT TENSE
Indicative

SING			PLURAL	
parātus, -a, -um	sum/es/est		parātī, -ae -a	sumus/estis/sunt
habitus, -a, -um	sum/es/est		habītī, -ae -a	sumus/estis/sunt
sūmptus, -a, -um	sum/es/est		sūmptī, -ae -a	sumus/estis/sunt
audītus, -a, -um	sum/es/est		audītī, -ae -a	sumus/estis/sunt

Subjunctive

SING			PLURAL	
parātus, -a, -um	sim/sīs/sit		parātī, -ae, -a	sumus/estis/sunt
habitus, -a, -um	sim/sīs/sit		habītī, -ae, -a	sumus/estis/sunt
sūmptus, -a, -um	sim/sīs/sit		sūmptī, -ae, -a	sumus/estis/sunt
audītus, -a, -um	sim/sīs/sit		audītī, -ae, -a	sumus/estis/sunt

PLUPERFECT TENSE
Indicative

SING			PLURAL	
parātus, -a, -um	eram/eras/erat		parātī, -ae, -a	eramus/eratis/erant
habitus, -a, -um	eram/eras/erat		habītī, -ae, -a	eramus/eratis/erant
sūmptus, -a, -um	eram/eras/erat		sūmptī, -ae, -a	eramus/eratis/erant
audītus, -a, -um	eram/eras/erat		audītī, -ae, -a	eramus/eratis/erant

Subjunctive

SING		PLURAL	
parātus, -a, -um	essem/essēs/esset	parātī, -ae, -a	essēmus/essētis/essent
habitus, -a, -um	essem/essēs/esset	habitī, -ae, -a	essēmus/essētis/essent
sūmptus, -a, -um	essem/essēs/esset	sūmptī, -ae, -a	essēmus/essētis/essent
audītus, -a, -um	essem/essēs/esset	audītī, -ae, -a	essēmus/essētis/essent

FUTURE PERFECT TENSE

Indicative

SING		PLURAL	
parātus, -a, -um	erō/eris/erit	parātī, -ae, -a	erimus/eritis/erunt
habitus, -a, -um	erō/eris/erit	habitī, -ae, -a	erimus/eritis/erunt
sūmptus, -a, -um	erō/eris/erit	sūmptī, -ae, -a	erimus/eritis/erunt
audītus, -a, -um	erō/eris/erit	audītī, -ae, -a	erimus/eritis/erunt

IMPERATIVE

Present

SING	parāre	habēre	sūmere	audīre
PLURAL	parāminī	habēminī	sūmiminī	audīminī

Future

SING				
2nd pers	parātor	habētor	sūmitor	audītor
3rd pers	parātor	habētor	sūmitor	audītor
PLURAL				
3rd pers	parantor	habentor	sūmuntor	audiuntor

INFINITIVE

Present

parārī	habērī	sūmī	audīrī

Perfect

parātus -a, -um, esse	habitus -a, -um, esse	sūmptus -a, -um, esse	audītus, -a, -um, esse

Future

parātum īrī	habitum īrī	sūmptum īrī	audītum īrī

VERBAL NOUNS AND ADJECTIVES

Present Participle Active

parāns	habēns	sūmēns	audiēns

Perfect Participle Passive

parātus	habitus	sūmptus	audītus

Future Participle Active

parātūrus	habitūrus	sūmptūrus	audītūrus

Gerund
(acc, gen, dat and abl)

parandum, -ī, -ō	habendum, -ī, -ō	sūmendum, -ī, -ō	audiendum, -ī, -ō

Gerundive

parandus	habendus	sūmendus	audiendus

Supines

1st	parātum	habitum	sūmptum	audītum
2nd	parātū	habitū	sūmptū	audītū

Note. *Some verbs of the 3rd conjugation have the present indicative ending in -io; e.g.* **capio,** *I capture.*

PRESENT TENSE

INDICATIVE		SUBJUNCTIVE	
Active	**Passive**	**Active**	**Passive**
capio	capior	capiam	capiar
capis	caperis	capias	capiāris
capit	capitur	capiat	capiātur
capimus	capimur	capiāmus	capiāmur
capitis	capiminī	capiātis	capiāminī
capiunt	capiuntur	capiant	capiantur

IMPERFECT TENSE

capiēbam *etc.*	capiēbar *etc.*	caperem *etc.*	caperer *etc.*

FUTURE TENSE

capiam	capiar
capiēs etc.	capiēris etc.

INFINITIVE MOOD

Present Active	capere
Present Passive	capī

PRESENT IMPERATIVE

Active		**Passive**	
cape	capite	capere	capiminī

	PARTICIPLE	GERUND	GERUNDIVE
Pres.	capiēns	capiendum	capiendus, -a, -um

In all other tenses and moods **capere** *is similar to* **sumere**.

IRREGULAR VERBS

	Esse *be*	**Posse** *be able*	**Velle** *wish*	**Ire** *go*
Present Indicative				
SING				
1ˢᵗ *pers*	sum	possum	volō	eō
2ⁿᵈ *pers*	es	potes	vīs	īs
3ʳᵈ *pers*	est	potest	vult, volt	it
PLURAL				
1ˢᵗ *pers*	sumus	possumus	volumus	īmus
2ⁿᵈ *pers*	estis	potestis	vultis, voltis	ītis
3ʳᵈ *pers*	sunt	possunt	volunt	eunt
Present Subjunctive				
SING				
1ˢᵗ *pers*	sim	possim	velim	eam
2ⁿᵈ *pers*	sīs	possīs	velīs	eās
3ʳᵈ *pers*	sit	possit	velit	eat
PLURAL				
1ˢᵗ *pers*	sīmus	possīmus	velīmus	eāmus
2ⁿᵈ *pers*	sītis	possītis	velītis	eātis
3ʳᵈ *pers*	sint	possint	velint	eant
Imperfect Indicative				
1ˢᵗ *pers*	eram	poteram	volēbam	ībam
Imperfect Subjunctive				
1ˢᵗ *pers*	essem	possem	vellem	īrem
Future Indicative				
1ˢᵗ *pers*	erō	poterō	volam	ībō
Future Subjunctive				
1ˢᵗ *pers*	futūrus, -a, -um sim *or* essem	—	—	itūrus, -a, -um sim *or* essem
Perfect Indicative				
1ˢᵗ *pers*	fuī	potuī	voluī	īvī, iī

Perfect Subjunctive

1st *pers*	fuerim	potuerim	voluerim	īverim, ierim

Pluperfect Indicative

1st *pers*	fueram	potueram	volueram	īveram, ieram

Pluperfect Subjunctive

1st *pers*	fuissem	potuissem	voluissem	īvissem, iissem

Future Perfect Indicative

1st *pers*	fuerō	potuerō	voluerō	īverō, ier

Present Imperative

SING	es	—	—	ī
PLURAL	este	—	—	īte

Future Imperative

SING	estō	—	—	ītō
PLURAL	estōte	—	—	ītōte

Infinitives

PRES	esse	posse	velle	īre
PERF	fuisse	potuisse	voluisse	īvisse, iisse
FUT	futūrus, -a, -um, esse	—	—	itūrus, -a, -um, esse

Participles

PRES	—	—	—	iēns, euntis
FUT	futūrus	—	—	itūrus

Gerund and Supine

GERUND	—	—	—	eundum
SUPINE	—	—	—	itum

Perfect Subjunctive

sum	possum	volo	eo
fuerim	potuerim	voluerim	iverim, ierim

Pluperfect Indicative

sum	possum	volo	eo
fueram	potueram	volueram	iveram, ieram

Pluperfect Subjunctive

sum	possum	volo	eo
fuissem	potuissem	voluissem	ivissem, iissem

Future Perfect Indicative

sum	possum	volo	eo
fuero	(potuero)	voluero	ivero, iero

Present Imperative

	sum	possum	volo	eo
SING.	es	—	—	i
PLURAL	este	—	—	ite

Future Imperative

	sum	possum	volo	eo
SING.	esto	—	—	ito
PLURAL	estote	—	—	itote

Infinitives

	sum	possum	volo	eo
PRES.	esse	posse	velle	ire
PERF.	fuisse	potuisse	voluisse	ivisse, iisse
FUT.	futurum, -a, -um, esse	—	—	iturum, -a, -um, esse

Participles

	sum	possum	volo	eo
PRES.	—	—	volens, -entis	iens, euntis
FUT.	futurus	—	—	iturus

Gerund and Supine

	sum	possum	volo	eo
GERUND	—	—	—	eundum
SUPINE	—	—	—	itum

LATIN – ENGLISH

Aa

ā prep (with abl) from; after, since; by, in respect of; **ab epistulīs, ā manū** secretary; **ab hāc parte** on this side; **ab integrō** afresh; **ā nōbīs** on our side; **ā tergō** in the rear; **cōpiōsus ā frūmentō** rich in corn; **usque ab** ever since

ā² interj ah!

ab prep see **ā¹**

abāctus ppp of **abigō**

abacus, -ī m tray; sideboard; gaming board; panel; counting table

abaliēnō, -āre, -āvī, -ātum vt to dispose of; to remove, estrange

Abantiadēs m Acrisius or Perseus

Abās, -antis m a king of Argos

abavus, -ī m great-great-grandfather

abbās, -ātis m abbot

abbātia f abbey

abbātissa f abbess

Abdēra, -ōrum or **-ae** ntpl, fs a town in Thrace

Abdērītānus adj see **Abdēra**

Abdērītēs m Democritus or Protagoras

abdicātiō, -ōnis f disowning, abdication

abdicō, -āre, -āvī, -ātum vt to disown; to resign; **sē abdicāre** abdicate

abdīcō, -īcere, -īxī, -ictum vt (AUG) to be unfavourable to

abditus ppp of **abdō**

abdō, -ere, -idī, -itum vt to hide; to remove

abdōmen, -inis nt paunch, belly; gluttony

abdūcō, -ūcere, -ūxī, -uctum vt to lead away, take away; to seduce

abductus ppp of **abdūcō**

abecedārium, -iī nt alphabet

abēgī perf of **abigō**

abeō, -īre, -iī, -itum vi to go away, depart; to pass away; to be changed; to retire (from an office); **sīc abīre** turn out like this

abequitō, -āre, -āvī, -ātum vi to ride away

aberrātiō, -ōnis f relief (from trouble)

aberrō, -āre, -āvī, -ātum vi to stray; to deviate; to have respite

abfore fut infin of **absum**

abfuī perf of **absum**

abfutūrus fut p of **absum**

abhinc adv since, ago

abhorreō, -ēre, -uī vi to shrink from; to differ; to be inconsistent

abiciō, -icere, -iēcī, -iectum vt to throw away, throw down; to abandon, degrade

abiectus ppp of **abiciō** ✦ adj despondent; contemptible

abiēgnus adj of fir

abiēns, -euntis pres p of **abeō**

abiēs, -etis f fir; ship

abigō, -igere, -ēgī, -āctum vt to drive away

abitus, -ūs m departure; exit

abiūdicō, -āre, -āvī, -ātum vt to take away (by judicial award)

abiūnctus ppp of **abiungō**

abiungō, -ungere, -ūnxī, -ūnctum vt to unyoke; to detach

abiūrō, -āre, -āvī, -ātum vt to deny on oath

ablātus ppp of **auferō**

ablēgātiō, -ōnis f sending away

ablēgō, -āre, -āvī, -ātum vt to send out of the way

abligurriō, -īre, -īvī, -ītum vt to spend extravagantly

ablocō, -āre, -āvī, -ātum vt to let (a house)

ablūdō, -dere, -sī, -sum vi to be unlike

abluō, -uere, -uī, -ūtum vt to wash clean; to remove

abnegō, -āre, -āvī, -ātum vt to refuse

abnepōs, -ōtis m great-great-grandson

abneptis f great-great-granddaughter

abnoctō, -āre vi to stay out all night

abnōrmis adj unorthodox

abnuō, -uere, -uī, -ūtum vt to refuse; to deny

aboleō, -ēre, -ēvī, -itum vt to abolish

abolēscō, -ēscere, -ēvī vi to vanish

abolitiō, -ōnis f cancelling

abolla, -ae f greatcoat

abōminātus adj accursed

abōminor, -ārī, -ātus vt to deprecate; to detest

Aborīginēs, -um mpl original inhabitants

aborior, -īrī, -tus vi to miscarry

abortiō, -ōnis f miscarriage

abortīvus adj born prematurely

abortus, -ūs m miscarriage

abrādō, -dere, -sī, -sum vt to scrape off, shave

abrāsus ppp of **abrādō**

abreptus ppp of **abripiō**

abripiō, -ipere, -ipuī, -eptum vt to drag away, carry off

abrogātiō, -ōnis f repeal

abrogō, -āre, -āvī, -ātum vt to annul

abrotonum, -ī nt southernwood

abrumpō, -umpere, -ūpī, -uptum vt to break off

abruptus ppp of **abrumpō** ✦ adj steep; abrupt, disconnected

abs etc see **ā¹**

1

abscēdō, **-ēdere**, **-essi**, **-essum** vi to depart, withdraw; to cease

abscīdō, **-dere**, **-dī**, **-sum** vt to cut off

abscindō, **-ndere**, **-dī**, **-ssum** vt to tear off, cut off

abscissus ppp of **abscindō**

abscīsus ppp of **abscīdō** ♦ adj steep; abrupt

abscondō, **-ere**, **-ī** and **-idī**, **-itum** vt to conceal; to leave behind

absēns, **-entis** pres p of **absum** ♦ adj absent

absentia, **-ae** f absence

absiliō, **-īre**, **-iī** and **-uī** vi to spring away

absimilis adj unlike

absinthium, **-ī** and **-iī** nt wormwood

absis, **-īdis** f vault; (ECCL) chancel

absistō, **-istere**, **-titī** vi to come away; to desist

absolūtē adv fully, unrestrictedly

absolūtiō, **-ōnis** f acquittal; perfection

absolūtus ppp of **absolvō** ♦ adj complete; (RHET) unqualified

absolvō, **-vere**, **-vī**, **-ūtum** vt to release, set free; (LAW) to acquit; to bring to completion, finish off; to pay off, discharge

absonus adj unmusical; incongruous; ~ ab not in keeping with

absorbeō, **-bēre**, **-buī**, **-ptum** vt to swallow up; to monopolize

absp- etc see **asp-**

absque prep (with abl) without, but for

abstēmius adj temperate

abstergeō, **-gēre**, **-sī**, **-sum** vt to wipe away; (fig) to banish

absterreō, **-ēre**, **-ui**, **-itum** vt to scare away, deter

abstinēns, **-entis** adj continent

abstinenter adv with restraint

abstinentia, **-ae** f restraint, self-control; fasting

abstineō, **-inēre**, **-inuī**, **-entum** vt to withhold, keep off ♦ vi to abstain, refrain; **sē abstinēre** refrain

abstitī perf of **absistō**

abstō, **-āre** vi to stand aloof

abstractus ppp of **abstrahō**

abstrahō, **-here**, **-xī**, **-ctum** vt to drag away, remove; to divert

abstrūdō, **-dere**, **-sī**, **-sum** vt to conceal

abstrūsus ppp of **abstrūdō** ♦ adj deep, abstruse; reserved

abstulī perf of **auferō**

absum, **abesse**, **āfuī** vi to be away, absent, distant; to keep clear of; to be different; to be missing, fail to assist; **tantum abest ut** so far from; **haud multum āfuit quīn** I was (they were etc) within an ace of

absūmō, **-ere**, **-psī**, **-ptum** vt to consume; to ruin, kill; (time) to spend

absurdē adv out of tune; absurdly

absurdus adj unmusical; senseless, absurd

Absyrtus, **-ī** m brother of Medea

abundāns, **-antis** adj overflowing; abundant; rich; abounding in

abundanter adv copiously

abundantia, **-ae** f abundance, plenty; wealth

abundē adv abundantly, more than enough

abundō, **-āre**, **-āvī**, **-ātum** vi to overflow; to abound, be rich in

abūsiō, **-ōnis** f (RHET) catachresis

abusque prep (with abl) all the way from

abūtor, **-tī**, **-sus** vi (with abl) to use up; to misuse

Abydēnus adj see **Abȳdos**

Abȳdos, **Abȳdus**, **-ī** m a town on Dardanelles

ac etc see **atque**

Acadēmia, **-ae** f Plato's Academy at Athens; Plato's philosophy; Cicero's villa

Acadēmica ntpl book of Cicero on philosophy

Acadēmus, **-ī** m an Athenian hero

acalanthis, **-dis** f thistlefinch

acanthus, **-ī** m bear's-breech

Acarnānes, **-um** mpl the Acarnanians

Acarnānia, **-iae** f a district of N.W. Greece

Acarnānicus adj see **Acarnānia**

Acca Larentia, **Accae Larentiae** f Roman goddess

accēdō, **-ēdere**, **-essī**, **-essum** vi to come, go to, approach; to attack; to be added; to agree with; (duty) to take up; **ad rem pūblicam accēdere** to enter politics; **prope ~ ad** to resemble; **accēdit quod**, **hūc accēdit ut** moreover

accelerō, **-āre**, **-āvī**, **-ātum** vt, vi to hasten

accendō, **-endere**, **-endī**, **-ēnsum** vt to set on fire, light; to illuminate; (fig) to inflame, incite

accēnseō, **-ēre**, **-uī**, **-um** vt to assign

accēnsī mpl (MIL) supernumeraries

accēnsus¹ ppp of **accendō**, **accēnseō**

accēnsus², **-ī** m officer attending a magistrate

accentus, **-ūs** m accent

accēpī perf of **accipiō**

acceptiō, **-ōnis** f receiving

acceptum nt credit side (of ledger); **in ~ referre** place to one's credit

acceptus ppp of **accipiō** ♦ adj acceptable

accersō etc see **arcessō**

accessiō, **-ōnis** f coming, visiting; attack; increase, addition

accessus, **-ūs** m approach, visit; flood tide; admittance, entrance

Acciānus adj see **Accius**

accidō, **-ere**, **-ī** vi to fall (at, on); (senses) to strike; (usu misfortune) to befall, happen

accīdō, **-dere**, **-dī**, **-sum** vt to fell, cut into; to eat up, impair

accingō, **-gere**, **-xī**, **-ctum** vt to gird on, arm; (fig) to make ready

acciō, **-īre**, **-īvī**, **-ītum** vt to summon; to procure

accipiō, **-ipere**, **-ēpī**, **-eptum** vt to take, receive, accept; (guest) to treat; (information) to hear; to interpret, take as; to suffer; to approve

accipiter, **-ris** m hawk

accīsus ppp of **accīdō**

accītus¹ ppp of **acciō**

accītus², **-ūs** m summons

Accius, **-ī** m Roman tragic poet

acclāmātiō, **-ōnis** f shout (of approval or disapproval)

acclāmō, **-āre**, **-āvī**, **-ātum** vi to cry out against; to hail

acclārō, **-āre**, **-āvī**, **-ātum** vt to make known

acclīnātus adj sloping

acclīnis adj leaning against; inclined

acclīnō, -āre, -āvī, -ātum vt to lean against; **sē acclīnāre** incline towards

acclīvis adj uphill

acclīvitās, -ātis f gradient

accola, -ae m neighbour

accolō, -olere, -oluī, -ultum vt to live near

accommodātē adv suitably

accommodātiō, -ōnis f fitting together; compliance

accommodātus adj suited

accommodō, -āre, -āvī, -ātum vt to fit, put on; to adjust, adapt, bring to; to apply; **sē accommodāre** devote oneself

accommodus adj suitable

accrēdō, -ere, -idī, -itum vi to believe

accrēscō, -ēscere, -ēvī, -ētum vi to increase, be added

accrētiō, -ōnis f increasing

accubitiō, -ōnis f reclining (at meals)

accubō, -āre vi to lie near; to recline (at meals)

accumbō, -mbere, -buī, -bitum vi to recline at table; **in sinū accumbere** sit next to

accumulātē adv copiously

accumulō, -āre, -āvī, -ātum vt to pile up, amass; to load

accūrātē adv painstakingly

accūrātiō, -ōnis f exactness

accūrātus adj studied

accūrō, -āre, -āvī, -ātum vt to attend to

accurrō, -rrere, -currī and **-rrī, -rsum** vi to hurry to

accursus, -ūs m hurrying

accūsābilis adj reprehensible

accūsātiō, -ōnis f accusation

accūsātor, -ōris m accuser, prosecutor

accūsātōriē adv like an accuser

accūsātōrius adj of the accuser

accūsō, -āre, -āvī, -ātum vt to accuse, prosecute; to reproach; **ambitūs accusāre** prosecute for bribery

acer, -is nt maple

ācer, -ris adj sharp; (sensation) keen, pungent; (emotion) violent; (mind) shrewd; (conduct) eager, brave; hasty, fierce; (circumstances) severe

acerbē adv see **acerbus**

acerbitās, -ātis f bitterness; (fig) harshness, severity; sorrow

acerbō, -āre, -āvī, -ātum vt to aggravate

acerbus adj bitter, sour; harsh; (fig) premature; (person) rough, morose, violent; (things) troublesome, sad

acernus adj of maple

acerra, -ae f incense box

acervātim adv in heaps

acervō, -āre, -āvī, -ātum vt to pile up

acervus, -ī m heap

acēscō, -ere, acuī vt to turn sour

Acestēs, -ae m a mythical Sicilian

acētum, -ī nt vinegar; (fig) wit

Achaemenēs, -is m first Persian king; type of Oriental wealth

Achaeus adj Greek

Achāia, -ae f a district in W. Greece; Greece; Roman province

Achāicus adj see **Achāia**

Achātēs, -ae m companion of Aeneas

Achelōius adj see **Achelōus**

Achelōus, -ī m river in N.W. Greece; river god

Acherōn, -ontis m river in Hades

Acherūsius adj see **Acherōn**

Achillēs, -is m Greek epic hero

Achillēus adj see **Achillēs**

Achīvus adj Greek

Acidālia, -ae f Venus

Acidālius adj see **Acidālia**

acidus adj sour, tart; (fig) disagreeable

aciēs, -ēī f sharp edge or point; (eye) sight, keen glance, pupil; (mind) power, apprehension; (MIL) line of troops, battle order, army, battle; (fig) debate; **prīma ~** van; **novissima ~** rearguard

acīnacēs, -is m scimitar

acinum, -ī nt berry, grape; fruit seed

acinus, -ī m berry, grape; fruit seed

acipēnser, -eris m sturgeon

acipēnsis, -is m sturgeon

aclys, -dis f javelin

aconītum, -ī nt monkshood; poison

acor, -ōris m sour taste

acquiēscō, -ēscere, -ēvī, -ētum vi to rest, die; to find pleasure (in); to acquiesce

acquīrō, -rere, -sīvī, -sītum vt to get in addition, acquire

Acragās, -antis m see **Agrigentum**

acrātophorum, -ī nt wine jar

acrēdula, -ae f a bird (unidentified)

ācriculus adj peevish

ācrimōnia, -ae f pungent taste; (speech, action) briskness, go

Acrisiōniadēs, -ae m Perseus

Acrisius, -ī m father of Danae

ācriter adv see **ācer**

ācroāma, -tis nt entertainment, entertainer

ācroāsis, -is f public lecture

Ācroceraunia, -ōrum ntpl a promontory in N.W. Greece

Ācrocorinthus, -ī f fortress of Corinth

acta, -ae f beach

ācta, -ōrum ntpl public records, proceedings; **~ diurna, ~ pūblica** daily gazette

Actaeus adj Athenian

āctiō, -ōnis f action, doing; official duties, negotiations; (LAW) action, suit, indictment, pleading, case, trial; (RHET) delivery; (drama) plot; **~ grātiārum** expression of thanks; **āctiōnem intendere, āctiōnem īnstituere** bring an action

āctitō, -āre, -āvī, -ātum vt to plead, act often

Actium, -ī and **-iī** nt a town in N.W. Greece; Augustus's great victory

Actius, Actiacus adj see **Actium**

āctivus adj of action, practical

āctor, -ōris m driver, performer; (LAW) plaintiff, pleader; (COMM) agent; (RHET) orator; (drama) actor; **~ pūblicus** manager of public property; **~ summārum** cashier

āctuāria f pinnace

āctuāriolum, -ī m small barge

āctuārius adj fast (ship)

āctuōsē adv actively

3

āctuōsus *adj* very active
āctus¹ *ppp of* **agō**
āctus², **-ūs** *m* moving, driving; right of way for cattle or vehicles; performance; *(drama)* playing a part, recital, act of a play
āctūtum *adv* immediately
acuī *perf of* **acēscō**; **acuō**
acula, **-ae** *f* small stream
aculeātus *adj* prickly; *(words)* stinging; quibbling
aculeus, **-ī** *m* sting, prickle, barb; *(fig)* sting
acūmen, **-inis** *nt* point, sting; *(fig)* shrewdness, ingenuity; trickery
acuō, **-uere**, **-uī**, **-ūtum** *vt* to sharpen; to exercise; *(the mind)* to stimulate; to rouse *(to action)*
acus, **-ūs** *f* needle, pin; **acū pingere** embroider; **rem acū tangere** hit the nail on the head
acūtē *adv see* **acūtus**
acūtulus *adj* rather subtle
acūtus *adj* sharp, pointed; *(senses)* keen; *(sound)* high-pitched; severe; intelligent
ad *prep (with acc)* to, towards, against; near, at; until; *(num)* about; with regard to, according to; for the purpose of, for; compared with; besides; **ad Castoris** to the temple of Castor; **ad dextram** on the right; **ad hōc** besides; **ad locum** on the spot; **ad manum** at hand; **ad rem** to the point; **ad summam** in short; **ad tempus** in time; **ad ūnum omnes** all without exception; **ad urbem esse** wait outside the city gates; **ad verbum** literally; **nīl ad** nothing to do with; **usque ad** right up to
adāctiō, **-ōnis** *f* enforcing
adāctus¹ *ppp of* **adigō**
adāctus², **-ūs** *m* snapping *(of teeth)*
adaequē *adv* equally
adaequō, **-āre**, **-āvī**, **-ātum** *vt* to make equal, level; to equal, match ♦ *vi* to be equal
adamantēus, **adamantinus** *adj see* **adamās**
adamās, **-antis** *m* adamant, steel; diamond
adamō, **-āre**, **-āvī**, **-ātum** *vt* to fall in love with
adaperiō, **-īre**, **-uī**, **-tum** *vt* to throw open
adapertilis *adj* openable
adaquō, **-āre**, **-āvī**, **-ātum** *vt (plants, animals)* to water
adaquor *vi* to fetch water
adauctus, **-ūs** *m* growing
adaugeō, **-gēre**, **-xī**, **-ctum** *vt* to aggravate; *(sacrifice)* to consecrate
adaugēscō, **-ere** *vi* to grow bigger
adbibō, **-ere**, **-ī** *vt* to drink; *(fig)* to drink in
adbītō, **-ere** *vi* to come near
adc- *etc see* **acc-**
addecet, **-ēre** *vt* it becomes
addēnseō, **-ēre** *vt* to close *(ranks)*
addīcō, **-īcere**, **-īxī**, **-ictum** *vi (AUG)* to be favourable ♦ *vt (LAW)* to award; *(auction)* to knock down; *(fig)* to sacrifice, devote
addictiō, **-ōnis** *f* award *(at law)*
addictus *ppp of* **addīcō** ♦ *m* bondsman
addiscō, **-scere**, **-dicī** *vt* to learn more
additāmentum, **-ī** *nt* increase
additus *ppp of* **addō**

addō, **-ere**, **-idī**, **-itum** *vt* to add, put to, bring to; to impart; to increase; **addere gradum** quicken pace; **adde quod** besides
addoceō, **-ēre**, **-uī**, **-tum** *vt* to teach new
addubitō, **-āre**, **-āvī**, **-ātum** *vi* to be in doubt ♦ *vt* to question
addūcō, **-ūcere**, **-ūxī**, **-uctum** *vt* to take, bring to; to draw together, pull taut, wrinkle; *(fig)* to induce; *(pass)* to be led to believe
adductus *ppp of* **addūcō** ♦ *adj* contracted; *(fig)* severe
adedō, **-edere**, **-ēdī**, **-ēsum** *vt* to begin to eat; to eat up; to use up; to wear away
adēmī *perf of* **adimō**
ademptiō, **-ōnis** *f* taking away
ademptus *ppp of* **adimō**
adeō¹, **-īre**, **-iī**, **-itum** *vt*, *vi* to go to, approach; to address; to undertake, submit to, enter upon
adeō² *adv* so; *(after pron)* just; *(after conj, adv, adj: for emphasis)* indeed, very; *(adding an explanation)* for, in fact, thus; or rather; **~ nōn ... ut** so far from; **atque ~**, **sīve ~** or rather; **usque ~** so far, so long, so much
adeps, **-ipis** *m/f* fat; corpulence
adeptiō, **-ōnis** *f* attainment
adeptus *ppa of* **adipīscor**
adequitō, **-āre**, **-āvī**, **-ātum** *vi* to ride up (to)
adesdum come here!
adesse *infin of* **adsum**
adēsus *ppp of* **adedō**
adfābilis *adj* easy to talk to
adfābilitās, **-ātis** *f* courtesy
adfabrē *adv* ingeniously
adfatim *adv* to one's satisfaction, enough, ad nauseam
adfātur, **-rī**, **-tus** *vt (defec)* to speak to
adfātus¹ *ppa of* **adfātur**
adfātus², **-ūs** *m* speaking to
adfectātiō, **-ōnis** *f* aspiring; *(RHET)* affectation
adfectātus *adj (RHET)* studied
adfectiō, **-ōnis** *f* frame of mind, mood; disposition; goodwill; *(ASTR)* relative position
adfectō, **-āre**, **-āvī**, **-ātum** *vt* to aspire to, aim at; to try to win over; to make pretence of; **viam adfectāre ad** try to get to
adfectus¹ *ppp of* **adficiō** ♦ *adj* affected with, experienced *(abl)*; *(person)* disposed; *(things)* weakened; *(undertakings)* well-advanced
adfectus², **-ūs** *m* disposition, mood; fondness; *(pl)* loved ones
adferō, **adferre**, **attulī**, **adlātum** *and* **allātum** *vt* to bring, carry to; to bring to bear, use against; to bring news; *(explanation)* to bring forward; to contribute *(something useful)*
adficiō, **-icere**, **-ēcī**, **-ectum** *vt* to affect; to endow, afflict with *(abl)*; **exsiliō adficere** banish; **honōre adficere** honour *(also used with other nouns to express the corresponding verbs)*
adfictus *ppp of* **adfingō**
adfīgō, **-gere**, **-xī**, **-xum** *vt* to fasten, attach; to impress *(on the mind)*
adfingō, **-ngere**, **-nxī**, **-ctum** *vt* to make, form *(as part of)*; invent
adfīnis, **-is** *m/f* neighbour; relation *(by marriage)* ♦ *adj* neighbouring; associated with *(dat, gen)*

adfinitās, -ātis f relationship (by marriage)
adfirmātē adv with assurance
adfirmātiō, -ōnis f declaration
adfirmō, -āre, -āvī, -ātum vt to declare; to confirm
adfīxus ppp of **adfīgō**
adflātus, -ūs m breath, exhalation; (fig) inspiration
adfleō, -ēre vi to weep (at)
adflīctātiō, -ōnis f suffering
adflīctō, -āre, -āvī, -ātum vt to harass, distress
adflīctor, -ōris m destroyer
adflīctus ppp of **adflīgō** ♦ adj distressed, ruined; dejected; depraved
adflīgō, -īgere, -īxī, -īctum vt to dash against, throw down; (fig) to impair, crush
adflō, -āre, -āvī, -ātum vt, vi to blow on, breathe upon
adfluēns, -entis adj rich (in)
adfluenter adv copiously
adfluentia, -ae f abundance
adfluō, -ere, -xī, -xum vi to flow; (fig) to flock in, abound in
adfore fut infin of **adsum**
adforem imperf subj of **adsum**
adfuī perf of **adsum**
adfulgeō, -gēre, -sī vi to shine on; to appear
adfundō, -undere, -ūdī, -ūsum vt to pour in; to rush (troops) to
adfūsus adj prostrate
adfutūrus fut p of **adsum**
adgemō, -ere vi to groan at
adglomerō, -āre vt to add on
adglūtinō, -āre vt to stick on
adgravēscō, -ere vi to become worse
adgravō, -āre, -āvī, -ātum vt to aggravate
adgredior, -dī, -ssus vt to approach, accost; to attack; (a task) to undertake, take up
adgregō, -āre, -āvī, -ātum vt to add, attach
adgressiō, -ōnis f introductory remarks
adgressus ppa of **adgredior**
adhaereō, -rēre, -sī, -sum vi to stick to; (fig) to cling to, keep close to
adhaerēscō, -ere vi to stick to or in; (speech) to falter
adhaesiō, -ōnis f clinging
adhaesus, -ūs m adhering
adhibeō, -ēre, -uī, -itum vt to bring, put, add; to summon, consult, treat; to use, apply (for some purpose)
adhinniō, -īre, -īvī, -ītum vi to neigh to; (fig) to go into raptures over
adhortātiō, -ōnis f exhortation
adhortātor, -ōris m encourager
adhortor, -ārī, -ātus vt to encourage, urge
adhūc adv so far; as yet, till now; still; ~ nōn not yet
adiaceō, -ēre, -uī vi to lie near, border on
adiciō, -icere, -iēcī, -iectum vt to throw to; to add; to turn towards (mind, eyes)
adiectiō, -ōnis f addition
adiectus' ppp of **adiciō**
adiectus², -ūs m bringing close

adigō, -igere, -ēgī, -āctum vt to drive (to); to compel; iūs iūrandum **adigere** put on oath; in verba **adigere** force to owe allegiance
adimō, -imere, -ēmī, -emptum vt to take away (from dat)
adipātum nt pastry
adipātus adj fatty; (fig) florid
adipīscor, -ipīscī, -eptus vt to overtake; to attain, acquire
aditus, -ūs m approach, access (to a person); entrance; (fig) avenue
adiūdicō, -āre, -āvī, -ātum vt to award (in arbitration); to ascribe
adiūmentum, -ī nt aid, means of support
adiūncta ntpl collateral circumstances
adiūnctiō, -ōnis f uniting; addition; (RHET) proviso; repetition
adiūnctus ppp of **adiungō** ♦ adj connected
adiungō, -ungere, -ūnxī, -ūnctum vt to yoke; to attach; (suspicion etc) to direct; (remark) to add
adiūrō, -āre, -āvī, -ātum vt, vi to swear, swear by
adiūtō, -āre, -āvī, -ātum vt to help
adiūtor, -ōris m helper; (MIL) adjutant; (POL) official; (THEAT) supporting cast
adiūtrīx, -rīcis f see **adiūtor**
adiūtus ppp of **adiuvō**
adiuvō, -uvāre, -ūvī, -ūtum vt to help; to encourage
adj- etc see **adi-**
adlābor, -bī, -psus vi to fall, move towards, come to
adlabōrō, -āre, -āvī, -ātum vi to work hard; to improve by taking trouble
adlacrimō, -āre, -āvī, -ātum vi to shed tears
adlāpsus' ppa of **adlābor**
adlāpsus², -ūs m stealthy approach
adlātrō, -āre, -āvī, -ātum vt to bark at; (fig) to revile
adlātus ppp of **adferō**
adlaudō, -āre, -āvī, -ātum vt to praise highly
adlectō, -āre, -āvī, -ātum vt to entice
adlectus ppp of **adliciō**
adlēctus ppp of **adlegō**
adlēgātī mpl deputies
adlēgātiō, -ōnis f mission
adlegō, -egere, -ēgī, -ēctum vt to elect
adlēgō, -āre, -āvī, -ātum vt to despatch, commission; to mention
adlevāmentum, -ī nt relief
adlevātiō, -ōnis f easing
adlevō, -āre, -āvī, -ātum vt to lift up; to comfort; to weaken
adliciō, -icere, -exī, -ectum vt to attract
adlīdō, -dere, -sī, -sum vt to dash (against); (fig) to hurt
adligō, -āre, -āvī, -ātum vt to tie up, bandage; (fig) to bind, lay under an obligation
adlinō, -inere, -ēvī, -itum vt to smear; (fig) to attach
adlīsus ppp of **adlīdō**
adlocūtiō, -ōnis f address, comforting words
adlocūtus ppa of **adloquor**
adloquium, -ī and **-iī** nt talk; encouragement
adloquor, -quī, -cūtus vt to speak to, address

adlūdiō, -āre, -āvī, -ātum vi to play (with)
adlūdō, -dere, -sī, -sum vi to joke, play
adluō, -ere, -ī vt to wash
adluviēs, -ēī f pool left by flood water
adluviō, -ōnis f alluvial land
admātūrō, -āre, -āvī, -atum vt to hurry on
admētior, -tīrī, -nsus vt to measure out
adminiculor, -ārī, -ātus vt to prop
adminiculum, -ī nt (AGR) stake; (fig) support
administer, -rī m assistant
administrātiō, -ōnis f services; management
administrātor, -ōris m manager
administrō, -āre, -āvī, -ātum vt to manage, govern
admīrābilis adj wonderful, surprising
admīrābilitās, -ātis f wonderfulness
admīrābiliter adv admirably; paradoxically
admīrātiō, -ōnis f wonder, surprise, admiration
admīror, -ārī, -ātus vt to wonder at, admire; to be surprised at
admīsceō, -scēre, -scuī, -xtum vt to mix in with, add to; (fig) to involve; **sē admīscēre** interfere
admissārius, -ī and **-iī** m stallion
admissum, -ī nt crime
admissus ppp of **admittō**
admittō, -ittere, -īsī, -issum vt to let in, admit; to set at a gallop; to allow; to commit (a crime); **equō admissō** charging
admixtiō, -ōnis f admixture
admixtus ppp of **admīsceō**
admoderātē adv suitably
admoderor, -ārī, -ātus vt to restrain
admodum adv very, quite; fully; yes; (with neg) at all
admoneō, -ēre, -uī, -itum vt to remind, suggest, advise, warn
admonitiō, -ōnis f reminder, suggestion, admonition
admonitor, -ōris m admonisher (male)
admonitrīx, -rīcis f admonisher (female)
admonitū at the suggestion, instance
admordeō, -dēre, -sum vt to bite into; (fig) to cheat
admorsus ppp of **admordeō**
admōtiō, -ōnis f applying
admōtus ppp of **admoveō**
admoveō, -ovēre, -ōvī, -ōtum vt to move, bring up, apply; to lend (an ear), direct (the mind)
admurmurātiō, -ōnis f murmuring
admurmurō, -āre, -āvī, -ātum vi to murmur (of a crowd approving or disapproving)
admutilō, -āre, -āvī, -ātum vt to clip close; (fig) to cheat
adnectō, -ctere, -xuī, -xum vt to connect, tie
adnexus, -ūs m connection
adnīsus ppa of **adnītor**
adnītor, -tī, -sus and **-xus** vi to lean on; to exert oneself
adnīxus ppa of **adnītor**
adnō, -āre vt, vi to swim to
adnotō, -āre, -āvī, -ātum vt to comment on
adnumerō, -āre, -āvī, -ātum vt to pay out; to reckon along with

adnuō, -uere, -uī, -ūtum vi to nod; to assent, promise; to indicate
adoleō, -olēre, -oluī, -ultum vt to burn; to pile with gifts
adolēscen- etc see **adulēscen-**
adolēscō, -ēscere, -ēvī vi to grow up, increase; to burn
Adōnis, -is and **-idis** m a beautiful youth loved by Venus
adopertus adj covered
adoptātiō, -ōnis f adopting
adoptiō, -ōnis f adoption
adoptīvus adj by adoption
adoptō, -āre, -āvī, -ātum vt to choose; to adopt
ador, -ōris and **-oris** nt spelt
adōrea f glory
adōreus adj see **ador**
adorior, -īrī, -tus vt to accost; to attack; to set about
adōrnō, -āre, -āvī, -ātum vt to get ready
adōrō, -āre, -āvī, -ātum vt to entreat; to worship, revere
adortus ppa of **adorior**
adp- etc see **app-**
adrādō, -dere, -sī, -sum vt to shave close
Adrastus, -ī m a king of Argos
adrāsus ppp of **adrādō**
adrēctus ppp of **adrigō +** adj steep
adrēpō, -ere, -sī, -tum vi to creep, steal into
adreptus ppp of **adripiō**
Adria etc see **Hadria** etc
adrīdeō, -dēre, -sī, -sum vt, vi to laugh, smile at; to please
adrigō, -igere, -ēxī, -ēctum vt to raise; (fig) to rouse
adripiō, -ipere, -ipuī, -eptum vt to seize; to appropriate; to take hold of; to learn quickly; (LAW) to arrest; to satirize
adrōdō, -dere, -sī, -sum vt to gnaw, nibble at
adrogāns, -antis adj arrogant, insolent
adroganter adv see **adrogāns**
adrogantia, -ae f arrogance, presumption, haughtiness
adrogātiō, -ōnis f adoption
adrogō, -āre, -āvī, -ātum vt to ask; to associate; to claim, assume; (fig) to award
adsc- etc see **asc-**
adsecla etc see **adsecula**
adsectātiō, -ōnis f attendance
adsectātor, -ōris m follower
adsector, -ārī, -ātus vt to attend on, follow (esp a candidate)
adsecula, -ae m follower (derogatory)
adsēdī perf of **adsideō; adsīdō**
adsēnsiō, -ōnis f assent, applause; (PHILOS) acceptance of the evidence of the senses
adsēnsor, -ōris m one in agreement
adsēnsus¹ ppa of **adsentiō**
adsēnsus², -ūs m assent, approval; echo; (PHILOS) acceptance of the evidence of the senses
adsentātiō, -ōnis f flattery
adsentātiuncula f trivial compliments
adsentātor, -ōris m flatterer (male)
adsentātōriē adv ingratiatingly

adsentātrīx, -rīcis f flatterer (female)

adsentiō, -entīre, -ēnsī, -ēnsum, adsentior, -entīrī, -ēnsus vi to agree, approve

adsentor, -ārī, -ātus vi to agree, flatter

adsequor, -quī, -cūtus vt to overtake; to attain; to grasp (by understanding)

adserō¹, -ere, -uī, -tum vt (LAW) to declare free (usu with manū), liberate (a slave), lay claim to, appropriate; **adsere in servitūtem** claim as a slave

adserō², -erere, -ēvī, -itum vt to plant near

adsertiō, -ōnis f declaration of status

adsertor, -ōris m champion

adserviō, -īre vi to assist

adservō, -āre, -āvī, -ātum vt to watch carefully; to keep, preserve

adsessiō, -ōnis f sitting beside

adsessor, -ōris m counsellor

adsessus, -ūs m sitting beside

adsevēranter adv emphatically

adsevērātiō, -ōnis f assertion; earnestness

adsevērō, -āre, -āvī, -ātum vt to do in earnest; to assert strongly

adsideō, -idēre, -ēdī, -essum vi to sit by; to attend, assist; to besiege; to resemble

adsīdō, -īdere, -ēdī vi to sit down

adsiduē adv continually

adsiduitās, -ātis f constant attendance; continuance, frequent recurrence

adsiduō adv continually

adsiduus¹ adj constantly in attendance, busy; continual, incessant

adsiduus², -ī m taxpayer

adsignātiō, -ōnis f allotment (of land)

adsignō, -āre, -āvī, -ātum vt to allot (esp land); to assign; to impute, attribute; to consign

adsiliō, -īīre, -iluī, -ultum vi to leap at or on to

adsimilis adj like

adsimiliter adv similarly

adsimulātus adj similar; counterfeit

adsimulō, -āre, -āvī, -ātum vt, vi to compare; to pretend, imitate

adsistō, -istere, -titī vi to stand (by); to defend

adsitus ppp of **adserō²**

adsoleō, -ēre vi to be usual

adsonō, -āre vi to respond

adsp- etc see **asp-**

adsternō, -ere vt to prostrate

adstipulātor, -ōris m supporter

adstipulor, -ārī, -ātus vi to agree with

adstitī perf of **adsistō; adstō**

adstō, -āre, -itī vi to stand near, stand up; to assist

adstrepō, -ere vi to roar

adstrictē adv concisely

adstrictus ppp of **adstringō** ◆ adj tight, narrow; concise; stingy

adstringō, -ngere, -nxī, -ctum vt to draw close, tighten; to bind, oblige; to abridge

adstruō, -ere, -xī, -ctum vt to build on; to add

adstupeō, -ēre vi to be astonished

adsuēfaciō, -acere, -ēcī, -actum vt to accustom, train

adsuēscō, -scere, -vī, -tum vi to accustom, train

adsuētūdō, -inis f habit

adsuētus ppp of **adsuēscō** ◆ adj customary

adsultō, -āre, -āvī, -ātum vi to jump; to attack

adsultus, -ūs m attack

adsum, -esse, -fuī vi to be present; to support, assist (esp at law); to come; to appear before (a tribunal); **animo adesse** pay attention; **iam aderō** I'll be back soon

adsūmō, -ere, -psī, -ptum vt to take for oneself, receive; to take also

adsūmptiō, -ōnis f taking up; (LOGIC) minor premise

adsūmptīvus adj (LAW) which takes its defence from extraneous circumstances

adsūmptum, -ī nt epithet

adsūmptus ppp of **adsūmō**

adsuō, -ere vt to sew on

adsurgō, -gere, -rēxī, -rēctum vi to rise, stand up; to swell, increase

adt- etc see **att-**

adūlātiō, -ōnis f (dogs) fawning; servility

adūlātor, -ōris m sycophant

adūlātōrius adj flattering

adulēscēns, -entis m/f young man or woman (usu from 15 to 30 years)

adulēscentia, -ae f youth (age 15 to 30)

adulēscentula, -ae f girl

adulēscentulus, -ī m quite a young man

adulō, -āre, -āvī, -ātum, adulor, -ārī, -ātus vt, vi to fawn upon, flatter, kowtow

adulter, -ī m, **adultera, -ae** f adulterer, adulteress ◆ adj adulterous

adulterīnus adj forged

adulterium, -ī and **-iī** nt adultery

adulterō, -āre, -āvī, -ātum vt, vi to commit adultery; to falsify

adultus ppp of **adolēscō** ◆ adj adult, mature

adumbrātim adv in outline

adumbrātiō, -ōnis f sketch; semblance

adumbrātus adj false

adumbrō, -āre, -āvī, -ātum vt to sketch; to represent, copy

aduncitās, -ātis f curvature

aduncus adj hooked, curved

adurgeō, -ēre vt to pursue closely

adūrō, -rere, -ssī, -stum vt to burn; to freeze; (fig) to fire

adusque prep (with acc) right up to ◆ adv entirely

adūstus ppp of **adūrō** ◆ adj brown

advectīcius adj imported

advectō, -āre vt to carry frequently

advectus¹ ppp of **advehō**

advectus², -ūs m bringing

advehō, -here, -xī, -ctum vt to carry, convey; (pass) to ride

advēlō, -āre vt to crown

advena, -ae m/f stranger ◆ adj foreign

adveniō, -enīre, -ēnī, -entum vi to arrive, come

adventīcius adj foreign, extraneous; unearned

adventō, -āre, -āvī, -ātum vi to come nearer and nearer, advance rapidly

adventor, -ōris m visitor

adventus, -ūs m arrival, approach

adversāria ntpl daybook

adversārius, -i and **-ii** m opponent ♦ adj
opposing
adversātrīx, -īcis f antagonist
adversiō, -ōnis f turning (the attention)
adversor, -ārī, -ātus vi to oppose, resist
adversum, -ī nt opposite; misfortune ♦ prep (+
acc) towards, against ♦ adv to meet
adversus ppp of **advertō** ♦ adj opposite, in front;
hostile; **adversō flūmine** upstream; **adversae
rēs** misfortune ♦ prep (+ acc) towards, against
♦ adv to meet
advertō, -tere, -tī, -sum vt to turn, direct
towards; to call attention; **animum advertere**
notice, perceive; (with **ad**) to attend to; (with **in**)
to punish
advesperāscit, -scere, -vit vi it is getting dark
advigilō, -āre vi to keep watch
advocātiō, -ōnis f legal assistance, counsel
advocātus, -ī m supporter in a lawsuit;
advocate, counsel
advocō, -āre, -āvī, -ātum vt to summon; (LAW)
to call in the assistance of
advolō, -āre, -āvī, -ātum vi to fly to, swoop
down upon
advolvō, -vere, -vī, -ūtum vt to roll to; to
prostrate
advor- etc see **adver-**
adytum, -ī nt sanctuary
Aeacidēs, -idae m Achilles; Pyrrhus
Aeacus, -ī m father of Peleus, and judge of the dead
Aeaea, -ae f Circe's island
Aeaeus adj of Circe
aedēs, -is f temple; (pl) house
aedicula, -ae f shrine; small house, room
aedificātiō, -ōnis f building
aedificātiuncula, -ae f little house
aedificātor, -ōris m builder
aedificium, -ī and **-ii** nt building
aedificō, -āre, -āvī, -ātum vt to build, construct
aedīlicius adj aedile's ♦ m ex-aedile
aedīlis, -is m aedile
aedīlitās, -ātis f aedileship
aedis, -is see **aedēs**
aeditumus, aedituus, -ī m temple-keeper
Aeduī, -ōrum mpl a tribe of central Gaul
Aeētēs, -ae m father of Medea
Aegaeus adj Aegean ♦ nt Aegean Sea
Aegātēs, -um fpl islands off Sicily
aeger, -rī adj ill, sick; sorrowful; weak
Aegīna, -ae f a Greek island
Aegīnēta, -ae m inhabitant of Aegina
aegis, -dis f shield of Jupiter or Athena, aegis
Aegisthus, -ī m paramour of Clytemnestra
aegocerōs, -ōtis m Capricorn
aegrē adv painfully; with displeasure; with
difficulty; hardly; ~ **ferre** be annoyed
aegrēscō, -ere vi to become ill; to be aggravated
aegrimōnia, -ae f distress of mind
aegritūdō, -inis f sickness; sorrow
aegror, -ōris m illness
aegrōtātiō, -ōnis f illness, disease
aegrōtō, -āre, -āvī, -ātum vi to be ill
aegrōtus adj ill, sick
Aegyptius adj see **Aegyptus**

Aegyptus, -ī f Egypt ♦ m brother of Danaus
aelinos, -ī m dirge
Aemiliānus adj esp Scipio, destroyer of Carthage
Aemilius, -ī Roman family name; **Via Aemilia** road
in N. Italy
aemulātiō, -ōnis f rivalry (good or bad); jealousy
aemulātor, -ōris m zealous imitator
aemulor, -ārī, -ātus vt to rival, copy; to be
jealous
aemulus, -ī m rival ♦ adj rivalling; jealous
Aeneadēs, -ae m Trojan; Roman
Aenēās, -ae m Trojan leader and hero of Virgil's epic
Aenēis, -idis and **-idos** f Aeneid
Aenēius adj see **Aenēās**
aēneus adj of bronze
aenigma, -tis nt riddle, mystery
aēnum, -ī nt bronze vessel
aēnus adj of bronze
Aeolēs, -um mpl the Aeolians
Aeolia f Lipari Island
Aeolidēs m a descendant of Aeolus
Aeolis¹, -idis f Aeolia (N.W. of Asia Minor)
Aeolis², -idis f daughter of Aeolus
Aeolius adj see **Aeolus**
Aeolus, -ī m king of the winds
aequābilis adj equal; consistent, even;
impartial
aequābilitās, -ātis f uniformity; impartiality
aequābiliter adv uniformly
aequaevus adj of the same age
aequālis adj equal, like; of the same age,
contemporary; uniform
aequālitās, -ātis f evenness; (in politics, age)
equality, similarity
aequāliter adv evenly
aequanimitās, -ātis f goodwill; calmness
aequātiō, -ōnis f equal distribution
aequē adv equally; (with 'ac', 'atque', 'et', 'quam')
just as; justly
Aequī, -ōrum mpl a people of central Italy
Aequicus, Aequiculus adj see **Aequī**
Aequimaelium, -ī and **-ii** nt an open space in Rome
aequinoctiālis adj see **aequinoctium**
aequinoctium, -ī and **-ii** nt equinox
aequiperābilis adj comparable
aequiperō, -āre, -āvī, -ātum vt to compare; to
equal
aequitās, -ātis f uniformity; fair dealing,
equity; calmness of mind
aequō, -āre, -āvī, -ātum vt to make equal, level;
to compare; to equal; **solō aequāre** raze to the
ground
aequor, -is nt a level surface, sea
aequoreus adj of the sea
aequum, -i nt plain; justice
aequus adj level, equal; favourable, friendly,
fair, just; calm; **aequō animō** patiently; **aequō
Marte** without deciding the issue; **aequum
est** it is reasonable; **ex aequō** equally
āēr, āeris m air, weather; mist
aerāria f mine
aerārium nt treasury

aerārius *adj* of bronze; of money ♦ *m a citizen of the lowest class at Rome;* **tribūnī aerāriī** paymasters; *a wealthy middle class at Rome*
aerātus *adj* of bronze
aereus *adj* of copper or bronze
aerifer, -ī *adj* carrying cymbals
aeripēs, -edis *adj* bronze-footed
āerius *adj* of the air; lofty
aerūgō, -inis *f* rust; (*fig*) envy, avarice
aerumna, -ae *f* trouble, hardship
aerumnōsus *adj* wretched
aes, aeris *nt* copper, bronze; money; (*pl*) objects made of copper or bronze (*esp statues, instruments, vessels; soldiers' pay*); **aes aliēnum** debt; **aes circumforāneum** borrowed money; **aes grave** *Roman coin, as*
Aeschylus, -ī *m Greek tragic poet*
Aesculāpius, -ī *m god of medicine*
aesculētum, -ī *nt* oak forest
aesculeus *adj see* **aesculus**
aesculus, -ī *f* durmast oak
Aesōn, -onis *m father of Jason*
Aesonidēs, -ae *m* Jason
Aesōpius *adj see* **Aesōpus**
Aesōpus, -ī *m Greek writer of fables*
aestās, -ātis *f* summer
aestifer, -ī *adj* heat-bringing
aestimātiō, -ōnis *f* valuation, assessment; **lītis ~** assessment of damages
aestimātor, -ōris *m* valuer
aestimō, -āre, -āvī, -ātum *vt* to value, estimate the value of; **māgnī aestimāre** think highly of
aestīva, -ōrum *ntpl* summer camp, campaign
aestīvus *adj* summer
aestuārium, -ī *and* **-iī** *nt* tidal waters, estuary
aestuō, -āre, -āvī, -ātum *vi* to boil, burn; (*movement*) to heave, toss; (*fig*) to be excited; to waver
aestuōsus *adj* very hot; agitated
aestus, -ūs *m* heat; surge of the sea; tide; (*fig*) passion; hesitation
aetās, -ātis *f* age, life; time
aetātem *adv* for life
aetātula, -ae *f* tender age
aeternitās, -ātis *f* eternity
aeternō, -āre *vt* to immortalize
aeternus *adj* eternal, immortal; lasting; **in aeternum** for ever
aethēr, -eris *m* sky, heaven; air
aetherius *adj* ethereal, heavenly; of air
Aethiops, -is *adj* Ethiopian; (*fig*) stupid
aethra, -ae *f* sky
Aetna, -ae *f* Etna (*in Sicily*)
Aetnaeus, Aetnēnsis *adj see* **Aetna**
Aetōlia, -iae *f a district of W. Greece*
Aetōlus, Aetōlicus *adj see* **Aetōlia**
aevitās, -ātis *old form of* **aetās**
aevum, -ī *nt* age, lifetime; eternity; **in ~** for ever
Āfer, -rī *adj* African
āfore *fut infin of* **absum**
Āfrānius, -ī *m Latin comic poet*
Āfrica, -ae *f Roman province (now Tunisia)*
Āfricānae *fpl* panthers
Āfricānus *adj name of two Scipios*

Āfricus *adj* African ♦ *m* south-west (wind)
āfuī, āfutūrus *perf, fut p of* **absum**
Agamēmnōn, -onis *m leader of Greeks against Troy*
Agamēmnonius *adj see* **Agamēmnōn**
Aganippē, -ēs *f a spring on Helicon*
agāsō, -ōnis *m* ostler, footman
age, agedum come on!, well then
agellus, -ī *m* plot of land
Agēnōr, -oris *m father of Europa*
Agēnoreus *adj see* **Agēnōr**
Agēnoridēs, -ae *m* Cadmus; Perseus
agēns, -entis *adj* (RHET) effective
ager, -rī *m* land, field; countryside; territory
agg- *etc see* **adg-**
agger, -is *m* rampart; mound, embankment, *any built-up mass*
aggerō¹, -āre, -āvī, -ātum *vt* to pile up; to increase
aggerō², -rere, -ssī, -stum *vt* to carry, bring
aggestus, -ūs *m* accumulation
agilis *adj* mobile; nimble, busy
agilitās, -ātis *f* mobility
agitābilis *adj* light
agitātiō, -ōnis *f* movement, activity
agitātor, -ōris *m* driver, charioteer
agitō, -āre, -āvī, -ātum *vt* (*animals*) to drive; to move, chase, agitate; (*fig*) to excite (*to action*); to persecute, ridicule; to keep (*a ceremony*) ♦ *vi* to live; to deliberate
agmen, -inis *nt* forward movement, procession, train; army on the march; **~ claudere** bring up the rear; **novissimum ~** rearguard; **prīmum ~ van**
agna, -ae *f* ewe lamb; lamb (*flesh*)
agnāscor, -scī, -tus *vi* to be born after
agnātus, -ī *m* relation (*by blood on father's side*)
agnellus, -ī *m* little lamb
agnīnus *adj* of lamb
agnitiō, -ōnis *f* recognition, knowledge
agnitus *ppp of* **agnōscō**
agnōmen, -inis *nt* an extra surname (*eg Africanus*)
agnōscō, -ōscere, -ōvī, -itum *vt* to recognize; to acknowledge, allow; to understand
agnus, -ī *m* lamb
agō, agere, ēgī, āctum *vt* to drive, lead; to plunder; to push forward, put forth; (*fig*) to move, rouse, persecute; to do, act, perform; (*time*) to pass, spend; (*undertakings*) to manage, wage; (*public speaking*) to plead, discuss; to negotiate, treat; (THEAT) to play, act the part of; **agere cum populō** address the people; **age** come on!, well then; **age age** all right!; **āctum est dē** it is all up with; **aliud agere** not attend; **animam agere** expire; **annum quartum agere** be three years old; **causam agere** plead a cause; **hōc age** pay attention; **id agere ut** aim at; **lēge agere** go to law; **nīl agis** it's no use; **quid agis?** how are you?; **rēs agitur** interests are at stake; **sē agere** go, come
agrāriī *mpl* the land reform party
agrārius *adj* of public land; **lēx agrāria** land law
agrestis *adj* rustic; boorish, wild, barbarous ♦ *m* countryman
agricola, -ae *m* countryman, farmer

Agricola, -ae m a Roman governor of Britain; his
biography by Tacitus

Agrigentīnus adj see **Agrigentum**

Agrigentum, -ī nt a town in Sicily

agripeta, -ae m landgrabber

Agrippa, -ae m Roman surname (esp Augustus's
minister)

Agrippīna, -ae f mother of Nero; **Colōnia ~**
or **Agrippīnēnsis** Cologne

Agyīeus, -eī and **-eos** m Apollo

āh interj ah! (in sorrow or joy)

aha interj expressing reproof or laughter

ahēn- etc see **aēn-**

Āiāx, -ācis m Ajax (name of two Greek heroes at Troy)

āiō vt (defec) to say, speak; **ain tū?/ain vērō?**
really?; **quid ais?** I say!

āla, -ae f wing; armpit; (MIL) wing of army

alabaster, -rī m perfume box

alacer, -ris adj brisk, cheerful

alacritās, -ātis f promptness, liveliness; joy,
rapture

alapa, -ae f slap on the face; a slave's freedom

ālāriī mpl allied troops

ālārius adj (MIL) on the wing

ālātus adj winged

alauda, -ae f lark; name of a legion of Caesar's

alāzōn, -onis m braggart

Alba Longa, Albae Longae f a Latin town
(precursor of Rome)

Albānus adj Alban; **Lacus ~, Mōns ~** lake and
mountain near Alba Longa

albātus adj dressed in white

albeō, -ēre vi to be white; to dawn

albēscō, -ere vi to become white; to dawn

albicō, -āre vi to be white

albidus adj white

Albiōn, -ōnis f ancient name for Britain

albitūdō, -inis f whiteness

Albula, -ae f old name for the Tiber

albulus adj whitish

album, -ī nt white; records

Albunea, -ae f a spring at Tibur; a sulphur spring near
Alban Lake

albus adj white, bright

Alcaeus, -ī m Greek lyric poet

alcēdō, -inis f kingfisher

alcēdōnia ntpl halcyon days

alcēs, -is f elk

Alcibiadēs, -is m brilliant Athenian politician

Alcīdēs, -ae m Hercules

Alcinous, -ī m king of Phaeacians in the Odyssey

ālea, -ae f gambling, dice; (fig) chance, hazard;
iacta ~ est the die is cast; **in āleam dare** to risk

āleātor, -ōris m gambler

āleātōrius adj in gambling

ālēc etc see **allēc**

āleō, -ōnis m gambler

** āles, -itis** adj winged; swift ♦ m/f bird; omen

alēscō, -ere vi to grow up

Alexander, -rī m a Greek name; Paris (prince of Troy);
Alexander (the Great) (king of Macedon)

Alexandrēa (later **-īa**), **-ēae** f Alexandria (in
Egypt)

alga, -ae f seaweed

algeō, -gēre, -sī vi to feel cold; (fig) to be
neglected

algēscō, -ere vi to catch cold

Algidus, -ī m mountain in Latium

algidus adj cold

algor, -ōris m cold

algū abl sg m with cold

aliā adv in another way

aliās adv at another time; at one time … at
another

alibī adv elsewhere; otherwise; in one place …
in another

alicubī adv somewhere

alicunde adv from somewhere

alid old form of **aliud**

aliēnātiō, -ōnis f transfer; estrangement

aliēnigena, -ae m foreigner

aliēnigenus adj foreign; heterogeneous

aliēnō, -āre, -āvī, -ātum vt to transfer (property
by sale); to alienate, estrange; (mind) to derange

aliēnus adj of another, of others; alien, strange;
(with abl or ab) unsuited to, different from;
hostile ♦ m stranger

āliger, -ī adj winged

alimentārius adj about food

alimentum, -ī nt nourishment, food; obligation
of children to parents; (fig) support

alimōnium, -i and **-iī** nt nourishment

aliō adv in another direction, elsewhere; one
way … another way

aliōquī, aliōquin adv otherwise, else; besides

aliōrsum adv in another direction; differently

ālipēs, -edis adj wing-footed; fleet

alīptēs, -ae m sports trainer

aliquā adv some way or other

aliquam adv: **~ diū** for some time; **~ multī** a
considerable number

aliquandō adv sometime, ever; sometimes;
once, for once; now at last

aliquantisper adv for a time

aliquantō adv (with comp) somewhat

aliquantulum nt a very little ♦ adv somewhat

aliquantulus adj quite small

aliquantum adj a good deal ♦ adv somewhat

aliquantus adj considerable

aliquātenus adv to some extent

aliquī, -quae, -quod adj some, any; some other

aliquid adv at all

aliquis, -quid pron somebody, something;
someone or something important

aliquō adv to some place, somewhere else

aliquot adj (indecl) some

aliquotiēns adv several times

aliter adv otherwise, differently; in one way …
in another

alitus ppp of **alō**

ālium, -i and **-iī** nt garlic

aliunde adv from somewhere else

alius, alia, aliud adj other, another; different;
~ … ~ some … others; **~ ex aliō** one after the
other; **in alia omnia īre** oppose a measure;
nihil aliud quam only

all- etc see **adl-**

allēc, -is nt fish pickle

allex, -icis m big toe

Allia, -ae f tributary of the Tiber (scene of a great Roman defeat)

Alliēnsis adj see **Allia**

Allobrogēs, -um mpl a people of S.E. Gaul

Allobrogicus adj see **Allobrogēs**

almus adj nourishing; kindly

alnus, -ī f alder

alō, -ere, -uī, -tum and **-itum** vt to nourish, rear; to increase, promote

Alpēs, -ium fpl Alps

Alphēus, -ī m river of Olympia in S.W. Greece

Alpīnus adj see **Alpēs**

alsī perf of **algeō**

alsius, alsus adj cold

altāria, -ium ntpl altars, altar; altar top

altē adv on high, from above; deeply; from afar

alter, -īus adj the one, the other (of two); second, the next; fellow man; different; ~ **ego**, ~ **īdem** a second self; **alterum tantum** twice as much; **ūnus et** ~ one or two

altercātiō, -ōnis f dispute, debate

altercor, -ārī, -ātus vi to wrangle, dispute; to cross-examine

alternīs adv alternately

alternō, -āre, -āvī, -ātum vt to do by turns, alternate

alternus adj one after the other, alternate; elegiac (verses)

alteruter, -īusutrīus adj one or the other

altilis adj fat (esp fowls)

altisonus adj sounding on high

altitonāns, -antis adj thundering on high

altitūdō, -inis f height, depth; (fig) sublimity; (mind) secrecy

altivolāns, -antis adj soaring on high

altor, -ōris m foster father

altrīnsecus adv on the other side

altrīx, -īcis f nourisher, foster mother

altum, -ī nt heaven; sea (usu out of sight of land); **ex altō repetītus** far-fetched

altus adj high, deep; (fig) noble; profound

ālūcinor, -ārī, -ātus vi to talk wildly; (mind) to wander

aluī perf of **alō**

alumnus, -ī m, **alumna, -ae** f foster child; pupil

alūta, -ae f soft leather; shoe, purse, face patch

alveārium, -ī and **-iī** nt beehive

alveolus, -ī m basin

alveus, -eī m hollow; trough; (ship) hold; bath tub; riverbed

alvus, -ī f bowels; womb; stomach

amābilis adj lovely, lovable

amābilitās, -ātis f charm

amābiliter adv see **amābilis**

Amalthēa, -ae f nymph or she-goat; **cornū Amalthēae** horn of plenty

Amalthēum, -ī nt Atticus's library

āmandātiō f sending away

āmandō, -āre, -āvī, -ātum vt to send away

amāns, -antis adj fond ♦ m lover

amanter adv affectionately

āmanuēnsis, -is m secretary

amāracinum, -inī nt marjoram ointment

amāracum, -ī nt, **amāracus, -ī** m/f sweet marjoram

amārē adv see **amārus**

amāritiēs, -ēī f, **amāritūdō, -inis** f, **amāror, -ōris** m bitterness

amārus adj bitter; (fig) sad; ill-natured

amāsius, -ī and **-iī** m lover

Amathūs, -ūntis f town in Cyprus

Amathūsia f Venus

amātiō, -ōnis f lovemaking

amātor, -ōris m lover, paramour

amātorculus m poor lover

amātōriē adv amorously

amātōrius adj of love, erotic

amātrīx, -rīcis f mistress

Amāzōn, -onis f Amazon, warrior woman

Amāzonidēs fpl Amazons

Amāzonius adj see **Amāzōn**

ambāctus, -ī m vassal

ambāgēs, -is f windings; (speech) circumlocution, quibbling; enigma

ambedō, -edere, -ēdī, -ēsum vt to consume

ambēsus ppp of **ambedō**

ambigō, -ere vt, vi to wander about; to be in doubt; to argue; to wrangle

ambiguē adv doubtfully

ambiguitās, -ātis f ambiguity

ambiguus adj changeable, doubtful, unreliable; ambiguous

ambiō, -īre, -iī, -ītum vt to go round, encircle; (POL) to canvass for votes; (fig) to court (for a favour)

ambitiō, -ōnis f canvassing for votes; currying favour; ambition

ambitiōsē adv ostentatiously

ambitiōsus adj winding; ostentatious, ambitious

ambitus, -ūs m circuit, circumference; circumlocution; canvassing, bribery; **lēx de ambitū** a law against bribery

ambītus ppp of **ambiō**

ambō, ambae, ambō num both, two

Ambracia, -ae f district of N.W. Greece

Ambraciēnsis, Ambraciēnsus adj see **Ambracia**

ambrosia, -ae f food of the gods

ambrosius adj divine

ambūbāia, -ae f Syrian flute-girl

ambulācrum, -ī nt avenue

ambulātiō, -ōnis f walk, walking; walk (place)

ambulātiuncula f short walk

ambulō, -āre, -āvī, -ātum vi to walk, go; to travel

ambūrō, -rere, -ssī, -stum vt to burn up; to make frostbitten; (fig) to ruin

ambūstus ppp of **ambūrō**

amellus, -ī m Michaelmas daisy

āmēns, -entis adj mad, frantic; stupid

āmentia, -ae f madness; stupidity

āmentum, -ī nt strap (for throwing javelin)

ames, -itis m fowler's pole

amfr- etc see **anfr-**

amīca, -ae f friend; mistress

amiciō, -īre, -tus vt to clothe, cover

amīciter, **-ē** *adv see* **amīcus**
amīcitia, **-ae** *f* friendship; alliance
amictus¹ *ppp of* **amiciō**
amictus², **-ūs** *m* (manner of) dress; clothing
amiculum, **-ī** *nt* cloak
amīculus, **-ī** *m* dear friend
amīcus, **-ī** *m* friend ♦ *adj* friendly, fond
āmissiō, **-ōnis** *f* loss
āmissus *ppp of* **āmittō**
amita, **-ae** *f* aunt (*on father's side*)
āmittō, **-ittere**, **-īsī**, **-issum** *vt* to let go, lose
Ammōn, **-is** *m* Egyptian god identified with Jupiter
Ammōniacus *adj see* **Ammōn**
amnicola, **-ae** *m/f* sth growing by a river
amniculus *m* brook
amnicus *adj see* **amnis**
amnis, **-is** *m* river
amō, **-āre**, **-āvī**, **-ātum** *vt* to love, like; (*colloq*) to be obliged to; **ita mē dī ament** bless my soul!; **amābō** please!
amoenitās, **-ātis** *f* delightfulness (*esp of scenery*)
amoenus *adj* delightful
āmōlior, **-īrī**, **-ītus** *vt* to remove
amōmum, **-ī** *nt* cardamom
amor, **-ōris** *m* love; (*fig*) strong desire; *term of endearment*; Cupid; (*pl*) love affairs
āmōtiō, **-ōnis** *f* removal
āmōtus *ppp of* **āmoveō**
āmoveō, **-ovēre**, **-ōvī**, **-ōtum** *vt* to remove; to banish
amphibolia, **-ae** *f* ambiguity
Amphīōn, **-onis** *m* musician and builder of Thebes
Amphīonius *adj see* **Amphīōn**
amphitheātrum, **-ī** *nt* amphitheatre
Amphitrītē, **-ēs** *f* sea goddess; the sea
Amphitryō, **-ōnis** *m* husband of Alcmena
Amphitryōniadēs *m* Hercules
amphora, **-ae** *f* a two-handled jar; liquid measure; (*NAUT*) measure of tonnage
Amphrȳsius *adj* of Apollo
Amphrȳsus, **-ī** *m* river in Thessaly
ample *adv see* **amplus**
amplector, **-ctī**, **-xus** *vt* to embrace, encircle; (*mind*) to grasp; (*speech*) to deal with; (*fig*) to cherish
amplexor, **-ārī**, **-ātus** *vt* to embrace, love
amplexus¹ *ppa of* **amplector**
amplexus², **-ūs** *m* embrace, encircling
amplificātiō, **-ōnis** *f* enlargement; (*RHET*) a passage elaborated for effect
amplificē *adv* splendidly
amplificō, **-āre**, **-āvī**, **-ātum** *vt* to increase, enlarge; (*RHET*) to enlarge upon
ampliō, **-āre**, **-āvī**, **-ātum** *vt* to enlarge; (*LAW*) to adjourn
ampliter *adv see* **amplus**
amplitūdō, **-inis** *f* size; (*fig*) distinction; (*RHET*) fullness
amplius *adv* more (*esp amount or number*), further, longer; ~ **ducentī** more than 200; ~ **nōn petere** take no further legal action; ~ **prōnūntiāre** adjourn a case
amplus *adj* large, spacious; great, abundant; powerful, splendid, eminent; (*superl*) distinguished

ampulla, **-ae** *f* a two-handled flask; (*fig*) high-flown language
ampullārius, **-ārī** *m* flask-maker
ampullor, **-ārī** *vi* to use high-flown language
amputātiō, **-ōnis** *f* pruning
amputatus *adj* (*RHET*) disconnected
amputō, **-āre**, **-āvī**, **-ātum** *vt* to cut off, prune; (*fig*) to lop off
Amūlius, **-ī** *m* king of Alba Longa, grand-uncle of Romulus
amurca, **-ae** *f* lees of olive oil
amussitātus *adj* nicely adjusted
Amȳclae, **-ārum** *fpl* town in S. Greece
Amȳclaeus *adj see* **Amȳclae**
amygdalum, **-ī** *nt* almond
amystis, **-dis** *f* emptying a cup at a draught
an *conj* or; perhaps; (*with single question*) surely not; **haud sciō an** I feel sure
Anacreōn, **-ontis** *m* Greek lyric poet
anadēma, **-tis** *nt* headband
anagnōstēs, **-ae** *m* reader
anapaestum, **-ī** *nt* poem in anapaests
anapaestus *adj*: ~ **pēs** anapaest
anas, **-tis** *f* duck
anaticula *f* duckling
anatīnus *adj see* **anas**
anatocismus, **-ī** *m* compound interest
Anaxagorās, **-ae** *m* early Greek philosopher
Anaximander, **-rī** *m* early Greek philosopher
anceps, **-ipitis** *adj* two-headed; double; wavering, doubtful; dangerous ♦ *nt* danger
Anchīsēs, **-ae** *m* father of Aeneas
Anchīsēus *adj* Aeneas
Anchīsiadēs *m* Aeneas
ancīle, **-is** *nt* oval shield (*esp one said to have fallen from heaven in Numa's reign*)
ancilla, **-ae** *f* servant
ancillāris *adj* of a young servant
ancillula *f* young servant
ancīsus *adj* cut round
ancora, **-ae** *f* anchor
ancorāle, **-is** *nt* cable
ancorārius *adj see* **ancora**
Ancus Marcius, **Anci Marcii** *m* 4th king of Rome
Ancȳra, **-ae** *f* Ankara (*capital of Galatia*)
andabata, **-ae** *m* blindfold gladiator
Andrius *adj see* **Andros**
androgynē, **-ēs** *f* hermaphrodite
androgynus, **-ī** *m* hermaphrodite
Andromachē, **-ēs** *f* wife of Hector
Andromeda, **-ae** *f* wife of Perseus; a constellation
Andronicus, **-ī** *m* Livius (*earliest Latin poet*)
Andros, **Andrus**, **-ī** *f* Aegean island
ānellus, **-ī** *m* little ring
anēthum, **-ī** *nt* fennel
ānfrāctus, **-ūs** *m* bend, orbit; roundabout way; (*words*) digression, prolixity
angelus, **-ī** *m* angel
angina, **-ae** *f* quinsy
angiportum, **-ī** *nt* alley
angiportus, **-ūs** *m* alley
angō, **-ere** *vt* to throttle; (*fig*) to distress, torment
angor, **-ōris** *m* suffocation; (*fig*) anguish

anguicomus *adj* with snakes for hair
anguiculus, -ī *m* small snake
anguifer, -ī *adj* snake-carrying
anguigena, -ae *m* one born of serpents; Theban
anguilla, -ae *f* eel
anguimanus *adj* with a trunk
anguipēs, -edis *adj* serpent-footed
anguis, -is *m/f* snake, serpent; (*constellation*)
Draco
Anguitenēns, -entis *m* Ophiuchus
angulātus *adj* angular
angulus, -ī *m* angle, corner; out-of-the-way
place; **ad parēs angulōs** at right angles
angustē *adv* close, within narrow limits;
concisely
angustiae, -ārum *fpl* defile, strait; (*time*)
shortness; (*means*) want; (*circumstances*)
difficulty; (*mind*) narrowness; (*words*) subtleties
angusticlāvius *adj* wearing a narrow purple
stripe
angustō, -āre *vt* to make narrow
angustum, -ī *nt* narrowness; danger
angustus *adj* narrow, close; (*time*) short;
(*means*) scanty; (*mind*) mean; (*argument*) subtle;
(*circumstances*) difficult
anhēlitus, -ūs *m* panting; breath, exhalation
anhēlō, -āre, -āvī, -ātum *vi* to breathe hard,
pant; to exhale
anhēlus *adj* panting
anicula, -ae *f* poor old woman
Aniēnsis, Aniēnus *adj* of the river Anio
Aniēnus *m* Anio
anīlis *adj* of an old woman
anīlitās, -tātis *f* old age
anīliter *adv* like an old woman
anima, -ae *f* wind, air; breath; life; soul, mind;
ghost, spirit; **animam agere, animam efflāre**
expire; **animam comprimere** hold one's
breath
animadversiō, -ōnis *f* observation; censure,
punishment
animadversor, -ōris *m* observer
animadvertō, -tere, -tī, -sum *vt* to pay
attention to, notice; to realise; to censure,
punish; **animadvertere in** punish
animal, -ālis *nt* animal; living creature
animālis *adj* of air; animate
animāns, -antis *m/f/nt* living creature; animal
animātiō, -ōnis *f* being
animātus *adj* disposed; *in a certain frame of mind*;
courageous
animō, -āre, -āvī, -ātum *vt* to animate; *to give a
certain temperament to*
animōsē *adv* boldly, eagerly
animōsus *adj* airy; lifelike; courageous, proud
animula, -ae *f* little soul
animulus, -ī *m* darling
animus, -ī *m* mind, soul; consciousness;
reason, thought, opinion, imagination; heart,
feelings, disposition; courage, spirit, pride,
passion; will, purpose; *term of endearment*;
animī in mind, in heart; **animī causā** for
amusement; **animō fingere** imagine; **animō
male est** I am fainting; **aequō animō esse**
be patient, calm; **bonō animō esse** take

courage; be well-disposed; **ex animō** sincerely;
ex animō effluere be forgotten; **in animō
habēre** purpose; **meō animō** in my opinion
Aniō, -ēnis *m* tributary of the Tiber
annālēs, -ium *mpl* annals, chronicle
annālis *adj* of a year; **lēx ~** law prescribing ages
for public offices
Anna Perenna, Annae Perennae *f* Roman
popular goddess
anne *etc see* **an**
anniculus *adj* a year old
anniversārius *adj* annual
annōn or not
annōna, -ae *f* year's produce; grain; price of
corn; the market
annōsus *adj* aged
annōtinus *adj* last year's
annus, -ī *m* year; **~ māgnus** astronomical great
year; **~ solidus** a full year
annuus *adj* a year's; annual
anquīrō, -rere, -sīvī, -sītum *vt* to search for; to
make inquiries; (*LAW*) to institute an inquiry
(**dē**) or prosecution (*abl, gen*)
ānsa, -ae *f* handle; (*fig*) opportunity
ānsātus *adj* with a handle; (*comedy*) with arms
akimbo
ānser, -is *m* goose
ānserīnus *adj see* **ānser**
ante *prep* (*with acc*) before (*in time, place,
comparison*) ♦ *adv* (*place*) in front; (*time*) before
anteā *adv* before, formerly
antecapiō, -apere, -ēpī, -eptum *vt* to take
beforehand, anticipate
antecēdō, -ēdere, -essī, -essum *vt* to precede;
to surpass
antecellō, -ere *vi* to excel, be superior
anteceptus *ppp of* **antecapiō**
antecessiō, -ōnis *f* preceding; antecedent
cause
antecessor, -ōris *m* forerunner
antecursor, -ōris *m* forerunner, pioneer
anteeō, -īre, -iī *vi* to precede, surpass
anteferō, -ferre, -tulī, -lātum *vt* to carry before;
to prefer; to anticipate
antefixus *adj* attached (in front) ♦ *ntpl*
ornaments on roofs of buildings
antegredior, -dī, -ssus *vt* to precede
antehabeō, -ēre *vt* to prefer
antehāc *adv* formerly, previously
antelātus *ppp of* **anteferō**
antelūcānus *adj* before dawn
antemerīdiānus *adj* before noon
antemittō, -ittere, -īsī, -issum *vt* to send on
in front
antenna, -ae *f* yardarm
antepīlānī, -ōrum *mpl* (*MIL*) the front ranks
antepōnō, -ōnere, -osuī, -ositum *vt* to set
before; to prefer
antequam *conj* before
Anterōs, -ōtis *m* avenger of slighted love
antēs, -ium *mpl* rows
antesignānus, -ī *m* (*MIL*) leader; (*pl*) defenders
of the standards

antestō, antistō, -āre, -ētī *vi* to excel, distinguish oneself

antestor, -ārī, -ātus *vi* to call a witness

anteveniō, -enīre, -ēnī, -entum *vt, vi* to anticipate; to surpass

antevertō, -tere, -tī, -sum *vt* to precede; to anticipate; to prefer

anticipātiō, -ōnis *f* foreknowledge

anticipō, -āre, -āvī, -ātum *vt* to take before, anticipate

antīcus *adj* in front

Antigonē, -ēs *f* daughter of Oedipus

Antigonus, -ī *m* name of Macedonian kings

Antiochēnsis *adj see* **Antiochīa**

Antiochīa, -īae *f* Antioch (*capital of Syria*)

Antiochus, -ī *m* name of kings of Syria

antīquārius, -ī *and* **-iī** *m* antiquary

antīquē *adv* in the old style

antīquitās, -ātis *f* antiquity, the ancients; integrity

antīquitus *adv* long ago, from ancient times

antīquō, -āre, -āvī, -ātum *vt* to vote against (*a bill*)

antīquus *adj* ancient, former, old; good old-fashioned, honest, illustrious; **antiquior** more important; **antiquissimus** most important

antistēs, -itis *m/f* high priest, chief priestess; (*fig*) master (*in any art*)

Antisthenēs, -is *and* **-ae** *m* founder of Cynic philosophy

antistita, -ae *f* chief priestess

antistō *etc see* **antestō**

antitheton, -ī *nt* (RHET) antithesis

Antōnīnus, -ī *m* name of Roman emperors (*esp Pius and Marcus Aurelius*)

Antōnius, -ī *m* Roman name (*esp the famous orator, and Mark Antony*)

antrum, -ī *nt* cave, hollow

ānulārius, -ī *m* ringmaker

ānulātus *adj* with rings on

ānulus, -ī *m* ring; equestrian rank

ānus, -ī *m* rectum; ring

anus, -ūs *f* old woman ◆ *adj* old

ānxiē *adv see* **ānxius**

ānxietās, -ātis *f* anxiety, trouble (*of the mind*)

ānxifer, -ī *adj* disquieting

ānxitūdō, -inis *f* anxiety

ānxius *adj* (*mind*) troubled; disquieting

Āones, -um *adj* Boeotian

Āonia *f* part of Boeotia

Āonius *adj* of Boeotia, of Helicon

Aornos, -ī *m/f* lake Avernus

apage *interj* away with!, go away!

apēliōtēs, -ae *m* east wind

Apellēs, -is *m* Greek painter

aper, -rī *m* boar

aperiō, -īre, -uī, -tum *vt* to uncover, disclose, open; (*country*) to open up; (*fig*) to unfold, explain, reveal

apertē *adv* clearly, openly

apertum, -ī *nt* open space; **in apertō esse** be well known; be easy

apertus *ppp of* **aperiō** ◆ *adj* open, exposed; clear, manifest; (*person*) frank

aperuī *perf of* **aperiō**

apex, -icis *m* summit; crown, priest's cap; (*fig*) crown

aphractus, -ī *f* a long open boat

apiārius, -ī *and* **-iī** *m* beekeeper

Apīcius, -ī *m* Roman epicure

apicula, -ae *f* little bee

apis, -is *f* bee

apīscor, -īscī, -tus *vt* to catch, get, attain

apium, -ī *and* **-iī** *nt* celery

aplustre, -is *nt* decorated stern of a ship

apoclētī, -ōrum *mpl* committee of the Aetolian League

apodytērium, -ī *and* **-iī** *nt* dressing room

Apollināris, -ineus *adj*: **lūdī Apollinārēs** Roman games in July

Apollō, -inis *m* Greek god of music, archery, prophecy, flocks and herds, and often identified with the sun

apologus, -ī *m* narrative, fable

apophorēta, -ōrum *ntpl* presents for guests to take home

apoproēgmena, -ōrum *ntpl* (PHILOS) what is rejected

apostolicus *adj see* **apostolus**

apostolus, -ī *m* (ECCL) apostle

apothēca, -ae *f* storehouse, wine store

apparātē *adv see* **apparātus¹**

apparātiō, -ōnis *f* preparation

apparātus¹ *adj* ready, well-supplied, sumptuous

apparātus², -ūs *m* preparation; equipment, munitions; pomp, ostentation

appāreō, -ēre, -uī, -itum *vi* to come in sight, appear; to be seen, show oneself; to wait upon (*an official*); **appāret** it is obvious

appāritiō, -ōnis *f* service; domestic servants

appāritor, -ōris *m* attendant

apparō, -āre, -āvī, -ātum *vt* to prepare, provide

appellātiō, -ōnis *f* accosting, appeal; title; pronunciation

appellātor, -ōris *m* appellant

appellitātus *adj* usually called

appellō¹, -āre, -āvī, -ātum *vt* to speak to; to appeal to; (*for money*) to dun; (LAW) to sue; to call, name; to pronounce

appellō², -ellere, -ulī, -ulsum *vt* to drive, bring (to); (NAUT) to bring to land

appendicula, -ae *f* small addition

appendix, -icis *f* supplement

appendō, -endere, -endī, -ensum *vt* to weigh, pay

appetēns, -entis *adj* eager; greedy

appetenter *adv see* **appetēns**

appetentia, -ae *f* craving

appetītiō, -ōnis *f* grasping, craving

appetītus¹ *ppp of* **appetō**

appetītus², -ūs *m* craving; natural desire (*as opposed to reason*)

appetō, -ere, -īvī, -ītum *vt* to grasp, try to get at; to attack; to desire ◆ *vi* to approach

Appius, -ī *m* Roman first name; **Via Appia** main road from Rome to Capua and Brundisium

applaudō, -dere, -sī, -sum *vt* to strike, clap ◆ *vi* to applaud

applicātiō, -ōnis f applying (of the mind); **iūs applicātiōnis** the right of a patron to inherit a client's effects

applicātus, applicitus ppp of **applicō**

applicō, -āre, -āvī and **-uī, ātum** and **itum** vt to attach, place close (to); (NAUT) to steer, bring to land; **sē applicāre, animum applicāre** devote self, attention (to)

applōrō, -āre vt to deplore

appōnō, -ōnere, -osuī, -ositum vt to put (to, beside); (meal) to serve; to add, appoint; to reckon

apporrēctus adj stretched nearby

apportō, -āre, -āvī, -ātum vt to bring, carry (to)

apposcō, -ere vt to demand also

appositē adv suitably

appositus ppp of **appōnō** ✦ adj situated near; (fig) bordering on; suitable

apposuī perf of **appōnō**

appōtus adj drunk

apprecor, -ārī, -ātus vt to pray to

apprehendō, -endere, -endī, -ēnsum vt to take hold of; (MIL) to occupy; (argument) to bring forward

apprīmē adv especially

apprimō, -imere, -essī, -essum vt to press close

approbātiō, -ōnis f acquiescence; proof

approbātor, -ōris m approver

approbē adv very well

approbō, -āre, -āvī, -ātum vt to approve; to prove; to perform to someone's satisfaction

apprōmittō, -ere vt to promise also

approperō, -āre, -āvī, -ātum vt to hasten ✦ vi to hurry up

appropinquō, -āre, -āvī, -ātum vi to approach

appropinquātiō, -ōnis f approach

appugnō, -āre vt to attack

appulsus[1] ppp of **appellō**[2]

appulsus[2], **-ūs** m landing; approach

aprīcātiō, -ōnis f basking

aprīcor, -ārī vi to bask

aprīcus adj sunny; basking; **in aprīcum prōferre** bring to light

Aprīlis adj April, of April

aprūgnus adj of the wild boar

aps- etc see **abs-**

aptē adv closely; suitably, rightly

aptō, -āre, -āvī, -ātum vt to fit, put on; (fig) to adapt; to prepare, equip

aptus adj attached, joined together, fitted (with); suitable

apud prep (with acc) 1. (with persons) beside, by, with, at the house of, among, in the time of; (speaking) in the presence of, to; (judgment) in the opinion of; (influence) with; (faith) in; (authors) in 2. (with places) near, at, in; **est ~ mē** I have; **sum ~ mē** I am in my senses

Āpūlia, -iae f district of S.E. Italy

Āpūlus adj see **Āpūlia**

aput prep see **apud**

aqua, -ae f water; **~ mihī haeret** I am in a fix; **~ intercus** dropsy; **aquam adspergere** revive; **aquam praebēre** entertain; **aquam et terram petere** demand submission; **aquā et ignī interdīcere** outlaw

aquae fpl medicinal waters, spa

aquaeductus, -ūs m aqueduct; right of leading water

aquāliculus m belly

aquālis, -is m/f washbasin

aquārius adj of water ✦ m water carrier, water inspector; a constellation

aquāticus adj aquatic; humid

aquātilis adj aquatic

aquātiō, -ōnis f fetching water; watering place

aquātor, -ōris m water carrier

aquila, -ae f eagle; standard of a legion; (ARCH) gable; a constellation; **aquilae senectūs** a vigorous old age

Aquileia, -ae f town in N. Italy

Aquileiēnsis adj see **Aquileia**

aquilifer, -i m chief standard-bearer

aquilīnus adj eagle's

aquilō, -ōnis m north wind; north

aquilōnius adj northerly

aquilus adj swarthy

Aquīnās, -ātis adj see **Aquīnum**

Aquīnum, -i nt town in Latium

Aquītānia, -iae f district of S.W. Gaul

Aquītānus adj see **Aquītānia**

aquor, -ārī, -ātus vi to fetch water

aquōsus adj humid, rainy

aquula, -ae f little stream

āra, -ae f altar; (fig) refuge; a constellation; **ārae et focī** hearth and home

arabarchēs, -ae m customs officer (in Egypt)

Arabia, -iae f Arabia

Arabicē adv with all the perfumes of Arabia

Arabicus, Arabicius, Arabus adj see **Arabia**

Arachnē, -s f Lydian woman changed into a spider

arānea, -ae f spider; cobweb

arāneola f, **-olus** m small spider

arāneōsus adj full of spiders' webs

arāneum, -ī nt spider's web

arāneus, -ī m spider ✦ adj of spiders

Arar, -is m (river) Saône

Arātēus adj see **Arātus**

arātiō, -ōnis f ploughing, farming; arable land

arātiuncula f small plot

arātor, -ōris m ploughman, farmer; (pl) cultivators of public land

arātrum, -ī nt plough

Arātus, -ī m Greek astronomical poet

Araxēs, -is m river in Armenia

arbiter, -rī m witness; arbiter, judge, umpire; controller; **~ bibendī** president of a drinking party

arbitra, -ae f witness

arbitrāriō adv with some uncertainty

arbitrārius adj uncertain

arbitrātus, -ūs m decision; **meō arbitrātū** in my judgment

arbitrium, -ī and **-iī** nt decision (of an arbitrator), judgment; mastery, control

arbitror, -ārī, -ātus vt, vi to be a witness of; to testify; to think, suppose

arbor, arbōs, -oris f tree; ship, mast, oar; **~ īnfēlix** gallows

arboreus adj of trees, like a tree

arbustum, -**ī** *nt* plantation, orchard; (*pl*) trees
arbustus *adj* wooded
arbuteus *adj* of the strawberry tree
arbutum, -**ī** *nt* fruit of strawberry tree
arbutus, -**ī** *f* strawberry tree
arca, -**ae** *f* box; moneybox, purse; coffin; prison cell; **ex arcā absolvere** pay cash
Arcades, -**um** *mpl* Arcadians
Arcadia, -**iae** *f* district of E. Greece
Arcadicus, -**ius** *adj see* **Arcadia**
arcānō *adv* privately
arcānum, -**ī** *nt* secret, mystery
arcānus *adj* secret; able to keep secrets
arceō, -**ēre**, -**uī**, -**tum** *vt* to enclose; to keep off, prevent
accessītū *abl sg m* at the summons
accessītus *ppp of* **accessō** ♦ *adj* far-fetched
accessō, -**ere**, -**īvī**, -**ītum** *vt* to send for, fetch; (*LAW*) to summon, accuse; (*fig*) to derive
archetypus, -**ī** *m* original
Archilochus, -**ī** *m* Greek iambic and elegiac poet
archimagīrus, -**ī** *m* chief cook
Archimēdēs, -**is** *m* famous mathematician of Syracuse
archipīrāta, -**ae** *m* pirate chief
architectōn, -**onis** *m* master builder; master in cunning
architector, -**ārī**, -**ātus** *vt* to construct; (*fig*) to devise
architectūra, -**ae** *f* architecture
architectus, -**ī** *m* architect; (*fig*) author
archōn, -**ontis** *m* Athenian magistrate
Archytās, -**ae** *m* Pythagorean philosopher of Tarentum
arcitenēns, -**entis** *adj* holding a bow ♦ *m* Apollo
Arctophylax, -**cis** *m* (*constellation*) Bootes
arctos, -**ī** *f* Great Bear, Little Bear; north, north wind; night
Arctūrus, -**ī** *m* brightest star in BoÐtes
arctus *etc see* **artus** *etc*
arcuī *perf of* **arceō**
arcula, -**ae** *f* casket; (*RHET*) ornament
arcuō, -**āre**, -**āvī**, -**ātum** *vt* to curve
arcus, -**ūs** *m* bow; rainbow; arch, curve; (*MATH*) arc
ardea, -**ae** *f* heron
Ardea, -**ae** *f* town in Latium
ardeliō, -**ōnis** *m* busybody
ārdēns, -**entis** *adj* hot, glowing, fiery; (*fig*) eager, ardent
ārdenter *adv* passionately
ārdeō, -**dēre**, -**sī**, -**sum** *vi* to be on fire, burn, shine; (*fig*) to be fired, burn
ārdēscō, -**ere** *vi* to catch fire, gleam; (*fig*) to become inflamed, wax hotter
ārdor, -**ōris** *m* heat, brightness; (*fig*) ardour, passion
arduum, -**ī** *nt* steep slope; difficulty
arduus *adj* steep, high; difficult, troublesome
ārea, -**ae** *f* vacant site, open space, playground; threshing-floor; (*fig*) scope (*for effort*)
ārefaciō, -**acere**, -**ēcī**, -**actum** *vt* to dry
arēna *etc see* **harēna**
ārēns, -**entis** *adj* arid; thirsty

āreō, -**ēre** *vi* to be dry
āreola, -**ae** *f* small open space
Areōpagītēs *m* member of the court
Areōpagus, -**ī** *m* Mars' Hill in Athens; a criminal court
Arēs, -**is** *m* Greek god of war
ārēscō, -**ere** *vi* to dry, dry up
Arestoridēs, -**ae** *m* Argus
aretālogus, -**ī** *m* braggart
Arethūsa, -**ae** *f* spring near Syracuse
Arethūsis *adj* Syracusan
Argēī, -**ōrum** *mpl* sacred places in Rome; effigies thrown annually into the Tiber
argentāria, -**ae** *f* bank, banking; silver mine
argentārius *adj* of silver, of money ♦ *m* banker
argentātus *adj* silver-plated; backed with money
argenteus *adj* of silver, adorned with silver; silvery (*in colour*); of the silver age
argentum, -**ī** *nt* silver, silver plate; money
Argēus, **Argīvus**, **Argolicus** *adj* Argive; Greek
Argīlētānus *adj see* **Argīlētum**
Argīlētum, -**ī** *nt* part of Rome (*noted for bookshops*)
argilla, -**ae** *f* clay
Argō, -**ūs** *f* Jason's ship
Argolis, -**olidis** *f* district about Argos
Argonautae, -**ārum** *mpl* Argonauts
Argonauticus *adj see* **Argonautae**
Argos *nt*, **Argī**, -**ōrum** *mpl* town in S.E. Greece
Argōus *adj see* **Argō**
argūmentātiō, -**ōnis** *f* adducing proofs
argūmentor, -**ārī**, -**ātus** *vt*, *vi* to prove, adduce as proof; to conclude
argūmentum, -**ī** *nt* evidence, proof; (*LIT*) subject matter, theme, plot (*of a play*); (*art*) subject, motif
arguō, -**uere**, -**uī**, -**ūtum** *vt* to prove, make known; to accuse, blame, denounce
Argus, -**ī** *m* monster with many eyes
argūtē *adv* subtly
argūtiae, -**ārum** *fpl* nimbleness, liveliness; wit, subtlety, slyness
argūtor, -**ārī**, -**ātus** *vi* to chatter
argūtulus *adj* rather subtle
argūtus *adj* (*sight*) clear, distinct, graceful; (*sound*) clear, melodious, noisy; (*mind*) acute, witty, sly
argyraspis, -**dis** *adj* silver-shielded
Ariadna, -**ae** *f* daughter of Minos of Crete
Ariadnaeus *adj see* **Ariadna**
āridulus *adj* rather dry
āridum, -**ī** *nt* dry land
āridus *adj* dry, withered; meagre; (*style*) flat
ariēs, -**etis** *m* ram; 1st sign of Zodiac; battering ram; beam used as a breakwater
arietō, -**āre** *vt*, *vi* to butt, strike hard
Ariōn, -**onis** *m* early Greek poet and musician
Ariōnius *adj see* **Ariōn**
arista, -**ae** *f* ear of corn
Aristaeus, -**ī** *m* legendary founder of beekeeping
Aristarchus, -**ī** *m* Alexandrian scholar; a severe critic
Aristīdēs, -**is** *m* Athenian statesman noted for integrity
Aristippēus *adj see* **Aristippus**
Aristippus, -**ī** *m* Greek hedonist philosopher

aristolochia, -ae f birthwort
Aristophanēs, -is m Greek comic poet
Aristophanēus, Aristophanīus adj see
　Aristophanēs
Aristotelēs, -is m Aristotle (founder of Peripatetic
　school of philosophy)
Aristotelēus, Aristotelīus adj see **Aristotelēs**
arithmētica, -ōrum ntpl arithmetic
āritūdō, -inis f dryness
Ariūsius adj of Ariusia (in Chios)
arma, -ōrum ntpl armour, shield; arms,
　weapons (of close combat only); warfare, troops;
　(fig) defence, protection; implements, ship's
　gear
armāmenta, -ōrum ntpl implements, ship's
　gear
armāmentārium, -ī and **-iī** nt arsenal
armāriolum, -ī nt small chest
armārium, -ī and **-iī** nt chest, safe
armātū abl m armour; **gravī ~** with heavy-
　armed troops
armatūra, -ae f armour, equipment; **levis**
　~ light-armed troops
armatus adj armed
Armenia, -ae f Armenia
Armeniaca, -acae f apricot tree
Armeniacum, -acī nt apricot
Armenius adj see **Armenia**
armentālis adj of the herd
armentārius, -ī and **-iī** m cattle herd
armentum, -ī nt cattle (for ploughing), herd (cattle
　etc)
armifer, -ī adj armed
armiger, -ī m armour-bearer ♦ adj armed;
　productive of warriors
armilla, -ae f bracelet
armillātus adj wearing a bracelet
armipotēns, -entis adj strong in battle
armisonus adj resounding with arms
armō, -āre, -āvī, -ātum vt to arm, equip; to
　rouse to arms (against)
armus, -ī m shoulder (esp of animals)
Arniēnsis adj see **Arnus**
Arnus, -ī m (river) Arno
arō, -āre, -āvī, -ātum vt to plough, cultivate; to
　live by farming; (fig: sea, brow) to furrow
Arpīnās, -ātis adj see **Arpīnum**
Arpīnum, -ī nt town in Latium (birthplace of Cicero)
arquātus adj jaundiced
arr- etc see **adr-**
arrabō, -ōnis m earnest money
ars, artis f skill (in any craft); the art (of any
　profession); science, theory; handbook; work of
　art; moral quality, virtue; artifice; fraud
ārsī perf of **ārdeō**
ārsus ppp of **ārdeō**
artē adv closely, soundly, briefly
artēria¹, -ae f windpipe; artery
artēria², -ōrum ntpl trachea
arthrīticus adj gouty
articulātim adv joint by joint; (speech) distinctly
articulō, -āre, -āvī, -ātum vt to articulate
articulōsus adj minutely subdivided

articulus, -ī m joint, knuckle; limb; (words)
　clause; (time) point, turning point; **in ipsō**
　articulō temporis in the nick of time
artifex, -icis m artist, craftsman, master;
　(fig) maker, author ♦ adj ingenious, artistic,
　artificial
artificiōsē adv skilfully
artificiōsus adj ingenious, artistic, artificial
artificium, -ī and **-iī** nt skill, workmanship;
　art, craft; theory, rule of an art; ingenuity,
　cunning
artō, -āre vt to compress, curtail
artolaganus, -ī m kind of cake
artopta, -ae m baker; baking tin
artus¹ adj close, narrow, tight; (sleep) deep; (fig)
　strict, straitened
artus², -ūs m joint; (pl) limbs, body; (fig)
　strength
ārula, -ae f small altar
arundō etc see **harundō** etc
arvīna, -ae f grease
arvum, -ī nt field; land, country, plain
arvus adj ploughed
arx, arcis f fortress, castle; height, summit; (fig)
　bulwark, stronghold; **arcem facere ē cloācā**
　make a mountain out of a molehill
ās, assis m (weight) pound; (coin) bronze unit, of low
　value; (inheritance) the whole (subdivided into 12
　parts); **ad assem** to the last farthing; **hērēs ex**
　asse sole heir
Ascānius, -ī m son of Aeneas
ascendō, -endere, -endī, -ēnsum vt, vi to go up,
　climb, embark; (fig) to rise
ascēnsiō, -ōnis f ascent; (fig) sublimity
ascēnsus, -ūs m ascent, rising; way up
ascia, -ae f axe; mason's trowel
asciō, -īre vt to admit
ascīscō, -īscere, -īvī, -ītum vt to receive with
　approval; to admit (to some kind of association); to
　appropriate, adopt (esp customs); to arrogate to
　oneself
ascītus adj acquired, alien
Ascra, -ae f birthplace of Hesiod in Boeotia
Ascraeus adj of Ascra; of Hesiod; of Helicon
ascrībō, -bere, -psī, -ptum vt to add (in writing);
　to attribute, ascribe; to apply (an illustration); to
　enrol, include
ascrīptīcius adj enrolled
ascrīptiō, -ōnis f addition (in writing)
ascrīptīvus adj (MIL) supernumerary
ascrīptor, -ōris m supporter
ascrīptus ppp of **ascrībō**
asella, -ae f young ass
asellus, -ī m young ass
Āsia, -ae f Roman province; Asia Minor; Asia
asīlus, -ī m gad fly
asinus, -ī m ass; fool
Āsis, -dis f Asia
Āsius, Āsiānus, Āsiāticus adj see **Āsia**
Āsōpus, -ī m river in Boeotia
asōtus, -ī m libertine
asparagus, -ī m asparagus
aspargō etc see **aspergō¹**
aspectābilis adj visible

aspectō, -āre vt to look at, gaze at; to pay heed to; (places) to face

aspectus¹ ppp of **aspiciō**

aspectus², -ūs m look, sight; glance, sense of sight; aspect, appearance

aspellō, -ere vt to drive away

asper, -ī adj rough; (taste) bitter; (sound) harsh; (weather) severe; (style) rugged; (person) violent, exasperated, unkind, austere; (animal) savage; (circumstances) difficult

asperē adv see asper

aspergō¹, -gere, -sī, -sum vt to scatter, sprinkle; to bespatter, besprinkle; **aquam aspergere** revive

aspergō², -inis f sprinkling; spray

asperitās, -ātis f roughness, unevenness, harshness, severity; (fig) ruggedness, fierceness; trouble, difficulty

aspernātiō, -ōnis f disdain

aspernor, -ārī, -ātus vt to reject, disdain

asperō, -āre, -āvī, -ātum vt to roughen, sharpen; to exasperate

aspersiō, -ōnis f sprinkling

aspersus ppp of **aspergō¹**

aspiciō, -icere, -exī, -ectum vt to catch sight of, look at; (places) to face; (fig) to examine, consider

aspīrātiō, -ōnis f breathing (on); evaporation; pronouncing with an aspirate

aspīrō, -āre, -āvī, -ātum vi to breathe, blow; to favour; to aspire, attain (to) ♦ vt to blow, instil

aspis, -dis f asp

asportātiō, -ōnis f removal

asportō, -āre vt to carry off

asprēta, -ōrum ntpl rough country

ass- etc see ads-

Assaracus, -ī m Trojan ancestor of Aeneas

asser, -is m pole, stake

assula, -ae f splinter

assulātim adv in splinters

assum, -ī nt roast; (pl) sweating-bath

assus adj roasted

Assyria, -ae f country in W. Asia

Assyrius adj Assyrian; oriental

ast conj (laws) and then; (vows) then; (strong contrast) and yet

ast- etc see adst-

Astraea, -ae f goddess of Justice

Astraeus, -ī m father of winds; **Astraeī frātrēs** the winds

astrologia, -ae f astronomy

astrologus, -ī m astronomer; astrologer

astrum, -ī nt star, heavenly body, constellation; a great height; heaven, immortality, glory

astu nt (indecl) city (esp Athens)

astus, -ūs m cleverness, cunning

astūtē adv cleverly

astūtia, -ae f slyness, cunning

astūtus adj artful, sly

Astyanax, -ctis m son of Hector and Andromache

asӯlum, -ī nt sanctuary

asymbolus adj with no contribution

at conj (adversative) but, on the other hand; (objecting) but it may be said; (limiting) at least, but at least; (continuing) then, thereupon; (transitional) now; (with passionate appeals) but oh!, look now!; **at enim** yes, but; **at tamen** nevertheless

Atābulus, -ī m sirocco

atat interj (expressing fright, pain, surprise) oh!

atavus, -ī m great-great-great-grandfather; ancestor

Atella, -ae f Oscan town in Campania

Ātellānicus, Atellānius adj see Atella

Atellānus adj: **fābula Atellāna** kind of comic show popular in Rome

āter, -rī adj black, dark; gloomy, dismal; malicious; **diēs ātrī** unlucky days

Athamantēus adj see Athamās

Athamantiadēs m Palaemon

Athamantis f Helle

Athamās, -antis m king of Thessaly (who went mad)

Athēnae, -ārum fpl Athens

Athēnaeus, Athēniēnsis adj see Athēnae

atheos, -ī m atheist

athlēta, -ae m wrestler, athlete

athlēticē adv athletically

Athos (dat **-ō**, acc **-ō, -on, -ōnem**) m mount Athos (in Macedonia)

Atlantiadēs m Mercury

Atlanticus adj: **mare Atlanticum** Atlantic Ocean

Atlantis f lost Atlantic island; a Pleiad

Atlās, -antis m giant supporting the sky; Atlas mountains

atomus, -ī m atom

atque (before consonants **ac**) conj (connecting words) and, and in fact; (connecting clauses) and moreover, and then, and so, and yet; (in comparison) as, than, to, from; **~ adeō** and that too; or rather; **~ nōn** and not rather; **~ sī** as if; **alius ~** different from; **contrā ~** opposite to; **idem ~** same as; **plūs ~** more than

atquī conj (adversative) and yet, nevertheless, yes but; (confirming) by all means; (minor premise) now; **~ sī** if now

ātrāmentum, -ī nt ink; blacking

ātrātus adj in mourning

Atreus, -eī m son of Pelops (king of Argos)

Atrīdēs m Agamemnon; Menelaus

ātriēnsis, -is m steward, major-domo

ātriolum, -ī nt anteroom

ātrium, -ī and **-iī** nt hall, open central room in Roman house; forecourt of a temple; hall (in other buildings)

atrōcitās, -ātis f hideousness; (mind) brutality; (PHILOS) severity

atrōciter adv savagely

Atropos, -ī f one of the Fates

atrōx, -ōcis adj hideous, dreadful; fierce, brutal, unyielding

attāctus¹ ppp of **attingō**

attāctus², -ūs m contact

attagēn, -is m heathcock

Attalica ntpl garments of woven gold

Attalicus adj of Attalus; of Pergamum; ornamented with gold cloth

Attalus, -ī m king of Pergamum (who bequeathed his kingdom to Rome)

attamen conj nevertheless

attat *see* **atat**

attegia, -ae *f* hut

attemperātē *adv* opportunely

attempto *etc see* **attentō**

attendō, -dere, -dī, -tum *vt* to direct (*the attention*); attend to, notice

attentē *adv* carefully

attentiō, -ōnis *f* attentiveness

attentō, -āre, -āvī, -ātum *vt* to test, try; (*loyalty*) to tamper with; to attack

attentus¹ *ppp of* **attendō** ♦ *adj* attentive, intent; businesslike, careful (*esp about money*)

attentus² *ppp of* **attineō**

attenuātē *adv* simply

attenuātus *adj* weak; (*style*) brief; refined; plain

attenuō, -āre, -āvī, -ātum *vt* to weaken, reduce; to diminish; to humble

atterō, -erere, -rīvī, -rītum *vt* to rub; to wear away; (*fig*) to impair, exhaust

attestor, -ārī, -ātus *vt* to confirm

attexō, -ere, -uī, -tum *vt* to weave on; (*fig*) to add on

Atthis, -dis *f* Attica

Attiānus *adj see* **Attius**

Attica, -ae *f* district of Greece about Athens

Atticē *adv* in the Athenian manner

Atticissō *vi* to speak in the Athenian manner

Atticus *adj* Attic, Athenian; (RHET) of a plain and direct style

attigī *perf of* **attingō**

attigō *see* **attingō**

attineō, -inēre, -inuī, -entum *vt* to hold fast, detain; to guard; to reach for ♦ *vi* to concern, pertain, be of importance, avail

attingō, -ingere, -igī, -āctum *vt* to touch; to strike, assault; to arrive at; to border on; to affect; to mention; to undertake; to concern, resemble

Attis, -dis *m* Phrygian priest of Cybele

Attius, -ī *m* Latin tragic poet

attollō, -ere *vt* to lift up, erect; (*fig*) to exalt, extol

attondeō, -ondēre, -ondī, -ōnsum *vt* to shear, prune, crop; (*fig*) to diminish; (*comedy*) to fleece

attonitus *adj* thunderstruck, terrified, astonished; inspired

attonō, -āre, -uī, -itum *vt* to stupefy

attōnsus *ppp of* **attondeō**

attorqueō, -ēre *vt* to hurl upwards

attractus *ppp of* **attrahō**

attrahō, -here, -xī, -ctum *vt* to drag by force, attract; (*fig*) to draw, incite

attrectō, -āre *vt* to touch, handle; to appropriate

attrepidō, -āre *vi* to hobble along

attribuō, -uere, -uī, -ūtum *vt* to assign, bestow; to add; to impute, attribute; to lay as a tax

attribūtiō, -ōnis *f* (*money*) assignment; (GRAM) predicate

attribūtum, -ī *nt* (GRAM) predicate

attribūtus *ppp of* **attribuō** ♦ *adj* subject

attrītus *ppp of* **atterō** ♦ *adj* worn; bruised; (*fig*) impudent

attulī *perf of* **adferō**

au *interj* (*expressing pain, surprise*) oh!

auceps, -upis *m* fowler; (*fig*) eavesdropper; a pedantic critic

auctārium, -ī *and* **-iī** *nt* extra

auctificus *adj* increasing

auctiō, -ōnis *f* increase; auction sale

auctiōnārius *adj* auction; **tabulae auctiōnāriae** catalogues

auctiōnor, -ārī, -ātus *vi* to hold an auction

auctitō, -āre *vt* to greatly increase

auctō, -āre *vt* to increase

auctor, -ōris *m/f* **1.** (*originator: of families*) progenitor; (*of buildings*) founder; (: *of deeds*) doer **2.** (*composer: of writings*) author, historian; (: *of knowledge*) investigator, teacher; (: *of news*) informant **3.** (*instigator: of action*) adviser; (: *of measures*) promoter; (: *of laws*) proposer, supporter; ratifier **4.** (*person of influence: in public life*) leader; (: *of conduct*) model; (: *of guarantees*) witness, bail; (: *of property*) seller; (: *of women and minors*) guardian; (: *of others' welfare*) champion; **mē auctōre** at my suggestion

auctōrāmentum, -ī *nt* contract; wages

auctōrātus *adj* bound (*by a pledge*); hired out (*for wages*)

auctōritās, -ātis *f* **1.** source; lead, responsibility **2.** judgment; opinion; advice, support; bidding, guidance; (*of senate*) decree; (*of people*) will **3.** power; (*person*) influence, authority, prestige; (*things*) importance, worth; (*conduct*) example; (*knowledge*) warrant, document, authority; (*property*) right of possession

auctumn- *etc see* **autumn-**

auctus¹ *ppp of* **augeō** ♦ *adj* enlarged, great

auctus², -ūs *m* growth, increase

aucupium, -ī *and* **-iī** *nt* fowling; birds caught; (*fig*) hunting (after); quibbling

aucupō, -āre *vt* to watch for

aucupor, -ārī, -ātus *vi* to go fowling ♦ *vt* to chase; (*fig*) to try to catch

audācia, -ae *f* daring, courage; audacity, impudence; (*pl*) deeds of daring

audācter, -ācius *adv see* **audāx**

audāx, -ācis *adj* bold, daring; rash, audacious; proud

audēns, -entis *adj* bold, brave

audenter *adv see* **audēns**

audentia, -ae *f* boldness, courage

audeō, -dēre, -sus *vt*, *vi* to dare, venture; to be brave

audiēns, -entis *m* hearer ♦ *adj* obedient

audientia, -ae *f* hearing; **audientiam facere** gain a hearing

audiō, -īre, -īvī *and* **-iī, -ītum** *vt* to hear; to learn, be told; to be called; to listen, attend to, study under (*a teacher*); to examine (*a case*); to agree with; to obey, heed; **bene/male audīre** have a good/bad reputation

audītiō, -ōnis *f* listening; hearsay, news

audītor, -ōris *m* hearer; pupil

audītōrium, -ī *and* **-iī** *nt* lecture room, law court; audience

audītus, -ūs *m* (sense of) hearing; a hearing; rumour

auferō, auferre, abstulī, ablātum *vt* to take away, carry away; to mislead, lead into a digression; to take by force, steal; to win, obtain (*as the result of effort*); **aufer** away with!

Aufidus, -ō *m river in Apulia*

aufugiō, -ugere, -ūgī *vi* to run away ♦ *vt* to flee from

Augēās, -ae *m king of Elis (whose stables Hercules cleaned)*

augeō, -gēre, -xī, -ctum *vt* to increase; to enrich, bless (with); to praise, worship ♦ *vi* to increase

augēscō, -ere *vi* to begin to grow, increase

augmen, -inis *nt* growth

augur, -is *m/f* augur; prophet, interpreter

augurāle, -is *nt part of camp where auspices were taken*

augurālis *adj* augur's

augurātiō, -ōnis *f* soothsaying

augurātō *adv* after taking auspices

augurātus, -ūs *m* office of augur

augurium, -ī *and* **-ī** *nt* augury; an omen; prophecy, interpretation; presentiment

augurius *adj* of augurs

augurō, -āre *vt, vi* to take auguries; to consecrate by auguries; to forebode

auguror, -ārī, -ātus *vt, vi* to take auguries; to foretell by omens; to predict, conjecture

Augusta, -ae *f title of the emperor's wife, mother, daughter or sister*

Augustālis *adj* of Augustus; **lūdī Augustālēs** games in October; **praefectus ~** governor of Egypt; **sodālēs Augustālēs** priests of deified Augustus

augustē *adv see* **augustus**

Augustus, -ī *m title given to C Octavius, first Roman emperor, and so to his successors* ♦ *adj* imperial; (*month*) August, of August

augustus *adj* venerable, august, majestic

aula¹, -ae *f* courtyard (*of a Greek house*); hall (*of a Roman house*); palace, royal court; courtiers; royal power

aula² *etc see* **olla**

aulaeum, -ī *nt* embroidered hangings, canopy, covering; (THEAT) curtain

aulicī, -ōrum *mpl* courtiers

aulicus *adj* of the court

Aulis, -idis *and* **-is** *f port in Boeotia from which the Greeks sailed for Troy*

auloedus, -ī *m* singer accompanied by flute

aura, -ae *f* breath of air, breeze, wind; air, upper world; vapour, odour, sound, gleam; (*fig*) winds (*of public favour*), breeze (*of prosperity*), air (*of freedom*), daylight (*of publicity*)

aurāria, -ae *f* gold mine

aurārius *adj* of gold

aurātus *adj* gilt, ornamented with gold; gold

Aurēlius, -ī *m Roman name;* **lēx Aurēlia** *law on the composition of juries;* **via Aurēlia** *main road running NW from Rome*

aureolus *adj* gold; beautiful, splendid

aureus *adj* gold, golden; gilded; (*fig*) beautiful, splendid ♦ *m* gold coin

aurichalcum, -ī *nt a precious metal*

auricomus *adj* golden-leaved

auricula, -ae *f* the external ear; ear

aurifer, -ī *adj* gold-producing

aurifex, -icis *m* goldsmith

aurīga, -ae *m* charioteer, driver; groom; helmsman; *a constellation*

aurigena, -ae *adj* gold-begotten

auriger, -ī *adj* gilded

aurīgō, -āre *vi* to compete in the chariot race

auris, -is *f* ear; (RHET) judgment; (AGR) earthboard (*of a plough*); **ad aurem admonēre** whisper; **in utramvis aurem dormīre** sleep soundly

aurītulus, -ī *m* "Long-Ears"

aurītus *adj* long-eared; attentive

aurōra, -ae *f* dawn, morning; *goddess of dawn;* the East

aurum, -ī *nt* gold; gold plate, jewellery, bit, fleece *etc*; money; lustre; the Golden Age

auscultātiō, -ōnis *f* obedience

auscultātor, -ōris *m* listener

auscultō, -āre, -āvī, -ātum *vt* to listen to; to overhear ♦ *vi* (*of servants*) to wait at the door; to obey

ausim *subj of* **audeō**

Ausones, -um *mpl indigenous people of central Italy*

Ausonia *f Italy*

Ausonidae, -um *mpl Italians*

Ausonius, -is *adj Italian*

auspex, -icis *m* augur, soothsayer; patron, commander; witness of a marriage contract

auspicātō *adv* after taking auspices; at a lucky moment

auspicātus *adj* consecrated; auspicious, lucky

auspicium, -ī *and* **-ī** *nt* augury, auspices; right of taking auspices; power, command; omen; **~ facere** give a sign

auspicō, -āre *vi* to take the auspices

auspicor, -ārī, -ātus *vi* to take the auspices; to make a beginning ♦ *vt* to begin, enter upon

auster, -rī *m* south wind; south

austērē *adv see* **austērus**

austēritās, -ātis *f* severity

austērus *adj* severe, serious; gloomy, irksome

austrālis *adj* southern

austrīnus *adj* from the south

ausum, -ī *nt* enterprise

ausus *ppa of* **audeō**

aut *conj* or; either ... or; or else, or at least, or rather

autem *conj* (*adversative*) but, on the other hand; (*in transitions, parentheses*) moreover, now, and; (*in dialogue*) indeed

authepsa, -ae *f* stove

autographus *adj* written with his own hand

Autolycus, -ī *m* a robber

automaton, -ī *nt* automaton

automatus *adj* spontaneous

Automedōn, -ontis *m* a charioteer

autumnālis *adj* autumn, autumnal

autumnus, -ī *m* autumn ♦ *adj* autumnal

autumō, -āre *vt* to assert

auxī *perf of* **augeō**

auxilia, -iōrum *ntpl* auxiliary troops; military force

auxiliāris *adj* helping, auxiliary; of the auxiliaries ♦ *mpl* auxiliary troops

auxiliārius *adj* helping; auxiliary

auxiliātor, **-ōris** *m* helper
auxiliātus, **-ūs** *m* aid
auxilior, **-ārī**, **-ātus** *vi* to aid, support
auxilium, **-ī** *and* **-iī** *nt* help, assistance
avārē, **avāriter** *adv see* **avārus**
avāritia, **-ae** *f* greed, selfishness
avāritiēs, **-ēī** *f* avarice
avārus *adj* greedy, covetous; eager
avē, **avēte**, **avētō** *impv* hail!, farewell!
āvehō, **-here**, **-xī**, **-ctum** *vt* to carry away; (*pass*) to ride away
āvellō, **-ellere**, **-ellī** *and* **-ulsī**, **(-olsī)**, **-ulsum**, **(-olsum)** *vt* to pull away, tear off; to take away (by force), remove
avēna, **-ae** *f* oats; (*music*) reed, shepherd's pipe
avēns, **-entis** *adj* eager
Aventīnum, **-ī** *nt* Aventine hill
Aventīnus, **-ī** *m* Aventine (hill) (*in Rome*) ✦ *adj* of Aventine
aveō, **-ēre** *vt* to desire, long for
Avernālis *adj* of lake Avernus
Avernus, **-ī** *m* lake near Cumae (*said to be an entrance to the lower world*); the lower world ✦ *adj* birdless; of Avernus; infernal
āverruncō, **-āre** *vt* to avert
āversābilis *adj* abominable
āversor¹, **-ārī**, **-ātus** *vi* to turn away ✦ *vt* to repulse, decline
āversor², **-ōris** *m* embezzler
āversum, **-ī** *nt* back
āversus *ppp of* **āvertō** ✦ *adj* in the rear, behind, backwards; hostile, averse

āvertō, **-tere**, **-tī**, **-sum** *vt* to turn aside, avert; to divert; to embezzle; to estrange ✦ *vi* to withdraw
avia¹, **-ae** *f* grandmother
avia², **-ōrum** *ntpl* wilderness
aviārium, **-ī** *nt* aviary, haunt of birds
aviārius *adj* of birds
avidē *adv see* **avidus**
aviditās, **-ātis** *f* eagerness, longing; avarice
avidus *adj* eager, covetous; avaricious, greedy; hungry; vast
avis, **-is** *f* bird; omen; ~ **alba** a rarity
avītus *adj* of a grandfather; ancestral
āvius *adj* out of the way, lonely, untrodden; wandering, astray
āvocāmentum, **-ī** *nt* relaxation
āvocātiō, **-ōnis** *f* diversion
āvocō, **-āre** *vt* to call off; to divert, distract; to amuse
āvolō, **-āre** *vi* to fly away, hurry away; to depart, vanish
āvolsus, **avulsus** *ppp of* **āvellō**
avunculus, **-ī** *m* uncle (*on mother's side*); ~ **magnus** great-uncle
avus, **-ī** *m* grandfather; ancestor
Axenus, **-ī** *m* Black Sea
axicia, **axitia**, **-ae** *f* scissors
āxilla, **-ae** *f* armpit
axis, **-is** *m* axle, chariot; axis, pole, sky, clime; plank
azȳmus *adj* unleavened

Bb

babae *interj (expressing wonder or joy)* oho!
Babylōn, -ōnis *f ancient city on the Euphrates*
Babylōnia *f the country under Babylon*
Babylōnicus, Babylōniēnsis *adj see* **Babylōnia**
Babylōnius *adj* Babylonian; Chaldaean; versed in astrology
bāca, -ae *f* berry; olive; fruit; pearl
bācātus *adj* of pearls
bacca *etc see* **bāca**
baccar, -is *nt* cyclamen
Baccha, -ae *f* Bacchante
Bacchānal, -ālis *nt place consecrated to Bacchus; (pl)* festival of Bacchus
bacchātiō, -ōnis *f* revel
Bacchēus, Bacchīcus, Bacchius *adj see* **Bacchus**
Bacchiadae, -ārum *mpl kings of Corinth (founders of Syracuse)*
bacchor, -ārī, -ātus *vi* to celebrate the festival of Bacchus; to revel, rave; to rage
Bacchus, -ī *m god of wine, vegetation, poetry, and religious ecstasy;* vine, wine
bācifer, -ī *adj* olive-bearing
bacillum, -ī *nt* stick, lictor's staff
Bactra, -ōrum *ntpl capital of Bactria in central Asia (now Balkh)*
Bactriāna *f* Bactria
Bactriānus, Bactrius *adj* Bactrian
baculum, -ī *nt,* **baculus, -ī** *m* stick, staff
Baetica *f Roman province (now Andalusia)*
Baeticus *adj see* **Baetis**
Baetis, -is *m river in Spain (now Guadalquivir)*
Bagrada, -ae *m river in Africa (now Medjerda)*
Bāiae, -ārum *fpl Roman spa on Bay of Naples*
Bāiānus *adj see* **Bāiae**
bāiulō, -āre *vt* to carry *(something heavy)*
bāiulus, -ī *m* porter
bālaena, -ae *f* whale
balanus, -ī *f* balsam *(from an Arabian nut);* a shellfish
balatrō, -ōnis *m* jester
bālātus, -ūs *m* bleating
balbus *adj* stammering
balbūtiō, -īre *vt, vi* to stammer, speak indistinctly; *(fig)* to speak obscurely
Baleārēs, -ium *fpl* Balearic islands
Baleāris, Baleāricus *adj see* **Baleārēs**
balineum *etc see* **balneum** *etc*
ballista, -ae *f (MIL)* catapult *for shooting stones and other missiles; (fig)* weapon
ballistārium, -ī and -iī *nt* catapult

balneae, -ārum *fpl* bath, baths
balneāria, -ōrum *ntpl* bathroom
balneārius *adj* of the baths
balneātor, -ōris *m* bath superintendent
balneolum, -ī *nt* small bath
balneum, -ī *nt* bath
bālō, -āre *vi* to bleat
balsamum, -ī *nt* balsam, balsam tree
baltea, -ōrum *ntpl* belt *(esp swordbelt; woman's girdle; strapping)*
balteus, -ī *m* belt *(esp swordbelt; woman's girdle; strapping)*
Bandusia, -ae *f spring near Horace's birthplace*
baptisma, -tis *nt* baptism
baptizō, -āre *vt (ECCL)* to baptize
barathrum, -ī *nt* abyss; the lower world; *(fig)* a greedy person
barba, -ae *f* beard
barbarē *adv* in a foreign language *(to a Greek),* in Latin; in an uncivilized way; roughly, cruelly
barbaria, -ae, barbariēs *(acc* **-em)** *f* a foreign country *(outside Greece or Italy); (words)* barbarism; *(manners)* rudeness, stupidity
barbaricus *adj* foreign, outlandish *(to a Greek),* Italian
barbarus *adj* foreign, barbarous; *(to a Greek)* Italian; rude, uncivilized; savage, barbarous ♦ *m* foreigner, barbarian
barbātulus *adj* with a little beard
barbātus *adj* bearded, adult; ancient *(Romans);* of philosophers
barbiger, -ī *adj* bearded
barbitos *(acc* **-on)** *m* lyre, lute
barbula, -ae *f* little beard
Barcās, -ae *m ancestor of Hannibal*
Barcīnus *adj see* **Barcās**
bardus¹ *adj* dull, stupid
bardus², -ī *m* Gallic minstrel
bārō, -ōnis *m* dunce
barrus, -ī *m* elephant
bascauda, -ae *f* basket *(for the table)*
bāsiātiō, -ōnis *f* kiss
basilica, -ae *f* public building used as exchange and law court
basilicē *adv* royally, in magnificent style
basilicum, -ī *nt* regal robe
basilicus *adj* royal, magnificent ♦ *m* highest throw at dice
bāsiō, -āre *vt* to kiss
basis, -is *f* pedestal, base
bāsium, -ī and -iī *nt* kiss

Bassareus, -eī m Bacchus
Batāvī, -ōrum mpl people of Batavia (now Holland)
batillum, -ī nt firepan
Battiadēs, -ae m Callimachus
bātuō, -ere, -ī vt to beat
baubor, -ārī vi (of dogs) to howl
Baucis, -idis f wife of Philemon
beātē adv see **beātus**
beātitās, -ātis f happiness
beātitūdō, -inis f happiness
beātulus, -ī m the blessed man
beātus adj happy; prosperous, well-off; rich,
   abundant
Bēdriacēnsis adj see **Bēdriācum**
Bēdriācum, -ī nt village in N. Italy
Belgae, -ārum mpl people of N. Gaul (now Belgium)
Bēlides, -um fpl Danaids
Bēlīdēs, -īdae m Danaus, Aegyptus, Lynceus
bellāria, -ōrum ntpl dessert, confectionery
bellātor, -ōris m warrior, fighter ♦ adj warlike
bellātōrius adj aggressive
bellātrīx, -īcis f warrioress ♦ adj warlike
bellē adv well, nicely; ~ **habēre** be well (in health)
Bellerophōn, -ontis m slayer of Chimaera, rider of
   Pegasus
Bellerophontēus adj see **Bellerophōn**
bellicōsus adj warlike
bellicus adj of war, military; **bellicum canere**
   give the signal for marching or attack
belliger, -ī adj martial
belligerō, -āre, -āvī, -ātum vi to wage war
bellipotēns, -entis adj strong in war
bellō, -āre, -āvī, -ātum vi to fight, wage war
Bellōna, -ae f goddess of war
bellor, -ārī vi to fight
bellulus adj pretty
bellum, -ī nt war, warfare; battle; ~ **gerere** wage
   war; **bellī** in war
bellus adj pretty, handsome; pleasant, nice
bēlua, -ae f beast, monster (esp large and fierce),
   any animal; (fig) brute; ~ **Gaetula** Indian
   elephant
bēluātus adj embroidered with animals
bēluōsus adj full of monsters
Bēlus, -ī m Baal; an oriental king
Bēnācus, -ī m lake in N. Italy (now Garda)
bene adv (compar **melius**, superl **optimē**) well;
   correctly; profitably; very ♦ interj bravo!, good!;
   ~ **dīcere** speak well; speak well of, praise;
   ~ **emere** buy cheap; ~ **est tibi** you are well off;
   ~ **facere** do well; do good to; ~ **facis** thank you;
   rem ~ **gerere** be successful; ~ **sē habēre** have
   a good time; ~ **habet** all is well, it's all right;
   ~ **merērī dē** do a service to; ~ **partum** honestly
   acquired; ~ **tē** your health!; ~ **vēndere** sell at a
   high price; ~ **vīvere** live a happy life
benedīcō, -īcere, -īxī, -ictum vt to speak well of,
   praise; (ECCL) to bless
benedictiō, -ōnis f (ECCL) blessing
beneficentia, -ae f kindness
beneficiāriī, -ōrum mpl privileged soldiers
beneficium, -ī and **-iī** nt benefit, favour; (POL, MIL)
   promotion; **beneficiō tuō** thanks to you
beneficus adj generous, obliging
Beneventānus adj see **Beneventum**

Beneventum, -ī nt town in S. Italy (now
   Benevento)
benevolē adv see **benevolus**
benevolēns, -entis adj kind-hearted
benevolentia, -ae f goodwill, friendliness
benevolus adj kindly, friendly; (of servants)
   devoted
benīgnē adv willingly, courteously; generously;
   (colloq) no thank you; ~ **facere** do a favour
benīgnitās, -ātis f kindness; liberality, bounty
benīgnus adj kind, friendly; favourable; liberal,
   lavish; fruitful, bounteous
beō, -āre, -āvī, -ātum vt to gladden, bless,
   enrich
Berecyntia f Cybele
Berecyntius adj of Berecyntus; of Cybele
Berecyntus, -ī m mountain in Phrygia sacred to
   Cybele
Berenīcē, -ēs f a queen of Egypt; **coma Berenīcēs**
   a constellation
bēryllus, -ī m beryl
bēs, bessis m two-thirds of the as; two-thirds
bēstia, -ae f beast; wild animal (for the arena)
bēstiārius adj of beasts ♦ m beast fighter (in the
   arena)
bēstiola, -ae f small animal
bēta¹, -ae f beet
bēta² nt indecl (Greek letter) beta
bibī perf of **bibō**
bibliopōla, -ae m bookseller
bibliothēca, -ae, bibliothēcē, -ēs f library
bibō, -ere, -ī vt to drink; to live on the banks
   of (a river); to drink in, absorb; (fig) to listen
   attentively, be imbued; **bibere aquas** be
   drowned; **Graecō mōre bibere** drink to someone's
   health
Bibulus, -ī m consul with Caesar in 59 BC
bibulus adj fond of drink, thirsty; (things) thirsty
biceps, -ipitis adj two-headed
biclīnium, -ī and **-iī** nt dining couch for two
bicolor, -ōris adj two-coloured
bicorniger, -ī adj two-horned
bicornis adj two-horned, two-pronged; (rivers)
   two-mouthed
bicorpor, -is adj two-bodied
bidēns, -entis adj with two teeth or prongs ♦ m
   hoe ♦ f sheep (or other sacrificial animal)
bidental, -ālis nt a place struck by lightning
biduum, -ī nt two days
biennium, -ī and **-iī** nt two years
bifāriam adv in two parts, twice
bifer, -ī adj flowering twice a year
bifidus adj split in two
biforis adj double-doored; double
bifōrmātus, bifōrmis adj with two forms
bifrōns, -ontis adj two-headed
bifurcus adj two-pronged, forked
bīgae, -ārum fpl chariot and pair
bīgātus adj stamped with a chariot and pair
biiugī, -ōrum mpl two horses yoked abreast;
   chariot with two horses
biiugis, biiugus adj yoked
bilībra, -ae f two pounds
bilībris adj holding two pounds

bilinguis *adj* double-tongued; bilingual; deceitful

bīlis, -is *f* bile, gall; (*fig*) anger, displeasure; ~ **ātra**, ~ **nigra** melancholy; madness

bilīx, -īcis *adj* double-stranded

bilūstris *adj* ten years

bimaris *adj* between two seas

bimarītus, -ī *m* bigamist

bimāter, -ris *adj* having two mothers

bimembris *adj* half man, half beast; (*pl*) Centaurs

bimēstris *adj* of two months, two months old

bimulus *adj* only two years old

bimus *adj* two years old, for two years

bīnī, bīnae, bīna *num* two each, two by two; a pair; (*with pl nouns having a meaning different from sg*) two

binoctium, -ī *and* **-iī** *nt* two nights

binōminis *adj* with two names

Biōn, -ōnis *m* satirical philosopher

Biōnēus *adj* satirical

bipalmis *adj* two spans long

bipartītō *adv* in two parts, in two directions

bipartītus *adj* divided in two

bipatēns, -entis *adj* double-opening

bipedālis *adj* two feet long, broad or thick

bipennifer, -ī *adj* wielding a battle-axe

bipennis *adj* two-edged ♦ *f* battle-axe

bipertītō *etc see* **bipartītō**

bipēs, -edis *adj* two-footed ♦ *m* biped

birēmis *adj* two-oared; with two banks of oars ♦ *f* two-oared skiff; galley with two banks of oars

bis *adv* twice, double; **bis ad eundem** make the same mistake twice; **bis diē, in diē** twice a day; **bis tantō, bis tantum** twice as much; **bis terque** frequently; **bis terve** seldom

bissextus, -ī *m intercalary day after 24th Feb*

Bistones, -um *mpl people of Thrace*

Bistonis *f Thracian woman, Bacchante*

Bistonius *adj Thracian*

bisulcilingua, -ae *adj* fork-tongued, deceitful

bisulcus *adj* cloven

Bīthȳnia, -iae *f province of Asia Minor*

Bīthȳnicus, Bīthȳnius *adj see* **Bīthȳnia**

bītō, -ere *vi* to go

bitūmen, -inis *nt* bitumen, *a kind of pitch*

bitūmineus *adj see* **bitūmen**

bivium *nt* two ways

bivius *adj* two-way

blaesus *adj* lisping, indistinct

blandē *adv see* **blandus**

blandidicus *adj* fair-spoken

blandiloquentia, -ae *f* attractive language

blandiloquus, blandiloquentulus *adj* fair-spoken

blandīmentum, -ī *nt* compliment, allurement

blandior, -īrī, -ītus *vi* to coax, caress; to flatter, pay compliments; (*things*) to please, entice

blanditia, -ae *f* caress, flattery; charm, allurement

blandītim *adv* caressingly

blandus *adj* smooth-tongued, flattering, fawning; charming, winsome

blaterō, -āre *vi* to babble

blatiō, -īre *vt* to babble

blatta, -ae *f* cockroach

blennus, -ī *m* idiot

bliteus *adj* silly

blitum, -ī *nt kind of spinach*

boārius *adj* of cattle; **forum boārium** cattle market in Rome

Bodotria, -ae *f* Firth of Forth

Boeōtarchēs *m chief magistrate of Boeotia*

Boeōtia, -iae *f district of central Greece*

Boeōtius, Boeōtus *adj see* **Boeōtia**

boiae, -ārum *fpl* collar

Boiī, -ōrum *mpl people of S.E. Gaul*

Boiohaemī, -ōrum *mpl* Bohemians

bōlētus, -ī *m* mushroom

bolus, -ī *m* (*dice*) throw; (*net*) cast; (*fig*) haul, piece of good luck; titbit

bombus, -ī *m* booming, humming, buzzing

bombȳcinus *adj* of silk

bombȳx, -ȳcis *m* silkworm; silk

Bona Dea, Bonae Deae *f goddess worshipped by women*

bonitās, -ātis *f* goodness; honesty, integrity; kindness, affability

Bonōnia, -ae *f town in N. Italy (now Bologna)*

Bonōniēnsis *adj see* **Bonōnia**

bonum, -ī *nt* a moral good; advantage, blessing; (*pl*) property; **cuī bonō?** who was the gainer?

bonus *adj* (*compar* **melior**, *superl* **optimus**) good; kind; brave; loyal; beneficial; lucky ♦ *mpl* upper class party, conservatives; **bona aetās** prime of life; **bonō animō** of good cheer; well-disposed; **bonae artēs** integrity; culture, liberal education; **bona dicta** witticisms; **bona fidēs** good faith; **bonī mōrēs** morality; **bonī nummī** genuine money; **bona pars** large part; conservative party; **bonae rēs** comforts, luxuries; prosperity; morality; **bonā veniā** with kind permission; **bona verba** words of good omen; well-chosen diction; **bona vōx** loud voice

boō, -āre *vi* to cry aloud

Boōtēs, -ae *nt constellation containing Arcturus*

Boreās, -ae *m* north wind; north

Boreus *adj see* **Boreās**

Borysthenēs, -is *m* (*river*) Dnieper

Borysthenidae *mpl dwellers near the Dnieper*

Borysthenius *adj see* **Borysthenidae**

bōs, bovis *m/f* ox, cow; kind of turbot; **bōs Lūca** elephant; **bovī clitellās impōnere** put a round peg in a square hole

Bosporānus, Bosporius *adj see* **Bosporus**

Bosporus, -ī *m strait from Black Sea to Sea of Marmora*

Bosporus Cimmerius *m strait from Sea of Azov to Black Sea*

Boudicca, -ae *f British queen (falsely called Boadicea)*

bovārius *etc see* **boārius**

Bovillae, -ārum *fpl ancient Latin town*

Bovillānus *adj see* **Bovillae**

bovillus *adj* of oxen

brācae, -ārum *fpl* trousers

brācātus, -ī *adj* trousered; barbarian (*esp of tribes beyond the Alps*)

bracchiālis *adj* of the arm

bracchiolum, **-ī** *nt* dainty arm
bracchium, **-ī** *and* **-iī** *nt* arm, forearm; *(shellfish)* claw; *(tree)* branch; *(sea)* arm; *(NAUT)* yardarm; *(MIL)* outwork, mole; **levī bracchiō, mollī bracchiō** casually
bractea *etc see* **brattea**
brassica, **-ae** *f* cabbage
brattea, **-ae** *f* gold leaf
bratteola, **-ae** *f* very fine gold leaf
Brennus, **-ī** *m Gallic chief who defeated the Romans*
brevī *adv* shortly, soon; briefly, in a few words
brevia, **-ium** *ntpl* shoals
breviārium, **-ī** *and* **-iī** *nt* summary, statistical survey, official report
breviculus *adj* shortish
breviloquēns, **-ēntis** *adj* brief
brevis *adj* short, small, shallow; brief, short-lived; concise
brevitās, **-ātis** *f* shortness, smallness; brevity, conciseness
breviter *adv* concisely
Brigantēs, **-um** *mpl British tribe in N. England*
Briganticus *adj see* **Brigantēs**
Brīsēis, **-idos** *f captive of Achilles*
Britannia, **-iae** *f* Britain; the British Isles
Britannicus *m son of emperor Claudius*
Britannus, **Britannicus** *adj see* **Britannia**
Bromius, **-ī** *and* **-iī** *m* Bacchus
brūma, **-ae** *f* winter solstice, midwinter; winter
brūmālis *adj* of the winter solstice; wintry; ~ **flexus** tropic of Capricorn
Brundisīnus *adj see* **Brundisium**
Brundisium, **-ī** *and* **-iī** *nt port in S.E. Italy (now* Brindisi)
Bruttiī, **-ōrum** *mpl people of the toe of Italy*
Bruttius *adj see* **Bruttiī**
Brūtus, **-ī** *m liberator of Rome from kings; murderer of Caesar*
brūtus *adj* heavy, unwieldy; stupid, irrational

bubīle, **-is** *nt* stall
būbo, **-ōnis** *m/f* owl
būbula, **-ae** *f* beef
bubulcitor, **-ārī** *vi* to drive oxen
bubulcus, **-ī** *m* ploughman
būbulus *adj* of cattle
būcaeda, **-ae** *m* flogged slave
bucca, **-ae** *f* cheek; mouth; ranter
buccō, **-ōnis** *m* babbler
buccula, **-ae** *f* visor
bucculentus *adj* fat-cheeked
būcerus *adj* horned
būcina, **-ae** *f* shepherd's horn; military trumpet; night watch
būcinātor, **-ōris** *m* trumpeter
būcolica, **-ōrum** *ntpl* pastoral poetry
būcula, **-ae** *f* young cow
būfō, **-ōnis** *m* toad
bulbus, **-ī** *m* bulb; onion
būlē, **-es** *f* Greek senate
būleuta *m* senator
būleutērium *nt* senate house
bulla, **-ae** *f* bubble; knob, stud; *gold charm worn round the neck by children of noblemen*
bullātus *adj* wearing the bulla; still a child
būmastus, **-ī** *f kind of vine*
būris, **-is** *m* plough-beam
Burrus *old form of* **Pyrrhus**
Busīris, **-idis** *m Egyptian king killed by Hercules*
bustirapus, **-ī** *m* graverobber
bustuārius *adj* at a funeral
bustum, **-ī** *nt* funeral place; tomb, grave
buxifer, **-ī** *adj* famed for its box trees
buxum, **-ī** *nt* boxwood; flute, top, comb, tablet
buxus, **-ī** *f* box tree; flute
Byzantium, **-ī** *and* **-iī** *nt city on Bosporus (later* Constantinople, now Istanbul)
Byzantius *adj see* **Byzantium**

Cc

caballīnus *adj* horse's

caballus, -ī *m* horse

cacātus *adj* impure

cachinnātiō, -ōnis *f* loud laughter

cachinnō¹, -āre *vi* to laugh, guffaw

cachinnō², -ōnis *m* scoffer

cachinnus, -ī *m* laugh, derisive laughter; (*waves*) splashing

cacō, -āre *vi* to evacuate the bowels

cacoēthes, -is *nt* (*fig*) itch

cacula, -ae *m* soldier's slave

cacūmen, -inis *nt* extremity, point, summit, treetop; (*fig*) height, limit

cacūminō, -āre *vt* to make pointed

Cācus, -ī *m* giant robber, son of Vulcan

cadāver, -is *nt* corpse, carcass

cadāverōsus *adj* ghastly

Cadmēa, -ēae *f* fortress of Thebes

Cadmēis, -ēidis *f* Agave; Ino; Semele

Cadmēus, Cadmēius *adj* of Cadmus; Theban

Cadmus, -ī *m* founder of Thebes

cadō, -ere, cecidī, cāsum *vi* to fall; to droop, die, be killed; (*ASTR*) to set; (*dice*) to be thrown; (*events*) to happen, turn out; (*money*) to be due; (*strength, speech, courage*) to diminish, cease, fail; (*wind, rage*) to subside; (*words*) to end; **cadere in** suit, agree with; come under; **cadere sub** be exposed to; **animīs cadere** be disheartened; **causā cadere** lose one's case

cādūceātor, -ōris *m* officer with flag of truce

cādūceus, -ī *m* herald's staff; Mercury's wand

cādūcifer, -ī *adj* with herald's staff

cadūcus *adj* falling, fallen; (*fig*) perishable, fleeting, vain; (*LAW*) without an heir ◆ *nt* property without an heir

Cadurcī, -ōrum *mpl* Gallic tribe

Cadurcum, -ī *nt* linen coverlet

cadus, -ī *m* jar, flask (*esp for wine*); urn

caecigenus *adj* born blind

Caeciliānus *adj see* **Caecilius**

Caecilius, -ī *m* Roman name (*esp early Latin comic poet*)

caecitās, -ātis *f* blindness

caecō, -āre, -āvī, -ātum *vt* to blind; to make obscure

Caecubum, -ī *nt* choice wine from the Ager Caecubus in S. Latium

caecus *adj* blind; invisible, secret; dark, obscure; (*fig*) aimless, unknown, uncertain; **appāret caecō** it's as clear as daylight; **domus caeca** a

house with no windows; **caecā diē emere** buy on credit; **caecum corpus** the back

caedēs, -is *f* murder, massacre; gore; the slain

caedō, -ere, cecīdī, caesum *vt* to cut; to strike; to kill, cut to pieces; (*animals*) to sacrifice

caelāmen, -inis *nt* engraved work

caelātor, -ōris *m* engraver

caelātūra, -ae *f* engraving in bas-relief

caelebs, -ibis *adj* unmarried (*bachelor or widower*); (*trees*) with no vine trained on

caeles, -itis *adj* celestial ◆ *mpl* the gods

caelestis, -is *adj* of the sky, heavenly; divine; glorious ◆ *mpl* the gods ◆ *ntpl* the heavenly bodies

Caeliānus *adj see* **Caelius**

caelibātus, -ūs *m* celibacy

caelicola, -ae *m* god

caelifer, -ī *adj* supporting the sky

Caelius, -ī *m* Roman name; Roman hill

caelō, -āre, -āvī, -ātum *vt* to engrave (*in relief on metals*), carve (*on wood*); (*fig*) to compose

caelum¹, -ī *nt* engraver's chisel

caelum², -ī *nt* sky, heaven; air, climate, weather; (*fig*) height of success, glory; ~ **ac terrās miscēre** create chaos; **ad ~ ferre** extol; **dē caelō dēlāpsus** a messiah; **dē caelō servāre** watch for omens; **dē caelō tangī** be struck by lightning; **digitō ~ attingere** be in the seventh heaven; **in caelumō esse** be overjoyed

caementum, -ī *nt* quarrystone, rubble

caenōsus *adj* muddy

caenum, -ī *nt* mud, filth

caepa, -ae *f,* **caepe, -is** *nt* onion

Caere (*gen* **-itis**, *abl* **-ēte**) *nt indecl, f* ancient Etruscan town

Caerēs, -itis *and* **-ētis** *adj*: **Caerite cērā dignī** like the disfranchised masses

caerimōnia, -ae *f* sanctity; veneration (*for gods*); religious usage, ritual

caeruleus, caerulus *adj* blue, dark blue, dark green, dusky ◆ *ntpl* the sea

Caesar, -is *m* Julius (*great Roman soldier, statesman, author*); Augustus; the emperor

Caesareus, Caesariānus, Caesarīnus *adj see* **Caesar**

caesariātus *adj* bushy-haired

caesariēs, -ēī *f* hair

caesīcius *adj* bluish

caesim *adv* with the edge of the sword; (*RHET*) in short clauses

caesius *adj* bluish grey, blue-eyed

caespes, -itis *m* sod, turf; mass of roots
caestus, -ūs *m* boxing glove
caesus *ppp of* **caedō**
caetra, -ae *f* targe
caetrātus *adj* armed with a targe
Caïcus, -ī *m* river in Asia Minor
Cāiēta, -ae, Cāiētē, -ēs *f* town in Latium
Cāius *etc see* **Gāius**[1]
Calaber, -rī *adj* Calabrian
Calabria *f* S.E. peninsula of Italy
Calamis, -idis *m* Greek sculptor
calamister, -rī *m*, **calamisterum, -rī** *nt* curling iron; (RHET) flourish
calamistrātus *adj* curled; foppish
calamitās, -ātis *f* disaster; (MIL) defeat; (AGR) damage, failure
calamitōsē *adv see* **calamitōsus**
calamitōsus *adj* disastrous, ruinous; blighted, unfortunate
calamus, -ī *m* reed; stalk; pen, pipe, arrow, fishing rod
calathiscus, -ī *m* small basket
calathus, -ī *m* wicker basket; bowl, cup
calātor, -ōris *m* servant
calcāneum, -ī *nt* heel
calcar, -āris *nt* spur
calceāmentum, -ī *nt* shoe
calceātus *ppp* shod
calceolārius, -ī *and* **-iī** *m* shoemaker
calceolus, -ī *m* small shoe
calceus, -ī *m* shoe
Calchās, -antis *m* Greek prophet at Troy
calcitrō, -āre *vi* to kick; (*fig*) to resist
calcō, -āre, -āvī, -ātum *vt* to tread, trample on; (*fig*) to spurn
calculus, -ī *m* pebble, stone; draughtsman, counting stone, reckoning, voting stone; **calculum redūcere** take back a move; **calculōs subdūcere** compute; **ad calculōs vocāre** subject to a reckoning
caldārius *adj* with warm water
caldus *etc see* **calidus**
Calēdonia, -ae *f* the Scottish Highlands
Calēdonius *adj see* **Calēdonia**
calefaciō, calfaciō, -facere, -fēcī, -factum *vt* to warm, heat; (*fig*) to provoke, excite
calefactō, -āre *vt* to warm
Calendae *see* **Kalendae**
Calēnus *adj* of Cales ♦ *nt* wine of Cales
caleō, -ēre *vi* to be warm, be hot, glow; (*mind*) to be inflamed; (*things*) to be pursued with enthusiasm; to be fresh
Calēs, -ium *fpl* town in Campania
calēscō, -ere, -uī *vi* to get hot; (*fig*) to become inflamed
calidē *adv* promptly
calidus *adj* warm, hot; (*fig*) fiery, eager; hasty; prompt ♦ *f* warm water ♦ *nt* warm drink
caliendrum, -ī *nt* headdress of hair
caliga, -ae *f* soldier's boot
caligātus *adj* heavily shod
cālīginōsus *adj* misty, obscure
cālīgō[1]**, -inis** *f* mist, fog; dimness, darkness; (*mind*) obtuseness; (*circumstances*) trouble

cālīgō[2]**, -āre** *vi* to be misty, be dim; to cause dizziness
Caligula, -ae *m* emperor Gaius
calix, -cis *m* wine cup; cooking pot
calleō, -ēre *vi* to be thick-skinned; (*fig*) to be unfeeling; to be wise, be skilful ♦ *vt* to know, understand
callidē *adv see* **callidus**
calliditās, -ātis *f* skill; cunning
callidus *adj* skilful, clever; crafty
Callimachus, -ī *m* Greek poet of Alexandria
Calliopē, -ēs, Calliopēa, -ēae *f* Muse of epic poetry
callis, -is *m* footpath, mountain track; pass; hill pastures
Callistō, -ūs *f* daughter of Lycaon; (*constellation*) Great Bear
callōsus *adj* hard-skinned; solid
callum, -ī *nt* hard or thick skin; firm flesh; (*fig*) callousness
cālō, -ōnis *m* soldier's servant; drudge
calō, -āre, -āvī, -ātum *vt* to convoke
calor, -ōris *m* warmth, heat; (*fig*) passion, love
Calpē, -ēs *f* Rock of Gibraltar
Calpurniānus *adj see* **Calpurnius**
Calpurnius, -ī *m* Roman name
caltha, -ae *f* marigold
calthula, -ae *f* yellow dress
caluī *perf of* **calēscō**
calumnia, -ae *f* chicanery, sharp practice; subterfuge; misrepresentation; (LAW) dishonest accusation, blackmail; being convicted of malicious prosecution; **calumniam iūrāre** swear that an action is brought in good faith
calumniātor, -ōris *m* legal trickster, slanderer
calumnior, -ārī, -ātus *vt* to misrepresent, slander; (LAW) to bring an action in bad faith; **sē calumniārī** deprecate oneself
calva, -ae *f* bald head
calvitium, -ī *and* **-iī** *nt* baldness
calvor, -ārī *vt* to deceive
calvus *adj* bald
calx[1]**, -cis** *f* heel; foot; **calce petere, calce ferīre** kick; **adversus stimulum calcēs** kicking against the pricks
calx[2]**, -cis** *f* pebble; lime, chalk; finishing line, end; **ad carcerēs ā calce revocārī** have to begin all over again
Calydōn, -ōnis *f* town in Aetolia
Calydōnis *adj* Calydonian
Calydōnius *f* Deianira; **~ amnis** Achelous; **~ hērōs** Meleager; **Calydōnia rēgna** Daunia in S. Italy
Calypsō, -ūs (*acc* **-ō**) *f* nymph who detained Ulysses in Ogygia
camēlīnus *adj* camel's
camella, -ae *f* wine cup
camēlus, -ī *m* camel
Camēna, -ae *f* Muse; poetry
camera, -ae *f* arched roof
Camerīnum, -ī *nt* town in Umbria
Camers, -tis, -tīnus *adj* of Camerinum
Camillus, -ī *m* Roman hero (who saved Rome from the Gauls)

camīnus, -ī *m* furnace, fire; forge; **oleum addere camīnō** add fuel to the flames

cammarus, -ī *m* lobster

Campānia, -iae *f district of W. Italy*

Campānicus, Campānicius *adj* Campanian, Capuan

campē, -ēs *f* evasion

campester, -ris *adj* of the plain; of the Campus Martius ♦ *nt* loincloth ♦ *ntpl* level ground

campus, -ī *m* plain; sports field; *any level surface;* (*fig*) theatre, arena (*of action, debate*); ~ **Martius** level ground by the Tiber (*used for assemblies, sports, military drills*)

Camulodūnum, -ī *nt town of Trinobantes (now* Colchester)

camur, -ī *adj* crooked

canālis, -is *m* pipe, conduit, canal

cancellī, -ōrum *mpl* grating, enclosure; barrier (*in public places*), bar of law court

cancer, -rī *m* crab; (*constellation*) Cancer; south, tropical heat; (MED) cancer

candefaciō, -ere *vt* to make dazzlingly white

candēla, -ae *f* taper, tallow candle; waxed cord; **candēlam appōnere valvīs** set the house on fire

candēlābrum, -ī *nt* candlestick, chandelier, lampstand

candēns, -entis *adj* dazzling white; white-hot

candeō, -ēre *vi* to shine, be white; to be white-hot

candēscō, -ere *vi* to become white; to grow white-hot

candidātōrius *adj* of a candidate

candidātus *adj* dressed in white ♦ *m* candidate for office

candidē *adv* in white; sincerely

candidulus *adj* pretty white

candidus *adj* white, bright; radiant, beautiful; clothed in white; (*style*) clear; (*mind*) candid, frank; (*circumstances*) happy; **candida sententia** acquittal

candor, -ōris *m* whiteness, brightness, beauty; (*fig*) brilliance, sincerity

cānēns, -entis *adj* white

cāneō, -ēre, -uī *vi* to be grey, be white

cānēscō, -ere *vi* to grow white; to grow old

canīcula, -ae *f* (*dog*) bitch; Dog Star, Sirius

canīnus *adj* dog's, canine; snarling, spiteful; **canīna littera** letter R

canis, -is *m/f* dog, bitch; (*fig*) shameless or angry person; hanger-on; (*dice*) lowest throw; (ASTR) Canis Major, Canis Minor; (*myth*) Cerberus

canistrum, -ī *nt* wicker basket

cānitiēs, -ēī *f* greyness; grey hair; old age

canna, -ae *f* reed; pipe; gondola

cannabis, -is *f* hemp

Cannae, -ārum *fpl village in Apulia (scene of great Roman defeat by Hannibal*)

Cannēnsis *adj see* **Cannae**

canō, canere, cecinī *vt, vi* to sing; to play; to sing about, recite, celebrate; to prophesy; (MIL) to sound; (*birds*) to sing, crow

canor, -ōris *m* song, tune, sound

canōrus *adj* musical, melodious; singsong ♦ *nt* melodiousness

Cantaber, -rī *m* Cantabrian

Cantabria, -riae *f district of N Spain*

Cantabricus *adj see* **Cantabria**

cantāmen, -inis *nt* charm

cantharis, -idis *f* beetle; Spanish fly

cantharus, -ī *m* tankard

canthērīnus *adj* of a horse

canthērius, -ī *and* **-iī** *m* gelding

canticum, -ī *nt* aria in Latin comedy; song

cantilēna, -ae *f* old song, gossip; **cantilēnam eandem canere** keep harping on the same theme

cantiō, -ōnis *f* song; charm

cantitō, -āre, -āvī, -atum *vt* to sing or play often

Cantium, -ī *and* **-iī** *nt* Kent

cantiunculae, -ārum *fpl* fascinating strains

cantō, -āre, -āvī, -ātum *vt, vi* to sing; to play; to sing about, recite, celebrate; to proclaim, harp on; to use magic spells; to sound; to drawl

cantor, -ōris *m,* **cantorīx, -rīcis** *f* singer, musician, poet; actor

cantus, -ūs *m* singing, playing, music; prophecy; magic spell

cānus *adj* white, grey, hoary; old ♦ *mpl* grey hairs

Canusīnus *adj see* **Canusium**

Canusium, -ī *nt town in Apulia (famous for wool*)

capācitās, -ātis *f* spaciousness

capāx, -ācis *adj* capable of holding, spacious, roomy; capable, able, fit

capēdō, -inis *f* sacrificial dish

capēduncula *f* small dish

capella, -ae *f* she-goat; (ASTR) bright star in Auriga

Capēna, -ae *f old Etruscan town*

Capēnās, Capēnus *adj:* **Porta Capēna** *Roman gate leading to the Via Appia*

caper, -rī *m* goat; odour of the armpits

caperrō, -āre *vi* to wrinkle

capessō, -ere, -īvī, -ītum *vt* to seize, take hold of, try to reach, make for; to take in hand, engage in; **rem pūblicam capessere** go in for politics

capillātus *adj* long-haired; ancient

capillus, -ī *m* hair (*of head or beard*), a hair

capiō, -ere, cēpī, captum *vt* to take, seize; to catch, capture; (MIL) to occupy, take prisoner; (NAUT) to make, reach (*a goal*); (*fig*) to captivate, charm, cheat; (*pass*) to be maimed, lose the use of; (*appearance*) to assume; (*habit*) to cultivate; (*duty*) to undertake; (*ideas*) to conceive, form; (*feeling*) to experience; (*harm*) to suffer; to receive, get, inherit; to contain, hold; (*fig*) to bear; (*mind*) to grasp; **cōnsilium capere** come to a decision; **impetum capere** gather momentum; **initium capere** start; **oculō capī** lose an eye; **mente captus** insane; **cupīdō eum cēpit** he felt a desire

capis, -dis *f sacrificial bowl with one handle*

capistrātus *adj* haltered

capistrum, -ī *nt* halter, muzzle

capital, -ālis *nt* capital crime

capitālis *adj* mortal, deadly, dangerous; (LAW) capital; important, excellent

capitō, -ōnis *m* bighead

Capitōlīnus adj of the Capitol; of Jupiter
Capitōlium, **-ī** nt Roman hill with temple of Jupiter
capitulātim adv summarily
capitulum, **-ī** nt small head; person, creature
Cappadocia, **-ae** f country of Asia Minor
capra, **-ae** f she-goat; odour of armpits; (ASTR) Capella
caprea, **-ae** f roe
Capreae, **-ārum** fpl island of Capri
capreolus, **-ī** m roebuck; (pl) crossbeams
Capricornus, **-ī** m (constellation) Capricorn (associated with midwinter)
caprificus, **-ī** f wild fig tree
caprigenus adj of goats
caprimulgus, **-ī** m goatherd, rustic
caprīnus adj of goats
capripēs, **-edis** adj goat-footed
capsa, **-ae** f box (esp for papyrus rolls)
capsō archaic fut of **capiō**
capsula, **-ae** f small box; **dē capsulā tōtus** out of a bandbox
Capta, **-ae** f Minerva
captātiō, **-ōnis** f catching at
captātor, **-ōris** m one who courts; legacy hunter
captiō, **-ōnis** f fraud; disadvantage; (argument) fallacy, sophism
captiōsē adv see **captiōsus**
captiōsus adj deceptive; dangerous; captious
captiuncula, **-ae** f quibble
captīvitās, **-ātis** f captivity; capture
captīvus adj captive, captured; of captives ♦ m/f prisoner of war
captō, **-āre**, **-āvī**, **-ātum** vt to try to catch, chase; to try to win, court, watch for; to deceive, trap
captus¹ ppp of **capiō** ♦ m prisoner
captus², **-ūs** m grasp, notion
Capua, **-ae** f chief town of Campania
capulāris adj due for a coffin
capulus, **-ī** m coffin; handle, hilt
caput, **-itis** nt head; top, extremity; (rivers) source; (more rarely) mouth; person, individual; life; civil rights; (person) chief, leader; (towns) capital; (money) principal; (writing) substance, chapter; principle, main point, the great thing; **cēnae** main dish; **capitis accūsāre** charge with a capital offence; **capitis damnāre** condemn to death; **capitis dēminūtiō** loss of political rights; **capitis poena** capital punishment; **capita cōnferre** confer in secret; **in capita** per head; **suprā ~ esse** be imminent
Cār, **-is** m Carian
carbaseus adj linen, canvas
carbasus, **-ī** f, **carbasa**, **-ōrum** ntpl Spanish flax, fine linen; garment, sail, curtain
carbō, **-ōnis** m charcoal, embers
carbōnārius, **-ī** and **-iī** m charcoal burner
carbunculus, **-ī** m small coal; precious stone
carcer, **-is** m prison; jailbird; barrier, starting place (for races); **ad carcerēs ā calce revocārī** have to begin all over again
carcerārius adj of a prison
carchēsium, **-ī** and **-iī** nt drinking cup; (NAUT) masthead

cardiacus, **-ī** m dyspeptic
cardō, **-inis** m hinge; (ASTR) pole, axis, cardinal point; (fig) juncture, critical moment
carduus, **-ī** m thistle
cārē adv see **cārus**
cārectum, **-ī** nt sedge
cāreō, **-ēre**, **-uī** vi (with abl) to be free from, not have, be without; to abstain from, be absent from; to want, miss
cārex, **-icis** f sedge
Cāria, **-ae** f district of S.W. Asia Minor
Cāricus adj Carian ♦ f dried fig
cariēs (acc **-em**, abl **-ē**) f dry rot
carīna, **-ae** f keel; ship
Carīnae, **-ārum** fpl district of Rome
carīnārius, **-ī** and **-iī** m dyer of yellow
cariōsus adj crumbling; (fig) withered
cāris, **-idis** f kind of crab
cāritās, **-ātis** f dearness, high price; esteem, affection
carmen, **-inis** nt song, tune; poem, poetry, verse; prophecy; (in law, religion) formula; moral text
Carmentālis adj see **Carmentis**
Carmentis, **-is**, **Carmentia**, **-ae** f prophetess, mother of Evander
carnārium, **-ī** and **-iī** nt fleshhook; larder
Carneadēs, **-is** m Greek philosopher (founder of the New Academy)
Carneadēus adj see **Carneadēs**
carnifex, **-icis** m executioner, hangman; scoundrel; murderer
carnificīna, **-ae** f execution; torture; **carnificīnam facere** be an executioner
carnificō, **-āre** vt to behead, mutilate
carnuf- etc see **carnif-**
cārō, **-ere** vt to card
carō, **-nis** f flesh
Carpathius adj see **Carpathus**
Carpathus, **-ī** f island between Crete and Rhodes
carpatina, **-ae** f leather shoe
carpentum, **-ī** nt two-wheeled coach
carpō, **-ere**, **-sī**, **-tum** vt to pick, pluck, gather; to tear off; to browse, graze on; (wool) to card; (fig) to enjoy, snatch; to carp at, slander; to weaken, wear down; to divide up; (journey) to go, travel
carptim adv in parts; at different points; at different times
carptor, **-ōris** m carver
carptus ppp of **carpō**
carrus, **-ī** m wagon
Carthāginiēnsis adj see **Carthāgō**
Carthāgō, **-inis** f Carthage (near Tunis); **~ Nova** town in Spain (now Cartagena)
caruncula, **-ae** f piece of flesh
cārus adj dear, costly; dear, beloved
Carystēus adj see **Carystos**
Carystos, **-ī** f town in Euboea (famous for marble)
casa, **-ae** f cottage, hut
cascus adj old
cāseolus, **-ī** m small cheese
cāseus, **-ī** m cheese
casia, **-ae** f cinnamon; spurge laurel
Caspius adj Caspian

Cassandra, -ae f Trojan princess and prophetess, doomed never to be believed

cassēs, -ium mpl net, snare; spider's web

Cassiānus adj see **Cassius**

cassida, -ae f helmet

Cassiopēa, -ae, Cassiopē, -ēs f mother of Andromeda; a constellation

cassis, -idis f helmet

Cassius, -ī m Roman family name

cassō, -āre vi to shake

cassus adj empty; devoid of, without (abl); vain, useless; ~ **lūmine** dead; **in cassum** in vain

Castalia, -ae f spring on Parnassus, sacred to Apollo and the Muses

Castalides, -dum fpl Muses

Castalius, -is adj see **Castalia**

castanea, -ae f chestnut tree; chestnut

castē adv see **castus**

castellānus adj of a fortress ♦ mpl garrison

castellātim adv in different fortresses

castellum, -ī nt fortress, castle; (fig) defence, refuge

castēria, -ae f rowers' quarters

castīgābilis adj punishable

castīgātiō, -ōnis f correction, reproof

castīgātor, -ōris m reprover

castīgātus adj small, slender

castīgō, -āre, -āvī, -ātum vt to correct, punish; to reprove; to restrain

castimōnia, -ae f purity, morality; chastity, abstinence

castitās, -ātis f chastity

Castor, -oris m twin brother of Pollux (patron of sailors); star in Gemini

castor, -oris m beaver

castoreum, -ī nt odorous secretion of the beaver

castra, -ōrum ntpl camp; day's march; army life; (fig) party, sect; ~ **movēre** strike camp; ~ **mūnīre** construct a camp; ~ **pōnere** pitch camp; **bīna** ~ two camps

castrēnsis adj of the camp, military

castrō, -āre vt to castrate; (fig) to weaken

castrum, -ī nt fort

castus adj clean, pure, chaste, innocent; holy, pious

cāsū adv by chance

casula, -ae f little cottage

cāsus, -ūs m fall, downfall; event, chance, accident; misfortune, death; opportunity; (time) end; (GRAM) case

Catadūpa, -ōrum ntpl Nile cataract near Syene

catagraphus adj painted

Catamītus, -ī m Ganymede

cataphractēs, -ae m coat of mail

cataphractus adj wearing mail

cataplus, -ī m ship arriving

catapulta, -ae f (MIL) catapult; (fig) missile

catapultārius adj thrown by catapult

cataracta, -ae f waterfall; sluice; drawbridge

catasta, -ae f stage, scaffold

catē adv see **catus**

catēia, -ae f javelin

catella, -ae f small chain

catellus, -ī m puppy

catēna, -ae f chain; fetter; (fig) bond, restraint; series

catēnātus adj chained, fettered

caterva, -ae f crowd, band; flock; (MIL) troop, body; (THEAT) company

catervātim adv in companies

cathedra, -ae f armchair, sedan chair; teacher's chair

catholicus adj (ECCL) orthodox, universal

Catilīna, -ae m Catiline (conspirator suppressed by Cicero)

Catilīnārius adj see **Catilīna**

catillō, -āre vt to lick a plate

catillus, -ī m small dish

catīnus, -ī m dish, pot

Catō, -ōnis m famous censor and author, idealized as the pattern of an ancient Roman; famous Stoic and republican leader against Caesar

Catōniānus adj see **Catō**

Catōnīnī mpl Cato's supporters

catōnium, -ī and **-iī** nt the lower world

Catulliānus adj see **Catullus**

Catullus, -ī m Latin lyric poet

catulus, -ī m puppy; cub, young of other animals

catus adj clever, wise; sly, cunning

Caucasius adj see **Caucasus**

Caucasus, -ī m Caucasus (mountains)

cauda, -ae f tail; **caudam iactāre** fawn; **caudam trahere** be made a fool of

caudeus adj wooden

caudex, -icis m trunk; block of wood; book, ledger; (fig) blockhead

caudicālis adj of woodcutting

Caudīnus adj see **Caudium**

Caudium, -ī nt Samnite town

caulae, -ārum fpl opening; sheepfold

caulis, -is m stalk; cabbage

Cauneus adj Caunian

Caunus, -ī f town in Caria ♦ fpl dried figs

caupō, -ōnis m shopkeeper, innkeeper

caupōna, -ae f shop, inn

caupōnius adj see **caupō**

caupōnor, -ārī vt to trade in

caupōnula, -ae f tavern

Caurus, -ī m north-west wind

causa, -ae f cause, reason; purpose, sake; excuse, pretext; opportunity; connection, case, position; (LAW) case, suit; (POL) cause, party; (RHET) subject matter; **causam agere, causam ōrāre** plead a case; **causam dēfendere** speak for the defence; **causam dīcere** defend oneself; **causā** for the sake of; **cum causā** with good reason; **quā dē causā** for this reason; **in causā esse** be responsible; **per causam** under the pretext

causārius adj (MIL) unfit for service

causia, -ae f Macedonian hat

causidicus, -ī m advocate

causificor, -ārī vi to make a pretext

causor, -ārī, -ātus vt, vi to pretend, make an excuse of

caussa etc see **causa**

causula, -ae f petty lawsuit; slight cause

cautē adv carefully, cautiously; with security

cautēla, -ae f caution

cautēs, -is f rock, crag

cautim adv warily

cautiō, -ōnis f caution, wariness; (LAW) security, bond, bail; **mihi ~ est** I must take care; **mea ~ est** I must see to it

cautor, -ōris m wary person; surety

cautus ppp of **caveō** ♦ adj wary, provident; safe, secure

cavaedium, -ī and **-iī** nt inner court (of a house)

cavea, -ae f cage, stall, coop, hive; (THEAT) auditorium; theatre; **prīma ~** upper class seats; **ultima ~** lower class seats

caveō, -ēre, cāvī, cautum vt to beware of, guard against ♦ vi (+ **ab** or abl) to be on one's guard against; (with dat) to look after; (with nē) to take care that ... not; (with ut) to take good care that; (with subj or inf) to take care not to, do not; (LAW) to stipulate, decree; (COMM) to get a guarantee, give a guarantee, stand security; **cavē** look out!

caverna, -ae f hollow, cave, vault; (NAUT) hold

cavilla, -ae f jeering

cavillātiō, -ōnis f jeering, banter; sophistry

cavillātor, -ōris m scoffer

cavillor, -ārī, -ātus vt to scoff at ♦ vi to jeer, scoff; to quibble

cavō, -āre, -āvī, -ātum vt to hollow, excavate

cavus adj hollow, concave, vaulted; (river) deep-channelled ♦ nt cavity, hole

Caystros, Caystrus, -ī m river in Lydia (famous for swans)

-ce demonstrative particle appended to pronouns and adverbs

Cēa, -ae f Aegean island (birthplace of Simonides)

cecidī perf of **cadō**

cecīdī perf of **caedō**

cecinī perf of **canō**

Cecropidēs, -idae m Theseus; Athenian

Cecropis, -idis f Aglauros; Procne; Philomela; Athenian, Attic

Cecropius adj Athenian ♦ f Athens

Cecrops, -is m ancient king of Athens

cedo (pl **cette**) impv give me, bring here; tell me; let me; look at!

cēdō, -ere, cessī, cessum vi to go, walk; to depart, withdraw, retreat; to pass away, die; (events) to turn out; to be changed (into); to accrue (to); to yield, be inferior (to) ♦ vt to give up, concede, allow; **cēdere bonīs, cēdere possessiōne** make over property (to); **cēdere forō** go bankrupt; **cēdere locō** leave one's post; **cēdere memoriā** be forgotten

cedrus, -ī f cedar, perfumed juniper; cedar oil

Celaenō, -ūs f a Harpy; a Pleiad

cēlāta ntpl secrets

celeber, -ris adj crowded, populous; honoured, famous; repeated

celebrātiō, -ōnis f throng; celebration

celebrātus adj full, much used; festive; famous

celebritās, -ātis f crowd; celebration; fame

celebrō, -āre, -āvī, -ātum vt to crowd, frequent; to repeat, practise; to celebrate, keep (a festival); to advertise, glorify

celer, -is adj quick, swift, fast; hasty

Celerēs, -um mpl royal bodyguard

celeripēs, -edis adj swift-footed

celeritās, -ātis f speed, quickness

celeriter adv see **celer**

celerō, -āre vt to quicken ♦ vi to make haste

cella, -ae f granary, stall, cell; garret, hut, small room; sanctuary (of a temple)

cellārius adj of the storeroom ♦ m steward

cellula, -ae f little room

cēlō, -āre, -āvī, -ātum vt to hide, conceal, keep secret; **id mē cēlat** he keeps me in the dark about it

celōx, -ōcis adj swift ♦ f fast ship, yacht

celsus adj high, lofty; (fig) great, eminent; haughty

Celtae, -ārum mpl Celts (esp of central Gaul) ♦ nt the Celtic nation

Celtibērī, -ōrum mpl people of central Spain

Celtibēria, -iae f Central Spain

Celtibēricus adj see **Celtibēria**

Celticus adj Celtic

cēna, -ae f dinner (the principal Roman meal); **inter cēnam** at table

cēnāculum, -ī nt dining-room; upper room, garret

cēnāticus adj of dinner

cēnātiō, -ōnis f dining-room

cēnātus ppa having dined, after dinner ♦ ppp spent in feasting

Cenchreae, -ārum fpl harbour of Corinth

cēnitō, -āre vi to be accustomed to dine

cēnō, -āre, -āvī, -ātum vi to dine ♦ vt to eat, dine on

cēnseō, -ēre, -uī, -um vt (census) to assess, rate, take a census, make a property return; (fig) to estimate, appreciate, celebrate; (senate or other body) to decree, resolve; (member) to express an opinion, move, vote; to advise; to judge, think, suppose, consider; **cēnsuī cēnsendō for** census purposes

cēnsiō, -ōnis f punishment; expression of opinion

cēnsor, -ōris m censor; (fig) severe judge, critic

cēnsōrius adj of the censors, to be dealt with by the censors; (fig) severe; **homō ~** an ex-censor

cēnsūra, -ae f censorship; criticism

cēnsus[1] ppp of **cēnseō**; **capite cēnsī** the poorest class of Roman citizens

cēnsus[2], -ūs m register of Roman citizens and their property, census; registered property; wealth; **cēnsum agere, cēnsum habēre** hold a census; **sine cēnsū** poor

centaurēum, -ī nt centaury

Centaurēus adj see **Centaurus**

Centaurus, -ī m Centaur, half man, half horse

centēnī, -um num a hundred each, a hundred

centēsimus adj hundredth ♦ f hundredth part; (interest) 1 per cent monthly (12 per cent per annum)

centiceps adj hundred-headed

centiēns, -ēs adv a hundred times

centimanus adj hundred-handed

centō, -ōnis m patchwork; **centōnēs sarcīre** tell tall stories

centum num a hundred

centumgeminus adj hundred-fold

centumplex adj hundred-fold

centumpondium, **-ī** *and* **-iī** *nt* a hundred pounds

centumvirālis *adj* of the centumviri

centumvirī, **-ōrum** *mpl* a bench of judges who heard special civil cases in Rome

centunculus, **-ī** *m* piece of patchwork, saddlecloth

centuria, **-ae** *f* (MIL) company; (POL) century (*a division of the Roman people according to property*)

centuriātim *adv* by companies, by centuries

centuriātus¹ *adj* divided by centuries; **comitia centuriāta** *assembly which voted by centuries*

centuriātus², **-ūs** *m* division into centuries; rank of centurion

centuriō¹, **-āre**, **-āvī**, **-ātum** *vt* (MIL) to assign to companies; (POL) to divide by centuries

centuriō², **-ōnis** *m* (MIL) captain, centurion

centussis, **-is** *m* a hundred asses

cēnula, **-ae** *f* little dinner

Cēōs (*acc* **-ō**) *see* **Cēa**

Cēphēis *f* Andromeda

Cēphēius *adj* of Cepheus

Cēpheus, **-eī** (*acc* **-ea**) *m* king of Ethiopia (*father of Andromeda*)

Cēphēus *adj* Ethiopian

Cēphīsis *adj see* **Cēphīsus**

Cēphīsius *m* Narcissus

Cēphīsus, **-ī** *m* river in central Greece

cēpī *perf of* **capiō**

cēra, **-ae** *f* wax; honey cells; writing tablet, notebook; seal; portrait of an ancestor; **prīma ~** first page

Cerāmīcus, **-ī** *m* Athenian cemetery

cērārium, **-ī** *and* **-iī** *nt* seal-duty

cerastēs, **-ae** *m* a horned serpent

cerasus, **-ī** *f* cherry tree; cherry

cērātus *adj* waxed

Ceraunia, **-ōrum** *nt*, **Cerauniī** *m* mountains in Epirus

Cerbereus *adj see* **Cerberus**

Cerberus, **-ī** *m* three-headed watchdog of Hades

cercopithēcus, **-ī** *m* monkey

cercūrus, **-ī** *m* Cyprian type of ship

cerdō, **-ōnis** *m* tradesman

Cereālia, **-ium** *ntpl* festival of Ceres

Cereālis *adj* of Ceres; of corn, of meal

cerebrōsus *adj* hot-headed

cerebrum, **-ī** *nt* brain; understanding; quick temper

Cerēs, **-eris** *f* goddess of agriculture; (*fig*) grain, bread

cēreus *adj* waxen; wax-coloured; (*fig*) supple, easily led ♦ *m* taper

cērāria, **-ae** *f* taper maker

cērina, **-ōrum** *ntpl* wax-coloured clothes

cērintha, **-ae** *f* honeywort

cernō, **-ere**, **-crēvī**, **crētum** *vt* to see, discern; to understand, perceive; to decide, determine; (LAW) to decide to take up (*an inheritance*)

cernuus *adj* face downwards

cērōma, **-atis** *nt* wrestlers' ointment

cērōmaticus *adj* smeared with wax ointment

cerrītus *adj* crazy

certāmen, **-inis** *nt* contest, match; battle, combat; (*fig*) struggle, rivalry

certātim *adv* emulously

certātiō, **-ōnis** *f* contest; debate; rivalry

certē *adv* assuredly, of course; at least

certō¹ *adv* certainly, really

certō², **-āre**, **-āvī**, **-ātum** *vi* to contend, compete; (MIL) to fight it out; (LAW) to dispute; (*with inf*) to try hard

certus *adj* determined, fixed, definite; reliable, unerring; sure, certain; **mihi certum est** I have made up my mind; **certum scīre**, **prō certō habēre** know for certain, be sure; **certiōrem facere** inform

cērula, **-ae** *f* piece of wax; **~ miniāta** red pencil

cērussa, **-ae** *f* white lead

cērussātus *adj* painted with white lead

cerva, **-ae** *f* hind, deer

cervīcal, **-ālis** *nt* pillow

cervīcula, **-ae** *f* slender neck

cervīnus *adj* deer's

cervīx, **-īcis** *f* neck; **in cervīcibus esse** be a burden (to), threaten

cervus, **-ī** *m* stag, deer; (MIL) palisade

cessātiō, **-ōnis** *f* delaying; inactivity, idleness

cessātor, **-ōris** *m* idler

cessī *perf of* **cēdō**

cessiō, **-ōnis** *f* giving up

cessō, **-āre**, **-āvī**, **-ātum** *vi* to be remiss, stop; to loiter, delay; to be idle, rest, do nothing; (*land*) to lie fallow; to err

cestrosphendonē, **-ēs** *f* (MIL) engine for shooting stones

cestus, **-ī** *m* girdle (*esp of Venus*)

cētārium, **-ī** *and* **-iī** *nt* fishpond

cētārius, **-ī** *and* **-iī** *m* fishmonger

cētera *adv* in other respects

cēterī, **-ōrum** *adj* the rest, the others; (*sg*) the rest of

cēterōquī, **cēterōquīn** *adv* otherwise

cēterum *adv* for the rest, otherwise; but for all that; besides

Cethēgus, **-ī** *m* a conspirator with Catiline

cētr- *etc see* **caetr-**

cette *etc see* **cedo**

cētus, **-ī** *m*, **cētē** *ntpl* sea monster, whale

ceu *adv* just as, as if

Cēus *adj see* **Cēa**

Cēyx, **-ȳcis** *m* husband of Alcyone, changed to a kingfisher

Chalcidēnsis, **Chalcidiscus** *adj see* **Chalcis**

Chalcis, **-dis** *f* chief town of Euboea

Chaldaeī, **-aeōrum** *mpl* Chaldeans; astrologers

Chaldāicus *adj see* **Chaldaeī**

chalybēius *adj* of steel

Chalybes, **-um** *mpl* a people of Pontus (*famous as ironworkers*)

chalybs, **-is** *m* steel

Chāones, **-um** *mpl* a people of Epirus

Chāonia, **-iae** *f* Epirus

Chāonius, **-is** *adj see* **Chāonia**

Chaos (*abl* **-ō**) *nt* empty space, the lower world, chaos

chara, **-ae** *f* an unidentified vegetable

charistia, **-ōrum** *ntpl* a Roman family festival

Charites, **-um** *fpl* the Graces

Charŏn, -ontis m Charon *(ferryman of Hades)*

charta, -ae f sheet of papyrus, paper; writing

chartula, -ae f piece of paper

Charybdis, -is f *monster personifying a whirlpool in the Straits of Messina;* (fig) peril

Chattī, -ōrum mpl *a people of central Germany*

Chēlae, -ārum fpl (ASTR) the Claws (of Scorpio), Libra

chelydrus, -ī m watersnake

chelys (acc -yn) f tortoise; lyre

cheragra, -ae f gout in the hands

Cherronēsus, Chersonēsus, -ī f Gallipoli peninsula; Crimea

chīliarchus, -ī m officer in charge of 1000 men; chancellor of Persia

Chimaera, -ae f *fire-breathing monster formed of lion, goat and serpent*

Chimaeriferus adj *birthplace of Chimaera*

Chios, -ī f *Aegean island (famous for wine)*

chīrographum, -ī nt handwriting; document

Chīrōn, -ōnis m *a learned Centaur (tutor of heroes)*

chīronomos, -ī m/f, **chīronomōn, -untis** and **-ontis** m mime actor

chīrūrgia, -ae f surgery; (fig) violent measures

Chīus adj Chian ♦ nt Chian wine; Chian cloth

chlamydātus adj wearing a military cloak

chlamys, -dis f Greek military cloak

Choerilus, -ī m *inferior Greek poet*

chorāgium, -ī and **-iī** nt producing of a chorus

chorāgus, -ī m *one who finances a chorus*

choraulēs, -ae m flute-player *(accompanying a chorus)*

chorda, -ae f string *(of an instrument)*; rope

chorēa, -ae f dance

chorēus, -ī m trochee

chorus, -ī m choral dance; chorus, choir of singers or dancers; band, troop

Christiānismus, -ī m Christianity

Christiānus adj Christian

Christus, -ī m Christ

Chrȳsēis, -ēidis f *daughter of Chrȳsȳs*

Chrȳsēs, -ae m *priest of Apollo in the Iliad*

Chrȳsippēus adj see **Chrȳsippus**

Chrȳsippus, -ī m *Stoic philosopher*

chrȳsolithos, -ī m/f topaz

chrȳsos, -ī m gold

cibārius adj food (in cpds) ♦ ntpl rations

cibātus, -ūs m food

cibōrium, -ī and **-iī** nt kind of drinking cup

cibus, -ī m food, fodder, nourishment

cicāda, -ae f cicada, cricket

cicātrīcōsus adj scarred

cicātrīx, -īcis f scar; (plants) mark of an incision

ciccus, -ī m pomegranate pip

cicer, -is nt chickpea

Cicerō, -ōnis m *great Roman orator and author*

Cicerōniānus adj see **Cicerō**

cichorēum, -ī nt chicory

Cicŏnes, -um mpl *people of Thrace*

** cicōnia, -ae** f stork

cicur, -is adj tame

cicūta, -ae f hemlock; pipe

cieŏ, ciēre, cīvī, citum vt to move, stir, rouse; to call, invoke; (fig) to give rise to, produce; **calcem ciēre** make a move (in chess)

Cilicia, -ae f *country in S. Asia Minor (famous for piracy)*

Ciliciēnsis, Ciliciēnsus adj see **Cilicia**

Cilix, -cis, Cilissa adj Cilician ♦ nt goats' hair garment

Cimbrī, -ōrum mpl *people of N. Germany*

Cimbricus adj see **Cimbrī**

cīmex, -icis m bug

Cimmeriī, -ōrum mpl *people of the Crimea; mythical race in caves near Cumae*

Cimmerius adj see **Cimmeriī**

cinaedius adj lewd

cinaedus, -ī m sodomite; lewd dancer

Cincinnātus, -ī m *ancient Roman dictator*

cincinnātus adj with curled hair

cincinnus, -ī m curled hair; (fig) rhetorical ornament

Cincius, -ī m *Roman tribune; Roman historian*

cincticulus, -ī m small girdle

cinctus¹ ppp of **cingō**

cinctus², -ūs m girding; ~ **Gabīnus** *a ceremonial style of wearing the toga*

cinctūtus adj girded

cinefactus adj reduced to ashes

cinerārius, -ī and **-iī** m hair curler

cingō, -gere, -xī, -ctum vt to surround, enclose; to gird, crown; (MIL) to besiege, fortify; to cover, escort; **ferrum cingor** I put on my sword

cingula, -ae f girth *(of animals)*

cingulum, -ī nt belt

cingulus, -ī m zone

ciniflō, -ōnis m hair curler

cinis, -eris m ashes; (fig) ruin

Cinna, -ae m *colleague of Marius; poet friend of Catullus*

cinnamōmum, cinnamum, -ī nt cinnamon

cinxī perf of **cingō**

Cīnyphius adj of the Cinyps *(river of N. Africa)*; African

Cinyrās, -ae m *father of Adonis*

Cinyrēius adj see **Cinyrās**

cippus, -ī m tombstone; (pl) palisade

circā adv around, round about ♦ prep (with acc) *(place)* round, in the vicinity of, in; (time, number) about; with regard to

Circaeus adj see **Circē**

circamoerium, -ī and **-iī** nt space on both sides of a wall

Circē, -ēs and **-ae** f *goddess with magic powers living in Aeaea*

circēnsēs, -ium mpl the games

circēnsis adj of the Circus

circinō, -āre vt to circle through

circinus, -ī m pair of compasses

circiter adv (time, number) about ♦ prep (with acc) about, near

circueō, circumeō, -īre, -īvī and **-iī, -itum** vt, vi to go round, surround; (MIL) to encircle; to visit, go round canvassing; to deceive

circuitiō, -ōnis f (MIL) rounds; (speech) evasiveness

circuitus¹ ppp of **circueō**

circuitus², **-ūs** *m* revolution; way round, circuit; (RHET) period, periphrasis

circulātor, **-ōris** *m* pedlar

circulor, **-ārī** *vi* to collect in crowds

circulus, **-ī** *m* circle; orbit; ring; social group

circum *adv* round about ♦ *prep (with acc)* round, about; near; ~ **īnsulās mittere** send to the islands round about

circumagō, **-agere**, **-ēgī**, **-āctum** *vt* to turn, move in a circle, wheel; (*pass, time*) to pass; (*mind*) to be swayed

circumarō, **-āre** *vt* to plough round

circumcaesūra, **-ae** *f* outline

circumcīdō, **-dere**, **-dī**, **-sum** *vt* to cut round, trim; to cut down, abridge

circumcircā *adv* all round

circumcīsus *ppp of* **circumcīdō** ♦ *adj* precipitous

circumclūdō, **-dere**, **-sī**, **-sum** *vt* to shut in, hem in

circumcolō, **-ere** *vt* to live round about

circumcursō, **-āre** *vi* to run about

circumdō, **-are**, **-edī**, **-atum** *vt* to put round; to surround, enclose

circumdūcō, **-ūcere**, **-ūxī**, **-uctum** *vt* to lead round, draw round; to cheat; (*speech*) to prolong, drawl

circumductus *ppp of* **circumdūcō**

circumeō *etc see* **circueō**

circumequitō, **-āre** *vt* to ride round

circumferō, **-ferre**, **-tulī**, **-lātum** *vt* to carry round, pass round; to spread, broadcast; to purify; (*pass*) to revolve

circumflectō, **-ctere**, **-xī**, **-xum** *vt* to wheel round

circumflō, **-āre** *vt* (*fig*) to buffet

circumfluō, **-ere**, **-xī**, **-xum** *vt, vi* to flow round; (*fig*) to overflow, abound

circumfluus *adj* flowing round; surrounded (*by water*)

circumforāneus *adj* itinerant; (*money*) borrowed

circumfundō, **-undere**, **-ūdī**, **-ūsum** *vt* to pour round, surround; (*fig*) to crowd round, overwhelm; (*pass*) to flow round

circumgemō, **-ere** *vt* to growl round

circumgestō, **-āre** *vt* to carry about

circumgredior, **-dī**, **-ssus** *vt, vi* to make an encircling move, surround

circumiaceō, **-ēre** *vi* to be adjacent

circumiciō, **-icere**, **-iēcī**, **-iectum** *vt* to throw round, put round; to surround

circumiecta *ntpl* neighbourhood

circumiectus¹ *adj* surrounding

circumiectus², **-ūs** *m* enclosure; embrace

circumit- *etc see* **circuit-**

circumitiō, **-ōnis** *f see* **circuitiō**

circumitus, **-ūs** *m see* **circuitus²**

circumlātus *ppp of* **circumferō**

circumligō, **-āre**, **-āvī**, **-ātum** *vt* to tie to, bind round

circumlinō, **-ere**, **-tum** *vt* to smear all over, bedaub

circumluō, **-ere** *vt* to wash

circumluviō, **-ōnis** *f* alluvial land

circummittō, **-ittere**, **-īsī**, **-issum** *vt* to send round

circummoeniō, **circummūniō**, **-īre**, **-īvī**, **-ītum** *vt* to fortify

circummūnītiō, **-ōnis** *f* investing

circumpadānus *adj* of the Po valley

circumpendeō, **-ēre** *vi* to hang round

circumplaudō, **-ere** *vt* to applaud on all sides

circumplector, **-ctī**, **-xus** *vt* to embrace, surround

circumplicō, **-āre**, **-āvī**, **-ātum** *vt* to wind round

circumpōnō, **-pōnere**, **-posuī**, **-positum** *vt* to put round

circumpōtātiō, **-ōnis** *f* passing drinks round

circumrētiō, **-īre**, **-īvī**, **-ītum** *vt* to ensnare

circumrōdō, **-rodere**, **-rosī** *vt* to nibble round about; (*fig*) to slander

circumsaepiō, **-īre**, **-sī**, **-tum** *vt* to fence round

circumscindō, **-ere** *vt* to strip

circumscrībō, **-bere**, **-psī**, **-ptum** *vt* to draw a line round; to mark the limits of; to restrict, circumscribe; to set aside; to defraud

circumscrīptē *adv* in periods

circumscrīptiō, **-ōnis** *f* circle, contour; fraud; (RHET) period

circumscrīptor, **-ōris** *m* defrauder

circumscrīptus *ppp of* **circumscrībō** ♦ *adj* restricted; (RHET) periodic

circumsecō, **-āre** *vt* to cut round

circumsedeō, **-edēre**, **-ēdī**, **-essum** *vt* to blockade, beset

circumsēpiō *etc see* **circumsaepiō**

circumsessiō, **-ōnis** *f* siege

circumsessus *ppp of* **circumsedeō**

circumsīdō, **-ere** *vt* to besiege

circumsiliō, **-īre** *vi* to hop about; (*fig*) to be rampant

circumsistō, **-sistere**, **-stetī** *vt* surround

circumsonō, **-āre** *vi* to resound on all sides ♦ *vt* to fill with sound

circumsonus *adj* noisy

circumspectātrīx, **-īcis** *f* spy

circumspectiō, **-ōnis** *f* caution

circumspectō, **-āre** *vt, vi* to look all round, search anxiously, be on the lookout

circumspectus¹ *ppp of* **circumspiciō** ♦ *adj* carefully considered, cautious

circumspectus², **-ūs** *m* consideration; view

circumspiciō, **-icere**, **-exī**, **-ectum** *vi* to look all round; to be careful ♦ *vt* to survey; (*fig*) to consider, search for

circumstantēs, **-antium** *mpl* bystanders

circumstetī *perf of* **circumsistō**; **circumstō**

circumstō, **-āre**, **-etī** *vt, vi* to stand round; to besiege; (*fig*) to encompass

circumstrepō, **-ere** *vt* to make a clamour round

circumsurgēns, **-entis** *pres p* rising on all sides

circumtentus *adj* covered tightly

circumterō, **-ere** *vt* to crowd round

circumtextus *adj* embroidered round the edge

circumtonō, **-āre**, **-uī** *vt* to thunder about

circumvādō, **-dere**, **-sī** *vt* to assail on all sides

circumvagus *adj* encircling

circumvallō, **-āre**, **-āvī**, **-ātum** *vt* to blockade, beset

circumvectiō, -ōnis f carrying about; (sun) revolution

circumvector, -ārī vi to travel round, cruise round; (fig) describe

circumvehor, -hī, -ctus vt, vi to ride round, sail round; (fig) to describe

circumvēlō, -āre vt to envelop

circumveniō, -enīre, -ēnī, -entum vt to surround, beset; to oppress; to cheat

circumvertō, circumvortō, -ere vt to turn round

circumvestiō, -īre vt to envelop

circumvinciō, -īre vt to lash about

circumvīsō, -ere vt to look at all round

circumvolitō, -āre, -āvī, -ātum vt, vi to fly round; to hover around

circumvolō, -āre vt to fly round

circumvolvō, -vere vt to roll round

circus, -ī m circle; the Circus Maximus (famous Roman racecourse), a racecourse

Cirrha, -ae f town near Delphi (sacred to Apollo)

Cirrhaeus adj see Cirrha

cirrus, -ī m curl of hair; fringe

cis prep (with acc) on this side of; (time) within

Cisalpīnus adj on the Italian side of the Alps, Cisalpine

cisium, -ī and **-iī** nt two-wheeled carriage

Cissēis, -dis f Hecuba

cista, -ae f box, casket; ballot box

cistella, -ae f small box

cistellātrīx, -īcis f keeper of the moneybox

cistellula, -ae f little box

cisterna, -ae f reservoir

cistophorus, -ī m an Asiatic coin

cistula, -ae f little box

citātus adj quick, impetuous

citerior (superl **-imus**) adj on this side, nearer

Cithaerōn, -ōnis m mountain range between Attica and Boeotia

cithara, -ae f lyre, lute

citharista, -ae m, **citharistria, -ae** f lyre player

citharizō, -āre vi to play the lyre

citharoedus, -ī m a singer who accompanies himself on the lyre

citimus adj nearest

cito (compar **-ius**, superl **-issimē**) adv quickly, soon; **nōn ~** not easily

citō, -āre, -āvī, -ātum vt to set in motion, rouse; to call (by name), appeal to, cite, mention

citrā adv on this side, this way, not so far ♦ prep (with acc) on this side of, short of; (time) before, since; apart from; **~ quam** before

citreus adj of citrus wood

citrō adv hither, this way; **ultrō citrōque** to and fro

citrus, -ī f citrus tree; citron tree

citus ppp of cieō ♦ adj quick

cīvicus adj civic, civil; **corōna cīvica** civic crown (for saving a citizen's life in war)

cīvīlis adj of citizens, civil; political, civilian; courteous, democratic; **iūs cīvīle** civil rights; Civil Law; code of legal procedure

cīvīlitās, -ātis f politics; politeness

cīvīliter adv like citizens; courteously

cīvis, -is m/f citizen, fellow citizen

cīvitās, -ātis f citizenship; community, state; city; **cīvitāte dōnāre** naturalize

clādēs, -is f damage, disaster, ruin; defeat; (fig) scourge; **dare clādem** make havoc

clam adv secretly; unknown ♦ prep (with acc) unknown to; **~ mē habēre** keep from me

clāmātor, -ōris m bawler

clāmitātiō, -ōnis f bawling

clāmitō, -āre, -āvī, -ātum vt, vi to bawl, screech, cry out

clāmō, -āre, -āvī, -ātum vt, vi to shout, cry out; to call upon, proclaim

clāmor, -ōris m shout, cry; acclamation

clāmōsus adj noisy

clanculum adv secretly ♦ prep (with acc) unknown to

clandestīnō adv see clandestīnus

clandestīnus adj secret

clangor, -ōris m clang, noise

clārē adv brightly, loudly, clearly, with distinction

clāreō, -ēre vi to be bright, be clear; to be evident; to be renowned

clārēscō, -ere, clāruī vi to brighten, sound clear; to become obvious; to become famous

clārigātiō, -ōnis f formal ultimatum to an enemy; fine for trespass

clārigō, -āre vi to deliver a formal ultimatum

clārisonus adj loud and clear

clāritās, -ātis f distinctness; (RHET) lucidity; celebrity

clāritūdō, -inis f brightness; (fig) distinction

Clarius adj of Claros ♦ m Apollo

clārō, -āre vt to illuminate; to explain; to make famous

Claros, -ī f town in Ionia (famous for worship of Apollo)

clārus adj (sight) bright; (sound) loud; (mind) clear; (person) distinguished; **~ intonāre** thunder from a clear sky; **vir clārissimus** a courtesy title for eminent men

classiārius adj naval ♦ mpl marines

classicula, -ae f flotilla

classicum, -ī nt battle-signal; trumpet

classicus adj of the first class; naval ♦ mpl marines

classis, -is f a political class; army; fleet

clāthrī, -ōrum mpl cage

clāthrātus adj barred

clātrī, -ōrum mpl see clāthrī

claudeō, -ēre vi to limp; (fig) to be defective

claudicātiō, -ōnis f limping

claudicō, -āre vi to be lame; to waver, be defective

Claudius[1], -ī m patrician family name (esp Appius Claudius Caecus, famous censor); Emperor Claudius

Claudius[2], Claudiānus, Claudiālis adj see Claudius[1]

claudō[1], -dere, -sī, -sum vt to shut, close; to cut off, block; to conclude; to imprison, confine, blockade; **agmen claudere** bring up the rear

claudō[2], -ere etc see claudeō

claudus adj lame; (verse) elegiac; (fig) wavering

clausī perf of claudō[1]

claustra, -ōrum ntpl bar, bolt, lock; barrier, barricade, dam

clausula, -ae f conclusion; (RHET) ending of a
 period
clausum, -ī nt enclosure
clausus ppp of **claudō¹**
clāva, -ae f club, knotty branch; (MIL) foil
clāvārium, -ī and **-iī** nt money for buying shoe
 nails
clāvātor, -ōris m cudgel-bearer
clāvicula, -ae f vine tendril
clāviger, -ī m (Hercules) club bearer; (Janus) key-
 bearer
clāvis, -is f key
clāvus, -ī m nail; tiller, rudder; purple stripe on the
 tunic (broad for senators, narrow for equites); **clāvum
 annī movēre** reckon the beginning of the year
Cleanthēs, -is m Stoic philosopher
clēmēns, -entis adj mild, gentle, merciful;
 (weather, water) mild, calm
clēmenter adv gently, indulgently; gradually
clēmentia, -ae f mildness, forbearance, mercy
Cleopatra, -ae f queen of Egypt
clepō, -ere, -sī, -tum vt to steal
clepsydra, -ae f waterclock (used for timing
 speakers); **clepsydram dare** give leave to speak;
 clepsydram petere ask leave to speak
clepta, -ae m thief
cliēns, -entis m client, dependant; follower;
 vassal-state
clienta, -ae f client
clientēla, -ae f clientship, protection; clients
clientulus, -ī m insignificant client
clīnāmen, -inis nt swerve
clīnātus adj inclined
Clīō, -ūs f Muse of history
clipeātus adj armed with a shield
clipeus, -ī m, **clipeum, -ī** nt round bronze shield;
 disc; medallion on a metal base
clitellae, -ārum fpl packsaddle (attribute of an ass)
clitellārius adj carrying packsaddles
Clitumnus, -ī m river in Umbria
clīvōsus adj hilly
clīvus, -ī m slope, hill; ~ **sacer** part of the Via Sacra
cloāca, -ae f sewer, drain
Cloācīna, -ae f Venus
Clōdius, -ī m Roman plebeian name (esp the tribune,
 enemy of Cicero)
Cloelia, -ae f Roman girl hostage (who escaped by
 swimming the Tiber)
Clōthō (acc **-ō**) f one of the Fates
clueō, -ēre, -eor, -ērī vi to be called, be famed
clūnis, -is m/f buttock
clūrīnus adj of apes
Clūsīnus adj see **Clūsium**
Clūsium, -ī nt old Etruscan town (now Chiusi)
Clūsius, -ī m Janus
Clytaemnēstra, -ae f wife of Agamemnon (whom
 she murdered)
Cnidius adj see **Cnidus**
Cnidus, -ī f town in Caria (famous for worship of Venus)
coacervātiō, -ōnis f accumulation
coacervō, -āre vt to heap, accumulate
coacēscō, -ēscere, -uī vi to become sour
coāctō, -āre vt to force
coāctor, -ōris m collector (of money)

coāctōrēs agminis rearguard
coāctum, -ī nt thick coverlet
coāctus¹ adj forced
coāctus² ppp of **cōgō**
coāctus³, -ūs m compulsion
coaedificō, -āre, -āvī, -ātum vt to build on
coaequō, -āre, -āvī, -ātum vt to make equal,
 bring down to the same level
coagmentātiō, -ōnis f combination
coagmentō, -āre, -āvī, -ātum vt to glue, join
 together
coagmentum, -ī nt joining, joint
coāgulum, -ī nt rennet
coalēscō, -ēscere, -uī, -itum vi to grow
 together; (fig) to agree together; to flourish
coangustō, -āre vt to restrict
coarct- etc see **coart-**
coarguō, -ere, -ī vt to convict, prove
 conclusively
coartātiō, -ōnis f crowding together
coartō, -āre, -āvī, -ātum vt to compress,
 abridge
coccineus, coccinus adj scarlet
coccum, -ī nt scarlet
cochlea, coclea, -ae f snail
cocleāre, -is nt spoon
cocles, -itis m man blind in one eye; surname of
 Horatius who defended the bridge
coctilis adj baked; of bricks
coctus ppp of **coquō** ✦ adj (fig) well considered
cocus etc see **coquus**
Cōcȳtius adj see **Cōcȳtos**
Cōcȳtos, -us, -ī m river in the lower world
cōda etc see **cauda**
cōdex etc see **caudex**
cōdicillī, -ōrum mpl letter, note, petition; codicil
Codrus, -ī m last king of Athens
coēgī perf of **cōgō**
coel- etc see **cael-**
coemō, -emere, -ēmī, -emptum vt to buy up
coemptiō, -ōnis f a form of Roman marriage; mock
 sale of an estate
coemptiōnālis adj used in a mock sale;
 worthless
coen- etc see **caen-** or **cēn-**
coeō, -īre, -īvī and **-iī, -itum** vi to meet, assemble;
 to encounter; to combine, mate; (wounds) to
 close; to agree, conspire ✦ vt: **coīre societātem**
 make a compact
coepiō, -ere, -ī, -tum vt, vi begin (esp in perf tenses);
 rēs agī coeptae sunt things began to be done;
 coepisse to begin
coeptō, -āre, -āvī, -ātum vt, vi to begin, attempt
coeptum, -ī nt beginning, undertaking
coeptus ppp of **coepiō**
coeptus², -ūs m beginning
coepulōnus, -ī m fellow-banqueter
coerātor etc see **cūrātor**
coerceō, -ēre, -uī, -itum vt to enclose; to
 confine, repress; (fig) to control, check, correct
coercitiō, -ōnis f coercion, punishment
coetus, coitus, -ūs m meeting, joining
 together; assembly, crowd
cōgitātē adv deliberately

cōgitātiō, -ōnis f thought, reflection; idea, plan; faculty of thought, imagination

cōgitātus adj deliberate ♦ ntpl ideas

cōgitō, -āre, -āvī, -ātum vt, vi to think, ponder, imagine; to feel disposed; to plan, intend

cognātiō, -ōnis f relationship (by blood); kin, family; (fig) affinity, resemblance

cognātus, -ī m, cognāta, -ae f relation ♦ adj related; (fig) connected, similar

cognitiō, -ōnis f acquiring of knowledge, knowledge; idea, notion; (LAW) judicial inquiry; (comedy) recognition

cognitor, -ōris m (LAW) attorney; witness of a person's identity; (fig) defender

cognitus[1] adj acknowledged

cognitus[2] ppp of cognōscō

cognōmen, -inis nt surname; name

cognōmentum, -ī nt surname, name

cognōminis adj with the same name

cognōminō, -āre, -āvī, -ātum vt to give a surname to; verba cognōmināta synonyms

cognōscō, -ōscere, -ōvī, -itum vt to get to know, learn, understand; to know, recognize, identify; (LAW) to investigate; (MIL) to reconnoitre

cōgō, -ere, coēgī, coāctum vt to collect, gather together; (liquids) to thicken, curdle; to contract, confine; to compel, force; to infer; agmen cōgere bring up the rear; senātum cōgere call a meeting of the senate

cohaerentia, -ae f coherence

cohaereō, -rēre, -sī, -sum vt to stick together, cohere; to cling to; (fig) to be consistent, harmonize; to agree, be consistent with

cohaerēscō, -ere vi to stick together

cohaesus ppp of cohaereō

cohērēs, -ēdis m/f co-heir

cohibeō, -ēre, -uī, -itum vt to hold together, encircle; to hinder, stop; (fig) to restrain, repress

cohonestō, -āre vt to do honour to

cohorrēscō, -ēscere, -uī vi to shudder all over

cohors, -tis f courtyard; (MIL) cohort (about 600 men); retinue (esp of the praetor in a province); (fig) company

cohortātiō, -ōnis f encouragement

cohorticula, -ae f small cohort

cohortor, -ārī, -ātus vt to encourage, urge

coitiō, -ōnis f encounter; conspiracy

coitus etc see coetus

colaphus, -ī m blow with the fist, box

Colchis[1], -idis f Medea's country (at the E. end of the Black Sea)

Colchis[2], Colchius, Colchicus adj Colchian

cōleus etc see culleus

cōlis etc see caulis

collabāscō, -ere vi to waver also

collabefactō, -āre vt to shake violently

collabefīō, -fierī, -factus vi to be destroyed

collābor, -bī, -psus vi to fall in ruin, collapse

collacerātus adj torn to pieces

collacrimātiō, -ōnis f weeping

collactea, -ae f foster-sister

collāpsus ppa of collābor

collāre, -is nt neckband

Collātia, -iae f ancient town near Rome

Collātīnus adj of Collatia ♦ m husband of Lucretia

collātiō, -ōnis f bringing together, combination; (money) contribution; (RHET) comparison; (PHILOS) analogy

collātor, -ōris m contributor

collātus ppp of cōnferō

collaudātiō, -ōnis f praise

collaudō, -āre, -āvī, -ātum vt to praise highly

collaxō, -āre vt to make porous

collēcta, -ae f money contribution

collēctīcius adj hastily gathered

collēctiō, -ōnis f gathering up; (RHET) recapitulation

collēctus[1] ppp of colligō[2]

collēctus[2], -ūs m accumulation

collēga, -ae m colleague; associate

collēgī perf of colligō[2]

collēgium, -ī and -iī nt association in office; college, guild (of magistrates, etc)

collībertus, -ī m fellow freedman

collibet, collubet, -uit and -itum est vi it pleases

collīdō, -dere, -sī, -sum vt to beat together, strike, bruise; (fig) to bring into conflict

colligātiō, -ōnis f connection

colligō[1], -āre, -āvī, -ātum vt to fasten, tie up; (fig) to combine; to restrain, check

colligō[2], -igere, -ēgī, -ēctum vt to gather, collect; to compress, draw together; to check; (fig) to acquire; to think about; to infer, conclude; animum colligere, mentem colligere recover, rally; sē colligere crouch; recover one's courage; vāsa colligere (MIL) pack up

Collīna Porta gate in N.E. of Rome

collīneō, -āre vt, vi to aim straight

collinō, -inere, -ēvī, -itum vt to besmear; (fig) to deface

colliquefactus adj dissolved

collis, -is m hill, slope

collīsī perf of collīdō

collīsus ppp of collīdō

collitus ppp of collinō

collocātiō, -ōnis f arrangement; giving in marriage

collocō, -āre, -āvī, -ātum vt to place, station, arrange; to give in marriage; (money) to invest; (fig) to establish; to occupy, employ

collocuplētō, -āre, -āvī vt to enrich

collocūtiō, -ōnis f conversation

colloquium, -ī and -iī nt conversation, conference

colloquor, -quī, -cūtus vi to converse, hold a conference with; to talk to

collubet etc see collibet

collūceō, -ēre vi to shine brightly; (fig) to be resplendent

collūdō, -dere, -sī, -sum vi to play together or with; to practise collusion

collum, -ī nt neck; ~ torquēre, ~ obtorquēre, ~ obstringere arrest

colluō, -uere, -uī, -ūtum vt to rinse, moisten

collus etc see collum

collūsiō, -ōnis f secret understanding

collūsor, -ōris *m* playmate, fellow gambler

collūstrō, -āre, -āvī, -ātum *vt* to light up; to survey

colluviō, -ōnis, colluviēs (*acc* -em, *abl* -ē) *f* sweepings, filth; (*fig*) dregs, rabble

collybus, -ī *m* money exchange, rate of exchange

collȳra, -ae *f* vermicelli

collȳricus *adj see* **collȳra**

collȳrium, -ī *and* **-iī** *nt* eye lotion

colō, -ere, -uī, cultum *vt* (AGR) to cultivate, work; (*place*) to live in; (*human affairs*) to cherish, protect, adorn; (*qualities, pursuits*) to cultivate, practise; (*gods*) to worship; (*men*) to honour, court; **vītam colere** live

colocāsia, -ae *f*, **colocāsia, -ōrum** *ntpl* Egyptian bean, caladium

colōna, -ae *f* country-woman

colōnia, -ae *f* settlement, colony; settlers

colōnicus *adj* colonial

colōnus, -ī *m* crofter, farmer; settler, colonist

color, colōs, -ōris *m* colour; complexion; beauty, lustre; (*fig*) outward show; (RHET) style, tone; colourful excuse; **colōrem mūtāre** blush, go pale; **homō nullīus colōris** an unknown person

colōrātus *adj* healthily tanned

colōrō, -āre, -āvī, -ātum *vt* to colour, tan; (*fig*) to give a colour to

colossus, -ī *m gigantic statue* (*esp that of Apollo at Rhodes*)

colostra, colustra, -ae *f* beestings

coluber, -rī *m* snake

colubra, -ae *f* snake

colubrifer, -ī *adj* snaky

colubrīnus *adj* wily

coluī *perf of* **colō**

cōlum, -ī *nt* strainer

columba, -ae *f* dove, pigeon

columbar, -āris *nt* kind of collar

columbārium, -ī *and* **-iī** *nt* dovecote

columbīnus *adj* pigeon's ♦ *m* little pigeon

columbus, -ī *m* dove, cock-pigeon

columella, -ae *f* small pillar

columen, -inis *nt* height, summit; pillar; (*fig*) chief; prop

columna, -ae *f* column, pillar; *a pillory in the Forum Romanum*; waterspout

columnārium, -ī *and* **-iī** *nt* pillar tax

columnārius, -ī *m* criminal

columnātus *adj* pillared

colurnus *adj* made of hazel

colus, -ī *and* **-ūs** *m/f* distaff

colȳphia, -ōrum *ntpl food of athletes*

coma, -ae *f* hair (*of the head*); foliage

comāns, -antis *adj* hairy, plumed; leafy

cōmarchus, -ī *m* burgomaster

comātus *adj* long-haired; leafy; **Gallia comāta** Transalpine Gaul

combibō¹, -ere, -ī *vt* to drink to the full, absorb

combibō², -ōnis *m* fellow-drinker

combūrō, -rere, -ssī, -stum *vt* to burn up; (*fig*) to ruin

combūstus *ppp of* **combūrō**

comedō, -ēsse, -ēdī, -ēsum *and* **-ēstum** *vt* to eat up, devour; (*fig*) to waste, squander; **sē comedēsse** pine away

Cōmēnsis *adj see* **Cōmum**

comes, -itis *m/f* companion, partner; attendant, follower; one of a magistrate's or emperor's retinue; (*medieval title*) count

comēs, comēst *pres of* **comedō**

comēstus, comēsus *ppp of* **comedō**

comētēs, -ae *m* comet

cōmicē *adv* in the manner of comedy

cōmicus, -ī *m* comedy actor, comedy writer ♦ *adj* of comedy, comic

cōmis *adj* courteous, friendly

cōmissābundus *adj* carousing

cōmissātiō, -ōnis *f* Bacchanalian revel

cōmissātor, -ōris *m* reveller

cōmissor, -ārī, -ātus *vi* to carouse, make merry

cōmitās, -ātis *f* kindness, affability

comitātus, -ūs *m* escort, retinue; company

cōmiter *adv see* **cōmis**

comitia, -iōrum *ntpl* assembly for the election of magistrates and other business (*esp the* **comitia centuriāta**); elections

comitiālis *adj* of the elections; **~ morbus** epilepsy

comitiātus, -ūs *m* assembly at the elections

comitium, -ī *and* **-iī** *nt* place of assembly

comitō, -āre, -āvī, -ātum *vt* to accompany

comitor, -ārī, -ātus *vt, vi* to attend, follow

commaculō, -āre, -āvī, -ātum *vt* to stain, defile

commanipulāris, -is *m* soldier in the same company

commeātus, -ūs *m* passage; leave, furlough; convoy (*of troops or goods*); (MIL) lines of communication, provisions, supplies

commeditor, -ārī *vt* to practise

commeminī, -isse *vt, vi* to remember perfectly

commemorābilis *adj* memorable

commemorātiō, -ōnis *f* recollection, recounting

commemorō, -āre, -āvī, -ātum *vt* to recall, remind; to mention, relate

commendābilis *adj* praiseworthy

commendātīcius *adj* of recommendation or introduction

commendātiō, -ōnis *f* recommendation; worth, excellence

commendātor, -ōris *m* commender (*male*)

commendātrīx, -rīcis *f* commender (*female*)

commendātus *adj* approved, valued

commendō, -āre, -āvī, -ātum *vt* to entrust, commit, commend (*to one's care or charge*), recommend, set off to advantage

commēnsus *ppa of* **commētior**

commentāriolum, -ī *nt* short treatise

commentārius, -ī *and* **-iī** *m*, **commentārium, -ī** *and* **-iī** *nt* notebook; commentary, memoir; (LAW) brief

commentātiō, -ōnis *f* studying, meditation

commentīcius *adj* fictitious, imaginary; false

commentor¹, -ārī, -ātus *vt, vi* to study, think over, prepare carefully; to invent, compose, write

commentor², -ōris *m* inventor

commentum, **-ī** nt invention, fiction; contrivance

commentus ppa of **comminīscor** ♦ adj feigned, fictitious

commeō, **-āre** vi to pass to and fro; to go or come often

commercium, **-ī** and **-iī** nt trade, commerce; right to trade; dealings, communication

commercor, **-ārī**, **-ātus** vt to buy up

commereō, **-ēre**, **-uī**, **-itum**, **commereor**, **-ērī**, **-itus** vt to deserve; to be guilty of

commētior, **-tīrī**, **-nsus** vt to measure

commētō, **-āre** vi to go often

commictus ppp of **commingō**

commigrō, **-āre**, **-āvī**, **-ātum** vi to remove, migrate

commīlitium, **-ī** and **-iī** nt service together

commīlitō, **-ōnis** m fellow soldier

comminātiō, **-ōnis** f threat

commingō, **-ingere**, **-īnxī**, **-īctum** vt to pollute

comminīscor, **-ī**, **commentus** vt to devise, contrive

comminor, **-ārī**, **-ātus** vt to threaten

comminuō, **-uere**, **-uī**, **-ūtum** vt to break up, smash; to diminish; to impair

comminus adv hand to hand; near at hand

commīsceō, **-scēre**, **-scuī**, **-xtum** vt to mix together, join together

commiserātiō, **-ōnis** f (RHET) passage intended to arouse pity

commiserēscō, **-ere** vt to pity

commiseror, **-ārī** vt to bewail ♦ vi (RHET) to try to excite pity

commissiō, **-ōnis** f start (of a contest)

commissum, **-ī** nt enterprise; offence, crime; secret

commissūra, **-ae** f joint, connection

commissus ppp of **committō**

committō, **-ittere**, **-īsī**, **-issum** vt to join, connect, bring together; to begin, undertake; (battle) to join, engage in; (offence) to commit, be guilty of; (punishment) to incur, forfeit; to entrust, trust; **sē urbī committere** venture into the city

commixtus ppp of **commīsceō**

commodē adv properly, well; aptly, opportunely; pleasantly

commoditās, **-ātis** f convenience, ease, fitness; advantage; (person) kindliness; (RHET) apt expression

commodō, **-āre**, **-āvī**, **-ātum** vt to adjust, adapt; to give, lend, oblige with; (with dat) to oblige

commodulē, **-um** adv conveniently

commodum[1], **-ī** nt convenience; advantage, interest; pay, salary; loan; **commodō tuō** at your leisure; **commoda vītae** the good things of life

commodum[2] adv opportunely; just

commodus adj proper, fit, full; suitable, easy, opportune; (person) pleasant, obliging

commōlior, **-īrī** vt to set in motion

commonefaciō, **-facere**, **-fēcī**, **-factum** vt to remind, recall

commoneō, **-ēre**, **-uī**, **-itum** vt to remind, impress upon

commōnstrō, **-āre** vt to point out

commorātiō, **-ōnis** f delay, residence; (RHET) dwelling (on a topic)

commoror, **-ārī**, **-ātus** vi to sojourn, wait; (RHET) to dwell ♦ vt to detain

commōtiō, **-ōnis** f excitement

commōtiuncula f slight indisposition

commōtus ppp of **commoveō** ♦ adj excited, emotional

commoveō, **-ovēre**, **-ōvī**, **-ōtum** vt to set in motion, move, dislodge, agitate; (mind) to unsettle, shake, excite, move, affect; (emotions) to stir up, provoke

commūne, **-is** nt common property; state; **in ~** for a common end; equally; in general

commūnicātiō, **-ōnis** f imparting; (RHET) making the audience appear to take part in the discussion

commūnicō, **-āre**, **-āvī**, **-ātum** vt to share (by giving or receiving); to impart, communicate; **cōnsilia commūnicāre cum** make common cause with

commūniō[1], **-īre**, **-īvī** and **-iī**, **-ītum** vt to build (a fortification), fortify, strengthen

commūniō[2], **-ōnis** f sharing in common, communion

commūnis adj common, general, universal; (person) affable, democratic; **commūnia loca** public places; **commūnēs locī** general topics; **~ sēnsus** popular sentiment; **aliquid commūne habēre** have something in common

commūnitās, **-ātis** f fellowship; sense of fellowship; affability

commūniter adv in common, jointly

commūnītiō, **-ōnis** f preparing the way

commurmuror, **-ārī**, **-ātus** vi to mutter to oneself

commūtābilis adj changeable

commūtātiō, **-iōnis** f change

commūtātus, **-ūs** m change

commūtō, **-āre**, **-āvī**, **-ātum** vt to change, exchange, interchange

cōmō, **-ere**, **-psī**, **-ptum** vt to arrange, dress, adorn

cōmoedia, **-ae** f comedy

cōmoedicē adv as in comedy

cōmoedus, **-ī** m comic actor

comōsus adj shaggy

compāctiō, **-ōnis** f joining together

compāctus ppp of **compingō**

compāgēs, **-is**, **compāgō**, **-inis** f joint, structure, framework

compār, **-aris** m/f comrade, husband, wife ♦ adj equal

comparābilis adj comparable

comparātē adv by bringing in a comparison

comparātiō, **-ōnis** f comparison; (ASTR) relative positions; agreement; preparation, procuring

comparātīvus adj based on comparison

compāreō, **-ēre** vi to be visible; to be present, be realized

comparō, **-āre**, **-āvī**, **-ātum** vt to couple together, match; to compare; (POL) to agree (*about respective duties*); to prepare, provide; (*custom*) to establish; to procure, purchase, get

compāscō, -ere vt to put (cattle) to graze in common

compāscuus *adj* for common pasture

compecīscor, -iscī, -tus vi to come to an agreement

compectum, -tī *nt* agreement

compediō, -īre, -ītum vt to fetter

compēgī *perf of* **compingō**

compellātiō, -ōnis *f* reprimand

compellō¹, -āre, -āvī, -ātum vt to call, address; to reproach; (LAW) to arraign

compellō², -ellere, -ulī, -ulsum vt to drive, bring together, concentrate; to impel, compel

compendiārius *adj* short

compendium, -ī *and* **-iī** *nt* saving; abbreviating; short cut; **compendiī facere** save; abridge; **compendiī fierī** be brief

compēnsātiō, -ōnis *f* (*fig*) compromise

compēnsō, -āre, -āvī, -ātum vt to balance (against), make up for

compercō, -cere, -sī vt, vi to save; to refrain

comperendinātiō, -iōnis *f* adjournment for two days

comperendinātus, -ūs *m* adjournment for two days

comperendinō, -āre vt to adjourn for two days

comperiō, -īre, -ī, -tum, comperior vt to find out, learn; **compertus** detected; found guilty; **compertum habēre** know for certain

compēs, -edis *f* fetter, bond

compēscō, -ere, -uī vt to check, suppress

competītor, -ōris *m*, **competītrīx, -rīcis** *f* rival candidate

competō, -ere, -īvī *and* **-iī, -ītum** vi to coincide, agree; to be capable

compīlātiō, -ōnis *f* plundering; compilation

compīlō, -āre, -āvī, -ātum vt to pillage

compingō, -ingere, -ēgī, -āctum vt to put together, compose; to lock up, hide away

compitālia, -ium *and* **-iōrum** *ntpl* festival in honour *of the Lares Compitales*

compitālicius *adj* of the Compitalia

compitālis *adj* of crossroads

compitum, -ī *nt* crossroads

complaceō, -ēre, -uī *and* **-itus sum** vi to please (someone else) as well, please very much

complānō, -āre vt to level, raze to the ground

complector, -ctī, -xus vt to embrace, clasp; to enclose; (*speech, writing*) to deal with, comprise; (*mind*) to grasp, comprehend; to honour, be fond of

complēmentum, -ī *nt* complement

compleō, -ēre, -ēvī, -ētum vt to fill, fill up; (MIL) to man, make up the complement of; (*time, promise, duty*) to complete, fulfil, finish

complētus *adj* perfect

complexiō, -ōnis *f* combination; (RHET) period; (LOGIC) conclusion of an argument; dilemma

complexus, -ūs *m* embrace; (*fig*) affection, close combat; (*speech*) connection

complicō, -āre vt to fold up

complōrātiō, -iōnis *f*, **complōrātus, -ūs** *m* loud lamentation

complōrō, -āre, -āvī, -ātum vt to mourn for

complūrēs, -ium *adj* several, very many

complūriēns *adv* several times

complūsculī, -ōrum *adj* quite a few

compluvium, -ī *and* **-iī** *nt* roof opening in a Roman house

compōnō, -ōnere, -osuī, -ositum vt to put together, join; to compose, construct; to compare, contrast; to match, oppose; to put away, store up, stow; (*dead*) to lay out, inter; to allay, quieten, reconcile; to adjust, settle, arrange; to devise, prepare ♦ vi to make peace

comportō, -āre vt to collect, bring in

compos, -tis *adj* in control, in possession; sharing; **vōtī ~** having got one's wish

compositē *adv* properly, in a polished manner

compositiō, -ōnis *f* compounding, system; (*words*) arrangement; reconciliation; matching (*of fighters*)

compositor, -ōris *m* arranger

compositūra, -ae *f* connection

compositus *ppp of* **compōnō** ♦ *adj* orderly, regular; adapted, assumed, ready; calm, sedate; (*words*) compound; **compositō, ex compositō** as agreed

compōtātiō, -ōnis *f* drinking party

compotiō, -īre vt to put in possession (of)

compōtor, -ōris *m*, **compōtrīx, -rīcis** *f* fellow drinker

comprānsor, -ōris *m* fellow guest

comprecātiō, -ōnis *f* public supplication

comprecor, -ārī, -ātus vt, vi to pray to; to pray for

comprehendō, comprendō, -endere, -endī, -ēnsum vt to grasp, catch; to seize, arrest, catch in the act; (*words*) to comprise, recount; (*thought*) to grasp, comprehend; to hold in affection; **numerō comprehendere** count

comprehēnsibilis *adj* conceivable

comprehēnsiō, -ōnis *f* grasping, seizing; perception, idea; (RHET) period

comprehēnsus, comprēnsus *ppp of* **comprehendō**

comprendō *etc see* **comprehendō**

compressī *perf of* **comprimō**

compressiō, -ōnis *f* embrace; (RHET) compression

compressus¹ *ppp of* **comprimō**

compressus², -ūs *m* compression, embrace

comprimō, -imere, -essī, -essum vt to squeeze, compress; to check, restrain; to suppress, withhold; **animam comprimere** hold one's breath; **compressīs manibus** with hands folded, idle

comprobātiō, -ōnis *f* approval

comprobātor, -ōris *m* supporter

comprobō, -āre, -āvī, -ātum vt to prove, make good; to approve

comprōmissum, -ī *nt* mutual agreement to abide by an arbitrator's decision

comprōmittō, -ittere, -īsī, -issum vt to undertake to abide by an arbitrator's decision

cōmpsī *perf of* **cōmō**

cōmptus¹ *ppp of* **cōmō** ♦ *adj* elegant

cōmptus², -ūs *m* coiffure; union

compulī *perf of* **compellō²**
compulsus *ppp of* **compellō²**
compungō, -ungere, -ūnxī, -ūnctum *vt* to prick, sting, tattoo
computō, -āre, -āvī, -ātum *vt* to reckon, number
Cōmum, -ī *nt* (*also* **Novum Cōmum**) *town in N. Italy* (*now* Como)
cōnāmen, -inis *nt* effort; support
cōnāta, -ōrum *ntpl* undertaking, venture
cōnātus, -ūs *m* effort; endeavour; inclination, impulse
concaedēs, -ium *fpl* barricade of felled trees
concalefaciō, -facere, -fēcī, -factum *vt* to warm well
concaleō, -ēre *vi* to be hot
concalēscō, -ēscere, -uī *vi* to become hot, glow
concallēscō, -ēscere, -uī *vi* to become shrewd; to become unfeeling
concastīgō, -āre *vt* to punish severely
concavō, -āre *vt* to curve
concavus *adj* hollow; vaulted, bent
concēdō, -ēdere, -essī, -essum *vi* to withdraw, depart; to disappear, pass away, pass; to yield, submit, give precedence, comply ♦ *vt* to give up, cede; to grant, allow; to pardon, overlook
concelebrō, -āre, -āvī, -ātum *vt* to frequent, fill, enliven; (*study*) to pursue eagerly; to celebrate; to make known
concēnātiō, -ōnis *f* dining together
concentiō, -ōnis *f* chorus
concenturiō, -āre *vt* to marshal
concentus, -ūs *m* chorus, concert; (*fig*) concord, harmony
conceptiō, -ōnis *f* conception; drawing up legal formulae
conceptīvus *adj* (*holidays*) movable
conceptus¹ *ppp of* **concipiō**
conceptus², -ūs *m* conception
concerpō, -ere, -sī, -tum *vt* to tear up; (*fig*) to abuse
concertātiō, -ōnis *f* controversy
concertātor, -ōris *m* rival
concertātōrius *adj* controversial
concertō, -āre, -āvī, -ātum *vi* to fight; to dispute
concessiō, -ōnis *f* grant, permission; (*LAW*) pleading guilty and asking indulgence
concessō, -āre *vi* to stop, loiter
concessus¹ *ppp of* **concēdō**
concessus², -ūs *m* permission
concha, -ae *f* mussel, oyster, murex; mussel shell, oyster shell, pearl; purple dye; trumpet, perfume dish
conchis, -is *f* kind of bean
conchīta, -ae *m* catcher of shellfish
conchȳliātus *adj* purple
conchȳlium, -ī *and* **-iī** *nt* shellfish, oyster, murex; purple
concidō, -ere, -ī *vi* to fall, collapse; to subside, fail, perish
concīdō, -dere, -dī, -sum *vt* to cut up, cut to pieces, kill; (*fig*) to ruin, strike down; (*RHET*) to dismember, enfeeble

conciō, -iēre, -īvī, -itum, conciō, -īre, -ītum *vt* to rouse, assemble; to stir up, shake; (*fig*) to rouse, provoke
conciliābulum, -ī *nt* place for public gatherings
conciliātiō, -ōnis *f* union; winning over (*friends, hearers*); (PHILOS) inclination
conciliātor, -ōris *m* promoter
conciliātrīx, -īcis *m*, **conciliātrīcula, -ae** *f* promoter, matchmaker
conciliātus¹, -ūs *m* combination
conciliātus² *adj* beloved; favourable
conciliō, -āre, -āvī, -ātum *vt* to unite; to win over, reconcile; to procure, purchase, bring about, promote
concilium, -ī *and* **-iī** *nt* gathering, meeting; council; (*things*) union
concinnē *adv see* **concinnus**
concinnitās, -ātis, concinnitūdō, -ūdinis *f* (RHET) rhythmical style
concinnō, -āre, -āvī, -ātum *vt* to arrange; to bring about, produce; (*with adj*) to make
concinnus *adj* symmetrical, beautiful; (*style*) polished, rhythmical; (*person*) elegant, courteous; (*things*) suited, pleasing
concinō, -ere, -uī *vi* to sing, play, sound together; (*fig*) to agree, harmonize ♦ *vt* to sing about, celebrate, prophesy
concio- *etc see* **contio-**
conciō *etc see* **conciō**
concipiō, -ipere, -ēpī, -eptum *vt* to take to oneself, absorb; (*women*) to conceive; (*senses*) to perceive; (*mind*) to conceive, imagine, understand; (*feelings, acts*) to harbour, foster, commit; (*words*) to draw up, intimate formally
concīsiō, -ōnis *f* breaking up into short clauses
concīsus *ppp of* **concīdō** ♦ *adj* broken up, concise
concitātē *adv see* **concitātus**
concitātiō, -ōnis *f* acceleration; (*mind*) excitement, passion; riot
concitātor, -ōris *m* agitator
concitātus *ppp of* **concitō** ♦ *adj* fast; excited
concitō, -āre, -āvī, -ātum *vt* to move rapidly, bestir, hurl; to urge, rouse, impel; to stir up, occasion
concitor, -ōris *m* instigator
concitus, concītus *ppp of* **conciō; conciō**
conclāmātiō, -ōnis *f* great shout
conclāmitō, -āre *vi* to keep on shouting
conclāmō, -āre, -āvī, -ātum *vt, vi* to shout, cry out; to call to help; (MIL) to give the signal; (*dead*) to call by name in mourning; **vāsa conclāmāre** give the order to pack up; **conclāmātum est** it's all over
conclāve, -is *nt* room
conclūdō, -dere, -sī, -sum *vt* to shut up, enclose; to include, comprise; to end, conclude, round off (*esp with a rhythmical cadence*); (PHILOS) to infer, demonstrate
conclūsē *adv* with rhythmical cadences
conclūsiō, -ōnis *f* (MIL) blockade; end, conclusion; (RHET) period, peroration; (LOGIC) conclusion
conclūsiuncula, -ae *f* quibble
conclūsum, -ī *nt* logical conclusion
conclūsus *ppp of* **conclūdō**

concoctus *ppp of* **concoquō**

concolor, -ōris *adj* of the same colour

concomitātus *adj* escorted

concoquō, -quere, -xī, -ctum *vt* to boil down; to digest; (*fig*) to put up with, stomach; (*thought*) to consider well, concoct

concordia, -ae *f* friendship, concord, union; *goddess of Concord*

concorditer *adv* amicably

concordō, -āre *vi* to agree, be in harmony

concors, -dis *adj* concordant, united, harmonious

concrēbrēscō, -ēscere, -uī *vi* to gather strength

concrēdō, -ere, -idī, -itum *vt* to entrust

concremō, -āre, -āvī, -ātum *vt* to burn

concrepō, -āre, -uī, -itum *vi* to rattle, creak, clash, snap (fingers) ♦ *vt* to beat

concrēscō, -scere, -vī, -tum *vi* to harden, curdle, congeal, clot; to grow, take shape

concrētiō, -ōnis *f* condensing; matter

concrētum, -ī *nt* solid matter, hard frost

concrētus *ppp of* **concrēscō** ♦ *adj* hard, thick, stiff, congealed; compounded

concrīminor, -ārī, -ātus *vi* to bring a complaint

concruciō, -āre *vt* to torture

concubīna, -ae *f* (*female*) concubine

concubīnātus, -ūs *m* concubinage

concubīnus, -ī *m* (*male*) concubine

concubitus, -ūs *m* reclining together (*at table*); sexual union

concubius *adj*: **concubiā nocte** during the first sleep ♦ *nt* the time of the first sleep

conculcō, -āre *vt* to trample under foot, treat with contempt

concumbō, -mbere, -buī, -bitum *vi* to lie together, lie with

concupīscō, -īscere, -īvī, -ītum *vt* to covet, long for, aspire to

concūrō, -āre *vt* to take care of

concurrō, -rere, -rī, -sum *vi* to flock together, rush in; (*things*) to clash, meet; (MIL) to join battle, charge; (*events*) to happen at the same time, concur

concursātiō, -ōnis *f* running together, rushing about; (MIL) skirmishing; (*dreams*) coherent design

concursātor, -ōris *m* skirmisher

concursiō, -ōnis *f* meeting, concourse; (RHET) repetition for emphasis

concursō, -āre *vi* to collide; to rush about, travel about; (MIL) to skirmish ♦ *vt* to visit, go from place to place

concursus, -ūs *m* concourse, gathering, collision; uproar; (*fig*) combination; (MIL) assault, charge

concussī *perf of* **concutiō**

concussus¹ *ppp of* **concutiō**

concussus², -ūs *m* shaking

concutiō, -tere, -ssī, -ssum *vt* to strike, shake, shatter; (*weapons*) to hurl; (*power*) to disturb, impair; (*person*) to agitate, alarm; (*self*) to search, examine; to rouse

condalium, -ī *and* **-iī** *nt* slave's ring

condecet, -ēre *vt impers* it becomes

condecorō, -āre *vt* to enhance

condemnātor, -ōris *m* accuser

condemnō, -āre, -āvī, -ātum *vt* to condemn, sentence; to urge the conviction of; to blame, censure; **ambitūs condemnāre** convict of bribery; **capitis condemnāre** condemn to death; **vōtī condemnātus** obliged to fulfil a vow

condēnsō, -āre, -eō, -ēre *vt* to compress, move close together

condēnsus *adj* very dense, close, thick

condiciō, -ōnis *f* arrangement, condition, terms; marriage contract, match; situation, position, circumstances; manner, mode; **eā condiciōne ut** on condition that; **sub condiciōne** conditionally; **hīs condiciōnibus** on these terms; **vītae** – way of life

condīcō, -īcere, -īxī, -ictum *vt, vi* to talk over, agree upon, promise; **ad cēnam condīcere** have a dinner engagement

condidī *perf of* **condō**

condignē *adv see* **condignus**

condignus *adj* very worthy

condīmentum, -ī *nt* spice, seasoning

condiō, -īre, -īvī, -ītum *vt* to pickle, preserve, embalm; to season; (*fig*) to give zest to, temper

condiscipulus, -ī *m* school-fellow

condiscō, -scere, -dicī *vt* to learn thoroughly, learn by heart

conditiō *etc see* **condiciō**

condītiō, -ōnis *f* preserving, seasoning

conditor, -ōris *m* founder, author, composer

condītōrium, -ī *and* **-iī** *nt* coffin, urn, tomb

conditus¹ *ppp of* **condō**

condītus² *ppp of* **condiō**

condītus¹ *adj* savoury; (*fig*) polished

condō, -ere, -idī, -itum *vt* 1. (*build, found: arts*) to make, compose, write; (: *institutions*) to establish 2. (*put away for keeping, store up: fruit*) to preserve; (: *person*) to imprison; (: *dead*) to bury; (: *memory*) to lay up; (: *time*) to pass, bring to a close 3. (*put out of sight, conceal: eyes*) to close; (: *sword*) to sheathe, plunge; (: *troops*) to place in ambush

condocefaciō, -ere *vt* to train

condoceō, -ēre, -uī, -tum *vt* to train

condolēscō, -ēscere, -uī *vi* to begin to ache, feel very sore

condōnātiō, -ōnis *f* giving away

condōnō, -āre, -āvī, -ātum *vt* to give, present, deliver up; (*debt*) to remit; (*offence*) to pardon, let off

condormīscō, -īscere, -īvī *vi* to fall fast asleep

condūcibilis *adj* expedient

condūcō, -ūcere, -ūxī, -uctum *vt* to bring together, assemble, connect; to hire, rent, borrow; (*public work*) to undertake, get the contract for; (*taxes*) to farm ♦ *vi* to be of use, profit

conductī, -ōrum *mpl* hirelings, mercenaries

conductīcius *adj* hired

conductiō, -ōnis *f* hiring, farming

conductor, -ōris *m* hirer, tenant; contractor

conductum, -ī *nt* anything hired or rented

conductus *ppp of* **condūcō**

conduplicō, -āre *vt* to double

condūrō, **-āre** vt to make very hard

condus, **-ī** m steward

cōnectō, **-ctere**, **-xuī**, **-xum** vt to tie, fasten, link, join; (LOGIC) to state a conclusion

cōnexum, **-ī** nt logical inference

cōnexus¹ ppp of **cōnectō** ♦ adj connected; (time) following

cōnexus², **-ūs** m combination

cōnfābulor, **-ārī**, **-ātus** vi to talk (to), discuss

cōnfarreātiō, **-ōnis** f the most solemn of Roman marriage ceremonies

cōnfarreō, **-āre**, **-ātum** vt to marry by confarreatio

cōnfātālis adj bound by the same destiny

cōnfēcī perf of **cōnficiō**

cōnfectiō, **-ōnis** f making, completion; (food) chewing

cōnfector, **-ōris** m maker, finisher; destroyer

cōnfectus ppp of **cōnficiō**

cōnferciō, **-cīre**, **-sī**, **-tum** vt to stuff, cram, pack closely

cōnferō, **-ferre**, **-tulī**, **-lātum** vt to gather together, collect; to contribute; to confer, talk over; (MIL) to oppose, engage in battle; to compare; (words) to condense; to direct, transfer; to transform (into), turn (to); to devote, bestow; to ascribe, assign, impute; (time) to postpone; **capita cōnferre** put heads together, confer; **gradum cōnferre cum** walk beside; **sē cōnferre** go, turn (to); **sermōnēs cōnferre** converse; **signa cōnferre** join battle

cōnfertim adv in close order

cōnfertus ppp of **cōnferciō** ♦ adj crowded, full; (MIL) in close order

cōnfervēscō, **-vēscere**, **-buī** vi to boil up, grow hot

cōnfessiō, **-ōnis** f acknowledgement, confession

cōnfessus ppa of **cōnfiteor** ♦ adj acknowledged, certain; **in cōnfessō esse/in cōnfessum venīre** be generally admitted

cōnfestim adv immediately

cōnficiō, **-icere**, **-ēcī**, **-ectum** vt to make, effect, complete, accomplish; to get together, procure; to wear out, exhaust, consume, destroy; (COMM) to settle; (space) to travel; (time) to pass, complete; (PHILOS) to be an active cause; (LOGIC) to deduce; (pass) it follows

cōnfictiō, **-ōnis** f fabrication

cōnfictus ppp of **cōnfingō**

cōnfīdēns, **-entis** pres p of **cōnfīdō** ♦ adj self-confident, bold, presumptuous

cōnfīdenter adv fearlessly, insolently

cōnfīdentia, **-ae** f confidence, self-confidence; impudence

cōnfīdentiloquus adj outspoken

cōnfīdō, **-dere**, **-sus sum** vi to trust, rely, be sure; **sibi cōnfīdere** be confident

cōnfīgō, **-gere**, **-xī**, **-xum** vt to fasten together; to pierce, shoot; (fig) to paralyse

cōnfingō, **-ingere**, **-inxī**, **-ictum** vt to make, invent, pretend

cōnfīnis adj adjoining; (fig) akin

cōnfīnium, **-ī** nt common boundary; (pl) neighbours; (fig) close connection, borderland between

cōnfiō, **-fierī** occ pass of **cōnficiō**

cōnfirmātiō, **-ōnis** f establishing; (person) encouragement; (fact) verifying; (RHET) adducing of proofs

cōnfirmātor, **-ōris** m guarantor (of money)

cōnfirmātus adj resolute; proved, certain

cōnfirmō, **-āre**, **-āvī**, **-ātum** vt to strengthen, reinforce; (decree) to confirm, ratify; (mind) to encourage; (fact) to corroborate, prove, assert; **sē cōnfirmāre** recover; take courage

cōnfiscō, **-āre** vt to keep in a chest; to confiscate

cōnfisiō, **-ōnis** f assurance

cōnfīsus ppa of **cōnfīdō**

cōnfiteor, **-itērī**, **-essus** vt, vi to confess, acknowledge; to reveal

cōnfīxus ppp of **cōnfīgō**

cōnflagrō, **-āre**, **-āvī**, **-ātum** vi to burn, be ablaze

cōnflictiō, **-ōnis** f conflict

cōnflictō, **-āre**, **-āvī**, **-ātum** vt to strike down, contend (with); (pass) to fight, be harassed, be afflicted

cōnflictus, **-ūs** m striking together

cōnflīgō, **-gere**, **-xī**, **-ctum** vt to dash together; (fig) to contrast ♦ vi to fight, come into conflict

cōnflō, **-āre**, **-āvī**, **-ātum** vt to ignite; (passion) to inflame; to melt down; (fig) to produce, procure, occasion

cōnfluēns, **-entis**, **cōnfluentēs**, **-entium** m confluence of two rivers

cōnfluō, **-ere**, **-xī** vi to flow together; (fig) to flock together, pour in

cōnfodiō, **-odere**, **-ōdī**, **-ossum** vt to dig; to stab

cōnfore fut infin of **cōnsum**

cōnfōrmātiō, **-ōnis** f shape, form; (words) arrangement; (voice) expression; (mind) idea; (RHET) figure

cōnfōrmō, **-āre**, **-āvī**, **-ātum** vt to shape, fashion

cōnfossus ppp of **cōnfodiō** ♦ adj full of holes

cōnfrāctus ppp of **cōnfringō**

cōnfragōsus adj broken, rough; (fig) hard

cōnfrēgī perf of **cōnfringō**

cōnfremō, **-ere**, **-uī** vi to murmur aloud

cōnfricō, **-āre** vt to rub well

cōnfringō, **-ingere**, **-ēgī**, **-āctum** vt to break in pieces, wreck; (fig) to ruin

cōnfugiō, **-ugere**, **-ūgī** vi to flee for help (to), take refuge (with); (fig) to have recourse (to)

cōnfugium, **-ī** and **-iī** nt refuge

cōnfundō, **-undere**, **-ūdī**, **-ūsum** vt to mix, mingle, join; to mix up, confuse, throw into disorder; (mind) to perplex, bewilder; to diffuse, spread over

cōnfūsē adv confusedly

cōnfūsiō, **-ōnis** f combination; confusion, disorder; **ōris** ~ going red in the face

cōnfūsus ppp of **cōnfundō** ♦ adj confused, disorderly, troubled

cōnfūtō, **-āre**, **-āvī**, **-ātum** vt to keep from boiling over; to repress; to silence, confute

congelō, **-āre**, **-āvī**, **-ātum** vt to freeze, harden ◆ vi to freeze over, grow numb

congeminō, **-āre**, **-āvī**, **-ātum** vt to double

congemō, **-ere**, **-uī** vi to groan, sigh ◆ vt to lament

conger, **-rī** m sea eel

congeriēs, **-ēī** f heap, mass, accumulation

congerō¹, **-rere**, **-ssī**, **-stum** vt to collect, accumulate, build; (missiles) to shower; (speech) to comprise; (fig) to heap (upon), ascribe

congerō², **-ōnis** m thief

congerrō, **-ōnis** m companion in revelry

congestīcius adj piled up

congestus¹ ppp of **congerō**¹

congestus², **-ūs** m accumulating; heap, mass

congiālis adj holding a congius

congiārium, **-ī** and **-iī** nt gift of food to the people, gratuity to the army

congius, **-ī** and **-iī** m Roman liquid measure (about 6 pints)

conglaciō, **-āre** vi to freeze up

conglīscō, **-ere** vi to blaze up

conglobātiō, **-ōnis** f mustering

conglobō, **-āre**, **-āvī**, **-ātum** vt to make round; to mass together

conglomerō, **-āre** vt to roll up

conglūtinātiō, **-ōnis** f gluing, cementing; (fig) combination

conglūtinō, **-āre**, **-āvī**, **-ātum** vt to glue, cement; (fig) to join, weld together; to contrive

congraecō, **-āre** vt to squander on luxury

congrātulor, **-ārī**, **-ātus** vi to congratulate

congredior, **-dī**, **-ssus** vt, vi to meet, accost; to contend, fight

congregābilis adj gregarious

congregātiō, **-ōnis** f union, society

congregō, **-āre**, **-āvī**, **-ātum** vt to collect, assemble, unite

congressiō, **-ōnis** f meeting, conference

congressus¹ ppa of **congredior**

congressus², **-ūs** m meeting, association, union; encounter, fight

congruēns, **-entis** adj suitable, consistent, proper; harmonious

congruenter adv in conformity

congruō, **-ere**, **-ī** vi to coincide; to correspond, suit; to agree, sympathize

congruus adj agreeable

coniciō, **-icere**, **-iēcī**, **-iectum** vt to throw together; to throw, hurl; to put, fling, drive, direct; to infer, conjecture; (AUG) to interpret; sē conicere rush, fly; devote oneself

coniectiō, **-ōnis** f throwing, conjecture, interpretation

coniectō, **-āre** vt to infer, conjecture, guess

coniector, **-ōris** m (male) interpreter, diviner

coniectrīx, **-rīcis** f (female) interpreter, diviner

coniectūra, **-ae** f inference, conjecture, guess; interpretation

coniectūrālis adj (RHET) involving a question of fact

coniectus¹ ppp of **coniciō**

coniectus², **-ūs** m heap, mass, concourse; throwing, throw, range; (eyes, mind) turning, directing

cōnifer, **cōniger**, **-ī** adj cone-bearing

cōnītor, **-tī**, **-sus** and **-xus** vi to lean on; to strive, struggle on; to labour

coniugālis adj of marriage, conjugal

coniugātiō, **-ōnis** f etymological relationship

coniugātor, **-ōris** m uniter

coniugiālis adj marriage- (in cpds)

coniugium, **-ī** and **-iī** nt union, marriage; husband, wife

coniugō, **-āre** vt to form (a friendship); **coniugāta verba** words related etymologically

coniūnctē adv jointly; on familiar terms; (LOGIC) hypothetically

coniūnctim adv together, jointly

coniūnctiō, **-ōnis** f union, connection, association; (minds) sympathy, affinity; (GRAM) conjunction

coniūnctum, **-ī** nt (RHET) connection; (PHILOS) inherent property (of a body)

coniūnctus ppp of **coniungō** ◆ adj near; connected, agreeing, conforming; related, friendly, intimate

coniungō, **-ungere**, **-ūnxī**, **-ūnctum** vt to yoke, join together, connect; (war) to join forces in; to unite in love, marriage, friendship; to continue without a break

coniūnx, **-ugis** m/f consort, wife, husband, bride

coniūrātī, **-ōrum** mpl conspirators

coniūrātiō, **-ōnis** f conspiracy, plot; alliance

coniūrātus adj (MIL) after taking the oath

coniūrō, **-āre**, **-āvī**, **-ātum** vi to take an oath; to conspire, plot

coniux etc see **coniūnx**

cōnīveō, **-vēre**, **-vī** and **-xī** vi to shut the eyes, blink; (fig) to be asleep; to connive at

conj- etc see **coni-**

conl- etc see **coll-**

conm- etc see **comm-**

conn- etc see **cōn-**

Conōn, **-is** m Athenian commander; Greek astronomer

cōnōpēum, **cōnōpeum**, **-ēī** nt mosquito net

cōnor, **-ārī**, **-ātus** vt to try, attempt, venture

conp- etc see **comp-**

conquassātiō, **-ōnis** f severe shaking

conquassō, **-āre**, **-ātum** vt to shake, upset, shatter

conqueror, **-rī**, **-stus** vt, vi to complain bitterly of, bewail

conquestiō, **-ōnis** f complaining; (RHET) appeal to pity

conquestus¹ ppa of **conqueror**

conquestus², **-ūs** m outcry

conquiēscō, **-scere**, **-vī**, **-tum** vi to rest, take a respite; (fig) to be at peace, find recreation; (things) to stop, be quiet

conquīnīscō, **-ere** vi to cower, squat, stoop down

conquīrō, **-rere**, **-sīvī**, **-sītum** vt to search for, collect

conquīsītē adv carefully

conquīsītiō, **-ōnis** f search; (MIL) levy

conquīsītor, **-ōris** m recruiting officer; (theatre) claqueur

conquīsītus ppp of **conquīrō** ◆ adj select, costly

conr- *etc see* **corr-**

cōnsaepiō, -īre, -sī, -tum *vt* to enclose, fence round

cōnsaeptum, -tī *nt* enclosure

cōnsalūtātiō, -ōnis *f* mutual greeting

cōnsalūtō, -āre, -āvī, -ātum *vt* to greet, hail

cōnsānēscō, -ēscere, -uī *vi* to heal up

cōnsanguineus *adj* brother, sister, kindred ♦ *mpl* relations

cōnsanguinitās, -ātis *f* relationship

cōnscelerātus *adj* wicked

cōnscelerō, -āre, -āvī, -ātum *vt* to disgrace

cōnscendō, -endere, -endī, -ēnsum *vt, vi* to climb, mount, embark

cōnscēnsiō, -ōnis *f* embarkation

cōnscēnsus *ppp of* **cōnscendō**

cōnscientia, -ae *f* joint knowledge, being in the know; (*sense of*) consciousness; moral sense, conscience, guilty conscience

cōnscindō, -ndere, -dī, -ssum *vt* to tear to pieces; (*fig*) to abuse

cōnsciō, -īre *vt* to be conscious of guilt

cōnscīscō, -scere, -vī *and* **-iī, -ītum** *vt* to decide on publicly; to inflict on oneself; **mortem (sibi) cōnscīscere** commit suicide

cōnscīssus *ppp of* **cōnscindō**

cōnscītus *ppp of* **cōnscīscō**

cōnscius *adj* sharing knowledge, privy, in the know; aware, conscious (of); conscious of guilt ♦ *m/f* confederate, confidant

cōnscreor, -ārī *vi* to clear the throat

cōnscrībō, -bere, -psī, -ptum *vt* to enlist, enrol; to write, compose, draw up, prescribe

cōnscrīptiō, -ōnis *f* document, draft

cōnscrīptus *ppp of* **cōnscrībō**; **patrēs cōnscrīptī** patrician and elected plebeian members; senators

cōnsecō, -āre, -uī, -tum *vt* to cut up

cōnsecrātiō, -ōnis *f* consecration, deification

cōnsecrō, -āre, -āvī, -ātum *vt* to dedicate, consecrate, deify; (*fig*) to devote; to immortalise; **caput cōnsecrāre** doom to death

cōnsectārius *adj* logical, consequent ♦ *ntpl* inferences

cōnsectātiō, -ōnis *f* pursuit

cōnsectātrīx, -īcis *f* (*fig*) follower

cōnsectiō, -ōnis *f* cutting up

cōnsector, -ārī, -ātus *vt* to follow, go after, try to gain; to emulate, imitate; to pursue, chase

cōnsecūtiō, -ōnis *f* (*PHILOS*) consequences, effect; (*RHET*) sequence

cōnsēdī *perf of* **cōnsīdō**

cōnsenēscō, -ēscere, -uī *vi* to grow old, grow old together; (*fig*) to fade, pine, decay, become obsolete

cōnsēnsiō, -ōnis *f* agreement, accord; conspiracy, plot

cōnsēnsū *adv* unanimously

cōnsēnsus¹ *ppp of* **cōnsentiō**

cōnsēnsus², -ūs *m* agreement, concord; conspiracy; (*PHILOS*) common sensation; (*fig*) harmony

cōnsentāneus *adj* agreeing, in keeping with; **cōnsentāneum est** it is reasonable

cōnsentiō, -entīre, -ēnsī, -ēnsum *vi* to agree, determine together; to plot, conspire;

(*PHILOS*) to have common sensations; (*fig*) to harmonize, suit, be consistent (with); **bellum cōnsentīre** vote for war

cōnsequēns, -entis *pres p of* **cōnsequor** ♦ *adj* coherent, reasonable; logical, consequent ♦ *nt* consequence

cōnsequor, -quī, -cūtus *vt* to follow, pursue; to overtake, reach; (*time*) to come after; (*example*) to follow, copy; (*effect*) to result, be the consequence of; (*aim*) to attain, get; (*mind*) to grasp, learn; (*events*) to happen to, come to; (*standard*) to equal, come up to; (*speech*) to do justice to

cōnserō¹, -erere, -ēvī, -itum *vt* to sow, plant; (*ground*) to sow with, plant with; (*fig*) to cover, fill

cōnserō², -ere, -uī, -tum *vt* to join, string together, twine; (*MIL*) to join battle; **manum/manūs ~** engage in close combat; **ex iūre manum ~** lay claim to (*in an action for possession*)

cōnsertē *adv* connectedly

cōnsertus *ppp of* **cōnserō²**

cōnserva, -ae *f* fellow slave

cōnservātiō, -ōnis *f* preserving

cōnservātor, -ōris *m* preserver

cōnservitium, -ī *and* **-iī** *nt* being fellow slaves

cōnservō, -āre, -āvī, -ātum *vt* to preserve, save, keep

cōnservus, -ī *m* fellow slave

cōnsessor, -ōris *m* companion at table, fellow spectator; (*LAW*) assessor

cōnsessus, -ūs *m* assembly; (*LAW*) court

cōnsēvī *perf of* **cōnserō¹**

cōnsīderātē *adv* cautiously, deliberately

cōnsīderātiō, -ōnis *f* contemplation

cōnsīderātus *adj* (*person*) circumspect; (*things*) well-considered

cōnsīderō, -āre, -āvī, -ātum *vt* to look at, inspect; to consider, contemplate

cōnsīdō, -īdere, -ēdī, -essum *vi* to sit down, take seats; (*courts*) to be in session; (*MIL*) to take up a position; (*residence*) to settle; (*places*) to subside, sink; (*fig*) to sink, settle down, subside

cōnsignō, -āre, -āvī, -ātum *vt* to seal, sign; to attest, vouch for; to record, register

cōnsilēscō, -ere *vi* to calm down

cōnsiliārius, -ī *and* **-iī** *m* adviser, counsellor; spokesman ♦ *adj* counselling

cōnsiliātor, -ōris *m* counsellor

cōnsilior, -ārī, -ātus *vi* to consult; (*with dat*) to advise

cōnsilium, -ī *and* **-iī** *nt* deliberation, consultation; deliberating body, council; decision, purpose; plan, measure, stratagem; advice, counsel; judgement, insight, wisdom; **~ capere, ~ inīre** come to a decision, resolve; **cōnsilii esse** be an open question; **cōnsiliō** intentionally; **eō cōnsiliō ut** with the intention of; **prīvātō cōnsiliō** for one's own purposes

cōnsimilis *adj* just like

cōnsipiō, -ere *vi* to be in one's senses

cōnsistō, -istere, -titī *vi* to stand, rest, take up a position; to consist (of), depend (on); to exist, be; (*fig*) to stand firm, endure; (*liquid*) to solidify, freeze; to stop, pause, halt, come to rest; (fig) to come to a standstill, come to an end

cōnsitiō, -ōnis f sowing, planting

cōnsitor, -ōris m sower, planter

cōnsitus ppp of **cōnserō¹**

cōnsōbrīnus, -ī m, **cōnsōbrīna, -ae** f cousin

cōnsociātiō, -ōnis f society

cōnsociō, -āre, -āvī, -ātum vt to share, associate, unite

cōnsōlābilis adj consolable

cōnsōlātiō, -ōnis f comfort, encouragement, consolation

cōnsōlātor, -ōris m comforter

cōnsōlātōrius adj of consolation

cōnsōlor, -ārī, -ātus vt to console, comfort, reassure; (things) to relieve, mitigate

cōnsomniō, -āre vt to dream about

cōnsonō, -āre, -uī vi to resound; (fig) to accord

cōnsonus adj concordant; (fig) suitable

cōnsōpiō, -īre, -īvī, -ītum vt to put to sleep

cōnsors, -tis adj sharing in common; (things) shared in common ♦ m/f partner, colleague

cōnsortiō, -ōnis f partnership, fellowship

cōnsortium, -ī and **-iī** nt society, participation

cōnspectus¹ ppp of **cōnspiciō** ♦ adj visible; conspicuous

cōnspectus², -ūs m look, view, sight; appearing on the scene; (fig) mental picture, survey; **in cōnspectum venīre** come in sight, come near

cōnspergō, -gere, -sī, -sum vt to besprinkle; (fig) to spangle

cōnspiciendus adj noteworthy, distinguished

cōnspiciō, -icere, -exī, -ectum vt to observe, catch sight of; to look at (esp with admiration), contemplate; (pass) to attract attention, be conspicuous, be notorious; (mind) to see, perceive

cōnspicor, -ārī, -ātus vt to observe, see, catch sight of

cōnspicuus adj visible; conspicuous, distinguished

cōnspīrātiō, -ōnis f concord, unanimity; plotting, conspiracy

cōnspīrō, -āre, -āvī, -ātum vi to agree, unite; to plot, conspire; (music) to sound together

cōnspōnsor, -ōris m co-guarantor

cōnspuō, -ere vt to spit upon

cōnspurcō, -āre vt to pollute

cōnspūtō, -āre vt to spit upon (with contempt)

cōnstabiliō, -īre, -īvī, -ītum vt to establish

cōnstāns, -antis pres p of **cōnstō** ♦ adj steady, stable, constant; consistent; faithful, steadfast

cōnstanter adv steadily, firmly, calmly; consistently

cōnstantia, -ae f steadiness, firmness; consistency, harmony; self-possession, constancy

cōnsternātiō, -ōnis f disorder, tumult; (horses) stampede; (mind) dismay, alarm

cōnsternō¹, -ernere, -rāvī, -rātum vt to spread, cover, thatch, pave; **cōnstrāta nāvis** decked ship

cōnsternō², -āre, -āvī, -ātum vt to startle, stampede; to alarm, throw into confusion

cōnstīpō, -āre vt to crowd together

cōnstitī perf of **cōnsistō**

cōnstituō, -uere, -uī, -ūtum vt to put, place, set down; (MIL) to station, post, halt; to establish, build, create; to settle, arrange, organize; to appoint, determine, fix; to resolve, decide; **bene cōnstitūtum corpus** a good constitution

cōnstitūtiō, -ōnis f state, condition; regulation, decree; definition, point at issue

cōnstitūtum, -ūtī nt agreement

cōnstō, -āre, -itī, -ātum vi to stand together; to agree, correspond, tally; to stand firm, remain constant; to exist, be; to consist (of); be composed (of); (facts) to be established, be well-known; (COMM) to cost; **sibi cōnstāre** be consistent; **inter omnēs cōnstat** it is common knowledge; **mihi cōnstat** I am determined; **ratiō cōnstat** the account is correct

cōnstrātum, -ī nt flooring, deck

cōnstrātus ppp of **cōnsternō¹**

cōnstringō, -ingere, -inxī, -ictum vt to tie up, bind, fetter; (fig) to restrain, restrict; (speech) to compress, condense

cōnstructiō, -ōnis f building up; (words) arrangement, sequence

cōnstruō, -ere, -xī, -ctum vt to heap up; to build, construct

cōnstuprātor, -ōris m debaucher

cōnstuprō, -āre vt to debauch, rape

cōnsuādeō, -ēre vi to advise strongly

Cōnsuālia, -ium ntpl festival of Consus

cōnsuāsor, -ōris m earnest adviser

cōnsūdō, -āre vi to sweat profusely

cōnsuēfaciō, -facere, -fēcī, -factum vt to accustom

cōnsuēscō, -scere, -vī, -tum vt to accustom, inure ♦ vi to get accustomed; to cohabit (with); (perf tenses) to be accustomed, be in the habit of

cōnsuētūdō, -inis f custom, habit; familiarity, social intercourse; love affair; (language) usage, idiom; **cōnsuētūdine/ex cōnsuētūdine** as usual; **epistulārum** ~ correspondence

cōnsuētus ppp of **cōnsuēscō** ♦ adj customary, usual

cōnsuēvī perf of **cōnsuēscō**

cōnsul, -is m consul; ~ **dēsignātus** consul elect; ~ **ōrdinārius** regular consul; ~ **suffectus** successor to a consul who has died during his term of office; ~ **iterum/tertium** consul for the second/third time; **cōnsulem creāre, cōnsulem dīcere, cōnsulem facere** elect to the consulship; **L. Domitiō App. Claudiō cōnsulibus** in the year 54 B.C.

cōnsulāris adj consular, consul's; of consular rank ♦ m ex-consul

cōnsulāriter adv in a manner worthy of a consul

cōnsulātus, -ūs m consulship; **cōnsulātum petere** stand for the consulship

cōnsulō, -ere, -uī, -tum vi to deliberate, take thought; (with dat) to look after, consult the interests of; (with dē or in) to take measures against, pass sentence on ♦ vt to consult, ask advice of; to consider; to advise (something); to decide; **bonī/optimī cōnsulere** take in good part, be satisfied with

cōnsultātiō, **-ōnis** *f* deliberation; inquiry; case
cōnsultē *adv* deliberately
cōnsultō¹ *adv* deliberately
cōnsultō², **-āre**, **-āvī**, **-ātum** *vt*, *vi* to deliberate, reflect; to consult; (*with dat*) to consult the interests of
cōnsultor, **-ōris** *m* counsellor; **consulter** client
cōnsultrīx, **-īcis** *f* protectress
cōnsultum, **-ī** *nt* decree (*esp of the Senate*); consultation; response (*from an oracle*)
cōnsultus *ppp of* **cōnsulō ♦** *adj* considered; experienced, skilled **♦** *m* lawyer; **iūris ~** lawyer
cōnsuluī *perf of* **cōnsulō**
(**cōnsum**), **-futūrum**, **-fore** *vi* to be all right
cōnsummātus *adj* perfect
cōnsummō, **-āre** *vt* to sum up; to complete, perfect
cōnsūmō, **-ere**, **-psī**, **-ptum** *vt* to consume, use up, eat up; to waste, squander; to exhaust, destroy, kill; to spend, devote
cōnsūmptiō, **-ōnis** *f* wasting
cōnsūmptor, **-ōris** *m* destroyer
cōnsūmptus *ppp of* **cōnsūmō**
cōnsuō, **-uere**, **-uī**, **-ūtum** *vt* to sew up; (*fig*) to contrive
cōnsurgō, **-gere**, **-rēxī**, **-rēctum** *vi* to rise, stand up; to be roused (to); to spring up, start
cōnsurrēctiō, **-ōnis** *f* standing up
Cōnsus, **-ī** *m* ancient Roman god (*connected with harvest*)
cōnsusurrō, **-āre** *vi* to whisper together
cōnsūtus *ppp of* **cōnsuō**
contābefaciō, **-ere** *vt* to wear out
contābēscō, **-ēscere**, **-uī** *vi* to waste away
contabulātiō, **-ōnis** *f* flooring, storey
contabulō, **-āre**, **-āvī**, **-ātum** *vt* to board over, build in storeys
contāctus¹ *ppp of* **contingō¹**
contāctus², **-ūs** *m* touch, contact; contagion, infection
contāgēs, **-is** *f* contact, touch
contāgiō, **-ōnis** *f*, **contāgium**, **-ī** *and* **-iī** *nt* contact; contagion, infection; (*fig*) contamination, bad example
contāminātus *adj* impure, vicious
contāminō, **-āre**, **-āvī**, **-ātum** *vt* to defile; (*fig*) to mar, spoil
contechnor, **-ārī**, **-ātus** *vi* to think out plots
contegō, **-egere**, **-ēxī**, **-ēctum** *vt* to cover up, cover over; to protect; to hide
contemerō, **-āre** *vt* to defile
contemnō, **-nere**, **-psī**, **-ptum** *vt* to think light of, have no fear of, despise, defy; to disparage
contemplātiō, **-ōnis** *f* contemplation, surveying
contemplātor, **-ōris** *m* observer
contemplātus, **-ūs** *m* contemplation
contemplō, **-āre**, **-āvī**, **-ātum**, **contemplor**, **-ārī**, **-ātus** *vt* to look at, observe, contemplate
contempsī *perf of* **contemnō**
contemptim *adv* contemptuously, slightingly
contemptiō, **-ōnis** *f* disregard, scorn, despising
contemptor, **-ōris** *m* (*male*) despiser, defier
contemptrīx, **-rīcis** *f* (*female*) despiser, defier

contemptus¹ *ppp of* **contemnō ♦** *adj* contemptible
contemptus², **-ūs** *m* despising, scorn; being slighted; **contemptuī esse** be despised
contendō, **-dere**, **-dī**, **-tum** *vt* to stretch, draw, tighten; (*instrument*) to tune; (*effort*) to strain, exert; (*argument*) to assert, maintain; (*comparison*) to compare, contrast; (*course*) to direct **♦** *vi* to exert oneself, strive; to hurry; to journey, march; to contend, compete, fight; to entreat, solicit
contentē¹ *adv* (*from* **contendō**) earnestly, intensely
contentē² *adv* (*from* **contineō**) closely
contentiō, **-ōnis** *f* straining, effort; striving (after); struggle, competition, dispute; comparison, contrast, antithesis
contentus¹ *ppp of* **contendō ♦** *adj* strained, tense; (*fig*) intent
contentus² *ppp of* **contineō ♦** *adj* content, satisfied
conterminus *adj* bordering, neighbouring
conterō, **-erere**, **-rīvī**, **-rītum** *vt* to grind, crumble; to wear out, waste; (*time*) to spend, pass; (*fig*) to obliterate
conterreō, **-ēre**, **-uī**, **-itum** *vt* to terrify
contestātus *adj* proved
contestor, **-ārī**, **-ātus** *vt* to call to witness; **lītem ~** open a lawsuit by calling witnesses
contexō, **-ere**, **-uī**, **-tum** *vt* to weave, interweave; to devise, construct; (*recital*) to continue
contextē *adv* in a connected fashion
contextus¹ *adj* connected
contextus², **-ūs** *m* connection, coherence
conticēscō, **conticīscō**, **-ēscere**, **-uī** *vi* to become quiet, fall silent; (*fig*) to cease, abate
contigī *perf of* **contingō¹**
contignātiō, **-ōnis** *f* floor, storey
contignō, **-āre** *vt* to floor
contiguus *adj* adjoining, near; within reach
continēns, **-entis** *pres p of* **contineō ♦** *adj* bordering, adjacent; unbroken, continuous; (*time*) successive, continual, uninterrupted; (*person*) temperate, continent **♦** *nt* mainland, continent; essential point (*in an argument*)
continenter *adv* (*place*) in a row; (*time*) continuously; (*person*) temperately
continentia, **-ae** *f* moderation, self-control
contineō, **-inēre**, **-inuī**, **-entum** *vt* to hold, keep together; to confine, enclose; to contain, include, comprise; (*pass*) to consist of, rest on; to control, check, repress
contingō¹, **-ingere**, **-igī**, **-āctum** *vt* to touch, take hold of, partake of; to be near, border on; to reach, come to; to contaminate; (*mind*) to touch, affect, concern **♦** *vi* to happen, succeed
contingō², **-ere** *vt* to moisten, smear
continuātiō, **-ōnis** *f* unbroken succession, series; (RHET) period
continuī *perf of* **contineō**
continuō *adv* immediately, without delay; (*argument*) necessarily

continuō², **-āre**, **-āvī**, **-ātum** vt to join together, make continuous; to continue without a break; **verba continuāre** form a sentence

continuus adj joined (to); continuous, successive, uninterrupted; **continuā nocte** the following night; **triduum continuum** three days running

cōntiō, **-ōnis** f public meeting; speech, address; rostrum; **cōntiōnem habēre** hold a meeting; deliver an address; **prō cōntiōne** in public

cōntiōnābundus adj delivering a harangue, playing the demagogue

cōntiōnālis adj suitable for a public meeting, demagogic

cōntiōnārius adj fond of public meetings

cōntiōnātor, **-ōris** m demagogue

cōntiōnor, **-ārī**, **-ātus** vi to address a public meeting, harangue; to declare in public; to come to a meeting

cōntiuncula, **-ae** f short speech

contorqueō, **-quēre**, **-sī**, **-tum** vt to twist, turn; (weapons) to throw, brandish; (words) to deliver forcibly

contortē adv intricately

contortiō, **-ōnis** f intricacy

contortor, **-ōris** m perverter

contortulus adj somewhat complicated

contortuplicātus adj very complicated

contortus ppp of **contorqueō** ♦ adj vehement; intricate

contrā adv (place) opposite, face to face; (speech) in reply; (action) to fight, in opposition, against (someone); (result, with esse) adverse, unsuccessful; (comparison) the contrary, conversely, differently; (argument) on the contrary, on the other hand; ~ atque, ~ quam contrary to what, otherwise than ♦ prep (with acc) facing, opposite to; against; contrary to, in violation of

contractiō, **-ōnis** f contracting; shortening; despondency

contractiuncula, **-ae** f slight despondency

contractus ppp of **contrahō** ♦ adj contracted, narrow; short; in seclusion

contrādīcō (usu two words), **-dīcere**, **-dīxī**, **-dictum** vt, vi to oppose, object; (LAW) to be counsel for the other side

contrādictiō, **-ōnis** f objection

contrahō, **-here**, **-xī**, **-ctum** vt to draw together, assemble; to bring about, achieve; (COMM) to contract, make a bargain; to shorten, narrow; to limit, depress; (blame) to incur; (brow) to wrinkle; (sail) to shorten; (sky) to overcast

contrāriē adv differently

contrārius adj opposite, from opposite; contrary; hostile, harmful ♦ nt opposite, reverse; **ex contrāriō** on the contrary

contrectābiliter adv so as to be felt

contrectātiō, **-ōnis** f touching

contrectō, **-āre**, **-āvī**, **-ātum** vt to touch, handle; (fig) to consider

contremīscō, **-īscere**, **-uī** vi to tremble all over; (fig) to waver ♦ vt to be afraid of

contremō, **-ere** vi to quake

contribuō, **-uere**, **-uī**, **-ūtum** vt to bring together, join, incorporate

contristō, **-āre**, **-āvī**, **-ātum** vt to sadden, darken, cloud

contrītus ppp of **conterō** ♦ adj trite, well-worn

contrōversia, **-ae** f dispute, argument, debate, controversy

contrōversiōsus adj much disputed

contrōversus adj disputed, questionable

contrucīdō, **-āre**, **-āvī**, **-ātum** vt to massacre

contrūdō, **-dere**, **-sī**, **-sum** vt to crowd together

contruncō, **-āre** vt to hack to pieces

contrūsus ppp of **contrūdō**

contubernālis, **-is** m/f tent companion; junior officer serving with a general; (fig) companion, mate

contubernium, **-ī** and **-iī** nt service in the same tent, mess; service as junior officer with a general; common tent, slaves' home

contueor, **-ērī**, **-itus** vt to look at, consider, observe

contuitus, **-ūs** m observing, view

contulī perf of **cōnferō**

contumācia, **-ae** f obstinacy, defiance

contumāciter adv see **contumāx**

contumāx, **-ācis** adj stubborn, insolent, pig-headed

contumēlia, **-ae** f (verbal) insult, libel, invective; (physical) assault, ill-treatment

contumēliōsē adv insolently

contumēliōsus adj insulting, outrageous

contumulō, **-āre** vt to bury

contundō, **-undere**, **-udī**, **-ūsum** vt to pound, beat, bruise; (fig) to suppress, destroy

contuor etc see **contueor**

conturbātiō, **-ōnis** f confusion, mental disorder

conturbātus adj distracted, diseased

conturbō, **-āre**, **-āvī**, **-ātum** vt to throw into confusion; (mind) to derange, disquiet; (money) to embarrass

contus, **-ī** m pole

contūsus ppp of **contundō**

contūtus see **contuitus**

cōnūbiālis adj conjugal

cōnūbium, **-ī** and **-iī** nt marriage; **iūs cōnūbiī** right of intermarriage

cōnus, **-ī** m cone; (helmet) apex

convador, **-ārī**, **-ātus** vt (LAW) to bind over

convalēscō, **-ēscere**, **-uī** vi to recover, get better; (fig) to grow stronger, improve

convallis, **-is** f valley with hills on all sides

convāsō, **-āre** vt to pack up

convectō, **-āre** vt to bring home

convector, **-ōris** m fellow passenger

convehō, **-here**, **-xī**, **-ctum** vt to bring in, carry

convellō, **-ellere**, **-ellī**, **-ulsum** and **-olsum** vt to wrench, tear away; to break up; (fig) to destroy, overthrow; **signa convellere** decamp

convena, **-ae** adj meeting

convenae, **-ārum** mpl/fpl crowd of strangers, refugees

conveniēns, **-entis** pres p of **conveniō** ♦ adj harmonious, consistent; fit, appropriate

convenienter *adv* in conformity (with), consistently; aptly

convenientia, -ae *f* conformity, harmony

conveniō, -enīre, -ēnī, -entum *vi* to meet, assemble; (*events*) to combine, coincide; (*person*) to agree, harmonize; (*things*) to fit, suit; (*impers*) to be suitable, be proper ♦ *vt* to speak to, interview

conventīcium, -ī *and* **-iī** *nt* payment for attendance at assemblies

conventīcius *adj* visiting regularly

conventiculum, -ī *nt* gathering; meeting place

conventiō, -ōnis *f* agreement

conventum, -ī *nt* agreement

conventus[1] *ppp of* **conveniō**

conventus[2], -ūs *m* meeting; (*LAW*) local assizes; (*COMM*) corporation; agreement; **conventūs agere** hold the assizes

converrō, -rere, -rī, -sum *vt* to sweep up, brush together; (*comedy*) to give a good beating to

conversātiō, -ōnis *f* associating (with)

conversiō, -ōnis *f* revolution, cycle; change over; (*RHET*) well-rounded period; verbal repetition at end of clauses

conversō, -āre *vt* to turn round

conversus *ppp* **converrō; convertō**

convertō, -tere, -tī, -sum *vt* to turn round, turn back; (*MIL*) to wheel; to turn, direct; to change, transform; (*writings*) to translate ♦ *vi* to return, turn, change

convestiō, -īre, -īvī, -ītum *vt* to clothe, encompass

convexus *adj* vaulted, rounded; hollow; sloping ♦ *nt* vault, hollow

convīciātor, -ōris *m* slanderer

convīcior, -ārī, -ātus *vt* to revile

convīcium, -ī *and* **-iī** *nt* loud noise, outcry; invective, abuse; reproof, protest

convīctiō, -ōnis *f* companionship

convīctor, -ōris *m* familiar friend

convīctus *ppp of* **convincō**

convīctus, -ūs *m* community life, intercourse; entertainment

convincō, -incere, -īcī, -ictum *vt* to refute, convict, prove wrong; to prove, demonstrate

convīsō, -ere *vt* to search, examine; to pervade

convītium *see* **convīcium**

convīva, -ae *m/f* guest

convīvālis *adj* festive, convivial

convīvātor, -ōris *m* host

convīvium, -ī *and* **-iī** *nt* banquet, entertainment; guests

convīvor, -ārī, -ātus *vi* to feast together, carouse

convocātiō, -ōnis *f* assembling

convocō, -āre, -āvī, -ātum *vt* to call a meeting of, muster

convolnerō *see* **convulnerō**

convolō, -āre, -āvī, -ātum *vi* to flock together

convolsus *see* **convulsus**

convolvō, -vere, -vī, -ūtum *vt* to roll up, coil up; to intertwine

convomō, -ere *vt* to vomit over

convorrō *see* **converrō**

convortō *see* **convertō**

convulnerō, -āre *vt* to wound seriously

convulsus *ppp of* **convellō**

cooperiō, -īre, -uī, -tum *vt* to cover over, overwhelm

cooptātiō, -ōnis *f* electing, nominating (*of new members*)

cooptō, -āre, -āvī, -ātum *vt* to elect (*as a colleague*)

coorior, -īrī, -tus *vi* to rise, appear; to break out, begin

coortus, -ūs *m* originating

cōpa, -ae *f* barmaid

cophinus, -ī *m* basket

cōpia, -ae *f* abundance, plenty, number; resources, wealth, prosperity; (*MIL, usu pl*) troops, force; (*words, thought*) richness, fulness, store; (*action*) opportunity, facility, means, access; **prō cōpiā** according to one's resources, as good as possible considering

cōpiolae, -ārum *fpl* small force

cōpiōsē *adv* abundantly, fully, at great length

cōpiōsus *adj* abounding, rich, plentiful; (*speech*) eloquent, fluent

cōpis *adj* rich

cōpula, -ae *f* rope, leash, grapnel; (*fig*) bond

cōpulātiō, -ōnis *f* coupling, union

cōpulātus *adj* connected, binding

cōpulō, -āre, -āvī, -ātum *vt* to couple, join; (*fig*) to unite, associate

coqua, -ae *f* cook

coquīnō, -āre *vi* to be a cook

coquīnus *adj* of cooking

coquō, -quere, -xī, -ctum *vt* to cook, boil, bake; to parch, burn; (*fruit*) to ripen; (*stomach*) to digest; (*thought*) to plan, concoct; (*care*) to disquiet, disturb

coquus, cocus, -ī *m* cook

cor, cordis *nt* heart; (*feeling*) heart, soul; (*thought*) mind, judgement; **cordī esse** please, be agreeable

cōram *adv* in one's presence; in person ♦ *prep* (*with abl*) in the presence of, before

corbis, -is *m/f* basket

corbīta, -ae *f* slow boat

corbula, -ae *f* little basket

corculum, -ī *nt* dear heart

Corcȳra, -ae *f* island off W. coast of Greece (now Corfu)

Corcȳraeus *adj see* **Corcȳra**

cordātē *adv see* **cordātus**

cordātus *adj* wise

cordolium, -ī *and* **-iī** *nt* sorrow

Corfīniēnsis *adj see* **Corfīnium**

Corfīnium, -ī *nt* town in central Italy

coriandrum, -ī *nt* coriander

Corinthiacus, Corinthiēnsis, Corinthius *adj*: **Corinthium aes** Corinthian brass (*an alloy of gold, silver and copper*)

Corinthus, -ī *f* Corinth

corium, -ī *and* **-iī** *nt*, **corius, -ī** *and* **-iī** *m* hide, skin; leather, strap

Cornēlia, -iae *f* mother of the Gracchi

Cornēliānus, Cornēlius *adj*: **lēgēs Cornēliae** Sulla's laws

Cornēlius, **-ī** m famous Roman family name (esp Scipios, Gracchi, Sulla)

corneolus adj horny

corneus¹ adj of horn

corneus² adj of the cornel tree, of cornel wood

cornicen, **-cinis** m horn-blower

cornīcula, **-ae** f little crow

corniculārius, **-ī** and **-iī** m adjutant

corniculum, **-ī** nt a horn-shaped decoration

corniger, **-ī** adj horned

cornipēs, **-edis** adj horn-footed

cornīx, **-īcis** f crow

cornū, **-ūs**, **cornum**, **-ī** nt horn; anything horn-shaped; (army) wing; (bay) arm; (book) roller-end; (bow) tip; (helmet) crest-socket; (land) tongue, spit; (lyre) arm; (moon) horn; (place) side; (river) branch; (yardarm) point; anything made of horn: bow, funnel, lantern; (music) horn; (oil) cruet; anything like horn, beak, hoof, wart; (fig) strength, courage; ~ cōpiae Amalthea's horn, symbol of plenty

cornum¹, **-ī** nt cornelian cherry

cornum² see cornū

cornus, **-ī** f cornelian cherry tree; javelin

corōlla, **-ae** f small garland

corōllārium, **-ī** and **-iī** nt garland for actors; present, gratuity

corōna, **-ae** f garland, crown; (ASTR) Corona Borealis; (people) gathering, bystanders; (MIL) cordon of besiegers or defenders; **sub corōnā vēndere**, **sub corōnā vēnīre** sell, be sold as slaves

Corōnaeus, **Corōnēus**, **Corōnēnsis** adj see Corōnēa

corōnārium aurum gold collected in the provinces for a victorious general

Corōnēa, **-ēae** f town in central Greece

corōnō, **-āre**, **-āvī**, **-ātum** vt to put a garland on, crown; to encircle

corporeus adj corporeal; of flesh

corpulentus adj corpulent

corpus, **-oris** nt body; substance, flesh; corpse; trunk, torso; person, individual; (fig) structure, corporation, body politic

corpusculum, **-ī** nt particle; term of endearment

corrādō, **-dere**, **-sī**, **-sum** vt to scrape together, procure

corrēctiō, **-ōnis** f amending, improving

corrēctor, **-ōris** m reformer, critic

corrēctus ppp of corrigō

corrēpō, **-ere**, **-sī** vi to creep, slink, cower

correptē adv briefly

correptus ppp of corripiō

corrīdeō, **-ēre** vi to laugh aloud

corrigia, **-ae** f shoelace

corrigō, **-igere**, **-ēxī**, **-ēctum** vt to make straight; to put right, improve, correct

corripiō, **-ipere**, **-ipuī**, **-eptum** vt to seize, carry off, get along quickly; (speech) to reprove, reproach, accuse; (passion) to seize upon, attack; (time, words) to cut short; **sē gradum corripere**, **sē viam corripere** hasten, rush

corrōborō, **-āre**, **-āvī**, **-ātum** vt to make strong, invigorate

corrōdō, **-dere**, **-sī**, **-sum** vt to nibble away

corrogō, **-āre** vt to gather by requesting

corrūgō, **-āre** vt to wrinkle

corrumpō, **-umpere**, **-ūpī**, **-uptum** vt to break up, ruin, waste; to mar, adulterate, falsify; (person) to corrupt, seduce, bribe

corruō, **-ere**, **-ī** vi to fall, collapse ♦ vt to overthrow, heap up

corruptē adv perversely; in a lax manner

corruptēla, **-ae** f corruption, bribery; seducer

corruptiō, **-ōnis** f bribing, seducing; corrupt state

corruptor, **-ōris** m, **corruptrīx**, **-rīcis** f corrupter, seducer

corruptus ppp of corrumpō ♦ adj spoiled, corrupt, bad

Corsus adj Corsican

cortex, **-icis** m/f bark, rind; cork

cortīna, **-ae** f kettle, cauldron; tripod of Apollo; (fig) vault, circle

corulus, **-ī** f hazel

Cōrus see Caurus

coruscō, **-āre** vt to butt; to shake, brandish ♦ vi to flutter, flash, quiver

coruscus adj tremulous, oscillating; shimmering, glittering

corvus, **-ī** m raven; (MIL) grapnel

Corybantēs, **-ium** mpl priests of Cybele

Corybantius adj see Corybantēs

cōrycus, **-ī** m punchball

corylētum, **-ī** nt hazel copse

corylus, **-ī** f hazel

corymbifer m Bacchus

corymbus, **-ī** m cluster (esp of ivy berries)

coryphaeus, **-ī** m leader

cōrytos, **cōrytus**, **-ī** m quiver

cōs, **cōtis** f hard rock, flint; grindstone

Cōs, **Coī** f Aegean island (famous for wine and weaving) ♦ nt Coan wine ♦ ntpl Coan clothes

cosmēta, **-ae** m master of the wardrobe

costa, **-ae** f rib; side, wall

costum, **-ī** nt an aromatic plant, perfume

cothurnātus adj buskined, tragic

cothurnus, **-ī** m buskin, hunting boot; tragedy, elevated style

cotīd- see cottīd-

cōtis f see cōs

cottabus, **-ī** m game of throwing drops of wine

cottana, **-ōrum** ntpl Syrian figs

cottīdiānō adv daily

cottīdiānus adj daily; everyday, ordinary

cottīdiē adv every day, daily

coturnīx, **-īcis** f quail

Cotyttia, **-ōrum** ntpl festival of Thracian goddess Cotytto

Cōus adj Coan

covinnārius, **-ī** and **-iī** m chariot fighter

covinnus, **-ī** m war chariot; coach

coxa, **-ae**, **coxendīx**, **-īcis** f hip

coxī perf of coquō

crābrō, **-ōnis** m hornet

crambē, **-ēs** f cabbage; ~ repetīta stale repetitions

Crantor, **-oris** m Greek Academic philosopher

crāpula, **-ae** f intoxication, hangover

crāpulārius adj for intoxication

crās *adv* tomorrow

crassē *adv* grossly, dimly

Crassiānus *adj see* **Crassus**

crassitūdō, -inis *f* thickness, density

crassus *adj* thick, gross, dense; (*fig*) dull, stupid

Crassus, -ī *m famous orator; wealthy politician, triumvir with Caesar and Pompey*

crāstinum, -ī *nt* the morrow

crāstinus *adj* of tomorrow; **diē crāstinī** tomorrow

crātēr, -is *m*, **crātēra, -ae** *f* bowl (*esp for mixing wine and water*); crater; *a constellation*

crātis, -is *f* wickerwork, hurdle; (AGR) harrow; (MIL) faggots for lining trenches; (*shield*) ribs; (*fig*) frame, joints

creātiō, -ōnis *f* election

creātor, -ōris *m*, **creātrīx, -rīcis** *f* creator, father, mother

creātus *m* (*with abl*) son of

crēber, -rī *adj* dense, thick, crowded; numerous, frequent; (*fig*) prolific, abundant

crēbrēscō, -ēscere, -uī *vi* to increase, become frequent

crēbritās, -ātis *f* frequency

crēbrō *adv* repeatedly

crēdibilis *adj* credible

crēdibiliter *adv see* **crēdibilis**

crēditor, -ōris *m* creditor

crēditum, -itī *nt* loan

crēdō, -ere, -idī, -itum *vt, vi* to entrust, lend; to trust, have confidence in; to believe; to think, suppose; **crēderēs** one would have thought

crēdulitās, -ātis *f* credulity

crēdulus *adj* credulous, trusting

cremō, -āre, -āvī, -ātum *vt* to burn, cremate

Cremōna, -ae *f town in N. Italy*

cremor, -ōris *m* juice, broth

creō, -āre, -āvī, -ātum *vt* to create, produce, beget; to elect (*to an office*), cause, occasion

creper, -ī *adj* dark; doubtful

crepida, -ae *f* sandal; **nē sūtor suprā crepidam** let the cobbler stick to his last

crepidātus *adj* wearing sandals

crepīdō, -inis *f* pedestal, base; bank, pier, dam

crepidula, -ae *f* small sandal

crepitācillum, -ī *nt* rattle

crepitō, -āre *vi* to rattle, chatter, rustle, creak

crepitus, -ūs *m* rattling, chattering, rustling, creaking

crepō, -āre, -uī, -itum *vi* to rattle, creak, snap (*fingers*) ✦ *vt* to make rattle, clap; to chatter about

crepundia, -ōrum *ntpl* rattle, babies' toys

crepusculum, -ī *nt* twilight, dusk; darkness

Crēs, -ētis *m* Cretan

crēscō, -scere, -vī, -tum *vi* to arise, appear, be born; to grow up, thrive, increase, multiply; to prosper, be promoted, rise in the world

Crēsius *adj* Cretan

Crēssa, -ae *f* Cretan

Crēta, -ae *f* Crete

crēta, -ae *f* chalk; good mark

Crētaeus, Crēticus, Crētis, -idis *adj see* **Crēta**

crētātus *adj* chalked; dressed in white

Crētē *see* **Crēta**

crēteus *adj* of chalk, of clay

crētiō, -ōnis *f declaration of accepting an inheritance*

crētōsus *adj* chalky, clayey

crētula, -ae *f* white clay for sealing

crētus *ppp of* **cernō** ✦ *ppa of* **crēscō** ✦ *adj* descended, born

Creūsa, -ae *f wife of Jason; wife of Aeneas*

crēvī *perf of* **cernō**; **crēscō**

crībrum, -ī *nt* sieve

crīmen, -inis *nt* accusation, charge, reproach; guilt, crime; cause of offence; **esse in crīmine** stand accused

crīminātiō, -ōnis *f* complaint, slander

crīminātor, -ōris *m* accuser

crīminō, -āre *vt* to accuse

crīminor, -ārī, -ātus *dep* to accuse, impeach; (*things*) to complain of, charge with

crīminōsē *adv* accusingly, slanderously

crīminōsus *adj* reproachful, slanderous

crīnālis *adj* for the hair, hair- (*in cpds*) ✦ *nt* hairpin

crīnis, -is *m* hair; (*comet*) tail

crīnītus *adj* long-haired; crested; **stēlla crīnīta** comet

crīspāns, -antis *adj* wrinkled

crīspō, -āre *vt* to curl, swing, wave

crīspus *adj* curled; curly-headed; wrinkled; tremulous

crista, -ae *f* cockscomb, crest; plume

cristātus *adj* crested, plumed

criticus, -ī *m* critic

croceus *adj* of saffron, yellow

crocinus *adj* yellow ✦ *nt* saffron oil

crōciō, -īre *vi* to croak

crocodīlus, -ī *m* crocodile

crocōtārius *adj* of saffron clothes

crocōtula, -ae *f* saffron dress

crocus, -ī *m*, **crocum, -ī** *nt* saffron; yellow

Croesus, -ī *m* king of Lydia (*famed for wealth*)

crotalistria, -ae *f* castanet dancer

crotalum, -ī *nt* rattle, castanet

cruciābilitās, -ātis *f* torment

cruciāmentum, -ī *nt* torture

cruciātus, -ūs *m* torture; instrument of torture; (*fig*) ruin, misfortune

cruciō, -āre, -āvī, -ātum *vt* to torture; to torment

crūdēlis *adj* hard-hearted, cruel

crūdēlitās, -ātis *f* cruelty, severity

crūdēliter *adv see* **crūdēlis**

crūdēscō, -ēscere, -uī *vi* to grow violent, grow worse

crūditās, -ātis *f* indigestion

crūdus *adj* bleeding; (*food*) raw, undigested; (*person*) dyspeptic; (*leather*) rawhide; (*fruit*) unripe; (*age*) immature, fresh; (*voice*) hoarse; (*fig*) unfeeling, cruel, merciless

cruentō, -āre *vt* to stain with blood, wound

cruentus *adj* bloody, gory; bloodthirsty, cruel; blood-red

crumēna, -ae *f* purse; money

crumilla, -ae *f* purse

cruor, -ōris *m* blood; bloodshed

cruppellāriī, -ōrum mpl mail-clad fighters

crūrifragius, -ī and **-iī** m one whose legs have been broken

crūs, -ūris nt leg, shin

crūsta, -ae f hard surface, crust; stucco, embossed or inlaid work

crūstulum, -ī nt small pastry

crūstum, -ī nt pastry

crux, -ucis f gallows, cross; (fig) torment; **abī in malam crucem** go and be hanged!

crypta, -ae f underground passage, grotto

cryptoporticus, -ūs f covered walk

crystallinus adj of crystal ♦ ntpl crystal vases

crystallum, -ī nt, **crystallus, -ī** m crystal

cubiculāris, cubiculārius adj of the bedroom ♦ m valet de chambre

cubiculum, -ī nt bedroom

cubīle, -is nt bed, couch; (animals) lair, nest; (fig) den

cubital, -ālis nt cushion

cubitālis adj a cubit long

cubitō, -āre vi to lie (in bed)

cubitum, -ī nt elbow; cubit

cubitus, -ūs m lying in bed

cubō, -āre, -uī, -itum vi to lie in bed; to recline at table; (places) to lie on a slope

cucullus, -ī m hood, cowl

cucūlus, -ī m cuckoo

cucumis, -eris m cucumber

cucurbita, -ae f gourd; cupping glass

cucurrī perf of **currō**

cūdō, -ere vt to beat, thresh; (metal) to forge; (money) to coin

cūiās, -tis pron of what country?, of what town?

cuicuimodī (gen of quisquis and modus) of whatever kind, whatever like

cūius pron (interrog) whose?; (rel) whose

culcita, -ae f mattress, pillow; eyepatch

cūleus see **culleus**

culex, -icis m/f gnat

culīna, -ae f kitchen; food

culleus, cūleus, -ī m leather bag for holding liquids; a fluid measure

culmen, -inis nt stalk; top, roof, summit; (fig) height, acme

culmus, -ī m stalk, straw

culpa, -ae f blame, fault; mischief; **in culpā sum, mea ~ est** I am at fault or to blame

culpātus adj blameworthy

culpitō, -āre vt to find fault with

culpō, -āre, -āvī, -ātum vt to blame, reproach

cultē adv in a refined manner

cultellus, -ī m small knife

culter, -rī m knife, razor

cultiō, -ōnis f cultivation

cultor, -ōris m cultivator, planter, farmer; inhabitant; supporter, upholder; worshipper

cultrīx, -īcis f inhabitant; (fig) nurse, fosterer

cultūra, -ae f cultivation, agriculture; (mind) care, culture; (person) courting

cultus¹ ppp of **colō** ♦ adj cultivated; (dress) well-dressed; (mind) polished, cultured ♦ ntpl cultivated land

cultus², -ūs m cultivation, care; (mind) training, culture; (dress) style, attire; (way of life) refinement, civilization; (gods) worship; (men) honouring

culullus, -ī m goblet

cūlus, -ī m buttocks

cum¹ prep (with abl) with; **cum decimō** tenfold; **cum eō quod, cum eō ut** with the proviso that; **cum prīmīs** especially; **cum māgnā calamitāte cīvitātis** to the great misfortune of the community; **cum perīculō suō** at one's own peril

cum² conj (time) when, whenever, while, as, after, since; (cause) since, as, seeing that; (concession) although; (condition) if; (contrast) while, whereas; **multī annī sunt cum in aere meō est** for many years now he has been in my debt; **aliquot sunt annī cum vōs dēlēgī** it is now some years since I chose you; **cum māximē** just when; just then, just now; **cum prīmum** as soon as; **cum ... tum** not only ... but also; both ... and

Cūmae, -ārum fpl town near Naples (famous for its Sibyl)

Cūmaeānum, -āni nt Cicero's Cumaean residence

Cūmaeus, -ānus adj see **Cūmae**

cumba, cymba, -ae f boat, skiff

cumera, -ae f grain chest

cumīnum, -ī nt cumin

cumque, quomque adv -ever, -soever; at any time

cumulātē adv fully, abundantly

cumulātus adj increased; complete

cumulō, -āre, -āvī, -ātum vt to heap up; to amass, increase; to fill up, overload; (fig) to fill, overwhelm, crown, complete

cumulus, -ī m heap, mass; crowning addition, summit

cūnābula, -ōrum ntpl cradle

cūnae, -ārum fpl cradle

cūnctābundus adj hesitant, dilatory

cūnctāns, -antis adj dilatory, reluctant; sluggish, tough

cūnctanter adv slowly

cūnctātiō, -ōnis f delaying, hesitation

cūnctātor, -ōris m loiterer; one given to cautious tactics (esp Q Fabius Maximus)

cūnctor, -ārī, -ātus vi to linger, delay, hesitate; to move slowly

cūnctus adj the whole of; (pl) all together, all

cuneātim adv in the form of a wedge

cuneātus adj wedge-shaped

cuneus, -ī m wedge; (MIL) wedge-shaped formation of troops; (theatre) block of seats

cunīculus, -ī m rabbit; underground passage; (MIL) mine

cunque see **cumque**

cūpa, -ae f vat, tun

cupidē adv eagerly, passionately

Cupīdineus adj see **Cupīdō**

cupiditās, -ātis f desire, eagerness, enthusiasm; passion, lust; avarice, greed; ambition; partisanship

cupīdō, -inis f desire, eagerness; passion, lust; greed

Cupīdō, -inis m Cupid (son of Venus)

cupidus *adj* desirous, eager; fond, loving; passionate, lustful; greedy, ambitious; partial

cupiēns, -ēntis *pres p of* **cupiō ✦** *adj* eager, desirous

cupienter *adv see* **cupiēns**

cupiō, -ere, -īvī *and* **-iī, -ītum** *vt* to wish, desire, long for; (*with dat*) to wish well

cupītor, -ōris *m* desirer

cupītus *ppp of* **cupiō**

cuppēdia¹, -ae *f* fondness for delicacies

cuppēdia², -ōrum *ntpl* delicacies

cuppēdinārius, -ī *m* confectioner

cuppēdō, -inis *f* longing, passion

cuppes, -dis *adj* fond of delicacies

cupressētum, -ī *nt* cypress grove

cupresseus *adj* of cypress wood

cupressifer, -ī *adj* cypress-bearing

cupressus, -ī *f* cypress

cūr *adv* why?; (*indirect*) why, the reason for

cūra, -ae *f* care, trouble, pains (bestowed); anxiety, concern, sorrow (felt); attention (to), charge (of), concern (for); (*MED*) treatment, cure; (*writing*) work; (*LAW*) trusteeship; (*poet*) love; (*person*) mistress, guardian; ~ **est** I am anxious; **cūrae esse** be attended to, looked after

cūrābilis *adj* troublesome

cūralium, -ī *and* **-iī** *nt* red coral

cūrātē *adv* carefully

cūrātiō, -ōnis *f* charge, management; office; treatment, healing

cūrātor, -ōris *m* manager, overseer; (*LAW*) guardian

cūrātūra, -ae *f* dieting

cūrātus *adj* cared for; earnest, anxious

curculiō, -ōnis *m* weevil

curculiunculus, -ī *m* little weevil

Curēnsis *adj see* **Curēs**

Curēs, -ium *mpl* ancient Sabine town

Cūrētēs, -um *mpl* attendants of Jupiter in Crete

Cūrētis, -idis *adj* Cretan

cūria, -ae *f* earliest division of the Roman people; meeting-place of a curia; senate house; senate

cūriālis, -is *m* member of a curia

cūriātim *adv* by curiae

cūriātus *adj* of the curiae; **comitia cūriāta** earliest Roman assembly

cūriō¹, -ōnis *m* president of a curia; ~ **māximus** head of all the curiae

cūriō², -ōnis *adj* emaciated

cūriōsē *adv* carefully; inquisitively

cūriōsitās, -ātis *f* curiosity

cūriōsus *adj* careful, thoughtful, painstaking; inquiring, inquisitive, officious; careworn

curis, -ītis *f* spear

cūrō, -āre, -āvī, -ātum *vt* to take care of, attend to; to bother about; (*with gerundive*) to get something done; (*with inf*) to take the trouble; (*with* **ut**) to see to it that; (*public life*) to be in charge of, administer; (*MED*) to treat, cure; (*money*) to pay, settle up; **aliud cūrā** never mind; **corpus/cutem ~** take it easy; **prōdigia ~** avert portents

curriculum, -ī *nt* running, race; course, lap; (*fig*) career; **curriculō** at full speed

currō, -ere, cucurrī, cursum *vi* to run; to hasten, fly ✦ *vt* to run through, traverse; **currentem incitāre** spur a willing horse

currus, -ūs *m* car, chariot; triumph; team of horses; ploughwheels

cursim *adv* quickly, at the double

cursitō, -āre *vi* to run about, fly hither and thither

cursō, -āre *vi* to run about

cursor, -ōris *m* runner, racer; courier

cursūra, -ae *f* running

cursus, -ūs *m* running, speed; passage, journey; course, direction; (*things*) movement, flow; (*fig*) rapidity, flow, progress; ~ **honōrum** succession of magistracies; ~ **rērum** course of events; **cursum tenēre** keep on one's course; **cursū** at a run; **māgnō cursū** at full speed

curtō, -āre *vt* to shorten

curtus *adj* short, broken off; incomplete

curūlis *adj* official, curule; **aedīlis ~** patrician aedile; **sella ~** magistrates' chair; **equī ~** horses provided for the games by the state

curvāmen, -inis *nt* bend

curvātūra, -ae *f* curve

curvō, -āre, -āvī, -ātum *vt* to curve, bend, arch; (*fig*) to move

curvus *adj* bent, curved, crooked; (*person*) aged; (*fig*) wrong

cuspis, -dis *f* point; spear, javelin, trident, sting

custōdēla, -ae *f* care, guard

custōdia, -ae *f* watch, guard, care; (*person*) sentry, guard; (*place*) sentry's post, guardhouse; custody, confinement, prison; **lībera ~** confinement in one's own house

custōdiō, -īre, -īvī *and* **-iī, -ītum** *vt* to guard, defend; to hold in custody, keep watch on; to keep, preserve, observe

custōs, -ōdis *m/f* guard, bodyguard, protector, protectress; jailer, warder; (*MIL*) sentry, spy; container

cutícula, -ae *f* skin

cutis, -is *f* skin; **cutem cūrāre** take it easy

cyathissō, -āre *vi* to serve wine

cyathus, -ī *m* wine ladle; (*measure*) one-twelfth of a pint

cybaea, -ae *f* kind of merchant ship

Cybēbē, Cybelē, -ēs *f* Phrygian mother-goddess, Magna Mater

Cybelēius *adj see* **Cybēbē**

Cyclades, -um *fpl* group of Aegean islands

cyclas, -adis *f* formal dress with a border

cyclicus *adj* of the traditional epic stories

Cyclōpius *adj see* **Cyclōps**

Cyclōps, -is *m* one-eyed giant (*esp Polyphemus*)

cycnēus *adj* of a swan, swan's

cycnus, -ī *m* swan

Cydōnius *adj* Cretan ✦ *ntpl* quinces

cygnus *see* **cycnus**

cylindrus, -ī *m* cylinder; roller

Cyllēnē, -ēs *and* **-ae** *f* mountain in Arcadia

Cyllēnēus, Cyllēnis, Cyllēnius *adj see* **Cyllēnē**

Cyllēnēus, -ī *m* Mercury

cymba *see* **cumba**

cymbalum, -ī *nt* cymbal

cymbium, **-ī** and **-iī** nt cup
Cynicē adv like the Cynics
Cynicus, **-ī** m a Cynic philosopher (esp Diogenes) ♦ adj Cynic
cynocephalus, **-ī** m dog-headed ape
Cynosūra, **-ae** f (constellation of) Ursa Minor
Cynosūris, **-idis** adj see **Cynosūra**
Cynthia, **-iae** f Diana
Cynthius, **-ī** m Apollo
Cynthus, **-ī** m hill in Delos (birthplace of Apollo and Diana)
cyparissus, **-ī** f cypress
Cypris, **-idis** f Venus
Cyprius adj Cyprian; copper
Cyprus, **-ī** f (island of) Cyprus (famed for its copper and the worship of Venus)
Cyrēnaeī, **Cyrēnaicī** mpl followers of Aristippus

Cyrēnaeus, **Cyrēnaicus**, **Cyrēnēnsis** adj see **Cyrēnē**
Cyrēnē, **-ēs** f, **Cyrēnae**, **-ārum** fpl town and province of N. Africa
Cyrnēus adj Corsican
Cȳrus, **-ī** m Persian king
Cytaeis, **-idis** f Medea
Cythēra, **-ae** f island S. of Greece (famed for its worship of Venus)
Cytherēa, **-ēae**, **Cytherēia**, **-ēiae**, **Cytherēis**, **-ēidis** f Venus
Cytherēus, **Cythēriacus** adj Cytherean; of Venus
cytisus, **-ī** m/f cytisus (a kind of clover)
Cyzicēnus adj see **Cyzicum**
Cyzicum, **-ī** nt, **Cyzicus**, **-ī**, **Cyzicos**, **-ī** f town on Sea of Marmora

Dd

Dăcī, -ōrum *mpl* Dacians (*a people on the lower Danube*)

Dăcia, -iae *f the country of the Dacians (now* Romania)

Dăcicus, -icī *m gold coin of Domitian's reign*

dactylicus *adj* dactylic

dactylus, -ī *m* dactyl

Daedalēus *adj see* **Daedalus**

Daedalus, -ī *m mythical Athenian craftsman and inventor*

daedalus *adj* artistic, skilful in creating; skilfully made, variegated

Dalmatae, -ārum *mpl* Dalmatians (*a people on the East coast of the Adriatic*)

Dalmatia, -iae *f* Dalmatia

Dalmaticus *adj see* **Dalmatia**

dăma, -ae *f* deer; venison

Damascēnus *adj see* **Damascus**

Damascus, -ī *f* Damascus

damma *f see* **dăma**

damnătiō, -ōnis *f* condemnation

damnătōrius *adj* condemnatory

damnătus *adj* criminal; miserable

damnificus *adj* pernicious

damnō, -āre, -āvī, -ātum *vt* to condemn, sentence; to procure the conviction of; (*heirs*) to oblige; to censure; **capitis/capite damnāre** condemn to death; **māiestātis damnāre** de **māiestāte damnāre** condemn for treason; **vōtī damnāre** oblige to fulfil a vow

damnōsē *adv* ruinously

damnōsus *adj* harmful, ruinous; spendthrift; wronged

damnum, -ī *nt* loss, harm, damage; (*LAW*) fine, damages; ~ **facere** suffer loss

Danaē, -ēs *f mother of Perseus*

Danaēius *adj see* **Danaē**

Danaī, -ōrum *and* **-um** *mpl* the Greeks

Danaides, -idum *fpl daughters of Danaus*

Danaus¹, -ī *m king of Argos and father of 50 daughters*

Danaus² *adj* Greek

danista, -ae *m* moneylender

danisticus *adj* moneylending

danō *see* **dō**

Dānuvius, -ī *m upper Danube*

Daphnē, -ēs *f nymph changed into a laurel tree*

Daphnis, -idis (*acc* **-im** *and* **-in**) *m mythical Sicilian shepherd*

dapinō, -āre *vt* to serve (*food*)

daps, dapis *f* religious feast; meal, banquet

dapsilis *adj* sumptuous, abundant

Dardania, -iae *f* Troy

Dardanidēs, -idae *m* Trojan (*esp Aeneas*)

Dardanus¹, -ī *m son of Jupiter and ancestor of Trojan kings*

Dardanus², Dardanius, Dardanis, -idis *adj* Trojan

Darēus, -ī *m* Persian king

datārius *adj* to give away

datătim *adv* passing from one to the other

datiō, -ōnis *f* right to give away; (*laws*) making

datō, -āre *vt* to be in the habit of giving

dator, -ōris *m* giver; (*sport*) bowler

Daulias, -adis *adj see* **Daulis**

Daulis, -dis *f town in central Greece (noted for the story of Procne and Philomela)*

Daunias, -iadis *f* Apulia

Daunius *adj* Rutulian; Italian

Daunus, -ī *m legendary king of Apulia (ancestor of Turnus)*

dē *prep (with abl)* (*movement*) down from, from; (*origin*) from, of, out of; (*time*) immediately after, in; (*thought, talk, action*) about, concerning; (*reason*) for, because of; (*imitation*) after, in accordance with; **dē industriā** on purpose; **dē integrō** afresh; **dē nocte** during the night; **diem dē diē** from day to day

dea, -ae *f* goddess

dealbō, -āre *vt* to whitewash, plaster

deambulātiō, -ōnis *f* walk

deambulō, -āre, -āvī, -ātum *vi* to go for a walk

deamō, -āre, -āvī, -ātum *vt* to be in love with; to be much obliged to

dearmātus *adj* disarmed

deartuō, -āre, -āvī, -ātum *vt* to dismember, ruin

deasciō, -āre *vt* to smooth with an axe; (*fig*) to cheat

dēbacchor, -ārī, -ātus *vi* to rage furiously

dēbellātor, -ōris *m* conqueror

dēbellō, -āre, -āvī, -ātum *vi* to bring a war to an end ✦ *vt* to subdue; to fight out

dēbeō, -ēre, -uī, -itum *vt* to owe; (*with inf*) to be bound, ought, should, must; to have to thank for, be indebted for; (*pass*) to be destined

dēbilis *adj* frail, weak

dēbilitās, -ātis *f* weakness, infirmity

dēbilitātiō, -ōnis *f* weakening

dēbilitō, -āre, -āvī, -ātum *vt* to cripple, disable; (*fig*) to paralyse, unnerve

dēbitiō, -ōnis *f* owing

dēbitor, -ōris *m* debtor

dēbitum, **-ī** nt debt

dēblaterō, **-āre** vt to blab

dēcantō, **-āre**, **-āvī**, **-ātum** vt to keep on repeating ♦ vi to stop singing

dēcēdō, **-ēdere**, **-essī**, **-essum** vi to withdraw, depart; to retire from a province (after term of office); to abate, cease, die; (rights) to give up, forgo; (fig) to go wrong, swerve (from duty); **viā dēcēdere** get out of the way

decem num ten

December, **-ris** adj of December ♦ m December

decempeda, **-ae** f ten-foot rule

decempedātor, **-ōris** m surveyor

decemplex, **-icis** adj tenfold

decemprīmī, **-ōrum** mpl civic chiefs of Italian towns

decemscalmus adj ten-oared

decemvirālis adj of the decemviri

decemvirātus, **-ūs** m office of decemvir

decemvirī, **-ōrum** and **-um** mpl commission of ten men (for public or religious duties)

decennis adj ten years'

decēns, **-entis** adj seemly, proper; comely, handsome

decenter adv with propriety

decentia, **-ae** f comeliness

dēceptus ppp of **dēcipiō**

dēcernō, **-ernere**, **-rēvī**, **-rētum** vt to decide, determine; to decree; to fight it out, decide the issue

dēcerpō, **-ere**, **-sī**, **-tum** vt to pluck off, gather; (fig) to derive, enjoy

dēcertātiō, **-ōnis** f deciding the issue

dēcertō, **-āre**, **-āvī**, **-ātum** vi to fight it out, decide the issue

dēcessiō, **-ōnis** f departure; retirement (from a province); deduction, disappearance

dēcessor, **-ōris** m retiring magistrate

dēcessus, **-ūs** m retirement (from a province); death; (tide) ebbing

decet, **-ēre**, **-uīt** vt, vi it becomes, suits; it is right, proper

dēcidō, **-ere**, **-ī** vi to fall down, fall off; to die; (fig) to fail, come down

dēcīdō, **-dere**, **-dī**, **-sum** vt to cut off; to settle, put an end to

deciēns, **deciēs** adv ten times

decimus, **decumus** adj tenth; **cum decimō** tenfold; **decimum** for the tenth time

dēcipiō, **-ipere**, **-ēpī**, **-eptum** vt to ensnare; to deceive, beguile, disappoint

dēcīsiō, **-ōnis** f settlement

dēcīsus ppp of **dēcīdō**

Decius¹, **-ī** m Roman plebeian name (esp P Decius Mus, father and son, who devoted their lives in battle)

Decius², **Deciānus** adj see **Decius¹**

dēclāmātiō, **-ōnis** f loud talking; rhetorical exercise on a given theme

dēclāmātor, **-ōris** m apprentice in public speaking

dēclāmātōrius adj rhetorical

dēclāmitō, **-āre** vi to practise rhetoric; to bluster ♦ vt to practise pleading

dēclāmō, **-āre**, **-āvī**, **-ātum** vi to practise public speaking, declaim; to bluster

dēclārātiō, **-ōnis** f expression, making known

dēclārō, **-āre**, **-āvī**, **-ātum** vt to make known; to proclaim, announce, reveal, express, demonstrate

dēclīnātiō, **-ōnis** f swerving; avoidance; (RHET) digression; (GRAM) inflection

dēclīnō, **-āre**, **-āvī**, **-ātum** vt to turn aside, deflect; (eyes) to close; to evade, shun ♦ vi to turn aside, swerve; to digress

declive nt slope, decline

dēclīvis adj sloping, steep, downhill

dēclīvitās, **-ātis** f sloping ground

dēcocta, **-ae** f a cold drink

dēcoctor, **-ōris** m bankrupt

dēcoctus ppp of **dēcoquō** ♦ adj (style) ripe, elaborated

dēcōlō, **-āre** vi to run out; (fig) to fail

dēcolor, **-ōris** adj discoloured, faded; **~ aetās** a degenerate age

dēcolōrātiō, **-ōnis** f discolouring

dēcolōrō, **-āre**, **-āvī**, **-ātum** vt to discolour, deface

dēcoquō, **-quere**, **-xī**, **-ctum** vt to boil down; to cook ♦ vi to go bankrupt

decor, **-ōris** m comeliness, ornament, beauty

decorē adv becomingly, beautifully

decorō, **-āre**, **-āvī**, **-ātum** vt to adorn, embellish; (fig) to distinguish, honour

decōrum, **-ī** nt propriety

decōrus adj becoming, proper; beautiful, noble; adorned

dēcrepitus adj decrepit

dēcrēscō, **-scere**, **-vī**, **-tum** vi to decrease, wane, wear away; to disappear

dēcrētum, **-ī** nt decree, resolution; (PHILOS) doctrine

dēcrētus ppp of **dēcernō**

dēcrēvī perf **dēcernō**; **dēcrēscō**

decuma, **-ae** f tithe; provincial land tax; largesse

decumāna, **-ae** f wife of a tithe-collector

decumānus adj paying tithes; (MIL) of the 10th cohort or legion ♦ m collector of tithes; **decumānī decumānōrum** mpl men of the 10th legion; **porta decumāna** main gate of a Roman camp

decumātēs, **-ium** adj, pl subject to tithes

dēcumbō, **-mbere**, **-buī** vi to lie down; to recline at table; to fall (in fight)

decumus see **decimus**

decuria, **-ae** f group of ten; panel of judges; social club

decuriātiō, **-ōnis** f, **decuriātus**, **-ūs** m dividing into decuriae

decuriō¹, **-āre**, **-āvī**, **-ātum** vt to divide into decuriae or groups

decuriō², **-ōnis** m head of a decuria; (MIL) cavalry officer; senator of a provincial town or colony

dēcurrō, **-rrere**, **-currī** and **-rrī**, **-rsum** vt, vi to run down, hurry, flow, sail down; to traverse; (MIL) to parade, charge; (time) to pass through; (fig) to have recourse to

dēcursiō¹, **-ōnis** f military manoeuvre

dēcursus¹ ppp of **dēcurrō**

dēcursus², **-ūs** m descent, downrush; (MIL) manoeuvre, attack; (time) career

dēcurtātus *adj* mutilated

decus, -oris *nt* ornament, glory, beauty; honour, virtue; (*pl*) heroic deeds

dēcussō, -āre *vt* to divide crosswise

dēcutiō, -tere, -ssī, -ssum *vt* to strike down, shake off

dēdecet, -ēre, -uit *vt* it is unbecoming to, is a disgrace to

dēdecorō, -āre *vt* to disgrace

dēdecōrus *adj* dishonourable

dēdecus, -oris *nt* disgrace, shame; vice, crime

dedī *perf of* **dō**

dēdicātiō, -ōnis *f* consecration

dēdicō, -āre, -āvī, -ātum *vt* to consecrate, dedicate; to declare (*property in a census return*)

dēdidī *perf of* **dēdō**

dēdignor, -ārī, -ātus *vt* to scorn, reject

dēdiscō, -scere, -dicī *vt* to unlearn, forget

dēdītīcius, -ī *and* **-iī** *m* one who has capitulated

dēditiō, -ōnis *f* surrender, capitulation

dēditus *ppp of* **dēdō** ♦ *adj* addicted, devoted; **dēditā operā** intentionally

dēdō, -ere, -idī, -itum *vt* to give up, yield, surrender; to devote

dēdoceō, -ēre *vt* to teach not to

dēdoleō, -ēre, -uī *vi* to cease grieving

dēdūcō, -ūcere, -ūxī, -uctum *vt* to bring down, lead away, deflect; (*MIL*) to lead, withdraw; (*bride*) to bring home; (*colony*) to settle; (*hair*) to comb out; (*important person*) to escort; (*LAW*) to evict, bring to trial; (*money*) to subtract; (*sail*) to unfurl; (*ship*) to launch; (*thread*) to spin out; (*writing*) to compose; (*fig*) to bring, reduce, divert, derive

dēductiō, -ōnis *f* leading off; settling a colony; reduction; eviction; inference

dēductor, -ōris *m* escort

dēductus *ppp of* **dēdūcō** ♦ *adj* finely spun

deerrō, -āre, -āvī, -ātum *vi* to go astray

deesse *infin of* **dēsum**

dēfaecō, -āre, -āvī, -ātum *vt* to clean; (*fig*) to make clear, set at ease

dēfatigātiō, -ōnis *f* tiring out; weariness

dēfatigō, -āre, -āvī, -ātum *vt* to tire out, exhaust

dēfatīscor *etc see* **dēfetīscor**

dēfectiō, -ōnis *f* desertion; failure, faintness; (*ASTR*) eclipse

dēfector, -ōris *m* deserter, rebel

dēfectus[1] *ppp of* **dēficiō** ♦ *adj* weak, failing

dēfectus[2], -ūs *m* failure; eclipse

dēfendō, -dere, -dī, -sum *vt* to avert, repel; to defend, protect; (*LAW*) to speak in defence, urge, maintain; (*THEAT*) to play (*a part*); **crīmen dēfendere** answer an accusation

dēfēnsiō, -ōnis *f* defence, speech in defence

dēfēnsitō, -āre *vt* to defend often

dēfēnsō, -āre *vt* to defend

dēfēnsor, -ōris *m* averter; defender, protector, guard

dēferō, -ferre, -tulī, -lātum *vt* to bring down, bring, carry; to bear away; (*power, honour*) to offer, confer; (*information*) to report; (*LAW*) to inform against, indict; to recommend (*for*

public services); **ad cōnsilium dēferre** take into consideration

dēfervēscō, -vēscere, -vī *and* **-buī** *vi* to cool down, calm down

dēfessus *adj* tired, exhausted

dēfetīgō *etc see* **dēfatīgō**

dēfetīscor, -tīscī, -ssus *vi* to grow weary

dēficiō, -icere, -ēcī, -ectum *vt, vi* to desert, forsake, fail; to be lacking, run short, cease; (*ASTR*) to be eclipsed; **animō dēficere** lose heart

dēfīgō, -gere, -xī, -xum *vt* to fix firmly; to drive in, thrust; (*eyes, mind*) to concentrate; (*fig*) to stupefy, astound; (*magic*) to bewitch

dēfingō, -ere *vt* to make, portray

dēfīniō, -īre, -īvī, -ītum *vt* to mark the limit of, limit; to define, prescribe; to restrict; to terminate

dēfīnītē *adv* precisely

dēfīnītiō, -ōnis *f* limiting, prescribing, definition

dēfīnītīvus *adj* explanatory

dēfīnītus *adj* precise

dēfīō, -ierī *vi* to fail

dēflagrātiō, -ōnis *f* conflagration

dēflagrō, -āre, -āvī, -ātum *vi* to be burned down, perish; to cool down, abate ♦ *vt* to burn down

dēflectō, -ctere, -xī, -xum *vt* to bend down, turn aside; (*fig*) to pervert ♦ *vi* to turn aside, deviate

dēfleō, -ēre, -ēvī, -ētum *vt* to lament bitterly, bewail ♦ *vi* to weep bitterly

dēflexus *ppp of* **dēflectō**

dēflōrēscō, -ēscere, -uī *vi* to shed blooms; (*fig*) to fade

dēfluō, -ere, -xī, -xum *vi* to flow down, float down; to fall, drop, droop; (*fig*) to come from, be derived; to flow past; (*fig*) to pass away, fail

dēfodiō, -odere, -ōdī, -ossum *vt* to dig, dig out; to bury; (*fig*) to hide away

dēfore *fut infin of* **dēsum**

dēfōrmis *adj* misshapen, disfigured, ugly; shapeless; (*fig*) disgraceful, disgusting

dēfōrmitās, -ātis *f* deformity, hideousness; baseness

dēfōrmō, -āre, -āvī, -ātum *vt* to form, sketch; to deform, disfigure; to describe; to mar, disgrace

dēfossus *ppp of* **dēfodiō**

dēfraudō, -āre *vt* to cheat, defraud; **genium dēfraudāre** deny oneself

dēfrēnātus *adj* unbridled

dēfricō, -āre, -uī, -ātum *and* **-tum** *vt* to rub down; (*fig*) to satirize

dēfringō, -ingere, -ēgī, -āctum *vt* to break off, break down

dēfrūdō *etc see* **dēfraudō**

dēfrutum, -ī *nt* new wine boiled down

dēfugiō, -ugere, -ūgī *vt* to run away from, shirk ♦ *vi* to flee

dēfuī *perf of* **dēsum**

dēfūnctus *ppa of* **dēfungor** ♦ *adj* discharged; dead

dēfundō, -undere, -ūdī, -ūsum *vt* to pour out

dēfungor, **-ungī**, **-ūnctus** vi (with abl) to discharge, have done with; to die

dēfutūrus fut p of **dēsum**

dēgener, **-is** adj degenerate, unworthy, base

dēgenerātum, **-ātī** nt degenerate character

dēgenerō, **-āre**, **-āvī**, **-ātum** vi to degenerate, deteriorate ♦ vt to disgrace

dēgerō, **-ere** vt to carry off

dēgō, **-ere**, **-ī** vt (time) to pass, spend; (war) wage ♦ vi to live

dēgrandinat it is hailing heavily

dēgravō, **-āre** vt to weigh down, overpower

dēgredior, **-dī**, **-ssus** vi to march down, descend, dismount

dēgrunniō, **-īre** vi to grunt hard

dēgustō, **-āre** vt to taste, touch; (fig) to try, experience

dehinc adv from here; from now, henceforth; then, next

dehīscō, **-ere** vi to gape, yawn

dehonestāmentum, **-ī** nt disfigurement

dehonestō, **-āre** vt to disgrace

dehortor, **-ārī**, **-ātus** vt to dissuade, discourage

Dēianīra, **-ae** f wife of Hercules

dēiciō, **-icere**, **-iēcī**, **-iectum** vt to throw down, hurl, fell; to overthrow, kill; (eyes) to lower, avert; (LAW) to evict; (MIL) to dislodge; (ship) to drive off its course; (hopes, honours) to foil, disappoint

dēiectiō, **-ōnis** f eviction

dēiectus¹ ppp of **dēiciō** ♦ adj low-lying; disheartened

dēiectus², **-ūs** m felling; steep slope

dēierō, **-āre**, **-āvī**, **-ātum** vi to swear solemnly

dein etc see **deinde**

deinceps adv successively, in order

deinde, **dein** adv from there, next; then, thereafter; next in order

Dēiotarus, **-ī** m king of Galatia (defended by Cicero)

Dēiphobus, **-ī** m son of Priam (second husband of Helen)

dēiungō, **-ere** vt to sever

dēiuvō, **-āre** vt to fail to help

dej- etc see **dei-**

dēlābor, **-bī**, **-psus** vi to fall down, fly down, sink; (fig) to come down, fall into

dēlacerō, **-āre** vt to tear to pieces

dēlāmentor, **-ārī** vt to mourn bitterly for

dēlāpsus ppa of **dēlābor**

dēlassō, **-āre** vt to tire out

dēlātiō, **-ōnis** f accusing, informing

dēlātor, **-ōris** m informer, denouncer

dēlectābilis adj enjoyable

dēlectāmentum, **-ī** nt amusement

dēlectātiō, **-ōnis** f delight

dēlectō, **-āre** vt to charm, delight, amuse

dēlectus¹ ppp of **dēligō**

dēlectus², **-ūs** m choice; see also **dīlēctus²**

dēlēgātiō, **-ōnis** f assignment

dēlēgī perf of **dēligō**

dēlēgō, **-āre**, **-āvī**, **-ātum** vt to assign, transfer, make over; to ascribe

dēlēnificus adj charming

dēlēnīmentum, **-ī** nt solace, allurement

dēlēniō, **-īre**, **-īvī**, **-ītum** vt to soothe, solace; to seduce, win over

dēlēnītor, **-ōris** m cajoler

dēleō, **-ēre**, **-ēvī**, **-ētum** vt to destroy, annihilate; to efface, blot out

Dēlia, **-ae** f Diana

Dēliacus adj of Delos

dēlīberābundus adj deliberating

dēlīberātiō, **-ōnis** f deliberating, consideration

dēlīberātīvus adj deliberative

dēlīberātor, **-ōris** m consulter

dēlīberātus adj determined

dēlīberō, **-āre**, **-āvī**, **-ātum** vt, vi to consider, deliberate, consult; to resolve, determine; **dēlīberārī potest** it is in doubt

dēlībō, **-āre**, **-āvī**, **-ātum** vt to taste, sip; to pick, gather; to detract from, mar

dēlibrō, **-āre** vt to strip the bark off

dēlibuō, **-uere**, **-uī**, **-ūtum** vt to smear, steep

dēlicātē adv luxuriously

dēlicātus adj delightful; tender, soft; voluptuous, spoiled, effeminate; fastidious

dēliciae, **-ārum** fpl delight, pleasure; whimsicalities, sport; (person) sweetheart, darling

dēliciolae, **-ārum** fpl darling

dēlicium, **-ī** and **-iī** nt favourite

dēlicō, **-āre** vt to explain

dēlictum, **-ī** nt offence, wrong

dēlicuus adj lacking

dēligō, **-āre**, **-āvī**, **-ātum** vt to tie up, make fast

dēligō, **-igere**, **-ēgī**, **-ēctum** vt to select, gather; to set aside

dēlingō, **-ere** vt to have a lick of

dēlīni- etc see **dēlēni-**

dēlinquō, **-inquere**, **-īquī**, **-ictum** vi to fail, offend, do wrong

dēliquēscō, **-uēscere**, **-cuī** vi to melt away; (fig) to pine away

dēliquiō, **-ōnis** f lack

dēlīrāmentum, **-ī** nt nonsense

dēlīrātiō, **-ōnis** f dotage

dēlīrō, **-āre** vi to be crazy, drivel

dēlīrus adj crazy

dēlitēscō, **-ēscere**, **-uī** vi to hide away, lurk; (fig) to skulk, take shelter under

dēlītigō, **-āre** vi to scold

Dēlius, **-iacus** adj see **Dēlos**

Delmatae see **Dalmatae**

Dēlos, **-ī** f sacred Aegean island (birthplace of Apollo and Diana)

Delphī, **-ōrum** mpl town in central Greece (famous for its oracle of Apollo); the Delphians

Delphicus adj see **Delphī**

delphīnus, **-ī**, **delphīn**, **-is** m dolphin

Deltōton, **-ī** nt (constellation) Triangulum

dēlubrum, **-ī** nt sanctuary, temple

dēluctō, **-āre**, **dēluctor**, **-ārī** vi to wrestle

dēlūdificō, **-āre** vt to make fun of

dēlūdō, **-dere**, **-sī**, **-sum** vt to dupe, delude

dēlumbis adj feeble

dēlumbō, **-āre** vt to enervate

dēmadēscō, **-ēscere**, **-uī** vi to be drenched

dēmandō, **-āre** vt to entrust, commit

dēmarchus, -ī *m* demarch (*chief of a village in Attica*)

dēmēns, -entis *adj* mad, foolish

dēmēnsum, -ī *nt* ration

dēmēnsus *ppa of* **dēmētior**

dēmenter *adv see* **dēmēns**

dēmentia, -ae *f* madness, folly

dēmentiō, -īre *vi* to rave

dēmereō, -ēre, -uī, -itum, dēmereor, -ērī *vt* to earn, deserve; to do a service to

dēmergō, -gere, -sī, -sum *vt* to submerge, plunge, sink; (*fig*) to overwhelm

dēmessus *ppp of* **dēmetō**

dēmētior, -tīrī, -nsus *vt* to measure out

dēmetō, -tere, -ssuī, -ssum *vt* to reap, harvest; to cut off

dēmigrātiō, -ōnis *f* emigration

dēmigrō, -āre *vi* to move, emigrate

dēminuō, -uere, -uī, -ūtum *vt* to make smaller, lessen, detract from; **capite dēminuere** deprive of citizenship

dēminūtiō, -ōnis *f* decrease, lessening; (*LAW*) right to transfer property; **capitis ~** loss of political rights

dēmīror, -ārī, -ātus *vt* to marvel at, wonder

dēmisse *adv* modestly, meanly

dēmissīcius *adj* flowing

dēmissiō, -ōnis *f* letting down; (*fig*) dejection

dēmissus *ppp of* **dēmittō ♦** *adj* low-lying; drooping; humble, unassuming; dejected; (*origin*) descended

dēmītigō, -āre *vt* to make milder

dēmittō, -ittere, -īsī, -issum *vt* to let down, lower, sink; to send down, plunge; (*beard*) to grow; (*ship*) to bring to land; (*troops*) to move down; (*fig*) to cast down, dishearten, reduce, impress; **sē dēmittere** stoop; descend; be disheartened

dēmiūrgus, -ī *m* chief magistrate in a Greek state

dēmō, -ere, -psī, -ptum *vt* to take away, subtract

Dēmocriticus, Dēmocritius, Dēmocritēus *adj see* **Dēmocritus**

Dēmocritus, -ī *m* Greek philosopher (*author of the atomic theory*)

dēmōlior, -īrī *vt* to pull down, destroy

dēmōlītiō, -ōnis *f* pulling down

dēmōnstrātiō, -ōnis *f* pointing out, explanation

dēmōnstrātīvus *adj* (*RHET*) for display

dēmōnstrātor, -ōris *m* indicator

dēmōnstrō, -āre, -āvī, -ātum *vt* to point out; to explain, represent, prove

dēmorior, -ī, -tuus *vi* to die, pass away ♦ *vt* to be in love with

dēmoror, -ārī, -ātus *vi* to wait ♦ *vt* to detain, delay

dēmortuus *ppa of* **dēmorior**

Dēmosthenēs, -is *m* greatest Athenian orator

dēmoveō, -ovēre, -ōvī, -ōtum *vt* to remove, turn aside, dislodge

dēmpsī *perf of* **dēmō**

dēmptus *ppp of* **dēmō**

dēmūgītus *adj* filled with lowing

dēmulceō, -cēre, -sī *vt* to stroke

dēmum *adv* (*time*) at last, not till; (*emphasis*) just, precisely; **ibi ~** just there; **modo ~** only now; **nunc ~** now at last; **post ~** not till after; **tum ~** only then

dēmurmurō, -āre *vt* to mumble through

dēmūtātiō, -ōnis *f* change

dēmūtō, -āre *vt* to change, make worse ♦ *vi* to change one's mind

dēnārius, -ī and -iī *m* Roman silver coin

dēnārrō, -āre *vt* to relate fully

dēnāsō, -āre *vt* to take the nose off

dēnatō, -āre *vi* to swim down

dēnegō, -āre, -āvī, ātum *vt* to deny, refuse, reject ♦ *vi* to say no

dēnī, -ōrum *adj* ten each, in tens; ten; tenth

dēnicālis *adj* for purifying after a death

dēnique *adv* at last, finally; (*enumerating*) lastly, next; (*summing up*) in short, briefly; (*emphasis*) just, precisely

dēnōminō, -āre *vt* to designate

dēnōrmō, -āre *vt* to make irregular

dēnotō, -āre, -āvī, -ātum *vt* to point out, specify; to observe

dēns, dentis *m* tooth; ivory; prong, fluke

dēnsē *adv* repeatedly

dēnsō, -āre, -āvī, -ātum, dēnseō, -ēre *vt* to thicken; (*ranks*) to close

dēnsus *adj* thick, dense, close; frequent; (*style*) concise

dentālia, -ium *ntpl* ploughbeam

dentātus *adj* toothed; (*paper*) polished

dentiō, -īre *vi* to cut one's teeth; (*teeth*) to grow

dēnūbō, -bere, -psī, -ptum *vi* to marry, marry beneath one

dēnūdō, -āre, -āvī, -ātum *vt* to bare, strip; (*fig*) to disclose

dēnūntiātiō, -ōnis *f* intimation, warning

dēnūntiō, -āre, -āvī, -ātum *vt* to intimate, give notice of, declare; to threaten, warn; (*LAW*) to summon as witness

dēnuō *adv* afresh, again, once more

deonerō, -āre *vt* to unload

deorsum, deorsus *adv* downwards

deōsculor, -ārī *vt* to kiss warmly

dēpacīscor *etc see* **dēpecīscor**

dēpāctus *adj* driven in firmly

dēpāscō, -scere, -vī, -stum, dēpāscor, dēpāscī *vt* to feed on, eat up; (*fig*) to devour, destroy, prune away

dēpecīscor, -īscī, -tus *vt* to bargain for, agree about

dēpectō, -ctere, -xum *vt* to comb; (*comedy*) to flog

dēpectus *ppa of* **dēpecīscor**

dēpecūlātor, -ōris *m* embezzler

dēpecūlor, -ārī, -ātus *vt* to plunder

dēpellō, -ellere, -ulī, -ulsum *vt* to expel, remove, cast down; (*MIL*) to dislodge; (*infants*) to wean; (*fig*) to deter, avert

dēpendeō, -ēre *vi* to hang down, hang from; to depend on; to be derived

dēpendō, -endere, -endī, -ēnsum *vt* to weigh, pay up

dēperdō, -ere, -idī, -itum *vt* to lose completely, destroy, ruin

dēpereō, -īre, -iī vi to perish, be completely destroyed; to be undone ✦ vt to be hopelessly in love with

dēpexus ppp of **dēpectō**

dēpingō, -ingere, -inxī, -ictum vt to paint; (fig) to portray, describe

dēplangō, -gere, -xī vt to bewail frantically

dēplexus adj grasping

dēplōrābundus adj weeping bitterly

dēplōrō, -āre, -āvī, -ātum vi to weep bitterly ✦ vt to bewail bitterly, mourn; to despair of

dēpluit, -ere vi to rain down

dēpōnō, -ōnere, -osuī, -ositum vt to lay down; to set aside, put away, get rid of; to wager; to deposit, entrust, commit to the care of; (fig) to give up

dēpopulātiō, -ōnis f ravaging

dēpopulātor, -ōris m marauder

dēpopulor, -ārī, -ātus, dēpopulō, -āre vt to ravage, devastate; (fig) to waste, destroy

dēportō, -āre, -āvī, -ātum vt to carry down, carry off; to bring home (from a province); (LAW) to banish for life; (fig) to win

dēposcō, -scere, -poscī vt to demand, require, claim

dēpositum, -ī nt trust, deposit

dēpositus ppp of **dēpōnō** ✦ adj dying, dead, despaired of

dēprāvātē adv perversely

dēprāvātiō, -ōnis f distorting

dēprāvō, -āre, -āvī, -ātum vt to distort; (fig) to pervert, corrupt

dēprecābundus adj imploring

dēprecātiō, -ōnis f averting by prayer; imprecation, invocation; plea for indulgence

dēprecātor, -ōris m intercessor

dēprecor, -ārī, -ātus vt to avert (by prayer); deprecate, intercede for

dēprehendō, dēprendō, -endere, -endī, -ēnsum vt to catch, intercept; to overtake, surprise; to catch in the act, detect; (fig) to perceive, discover

dēprehēnsiō, -ōnis f detection

dēprehēnsus, dēprēnsus ppp of **dēprehendō**

dēpressī perf of **dēprimō**

dēpressus ppp of **dēprimō** ✦ adj low

dēprimō, -imere, -essī, -essum vt to press down, weigh down; to dig deep; (ship) to sink; (fig) to suppress, keep down

dēproelior, -ārī vi to fight it out

dēprōmō, -ere, psī, -ptum vt to fetch, bring out, produce

dēproperō, -āre vi to hurry up ✦ vt to hurry and make

depsō, -ere vt to knead

dēpudet, -ēre, -uit v impers not to be ashamed

dēpūgis adj thin-buttocked

dēpugnō, -āre, -āvī, -ātum vi to fight it out, fight hard

dēpulī perf of **dēpellō**

dēpulsiō, -ōnis f averting; defence

dēpulsō, -āre vt to push out of the way

dēpulsor, -ōris m repeller

dēpulsus ppp of **dēpellō**

dēpūrgō, -āre vt to clean

dēputō, -āre vt to prune; to consider, reckon

dēpȳgis etc see **dēpūgis**

dēque adv down

dērēctā, dērēctē, dērēctō adv straight

dērēctus ppp of **dērigō** ✦ adj straight, upright, at right angles; straightforward

dērelictiō, -ōnis f disregarding

dērelinquō, -inquere, -īquī, -ictum vt to abandon, forsake

dērepente adv suddenly

dērēpō, -ere vi to creep down

dēreptus ppp of **dēripiō**

dērīdeō, -dēre, -sī, -sum vt to laugh at, deride

dērīdiculum, -ī nt mockery, absurdity; object of derision

dērīdiculus adj laughable

dērigēscō, -ēscere, -uī vi to stiffen, curdle

dērigō, -igere, -ēxī, -ēctum vt to turn, aim, direct; (fig) to regulate

dēripiō, -ipere, -ipuī, -eptum vt to tear off, pull down

dērīsor, -ōris m scoffer

dērīsus¹ ppp of **dērīdeō**

dērīsus², -ūs m scorn, derision

dērīvātiō, -ōnis f diverting

dērīvō, -āre, -āvī, -ātum vt to lead off, draw off

dērogō, -āre vt (LAW) to propose to amend; (fig) to detract from

dērōsus adj gnawed away

dēruncinō, -āre vt to plane off; (comedy) to cheat

dēruō, -ere, -ī, -tum vt to demolish

dēruptus adj steep ✦ ntpl precipice

dēsaeviō, -īre vi to rage furiously; to cease raging

dēscendō, -endere, -endī, -ēnsum vi to come down, go down, descend, dismount; (MIL) to march down; (things) to fall, sink, penetrate; (fig) to stoop (to), lower oneself

dēscēnsiō, -ōnis f going down

dēscēnsus, -ūs m way down

dēscīscō, -īscere, -īvī and **-iī, -ītum** vi to desert, revolt; to deviate, part company

dēscrībō, -bere, -psī, -ptum vt to copy out; to draw, sketch; to describe; see also **dīscrībō**

dēscrīptiō, -ōnis f copy; drawing, diagram; description

dēscrīptus ppp of **dēscrībō**; see also **dīscrīptus**

dēsecō, -āre, -uī, -tum vt to cut off

dēserō, -ere, -uī, -tum vt to desert, abandon, forsake; (bail) to forfeit

dēsertor, -ōris m deserter

dēsertus ppp of **dēserō** ✦ adj desert, uninhabited ✦ ntpl deserts

dēserviō, -īre vi to be a slave (to), serve

dēses, -idis adj idle, inactive

dēsiccō, -āre vt to dry, drain

dēsideō, -idēre, -ēdī vi to sit idle

dēsīderābilis adj desirable

dēsīderātiō, -ōnis f missing

dēsīderium, -ī and **-iī** nt longing, sense of loss; want; petition; mē ~ tenet urbis I miss Rome

dēsīderō, -āre, -āvī, -ātum vt to feel the want of, miss; to long for, desire; (casualties) to lose

dēsidia, -ae f idleness, apathy

dēsidiōsē adv idly

dēsidiōsus *adj* lazy, idle; relaxing

dēsīdō, -īdere, -ēdī *vi* to sink, settle down; (*fig*) to deteriorate

dēsignātiō, -ōnis *f* specifying; election (*of magistrates*)

dēsignātor *etc see* **dissignātor**

dēsignātus *adj* elect

dēsignō, -āre, -āvī, -ātum *vt* to trace out; to indicate, define; (POL) to elect; (*art*) to depict

dēsiī *perf of* **dēsinō**

dēsiliō, -īlīre, -iluī, -ultum *vi* to jump down, alight

dēsinō, -nere, -ī *vt* to leave off, abandon ♦ *vi* to stop, desist; to end (*in*)

dēsipiēns, -ientis *adj* silly

dēsipientia, -ae *f* folly

dēsipiō, -ere *vi* to be stupid, play the fool

dēsistō, -istere, -titī, -titum *vi* to stop, leave off, desist

dēsitus *ppp of* **dēsinō**

dēsōlō, -āre, -āvī, -ātum *vt* to leave desolate, abandon

dēspectō, -āre *vt* to look down on, command a view of; to despise

dēspectus¹ *ppp of* **dēspiciō** ♦ *adj* contemptible

dēspectus², -ūs *m* view, prospect

dēspēranter *adv* despairingly

dēspērātiō, -ōnis *f* despair

dēspērātus *adj* despaired of, hopeless; desperate, reckless

dēspērō, -āre, -āvī, -ātum *vt, vi* to despair, give up hope of

dēspexī *perf of* **dēspiciō**

dēspicātiō, -ōnis *f* contempt

despicātus *adj* despised, contemptible

dēspicātus, -ūs *m* contempt

dēspicientia, -ae *f* contempt

dēspiciō, -icere, -exī, -ectum *vt* to look down on; to despise ♦ *vi* to look down

dēspoliātor, -ōris *m* robber

dēspoliō, -āre *vt* to rob, plunder

dēspondeō, -ondēre, -ondī and -opondī, -ōnsum *vt* to pledge, promise; to betroth; to devote; to give up, despair of; **animum dēspondēre** despair

dēspūmō, -āre *vt* to skim off

dēspuō, -ere *vi* to spit on the ground ♦ *vt* to reject

dēsquāmō, -āre *vt* to scale, peel

dēstillō, -āre *vi* to drop down ♦ *vt* to distil

dēstimulō, -āre *vt* to run through

dēstinātiō, -ōnis *f* resolution, appointment

dēstinātus *adj* fixed, decided

dēstinō, -āre, -āvī, -ātum *vt* to make fast; to appoint, determine, resolve; (*archery*) to aim at; (*fig*) to intend to buy ♦ *nt ppp* mark; intention; **dēstinātum est mihi** I have decided

dēstitī *perf of* **dēsistō**

dēstituō, -uere, -uī, -ūtum *vt* to set apart, place; to forsake, leave in the lurch

dēstitūtiō, -ōnis *f* defaulting

dēstitūtus *ppp of* **dēstituō**

dēstrictus *ppp of* **dēstringō** ♦ *adj* severe

dēstringō, -ingere, -inxī, -ictum *vt* (*leaves*) to strip; (*body*) to rub down; (*sword*) to draw; to graze, skim; (*fig*) to censure

dēstruō, -ere, -xī, -ctum *vt* to demolish; to destroy

dēsubitō *adv* all of a sudden

dēsūdāscō, -ere *vi* to sweat all over

dēsūdō, -āre *vi* to exert oneself

dēsuēfactus *adj* unaccustomed

dēsuētūdō, -inis *f* disuse

dēsuētus *adj* unaccustomed, unused

dēsultor, -ōris *m* circus rider; (*fig*) fickle lover

dēsultūra, -ae *f* jumping down

dēsum, deesse, -fuī *vi* to be missing, fail, fail in one's duty

dēsūmō, -ere, -psī, -ptum *vt* to select

dēsuper *adv* from above

dēsurgō, -ere *vi* to rise

dētegō, -egere, -ēxī, -ēctum *vt* to uncover, disclose; (*fig*) to reveal, detect

dētendō, -endere, -ēnsum *vt* (*tent*) to strike

dētentus *ppp of* **dētineō**

dētergō, -gere, -sī, -sum *vt* to wipe away, clear away; to clean; to break off

dēterior, -ōris *adj* lower; inferior, worse

dēterius *adv* worse

dēterminātiō, -ōnis *f* boundary, end

dēterminō, -āre, -āvī, -ātum *vt* to bound, limit; to settle

dēterō, -erere, -rīvī, -rītum *vt* to rub, wear away; (*style*) to polish; (*fig*) to weaken

dēterreō, -ēre, -uī, -itum *vt* to frighten away; to deter, discourage, prevent

dētersus *ppp of* **dētergō**

dētestābilis *adj* abominable

dētestātiō, -ōnis *f* execration, curse; averting

dētestor, -ārī, -ātus *vt* to invoke, invoke against; to curse, execrate; to avert, deprecate

dētexō, -ere, -uī, -tum *vt* to weave, finish weaving; (*comedy*) to steal; (*fig*) to describe

dētineō, -inēre, -inuī, -entum *vt* to hold back, detain; to keep occupied

dētondeō, -ondēre, -ondī, -ōnsum *vt* to shear off, strip

dētonō, -āre, -uī *vi* to cease thundering

dētorqueō, -quēre, -sī, -tum *vt* to turn aside, direct; to distort, misrepresent

dētractātiō, -ōnis *f* declining

dētractiō, -ōnis *f* removal, departure

dētractō *etc see* **dētrectō**

dētractus *ppp of* **dētrahō**

dētrahō, -here, -xī, -ctum *vt* to draw off, take away, pull down; to withdraw, force to leave; to detract, disparage

dētrectātor, -ōris *m* disparager

dētrectō, -āre, -āvī, -ātum *vt* to decline, shirk; to detract from, disparage

dētrīmentōsus *adj* harmful

dētrīmentum, -ī *nt* loss, harm; (MIL) defeat; **~ capere** suffer harm

dētrītus *ppp of* **dēterō**

dētrūdō, -dere, -sī, -sum *vt* to push down, thrust away; to dislodge, evict; to postpone; (*fig*) to force

61

dētruncō, -āre, -āvī, -ātum vt to cut off, behead, mutilate

dētrūsus ppp of **dētrūdō**

dēturbō, -āre, -āvī, -ātum vt to dash down, pull down; (fig) to cast down, deprive

Deucaliōn, -ōnis m son of Prometheus (survivor of the Flood)

Deucaliōnēus adj see **Deucaliōn**

deūnx, -cis m eleven twelfths

deūrō, -rere, -ssī, -stum vt to burn up; to frost

deus, -ī (voc **deus**, pl **dī, deos, deum, dis**) m god; **dī meliōra** Heaven forbid!; **dī tē ament** bless you!

deūstus ppp of **deūrō**

deūtor, -ī vi to maltreat

dēvastō, -āre vt to lay waste

dēvehō, -here, -xī, -ctum vt to carry down, convey; (pass) to ride down, sail down

dēvellō, -ellere, -ellī and **-olsī, -ulsum** vt to pluck, pull out

dēvēlō, -āre vt to unveil

dēveneror, -ārī vt to worship; to avert by prayers

dēveniō, -enīre, -ēnī, -entum vi to come, reach, fall into

dēverberō, -āre, -āvī, -ātum vt to thrash soundly

dēversor¹, -ārī vi to lodge, stay (as guest)

dēversor², -ōris m guest

dēversōriolum, -ī nt small lodging

dēversōrium, -ī and **-iī** nt inn, lodging

dēversōrius adj for lodging

dēverticulum, -ī nt by-road, by-pass; digression; lodging place; (fig) refuge

dēvertō, -tere, -tī, -sum vi to turn aside, put up; to have recourse to; to digress

dēvertor, -tī, -versus vi see **dēvertō**

dēvexus adj sloping, going down, steep

dēvinciō, -cīre, -xī, -ctum vt to tie up; (fig) to bind, lay under an obligation

dēvincō, -incere, -īcī, -ictum vt to defeat completely, win the day

dēvītātiō, -ōnis f avoiding

dēvītō, -āre vt to avoid

dēvius adj out of the way, devious; (person) solitary, wandering off the beaten track; (fig) inconstant

dēvocō, -āre, -āvī, -ātum vt to call down, fetch; to entice away

dēvolō, -āre vi to fly down

dēvolvō, -vere, -vī, -ūtum vt to roll down, fall; (wool) to spin off

dēvorō, -āre, -āvī, -ātum vt to swallow, gulp down; to engulf, devour; (money) to squander; (tears) to repress; (trouble) to endure patiently

dēvors-, dēvort- see **dēvers-, dēvert-**

dēvortia, -ōrum ntpl byways

dēvōtiō, -ōnis f devoting; (magic) spell

dēvōtō, -āre vt to bewitch

dēvōtus ppp of **dēvoveō** ♦ adj faithful; accursed

dēvoveō, -ovēre, -ōvī, -ōtum vt to devote, vow, dedicate; to give up; to curse; to bewitch

dēvulsus ppp of **dēvellō**

dextella, -ae f little right hand

dexter, -erī and **-rī** adj right, right-hand; handy, skilful; favourable

dexteritās, -ātis f adroitness

dextrā prep (with acc) on the right of

dextra f right hand, right-hand side; hand; pledge of friendship

dextrē (compar **-erius**) adv adroitly

dextrōrsum, dextrōrsus, dextrōvorsum adv to the right

dī pl of **deus**

diabathrārius, -ī and **-iī** m slipper maker

diabolus, -ī m devil

diāconus, -ī m (ECCL) deacon

diadēma, -tis nt royal headband, diadem

diaeta, -ae f diet; living room

dialectica, -ae, dialecticē, -ēs f dialectic, logic ♦ ntpl logical questions

dialecticē adv dialectically

dialecticus adj dialectical ♦ m logician

Diālis adj of Jupiter ♦ m high priest of Jupiter

dialogus, -ī m dialogue, conversation

Diāna, -ae f virgin goddess of hunting (also identified with the moon and Hecate, and patroness of childbirth)

Diānius adj of Diana ♦ nt sanctuary of Diana

diāria, -ōrum ntpl daily allowance of food or pay

dibaphus, -ī f Roman state robe

dica, -ae f lawsuit

dicācitās, -ātis f raillery, repartee

dicāculus adj pert

dicātiō, -ōnis f declaration of citizenship

dicāx, -ācis adj witty, smart

dichorēus, -ī m double trochee

diciō, -ōnis f power, sway, authority

dicis causā for the sake of appearance

dicō, -āre, -āvī, -ātum vt to dedicate, consecrate; to deify; to devote, give over

dīcō, -cere, -xī, dictum vt to say, tell; to mention, mean, call, name; to pronounce; (RHET) to speak, deliver; (LAW) to plead; (poetry) to describe, celebrate; (official) to appoint; (time, place) to settle, fix ♦ vi to speak (in public); **causam dīcere** plead; **iūs dīcere** deliver judgment; **sententiam dīcere** vote; ~ namely; **dīxī** I have finished; **dictum factum** no sooner said than done

dicrotum, -ī nt bireme

Dictaeus adj Cretan

dictamnus, -ī f dittany (a kind of wild marjoram)

dictāta, -ōrum ntpl lessons, rules

dictātor, -ōris m dictator

dictātōrius adj dictator's

dictātūra, -ae f dictatorship

Dictē, -ēs f mountain in Crete (where Jupiter was brought up)

dictiō, -ōnis f speaking, declaring; style, expression, oratory; (oracle) response

dictitō, -āre vt to keep saying, assert; to plead often

dictō, -āre, -āvī, -ātum vt to say repeatedly; to dictate; to compose

dictum, -ī nt saying, word; proverb; bon mot, witticism; command

dictus ppp of **dīcō**

Dictynna, -ae f Britomartis; Diana

Dictynnaeus adj see **Dictynna**

didicī *perf of* **discō**

Dīdō, -ūs *and* **-ōnis** *(acc* **-ō)** *f* Queen of Carthage

dīdō, -ere, -idī, -itum *vt* to distribute, broadcast

dīdūcō, -ūcere, -ūxī, -uctum *vt* to separate, split, open up; *(MIL)* to disperse; *(fig)* to part, divide

diēcula, -ae *f* one little day

diērēctus *adj* crucified; **abī ~** go and be hanged

diēs, -ēī *m/f* day; set day *(usu fem)*; a day's journey; *(fig)* time; **~ meus** my birthday; **diem dīcere** impeach; **diem obīre** die; **diem dē diē, diem ex diē** from day to day; **in diem** to a later day; for today; **in diēs** daily

Diēspiter, -ris *m* Jupiter

diffāmō, -āre, -āvī, -ātum *vt* to divulge; to malign

differentia, -ae *f* difference, diversity; species

differitās, -ātis *f* difference

differō, -erre, distulī, dīlātum *vt* to disperse; to divulge, publish; *(fig)* to distract, disquiet; *(time)* to put off, delay ♦ *vi* to differ, be distinguished

differtus *adj* stuffed, crammed

difficilis *adj* difficult; *(person)* awkward, surly

difficiliter *adv* with difficulty

difficultās, -ātis *f* difficulty, distress, hardship; surliness

difficulter *adv* with difficulty

diffīdēns, -entis *adj* nervous

diffīdenter *adv* without confidence

diffīdentia, -ae *f* mistrust, diffidence

diffīdō, -dere, -sus *vi* to distrust, despair

diffindō, -ndere, -dī, -ssum *vt* to split, open up; *(fig)* to break off

diffingō, -ere *vt* to remake

diffissus *ppp of* **diffindō**

diffisus *ppa of* **diffīdō**

diffiteor, -ērī *vt* to disown

diffluēns, -entis *adj* *(RHET)* loose

diffluō, -ere *vi* to flow away; to melt away; *(fig)* to wallow

diffringō, -ere *vt* to shatter

diffugiō, -ugere, -ūgī *vi* to disperse, disappear

diffugium, -ī *and* **-iī** *nt* dispersion

diffunditō, -āre *vt* to pour out, waste

diffundō, -undere, -ūdī, -ūsum *vt* to pour off; to spread, diffuse; to cheer, gladden

diffūsē *adv* expansively

diffūsilis *adj* diffusive

diffūsus *ppp of* **diffundō** ♦ *adj* spreading; *(writing)* loose

Dīgentia, -ae *f* tributary of the Anio *(near Horace's villa)*

dīgerō, -rere, -ssī, -stum *vt* to divide, distribute; to arrange, set out; to interpret

dīgestiō, -ōnis *f* *(RHET)* enumeration

dīgestus *ppp of* **dīgerō**

digitulus, -ī *m* little finger

digitus, -ī *m* finger; toe; inch; *(pl)* skill in counting; **digitum porrigere, digitum prōferre** take the slightest trouble; **digitum trānsversum nōn discēdere** not swerve a finger's breadth; **attingere caelum digitō** reach the height of happiness; **licērī digitō** bid at an auction; **mōnstrārī digitō** be a

celebrity; **extrēmī digitī, summī digitī** the fingertips; **concrepāre digitīs** snap the fingers

dīgladior, -ārī *vi* to fight fiercely

dignātiō, -ōnis *f* honour, dignity

dignē *adv see* **dignus**

dignitās, -ātis *f* worth, worthiness; dignity, rank, position; political office

dignō, -āre *vt* to think worthy

dignor, -ārī *vt* to think worthy; to deign

dīgnōscō, -ere, -ōvī *vt* to distinguish

dignus *adj* worth, worthy; *(things)* fitting, proper

dīgredior, -dī, -ssus *vi* to separate, part; to deviate, digress

dīgressiō, -ōnis *f* parting; deviation, digression

dīgressus' *ppa of* **dīgredior**

dīgressus², -ūs *m* parting

dīiūdicātiō, -ōnis *f* decision

dīiūdicō, -āre *vt* to decide; to discriminate

dīiun- *etc see* **disiun-**

dīlābor, -bī, -psus *vi* to dissolve, disintegrate; to flow away; *(troops)* to disperse; *(fig)* to decay, vanish

dīlacerō, -āre *vt* to tear to pieces

dīlāminō, -āre *vt* to split in two

dīlaniō, -āre, -āvī, -ātum *vt* to tear to shreds

dīlapidō, -āre *vt* to demolish

dīlāpsus *ppa of* **dīlābor**

dīlargior, -īrī *vt* to give away liberally

dīlātiō, -ōnis *f* putting off, adjournment

dīlātō, -āre, -āvī, -ātum *vt* to expand; *(pronunciation)* to broaden

dīlātor, -ōris *m* procrastinator

dīlātus *ppp of* **differō**

dīlaudō, -āre *vt* to praise extravagantly

dīlēctus' *ppp of* **dīligō** ♦ *adj* beloved

dīlēctus², -ūs *m* selection, picking; *(MIL)* levy; **dīlēctum habēre** hold a levy, recruit

dīlēxī *perf of* **dīligō**

dīligēns, -entis *adj* painstaking, conscientious, attentive (to); thrifty

dīligenter *adv see* **dīligēns**

dīligentia, -ae *f* carefulness, attentiveness; thrift

dīligō, -igere, -ēxī, -ēctum *vt* to prize especially, esteem, love

dīlōricō, -āre *vt* to tear open

dīlūceō, -ēre *vi* to be evident

dīlūcēscit, -cēscere, -xit *vi* to dawn, begin to grow light

dīlūcidē *adv see* **dīlūcidus**

dīlūcidus *adj* clear, distinct

dīlūculum, -ī *nt* dawn

dīlūdium, -ī *and* **-iī** *nt* interval

dīluō, -uere, -uī, -ūtum *vt* to wash away, dissolve, dilute; to explain; *(fig)* to weaken, do away with

dīluviēs, -iēī *f*, **dīluvium, -ī** *and* **-iī** *nt* flood, deluge

dīluviō, -āre *vt* to inundate

dīmānō, -āre *vi* to spread abroad

dīmēnsiō, -ōnis *f* measuring

dīmēnsus *adj* measured

dīmētior, -tīrī, -nsus *vt* to measure out

dīmētō, -āre, dīmētor, -ārī vt to mark out
dīmicātiō, -ōnis f fighting, struggle
dīmicō, -āre, -āvī, -ātum vi to fight, struggle, contend
dīmidiātus adj half, halved
dīmidius adj half ♦ nt half
dīmissiō, -ōnis f sending away; discharging
dīmissus ppp of **dīmittō**
dīmittō, -ittere, -īsī, -issum vt to send away, send round; to let go, lay down; (meeting) to dismiss; (MIL) to disband, detach; (fig) to abandon, forsake
dimminuō, -ere vt to dash to pieces
dīmoveō, -ovēre, -ōvī, -ōtum vt to part, separate; to disperse; to entice away
Dindymēnē, -ēnēs f Cybele
Dindymus, -ī m mountain in Mysia (sacred to Cybele)
dīnōscō see **dīgnōscō**
dīnumerātiō, -ōnis f reckoning up
dīnumerō, -āre vt to count, reckon up; to pay out
diōbolāris adj costing two obols
dioecēsis, -is f district; (ECCL) diocese
dioecētēs, -ae m treasurer
Diogenēs, -is m famous Cynic philosopher; a Stoic philosopher
Diomēdēs, -is m Greek hero at the Trojan War
Diomēdēus adj see **Diomēdēs**
Diōnaeus adj see **Diōnē**
Diōnē, -ēs, Diōna, -ae f mother of Venus; Venus
Diōnӯsia, -iōrum ntpl Greek festival of Bacchus
Diōnӯsius, -ī m tyrant of Syracuse
Diōnӯsus, -ī m Bacchus
diōta, -ae f a two-handled wine jar
diplōma, -tis nt letter of recommendation
Dipylon, -ī nt Athenian gate
Dircaeus adj Boeotian
Dircē, -ēs f famous spring in Boeotia
dīrēctus ppp of **dīrigō** ♦ adj straight; straightforward, simple; see also **dērēctus**
dīrēmī perf of **dirimō**
diremptus¹ ppp of **dirimō**
diremptus², -ūs m separation
dīreptiō, -ōnis f plundering
dīreptor, -ōris m plunderer
dīreptus ppp of **dīripiō**
dīrēxī perf of **dīrigō**
dīribeō, -ēre vt to sort out (votes taken from ballot-boxes)
dīribitiō, -ōnis f sorting
dīribitor, -ōris m ballot-sorter
dīrigō, -igere, -ēxī, -ēctum vt to put in line, arrange; see also **dērigō**
dirimō, -imere, -ēmī, -emptum vt to part, divide; to interrupt, break off; to put an end to
dīripiō, -ipere, -ipuī, -eptum vt to tear in pieces; to plunder, ravage; to seize; (fig) to distract
dīritās, -ātis f mischief, cruelty
dīrumpō, disrumpō, -umpere, -ūpī, -uptum vt to burst, break in pieces; (fig) to break off; (pass) to burst (with passion)

dīruō, -ere, -ī, -tum vt to demolish; to scatter; **aere dīrutus** having one's pay stopped
dīruptus ppp of **dīrumpō**
dīrus adj ominous, fearful; (person) dread, terrible ♦ fpl bad luck; the Furies ♦ ntpl terrors
dīrutus ppp of **dīruō** ♦ adj bankrupt
Dīs, Dītis m Pluto
dīs, dītis adj rich
discēdō, -ēdere, -essī, -essum vi to go away, depart; to part, disperse; (MIL) to march away; (result of battle) to come off; (POL) to go over (to a different policy); to pass away, disappear; to leave out of consideration; **ab signīs discēdere** break the ranks; **victor discēdere** come off best
disceptātiō, -ōnis f discussion, debate
disceptātor, -ōris m, **disceptātrīx, -rīcis** f arbitrator
disceptō, -āre vt to debate, discuss; (LAW) to decide
discernō, -ernere, -rēvī, -rētum vt to divide, separate; to distinguish between
discerpō, -ere, -sī, -tum vt to tear apart, disperse; (fig) to revile
discessiō, -ōnis f separation, departure; (senate) division
discessus, -ūs m parting; departure; marching away
discidium, -i and -iī nt disintegration; separation, divorce; discord
discīdō, -ere vt to cut in pieces
discinctus ppp of **discingō** ♦ adj ungirt; negligent; dissolute
discindō, -ndere, -dī, -ssum vt to tear up, cut open
discingō, -gere, -xī, -ctum vt to ungird
disciplīna, -ae f teaching, instruction; learning, science, school, system; training, discipline; habits
discipulus, -ī m, **discipula, -ae** f pupil, apprentice
discissus ppp of **discindō**
disclūdō, -dere, -sī, -sum vt to keep apart, separate out
discō, -ere, didicī vt to learn, be taught, be told
discolor, -ōris adj of a different colour; variegated; different
discondūcit it is not worthwhile
disconveniō, -īre vi to disagree, be inconsistent
discordābilis adj disagreeing
discordia, -ae f discord, disagreement
discordiōsus adj seditious
discordō, -āre vi to disagree, quarrel; to be unlike
discors, -dis adj discordant, at variance; inconsistent
discrepantia, -ae f disagreement
discrepātiō, -ōnis f dispute
discrepitō, -āre vi to be quite different
discrepō, -āre, -uī vi to be out of tune; to disagree, differ; to be disputed
discrētus ppp of **discernō**
dīscrībō, -bere, -psī, -ptum vt to distribute, apportion, classify

discrīmen, -inis *nt* interval, dividing line; distinction, difference; turning point, critical moment; crisis, danger

discrīminō, -āre *vt* to divide

dīscrīptē *adv* in good order

dīscrīptiō, -ōnis *f* apportioning, distributing

dīscrīptus *ppp of* **dīscrībō** ♦ *adj* secluded; well-arranged

discruciō, -āre *vt* to torture; (*fig*) to torment, trouble

discumbō, -mbere, -buī, -bitum *vi* to recline at table; to go to bed

discupiō, -ere *vi* to long

discurrō, -rrere, -currī *and* **-rrī, -rsum** *vi* to run about, run different ways

discursus, -ūs *m* running hither and thither

discus, -ī *m* quoit

discussus *ppp of* **discutiō**

discutiō, -tere, -ssī, -ssum *vt* to dash to pieces, smash; to scatter; to dispel

disertē, disertim *adv* distinctly; eloquently

disertus *adj* fluent, eloquent, explicit

disiciō, -icere, -iēcī, -iectum *vt* to scatter, cast asunder; to break up, destroy; (*MIL*) to rout

disiectō, -āre *vt* to toss about

disiectus¹ *ppp of* **disiciō**

disiectus², -ūs *m* scattering

disiūnctiō, -ōnis *f* separation, differing; (*LOGIC*) statement of alternatives; (*RHET*) a sequence of short co-ordinate clauses

disiūnctius *adv* rather in the manner of a dilemma

disiūnctus *ppp of* **disiungō** ♦ *adj* distinct, distant, removed; (*speech*) disjointed; (*LOGIC*) opposite

disiungō, -ungere, -ūnxī, -ūnctum *vt* to unyoke; to separate, remove

dispālēscō, -ere *vi* to be noised abroad

dispandō, -āndere, -andī, -ānsum *and* **-essum** *vt* to spread out

dispār, -aris *adj* unlike, unequal

disparilis *adj* dissimilar

disparō, -āre, -āvī, -ātum *vt* to segregate

dispart- *etc see* **dispert-**

dispectus *ppp of* **dispiciō**

dispellō, -ellere, -ulī, -ulsum *vt* to scatter, dispel

dispendium, -ī *and* **-iī** *nt* expense, loss

dispennō *etc see* **dispandō**

dispēnsātiō, -ōnis *f* management, stewardship

dispēnsātor, -ōris *m* steward, treasurer

dispēnsō, -āre, -āvī, -ātum *vi* to weigh out, pay out; to manage, distribute; (*fig*) to regulate

dispercutiō, -ere *vt* to dash out

disperdō, -ere, -idī, -itum *vt* to ruin, squander

dispereō, -īre, -iī *vi* to go to ruin, be undone

dispergō, -gere, -sī, -sum *vt* to disperse, spread over, space out

dispersē *adv* here and there

dispersus *ppp of* **dispergō**

dispertiō, -īre, -īvī, -ītum, dispertior, -īrī *vt* to apportion, distribute

dispertītiō, -ōnis *f* division

dispessus *ppp of* **dispandō**

dispiciō, -icere, -exī, -ectum *vt* to see clearly, see through; to distinguish, discern; (*fig*) to consider

displiceō, -ēre *vi* (*with dat*) to displease; **sibi displicēre** be in a bad humour

displōdō, -dere, -sī, -sum *vt* to burst with a crash

dispōnō, -ōnere, -osuī, -ositum *vt* to set out, arrange; (*MIL*) to station

dispositē *adv* methodically

dispositiō, -ōnis *f* arrangement

dispositūra, -ae *f* arrangement

dispositus¹ *ppp of* **dispōnō** ♦ *adj* orderly

dispositus², -ūs *m* arranging

dispudet, -ēre, -uit *v impers* to be very ashamed

dispulsus *ppp of* **dispellō**

disputātiō, -ōnis *f* argument

disputātor, -ōris *m* debater

disputō, -āre, -āvī, -ātum *vt* to calculate; to examine, discuss

disquīrō, -ere *vt* to investigate

disquīsītiō, -ōnis *f* inquiry

disrumpō *etc see* **dīrumpō**

dissaepiō, -īre, -sī, -tum *vt* to fence off, separate off

dissaeptum, -ī *nt* partition

dissāvior, -ārī *vt* to kiss passionately

dissēdī *perf of* **dissideō**

dissēminō, -āre *vt* to sow, broadcast

dissēnsiō, -ōnis *f* disagreement, conflict

dissēnsus, -ūs *m* dissension

dissentāneus *adj* contrary

dissentiō, -entīre, -ēnsī, -ēnsum *vi* to disagree, differ; to be unlike, be inconsistent

dissēp- *etc see* **dissaep-**

disserēnō, -āre *vi* to clear up

disserō¹, -erere, -ēvī, -itum *vt* to sow, plant at intervals

disserō², -ere, -uī, -tum *vt* to set out in order, arrange; to examine, discuss

disserpō, -ere *vi* to spread imperceptibly

dissertō, -āre *vt* to discuss, dispute

dissideō, -idēre, -ēdī, -essum *vi* to be distant; to disagree, quarrel; to differ, be unlike, be uneven

dissignātiō, -ōnis *f* arrangement

dissignātor, -ōris *m* master of ceremonies; undertaker

dissignō, -āre *vt* to arrange, regulate; *see also* **dēsignō**

dissiliō, -īre, -uī *vi* to fly apart, break up

dissimilis *adj* unlike, different

dissimiliter *adv* differently

dissimilitūdō, -inis *f* unlikeness

dissimulanter *adv* secretly

dissimulantia, -ae *f* dissembling

dissimulātiō, -ōnis *f* disguising, dissembling; Socratic irony

dissimulātor, -ōris *m* dissembler

dissimulō, -āre, -āvī, -ātum *vt* to dissemble, conceal, pretend that ... not, ignore

dissipābilis *adj* diffusible

dissipātiō, -ōnis *f* scattering, dispersing

dissipō, dissupō, -āre, -āvī, -ātum vt to scatter, disperse; to spread, broadcast; to squander, destroy; (MIL) to put to flight

dissitus ppp of **disserō**[1]

dissociābilis adj disuniting; incompatible

dissociātiō, -ōnis f separation

dissociō, -āre, -āvī, -ātum vt to disunite, estrange

dissolūbilis adj dissoluble

dissolūtē adv loosely, negligently

dissolūtiō, -ōnis f breaking up, destruction; looseness; (LAW) refutation; (person) weakness

dissolūtum, -ī nt asyndeton

dissolūtus ppp of **dissolvō** ◆ adj loose; lax, careless; licentious

dissolvō, -vere, -vī, -ūtum vt to unloose, dissolve; to destroy, abolish; to refute; to pay up, discharge (debt); to free, release

dissonus adj discordant, jarring, disagreeing, different

dissors, -tis adj not shared

dissuādeō, -dēre, -sī, -sum vt to advise against, oppose

dissuāsiō, -ōnis f advising against

dissuāsor, -ōris m opposer

dissultō, -āre vi to fly asunder

dissuō, -ere vt to undo, open up

dissupō etc see **dissipō**

distaedet, -ēre v impers to weary, disgust

distantia, -ae f diversity

distendō, distenō, -dere, -dī, -tum vt to stretch out, swell

distentus ppp of **distendō** ◆ adj full ◆ ppp of **distineō** ◆ adj busy

disterminō, -āre vt to divide, limit

distichon, -ī nt couplet

distinctē adv distinctly, lucidly

distinctiō, -ōnis f differentiating, difference; (GRAM) punctuation; (RHET) distinction between words

distinctus[1] ppp of **distinguō** ◆ adj separate, distinct; ornamented, set off; lucid

distinctus[2] **, -ūs** m difference

distineō, -inēre, -inuī, -entum vt to keep apart, divide; to distract; to detain, occupy; to prevent

distinguō, -guere, -xī, -ctum vt to divide, distinguish, discriminate; to punctuate; to adorn, set off

distō, -āre vi to be apart, be distant; to be different

distorqueō, -quēre, -sī, -tum vt to twist, distort

distortiō, -ōnis f contortion

distortus ppp of **distorqueō** ◆ adj deformed

distractiō, -ōnis f parting, variance

distractus ppp of **distrahō** ◆ adj separate

distrahō, -here, -xī, -ctum vt to tear apart, separate, estrange; to sell piecemeal, retail; (mind) to distract, perplex; **aciem distrahere** break up a formation; **contrōversiās distrahere** end a dispute; **vōcēs distrahere** leave a hiatus

distribuō, -uere, -uī, -ūtum vt to distribute, divide

distribūtē adv methodically

distribūtiō, -ōnis f distribution, division

districtus ppp of **distringō** ◆ adj busy, occupied; perplexed; severe

distringō, -ngere, -nxī, -ctum vt to draw apart; to engage, distract; (MIL) to create a diversion against

distruncō, -āre vt to cut in two

distulī perf of **differō**

disturbō, -āre, -āvī, -ātum vt to throw into confusion; to demolish; to frustrate, ruin

dītēscō, -ere vi to grow rich

dīthyrambicus adj dithyrambic

dīthyrambus, -ī m dithyramb

dītiae, -ārum fpl wealth

dītiō etc see **diciō**

dītō, -āre vt to enrich

diū (compar **diūtius**, superl **diūtissimē**) adv long, for a long time; long ago; by day

diurnum, -ī nt day-book; **ācta diurna** Roman daily gazette

diurnus adj daily, for a day; by day, day- (in cpds)

dīus adj divine, noble

diūtinē adv long

diūtinus adj long, lasting

diūtissimē, -ius etc see **diū**

diūturnitās, -ātis f long time, long duration

diūturnus adj long, lasting

dīva, -ae f goddess

dīvāricō, -āre vt to spread

dīvellō, -ellere, -ellī, -ulsum vt to tear apart, tear in pieces; (fig) to tear away, separate, estrange

dīvēndō, -ere, -itum vt to sell in lots

dīverberō, -āre vt to divide, cleave

dīverbium, -ī and **-iī** nt (comedy) passage in dialogue

dīversē adv in different directions, variously

dīversitās, -ātis f contradiction, disagreement, difference

dīversus, dīvorsus ppp of **dīvertō** ◆ adj in different directions, apart; different; remote, opposite, conflicting; hostile ◆ mpl individuals

dīvertō, -tere, -tī, -sum vi to turn away; differ

dīves, -itis adj rich

dīvexō, -āre vt to pillage

dīvidia, -ae f worry, concern

dīvidō, -idere, -īsī, -īsum vt to divide, break open; to distribute, apportion; to separate, keep apart; to distinguish; (jewel) to set off; **sententiam dīvidere** take the vote separately on the parts of a motion

dīviduus adj divisible; divided

dīvīnātiō, -ōnis f foreseeing the future, divination; (LAW) inquiry to select the most suitable prosecutor

dīvīnē adv by divine influence; prophetically; admirably

dīvīnitās, -ātis f divinity; divination; divine quality

dīvīnitus adv from heaven, by divine influence; excellently

dīvīnō, -āre, -āvī, -ātum vt to foresee, prophesy

dīvīnus adj divine, of the gods; prophetic; superhuman, excellent ♦ m soothsayer ♦ nt sacrifice; oath; **rēs dīvīna** religious service, sacrifice; **dīvīna hūmānaque** all things in heaven and earth; **dīvīnī crēdere** believe on oath

dīvīsī perf of **dīvidō**

dīvīsiō, -ōnis f division; distribution

dīvīsor, -ōris m distributor; bribery agent

dīvīsus¹ ppp of **dīvidō** ♦ adj separate

dīvīsus², -ūs m division

dīvitiae, -ārum fpl wealth; (fig) richness

dīvor- etc see **dīver-**

dīvortium, -ī and **-iī** nt separation; divorce (by consent), road fork, watershed

dīvulgātus adj widespread

dīvulgō, -āre, -āvī, -ātum vt to publish, make public

dīvulsus ppp of **dīvellō**

dīvum, -ī nt sky; **sub dīvō** in the open air

dīvus adj divine; deified ♦ m god

dīxī perf of **dīcō**

dō, dare, dedī, datum vt to give; to permit, grant; to put, bring, cause, make; to give up, devote; to tell; to impute; **fābulam dare** produce a play; **in fugam dare** put to flight; **litterās dare** post a letter; **manūs dare** surrender; **nōmen dare** enlist; **operam dare** take pains, do one's best; **poenās dare** pay the penalty; **vēla dare** set sail; **verba dare** cheat

doceō, -ēre, -uī, -tum vt to teach; to inform, tell; **fābulam docēre** produce a play

dochmius, -ī and **-iī** m dochmiac foot

docilis adj easily trained, docile

docilitās, -ātis f aptness for being taught

doctē adv skilfully, cleverly

doctor, -ōris m teacher, instructor

doctrīna, -ae f instruction, education, learning; science

doctus ppp of **doceō** ♦ adj learned, skilled; cunning, clever

documentum, -ī nt lesson, example, proof

Dōdōna, -ae f town in Epirus (famous for its oracle of Jupiter)

Dōdōnaeus, Dōdōnaeis, -idis adj see **Dōdōna**

dōdrāns, -antis m three-fourths

dogma, -tis nt philosophical doctrine

dolābra, -ae f pickaxe

dolēns, -entis pres p of **doleō** ♦ adj painful

dolenter adv sorrowfully

doleō, -ēre, -uī, -itum vt, vi to be in pain, be sore; to grieve, lament, be sorry (for); to pain; **cui dolet meminit** once bitten, twice shy

dōliāris adj tubby

dōliolum, -ī nt small cask

dōlium, -ī and **-iī** nt large wine jar

dolō¹, -āre, -āvī, -ātum vt to hew, shape with an axe

dolō², -ōnis m pike; sting; fore-topsail

Dolopes, -um mpl people of Thessaly

Dolopia, -iae f the country of the people of Thessaly

dolor, -ōris m pain, pang; sorrow, trouble; indignation, resentment; (RHET) pathos

dolōsē adv see **dolōsus**

dolōsus adj deceitful, crafty

dolus, -ī m deceit, guile, trick; ~ **malus** wilful fraud

domābilis adj tameable

domesticus adj domestic, household; personal, private; of one's own country, internal ♦ mpl members of a household; **bellum domesticum** civil war

domī adv at home

domicilium, -ī and **-iī** nt dwelling

domina, -ae f mistress, lady of the house; wife, mistress; (fig) lady

domināns, -antis pres p of **dominor** ♦ adj (words) literal ♦ m tyrant

dominātiō, -ōnis f mastery, tyranny

dominātor, -ōris m lord

dominātrīx, -rīcis f queen

dominātus, -ūs m mastery, sovereignty

dominicus adj (ECCL) the Lord's

dominium, -ī and **-iī** nt absolute ownership; feast

dominor, -ārī, -ātus vi to rule, be master; (fig) to lord it

dominus, -ī m master, lord; owner; host; despot; (ECCL) the Lord

Domitiānus adj, m Roman Emperor

Domitius, -ī m Roman plebeian name (esp with surname Ahenobarbus)

domitō, -āre vt to break in

domitor, -ōris m, **domitrīx, -rīcis** f tamer; conqueror

domitus¹ ppp of **domō**

domitus², -ūs m taming

domō, -āre, -uī, -itum vt to tame, break in; to conquer

domus, -ūs and **-ī** f house (esp in town); home, native place; family; (PHILOS) sect; **domī** at home; in peace; **domī habēre** have of one's own, have plenty of; **domum** home(wards); **domō** from home

dōnābilis adj deserving a present

dōnārium, -ī and **-iī** nt offering; altar, temple

dōnātiō, -ōnis f presenting

dōnātīvum, -ī nt largesse, gratuity

dōnec, dōnicum, dōnique conj until; while, as long as

dōnō, -āre, -āvī, -ātum vt to present, bestow; to remit, condone (for another's sake); (fig) to sacrifice

dōnum, -ī nt gift; offering

dorcas, -dis f gazelle

Dōrēs, -um mpl Dorians (mostly the Greeks of the Peloponnese)

Dōricus adj Dorian; Greek

Dōris, -dis f a sea nymph; the sea

dormiō, -īre, -īvī, -ītum vi to sleep, be asleep

dormītātor, -ōris m dreamer

dormītō, -āre vi to be drowsy, nod

dorsum, -ī nt back; mountain ridge

dōs, dōtis f dowry; (fig) gift, talent

Dossēnus, -ī m hunchback, clown

dōtālis adj dowry (in cpds), dotal

dōtātus adj richly endowed

dōtō, -āre vt to endow

drachma, drachuma, -ae f a Greek silver coin

draco, -ōnis *m* serpent, dragon; (ASTR) Draco

dracōnigena, -ae *adj* sprung from dragon's teeth

drăpeta, -ae *m* runaway slave

Drepanum, -ī, Drepana, -ōrum *nt town in W. Sicily*

dromas, -dis *m* dromedary

dromos, -ī *m* racecourse (*at Sparta*)

Druidēs, -um, Druidae, -ārum *mpl* Druids

Drūsiānus *adj see* **Drūsus**

Drūsus, -ī *m* Roman surname (*esp famous commander in Germany under Augustus*)

Dryades, -um *fpl* woodnymphs, Dryads

Dryopes, -um *mpl a people of Epirus*

dubiē *adv* doubtfully

dubitābilis *adj* doubtful

dubitanter *adv* doubtingly, hesitatingly

dubitātiō, -ōnis *f* wavering, uncertainty, doubting; hesitancy, irresolution; (RHET) misgiving

dubitō, -āre, -āvī, -ātum *vt, vi* to waver, be in doubt, wonder, doubt; to hesitate, stop to think

dubium *nt* doubt

dubius *adj* wavering, uncertain; doubtful, indecisive; precarious; irresolute ♦ *nt* doubt; **in dubium vocāre** call in question; **in dubium venīre** be called in question; **sine dubiō, haud dubiē** undoubtedly

ducēnī, -ōrum *adj* 200 each

ducentēsima, -ae *f* one-half per cent

ducentī, -ōrum *num* two hundred

ducentiēs, -iēns *adv* 2 times

dūcō, -cere, -xī, ductum *vt* to lead, guide, bring, take; to draw, draw out; to reckon, consider; (MIL) to lead, march, command; (*breath*) to inhale; (*ceremony*) to conduct; (*changed aspect*) to take on, receive; (*dance*) to perform; (*drink*) to quaff; (*metal*) to shape, beat out; (*mind*) to attract, induce, deceive; (*oars*) to pull; (*origin*) to derive, trace; (*time*) to prolong, put off, pass; (*udders*) to milk; (*wool*) to spin; (*a work*) to construct, compose, make; (COMM) to calculate; **ilia dūcere** become broken-winded; **in numerō hostium dūcere** regard as an enemy; **ōs dūcere** make faces; **parvī dūcere** think little of; **ratiōnem dūcere** have regard for; **uxōrem dūcere** marry

ductim *adv* in streams

ductitō, -āre *vt* to lead on, deceive; to marry

ductō, -āre *vt* to lead, draw; to take home; to cheat

ductor, -ōris *m* leader, commander; guide, pilot

ductus¹ *ppp of* **dūcō**

ductus², -ūs *m* drawing, drawing off; form; command, generalship

dūdum *adv* a little while ago, just now; for long; **haud ~** not long ago; **iam ~ adsum** I have been here a long time; **quam ~** how long

duellum *etc see* **bellum**

Duillius, -ī *m* consul who defeated the Carthaginians at sea

duim *pres subj of* **dō**

dulce, dulciter *adv see* **dulcis**

dulcēdō, -inis *f* sweetness; pleasantness, charm

dulcēscō, -ere *vi* to become sweet

dulciculus *adj* rather sweet

dulcifer, -ī *adj* sweet

dulcis *adj* sweet; pleasant, lovely; kind, dear

dulcitūdō, -inis *f* sweetness

dūlicē *adv* like a slave

Dūlichium, -ī *nt island in the Ionian Sea near Ithaca*

Dūlichius *adj* of Dulichium; of Ulysses

dum *conj* while, as long as; provided that, if only; until ♦ *adv* (*enclitic*) now, a moment; (*with neg*) yet

dūmētum, -ī *nt* thicket, thornbushes

dummodo *conj* provided that

dūmōsus *adj* thorny

dumtaxat *adv* at least; only, merely

dūmus, -ī *m* thornbush

duo, duae, duo *num* two

duodeciēns, -ēs *adv* twelve times

duodecim *num* twelve

duodecimus *adj* twelfth

duodēnī, -ōrum *adj* twelve each, in dozens

duodēquadrāgēsimus *adj* thirty-eighth

duodēquadrāgintā *num* thirty-eight

duodēquīnquāgēsimus *adj* forty-eighth

duodētrīciēns *adv* twenty-eight times

duodētrīgintā *num* twenty-eight

duodēvīcēnī *adj* eighteen each

duodēvīgintī *num* eighteen

duoetvīcēsimānī, -ānōrum *mpl* soldiers of the 22nd legion

duoetvīcēsimus *adj* twenty-second

duovirī, duumvirī, -ōrum *mpl* a board of two men; colonial magistrates; **~ nāvālēs** naval commissioners (*for supply and repair*); **~ sacrōrum** keepers of the Sibylline Books

duplex, -icis *adj* double, twofold; both; (*person*) false

duplicārius, -ī *and* **-iī** *m* soldier receiving double pay

dupliciter *adv* doubly, on two accounts

duplicō, -āre, -āvī, -ātum *vt* to double, increase; to bend

duplus *adj* double, twice as much ♦ *nt* double ♦ *f* double the price

dupondius, -ī *and* **-iī** *m* coin worth two asses

dūrābilis *adj* lasting

dūrāmen, -inis *nt* hardness

dūrateus *adj* wooden

dūrē, dūriter *adv* stiffly; hardily; harshly, roughly

dūrēscō, -ēscere, -uī *vi* to harden

dūritās, -ātis *f* harshness

dūritia, -ae, dūritiēs, -ēī *f* hardness; hardiness; severity; want of feeling

dūrō, -āre, -āvī, -ātum *vt* to harden, stiffen; to make hardy, inure; (*mind*) to dull ♦ *vi* to harden; to be patient, endure; to hold out, last; (*mind*) to be steeled

dūruī *perf of* **dūrēscō**
dūrus *adj* hard, harsh, rough; hardy,
    tough; rude, uncultured; (*character*) severe,
    unfeeling, impudent, miserly; (*circumstances*)
    hard, cruel
duumvirī *etc see* **duovirī**
dux, ducis *m* leader, guide; chief, head; (MIL)
    commander, general

dūxī *perf of* **dūcō**
Dymantis, -antidis *f* Hecuba
Dymās, -antis *m father of Hecuba*
dynamis, -is *f* plenty
dynastēs, -ae *m* ruler, prince
Dyrrhachīnus *adj see* **Dyrrhachium**
Dyrrhachium, Dyrrachium, -ī *nt Adriatic port*
    (*now* Durrës)

Ee

ē *prep see* **ex**
eā *adv* there, that way
ea *f, pron* she, it ♦ *adj see* **is**
eadem *f, pron see* **īdem**
eādem *adv* the same way; at the same time
eaīdem, eapse *f of* **ipse**
eapse *f of* **ipse**
eātenus *adv* so far
ebenus *etc see* **hebenus**
ēbibō, -ere, -ī *vt* to drink up, drain; to squander; to absorb
ēblandior, -īrī *vt* to coax out, obtain by flattery; **ēblandītus** obtained by flattery
Eborācum, -ī *nt* York
ēbrietās, ātis *f* drunkenness
ēbriolus *adj* tipsy
ēbriōsitās, -ātis *f* addiction to drink
ēbriōsus *adj* drunkard; (*berry*) juicy
ēbrius *adj* drunk; full; (*fig*) intoxicated
ēbulliō, -īre *vi* to bubble up ♦ *vt* to brag about
ebulus, -ī *m*, **ebulum, -ī** *nt* danewort, dwarf elder
ebur, -is *nt* ivory; ivory work
Eburācum, -ī *nt* York
eburātus *adj* inlaid with ivory
eburneolus *adj* of ivory
eburneus, eburnus *adj* of ivory; ivory-white
ēcastor *interj* by Castor!
ecce *adv* look!, here is!, there is!; lo and behold!; **ecca, eccam, eccillam, eccistam** here she is!; **eccum, eccillum** here he is!; **eccōs, eccās** here they are!
eccerē *interj* there now!
eccheuma, -tis *nt* pouring out
ecclēsia, -ae *f* a Greek assembly; (*ECCL*) congregation, church
eccum *etc see* **ecce**
ecdicus, -ī *m* civic lawyer
ecf- *see* **eff-**
echidna, -ae *f* viper; ~ **Lernaea** hydra
echīnus, -ī *m* sea-urchin; hedgehog; a rinsing bowl
Echīōn, -onis *m* Theban hero
Echīonidēs *m* Pentheus
Echīonius *adj* Theban
Ēchō, -us *f* wood nymph; echo
ecloga, -ae *f* selection; eclogue
ecquandō *adv* ever
ecquī, -ae, -od *adj interrog* any
ecquid, ecquidī *adv* whether
ecquis, -id *pron interrog* anyone, anything

ecquō *adv* anywhere
eculeus, -ī *m* foal; rack
edācitās, -ātis *f* gluttony
edāx, -ācis *adj* gluttonous; (*fig*) devouring, carking
ēdentō, -āre *vt* to knock the teeth out of
ēdentulus *adj* toothless; old
edepol *interj* by Pollux, indeed
ēdī *perf of* **edō**
ēdīcō, -īcere, -īxī, -ictum *vt* to declare; to decree, publish by an edict
ēdictiō, -ōnis *f* decree
ēdictō, -āre *vt* to proclaim
ēdictum, -ī *nt* proclamation, edict (*esp a praetor's*)
ēdidī *perf of* **ēdō**
ēdiscō, -ere, ēdidicī *vt* to learn well, learn by heart
ēdisserō, -ere, -uī, -tum *vt* to explain in detail
ēdissertō, -āre *vt* to explain fully
ēditīcius *adj* chosen by the plaintiff
ēditiō, -ōnis *f* publishing, edition; statement; (*LAW*) designation of a suit
ēditus *ppp of* **ēdō** ♦ *adj* high; descended ♦ *nt* height; order
edō, edere *and* **ēsse, ēdī, ēsum** *vt* to eat; (*fig*) to devour
ēdō, -ere, -idī, -itum *vt* to put forth, discharge; to emit; to give birth to, produce; (*speech*) to declare, relate, utter; (*action*) to cause, perform; (*book*) to publish; (*POL*) to promulgate; **lūdōs ēdere** put on a show; **tribūs ēdere** nominate tribes of jurors
ēdoceō, -ēre, -uī, -ctum *vt* to instruct clearly, teach thoroughly
ēdomō, -āre, -uī, -itum *vt* to conquer, overcome
Ēdōnus *adj* Thracian
ēdormiō, -īre *vi* to have a good sleep ♦ *vt* to sleep off
ēdormīscō, -ere *vt* to sleep off
ēducātiō, -ōnis *f* bringing up, rearing
ēducātor, -ōris *m* foster father, tutor
ēducātrīx, -īcis *f* nurse
ēducō, -āre, -āvī, -ātum *vt* to bring up, rear, train; to produce
ēdūcō, -ūcere, -ūxī, -uctum *vt* to draw out, bring away; to raise up, erect; (*LAW*) to summon; (*MIL*) to lead out, march out; (*ship*) to put to sea; (*young*) to hatch, rear, train
edūlis *adj* edible
ēdūrō, -āre *vi* to last out
ēdūrus *adj* very hard

effarciō *etc see* **efferciō**

effātus *ppa (occ pass) of* **effor** ♦ *adj* solemnly pronounced, declared ♦ *nt* axiom; (*pl*) predictions

effectiō, -ōnis *f* performing; efficient cause

effector, -ōris *m*, **effectrix, -rīcis** *f* producer, author

effectus¹ *ppp of* **efficiō**

effectus², -ūs *m* completion, performance; effect

effēminātē *adv see* **effēminātus**

effēminātus *adj* effeminate

effēminō, -āre, -āvī, -ātum *vt* to make a woman of; to enervate

efferātus *adj* savage

efferciō, -cīre, -sī, -tum *vt* to cram full

efferitās, -ātis *f* wildness

efferō¹, -āre, -āvī, -ātum *vt* to make wild; (*fig*) to exasperate

efferō², ecferō, -re, extulī, ēlātum *vt* to bring out, carry out; to lift up, raise; (*dead*) to carry to the grave; (*emotion*) to transport; (*honour*) to exalt; (*news*) to spread abroad; (*soil*) to produce; (*trouble*) to endure to the end; **sē efferre** rise; be conceited

effertus *ppp of* **efferciō** ♦ *adj* full, bulging

efferus *adj* savage

effervēscō, -vēscere, -buī *vi* to boil over; (*fig*) to rage

effervō, -ere *vi* to boil up

effētus *adj* exhausted

efficācitās, -ātis *f* power

efficāciter *adv* effectually

efficāx, -ācis *adj* capable, effective

efficiēns, -entis *pres p of* **efficiō** ♦ *adj* effective, efficient

efficienter *adv* efficiently

efficientia, -ae *f* power, efficacy

efficiō, -icere, -ēcī, -ectum *vt* to make, accomplish; to cause, bring about; (*numbers*) to amount to; (*soil*) to yield; (*theory*) to make out, try to prove

effictus *ppp of* **effingō**

effigiēs, -ēī, effigia, -ae *f* likeness, copy; ghost; portrait, statue; (*fig*) image, ideal

effingō, -ngere, -nxī, -ctum *vt* to form, fashion; to portray, represent; to wipe clean; to fondle

efflāgitātiō, -ōnis *f* urgent demand

efflāgitātus, -ūs *m* urgent request

efflāgitō, -āre *vt* to demand urgently

efflictim *adv* desperately

efflictō, -āre *vt* to strike dead

effligō, -gere, -xī, -ctum *vt* to exterminate

efflō, -āre, -āvī, -ātum *vt* to breathe out, blow out ♦ *vi* to billow out; **animam efflāre** expire

efflōrēscō, -ēscere, -uī *vi* to blossom forth

effluō, -ere, -xī *vi* to run out, issue, emanate; (*fig*) to pass away, vanish; (*rumour*) to get known; **ex animō effluere** become forgotten

effluvium, -ī *and* **-iī** *nt* outlet

effodiō, -odere, -ōdī, -ossum *vt* to dig up; (*eyes*) to gouge out; (*house*) to ransack

effor, -ārī, -ātus *vt* to speak, utter; (*AUG*) to ordain; (*LOGIC*) to state a proposition

effossus *ppp of* **effodiō**

effrēnātē *adv see* **effrēnātus**

effrēnātiō, -ōnis *f* impetuousness

effrēnātus *adj* unbridled, violent, unruly

effrēnus *adj* unbridled

effringō, -ingere, -ēgī, -āctum *vt* to break open, smash

effugiō, -ugere, -ūgī *vi* to run away, escape ♦ *vt* to flee from, escape; to escape the notice of

effugium, -ī *and* **-iī** *nt* flight, escape; means of escape

effulgeō, -gēre, -sī *vi* to shine out, blaze

effultus *adj* supported

effundō, -undere, -ūdī, -ūsum *vt* to pour forth, pour out; (*crops*) to produce in abundance; (*missiles*) to shoot; (*rider*) to throw; (*speech*) to give vent to; (*effort*) to waste; (*money*) to squander; (*reins*) to let go; **sē effundere, sē effundī** rush out; indulge (in)

effūsē *adv* far and wide; lavishly, extravagantly

effūsiō, -ōnis *f* pouring out, rushing out; profusion, extravagance; exuberance

effūsus *ppp of* **effundō** ♦ *adj* vast, extensive; loose, straggling; lavish, extravagant

effūtiō, -īre *vt* to blab, chatter

ēgelidus *adj* mild, cool

egēns, -entis *pres p of* **egeō** ♦ *adj* needy

egēnus *adj* destitute

egeō, -ēre, -uī *vi* to be in want; (*with abl or gen*) to need, want

Ēgeria, -ae *f* nymph *who taught Numa*

ēgerō, -rere, -ssī, -stum *vt* to carry out; to discharge, emit

egestās, -ātis *f* want, poverty

ēgestus *ppp of* **ēgerō**

ēgī *perf of* **agō**

ego *pron* I; **egomet** I (*emphatic*)

ēgredior, -dī, -ssus *vi* to go out, come out; to go up, climb; (*MIL*) to march out; (*NAUT*) to disembark, put to sea; (*speech*) to digress ♦ *vt* to go beyond, quit; (*fig*) to overstep, surpass

ēgregiē *adv* uncommonly well, singularly

ēgregius *adj* outstanding, surpassing; distinguished, illustrious

ēgressus¹ *ppa of* **ēgredior**

ēgressus², -ūs *m* departure; way out; digression; (*NAUT*) landing; (*river*) mouth

eguī *perf of* **egeō**

ēgurgitō, -āre *vt* to lavish

ehem *interj* (*expressing surprise*) ha!, so!

ēheu *interj* (*expressing pain*) alas!

eho *interj* (*expressing rebuke*) look here!

ei *interj* (*expressing alarm*) oh!

eī *dat of* **is**

eia *interj* (*expressing delight, playful remonstrance, encouragement*) aha!, come now!, come on!

ēiaculor, -ārī *vt* to shoot out

ēiciō, -icere, -iēcī, -iectum *vt* to throw out, drive out, put out; (*joint*) to dislocate; (*mind*) to banish; (*NAUT*) to bring to land, run aground, wreck; (*rider*) to throw; (*speech*) to utter; (*THEAT*) to hiss off; **sē ēicere** rush out, break out

ēiectāmenta, -ōrum *ntpl* refuse

ēiectiō, -ōnis *f* banishment

ēiectō, -āre *vt* to throw up

ēiectus¹ *ppp of* **ēiciō** ♦ *adj* shipwrecked

71

ēiectus², **-ūs** *m* emitting

ēierō, **ēiūrō**, **-āre** *vt* to abjure, reject on oath, forswear; *(office)* to resign; **bonam cōpiam ēierāre** declare oneself bankrupt

ēiulātiō, **-ōnis** *f*, **ēiulātus**, **-ūs** *m* wailing

ēiulō, **-āre** *vi* to wail, lament

ēius *pron* his, her, its; **ēiusmodī** such

ej- *etc see* **ei-**

ēlābor, **-bī**, **-psus** *vi* to glide away, slip off; to escape, get off; to pass away

ēlabōrātus *adj* studied

ēlabōrō, **-āre**, **-āvī**, **-ātum** *vi* to exert oneself, take great pains ♦ *vt* to work out, elaborate

ēlāmentābilis *adj* very mournful

ēlanguēscō, **-ēscere**, **-ī** *vi* to grow faint; to relax

ēlāpsus *ppa of* **ēlābor**

ēlātē *adv* proudly

ēlātiō, **-ōnis** *f* ecstasy, exaltation

ēlātrō, **-āre** *vt* to bark out

ēlātus *ppp of* **efferō²** ♦ *adj* high; exalted

ēlavō, **-avāre**, **-āvī**, **-autum** *and* **-ōtum** *vt* to wash clean; *(comedy)* to rob

Ēlea, **-ae** *f* town in S. Italy (*birthplace of Parmenides*)

Ēleātēs, **Ēleāticus** *adj see* **Ēlea**

ēlecebra, **-ae** *f* snare

ēlēctē *adv* choicely

ēlēctilis *adj* choice

ēlēctiō, **-ōnis** *f* choice, option

ēlēctō, **-āre** *vt* to coax out

ēlēctō, **-āre** *vt* to select

Ēlectra, **-ae** *f* a Pleiad (*daughter of Atlas; sister of Orestes*)

ēlēctrum, **-ī** *nt* amber; an alloy of gold and silver

ēlēctus¹ *ppp of* **ēligō** ♦ *adj* select, choice

ēlēctus², **-ūs** *m* choice

ēlegāns, **-antis** *adj* tasteful, refined, elegant; fastidious; *(things)* fine, choice

ēleganter *adv* with good taste

ēlegantia, **-ae** *f* taste, finesse, elegance; fastidiousness

elegī, **-ōrum** *mpl* elegiac verses

ēlēgī *perf of* **ēligō**

elegīa, **-ae** *f* elegy

Eleleides, **-eidum** *fpl* Bacchantes

Eleleus, **-eī** *m* Bacchus

elementum, **-ī** *nt* element; *(pl)* first principles, rudiments; beginnings; letters (*of alphabet*)

elenchus, **-ī** *m* a pear-shaped pearl

elephantomacha, **-ae** *m* fighter mounted on an elephant

elephantus, **-ī**, **elephās**, **-antis** *m* elephant; ivory

Ēlēus, **Ēlēius**, **Ēlēias** *adj* Elean; Olympian

Eleusīn, **-is** *f* Eleusis (*Attic town famous for its mysteries of Demeter*)

Eleusīus *adj see* **Eleusīn**

eleutheria, **-ae** *f* liberty

ēlevō, **-āre** *vt* to lift, raise; to alleviate; to make light of, lessen, disparage

ēliciō, **-ere**, **-uī**, **-itum** *vt* to lure out, draw out; (*god*) to call down; (*spirit*) to conjure up; (*fig*) to elicit, draw

ēlīdō, **-dere**, **-sī**, **-sum** *vt* to dash out, squeeze out; to drive out; to crush, destroy

ēligō, **-igere**, **-ēgī**, **-ēctum** *vt* to pick, pluck out; to choose

ēlīminō, **-āre** *vt* to carry outside

ēlīmō, **-āre** *vt* to file; (*fig*) to perfect

ēlinguis *adj* speechless; not eloquent

ēlinguō, **-āre** *vt* to tear the tongue out of

Ēlis, **-idis** *f* district and town in W. Peloponnese (*famous for Olympia*)

Elissa, **-ae** *f* Dido

ēlīsus *ppp of* **ēlīdō**

ēlixus *adj* boiled

elleborōsus *adj* quite mad

elleborus, **-ī** *m*, **elleborum**, **-ī** *nt* hellebore

ellum, **ellam** there he/she is!

ēlocō, **-āre** *vt* to lease, farm out

ēlocūtiō, **-ōnis** *f* delivery, style

ēlocūtus *ppa of* **ēloquor**

ēlogium, **-ī** *and* **-iī** *nt* short saying; inscription; (*will*) clause

ēloquēns, **-entis** *adj* eloquent

ēloquenter *adv see* **ēloquēns**

ēloquentia, **-ae** *f* eloquence

ēloquium, **-ī** *and* **-iī** *nt* eloquence

ēloquor, **-quī**, **-cūtus** *vt*, *vi* to speak out, speak eloquently

ēlūceō, **-cēre**, **-xī** *vi* to shine out, glitter

ēluctor, **-ārī**, **-ātus** *vi* to struggle, force a way out ♦ *vt* to struggle out of, surmount

ēlūcubrō, **-āre**, **ēlūcubror**, **-ārī**, **-ātus** *vt* to compose by lamplight

ēlūdificor, **-ārī**, **-ātus** *vt* to cheat, play up

ēlūdō, **-dere**, **-sī**, **-sum** *vt* to parry, ward off, foil; to win off at play; to outplay, outmanoeuvre; to cheat, make fun of ♦ *vi* to finish one's sport

ēlūgeō, **-gēre**, **-xī** *vt* to mourn for

ēlumbis *adj* feeble

ēluō, **-uere**, **-uī**, **-ūtum** *vt* to wash clean; (*money*) to squander; (*fig*) to wash away, get rid of

ēlūsus *ppp of* **ēlūdō**

ēlūtus *ppp of* **ēluō** ♦ *adj* insipid

ēluviēs (*acc* **-em**, *abl* **-ē**) discharge; overflowing

ēluviō, **-ōnis** *f* deluge

Ēlysium, **-ī** *nt* Elysium

Ēlysius *adj* Elysian

em *interj* there you are!

ēmancipātiō, **-ōnis** *f* giving a son his independence; conveyance (*of property*)

ēmancipō, **-āre** *vt* to declare independent; to transfer, give up, sell

ēmānō, **-āre**, **-āvī**, **-ātum** *vi* to flow out; to spring (from); (*news*) to leak out, become known

Ēmathia, **-ae** *f* district of Macedonia; Macedonia, Thessaly

Ēmathides, **-idum** *fpl* Muses

Ēmathius *adj* Macedonian, Pharsalian

ēmātūrēscō, **-ēscere**, **-uī** *vi* to soften

emāx, **-ācis** *adj* fond of buying

emblēma, **-tis** *nt* inlaid work, mosaic

embolium, **-ī** *and* **-iī** *nt* interlude

ēmendābilis *adj* corrigible

ēmendātē *adv see* **ēmendātus**

ēmendātiō, **-ōnis** *f* correction

ēmendātor, -ōris m, **ēmendātrix, -rīcis** f
  corrector
ēmendātus adj faultless
ēmendō, -āre, -āvī, -ātum vt to correct,
  improve
ēmēnsus ppa of **ēmētior** ♦ adj traversed
ēmentior, -īrī, -ītus vi to tell lies ♦ vt to pretend,
  fabricate; **ēmentītus** pretended
ēmercor, -ārī vt to purchase
ēmereō, -ēre, -uī, -itum, ēmereor, ēmerērī
  vt to earn fully, deserve; to lay under an
  obligation; to complete one's term of service
ēmergō, -gere, -sī, -sum vt to raise out; (fig) to
  extricate ♦ vi to rise, come up, emerge; (fig) to
  get clear, extricate oneself; (impers) it becomes
  evident
ēmeritus ppa of **ēmereor** ♦ adj superannuated,
  worn-out ♦ m veteran
ēmersus ppp of **ēmergō**
emetica, -ae f emetic
ēmētior, -tīrī, -nsus vt to measure out; to
  traverse, pass over; (time) to live through; (fig)
  to impart
ēmetō, -ere vt to harvest
ēmī perf of **emō**
ēmicō, -āre, -uī, -ātum vi to dart out, dash out,
  flash out; (fig) to shine
ēmigrō, -āre, -āvī, -ātum vi to remove, depart
ēminēns, -entis pres p of **ēmineō** ♦ adj high,
  projecting; (fig) distinguished, eminent
ēminentia, -ae f prominence; (painting) light
ēmineō, -ēre, -uī vi to stand out, project; to
  be prominent, be conspicuous, distinguish
  oneself
ēminor, -ārī vi to threaten
ēminus adv at or from a distance
ēmīror, -ārī vt to marvel at
ēmissārium, -ī and **-iī** nt outlet
ēmissārius, -ī and **-iī** m scout
ēmissīcius adj prying
ēmissiō, -ōnis f letting go, discharge
ēmissus¹ ppp of **ēmittō**
ēmissus², -ūs m emission
ēmittō, -ittere, -īsī, -issum vt to send out, let
  out; to let go, let slip; (missile) to discharge;
  (person) to release, free; (sound) to utter; (writing)
  to publish
emō, -ere, ēmī, emptum vt to buy, procure; to
  win over; **bene emere** buy cheap; **male emere**
  buy dear; **in diem emere** buy on credit
ēmoderor, -ārī vt to give expression to
ēmodulor, -ārī vt to sing through
ēmōlior, -īrī vt to accomplish
ēmolliō, -īre, -iī, -ītum vt to soften; to mollify;
  to enervate
ēmolumentum, -ī nt profit, advantage
ēmoneō, -ēre vt to strongly advise
ēmorior, -ī, -tuus vi to die; (fig) to pass away
ēmortuālis adj of death
ēmoveō, -ovēre, -ōvī, -ōtum vt to remove,
  drive away
Empedoclēs, -is m Sicilian philosopher
Empedoclēus adj see **Empedoclēs**
empīricus, -ī m empirical doctor
emporium, -ī and **-iī** nt market, market town

emptiō, -ōnis f buying; a purchase
emptitō, -āre vt to often buy
emptor, -ōris m purchaser
emptus ppp of **emō**
ēmulgeō, -ēre vt to drain
ēmunctus ppp of **ēmungō** ♦ adj discriminating
ēmungō, -gere, -xī, -ctum vt to blow the nose
  of; (comedy) to cheat
ēmūniō, -īre, -īvī, -ītum vt to strengthen,
  secure; to build up; to make roads through
ēn interj (drawing attention) look!, see!; (excited
  question) really, indeed; (command) come now!
ēnārrābilis adj describable
ēnārrō, -āre, -āvī, -ātum vt to describe in detail
ēnāscor, -scī, -tus vi to sprout, grow
ēnatō, -āre vi to swim ashore; (fig) to escape
ēnātus ppa of **ēnāscor**
ēnāvigō, -āre vi to sail clear, clear ♦ vt to sail
  over
Enceladus, -ī m giant under Etna
endromis, -dis f sports wrap
Endymiōn, -ōnis m a beautiful youth loved by the
  Moon, and doomed to lasting sleep
ēnecō, -āre, -uī and **-āvī, -tum** and **-ātum** vt to
  kill; to wear out; to torment
ēnervātus adj limp
ēnervis adj enfeebled
ēnervō, -āre, -āvī, -ātum vt to weaken, unman
ēnicō etc see **ēnecō**
enim conj (affirming) yes, truly, in fact; (explaining)
  for, for instance, of course; **at ~** but it will be
  objected; **quid ~?** well?; **sed ~** but actually
enimvērō conj certainly, yes indeed
Enīpeus, -eī m river in Thessaly
ēnīsus ppa of **ēnītor**
ēniteō, -ēre, -uī vi to shine, brighten up; (fig) to
  be brilliant, distinguish oneself
ēnitēscō, -ēscere, -uī vi to shine, be brilliant
ēnītor, -tī, -sus and **-xus** vi to struggle up, climb;
  to strive, make a great effort ♦ vt to give birth
  to; to climb
ēnīxē adv earnestly
ēnīxus ppa of **ēnītor** ♦ adj strenuous
Enniānus adj see **Ennius**
Ennius, -ī m greatest of the early Latin poets
Ennosigaeus, -ī m Earthshaker, Neptune
ēnō, -āre, -āvī vi to swim out, swim ashore; to
  fly away
ēnōdātē adv lucidly
ēnōdātiō, -ōnis f unravelling
ēnōdis adj free from knots; plain
ēnōdō, -āre, -āvī, -ātum vt to elucidate
ēnōrmis adj irregular; immense
ēnōtēscō, -ēscere, -uī vi to get known
ēnotō, -āre vt to make a note of
ēnsiculus, -ī m little sword
ēnsiger, -ī adj with his sword
ēnsis, -is m sword
enthymēma, -tis nt argument
ēnūbō, -bere, -psī vi to marry out of one's
  station; to marry and go away
ēnucleātē adv plainly
ēnucleātus adj (style) straightforward; (votes)
  honest

ēnucleō, -āre vt to elucidate
ēnumerātiō, -ōnis f enumeration; (RHET) recapitulation
ēnumerō, -āre vt to count up; to pay out; to relate
ēnūntiātiō, -ōnis f proposition
ēnūntiātum, -ī nt proposition
ēnūntiō, -āre vt to disclose, report; to express; to pronounce
ēnūptiō, -ōnis f marrying out of one's station
ēnūtriō, -īre vt to feed, bring up
eō¹, īre, īvī and **iī, itum** vi to go; (MIL) to march; (time) to pass; (event) to proceed, turn out; **in alia omnia īre** vote against a bill; **in sententiam īre** support a motion; **sīc eat** so may he fare!; **ī** (mocking) go on!
eō² adv (place) thither, there; (purpose) with a view to; (degree) so far, to such a pitch; (time) so long; (cause) on that account, for the reason; (with comp) the; **accēdit eō** besides; **rēs erat eō locī** such was the state of affairs; **eō magis** all the more
eōdem adv to the same place, purpose or person; **~ locī** in the same place
Eōs f dawn
Eōus adj at dawn, eastern ◆ m morning star; Oriental
Epamīnōndās, -ae m Theban general
epāstus adj eaten up
ephēbus, -ī m youth (18 to 20)
ephēmeris, -idis f diary
Ephesius adj see **Ephesus**
Ephesus, -ī f Ionian town in Asia Minor
ephippiātus adj riding a saddled horse
ephippium, -ī and **-iī** nt saddle
ephorus, -ī m a Spartan magistrate, ephor
Ephyra, -ae, Ephyrē, -ēs f Corinth
Ephyrēius adj see **Ephyra**
Epicharmus, -ī m Greek philosopher and comic poet
epichysis, -is f kind of jug
epicōpus adj rowing
Epicūrēus adj Epicurean
Epicūrus, -ī m famous Greek philosopher
epicus adj epic
Epidaurius adj see **Epidaurus**
Epidaurus, -ī f town in E. Peloponnese
epidīcticus adj (RHET) for display
epigramma, -tis nt inscription; epigram
epilogus, -ī m peroration
epimēnia, -ōrum ntpl a month's rations
Epimēthis, -dis f Pyrrha (daughter of Epimetheus)
epirēdium, -ī and **-iī** nt trace
Ēpīrōtēs, -ōtae m native of Epirus
Ēpīrōticus, Ēpīrēnsis adj see **Ēpīrus**
Ēpīrus, Ēpīros, -ī f district of N.W. Greece
episcopus, -ī m bishop
epistolium, -ī and **-iī** nt short note
epistula, -ae f letter; **ab epistulīs** secretary
epitaphium, -ī and **-iī** nt funeral oration
epithēca, -ae f addition
epitoma, -ae, epitomē, -ēs f abridgement
epityrum, -ī nt olive salad
epops, -is m hoopoe
epos (pl **-ē**) nt epic

ēpōtō, -āre, -āvī, -um vt to drink up, drain; to waste in drink; to absorb
epulae, -ārum fpl dishes; feast, banquet
epulāris adj at a banquet
epulō, -ōnis m guest at a feast; priest in charge of religious banquets
epulor, -ārī, -ātus vi to be at a feast ◆ vt to feast on
epulum, -ī nt banquet
equa, -ae f mare
eques, -itis m horseman, trooper; (pl) cavalry; knight, member of the equestrian order
equester, -ris adj equestrian, cavalry- (in cpds)
equidem adv (affirming) indeed, of course, for my part; (concessive) to be sure
equīnus adj horse's
equīria, -ōrum ntpl horseraces
equitātus, -ūs m cavalry
equitō, -āre vi to ride
equuleus etc see **eculeus**
equulus, -ī m colt
equus, -ī m horse; (ASTR) Pegasus; **~ bipēs** seahorse; **equō merēre** serve in the cavalry; **equīs virīsque** with might and main
era, -ae f mistress (of the house); (goddess) Lady
ērādīcō, -āre vt to root out, destroy
ērādō, -dere, -sī, -sum vt to erase, obliterate
Eratō f Muse of lyric poetry
Eratosthenēs, -is m famous Alexandrian geographer
Erebēus adj see **Erebus**
Erebus, -ī m god of darkness; the lower world
Erechtheus, -eī m legendary king of Athens
Erechthēus adj see **Erechtheus**
Erechthīdae mpl Athenians
Erechthis, -idis f Orithyia; Procris
ērēctus ppp of **ērigō** ◆ adj upright, lofty; noble, haughty; alert, tense; resolute
ērēpō, -ere, -sī vi to creep out, clamber up ◆ vt to crawl over, climb
ēreptiō, -ōnis f seizure, robbery
ēreptor, -ōris m robber
ēreptus ppp of **ēripiō**
ergā prep (with acc) towards; against
ergastulum, -ī nt prison (esp for slaves); (pl) convicts
ergō adv therefore, consequently; (questions, commands) then, so; (resuming) well then; (with gen) for the sake of, because of
Erichthonius, -ī m a king of Troy; a king of Athens ◆ adj Trojan; Athenian
ēricius, -ī and **-iī** m hedgehog; (MIL) beam with iron spikes
Ēridanus, -ī m mythical name of river Po
erifuga, -ae m runaway slave
ērigō, -igere, -ēxī, -ēctum vt to make upright, raise up, erect; to excite; to encourage
Ērigonē, -ēs f (constellation) Virgo
Ērigonēius adj see **Ērigonē**
erīlis adj the master's, the mistress's
Erīnȳs, -yos f Fury; (fig) curse, frenzy
Eriphȳla, -ae f mother of Alcmaeon (who killed her)
ēripiō, -ipere, -ipuī, -eptum vt to tear away, pull away, take by force; to rob; to rescue; **sē ēripere** escape
ērogātiō, -ōnis f paying out

ērogitō, -āre *vt* to enquire

ērogō, -āre, -āvī, -ātum *vt* to pay out, expend; to bequeath

errābundus *adj* wandering

errāticus *adj* roving, shifting

errātiō, -ōnis *f* wandering, roving

errātum, -ī *nt* mistake, error

errātus, -ūs *m* wandering

errō¹, -āre, -āvī, -ātum *vi* to wander, stray, lose one's way; to waver; to make a mistake, err ♦ *vt* to traverse; **stēllae errantēs** planets

errō², -ōnis *m* vagabond

error, -ōris *m* wandering; meander, maze; uncertainty; error, mistake, delusion; deception

ērubēscō, -ēscere, -uī *vi* to blush; to feel ashamed ♦ *vt* to blush for, be ashamed of; to respect

ērūca, -ae *f* colewort

ēructō, -āre *vt* to belch, vomit; to talk drunkenly about; to throw up

ērudiō, -īre, -iī, -ītum *vt* to educate, instruct

ērudītē *adv* learnedly

ērudītiō, -ōnis *f* education, instruction; learning, knowledge

ērudītulus *adj* somewhat skilled

ērudītus *ppp of* **ērudiō** ♦ *adj* learned, educated, accomplished

ērumpō, -umpere, -ūpī, -uptum *vt* to break open; to make break out ♦ *vi* to burst out, break through; to end (in)

ēruō, -ere, -ī, -tum *vt* to uproot, tear out; to demolish, destroy; to elicit, draw out; to rescue

ēruptiō, -ōnis *f* eruption; (MIL) sally

ēruptus *ppp of* **ērumpō**

erus, -ī *m* master (of the house); owner

ērutus *ppp of* **ēruō**

ervum, -ī *nt* vetch

Erycīnus *adj* of Eryx; of Venus; Sicilian ♦ *f* Venus

Erymanthius, -is *adj see* **Erymanthus**

Erymanthus, Erymanthī *m* mountain range in Arcadia (where Hercules killed the boar)

Eryx, -cis *m* town and mountain in the extreme W. of Sicily

esca, -ae *f* food, titbits; bait

escārius *adj* of food; of bait ♦ *ntpl* dishes

ēscendō, -endere, -endī, -ēnsum *vi* to climb up, go up ♦ *vt* to mount

ēscēnsiō, -ōnis *f* raid (from the coast), disembarkation

esculentus *adj* edible, tasty

Esquiliae, -iārum *fpl* Esquiline hill (in Rome)

Esquilīnus *adj* Esquiline ♦ *f* Esquiline gate

essedārius, -ī and -iī *m* chariot fighter

essedum, -ī *nt* war chariot

essitō, -āre *vt* to usually eat

ēst *pres of* **edō**

ēstrīx, -īcis *f* glutton

ēsuriālis *adj* of hunger

ēsuriō, -īre, -ītum *vi* to be hungry ♦ *vt* to hunger for

ēsurītiō, -ōnis *f* hunger

ēsus *ppp of* **edō**

et *conj* and; (repeated) both ... and; (adding emphasis) in fact, yes; (comparing) as, than ♦ *adv* also, too; even

etenim *conj* (adding an explanation) and as a matter of fact, in fact

etēsiae, -ārum *fpl* Etesian winds

etēsius *adj see* **etēsiae**

ēthologus, -ī *m* mimic

etiam *adv* also, besides; (emphatic) even, actually; (affirming) yes, certainly; (indignant) really!; (time) still, as yet; again; ~ **atque** ~ again and again; ~ **cavēs** do be careful!; **nihil** ~ nothing at all

etiamdum *adv* still, as yet

etiamnum, etiamnunc *adv* still, till now, till then; besides

etiamsī *conj* even if, although

etiamtum, etiamtunc *adv* till then, still

Etrūria, -ae *f* district of Italy north of Rome

Etruscus *adj* Etruscan

etsī *conj* even if, though; and yet

etymologia, -ae *f* etymology

eu *interj* well done!, bravo!

Euan *m* Bacchus

Euander, Euanderus, -rī *m* Evander (ancient king on the site of Rome)

Euandrius *adj see* **Euander**

euax *interj* hurrah!

Euboea, -oeae *f* Greek island

Euboicus *adj* Euboean

euge, eugepae *interj* bravo!, cheers!

Euhan *m* Bacchus

euhāns, -antis *adj* shouting the Bacchic cry

Euhias *f* Bacchante

Euhius, -ī *m* Bacchus

euhoe *interj* ecstatic cry of Bacchic revellers

Euius, -ī *m* Bacchus

Eumenides, -um *fpl* Furies

eunūchus, -ī *m* eunuch

Euphrātēs, -is *m* (river) Euphrates

Eupolis, -dis *m* Athenian comic poet

Eurīpidēs, -is *m* Athenian tragic poet

Eurīpidēus *adj see* **Eurīpidēs**

Eurīpus, -ī *m* strait between Euboea and mainland; a channel, conduit

Eurōpa, -ae, Eurōpē, -ēs *f* mythical princess of Tyre (who was carried by a bull to Crete); (continent of) Europe

Eurōpaeus *adj see* **Eurōpa**

Eurōtās, -ae *m* river of Sparta

Eurōus *adj* eastern

Eurus, -ī *m* east wind; south-east wind

Eurydicē, -ēs *f* wife of Orpheus

Eurystheus, -eī *m* king of Mycenae (who imposed the labours on Hercules)

euschēmē *adv* gracefully

Euterpē, -ēs *f* Muse of music

Euxīnus *m* the Black (Sea)

ēvādō, -dere, -sī, -sum *vi* to come out; to climb up; to escape; to turn out, result, come true ♦ *vt* to pass, mount; to escape from

ēvagor, -ārī, -ātus *vi* (MIL) to manoeuvre; (fig) to spread ♦ *vt* to stray beyond

ēvalēscō, -ēscere, -uī *vi* to grow, increase; to be able; to come into vogue

Ēvander *etc see* **Euander**

ēvānēscō, -ēscere, -uī *vi* to vanish, die away, lose effect

ēvangelium, -ī *and* **-iī** *nt* (ECCL) Gospel

ēvānidus *adj* vanishing

ēvāsī *perf of* **ēvādō**

ēvastō, -āre *vt* to devastate

ēvehō, -here, -xī, -ctum *vt* to carry out; to raise up, exalt; to spread abroad; (*pass*) to ride, sail, move out

ēvellō, -ellere, -ellī, -ulsum *vt* to tear out, pull out; to eradicate

ēveniō, -enīre, -ēnī, -entum *vi* to come out; to turn out, result; to come to pass, happen, befall

ēventum, -ī *nt* result, issue; occurrence, event; fortune, experience

ēventus, -ūs *m* result, issue; success; fortune, fate

ēverberō, -āre *vt* to beat violently

ēverriculum, -ī *nt* dragnet

ēverrō, -rere, -rī, -sum *vt* to sweep out, clean out

ēversiō, -ōnis *f* overthrow, destruction

ēversor, -ōris *m* destroyer

ēversus *ppp of* **ēverrō; ēvertō**

ēvertō, -tere, -tī, -sum *vt* to turn out, eject; to turn up, overturn; to overthrow, ruin, destroy

ēvestīgātus *adj* tracked down

ēvictus *ppp of* **ēvincō**

ēvidēns, -entis *adj* visible, plain, evident

ēvidenter *adv see* **ēvidēns**

ēvidentia, -ae *f* distinctness

ēvigilō, -āre, -āvī, -ātum *vi* to be wide awake ♦ *vt* to compose carefully

ēvīlēscō, -ere *vi* to become worthless

ēvinciō, -cīre, -xī, -ctum *vt* to garland, crown

ēvincō, -incere, -īcī, -ictum *vt* to overcome, conquer; to prevail over; to prove

ēvirō, -āre *vt* to castrate

ēviscerō, -āre *vt* to disembowel, tear to pieces

ēvītābilis *adj* avoidable

ēvītō, -āre, -āvī, -ātum *vt* to avoid, clear

ēvocātī, -ōrum *mpl* veteran volunteers

ēvocātor, -ōris *m* enlister

ēvocō, -āre, -āvī, -ātum *vt* to call out, summon; to challenge; to call up; to call forth, evoke

ēvolō, -āre, -āvī, -ātum *vi* to fly out, fly away; to rush out; (*fig*) to rise, soar

ēvolūtiō, -ōnis *f* unrolling (*a book*)

ēvolvō, -vere, -vī, -ūtum *vt* to roll out, roll along; to unroll, unfold; (*book*) to open, read; (*fig*) to disclose, unravel, disentangle

ēvomō, -ere, -uī, -itum *vt* to vomit up, disgorge

ēvulgō, -āre, -āvī, -ātum *vt* to divulge, make public

ēvulsiō, -ōnis *f* pulling out

ēvulsus *ppp of* **ēvellō**

ex, ē *prep* (*with abl*) (*place*) out of, from, down from; (*person*) from; (*time*) after, immediately after, since; (*change*) from being; (*source, material*) of; (*cause*) by reason of, through; (*conformity*) in accordance with; **ex itinere** on the march; **ex parte** in part; **ex quō** since; **ex rē** for the good of; **ex ūsū** for the good of; **ē rē pūblicā** constitutionally; **ex sententiā**

to one's liking; **aliud ex aliō** one thing after another; **ūnus ex** one of

exacerbō, -āre *vt* to exasperate

exāctiō, -ōnis *f* expulsion; supervision; tax; (*debts*) calling in

exāctor, -ōris *m* expeller; superintendent; tax collector

exāctus *ppp of* **exigō** ♦ *adj* precise, exact

exacuō, -uere, -uī, -ūtum *vt* to sharpen; (*fig*) to quicken, inflame

exadversum, exadversus *adv, prep* (*with acc*) right opposite

exaedificātiō, -ōnis *f* construction

exaedificō, -āre *vt* to build up; to finish the building of

exaequātiō, -ōnis *f* levelling

exaequō, -āre, -āvī, -ātum *vt* to level out; to compensate; to put on an equal footing; to equal

exaestuō, -āre *vi* to boil up

exaggerātiō, -ōnis *f* exaltation

exaggerō, -āre, -āvī, -ātum *vt* to pile up; (*fig*) to heighten, enhance

exagitātor, -ōris *m* critic

exagitō, -āre, -āvī, -ātum *vt* to disturb, harass; to scold, censure; to excite, incite

exagōga, -ae *f* export

exalbēscō, -ēscere, -uī *vi* to turn quite pale

exāmen, -inis *nt* swarm, crowd; tongue (*of a balance*); examining

exāminō, -āre, -āvī, -ātum *vt* to weigh; to consider, test

examussim *adv* exactly, perfectly

exanclō, -āre *vt* to drain; to endure to the end

exanimālis *adj* dead; deadly

exanimātiō, -ōnis *f* panic

exanimis *adj* lifeless, breathless; terrified

exanimō, -āre, -āvī, -ātum *vt* to wind; to kill; to terrify, agitate; (*pass*) to be out of breath

exanimus *see* **exanimis**

exārdēscō, -dēscere, -sī, -sum *vi* to catch fire, blaze up; (*fig*) to be inflamed, break out

exārēscō, -ēscere, -uī *vi* to dry, dry up

exarmō, -āre *vt* to disarm

exarō, -āre, -āvī, -ātum *vt* to plough up; to cultivate, produce; (*brow*) to furrow; (*writing*) to pen

exārsī *perf of* **exārdēscō**

exasciātus *adj* hewn out

exasperō, -āre, -āvī, -ātum *vt* to roughen; (*fig*) to provoke

exauctōrō, -āre, -āvī, -ātum *vt* (MIL) to discharge, release; to cashier

exaudiō, -īre, -īvī, -ītum *vt* to hear clearly; to listen to; to obey

exaugeō, -ēre *vt* to increase

exaugurātiō, -ōnis *f* desecrating

exaugurō, -āre *vt* to desecrate

exauspicō, -āre *vi* to take an omen

exbibō *etc see* **ēbibō**

excaecō, -āre *vt* to blind; (*river*) to block up

excandēscentia, -ae *f* growing anger

excandēscō, -ēscere, -uī *vi* to burn, be inflamed

excantō, -āre *vt* to charm out, spirit away

excarnificō, -āre vt to tear to pieces
excavō, -āre vt to hollow out
excēdō, -ēdere, -essī, -essum vi to go out, go away; to die, disappear; to advance, proceed (to); to digress ♦ vt to leave; to overstep, exceed
excellēns, -entis presp of **excellō** ♦ adj outstanding, excellent
excellenter adv see **excellēns**
excellentia, -ae f superiority, excellence
excellō, -ere vi to be eminent, excel
excelsē adv loftily
excelsitās, -ātis f loftiness
excelsum, -ī nt height
excelsus adj high, elevated; eminent, illustrious
exceptiō, -ōnis f exception, restriction; (LAW) objection
exceptō, -āre vt to catch, take out
exceptus ppp of **excipiō**
excernō, -ernere, -rēvī, -rētum vt to sift out, separate
excerpō, -ere, -sī, -tum vt to take out; to select, copy out extracts; to leave out, omit
excessus, -ūs m departure, death
excetra, -ae f snake
excidiō, -ōnis f destruction
excidium, -ī and **-iī** nt overthrow, destruction
excidō, -ere, -ī vi to fall out, fall; (speech) to slip out, escape; (memory) to get forgotten, escape; (person) to fail, lose; (things) to disappear, be lost
excīdō, -dere, -dī, -sum vt to cut off, hew out, fell; to raze; (fig) to banish
excieō vt see **exciō**
exciō, -īre, -īvī and **-iī, -itum** and **-ītum** vt to call out, rouse, summon; to occasion, produce; to excite
excipiō, -ipere, -ēpī, -eptum vt to take out, remove; to exempt, make an exception of, mention specifically; to take up, catch, intercept, overhear; to receive, welcome, entertain; to come next to, follow after, succeed
excīsiō, -ōnis f destroying
excīsus ppp of **excīdō**
excitātus adj loud, strong
excitō, -āre, -āvī, -ātum vt to rouse, wake up, summon; to raise, build; to call on (to stand up); (fig) to encourage, revive, excite
excitus, excītus ppp of **exciō**
exclāmātiō, -ōnis f exclamation
exclāmō, -āre, -āvī, -ātum vi to cry out, shout ♦ vt to exclaim, call
exclūdō, -dere, -sī, -sum vt to shut out, exclude; to shut off, keep off; (egg) to hatch out; (eye) to knock out; (fig) to prevent, except
exclūsiō, -ōnis f shutting out
exclūsus ppp of **exclūdō**
excoctus ppp of **excoquō**
excōgitātiō, -ōnis f thinking out, devising
excōgitō, -āre, -āvī, -ātum vt to think out, contrive
excolō, -olere, -oluī, -ultum vt to work carefully; to perfect, refine
excoquō, -quere, -xī, -ctum vt to boil away; to remove with heat, make with heat; to dry up

excors, -dis adj senseless, stupid
excrēmentum, -ī nt excretion
excreō etc see **exscreō**
excrēscō, -scere, -vī, -tum vi to grow, rise up
excrētus ppp of **excernō**
excruciō, -āre, -āvī, -ātum vt to torture, torment
excubiae, -ārum fpl keeping guard, watch; sentry
excubitor, -ōris m sentry
excubō, -āre, -uī, -itum vi to sleep out of doors; to keep watch; (fig) to be on the alert
excūdō, -dere, -dī, -sum vt to strike out, hammer out; (egg) to hatch; (fig) to make, compose
exculcō, -āre vt to beat, tramp down
excultus ppp of **excolō**
excurrō, -rrere, -currī and **-rrī, -rsum** vi to run out, hurry out; to make an excursion; (MIL) to make a sortie; (place) to extend, project; (fig) to expand
excursiō, -ōnis f raid, sortie; (gesture) stepping forward; (fig) outset
excursor, -ōris m scout
excursus, -ūs m excursion, raid, charge
excūsābilis adj excusable
excūsātē adv excusably
excūsātiō, -ōnis f excuse, plea
excūsō, -āre, -āvī, -ātum vt to excuse; to apologize for; to plead as an excuse
excussus ppp of **excutiō**
excūsus ppp of **excūdō**
excutiō, -tere, -ssī, -ssum vt to shake out, shake off; to knock out, drive out, cast off; (fig) to discard, banish; to examine, inspect
exdorsuō, -āre vt to fillet
exec- etc see **exsec-**
exedō, -ēsse, -ēdī, -ēsum vt to eat up; to wear away, destroy; (feelings) to prey on
exedra, -ae f hall, lecture room
exedrium, -ī and **-iī** nt sitting room
exēmī perf of **eximō**
exemplar, -āris nt copy; likeness; model, ideal
exemplārēs mpl copies
exemplum, -ī nt copy; example, sample, precedent, pattern; purport, nature; warning, object lesson; ~ **dare** set an example; **exemplī causā, exemplī grātiā** for instance
exemptus ppp of **eximō**
exenterō, -āre vt (comedy) to empty, clean out; to torture
exeō, -īre, -iī, -itum vi to go out, leave; to come out, issue; (MIL) to march out; (time) to expire; to spring up, rise ♦ vt to pass beyond; to avoid; **exīre ex potestāte** lose control
exeq- etc see **exseq-**
exerceō, -ēre, -uī, -itum vt to keep busy, supervise; (ground) to work, cultivate; (MIL) to drill, exercise; (mind) to engage, employ; (occupation) to practise, follow, carry on; (trouble) to worry, harass; **sē exercēre** practise, exercise
exercitātiō, -ōnis f practice, exercise, experience
exercitātus adj practised, trained, versed; troubled

exercitium, -ī *and* -iī *nt* exercising

exercitō, -āre *vt* to exercise

exercitor, -ōris *m* trainer

exercitus' *ppp of* **exerceō** ♦ *adj* disciplined; troubled; troublesome

exercitus², -ūs *m* army (*esp the infantry*); assembly; troop, flock; exercise

exerō *etc see* **exserō**

exēsor, -ōris *m* corroder

exēsus *ppp of* **exedō**

exhālātiō, -ōnis *f* vapour

exhālō, -āre *vt* to exhale, breathe out ♦ *vi* to steam; to expire

exhauriō, -rīre, -sī, -stum *vt* to drain off; to empty; to take away, remove; (*fig*) to exhaust, finish; (*trouble*) to undergo, endure to the end

exhērēdō, -āre *vt* to disinherit

exhērēs, -ēdis *adj* disinherited

exhibeō, -ere, -uī, -itum *vt* to hold out, produce (*in public*); to display, show; to cause, occasion

exhilarātus *adj* delighted

exhorrēscō, -ēscere, -uī *vi* to be terrified ♦ *vt* to be terrified at

exhortātiō, -ōnis *f* encouragement

exhortor, -ārī, -ātus *vt* to encourage

exigō, -igere, -ēgī, -āctum *vt* to drive out, thrust; (*payment*) to exact, enforce; to demand, claim; (*goods*) to dispose of; (*time*) to pass, complete; (*work*) to finish; (*news*) to ascertain; to test, examine, consider

exiguē *adv* briefly, slightly, hardly

exiguitās, -ātis *f* smallness, meagreness

exiguus *adj* small, short, meagre ♦ *nt* a little bit

exiliō *etc see* **exsiliō**

exīlis *adj* thin, small, meagre; poor; (*style*) flat, insipid

exīlitās, -ātis *f* thinness, meagreness

exīliter *adv* feebly

exilium *etc see* **exsilium**

exim *see* **exinde**

eximiē *adv* exceptionally

eximius *adj* exempt; select; distinguished, exceptional

eximō, -imere, -ēmī, -emptum *vt* to take out, remove; to release, free; to exempt; (*time*) to waste; (*fig*) to banish

exin *see* **exinde**

exināniō, -īre, -iī, -ītum *vt* to empty; to pillage

exinde *adv* (*place*) from there, next; (*time*) then, thereafter, next; (*measure*) accordingly

exīstimātiō, -ōnis *f* opinion, judgment; reputation, character; (*money*) credit

exīstimātor, -ōris *m* judge, critic

exīstimō, -āre, -āvī, -ātum *vt* to value, estimate, judge, think, consider

existō *etc see* **exsistō**

exīstumō *vt see* **exīstimō**

exitiābilis *adj* deadly, fatal

exitiālis *adj* deadly

exitiōsus *adj* pernicious, fatal

exitium, -ī *and* -iī *nt* destruction, ruin

exitus, -ūs *m* departure; way out, outlet; conclusion, end; death; outcome, result

exlēx, -ēgis *adj* above the law, lawless

exoculō, -āre *vt* to knock the eyes out of

exodium, -ī *and* -iī *nt* afterpiece

exolēscō, -scere, -vī, -tum *vi* to decay, become obsolete

exolētus *adj* full-grown

exonerō, -āre, -āvī, -ātum *vt* to unload, discharge; (*fig*) to relieve, exonerate

exoptātus *adj* welcome

exoptō, -āre, -āvī, -ātum *vt* to long for, desire

exōrābilis *adj* sympathetic

exōrātor, -ōris *m* successful pleader

exōrdior, -dīrī, -sus *vt* to lay the warp; to begin

exōrdium, -ī *and* -iī *nt* beginning; (RHET) introductory section

exorior, -īrī, -tus *vi* to spring up, come out, rise; to arise, appear, start

exōrnātiō, -ōnis *f* embellishment

exōrnātor, -ōris *m* embellisher

exōrnō, -āre, -āvī, -ātum *vt* to equip, fit out; to embellish, adorn

exōrō, -āre, -āvī, -ātum *vt* to prevail upon, persuade; to obtain, win by entreaty

exōrsus' *ppa of* **exōrdior** ♦ *adj* begun ♦ *ntpl* preamble

exōrsus², -ūs *m* beginning

exortus' *ppa of* **exorior**

exortus², -ūs *m* rising; east

exos, -ossis *adj* boneless

exōsculor, -ārī, -ātus *vt* to kiss fondly

exossō, -āre *vt* to bone

exōstra, -ae *f* stage mechanism; (*fig*) public

exōsus *adj* detesting

exōticus *adj* foreign

expallēscō, -ēscere, -uī *vi* to turn pale, be afraid

expalpō, -āre *vt* to coax out

expandō, -ere, -nsī, -nsum *and* -ssum *vt* to unfold

expatrō, -āre *vt* to squander

expavēscō, -ere, expāvī *vi* to be terrified ♦ *vt* to dread

expect- *etc see* **exspect-**

expediō, -īre, -īvī *and* -iī, -ītum *vt* to free, extricate, disentangle; to prepare, clear (for action); to put right, settle; to explain, relate; (*impers*) it is useful, expedient

expedītē *adv* readily, freely

expedītiō, -ōnis *f* (MIL) expedition, enterprise

expedītus *ppp of* **expediō** ♦ *adj* light-armed; ready, prompt; at hand ♦ *m* light-armed soldier; **in expedītō esse habēre** be, have in readiness

expellō, -ellere, -ulī, -ulsum *vt* to drive away, eject, expel; to remove, repudiate

expendō, -endere, -endī, -ēnsum *vt* to weigh out; to pay out; (*penalty*) to suffer; (*mind*) to ponder, consider, judge

expēnsum, -ī *nt* payment, expenditure

expergēfaciō, -facere, -fēcī, -factum *vt* to rouse, excite

expergīscor, -gīscī, -rēctus *vi* to wake up; to bestir oneself

expergō, -ere, -ī, -itum *vt* to awaken

experiēns, -entis *pres p of* **experior** ♦ *adj* enterprising

experientia, -ae f experiment; endeavour; experience, practice

experīmentum, -ī nt proof, test; experience

experior, -īrī, -tus vt to test, make trial of; to attempt, experience; (LAW) to go to law; (perf tenses) to know from experience

experrēctus ppa of **expergīscor**

expers, -tis adj having no part in, not sharing; free from, without

expertus ppa (occ pass) of **experior** ♦ adj proved, tried; experienced

expetessō, -ere vt to desire

expetō, -ere, -īvī and **-iī, -ītum** vt to aim at, tend towards; to desire, covet; to attack; to demand, require ♦ vi to befall, happen

expiātiō, -ōnis f atonement

expictus ppp of **expingō**

expīlātiō, -ōnis f pillaging

expīlātor, -ōris m plunderer

expīlō, -āre, -āvī, -ātum vt to rob, plunder

expingō, -ingere, -inxī, -ictum vt to portray

expiō, -āre, -āvī, -ātum vt to purify; to atone for, make amends for; to avert (evil)

expīrō etc see **exspīrō**

expiscor, -ārī, -ātus vt to try to find out, ferret out

explānātē adv see **explānātus**

explānātiō, -ōnis f explanation

explānātor, -ōris m interpreter

explānātus adj distinct

explānō, -āre, -āvī, -ātum vt to state clearly, explain; to pronounce clearly

explaudō etc see **explōdō**

explēmentum, -ī nt filling

expleō, -ēre, -ēvī, -ētum vt to fill up; to complete; (desire) to satisfy, appease; (duty) to perform, discharge; (loss) to make good; (time) to fulfil, complete

explētiō, -ōnis f satisfying

explētus ppp of **expleō** ♦ adj complete

explicātē adv plainly

explicātiō, -ōnis f uncoiling; expounding, analysing

explicātor, -ōris m, **explicātrīx, -rīcis** f expounder

explicātus¹ adj spread out; plain, clear

explicātus², -ūs m explanation

explicitus adj easy

explicō, -āre, -āvī and **-uī, -ātum** and **-itum** vt to unfold, undo, spread out; (book) to open; (MIL) to deploy, extend; (difficulty) to put in order, settle; (speech) to develop, explain; to set free

explōdō, -dere, -sī, -sum vt to hiss off, drive away; (fig) to reject

explōrātē adv with certainty

explōrātiō, -ōnis f spying

explōrātor, -ōris m spy, scout

explōrātus adj certain, sure

explōrō, -āre, -āvī, -ātum vt to investigate, reconnoitre; to ascertain; to put to the test

explōsī perf of **explōdō**

explōsiō, -ōnis f driving off (the stage)

explōsus ppp of **explōdō**

expoliō, -īre, -īvī, -ītum vt to smooth off, polish; (fig) to refine, embellish

expolītiō, -ōnis f smoothing off; polish, finish

expōnō, -ōnere, -osuī, -ositum vt to set out, put out; (child) to expose; (NAUT) to disembark; (money) to offer; (fig) to set forth, expose, display; (speech) to explain, expound

exporrigō, -igere, -ēxī, -ēctum vt to extend, smooth out

exportātiō, -ōnis f exporting

exportō, -āre, -āvī, -ātum vt to carry out, export

exposcō, -ere, expoposcī vt to implore, pray for; to demand

expositīcius adj foundling

expositiō, -ōnis f narration, explanation

expositus ppp of **expōnō** ♦ adj open, affable; vulgar

expostulātiō, -ōnis f complaint

expostulō, -āre, -āvī, -ātum vt to demand urgently; to complain of, expostulate

expōtus ppp of **ēpōtō**

expressus ppp of **exprimō** ♦ adj distinct, prominent

exprimō, -imere, -essī, -essum vt to squeeze out, force out; to press up; (fig) to extort, wrest; (art) to mould, model; (words) to imitate, portray, translate, pronounce

exprobrātiō, -ōnis f reproach

exprobrō, -āre, -āvī, -ātum vt to reproach, cast up

exprōmō, -ere, -psī, -ptum vt to bring out, fetch out; (acts) to exhibit, practise; (feelings) to give vent to; (speech) to disclose, state

expugnābilis adj capable of being taken by storm

expugnācior, -ōris adj more effective

expugnātiō, -ōnis f storming, assault

expugnātor, -ōris m stormer

expugnō, -āre, -āvī, -ātum vt to storm, reduce; to conquer; (fig) to overcome, extort

expulī perf of **expellō**

expulsiō, -ōnis f expulsion

expulsor, -ōris m expeller

expulsus ppp of **expellō**

expultrīx, -īcis f expeller

expungō, -ungere, -ūnxī, -ūnctum vt to prick out, cancel

expūrgātiō, -ōnis f excuse

expūrgō, -āre vt to purify; to justify

exputō, -āre vt to consider, comprehend

exquīrō, -rere, -sīvī, -sītum vt to search out, investigate; to inquire; to devise

exquīsītē adv with particular care

exquīsītus ppp of **exquīrō** ♦ adj well thought out, choice

exsaeviō, -īre vi to cease raging

exsanguis adj bloodless, pale; feeble

exsarciō, -cīre, -tum vt to repair

exsatiō, -āre vt to satiate, satisfy

exsaturābilis adj appeasable

exsaturō, -āre vt to satiate

exsce- etc see **esce-**

exscindō, -ndere, -dī, -ssum vt to extirpate

exscreō, -āre vt to cough up

exscrībō, -bere, -psī, -ptum vt to copy out; to note down

exsculpō – extin-

exsculpō, -ere, -sī, -tum vt to carve out; to erase; (fig) to extort

exsecō, -āre, -uī, -tum vt to cut out; to castrate

exsecrābilis adj cursing, deadly

exsecrātiō, -ōnis f curse; solemn oath

exsecrātus adj accursed

exsecror, -ārī, -ātus vt to curse; to take an oath

exsectiō, -ōnis f cutting out

exsecūtiō, -ōnis f management; discussion

exsecūtus ppa of **exsequor**

exsequiae, -ārum fpl funeral, funeral rites

exsequiālis adj funeral

exsequor, -quī, -cūtus vt to follow, pursue; to follow to the grave; (duty) to carry out, accomplish; (speech) to describe, relate; (suffering) to undergo; (wrong) to avenge, punish

exserciō vt see **exsarciō**

exserō, -ere, -uī, -tum vt to put out, stretch out; to reveal

exsertō, -āre vt to stretch out repeatedly

exsertus ppp of **exserō** ♦ adj protruding

exsībilō, -āre vt to hiss off

exsiccātus adj (style) uninteresting

exsiccō, -āre, -āvī, -ātum vt to dry up; to drain

exsicō etc see **exsecō**

exsignō, -āre vt to write down in detail

exsiliō, -īre, -uī, -sultum vi to jump up, spring out; to start

exsilium, -ī and **-iī** nt banishment, exile; retreat

exsistō, -istere, -titī, -titum vi to emerge, appear; to arise, spring (from); to be, exist

exsolvō, -vere, -vī, -ūtum vt to undo, loosen, open; to release, free; to get rid of, throw off; (debt, promise) to discharge, fulfil, pay up; (words) to explain

exsomnis adj sleepless, watchful

exsorbeō, -ēre, -uī vt to suck, drain; to devour, endure

exsors, -tis adj chosen, special; free from

exspargō etc see **exspergō**

exspatior, -ārī, -ātus vi to go off the course

exspectābilis adj to be expected

exspectātiō, -ōnis f waiting, expectation

exspectātus adj looked for, welcome

exspectō, -āre, -āvī, -ātum vt to wait for/till; to see; to expect; to hope for, dread; to require

exspergō, -gere, -sum vt to scatter; to diffuse

exspēs adj despairing

exspīrātiō, -ōnis f exhalation

exspīrō, -āre, -āvī, -ātum vt to breathe out, exhale; to emit ♦ vi to rush out; to expire, come to an end

exsplendēscō, -ere vi to shine

exspoliō, -āre vt to pillage

exspuō, -uere, -uī, -ūtum vt to spit out, eject; (fig) to banish

exsternō, -āre vt to terrify

exstillō, -āre vi to drip

exstimulātor, -ōris m instigator

exstimulō, -āre vt to goad on; to excite

exstinctiō, -ōnis f annihilation

exstinctor, -ōris m extinguisher; destroyer

exstinguō, -guere, -xī, -ctum vt to put out, extinguish; to kill, destroy, abolish

exstirpō, -āre vt to root out, eradicate

exstitī perf of **exsistō**

exstō, -āre vi to stand out, project; to be conspicuous, be visible; to be extant, exist, be

exstructiō, -ōnis f erection

exstruō, -ere, -xī, -ctum vt to heap up; to build up, construct

exsūdō, -āre vi to come out in sweat ♦ vt (fig) to toil through

exsūgō, -gere, -xī, -ctum vt to suck out

exsul, -is m/f exile

exsulō, -āre, -āvī, -ātum vi to be an exile

exsultātiō, -ōnis f great rejoicing

exsultim adv friskily

exsultō, -āre, -āvī, -ātum vi to jump up, prance; (fig) to exult, run riot, boast; (speech) to range at will

exsuperābilis adj superable

exsuperantia, -ae f superiority

exsuperō, -āre, -āvi, -ātum vi to mount up; to gain the upper hand, excel ♦ vt to go over; to surpass; to overpower

exsurdō, -āre vt to deafen; (fig) to dull

exsurgō, -gere, -rēxī, -rēctum vi to rise, stand up; to recover

exsuscitō, -āre vt to wake up; (fire) to fan; (mind) to excite

exta, -ōrum ntpl internal organs

extābēscō, -ēscere, -uī vi to waste away; to vanish

extāris adj sacrificial

extemplō adv immediately, on the spur of the moment; **quom ~** as soon as

extemporālis adj extempore

extempulō see **extemplō**

extendō, -dere, -dī, -tum and **extēnsum** vt to stretch out, spread, extend; to enlarge, increase; (time) to prolong; **sē extendere** exert oneself; **īre per extentum fūnem** walk the tightrope

extēnsus ppp of **extendō**

extentō, -āre vt to strain, exert

extentus ppp of **extendō** ♦ adj broad

extenuātiō, -ōnis f (RHET) diminution

extenuō, -āre, -āvī, -ātum vt to thin out, rarefy; to diminish, weaken

exter adj from outside; foreign

exterebrō, -āre vt to bore out; to extort

extergeō, -gēre, -sī, -sum vt to wipe off, clean; to plunder

exterior, -ōris adj outer, exterior

exterius adv on the outside

exterminō, -āre vt to drive out, banish; (fig) to put aside

externus adj outward, external; foreign, strange

exterō, -erere, -rīvī, -rītum vt to rub out, wear away

exterreō, -ēre, -uī, -itum vt to frighten

extersus ppp of **extergeō**

exterus see **exter**

extexō, -ere vt to unweave; (fig) to cheat

extimēscō, -ēscere, -uī vi to be very frightened ♦ vt to be very afraid of

extimus adj outermost, farthest

extin- etc see **exstin-**

extispex, -icis m diviner

extollō, -ere, -tulī vt to lift up, raise; (fig) to exalt, beautify; (time) to defer

extorqueō, -quēre, -sī, -tum vt to wrench out, wrest; to dislocate; (fig) to obtain by force, extort

extorris adj banished, in exile

extortor, -ōris m extorter

extortus ppp of **extorqueō**

extrā adv outside; ~ quam except that, unless ♦ prep (with acc) outside, beyond; free from; except

extrahō, -here, -xī, -ctum vt to draw out, pull out; to extricate, rescue; to remove; (time) to prolong, waste

extrāneus, -ī m stranger ♦ adj external, foreign

extraōrdinārius adj special, unusual

extrārius adj external; unrelated ♦ m stranger

extrēmitās, -ātis f extremity, end

extrēmum¹, -ī nt end; ad ~ at last

extrēmum² adv for the last time

extrēmus adj outermost, extreme; last; utmost, greatest, meanest

extrīcō, -āre, -āvī, -ātum vt to disentangle, extricate; to clear up

extrīnsecus adv from outside, from abroad; on the outside

extrītus ppp of **exterō**

extrūdō, -dere, -sī, -sum vt to drive out; to keep out; (sale) to push

extulī perf of **efferō²**

extumeō, -ēre vi to swell up

extundō, -undere, -udī, -ūsum vt to beat out, hammer out; (comedy) to extort; (fig) to form, compose

exturbō, -āre, -āvī, -ātum vt to drive out, throw out, knock out; (wife) to put away; (fig) to banish, disturb

exūberō, -āre vi to abound

exul etc see **exsul**

exulcerō, -āre, -āvī, -ātum vt to aggravate

exululō, -āre vi to howl wildly ♦ vt to invoke with cries

exūnctus ppp of **exungō**

exundō, -āre vi to overflow; to be washed up

exungō, -ere vt to anoint liberally

exuō, -uere, -uī, -ūtum vt to draw out, put off; to lay aside; to strip

exūrō, -rere, -ssī, -stum vt to burn up; to dry up; to burn out; (fig) to inflame

exūstiō, -ōnis f conflagration

exūtus ppp of **exuō**

exuviae, -ārum fpl clothing, arms; hide; spoils

Ff

faba, -ae f bean

fabālis adj bean- (in cpds)

fābella, -ae f short story, fable; play

faber, -rī m craftsman (in metal, stone, wood), tradesman, smith; (MIL) artisan; ~ **ferrārius** blacksmith; ~ **tignārius** carpenter ♦ adj skilful

Fabius¹, -ī m Roman family name (esp Q F Maximus Cunctator, dictator against Hannibal)

Fabius², Fabiānus adj see **Fabius¹**

fabrē adv skilfully

fabrēfaciō, -facere, -fēcī, -factum vt to make, build, forge

fabrica, -ae f art, trade; work of art; workshop; (comedy) trick

fabricātiō, -ōnis f structure

fabricātor, -ōris m artificer

Fabricius¹, -ī m Roman family name (esp C F Luscinus, incorruptible commander against Pyrrhus)

Fabricius², Fabriciānus adj see **Fabricius¹**

fabricō, -āre, fabricor, -ārī, -ātus vt to make, build, forge

fabrīlis adj artificer's ♦ ntpl tools

fābula, -ae f story; common talk; play, drama; fable; **fābulae** nonsense!; **lupus in fābulā** talk of the devil!

fābulor, -ārī, -ātus vi to talk, converse ♦ vt to say, invent

fābulōsus adj legendary

facessō, -ere, -īvī, -ītum vt to perform, carry out; to cause (trouble) ♦ vi to go away, retire

facētē adv humorously; brilliantly

facētiae, -ārum fpl wit, clever talk, humour

facētus adj witty, humorous; fine, genteel, elegant

faciēs, -ēī f form, shape; face, looks; appearance, aspect, character

facile adv easily; unquestionably; readily; pleasantly

facilis adj easy; well-suited; ready, quick; (person) good-natured, approachable; (fortune) prosperous

facilitās, -ātis f ease, readiness; (speech) fluency; (person) good nature, affability

facinorōsus adj criminal

facinus, -oris nt deed, action; crime

faciō, -ere, fēcī, factum (impv **fac**, pass **fīō**) vt to make, create, compose, cause; to do, perform; (profession) to practise; (property) to put under; (value) to regard, think of; (words) to represent, pretend, suppose ♦ vi to do, act; (religion) to offer (sacrifice); (with **ad** or **dat**) to be of use; **cōpiam facere** afford an opportunity;

damnum facere suffer loss; **metum facere** excite fear; **proelium facere** join battle; **rem facere** make money; **verba facere** talk; **māgnī facere** think highly of; **quid tibi faciam?** how am I to answer you?; **quid tē faciam?** what am I to do with you?; **fac sciam** let me know; **fac potuisse** suppose one could have

factiō, -ōnis f making, doing; group, party, faction (esp in politics and chariot racing)

factiōsus adj factious, oligarchical

factitō, -āre, -āvī, -ātum vt to keep making or doing; to practise; to declare (to be)

factor, -ōris m (sport) batsman

factum, -ī nt deed, exploit

factus ppp of **faciō**

facula, -ae f little torch

facultās, -ātis f means, opportunity; ability; abundance, supply, resources

fācundē adv see **fācundus**

fācundia, -ae f eloquence

fācundus adj fluent, eloquent

faeceus adj impure

faecula, -ae f wine lees

faenebris adj of usury

faenerātiō, -ōnis f usury

faenerātō adv with interest

faenerātor, -ōris m moneylender

faenerō, -āre, faeneror, -ārī, -ātus vt to lend at interest; to ruin with usury; (fig) to trade in

faenīlia, -um ntpl hayloft

faenum, -ī nt hay; ~ **habet in cornū** he is dangerous

faenus, -oris nt interest; capital lent at interest; (fig) profit, advantage

faenusculum, -ī nt a little interest

Faesulae, -ārum fpl town in Etruria (now Fiesole)

Faesulānus adj see **Faesulae**

faex, faecis f sediment, lees; brine (of pickles); (fig) dregs

fāgineus, fāginus adj of beech

fāgus, -ī f beech

fala, -ae f siege tower (used in assaults); (Circus) pillar

falārica, -ae f a missile, firebrand

falcārius, -ī and -iī m sicklemaker

falcātus adj scythed; sickle-shaped

falcifer, -ī adj scythe-carrying

Falernus adj Falernian (of a district in N. Campania famous for its wine) ♦ nt Falernian wine

Faliscī, -ōrum mpl a people of S.E. Etruria (with chief town Falerii)

Faliscus *adj see* **Faliscī**
fallācia, -ae *f* trick, deception
fallāciter *adv see* **fallāx**
fallāx, -ācis *adj* deceitful, deceptive
fallō, -lere, fefellī, -sum *vt* to deceive, cheat,
beguile; to disappoint, fail, betray; (*promise*) to
break; to escape the notice of, be unknown to;
(*pass*) to be mistaken; **mē fallit** I am mistaken;
I do not know
falsē *adv* wrongly, by mistake; fraudulently
falsidicus *adj* lying
falsificus *adj* deceiving
falsiiūrius *adj* perjurious
falsiloquus *adj* lying
falsiparēns, -entis *adj* with a pretended father
falsō *adv see* **falsē**
falsus *ppp of* **fallō** ♦ *adj* false, mistaken;
deceitful; forged, falsified; sham, fictitious
♦ *nt* falsehood, error
falx, falcis *f* sickle, scythe; pruning hook; (MIL)
siege hook
fāma, -ae *f* talk, rumour, tradition; public
opinion; reputation, fame; infamy
famēlicus *adj* hungry
famēs, -is *f* hunger; famine; (*fig*) greed; (RHET)
poverty of expression
fāmigerātiō, -ōnis *f* rumour
fāmigerātor, -ōris *m* telltale
familia, -ae *f* domestics, slaves of a household;
family property, estate; family, house; school,
sect; **pater familiās** master of a household;
familiam dūcere be head of a sect, company
etc
familiāris *adj* domestic, household, family;
intimate, friendly; (*entrails*) relating to the
sacrificer ♦ *m* servant; friend
familiāritās, -ātis *f* intimacy, friendship
familiāriter *adv* on friendly terms
fāmōsus *adj* celebrated; infamous; slanderous
famula, -ae *f* maidservant, handmaid
famulāris *adj* of servants
famulātus, -ūs *m* slavery
famulor, -ārī *vi* to serve
famulus, -ī *m* servant, attendant ♦ *adj*
serviceable
fānāticus *adj* inspired; frantic, frenzied
fandī *gerund of* **for**
fandum, -ī *nt* right
fānum, -ī *nt* sanctuary, temple
fār, farris *nt* spelt; corn; meal
farciō, -cīre, -sī, -tum *vt* to stuff, fill full
farīna, -ae *f* meal, flour
farrāgō, -inis *f* mash, hotch-potch; medley
farrātus *adj* of corn; filled with corn
farsī *perf of* **farciō**
fartem, -im *f acc* filling; mincemeat
fartor, -ōris *m* fattener, poulterer
fartus *ppp of* **farciō**
fās *nt* divine law; right; **fās est** it is lawful,
possible
fascia, -ae *f* band, bandage; streak of cloud
fasciculus, -ī *m* bundle, packet
fascinō, -āre *vt* to bewitch (*esp with the evil eye*)
fascinum, -ī *nt*, **fascinus, -ī** *m* charm
fasciola, -ae *f* small bandage

fascis, -is *m* bundle, faggot; soldier's pack,
burden; (*pl*) rods and axe (*carried before the highest
magistrates*); high office (*esp the consulship*)
fassus *ppa of* **fateor**
fāstī, -ōrum *mpl register of days for legal and public
business*; calendar; *registers of magistrates and other
public records*
fastīdiō, -īre, -īī, -ītum *vt* to loathe, dislike,
despise ♦ *vi* to feel squeamish, be disgusted; to
be disdainful
fastīdiōsē *adv* squeamishly; disdainfully
fastīdiōsus *adj* squeamish, disgusted;
fastidious, nice; disagreeable
fastīdium, -ī *and* **-iī** *nt* squeamishness, distaste;
disgust, aversion; disdain, pride
fastīgātē *adv* in a sloping position
fastīgātus *adj* sloping up or down
fastīgium, -ī *and* **-iī** *nt* gable, pediment; slope;
height, depth; top, summit; (*fig*) highest
degree, acme, dignity; (*speech*) main headings
fāstus *adj* lawful for public business
fastus, -ūs *m* disdain, pride
Fāta *ntpl* the Fates
fātālis *adj* fateful, destined; fatal, deadly
fātāliter *adv* by fate
fateor, -tērī, -ssus *vt* to confess, acknowledge;
to reveal, bear witness to
fāticanus, -inus *adj* prophetic
fātidicus *adj* prophetic ♦ *m* prophet
fātifer, -ī *adj* deadly
fatīgātiō, -ōnis *f* weariness
fatīgō, -āre, -āvī, -ātum *vt* to tire, exhaust; to
worry, importune; to wear down, torment
fātiloqua, -ae *f* prophetess
fatīscō, -ere, fatīscor, -ī *vi* to crack, split; (*fig*) to
become exhausted
fatuitās, -ātis *f* silliness
fātum, -ī *nt* divine word, oracle; fate, destiny;
divine will; misfortune, doom, death; **fātō
obīre** die a natural death
fātur, fātus *3rd pers and ppa of* **for**
fatuus *adj* silly; unwieldy ♦ *m* fool
faucēs, -ium *fpl* throat; pass, narrow channel,
chasm; (*fig*) jaws
Faunus, -ī *m father of Latinus (god of forests and
herdsmen, identified with Pan)*; (*pl*) woodland
spirits, Fauns
faustē *adv see* **faustus**
faustitās, -ātis *f* good fortune, fertility
faustus *adj* auspicious, lucky
fautor, -ōris *m* supporter, patron
fautrīx, -icis *f* protectress
favea, -ae *f* pet slave
faveō, -ēre, fāvī, fautum *vi* (*with dat*) to favour,
befriend, support; **favēre linguīs** keep silence
favilla, -ae *f* embers, ashes; (*fig*) spark
favitor *etc see* **fautor**
Favōnius, -ī *m* west wind, zephyr
favor, -ōris *m* favour, support; applause
favōrābilis *adj* in favour; pleasing
favus, -ī *m* honeycomb
fax, facis *f* torch, wedding torch, funeral torch;
marriage, death; (ASTR) meteor; (*fig*) flame,
fire, instigator; guide; **facem praeferre** act
as guide

faxim, faxō *archaic subj and fut of* **faciō**
febrĭcula, -ae *f* slight fever
febris, -is *f* fever
Februārius, -ī *m* February ♦ *adj* of February
februum, -ī *nt* purification; **Februa** *pl festival of purification in February*
fēcī *perf of* **faciō**
fēcundĭtās, -ātis *f* fertility; (*style*) exuberance
fēcundō, -āre *vt* to fertilize
fēcundus *adj* fertile, fruitful; fertilizing; (*fig*) abundant, rich, prolific
fefellī *perf of* **fallō**
fel, fellis *nt* gall bladder, bile; poison; (*fig*) animosity
fēlēs, -is *f* cat
fēlīcĭtās, -ātis *f* happiness, good luck
fēlīciter *adv* abundantly; favourably; happily
fēlīx, -icis *adj* fruitful; auspicious, favourable; fortunate, successful
fēmella, -ae *f* girl
fēmina, -ae *f* female, woman
fēmineus *adj* woman's, of women; unmanly
femur, -oris *and* **-inis** *nt* thigh
fēn- *etc see* **faen-**
fenestra, -ae *f* window; (*fig*) loophole
fera, -ae *f* wild beast
ferācius *adv* more fruitfully
fērālis *adj* funereal; of the Feralia; deadly ♦ *ntpl festival of the dead in February*
ferāx, -ācis *adj* fruitful, productive
ferbuī *perf of* **ferveō**
ferculum, -ī *nt* litter, barrow; dish, course
ferē *adv* almost, nearly, about; quite, just; usually, generally, as a rule; (*with neg*) hardly; **nihil ~** hardly anything
ferentārius, -ī *and* **-iī** *m* a light-armed soldier
Feretrius, -ī *m* an epithet of Jupiter
feretrum, -ī *nt* bier
fēriae, -ārum *fpl* festival, holidays; (*fig*) peace, rest
fēriātus *adj* on holiday, idle
ferīnus *adj* of wild beasts ♦ *f* game
feriō, -īre *vt* to strike, hit; to kill, sacrifice; (*comedy*) to cheat; **foedus ferīre** conclude a treaty
ferĭtās, -ātis *f* wildness, savagery
fermē *see* **ferē**
fermentum, -ī *nt* yeast; beer; (*fig*) passion, vexation
ferō, ferre, tulī, lātum *vt* to carry, bring, bear; to bring forth, produce; to move, stir, raise; to carry off, sweep away, plunder; (*pass*) to rush, hurry, fly, flow, drift; (*road*) to lead; (*trouble*) to endure, suffer, sustain; (*feelings*) to exhibit, show; (*speech*) to talk about, give out, celebrate; (*bookkeeping*) to enter; (*circumstances*) to allow, require; **sē ferre** rush, move; profess to be, boast; **condiciōnem ferre, lēgem ferre** propose terms, a law; **iūdicem ferre** sue; **sententiam ferre, suffrāgium ferre** vote; **signa ferre** march; attack; **aegrē ferre, graviter ferre** be annoyed at; **laudibus ferre** extol; **in oculīs ferre** be very fond of; **prae sē ferre** show, declare; **fertur, ferunt** it is said, they say; **ut mea fert opīniō** in my opinion

ferōcia, -ae *f* courage; spirit; pride, presumption
ferōcĭtās, -ātis *f* high spirits, aggressiveness; presumption
ferōciter *adv* bravely; insolently
Fērōnia, -ae *f* old Italian goddess
ferōx, -ōcis *adj* warlike, spirited, daring; proud, insolent
ferrāmentum, -ī *nt* tool, implement
ferrārius *adj* of iron; **faber ~** blacksmith ♦ *f* iron-mine, iron-works
ferrātus *adj* ironclad, ironshod ♦ *mpl* men in armour
ferreus *adj* of iron, iron; (*fig*) hard, cruel; strong, unyielding
ferrūgineus *adj* rust-coloured, dark
ferrūgō, -inis *f* rust; dark colour; gloom
ferrum, -ī *nt* iron; sword; *any iron implement*; force of arms; **~ et ignis** devastation
fertilis *adj* fertile, productive; fertilizing
fertilĭtās, -ātis *f* fertility
ferula, -ae *f* fennel; staff, rod
ferus *adj* wild; uncivilized; cruel ♦ *m* beast
fervēfaciō, -ere, -fēcī, -factum *vt* to boil
fervēns, -entis *pres p of* **ferveō** ♦ *adj* hot; raging; (*fig*) impetuous, furious
ferventer *adv* hotly
ferveō, -vēre, -buī *vi* to boil, burn; (*fig*) to rage, bustle, be agitated
fervēscō, -ere *vi* to boil up, grow hot
fervidus *adj* hot, raging; (*fig*) fiery, violent
fervō, -vere, -vī *vi see* **ferveō**
fervor, -ōris *m* seething; heat; (*fig*) ardour, passion
Fescennīnus *adj* Fescennine (*a kind of ribald song, perhaps from Fescennium in Etruria*)
fessus *adj* tired, worn out
festīnanter *adv* hastily
festīnātiō, -ōnis *f* haste, hurry
festīnō, -āre *vi* to hurry, be quick ♦ *vt* to hasten, accelerate
festīnus *adj* hasty, quick
fēstīvē *adv* gaily; humorously
fēstīvĭtās, -ātis *f* gaiety, merriment; humour, fun
fēstīvus *adj* gay, jolly; delightful; (*speech*) humorous
festūca, -ae *f* rod (*with which slaves were manumitted*)
fēstus *adj* festal, on holiday ♦ *nt* holiday; feast
fētiālis, -is *m* priest who carried out the ritual in making war and peace
fētūra, -ae *f* breeding; brood
fētus¹ *adj* pregnant; newly delivered; (*fig*) productive, full of
fētus², -ūs *m* breeding, bearing, producing; brood, young; fruit, produce; (*fig*) production
fiber, -rī *m* beaver
fibra, -ae *f* fibre; section of lung or liver; entrails
fībula, -ae *f* clasp, brooch; clamp
ficedula, -ae *f* fig pecker
fictē *adv* falsely
fictilis *adj* clay, earthen ♦ *nt* jar; clay figure
fictor, -ōris *m* sculptor; maker, inventor
fictrīx, -īcis *f* maker

fictūra, **-ae** f shaping, invention

fictus ppp of **fingō** ♦ adj false, fictitious ♦ nt falsehood

ficulnus adj of the fig tree

ficus, **-ī** and **-ūs** f fig tree; fig

fidēle adv faithfully, surely, firmly

fidēlia, **-ae** f pot, pail; **dē eādem fidēliā duōs parietēs dealbāre** kill two birds with one stone

fidēlis adj faithful, loyal; trustworthy, sure

fidēlitās, **-ātis** f faithfulness, loyalty

fidēliter adv faithfully, surely, firmly

Fīdēnae, **-ārum** fpl ancient Latin town

Fīdēnās, **-ātis** adj see **Fīdēnae**

fidens, **-entis** pres p of **fīdō** ♦ adj bold, resolute

fidenter adv see **fidens**

fidentia, **-ae** f self-confidence

fidēs¹, **-eī** f trust, faith, belief; trustworthiness, honour, loyalty, truth; promise, assurance, word; guarantee, safe-conduct, protection; (COMM) credit; (LAW) good faith; **~ mala** dishonesty; **rēs fidēsque** entire resources; **fidem facere** convince; **fidem servāre ergā** keep faith with; **dī vostram fidem** for Heaven's sake!; **ex fidē bonā** in good faith

fidēs², **-is** f (usu pl) stringed instrument, lyre, lute; (ASTR) Lyra

fidī perf of **findō**

fidicen, **-inis** m musician; lyric poet

fidicina, **-ae** f music girl

fidicula, **-ae** f small lute

Fidius, **-ī** m an epithet of Jupiter

fīdō, **-dere**, **-sus** vi (with dat or abl) to trust, rely on

fidūcia, **-ae** f confidence, assurance; self-confidence; (LAW) trust, security

fidūciārius adj to be held in trust

fidus adj trusty, reliable; sure, safe

fīgō, **-gere**, **-xī**, **-xum** vt to fix, fasten, attach; to drive in, pierce; (speech) to taunt

figulāris adj a potter's

figulus, **-ī** m potter; builder

figūra, **-ae** f shape, form; nature, kind; phantom; (RHET) figure of speech

figūrō, **-āre** vt to form, shape

fīlātim adv thread by thread

fīlia, **-ae** f daughter

fīlicātus adj with fern patterns

fīliola, **-ae** f little daughter

fīliolus, **-ī** m little son

fīlius, **-ī** and **-iī** m son; **terrae ~** a nobody

filix, **-cis** f fern

fīlum, **-ī** nt thread; band of wool, fillet; string, shred, wick; contour, shape; (speech) texture, quality

fimbriae, **-ārum** fpl fringe, end

fimus, **-ī** m dung; dirt

findō, **-ndere**, **-dī**, **-ssum** vt to split, divide; to burst

fingō, **-ere**, **finxī**, **fictum** vt to form, shape, make; to mould, model; to dress, arrange; to train; (mind, speech) to imagine, suppose, represent, sketch; to invent, fabricate; **vultum fingere** compose the features

fīniō, **-īre**, **-īvī**, **-ītum** vt to bound, limit; to restrain; to prescribe, define, determine; to end, finish, complete ♦ vi to finish, die

finis, **-is** m/f boundary, border; (pl) territory; bound, limit; end; death; highest point, summit; aim, purpose; **~ bonōrum** the chief good; **quem ad fīnem?** how long?; **fīne genūs** up to the knee

finītē adv within limits

finītimus adj neighbouring, adjoining; akin, like ♦ mpl neighbours

finītor, **-ōris** m surveyor

finītumus adj see **finītimus**

finītus ppp of **fīniō** ♦ adj (RHET) well-rounded

finxī perf of **fingō**

fīō, fierī, factus vi to become, arise; to be made, be done; to happen; **quī fit ut?** how is it that?; **ut fit** as usually happens; **quid mē fiet?** what will become of me?

firmāmen, **-inis** nt support

firmāmentum, **-ī** nt support, strengthening; (fig) mainstay

firmātor, **-ōris** m establisher

firmē adv powerfully, steadily

firmitās, **-ātis** f firmness, strength; steadfastness, stamina

firmiter adv see **firmē**

firmitūdō, **-inis** f strength, stability

firmō, **-āre**, **-āvī**, **-ātum** vt to strengthen, support, fortify; (mind) to encourage, steady; (fact) to confirm, prove, assert

firmus adj strong, stable, firm; (fig) powerful, constant, sure, true

fiscella, **-ae** f wicker basket

fiscina, **-ae** f wicker basket

fiscus, **-ī** m purse, moneybox; public exchequer; imperial treasury, the emperor's privy purse

fissilis adj easy to split

fissiō, **-ōnis** f dividing

fissum, **-ī** nt slit, fissure

fissus ppp of **findō**

fistūca, **-ae** f rammer

fistula, **-ae** f pipe, tube; panpipes; (MED) ulcer

fistulātor, **-ōris** m panpipe player

fisus ppa of **fīdō**

fīxī perf of **fīgō**

fīxus ppp of **fīgō** ♦ adj fixed, fast, permanent

flābellifera, **-ae** f fanbearer

flābellum, **-ī** nt fan

flābilis adj airy

flābra, **-ōrum** ntpl blasts, gusts; wind

flacceō, **-ēre** vi to flag, lose heart

flaccēscō, **-ere** vi to flag, droop

flaccidus adj flabby, feeble

flaccus adj flap-eared

Flaccus, **-ī** m surname of Horace

flagellō, **-āre** vt to whip, lash

flagellum, **-ī** nt whip, lash; strap, thong; (vine) shoot; (polyp) arm; (feelings) sting

flāgitātiō, **-ōnis** f demand

flāgitātor, **-ōris** m demander, dun

flāgitiōsē adv infamously

flāgitiōsus adj disgraceful, profligate

flāgitium, **-ī** and **-iī** nt offence, disgrace, shame; scoundrel

flăgitō, -āre, -āvī, -ātum vt to demand, importune, dun; (*LAW*) to summon

flagrāns, -antis pres p of **flagrō ♦** adj hot, blazing; brilliant; passionate

flagranter adv passionately

flagrantia, -ae f blazing; (*fig*) shame

flagrō, -āre vi to blaze, burn, be on fire; (*feelings*) to be excited, be inflamed; (*ill-will*) to be the victim of

flagrum, -ī nt whip, lash

flāmen¹, -inis m priest (*of a particular deity*)

flāmen², -inis nt blast, gale, wind

flāminica, -ae f wife of a priest

Flāminīnus, -ī m Roman surname (*esp the conqueror of Philip V of Macedon*)

flāminium, -ī and **-iī** nt priesthood

Flāminius¹, -ī m Roman family name (*esp the consul defeated by Hannibal*)

Flāminius², Flāminiānus adj: **Via Flāminia** road from Rome N.E. to Ariminum

flamma, -ae f flame, fire; torch, star; fiery colour; (*fig*) passion; danger, disaster

flammeolum, -ī nt bridal veil

flammēscō, -ere vi to become fiery

flammeus adj fiery, blazing; flame-coloured ♦ nt bridal veil

flammifer, -ī adj fiery

flammō, -āre, -āvī, -ātum vi to blaze ♦ vt to set on fire, burn; (*fig*) to inflame, incense

flammula, -ae f little flame

flātus, -ūs m blowing, breath; breeze; (*fig*) arrogance

flāvēns, -entis adj yellow, golden

flāvēscō, -ere vi to turn yellow

Flāviānus adj see **Flāvius**

Flāvius, -ī m Roman family name (*esp the emperors Vespasian, Titus and Domitian*)

flāvus adj yellow, golden

flēbilis adj lamentable; tearful, mournful

flēbiliter adv see **flēbilis**

flectō, -ctere, -xī, -xum vt to bend, turn; to turn aside, wheel; (*promontory*) to round; (*mind*) to direct, persuade, dissuade ♦ vi to turn, march

fleō, -ēre, -ēvī, -ētum vi to weep, cry ♦ vt to lament, mourn for

flētus, -ūs m weeping, tears

flexanimus adj moving

flexī perf of **flectō**

flexibilis adj pliant, flexible; fickle

flexilis adj pliant

flexiloquus adj ambiguous

flexiō, -ōnis f bending, winding; (*voice*) modulation

flexipēs, -edis adj twining

flexuōsus adj tortuous

flexūra, -ae f bending

flexus¹ ppp of **flectō ♦** adj winding

flexus², -ūs m winding, bending; change

flīctus, -ūs m collision

flō, -āre, -āvī, -ātum vt, vi to blow; (*money*) to coin

floccus, -ī m bit of wool; triviality; **floccī nōn faciō** I don't care a straw for

Flōra, -ae f goddess of flowers

Flōrālis adj see **Flōra**

flōrēns, -entis pres p of **flōreō ♦** adj in bloom; bright; prosperous, flourishing

flōreō, -ēre, -uī vi to blossom, flower; (*age*) to be in one's prime; (*wine*) to froth; (*fig*) to flourish, prosper; (*places*) to be gay with

flōrēscō, -ere vi to begin to flower; to grow prosperous

flōreus adj of flowers, flowery

flōridulus adj pretty little

flōridus adj of flowers, flowery; fresh, pretty; (*style*) florid, ornate

flōrifer, -ī adj flowery

flōrilegus adj flower-sipping

flōrus adj beautiful

flōs, -ōris m flower, blossom; (*wine*) bouquet; (*age*) prime, heyday; (*youth*) downy beard, youthful innocence; (*fig*) crown, glory; (*speech*) ornament

flōsculus, -ī m little flower; (*fig*) pride, ornament

flūctifragus adj surging

flūctuātiō, -ōnis f wavering

flūctuō, -āre vi to toss, wave; (*fig*) to rage, swell, waver

flūctuōsus adj stormy

flūctus, -ūs m wave; flowing, flood; (*fig*) disturbance; **flūctūs in simpulō** a storm in a teacup

fluēns, -entis pres p of **fluō ♦** adj lax, loose, enervated; (*speech*) fluent

fluenta, -ōrum ntpl stream, flood

fluenter adv in a flowing manner

fluentisonus adj wave-echoing

fluidus adj flowing, fluid; lax, soft; relaxing

fluitō, -āre vi to flow, float about; to wave, flap, move unsteadily; (*fig*) to waver

flūmen, -inis nt stream, river; (*fig*) flood, flow, fluency; **adversō flūmine** upstream; **secundō flūmine** downstream

flūmineus adj river- (*in cpds*)

fluō, -ere, -xī, -xum vi to flow; to overflow, drip; (*fig*) to fall in, fall away, vanish; (*speech*) to run evenly; (*circumstances*) to proceed, tend

flūtō etc see **fluitō**

fluviālis adj river- (*in cpds*)

fluviātilis adj river- (*in cpds*)

flūvidus etc see **fluidus**

fluvius, -ī and **-iī** m river, stream

fluxī perf of **fluō**

fluxus adj flowing, loose, leaky; (*person*) lax, dissolute; (*thing*) frail, fleeting, unreliable

fōcāle, -is nt scarf

foculus, -ī m stove, fire

focus, -ī m hearth, fireplace; pyre, altar; (*fig*) home

fodicō, -āre vt to nudge, jog

fodiō, -ere, fōdī, fossum vt to dig; to prick, stab; (*fig*) to goad

foedē adv see **foedus¹**

foederātus adj confederated

foedifragus adj perfidious

foeditās, -ātis f foulness, hideousness

foedō, -āre, -āvī, -ātum vt to mar, disfigure; to disgrace, sully

foedus¹ adj foul, hideous, revolting; vile, disgraceful

foedus², **-eris** nt treaty, league; agreement, compact; law

foen- etc see **faen-**

foeteō, **-ēre** vi to stink

foetidus adj stinking

foetor, **-ōris** m stench

foetu- etc see **fētu-**

foliātum, **-ī** nt nard oil

folium, **-ī** and **-iī** nt leaf

folliculus, **-ī** m small bag; eggshell

follis, **-is** m bellows; punchball; purse

fōmentum, **-ī** nt poultice, bandage; (fig) alleviation

fōmes, **-itis** m tinder, kindling

fōns, **fontis** m spring, source; water; (fig) origin, fountainhead

fontānus adj spring- (in cpds)

fonticulus, **-ī** m little spring

for, **fārī**, **fātus** vt, vi to speak, utter

forābilis adj penetrable

forāmen, **-inis** nt hole, opening

forās adv out, outside

forceps, **-ipis** m/f tongs, forceps

forda, **-ae** f cow in calf

fore, **forem** fut infin and imperf subj of **sum**

forēnsis adj public, forensic; of the marketplace

foris, **-is** f (usu pl) door; (fig) opening, entrance

foris adv out of doors, outside, abroad; from outside, from abroad; ~ **cēnāre** dine out

fōrma, **-ae** f form, shape, appearance; mould, stamp, last; (person) beauty; (fig) idea, nature, kind

fōrmāmentum, **-ī** nt shape

fōrmātūra, **-ae** f shaping

Formiae, **-ārum** fpl town in S. Latium

Formiānus adj of Formiae ♦ nt villa at Formiae

formīca, **-ae** f ant

formīcinus adj crawling

formīdābilis adj terrifying

formīdō¹, **-āre**, **-āvī**, **-ātum** vt, vi to fear, be terrified

formīdō², **-inis** f terror, awe, horror; scarecrow

formīdolōsē adv see **formīdolōsus**

formīdolōsus adj fearful, terrifying; afraid

fōrmō, **-āre**, **-āvī**, **-ātum** vt to shape, fashion, form

fōrmōsitās, **-ātis** f beauty

fōrmōsus adj beautiful, handsome

fōrmula, **-ae** f rule, regulation; (LAW) procedure, formula; (PHILOS) principle

fornācula, **-ae** f small oven

fornāx, **-ācis** f furnace, oven, kiln

fornicātus adj arched

fornix, **-icis** m arch, vault; brothel

forō, **-āre** vt to pierce

Foroiūliēnsis adj see **Forum Iūli**

fors, **fortis** f chance, luck ♦ adv perchance; forte by chance, as it happened; perhaps; nē forte in case; sī forte if perhaps; in the hope that

forsan, **forsit**, **forsitan** adv perhaps

fortasse, **-is** adv perhaps, possibly; (irony) very likely

forticulus adj quite brave

fortis adj strong, sturdy; brave, manly, resolute

fortiter adv vigorously; bravely

fortitūdō, **-inis** f courage, resolution; strength

fortuītō adv by chance

fortuītus adj casual, accidental

fortūna, **-ae** f chance, luck, fortune; good luck, success; misfortune; circumstances, lot; (pl) possessions; **fortūnae fīlius** Fortune's favourite; **fortūnam habēre** be successful

fortūnātē adv see **fortūnātus**

fortūnātus adj happy, lucky; well off, rich, blessed

fortūnō, **-āre** vt to bless, prosper

forulī, **-ōrum** mpl bookcase

forum, **-ī** nt public place, market; market town; Roman Forum between the Palatine and Capitol; public affairs, law courts, business; ~ **boārium** cattle market; ~ **olitōrium** vegetable market; ~ **piscātōrium** fish market; ~ **agere** hold an assize; ~ **attingere** enter public life; **cēdere forō** go bankrupt; **utī forō** take advantage of a situation

Forum Iūlī colony in S. Gaul (now Fréjus)

forus, **-ī** m gangway; block of seats; (bees) cell frame

fossa, **-ae** f ditch, trench

fossiō, **-ōnis** f digging

fossor, **-ōris** m digger

fossus ppp of **fodiō**

fōtus ppp of **foveō**

fovea, **-ae** f pit, pitfall

foveō, **-ēre**, **fōvī**, **fōtum** vt to warm, keep warm; (MED) to foment; to fondle, keep; (fig) to cherish, love, foster, pamper, encourage; **castra fovēre** remain in camp

frāctus ppp of **frangō** ♦ adj weak, faint

frāga, **-ōrum** ntpl strawberries

fragilis adj brittle, fragile; frail, fleeting

fragilitās, **-ātis** f frailness

fragmen, **-inis** nt (pl) fragments, ruins, wreck

fragmentum, **-ī** nt fragment, remnant

fragor, **-ōris** m crash, din; disintegration

fragōsus adj crashing, roaring, breakable; rough

frāgrāns, **-antis** adj fragrant

framea, **-ae** f German spear

frangō, **-angere**, **-ēgī**, **-āctum** vt to break, shatter, wreck; to crush, grind; (fig) to break down, weaken, humble; (emotion) to touch, move; **cervicem frangere** strangle

frāter, **-ris** m brother; cousin; (fig) friend, ally

frāterculus, **-ī** m brother

frāternē adv like a brother

frāternitās, **-ātis** f brotherhood

frāternus adj brotherly, a brother's, fraternal

frātricīda, **-ae** m fratricide

fraudātiō, **-ōnis** f deceit, fraud

fraudātor, **-ōris** m swindler

fraudō, **-āre**, **-āvī**, **-ātum** vt to cheat, defraud; to steal, cancel

fraudulentus adj deceitful, fraudulent

fraus, **-audis** f deceit, fraud; delusion, error; offence, wrong; injury, damage; **lēgī fraudem**

facere evade the law; **in fraudem incidere** be disappointed; **sine fraude** without harm

fraxineus, fraxinus adj of ash

fraxinus, -ī f ash tree; ashen spear

Fregellae, -ārum fpl town in S. Latium

Fregellānus adj see **Fregellae**

frēgī perf of **frangō**

fremebundus adj roaring

fremitus, -ūs m roaring, snorting, noise

fremō, -ere, -uī, -itum vi to roar, snort, grumble ♦ vt to shout for, complain

fremor, -ōris m murmuring

frendō, -ere vi to gnash the teeth

frēnō, -āre, -āvī, -ātum vt to bridle; (fig) to curb, restrain

frēnum, -ī nt (pl -a, -ōrum nt, -ī, -ōrum m) bridle, bit; (fig) curb, check; **frēnōs dare** give vent to; **~ mordēre** take the bit between one's teeth

frequēns, -entis adj crowded, numerous, populous; regular, repeated, frequent; **~ senatus** a crowded meeting of the senate

frequentātiō, -ōnis f accumulation

frequenter adv in large numbers; repeatedly, often

frequentia, -ae f full attendance, throng, crowd

frequentō, -āre, -āvī, -ātum vt to crowd, populate; to visit repeatedly, frequent; to repeat; (festival) to celebrate, keep

fretēnsis adj of the Straits of Messina

fretum, -ī nt strait; sea; (fig) violence; **~ Siciliēnse** Straits of Messina

fretus, -ūs m strait

frētus adj relying, confident

fricō, -āre, -uī, -tum vt to rub, rub down

frictus ppp of **frigō**

frīgefactō, -āre vt to cool

frīgeō, -ēre vi to be cold; (fig) to be lifeless, flag; to be coldly received, fall flat

frīgerāns adj cooling

frīgēscō, -ere, frixī vi to grow cold; to become inactive

frīgida, -ae f cold water

frīgidē adv feebly

frīgidulus adj rather cold, faint

frīgidus adj cold, cool; chilling; (fig) dull, torpid; (words) flat, uninteresting

frīgō, -gere, -xī, -ctum vt to roast, fry

frīgus, -oris nt cold; cold weather, winter; death; (fig) dullness, inactivity; coldness, indifference

friguttiō, -īre vi to stammer

friō, -āre vt to crumble

fritillus, -ī m dice box

frīvolus adj empty, paltry

frīxī perf of **frigō**

frondātor, -ōris m vinedresser, pruner

frondeō, -ēre vi to be in leaf

frondēscō, -ere vi to become leafy, shoot

frondeus adj leafy

frondifer, -ī adj leafy

frondōsus adj leafy

frōns[1], -ondis f leaf, foliage; garland of leaves

frōns[2], -ontis f forehead, brow; front, facade; (fig) look, appearance, exterior; **frontem**

contrahere frown; **ā fronte** in front; **in fronte** in breadth

frontālia, -um ntpl frontlet

frontō, -ōnis m a broad-browed man

frūctuārius adj productive; paid for out of produce

fructuōsus adj productive; profitable

frūctus[1] ppa of **fruor**

frūctus[2], -ūs m enjoyment; revenue, income; produce, fruit; (fig) consequence, reward; **frūctuī esse** be an asset (to); **frūctum percipere** reap the fruits (of)

frūgālis adj thrifty, worthy

frūgālitās, -ātis f thriftiness, restraint

frūgāliter adv temperately

frūgēs etc see **frūx**

frūgī adj (indecl) frugal, temperate, honest; useful

frūgifer, -ī adj fruitful, fertile

frūgiferēns, -entis adj fruitful

frūgilegus adj food-gathering

frūgiparus adj fruitful

frūmentārius adj of corn, corn- (in cpds) ♦ m corn dealer; **lēx frūmentāria** law about the distribution of corn; **rēs frūmentāria** commissariat

frūmentātiō, -ōnis f foraging

frūmentātor, -ōris m corn merchant, forager

frūmentor, -ārī, -ātus vi to go foraging

frūmentum, -ī nt corn, grain; (pl) crops

frūniscor, -ī vt to enjoy

fruor, -uī, -ūctus vt, vi (usu with abl) to enjoy, enjoy the company of; (LAW) to have the use and enjoyment of

frūstillātim adv in little bits

frūstrā adv in vain, for nothing; groundlessly; in error; **~ esse** be deceived; **~ habēre** foil

frūstrāmen, -inis nt deception

frūstrātiō, -ōnis f deception, frustration

frūstrō, -āre, frūstror, -ārī, -ātus vt to deceive, trick

frūstulentus adj full of crumbs

frūstum, -ī nt bit, scrap

frutex, -icis m bush, shrub; (comedy) blockhead

fruticētum, -ī nt thicket

fruticor, -ārī vi to sprout

fruticōsus adj bushy

frūx, -ūgis f, -**ūgēs, -ūgum** pl fruits of the earth, produce; (fig) reward, success; virtue; **sē ad frūgem bonam recipere** reform

fuam old pres subj of **sum**

fūcātus adj counterfeit, artificial

fūcō, -āre, -āvī, -ātum vt to paint, dye (esp red)

fūcōsus adj spurious

fūcus[1], -ī m red dye, rouge; bee glue; (fig) deceit, pretence

fūcus[2], -ī m drone

fūdī perf of **fundō[2]**

fuga, -ae f flight, rout; banishment; speed, swift passing; refuge; (fig) avoidance, escape; **fugam facere, in fugam dare** put to flight

fugācius adv more timidly

fugāx, -ācis adj timorous, shy, fugitive; swift, transient; (with gen) avoiding

fūgī perf of **fugiō**

fugiēns, -entis *pres p of* **fugiō** ♦ *adj* fleeting, dying; averse (to)

fugiō, -ere, fūgī, -itum *vi* to flee, run away, escape; to go into exile; *(fig)* to vanish, pass swiftly ♦ *vt* to flee from, escape from; to shun, avoid; *(fig)* to escape, escape notice of; **fuge quaerere** do not ask; **mē fugit** I do not notice or know

fugitīvus, -ī *m* runaway slave, truant, deserter ♦ *adj* fugitive

fugitō, -āre *vt* to flee from, shun

fugō, -āre, -āvī, -ātum *vt* to put to flight; to banish; to rebuff

fulcīmen, -inis *nt* support

fulciō, -cīre, -sī, -tum *vt* to prop, support; to strengthen, secure; *(fig)* to sustain, bolster up

fulcrum, -ī *nt* bedpost; couch

fulgeō, -gēre, -sī *vi* to flash, lighten; to shine; *(fig)* to be illustrious

fulgidus *adj* flashing

fulgō *etc see* **fulgeō**

fulgor, -ōris *m* lightning; flash, brightness; *(fig)* splendour

fulgur, -is *nt* lightning; thunderbolt; splendour

fulgurālis *adj* of lightning *(as an omen)*

fulgurātor, -ōris *m* interpreter of lightning

fulgurītus *adj* struck by lightning

fulgurō, -āre *vi* to lighten

fulica, -ae *f* coot

fūlīgō, -inis *f* soot; black paint

fulix, -cis *f see* **fulica**

fullō, -ōnis *m* fuller

fullōnius *adj* fuller's

fulmen, -inis *nt* thunderbolt; *(fig)* disaster

fulmenta, -ae *f* heel *(of a shoe)*

fulmineus *adj* of lightning; *(fig)* deadly

fulminō, -āre *vi* to lighten; *(fig)* to threaten

fulsī *perf of* **fulciō**; **fulgeō**

fultūra, -ae *f* support

fultus *ppp of* **fulciō**

Fulvia, -iae *f wife of M. Antony*

Fulvius, -ī *m Roman family name*

fulvus *adj* yellow, tawny, dun

fūmeus *adj* smoking

fūmidus *adj* smoky, smoking

fūmifer, -ī *adj* smoking

fūmificō, -āre *vi* to burn incense

fūmificus *adj* steaming

fūmō, -āre *vi* to smoke, steam

fūmōsus *adj* smoky, smoked

fūmus, -ī *m* smoke, steam

fūnāle, -is *nt* cord; wax torch; chandelier

fūnambulus, -ī *m* tightrope walker

fūnctiō, -ōnis *f* performance

fūnctus *ppa of* **fungor**

fūnda, -ae *f* sling; dragnet

fundāmen, -inis *nt* foundation

fundāmentum, -ī *nt* foundation; **fundāmenta agere, fundāmenta iacere** lay the foundations

Fundānus *adj see* **Fundī**

fundātor, -ōris *m* founder

Fundī, -ōrum *mpl coast town in Latium*

funditō, -āre *vt* to sling

funditor, -ōris *m* slinger

funditus *adv* utterly, completely; at the bottom

fundō¹, -āre, -āvī, -ātum *vt* to found; to secure; *(fig)* to establish, make secure

fundō², -ere, fūdī, fūsum *vt* to pour, shed, spill; *(metal)* to cast; *(solids)* to hurl, scatter, shower; *(MIL)* to rout; *(crops)* to produce in abundance; *(speech)* to utter; *(fig)* to spread, extend

fundus, -ī *m* bottom; farm, estate; *(LAW)* authorizer

fūnebris *adj* funeral- *(in cpds)*; murderous

fūnerātus *adj* killed

fūnereus *adj* funeral- *(in cpds)*, fatal

fūnestō, -āre *vt* to pollute with murder, desecrate

fūnestus *adj* deadly, fatal; sorrowful, in mourning

fungīnus *adj* of a mushroom

fungor, -gi, fūnctus *vt, vi (usu with abl)* to perform, discharge, do; to be acted on

fungus, -ī *m* mushroom, fungus; *(candle)* clot on the wick

fūniculus, -ī *m* cord

fūnis, -is *m* rope, rigging; **fūnem dūcere** be the master

fūnus, -eris *nt* funeral; death; corpse; ruin, destruction

fūr, fūris *m* thief; slave

fūrācissimē *adv* most thievishly

fūrāx, -ācis *adj* thieving

furca, -ae *f* fork; fork-shaped pole; pillory

furcifer, -ī *m* gallows rogue

furcilla, -ae *f* little fork

furcillō, -āre *vt* to prop up

furcula, -ae *f* forked prop; **furculae Caudīnae** Pass of Caudium

furenter *adv* furiously

furfur, -is *m* bran; scurf

Furia, -ae *f* Fury, avenging spirit; madness, frenzy, rage

furiālis *adj* of the Furies; frantic, fearful; infuriating

furiāliter *adv* madly

furibundus *adj* mad, frenzied

furiō, -āre, -āvī, -ātum *vt* to madden

furiōsē *adv* in a frenzy

furiōsus *adj* mad, frantic

furnus, -ī *m* oven

furō, -ere *vi* to rave, rage, be mad, be crazy

furor, -ōris *m* madness, frenzy, passion

fūror, -ārī, -ātus *vt* to steal; to pillage; to impersonate

fūrtificus *adj* thievish

fūrtim *adv* by stealth, secretly

fūrtīvē *adv* secretly

fūrtīvus *adj* stolen; secret, furtive

fūrtō *adv* secretly

fūrtum, -ī *nt* theft, robbery; *(pl)* stolen goods; *(fig)* trick, intrigue

fūrunculus, -ī *m* pilferer

furvus *adj* black, dark

fuscina, -ae *f* trident

fuscō, -āre *vt* to blacken

fuscus *adj* dark, swarthy; *(voice)* husky, muffled

fūsē *adv* diffusely

fūsilis *adj* molten, softened
fūsiō, -ōnis *f* outpouring
fūstis, -is *m* stick, club, cudgel; (MIL) beating to death
fūstuārium, -ī and -iī *nt* beating to death
fūsus¹ *ppp of* **fundō** ♦ *adj* broad, diffuse; copious

fūsus², -ī *m* spindle
futile *adv* in vain
futilis *adj* brittle; worthless
futilitās, -ātis *f* futility
futūrum, -ī *nt* future
futūrus *fut p of* **sum** ♦ *adj* future, coming

Gg

Gabiī, -iōrum *mpl* ancient town in Latium
Gabinius¹, -ī *m* Roman family name (*esp Aulus, tribune 67 B.C.*)
Gabinius², Gabiniānus *adj*: **lēx Gabinia** law giving Pompey command against the pirates
Gabīnus *adj see* **Gabiī**
Gādēs, -ium *fpl* town in Spain (now Cadiz)
Gāditānus *adj see* **Gādēs**
gaesum, -ī *nt* Gallic javelin
Gaetūlī, -ōrum *mpl* African people N. of Sahara
Gaetūlus, -icus *adj* Gaetulian; African
Gāius¹, -ī *m* Roman praenomen (*esp emperor Caligula*)
Gāius², Gāia *m/f* (*wedding ceremony*) bridegroom, bride
Galatae, -ārum *mpl* Galatians of Asia Minor
Galatia, -iae *f* Galatia
Galba, -ae *m* Roman surname (*esp emperor 68–9*)
galbaneus *adj* of galbanum (*a Syrian plant*)
galbinus *adj* greenish-yellow ♦ *ntpl* pale green clothes
galea, -ae *f* helmet
galeātus *adj* helmeted
galērītus *adj* rustic
galērum, -ī *nt*, **galērus, -ī** *m* leather hood, cap; wig
galla, -ae *f* oak apple
Gallī, -ōrum *mpl* Gauls (*people of what is now France and N. Italy*)
Gallia, -iae *f* Gaul
Gallicānus *adj* of Italian Gaul
Gallicus *adj* Gallic ♦ *f* a Gallic shoe
gallīna, -ae *f* hen; **gallīnae albae fīlius** fortune's favourite
gallīnāceus *adj* of poultry
gallīnārius, -ī *and* **-iī** *m* poultry farmer
Gallograecī, -ōrum *mpl* Galatians
Gallograecia, -iae *f* Galatia
Gallus, -ī *m* Gaul; Roman surname (*esp the lyric poet*); priest of Cybele
gallus, -ī *m* cock
ganēa, -ae *f* low eating house
ganeō, -ōnis *m* profligate
ganeum, -ī *nt* low eating house
Gangaridae, -ārum *mpl* a people on the Ganges
Gangēs, -is *m* (river) Ganges
Gangēticus *adj see* **Gangēs**
ganniō, -īre *vi* to yelp; (*fig*) to grumble
gannītus, -ūs *m* yelping
Ganymēdēs, -is *m* Ganymede (*cup bearer in Olympus*)
Garamantes, -um *mpl* N. African tribe

Garamantis, -idis *adj see* **Garamantes**
Gargānus, -ī *m* mountain in S. Italy
garriō, -īre *vi* to chatter
garrulitās, -ātis *f* chattering
garrulus *adj* talkative, babbling
garum, -ī *nt* fish sauce
Garumna, -ae *f* (river) Garonne
gaudeō, -ēre, gāvīsus *vt*, *vi* to rejoice, be pleased, delight (in); **in sē gaudēre, in sinū gaudēre** be secretly pleased
gaudium, -ī *and* **-iī** *nt* joy, delight, enjoyment
gaulus, -ī *m* bucket
gausapē, -is *nt*, **gausapa, -ōrum** *pl* a woollen cloth, frieze
gāvīsus *ppa of* **gaudeō**
gāza, -ae *f* treasure, riches
gelidē *adv* feebly
gelidus *adj* cold, frosty; stiff, numb; chilling ♦ *f* cold water
gelō, -āre *vt* to freeze
Gelōnī, -ōrum *mpl* Scythian tribe (*in what is now Ukraine*)
gelū, -ūs *nt* frost, cold; chill
gemebundus *adj* groaning
gemellipara, -ae *f* mother of twins
gemellus *adj* twin, double; alike ♦ *m* twin
geminātiō, -ōnis *f* doubling
geminō, -āre, -āvī, -ātum *vt* to double, bring together; to repeat ♦ *vi* to be double
geminus *adj* twin, double, both; similar ♦ *mpl* twins (*esp Castor and Pollux*)
gemitus, -ūs *m* groan, sigh, moaning sound
gemma, -ae *f* bud, precious stone, jewel; jewelled cup, signet
gemmātus *adj* bejewelled
gemmeus *adj* jewelled; sparkling
gemmifer, -ī *adj* gem-producing
gemmō, -āre *vi* to bud, sprout; to sparkle
gemō, -ere, -uī, -itum *vi* to sigh, groan, moan ♦ *vt* to bewail
Gemōniae, -ārum *fpl* steps in Rome on which bodies of criminals were thrown
genae, -ārum *fpl* cheeks; eyes, eye sockets
geneālogus, -ī *m* genealogist
gener, -ī *m* son-in-law
generālis *adj* of the species; universal
generāliter *adv* generally
generāscō, -ere *vi* to be produced
generātim *adv* by species, in classes; in general
generātor, -ōris *m* producer
generō, -āre, -āvī, -ātum *vt* to breed, procreate

generōsus *adj* high-born, noble; well-stocked; generous, chivalrous; (*things*) noble, honourable

genesis, -is *f* birth; horoscope

genethliacon, -ī *nt* birthday poem

genetīvus *adj* native, inborn

genetrīx, -īcis *f* mother

geniālis *adj* nuptial; joyful, genial

geniāliter *adv* merrily

geniculātus *adj* jointed

genista, -ae *f* broom

genitābilis *adj* productive

genitālis *adj* fruitful, generative; of birth

genitāliter *adv* fruitfully

genitor, -ōris *m* father, creator

genitus *ppp of* **gignō**

genius, -ī *and* **-iī** *m* guardian spirit; enjoyment, inclination; talent; **geniō indulgēre** enjoy oneself

gēns, gentis *f* clan, family, stock, race; tribe, people, nation; descendant; (*pl*) foreign peoples; **minimē gentium** by no means; **ubi gentium** where in the world

genticus *adj* national

gentīlicius *adj* family

gentīlis *adj* family, hereditary; national ♦ *m* kinsman

gentīlitās, -ātis *f* clan relationship

genū, -ūs *nt* knee

genuālia, -um *ntpl* garters

genuī *perf of* **gignō**

genuīnus[1] *adj* natural

genuīnus[2] *adj* of the cheek ♦ *mpl* back teeth

genus, -eris *nt* birth, descent, noble birth, descendant, race; kind, class, species, respect, way; (*LOGIC*) genus, general term; **id ~** of that kind; **in omnī genere** in all respects

geōgraphia, -ae *f* geography

geōmetrēs, -ae *m* geometer

geōmetria, -ae *f* geometry

geōmetricus *adj* geometrical ♦ *ntpl* geometry

germānē *adv* sincerely

Germānī, -ōrum *mpl* Germans

Germānia, -iae *f* Germany

Germānicus *adj, m* cognomen of Nero Claudius Drusus and his son

germānitās, -ātis *f* brotherhood, sisterhood; relation of sister colonies

germānus *adj* of the same parents, full (brother, sister); genuine, true ♦ *m* full brother ♦ *f* full sister

germen, -inis *nt* bud, shoot; embryo; (*fig*) germ

gerō[1]**, -rere, -ssī, -stum** *vt* to carry, wear; to bring; (*plants*) to bear, produce; (*feelings*) to entertain, show; (*activity*) to conduct, manage, administer, wage; (*time*) spend; **mōrem gerere** comply, humour; **persōnam gerere** play a part; **sē gerere** behave; **sē medium gerere** be neutral; **prae sē gerere** exhibit; **rēs gestae** exploits

gerō[2]**, -ōnis** *nt* carrier

gerrae, -ārum *fpl* trifles, nonsense

gerrō, -ōnis *m* idler

gerulus, -ī *m* carrier

Gēryōn, -onis *m* mythical three-bodied king killed by Hercules

gessī *perf of* **gerō**[1]

gestāmen, -inis *nt* arms, ornaments, burden; litter, carriage

gestiō[1]**, -ōnis** *f* performance

gestiō[2]**, -īre** *vi* to jump for joy, be excited; to be very eager

gestitō, -āre *vt* to always wear *or* carry

gestō, -āre *vt* to carry about, usually wear; to fondle; to blab; (*pass*) to go for a ride, drive, sail

gestor, -ōris *m* telltale

gestus[1] *ppp of* **gerō**[1]

gestus[2]**, -ūs** *m* posture, gesture; gesticulation

Getae, -ārum *mpl* Thracian tribe on the lower Danube

Geticus *adj* Getan, Thracian

gibbus, -ī *m* hump

Gigantēs, -um *mpl* Giants, sons of Earth

Gigantēus *adj see* **Gigantes**

gignō, -ere, genuī, genitum *vt* to beget, bear, produce; to cause

gilvus *adj* pale yellow, dun

gingīva, -ae *f* gum

glaber, -rī *adj* smooth, bald ♦ *m* favourite slave

glaciālis *adj* icy

glaciēs, -ēī *f* ice

glaciō, -āre *vt* to freeze

gladiātor, -ōris *m* gladiator; (*pl*) gladiatorial show

gladiātōrius *adj* of gladiators ♦ *nt* gladiators' pay

gladiātūra, -ae *f* gladiator's profession

gladius, -ī *and* **-iī** *m* sword; (*fig*) murder, death; **gladium stringere** draw the sword; **suō sibi gladiō iugulāre** beat at his own game

glaeba, -ae *f* sod, clod of earth; soil; lump

glaebula, -ae *f* small lump; small holding

glaesum *etc see* **glēsum**

glandifer, -ī *adj* acorn-bearing

glandium, -ī *and* **-iī** *nt* glandule (in meat)

glāns, -andis *f* acorn, nut; bullet

glārea, -ae *f* gravel

glāreōsus *adj* gravelly

glaucuma, -ae *f* cataract; **glaucōmam ob oculōs obicere** throw dust in the eyes of

glaucus *adj* bluish grey

glēba *etc see* **glaeba**

glēsum, -ī *nt* amber

glīs, -īris *m* dormouse

glīscō, -ere *vi* to grow, swell, blaze up

globōsus *adj* spherical

globus, -ī *m* ball, sphere; (*MIL*) troop; mass, crowd, cluster

glōmerāmen, -inis *nt* ball

glomerō, -āre, -āvī, -ātum *vt* to form into a ball, gather, accumulate

glomus, -eris *nt* ball of thread, clue

glōria, -ae *f* glory, fame; ambition, pride, boasting; (*pl*) glorious deeds

glōriātiō, -ōnis *f* boasting

glōriola, -ae *f* a little glory

glōrior, -ārī, -ātus *vt, vi* to boast, pride oneself

glōriōsē *adv see* **glōriōsus**

glōriōsus *adj* famous, glorious; boastful

glūten, -inis nt glue
glūtinātor, -ōris m bookbinder
gluttiō, -īre vt to gulp down
gnāruris, gnārus adj knowing, expert; known
gnātus see **nātus**
gnāvus see **nāvus**
Gnōsis, -idis f Ariadne
Gnōsius, Gnōsiacus, Gnōsias adj of Cnossos, Cretan ♦ f Ariadne
Gnōsus, -ī f Cnossos (ancient capital of Crete)
gōbiō, -ōnis, gōbius, -ī and **-iī** m gudgeon
Gorgiās, -ae m Sicilian sophist and teacher of rhetoric
Gorgō, -ōnis f mythical monster capable of turning men to stone, Medusa
Gorgoneus adj: **equus ~** Pegasus; **lacus ~** Hippocrene
Gortȳna, -ae f Cretan town
Gortȳnius, Gortȳniacus adj Gortynian, Cretan
gōrȳtos, -ī m quiver
grabātus, -ī m camp bed, low couch
Gracchānus adj see **Gracchus**
Gracchus, -ī m Roman surname (esp the famous tribunes Tiberius and Gaius)
gracilis adj slender, slight, meagre, poor; (style) plain
gracilitās, -ātis f slimness, leanness; (style) simplicity
grāculus, -ī m jackdaw
gradātim adv step by step, gradually
gradātiō, -ōnis f (RHET) climax
gradior, -adī, -essus vi to step, walk
Grādīvus, -ī m Mars
gradus, -ūs m step, pace; stage, step towards; firm stand, position, standing; (pl) stair, steps; (hair) braid; (MATH) degree; (fig) degree, rank; **citātō gradū, plēnō gradū** at the double; **suspēnsō gradū** on tiptoe; **dē gradū deicī** be disconcerted
Graecē adv in Greek
Graecia, -iae f Greece; **Māgna ~** S. Italy
graecissō, -āre vi to ape the Greeks
graecor, -ārī vi to live like Greeks
Graeculus adj (contemptuous) Greek
Graecus adj Greek
Grāiugena, -ae m Greek
Grāius adj Greek
grallātor, -ōris m stiltwalker
grāmen, -inis nt grass; herb
grāmineus adj grassy; of cane
grammaticus adj literary, grammatical ♦ m teacher of literature and language ♦ f, ntpl grammar, literature, philology
grānāria, -ōrum ntpl granary
grandaevus adj aged, very old
grandēscō, -ere vi to grow
grandiculus adj quite big
grandifer, -ī adj productive
grandiloquus, -ī m grand speaker; boaster
grandinat, -āre vi it hails
grandis adj large, great, tall; old; strong; (style) grand, sublime; **~ nātū** old
granditās, -ātis f grandeur
grandō, -inis f hail
grānifer, -ī adj grain-carrying

grānum, -ī nt seed, grain
graphicē adv nicely
graphicus adj fine, masterly
graphium, -ī and **-iī** nt stilus, pen
grassātor, -ōris m vagabond; robber, footpad
grassor, -ārī, -ātus vi to walk about, prowl, loiter; (action) to proceed; (fig) to attack, rage against
grātē adv with pleasure; gratefully
grātēs fpl thanks
grātia, -ae f charm, grace; favour, influence, regard, friendship; kindness, service; gratitude, thanks; **grātiam facere** excuse; **grātiam referre** return a favour; **in grātiam redīre cum** be reconciled to; **grātiās agere** thank; **grātiās habēre** feel grateful; **grātiā** (with gen) for the sake of; **eā grātiā** on that account; **grātiīs** for nothing
Grātiae, -ārum fpl the three Graces
grātificātiō, -ōnis f obligingness
grātificor, -ārī vi to do a favour, oblige ♦ vt to make a present of
grātiīs, grātīs adv for nothing
grātiōsus adj in favour, popular; obliging
grātor, -ārī, -ātus vi to rejoice, congratulate
grātuītō adv for nothing
grātuītus adj free, gratuitous
grātulābundus adj congratulating
grātulātiō, -ōnis f rejoicing; congratulation; public thanksgiving
grātulor, -ārī, -ātus vt, vi to congratulate; to give thanks
grātus adj pleasing, welcome, dear; grateful, thankful; (acts) deserving thanks; **grātum facere** do a favour
gravātē adv reluctantly, grudgingly
gravātim adv unwillingly
gravēdinōsus adj liable to colds
gravēdō, -inis f cold in the head
graveolēns, -entis adj strong-smelling
gravēscō, -ere vi to become heavy; to grow worse
graviditās, -ātis f pregnancy
gravidō, -āre vt to impregnate
gravidus adj pregnant; loaded, full
gravis adj heavy; loaded, pregnant; (smell) strong, offensive; (sound) deep, bass; (body) sick; (food) indigestible; (fig) oppressive, painful, severe; important, influential, dignified
gravitās, -ātis f weight, severity, sickness; importance, dignity, seriousness; **annōnae ~** high price of corn
graviter adv heavily; strongly, deeply; severely, seriously, violently; gravely, with dignity; **~ ferre** be vexed at
gravō, -āre vt to load, weigh down; to oppress, aggravate
gravor, -ārī vt, vi to feel annoyed, object to, disdain
gregālis adj of the herd, common ♦ m comrade
gregārius adj; (MIL) private
gregātim adv in crowds
gremium, -ī nt bosom, lap
gressus¹ ppa of **gradior**

93

gressus², **-ūs** *m* step; course
grex, **-egis** *m* flock, herd; company, troop
grunniō, **-īre** *vi* to grunt
grunnītus, **-ūs** *m* grunting
grūs, **-uis** *f* crane
grȳps, **-ȳpis** *m* griffin
gubernāclum, **gubernāculum**, **-ī** *nt* rudder, tiller; helm, government
gubernātiō, **-ōnis** *f* steering, management
gubernātor, **-ōris** *m* steersman, pilot, governor
gubernātrīx, **-īcis** *f* directress
gubernō, **-āre**, **-āvī**, **-ātum** *vt* to steer, pilot; to manage, govern
gula, **-ae** *f* gullet, throat; gluttony, palate
gulōsus *adj* dainty
gurges, **-itis** *m* abyss, deep water, flood; (*person*) spendthrift
gurguliō, **-ōnis** *f* gullet, windpipe
gurgustium, **-ī** *and* **-iī** *nt* hovel, shack
gustātus, **-ūs** *m* sense of taste; flavour

gustō, **-āre**, **-āvī**, **-ātum** *vt* to taste; to have a snack; (*fig*) to enjoy, overhear; **prīmīs labrīs gustāre** have a superficial knowledge of
gustus, **-ūs** *m* tasting; preliminary dish
gutta, **-ae** *f* drop; spot, speck
guttātim *adv* drop by drop
guttur, **-is** *nt* throat, gluttony
gūttus, **-ī** *m* flask
Gyās, **-ae** *m* giant with a hundred arms
Gȳgaeus *adj see* **Gȳgēs**
Gȳgēs, **-is** *and* **-ae** *m* king of Lydia (famed for his magic ring)
gymnasiarchus, **-ī** *m* master of a gymnasium
gymnasium, **-ī** *and* **-iī** *nt* sports ground, school
gymnasticus *adj* gymnastic
gymnicus *adj* gymnastic
gynaecēum, **-ēī**, **gynaecīum**, **-iī** *nt* women's quarters
gypsātus *adj* coated with plaster
gypsum, **-ī** *nt* plaster of Paris; a plaster figure
gȳrus, **-ī** *m* circle, coil, ring; course

Hh

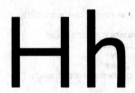

ha *interj* (*expressing joy or laughter*) hurrah!, ha ha!

habēna, -ae *f* strap; (*pl*) reins; (*fig*) control; **habēnās dare, habēnās immittere** allow to run freely

habeō, -ēre, -uī, -itum *vt* to have, hold; to keep, contain, possess; (*fact*) to know; (*with inf*) to be in a position to; (*person*) to treat, regard, consider; (*action*) to make, hold, carry out ♦ *vi* to have possessions; **ōrātiōnem habēre** make a speech; **in animō habēre** intend; **prō certō habēre** be sure; **sē habēre** find oneself, be; **sibi habēre** keep to oneself; (*fight*); **habet** a hit!; **bene habet** it is well; **sīc habet** so it is; **sīc habētō** be sure of this

habilis *adj* manageable, handy; suitable, nimble, expert

habilitās, -ātis *f* aptitude

habitābilis *adj* habitable

habitātiō, -ōnis *f* dwelling, house

habitātor, -ōris *m* tenant, inhabitant

habitō, -āre, -āvī, -ātum *vt* to inhabit ♦ *vi* to live, dwell; to remain, be always (in)

habitūdō, -inis *f* condition

habitus¹ *ppp of* **habeō** ♦ *adj* stout; in a humour

habitus², -ūs *m* condition, appearance; dress; character, quality; disposition, feeling

hāc *adv* this way

hāctenus *adv* thus far, so far; till now

Hadria, -ae *f* town in N. Italy; Adriatic Sea

Hadriānus, -ānī *m* (emperor) Hadrian

Hadriāticus, Hadriacus *adj* of (emperor) Hadrian

haedilia, -ae *f* little kid

haedinus *adj* kid's

haedulus, -ī *m* little kid

haedus, -ī *m* kid; (*ASTR, usu pl*) the Kids (*a cluster in Auriga*)

Haemonia, -ae *f* Thessaly

Haemonius *adj* Thessalian

Haemus, -ī *m* mountain range in Thrace

haereō, -rēre, -sī, -sum *vi* to cling, stick, be attached; (*nearness*) to stay close, hang on; (*continuance*) to linger, remain (at); (*stoppage*) to stick fast, come to a standstill, be at a loss

haerēscō, -ere *vi* to adhere

haeresis, -is *f* sect

haesī *perf of* **haereō**

haesitantia, -ae *f* stammering

haesitātiō, -ōnis *f* stammering; indecision

haesitō, -āre *vi* to get stuck; to stammer; to hesitate, be uncertain

hahae, hahahae *see* **ha**

haliaeetos, -ī *m* osprey

hālitus, -ūs *m* breath, vapour

hallex, -icis *m* big toe

hāllūcinor *etc see* **ālūcinor**

hālō, -āre *vi* to be fragrant ♦ *vt* to exhale

hālūcinor *etc see* **ālūcinor**

hama, -ae *f* water bucket

Hamādryas, -adis *f* woodnymph

hāmātilis *adj* with hooks

hāmātus *adj* hooked

Hamilcar, -is *m* father of Hannibal

hāmus, -ī *m* hook; talons

Hannibal, -is *m* famous Carthaginian general in 2nd Punic War

hara, -ae *f* sty, pen

harēna, -ae *f* sand; desert, seashore; arena (*in the amphitheatre*)

harēnōsus *adj* sandy

hariola, -ae *f*, **hariolus, -ī** *m* soothsayer

hariolor, -ārī *vi* to prophesy; to talk nonsense

harmonia, -ae *f* concord, melody; (*fig*) harmony

harpagō¹, -āre *vt* to steal

harpagō², -ōnis *m* grappling hook; (*person*) robber

harpē, -ēs *f* scimitar

Harpȳiae, -ārum *fpl* Harpies (*mythical monsters, half woman, half bird*)

harundifer, -ī *adj* reed-crowned

harundineus *adj* reedy

harundinōsus *adj* abounding in reeds

harundō, -inis *f* reed, cane; fishing rod; shaft, arrow; (*fowling*) limed twig; (*music*) pipe, flute; (*toy*) hobbyhorse; (*weaving*) comb; (*writing*) pen

haruspex, -icis *m* diviner (*from entrails*); prophet

haruspica, -ae *f* soothsayer

haruspicīnus *adj* of divination by entrails ♦ *f* art of such divination

haruspicium, -ī and -iī *nt* divination

Hasdrubal, -is *m* brother of Hannibal

hasta, -ae *f* spear, pike; *sign of an auction sale*; **sub hastā vēndere** put up for auction

hastātus *adj* armed with a spear ♦ *mpl* first line of Roman army in battle; **prīmus ~** 1st company of hastati

hastīle, -is *nt* shaft, spear, javelin; vine prop

hau, haud *adv* not, not at all

hauddum *adv* not yet

haudquāquam *adv* not at all, not by any means

haurió, -ríre, -sí, -stum vt to draw, draw off, derive; to drain, empty, exhaust; to take in, drink, swallow, devour

haustus' ppp of **haurió**

haustus², -ús m drawing (water); drinking; drink, draught

haut see **hau**

hebdomas, -dis f week

Hébé, -és f goddess of youth (cup bearer to the gods)

hebenus, -í f ebony

hebeó, -ére vi to be blunt, dull, sluggish

hebes, -tis adj blunt, dull, sluggish; obtuse, stupid

hebéscó, -ere vi to grow dim or dull

hebetó, -áre vt to blunt, dull, dim

Hebrus, -í m Thracian river (now Maritza)

Hecaté, -és f goddess of magic (and often identified with Diana)

Hecatéius, Hecatéis adj see **Hecaté**

hecatombé, -és f hecatomb

Hector, -is m son of Priam (chief warrior of the Trojans against the Greeks)

Hectoreus adj of Hector; Trojan

Hecuba, -ae, Hecubé, -és f wife of Priam

hedera, -ae f ivy

hederiger, -í adj wearing ivy

hederósus adj covered with ivy

hédychrum, -í nt a cosmetic perfume

hei, heia see **eia**

Helena, -ae, Helené, -és f Helen (wife of Menelaus, abducted by Paris)

Helenus, -í m son of Priam (with prophetic powers)

Héliades, -um fpl daughters of the Sun (changed to poplars or alders, and their tears to amber)

Helicé, -és f the Great Bear

Helicón, -ónis m mountain in Greece sacred to Apollo and the Muses

Helicóniades, -um fpl the Muses

Helicónius adj see **Helicón**

Hellas, -dis f Greece

Hellé, -és f mythical Greek princess (carried by the golden-fleeced ram, and drowned in the Hellespont)

Helléspontius, Helléspontiacus adj see **Helléspontus**

Helléspontus, -í m Hellespont (now Dardanelles)

helluó, -ónis m glutton

helluor, -árí vi to be a glutton

helvella, -ae f a savoury herb

Helvétií, -órum mpl people of E. Gaul (now Switzerland)

Helvétius, Helvéticus adj see **Helvétií**

hem interj (expressing surprise) eh?, well well!

hémerodromus, -í m express courier

hémicillus, -í m mule

hémicyclium, -í and **-íí** nt semicircle with seats

hémína, -ae f half a pint

hendecasyllabí, -órum mpl hendecasyllabics, verses of eleven syllables per line

heptéris, -is f ship with seven banks of oars

hera etc see **era**

Héra, -ae f Greek goddess identified with Juno

Héraclítus, -í m early Greek philosopher

Héraea, -aeórum ntpl festival of Hera

herba, -ae f blade, young plant; grass, herb, weed

herbéscó, -ere vi to grow into blades

herbeus adj grass-green

herbidus adj grassy

herbifer, -í adj grassy

herbósus adj grassy, made of turf; made of herbs

herbula, -ae f little herb

hercíscó, -ere vt to divide an inheritance

hercle interj by Hercules!

herctum, -í nt inheritance

Hercule interj by Hercules!

Herculés, -is and **-í** m mythical Greek hero, later deified

Herculeus adj: **arbor ~** poplar; **urbs ~** Herculaneum

here see **herí**

héréditárius adj inherited; about an inheritance

héréditás, -átis f inheritance; **~ sine sacris** a gift without awkward obligations

hérédium, -í and **-íí** nt inherited estate

hérés, -édis m/f heir, heiress; (fig) master, successor

herí adv yesterday

herílis etc see **erílis**

Hermés, -ae m Greek god identified with Mercury; Hermes pillar

Hernicí, -órum mpl people of central Italy

Hernicus adj see **Hernicí**

Héerodotus, -í m first Greek historian

héróicus adj heroic, epic

héróina, -ae f demigoddess

héróis, -dis f demigoddess

hérós, -is m demigod, hero

héróus adj heroic, epic

herus etc see **erus**

Hésiodéus, -íus adj see **Hésiodus**

Hésiodus, -í m Hesiod (Greek didactic poet)

Hesperia, -iae f Italy; Spain

Hesperides, -idum fpl keepers of a garden in the far West

Hesperius, -is adj western

Hesperus, -í m evening star

hesternus adj of yesterday

heu interj (expressing dismay or pain) oh!, alas!

heus interj (calling attention) ho!, hallo!

hexameter, -rí m hexameter verse

hexéris, -is f ship with six banks of oars

hiátus, -ús m opening, abyss; open mouth, gaping; (GRAM) hiatus

Hibéres, -um mpl Spaniards

Hibéria, -iae f Spain

híberna, -órum ntpl winter quarters

híbernácula, -órum ntpl winter tents

Hibernia, -ae f Ireland

híbernó, -áre vi to winter, remain in winter quarters

híbernus adj winter, wintry

Hibérus', Hibéricus adj Spanish

Hibérus², -í m (river) Ebro

hibíscum, -í nt marsh mallow

hibrida, hybrida, -ae m/f (dog) mongrel

hīc¹, **haec**, **hōc** *pron, adj* this; he, she, it; my, the latter, the present; **hīc homō** I; **hōc magis** the more; **hōc est** that is

hīc² *adv* here; herein; (*time*) at this point

hīce, **haece**, **hōce** *emphatic forms of* **hīc¹**, **haec**, **hōc**

hīcine, **haecine**, **hōcine** *emphatic forms of* **hīc¹**, **haec**, **hōc**

hiemālis *adj* winter, stormy

hiemō, **-āre** *vi* to pass the winter; to be wintry, stormy

hiems, **(hiemps)**, **-is** *f* winter; stormy weather, cold

Hierōnymus, **-ī** *m* Jerome

Hierosolyma, **-ōrum** *ntpl* Jerusalem

Hierosolymārius *adj see* **Hierosolyma**

hietō, **-āre** *vi* to yawn

hilare *adv see* **hilaris**

hilaris *adj* cheerful, merry

hilaritās, **-ātis** *f* cheerfulness

hilaritūdō, **-inis** *f* merriment

hilarō, **-āre** *vt* to cheer, gladden

hilarulus *adj* a gay little thing

hilarus *etc see* **hilaris**

hīllae, **-ārum** *fpl* smoked sausage

Hīlōtae, **-ārum** *mpl* Helots (*of Sparta*)

hīlum, **-ī** *nt* something, a whit

hinc *adv* from here, hence; on this side; from this source, for this reason; (*time*) henceforth

hinniō, **-īre** *vi* to neigh

hinnītus, **-ūs** *m* neighing

hinnuleus, **-ī** *m* fawn

hiō, **-āre** *vi* to be open, gape, yawn; (*speech*) to be disconnected, leave a hiatus ♦ *vt* to sing

hippagōgī, **-ōrum** *fpl* cavalry transports

hippocentaurus, **-ī** *m* centaur

hippodromos, **-ī** *m* racecourse

Hippolytus, **-ī** *m* son *of Theseus* (*slandered by stepmother Phaedra*)

hippomanes, **-is** *nt* mare's fluid; membrane on foal's forehead

Hippōnactēus *adj* of Hipponax ♦ *m* iambic verse used by Hipponax

Hippōnax, **-ctis** *m* Greek satirist

hippotoxotae, **-ārum** *mpl* mounted archers

hīra, **-ae** *f* the empty gut

hircīnus *adj* of a goat

hircōsus *adj* goatish

hircus, **-ī** *m* he-goat; goatish smell

hirnea, **-ae** *f* jug

hirq- *etc see* **hirc-**

hirsūtus *adj* shaggy, bristly; uncouth

hirtus *adj* hairy, shaggy; rude

hirūdō, **-inis** *f* leech

hirundinīnus *adj* swallows'

hirundō, **-inis** *f* swallow

hīscō, **-ere** *vi* to gape; to open the mouth ♦ *vt* to utter

Hispānia, **-iae** *f* Spain

Hispāniēnsis, **Hispānus** *adj* Spanish

hispidus *adj* hairy, rough

Hister, **-rī** *m* lower Danube

historia, **-ae** *f* history, inquiry; story

historicus *adj* historical ♦ *m* historian

histricus *adj* of the stage

histriō, **-ōnis** *m* actor

histriōnālis *adj* of an actor

histriōnia, **-ae** *f* acting

hiulcē *adv* with hiatus

hiulcō, **-āre** *vt* to split open

hiulcus *adj* gaping, open; (*speech*) with hiatus

hodiē *adv* today; nowadays, now; up to the present

hodiernus *adj* today's

holitor, **-ōris** *m* market gardener

holitōrius *adj* for market gardeners

holus, **-eris** *nt* vegetables

holusculum, **-ī** *nt* small cabbage

Homēricus *adj see* **Homērus**

Homērus, **-ī** *m* Greek epic poet, Homer

homicīda, **-ae** *m* killer, murderer

homicīdium, **-ī** *and* **-iī** *nt* murder

homō, **-inis** *m/f* human being, man; (*pl*) people, the world; (*derogatory*) fellow, creature; **inter hominēs esse** be alive; see the world

homullus, **-ī**, **homunciō**, **-ōnis**, **homunculus**, **-ī** *m* little man, poor creature, mortal

honestās, **-ātis** *f* good character, honourable reputation; sense of honour, integrity; (*things*) beauty

honestē *adv* decently, virtuously

honestō, **-āre** *vt* to honour, dignify, embellish

honestus *adj* honoured, respectable; honourable, virtuous; (*appearance*) handsome ♦ *m* gentleman ♦ *nt* virtue, good; beauty

honor, **-ōris** *m* honour, esteem; public office, position, preferment; award, tribute, offering; ornament, beauty; **honōris causā** out of respect; **honōrem praefārī** apologize for a remark

honōrābilis *adj* as a mark of respect

honōrārius *adj* done out of respect, honorary

honōrātē *adv* honourably

honōrātus *adj* esteemed, distinguished; in high office; complimentary

honōrificē *adv* in complimentary terms

honōrificus *adj* complimentary

honōrō, **-āre**, **-āvī**, **-ātum** *vt* to do honour to, embellish

honōrus *adj* complimentary

honōs *etc see* **honor**

hōra, **-ae** *f* hour; time, season; (*pl*) clock; **in hōrās** hourly; **in hōram vīvere** live from hand to mouth

hōraeum, **-ī** *nt* pickle

Horātius¹, **-ī** *m* Roman family name (*esp the defender of Rome against Porsenna*); the lyric poet Horace

Horātius² *adj see* **Horātius¹**

hordeum, **-ī** *nt* barley

horia, **-ae** *f* fishing smack

hōrnō *adv* this year

hōrnōtinus *adj* this year's

hōrnus *adj* this year's

hōrologium, **-ī** *and* **-iī** *nt* clock

horrendus *adj* fearful, terrible; awesome

horrēns, -entis *pres p of* **horreō ♦** *adj* bristling, shaggy

horreō, -ēre, -uī *vi* to stand stiff, bristle; to shiver, shudder, tremble **♦** *vt* to dread; to be afraid, be amazed

horrēscō, -ere, horruī *vi* to stand on end, become rough; to begin to quake; to start, be terrified **♦** *vt* to dread

horreum, -ī *nt* barn, granary, store

horribilis *adj* terrifying; amazing

horridē *adv see* **horridus**

horridulus *adj* protruding a little; unkempt; (*fig*) uncouth

horridus *adj* bristling, shaggy, rough, rugged; shivering; (*manners*) rude, uncouth; frightening

horrifer, -ī *adj* chilling; terrifying

horrificē *adv* in awesome manner

horrificō, -āre *vt* to ruffle; to terrify

horrificus *adj* terrifying

horrisonus *adj* dread-sounding

horror, -ōris *m* bristling; shivering, ague; terror, fright, awe, a terror

hōrsum *adv* this way

hortāmen, -inis *nt* encouragement

hortāmentum, -ī *nt* encouragement

hortātiō, -ōnis *f* harangue, encouragement

hortātor, -ōris *m* encourager

hortātus, -ūs *m* encouragement

Hortēnsius, -ī *m* Roman family name (*esp an orator in Cicero's time*)

hortor, -ārī, -ātus *vt* to urge, encourage, exhort, harangue

hortulus, -ī *m* little garden

hortus, -ī *m* garden; (*pl*) park

hospes, -itis *m*, **hospita, -ae** *f* host, hostess; guest, friend; stranger, foreigner **♦** *adj* strange

hospitālis *adj* host's, guest's; hospitable

hospitālitās, -ātis *f* hospitality

hospitāliter *adv* hospitably

hospitium, -ī *and* **-iī** *nt* hospitality, friendship; lodging, inn

hostia, -ae *f* victim, sacrifice

hostiātus *adj* provided with victims

hosticus *adj* hostile; strange **♦** *nt* enemy territory

hostīlis *adj* of the enemy, hostile

hostīliter *adv* in hostile manner

hostīmentum, -ī *nt* recompense

hostiō, -īre *vt* to requite

hostis, -is *m/f* enemy

hūc *adv* hither, here; to this, to such a pitch; **hūc illūc** hither and thither

hui *interj* (*expressing surprise*) ho!, my word!

hūiusmodī such

hūmānē, hūmāniter *adv* humanly; gently, politely

hūmānitās, -ātis *f* human nature, mankind; humanity, kindness, courtesy; culture, refinement

hūmānitus *adv* in accordance with human nature; kindly

hūmānus *adj* human, humane, kind, courteous; cultured, refined, well-educated; **hūmānō māior** superhuman

humātiō, -ōnis *f* burying

hūme-, hūmi- *see* **ūme-, ūmi-**

humilis *adj* low, low-lying, shallow; (*condition*) lowly, humble, poor; (*language*) commonplace; (*mind*) mean, base

humilitās, -ātis *f* low position, smallness, shallowness; lowliness, insignificance; meanness, baseness

humiliter *adv* meanly, humbly

humō, -āre, -āvī, -ātum *vt* to bury

humus, -ī *f* earth, ground; land; **humī** on the ground

hyacinthinus *adj* of the hyacinthus

hyacinthus, -ī *m* iris, lily

Hyades, -um *fpl* Hyads (*a group of stars in Taurus*)

hyaena, -ae *f* hyena

hyalus, -ī *m* glass

Hybla, -ae *f* mountain in Sicily (*famous for bees*)

Hyblaeus *adj see* **Hybla**

hybrida *etc see* **hibrida**

Hydaspēs, -is *m* tributary of river Indus (*now* Jhelum)

Hўdra, -ae *f* hydra (*a mythical dragon with seven heads*)

hydraulus, -ī *m* water organ

hydria, -ae *f* ewer

Hydrochous, -ī *m* Aquarius

hydrōpicus *adj* suffering from dropsy

hydrōps, -is *m* dropsy

hydrus, -ī *m* serpent

Hylās, -ae *m* a youth loved by Hercules

Hymēn, -enis, Hymenaeus, -ī *m* god of marriage; wedding song; wedding

Hymettius *adj see* **Hymettus**

Hymettus, -ī *m* mountain near Athens (*famous for honey and marble*)

Hypanis, -is *m* river of Sarmatia (*now* Bug)

Hyperboreī, -ōrum *mpl* fabulous people in the far North

Hyperboreus *adj see* **Hyperboreī**

Hyperīōn, -onis *m* father of the Sun; the Sun

hypodidascalus, -ī *m* assistant teacher

hypomnēma, -tis *nt* memorandum

Hyrcānī, -ōrum *mpl* people on the Caspian Sea

Hyrcānus *adj* Hyrcanian

Ii

Iacchus, -ī *m* Bacchus; wine
iaceō, -ēre, -uī *vi* to lie; to be ill, lie dead;
(*places*) to be situated, be flat or low-lying,
be in ruins; (*dress*) to hang loose; (*fig*) to be
inactive, be downhearted; (*things*) to be
dormant, neglected, despised
iaciō, -ere, iēcī, iactum *vt* to throw; to lay,
build; (*seed*) to sow; (*speech*) to cast, let fall,
mention
iactāns, -antis *pres p of* **iactō ♦** *adj* boastful
iactanter *adv* ostentatiously
iactantia, -ae *f* boasting, ostentation
iactātiō, -ōnis *f* tossing, gesticulation;
boasting, ostentation; ~ **populāris** publicity
iactātus, -ūs *m* waving
iactitō, -āre *vt* to mention, bandy
iactō, -āre, -āvī, -ātum *vt* to throw, scatter; to
shake, toss about; (*mind*) to disquiet; (*ideas*) to
consider, discuss, mention; (*speech*) to boast
of; **sē iactāre** waver, fluctuate; to behave
ostentatiously, be officious
iactūra, -ae *f* throwing overboard; loss,
sacrifice
iactus¹ *ppp of* **iaciō**
iactus², -ūs *m* throwing, throw; **intrā tēlī
iactum** within spear's range
iacuī *perf of* **iaceō**
iaculābilis *adj* missile
iaculātor, -ōris *m* thrower, shooter; light-
armed soldier
iaculātrīx, -īcis *f* huntress
iaculor, -ārī, -ātus *vt* to throw, hurl, shoot; to
throw the javelin; to shoot at, hit; (*fig*) to aim
at, attack
iaculum, -ī *nt* javelin; fishing net
iāien- *etc see* **iēn-**
iam *adv* (*past*) already, by then; (*present*)
now, already; (*future*) directly, very soon;
(*emphasis*) indeed, precisely; (*inference*)
therefore, then surely; (*transition*) moreover,
next; **iam dūdum** for a long time, long
ago; immediately; **iam iam** right now, any
moment now; **non iam** no longer; **iam …
iam** at one time … at another; **iam nunc** just
now; **iam prīdem** long ago, for a long time;
iam tum even at that time; **sī iam** supposing
for the purpose of argument
iambēus *adj* iambic
iambus, -ī *m* iambic foot; iambic poetry
iānālis *adj see* **iānus**
iāniculum, -ī *nt* Roman hill across the Tiber

iānitor, -ōris *m* doorkeeper, porter
iānua, -ae *f* door; entrance; (*fig*) key
iānuārius *adj* of January **♦** *m* January
iānus, -ī *m* god of gateways and beginnings;
archway, arcade
Iapetīonidēs, -ae *m* Atlas
Iapetus, -ī *m* a Titan (*father of Atlas and
Prometheus*)
Iāpyx, -gis *adj* Iapygian; Apulian **♦** *m* west-
north-west wind from Apulia
Iāsōn, -onis *m* Jason (*leader of Argonauts, husband
of Medea*)
Iāsonius *adj see* **Iāsōn**
iaspis, -dis *f* jasper
Ībēr- *etc see* **Hībēr-**
ibi *adv* there; then; in this, at it
ibīdem *adv* in the same place; at that very
moment
ibis, -is *and* **-idis** *f* ibis
Īcarium, -ī *nt* Icarian (Sea)
Īcarius *adj see* **Īcarus**
Īcarus, -ī *m* son of Daedalus (*drowned in the Aegean*)
īcō, -ere, -ī, ictum *vt* to strike; **foedus īcere**
make a treaty
ictericus *adj* jaundiced
ictis, -dis *f* weasel
ictus¹ *ppp of* **īcō**
ictus², -ūs *m* stroke, blow; wound; (*metre*) beat
Īda, -ae, Īdē, -ēs *f* mountain in Crete; mountain
near Troy
Īdaeus *adj* Cretan; Trojan
idcircō *adv* for that reason; for the purpose
īdem, eadem, idem *pron* the same; also,
likewise
identidem *adv* repeatedly, again and again
ideō *adv* therefore, for this reason, that is why
idiōta, -ae *m* ignorant person, layman
īdōlon, -ī *nt* apparition
idōneē *adv see* **idōneus**
idōneus *adj* fit, proper, suitable, sufficient
Īdūs, -uum *fpl* Ides (*the 15th March, May, July,
October, the 13th of other months*)
iēcī *perf of* **iaciō**
iecur, -oris *and* **-inoris** *nt* liver; (*fig*) passion
iecusculum, -ī *nt* small liver
ieiūniōsus *adj* hungry
ieiūnitās, -ātis *f* fasting; (*fig*) meagreness
ieiūnium, -ī *and* **-iī** *nt* fast; hunger; leanness
ieiūnus *adj* fasting, hungry; (*things*) barren,
poor, meagre; (*style*) feeble

99

iēntāculum, -ī *nt* breakfast
igitur *adv* therefore, then, so
ignārus *adj* ignorant, unaware; unknown
ignāvē, ignāviter *adv* without energy
ignāvia, -ae *f* idleness, laziness; cowardice
ignāvus *adj* idle, lazy, listless; cowardly; relaxing
ignēscō, -ere *vi* to take fire, burn
igneus *adj* burning, fiery
igniculus, -ī *m* spark; (*fig*) fire, vehemence
ignifer, -ī *adj* fiery
ignigena, -ae *m* the fireborn (*Bacchus*)
ignipēs, -edis *adj* fiery-footed
ignipotēns, -entis *adj* fire-working (*Vulcan*)
ignis, -is *m* fire, a fire; firebrand, lightning; brightness, redness; (*fig*) passion, love
ignōbilis *adj* unknown, obscure; low-born
ignōbilitās, -ātis *f* obscurity; low birth
ignōminia, -ae *f* dishonour, disgrace
ignōminiōsus *adj* (*person*) degraded, disgraced; (*things*) shameful
ignōrābilis *adj* unknown
ignōrantia, -ae *f* ignorance
ignōrātiō, -ōnis *f* ignorance
ignōrō, -āre, -āvī, -ātum *vt* to not know, be unacquainted with; to disregard
ignōscō, -scere, -vī, -tum *vt, vi* to forgive, pardon
ignōtus *adj* unknown; low-born; ignorant
īlex, -icis *f* holm oak
Īlia, -ae *f* mother of Romulus and Remus
īlia, -um *ntpl* groin; entrails; ~ dūcere become broken-winded
Īliadēs, -adae *m* son of Ilia; Trojan
Īlias, -dis *f* the Iliad; a Trojan woman
īlicet *adv* it's all over, let us go; immediately
īlicō *adv* on the spot; instantly
īlignus *adj* of holm oak
Īlīthyia, -ae *f* Greek goddess of childbirth
Īlium, -ī *nt*, **Īlion, -ī** *nt*, **Īlios, -ī** *f* Troy
Īlius, Īliacus *adj* Trojan
illā *adv* that way
illābefactus *adj* unbroken
illābor, -bī, -psus *vi* to flow into, fall down
illabōrō, -āre *vi* to work (at)
illāc *adv* that way
illacessītus *adj* unprovoked
illacrimābilis *adj* unwept; inexorable
illacrimō, -āre, illacrimor, -ārī *vi* to weep over, lament; to weep
illaesus *adj* unhurt
illaetābilis *adj* cheerless
illāpsus *ppa of* **illābor**
illaqueō, -āre *vt* to ensnare
illātus *ppp of* **īnferō**
illaudātus *adj* wicked
ille, -a, -ud *pron, adj* that, that one; he, she, it; the famous; the former, the other; ex illō since then
illecebra, -ae *f* attraction, lure, bait, decoy bird
illecebrōsus *adj* seductive
illectus *ppp of* **illiciō**

illēctus *adj* unread
illepidē *adv see* **illepidus**
illepidus *adj* inelegant, churlish
illex, -icis *m/f* lure
illēx, -ēgis *adj* lawless
illexī *perf of* **illiciō**
illībātus *adj* unimpaired
illīberālis *adj* ungenerous, mean, disobliging
illīberālitās, -ātis *f* meanness
illīberāliter *adv see* **illīberālis**
illic, -aec, -ūc *pron* he, she, it; that
illīc *adv* there, yonder; in that matter
illiciō, -icere, -exī, -ectum *vt* to seduce, decoy, mislead
illicitātor, -ōris *m* sham bidder (*at an auction*)
illicitus *adj* unlawful
illīdō, -dere, -sī, -sum *vt* to strike, dash against
illigō, -āre, -āvī, -ātum *vt* to fasten on, attach; to connect; to impede, encumber, oblige
illim *adv* from there
illīmis *adj* clear
illinc *adv* from there; on that side
illinō, -inere, -ēvī, -itum *vt* to smear over, cover, bedaub
illiquefactus *adj* melted
illīsī *perf of* **illīdō**
illisus *ppp of* **illīdō**
illitterātus *adj* uneducated, uncultured
illitus *ppp of* **illinō**
illō *adv* (to) there; to that end
illōtus *adj* dirty
illūc *adv* (to) there; to that; to him/her
illūceō, -ēre *vi* to blaze
illūcēscō, -cēscere, -xī *vi* to become light, dawn
illūdō, -dere, -sī, -sum *vt, vi* to play, amuse oneself; to abuse; to jeer at, ridicule
illūminātē *adv* luminously
illūminō, -āre, -āvī, -ātum *vt* to light up; to enlighten; to embellish
illūsiō, -ōnis *f* irony
illūstris *adj* bright, clear; distinct, manifest; distinguished, illustrious
illūstrō, -āre, -āvī, -ātum *vt* to illuminate; to make clear, explain; to make famous
illūsus *ppp of* **illūdō**
illuviēs, -ēī *f* dirt, filth; floods
Illyria, -ae *f*, **Illyricum, -cī** *nt* Illyria
Illyricus, Illyrius *adj see* **Illyria**
Illyriī, -ōrum *mpl* people E. of the Adriatic
Ilva, -ae *f* Italian island (*now* Elba)
imāginārius *adj* fancied
imāginātiō, -ōnis *f* fancy
imāginor, -ārī *vt* to picture to oneself
imāgō, -inis *f* likeness, picture, statue; portrait of ancestor; apparition, ghost; echo, mental picture, idea; (*fig*) semblance, mere shadow; (RHET) comparison
imbēcillē *adv* faintly
imbēcillitās, -ātis *f* weakness, helplessness
imbēcillus *adj* weak, frail; helpless
imbellis *adj* non-combatant; peaceful; cowardly

imber, **-ris** *m* rain, heavy shower; water; (*fig*) stream, shower

imberbis, **imberbus** *adj* beardless

imbibō, **-ere**, **-ī** *vt* (*mind*) to conceive; to resolve

imbrex, **-icis** *f* tile

imbricus *adj* rainy

imbrifer, **-ī** *adj* rainy

imbuō, **-uere**, **-uī**, **-ūtum** *vt* to wet, steep, dip; (*fig*) to taint, fill; to inspire, accustom, train; to begin, be the first to explore

imitābilis *adj* imitable

imitāmen, **-inis** *nt* imitation; likeness

imitāmenta, **-ōrum** *ntpl* pretence

imitātiō, **-ōnis** *f* imitation

imitātor, **-ōris** *m*, **imitātrīx**, **-rīcis** *f* imitator

imitātus *adj* copied

imitor, **-ārī**, **-ātus** *vt* to copy, portray; to imitate, act like

immadēscō, **-ēscere**, **-uī** *vi* to become wet

immāne *adv* savagely

immānis *adj* enormous, vast; monstrous, savage, frightful

immānitās, **-ātis** *f* vastness; savageness, barbarism

immānsuētus *adj* wild

immātūritās, **-ātis** *f* over-eagerness

immātūrus *adj* untimely

immedicābilis *adj* incurable

immemor, **-is** *adj* unmindful, forgetful, negligent

immemorābilis *adj* indescribable, not worth mentioning

immemorātus *adj* hitherto untold

immēnsitās, **-ātis** *f* immensity

immēnsum, **-ī** *nt* infinity, vast extent ♦ *adv* exceedingly

immēnsus *adj* immeasurable, vast, unending

immerēns, **-entis** *adj* undeserving

immergō, **-gere**, **-sī**, **-sum** *vt* to plunge, immerse

immeritō *adv* unjustly

immeritus *adj* undeserving, innocent; undeserved

immersābilis *adj* never foundering

immersus *ppp of* **immergō**

immētātus *adj* unmeasured

immigrō, **-āre**, **-āvī**, **-ātum** *vi* to move (into)

immineō, **-ēre**, **-uī** *vi* to overhang, project; to be near, adjoin, impend; to threaten, be a menace to; to long for, grasp at

imminuō, **-uere**, **-uī**, **-ūtum** *vt* to lessen, shorten; to impair; to encroach on, ruin

imminūtiō, **-ōnis** *f* mutilation; (*RHET*) understatement

immisceō, **-scēre**, **-scuī**, **-xtum** *vt* to intermingle, blend; **sē immiscēre** join, meddle with

immiserābilis *adj* unpitied

immisericorditer *adv* unmercifully

immisericors, **-dis** *adj* pitiless

immissiō, **-ōnis** *f* letting grow

immissus *ppp of* **immittō**

immītis *adj* unripe; severe, inexorable

immittō, **-ittere**, **-īsī**, **-issum** *vt* to let in, put in; to graft on; to let go, let loose, let grow; to launch, throw; to incite, set on

immīxtus *ppp of* **immisceō**

immo *adv* (*correcting preceding words*) no, yes; on the contrary, or rather; **~ sī** ah, if only

immōbilis *adj* motionless; immovable

immoderātē *adv* extravagantly

immoderātiō, **-ōnis** *f* excess

immoderātus *adj* limitless; excessive, unbridled

immodestē *adv* extravagantly

immodestia, **-ae** *f* licence

immodestus *adj* immoderate

immodicē *adv see* **immodicus**

immodicus *adj* excessive, extravagant, unruly

immodulātus *adj* unrhythmical

immolātiō, **-ōnis** *f* sacrifice

immolātor, **-ōris** *m* sacrificer

immōlītus *adj* erected

immolō, **-āre**, **-āvī**, **-ātum** *vt* to sacrifice; to slay

immorior, **-ī**, **-tuus** *vi* to die upon; to waste away

immorsus *adj* bitten; (*fig*) stimulated

immortālis *adj* immortal, everlasting

immortālitās, **-ātis** *f* immortality; lasting fame

immortāliter *adv* infinitely

immōtus *adj* motionless, unmoved, immovable

immūgiō, **-īre**, **-īī** *vi* to roar (in)

immulgeō, **-ēre** *vt* to milk

immundus *adj* unclean, dirty

immūniō, **-īre**, **-īvī** *vt* to strengthen

immūnis *adj* with no public obligations, untaxed, free from office; exempt, free (from)

immūnitās, **-ātis** *f* exemption, immunity, privilege

immūnītus *adj* undefended; (*roads*) unmetalled

immurmurō, **-āre** *vi* to murmur (at)

immūtābilis *adj* unalterable

immūtābilitās, **-ātis** *f* immutability

immūtātiō, **-ōnis** *f* exchange; (*RHET*) metonymy

immūtātus *adj* unchanged

immūtō, **-āre**, **-āvī**, **-ātum** *vt* to change; (*words*) to substitute by metonymy

impācātus *adj* aggressive

impāctus *ppp of* **impingō**

impār, **-aris** *adj* unequal, uneven, unlike; no match for, inferior; (*metre*) elegiac

imparātus *adj* unprepared, unprovided

impariter *adv* unequally

impāstus *adj* hungry

impatiēns, **-entis** *adj* unable to endure, impatient

impatienter *adv* intolerably

impatientia, **-ae** *f* want of endurance

impavidē *adv see* **impavidus**

impavidus *adj* fearless, undaunted

impedīmentum, **-ī** *nt* hindrance, obstacle; (*pl*) baggage, luggage, supply train

impediō, **-īre**, **-īvī** *and* **-iī**, **-ītum** *vt* to hinder, entangle; to encircle; (*fig*) to embarrass, obstruct, prevent

impedītiō, **-ōnis** *f* obstruction

impedītus *adj* (MIL) hampered with baggage, in difficulties; (*place*) difficult, impassable; (*mind*) busy, obsessed

impēgī *perf of* **impingō**

impellō, **-ellere**, **-ulī**, **-ulsum** *vt* to strike, drive; to set in motion, impel, shoot; to incite, urge on; (*fig*) to overthrow, ruin

impendeō, **-ēre** *vi* to overhang; to be imminent, threaten

impendiō *adv* very much

impendium, **-ī** *and* **-iī** *nt* expense, outlay; interest on a loan

impendō, **-endere**, **-endī**, **-ēnsum** *vt* to weigh out, pay out, spend; (*fig*) to devote

impenetrābilis *adj* impenetrable

impēnsa, **-ae** *f* expense, outlay

impēnsē *adv* very much; earnestly

impēnsus *ppp of* **impendō** ♦ *adj* (*cost*) high, dear; (*fig*) great, earnest

imperātor, **-ōris** *m* commander-in-chief, general; emperor; chief, master

imperātōrius *adj* of a general; imperial

imperātum, **-ī** *nt* order

imperceptus *adj* unknown

impercussus *adj* noiseless

imperditus *adj* not slain

imperfectus *adj* unfinished, imperfect

imperfōssus *adj* not stabbed

imperiōsus *adj* powerful, imperial; tyrannical

imperītē *adv* awkwardly

imperītia, **-ae** *f* inexperience

imperītō, **-āre** *vt, vi* to rule, command

imperītus *adj* inexperienced, ignorant

imperium, **-ī** *and* **-iī** *nt* command, order; mastery, sovereignty, power; military command, supreme authority; empire; (*pl*) those in command, the authorities

impermissus *adj* unlawful

imperō, **-āre**, **-āvī**, **-ātum** *vt, vi* to order, command; to requisition, demand; to rule, govern, control; to be emperor

imperterritus *adj* undaunted

impertiō, **-īre**, **-īvī** *and* **-iī**, **-ītum** *vt* to share, communicate, impart

imperturbātus *adj* unruffled

impervius *adj* impassable

impetibilis *adj* intolerable

impetis (*gen*) (*abl* **-e**) *m* force; extent

impetrābilis *adj* attainable; successful

impetrātiō, **-ōnis** *f* favour

impetriō, **-īre** *vt* to succeed with the auspices

impetrō, **-āre**, **-āvī**, **-ātum** *vt* to achieve; to obtain, secure (*a request*)

impetus, **-ūs** *m* attack, onset; charge; rapid motion, rush; (*mind*) impulse, passion

impexus *adj* unkempt

impiē *adv* wickedly

impietās, **-ātis** *f* impiety, disloyalty, unfilial conduct

impiger, **-rī** *adj* active, energetic

impigrē *adv see* **impiger**

impigritās, **-ātis** *f* energy

impingō, **-ingere**, **-ēgī**, **-āctum** *vt* to dash, force against; to force upon; (*fig*) to bring against, drive

impiō, **-āre** *vt* to make sinful

impius *adj* (*to gods*) impious; (*to parents*) undutiful; (*to country*) disloyal; wicked, unscrupulous

implācābilis *adj* implacable

implācābiliter *adv see* **implācābilis**

implācātus *adj* unappeased

implacidus *adj* savage

impleō, **-ēre**, **-ēvī**, **-ētum** *vt* to fill; to satisfy; (*time, number*) to make up, complete; (*duty*) to discharge, fulfil

implexus *adj* entwined; involved

implicātiō, **-ōnis** *f* entanglement

implicātus *adj* complicated, confused

implicitē *adv* intricately

implicō, **-āre**, **-āvī** *and* **-uī**, **-ātum** *and* **-itum** *vt* to entwine, enfold, clasp; (*fig*) to entangle, involve; to connect closely, join

implōrātiō, **-ōnis** *f* beseeching

implōrō, **-āre**, **-āvī**, **-ātum** *vt* to invoke, entreat, appeal to

implūmis *adj* unfledged

impluō, **-ere** *vi* to rain upon

impluvium, **-ī** *and* **-iī** *nt* roof-opening of the Roman atrium; rain basin in the atrium

impolītē *adv* without ornament

impolītus *adj* unpolished, inelegant

impollūtus *adj* unstained

impōnō, **-ōnere**, **-osuī**, **-ositum** *vt* to put in, lay on, place; to embark; (*fig*) to impose, inflict, assign; to put in charge; (*tax*) to impose; (*with dat*) to impose upon, cheat

importō, **-āre**, **-āvī**, **-ātum** *vt* to bring in, import; (*fig*) to bring upon, introduce

importūnē *adv see* **importūnus**

importūnitās, **-ātis** *f* insolence, ill nature

importūnus *adj* unsuitable; troublesome; ill-natured, uncivil, bullying

importuōsus *adj* without a harbour

impos, **-tis** *adj* not master (of)

impositus, **impostus** *ppp of* **impōnō**

impotēns, **-entis** *adj* powerless, weak; with no control over; headstrong, violent

impotenter *adv* weakly; violently

impotentia, **-ae** *f* poverty; want of self-control, violence

impraesentiārum *adv* at present

imprānsus *adj* fasting, without breakfast

imprecor, **-ārī** *vt* to invoke

impressiō, **-ōnis** *f* (MIL) thrust, raid; (*mind*) impression; (*speech*) emphasis; (*rhythm*) beat

impressus *ppp of* **imprimō**

imprīmīs *adv* especially

imprimō, **-imere**, **-essī**, **-essum** *vt* to press upon, impress, imprint, stamp

improbātiō, **-ōnis** *f* blame

improbē *adv* badly, wrongly; persistently

improbitās, **-ātis** *f* badness, dishonesty

improbō, -āre, -āvī, -ātum *vt* to disapprove, condemn, reject

improbulus *adj* a little presumptuous

improbus *adj* bad, inferior (*in quality*); wicked, perverse, cruel; unruly, persistent, rebellious

imprōcērus *adj* undersized

imprōdictus *adj* not postponed

imprōmptus *adj* unready, slow

improperātus *adj* lingering

improsper, -ī *adj* unsuccessful

improsperē *adv* unfortunately

imprōvidē *adv see* **imprōvidus**

imprōvidus *adj* unforeseeing, thoughtless

imprōvīsus *adj* unexpected; **imprōvīsō, de imprōvīsō, ex imprōvīsō** unexpectedly

imprūdēns, -entis *adj* unforeseeing, not expecting; ignorant, unaware

imprūdenter *adv* thoughtlessly, unawares

imprūdentia, -ae *f* thoughtlessness; ignorance; aimlessness

impūbēs, -eris *and* **-is** *adj* youthful; chaste

impudens, -entis *adj* shameless, impudent

impudenter *adv see* **impudens**

impudentia, -ae *f* impudence

impudīcitia, -ae *f* lewdness

impudīcus *adj* shameless; immodest

impugnātiō, -ōnis *f* assault

impugnō, -āre, -āvī, -ātum *vt* to attack; (*fig*) to oppose, impugn

impulī *perf of* **impellō**

impulsiō, -ōnis *f* pressure; (*mind*) impulse

impulsor, -ōris *m* instigator

impulsus¹ *ppp of* **impellō**

impulsus², -ūs *m* push, pressure, impulse; (*fig*) instigation

impūne *adv* safely, with impunity

impūnitās, -ātis *f* impunity

impūnītē *adv* with impunity

impūnītus *adj* unpunished

impūrātus *adj* vile

impūrē *adv see* **impūrus**

impūritās, -ātis *f* uncleanness

impūrus *adj* unclean; infamous, vile

imputātus *adj* unpruned

imputō, -āre, -āvī, -ātum *vt* to put to one's account; to ascribe, credit, impute

īmulus *adj* little tip of

īmus *adj* lowest, deepest, bottom of; last

in *prep* (*with abl*) in, on, at; among; in the case of; (*time*) during; (*with acc*) into, on to, to, towards; against; (*time*) for, till; (*purpose*) for; **in armīs** under arms; **in equō** on horseback; **in eō esse ut** be in the position of; be on the point of; **in hōrās** hourly; **in modum** in the manner of; **in rem** of use; **in universum** in general

inaccessus *adj* unapproachable

inacēscō, -ere *vi* to turn sour

Īnachidēs, -idae *m* Perseus; Epaphus

Īnachis, -idis *f* Io

Īnachius *adj* of Inachus, Argive, Greek

Īnachus, -ī *m first king of Argos*

inadsuētus *adj* unaccustomed

inadūstus *adj* unsinged

inaedificō, -āre, -āvī, -ātum *vt* to build on, erect; to wall up, block up

inaequābilis *adj* uneven

inaequālis *adj* uneven; unequal; capricious

inaequāliter *adv see* **inaequālis**

inaequātus *adj* unequal

inaequō, -āre *vt* to level up

inaestimābilis *adj* incalculable; invaluable; valueless

inaestuō, -āre *vi* to rage in

inamābilis *adj* hateful

inamārēscō, -ere *vi* to become bitter

inambitiōsus *adj* unambitious

inambulātiō, -ōnis *f* walking about

inambulō, -āre *vi* to walk up and down

inamoenus *adj* disagreeable

inanimus *adj* lifeless, inanimate

ināniō, -īre *vt* to make empty

inānis *adj* empty, void; poor, unsubstantial; useless, worthless, vain, idle ◆ *nt* (*PHILOS*) space; (*fig*) vanity

inānitās, -ātis *f* empty space; inanity

ināniter *adv* idly, vainly

inarātus *adj* fallow

inārdēscō, -dēscere, -sī *vi* to be kindled, flare up

inass- *etc see* **inads-**

inattenuātus *adj* undiminished

inaudāx, -ācis *adj* timorous

inaudiō, -īre *vt* to hear of, learn

inaudītus *adj* unheard of, unusual; without a hearing

inaugurātō *adv* after taking the auspices

inaugurō, -āre *vi* to take auspices ◆ *vt* to consecrate, inaugurate

inaurēs, -ium *fpl* earrings

inaurō, -āre, -āvi, -ātum *vt* to gild; (*fig*) to enrich

inauspicātō *adv* without taking the auspices

inauspicātus *adj* done without auspices

inausus *adj* unattempted

incaeduus *adj* uncut

incalēscō, -ēscere, -uī *vi* to grow hot; (*fig*) to warm, glow

incalfaciō, -ere *vt* to heat

incallidē *adv* unskilfully

incallidus *adj* stupid, simple

incandēscō, -ēscere, -uī *vi* to become hot; to turn white

incānēscō, -ēscere, -uī *vi* to grow grey

incantātus *adj* enchanted

incānus *adj* grey

incassum *adv* in vain

incastīgātus *adj* unrebuked

incautē *adv* negligently

incautus *adj* careless, heedless; unforeseen, unguarded

incēdō, -ēdere, -ēssī, -ēssum *vi* to walk, parade, march; (*MIL*) to advance; (*feelings*) to come upon

incelebrātus *adj* not made known

incēnātus *adj* supperless

incendiārius, -ī *and* **-iī** *m* incendiary

incendium, **-ī** and **-iī** nt fire, conflagration; heat; (fig) fire, vehemence, passion

incendō, **-ere**, **-ī**, **incēnsum** vt to set fire to, burn; to light, brighten; (fig) to inflame, rouse, incense

incēnsiō, **-ōnis** f burning

incēnsus¹ ppp of **incendō**

incēnsus² adj not registered

incēpī perf of **incipiō**

inceptiō, **-ōnis** f undertaking

inceptō, **-āre** vt to begin, attempt

inceptor, **-ōris** m originator

inceptum, **-ī** nt beginning, undertaking, attempt

inceptus ppp of **incipiō**

incērō, **-āre** vt to cover with wax

incertō adv not for certain

incertus adj uncertain, doubtful, unsteady ♦ nt uncertainty

incēssō, **-ere**, **-īvī** vt to attack; (fig) to assail

incēssus, **-ūs** m gait, pace, tramp; invasion; approach

incestē adv see **incestus¹**

incestō, **-āre** vt to pollute, dishonour

incestus¹ adj sinful; unchaste, incestuous ♦ nt incest

incestus², **-ūs** m incest

incho- etc see **incoh-**

incidō, **-idere**, **-idī**, **-āsum** vi to fall upon, fall into; to meet, fall in with, come across; to befall, occur, happen; **in mentem incidere** occur to one

incīdō, **-dere**, **-dī**, **-sum** vt to cut open; to cut up; to engrave, inscribe; to interrupt, cut short

incīle, **-is** nt ditch

incīlō, **-āre** vt to rebuke

incingō, **-gere**, **-xī**, **-ctum** vt to gird, wreathe; to surround

incinō, **-ere** vt to sing, play

incipiō, **-ipere**, **-ēpī**, **-eptum** vt, vi to begin

incipissō, **-ere** vt to begin

incīsē adv in short clauses

incīsim adv in short clauses

incīsiō, **-ōnis** f clause

incīsum, **-ī** nt clause

incīsus ppp of **incīdō**

incitāmentum, **-ī** nt incentive

incitātē adv impetuously

incitātiō, **-ōnis** f inciting, rapidity

incitātus ppp of **incitō** ♦ adj swift, rapid; **equō incitātō** at a gallop

incitō, **-āre**, **-āvī**, **-ātum** vt to urge on, rush; to rouse, encourage, excite; to inspire; to increase; **sē incitāre** rush; **currentem incitāre** spur a willing horse

incitus¹ adj swift

incitus² adj immovable; **ad incitās redigere**, **ad incita redigere** bring to a standstill

inclāmō, **-āre** vt, vi to call out, cry out to; to scold, abuse

inclārēscō, **-ēscere**, **-uī** vi to become famous

inclēmēns, **-entis** adj severe

inclēmenter adv harshly

inclēmentia, **-ae** f severity

inclīnātiō, **-ōnis** f leaning, slope; (fig) tendency, inclination, bias; (circumstances) change; (voice) modulation

inclīnātus adj inclined, prone; falling; (voice) deep

inclīnō, **-āre**, **-āvī**, **-ātum** vt to bend, turn; to turn back; (fig) to incline, direct, transfer; to change ♦ vi to bend, sink; (MIL) to give way; (fig) to change, deteriorate; to incline, tend, turn in favour

inclitus etc see **inclutus**

inclūdō, **-dere**, **-sī**, **-sum** vt to shut in, keep in, enclose; to obstruct, block; (fig) to include; (time) to close, end

inclūsiō, **-ōnis** f imprisonment

inclūsus ppp of **inclūdō**

inclutus adj famous, glorious

incoctus¹ ppp of **incoquō**

incoctus² adj uncooked, raw

incōgitābilis adj thoughtless

incōgitāns, **-antis** adj thoughtless

incōgitantia, **-ae** f thoughtlessness

incōgitō, **-āre** vt to contrive

incognitus adj unknown, unrecognized; (LAW) untried

incohātus adj unfinished

incohō, **-āre**, **-āvī**, **-ātum** vt to begin, start

incola, **-ae** m/f inhabitant, resident

incolō, **-ere**, **-uī** vt to live in, inhabit ♦ vi to live, reside

incolumis adj safe and sound, unharmed

incolumitās, **-ātis** f safety

incomitātus adj unaccompanied

incommendātus adj unprotected

incommodē adv inconveniently, unfortunately

incommoditās, **-ātis** f inconvenience, disadvantage

incommodō, **-āre** vi to be inconvenient, annoy

incommodum, **-ī** nt inconvenience, disadvantage, misfortune

incommodus adj inconvenient, troublesome

incommūtābilis adj unchangeable

incompertus adj unknown

incompositē adv see **incompositus**

incompositus adj in disorder, irregular

incōmptus adj undressed, inelegant

inconcēssus adj forbidden

inconciliō, **-āre** vt to win over (by guile); trick, inveigle, embarrass

inconcinnus adj inartistic, awkward

inconcussus adj unshaken, stable

inconditē adv confusedly

inconditus adj undisciplined, not organized; (language) artless

incōnsīderātē adv see **incōnsīderātus**

incōnsīderātus adj thoughtless, ill-advised

incōnsōlābilis adj incurable

incōnstāns, **-antis** adj fickle, inconsistent

incōnstanter adv inconsistently

incōnstantia, **-ae** f fickleness, inconsistency

incōnsultē adv indiscreetly

incōnsultū without consulting
incōnsultus *adj* indiscreet, ill-advised; unanswered; not consulted
incōnsūmptus *adj* unconsumed
incontāminātus *adj* untainted
incontentus *adj* untuned
incontinēns, -entis *adj* intemperate
incontinenter *adv* without self-control
incontinentia, -ae *f* lack of self-control
inconveniēns, -entis *adj* ill-matched
incoquō, -quere, -xī, -ctum *vt* to boil; to dye
incorrēctus *adj* unrevised
incorruptē *adv* justly
incorruptus *adj* unspoiled; uncorrupted, genuine
incrēbrēscō, incrēbēscō, -ēscere, -uī *vi* to increase, grow, spread
incrēdibilis *adj* incredible, extraordinary
incrēdibiliter *adv see* **incrēdibilis**
incrēdulus *adj* incredulous
incrēmentum, -ī *nt* growth, increase; addition; offspring
increpitō, -āre *vt* to rebuke; to challenge
increpō, -āre, -uī, -itum *vi* to make a noise, sound; *(news)* to be noised abroad ♦ *vt* to cause to make a noise; to exclaim against, rebuke
incrēscō, -scere, -vī *vi* to grow in, increase
incrētus *adj* sifted in
incruentātus *adj* unstained with blood
incruentus *adj* bloodless, without bloodshed
incrūstō, -āre *vt* to encrust
incubō, -āre, -uī, -itum *vi* to lie in or on; *(fig)* to brood over
incubuī *perf of* **incubō**; **incumbō**
inculcō, -āre, -āvī, -ātum *vt* to force in; to force upon, impress on
inculpātus *adj* blameless
incultē *adv* uncouthly
incultus¹ *adj* uncultivated; *(fig)* neglected, uneducated, rude
incultus², -ūs *m* neglect, squalor
incumbō, -mbere, -buī, -bitum *vi* to lean, recline on; to fall upon, throw oneself upon; to oppress, lie heavily upon; *(fig)* to devote attention to, take pains with; to incline
incūnābula, -ōrum *ntpl* swaddling clothes; *(fig)* cradle, infancy, birthplace, origin
incūrātus *adj* neglected
incūria, -ae *f* negligence
incūriōsē *adv* carelessly
incūriōsus *adj* careless, indifferent
incurrō, -rrere, -rrī *and* **-curri, -rsum** *vi* to run into, rush, attack; to invade; to meet with, get involved in; *(events)* to occur, coincide
incursiō, -ōnis *f* attack; invasion, raid; collision
incursō, -āre *vt, vi* to run into, assault; to frequently invade; *(fig)* to meet, strike
incursus, -ūs *m* assault, striking; *(mind)* impulse
incurvō, -āre *vt* to bend, crook
incurvus *adj* bent, crooked
incūs, -ūdis *f* anvil
incūsātiō, -ōnis *f* blaming

incūsō, -āre, -āvī, -ātum *vt* to find fault with, accuse
incussī *perf of* **incutiō**
incussus¹ *ppp of* **incutiō**
incussus², -ūs *m* shock
incustōdītus *adj* unguarded, unconcealed
incūsus *adj* forged
incutiō, -tere, -ssī, -ssum *vt* to strike, dash against; to throw; *(fig)* to strike into, inspire with
indāgātiō, -ōnis *f* search
indāgātor, -ōris *m* explorer
indāgātrīx, -rīcis *f* female explorer
indāgō¹, -āre *vt* to track down; *(fig)* to trace, investigate
indāgō², -inis *f (hunt)* drive, encirclement
indaudiō *etc see* **inaudiō**
inde *adv* from there, from that, from them; on that side; from then, ever since; after that, then
indēbitus *adj* not due
indēclīnātus *adj* constant
indecor, -is *adj* dishonourable, a disgrace
indecorē *adv* indecently
indecorō, -āre *vt* to disgrace
indecōrus *adj* unbecoming, unsightly
indēfēnsus *adj* undefended
indēfessus *adj* unwearied, tireless
indēflētus *adj* unwept
indēiectus *adj* undemolished
indēlēbilis *adj* imperishable
indēlībātus *adj* unimpaired
indemnātus *adj* unconvicted
indēplōrātus *adj* unlamented
indēprēnsus *adj* undetected
indeptus *ppa of* **indipīscor**
indēsertus *adj* unforsaken
indēstrictus *adj* unscathed
indētōnsus *adj* unshorn
indēvītātus *adj* unerring
index, -icis *m* forefinger; witness, informer; *(book, art)* title, inscription; *(stone)* touchstone; *(fig)* indication, pointer, sign
India, -iae *f* India
indicātiō, -ōnis *f* value
indīcente mē without my telling
indicium, -ī *and* **-iī** *nt* information, evidence; reward for information; indication, sign, proof; ~ **profitērī**, ~ **offerre** turn King's evidence; ~ **postulāre**, ~ **dare** ask, grant permission to give evidence
indicō, -āre, -āvī, -ātum *vt* to point out; to disclose, betray; to give information, give evidence; to put a price on
indīcō, -īcere, -īxī, -ictum *vt* to declare, proclaim, appoint
indictus¹ *ppp of* **indīcō**
indictus², -ī *adj* not said, unsung; **causā indictā** without a hearing
Indicus *adj see* **India**
indidem *adv* from the same place or thing
indidī *perf of* **indō**
indifferēns, -entis *adj* neither good nor bad
indigena, -ae *m* native ♦ *adj* native

indigēns, -entis *adj* needy

indigentia, -ae *f* need; craving

indigeō, -ēre, -uī *vi* (*with abl*) to need, want, require; to crave

indiges, -etis *m* national deity

indīgestus *adj* confused

indignābundus *adj* enraged

indignans, -antis *adj* indignant

indignātiō, -ōnis *f* indignation

indignē *adv* unworthily; indignantly

indignitās, -ātis *f* unworthiness, enormity; insulting treatment; indignation

indignor, -ārī, -ātus *vt* to be displeased with, be angry at

indignus *adj* unworthy, undeserving; shameful, severe; undeserved

indigus *adj* in want

indīligēns, -entis *adj* careless

indīligenter *adv see* **indīligēns**

indīligentia, -ae *f* carelessness

indipīscor, -ī, indeptus *vt* to obtain, get, reach

indīreptus *adj* unplundered

indiscrētus *adj* closely connected, indiscriminate, indistinguishable

indisertē *adv* without eloquence

indisertus *adj* not eloquent

indispositus *adj* disorderly

indissolūbilis *adj* imperishable

indistinctus *adj* confused, obscure

inditus *ppp of* **indō**

indīviduus *adj* indivisible; inseparable ♦ *nt* atom

indō, -ere, -idī, -itum *vt* to put in or on; to introduce; to impart, impose

indocilis *adj* difficult to teach, hard to learn; untaught

indoctē *adv* unskilfully

indoctus *adj* untrained, illiterate, ignorant

indolentia, -ae *f* freedom from pain

indolēs, -is *f* nature, character, talents

indolēscō, -ēscere, -uī *vi* to feel sorry

indomitus *adj* untamed, wild; ungovernable

indormiō, -īre *vi* to sleep on; to be careless

indōtātus *adj* with no dowry; unhonoured; (*fig*) unadorned

indubitō, -āre *vi* to begin to doubt

indubius *adj* undoubted

indūcō, -ūcere, -ūxī, -uctum *vt* to bring in, lead on; to introduce; to overlay, cover over; (*fig*) to move, persuade, seduce; (*book-keeping*) to enter; (*dress*) to put on; (*public show*) to exhibit; (*writing*) to erase; **animum indūcere, in animum indūcere** determine, imagine

inductiō, -ōnis *f* leading, bringing on; (*mind*) purpose, intention; (*LOGIC*) induction

inductus *ppp of* **indūcō**

indugredior *etc see* **ingredior**

induī *perf of* **induō**

indulgēns, -entis *pres p of* **indulgeō** ♦ *adj* indulgent, kind

indulgenter *adv* indulgently

indulgentia, -ae *f* indulgence, gentleness

indulgeō, -gēre, -si *vi* (*with dat*) to be kind to, indulge, give way to; to indulge in ♦ *vt* to concede; **sibi indulgēre** take liberties

induō, -uere, -uī, -ūtum *vt* (*dress*) to put on; (*fig*) to assume, entangle

indup- *etc see* **imp-**

indūrēscō, -ēscere, -uī *vi* to harden

indūrō, -āre *vt* to harden

Indus¹, -ī *m* Indian; Ethiopian; mahout

Indus² *adj see* **India**

industria, -ae *f* diligence; **dē industriā, ex industriā** on purpose

industriē *adv see* **industrius**

industrius *adj* diligent, painstaking

indūtiae, -ārum *fpl* truce, armistice

indūtus¹ *ppp of* **induō**

indūtus², -us *m* wearing

induviae, -ārum *fpl* clothes

indūxī *perf of* **indūcō**

inēbriō, -āre *vt* to intoxicate; (*fig*) to saturate

inedia, -ae *f* starvation

inēditus *adj* unpublished

inēlegāns, -antis *adj* tasteless

inēleganter *adv* without taste

inēluctābilis *adj* inescapable

inēmorior, -ī *vi* to die in

inemptus *adj* unpurchased

inēnārrābilis *adj* indescribable

inēnōdābilis *adj* inexplicable

ineō, -īre, -īvī and -iī, -itum *vi* to go in, come in; to begin ♦ *vt* to enter; to begin, enter upon, form, undertake; **cōnsilium inīre** form a plan; **grātiam inīre** win favour; **numerum inīre** enumerate; **ratiōnem inīre** calculate, consider, contrive; **suffrāgium inīre** vote; **viam inīre** find out a way

ineptē *adv see* **ineptus**

ineptia, -ae *f* stupidity; (*pl*) nonsense

ineptiō, -īre *vi* to play the fool

ineptus *adj* unsuitable; silly, tactless, absurd

inermis, inermus *adj* unarmed, defenceless; harmless

inerrāns, -antis *adj* fixed

inerrō, -āre *vi* to wander about in

iners, -tis *adj* unskilful; inactive, indolent, timid; insipid

inertia, -ae *f* lack of skill; idleness, laziness

inērudītus *adj* uneducated

inescō, -āre *vt* to entice, deceive

inēvectus *adj* mounted

inēvītābilis *adj* inescapable

inexcītus *adj* peaceful

inexcūsābilis *adj* with no excuse

inexercitātus *adj* untrained

inexhaustus *adj* unexhausted

inexōrābilis *adj* inexorable; (*things*) severe

inexperrēctus *adj* unawakened

inexpertus *adj* inexperienced; untried

inexpiābilis *adj* inexpiable; implacable

inexplēbilis *adj* insatiable

inexplētus *adj* incessant

inexplicābilis *adj* inexplicable; impracticable, unending

inexplōrātō *adv* without making a reconnaissance

inexplōrātus *adj* unreconnoitred

inexpugnābilis *adj* impregnable, safe

inexspectātus *adj* unexpected

inexstinctus *adj* unextinguished; insatiable, imperishable

inexsuperābilis *adj* insurmountable

inextrīcābilis *adj* inextricable

īnfabrē *adv* unskilfully

īnfabricātus *adj* unfashioned

īnfacētus *adj* not witty, crude

īnfācundus *adj* ineloquent

īnfāmia, -ae *f* disgrace, scandal

īnfāmis *adj* infamous, disreputable

īnfāmō, -āre, -āvī, -ātum *vt* to disgrace, bring into disrepute

īnfandus *adj* unspeakable, atrocious

īnfāns, -antis *adj* mute, speechless; young, infant; tongue-tied; childish ♦ *m/f* infant, child

īnfantia, -ae *f* inability to speak; infancy; lack of eloquence

īnfatuō, -āre *vt* to make a fool of

īnfaustus *adj* unlucky

īnfector, -ōris *m* dyer

īnfectus' *ppp of* **īnficiō**

īnfectus² *adj* undone, unfinished; **rē īnfectā** without achieving one's purpose

īnfēcunditās, -ātis *f* infertility

īnfēcundus *adj* unfruitful

īnfēlīcitās, -ātis *f* misfortune

īnfēlīciter *adv see* **īnfēlīx**

īnfēlīcō, -āre *vt* to make unhappy

īnfēlīx, -īcis *adj* unfruitful; unhappy, unlucky

īnfēnsē *adv* aggressively

īnfēnsō, -āre *vt* to make dangerous, make hostile

īnfēnsus *adj* hostile, dangerous

īnferciō, -īre *vt* to cram in

īnferiae, -ārum *fpl* offerings to the dead

īnferior, -ōris *compar of* **īnferus**

īnferius *compar of* **īnfrā**

īnfernē *adv* below

īnfernus *adj* beneath; of the lower world, infernal ♦ *mpl* the shades ♦ *ntpl* the lower world

īnferō, -re, intulī, illātum *vt* to carry in, bring to, put on; to move forward; (*fig*) to introduce, cause; (*book-keeping*) to enter; (*LOGIC*) to infer; **bellum īnferre** make war (on); **pedem īnferre** advance; **sē īnferre** repair, rush, strut about; **signa īnferre** attack, charge

īnferus (*compar* **īnferior,** *superl* **īnfimus**) *adj* lower, below ♦ *mpl* the dead, the lower world ♦ *compar* lower; later; inferior ♦ *superl* lowest, bottom of; meanest, humblest

īnfervēscō, -vēscere, -buī *vi* to boil

īnfestē *adv* aggressively

īnfestō, -āre *vt* to attack

īnfestus *adj* unsafe; dangerous, aggressive

īnficēt- *see* **īnfacēt-**

īnficiō, -icere, -ēcī, -ectum *vt* to dip, dye, discolour; to taint, infect; (*fig*) to instruct, corrupt, poison

īnfidēlis *adj* faithless

īnfidēlitās, -ātis *f* disloyalty

īnfidēliter *adv* treacherously

īnfidus *adj* unsafe, treacherous

īnfīgō, -gere, -xī, -xum *vt* to thrust, drive in; (*fig*) to impress, imprint

īnfimus *superl of* **īnferus**

īnfindō, -ere *vt* to cut into, plough

īnfinitās, -ātis *f* boundless extent, infinity

īnfīnītē *adv* without end

īnfīnītiō, -ōnis *f* infinity

īnfīnītus *adj* boundless, endless, infinite; indefinite

īnfirmātiō, -ōnis *f* invalidating, refuting

īnfirmē *adv* feebly

īnfirmitās, -ātis *f* weakness; infirmity, sickness

īnfirmō, -āre *vt* to weaken; to invalidate, refute

īnfirmus *adj* weak, indisposed; weak-minded; (*things*) trivial

īnfit *vi* (*defec*) begins

īnfitiālis *adj* negative

īnfitiās eō deny

īnfitiātiō, -ōnis *f* denial

īnfitiātor, -ōris *m* denier (of a debt)

īnfitior, -ārī, -ātus *vt* to deny, repudiate

īnfīxus *ppp of* **īnfīgō**

īnflammātiō, -ōnis *f* (*fig*) exciting

īnflammō, -āre, -āvī, -ātum *vt* to set on fire, light; (*fig*) to inflame, rouse

īnflātē *adv* pompously

īnflātiō, -ōnis *f* flatulence

īnflātus, -ūs *m* blow; inspiration ♦ *adj* blown up, swollen; (*fig*) puffed up, conceited; (*style*) turgid

īnflectō, -ctere, -xī, -xum *vt* to bend, curve; to change; (*voice*) to modulate; (*fig*) to affect, move

īnflētus *adj* unwept

īnflexiō, -ōnis *f* bending

īnflexus *ppp of* **īnflectō**

īnflīgō, -gere, -xī, -ctum *vt* to dash against, strike; to inflict

īnflō, -āre, -āvī, -ātum *vt* to blow, inflate; (*fig*) to inspire, puff up

īnfluō, -ere, -xī, -xum *vi* to flow in; (*fig*) to stream, pour in

īnfodiō, -odere, -ōdī, -ossum *vt* to dig in, bury

īnfōrmātiō, -ōnis *f* sketch, idea

īnfōrmis *adj* shapeless; hideous

īnfōrmō, -āre, -āvī, -ātum *vt* to shape, fashion; to sketch; to educate

īnfortūnātus *adj* unfortunate

īnfortūnium, -ī and -iī *nt* misfortune

īnfossus *ppp of* **īnfodiō**

īnfrā (*compar* **īnferius**) *adv* underneath, below ♦ *compar* lower down ♦ *prep* (*with acc*) below, beneath, under; later than

īnfrāctiō, -ōnis *f* weakening

īnfrāctus *ppp of* **īnfringō**

īnfragilis *adj* strong
īnfremō, -ere, -uī *vi* to growl
īnfrēnātus[1] *ppp of* **īnfrēnō**
īnfrēnātus[2] *adj* without a bridle
īnfrendō, -ere *vi* to gnash
īnfrēnis, -us *adj* unbridled
īnfrēnō, -āre, -āvī, -ātum *vt* to put a bridle on, harness; (*fig*) to curb
īnfrequēns, -entis *adj* not crowded, infrequent; badly attended
īnfrequentia, -ae *f* small number; emptiness
īnfringō, -ingere, -ēgī, -āctum *vt* to break, bruise; (*fig*) to weaken, break down, exhaust
īnfrōns, -ondis *adj* leafless
īnfūcātus *adj* showy
īnfula, -ae *f* woollen band, fillet, badge of honour
īnfumus *etc see* **īnfimus**
īnfundō, -undere, -ūdī, -ūsum *vt* to pour in or on; to serve; (*fig*) to spread
īnfuscō, -āre *vt* to darken; to spoil, tarnish
īnfūsus *ppp of* **īnfundō**
ingeminō, -āre *vt* to redouble ♦ *vi* to be redoubled
ingemīscō, -īscere, -uī *vi* to groan, sigh ♦ *vt* to sigh over
ingemō, -ere, -uī *vt*, *vi* to sigh for, mourn
ingenerō, -āre, -āvī, -ātum *vt* to engender, produce, create
ingeniātus *adj* with a natural talent
ingeniōsē *adv* cleverly
ingeniōsus *adj* talented, clever; (*things*) naturally suited
ingenitus *ppp of* **ingignō** ♦ *adj* inborn, natural
ingenium, -ī *and* **-iī** *nt* nature; (*disposition*) bent, character; (*intellect*) ability, talent, genius; (*person*) genius
ingēns, -entis *adj* huge, mighty, great
ingenuē *adv* liberally, frankly
ingenuitās, -ātis *f* noble birth, noble character
ingenuus *adj* native, innate; free-born; noble, frank; delicate
ingerō, -rere, -ssī, -stum *vt* to carry in; to heap on; to throw, hurl; (*fig*) to press, obtrude
ingignō, -ignere, -enuī, -enitum *vt* to engender, implant
inglōrius *adj* inglorious
ingluviēs, -ēī *f* maw; gluttony
ingrātē *adv* unwillingly; ungratefully
ingrātīīs, ingrātīs *adv* against one's will
ingrātus *adj* disagreeable, unwelcome; ungrateful, thankless
ingravēscō, -ere *vi* to grow heavy, become worse, increase
ingravō, -āre *vt* to weigh heavily on; to aggravate
ingredior, -dī, -ssus *vt*, *vi* to go in, enter; to walk, march; to enter upon, engage in; to commence, begin to speak
ingressiō, -ōnis *f* entrance; beginning; pace
ingressus, -ūs *m* entrance; (MIL) inroad; beginning; walking, gait
ingruō, -ere, -ī *vi* to fall upon, assail

inguen, -inis *nt* groin
ingurgitō, -āre *vt* to pour in; **sē ingurgitāre** gorge oneself; (*fig*) to be absorbed in
ingustātus *adj* untasted
inhabilis *adj* unwieldy, awkward; unfit
inhabitābilis *adj* uninhabitable
inhabitō, -āre *vt* to inhabit
inhaereō, -rēre, -sī, -sum *vi* to stick in, cling to; to adhere, be closely connected with; to be always in
inhaerēscō, -ere *vi* to take hold, cling fast
inhālō, -āre *vt* to breathe on
inhibeō, -ēre, -uī, -itum *vt* to check, restrain, use, practise; **inhibēre rēmīs/nāvem** back water
inhibitiō, -ōnis *f* backing water
inhiō, -āre *vi* to gape ♦ *vt* to gape at, covet
inhonestē *adv see* **inhonestus**
inhonestō, -āre *vt* to dishonour
inhonestus *adj* dishonourable, inglorious; ugly
inhonōrātus *adj* unhonoured; unrewarded
inhonōrus *adj* unhonoured; ugly
inhorreō, -ēre, -uī *vt* to stand erect, bristle
inhorrēscō, -ēscere, -uī *vi* to bristle up; to shiver, shudder, tremble
inhospitālis *adj* inhospitable
inhospitālitās, -ātis *f* inhospitality
inhospitus *adj* inhospitable
inhūmānē *adv* savagely; uncivilly
inhūmānitās, -ātis *f* barbarity; discourtesy, churlishness, meanness
inhūmāniter *adv* = **inhūmānē**
inhūmānus *adj* savage, brutal; ill-bred, uncivil, uncultured
inhumātus *adj* unburied
inibi *adv* there, therein; about to happen
iniciō, -icere, -iēcī, -iectum *vt* to throw into, put on; (*fig*) to inspire, cause; (*speech*) to hint, mention; **manum inicere** take possession
iniectus, -ūs *m* putting in, throwing over
inimīcē *adv* hostilely
inimīcitia, -ae *f* enmity
inimīcō, -āre *vt* to make enemies
inimīcus *adj* unfriendly, hostile; injurious ♦ *m/f* enemy; **inimīcissimus** greatest enemy
inīquē *adv* unequally, unjustly
inīquitās, -ātis *f* unevenness; difficulty; injustice, unfair demands
inīquus *adj* unequal, uneven; adverse, unfavourable, injurious; unfair, unjust; excessive; impatient, discontented ♦ *m* enemy
initiō, -āre *vt* to initiate
initium, -ī *and* **-iī** *nt* beginning; (*pl*) elements, first principles; holy rites, mysteries
initus[1] *ppp of* **ineō**
initus[2], **-ūs** *m* approach; beginning
iniūcundē *adv see* **iniūcundus**
iniūcunditās, -ātis *f* unpleasantness
iniūcundus *adj* unpleasant
iniungō, -ungere, -ūnxī, -ūnctum *vt* to join, attach; (*fig*) to impose, inflict
iniūrātus *adj* unsworn

iniūria, -ae f wrong, injury, injustice; insult, outrage; severity, revenge; unjust possession; **iniūriā** unjustly

iniūriōsē adv wrongfully

iniūriōsus adj unjust, wrongful; harmful

iniūrius adj wrong, unjust

iniūssū without orders (from)

iniūssus adj unbidden

iniūstē adv see **iniūstus**

iniūstitia, -ae f injustice, severity

iniūstus adj unjust, wrong; excessive, severe

inl- etc see **ill-**

inm- etc see **imm-**

innābilis adj that none may swim

innāscor, -scī, -tus vi to be born in, grow up in

innatō, -āre vt to swim in, float on; to swim, flow into

innātus ppa of **innāscor** ♦ adj innate, natural

innāvigābilis adj unnavigable

innectō, -ctere, -xuī, -xum vt to tie, fasten together, entwine; (fig) to connect; to contrive

innītor, -tī, -xus and **-sus** vi to rest, lean on; to depend

innō, -āre vi to swim in, float on, sail on

innocēns, -entis adj harmless; innocent; upright, unselfish

innocenter adv blamelessly

innocentia, -ae f innocence; integrity, unselfishness

innocuē adv innocently

innocuus adj harmless; innocent; unharmed

innōtēscō, -ēscere, -uī vi to become known

innovō, -āre vt to renew; **sē innovāre** return

innoxius adj harmless, safe; innocent; unharmed

innuba, -ae adj unmarried

innūbilus adj cloudless

innūbō, -bere, -psī vi to marry into

innumerābilis adj countless

innumerābilitās, -ātis f countless number

innumerābiliter adv innumerably

innumerālis adj numberless

innumerus adj countless

innuō, -ere, -ī vi to give a nod

innūpta, -ae adj unmarried

Īnō, -ūs f daughter of Cadmus

inoblītus adj unforgetful

inobrutus adj not overwhelmed

inobservābilis adj unnoticed

inobservātus adj unobserved

inoffēnsus adj without hindrance, uninterrupted

inofficiōsus adj irresponsible; disobliging

inolēns, -entis adj odourless

inolēscō, -scere, -vī vi to grow in

inōminātus adj inauspicious

inopia, -ae f want, scarcity, poverty, helplessness

inopīnāns, -antis adj unaware

inopīnātō adv unexpectedly

inopīnātus adj unexpected; off one's guard

inopīnus adj unexpected

inopiōsus adj in want

inops, -is adj destitute, poor, in need (of); helpless, weak; (speech) poor in ideas

inōrātus adj unpleaded

inōrdinātus adj disordered, irregular

inōrnātus adj unadorned, plain; uncelebrated

Īnōus adj see **Īnō**

inp- etc see **imp-**

inquam vt (defec) to say; (emphatic) I repeat, maintain

inquiēs, -ētis adj restless

inquiētō, -āre vt to unsettle, make difficult

inquiētus adj restless, unsettled

inquilīnus, -ī m inhabitant, tenant

inquinātē adv filthily

inquinātus adj filthy, impure

inquinō, -āre, -āvī, -ātum vt to defile, stain, contaminate

inquīrō, -rere, -sīvī, -sītum vt to search for, inquire into; (LAW) to collect evidence

inquīsītiō, -ōnis f searching, inquiry; (LAW) inquisition

inquīsītor, -ōris m searcher, spy; investigator

inquīsītus[1] ppp of **inquīrō**

inquīsītus[2] adj not investigated

inr- etc see **irr-**

īnsalūtātus adj ungreeted

īnsānābilis adj incurable

īnsānē adv madly

īnsānia, -ae f madness; folly, mania, poetic rapture

īnsāniō, -īre, -īvī, -ītum vi to be mad, rave; to rage; to be inspired

īnsānitās, -ātis f unhealthiness

īnsānum adv (slang) frightfully

īnsānus adj mad; frantic, furious; outrageous

īnsatiābilis adj insatiable; never cloying

īnsatiābiliter adv see **īnsatiābilis**

īnsatietās, -ātis f insatiateness

īnsaturābilis adj insatiable

īnsaturābiliter adv see **īnsaturābilis**

īnscendō, -endere, -endī, -ēnsum vt, vi to climb up, mount, embark

īnscēnsiō, -ōnis f going on board

īnscēnsus ppp of **īnscendō**

īnsciēns, -entis adj unaware; stupid

īnscienter adv ignorantly

īnscientia, -ae f ignorance, inexperience; neglect

īnscītē adv clumsily

īnscītia, -ae f ignorance, stupidity, inattention

īnscītus adj ignorant, stupid

īnscius adj unaware, ignorant

īnscrībō, -bere, -psī, -ptum vt to write on, inscribe; to ascribe, assign; (book) to entitle; (for sale) to advertise

īnscrīptiō, -ōnis f inscribing, title

īnscrīptus ppp of **īnscrībō**

īnsculpō, -ere, -sī, -tum vt to carve in, engrave on

īnsectātiō, -ōnis f hot pursuit; (words) abusing, persecution

īnsectātor, -ōris m persecutor

īnsector, -ārī, -ātus, īnsectō, -āre vt to pursue, attack, criticise

īnsectus adj notched

īnsēdābiliter adv incessantly

īnsēdī perf of **īnsīdō**

īnsenēscō, -ēscere, -uī vi to grow old in

īnsēnsilis adj imperceptible

īnsepultus adj unburied

īnsequēns, -entis pres p of **īnsequor** ♦ adj the following

īnsequor, -quī, -cūtus vt to follow, pursue hotly; to proceed; (time) to come after, come next; (fig) to attack, persecute

īnserō¹, -erere, -ēvī, -itum vt to graft; (fig) to implant

īnserō², -ere, -uī, -tum vt to let in, insert; to introduce, mingle, involve

īnsertō, -āre vt to put in

īnsertus ppp of **īnserō²**

īnserviō, -īre, -iī, -ītum vt, vi to be a slave (to); to be devoted, submissive (to)

īnsessus ppp of **īnsīdō**

īnsībilō, -āre vi to whistle in

īnsideō, -ēre vi to sit on or in; to remain fixed ♦ vt to hold, occupy

īnsidiae, -ārum fpl ambush; (fig) trap, trickery

īnsidiātor, -ōris nt soldier in ambush; (fig) waylayer, plotter

īnsidior, -ārī, -ātus vi to lie in ambush; (with dat) to lie in wait for, plot against

īnsidiōsē adv insidiously

īnsidiōsus adj artful, treacherous

īnsīdō, -īdere, -ēdī, -essum vi to settle on; (fig) to become fixed, rooted in ♦ vt to occupy

īnsigne, -is nt distinguishing mark, badge, decoration; (pl) insignia, honours; (speech) purple passages

īnsigniō, -īre vt to distinguish

īnsignis adj distinguished, conspicuous

īnsignītē adv remarkably

īnsilia, -um ntpl treadle (of a loom)

īnsiliō, -īre, -uī vi to jump into or onto

īnsimulātiō, -ōnis f accusation

īnsimulō, -āre, -āvī, -ātum vt to charge, accuse, allege (esp falsely)

īnsincērus adj adulterated

īnsinuātiō, -ōnis f ingratiating

īnsinuō, -āre, -āvī, -ātum vt to bring in, introduce stealthily ♦ vi to creep in, worm one's way in, penetrate; sē īnsinuāre ingratiate oneself; to make one's way into

īnsipiēns, -entis adj senseless, foolish

īnsipienter adv foolishly

īnsipientia, -ae f folly

īnsistō, -istere, -titī vi to stand on, step on; to stand firm, halt, pause; to tread on the heels, press on, pursue; to enter upon, apply oneself to, begin; to persist, continue

īnsitiō, -ōnis f grafting; grafting time

īnsitīvus adj grafted; (fig) spurious

īnsitor, -ōris m grafter

īnsitus ppp of **īnserō¹** ♦ adj innate; incorporated

īnsociābilis adj incompatible

īnsōlābiliter adv unconsolably

īnsolēns, -entis adj unusual, unaccustomed; excessive, extravagant, insolent

īnsolenter adv unusually; immoderately, insolently

īnsolentia, -ae f inexperience, novelty, strangeness; excess, insolence

īnsolēscō, -ere vi to become insolent, elated

īnsolidus adj soft

īnsolitus adj unaccustomed, unusual

īnsomnia, -ae f sleeplessness

īnsomnis adj sleepless

īnsomnium, -ī and -iī nt dream

īnsonō, -āre, -uī vi to resound, sound; to make a noise

īnsōns, -ontis adj innocent; harmless

īnsōpītus adj sleepless

īnspectō, -āre vt to look at

īnspectus ppp of **īnspiciō**

īnspērāns, -antis adj not expecting

īnspērātus adj unexpected; īnspērātō, ex īnspērātō unexpectedly

īnspergō, -gere, -sī, -sum vt to sprinkle on

īnspiciō, -icere, -exī, -ectum vt to look into; to examine, inspect; (MIL) to review; (mind) to consider, get to know

īnspīcō, -āre vt to sharpen

īnspīrō, -āre, -āvī, -ātum vt, vi to blow on, breathe into

īnspoliātus adj unpillaged

īnspūtō, -āre vt to spit on

īnstābilis adj unsteady, not firm; (fig) inconstant

īnstāns, -antis pres p of **īnstō** ♦ adj present; urgent, threatening

īnstanter adv vehemently

īnstantia, -ae f presence; vehemence

īnstar nt (indecl) likeness, appearance; as good as, worth

īnstaurātiō, -ōnis f renewal

īnstaurātīvus adj renewed

īnstaurō, -āre, -āvī, -ātum vt to renew, restore; to celebrate; to requite

īnsternō, -ernere, -rāvī, -rātum vt to spread over, cover

īnstīgātor, -ōris m instigator

īnstīgātrīx, -rīcis f female instigator

īnstīgō, -āre vt to goad, incite, instigate

īnstillō, -āre vt to drop on, instil

īnstimulātor, -ōris m instigator

īnstimulō, -āre vt to urge on

īnstinctor, -ōris m instigator

īnstinctus¹ adj incited, inspired

īnstinctus², -ūs m impulse, inspiration

īnstipulor, -ārī, -ātus vi to bargain for

īnstita, -ae f flounce (of a lady's tunic)

īnstitī perf of **īnsistō**

īnstitiō, -ōnis f stopping

īnstitor, -ōris m pedlar

īnstituō, -uere, -uī, -ūtum vt to set, implant; to set up, establish, build, appoint; to marshal, arrange, organize; to teach, educate; to undertake, resolve on

īnstitūtiō, -ōnis f custom; arrangement; education; (pl) principles of education

īnstitūtum, **-ī** *nt* way of life, tradition, law; stipulation, agreement; purpose; (*pl*) principles

īnstō, **-āre**, **-itī** *vi* to stand on or in; to be close, be hard on the heels of, pursue; (*events*) to approach, impend; (*fig*) to press on, work hard at; (*speech*) to insist, urge

īnstrātus *ppp of* **īnsternō**

īnstrēnuus *adj* languid, slow

īnstrepō, **-ere** *vi* to creak

īnstructiō, **-ōnis** *f* building; setting out

īnstructius *adv* in better style

īnstructor, **-ōris** *m* preparer

īnstructus¹ *ppp of* **īnstruō** ✦ *adj* provided, equipped; prepared, versed

īnstructus², **-ūs** *m* equipment

īnstrūmentum, **-ī** *nt* tool, instrument; equipment, furniture, stock; (*fig*) means, provision; dress, embellishment

īnstruō, **-ere**, **-xī**, **-ctum** *vt* to erect, build up; (MIL) to marshal, array; to equip, provide, prepare; (*fig*) to teach, train

īnsuāsum, **-ī** *nt* a dark colour

īnsuāvis *adj* disagreeable

īnsūdō, **-āre** *vi* to perspire on

īnsuēfactus *adj* accustomed

īnsuēscō, **-scere**, **-vī**, **-tum** *vt* to train, accustom ✦ *vi* to become accustomed

īnsuētus¹ *ppp of* **īnsuēscō**

īnsuētus² *adj* unaccustomed, unused; unusual

īnsula, **-ae** *f* island; block (of houses)

īnsulānus, **-ī** *m* islander

īnsulsē *adv see* **īnsulsus**

īnsulsitās, **-ātis** *f* lack of taste, absurdity

īnsulsus *adj* tasteless, absurd, dull

īnsultō, **-āre** *vt*, *vi* to jump on, leap in; (*fig*) to exult, taunt, insult

īnsultūra, **-ae** *f* jumping on

īnsum, **inesse**, **īnfuī** *vi* to be in or on; to belong to

īnsūmō, **-ere**, **-psī**, **-ptum** *vt* to spend, devote

īnsuō, **-uere**, **-uī**, **-ūtum** *vt* to sew in, sew up in

īnsuper *adv* above, on top; besides, over and above ✦ *prep* (*abl*) besides

īnsuperābilis *adj* unconquerable, impassable

īnsurgō, **-gere**, **-rēxī**, **-rēctum** *vi* to stand up, rise to; to rise, grow, swell; to rise against

īnsusurrō, **-āre** *vt*, *vi* to whisper

īnsūtus *ppp of* **īnsuō**

intābēscō, **-ēscere**, **-uī** *vi* to melt away, waste away

intāctilis *adj* intangible

intāctus *adj* untouched, intact; untried; undefiled, chaste

intāminātus *adj* unsullied

intēctus¹ *ppp of* **integō**

intēctus² *adj* uncovered, unclad; frank

integellus *adj* fairly whole or pure

integer, **-rī** *adj* whole, complete, unimpaired, intact; sound, fresh, new; (*mind*) unbiased, free; (*character*) virtuous, pure, upright; (*decision*) undecided, open; **in integrum restituere** restore to a former state; **ab**

integrō, **dē integrō**, **ex integrō** afresh; **integrum est mihi** I am at liberty (to)

integō, **-egere**, **-ēxī**, **-ēctum** *vt* to cover over; to protect

integrāscō, **-ere** *vi* to begin all over again

integrātiō, **-ōnis** *f* renewing

integrē *adv* entirely; honestly; correctly

integritās, **-ātis** *f* completeness, soundness; integrity, honesty; (*language*) correctness

integrō, **-āre** *vt* to renew, replenish, repair; (*mind*) to refresh

integumentum, **-ī** *nt* cover, covering, shelter

intellēctus¹ *ppp of* **intellegō**

intellēctus², **-ūs** *m* understanding; (*word*) meaning

intellegēns, **-entis** *pres p of* **intellegō** ✦ *adj* intelligent, a connoisseur

intellegenter *adv* intelligently

intellegentia, **-ae** *f* discernment, understanding; taste

intellegō, **-egere**, **-ēxī**, **-ēctum** *vt* to understand, perceive, realize; to be a connoisseur

intemerātus *adj* pure, undefiled

intemperāns, **-antis** *adj* immoderate, extravagant; incontinent

intemperanter *adv* extravagantly

intemperantia, **-ae** *f* excess, extravagance; arrogance

intemperātē *adv* dissolutely

intemperātus *adj* excessive

intemperiae, **-ārum** *fpl* inclemency; madness

intemperiēs, **-ēī** *f* inclemency, storm; (*fig*) fury

intempestīvē *adv* inopportunely

intempestīvus *adj* unseasonable, untimely

intempestus *adj* (*night*) the dead of; unhealthy

intemptātus *adj* untried

intendō, **-dere**, **-dī**, **-tum** *vt* to stretch out, strain, spread; (*weapon*) to aim; (*tent*) to pitch; (*attention*, *course*) to direct, turn; (*fact*) to increase, exaggerate; (*speech*) to maintain; (*trouble*) to threaten ✦ *vi* to make for, intend; **animō intendere** purpose; **sē intendere** exert oneself

intentē *adv* strictly

intentiō, **-ōnis** *f* straining, tension; (*mind*) exertion, attention; (LAW) accusation

intentō, **-āre** *vt* to stretch out, aim; (*fig*) to threaten with, attack

intentus¹ *ppp of* **intendō** ✦ *adj* taut; attentive, intent; strict; (*speech*) vigorous

intentus², **-ūs** *m* stretching out

intepeō, **-ēre** *vi* to be warm

intepēscō, **-ēscere**, **-uī** *vi* to be warmed

inter *prep* (*with acc*) between, among, during, in the course of; in spite of; ~ **haec** meanwhile; ~ **manūs** within reach; ~ **nōs** confidentially; ~ **sē** mutually, one another; ~ **sīcāriōs** in the murder court; ~ **viam** on the way

interāmenta, **-ōrum** *ntpl* ship's timbers

interaptus *adj* joined together

interārēscō, **-ere** *vi* to wither away

interbibō, **-ere** *vi* to drink up
interbītō, **-ere** *vi* to fall through
intercalāris *adj* intercalary
intercalārius *adj* intercalary
intercalō, **-āre** *vt* to intercalate
intercapēdō, **-inis** *f* interruption, respite
intercēdō, **-ēdere**, **-ēssī**, **-ēssum** *vi* to come between, intervene; to occur; to become surety; to interfere, obstruct; (*tribune*) to protest, veto
interceptiō, **-ōnis** *f* taking away
interceptor, **-ōris** *m* embezzler
interceptus *ppp of* **intercipiō**
intercēssiō, **-ōnis** *f* (LAW) becoming surety; (*tribune*) veto
intercēssor, **-ōris** *m* mediator, surety; interposer of the veto; obstructor
intercidō, **-ere**, **-ī** *vi* to fall short; to happen in the meantime; to get lost, become obsolete, be forgotten
intercīdō, **-dere**, **-dī**, **-sum** *vt* to cut through, sever
intercinō, **-ere** *vt* to sing between
intercipiō, **-ipere**, **-ēpi**, **-eptum** *vt* to intercept; to embezzle, steal; to cut off, obstruct
intercīsē *adv* piecemeal
intercīsus *ppp of* **intercīdō**
interclūdō, **-dere**, **-sī**, **-sum** *vt* to cut off, block, shut off, prevent; **animam interclūdere** suffocate
interclūsiō, **-ōnis** *f* stoppage
interclūsus *ppp of* **interclūdō**
intercolumnium, **-ī** *and* **-iī** *nt* space between two pillars
intercurrō, **-ere** *vi* to mingle with; to intercede; to hurry in the meantime
intercursō, **-āre** *vi* to crisscross; to attack between the lines
intercursus, **-ūs** *m* intervention
intercus, **-tis** *adj*: **aqua ~** dropsy
interdīcō, **-īcere**, **-īxī**, **-ictum** *vt*, *vi* to forbid, interdict; (*praetor*) to make a provisional order; **aquā et īgnī interdīcere** banish
interdictiō, **-ōnis** *f* prohibiting, banishment
interdictum, **-ī** *nt* prohibition; provisional order (*by a praetor*)
interdiū *adv* by day
interdō, **-are** *vt* to make at intervals; to distribute; **nōn interdōuim** I wouldn't care
interductus, **-ūs** *m* punctuation
interdum *adv* now and then, occasionally
intereā *adv* meanwhile, in the meantime; nevertheless
interēmī *perf of* **interimō**
interemptus *ppp of* **interimō**
intereō, **-īre**, **-iī**, **-itum** *vi* to be lost, perish, die
interequitō, **-āre** *vt*, *vi* to ride between
interesse *infin of* **intersum**
interfātiō, **-ōnis** *f* interruption
interfātur, **-ārī**, **-ātus** *vi* to interrupt
interfectiō, **-ōnis** *f* killing
interfector, **-ōris** *m* murderer
interfectrīx, **-rīcis** *f* murderess

interfectus *ppp of* **interficiō**
interficiō, **-icere**, **-ēcī**, **-ectum** *vt* to kill, destroy
interfīō, **-ierī** *vi* to pass away
interfluō, **-ere**, **-xī**, **-xum** *vt*, *vi* to flow between
interfodiō, **-ere** *vt* to pierce
interfugiō, **-ere** *vi* to flee among
interfuī *perf of* **intersum**
interfulgeō, **-ēre** *vi* to shine amongst
interfūsus *ppp* lying between; marked here and there
interiaceō, **-ēre** *vi* to lie between
interibi *adv* in the meantime
intericiō, **-icere**, **-iēcī**, **-iectum** *vt* to put amongst or between, interpose, mingle; **annō interiectō** after a year
interiectus, **-ūs** *m* coming in between; interval
interiī *perf of* **intereō**
interim *adv* meanwhile, in the meantime; sometimes; all the same
interimō, **-imere**, **-ēmī**, **-emptum** *vt* to abolish, destroy, kill
interior, **-ōris** *adj* inner, interior; nearer, on the near side; secret, private; more intimate, more profound
interitiō, **-ōnis** *f* ruin
interitus, **-ūs** *m* destruction, ruin, death
interiūnctus *adj* joined together
interius *adv* inwardly; too short
interlābor, **-ī** *vi* to glide between
interlegō, **-ere** *vt* to pick here and there
interlinō, **-inere**, **-ēvī**, **-itum** *vt* to smear in parts; to erase here and there
interloquor, **-quī**, **-cūtus** *vi* to interrupt
interlūceō, **-cēre**, **-xī** *vi* to shine through, be clearly seen
interlūnia, **-ōrum** *ntpl* new moon
interluō, **-ere** *vt* to wash, flow between
intermēnstruus *adj* of the new moon ♦ *nt* new moon
interminātus¹ *ppa* (*occ pass*) *of* **interminor** ♦ *adj* forbidden
interminātus² *adj* endless
interminor, **-ārī**, **-ātus** *vi* to threaten; to forbid threateningly
intermisceō, **-scēre**, **-scuī**, **-xtum** *vt* to mix, intermingle
intermissiō, **-ōnis** *f* interruption
intermittō, **-ittere**, **-īsī**, **-issum** *vt* to break off; to interrupt; to omit, neglect; to allow to elapse ♦ *vi* to cease, pause
intermixtus *ppp of* **intermisceō**
intermorior, **-ī**, **-tuus** *vi* to die suddenly
intermortuus *adj* falling unconscious
intermundia, **-ōrum** *ntpl* space between worlds
intermūrālis *adj* between two walls
internātus *adj* growing among
internecīnus *adj* murderous, of extermination
interneciō, **-ōnis** *f* massacre, extermination
internecīvus *adj* = **internecīnus**
internectō, **-ere** *vt* to enclasp

internōdia, -ōrum *ntpl* space between joints
internōscō, -scere, -vī, -tum *vt* to distinguish between
internūntia, -iae *f* messenger, mediator, go-between
internūntiō, -āre *vi* to exchange messages
internūntius, -ī *and* **-iī** *m* messenger, mediator, go-between
internus *adj* internal, civil ✦ *ntpl* domestic affairs
interō, -erere, -rīvī, -rītum *vt* to rub in; (*fig*) to concoct
interpellātiō, -ōnis *f* interruption
interpellātor, -ōris *m* interrupter
interpellō, -āre, -āvī, -ātum *vt* to interrupt; to disturb, obstruct
interpolis *adj* made up
interpolō, -āre *vt* to renovate, do up; (*writing*) to falsify
interpōnō, -ōnere, -osuī, -ositum *vt* to put between *or* amongst, insert; (*time*) to allow to elapse; (*person*) to introduce, admit; (*pretext etc*) to put forward, interpose; **fidem interpōnere** pledge one's word; **sē interpōnere** interfere, become involved
interpositiō, -ōnis *f* introduction
interpositus¹ *ppp of* **interpōnō**
interpositus², -ūs *m* obstruction
interpres, -tis *m/f* agent, negotiator; interpreter, explainer, translator
interpretātiō, -ōnis *f* interpretation, exposition, meaning
interpretātus *adj* translated
interpretor, -ārī, -ātus *vt* to interpret, explain, translate, understand
interprimō, -imere, -essī, -essum *vt* to squeeze
interpūnctiō, -ōnis *f* punctuation
interpūnctus *adj* well-divided ✦ *ntpl* punctuation
interquiēscō, -scere, -vī *vi* to rest awhile
interrēgnum, -ī *nt* regency, interregnum; interval between consuls
interrēx, -ēgis *m* regent; deputy consul
interritus *adj* undaunted, unafraid
interrogātiō, -ōnis *f* question; (*LAW*) cross-examination; (*LOGIC*) syllogism
interrogātiuncula, -ae *f* short argument
interrogō, -āre, -āvī, -ātum *vt* to ask, put a question; (*LAW*) to cross-examine, bring to trial
interrumpō, -umpere, -ūpī, -uptum *vt* to break up, sever; (*fig*) to break off, interrupt
interruptē *adv* interruptedly
intersaepiō, -īre, -sī, -tum *vt* to shut off, close
interscindō, -ndere, -dī, -ssum *vt* to cut off, break down
interserō¹, -erere, -ēvī, -itum *vt* to plant at intervals
interserō², -ere, -uī, -tum *vt* to interpose
intersitus *ppp of* **interserō¹**
interspīrātiō, -ōnis *f* pause for breath
interstinguō, -guere, -ctum *vt* to mark, spot; to extinguish

interstringō, -ere *vt* to strangle
intersum, -esse, -fuī *vi* to be between; to be amongst, be present at; (*time*) to elapse; **interest** there is a difference; it is of importance, it concerns, it matters; **meā interest** it is important for me
intertextus *adj* interwoven
intertrahō, -here, -xī *vt* to take away
intertrīmentum, -ī *nt* wastage; loss, damage
interturbātiō, -ōnis *f* confusion
intervallum, -ī *nt* space, distance, interval; (*time*) pause, interval, respite; difference
intervellō, -ere *vt* to pluck out; to tear apart
interveniō, -enīre, -ēnī, -entum *vi* to come on the scene, intervene; to interfere (with), interrupt; to happen, occur
interventor, -ōris *m* intruder
interventus, -ūs *m* appearance, intervention; occurrence
intervertō, -tere, -tī, -sum *vt* to embezzle; to rob, cheat
intervīsō, -ere, -ī, -um *vt* to have a look at, look and see; to visit occasionally
intervolitō, -āre *vi* to fly about, amongst
intervomō, -ere *vt* to throw up (amongst)
intervortō *vt see* **intervortō**
intestābilis *adj* infamous, wicked
intestātō *adv* without making a will
intestātus *adj* intestate; not convicted by witnesses
intestīnus *adj* internal ✦ *nt, ntpl* intestines, entrails
intexō, -ere, -uī, -tum *vt* to inweave, embroider, interlace
intibum, -ī *nt* endive
intimē *adv* most intimately, cordially
intimus *adj* innermost; deepest, secret; intimate ✦ *m* most intimate friend
intingō, intinguō, -gere, -xī, -ctum *vt* to dip in
intolerābilis *adj* unbearable; irresistible
intolerandus *adj* intolerable
intolerāns, -antis *adj* impatient; unbearable
intoleranter *adv* excessively
intolerantia, -ae *f* insolence
intonō, -āre, -uī, -ātum *vi* to thunder, thunder out
intōnsus *adj* unshorn, unshaven; long-haired, bearded; uncouth
intorqueō, -quēre, -sī, -tum *vt* to twist, wrap round; to hurl at
intortus *ppp of* **intorqueō** ✦ *adj* twisted, curled; confused
intrā *adv* inside, within ✦ *prep* (*with acc*) inside, within; (*time*) within, during; (*amount*) less than, within the limits of
intrābilis *adj* navigable
intractābilis *adj* formidable
intractātus *adj* not broken in; unattempted
intremīscō, -īscere, -uī *vi* to begin to shake
intremō, -ere *vi* to tremble
intrepidē *adv see* **intrepidus**
intrepidus *adj* calm, brave; undisturbed
intrīcō, -āre *vt* to entangle

intrīnsecus *adv* on the inside

intrītus *adj* not worn out

intrīvī *perf of* **interō**

intrō¹ *adv* inside, in

intrō², **-āre**, **-āvī**, **-ātum** *vt*, *vi* to go in, enter; to penetrate

intrōdūcō, **-ūcere**, **-ūxī**, **-uctum** *vt* to bring in, introduce, escort in; to institute

intrōductiō, **-ōnis** *f* bringing in

introeō, **-īre**, **-iī**, **-itum** *vi* to go into, enter

intrōferō, **-ferre**, **-tulī**, **-lātum** *vt* to carry inside

intrōgredior, **-dī**, **-ssus** *vi* to step inside

introitus, **-ūs** *m* entrance; beginning

intrōlātus *ppp of* **intrōferō**

intrōmittō, **-ittere**, **-īsī**, **-issum** *vt* to let in, admit

intrōrsum, **intrōrsus** *adv* inwards, inside

intrōrumpō, **-ere** *vi* to break into

intrōspectō, **-āre** *vt* to look in at

intrōspiciō, **-icere**, **-exī**, **-ectum** *vt* to look inside; to look at, examine

intubum *etc see* **intibum**

intueor, **-ērī**, **-itus** *vt* to look at, watch; to contemplate, consider; to admire

intumēscō, **-ēscere**, **-uī** *vi* to begin to swell, rise; to increase; to become angry

intumulātus *adj* unburied

intuor *etc see* **intueor**

inturbidus *adj* undisturbed; quiet

intus *adv* inside, within, in; from within

intūtus *adj* unsafe; unguarded

inula, **-ae** *f* elecampane

inultus *adj* unavenged; unpunished

inumbrō, **-āre** *vt* to shade; to cover

inundō, **-āre**, **-āvī**, **-ātum** *vt*, *vi* to overflow, flood

inunguō, **-unguere**, **-ūnxī**, **-ūnctum** *vt* to anoint

inurbānē *adv see* **inurbānus**

inurbānus *adj* rustic, unmannerly, unpolished

inurgeō, **-ēre** *vi* to push, butt

inūrō, **-rere**, **-ssī**, **-stum** *vt* to brand; (*fig*) to brand, inflict

inūsitātē *adv* strangely

inūsitātus *adj* unusual, extraordinary

inūstus *ppp of* **inūrō**

inūtilis *adj* useless; harmful

inūtilitās, **-ātis** *f* uselessness, harmfulness

inūtiliter *adv* unprofitably

invādō, **-dere**, **-sī**, **-sum** *vt*, *vi* to get in, make one's way in; to enter upon; to fall upon, attack, invade; to seize, take possession of

invalēscō, **-ēscere**, **-uī** *vi* to grow stronger

invalidus *adj* weak; inadequate

invāsī *perf of* **invādō**

invectiō, **-ōnis** *f* importing; invective

invectus *ppp of* **invehō**

invehō, **-here**, **-xī**, **-ctum** *vt* to carry in, bring in; **sē invehere** attack

invehor, **-hī**, **-ctus** *vi* to ride, drive, sail in or into, enter; to attack; to inveigh against

invēndibilis *adj* unsaleable

inveniō, **-enīre**, **-ēnī**, **-entum** *vt* to find, come upon; to find out, discover; to invent, contrive; to win, get

inventiō, **-ōnis** *f* invention; (RHET) compiling the subject-matter

inventor, **-ōris** *m* inventor, discoverer

inventrīx, **-rīcis** *f* inventor, discoverer

inventus *ppp of* **inveniō** ✦ *nt* invention, discovery

invenustus *adj* unattractive; unlucky in love

inverēcundus *adj* immodest, shameless

invergō, **-ere** *vt* to pour upon

inversiō, **-ōnis** *f* transposition; irony

inversus *ppp of* **invertō** ✦ *adj* upside down, inside out; perverted

invertō, **-tere**, **-tī**, **-sum** *vt* to turn over, invert; to change, pervert

invesperāscit, **-ere** *vi* it is dusk

investīgātiō, **-ōnis** *f* search

investīgātor, **-ōris** *m* investigator

investīgō, **-āre**, **-āvī**, **-ātum** *vt* to follow the trail of; (*fig*) to track down, find out

inveterāscō, **-scere**, **-vī** *vi* to grow old (in); to become established, fixed, inveterate; to grow obsolete

inveterātiō, **-ōnis** *f* chronic illness

inveterātus *adj* of long standing, inveterate

invexī *perf of* **invehō**

invicem *adv* in turns, alternately; mutually, each other

invictus *adj* unbeaten; unconquerable

invidentia, **-ae** *f* envy

invideō, **-idēre**, **-īdī**, **-īsum** *vt*, *vi* to cast an evil eye on; (*with dat*) to envy, grudge; to begrudge

invidia, **-ae** *f* envy, jealousy, ill-will; unpopularity

invidiōsē *adv* spitefully

invidiōsus *adj* envious, spiteful; enviable; invidious, hateful

invidus *adj* envious, jealous, hostile

invigilō, **-āre** *vi* to be awake over; to watch over, be intent on

inviolābilis *adj* invulnerable; inviolable

inviolātē *adv* inviolately

inviolātus *adj* unhurt; inviolable

invīsitātus *adj* unseen, unknown, strange

invīsō, **-ere**, **-ī**, **-um** *vt* to go and see, visit, have a look at; to inspect

invīsus¹ *adj* hateful, detested; hostile

invīsus² *adj* unseen

invītāmentum, **-ī** *nt* attraction, inducement

invītātiō, **-ōnis** *f* invitation; entertainment

invītātus, **-ūs** *m* invitation

invītē *adv* unwillingly

invītō, **-āre**, **-āvī**, **-ātum** *vt* to invite; to treat, entertain; to summon; to attract, induce

invītus *adj* against one's will, reluctant

invius *adj* trackless, impassable; inaccessible

invocātus¹ *ppp of* **invocō**

invocātus² *adj* unbidden, uninvited

invocō, **-āre**, **-āvī**, **-ātum** *vt* to call upon, invoke; to appeal to; to call

involātus, **-ūs** *m* flight

involitō, **-āre** *vi* to play upon

involō, **-āre** *vi* to fly at, pounce on, attack

involūcre, **-is** *nt* napkin

involūcrum, **-ī** *nt* covering, case

involūtus *ppp of* **involvō** ♦ *adj* complicated

involvō, **-vere**, **-vī**, **-ūtum** *vt* to roll on; to wrap up, envelop, entangle

involvolus, **-ī** *m* caterpillar

invulnerātus *adj* unwounded

iō *interj* (*joy*) hurrah!; (*pain*) oh!; (*calling*) ho there!

Iŏannēs, **-is** *m* John

iocātiō, **-ōnis** *f* joke

iocor, **-ārī**, **-ātus** *vt, vi* to joke, jest

iocōsē *adv* jestingly

iocōsus *adj* humorous, playful

ioculāris *adj* laughable, funny ♦ *ntpl* jokes

ioculārius *adj* ludicrous

ioculātor, **-ōris** *m* jester

ioculor, **-ārī** *vi* to joke

ioculus, **-ī** *m* a bit of fun

iocus, **-ī** *m*, **ioca**, **-ōrum** *ntpl* joke, jest; **extrā iocum** joking apart; **per iocum** for fun

Iōnes, **-um** *mpl* Ionians

Iōnia, **-iae** *f* Ionia, *coastal district of Asia Minor*

Iōnium, **-ī** *nt* Ionian Sea (*W. of Greece*)

Iōnius, **iōnicus** *adj* Ionian

iōta *nt indecl* Greek letter I

Iovis *gen of* **Iuppiter**

Īphianassa, **-ae** *f* Iphigenia

Īphigenīa, **-ae** *f daughter of Agamemnon (who sacrificed her at Aulis to Diana)*

ipse, **-a**, **-um**, **-īus** *pron* self, himself *etc*; in person, for one's own part, of one's own accord, by oneself; just, precisely, very; the master, the host

ipsissimus his very own self; **nunc ipsissimum** right now

īra, **-ae** *f* anger, rage; object of indignation

īrācundē *adv* angrily

īrācundia, **-ae** *f* irascibility, quick temper; rage, resentment

īrācundus *adj* irascible, choleric; resentful

īrāscor, **-ī** *vi* to be angry, get furious

īrātē *adv see* **īrātus**

īrātus *adj* angry, furious

īre *infin of* **eō**

Īris, **-dis** (*acc* **-m**) *f messenger of the gods*; the rainbow

īrōnīa, **-ae** *f* irony

irrāsus *adj* unshaven

irraucēscō, **-cēscere**, **-sī** *vi* to become hoarse

irredivīvus *adj* irreparable

irreligātus *adj* not tied

irreligiōsē *adv see* **irreligiōsus**

irreligiōsus *adj* impious

irremeābilis *adj* from which there is no returning

irreparābilis *adj* irretrievable

irrepertus *adj* undiscovered

irrēpō, **-ere**, **-sī** *vi* to steal into, insinuate oneself into

irreprehēnsus *adj* blameless

irrequiētus *adj* restless

irresectus *adj* unpared

irresolūtus *adj* not slackened

irrētiō, **-īre**, **-īī**, **-ītum** *vt* to ensnare, entangle

irretortus *adj* not turned back

irreverentia, **-ae** *f* disrespect

irrevocābilis *adj* irrevocable; implacable

irrevocātus *adj* without an encore

irrīdeō, **-dēre**, **-sī**, **-sum** *vi* to laugh, joke ♦ *vt* to laugh at, ridicule

irrīdiculē *adv* unwittily

irrīdiculum, **-ī** *nt* laughing stock

irrigātiō, **-ōnis** *f* irrigation

irrigō, **-āre**, **-āvī**, **-ātum** *vt* to water, irrigate; to inundate; (*fig*) to shed over, flood, refresh

irriguus *adj* well-watered, swampy; refreshing

irrīsiō, **-ōnis** *f* ridicule, mockery

irrīsor, **-ōris** *m* scoffer

irrīsus¹ *ppp of* **irrīdeō**

irrīsus², **-ūs** *m* derision

irrītābilis *adj* excitable

irrītāmen, **-inis** *nt* excitement, provocation

irrītātiō, **-ōnis** *f* incitement, irritation

irrītō, **-āre**, **-āvī**, **-ātum** *vt* to provoke, incite, enrage

irritus *adj* invalid, null and void; useless, vain, ineffective; (*person*) unsuccessful; **ad irritum cadere** come to nothing

irrogātiō, **-ōnis** *f* imposing

irrogō, **-āre** *vt* to propose (*a measure*) against; to impose

irrōrō, **-āre** *vt* to bedew

irrumpō, **-umpere**, **-ūpī**, **-uptum** *vt, vi* to rush in, break in; to intrude, invade

irruō, **-ere**, **-ī** *vi* to force a way in, rush in, attack; (*speech*) to make a blunder

irruptiō, **-ōnis** *f* invasion, raid

irruptus¹ *ppp of* **irrumpō**

irruptus² *adj* unbroken

is, **ea**, **id** *pron* he, she, it; this, that, the; such; **nōn is sum quī** I am not the man to; **id** (*with vi*) for this reason; **id quod** what; **id eō est** hitherto; for the purpose; besides; **in eō est** it has come to this; one is on the point of; it depends on this

Ismara, **-ōrum** *ntpl*, **Ismarus**, **-ī** *m* Mt Ismarus (in Thrace)

Ismarius *adj* Thracian

Īsocratēs, **-is** *m Athenian orator and teacher of rhetoric*

istāc *adv* that way

iste, **-a**, **-ud**, **-īus** *pron* that of yours; (*LAW*) your client, the plaintiff, the defendant; (*contemptuous*) the fellow; that, such

Isthmius *adj* Isthmian ♦ *ntpl* the Isthmian Games

Isthmus, **Isthmos**, **-ī** *m* Isthmus of Corinth

istic, **-aec**, **-uc** *and* **-oc** *pron* that of yours, that

istīc *adv* there; in this, on this occasion

istinc *adv* from there; of that

istīusmodī such, of that kind

istō, **istōc** *adv* to you, there, yonder

istōrsum *adv* in that direction

istūc *adv* (to) there, to that

ita *adv* thus, so; as follows; yes; accordingly; **itane** really?; **nōn ita** not so very; **ita ut** just as; **ita ... ut** so, to such an extent that; on condition that; only in so far as; **ita ... ut nōn** without; **ut ... ita** just as ... so; although ... nevertheless

Ītalī, -ōrum *mpl* Italians

Ītalia, -iae *f* Italy

Ītalicus, Ītalus *adj* Italian

itaque *conj* and so, therefore, accordingly

item *adv* likewise, also

iter, -ineris *nt* way, journey, march; a day's journey or march; route, road, passage; *(fig)* way, course; **~ mihi est** I have to go to; **~ dare** grant a right of way; **~ facere** to journey, march, travel; **ex itinere, in itinere** on the way, on the march; **māgnīs itineribus** by forced marches

iterātiō, -ōnis *f* repetition

iterō, -āre, -āvī, -ātum *vt* to repeat, renew; to plough again

iterum *adv* again, a second time; **~ atque ~** repeatedly

Ithaca, -ae, Ithacē, -ēs *f* island W. of Greece (home of Ulysses)

Ithacēnsis, Ithacus *adj* Ithacan

Ithacus, -ī *m* Ulysses

itidem *adv* in the same way, similarly

itiō, -ōnis *f* going

itō, -āre *vi* to go

itus, -ūs *m* going, movement, departure

iuba, -ae *f* mane; crest

Iuba, -ae *m* king of Numidia (supporter of Pompey)

iubar, -is *nt* brightness, light

iubātus *adj* crested

iubeō, -bēre, -ssī, -ssum *vt* to order, command, tell; *(greeting)* to bid; *(MED)* to prescribe; *(POL)* to decree, ratify, appoint

iūcundē *adv* agreeably

iūcunditās, -ātis *f* delight, enjoyment

iūcundus *adj* delightful, pleasing

Iūdaea, -ae *f* Judaea, Palestine

Iūdaeus¹, -ī *m* Jew

Iūdaeus², Iūdaicus *adj* Jewish

iūdex, -icis *m* judge; *(pl)* panel of jurors; *(fig)* critic

iūdicātiō, -ōnis *f* judicial inquiry; opinion

iūdicātum, -ī *nt* judgment, precedent

iūdicātus, -ūs *m* office of judge

iūdiciālis *adj* judicial, forensic

iūdiciārius *adj* judiciary

iūdicium, -ī and -iī *nt* trial; court of justice; sentence; judgment, opinion; discernment, taste, tact; **in ~ vocāre, iūdiciō arcessere** sue, summon

iūdicō, -āre, -āvī, -ātum *vt* to judge, examine, sentence, condemn; to form an opinion of, decide; to declare

iugālis *adj* yoked together; nuptial

iugātiō, -ōnis *f* training (of a vine)

iūgerum, -ī *nt* a land measure (240 × 120 feet)

iūgis *adj* perpetual, never-failing

iūglāns, -andis *f* walnut tree

iugō, -āre, -āvī, -ātum *vt* to couple, marry

iugōsus *adj* hilly

Iugulae, -ārum *fpl* Orion's Belt

iugulō, -āre, -āvī, -ātum *vt* to cut the throat of, kill, murder

iugulus, -ī *m*, **iugulum, -ī** *nt* throat

iugum, -ī *nt* (animals) yoke, collar; pair, team; *(MIL)* yoke of subjugation; *(mountain)* ridge, height, summit; *(ASTR)* Libra; *(loom)* crossbeam; *(ship)* thwart; *(fig)* yoke, bond

Iugurtha, -ae *m* king of Numidia (rebel against Rome)

Iugurthīnus *adj see* **Iugurtha**

Iūlēus *adj* of Iulus; of Caesar; of July

Iūlius¹, -ī *m* Roman family name (esp Caesar); *(month)* July

Iūlius², Iūliānus *adj see* **Iūlius¹**

Iūlus, -ī *m* son of Aeneas, Ascanius

iūmentum, -ī *nt* beast of burden, packhorse

iunceus *adj* of rushes; slender

iuncōsus *adj* rushy

iūnctiō, -ōnis *f* union

iūnctūra, -ae *f* joint; combination; relationship

iūnctus *ppp of* **iungō** ♦ *adj* connected, attached

iuncus, -ī *m* rush

iungō, -gere, iūnxī, iūnctum *vt* to join together, unite; to yoke, harness; to mate; *(river)* to span, bridge; *(fig)* to bring together, connect, associate; *(agreement)* to make; *(words)* to compound

iūnior, -ōris *adj* younger

iūniperus, -ī *f* juniper

Iūnius¹, -ī *m* Roman family name; *(month)* June

Iūnius² *adj* of June

Iūnō, -ōnis *f* Roman goddess, wife of Jupiter, patroness of women and marriage

Iūnōnālis *adj see* **Iūnō**

Iūnōnicola, -ae *m/f* worshipper of Juno

Iūnōnigena, -ae *m* Vulcan

Iūnōnius *adj* = **Iūnōnālis**

Iuppiter, Iovis *m* Jupiter (king of the gods, god of sky and weather); **~ Stygius** Pluto; **sub Iove** in the open air

iūrātor, -ōris *m* sworn judge

iūrecōnsultus *etc see* **iūriscōnsultus**

iūreiūrō, -āre *vi* to swear

iūreperītus *etc see* **iūrisperītus**

iūrgium, -ī and -iī *nt* quarrel, brawl

iūrgō, -āre *vi* to quarrel, squabble ♦ *vt* to scold

iūridiciālis *adj* of law, juridical

iūriscōnsultus, -ī *m* lawyer

iūrisdictiō, -ōnis *f* administration of justice; authority

iūrisperītus *adj* versed in the law

iūrō, -āre, -āvī, -ātum *vi, vt* to swear, take an oath; to conspire; **in nōmen ~** swear allegiance to; **in verba ~** take a prescribed form of oath; **iūrātus** having sworn, under oath

iūs¹, iūris *nt* broth, soup

iūs², iūris *nt* law, right, justice; law court; jurisdiction, authority; **iūs gentium** international law; **iūs pūblicum** constitutional law; **summum iūs** the strict letter of the law; **iūs dīcere** administer justice; **suī iūris** independent; **iūre** rightly, justly

iūsiūrandum, iūrisiūrandī *nt* oath

iussī *perf of* **iubeō**

iussū *abl m* by order

iussus *ppp of* **iubeō** ✦ *nt* order, command, prescription

iūstē *adv* duly, rightly

iūstificus *adj* just dealing

iūstitia, -ae *f* justice, uprightness, fairness

iūstitium, -ī *and* **-iī** *nt* cessation of legal business

iūstus *adj* just, fair; lawful, right; regular, proper ✦ *nt* right ✦ *ntpl* rights; formalities, obsequies

iūtus *ppp of* **iuvō**

iuvenālis *adj* youthful ✦ *ntpl* youthful games

Iuvenālis, -is *m* Juvenal (*Roman satirist*)

iuvenāliter *adv* vigorously, impetuously

iuvenca, -ae *f* heifer; girl

iuvencus, -ī *m* bullock; young man ✦ *adj* young

iuvenēscō, -ēscere, -uī *vi* to grow up; to grow young again

iuvenīlis *adj* youthful

iuvenīliter *adv see* **iuvenīlis**

iuvenis *adj* young ✦ *m/f* young man or woman (*20-45 years*), man, warrior

iuvenor, -ārī *vi* to behave indiscreetly

iuventa, -ae *f* youth

iuventās, -ātis *f* youth

iuventūs, -ūtis *f* youth, manhood; men, soldiers

iuvō, -āre, iūvī, iūtum *vt* to help, be of use to; to please, delight; **iuvat mē** I am glad

iuxtā *adv* near by, close; alike, just the same ✦ *prep* (*with acc*) close to, hard by; next to; very like, next door to; **~ ac, ~ cum, ~ quam** just the same as

iuxtim *adv* near; equally

īvī *perf of* **eō**

Ixīōn, -onis *m* Lapith king (*bound to a revolving wheel in Tartarus*)

Ixīoneus *adj see* **Ixīōn**

Ixīonidae, -ārum *mpl* Centaurs

Ixīonidēs, -ae *m* Pirithous

J- see **I-**

Kk

Kalendae, -ārum Kalends, first day (*of each month*)

Karthāgō *see* **Carthāgō**

LI

labāscō, -ere vi to totter, waver
lābēcula, -ae f aspersion
labefaciō, -facere, -fēcī, -factum (pass **-fiō**) vt to shake; (fig) to weaken, ruin
labefactō, -āre, -āvī, -ātum vt to shake; (fig) to weaken, destroy
labellum, -ī nt lip
lābellum, -ī nt small basin
Labērius, -ī m Roman family name (esp a writer of mimes)
lābēs¹, -is f sinking, fall; ruin, destruction
lābēs², -is f spot, blemish; disgrace, stigma; (person) blot
labia, -iae f lip
Labiēnus, -ī m Roman surname (esp Caesar's officer who went over to Pompey)
labiōsus adj large-lipped
labium, -ī and -iī nt lip
labō, -āre vi to totter, be unsteady, give way; to waver, hesitate, collapse
lābor, -bī, -psus vi to slide, glide; to sink, fall; to slip away, pass away; (fig) to fade, decline, perish; to be disappointed, make a mistake
labor, labōs, -ōris m effort, exertion, labour; work, task; hardship, suffering, distress; (ASTR) eclipse
labōrifer, -ī adj sore afflicted
labōriōsē adv laboriously, with difficulty
labōriōsus adj troublesome, difficult; industrious
labōrō, -āre, -āvī, -ātum vi to work, toil, take pains; to suffer, be troubled (with), be in distress; to be anxious, worried ♦ vt to work out, make, produce
labōs etc see **labor**
labrum, -i nt lip; edge, rim; **primīs labrīs gustāre** acquire a smattering of
lābrum, -ī nt tub, vat; bath
lābrusca, -ae f wild vine
lābruscum, -ī nt wild grape
labyrinthēus adj labyrinthine
labyrinthus, -ī m labyrinth, maze (esp that of Cnossos in Crete)
lac, lactis nt milk
Lacaena, -ae f Spartan woman ♦ adj Spartan
Lacedaemōn, Lacedaemō, -onis (acc **-ona**) f Sparta
Lacedaemonius adj Spartan
lacer, -ī adj torn, mangled, lacerated; tearing
lacerātiō, -ōnis f tearing
lacerna, -ae f cloak (worn in cold weather)

lacernātus adj cloaked
lacerō, -āre, -āvī, -ātum vt to tear, lacerate, mangle; (ship) to wreck; (speech) to slander, abuse; (feeling) to torture, distress; (goods, time) to waste, destroy
lacerta, -ae f lizard; a seafish
lacertōsus adj brawny
lacertus¹, -ī m upper arm, arm; (pl) brawn, muscle
lacertus², -ī m lizard; a sea fish
lacessō, -ere, -īvī and -iī, -ītum vt to strike, provoke, challenge; (fig) to incite, exasperate
Lachesis, -is f one of the Fates
lacinia, -ae f flap, corner (of dress)
Lacīnium, -ī nt promontory in S. Italy, with a temple of Juno
Lacīnius adj see **Lacīnium**
Lacō, Lacōn, -ōnis m Spartan; Spartan dog
Lacōnicus adj Spartan ♦ nt sweating bath
lacrima, -ae f tear; (plant) gumdrop
lacrimābilis adj mournful
lacrimābundus adj bursting into tears
lacrimō, -āre, -āvī, -ātum vt, vi to weep, weep for
lacrimōsus adj tearful; lamentable
lacrimula, -ae f tear, crocodile tear
lacrum- etc see **lacrim-**
lactāns, -antis adj giving milk; sucking
lactātiō, -ōnis f allurement
lactēns, -entis adj sucking; milky, juicy
lacteolus adj milk-white
lactēs, -ium fpl guts, small intestines
lactēscō, -ere vi to turn to milk
lacteus adj milky, milk-white
lactō, -āre vt to dupe, wheedle
lactūca, -ae f lettuce
lacūna, -ae f hole, pit; pool, pond; (fig) deficiency
lacūnar, -āris nt panelled ceiling
lacūnō, -āre vt to panel
lacūnōsus adj sunken
lacus, -ūs m vat, tank; lake; reservoir, cistern
laedō, -dere, -sī, -sum vt to hurt, strike, wound; (fig) to offend, annoy, break
Laelius, -ī m Roman family name (esp the friend of Scipio)
laena, -ae f a lined cloak
Lāërtēs, -ae m father of Ulysses
Lāërtiadēs m Ulysses
Lāërtius adj see **Lāërtēs**
laesī perf of **laedō**

laesiō, -ōnis *f* attack
Laestrygonēs, -um *mpl fabulous cannibals of Campania, founders of Formiae*
Laestrygonius *adj see* **Laestrygonēs**
laesus *ppp of* **laedō**
laetābilis *adj* joyful
laetē *adv* gladly
laetificō, -āre *vt* to gladden
laetificus *adj* glad, joyful
laetitia, -ae *f* joy, delight, exuberance
laetor, -ārī, -ātus *vi* to rejoice, be glad
laetus *adj* glad, cheerful; delighting (in); pleasing, welcome; (*growth*) fertile, rich; (*style*) exuberant
laevē *adv* awkwardly
laevus *adj* left; stupid; ill-omened, unfortunate; (*AUG*) lucky, favourable ♦ *f* left hand
laganum, -ī *nt a kind of oilcake*
lagēos, -ī *f* a Greek vine
lagoena, -ae *f* flagon
lagōis, -idis *f a kind of grouse*
lagōna, -ae *f* flagon
Lāiadēs, -ae *m* Oedipus
Lāius, -ī *m* father of Oedipus
lallō, -āre *vi* to sing a lullaby
lāma, -ae *f* bog
lamberō, -āre *vt* to tear to pieces
lambō, -ere, -ī *vt* to lick, touch; (*river*) to wash
lāmenta, -ōrum *ntpl* lamentation
lāmentābilis *adj* mournful, sorrowful
lāmentārius *adj* sorrowful
lāmentātiō, -ōnis *f* weeping, lamentation
lāmentor, -ārī, -ātus *vi* to weep, lament ♦ *vt* to weep for, bewail
lamia, -ae *f* witch
lāmina, lammina, lāmna, -ae *f* plate, leaf (*of metal, wood*); blade; coin
lampas, -dis *f* torch; brightness, day
Lamus, -ī *m* Laestrygonian king
lāna, -ae *f* wool
lānārius, -ī *and* **-iī** *m* wool-worker
lānātus *adj* woolly
lancea, -ae *f* spear, lance
lancinō, -āre *vt* to tear up; to squander
lāneus *adj* woollen
languefaciō, -ere *vt* to make weary
langueō, -ēre *vi* to be weary, be weak, droop; to be idle, dull
languēscō, -ēscere, -uī *vi* to grow faint, droop
languidē *adv see* **languidus**
languidulus *adj* languid
languidus *adj* faint, languid, sluggish; listless, feeble
languor, -ōris *m* faintness, fatigue, weakness; dullness, apathy
laniātus, -ūs *m* mangling; (*mind*) anguish
laniēna, -ae *f* butcher's shop
lānificium, -ī *and* **-iī** *nt* wool-working
lānificus *adj* wool-working
lāniger, -ī *adj* fleecy ♦ *m/f* ram, sheep
laniō, -āre, -āvī, -ātum *vt* to tear to pieces, mangle
lanista, -ae *m* trainer of gladiators, fencing master; (*fig*) agitator

lānitium, -ī *and* **-iī** *nt* woolgrowing
lanius, -ī *and* **-iī** *m* butcher
lanterna, -ae *f* lamp
lanternārius, -ī *and* **-iī** *m* guide
lānūgō, -inis *f* down, woolliness
Lānuvīnus *adj see* **Lānuvium**
Lānuvium, -ī *nt Latin town on the Appian Way*
lānx, lancis *f* dish, platter; (*balance*) scale
Lāomedōn, -ontis *m* king of Troy (*father of Priam*)
Lāomedontēus *adj,* **Lāomedontiadēs, -ae** *m* son of Lāomedōn; (*pl*) Trojans
Lāomedontius *adj* Trojan
lapathum, -ī *nt,* **lapathus, -ī** *f* sorrel
lapicīda, -ae *m* stonecutter
lapicīdīnae, -ārum *fpl* quarries
lapidārius *adj* stone- (*in cpds*)
lapidātiō, -ōnis *f* throwing of stones
lapidātor, -ōris *m* stone thrower
lapideus *adj* of stones, stone- (*in cpds*)
lapidō, -āre *vt* to stone ♦ *vi* to rain stones
lapidōsus *adj* stony; hard as stone
lapillus, -ī *m* stone, pebble; precious stone, mosaic piece
lapis, -dis *m* stone; milestone, boundary stone, tombstone; precious stone; marble; auctioneer's stand; (*abuse*) blockhead; **bis ad eundem lapidem (offendere)** make the same mistake twice; **Juppiter ~** the Jupiter stone
Lapithae, -ārum *and* **-um** *mpl* Lapiths, *mythical people of Thessaly*
Lapithaeus, -ēius *adj see* **Lapithae**
lappa, -ae *f* goosegrass
lāpsiō, -ōnis *f* tendency
lāpsō, -āre *vi* to slip, stumble
lāpsus¹ *ppa of* **lābor**
lāpsus², -ūs *m* fall, slide, course, flight; error, failure
laqueāria, -ium *ntpl* panelled ceiling
laqueātus *adj* panelled, with a panelled ceiling
laqueus, -ī *m* noose, snare, halter; (*fig*) trap
Lār, Laris *m* tutelary deity, household god; hearth, home
lārdum *etc see* **lāridum**
largē *adv* plentifully, generously, very much
largificus *adj* bountiful
largifluus *adj* copious
largiloquus *adj* talkative
largior, -īrī, -ītus *vt* to give freely, lavish; to bestow, confer ♦ *vi* to give largesse
largitās, -ātis *f* liberality, abundance
largiter *adv* = **largē**
largītiō, -ōnis *f* giving freely, distributing; bribery
largītor, -ōris *m* liberal giver, dispenser; spendthrift; briber
largus *adj* copious, ample; liberal, bountiful
lāridum, -ī *nt* bacon fat
Lārissa, Lārīsa, -ae *f town in Thessaly*
Lārissaeus, -ēnsis *adj see* **Lārissa**
Lārius, -ī *m* lake Como
larix, -cis *f* larch
larva, -ae *f* ghost; mask
larvātus *adj* bewitched
lasanum, -ī *nt* pot

lasārpīcifer, -ī *adj* producing asafoetida
lascīvia, -ae *f* playfulness; impudence, lewdness
lascīviō, -īre *vi* to frolic, frisk; to run wild, be irresponsible
lascīvus *adj* playful, frisky; impudent, lustful
laserpīcium, -ī *and* **-iī** *nt* silphium
lassitūdō, -inis *f* fatigue, heaviness
lassō, -āre *vt* to tire, fatigue
lassulus *adj* rather weary
lassus *adj* tired, exhausted
lātē *adv* widely, extensively; **longē lātēque** far and wide, everywhere
latebra, -ae *f* hiding place, retreat; *(fig)* loophole, pretext
latebricola, -ae *adj* low-living
latebrōsē *adv* in hiding
latebrōsus *adj* secret, full of coverts; porous
latēns, -entis *pres p of* **lateō ♦** *adj* hidden, secret
latenter *adv* in secret
lateō, -ēre, -uī *vi* to lie hid, lurk, skulk; to be in safety, live a retired life; to be unknown, escape notice
later, -is *m* brick, tile; **laterem lavāre** waste one's time
laterāmen, -inis *nt* earthenware
laterculus, -ī *m* small brick, tile; *kind of cake*
latericius *adj* of bricks ♦ *nt* brickwork
lāterna *etc see* **lanterna**
latēscō, -ere *vi* to hide oneself
latex, -icis *m* water; *any other liquid*
Latiar, -iaris *nt festival of Jupiter Latiaris*
Latiaris *adj* Latin
latibulum, -ī *nt* hiding place, den, lair
lāticlāvius *adj* with a broad purple stripe ♦ *m* senator, patrician
lātifundium, -ī *and* **-iī** *nt* large estate
Latīnē *adv* in Latin, into Latin; **~ loquī** speak Latin, speak plainly, speak correctly; **~ reddere** translate into Latin
Latīnitās, -ātis *f* good Latin, Latinity; Latin rights
Latīnus *adj* Latin ♦ *m legendary king of the Laurentians*
lātiō, -ōnis *f* bringing; proposing
latitō, -āre *vi* to hide away, lurk, keep out of the way
lātitūdō, -inis *f* breadth, width; size; broad pronunciation
Latium, -ī *nt district of Italy including Rome; Latin rights*
Latius = Latiaris; Latīnus
Lātōis¹, -idis *f* Diana
Lātōis², -ius *adj see* **Lātōis¹**
lātom- *etc see* **lautum-**
Lātōna, -ae *f mother of Apollo and Diana*
Lātōnigenae, -ārum *pl* Apollo and Diana
Lātōnius *adj, f* Diana
lātor, -ōris *m* proposer
Lātōus *adj of* Latona ♦ *m* Apollo
lātrātor, -ōris *m* barker
lātrātus, -ūs *m* barking
lātrō, -āre *vi* to bark; to rant, roar ♦ *vt* to bark at; to clamour for

latrō, -ōnis *m* mercenary soldier; bandit, brigand; *(chess)* man
latrōcinium, -ī *and* **-iī** *nt* highway robbery, piracy
latrōcinor, -ārī, -ātus *vi* to serve as a mercenary; to be a brigand or pirate
latrunculus, -ī *m* brigand; *(chess)* man
lātumiae *etc see* **lautumiae**
lātus¹ *ppp of* **ferō**
lātus² *adj* broad, wide; extensive; *(pronunciation)* broad; *(style)* diffuse
latus, -eris *nt* side, flank; lungs; body; **~ dare** expose oneself; **~ tegere** walk beside; **lateris dolor** pleurisy; **ab latere** on the flank
latusculum, -ī *nt* little side
laudābilis *adj* praiseworthy
laudābiliter *adv* laudably
laudātiō, -ōnis *f* commendation, eulogy; panegyric, testimonial
laudātor, -ōris *m*, **laudātrīx, -rīcis** *f* praiser, eulogizer; speaker of a funeral oration
laudātus *adj* excellent
laudō, -āre, -āvī, -ātum *vt* to praise, commend, approve; to pronounce a funeral oration over; to quote, name
laurea, -ae *f* bay tree; crown of bay; triumph
laureātus *adj* crowned with bay; *(despatches)* victorious
Laurentēs, -um *mpl* Laurentians *(people of ancient Latium)*
Laurentius *adj see* **Laurentēs**
laureola, -ae *f* triumph
laureus *adj* of bay
lauricomus *adj* bay-covered
lauriger, -ī *adj* crowned with bay
laurus, -ī *f* bay tree; bay crown; victory, triumph
laus, laudis *f* praise, approval; glory, fame; praiseworthy act, merit, worth
lautē *adv* elegantly, splendidly; excellently
lautia, -ōrum *ntpl* State banquet
lautitia, -ae *f* luxury
lautumiae, -ārum *fpl* stone quarry; prison
lautus *ppp of* **lavō ♦** *adj* neat, elegant, sumptuous; fine, grand, distinguished
lavābrum, -ī *nt* bath
lavātiō, -ōnis *f* washing, bath; bathing gear
Lāvīnium, -ī *nt town of ancient Latium*
Lāvīnius *adj see* **Lāvīnium**
lavō, -āre, lāvī, lautum, lavātum, lōtum *vt* to wash, bathe; to wet, soak, wash away
laxāmentum, -ī *nt* respite, relaxation
laxē *adv* loosely, freely
laxitās, -ātis *f* roominess
laxō, -āre, -āvī, -ātum *vt* to extend, open out; to undo; to slacken; *(fig)* to release, relieve; to relax, abate ♦ *vi (price)* to fall off
laxus *adj* wide, loose, roomy; *(time)* deferred; *(fig)* free, easy
lea, -ae *f* lioness
leaena, -ae *f* lioness
Lēander, -rī *m* Hero's lover *(who swam the Hellespont)*
lebēs, -ētis *m* basin, pan, cauldron
lectīca, -ae *f* litter, sedan chair
lectīcārius, -ī *and* **-iī** *m* litter-bearer
lectīcula, -ae *f* small litter; bier

lēctiō, -ōnis f selecting; reading, calling the roll

lectisterniātor, -ōris m arranger of couches

lectisternium, -ī and **-iī** nt religious feast

lēctitō, -āre vt to read frequently

lēctiuncula, -ae f light reading

lēctor, -ōris m reader

lectulus, -ī m couch, bed

lectus, -ī m couch, bed; bier

lēctus ppp of **legō ♦** adj picked; choice, excellent

Lēda, -ae, Lēdē, -ēs f mother of Castor, Pollux, Helen and Clytemnestra

Lēdaeus adj see **Lēda**

lēgātiō, -ōnis f mission, embassy; members of a mission; (MIL) staff appointment, command of a legion; **lībera** ~ free commission to visit provinces; **vōtīva** ~ free commission for paying a vow in a province

lēgātor, -ōris m testator

lēgātum, -ī nt legacy, bequest

lēgātus, -ī m delegate, ambassador; deputy, lieutenant; commander (of a legion)

lēgifer, -ī adj law-giving

legiō, -ōnis f legion (up to 6000 men); (pl) troops, army

legiōnārius adj legionary

lēgirupa, -ae, lēgirupiō, -iōnis m lawbreaker

lēgitimē adv lawfully, properly

lēgitimus adj lawful, legal; right, proper

legiuncula, -ae f small legion

legō, -ere, lēgī, lēctum vt to gather, pick; to choose, select; (sail) to furl; (places) to traverse, pass, coast along; (view) to scan; (writing) to read, recite; **senātum legere** call the roll of the senate

lēgō, -āre, -āvī, -ātum vt to send, charge, commission; to appoint as deputy or lieutenant; (will) to leave, bequeath

lēgulēius, -ī and **-iī** m pettifogging lawyer

legūmen, -inis nt pulse, bean

lembus, -ī m pinnace, cutter

Lemnias f Lemnian woman

Lemnicola, -ae m Vulcan

lēmniscātus adj beribboned

lēmniscus, -ī m ribbon (hanging from a victor's crown)

Lēmnius adj see **Lēmnos**

Lēmnos, Lēmnus, -ī f Aegean island, abode of Vulcan

Lemurēs, -um mpl ghosts

lēna, -ae f procuress; seductress

Lēnaeus adj Bacchic ♦ m Bacchus

lēnīmen, -inis nt solace, comfort

lēnīmentum, -ī nt sop

lēniō, -īre, -īvī and **-iī, -ītum** vt to soften, soothe, heal, calm

lēnis adj soft, smooth, mild, gentle, calm

lēnitās, -ātis f softness, smoothness, mildness, tenderness

lēniter adv softly, gently; moderately, half-heartedly

lēnitūdō, -inis f smoothness, mildness

lēnō, -ōnis m pander, brothel keeper; go-between

lēnōcinium, -ī and **-iī** nt pandering; allurement; meretricious ornament

lēnōcinor, -ārī, -ātus vi to pay court to; to promote

lēnōnius adj pander's

lēns, lentis f lentil

lentē adv slowly; calmly, coolly

lentēscō, -ere vi to become sticky, soften; to relax

lentiscifer, -ī adj bearing mastic trees

lentiscus, -ī f mastic tree

lentitūdō, -inis f slowness, dullness, apathy

lentō, -āre vt to bend

lentulus adj rather slow

lentus adj sticky, sluggish; pliant; slow, lasting, lingering; (person) calm, at ease, indifferent

lēnunculus, -ī m skiff

leō, -ōnis m lion

Leōnidās, -ae m Spartan king who fell at Thermopylae

leōnīnus adj lion's

Leontīnī, -ōrum mpl town in Sicily

Leontīnus adj see **Leontīnī**

lepas, -dis f limpet

lepidē adv neatly, charmingly; (reply) very well, splendidly

lepidus adj pleasant, charming, neat, witty

lepōs, lepor, -ōris m pleasantness, charm; wit

lepus, -oris m hare

lepusculus, -ī m young hare

Lerna, -ae, Lernē, -ēs f marsh near Argos (where Hercules killed the Hydra)

Lernaeus adj Lernaean

Lesbias, -iadis f Lesbian woman

Lesbis, Lesbius, Lesbōus, Lesbiacus adj see **Lesbos**

Lesbos, Lesbus, -ī f Aegean island (home of Alcaeus and Sappho)

lētālis adj deadly

Lēthaeus adj of Lethe; infernal; soporific

lēthargicus, -ī m lethargic person

lēthargus, -ī m drowsiness

Lēthē, -ēs f river in the lower world, which caused forgetfulness

lētifer, -ī adj fatal

lētō, -āre vt to kill

lētum, -ī nt death; destruction

Leucadius adj see **Leucas**

Leucas, -dis, Leucadia, -diae f island off W. Greece

Leucothea, -ae, Leucotheē, -ēs f Ino (a sea goddess)

Leuctra, -ōrum ntpl battlefield in Boeotia

Leuctricus adj see **Leuctra**

levāmen, -inis nt alleviation, comfort

levāmentum, -ī nt mitigation, consolation

levātiō, -ōnis f relief; diminishing

lēvī perf of **linō**

leviculus adj rather vain

levidēnsis adj slight

levipēs, -edis adj light-footed

levis adj (weight) light; (MIL) light-armed; (fig) easy, gentle; (importance) slight, trivial; (motion) nimble, fleet; (character) fickle, unreliable

lēvis adj smooth; (youth) beardless, delicate

levisomnus adj light-sleeping

levitās, -ātis f lightness; nimbleness; fickleness, frivolity

lēvĭtās, -ātis f smoothness; fluency
leviter adv lightly; slightly; easily
levŏ, -āre vt to lighten, ease; (fig) to alleviate, lessen; to comfort, relieve; to impair; (danger) to avert; **sē levāre** rise
lēvŏ, -āre vt to smooth, polish
lēvor, -ōris m smoothness
lēx, lēgis f law, statute; bill; rule, principle; contract, condition; **lēgem ferre** propose a bill; **lēgem perferre** carry a motion; **lēge agere** proceed according to law; **sine lēge** out of control
lībāmen, -inis nt offering, libation
lībāmentum, -ī nt offering, libation
lībātiŏ, -ōnis f libation
lībella, -ae f small coin, as; level; **ad lībellam** exactly; **ex lībellā** sole heir
libellus, -ī m small book; notebook, diary, letter; notice, programme, handbill; petition, complaint; lampoon
libēns, -entis adj willing, glad
libenter adv willingly, with pleasure
liber, -rī m inner bark (of a tree); book; register
Līber, -ī m Italian god of fertility (identified with Bacchus)
līber, -ī adj free, open, unrestricted, undisturbed; (with abl) free from; (speech) frank; (POL) free, not slave, democratic
Lībera, -ae f Proserpine; Ariadne
Līberālia, -ālium ntpl festival of Liber in March
līberālis adj of freedom, of free citizens, gentlemanly, honourable; generous, liberal; handsome
līberālitās, -ātis f courtesy, kindness; generosity; bounty
līberāliter adv courteously, nobly; generously
līberātiŏ, -ōnis f delivery, freeing; (LAW) acquittal
līberātor, -ōris m liberator, deliverer
līberē adv freely, frankly, boldly
līberī, -ōrum mpl children
līberŏ, -āre, -āvī, -ātum vt to free, set free, release; to exempt; (LAW) to acquit; (slave) to give freedom to; **fidem līberāre** keep one's promise; **nōmina līberāre** cancel debts
līberta, -ae f freedwoman
lībertās, -ātis f freedom, liberty; status of a freeman; (POL) independence; freedom of speech, outspokenness
lībertīnus adj of a freedman, freed ♦ m freedman ♦ f freedwoman
lībertus, -ī m freedman
libet, lubet, -ēre, -uit and **-itum est** vi (impers) it pleases; **mihi ~ I** like; **ut ~** as you please
lībīdinōsē adv wilfully
lībīdinōsus adj wilful, arbitrary, extravagant; sensual, lustful
lībīdŏ, lubīdŏ, -inis f desire, passion; wilfulness, caprice; lust
libita, -ōrum ntpl pleasure, fancy
Libitīna, -ae f goddess of burials
lībŏ, -āre, -āvī, -ātum vt to taste, sip, touch; to pour (a libation), offer; to extract, take out; to impair

lībra, -ae f pound; balance, pair of scales; **ad lībram** of equal size
lībrāmentum, -ī nt level surface, weight (to give balance or movement); (water) fall
lībrāria, -ae f head spinner
lībrāriolus, -ī m copyist
lībrārium, -ī and **-iī** nt bookcase
lībrārius adj of books ♦ m copyist
lībrātus adj level; powerful
lībrīlis adj weighing a pound
lībritor, -ōris m slinger
lībrŏ, -āre, -āvī, -ātum vt to poise, hold balanced; to swing, hurl
lībum, -ī nt cake
Liburna, -ae f a fast galley, frigate
Liburnī, -ōrum mpl people of Illyria
Liburnus adj Liburnian
Libya, -ae, Libyē, -ēs f Africa
Libycus adj African
Libyes, -um mpl Libyans, people in N. Africa
Libyssus, Libystinus, Libystis adj = **Libycus**
licēns, -entis adj free, bold, unrestricted
licenter adv freely, lawlessly
licentia, -ae f freedom, license; lawlessness, licentiousness
liceŏ, -ēre, -uī vi to be for sale, value at
liceor, -ērī, -itus vt, vi to bid (at an auction), bid for
licet, -ēre, -uit and **-itum est** vi (impers) it is permitted, it is lawful; (reply) all right ♦ conj although; **mihi ~ I may**
Licinius¹, -ī m Roman family name (esp with surname Crassus)
Licinius² adj see **Licinius¹**
licitātiŏ, -ōnis f bidding (at a sale)
licitor, -ārī vi to make a bid, bid
licitus adj lawful
licium, -ī and **-iī** nt thread
lictor, -ōris m lictor (an attendant with fasces preceding a magistrate)
licuī perf of **liceŏ; liquēscŏ**
liēn, -ēnis m spleen
ligāmen, -inis nt band, bandage
ligāmentum, -ī nt bandage
Liger, -is m (river) Loire
lignārius, -ī and **-iī** m carpenter
lignātiŏ, -ōnis f fetching wood
lignātor, -ōris m woodcutter
ligneolus adj wooden
ligneus adj wooden
lignor, -ārī vi to fetch wood
lignum, -ī nt wood, firewood, timber; **in silvam ligna ferre** carry coals to Newcastle
ligŏ¹, -āre, -āvī, -ātum vt to tie up, bandage; (fig) to unite
ligŏ², -ōnis m mattock, hoe
ligula, -ae f shoestrap
Ligur, -ris m/f Ligurian
Liguria, -riae f district of N.W. Italy
ligūriŏ, ligurriŏ, -īre vt to lick; to eat daintily; (fig) to feast on, lust after
ligūrītiŏ, -ōnis f daintiness
Ligus, -ris m/f Ligurian
Ligusticus, -stīnus adj see **Ligus**

ligustrum, **-ī** *nt* privet
līlium, **-ī** *and* **-iī** *nt* lily; (MIL) spiked pit
līma, **-ae** *f* file; (*fig*) revision
līmātius *adv* more elegantly
līmātulus *adj* refined
līmāx, **-ācis** *f* slug, snail
limbus, **-ī** *m* fringe, hem
līmen, **-inis** *nt* threshold, lintel; doorway; entrance; house, home; (*fig*) beginning
līmes, **-itis** *m* path between fields; boundary; path, track, way; frontier, boundary line
līmō, **-āre**, **-āvī**, **-ātum** *vt* to file; (*fig*) to polish, refine; to file down, investigate carefully; to take away from
līmōsus *adj* muddy
limpidus *adj* clear, limpid
līmus¹ *adj* sidelong, askance
līmus², **-ī** *m* mud, slime, dirt
līmus³, **-ī** *m* ceremonial apron
līnea, **-ae** *f* line, string; plumbline; boundary; **ad līneam, rectā līneā** vertically; **extrēmā līneā amāre** love at a distance
līneāmentum, **-ī** *nt* line; feature; outline
līneus *adj* flaxen, linen
lingō, **-ere** *vt* to lick
lingua, **-ae** *f* tongue; speech, language; tongue of land; **~ Latīna** Latin
lingula, **-ae** *f* tongue of land
līniger, **-ī** *adj* linen-clad
linō, **-ere**, **lēvī**, **litum** *vt* to daub, smear; to overlay; (*writing*) to rub out; (*fig*) to befoul
linquō, **-ere**, **līquī** *vt* to leave, quit; to give up, let alone; (*pass*) to faint, swoon; **linquitur ut it** remains to
linteātus *adj* canvas
linteō, **-ōnis** *m* linen weaver
linter, **-ris** *f* boat; trough
linteum, **-ī** *nt* linen cloth, canvas; sail
linteus *adj* linen
lintriculus, **-ī** *m* small boat
līnum, **-ī** *nt* flax; linen; thread, line, rope; net
Lipara, **-ae**, **Liparē**, **-ēs** *f* island N. of Sicily (*now* Lipari)
Liparaeus, **-ēnsis** *adj see* **Lipara**
lippiō, **-īre** *vi* to have sore eyes
lippitūdō, **-inis** *f* inflammation of the eyes
lippus *adj* blear-eyed, with sore eyes; (*fig*) blind
liquefaciō, **-facere**, **-fēcī**, **-factum** (*pass* **-fīō**) *vt* to melt, dissolve; to decompose; (*fig*) to enervate
liquēns, **-entis** *adj* fluid, clear
liquēscō, **-ere**, **licuī** *vi* to melt; to clear; (*fig*) to grow soft, waste away
liquet, **-ēre**, **licuit** *vi* (*impers*) it is clear, it is evident; **nōn ~** not proven
līquī *perf of* **linquō**
liquidō *adv* clearly
liquidus *adj* fluid, liquid, flowing; clear, transparent, pure; (*mind*) calm, serene ♦ *nt* liquid water
liquō, **-āre** *vt* to melt; to strain
liquor, **-ōris** *m* fluidity; liquid, the sea
līquor, **-ī** *vi* to flow; (*fig*) to waste away
Līris, **-is** *m* river between Latium and Campania

līs, **lītis** *f* quarrel, dispute; lawsuit; matter in dispute; **lītem aestimāre** assess damages
litātiō, **-ōnis** *f* favourable sacrifice
lītera *etc see* **littera**
lītigātor, **-ōris** *m* litigant
lītigiōsus *adj* quarrelsome, contentious; disputed
lītigium, **-ī** *and* **-iī** *nt* quarrel
lītigō, **-āre** *vi* to quarrel; to go to law
litō, **-āre**, **-āvī**, **-ātum** *vi* to offer an acceptable sacrifice, obtain favourable omens; (*with dat*) to propitiate ♦ *vt* to offer successfully
lītorālis *adj* of the shore
lītoreus *adj* of the shore
littera, **-ae** *f* letter (*of the alphabet*)
litterae, **-ārum** *fpl* writing; letter, dispatch; document, ordinance; literature; learning, scholarship; **litterās discere** learn to read and write; **homō trium litterārum** thief (*from fur*); **sine litterīs** uncultured
litterārius *adj* of reading and writing
litterātē *adv* in clear letters; literally
litterātor, **-ōris** *m* grammarian
litterātūra, **-ae** *f* writing, alphabet
litterātus *adj* with letters on it, branded; educated, learned
litterula, **-ae** *f* small letter; short note; (*pl*) studies
litūra, **-ae** *f* correction, erasure, blot
litus *ppp of* **linō**
lītus, **-oris** *nt* shore, beach, coast; bank; **~ arāre** labour in vain
lituus, **-ī** *m* augur's staff; trumpet; (*fig*) starter
līvēns, **-entis** *pres p of* **līveō** ♦ *adj* bluish, black and blue
līveō, **-ēre** *vi* to be black and blue; to envy
līvēscō, **-ere** *vi* to turn black and blue
Līviānus *adj* = **Līvius²**
līvidulus *adj* a little jealous
līvidus *adj* bluish, black and blue; envious, malicious
Līvius¹, **-ī** *m* Roman family name (*esp the first Latin poet); the famous historian, Livy*
Līvius² *adj see* **Līvius¹**
līvor, **-ōris** *m* bluish colour; envy, malice
lixa, **-ae** *m* sutler, camp-follower
locātiō, **-ōnis** *f* leasing; lease, contract
locātōrius *adj* concerned with leases
locitō, **-āre** *vt* to let frequently
locō, **-āre**, **-āvī**, **-ātum** *vt* to place, put; to give in marriage; to let, lease, hire out; to contract for; (*money*) to invest
loculus, **-ī** *m* little place; (*pl*) satchel, purse
locuplēs, **-ētis** *adj* rich, opulent; reliable, responsible
locuplētō, **-āre** *vt* to enrich
locus, **-ī** (*pl* **-ī** *m and* **-a** *nt*) *m* place, site, locality, region; (MIL) post; (*theatre*) seat; (*book*) passage; (*speech*) topic, subject, argument; (*fig*) room, occasion; situation, state; rank, position; **locī** individual spots; **loca** regions, ground; **locī commūnēs** general arguments; **locō** (*with gen*) instead of; **in locō** opportunely; **eō locī** in the position; **intereā locī** meanwhile
lōcusta, **-ae** *f* locust

locūtiō, -ōnis f speech; pronunciation
locūtus ppa of **loquor**
lōdīx, -īcis f blanket
logica, -ōrum ntpl logic
logos, logus, -ī m word; idle talk; witticism
lōlīg- etc see **lollīg-**
lolium, -ī and **-iī** nt darnel
lollīgō, -inis f cuttlefish
lōmentum, -ī nt face cream
Londinium, -ī nt London
longaevus adj aged
longē adv far, far off; (time) long; (compar) by
  far, very much; ~ **esse** be far away, of no avail;
  ~ **latēque** everywhere
longinquitās, -ātis f length; distance; duration
longinquus adj distant, remote; foreign,
  strange; lasting, wearisome; (hope) long
  deferred
longitūdō, -inis f length; duration; **in
  longitūdinem** lengthwise
longiusculus adj rather long
longulē adv rather far
longulus adj rather long
longurius, -ī and **-iī** m long pole
longus adj long; vast; (time) long, protracted,
  tedious; (hope) far-reaching; **longa nāvis**
  warship; **longum est** it would be tedious; **nē
  longum faciam** to cut a long story short
loquācitās, -ātis f talkativeness
loquāciter adv see **loquāx**
loquāculus adj somewhat talkative
loquāx, -ācis adj talkative, chattering
loquella, -ae f language, words
loquor, -quī, cūtus vt, vi to speak, talk, say;
  to talk about, mention; (fig) to indicate; **rēs
  loquitur ipsa** the facts speak for themselves
lōrārius, -ī and **-iī** m flogger
lōrātus adj strapped
lōreus adj of leather strips
lōrīca, -ae f breastplate; parapet
lōrīcātus adj mailed
lōripēs, -edis adj bandylegged
lōrum, -ī nt strap; whip, lash; leather charm;
  (pl) reins
lōtos, lōtus, -ī f lotus
lōtus ppp of **lavō**
lubēns see **libēns**
lubentia, -ae f pleasure
lubet, lubīdō see **libet, libīdō**
lūbricō, -āre vt to make slippery
lūbricus adj slippery, slimy; gliding, fleeting;
  (fig) dangerous, hazardous
Lūca bōs f elephant
Lūcania, -iae f district of S. Italy
Lūcanica f kind of sausage
Lūcanus adj Lucanian ♦ m the epic poet Lucan
lūcar, -āris nt forest tax
lucellum, -ī nt small gain
lūceō, -cēre, -xī vi to shine, be light; (impers)
  to dawn, be daylight; (fig) to shine, be clear;
  meridiē nōn lūcēre (argue) that black is
  white
Lūcerēs, -um mpl a Roman patrician tribe
Lūceria, -iae f town in Apulia

Lūcerīnus adj see **Lūceria**
lucerna, -ae f lamp; (fig) midnight oil
lūcēscō, -ere vi to begin to shine, get light,
  dawn
lūcidē adv clearly
lūcidus adj bright, clear; (fig) lucid
lūcifer, -ī adj light-bringing ♦ m morning star,
  Venus; day
lūcifugus adj shunning the light
Lūcīlius, -ī m Roman family name (esp the first Latin
  satirist)
Lūcīna, -ae f goddess of childbirth
lūciscō etc see **lūcēscō**
Lucmō, Lucumō, -ōnis m Etruscan prince or
  priest
Lucrētia, -iae f wife of Collatinus, ravished by Tarquin
Lucrētius, -ī m Roman family name (esp the
  philosophic poet)
lucrifuga, -ae m non-profiteer
Lucrīnēnsis adj see **Lucrīnus**
Lucrīnus, -ī m lake near Baiae (famous for oysters)
lucror, -ārī, -ātus vt to gain, win, acquire
lucrōsus adj profitable
lucrum, -ī nt profit, gain; greed; wealth; **lucrī
  facere** gain, get the credit of; **lucrō esse** be of
  advantage; **in lucrīs pōnere** count as gain
luctāmen, -inis nt struggle, exertion
luctātiō, -ōnis f wrestling; fight, contest
luctātor, -ōris m wrestler
lūctificus adj baleful
lūctisonus adj mournful
luctor, -ārī, -ātus vi to wrestle; to struggle, fight
lūctuōsus adj sorrowful, lamentable
lūctus, -ūs m mourning, lamentation;
  mourning (dress)
lūcubrātiō, -ōnis f work by lamplight,
  nocturnal study
lūcubrō, -āre, -āvī, -ātum vi to work by night
  ♦ vt to compose by night
lūculentē adv splendidly, right
lūculenter adv very well
lūculentus adj bright; (fig) brilliant, excellent,
  rich, fine
Lūcullus, -ī m Roman surname (esp the conqueror of
  Mithridates)
lūcus, -ī m grove; wood
lūdia, -ae f woman gladiator
lūdibrium, -ī and **-iī** nt mockery, derision;
  laughing stock; sport, play; **lūdibriō habēre**
  make fun of
lūdibundus adj playful; safely, easily
lūdicer, -rī adj playful; theatrical
lūdicum, -ī nt public show, play; sport
lūdificātiō, -ōnis f ridicule; tricking
lūdificātor, -ōris m mocker
lūdificō, -āre, lūdificor, -ārī, -ātus vt to make a
  fool of, ridicule; to delude, thwart
lūdiō, -ōnis m actor
lūdius, -ī and **-iī** m actor; gladiator
lūdō, -dere, -sī, -sum vi to play; to sport, frolic;
  to dally, make love ♦ vt to play at; to amuse
  oneself with; to mimic, imitate; to ridicule,
  mock; to delude
lūdus, -ī m game, sport, play; (pl) public
  spectacle, games; school; (fig) child's play; fun,

jest; (love) dalliance; **lūdum dare** humour; **lūdōs facere** put on a public show; make fun of

luella, **-ae** f atonement

luēs, **-is** f plague, pest; misfortune

Lugdūnēnsis adj see **Lugdūnum**

Lugdūnum, **-ī** nt town in S. Gaul (now Lyon)

lūgeō, **-gēre**, **-xī**, **-ctum** vt, vi to mourn; to be in mourning

lūgubris adj mourning; disastrous; (sound) plaintive ♦ ntpl mourning dress

lumbī, **-ōrum** mpl loins

lumbrīcus, **-ī** m worm

lūmen, **-inis** nt light; lamp, torch; day; eye; life; (fig) ornament, glory; clarity

lūmināre, **-is** nt window

lūminōsus adj brilliant

lūna, **-ae** f moon; month; crescent

lūnāris adj of the moon

lūnātus adj crescent-shaped

lūnō, **-āre** vt to bend into a crescent

luō, **-ere**, **-ī** vt to pay; to atone for; to avert by expiation

lupa, **-ae** f she-wolf; prostitute

lupānar, **-āris** nt brothel

lupātus adj toothed ♦ m, ntpl curb

Lupercal, **-ālis** nt a grotto sacred to Pan

Lupercālia, **-ālium** ntpl festival of Pan in February

Lupercus, **-ī** m Pan; priest of Pan

lupīnum, **-ī** nt lupin; sham money, counters

lupīnus[1] adj wolf's

lupīnus[2], **-ī** m lupin; sham money, counters

lupus, **-ī** m wolf; (fish) pike; toothed bit; grapnel; ~ **in fābulā** talk of the devil

lūridus adj pale yellow, ghastly pallid

lūror, **-ōris** m yellowness

lūscinia, **-ae** f nightingale

luscitiōsus adj purblind

luscus adj one-eyed

lūsiō, **-ōnis** f play

Lūsitānia, **-iae** f part of W. Spain (including what is now Portugal)

Lūsitānus adj see **Lūsitānia**

lūsitō, **-āre** vi to play

lūsor, **-ōris** m player; humorous writer

lūstrālis adj lustral, propitiatory; quinquennial

lūstrātiō, **-ōnis** f purification; roving

lūstrō, **-āre**, **-āvī**, **-ātum** vt to purify; (motion) to go round, encircle, traverse; (MIL) to review; (eyes) to scan, survey; (mind) to consider; (light) to illuminate

lustror, **-ārī** vi to frequent brothels

lustrum, **-ī** nt den, lair; (pl) wild country; (fig) brothels; debauchery

lūstrum, **-ī** nt purificatory sacrifice; (time) five years

lūsus[1] ppp of **lūdō**

lūsus[2], **-ūs** m play, game, sport; dalliance

lūteolus adj yellow

Lutetia, **-ae** f town in N. Gaul (now Paris)

luteus adj of clay; muddy, dirty; (fig) vile

lūteus adj yellow, orange

lutitō, **-āre** vt to throw mud at

lutulentus adj muddy, filthy; (fig) foul

lutum, **-ī** nt mud, mire; clay

lūtum, **-ī** nt dyer's weed; yellow

lūx, **lūcis** f light; daylight; day; life; (fig) public view; glory, encouragement, enlightenment; **lūce** in the daytime; **prīmā lūce** at daybreak; **lūce carentēs** the dead

lūxī perf of **lūceō**; **lūgeō**

luxor, **-ārī** vi to live riotously

luxuria, **-ae**, **luxuriēs**, **-ēī** f rankness, profusion; extravagance, luxury

luxuriō, **-āre**, **luxurior**, **-ārī** vi to grow to excess, be luxuriant; (fig) to be exuberant, run riot

luxuriōsē adv voluptuously

luxuriōsus adj luxuriant; excessive, extravagant; voluptuous

luxus, **-ūs** m excess, debauchery, pomp

Lyaeus, **-ī** m Bacchus; wine

Lycaeus, **-ī** m mountain in Arcadia (sacred to Pan)

Lycāōn, **-onis** m father of Callisto, the Great Bear

Lycāonius adj see **Lycāōn**

Lycēum, **Lycīum**, **-ī** nt Aristotle's school at Athens

lychnūchus, **-ī** m lampstand

lychnus, **-ī** m lamp

Lycia, **-ae** f country in S.W. Asia Minor

Lycius adj Lycian

Lyctius adj Cretan

Lycurgus, **-ī** m Thracian king killed by Bacchus; Spartan lawgiver; Athenian orator

Lӯdia, **-iae** f country of Asia Minor

Lӯdius adj Lydian; Etruscan

Lӯdus, **-ī** m Lydian

lympha, **-ae** f water

lymphāticus adj crazy, frantic

lymphātus adj distracted

Lynceus, **-eī** m keen-sighted Argonaut

lynx, **lyncis** m/f lynx

lyra, **-ae** f lyre; lyric poetry

lyricus adj of the lyre, lyrical

Lysiās, **-ae** m Athenian orator

Mm

Macedō, -onis *m* Macedonian

Macedonia *f* Macedonia

Macedonicus, -onius *adj see* **Macedonia**

macellum, -ī *nt* market

maceō, -ēre *vi* to be lean

macer, -rī *adj* lean, meagre; poor

māceria, -ae *f* wall

mācerō, -āre *vt* to soften; *(body)* to enervate; *(mind)* to distress

macēscō, -ere *vi* to grow thin

machaera, -ae *f* sword

machaerophorus, -ī *m* soldier armed with a sword

Machāōn, -onis *m legendary Greek surgeon*

Machāonius *adj see* **Machāōn**

māchina, -ae *f* machine, engine; *(fig)* scheme, trick

māchināmentum, -ī *nt* engine

māchinātiō, -ōnis *f* mechanism, machine; *(fig)* contrivance

māchinātor, -ōris *m* engineer; *(fig)* contriver

māchinor, -ārī, -ātus *vt* to devise, contrive; *(fig)* to plot, scheme

maciēs, -ēī *f* leanness, meagreness; poorness

macilentus *adj* thin

macrēscō, -ere *vi* to grow thin

macritūdō, -inis *f* leanness

macrocollum, -ī *nt* large size of paper

mactābilis *adj* deadly

mactātus, -ūs *m* sacrifice

macte blessed; well done!

mactō[1], -āre, -āvī, -ātum *vt* to sacrifice; to punish, kill

mactō[2], -āre *vt* to glorify

macula, -ae *f* spot, stain; *(net)* mesh; *(fig)* blemish, fault

maculō, -āre, -āvī, -ātum *vt* to stain, defile

maculōsus *adj* dappled, mottled; stained, polluted

madefaciō, -facere, -fēcī, -factum *(pass* **-fīō)** *vt* to wet, soak

madeō, -ēre *vi* to be wet, be drenched; to be boiled soft; *(comedy)* to be drunk; *(fig)* to be steeped in

madēscō, -ere *vi* to get wet, become moist

madidus *adj* wet, soaked; sodden; drunk

madulsa, -ae *m* drunkard

Maeander, Maeandros, -rī *m a winding river of Asia Minor;* winding, wandering

Maecēnās, -ātis *m friend of Augustus, patron of poets*

maena, -ae *f* sprat

Maenala, -ōrum *ntpl mountain range in Arcadia*

Maenalis, -ius *adj* of Maenalus; Arcadian

Maenalus, Maenalos, -ī *m* Maenala

Maenas, -dis *f* Bacchante

Maeniānum *nt* balcony

Maenius, -ī *m Roman family name;* **Maenia columna** whipping post in the Forum

Maeonia, -ae *f* Lydia

Maeonidēs, -dae *m* Homer

Maeonius *adj* Lydian; Homeric; Etruscan

Maeōticus, Maeōtius *adj* Scythian, Maeotic

Maeōtis, -dis *f* Sea of Azov

maereō, -ēre *vi* to mourn, be sad

maeror, -ōris *m* mourning, sorrow, sadness

maestiter *adv see* **maestus**

maestitia, -ae *f* sadness, melancholy

maestus *adj* sad, sorrowful; gloomy; mourning

māgālia, -um *ntpl* huts

mage *etc see* **magis**

magicus *adj* magical

magis, mage *adv* more; **eō ~** the more, all the more

magister, -rī *m* master, chief, director; *(school)* teacher; *(fig)* instigator; **~ equitum** chief of cavalry, second in command *(to a dictator);* **~ mōrum** censor; **~ sacrōrum** chief priest

magisterium, -ī *and* **-iī** *nt* presidency, tutorship

magistra, -ae *f* mistress, instructress

magistrātus, -ūs *m* magistracy, office; magistrate, official

magnanimitās, -ātis *f* greatness

magnanimus *adj* great, brave

Magnēs, -ētis *m* Magnesian; magnet

Magnēsia *f district of Thessaly*

Magnēsius, Magnēssus, Magnētis *adj see* **Magnēsia**

magnidicus *adj* boastful

magnificē *adv* grandly; pompously

magnificentia, -ae *f* greatness, grandeur; pomposity

magnificō, -āre *vt* to esteem highly

magnificus *(compar* **-entior,** *superl* **-entissimus)** *adj* great, grand, splendid; pompous

magniloquentia, -ae *f* elevated language; pomposity

magniloquus *adj* boastful

magnitūdō, -inis *f* greatness, size, large amount; dignity

magnopere *adv* greatly, very much

magnus *(compar* **māior,** *superl* **māximus)** *adj* great, large, big, tall; *(voice)* loud; *(age)* advanced; (*value*) high, dear; (*fig*) grand, noble, important; **avunculus** ~ great-uncle; **magna loquī** boast; **magnī aestimāre** think highly of; **magnī esse** be highly esteemed; **magnō stāre** cost dear; **magnō opere** very much

magus, -ī *m* wise man; magician ♦ *adj* magic

Māia, -ae *f* mother of Mercury

māiestās, -ātis *f* greatness, dignity, majesty; treason; **māiestātem laedere, māiestātem minuere** offend against the sovereignty of; **lēx māiestātis** law against treason

māior, -ōris *compar of* **magnus**; ~ **nātū** older, elder; **in māius crēdere/ferre** exaggerate

māiōrēs, -ōrum *mpl* ancestors

Māius, -ī *m* May ♦ *adj* of May

māiusculus *adj* somewhat greater; a little older

māla, -ae *f* cheek, jaw

malacia, -ae *f* dead calm

malacus *adj* soft

male (*compar* **pēius**, *superl* **pessimē**) *adv* badly, wrongly, unfortunately; not; (*with words having bad sense*) very much; ~ **est animō** I feel ill; ~ **sānus** insane; ~ **dīcere** abuse, curse; ~ **facere** harm

maledicē *adv* abusively

maledictiō, -ōnis *f* abuse

maledictum, -ī *nt* curse

maledicus *adj* scurrilous

malefactum, -ī *nt* wrong

maleficē *adv see* **maleficus**

maleficium, -ī *and* **-iī** *nt* misdeed, wrong, mischief

maleficus *adj* wicked ♦ *m* criminal

malesuādus *adj* seductive

malevolēns, -entis *adj* spiteful

malevolentia, -ae *f* ill-will

malevolus *adj* ill-disposed, malicious

mālifer, -ī *adj* apple-growing

malignē *adv* spitefully; grudgingly

malignitās, -ātis *f* malice; stinginess

malignus *adj* unkind, ill-natured, spiteful; stingy; (*soil*) unfruitful; (*fig*) small, scanty

malitia, -ae *f* badness, malice; roguishness

malitiōsē *adv see* **malitiōsus**

malitiōsus *adj* wicked, crafty

maliv- *etc see* **malev-**

mālle *infin of* **mālō**

malleolus, -ī *m* hammer; (MIL) fire-brand

malleus, -ī *m* hammer, mallet, maul

mālō, -le, -uī *vt* to prefer; would rather

malobathrum, -ī *nt* an oriental perfume

māluī *perf of* **mālō**

malum, -ī *nt* evil, wrong, harm, misfortune; (*interj*) mischief

mālum, -ī *nt* apple, fruit

malus (*compar* **pēior**, *superl* **pessimus**) *adj* bad, evil, harmful; unlucky; ugly; **ī in malam rem** go to hell!

mālus¹, -ī *f* apple tree

mālus², -ī *m* mast, pole

malva, -ae *f* mallow

Māmers, -tis *m* Mars

Māmertīnī, -ōrum *mpl* mercenary troops who occupied Messana

mamma, -ae *f* breast; teat

mammilla, -ae *f* breast

mānābilis *adj* penetrating

manceps, -ipis *m* purchaser; contractor

mancipium, -ī *and* **-iī** *nt* formal purchase; property; slave

mancipō, -āre *vt* to sell, deliver up

mancup- *etc see* **mancip-**

mancus *adj* crippled

mandātum, -ī *nt* commission, command; (LAW) contract

mandātus, -ūs *m* command

mandō¹, -āre, -āvī, -ātum *vt* to entrust, commit; to commission, command

mandō², -ere, -ī, mānsum *vt* to chew, eat, devour

mandra, -ae *f* drove of cattle

mandūcus, -ī *m* masked figure of a glutton

māne *nt* (*indecl*) morning ♦ *adv* in the morning, early

maneō, -ēre, mānsī, mānsum *vi* to remain; to stay, stop; to last, abide, continue ♦ *vt* to wait for, await; **in condiciōne manēre** abide by an agreement

Mānēs, -ium *mpl* ghosts, shades of the dead; the lower world; bodily remains

mangō, -ōnis *m* dealer

manicae, -ārum *fpl* sleeves, gloves; handcuffs

manicātus *adj* with long sleeves

manicula, -ae *f* little hand

manifestō¹, -āre *vt* to disclose

manifestō² *adv* clearly, evidently

manifestus *adj* clear, obvious; convicted, caught

manip- *etc see* **manipul-**

manipulāris *adj* of a company ♦ *m* private (*in the ranks*); fellow soldier

manipulātim *adv* by companies

manipulus, -ī *m* bundle (*esp of hay*); (MIL) company

Manlius¹, -ī *m* Roman family name (*esp the saviour of the Capitol from the Gauls*); a severe disciplinarian

Manlius², Manliānus *adj see* **Manlius¹**

mannus, -ī *m* Gallic horse

mānō, -āre, -āvī, -ātum *vi* to flow, drip, stream; (*fig*) to spread, emanate

mānsī *perf of* **maneō**

mānsiō, -ōnis *f* remaining, stay

mānsitō, -āre *vi* to stay on

mānsuēfaciō, -facere, -fēcī, -factum (*pass* **-fīō**) *vt* to tame

mānsuēscō, -scere, -vī, -tum *vt* to tame ♦ *vi* to grow tame, grow mild

mānsuētē *adv see* **mānsuētus**

mānsuētūdō, -inis *f* tameness; gentleness

mānsuētus *ppp of* **mānsuēscō** ♦ *adj* tame; mild, gentle

mānsus *ppp of* **mandō²**; **maneō**

mantēle, -is *nt* napkin, towel

mantēlum, -ī *nt* cloak

mantica, -ae *f* knapsack

manticinor, -ārī, -ātus *vi* to be a prophet

mantō, -āre *vt* to remain, wait

Mantua, -ae *f* birthplace of Vergil in N. Italy

manuālis *adj* for the hand

manubiae, -ārum *fpl* money from sale of booty

manūbrium, **-ī** *and* **-iī** *nt* handle, haft
manuleātus *adj* with long sleeves
manūmissiō, **-ōnis** *f* emancipation (*of a slave*)
manūmittō, **-ittere**, **-īsī**, **-issum** *vt* to emancipate, make free
manupretium, **-ī** *and* **-iī** *nt* pay, wages, reward
manus, **-ūs** *f* hand; corps, band, company; (*elephant*) trunk; (*art*) touch; (*work*) handiwork, handwriting; (*war*) force, valour, hand to hand fighting; (*fig*) power; **~ extrēma** finishing touch; **~ ferrea** grappling iron; **manum dare** give up, yield; **manū** artificially; **manū mittere** emancipate; **ad manum** at hand; **in manū** obvious; subject; **in manūs venīre** come to hand; **in manibus** well known; at hand; **in manibus habēre** be engaged on; fondle; **per manūs** forcibly; **per manūs trādere** hand down
mapālia, **-um** *ntpl* huts
mappa, **-ae** *f* napkin, cloth
Marathōn, **-ōnis** *f* Attic village famous for Persian defeat
Marathōnius *adj see* **Marathōn**
Marcellia, **-iōrum** *ntpl* festival of the Marcelli
Marcellus, **-ī** *m* Roman surname (*esp the captor of Syracuse*)
marceō, **-ēre** *vi* to droop, be faint
marcēscō, **-ere** *vi* to waste away, grow feeble
Marciānus *adj see* **Marcius¹**
marcidus *adj* withered; enervated
Marcius¹, **-ī** *m* Roman family name (*esp Ancus, fourth king*)
Marcius² *adj see* **Marcius¹**
mare, **-is** *nt* sea; **~ nostrum** Mediterranean; **~ inferum** Tyrrhenian Sea; **~ superum** Adriatic
Mareōticus *adj* Mareotic; Egyptian
margarīta, **-ae** *f* pearl
marginō, **-āre** *vt* to put a border or kerb on
margō, **-inis** *m/f* edge, border, boundary; **~ cēnae** side dishes
Mariānus *adj see* **Marius¹**
Marīca, **-ae** *f* nymph of Minturnae
marīnus *adj* of the sea
marītālis *adj* marriage- (*in cpds*)
maritimus *adj* of the sea, maritime, coastal ♦ *ntpl* coastal area
marītō, **-āre** *vt* to marry
marītus, **-ī** *m* husband ♦ *adj* nuptial
Marius¹, **-ī** *m* Roman family name (*esp the victor over Jugurtha and the Teutons*)
Marius² *adj see* **Marius¹**
marmor, **-is** *nt* marble; statue, tablet; sea
marmoreus *adj* of marble; like marble
Marō, **-ōnis** *m* surname of Vergil
marra, **-ae** *f* kind of hoe
Mars, **Martis** *m* god of war, father of Romulus and Remus; war, conflict; planet Mars; **aequō Marte** on equal terms; **suō Marte** by one's own exertions
Marsī, **-ōrum** *mpl* people of central Italy, famous as fighters
Marsicus, **Marsus** *adj* Marsian
marsuppium, **-ī** *and* **-iī** *nt* purse
Mārtiālis *adj* of Mars

Mārticola, **-ae** *m* worshipper of Mars
Mārtigena, **-ae** *m* son of Mars
Mārtius *adj* of Mars; of March; warlike
mās, **maris** *m* male, man ♦ *adj* male; manly
māsculus *adj* male, masculine; manly
Masinissa, **-ae** *m* king of Numidia
massa, **-ae** *f* lump, mass
Massicum, **-ī** *nt* Massic wine
Massicus, **-ī** *m* mountain in Campania, famous for vines
Massilia, **-ae** *f* Greek colony in Gaul (*now Marseille*)
Massiliēnsis *adj see* **Massilia**
mastīgia, **-ae** *nt* scoundrel
mastrūca, **-ae** *f* sheepskin
mastrūcātus *adj* wearing sheepskin
matara, **-ae**, **mataris**, **-is** *f* Celtic javelin
matelliō, **-ōnis** *m* pot
māter, **-ris** *f* mother; **Magna ~** Cybele
mātercula, **-ae** *f* poor mother
māteria, **-ae**, **māteriēs**, **-ēī** *f* matter, substance; wood, timber; (*fig*) subject matter, theme; occasion, opportunity; (*person*) ability, character
māteriārius, **-ī** *and* **-iī** *m* timber merchant
māteriātus *adj* timbered
māteriēs *etc see* **māteria**
māterior, **-ārī** *vi* to fetch wood
māternus *adj* mother's
mātertera, **-ae** *f* aunt (*maternal*)
mathēmaticus, **-ī** *m* mathematician; astrologer
mātricīda, **-ae** *m* matricide
mātricīdium, **-ī** *and* **-iī** *nt* a mother's murder
mātrimōnium, **-ī** *and* **-iī** *nt* marriage
mātrimus *adj* whose mother is still alive
mātrōna, **-ae** *f* married woman, matron, lady
mātrōnālis *adj* a married woman's
matula, **-ae** *f* pot
mātūrē *adv* at the right time; early, promptly
mātūrēscō, **-ēscere**, **-uī** *vi* to ripen
mātūritās, **-ātis** *f* ripeness; (*fig*) maturity, perfection, height
mātūrō, **-āre**, **-āvī**, **-ātum** *vt* to bring to maturity; to hasten, be too hasty with ♦ *vi* to make haste
mātūrus *adj* ripe, mature; timely, seasonable; early
Mātūta, **-ae** *f* goddess of dawn
mātūtīnus *adj* morning, early
Mauritānia, **-ae** *f* Mauretania (*now Morocco*)
Maurus, **-ī** *m* Moor ♦ *adj* Moorish, African
Maurūsius *adj see* **Maurus**
Māvors, **-tis** *m* Mars
Māvortius *adj see* **Māvors**
maxilla, **-ae** *f* jaw
maximē *adv* most, very much, especially; precisely, just; certainly, yes; **cum ~** just as; **quam ~** as much as possible
maximitās, **-ātis** *f* great size
maximus *superl of* **magnus**
māxum- *etc see* **māxim-**
māzonomus, **-ī** *m* dish
meāpte my own
meātus, **-ūs** *m* movement, course

mēcastor *interj* by Castor!

mēcum with me

meddix tuticus *m* senior Oscan magistrate

Mēdēa, -ae *f* Colchian wife of Jason, expert in magic

Mēdēis *adj* magical

medentēs, -entum *mpl* doctors

medeor, -ērī *vi* (*with dat*) to heal, remedy

mediastīnus, -ī *m* drudge

mēdica, -ae *f* lucern (*kind of clover*)

medicābilis *adj* curable

medicāmen, -inis *nt* drug, medicine; cosmetic; (*fig*) remedy

medicāmentum, -ī *nt* drug, medicine; potion, poison; (*fig*) relief; embellishment

medicātus, -ūs *m* charm

medicīna, -ae *f* medicine; cure; (*fig*) remedy, relief

medicō, -āre, -āvī, -ātum *vt* to cure; to steep, dye

medicor, -ārī *vt, vi* to cure

medicus *adj* healing ♦ *m* doctor

medietās, -ātis *f* mean

medimnum, -ī *nt*, **medimnus, -ī** *m* bushel

mediocris *adj* middling, moderate, average

mediocritās, -ātis *f* mean, moderation; mediocrity

mediocriter *adv* moderately, not particularly; calmly

Mediolānēnsis *adj see* **Mediolānum**

Mediolānum, -ī *nt* town in N. Italy (*now* Milan)

meditāmentum, -ī *nt* preparation, drill

meditātiō, -ōnis *f* thinking about; preparation, practice

meditātus *adj* studied

mediterrāneus *adj* inland

meditor, -ārī, -ātus *vt, vi* to think over, contemplate, reflect; to practise, study

medius *adj* middle, the middle of; intermediate; intervening; middling, moderate; neutral ♦ *nt* middle; public ♦ *m* mediator; **medium complectī** clasp round the waist; **medium sē gerere** be neutral; **mediō** midway; **mediō temporis** meanwhile; **in medium** for the common good; **in medium prōferre** publish; **dē mediō tollere** do away with; **ē mediō abīre** die, disappear; **in mediō esse** be public; **in mediō positus** open to all; **in mediō relinquere** leave undecided

medius fidius *interj* by Heaven!

medix tuticus *see* **meddix tuticus**

medulla, -ae *f* marrow, pith

medullitus *adv* from the heart

medullula, -ae *f* marrow

Mēdus¹, -ī *m* Mede, Persian

Mēdus² *adj see* **Mēdus¹**

Medūsa, -ae *f* Gorgon, whose look turned everything to stone

Medūsaeus *adj*: ~ **equus** Pegasus

Megalēnsia, Megalēsia, -um *ntpl* festival of Cybele in April

Megara, -ae *f*, **Megara, -ōrum** *ntpl* town in Greece near the Isthmus

Megarēus, Megarīcus *adj* Megarean

megistānes, -um *mpl* grandees

mehercle, mehercule, mehercules *interj* by Hercules!

mēiō, -ere *vi* to make water

mel, mellis *nt* honey

melancholicus *adj* melancholy

melē *pl of* **melos**

Meleager, Meleagros, -rī *m* prince of Calydon

melicus *adj* musical; lyrical

melilōtos, -ī *f* kind of clover

melimēla, -ōrum *ntpl* honey apples

Mēlīnum, -ī *nt* Melian white

melior, -ōris *adj* better

melisphyllum, -ī *nt* balm

Melita, -ae *f* Malta

Melitēnsis *adj* Maltese

melius *nt of* **melior** ♦ *adv* better

meliusculē *adv* fairly well

meliusculus *adj* rather better

mellifer, -ī *adj* honey-making

mellītus *adj* honeyed; sweet

melos, -ī *nt* tune, song

Melpomenē, -ēs *f* Muse of tragedy

membrāna, -ae *f* skin, membrane, slough; parchment

membrānula, -ae *f* piece of parchment

membrātim *adv* limb by limb; piecemeal; in short sentences

membrum, -ī *nt* limb, member; part, division; clause

mēmet me (*emphatic*)

meminī, -isse *vi* (*with gen*) to remember, think of; to mention

Memnōn, -onis *m* Ethiopian king, killed at Troy

Memnonius *adj see* **Memnōn**

memor, -is *adj* mindful, remembering; in memory (of)

memorābilis *adj* memorable, remarkable

memorandus *adj* noteworthy

memorātus¹, -ūs *m* mention

memorātus² *adj* famed

memoria, -ae *f* memory, remembrance; time, lifetime; history; **haec ~** our day; **memoriae prōdere** hand down to posterity; **post hominum memoriam** since the beginning of history

memoriola, -ae *f* weak memory

memoriter *adv* from memory; accurately

memorō, -āre, -āvī, -ātum *vt* to mention, say, speak

Memphis, -is *and* **-idos** *f* town in middle Egypt

Memphītēs, Memphītis, Memphītīticus *adj* of Memphis; Egyptian

Menander, Menandros, -rī *m* Greek writer of comedy

Menandrēus *adj see* **Menander**

menda, -ae *f* fault

mendācium, -ī *and* **-iī** *nt* lie

mendāciunculum, -ī *nt* fib

mendāx, -ācis *adj* lying; deceptive, unreal ♦ *m* liar

mendīcitās, -ātis *f* beggary

mendīcō, -āre, mendīcor, -ārī *vi* to beg, go begging

mendīcus *adj* beggarly, poor ♦ *m* beggar

mendōsē *adv see* **mendōsus**
mendōsus *adj* faulty; wrong, mistaken
mendum, -ī *nt* fault, blunder
Menelāēus *adj see* **Menelāus**
Menelāus, -ī *m* brother of Agamemnon, husband of Helen
Menoetiadēs, -ae *m* Patroclus
mēns, mentis *f* mind, understanding; feelings, heart; idea, plan, purpose; courage; **venit in mentem** it occurs; **mente captus** insane; **eā mente ut** with the intention of
mēnsa, -ae *f* table; meal, course; counter, bank; **secunda ~** dessert
mēnsārius, -ī *and* **-iī** *m* banker
mēnsiō, -ōnis *f* (*metre*) quantity
mēnsis, -is *m* month
mēnsor, -ōris *m* measurer, surveyor
mēnstruālis *adj* for a month
mēnstruus *adj* monthly; for a month ♦ *nt* a month's provisions
mēnsula, -ae *f* little table
mēnsūra, -ae *f* measure, measurement; standard, standing; amount, size, capacity
mēnsus *ppa of* **mētior**
menta, -ae *f* mint
mentiēns, -ientis *m* fallacy
mentiō, -ōnis *f* mention, hint
mentior, -īrī, -ītus *vi* to lie, deceive ♦ *vt* to say falsely; to feign, imitate
mentītus *adj* lying, false
Mentor, -is *m* artist in metalwork; ornamental cup
Mentoreus *adj see* **Mentor**
mentum, -ī *nt* chin
meō, -āre *vi* to go, pass
mephītis, -is *f* noxious vapour, malaria
merācus *adj* pure
mercābilis *adj* buyable
mercātor, -ōris *m* merchant, dealer
mercātūra, -ae *f* commerce; purchase; goods
mercātus, -ūs *m* trade, traffic; market, fair
mercēdula, -ae *f* poor wages, small rent
mercēnārius *adj* hired, mercenary ♦ *m* servant
mercēs, -ēdis *f* pay, wages, fee; bribe; rent; (*fig*) reward, retribution, cost
mercimōnium, -ī *and* **-iī** *nt* wares, goods
mercor, -ārī, -ātus *vt* to trade in, purchase
Mercuriālis *adj see* **Mercurius**
Mercurius, -ī *m* messenger of the gods, god of trade, thieves, speech and the lyre; **stēlla Mercuriī** planet Mercury
merda, -ae *f* dung
merenda, -ae *f* lunch
mereō, -ēre, -uī, mereor, -ērī, -itus *vt, vi* to deserve; to earn, win, acquire; (MIL) to serve; **bene merēre dē** do a service to, serve well; **merēre equō** serve in the cavalry
meretrīcius *adj* a harlot's
meretrīcula, -ae *f* pretty harlot
meretrīx, -īcis *f* harlot
mergae, -ārum *fpl* pitchfork
merges, -itis *f* sheaf
mergō, -gere, -sī, -sum *vt* to dip, immerse, sink; (*fig*) to bury, plunge, drown
mergus, -ī *m* (*bird*) diver

merīdiānus *adj* midday; southerly
merīdiātiō, -ōnis *f* siesta
merīdiēs, -ēī *f* midday, noon; south
merīdiō, -āre *vi* to take a siesta
meritō¹, -āre *vt* to earn
meritō² *adv* deservedly
meritōrius *adj* money-earning ♦ *ntpl* lodgings
meritum, -ī *nt* service, kindness, merit; blame
meritus *ppp of* **mereō** ♦ *adj* deserved, just
merops, -is *f* bee-eater
mersī *perf of* **mergō**
mersō, -āre *vt* to immerse, plunge; to overwhelm
mersus *ppp of* **mergō**
merula, -ae *f* blackbird
merum, -ī *nt* neat wine
merus *adj* pure, undiluted; bare, mere
merx, mercis *f* goods, wares
Messalla, -ae *m* Roman surname (*esp* Messalla Corvīnus Augustan orator, soldier and literary patron)
Messallīna, -īnae *f* wife of emperor Claudius; wife of Nero
Messāna, -ae *f* Sicilian town (*now* Messina)
messis, -is *f* harvest
messor, -ōris *m* reaper
messōrius *adj* a reaper's
messuī *perf of* **metō**
messus *ppp of* **metō**
mēta, -ae *f* pillar at each end of the Circus course; turning point, winning post; (*fig*) goal, end, limit
metallum, -ī *nt* mine, quarry; metal
mētātor, -ōris *m* surveyor
Metaurus, -ī *m* river in Umbria, famous for the defeat of Hasdrubal
Metellus, -ī *m* Roman surname (*esp* the commander against Jugurtha)
Mēthymna, -ae *f* town in Lesbos
Mēthymnaeus *adj see* **Mēthymna**
mētior, -tīrī, -nsus *vt* to measure, measure out; to traverse; (*fig*) to estimate, judge
metō, -tere, -ssuī, -ssum *vt* to reap, gather; to mow, cut down
mētor, -ārī, -ātus *vt* to measure off, lay out
metrēta, -ae *f* liquid measure (about 9 gallons)
metuculōsus *adj* frightful
metuō, -uere, -uī, -ūtum *vt* to fear, be apprehensive
metus, -ūs *m* fear, alarm, anxiety
meus *adj* my, mine
mī *dat of* **ego** ♦ *voc and mpl of* **meus**
mīca, -ae *f* crumb, grain
micō, -āre, -uī *vi* to quiver, flicker, beat, flash, sparkle
Midās, -ae *m* Phrygian king whose touch turned everything to gold
migrātiō, -ōnis *f* removal, change
migrō, -āre, -āvī, -ātum *vi* to remove, change, pass away ♦ *vt* to transport, transgress
mīles, -itis *m* soldier, infantryman; army, troops
Mīlēsius *adj see* **Mīlētus**
Mīlētus, -tī *f* town in Asia Minor
mīlia, -um *ntpl* thousands; ~ **passuum** miles

mīliārium, milliārium, -ī *and* **-iī** *nt* milestone
mīlitāris *adj* military, a soldier's
mīlitāriter *adv* in a soldierly fashion
mīlitia, -ae *f* military service, war; the army; militiae on service; **domī mīlitiaeque** at home and abroad
mīlitō, -āre *vi* to serve, be a soldier
milium, -ī *and* **-iī** *nt* millet
mīlle (*pl* **mīlia**) *num* a thousand; ~ **passūs** a mile
mīllensimus, mīllēsimus *adj* thousandth
mīllia *etc see* **mīlia**
mīlliārium *etc see* **mīliārium**
mīlliēns, mīlliēs *adv* a thousand times
Milō, -ōnis *m* tribune who killed Clodius and was defended by Cicero
Milōniānus *adj see* **Milō**
Miltiadēs, -is *m* Athenian general, victor at Marathon
mīluīnus *adj* resembling a kite; rapacious
mīluus, mīlvus, -ī *m* kite; gurnard
mīma, -ae *f* actress
Mimallonis, -dis *f* Bacchante
mīmicē *adv see* **mīmicus**
mīmicus *adj* farcical
Mimnermus, -ī *m* Greek elegiac poet
mīmula, -ae *f* actress
mīmus, -ī *m* actor; mime, farce
mina, -ae *f* Greek silver coin
mināciter *adv see* **mināx**
minae, -ārum *fpl* threats; (wall) pinnacles
minanter *adv* threateningly
minātiō, -ōnis *f* threat
mināx, -ācis *adj* threatening; projecting
Minerva, -ae *f* goddess of wisdom and arts, esp weaving; (fig) talent, genius; working in wool; **sūs Minervam** "teach your grandmother!"
miniātulus *adj* painted red
miniātus *adj* red-leaded
minimē *adv* least, very little; (reply) no, not at all
minimus *adj* least, smallest, very small; youngest
miniō, -āre, -āvī, -ātum *vt* to colour red
minister, -rī *m*, **ministra, ministrae** *f* attendant, servant; helper, agent, tool
ministerium, -ī *and* **-iī** *nt* service, office, duty; retinue
ministrātor, -ōris *m*, **ministrātorrīx, ministrātorrīcis** *f* assistant, handmaid
ministrō, -āre *vt* to serve, supply; to manage
minitābundus *adj* threatening
minitor, -ārī, minitō, -āre *vt, vi* to threaten
minium, -ī *and* **-iī** *nt* vermilion, red lead
Mīnōis, -idis *f* Ariadne
Mīnōius, Mīnōus *adj see* **Mīnōs**
minor¹, -ārī, -ātus *vt, vi* to threaten; to project
minor², -ōris *adj* smaller, less, inferior; younger; (pl) descendants
Mīnōs, -is *m* king of Crete, judge in the lower world
Mīnōtaurus, -ī *m* monster of the Cretan labyrinth, half bull, half man
Minturnae, -ārum *fpl* town in S. Latium
Minturnēnsis *adj see* **Minturnae**
minum- *etc see* **minim-**

minuō, -uere, -uī, -ūtum *vt* to make smaller, lessen; to chop up; to reduce, weaken ♦ *vi* (*tide*) to ebb
minus *nt* = **minor²** ♦ *adv* less; not, not at all; **quō** ~ (*prevent*) from
minusculus *adj* smallish
minūtal, -ālis *nt* mince
minūtātim *adv* bit by bit
minūtē *adv* in a petty manner
minūtus *ppp of* **minuō** ♦ *adj* small; paltry
mīrābilis *adj* wonderful, extraordinary
mīrābiliter *adv see* **mīrābilis**
mīrābundus *adj* astonished
mīrāculum, -ī *nt* marvel, wonder; amazement
mīrandus *adj* wonderful
mīrātiō, -ōnis *f* wonder
mīrātor, -ōris *m* admirer
mīrātrīx, -īcis *adj* admiring
mīrē *adv see* **mīrus**
mīrificē *adv see* **mīrificus**
mīrificus *adj* wonderful
mirmillō *see* **murmillō**
mīror, -ārī, -ātus *vt* to wonder at, be surprised at, admire ♦ *vi* to wonder, be surprised
mīrus *adj* wonderful, strange; **mīrum quam, mīrum quantum** extraordinarily
miscellānea, -ōrum *ntpl* (food) hotchpotch
misceō, -scēre, -scuī, -xtum *vt* to mix, mingle, blend; to join, combine; to confuse, embroil
misellus *adj* poor little
Mīsēnēnsis *adj see* **Mīsēnum**
Mīsēnum, -ī *nt* promontory and harbour near Naples
miser, -ī *adj* wretched, poor, pitiful, sorry
miserābilis *adj* pitiable, sad, plaintive
miserābiliter *adv see* **miserābilis**
miserandus *adj* deplorable
miserātiō, -ōnis *f* pity, compassion, pathos
miserē *adv see* **miser**
misereō, -ēre, -uī, misereor, -ērī, -itus *vt, vi* (with gen) to pity, sympathize with; **miseret mē** I pity, I am sorry
miserēscō, -ere *vi* to feel pity
miseria, -ae *f* misery, trouble, distress
misericordia, -ae *f* pity, sympathy, mercy
misericors, -dis *adj* sympathetic, merciful
miseriter *adv* sadly
miseror, -ārī, -ātus *vt* to deplore; to pity
mīsī *perf of* **mittō**
missa, -ae *f* (ECCL) mass
missilis *adj* missile
missiō, -ōnis *f* sending; release; (MIL) discharge; (gladiators) quarter; (events) end; **sine missiōne** to the death
missitō, -āre *vt* to send repeatedly
missus¹ *ppp of* **mittō**
missus², -ūs *m* sending; throwing; ~ **sagittae** bowshot
mitella, -ae *f* turban
mītēscō, -ere *vi* to ripen; to grow mild
Mithridātēs, -is *m* king of Pontus, defeated by Pompey
Mithridātēus, Mithridāticus *adj see* **Mithridātēs**
mītigātiō, -ōnis *f* soothing

mītigō, -āre, -āvī, -ātum *vt* to ripen, soften; to calm, pacify

mītis *adj* ripe, mellow; soft, mild; gentle

mitra, -ae *f* turban

mittō, -ere, mīsi, missum *vt* to send, dispatch; to throw, hurl; to let go, dismiss; to emit, utter; (*news*) to send word; (*gift*) to bestow; (*event*) to end; (*speech*) to omit, stop; **sanguinem mittere** bleed; **ad cēnam mittere** invite to dinner; **missum facere** forgo

mītulus, -ī *m* mussel

mixtim *adv* promiscuously

mixtūra, -ae *f* mingling

Mnēmosynē, -ēs *f* mother of the Muses

mnēmosynon, -ī *nt* souvenir

mōbilis *adj* movable; nimble, fleet; excitable, fickle

mōbilitās, -ātis *f* agility, rapidity; fickleness

mōbiliter *adv* rapidly

mōbilitō, -āre *vt* to make rapid

moderābilis *adj* moderate

moderāmen, -inis *nt* control; government

moderanter *adv* with control

moderātē *adv* with restraint

moderātim *adv* gradually

moderātiō, -ōnis *f* control, government; moderation; rules

moderātor, -ōris *m* controller, governor

moderātrīx, -īcis *f* mistress, controller

moderātus *adj* restrained, orderly

moderor, -ārī, -ātus *vt* (*with dat*) to restrain, check; (*with acc*) to manage, govern, guide

modestē *adv* with moderation; humbly

modestia, -ae *f* temperate behaviour; discipline; humility

modestus *adj* sober, restrained; well-behaved, disciplined; modest, unassuming

modiālis *adj* holding a peck

modicē *adv* moderately; slightly

modicus *adj* moderate; middling, small, mean

modificātus *adj* measured

modius, -ī and -iī *m* corn measure, peck

modo *adv* only; at all, in any way; (*with imp*) just; (*time*) just now, a moment ago, in a moment ♦ *conj* if only; **nōn ~** not only; **non ~ ... sed** not only ... but also ...; **~ nōn** all but, almost; **~ ... ~** sometimes ... sometimes; **~ ... tum** at first ... then

modulātē *adv* melodiously

modulātor, -ōris *m* musician

modulātus *adj* played, measured

modulor, -ārī, -ātus *vt* to modulate, play, sing

modulus, -ī *m* measure

modus, -ī *m* measure; size; metre; music; way, method; limit, end; **ēius modī** such; **modō, in modum** like

moecha, -ae *f* adulteress

moechor, -ārī *vi* to commit adultery

moechus, -ī *m* adulterer

moenera *etc see* **mūnus**

moenia, -um *ntpl* defences, walls; town, stronghold

moeniō *etc see* **mūniō**

Moesī, -ōrum *mpl people on lower Danube (now Bulgaria)*

mola, -ae *f* millstone, mill; grains of spelt

molāris, -is *m* millstone; (*tooth*) molar

mōlēs, -is *f* mass, bulk, pile; dam, pier, massive structure; (*fig*) greatness, weight, effort, trouble

molestē *adv see* **molestus**

molestia, -ae *f* trouble, annoyance, worry; (*style*) affectation

molestus *adj* irksome, annoying; (*style*) laboured

mōlīmen, -inis *nt* exertion, labour; importance

mōlīmentum, -ī *nt* great effort

mōlior, -īrī, -ītus *vt* to labour at, work, build; to wield, move, heave; to undertake, devise, occasion ♦ *vi* to exert oneself, struggle

mōlītiō, -ōnis *f* laborious work

mōlītor, -ōris *m* builder

mollēscō, -ere *vi* to soften, become effeminate

molliculus *adj* tender

molliō, -īre, -īvī, -ītum *vt* to soften, make supple; to mitigate, make easier; to demoralize

mollis *adj* soft, supple; tender, gentle; (*character*) sensitive, weak, unmanly; (*poetry*) amatory; (*opinion*) changeable; (*slope*) easy

molliter *adv* softly, gently; calmly; voluptuously

mollitia, -ae, mollitiēs, -ēī *f* softness, suppleness; tenderness, weakness, effeminacy

mollitūdō, -inis *f* softness; susceptibility

molō, -ere *vt* to grind

Molossī, -ōrum *mpl Molossians, people in Epirus*

Molossicus, Molossus *adj see* **Molossī**

Molossis, -idis *f country of the Molossians*

Molossus, -ī *m* Molossian hound

mōly, -os *nt a magic herb*

mōmen, -inis *nt* movement, momentum

mōmentum, -ī *nt* movement; change; (*time*) short space, moment; (*fig*) cause, influence, importance; **nullīus mōmentī** unimportant

momordī *perf of* **mordeō**

Mona, -ae *f Isle of Man; Anglesey*

monachus, -ī *m* monk

monēdula, -ae *f* jackdaw

moneō, -ēre, -uī, -itum *vt* to remind, advise, warn; to instruct, foretell

monēris, -is *f* galley with one bank of oars

monērula *etc see* **monēdula**

monēta, -ae *f* mint; money; stamp

monīle, -is *nt* necklace, collar

monim- *etc see* **monum-**

monitiō, -ōnis *f* admonishing

monitor, -ōris *m* admonisher; prompter; teacher

monitum, -ī *nt* warning; prophecy

monitus, -ūs *m* admonition; warning

monogrammus *adj* shadowy

monopodium, -ī and -iī *nt* table with one leg

mōns, montis *m* mountain

mōnstrātor, -ōris *m* shower, inventor

mōnstrātus *adj* distinguished

mōnstrō, -āre, -āvī, -ātum *vt* to point out, show; to inform, instruct; to appoint; to denounce

mōnstrum, -ī *nt* portent, marvel; monster

mōnstruōsus *adj* unnatural

montānus *adj* mountainous, mountain- (*in cpds*), highland
monticola, -ae *m* highlander
montivagus *adj* mountain-roving
montuōsus, montōsus *adj* mountainous
monumentum, -ī *nt* memorial, monument; record
Mopsopius *adj* Athenian
mora¹, -ae *f* delay, pause; hindrance; space of time, sojourn; **moram facere** put off
mora², -ae *f* division of the Spartan army
mōrālis *adj* moral
morātor, -ōris *m* delayer
mōrātus *adj* mannered, of a nature; (*writing*) in character
morbidus *adj* unwholesome
morbus, -ī *m* illness, disease; distress
mordāciter *adv see* **mordāx**
mordāx, -ācis *adj* biting, sharp, pungent; (*fig*) snarling, carking
mordeō, -dēre, momordī, -sum *vt* to bite; to bite into, grip; (*cold*) to nip; (*words*) to sting, hurt, mortify
mordicus *adv* with a bite; (*fig*) doggedly
mōrēs *pl of* **mōs**
morētum, -ī *nt* salad
moribundus *adj* dying, mortal; deadly
mōrigeror, -ārī, -ātus *vi* (*with dat*) to gratify, humour
mōrigerus *adj* obliging, obedient
morior, -ī, -tuus *vi* to die; to decay, fade
moritūrus *fut p of* **morior**
mōrologus *adj* foolish
moror, -ārī, -ātus *vi* to delay, stay, loiter ♦ *vt* to detain, retard; to entertain; (*with neg*) to heed, object; **nihil morārī, nīl morārī** have no objection to; to not care for; to withdraw a charge against
mōrōsē *adv see* **mōrōsus**
mōrōsitās, -ātis *f* peevishness
mōrōsus *adj* peevish, difficult
Morpheus, -eos *m* god of dreams
mors, mortis *f* death; corpse; **mortem sibi cōnscīscere** commit suicide; **mortis poena** capital punishment
morsiuncula, -ae *f* little kiss
morsus¹ *ppp of* **mordeō** ♦ *ntpl* little bits
morsus², -ūs *m* bite; grip; (*fig*) sting, vexation
mortālis *adj* mortal; transient; man-made ♦ *m* human being
mortālitās, -ātis *f* mortality, death
mortārium, -ī and -iī *nt* mortar
mortifer, -ī *adj* fatal
mortuus *ppa of* **morior** ♦ *adj* dead ♦ *m* dead man
mōrum, -ī *nt* blackberry, mulberry
mōrus¹, -ī *f* black mulberry tree
mōrus² *adj* foolish ♦ *m* fool
mōs, mōris *m* nature, manner; humour, mood; custom, practice, law; (*pl*) behaviour, character, morals; **mōs māiōrum** national tradition; **mōrem gerere** oblige, humour; **mōre, in mōrem** like
Mosa, -ae *m* (river) Meuse
Mōsēs, -is *m* Moses
mōtiō, -ōnis *f* motion

mōtō, -āre *vt* to keep moving
mōtus¹ *ppp of* **moveō**
mōtus², -ūs *m* movement; dance, gesture; (*mind*) impulse, emotion; (POL) rising, rebellion; **terrae ~** earthquake
movēns, -entis *pres p of* **moveō** ♦ *adj* movable ♦ *ntpl* motives
moveō, -ēre, mōvī, mōtum *vt* to move, set in motion; to disturb; to change; to dislodge, expel; to occasion, begin; (*opinion*) to shake; (*mind*) to affect, influence, provoke ♦ *vi* to move; **castra movēre** strike camp; **sē movēre** budge; to dance
mox *adv* presently, soon, later on; next
Mōysēs *see* **Mōsēs**
mūcidus *adj* snivelling; mouldy
Mūcius, -ī *m* Roman family name (*esp Scaevola, who burned his right hand before Porsena*)
mūcrō, -ōnis *m* point, edge; sword
mūcus, -ī *m* mucus
mūgilis, -is *m* mullet
muginor, -ārī *vi* to hesitate
mūgiō, -īre *vi* to bellow, groan
mūgītus, -ūs *m* lowing, roaring
mūla, -ae *f* she-mule
mulceō, -cēre, -sī, -sum *vt* to stroke, caress; to soothe, alleviate, delight
Mulciber, -is *and* **-ī** *m* Vulcan
mulcō, -āre, -āvī, -ātum *vt* to beat, ill-treat, damage
mulctra, -ae *f*, **mulctrārium, -ārī** *and* **-āriī**, **mulctrum, -ī** *nt* milkpail
mulgeō, -ēre, mulsī *vt* to milk
muliebris *adj* woman's, feminine; effeminate
muliebriter *adv* like a woman; effeminately
mulier, -is *f* woman; wife
mulierārius *adj* woman's
muliercula, -ae *f* girl
mulierōsitās, -ātis *f* fondness for women
mulierōsus *adj* fond of women
mūlīnus *adj* mulish
mūliō, -ōnis *m* mule driver
mūliōnius *adj* mule driver's
mullus, -ī *m* red mullet
mulsī *perf of* **mulceō**; **mulgeō**
mulsus¹ *ppp of* **mulceō**
mulsus² *adj* honeyed, sweet ♦ *nt* honey-wine, mead
multa, -ae *f* penalty, fine; loss
multangulus *adj* many-angled
multātīcius *adj* fine- (*in cpds*)
multātiō, -ōnis *f* fining
multēsimus *adj* very small
multicavus *adj* many-holed
multīcia, -ōrum *ntpl* transparent garments
multifāriam *adv* in many places
multifidus *adj* divided into many parts
multifōrmis *adj* of many forms
multiforus *adj* many-holed
multigeneris, multigenus *adj* of many kinds
multiiugis, multiiugus *adj* yoked together; complex
multiloquium, -ī *and* **-iī** *nt* talkativeness
multiloquus *adj* talkative

multimodīs *adv* variously

multiplex, -icis *adj* with many folds, tortuous; many-sided, manifold, various; (*comparison*) far greater; (*character*) fickle, sly

multiplicō, -āre, -āvī, -ātum *vt* to multiply, enlarge

multipotēns, -entis *adj* very powerful

multitūdō, -inis *f* great number, multitude, crowd

multivolus *adj* longing for much

multō¹ *adv* much, far, by far; (*time*) long

multō², -āre, -āvī, -ātum *vt* to punish, fine

multum *adv* much, very, frequently

multus (*compar* **plūs,** *superl* **plūrimus**) *adj* much, many; (*speech*) lengthy, tedious; (*time*) late; **multā nocte** late at night; **nē multa** to cut a long story short

mūlus, -ī *m* mule

Mulvius *adj* Mulvian (*a Tiber bridge above Rome*)

mundānus, -ī *m* world citizen

munditia, -ae, munditiēs, -ēī *f* cleanness; neatness, elegance

mundus¹ *adj* clean, neat, elegant; **in mundō esse** be in readiness

mundus², -ī *m* toilet gear; universe, world, heavens; mankind

mūnerigerulus, -ī *m* bringer of presents

mūnerō, -āre, mūneror, -ārī *vt* to present, reward

mūnia, -ōrum *ntpl* official duties

mūniceps, -ipis *m/f* citizen (*of a municipium*), fellow-citizen

mūnicipālis *adj* provincial

mūnicipium, -ī *and* **-iī** *nt* provincial town, burgh

mūnificē *adv see* **mūnificus**

mūnificentia, -ae *f* liberality

mūnificō, -āre *vt* to treat generously

mūnificus *adj* liberal

mūnīmen, -inis *nt* defence

mūnīmentum, -ī *nt* defencework, protection

mūniō, -īre, -īī, -ītum *vt* to fortify, secure, strengthen; (*road*) to build; (*fig*) to protect

mūnis *adj* ready to oblige

mūnītiō, -ōnis *f* building; fortification; (*river*) bridging

mūnītō, -āre *vt* (*road*) to open up

mūnītor, -ōris *m* sapper, builder

mūnus, -eris *nt* service, duty; gift; public show; entertainment; tax; (*funeral*) tribute; (*book*) work

mūnusculum, -ī *nt* small present

mūraena, -ae *f a fish*

mūrālis *adj* wall- (*in cpds*), mural, for fighting from or attacking walls

mūrex, -icis *m* purple-fish; purple dye, purple; jagged rock

muria, -ae *f* brine

murmillō, -ōnis *m* kind of gladiator

murmur, -is *nt* murmur, hum, rumbling, roaring

murmurillum, -ī *nt* low murmur

murmurō, -āre *vi* to murmur, rumble; to grumble

murra, -ae *f* myrrh

murreus *adj* perfumed; *made of the stone called murra*

murrina¹, -ae *f* myrrh wine

murrina², -ōrum *ntpl* murrine vases

murt- *etc see* **myrt-**

mūrus, -ī *m* wall; dam; defence

mūs, mūris *m/f* mouse, rat

Mūsa, -ae *f goddess inspiring an art*; poem; (*pl*) studies

mūsaeus *adj* poetic, musical

musca, -ae *f* fly

mūscipula, -ae *f*, **mūscipulum, -ī** *nt* mousetrap

mūscōsus *adj* mossy

mūsculus, -ī *m* mouse; muscle; (*MIL*) shed

mūscus, -ī *m* moss

mūsicē *adv* very pleasantly

mūsicus *adj* of music, of poetry ♦ *m* musician ♦ *f* music, culture ♦ *ntpl* music

mussitō, -āre *vi* to say nothing; to mutter ♦ *vt* to bear in silence

mussō, -āre *vt, vi* to say nothing, brood over; to mutter, murmur

mustāceum, -ī *nt*, **mustāceus, -ī** *m* wedding cake

mūstēla, -ae *f* weasel

mustum, -ī *nt* unfermented wine, must; vintage

mūtābilis *adj* changeable, fickle

mūtābilitās, -ātis *f* fickleness

mūtātiō, -ōnis *f* change, alteration; exchange

mutilō, -āre, -āvī, -ātum *vt* to cut off, maim; to diminish

mutilus *adj* maimed

Mutina, -ae *f* town in N. Italy (*now* Modena)

Mutinēnsis *adj see* **Mutina**

mūtiō *etc see* **muttiō**

mūtō, -āre, -āvī, -ātum *vt* to shift; to change, alter; to exchange, barter ♦ *vi* to change; **mūtāta verba** figurative language

muttiō, -īre *vi* to mutter, mumble

mūtuātiō, -ōnis *f* borrowing

mūtuē *adv* mutually, in turns

mūtuitō, -āre *vt* to try to borrow

mūtūō *adv* = **mūtuē**

mūtuor, -ārī, -ātus *vt* to borrow

mūtus *adj* dumb, mute; silent, still

mūtuum, -ī *nt* loan

mūtuus *adj* borrowed, lent; mutual, reciprocal; **mūtuum dare** lend; **mūtuum sūmere** borrow; **mūtuum facere** return like for like

Mycēnae, -ārum *fpl* Agamemnon's capital in S. Greece

Mycēnaeus, Mycēnēnsis *adj see* **Mycēnae**

Mycēnis, -idis *f* Mycenaean woman; Iphigenia

Mygdonius *adj* Phrygian

myoparō, -ōnis *m* pirate galley

myrīca, -ae *f* tamarisk

Myrmidones, -um *mpl* followers of Achilles

Myrōn, -ōnis *m* famous Greek sculptor

myropōla, -ae *m* perfumer

myropōlium, -ī *and* **-iī** *nt* perfumer's shop

myrothēcium, -ī *and* **-iī** *nt* perfume-box

myrrh- *etc see* **murr-**

myrtētum, -ī nt myrtle grove
myrteus adj myrtle- (in cpds)
Myrtōum mare sea N.W. of Crete
myrtum, -ī nt myrtle-berry
myrtus, -ī and **-ūs** f myrtle
Mȳsia, -iae f country of Asia Minor
Mȳsius, Mȳsios adj see **MÐsia**
mysta, -ae m priest of mysteries

mystagōgus, -ī m initiator
mystērium, -ī and **-iī** nt secret religion, mystery;
secret
mysticus adj mystic
Mytilēnae, -ārum fpl, **Mytilēnē, -es** f capital
of Lesbos
Mytilēnaeus adj see **Mytilēnae**
Mytilēnēnsis adj see **Mytilēnae**

Nn

nablium, -ī and **-iī** nt kind of harp
nactus ppa of **nancīscor**
nae etc see **nē**
naenia etc see **nēnia**
Naeviānus adj see **Naevius**
Naevius, -ī m early Latin poet
naevus, -ī m mole (on the body)
Nāias, -adis, Nāis, -dis f water nymph, Naiad
Nāicus adj see **Nāias**
nam conj (explaining) for; (illustrating) for example; (transitional) now; (interrog) but; (enclitic) an emphatic particle
namque conj for, for indeed, for example
nancīscor, -ī, nactus and **nanctus** vt to obtain, get; to come upon, find
nānus, -ī m (with plants) dwarf
Napaeae, -ārum fpl dell nymphs
nāpus, -ī m turnip
Narbō, -ōnis m town in S. Gaul
Narbōnēnsis adj see **Narbō**
narcissus, -ī m narcissus
nardus, -ī f, **nardum, -ī** nt nard, nard oil
nāris, -is f nostril; (pl) nose; (fig) sagacity, scorn
nārrābilis adj to be told
nārrātiō, -ōnis f narrative
nārrātor, -ōris m storyteller, historian
nārrātus, -ūs m narrative
nārrō, -āre, -āvī, -ātum vt to tell, relate, say; **male nārrāre** bring bad news
narthēcium, -ī and **-iī** nt medicine chest
nāscor, -scī, -tus vi to be born; to originate, grow, be produced
Nāsō, -ōnis m surname of Ovid
nassa, -ae f wicker basket for catching fish; (fig) snare
nasturtium, -ī and **-iī** nt cress
nāsus, -ī m nose
nāsūtē adv sarcastically
nāsūtus adj big-nosed; satirical
nāta, -ae f daughter
nātālicius adj of one's birthday, natal ◆ ntpl birthday party
nātālis adj of birth, natal ◆ m birthday ◆ mpl birth, origin
nātātiō, -ōnis f swimming
natātor, -ōris m swimmer
nātiō, -ōnis f tribe, race; breed, class
natis, -is f (usu pl) buttocks
nātīvus adj created; inborn, native, natural
natō, -āre vi to swim, float; to flow, overflow; (eyes) to swim, fail; (fig) to waver
nātrīx, -icis f watersnake

nātū abl m by birth, in age; **grandis ~, māgnō ~** quite old; **māior ~** older; **māximus ~** oldest
nātūra, -ae f birth; nature, quality, character; natural order of things; the physical world; (physics) element; **rērum ~** Nature
nātūrālis adj by birth; by nature, natural
nātūrāliter adv by nature
nātus ppa of **nāscor** ◆ m son ◆ adj born, made (for); old, of age; **prō rē nātā, ē rē nātā** under the circumstances, as things are; **annōs vīgintī ~** 20 years old
nauarchus, -ī m captain
naucī: nōn ~ esse, nōn ~ facere, nōn ~ habēre to be worthless, consider worthless
nauclēricus adj skipper's
nauclērus, -ī m skipper
naufragium, -ī and **-iī** nt shipwreck, wreck; **~ facere** be shipwrecked
naufragus adj shipwrecked, wrecked; (sea) dangerous to shipping ◆ m shipwrecked man; (fig) ruined man
naulum, -ī nt fare
naumachia, -ae f mock sea fight
nausea, -ae f seasickness
nauseō, -āre vi to be sick; (fig) to disgust
nauseola, -ae f squeamishness
nauta, nāvita, -ae m sailor, mariner
nauticus adj nautical, sailors' ◆ mpl seamen
nāvālis adj naval, of ships ◆ nt, ntpl dockyard; rigging
nāvicula, -ae f boat
nāviculāria, -ae f shipping business
nāviculārius, -ī and **-iī** m ship-owner
nāvifragus adj dangerous
nāvigābilis adj navigable
nāvigātiō, -ōnis f voyage
nāviger, -ī adj ship-carrying
nāvigium, -ī and **-iī** nt vessel, ship
nāvigō, -āre, -āvī, -ātum vi to sail, put to sea ◆ vt to sail across, navigate
nāvis, -is f ship; **~ longa** warship; **~ mercātōria** merchantman; **~ onerāria** transport; **~ praetōria** flagship; **nāvem dēdūcere** launch; **nāvem solvere** set sail; **nāvem statuere** heave to; **nāvem subdūcere** beach; **nāvibus atque quadrīgīs** with might and main
nāvita etc see **nauta**
nāvitās, -ātis f energy
nāviter adv energetically; absolutely

nāvō, -āre vt to perform energetically; **operam nāvāre** be energetic; to come to the assistance (of)

nāvus adj energetic

Naxos, -ī f Aegean island (famous for wines and the story of Ariadne)

nē¹ interj truly, indeed

nē² adv not ♦ conj that not, lest; (fear) that; (purpose) so that ... not, to avoid, to prevent

-ne enclitic introducing a question

Neāpolis, -is f Naples

Neāpolītānus adj see **Neāpolis**

nebula, -ae f mist, vapour, cloud

nebulō, -ōnis m idler, good-for-nothing

nebulōsus adj misty, cloudy

nec etc see **neque**

necdum adv and not yet

necessāriē, necessāriō adv of necessity, unavoidably

necessārius adj necessary, inevitable; indispensable; (kin) related ♦ m/f relative ♦ ntpl necessities

necesse adj (indecl) necessary, inevitable; needful

necessitās, -ātis f necessity, compulsion; requirement, want; relationship, connection

necessitūdō, -inis f necessity, need, want; connection; friendship; (pl) relatives

necessum etc see **necesse**

necne adv or not

necnōn adv also, besides

necō, -āre, -āvī, -ātum vt to kill, murder

necopīnāns, -antis adj unaware

necopīnātō adv see **necopīnātus**

necopīnātus adj unexpected

necopīnus adj unexpected; unsuspecting

nectar, -is nt nectar (the drink of the gods)

nectareus adj of nectar

nectō, -ctere, -xī and **-xuī, -xum** vt to tie, fasten, connect; to weave; (fig) to bind, enslave (esp for debt); to contrive, frame

nēcubi conj so that nowhere

nēcunde conj so that from nowhere

nēdum adv much less, much more

nefandus adj abominable, impious

nefāriē adv see **nefārius**

nefārius adj heinous, criminal

nefās nt indecl wickedness, sin, wrong ♦ interj horror!, shame!

nefāstus adj wicked; unlucky; (days) closed to public business

negātiō, -ōnis f denial

negitō, -āre vt to deny, refuse

neglēctiō, -ōnis f neglect

neglēctus¹ ppp of **neglegō**

neglēctus², -ūs m neglecting

neglegēns, -entis pres p of **neglegō** ♦ adj careless, indifferent

neglegenter adv carelessly

neglegentia, -ae f carelessness, neglect, coldness

neglegō, -egere, -ēxī, -ēctum vt to neglect, not care for; to slight, disregard; to overlook

negō, -āre, -āvī, -ātum vt, vi to say no; to say not, deny; to refuse, decline

negōtiālis adj business- (in cpds)

negōtiāns, -antis m businessman

negōtiātiō, -ōnis f banking business

negōtiātor, -ōris m businessman, banker

negōtiolum, -ī nt trivial matter

negōtior, -ārī, -ātus vi to do business, trade

negōtiōsus adj busy

negōtium, -ī and **-iī** nt business, work; trouble; matter, thing; **quid est negōtiī?** what is the matter?

Nēlēius adj see **Nēleus¹**

Nēleus¹, -eī m father of Nestor

Nēleus² adj see **Nēleus¹**

Nemea¹, -ae f town in S. Greece, where Hercules killed the lion

Nemea², -ōrum ntpl Nemean Games

Nemeaeus adj Nemean

nēmō, -inis m/f no one, nobody ♦ adj no; ~ **nōn** everybody; **nōn** ~ many; ~ **ūnus** not a soul

nemorālis adj sylvan

nemorēnsis adj of the grove

nemoricultrīx, -īcis f forest dweller

nemorivagus adj forest-roving

nemorōsus adj well-wooded; leafy

nempe adv (confirming) surely, of course, certainly; (in questions) do you mean?

nemus, -ōris nt wood, grove

nēnia, -ae f dirge; incantation; song, nursery rhyme

neō, nēre, nēvī, nētum vt to spin; to weave

Neoptolemus, -ī m Pyrrhus (son of Achilles)

nepa, -ae f scorpion

nepōs, -ōtis m grandson; descendant; spendthrift

nepōtīnus, -ī m little grandson

neptis, -is f granddaughter

Neptūnius adj: ~ **hērōs** Theseus

Neptūnus, -ī m Neptune (god of the sea); sea

nēquam adj (indecl) worthless, bad

nēquāquam adv not at all, by no means

neque, nec adv not ♦ conj and not, but not; neither, nor; ~ ... **et** not only not ... but also

nequeō, -īre, -īvī, -ītum vi to be unable, cannot

nēquior, nēquissimus compar, superl of **nēquam**

nēquīquam adv fruitlessly, for nothing; without good reason

nēquiter adv worthlessly, wrongly

nēquitia, -ae, nēquitiēs, -ēi f worthlessness, badness

Nērēis, -ēidis f Nereid, sea nymph

Nērēius adj see **Nērēis**

Nēreus, -eī m a sea god; the sea

Nēritius adj of Neritos; Ithacan

Nēritos, -ī m island near Ithaca

Nerō, -ōnis m Roman surname (esp the emperor)

Nerōniānus adj see **Nerō**

nervōsē adv vigorously

nervōsus adj sinewy, vigorous

nervulī, -ōrum mpl energy

nervus, -ī m sinew; string; fetter, prison; (shield) leather; (pl) strength, vigour, energy

nesciō, -īre, -īvī and **-iī, -ītum** vt to not know, be ignorant of; to be unable; ~ **quis,** ~ **quid** somebody, something; ~ **an** probably

nescius *adj* ignorant, unaware; unable; unknown

Nestor, -oris *m* Greek leader at Troy *(famous for his great age and wisdom)*

neu *etc see* **nēve**

neuter, -rī *adj* neither; neuter

neutiquam *adv* by no means, certainly not

neutrō *adv* neither way

nēve, neu *conj* and not; neither, nor

nēvī *perf of* **neō**

nex, necis *f* murder, death

nexilis *adj* tied together

nexum, -ī *nt* personal enslavement

nexus¹ *ppp of* **nectō**

nexus², -ūs *m* entwining, grip; (LAW) bond, obligation *(esp enslavement for debt)*

nī *adv* not ♦ *conj* if not, unless; that not; **quid nī?** why not?

nīcētērium, -ī *and* **-iī** *nt* prize

nictō, -āre *vi* to wink

nīdāmentum, -ī *nt* nest

nīdor, -ōris *m* steam, smell

nīdulus, -ī *m* little nest

nīdus, -ī *m* nest; *(pl)* nestlings; *(fig)* home

niger, -rī *adj* black, dark; dismal, ill-omened; *(character)* bad

nigrāns, -antis *adj* black, dusky

nigrēscō, -ere *vi* to blacken, grow dark

nigrō, -āre *vi* to be black

nigror, -ōris *m* blackness

nihil, nīl *nt indecl* nothing ♦ *adv* not; ~ **ad nōs** it has nothing to do with us; ~ **est** it's no use; ~ **est quod** there is no reason why; ~ **nisi** nothing but, only; ~ **nōn** everything; **nōn** ~ something

nihilum, -ī *nt* nothing; **nihilī esse** be worthless; **nihilō minus** none the less

nīl, nīlum *see* **nihil, nihilum**

Nīliacus *adj* of the Nile; Egyptian

Nīlus, -ī *m* Nile; conduit

nimbifer, -ī *adj* stormy

nimbōsus *adj* stormy

nimbus, -ī *m* cloud, rain, storm

nimiō *adv* much, far

nīmīrum *adv* certainly, of course

nimis *adv* too much, very much; **nōn** ~ not very

nimium *adv* too, too much; very, very much

nimius *adj* too great, excessive; very great ♦ *nt* excess

ningit, ninguit, -ere *vi* it snows

ninguēs, -ium *fpl* snow

Nioba, -ae, Niobē, -ēs *f* daughter of Tantalus *(changed to a weeping rock)*

Niobēus *adj see* **Nioba**

Nīreus, -eī *and* **-eos** *m* handsomest of the Greeks at Troy

Nīsaeus, Nīsēius *adj see* **Nīsus**

Nīsēis, -edis *f* Scylla

nisi *conj* if not, unless; except, but

Nīsus, -ī *m* father of Scylla

nīsus¹ *ppa of* **nītor**

nīsus², -ūs *m* pressure, effort; striving, soaring

nītēdula, -ae *f* dormouse

nitēns, -entis *pres p of* **niteō** ♦ *adj* bright; brilliant, beautiful

niteō, -ēre *vi* to shine, gleam; to be sleek, be greasy; to thrive, look beautiful

nitēscō, -ere, nituī *vi* to brighten, shine, glow

nitidē *adv* magnificently

nitidiusculē *adv* rather more finely

nitidiusculus *adj* a little shinier

nitidus *adj* bright, shining; sleek; blooming; smart, spruce; *(speech)* refined

nitor, -ōris *m* brightness, sheen; sleekness, beauty; neatness, elegance

nītor, -tī, -sus *and* **-xus** *vi* to rest on, lean on; to press, stand firmly; to press forward, climb; to exert oneself, strive, labour; to depend on

nitrum, -ī *nt* soda

nivālis *adj* snowy

niveus *adj* of snow, snowy, snow-white

nivōsus *adj* snowy

nix, nivis *f* snow

nīxor, -ārī *vi* to rest on; to struggle

nīxus¹ *ppp of* **nītor**

nīxus², -ūs *m* pressure; labour

nō, nāre, nāvī *vi* to swim, float; to sail, fly

nōbilis *adj* known, noted, famous, notorious; noble, high-born; excellent

nōbilitās, -ātis *f* fame; noble birth; the nobility; excellence

nōbilitō, -āre, -āvī, -ātum *vt* to make famous or notorious

nocēns, -entis *pres p of* **noceō** ♦ *adj* harmful; criminal, guilty

noceō, -ēre, -uī, -itum *vi* *(with dat)* to harm, hurt

nocīvus *adj* injurious

noctifer, -ī *m* evening star

noctilūca, -ae *f* moon

noctivagus *adj* night-wandering

noctū *adv* by night

noctua, -ae *f* owl

noctuābundus *adj* travelling by night

nocturnus *adj* night- *(in cpds)*, nocturnal

nōdō, -āre, -āvī, -ātum *vt* to knot, tie

nōdōsus *adj* knotty

nōdus, -ī *m* knot; knob; girdle; *(fig)* bond, difficulty

nōlō, -le, -uī *vt, vi* to not wish, be unwilling, refuse; **nōlī, nōlīte** do not

Nomas, -dis *m/f* nomad; Numidian

nōmen, -inis *nt* name; title; (COMM) demand, debt; (GRAM) noun; *(fig)* reputation, fame; account, pretext; ~ **dare**, ~ **profitērī** enlist; ~ **dēferre** accuse; **nōmina facere** enter the items of a debt

nōmenclātor, -ōris *m* slave who told his master the names of people

nōminātim *adv* by name, one by one

nōminātiō, -ōnis *f* nomination

nōminitō, -āre *vt* to usually name

nōminō, -āre, -āvī, -ātum *vt* to name, call; to mention; to make famous; to nominate; to accuse, denounce

nomisma, -tis *nt* coin

nōn *adv* not; no

Nōnae, -ārum *fpl* Nones *(7th day of March, May, July, October, 5th of other months)*

nōnāgēsimus *adj* ninetieth
nōnāgiēns, nōnāgiēs *adv* ninety times
nōnāgintā *num* ninety
nōnānus *adj* of the ninth legion
nōndum *adv* not yet
nōngentī, -ōrum *num* nine hundred
nonna, -ae *f* nun
nōnne *adv* do not?, is not? *etc*; (*indirect*) whether not
nōnnullus *adj* some
nōnnunquam *adv* sometimes
nōnus *adj* ninth ♦ *f* ninth hour
nōnusdecimus *adj* nineteenth
Nōricum, -ī *nt country between the Danube and the Alps*
Nōricus *adj see* **Nōricum**
nōrma, -ae *f* rule
nōs *pron* we, us; I, me
nōscitō, -āre *vt* to know, recognize; to observe, examine
nōscō, -scere, -vī, -tum *vt* to get to know, learn; to examine; to recognize, allow; (*perf*) to know
nōsmet *pron* (*emphatic*)*see* **nōs**
noster, -rī *adj* our, ours; for us; my; (*with names*) my dear, good old ♦ *m* our friend ♦ *mpl* our side, our troops; **nostrī, nostrum** of us
nostrās, -ātis *adj* of our country, native
nota, -ae *f* mark, sign, note; (*writing*) note, letter; (*pl*) memoranda, shorthand, secret writing; (*books*) critical mark, punctuation; (*wine, etc*) brand, quality; (*gesture*) sign; (*fig*) sign, token; (*censor's*) black mark; (*fig*) stigma, disgrace
notābilis *adj* remarkable; notorious
notābiliter *adv* perceptibly
notārius, -ī and -iī *m* shorthand writer; secretary
notātiō, -ōnis *f* marking; choice; observation; (*censor*) stigmatizing; (*words*) etymology
nōtēscō, -ere, nōtuī *vi* to become known
nothus *adj* bastard; counterfeit
nōtiō, -ōnis *f* (*LAW*) cognisance, investigation; (*PHILOS*) idea
nōtitia, -ae, nōtitiēs, -ēī *f* fame; acquaintance; (*PHILOS*) idea, preconception
notō, -āre, -āvī, -ātum *vt* to mark, write; to denote; to observe; to brand, stigmatize
nōtuī *perf of* **nōtēscō**
Notus, Notos, -ī *m* south wind
nōtus *ppp of* **nōscō** ♦ *adj* known, familiar; notorious ♦ *mpl* acquaintances
novācula, -ae *f* razor
novālis, -is *f*, **novāle, -is** *nt* fallow land; field; crops
novātrīx, -īcis *f* renewer
novē *adv* unusually
novellus *adj* young, fresh, new
novem *num* nine
November, -ris *adj* of November ♦ *m* November
novendecim *num* nineteen
novendiālis *adj* nine days'; on the ninth day
novēnī, -ōrum *adj* in nines; nine
Novēnsilēs, -ium *mpl* new gods
noverca, -ae *f* stepmother
novercālis *adj* stepmother's
nōvī *perf of* **nōscō**
novīcius *adj* new

noviēns, noviēs *adv* nine times
novissimē *adv* lately; last of all
novissimus *adj* latest, last, rear
novitās, -ātis *f* newness, novelty; strangeness
novō, -āre, -āvī, -ātum *vt* to renew, refresh; to change; (*words*) to coin; **rēs novāre** effect a revolution
novus *adj* new, young, fresh, recent; strange, unusual; inexperienced; ~ **homō** upstart, first of his family to hold curule office; **novae rēs** revolution; **novae tabulae** cancellation of debts; **quid novī** what news?
nox, noctis *f* night; darkness, obscurity; **nocte, noctū** by night; **dē nocte** during the night
noxa, -ae *f* hurt, harm; offence, guilt; punishment
noxia, -ae *f* harm, damage; guilt, fault
noxius *adj* harmful; guilty
nūbēcula, -ae *f* cloudy look
nūbēs, -is *f* cloud; (*fig*) gloom; veil
nūbifer, -ī *adj* cloud-capped; cloudy
nūbigena, -ae *m* cloudborn, Centaur
nūbilis *adj* marriageable
nūbilus *adj* cloudy; gloomy, sad ♦ *ntpl* clouds
nūbō, -bere, -psī, -ptum *vi* (*women*) to be married
nucleus, -ī *m* nut, kernel
nūdius day since, days ago; ~ **tertius** the day before yesterday
nūdō, -āre, -āvī, -ātum *vt* to bare, strip, expose; (*MIL*) to leave exposed; to plunder; (*fig*) to disclose, betray
nūdus *adj* naked, bare; exposed, defenceless; wearing only a tunic; (*fig*) destitute, poor; mere; unembellished, undisguised; **vestīmenta dētrahere nūdō** draw blood from a stone
nūgae, -ārum *fpl* nonsense, trifles; (*person*) waster
nūgātor, -ōris *m* silly creature, liar
nūgātōrius *adj* futile
nūgāx, -ācis *adj* frivolous
nūgor, -ārī, -ātus *vi* to talk nonsense; to cheat
nullus (*gen* **-īus**, *dat* **-ī**) *adj* no, none; not, not at all; non-existent, of no account ♦ *m/f* nobody
num *interrog particle* surely not?; (*indirect*) whether, if
Numa, -ae *m second king of Rome*
nūmen, -inis *nt* nod, will; divine will, power; divinity, god
numerābilis *adj* easy to count
numerātus *adj* in cash ♦ *nt* ready money
numerō¹, -āre, -āvī, -ātum *vt* to count, number; (*money*) to pay out; (*fig*) to reckon, consider as
numerō² *adv* just now, quickly, too soon
numerōsē *adv* rhythmically
numerōsus *adj* populous; rhythmical
numerus, -ī *m* number; many, numbers; (*MIL*) troop; (*fig*) a cipher; (*pl*) mathematics; rank, category, regard; rhythm, metre, verse; **in numerō esse, in numerō habērī** be reckoned as; **nullō numerō** of no account
Numida *adj see* **Numidae**
Numidae, -ārum *mpl* Numidians (*people of N. Africa*)

Numidia, -iae f the country of the Numidians
Numidicus adj see **Numidia**
Numitor, -ōris m king of Alba (grandfather of Romulus)
nummārius adj money- (in cpds), financial; mercenary
nummātus adj moneyed
nummulī, -ōrum mpl some money, cash
nummus, -ī m coin, money, cash; (Roman coin) sestertius; (Greek coin) two-drachma piece
numnam, numne see **num**
numquam adv never; ~ nōn always; nōn ~ sometimes
numquid (question) do you? does he? etc; (indirect) whether
nunc adv now; at present, nowadays; but as it is; ~ ... ~ at one time ... at another
nuncupātiō, -ōnis f pronouncing
nuncupō, -āre, -āvī, -ātum vt to call, name; to pronounce formally
nūndinae, -ārum fpl market day; market; trade
nūndinātiō, -ōnis f trading
nūndinor, -ārī vi to trade, traffic; to flock together ♦ vt to buy
nūndinum, -ī nt market time; trīnum ~ 17 days
nunq- etc see **numq-**
nūntiātiō, -ōnis f announcing
nūntiō, -āre, -āvī, -ātum vt to announce, report, tell

nūntius adj informative, speaking ♦ m messenger; message, news; injunction; notice of divorce ♦ nt message
nūper adv recently, lately
nūpsī perf of **nūbō**
nūpta, -ae f bride, wife
nūptiae, -ārum fpl wedding, marriage
nūptiālis adj wedding- (in cpds), nuptial
nurus, -ūs f daughter-in-law; young woman
nūsquam adv nowhere; in nothing, for nothing
nūtō, -āre vi to nod; to sway, totter, falter
nūtrīcius, -ī m tutor
nūtrīcō, -āre, nūtrīcor, -ārī vt to nourish, sustain
nūtrīcula, -ae f nurse
nūtrīmen, -inis nt nourishment
nūtrīmentum, -ī nt nourishment, support
nūtriō, -īre, -īvī, -ītum vt to suckle, nourish, rear, nurse
nūtrīx, -īcis f nurse, foster mother
nūtus, -ūs m nod; will, command; (physics) gravity
nux, nucis f nut; nut tree, almond tree
Nyctēis, -idis f Antiopa
nympha, -ae, nymphē, -ēs f bride; nymph; water
Nysa, -ae f birthplace of Bacchus
Nysaeus, Nysaēis, Nysaius adj see **Nysa**

Oo

ō *interj (expressing joy, surprise, pain, etc)* oh!; *(with voc)* O!

ob *prep (with acc)* in front of; for, on account of, for the sake of; **quam ob rem** accordingly

obaerātus *adj* in debt ♦ *m* debtor

obambulō, -āre *vi* to walk past, prowl about

obarmō, -āre *vt* to arm *(against)*

obarō, -āre *vt* to plough up

obc- *etc see* **occ-**

obdō, -ere, -idī, -itum *vt* to shut; to expose

obdormīscō, -īscere, -īvī *vi* to fall asleep ♦ *vt* to sleep off

obdūcō, -ūcere, -ūxī, -uctum *vt* to draw over, cover; to bring up; *(drink)* to swallow; *(time)* to pass

obductiō, -ōnis *f* veiling

obductō, -āre *vt* to bring as a rival

obductus *ppp of* **obdūcō**

obdūrēscō, -ēscere, -uī *vi* to harden; to become obdurate

obdūrō, -āre *vi* to persist, stand firm

obeō, -īre, -īvī *and* **-iī, -itum** *vi* to go to, meet; to die; *(ASTR)* to set ♦ *vt* to visit, travel over; to survey, go over; to envelop; *(duty)* to engage in, perform; *(time)* to meet; **diem obīre** die; *(LAW)* to appear on the appointed day

obequitō, -āre *vi* to ride up to

oberrō, -āre *vi* to ramble about; to make a mistake

obēsus *adj* fat, plump; coarse

ōbex, -icis *m/f* bolt, bar, barrier

obf- *etc see* **off-**

obg- *etc see* **ogg-**

obhaerēscō, -rēscere, -sī *vi* to stick fast

obiaceō, -ēre *vi* to lie over against

obiciō, -icere, -iēcī, -iectum *vt* to throw to, set before; *(defence)* to put up, throw against; *(fig)* to expose, give up; *(speech)* to taunt, reproach

obiectātiō, -ōnis *f* reproach

obiectō, -āre *vt* to throw against; to expose, sacrifice; to reproach; *(hint)* to let on

obiectus¹ *ppp of* **obiciō** ♦ *adj* opposite, in front of; exposed ♦ *ntpl* accusations

obiectus², -ūs *m* putting in the way, interposing

obīrātus *adj* angered

obiter *adv* on the way; incidentally

obitus¹ *ppp of* **obeō**

obitus², -ūs *m* death, ruin; *(ASTR)* setting; visit

obiūrgātiō, -ōnis *f* reprimand

obiūrgātor, -ōris *m* reprover

obiūrgātōrius *adj* reproachful

obiūrgitō, -āre *vt* to keep on reproaching

obiūrgō, -āre, -āvī, -ātum *vt* to scold, rebuke; to deter by reproof

oblanguēscō, -ēscere, -uī *vi* to become feeble

oblātrātrīx, -īcis *f* nagging woman

oblātus *ppp of* **offerō**

oblectāmentum, -ī *nt* amusement

oblectātiō, -ōnis *f* delight

oblectō, -āre, -āvī, -ātum *vt* to delight, amuse, entertain; to detain; *(time)* to spend pleasantly; **sē oblectāre** enjoy oneself

oblīdō, -dere, -sī, -sum *vt* to crush, strangle

obligātiō, -ōnis *f* pledge

obligō, -āre, -āvī, -ātum *vt* to tie up, bandage; to put under an obligation, embarrass; *(LAW)* to render liable, make guilty; to mortgage

oblimō, -āre *vt* to cover with mud

oblinō, -inere, -ēvī, -itum *vt* to smear over; to defile; *(fig)* to overload

oblīquē *adv* sideways; indirectly

oblīquō, -āre *vt* to turn aside, veer

oblīquus *adj* slanting, downhill; from the side, sideways; *(look)* askance, envious; *(speech)* indirect

oblīsus *ppp of* **oblīdō**

oblītēscō, -ere *vi* to hide away

oblitterō, -āre, -āvī, -ātum *vt* to erase, cancel; *(fig)* to consign to oblivion

oblitus *ppp of* **oblinō**

oblītus *ppa of* **oblīvīscor**

oblīviō, -ōnis *f* oblivion, forgetfulness

oblīviōsus *adj* forgetful

oblīvīscor, -vīscī, -tus *vt, vi* to forget

oblīvium, -ī *and* **-iī** *nt* forgetfulness, oblivion

oblocūtor, -ōris *m* contradicter

oblongus *adj* oblong

obloquor, -quī, -cūtus *vi* to contradict, interrupt; to abuse; *(music)* to accompany

obluctor, -ārī *vi* to struggle against

obmōlior, -īrī *vt* to throw up *(as a defence)*

obmurmurō, -āre *vi* to roar in answer

obmūtēscō, -ēscere, -uī *vi* to become silent; to cease

obnātus *adj* growing on

obnītor, -tī, -xus *vi* to push against, struggle; to stand firm, resist

obnīxē *adv* resolutely

obnīxus *ppa of* **obnītor** ♦ *adj* steadfast

obnoxiē *adv* slavishly

obnoxiōsus *adj* submissive

obnoxius *adj* liable, addicted; culpable; submissive, slavish; under obligation, indebted; exposed (*to danger*)

obnūbō, -bere, -psī, -ptum *vt* to veil, cover

obnūntiātiō, -ōnis *f* announcement of an adverse omen

obnūntiō, -āre *vt* to announce an adverse omen

oboediēns, -entis *pres p of* **oboediō** ♦ *adj* obedient

oboedienter *adv* readily

oboedientia, -ae *f* obedience

oboediō, -īre *vi* to listen; to obey, be subject to

oboleō, -ēre, -uī *vt* to smell of

oborior, -īrī, -tus *vi* to arise, spring up

obp- *etc see* **opp-**

obrēpō, -ere, -sī, -tum *vt, vi* to creep up to, steal upon, surprise; to cheat

obrētiō, -īre *vt* to entangle

obrigēscō, -ēscere, -uī *vi* to stiffen

obrogō, -āre, -āvī, -ātum *vt* to invalidate (*by making a new law*)

obruō, -ere, -ī, -tum *vt* to cover over, bury, sink; to overwhelm, overpower ♦ *vi* to fall to ruin

obrussa, -ae *f* test, touchstone

obrutus *ppp of* **obruō**

obsaepiō, -īre, -sī, -tum *vt* to block, close

obsaturō, -āre *vt* to sate, glut

obscaen- *etc see* **obscen-**

obscēnē *adv* indecently

obscēnitās, -ātis *f* indecency

obscēnus *adj* filthy; indecent; ominous

obscūrātiō, -ōnis *f* darkening, disappearance

obscūrē *adv* secretly

obscūritās, -ātis *f* darkness; (*fig*) uncertainty; (*rank*) lowliness

obscūrō, -āre, -āvī, -ātum *vt* to darken; to conceal, suppress; (*speech*) to obscure; (*pass*) to become obsolete

obscūrus *adj* dark, shady, hidden; (*fig*) obscure, indistinct; unknown, ignoble; (*character*) reserved

obsecrātiō, -ōnis *f* entreaty; public prayer

obsecrō, -āre *vt* to implore, appeal to

obsecundō, -āre *vi* to comply with, back up

obsēdī *perf of* **obsideō**

obsēp- *etc see* **obsaep-**

obsequēns, -entis *pres p of* **obsequor** ♦ *adj* compliant; (*gods*) gracious

obsequenter *adv* compliantly

obsequentia, -ae *f* complaisance

obsequiōsus *adj* complaisant

obsequium, -ī *and* **-iī** *nt* compliance, indulgence; obedience, allegiance

obsequor, -quī, -cūtus *vi* to comply with, yield to, indulge

obserō¹, -āre *vt* to bar, close

obserō², -erere, -ēvī, -itum *vt* to sow, plant; to cover thickly

observāns, -antis *pres p of* **observō** ♦ *adj* attentive, respectful

observantia, -ae *f* respect

observātiō, -ōnis *f* watching; caution

observitō, -āre *vt* to observe carefully

observō, -āre, -āvī, -ātum *vt* to watch, watch for; to guard; (*laws*) to keep, comply with; (*person*) to pay respect to

obses, -idis *m/f* hostage; guarantee

obsessiō, -ōnis *f* blockade

obsessor, -ōris *m* frequenter; besieger

obsessus *ppp of* **obsideō**

obsideō, -idēre, -ēdī, -essum *vt* to sit at, frequent; (*MIL*) to blockade, besiege; to block, fill, take up; to guard, watch for ♦ *vi* to sit

obsidiō, -ōnis *f* siege, blockade; (*fig*) imminent danger

obsidium, -ī *and* **-iī** *nt* siege, blockade; hostageship

obsīdō, -ere *vt* to besiege, occupy

obsignātor, -ōris *m* sealer; witness

obsignō, -āre, -āvī, -ātum *vt* to seal up; to sign and seal; (*fig*) to stamp

obsistō, -istere, -titī, -titum *vi* to put oneself in the way, resist

obsitus *ppp of* **obserō²**

obsolefiō, -fierī *vi* to wear out, become degraded

obsolēscō, -scere, -vī, -tum *vi* to wear out, become out of date

obsolētius *adv* more shabbily

obsolētus *ppa of* **obsolēscō** ♦ *adj* worn out, shabby; obsolete; (*fig*) ordinary, mean

obsōnātor, -ōris *m* caterer

obsōnātus, -ūs *m* marketing

obsōnium, -ī *and* **-iī** *nt* food eaten with bread (*usu fish*)

obsonō, -āre *vi* to interrupt

obsōnō, -āre, obsōnor, -ārī *vi* to cater, buy provisions; to provide a meal

obsorbeō, -ēre *vt* to swallow, bolt

obstantia, -ium *ntpl* obstructions

obstetrīx, -īcis *f* midwife

obstinātē *adv* firmly, obstinately

obstinātiō, -ōnis *f* determination, stubbornness

obstinātus *adj* firm, resolute; stubborn

obstinō, -āre *vi* to be determined, persist

obstipēscō *etc see* **obstupēscō**

obstīpus *adj* bent, bowed, drawn back

obstitī *perf of* **obsistō**; **obstō**

obstō, -āre, -itī *vi* to stand in the way; to obstruct, prevent

obstrepō, -ere, -uī, -itum *vi* to make a noise; to shout against, cry down, molest ♦ *vt* to drown (*in noise*), fill with noise

obstrictus *ppp of* **obstringō**

obstringō, -ingere, -inxī, -ictum *vt* to bind up, tie round; (*fig*) to confine, hamper; to lay under an obligation

obstructiō, -ōnis *f* barrier

obstructus *ppp of* **obstruō**

obstrūdō, obtrūdō, -dere, -sī, -sum *vt* to force on to; to gulp down

obstruō, -ere, -xī, -ctum *vt* to build up against, block; to shut, hinder

obstupefaciō, -facere, -fēcī, -factum (*pass* **-fiō**) *vt* to astound, paralyse

obstupēscō, -ēscere, -uī *vi* to be astounded, paralysed

obstupidus *adj* stupefied

obsum, -esse, -fuī *vi* to be against, harm

obsuō, -uere, -uī, -ūtum *vt* to sew on, sew up

obsurdēscō, -ēscere, -uī *vi* to grow deaf; to turn a deaf ear

obsūtus *ppp of* **obsuō**

obtegō, -egere, -ēxī, -ēctum *vt* to cover over; to conceal

obtemperātiō, -ōnis *f* obedience

obtemperō, -āre, -āvī, -ātum *vi* (*with dat*) to comply with, obey

obtendō, -dere, -dī, -tum *vt* to spread over, stretch over against; to conceal; to make a pretext of

obtentus¹ *ppp of* **obtendō; obtineō**

obtentus², -ūs *m* screen; pretext

obterō, -erere, -rīvī, -rītum *vt* to trample on, crush; to disparage

obtestātiō, -ōnis *f* adjuring; supplication

obtestor, -ārī, -ātus *vt* to call to witness; to entreat

obtexō, -ere, -uī *vt* to overspread

obticeō, -ēre *vi* to be silent

obticēscō, -ēscere, -uī *vi* to be struck dumb

obtigī *perf of* **obtingō**

obtigō *see* **obtegō**

obtineō, -inēre, -inuī, -entum *vt* to hold, possess; to maintain; to gain, obtain ♦ *vi* to prevail, continue

obtingō, -ngere, -gī *vi* to fall to one's lot; to happen

obtorpēscō, -ēscere, -uī *vi* to become numb, lose feeling

obtorqueō, -quēre, -sī, -tum *vt* to twist about, wrench

obtrectātiō, -ōnis *f* disparagement

obtrectātor, -ōris *m* disparager

obtrectō, -āre *vt, vi* to detract, disparage

obtrītus *ppp of* **obterō**

obtrūdō *etc see* **obstrūdō**

obtruncō, -āre *vt* to cut down, slaughter

obtueor, -ērī, -or, -ī *vt* to gaze at, see clearly

obtulī *perf of* **offerō**

obtundō, -undere, -udī, -ūsum *and* **-ūnsum** *vt* to beat, thump; to blunt; (*speech*) to deafen, annoy

obturbō, -āre *vt* to throw into confusion; to bother, distract

obturgēscō, -ere *vi* to swell up

obtūrō, -āre *vt* to stop up, close

obtūsus, obtūnsus *ppp of* **obtundō** ♦ *adj* blunt; (*fig*) dulled, blurred, unfeeling

obtūtus, -ūs *m* gaze

obumbrō, -āre *vt* to shade, darken; (*fig*) to cloak, screen

obuncus *adj* hooked

obūstus *adj* burnt, hardened in fire

obvallātus *adj* fortified

obveniō, -enīre, -ēnī, -entum *vi* to come up; to fall to; to occur

obversor, -ārī *vi* to move about before; (*visions*) to hover

obversus *ppp of* **obvertō** ♦ *adj* turned towards ♦ *mpl* enemy

obvertō, -tere, -tī, -sum *vt* to direct towards, turn against

obviam *adv* to meet, against; ~ **ire** to go to meet

obvius *adj* in the way, to meet; opposite, against; at hand, accessible; exposed

obvolvō, -vere, -vī, -ūtum *vt* to wrap up, muffle up; (*fig*) to cloak

occaecō, -āre, -āvī, -ātum *vt* to blind, obscure, conceal; to benumb

occallēscō, -ēscere, -uī *vi* to grow a thick skin; to become hardened

occanō, -ere *vi* to sound the attack

occāsiō, -ōnis *f* opportunity, convenient time; (*MIL*) surprise

occāsiuncula, -ae *f* opportunity

occāsus, -ūs *m* setting; west; downfall, ruin

occātiō, -ōnis *f* harrowing

occātor, -ōris *m* harrower

occēdō, -ere *vi* to go up to

occentō, -āre *vt, vi* to serenade; to sing a lampoon

occēpī *perf of* **occipiō**

occepsō *archaic fut of* **occipiō**

occeptō, -āre *vt* to begin

occidēns, -entis *pres p of* **occidō** ♦ *m* west

occīdiō, -ōnis *f* massacre; **occīdiōne occīdere** annihilate

occidō, -idere, -idī, -āsum *vi* to fall; to set; to die, perish, be ruined

occīdō, -dere, -dī, -sum *vt* to fell; to cut down, kill; to pester

occiduus *adj* setting; western; failing

occinō, -ere, -uī *vi* to sing inauspiciously

occipiō, -ipere, -ēpī, -eptum *vt, vi* to begin

occipitium, -ī *and* **-iī** *nt* back of the head

occīsiō, -ōnis *f* massacre

occīsor, -ōris *m* killer

occīsus *ppp of* **occīdō**

occlāmitō, -āre *vi* to bawl

occlūdō, -dere, -sī, -sum *vt* to shut up; to stop

occō, -āre *vt* to harrow

occubō, -āre *vi* to lie

occulcō, -āre *vt* to trample down

occulō, -ere, -uī, -tum *vt* to cover over, hide

occultātiō, -ōnis *f* concealment

occultātor, -ōris *m* hider

occultē *adv* secretly

occultō, -āre, -āvī, -ātum *vt* to conceal, secrete

occultus *ppp of* **occulō** ♦ *adj* hidden, secret; (*person*) reserved, secretive ♦ *nt* secret, hiding

occumbō, -mbere, -buī, -bitum *vi* to fall, die

occupātiō, -ōnis *f* taking possession; business; engagement

occupātus *adj* occupied, busy

occupō, -āre, -āvī, -ātum *vt* to take possession of, seize; to occupy, take up; to surprise, anticipate; (*money*) to lend, invest

occurrō, -rere, -rī, -sum *vi* to run up to, meet; to attack; to fall in with; to hurry to; (*fig*) to obviate, counteract; (*words*) to object; (*thought*) to occur, suggest itself

occursātiō, -ōnis *f* fussy welcome

occursō, -āre *vi* to run to meet, meet; to oppose; (*thought*) to occur

occursus, -ūs *m* meeting

Ōceanītis, -ītidis f daughter of Ocean

Ōceanus, -ī m Ocean, a stream encircling the earth; the Atlantic

ocellus, -ī m eye; darling, gem

ōcior, -ōris adj quicker, swifter

ōcius adv more quickly; sooner, rather; quickly

ocrea, -ae f greave

ocreātus adj greaved

Octāviānus adj of Octavius ♦ m Octavian (a surname of Augustus)

Octāvius, -ī m Roman family name (esp the emperor Augustus; his father)

octāvum adv for the eighth time

octāvus adj eighth ♦ f eighth hour

octāvusdecimus adj eighteenth

octiēns, octiēs adv eight times

octingentēsimus adj eight hundredth

octingentī, -ōrum num eight hundred

octipēs, -edis adj eight-footed

octō num eight

Octōber, -ris adj of October ♦ m October

octōgēnī, -ōrum adj eighty each

octōgēsimus adj eightieth

octōgiēns, octōgiēs adv eighty times

octōgintā num eighty

octōiugis adj eight together

octōnī, -ōrum adj eight at a time, eight each

octōphoros adj (litter) carried by eight bearers

octuplicātus adj multiplied by eight

octuplus adj eightfold

octussis, -is m eight asses

oculātus adj with eyes; visible; **oculātā diē vēndere** sell for cash

oculus, -ī m eye; sight; (plant) bud; (fig) darling, jewel; **oculōs adicere ad** glance at, covet; **ante oculōs pōnere** imagine; **ex oculis** out of sight; **esse in oculīs** be in view; be a favourite

ōdī, -isse vt to hate, dislike

odiōsē adv see **odiōsus**

odiōsus adj odious, unpleasant

odium, -ī and **-iī** nt hatred, dislike, displeasure; insolence; **odiō esse** be hateful, be disliked

odor, odōs, -ōris m smell, perfume, stench; (fig) inkling, suggestion

odōrātiō, -ōnis f smelling

odōrātus¹ adj fragrant, perfumed

odōrātus², -ūs m sense of smell; smelling

odōrifer, -ī adj fragrant; perfume-producing

odōrō, -āre vt to perfume

odōror, -ārī, -ātus vt to smell, smell out; (fig) to search out; to aspire to; to get a smattering of

odōrus adj fragrant; keen-scented

odōs etc see **odor**

Odrysius adj Thracian

Odyssēa, -ae f Odyssey

Oeagrius adj Thracian

Oebalia, -iae f Tarentum

Oebalidēs, -idae m Castor, Pollux

Oebalis, -idis f Helen

Oebalius adj Spartan

Oebalus, -ī m king of Sparta

Oedipūs, -odis and **-ī** m king of Thebes; solver of riddles

oenophorum, -ī nt wine basket

Oenopia, -ae f Aegina

Oenotria, -ae f S.E. Italy

Oenotrius adj Italian

oestrus, -ī m gadfly; (fig) frenzy

Oeta, -ae, Oetē, -ēs f mountain range in Thessaly, associated with Hercules

Oetaeus adj see **Oeta**

ofella, -ae f morsel

offa, -ae f pellet, lump; swelling

offectus ppp of **officiō**

offendō, -endere, -endī, -ēnsum vt to hit; to hit on, come upon; to offend, blunder; to take offence; to fail, come to grief

offēnsa, -ae f displeasure, enmity; offence, injury

offēnsiō, -ōnis f stumbling; stumbling block; misfortune, indisposition; offence, displeasure

offēnsiuncula, -ae f slight displeasure; slight check

offēnsō, -āre vt, vi to dash against

offēnsus¹ ppp of **offendō** ♦ adj offensive; displeased ♦ nt offence

offēnsus², -ūs m shock; offence

offerō, -re, obtulī, oblātum vt to present, show; to bring forward, offer; to expose; to cause, inflict; **sē offerre** encounter

offerumenta, -ae f present

officīna, -ae f workshop, factory

officiō, -icere, -ēcī, -ectum vi to obstruct; to interfere with; to hurt, prejudice

officiōsē adv courteously

officiōsus adj obliging; dutiful

officium, -ī and **-iī** nt service, attention; ceremonial; duty, sense of duty; official duty, function

offigō, -ere vt to fasten, drive in

offirmātus adj determined

offirmō, -āre vt, vi to persevere in

offlectō, -ere vt to turn about

offrēnātus adj checked

offūcia, -ae f (cosmetic) paint; (fig) trick

offulgeō, -gēre, -sī vi to shine on

offundō, -undere, -ūdī, -ūsum vt to pour out to; to pour over; to spread; to cover, fill

offūsus ppp of **offundō**

oggannīō, -īre vi to growl at

oggerō, -ere vt to bring, give

Ōgygius adj Theban

oh interj (expressing surprise, joy, grief) oh!

ohē interj (expressing surfeit) stop!, enough!

oi interj (expressing complaint, weeping) oh!, oh dear!

oiei interj (lamenting) oh dear!

Oīleus, -eī m father of the less famous Ajax

olea, -ae f olive; olive tree

oleāginus adj of the olive tree

oleārius adj oil- (in cpds) ♦ m oil seller

oleaster, -rī m wild olive

olēns, -entis pres p of **oleō** ♦ adj fragrant; stinking, musty

oleō, -ēre, -uī vt, vi to smell, smell of; (fig) to betray

oleum, -ī nt olive oil, oil; wrestling school; ~ **et operam perdere** waste time and trouble

olfaciō, -facere, -fēcī, -factum *vt* to smell, scent

olfactō, -āre *vt* to smell at

olidus *adj* smelling, rank

ōlim *adv* once, once upon a time; at the time, at times; for a good while; one day (*in the future*)

olit- *etc see* **holit-**

olīva, -ae *f* olive, olive tree; olive branch, olive staff

olīvētum, -ī *nt* olive grove

olīvifer, -ī *adj* olive-bearing

olīvum, -ī *nt* oil; wrestling school; perfume

olla, -ae *f* pot, jar

olle, ollus *see* **ille**

olor, -ōris *m* swan

olōrīnus *adj* swan's

olus *etc see* **holus**

Olympia[1], -ae *f* site of the Greek games in Elis

Olympia[2], -ōrum *ntpl* Olympic Games

Olympiacus *adj* = **Olympicus**

Olympias, -adis *f* Olympiad, period of four years

Olympicus, Olympius *adj* Olympic

Olympionīcēs, -ae *m* Olympic winner

Olympus, -ī *m* mountain in N. Greece, abode of the gods; heaven

omāsum, -ī *nt* tripe; paunch

ōmen, -inis *nt* omen, sign; solemnity

ōmentum, -ī *nt* bowels

ōminor, -ārī, -ātus *vt* to forebode, prophesy

ōmissus *ppp of* **ōmittō ♦** *adj* remiss

ōmittō, -ittere, -īsī, -issum *vt* to let go; to leave off, give up; to disregard, overlook; (*speech*) to pass over, omit

omnifer, -ī *adj* all-sustaining

omnigenus *adj* of all kinds

omnimodīs *adv* wholly

omnīnō *adv* entirely, altogether, at all; in general; (*concession*) to be sure, yes; (*number*) in all, just; ~ **nōn** not at all

omniparēns, -entis *adj* mother of all

omnipotēns, -entis *adj* almighty

omnis *adj* all, every, any; every kind of; the whole of **♦** *nt* the universe **♦** *mpl* everybody **♦** *ntpl* everything

omnituēns, -entis *adj* all-seeing

omnivagus *adj* roving everywhere

omnivolus *adj* willing everything

onager, -rī *m* wild ass

onerārius *adj* (*beast*) of burden; (*ship*) transport

onerō, -āre, -āvī, -ātum *vt* to load, burden; (*fig*) to overload, oppress; to aggravate

onerōsus *adj* heavy, burdensome, irksome

onus, -eris *nt* load, burden, cargo; (*fig*) charge, difficulty

onustus *adj* loaded, burdened; (*fig*) filled

onyx, -chis *m/f* onyx; onyx box

opācitās, -ātis *f* shade

opācō, -āre *vt* to shade

opācus *adj* shady; dark

ope *abl of* **ops**

opella, -ae *f* light work, small service

opera, -ae *f* exertion, work; service; care, attention; leisure, time; (*person*) workman, hired rough; **operam dare** pay attention;

do one's best; **operae pretium** worth while; **operā meā** thanks to me

operārius *adj* working **♦** *m* workman

operculum, -ī *nt* cover, lid

operīmentum, -ī *nt* covering

operiō, -īre, -uī, -tum *vt* to cover; to close; (*fig*) to overwhelm, conceal

operor, -ārī, -ātus *vi* to work, take pains, be occupied

operōsē *adv* painstakingly

operōsus *adj* active, industrious; laborious, elaborate

opertus *ppp of* **operiō ♦** *adj* covered, hidden **♦** *nt* secret

opēs *pl of* **ops**

opicus *adj* barbarous, boorish

opifer, -ī *adj* helping

opifex, -icis *m/f* maker; craftsman, artisan

ōpiliō, -ōnis *m* shepherd

opīmitās, -ātis *f* abundance

opīmus *adj* rich, fruitful, fat; copious, sumptuous; (*style*) overloaded; **spolia opīma** spoils of an enemy commander killed by a Roman general

opīnābilis *adj* conjectural

opīnātiō, -ōnis *f* conjecture

opīnātor, -ōris *m* conjecturer

opīnātus, -ūs *m* supposition

opīniō, -ōnis *f* opinion, conjecture, belief; reputation, esteem; rumour; **contrā** opīniōnem, **praeter opīniōnem** contrary to expectation

opīniōsus *adj* dogmatic

opīnor, -ārī, -ātus *vi* to think, suppose, imagine **♦** *adj* imagined

opiparē *adv see* **opiparus**

opiparus *adj* rich, sumptuous

opitulor, -ārī, -ātus *vi* (*with dat*) to help

oportet, -ēre, -uit *vt* (*impers*) ought, should

oppēdō, -ere *vi* to insult

opperior, -īrī, -tus *vt, vi* to wait, wait for

oppetō, -ere, -īvī, -ītum *vt* to encounter; to die

oppidānus *adj* provincial **♦** *mpl* townsfolk

oppidō *adv* quite, completely, exactly

oppidulum, -ī *nt* small town

oppidum, -ī *nt* town

oppignerō, -āre *vt* to pledge

oppīlō, -āre *vt* to stop up

oppleō, -ēre, -ēvī, -ētum *vt* to fill, choke up

oppōnō, -ōnere, -osuī, -ositum *vt* to put against, set before; to expose; to present; (*argument*) to adduce, reply, oppose; (*property*) to pledge, mortgage

opportūnē *adv* opportunely

opportūnitās, -ātis *f* suitableness, advantage; good opportunity

opportūnus *adj* suitable, opportune; useful; exposed

oppositiō, -ōnis *f* opposing

oppositus[1] *ppp of* **oppōnō ♦** *adj* against, opposite

oppositus[2], -ūs *m* opposing

oppressiō, -ōnis *f* violence; seizure; overthrow

oppressus[1] *ppp of* **opprimō**

oppressus[2], -ūs *m* pressure

opprimō, -imere, -essī, -essum vt to press down, crush; to press together, close; to suppress, overwhelm, overthrow; to surprise, seize

opprobrium, -ī and **-iī** nt reproach, disgrace, scandal

opprobrō, -āre vt to taunt

oppsuī perf of **oppōnō**

oppugnātiō, -ōnis f attack, assault

oppugnātor, -ōris m assailant

oppugnō, -āre, -āvī, -ātum vt to attack, assault

ops, opis f power, strength; help; (pl) resources, wealth

Ops goddess of plenty

ops- etc see **obs-**

optābilis adj desirable

optātiō, -ōnis f wish

optātus adj longed for ♦ nt wish; **optātō** according to one's wish

optimās, -ātis adj aristocratic ♦ mpl the nobility

optimē adv best, very well; just in time

optimus adj best, very good; excellent; **optimō iūre** deservedly

optiō, -ōnis f choice ♦ m assistant

optīvus adj chosen

optō, -āre, -āvī, -ātum vt to choose; to wish for

optum- etc see **optim-**

opulēns, -entis adj rich

opulentē, -er adv sumptuously

opulentia, -ae f wealth; power

opulentō, -āre vt to enrich

opulentus adj rich, sumptuous, powerful

opus, -eris nt work, workmanship; (art) work, building, book; (MIL) siege work; (colloq) business; (with esse) need; **virō ~ est** a man is needed; **māgnō opere** much, greatly

opusculum, -ī nt little work

ōra, -ae f edge, boundary; coast; country; region; (NAUT) hawser

ōrāculum, -ī nt oracle, prophecy

ōrātiō, -ōnis f speech, language; a speech, oration; eloquence; prose; emperor's message; **ōrātiōnem habēre** deliver a speech

ōrātiuncula, -ae f short speech

ōrātor, -ōris m speaker, spokesman, orator

ōrātōrius adj oratorical

ōrātrīx, -īcis f suppliant

ōrātus, -ūs m request

orbātor, -ōris m bereaver

orbiculātus adj round

orbis, -is m circle, ring, disc, orbit; world; (movement) cycle, rotation; (style) rounding off; **~ lacteus** Milky Way; **~ signifer** Zodiac; **~ fortūnae** wheel of Fortune; **~ terrārum** the earth, world; **in orbem cōnsistere** form a circle; **in orbem īre** go the rounds

orbita, -ae f rut, track, path

orbitās, -ātis f childlessness, orphanhood, widowhood

orbitōsus adj full of ruts

orbō, -āre, -āvī, -ātum vt to bereave, orphan, make childless

orbus adj bereaved, orphan, childless; destitute

orca, -ae f vat

orchas, -dis f kind of olive

orchēstra, -ae f senatorial seats (in the theatre)

Orcus, -ī m Pluto; the lower world; death

ōrdinārius adj regular

ōrdinātim adv in order, properly

ōrdinātiō, -ōnis f orderly arrangement

ōrdinātus adj appointed

ōrdinō, -āre, -āvī, -ātum vt to arrange, regulate, set in order

ōrdior, -dīrī, -sus vt, vi to begin, undertake

ōrdō, -inis m line, row, series; order, regularity, arrangement; (MIL) rank, line, company; (pl) captains; (building) course, layer; (seats) row; (POL) class, order, station; **ex ōrdine** in order, in one's turn; one after the other; **extrā ōrdinem** irregularly, unusually

Orēas, -dis f mountain nymph

Orestēs, -is and **-ae** m son of Agamemnon, whom he avenged by killing his mother

Orestēus adj see **Orestēs**

orexis, -is f appetite

organum, -ī nt instrument, organ

orgia, -ōrum ntpl Bacchic revels; orgies

orichalcum, -ī nt copper ore, brass

ōricilla, -ae f lobe

oriēns, -entis pres p of **orior** ♦ m morning; east

orīgō, -inis f beginning, source; ancestry, descent; founder

Ōriōn, -onis and **-ōnis** m mythical hunter and constellation

orior, -īrī, -tus vi to rise; to spring, descend

oriundus adj descended, sprung

ōrnāmentum, -ī nt equipment, dress; ornament, decoration; distinction, pride of

ōrnātē adv elegantly

ōrnātus¹ ppp of **ōrnō** ♦ adj equipped, furnished; embellished, excellent

ōrnātus², -ūs m preparation; dress, equipment; embellishment

ōrnō, -āre, -āvī, -ātum vt to fit out, equip, dress, prepare; to adorn, embellish, honour

ornus, -ī f manna ash

ōrō, -āre, -āvī, -ātum vt to speak, plead; to beg, entreat; to pray

Orontēs, -is and **-ī** m river of Syria

Orontēus adj Syrian

Orpheus, -eī and **-eos** (acc **-ea**) m legendary Thracian singer, who went down to Hades for Eurydice

Orphēus, Orphēicus adj see **Orpheus**

ōrsus¹ ppa of **ōrdior** ♦ ntpl beginning; utterance

ōrsus², -ūs m beginning

ortus¹ ppa of **orior** ♦ adj born, descended

ortus², -ūs m rising; east; origin, source

Ortygia, -ae, Ortygiē, -ēs f Delos

Ortygius adj see **Ortygia**

oryx, -gis m gazelle

oryza, -ae f rice

os, ossis nt bone; (fig) very soul

ōs, ōris nt mouth; face; entrance, opening; effrontery; **ūnō ōre** unanimously; **in ōre esse** be talked about; **quō ōre redībō** how shall I have the face to go back?

oscen, -inis m bird of omen

ōscillum, -ī nt little mask

ōscitāns, **-antis** *pres p of* **ōscitō** ✦ *adj* listless, drowsy

ōscitanter *adv* half-heartedly

ōscitō, **-āre**, **ōscitor**, **-ārī** *vi* to yawn, be drowsy

ōsculātiō, **-ōnis** *f* kissing

ōsculor, **-ārī**, **-ātus** *vt* to kiss; to make a fuss of

ōsculum, **-ī** *nt* sweet mouth; kiss

Oscus *adj* Oscan

Osīris, **-is** *and* **-idis** *m* Egyptian god, husband of Isis

Ossa, **-ae** *f* mountain in Thessaly

osseus *adj* bony

ossifraga, **-ae** *f* osprey

ostendō, **-dere**, **-dī**, **-tum** *vt* to hold out, show, display; to expose; to disclose, reveal; (*speech*) to say, make known

ostentātiō, **-ōnis** *f* display; showing off, ostentation; pretence

ostentātor, **-ōris** *m* displayer, boaster

ostentō, **-āre** *vt* to hold out, proffer, exhibit; to show off, boast of; to make known, indicate

ostentum, **-ī** *nt* portent

ostentus[1] *ppp of* **ostendō**

ostentus[2], **-ūs** *m* display, appearance; proof

Ōstia, **-ae** *f*, **Ōstia**, **-ōrum** *ntpl* port at the Tiber mouth

ōstiārium, **-ī** *and* **-iī** *nt* door tax

ōstiātim *adv* from door to door

Ōstiēnsis *adj see* **Ōstia**

ōstium, **-ī** *and* **-iī** *nt* door; entrance, mouth

ostrea, **-ae** *f* oyster

ostreōsus *adj* rich in oysters

ostreum, **-ī** *nt* oyster

ostrifer, **-ī** *adj* oyster-producing

ostrīnus *adj* purple

ostrum, **-ī** *nt* purple; purple dress or coverings

ōsus, **ōsūrus** *ppa and fut p of* **ōdī**

Othō, **-ōnis** *m* author of a law giving theatre seats to Equites; Roman emperor after Galba

Othōniānus *adj see* **Othō**

ōtiolum, **-ī** *nt* bit of leisure

ōtior, **-ārī** *vi* to have a holiday, be idle

ōtiōsē *adv* leisurely; quietly; fearlessly

ōtiōsus *adj* at leisure, free; out of public affairs; neutral, indifferent; quiet, unexcited; (*things*) free, idle ✦ *m* private citizen, civilian

ōtium, **-ī** *and* **-iī** *nt* leisure, time (for), idleness, retirement; peace, quiet

ovātiō, **-ōnis** *f* minor triumph

ovīle, **-is** *nt* sheep fold, goat fold

ovillus *adj* of sheep

ovis, **-is** *f* sheep

ovō, **-āre** *vi* to rejoice; to celebrate a minor triumph

ōvum, **-ī** *nt* egg

Pp

păbulātiō, -ōnis *f* foraging
păbulātor, -ōris *m* forager
păbulor, -ārī *vi* to forage
păbulum, -ī *nt* food, fodder
păcālis *adj* of peace
păcātus *adj* peaceful, tranquil ♦ *nt* friendly country
Pachȳnum, -ī *nt S.E. point of Sicily (now Cape Passaro)*
păcifer, -ī *adj* peace-bringing
păcificātiō, -ōnis *f* peacemaking
păcificātor, -ōris *m* peacemaker
păcificātōrius *adj* peacemaking
păcificō, -āre *vi* to make a peace ♦ *vt* to appease
păcificus *adj* peacemaking
pacīscor, -īscī, -tus *vi* to make a bargain, agree ♦ *vt* to stipulate for; to barter
păcō, -āre, -āvī, -ātum *vt* to pacify, subdue
pactiō, -ōnis *f* bargain, agreement, contract; collusion; (words) formula
Pactōlus, -ī *m river of Lydia (famous for its gold)*
pactor, -ōris *m* negotiator
pactum, -ī *nt* agreement, contract
pactus *ppa of* **pacīscor** ♦ *adj* agreed, settled; betrothed
Pācuvius, -ī *m Latin tragic poet*
Padus, -ī *m* (river) Po
paeān, -ānis *m* healer, *epithet of Apollo*; hymn of praise, shout of joy; (metre) paeon
paedagōgus, -ī *m slave who took children to school*
paedor, -ōris *m* filth
paelex, -icis *f* mistress, concubine
paelicātus, -ūs *m* concubinage
Paelignī, -ōrum *mpl people of central Italy*
Paelignus *adj see* **Paelignī**
paene *adv* almost, nearly
paenīnsula, -ae *f* peninsula
paenitendus *adj* regrettable
paenitentia, -ae *f* repentance
paenitet, -ēre, -uit *vt, vi* (impers) to repent, regret, be sorry; to be dissatisfied; **an ~** is it not enough?
paenula, -ae *f* travelling cloak
paenulātus *adj* wearing a cloak
paeōn, -ōnis *m metrical foot of one long and three short syllables*
paeōnius *adj* healing
Paestānus *adj see* **Paestum**
Paestum, -ī *nt town in S. Italy*
paetulus *adj* with a slight cast in the eye
paetus *adj* with a cast in the eye

pāgānus *adj* rural ♦ *m* villager, yokel
pāgātim *adv* in every village
pāgella, -ae *f* small page
pāgina, -ae *f* (book) page, leaf
pāginula, -ae *f* small page
pāgus, -ī *m* village, country district; canton
pāla, -ae *f* spade; (ring) bezel
palaestra, -ae *f* wrestling school, gymnasium; exercise, wrestling; (RHET) exercise, training
palaestricē *adv* in gymnastic fashion
palaestricus *adj* of the wrestling school
palaestrīta, -ae *m* head of a wrestling school
palam *adv* openly, publicly, well-known ♦ *prep* (with abl) in the presence of
Palātīnus *adj* Palatine; imperial
Palātium, -ī *nt* Palatine Hill (in Rome); palace
palātum, -ī *nt* palate; taste, judgment
palea, -ae *f* chaff
paleāria, -ium *ntpl* dewlap
Palēs, -is *f goddess of shepherds*
Palīlis *adj* of Pales ♦ *ntpl festival of Pales*
palimpsēstus, -ī *m* palimpsest
Palinūrus, -ī *m pilot of Aeneas; promontory in S. Italy*
paliūrus, -ī *m* Christ's thorn
palla, -ae *f* woman's robe; tragic costume
Palladium, -dī *nt* image of Pallas
Palladius *adj* of Pallas
Pallantēus *adj see* **Pallas**
Pallas, -dis *and* **-dos** *f* Athene, Minerva; oil; olive tree
Pallās, -antis *m ancestor or son of Evander*
pallēns, -entis *pres p of* **palleō** ♦ *adj* pale; greenish
palleō, -ēre, -uī *vi* to be pale or yellow; to fade; to be anxious
pallēscō, -escere, -uī *vi* to turn pale, turn yellow
palliātus *adj* wearing a Greek cloak
pallidulus *adj* palish
pallidus *adj* pale, pallid, greenish; in love
palliolum, -ī *nt* small cloak, cape, hood
pallium, -ī *and* **-iī** *nt* coverlet; Greek cloak
pallor, -ōris *m* paleness, fading; fear
palma, -ae *f* (hand) palm, hand; (oar) blade; (tree) palm, date; branch; (fig) prize, victory, glory
palmāris *adj* excellent
palmārius *adj* prizewinning
palmātus *adj* palm-embroidered
palmes, -itis *m* pruned shoot, branch
palmētum, -ī *nt* palm grove
palmifer, -ī *adj* palm-bearing

palmōsus *adj* palm-clad

palmula, -ae *f* oar blade

pālor, -ārī, -ātus *vi* to wander about, straggle

palpātiō, -ōnis *f* flatteries

palpātor, -ōris *m* flatterer

palpebra, -ae *f* eyelid

palpitō, -āre *vi* to throb, writhe

palpō, -āre, palpor, -ārī *vt* to stroke; to coax, flatter

palpus, -ī *m* coaxing

palūdāmentum, -ī *nt* military cloak

palūdātus *adj* in a general's cloak

palūdōsus *adj* marshy

palumbēs, -is *m/f* wood pigeon

pālus, -ī *m* stake, pale

palūs, -ūdis *f* marsh, pool, lake

palūster, -ris *adj* marshy

pampineus *adj* of vineshoots

pampinus, -ī *m* vineshoot

Pān, -ānos (*acc* -**āna**) *m* Greek god of shepherds, hills and woods, esp associated with Arcadia

panacēa, -ae *f* a herb supposed to cure all diseases

Panaetius, -ī *m* Stoic philosopher

Panchāeus, Panchāāius *adj see* **Panchāia**

Panchāia, -iae *f part of Arabia*

panchrēstus *adj* good for everything

pancratium, -i *and* -**iī** *nt* all-in boxing and wrestling match

pandiculor, -āre *vi* to stretch oneself

Pandīōn, -onis *m* king of Athens, father of Procne and Philomela

Pandīonius *adj see* **Pandīōn**

pandō, -ere, -ī, pānsum *and* **passum** *vt* to spread out, stretch, extend; to open; (*fig*) to disclose, explain

pandus *adj* curved, bent

pangō, -ere, panxī *and* **pepigī, pāctum** *vt* to drive in, fasten; to make, compose; to agree, settle

pānicula, -ae *f* tuft

pānicum, -ī *nt* Italian millet

pānis, -is *m* bread, loaf

Pāniscus, -ī *m* little Pan

panniculus, -ī *m* rag

Pannonia, -ae *f country on the middle Danube*

Pannonius *adj see* **Pannonia**

pannōsus *adj* ragged

pannus, -ī *m* piece of cloth, rag, patch

Panormus, -ī *f town in Sicily (now Palermo)*

pānsa *adj* splayfoot

pānsus *ppp of* **pandō**

panthēra, -ae *f* panther

Panthoidēs, -ae *m* Euphorbus

Panthūs, -ī *m priest of Apollo at Troy*

panticēs, -um *mpl* bowels; sausages

panxī *perf of* **pangō**

papae *interj (expressing wonder)* ooh!

pāpas, -ae *m* tutor

papāver, -is *nt* poppy

papāvereus *adj see* **papāver**

Paphius *adj see* **Paphos**

Paphos, -ī *f town in Cyprus, sacred to Venus*

pāpiliō, -ōnis *m* butterfly

papilla, -ae *f* teat, nipple; breast

pappus, -ī *m* woolly seed

papula, -ae *f* pimple

papȳrifer, -ī *adj* papyrus-bearing

papȳrum, -ī *nt* papyrus; paper

papȳrus, -ī *m/f* papyrus; paper

pār, paris *adj* equal, like; a match for; proper, right ♦ *m* peer, partner, companion ♦ *nt* pair; **pār parī respondēre** return like for like; **parēs cum paribus facillimē congregantur** birds of a feather flock together; **lūdere pār impār** play at evens and odds

parābilis *adj* easy to get

parasīta, -ae *f* woman parasite

parasītaster, -rī *m* sorry parasite

parasīticus *adj* of a parasite

parasītus, -ī *m* parasite, sponger

parātē *adv* with preparation; carefully; promptly

parātiō, -ōnis *f* trying to get

paratragoedō, -āre *vi* to talk theatrically

parātus¹ *ppp of* **parō** ♦ *adj* ready; equipped; experienced

parātus², -ūs *m* preparation, equipment

Parca, -ae *f* Fate

parcē *adv* frugally; moderately

parcō, -cere, pepercī, -sum *vt, vi (with dat)* to spare, economize; to refrain from, forgo; (*with inf*) to forbear, stop

parcus *adj* sparing, thrifty; niggardly, scanty; chary

pardus, -ī *m* panther

pārēns, -entis *pres p of* **pāreō** ♦ *adj* obedient ♦ *mpl* subjects

parēns, -entis *m/f* parent, father, mother; ancestor; founder

parentālis *adj* parental ♦ *ntpl* festival in honour of dead ancestors and relatives

parentō, -āre *vi* to sacrifice in honour of dead parents or relatives; to avenge (*with the death of another*)

pāreō, -ēre, -uī, -itum *vi* to be visible, be evident; (*with dat*) to obey, submit to, comply with; **pāret** it is proved

pariēs, -etis *m* wall

parietinae, -ārum *fpl* ruins

Parīlia, -ium *ntpl festival of Pales*

parīlis *adj* equal

pariō, -ere, peperī, -tum *vt* to give birth to; to produce, create, cause; to procure

Paris, -idis *m son of Priam, abductor of Helen*

pariter *adv* equally, alike; at the same time, together

paritō, -āre *vt* to get ready

Parius *adj see* **Paros**

parma, -ae *f* shield, buckler

parmātus *adj* armed with a buckler

parmula, -ae *f* little shield

Parnāsis, -idis *adj* Parnassian

Parnāsius *adj* = **Parnāsis**

Parnāsus, -ī *m Mount Parnassus in central Greece, sacred to the Muses*

parō, -āre, -āvī, -ātum *vt* to prepare, get ready, provide; to intend, set about; to procure, get, buy; to arrange

parocha, -ae *f* provision of necessaries (*to officials travelling*)

parochus, -ī *m* purveyor; host

paropsis, -dis *f* dish

Paros, -ī *f* Aegean island *(famous for white marble)*

parra, -ae *f* owl

Parrhasis, -idis, Parrhasius *adj* Arcadian

parricīda, -ae *m* parricide, assassin; traitor

parricīdium, -ī *and* **-iī** *nt* parricide, murder; high treason

pars, -tis *f* part, share, fraction; party, side; direction; respect, degree; *(with pl verb)* some; *(pl)* stage part, role; duty, function; **māgna ~ the majority; māgnam partem** largely; **in eam partem** in that direction, on that side, in that sense; **nullā parte** not at all; **omnī parte** entirely; **ex parte** partly; **ex alterā parte** on the other hand; **ex māgnā parte** to a large extent; **prō parte** to the best of one's ability; **partēs agere** play a part; **duae partēs** two-thirds; **trēs partēs** three-fourths; **multīs partibus** a great deal

parsimōnia, -ae *f* thrift, frugality

parthenicē, -ēs *f* a plant

Parthenopē, -ēs *f* old name of Naples

Parthenopēius *adj see* **Parthenopē**

Parthī, -ōrum *mpl* Parthians *(Rome's great enemy in the East)*

Parthicus, Parthus *adj see* **Parthī**

particeps, -ipis *adj* sharing, partaking ♦ *m* partner

participō, -āre *vt* to share, impart, inform

particula, -ae *f* particle

partim *adv* partly, in part; mostly; some ... others

partiō, -īre, -īvī, -ītum, partior, -īrī *vt* to share, distribute, divide

partītē *adv* methodically

partītiō, -ōnis *f* distribution, division

parturiō, -īre *vi* to be in labour; *(fig)* to be anxious ♦ *vt* to teem with, be ready to produce; *(mind)* to brood over

partus¹ *ppp of* **pariō** ♦ *ntpl* possessions

partus², -ūs *m* birth; young

parum *adv* too little, not enough; not very, scarcely

parumper *adv* for a little while

parvitās, -ātis *f* smallness

parvulus, parvolus *adj* very small, slight; quite young ♦ *m* child

parvus *(compar* **minor,** *superl* **minimus)** *adj* small, little, slight; *(time)* short; *(age)* young; **parvī esse** be of little value

Pascha, -ae *f* Easter

pāscō, -scere, -vī, -stum *vt* to feed, put to graze; to keep, foster; *(fig)* to feast, cherish ♦ *vi* to graze, browse

pāscuus *adj* for pasture ♦ *nt* pasture

Pāsiphaē, -ēs *f* wife of Minos *(mother of the Minotaur)*

passer, -is *m* sparrow; *(fish)* plaice; **~ marīnus** ostrich

passerculus, -ī *m* little sparrow

passim *adv* here and there, at random; indiscriminately

passum, -ī *nt* raisin wine

passus¹ *ppp of* **pandō** ♦ *adj* spread out, dishevelled; dried

passus² *ppa of* **patior**

passus³, -ūs *m* step, pace; footstep; **mille passūs** mile; **mīlia passuum** miles

pastillus, -ī *m* lozenge

pāstor, -ōris *m* shepherd

pāstōrālis *adj* shepherd's, pastoral

pāstōricius, pāstōrius *adj* shepherd's

pāstus¹ *ppp of* **pāscō**

pāstus², -ūs *m* pasture, food

Patara, -ae *f* town in Lycia *(with oracle of Apollo)*

Pataraeus, Patareus *adj see* **Patara**

Patavīnus *adj see* **Patavium**

Patavium, -ī *nt* birthplace of Livy *(now Padua)*

patefaciō, -facere, -fēcī, -factum *(pass* **-fīō)** *vt* to open, open up; to disclose

patefactiō, -ōnis *f* disclosing

patefīō *etc see* **patefaciō**

patella, -ae *f* small dish, plate

patēns, -entis *pres p of* **pateō** ♦ *adj* open, accessible, exposed; broad; evident

patenter *adv* clearly

pateō, -ēre, -uī *vi* to be open, accessible, exposed; to extend; to be evident, known

pater, -ris *m* father; *(pl)* forefathers; senators

patera, -ae *f* dish, saucer, bowl

paterfamiliās, patrisfamiliās *m* master of the house

paternus *adj* father's, paternal; native

patēscō, -ere *vi* to open out; to extend; to become evident

patibilis *adj* endurable; sensitive

patibulātus *adj* pilloried

patibulum, -ī *nt* fork-shaped yoke, pillory

patiēns, -entis *pres p of* **patior** ♦ *adj* able to endure; patient; unyielding

patienter *adv* patiently

patientia, -ae *f* endurance, stamina; forbearance; submissiveness

patina, -ae *f* dish, pan

patior, -tī, -ssus *vt* to suffer, experience; to submit to; to allow, put up with; **facile patī** be well pleased with; **aegrē patī** be displeased with

Patrae, -ārum *fpl* Greek seaport *(now Patras)*

patrātor, -ōris *m* doer

patrātus *adj:* **pater ~** officiating priest

Patrēnsis *adj see* **Patrae**

patria, -ae *f* native land, native town, home

patricius *adj* patrician ♦ *m* aristocrat

patrimōnium, -ī *and* **-iī** *nt* inheritance, patrimony

patrimus *adj* having a father living

patrissō, -āre *vi* to take after one's father

patrītus *adj* of one's father

patrius *adj* father's; hereditary, native

patrō, -āre, -āvī, -ātum *vt* to achieve, execute, complete

patrōcinium, -ī *and* **-iī** *nt* patronage, advocacy, defence

patrōcinor, -ārī *vi (with dat)* to defend, support

patrōna, -ae *f* patron goddess; protectress, safeguard

patrōnus, **-ī** m patron, protector; (LAW) advocate, counsel
patruēlis adj cousin's ♦ m cousin
patruus, **-ī** m (paternal) uncle ♦ adj uncle's
patulus adj open; spreading, broad
paucitās, **-ātis** f small number, scarcity
pauculus adj very few
paucus adj few, little ♦ mpl a few, the select few ♦ ntpl a few words
paulātim adv little by little, gradually
paulisper adv for a little while
Paullus, **-ī** m = **Paulus**
paulō adv a little, somewhat
paululus adj very little ♦ nt a little bit
paulum adv = **paulō**
paulus adj little
Paulus, **-ī** m Roman surname (esp victor of Pydna)
pauper, **-is** adj poor; meagre ♦ mpl the poor
pauperculus adj poor
pauperiēs, **-ēī** f poverty
pauperō, **-āre** vt to impoverish; to rob
paupertās, **-ātis** f poverty, moderate means
pausa, **-ae** f stop, end
pauxillātim adv bit by bit
pauxillulus adj very little
pauxillus adj little
pavefactus adj frightened
paveō, **-ēre**, **pāvī** vi to be terrified, quake ♦ vt to dread, be scared of
pavēscō, **-ere** vt, vi to become alarmed (at)
pāvī perf of **pāscō**
pavidē adv in a panic
pavidus adj quaking, terrified
pavīmentātus adj paved
pavīmentum, **-ī** nt pavement, floor
paviō, **-īre** vt to strike
pavitō, **-āre** vi to be very frightened; to shiver
pāvō, **-ōnis** m peacock
pavor, **-ōris** m terror, panic
pāx, **pācis** f peace; (gods) grace; (mind) serenity ♦ interj enough!; **pāce tuā** by your leave
peccātum, **-ī** nt mistake, fault, sin
peccō, **-āre**, **-āvī**, **-ātum** vi to make a mistake, go wrong, offend
pecorōsus adj rich in cattle
pecten, **-inis** m comb; (fish) scallop; (loom) reed; (lyre) plectrum
pectō, **-ctere**, **-xī**, **-xum** vt to comb
pectus, **-oris** nt breast; heart, feeling; mind, thought
pecū nt flock of sheep; (pl) pastures
pecuārius adj of cattle ♦ m cattle breeder ♦ ntpl herds
pecūlātor, **-ōris** m embezzler
pecūlātus, **-ūs** m embezzlement
pecūliāris adj one's own; special
pecūliātus adj provided with money
pecūliōsus adj with private property
pecūlium, **-ī** and **-iī** nt small savings, private property
pecūnia, **-ae** f property; money
pecūniārius adj of money
pecūniōsus adj moneyed, well-off
pecus¹, **-oris** nt cattle, herd, flock; animal

pecus², **-udis** f sheep, head of cattle, beast
pedālis adj a foot long
pedārius adj (senator) without full rights
pedes, **-itis** m foot soldier, infantry ♦ adj on foot
pedester, **-ris** adj on foot, pedestrian; infantry- (in cpds), on land; (writing) in prose, prosaic
pedetemptim adv step by step, cautiously
pedica, **-ae** f fetter, snare
pedis, **-is** m louse
pedisequa, **-ae** f handmaid
pedisequus, **-ī** m attendant, lackey
peditātus, **-ūs** m infantry
pedum, **-ī** nt crook
Pēgaseus, **Pēgasis**, **-idis** adj Pegasean
Pēgasus, **-ī** m mythical winged horse (associated with the Muses)
pēgma, **-tis** nt bookcase; stage elevator
pēierō, **-āre** vi to perjure oneself
pēior, **-ōris** compar of **malus**
pēius adv worse
pelagius adj of the sea
pelagus, **-ī** (pl **-ē**) nt sea, open sea
pelamys, **-dis** f young tuna fish
Pelasgī, **-ōrum** mpl Greeks
Pelasgias, **Pelasgis**, **Pelasgus** adj Grecian
Pēleus, **-eī** and **-eos** (acc **-ea**) m king of Thessaly (father of Achilles)
Peliās, **-ae** m uncle of Jason
Pēlias, **Pēliacus**, **Pēlius** adj see **Pēlion**
Pēlīdēs, **-īdae** m Achilles; Neoptolemus
Pēlion, **-ī** nt mountain in Thessaly
Pella, **-ae**, **Pellē**, **-ēs** f town of Macedonia (birthplace of Alexander)
pellācia, **-ae** f attraction
Pellaeus adj of Pella; Alexandrian; Egyptian
pellāx, **-ācis** adj seductive
pellēctiō, **-ōnis** f reading through
pellectus ppp of **pelliciō**
pellegō etc see **perlegō**
pelliciō, **-icere**, **-exī**, **-ectum** vt to entice, inveigle
pellicula, **-ae** f skin, fleece
polliō, **-ōnis** m furrier
pellis, **-is** f skin, hide; leather, felt; tent
pellītus adj wearing skins, with leather coats
pellō, **-ere**, **pepulī**, **pulsum** vt to push, knock, drive; to drive off, rout, expel; (lyre) to play; (mind) to touch, affect; (feeling) to banish
pellūc- etc see **perlūc-**
Pelopēis, **Pelopēias**, **Pelopēius**, **Pelopēus** adj see **Pelops**
Pelopidae, **-idārum** mpl house of Pelops
Peloponnēsiacus, **-ius** adj see **Peloponnēsus**
Peloponnēsus, **-ī** f Peloponnese, S. Greece
Pelops, **-is** m son of Tantalus (grandfather of Agamemnon)
pelōris, **-idis** f a large mussel
pelta, **-ae** f light shield
peltastae, **-ārum** mpl peltasts
peltātus adj armed with the pelta
Pēlūsiacus adj see **Pēlūsium**
Pēlūsium, **-ī** nt Egyptian town at the E. mouth of the Nile
Pēlūsius adj see **Pēlūsium**

pelvis, **-is** f basin

penārius adj provision- (in cpds)

Penātēs, **-ium** mpl spirits of the larder, household gods; home

penātiger, **-ī** adj carrying his home gods

pendeō, **-ēre**, **pependī** vi to hang; to overhang, hover; to hang down, be flabby; (fig) to depend; to gaze, listen attentively; (mind) to be in suspense, be undecided

pendō, **-ere**, **pependī**, **pēnsum** vt to weigh; to pay; (fig) to ponder, value ♦ vi to weigh

pendulus adj hanging; in doubt

Pēnēis, **Pēnēius** adj see **Pēnēus**

Pēnelopē, **-ēs**, **Pēnelopa**, **-ae** f wife of Ulysses (famed for her constancy)

Pēnelopēus adj see **Pēnelopē**

penes prep (with acc) in the power or possession of; in the house of, with

penetrābilis adj penetrable; piercing

penetrālis adj penetrating; inner, inmost ♦ ntpl inner room, interior, sanctuary; remote parts

penetrō, **-āre**, **-āvī**, **-ātum** vt, vi to put into, penetrate, enter

Pēnēus, **-ī** m chief river of Thessaly

pēnicillus, **-ī** m painter's brush, pencil

pēniculus, **-ī** m brush; sponge

pēnis, **-is** m penis

penitē adj inwardly

penitus adv inside, deep within; deeply, from the depths; utterly, thoroughly

penna, **pinna**, **-ae** f feather, wing; flight

pennātus adj winged

penniger, **-ī** adj feathered

pennipotēns, **-entis** adj winged

pennula, **-ae** f little wing

pēnsilis adj hanging, pendent

pēnsiō, **-ōnis** f payment, instalment

pēnsitō, **-āre** vt to pay; to consider

pēnsō, **-āre**, **-āvī**, **-ātum** vt to weight out; to compensate, repay; to consider, judge

pēnsum, **-ī** nt spinner's work; task, duty; weight, value; **pēnsī esse** be of importance; **pēnsī habēre** care at all about

pēnsus ppp of **pendō**

pentēris, **-is** f quinquereme

Pentheus, **-eī** and **-eos** m king of Thebes (killed by Bacchantes)

pēnūria, **-ae** f want, need

penus, **-ūs** and **-ī** m/f, **penum**, **-ī** nt, **penus**, **-oris** nt provisions, store of food

pependī perf of **pendeō**; **pendō**

pepercī perf of **parcō**

peperī perf of **pariō**

pepigī perf of **pangō**

peplum, **-ī** nt, **peplus**, **-ī** m state robe of Athena

pepulī perf of **pellō**

per prep (with acc, space) through, all over; (time) throughout, during; (means) by, by means of; (cause) by reason of, for the sake of; **per īram** in anger; **per manūs** from hand to hand; **per mē** as far as I am concerned; **per vim** forcibly; **per ego tē deōs ōrō** in Heaven's name I beg you

pēra, **-ae** f bag

perabsurdus adj very absurd

peraccommodātus adj very convenient

perācer, **-ris** adj very sharp

peracerbus adj very sour

peracēscō, **-ēscere**, **-uī** vi to get vexed

perāctiō, **-ōnis** f last act

perāctus ppp of **peragō**

peracūtē adv very acutely

peracūtus adj very sharp, very clear

peradulēscēns, **-entis** adj very young

peraequē adv quite equally, uniformly

peragitātus adj harried

peragō, **-agere**, **-ēgī**, **-āctum** vt to carry through, complete; to pass through, pierce; to disturb; (LAW) to prosecute to a conviction; (words) to go over, describe

peragrātiō, **-ōnis** f travelling

peragrō, **-āre**, **-āvī**, **-ātum** vt to travel through, traverse

peramāns, **-antis** adj very fond

peramanter adv devotedly

perambulō, **-āre** vt to walk through, traverse

peramoenus adj very pleasant

peramplus adj very large

perangustē adv see **perangustus**

perangustus adj very narrow

perantīquus adj very old

perappositus adj very suitable

perarduus adj very difficult

perargūtus adj very witty

perarō, **-āre** vt to furrow; to write (on wax)

perattentē adv see **perattentus**

perattentus adj very attentive

peraudiendus adj to be heard to the end

perbacchor, **-ārī** vt to carouse through

perbeātus adj very happy

perbellē adv very nicely

perbene adv very well

perbenevolus adj very friendly

perbenignē adv very kindly

perbibō, **-ere**, **-ī** vt to drink up, imbibe

perbītō, **-ere** vi to perish

perblandus adj very charming

perbonus adj very good

perbrevis adj very short

perbreviter adv very briefly

perca, **-ae** f perch

percalefactus adj quite hot

percalēscō, **-ēscere**, **-uī** vi to become quite hot

percallēscō, **-ēscere**, **-uī** vi to become quite hardened ♦ vt to become thoroughly versed in

percārus adj very dear

percautus adj very cautious

percelebrō, **-āre** vt to talk much of

perceler, **-is** adj very quick

perceleriter adv see **perceler**

percellō, **-ellere**, **-ulī**, **-ulsum** vt to knock down, upset; to strike; (fig) to ruin, overthrow; to discourage, unnerve

percēnseō, **-ēre**, **-uī** vt to count over; (place) to travel through; (fig) to review

perceptiō, **-ōnis** f harvesting; understanding, idea

perceptus ppp of **percipiō**

percieō, **-iēre**, **-iō**, **-īre** vt to rouse, excite

percipiō, **-ipere**, **-ēpī**, **-eptum** *vt* to take, get hold of; to gather in; (*senses*) to feel; (*mind*) to learn, grasp, understand

percitus *ppp of* **percieō** ♦ *adj* roused, excited; excitable

percoctus *ppp of* **percoquō**

percolō¹, **-āre** *vt* to filter through

percolō², **-olere**, **-oluī**, **-ultum** *vt* to embellish; to honour

percōmis *adj* very friendly

percommodē *adv* very conveniently

percommodus *adj* very suitable

percontātiō, **-ōnis** *f* asking questions

percontātor, **-ōris** *m* inquisitive person

percontor, **-ārī**, **-ātus** *vt* to question, inquire

percontumāx, **-ācis** *adj* very obstinate

percoquō, **-quere**, **-xī**, **-ctum** *vt* to cook thoroughly, heat, scorch, ripen

percrēbēscō, **percrēbrēscō**, **-ēscere**, **-uī** *vi* to be spread abroad

percrepō, **-āre**, **-uī** *vi* to resound

perculī *perf of* **percellō**

perculsus *ppp of* **percellō**

percultus *ppp of* **percolō²**

percunct- *etc see* **percont-**

percupidus *adj* very fond

percupiō, **-ere** *vi* to wish very much

percūriōsus *adj* very inquisitive

percūrō, **-āre** *vt* to heal completely

percurrō, **-rrere**, **-currī** *and* **-rrī**, **-rsum** *vt* to run through, hurry over; (*fig*) to run over, look over ♦ *vi* to run along; to pass

percursātiō, **-ōnis** *f* travelling through

percursiō, **-ōnis** *f* running over

percursō, **-āre** *vi* to rove about

percursus *ppp of* **percurrō**

percussiō, **-ōnis** *f* beating; (*fingers*) snapping; (*music*) time

percussor, **-ōris** *m* assassin

percussus¹ *ppp of* **percutiō**

percussus², **-ūs** *m* striking

percutiō, **-tere**, **-ssī**, **-ssum** *vt* to strike, beat; to strike through, kill; (*feeling*) to shock, impress, move; (*colloq*) to trick

perdēlīrus *adj* quite crazy

perdidī *perf of* **perdō**

perdifficilis *adj* very difficult

perdifficiliter *adv* with great difficulty

perdignus *adj* most worthy

perdīligēns, **-entis** *adj* very diligent

perdīligenter *adv see* **perdīligēns**

perdiscō, **-scere**, **-dicī** *vt* to learn by heart

perdisertē *adv* very eloquently

perdītē *adv* desperately; recklessly

perditor, **-ōris** *m* destroyer

perditus *ppp of* **perdō** ♦ *adj* desperate, ruined; abandoned, profligate

perdiū *adv* for a very long time

perdiūturnus *adj* protracted

perdīves, **-itis** *adj* very rich

perdīx, **-icis** *m/f* partridge

perdō, **-ere**, **-idī**, **-itum** *vt* to destroy, ruin; to squander, waste; to lose; **dī tē perduint** curse you!

perdoceō, **-ēre**, **-uī**, **-tum** *vt* to teach thoroughly

perdolēscō, **-ēscere**, **-uī** *vi* to take it to heart

perdomō, **-āre**, **-uī**, **-itum** *vt* to subjugate, tame completely

perdormīscō, **-ere** *vi* to sleep on

perdūcō, **-ūcere**, **-ūxī**, **-uctum** *vt* to bring, guide to; to induce, seduce; to spread over; to prolong, continue

perductō, **-āre** *vt* to guide

perductor, **-ōris** *m* guide; pander

perductus *ppp of* **perdūcō**

perduelliō, **-ōnis** *f* treason

perduellis, **-is** *m* enemy

perduim *archaic subj of* **perdō**

perdūrō, **-āre** *vi* to endure, hold out

peredō, **-edere**, **-ēdī**, **-ēsum** *vt* to consume, devour

peregrē *adv* away from home, abroad; from abroad

peregrīnābundus *adj* travelling

peregrīnātiō, **-ōnis** *f* living abroad, travel

peregrīnātor, **-ōris** *m* traveller

peregrīnitās, **-ātis** *f* foreign manners

peregrīnor, **-ārī**, **-ātus** *vi* to be abroad, travel; to be a stranger

peregrīnus *adj* foreign, strange ♦ *m* foreigner, alien

perēlegāns, **-antis** *adj* very polished

perēleganter *adv* in a very polished manner

perēloquēns, **-entis** *adj* very eloquent

perēmī *perf of* **perimō**

peremnia, **-ium** *ntpl* auspices taken on crossing a river

peremptus *ppp of* **perimō**

perendiē *adv* the day after tomorrow

perendinus *adj* (*the day*) after tomorrow

perennis *adj* perpetual, unfailing

perennitās, **-ātis** *f* continuance

perennō, **-āre** *vi* to last a long time

pereō, **-īre**, **-iī**, **-itum** *vi* to be lost, pass away, perish, die; (*fig*) to be wasted, be in love, be undone

perequitō, **-āre** *vt*, *vi* to ride up and down

pererrō, **-āre**, **-āvī**, **-ātum** *vt* to roam over, cover

perērudītus *adj* very learned

perēsus *ppp of* **peredō**

perexcelsus *adj* very high

perexiguē *adv* very meagrely

perexiguus *adj* very small, very short

perfacētē *adv* very wittily

perfacētus *adj* very witty

perfacile *adv* very easily

perfacilis *adj* very easy; very courteous

perfamiliāris *adj* very intimate ♦ *m* very close friend

perfectē *adv* fully

perfectiō, **-ōnis** *f* completion, perfection

perfector, **-ōris** *m* perfecter

perfectus *ppp of* **perficiō** ♦ *adj* complete, perfect

perferō, **-ferre**, **-tulī**, **-lātum** *vt* to carry through, bring, convey; to bear, endure, put up with; (*work*) to finish, bring to completion; (*LAW*) to get passed; (*message*) to bring news

perficiō, -icere, -ēcī, -ectum vt to carry out, finish, complete; to perfect; to cause, make
perficus adj perfecting
perfidēlis adj very loyal
perfidia, -ae f treachery, dishonesty
perfidiōsē adv see **perfidiōsus**
perfidiōsus adj treacherous, dishonest
perfidus adj treacherous, faithless
perfigō, -gere, -xī, -xum vt to pierce
perflābilis adj that can be blown through
perflāgitiōsus adj very wicked
perflō, -āre vt to blow through, blow over
perfluctuō, -āre vt to flood through
perfluō, -ere, -xī vi to run out, leak
perfodiō, -odere, -ōdī, -ossum vt to dig through, excavate, pierce
perforō, -āre, -āvī, -ātum vt to bore through, pierce
perfortiter adv very bravely
perfossor, -ōris m: ~ parietum burglar
perfossus ppp of **perfodiō**
perfrāctus ppp of **perfringō**
perfrēgī perf of **perfringō**
perfremō, -ere vi to snort along
perfrequēns, -entis adj much frequented
perfricō, -āre, -uī, -tum and **-ātum** vt to rub all over; ōs perfricāre put on a bold face
perfrīgefaciō, -ere vt to make shudder
perfrīgēscō, -gēscere, -xī vi to catch a bad cold
perfrīgidus adj very cold
perfringō, -ingere, -ēgī, -āctum vt to break through, fracture, wreck; (fig) to violate; to affect powerfully
perfrīxī perf of **perfrīgēscō**
perfrūctus ppa of **perfruor**
perfruor, -uī, -ūctus vi (with abl) to enjoy to the full; to fulfil
perfuga, -ae m deserter
perfugiō, -ugere, -ūgī vi to flee for refuge, desert to
perfugium, -ī and **-iī** nt refuge, shelter
perfūnctiō, -ōnis f performing
perfūnctus ppa of **perfungor**
perfundō, -undere, -ūdī, -ūsum vt to pour over, drench, besprinkle; to dye; (fig) to flood, fill
perfungor, -gī, perfūnctus vi (with abl) to perform, discharge; to undergo
perfurō, -ere vi to rage furiously
perfūsus ppp of **perfundō**
Pergama, -ōrum ntpl Troy
Pergamēnus adj see **Pergama**
Pergameus adj Trojan
Pergamum, -ī nt town in Mysia (famous for its library)
pergaudeō, -ēre vi to be very glad
pergō, -gere, -rēxī, -rēctum vi to proceed, go on, continue ♦ vt to go on with, continue
pergraecor, -ārī vi to have a good time
pergrandis adj very large; very old
pergraphicus adj very artful
pergrātus adj very pleasant
pergravis adj very weighty
pergraviter adv very seriously
pergula, -ae f balcony; school; brothel
perhibeō, -ēre, -uī, -itum vt to assert, call, cite

perhīlum adv very little
perhonōrificē adv very respectfully
perhonōrificus adj very complimentary
perhorrēscō, -ēscere, -uī vi to shiver, tremble violently ♦ vt to have a horror of
perhorridus adj quite horrible
perhūmāniter adv see **perhūmānus**
perhūmānus adj very polite
Periclēs, -is and **-ī** m famous Athenian statesman and orator
perīclitātiō, -ōnis f experiment
perīclitor, -ārī, -ātus vt to test, try; to risk, endanger ♦ vi to attempt, venture; to run a risk, be in danger
perīculōsē adv see **perīculōsus**
perīculōsus adj dangerous, hazardous
perīculum, perīclum, -ī nt danger, risk; trial, attempt; (LAW) lawsuit, writ
peridōneus adj very suitable
periī perf of **pereō**
perillūstris adj very notable; highly honoured
perimbēcillus adj very weak
perimō, -imere, -ēmī, -emptum vt to destroy, prevent, kill
perincommodē adv see **perincommodus**
perincommodus adj very inconvenient
perinde adv just as, exactly as
perindulgēns, -entis adj very tender
perīnfirmus adj very feeble
peringeniōsus adj very clever
perinīquus adj very unfair; very discontented
perinsignis adj very conspicuous
perinvītus adj very unwilling
periodus, -ī f sentence, period
Peripatēticī, -ōrum mpl Peripatetics (followers of Aristotle)
peripetasmata, -um ntpl curtains
perīrātus adj very angry
periscelis, -dis f anklet
peristrōma, -atis nt coverlet
peristylum, -ī nt colonnade, peristyle
perītē adv expertly
perītia, -ae f practical knowledge, skill
perītus adj experienced, skilled, expert
periūcundē adv see **periūcundus**
periūcundus adj very enjoyable
periūrium, -ī and **-iī** nt perjury
periūrō see **pēierō**
periūrus adj perjured, lying
perlābor, -bī, -psus vi to glide along or through, move on
perlaetus adj very glad
perlāpsus ppa of **perlābor**
perlātē adv extensively
perlateō, -ēre vi to lie quite hidden
perlātus ppp of **perferō**
perlegō, -egere, -ēgī, -ēctum vt to survey; to read through
perlevis adj very slight
perleviter adv see **perlevis**
perlibēns, -entis adj very willing
perlibenter adv see **perlibēns**
perlīberālis adj very genteel
perlīberāliter adv very liberally

perlibet, -ēre vi (impers) (I) should very much like

perliciō etc see **pellicio**

perlītō, -āre, -āvī, -ātum vi to sacrifice with auspicious results

perlongē adv very far

perlongus adj very long, very tedious

perlub- etc see **perlib-**

perlūceō, -cēre, -xī vi to shine through, be transparent; (fig) to be quite intelligible

perlūcidulus adj transparent

perlūcidus adj transparent; very bright

perlūctuōsus adj very mournful

perluō, -ere vt to wash thoroughly; (pass) to bathe

perlūstrō, -āre vt to traverse; (fig) to survey

permāgnus adj very big, very great

permānanter adv by flowing through

permānāscō, -ere vi to penetrate

permaneō, -anēre, -ānsī, -ānsum vi to last, persist, endure to the end

permānō, -āre, -āvī, -ātum vi to flow or ooze through, penetrate

permānsiō, -ōnis f continuing, persisting

permarīnus adj of seafaring

permātūrēscō, -ēscere, -uī vi to ripen fully

permediocris adj very moderate

permēnsus ppa of **permētior**

permeō, -āre vt, vi to pass through, penetrate

permētior, -tīrī, -nsus vt to measure out; to traverse

permīrus adj very wonderful

permisceō, -scēre, -scuī, -xtum vt to mingle, intermingle; to throw into confusion

permissiō, -ōnis f unconditional surrender; permission

permissus¹ ppp of **permittō**

permissus², -ūs m leave, permission

permitiālis adj destructive

permitiēs, -ēī f ruin

permittō, -ittere, -īsī, -issum vt to let go, let pass; to hurl; to give up, entrust, concede; to allow, permit

permixtē adv see **permixtus**

permixtiō, -ōnis f mixture; disturbance

permixtus ppp of **permisceō ✦** adj promiscuous, disordered

permodestus adj very moderate

permolestē adv with much annoyance

permolestus adj very troublesome

permōtiō, -ōnis f excitement; emotion

permōtus ppp of **permoveō**

permoveō, -ovēre, -ōvī, -ōtum vt to stir violently; (fig) to influence, induce; to excite, move deeply

permulceō, -cēre, -sī, -sum vt to stroke, caress; (fig) to charm, flatter; to soothe, appease

permulsus ppp of **permulceō**

permultus adj very much, very many

permūniō, -īre, -īvī, -ītum vt to finish fortifying; to fortify strongly

permūtātiō, -ōnis f change, exchange

permūtō, -āre, -āvī, -ātum vt to change completely; to exchange; (money) to remit by bill of exchange

perna, -ae f ham

pernecessārius adj very necessary; very closely related

pernecesse adj indispensable

pernegō, -āre vi to deny flatly

perniciābilis adj ruinous

perniciēs, -ēī f destruction, ruin, death

perniciōsē adv see **perniciōsus**

perniciōsus adj ruinous

pernīcitās, -ātis f agility, swiftness

perniciter adv nimbly

pernimius adj much too much

pernīx, -īcis adj nimble, agile, swift

pernōbilis adj very famous

pernoctō, -āre vi to stay all night

pernōscō, -scere, -vī, -tum vt to examine thoroughly; to become fully acquainted with, know thoroughly

pernōtēscō, -ēscere, -uī vi to become generally known

pernōtus ppp of **pernōscō**

pernox, -octis adj all night long

pernumerō, -āre vt to count up

pērō, -ōnis m rawhide boot

perobscūrus adj very obscure

perodiōsus adj very troublesome

perofficiōsē adv very attentively

peroleō, -ēre vi to give off a strong smell

peropportūnē adv very opportunely

peropportūnus adj very timely

peroptātō adv very much to one's wish

peropus est it is most essential

perōrātiō, -ōnis f peroration

perōrnātus adj very ornate

perōrnō, -āre vt to give great distinction to

perōrō, -āre, -āvī, -ātum vt to plead at length; (speech) to bring to a close; to conclude

perōsus adj detesting

perpācō, -āre vt to quieten completely

perparcē adv very stingily

perparvulus adj very tiny

perparvus adj very small

perpāstus adj well fed

perpauculus adj very very few

perpaucus adj very little, very few

perpaulum, -ī nt a very little

perpauper, -is adj very poor

perpauxillum, -ī nt a very little

perpellō, -ellere, -ulī, -ulsum vt to urge, force, influence

perpendiculum, -ī nt plumbline; **ad ~** perpendicularly

perpendō, -endere, -endī, -ēnsum vt to weigh carefully, judge

perperam adv wrongly, falsely

perpes, -etis adj continuous

perpessiō, -ōnis f suffering, enduring

perpessus ppa of **perpetior**

perpetior, -tī, -ssus vt to endure patiently, allow

perpetrō, -āre, -āvī, -ātum vt to perform, carry out

perpetuitās, -ātis f continuity, uninterrupted duration

perpetuō[1] *adv* without interruption, forever, utterly

perpetuō[2], **-āre** *vt* to perpetuate, preserve

perpetuus *adj* continuous, entire; universal; **in perpetuum** forever

perplaceō, **-ēre** *vi* to please greatly

perplexē *adv* obscurely

perplexor, **-ārī** *vi* to cause confusion

perplexus *adj* confused, intricate, obscure

perplicātus *adj* interlaced

perpluō, **-ere** *vi* to let the rain through, leak

perpoliō, **-īre**, **-īvī**, **-ītum** *vt* to polish thoroughly

perpolītus *adj* finished, refined

perpopulor, **-ārī**, **-ātus** *vt* to ravage completely

perpōtātiō, **-ōnis** *f* drinking bout

perpōtō, **-āre** *vi* to drink continuously ♦ *vt* to drink off

perprimō, **-ere** *vt* to lie on

perpugnāx, **-ācis** *adj* very pugnacious

perpulcher, **-rī** *adj* very beautiful

perpulī *perf of* **perpellō**

perpūrgō, **-āre**, **-āvī**, **-ātum** *vt* to make quite clean; to explain

perpusillus *adj* very little

perquam *adv* very, extremely

perquīrō, **-rere**, **-sīvī**, **-sītum** *vt* to search for, inquire after; to examine carefully

perquīsītius *adv* more accurately

perrārō *adv* very seldom

perrārus *adj* very uncommon

perreconditus *adj* very abstruse

perrēpō, **-ere** *vt* to crawl over

perrēptō, **-āre**, **-āvī**, **-ātum** *vt*, *vi* to creep about or through

perrēxī *perf of* **pergō**

perrīdiculē *adv see* **perrīdiculus**

perrīdiculus *adj* very laughable

perrogātiō, **-ōnis** *f* passing (*of a law*)

perrogō, **-āre** *vt* to ask one after another

perrumpō, **-umpere**, **-ūpī**, **-uptum** *vt*, *vi* to break through, force a way through; (*fig*) to break down

perruptus *ppp of* **perrumpō**

Persae, **-ārum** *mpl* Persians

persaepe *adv* very often

persalsē *adv see* **persalsus**

persalsus *adj* very witty

persalūtātiō, **-ōnis** *f* greeting everyone in turn

persalūtō, **-āre** *vt* to greet in turn

persānctē *adv* most solemnly

persapiēns, **-entis** *adj* very wise

persapienter *adv see* **persapiēns**

perscienter *adv* very discreetly

perscindō, **-ndere**, **-dī**, **-ssum** *vt* to tear apart

perscītus *adj* very smart

perscrībō, **-bere**, **-psī**, **-ptum** *vt* to write in full; to describe, report; (*record*) to enter; (*money*) to make over in writing

perscrīptiō, **-ōnis** *f* entry; assignment

perscrīptor, **-ōris** *m* writer

perscrīptus *ppp of* **perscrībō**

perscrūtor, **-ārī**, **-ātus** *vt* to search, examine thoroughly

persecō, **-āre**, **-uī**, **-tum** *vt* to dissect; to do away with

persector, **-ārī** *vt* to investigate

persecūtiō, **-ōnis** *f* (*LAW*) prosecution

persecūtus *ppa of* **persequor**

persedeō, **-edēre**, **-ēdī**, **-essum** *vi* to remain sitting

persegnis *adj* very slow

Persēius *adj see* **Perseus**

persentiō, **-entīre**, **-ēnsī** *vt* to see clearly; to feel deeply

persentīscō, **-ere** *vi* to begin to see; to begin to feel

Persephonē, **-ēs** *f* Proserpine

persequor, **-quī**, **-cūtus** *vt* to follow all the way; to pursue, chase, hunt after; to overtake; (*pattern*) to be a follower of, copy; (*enemy*) to proceed against, take revenge on; (*action*) to perform, carry out; (*words*) to write down, describe

Persēs[1], **-ae** *m* last king of Macedonia

Persēs[2], **-ae** *m* Persian

Perseus, **-eī** *and* **-eos** (*acc* **-ea**) *m* son of Danaë (killer of Medusa, rescuer of Andromeda)

Persēus *adj see* **Perseus**

persevērāns, **-antis** *pres p of* **persevērō** ♦ *adj* persistent

persevēranter *adv see* **persevērāns**

persevērantia, **-ae** *f* persistence

persevērō, **-āre**, **-āvī**, **-ātum** *vi* to persist ♦ *vt* to persist in

persevērus *adj* very strict

Persicum *nt* peach

Persicus *adj* Persian; of Perses

persīdō, **-īdere**, **-ēdī**, **-essum** *vi* to sink down into

persignō, **-āre** *vt* to record

persimilis *adj* very like

persimplex, **-icis** *adj* very simple

Persis, **-idis** *f* Persia

persistō, **-istere**, **-titī** *vi* to persist

persōlus *adj* one and only

persolūtus *ppp of* **persolvō**

persolvō, **-vere**, **-vī**, **-ūtum** *vt* to pay, pay up; to explain

persōna, **-ae** *f* mask; character, part; person, personality

persōnātus *adj* masked; in an assumed character

personō, **-āre**, **-uī**, **-itum** *vi* to resound, ring (with); to play ♦ *vt* to make resound; to cry aloud

perspectē *adv* intelligently

perspectō, **-āre** *vt* to have a look through

perspectus *ppp of* **perspiciō** ♦ *adj* well-known

perspeculor, **-ārī** *vt* to reconnoitre

perspergō, **-gere**, **-sī**, **-sum** *vt* to besprinkle

perspicāx, **-ācis** *adj* sharp, shrewd

perspicientia, **-ae** *f* full understanding

perspiciō, **-icere**, **-exī**, **-ectum** *vt* to see through; to examine, observe

perspicuē *adv* clearly

perspicuitās, **-ātis** *f* clarity

perspicuus *adj* transparent; clear, evident

persternō, -ernere, -rāvī, -rātum *vt* to pave all over

perstimulō, -āre *vt* to rouse violently

perstitī *perf of* **persistō; perstō**

perstō, -āre, -itī, -ātum *vi* to stand fast; to last; to continue, persist

perstrātus *ppp of* **persternō**

perstrepō, -ere *vi* to make a lot of noise

perstrictus *ppp of* **perstringō**

perstringō, -ingere, -inxī, -ictum *vt* to graze, touch lightly; (*words*) to touch on, belittle, censure; (*senses*) to dull, deaden

perstudiōsē *adv* very eagerly

perstudiōsus *adj* very fond

persuādeō, -dēre, -sī, -sum *vi* (*with dat*) to convince, persuade; **persuāsum habeō, mihi persuāsum est** I am convinced

persuāsiō, -ōnis *f* convincing

persuāsus, -ūs *m* persuasion

persubtīlis *adj* very fine

persultō, -āre *vt, vi* to prance about, frisk over

pertaedet, -dēre, -sum est *vt* (*impers*) to be weary of, be sick of

pertegō, -egere, -ēxī, -ēctum *vt* to cover over

pertemptō, -āre *vt* to test carefully; to consider well; to pervade, seize

pertendō, -ere, -ī *vi* to push on, persist ♦ *vt* to go on with

pertenuis *adj* very small, very slight

perterebrō, -āre *vt* to bore through

pertergēō, -gēre, -sī, -sum *vt* to wipe over; to touch lightly

perterrefaciō, -ere *vt* to scare thoroughly

perterreō, -ēre, -uī, -itum *vt* to frighten thoroughly

perterricrepus *adj* with a terrifying crash

perterritus *adj* terrified

pertexō, -ere, -uī, -tum *vt* to accomplish

pertica, -ae *f* pole, staff

pertimefactus *adj* very frightened

pertiméscō, -ēscere, -uī *vt, vi* to be very alarmed, be very afraid of

pertinācia, -ae *f* perseverance, stubbornness

pertināciter *adv see* **pertināx**

pertināx, -ācis *adj* very tenacious; unyielding, stubborn

pertineō, -ēre, -uī *vi* to extend, reach; to tend, lead to, concern; to apply, pertain, belong; **quod pertinet ad** as far as concerns

pertingō, -ere *vi* to extend

pertolerō, -āre *vt* to endure to the end

pertorqueō, -ēre *vt* to distort

pertractātē *adv* in a hackneyed fashion

pertractātiō, -ōnis *f* handling

pertractō, -āre *vt* to handle, feel all over; (*fig*) to treat, study

pertractus *ppp of* **pertrahō**

pertrahō, -here, -xī, -ctum *vt* to drag across, take forcibly; to entice

pertrect- *etc see* **pertract-**

pertristis *adj* very sad, very morose

pertulī *perf of* **perferō**

pertumultuōsē *adv* very excitedly

pertundō, -undere, -udī, -ūsum *vt* to perforate

perturbātē *adv* in confusion

perturbātiō, -ōnis *f* confusion, disturbance; emotion

perturbātrīx, -īcis *f* disturber

perturbātus *ppp of* **perturbō** ♦ *adj* troubled; alarmed

perturbō, -āre, -āvī, -ātum *vt* to throw into disorder, upset, alarm

perturpis *adj* scandalous

pertūsus *ppp of* **pertundō** ♦ *adj* in holes, leaky

perungō, -ungere, -ūnxī, -ūnctum *vt* to smear all over

perurbānus *adj* very refined; over-fine

perūrō, -rere, -ssi, -stum *vt* to burn up, scorch; to inflame, chafe; to freeze, nip

Perusia, -iae *f* Etruscan town (*now* Perugia)

Perusīnus *adj see* **Perusia**

perūstus *ppp of* **perūrō**

perūtilis *adj* very useful

pervādō, -dere, -sī, -sum *vt, vi* to pass through, spread through; to penetrate, reach

pervagātus *adj* widespread, well-known; general

pervagor, -ārī, -ātus *vi* to range, rove about; to extend, spread ♦ *vt* to pervade

pervagus *adj* roving

pervariē *adv* very diversely

pervastō, -āre, -āvī, -ātum *vt* to devastate

pervāsus *ppp of* **pervādō**

pervectus *ppp of* **pervehō**

pervehō, -here, -xī, -ctum *vt* to carry, convey, bring through; (*pass*) to ride, drive, sail through; to attain

pervellō, -ere, -ī *vt* to pull, twitch, pinch; to stimulate; to disparage

perveniō, -enīre, -ēnī, -entum *vi* to come to, arrive, reach; to attain to

pervēnor, -ārī *vi* to chase through

perversē *adv* perversely

perversitās, -ātis *f* perverseness

perversus, pervorsus *ppp of* **pervertō** ♦ *adj* awry, squint; wrong, perverse

pervertō, -tere, -tī, -sum *vt* to overturn, upset; to overthrow, undo; (*speech*) to confute

pervesperī *adv* very late

pervestīgātiō, -ōnis *f* thorough search

pervestīgō, -āre, -āvī, -ātum *vt* to track down; to investigate

pervetus, -eris *adj* very old

pervetustus *adj* antiquated

pervicācia, -ae *f* obstinacy; firmness

pervicāciter *adv see* **pervicāx**

pervicāx, -ācis *adj* obstinate, wilful; dogged

pervictus *ppp of* **pervincō**

pervideō, -idēre, -īdī, -īsum *vt* to look over, survey; to consider; to discern

pervigeō, -ēre, -uī *vi* to continue to flourish

pervigil, -is *adj* awake, watchful

pervigilātiō, -ōnis *f* vigil

pervigilium, -ī *and* **-iī** *nt* vigil

pervigilō, -āre, -āvī, -ātum *vt, vi* to stay awake all night, keep vigil

pervīlis *adj* very cheap

pervincō, -incere, -īcī, -ictum *vt, vi* to conquer completely; to outdo, surpass; to prevail upon, effect; (*argument*) to carry a point, maintain, prove

pervius *adj* passable, accessible

pervīvō, -ere *vi* to survive

pervolgō *etc see* **pervulgō**

pervolitō, -āre *vt, vi* to fly about

pervolō¹, -āre, -āvī, -ātum *vt, vi* to fly through or over, fly to

pervolō², -elle, -oluī *vi* to wish very much

pervolūtō, -āre *vt* (*books*) to read through

pervolvō, -vere, -vī, -ūtum *vt* to tumble about; (*book*) to read through; (*pass*) to be very busy (with)

pervor- *etc see* **perver-**

pervulgātus *adj* very common

pervulgō, -āre, -āvī, -ātum *vt* to make public, impart; to haunt

pēs, pedis *m* foot; (*length*) foot; (*verse*) foot, metre; (*sailrope*) sheet; **pedem cōnferre** come to close quarters; **pedem referre** go back; **ante pedēs** self-evident; **pedibus** on foot, by land; **pedibus īre in sententiam** take sides; **pedibus aequīs** (NAUT) with the wind right aft; **servus ā pedibus** footman

pessimē *superl of* **male**

pessimus *superl of* **malus**

pessulus, -ī *m* bolt

pessum *adv* to the ground, to the bottom; ~ **dare** put an end to, ruin, destroy; ~ **īre** sink, perish

pestifer, -ī *adj* pestilential; baleful, destructive

pestilēns, -entis *adj* unhealthy; destructive

pestilentia, -ae *f* plague, pest; unhealthiness

pestilitās, -ātis *f* plague

pestis, -is *f* plague, pest; ruin, destruction

petasātus *adj* wearing the petasus

petasunculus, -ī *m* small leg of pork

petasus, -ī *m* broadbrimmed hat

petessō, -ere *vt* to be eager for

petītiō, -ōnis *f* thrust, attack; request, application; (*office*) candidature, standing for; (LAW) civil suit, right of claim

petītor, -ōris *m* candidate; plaintiff

petīturiō, -īre *vt* to long to be a candidate

petītus¹ *ppp of* **petō**

petītus², -ūs *m* falling to

petō, -ere, -īvī *and* **-iī, -ītum** *vt* to aim at, attack; (*place*) to make for, go to; to seek, look for, demand, ask; to go and fetch; (LAW) to sue; (*love*) to court; (*office*) to stand for

petorritum, -ī *nt* carriage

petrō, -ōnis *m* yokel

Petrōnius, -ī *m* arbiter of fashion under Nero

petulāns, -antis *adj* pert, impudent, lascivious

petulanter *adv see* **petulāns**

petulantia, -ae *f* pertness, impudence

petulcus *adj* butting

pexus *ppp of* **pectō**

Phaeāces, -cum *mpl* fabulous islanders in the Odyssey

Phaeācius, Phaeācus, Phaeax *adj* Phaeacian

Phaedra, -ae *f* stepmother of Hippolytus

Phaedrus, -ī *m* pupil of Socrates; writer of Latin fables

Phaethōn, -ontis *m* son of the Sun (*killed while driving his father's chariot*)

Phaethonteus *adj see* **Phaethōn**

Phaethontiades, -um *fpl* sisters of Phaethon

phalangae, -ārum *fpl* wooden rollers

phalangītae, -ārum *mpl* soldiers of a phalanx

phalanx, -gis *f* phalanx; troops, battle order

Phalaris, -dis *m* tyrant of Agrigentum

phalerae, -ārum *fpl* medallions, badges; (*horse*) trappings

phalerātus *adj* wearing medallions; ornamented

Phalēreus, -icus *adj see* **Phalērum**

Phalērum, -ī *nt* harbour of Athens

pharetra, -ae *f* quiver

pharetrātus *adj* wearing a quiver

Pharius *adj see* **Pharus**

pharmaceutria, -ae *f* sorceress

pharmacopōla, -ae *m* quack doctor

Pharsālicus, -ius *adj see* **Pharsālus**

Pharsālus, Pharsālos, -ī *f* town in Thessaly (*where Caesar defeated Pompey*)

Pharus, Pharos, -ī *f* island off Alexandria with a famous lighthouse; lighthouse

phasēlus, -ī *m/f* French bean; (*boat*) pinnace

Phāsiacus *adj* Colchian

Phāsiānus, -āna *m/f* pheasant

Phāsis¹, -dis *and* **-dos** *m* river of Colchis

Phāsis² *adj see* **Phāsis¹**

phasma, -tis *nt* ghost

Pherae, -ārum *fpl* town in Thessaly (*home of Admetus*)

Pheraeus *adj see* **Pherae**

phiala, -ae *f* saucer

Phīdiacus *adj see* **Phīdiās**

Phīdiās, -ae *m* famous Athenian sculptor

philēma, -tis *nt* kiss

Philippēus *adj see* **Philippus**

Philippī, -ōrum *mpl* town in Macedonia (*where Brutus and Cassius were defeated*)

Philippicae *fpl* Cicero's speeches against Antony

Philippicus *adj see* **Philippus**

Philippus, -ī *m* king of Macedonia; gold coin

philitia, phīditia, -ōrum *ntpl* public meals at Sparta

Philō, Philōn, -ōnis *m* Academic philosopher (*teacher of Cicero*)

Philoctētēs, -ae *m* Greek archer who gave Hercules poisoned arrows

philologia, -ae *f* study of literature

philologus *adj* scholarly, literary

Philomēla, -ae *f* sister of Procne; nightingale

philosophē *adv see* **philosophus**

philosophia, -ae *f* philosophy

philosophor, -ārī, -ātus *vi* to philosophize

philosophus, -ī *m* philosopher ♦ *adj* philosophical

philtrum, -ī *nt* love potion

philyra, -ae *f* inner bark of the lime tree

phīmus, -ī *m* dice box

Phlegethōn, -ontis *m* a river of Hades

Phlegethontis *adj see* **Phlegethōn**

Phlīāsius *adj see* **Phlīūs**

Phlīūs, -ūntis *f* town in Peloponnese

phōca, -ae *f* seal

Phōcaicus *adj see* **Phōcis**

Phōcēus *adj see* **Phōcis**

Phōcis, -idis f country of central Greece
Phōcius adj see **Phōcis**
Phoebas, -adis f prophetess
Phoebē, -ēs f Diana, the moon
Phoebēius, -ēus adj see **Phoebus**
Phoebigena, -ae m son of Phoebus, Aesculapius
Phoebus, -ī m Apollo; the sun
Phoenīcē, -cēs f Phoenicia
Phoenīces, -cum mpl Phoenicians
phoenīcopterus, -ī m flamingo
Phoenīssus adj Phoenician ♦ f Dido
phoenīx, -īcis m phoenix
Phoenīx, -īcis m friend of Achilles
Phorcis, -idos = **Phorcȳnis**
Phorcus, -ī m son of Neptune (father of Medusa)
Phorcȳnis, -ȳnidos f Medusa
Phraātēs, -ae m king of Parthia
phrenēsis, -is f delirium
phrenēticus adj mad, delirious
Phrixēus adj see **Phrixus**
Phrixus, -ī m Helle's brother (who took the ram with the golden fleece to Colchis)
Phryges, -um mpl Phrygians; Trojans
Phrygia, -iae f Phrygia (country of Asia Minor); Troy
Phrygius adj Phrygian, Trojan
Phthia, -ae f home of Achilles in Thessaly
Phthīōta, -ōtēs, -ōtae m native of Phthia
phthisis f consumption
Phthīus adj see **Phthīa**
phy interj bah!
phylaca, -ae f prison
phylarchus, -ī m chieftain
physica, -ae, physicē, -ēs f physics
physicē adv scientifically
physicus adj of physics, natural ♦ m natural philosopher ♦ ntpl physics
physiognōmōn, -onis m physiognomist
physiologia, -ae f natural philosophy, science
piābilis adj expiable
piāculāris adj atoning ♦ ntpl sin offerings
piāculum, -ī nt sin offering; victim; atonement, punishment; sin, guilt
piāmen, -inis nt atonement
pīca, -ae f magpie
picāria, -ae f pitch hut
picea, -ae f pine
Picēns, -entis adj = **Picēnus**
Picēnum, -ēnī nt Picenum
Picēnus adj of Picenum in E. Italy
piceus adj pitch black; of pitch
pictor, -ōris m painter
pictūra, -ae f painting; picture
pictūrātus adj feathered; embroidered
pictus ppp of **pingō** ♦ adj coloured, tattooed; (style) ornate; (fear) unreal
pīcus, -ī m woodpecker
piē adv religiously, dutifully
Pīeris, -dis f Muse
Pīerius adj of the Muses, poetic
pietās, -ātis f sense of duty (to gods, family, country), piety, filial affection, love, patriotism
piger, -rī adj reluctant, slack, slow; numbing, dull

piget, -ēre, -uit vt (impers) to be annoyed, dislike; to regret, repent
pigmentārius, -ī and **-iī** m dealer in paints
pigmentum, -ī nt paint, cosmetic; (style) colouring
pignerātor, -ōris m mortgagee
pignerō, -āre vt to pawn, mortgage
pigneror, -ārī, -ātus vt to claim, accept
pignus, -oris and **-eris** nt pledge, pawn, security; wager, stake; (fig) assurance, token; (pl) children, dear ones
pigritia, -ae, pigritiēs, -ēī f sluggishness, indolence
pigrō, -āre, pigror, -ārī vi to be slow, be slack
pila, -ae f ball, ball game
pīla¹, -ae f mortar
pīla², -ae f pillar; pier
pīlānus, -ī m soldier of the third line
pīlātus adj armed with javelins
pīlentum, -ī nt carriage
pilleātus adj wearing the felt cap
pilleolus, -ī m skullcap
pilleum, -ī nt, **pilleus, -ī** m felt cap presented to freed slaves; (fig) liberty
pilōsus adj hairy
pīlum, -ī nt javelin
pilus, -ī m hair; a whit
pīlus, -ī m division of triarii; **prīmus ~** chief centurion
Pimplēa, -ae, Pimplēis, -idis f Muse
Pimplēus adj of the Muses
Pindaricus adj see **Pindarus**
Pindarus, -ī m Pindar (Greek lyric poet)
Pindus, -ī m mountain range in Thessaly
pīnētum, -ī nt pine wood
pīneus adj pine- (in cpds)
pingō, -ere, pinxī, pictum vt to paint, embroider; to colour; (fig) to embellish, decorate
pinguēscō, -ere vi to grow fat, become fertile
pinguis adj fat, rich, fertile; (mind) gross, dull; (ease) comfortable, calm; (weather) thick ♦ nt grease
pīnifer, -ī, pīniger, -ī adj pine-clad
pinna, -ae f feather; wing, arrow; battlement; (fish) fin
pinnātus adj feathered, winged
pinniger, -ī adj winged; finny
pinnipēs, -edis adj wing-footed
pinnirapus, -ī m plume-snatcher
pinnula, -ae f little wing
pīnotērēs, -ae m hermit crab
pīnsō, -ere vt to beat, pound
pīnus, -ūs and **-ī** f stone pine, Scots fir; ship, torch, wreath
pinxī perf of **pingō**
piō, -āre vt to propitiate, worship; to atone for, avert; to avenge
piper, -is nt pepper
pīpilō, -āre vi to chirp
Pīraea, -ōrum ntpl Piraeus (main port of Athens)
Pīraeus, Pīraeus, -ī m main port of Athens
Pīraeus adj see **Pīraeus**
pīrāta, -ae m pirate**

pīrāticus *adj* pirate ♦ *f* piracy
Pīrēnē, -ēs *f spring in Corinth*
Pīrēnis, -idis *adj see* **Pīrēnē**
Pīrithous, -ī *m king of the Lapiths*
pirum, -ī *nt* pear
pirus, -ī *f* pear tree
Pīsa, -ae *f Greek town near the Olympic Games site*
Pīsae, -ārum *fpl town in Etruria (now Pisa)*
Pīsaeus *adj see* **Pīsae**
Pīsānus *adj see* **Pīsae**
piscārius *adj* fish- (*in cpds*), fishing- (*in cpds*)
piscātor, -ōris *m* fisherman
piscātōrius *adj* fishing- (*in cpds*)
piscātus, -ūs *m* fishing; fish; catch, haul
pisciculus, -ī *m* little fish
piscīna, -ae *f* fishpond; swimming pool
piscīnārius, -ī *and* **-iī** *m* person keen on fish ponds
piscis, -is *m* fish; (ASTR) Pisces
piscor, -ārī, -ātus *vi* to fish
piscōsus *adj* full of fish
pisculentus *adj* full of fish
Pīsistratidae, -idārum *mpl* sons of Pisistratus
Pīsistratus, -ī *m tyrant of Athens*
pistillum, -ī *nt* pestle
pistor, -ōris *m* miller; baker
pistrilla, -ae *f* little mortar
pistrīnum, -ī *nt* mill, bakery; drudgery
pistris, -is, pistrīx, -īcis *f* sea monster, whale; swift ship
pithēcium, -ī *and* **-iī** *nt* little ape
pītuīta, -ae *f* phlegm; catarrh, cold in the head
pītuītōsus *adj* phlegmatic
pius *adj* dutiful, conscientious; godly, holy; filial, affectionate; patriotic; good, upright ♦ *mpl* the blessed dead
pix, picis *f* pitch
plācābilis *adj* easily appeased
plācābilitās, -ātis *f* readiness to condone
plācāmen, -inis, plācāmentum, -ī *nt* peace-offering
plācātē *adv* calmly
plācātiō, -ōnis *f* propitiating
plācātus *ppp of* **plācō** ♦ *adj* calm, quiet, reconciled
placenta, -ae *f* cake
Placentia, -iae *f town in N. Italy (now Piacenza)*
Placentīnus *adj see* **Placentia**
placeō, -ēre, -uī, -itum *vi* (*with dat*) to please, satisfy; **placet** it seems good, it is agreed, resolved; **mihi ~** I am pleased with myself
placidē *adv* peacefully, gently
placidus *adj* calm, quiet, gentle
placitum, -ī *nt* belief
placitus *ppa of* **placeō** ♦ *adj* pleasing; agreed on
plācō, -āre, -āvī, -ātum *vt* to calm, appease, reconcile
plaga¹, -ae *f* region, zone
plaga², -ae *f* hunting net, snare, trap
plāga, -ae *f* blow, stroke, wound
plagiārius, -ī *and* **-iī** *m* plunderer, kidnapper
plāgigerulus *adj* much flogged
plāgōsus *adj* fond of punishing
plagula, -ae *f* curtain

planctus, -ūs *m* beating the breast, lamentation
plānē *adv* plainly, clearly; completely, quite; certainly
plangō, -gere, -xī, -ctum *vt, vi* to beat noisily; to beat in grief; to lament loudly, bewail
plangor, -ōris *m* beating; loud lamentation
plānipēs, -edis *m* ballet dancer
plānitās, -ātis *f* perspicuity
plānitiēs, -ēī, plānitia, -ae *f* level ground, plain
planta, -ae *f* shoot, slip; sole, foot
plantāria, -ium *ntpl* slips, young trees
planus, -ī *m* impostor
plānus *adj* level, flat; plain, clear ♦ *nt* level ground; **dē plānō** easily
platalea, -ae *f* spoonbill
platea, -ae *f* street
Platō, -ōnis *m* Plato (*founder of the Academic school of philosophy*)
Platōnicus *adj see* **Platō**
plaudō, -dere, -sī, -sum *vt* to clap, beat, stamp ♦ *vi* to clap, applaud; to approve, be pleased with
plausibilis *adj* praiseworthy
plausor, -ōris *m* applauder
plaustrum, -ī *nt* wagon, cart; (ASTR) Great Bear; **~ percellere** upset the applecart
plausus¹ *ppp of* **plaudō**
plausus², -ūs *m* flapping; clapping, applause
Plautīnus *adj see* **Plautus**
Plautus, -ī *m early Latin comic poet*
plēbēcula, -ae *f* rabble
plēbēius *adj* plebeian; common, low
plēbicola, -ae *m* friend of the people
plēbiscītum, -ī *nt* decree of the people
plēbs, plēbēs, -is *f* common people, plebeians; lower classes, masses
plēctō, -ere *vt* to punish
plēctrum, -ī *nt* plectrum; lyre, lyric poetry
Plēias, -dis *f* Pleiad; (*pl*) the Seven Sisters
plēnē *adv* fully, entirely
plēnus *adj* full, filled; (*fig*) sated; (*age*) mature; (*amount*) complete; (*body*) stout, plump; (*female*) pregnant; (*matter*) solid; (*style*) copious; (*voice*) loud; **ad plēnum** abundantly
plērumque *adv* generally, mostly
plērusque *adj* a large part, most; (*pl*) the majority, the most; very many
plexus *adj* plaited, interwoven
Plīas see Plēias
plicātrīx, -īcis *f* clothes folder
plicō, -āre, -āvī *and* **-uī, -ātum** *and* **-itum** *vt* to fold, coil
Plīnius, -ī *m Roman family name (esp Pliny the Elder, who died in the eruption of Vesuvius); Pliny the Younger, writer of letters*
plōrātus, -ūs *m* wailing
plōrō, -āre, -āvī, -ātum *vi* to wail, lament ♦ *vt* to weep for, bewail
plōstellum, -ī *nt* cart
ploxenum, -ī *nt* cart box
pluit, -ere, -it *vi* (*impers*) it is raining
plūma, -ae *f* soft feather, down
plumbeus *adj* of lead; (*fig*) heavy, dull, worthless

plumbum, -ī *nt* lead; bullet, pipe, ruler; ~ **album** tin

plūmeus *adj* down, downy

plūmipēs, -edis *adj* feather-footed

plūmōsus *adj* feathered

plūrimus *superl of* **multus**

plūs, -ūris *compar of* **multus** ♦ *adv* more

plūsculus *adj* a little more

pluteus, -ī *m* shelter, penthouse; parapet; couch; bookcase

Plūtō, -ōnis *m* king of the lower world

Plūtōnius *adj see* **Plūtō**

pluvia, -ae *f* rain

pluviālis *adj* rainy

pluvius *adj* rainy, rain- (*in cpds*)

pōcillum, -ī *nt* small cup

pōculum, -ī *nt* cup; drink, potion

podagra, -ae *f* gout

podagrōsus *adj* gouty

podium, -ī and -iī *nt* balcony

poēma, -tis *nt* poem

poena, -ae *f* penalty, punishment; **poenas dare** to be punished

Poenī, -ōrum *mpl* Carthaginians

Poenus, Pūnicus *adj* Punic

poēsis, -is *f* poetry, poem

poēta, -ae *m* poet

poēticē *adv* poetically

poēticus *adj* poetic ♦ *f* poetry

poētria, -ae *f* poetess

pol *interj* by Pollux!, truly

polenta, -ae *f* pearl barley

poliō, -īre, -īvī, -ītum *vt* to polish; to improve, put in good order

polītē *adv* elegantly

polītia, -ae *f* Plato's Republic

politicus *adj* political

polītus *adj* polished, refined, cultured

pollen, -inis *nt* fine flour, meal

pollēns, -entis *pres p of* **polleō** ♦ *adj* powerful, strong

pollentia, -ae *f* power

polleō, -ēre *vi* to be strong, be powerful

pollex, -icis *m* thumb

polliceor, -ērī, -itus *vt* to promise, offer

pollicitātiō, -ōnis *f* promise

pollicitor, -ārī, -ātus *vt* to promise

pollicitum, -ī *nt* promise

Polliō, -ōnis *m* Roman surname (*esp C. Asinius, soldier, statesman and literary patron under Augustus*)

pollis, -inis *m/f see* **pollen**

pollūcibiliter *adv* sumptuously

pollūctus *adj* offered up ♦ *nt* offering

polluō, -uere, -uī, -ūtum *vt* to defile, pollute, dishonour

Pollūx, -ūcis *m* twin brother of Castor (*famous as a boxer*)

polus, -ī *m* pole, North pole; sky

Polyhymnia, -ae *f a Muse*

Polyphēmus, -ī *m* one-eyed Cyclops

pōlypus, -ī *m* polypus

pōmārium, -i and -iī *nt* orchard

pōmārius, -ī and -iī *m* fruiterer

pōmerīdiānus *adj* afternoon

pōmērium, -ī and -iī *nt* free space round the city boundary

pōmifer, -ī *adj* fruitful

pōmoerium *see* **pōmērium**

pōmōsus *adj* full of fruit

pompa, -ae *f* procession; retinue, train; ostentation

Pompeiānus *adj see* **Pompeiī**

Pompeiī, -ōrum *mpl* Campanian town buried by an eruption of Vesuvius

Pompeius¹, -ī *m* Roman family name (*esp Pompey the Great*)

Pompeius², -ānus *adj see* **Pompeius¹**

Pompilius¹, -ī *m* Numa (*second king of Rome*)

Pompilius² *adj see* **Pompilius¹**

Pomptīnus *adj* Pomptine (*name of marshy district in S. Latium*)

pōmum, -ī *nt* fruit; fruit tree

pōmus, -ī *f* fruit tree

ponderō, -āre *vt* to weigh; to consider, reflect on

ponderōsus *adj* heavy, weighty

pondō *adv* in weight; pounds

pondus, -eris *nt* weight; mass, burden; (*fig*) importance, authority; (*character*) firmness; (*pl*) balance

pōne *adv* behind

pōnō, -ere, posuī, positum *vt* to put, place, lay, set; to lay down, lay aside; (*fig*) to regard, reckon; (*art*) to make, build; (*camp*) to pitch; (*corpse*) to lay out, bury; (*example*) to take; (*food*) to serve; (*hair*) to arrange; (*hope*) to base, stake; (*hypothesis*) to suppose, assume; (*institution*) to lay down, ordain; (*money*) to invest; (*sea*) to calm; (*theme*) to propose; (*time*) to spend, devote; (*tree*) to plant; (*wager*) to put down ♦ *vi* (*wind*) to abate

pōns, pontis *m* bridge; drawbridge; (*ship*) gangway, deck

ponticulus, -ī *m* small bridge

Ponticus *adj see* **Pontus**

pontifex, -icis *m* high priest, pontiff

pontificālis *adj* pontifical

pontificātus, -ūs *m* high priesthood

pontificius *adj* pontiff's

pontō, -ōnis *m* ferryboat

Pontus, -ī *m* Black Sea; kingdom of Mithridates in Asia Minor

pontus, -ī *m* sea

popa, -ae *m* minor priest

popanum, -ī *nt* sacrificial cake

popellus, -ī *m* mob

popīna, -ae *f* eating house, restaurant

popīnō, -ōnis *m* glutton

popl- *etc see* **pūbl-**

poples, -itis *m* knee

poposcī *perf of* **poscō**

poppysma, -tis *nt* clicking of the tongue

populābilis *adj* destroyable

populābundus *adj* ravaging

populāris *adj* of, from, for the people; popular, democratic; native ♦ *m* fellow countryman ♦ *mpl* the people's party, the democrats

populāritās, -ātis *f* courting popular favour

populāriter *adv* vulgarly; democratically

populātiō, -ōnis f plundering; plunder
populātor, -ōris m ravager
pōpuleus adj poplar- (in cpds)
pōpulifer, -ī adj rich in poplars
populor, -ārī, -ātus, populō, -āre vt to ravage, plunder; to destroy, ruin
populus, -ī m people, nation; populace, the public; large crowds; district
pōpulus, -ī f poplar tree
porca, -ae f sow
porcella, -ae f, **porcellus, -ī** m little pig
porcīna, -ae f pork
porcīnārius, -ī and **-iī** m pork seller
Porcius¹, -ī m family name of Cato
Porcius² adj see **Porcius¹**
porculus, -ī m porker
porcus, -ī m pig, hog
porgō etc see **porrigō**
Porphyriōn, -ōnis m a Giant
porrēctiō, -ōnis f extending
porrēctus ppp of **porrigō** ✦ adj long, protracted; dead
porrēxī perf of **porrigō**
porriciō, -ere vt to make an offering of; **inter caesa et porrēcta** at the eleventh hour
porrigō, -igere, -ēxī, -ēctum vt to stretch, spread out, extend; to offer, hold out
porrīgō, -inis f scurf, dandruff
porrō adv forward, a long way off; (time) in future, long ago; (sequence) next, moreover, in turn
porrum, -ī nt leek
Porsena, Porsenna, Porsinna, -ae f king of Clusium in Etruria
porta, -ae f gate; entrance, outlet
portātiō, -ōnis f carrying
portendō, -dere, -dī, -tum vt to denote, predict
portentificus adj marvellous
portentōsus adj unnatural
portentum, -ī nt omen, unnatural happening; monstrosity, monster; (story) marvel
porthmeus, -eī and **-eos** m ferryman
porticula, -ae f small gallery
porticus, -ūs m portico, colonnade; (MIL) gallery; (PHILOS) Stoicism
portiō, -ōnis f share, instalment; **prō portiōne** proportionally
portitor¹, -ōris m customs officer
portitor², -ōris m ferryman
portō, -āre, -āvī, -ātum vt to carry, convey, bring
portōrium, -ī and **-iī** nt customs duty, tax
portula, -ae f small gate
portuōsus adj well-off for harbours
portus, -ūs m harbour, port; (fig) safety, haven
pōsca, -ae f a vinegar drink
poscō, -ere, poposcī vt to ask, require, demand; to call on
Posīdōnius, -ī m Stoic philosopher (teacher of Cicero)
positiō, -ōnis f position, climate
positor, -ōris m builder
positūra, -ae f position; formation

positus ppp of **pōnō** ✦ adj situated
posse infin of **possum**
possēdī perf of **possideō**; **possīdō**
possessiō, -ōnis f seizing; occupation; possession, property
possessiuncula, -ae f small estate
possessor, -ōris m occupier, possessor
possessus ppp of **possideō**; **possīdō**
possideō, -idēre, -ēdī, -essum vt to hold, occupy; to have, possess
possīdō, -īdere, -ēdī, -essum vt to take possession of
possum, -sse, -tuī vi to be able, can; to have power, avail
post adv (place) behind; (time) after; (sequence) next ✦ prep (with acc) behind; after, since; **paulō ~** soon after; **~ urbem conditam** since the foundation of the city
posteā adv afterwards, thereafter; next, then; **~ quam** conj after
posterior, -ōris adj later, next; inferior, less important
posteritās, -ātis f posterity, the future
posterius adv later
posterus adj next, following ✦ mpl posterity
postferō, -re vt to put after, sacrifice
postgenitī, -ōrum mpl later generations
posthabeō, -ēre, -uī, -itum vt to put after, neglect
posthāc adv hereafter, in future
postibi adv then, after that
postīculum, -ī nt small back building
postīcus adj back- (in cpds), hind- (in cpds) ✦ nt back door
postideā adv after that
postillā adv afterwards
postis, -is m doorpost, door
postlīminium, -ī and **-iī** nt right of recovery
postmerīdiānus adj in the afternoon
postmodo, postmodum adv shortly, presently
postpōnō, -ōnere, -osuī, -ositum vt to put after, disregard
postputō, -āre vt to consider less important
postquam conj after, when
postrēmō adv finally
postrēmus adj last, rear; lowest, worst
postrīdiē adv next day, the day after
postscaenium, -ī and **-iī** nt behind the scenes
postscrībō, -ere vt to write after
postulātiō, -ōnis f demand, claim; complaint
postulātum, -ī nt demand, claim
postulātus, -ūs m claim
postulō, -āre, -āvī, -ātum vt to demand, claim; (LAW) to summon, prosecute; to apply for a writ (to prosecute)
postumus adj last, last-born
postus etc see **positus**
posuī perf of **pōnō**
pōtātiō, -ōnis f drinking
pōtātor, -ōris m toper
pote etc see **potis**
potēns, -entis adj able, capable; powerful, strong, potent; master of, ruling over; successful in carrying out

potentātus, -ūs *m* political power
potenter *adv* powerfully; competently
potentia, -ae *f* power, force, efficacy; tyranny
potērium, -ī *and* **-iī** *nt* goblet
potesse *archaic infin of* **possum**
potestās, -ātis *f* power, ability; control,
sovereignty, authority; opportunity,
permission; (*person*) magistrate; (*things*)
property; **potestātem suī facere** allow access
to oneself
potin can (you)?, is it possible?
potiō, -īre *vt* to put into the power of
pōtiō, -ōnis *f* drink, draught, philtre
potior¹, -īrī, -ītus *vi* (*with gen and abl*) to take
possession of, get hold of, acquire; to be
master of
potior², -ōris *adj* better, preferable
potis *adj* (*indecl*) able; possible
potissimum *adv* especially
potissimus *adj* chief, most important
pōtitō, -āre *vt* to drink much
potius *adv* rather, more
pōtō, -āre, -āvī, -ātum *and* **-um** *vt* to drink
pōtor, -ōris *m* drinker
pōtrīx, -īcis *f* woman tippler
potuī *perf of* **possum**
pōtulenta, -ōrum *ntpl* drinks
pōtus¹ *ppp of* **pōtō** ♦ *adj* drunk
pōtus², -ūs *m* drink
prae *adv* in front, before; in comparison ♦ *prep*
(*with abl*) in front of; compared with; (*cause*)
because of, for; **~ sē** openly; **~ sē ferre** display;
~ manū to hand
praeacūtus *adj* pointed
praealtus *adj* very high, very deep
praebeō, -ēre, -uī, -itum *vt* to hold out,
proffer; to give, supply; to show, represent; **sē**
praebēre behave, prove
praebibō, -ere, -ī *vt* to toast
praebitor, -ōris *m* purveyor
praecalidus *adj* very hot
praecānus *adj* prematurely grey
praecautus *ppp of* **praecaveō**
praecaveō, -avēre, -āvī, -autum *vt* to guard
against ♦ *vi* to beware, take precautions
praecēdō, -dere, -ssī, -ssum *vt* to go before; to
surpass ♦ *vi* to lead the way; to excel
praecellō, -ere *vi* to excel, be distinguished
♦ *vt* to surpass
praecelsus *adj* very high
praecentiō, -ōnis *f* prelude
praecentō, -āre *vi* to sing an incantation for
praeceps, -ipitis *adj* head first, headlong;
going down, precipitous; rapid, violent,
hasty; inclined (to); dangerous ♦ *nt* edge of
an abyss, precipice; danger ♦ *adv* headlong;
into danger
praeceptiō, -ōnis *f* previous notion; precept
praeceptor, -ōris *m* teacher
praeceptrīx, -rīcis *f* teacher
praeceptum, -ī *nt* maxim, precept; order
praeceptus *ppp of* **praecipiō**
praecerpō, -ere, -sī, -tum *vt* to gather
prematurely; to forestall

praecīdō, -dere, -dī, -sum *vt* to cut off,
damage; (*fig*) to cut short, put an end to
praecinctus *ppp of* **praecingō**
praecingō, -ingere, -inxī, -inctum *vt* to gird
in front; to surround
praecinō, -inere, -inuī, -entum *vt* to play
before; to chant a spell ♦ *vt* to predict
praecipiō, -ipere, -ēpī, -ēptum *vt* to take
beforehand, get in advance; to anticipate; to
teach, admonish, order
praecipitanter *adv* at full speed
praecipitem *acc of* **praeceps**
praecipitō, -āre, -āvī, -ātum *vt* to throw
down, throw away, hasten; (*fig*) to remove,
carry away, ruin ♦ *vi* to rush headlong, fall;
to be hasty
praecipuē *adv* especially, chiefly
praecipuus *adj* special; principal,
outstanding
praecīsē *adv* briefly, absolutely
praecīsus *ppp of* **praecīdō** ♦ *adj* steep
praeclārē *adv* very clearly; excellently
praeclārus *adj* very bright; beautiful,
splendid; distinguished, noble
praeclūdō, -dere, -sī, -sum *vt* to close, shut
against; to close to, impede
praecō, -ōnis *m* crier, herald; auctioneer
praecōgitō, -āre *vt* to premeditate
praecognitus *adj* foreseen
praecolō, -olere, -oluī, -ultum *vt* to cultivate
early
praecompositus *adj* studied
praecōnium, -ī *and* **-iī** *nt* office of a crier;
advertisement; commendation
praecōnius *adj* of a public crier
praecōnsūmō, -ere, -ptum *vt* to use up
beforehand
praecontrectō, -āre *vt* to consider
beforehand
praecordia, -ōrum *ntpl* midriff; stomach;
breast, heart; mind
praecorrumpō, -umpere, -ūpī, -uptum *vt* to
bribe beforehand
praecox, -cis *adj* early, premature
praecultus *ppp of* **praecolō**
praecurrentia, -ium *ntpl* antecedents
praecurrō, -rrere, -currī *and* **-rrī, -rsum** *vi*
to hurry on before, precede; to excel ♦ *vt* to
anticipate; to surpass
praecursiō, -ōnis *f* previous occurrence; (RHET)
preparation
praecursor, -ōris *m* advance guard; scout
praecutiō, -ere *vt* to brandish before
praeda, -ae *f* booty, plunder; (*animal*) prey;
(*fig*) gain
praedābundus *adj* plundering
praedamnō, -āre *vt* to condemn beforehand
praedātiō, -ōnis *f* plundering
praedātor, -ōris *m* plunderer
praedātōrius *adj* marauding
praedēlassō, -āre *vt* to weaken beforehand
praedēstinō, -āre *vt* to predetermine
praediātor, -ōris *m* buyer of landed estates
praediātōrius *adj* relating to the sale of
estates

praedicābilis *adj* laudatory

praedicātiō, -ōnis *f* proclamation; commendation

praedicātor, -ōris *m* eulogist

praedicō, -āre, -āvī, -ātum *vt* to proclaim, make public; to declare; to praise, boast

praedīcō, -īcere, -īxī, -ictum *vt* to mention beforehand, prearrange; to foretell; to warn, command

praedictiō, -ōnis *f* foretelling

praedictum, -ī *nt* prediction; command; prearrangement

praedictus *ppp of* **praedīcō**

praediolum, -ī *nt* small estate

praediscō, -ere *vt* to learn beforehand

praedispositus *adj* arranged beforehand

praeditus *adj* endowed, provided

praedium, -ī *and* **-iī** *nt* estate

praedīves, -itis *adj* very rich

praedō, -ōnis *m* robber, pirate

praedor, -ārī, -ātus *vt, vi* to plunder, rob; (*fig*) to profit

praedūcō, -ūcere, -ūxī, -uctum *vt* to draw in front

praedulcis *adj* very sweet

praedūrus *adj* very hard, very tough

praeēmineō, -ēre *vt* to surpass

praeeō, -īre, -īvī *and* **-iī, -itum** *vi* to lead the way, go first; (*formula*) to dictate, recite first ♦ *vt* to precede, outstrip

praeesse *infin of* **praesum**

praefātiō, -ōnis *f* formula; preface

praefātus *ppa of* **praefor**

praefectūra, -ae *f* superintendence; governorship; *Italian town governed by Roman edicts*, prefecture; district, province

praefectus *ppp of* **praeficiō** ♦ *m* overseer, director, governor, commander; ~ **classis** admiral; ~ **legiōnis** colonel; ~ **urbis** *or* **urbī** city prefect (*of Rome*)

praeferō, -ferre, -tulī, -lātum *vt* to carry in front, hold out; to prefer; to show, display; to anticipate; (*pass*) to hurry past, outflank

praeferōx, -ōcis *adj* very impetuous, very insolent

praefervidus *adj* very hot

praefestīnō, -āre *vi* to be too hasty; to hurry past

praefica, -ae *f* hired mourner

praeficiō, -icere, -ēcī, -ectum *vt* to put in charge, give command over

praefidēns, -entis *adj* over-confident

praefigō, -gere, -xī, -xum *vt* to fasten in front, set up before; to tip, point; to transfix

praefiniō, -īre, -īvī *and* **-iī, -ītum** *vt* to determine, prescribe

praefiscinē, -ī *adv* without offence

praeflōrō, -āre *vt* to tarnish

praefluō, -ere *vt, vi* to flow past

praefocō, -āre *vt* to choke

praefodiō, -odere, -ōdī *vt* to dig in front of; to bury beforehand

praefor, -ārī, -ātus *vt, vi* to say in advance, preface; to pray beforehand; to predict

praefrāctē *adv* resolutely

praefrāctus *ppp of* **praefringō** ♦ *adj* abrupt; stern

praefrīgidus *adj* very cold

praefringō, -ingere, -ēgī, -āctum *vt* to break off, shiver

praefuī *perf of* **praesum**

praefulciō, -cīre, -sī, -tum *vt* to prop up; to use as a prop

praefulgeō, -ulgēre, -ulsī *vt* to shine conspicuously; to outshine

praegelidus *adj* very cold

praegestiō, -īre *vi* to be very eager

praegnāns, -antis *adj* pregnant; full

praegracilis *adj* very slim

praegrandis *adj* very large, very great

praegravis *adj* very heavy; very wearisome

praegravō, -āre *vt* to weigh down; to eclipse

praegredior, -dī, -ssus *vt, vi* to go before; to go past; to surpass

praegressiō, -ōnis *f* precession, precedence

praegustātor, -ōris *m* taster

praegustō, -āre *vt* to taste beforehand

praehibeō, -ēre *vt* to offer, give

praeiaceō, -ēre *vt* to lie in front of

praeiūdicium, -ī *and* **-iī** *nt* precedent, example; prejudgment

praeiūdicō, -āre, -āvī, -ātum *vt* to prejudge, decide beforehand

praeiuvō, -āre *vt* to give previous assistance to

praelabor, -bī, -psus *vt, vi* to move past, move along

praelambō, -ere *vt* to lick first

praelātus *ppp of* **praeferō**

praelegō, -ere *vt* to coast along

praeligō, -āre *vt* to bind, tie up

praelongus *adj* very long, very tall

praeloquor, -quī, -cūtus *vi* to speak first

praelūceō, -cēre, -xī *vi* to light, shine; to outshine

praelūstris *adj* very magnificent

praemandāta *ntpl* warrant of arrest

praemandō, -āre, -āvī, -ātum *vt* to bespeak

praemātūrē *adv* too soon

praemātūrus *adj* too early, premature

praemedicātus *adj* protected by charms

praemeditātiō, -ōnis *f* thinking over the future

praemeditātus *adj* premeditated

praemeditor, -ārī, -ātus *vt* to think over, practise

praemetuenter *adv* anxiously

praemetuō, -ere *vi* to be anxious ♦ *vt* to fear the future

praemissus *ppp of* **praemittō**

praemittō, -ittere, -īsī, -issum *vt* to send in advance

praemium, -ī *and* **-iī** *nt* prize, reward

praemolestia, -ae *f* apprehension

praemōlior, -īrī *vt* to prepare thoroughly

praemoneō, -ēre, -uī, -itum *vt* to forewarn, foreshadow

praemonitus, -ūs *m* premonition

praemōnstrātor, -ōris *m* guide

praemōnstrō, **-āre** vt to guide; to predict
praemordeō, **-ēre** vt to bite off; to pilfer
praemorior, **-ī**, **-tuus** vi to die too soon
praemūniō, **-īre**, **-īvī**, **-ītum** vt to fortify, strengthen, secure
praemūnītiō, **-ōnis** f (RHET) preparation
praenārrō, **-āre** vt to tell beforehand
praenatō, **-āre** vt to flow past
Praeneste, **-is** nt/f Latin town (now Palestrina)
Praenestīnus adj see **Praeneste**
praeniteō, **-ēre**, **-uī** vi to seem more attractive
praenōmen, **-inis** nt first name
praenōscō, **-ere** vt to foreknow
praenōtiō, **-ōnis** f preconceived idea
praenūbilus adj very gloomy
praenūntia, **-iae** f harbinger
praenūntiō, **-āre** vt to foretell
praenūntius, **-ī** and **-iī** m harbinger
praeoccupō, **-āre**, **-āvī**, **-ātum** vt to take first, anticipate
praeolit mihi I get a hint of
praeoptō, **-āre**, **-āvī**, **-ātum** vt to choose rather, prefer
praepandō, **-ere** vt to spread out; to expound
praeparātiō, **-ōnis** f preparation
praeparō, **-āre**, **-āvī**, **-ātum** vt to prepare, prepare for; **ex praeparātō** by arrangement
praepediō, **-īre**, **-īvī**, **-ītum** vt to shackle, tether; to hamper
praependeō, **-ēre** vi to hang down in front
praepes, **-etis** adj swift, winged; of good omen
   ♦ f bird
praepilātus adj tipped with a ball
praepinguis adj very rich
praepolleō, **-ēre** vi to be very powerful, be superior
praeponderō, **-āre** vt to outweigh
praepōnō, **-ōnere**, **-osuī**, **-ositum** vt to put first, place in front; to put in charge, appoint commander; to prefer
praeportō, **-āre** vt to carry before
praepositiō, **-ōnis** f preference; (GRAM) preposition
praepositus ppp of **praepōnō** ♦ m overseer, commander
praepossum, **-sse**, **-tuī** vi to gain the upper hand
praeposterē adv the wrong way round
praeposterus adj inverted, perverted; absurd
praepotēns, **-entis** adj very powerful
praeproperanter adv too hastily
praeproperē adv too hastily
praeproperus adj overhasty, rash
praepūtium, **-ī** and **-iī** nt foreskin
praequam adv compared with
praequestus adj complaining beforehand
praeradiō, **-āre** vt to outshine
praerapidus adj very swift
praereptus ppp of **praeripiō**
praerigēscō, **-ēscere**, **-uī** vi to become very stiff
praeripiō, **-ipere**, **-ipuī**, **-eptum** vt to take before, forestall; to carry off prematurely; to frustrate

praerōdō, **-dere**, **-sum** vt to bite the end of, nibble off
praerogātīva, **-ae** f tribe or century with the first vote, the first vote; previous election; omen, sure token
praerogātīvus adj voting first
praerōsus ppp of **praerōdō**
praerumpō, **-umpere**, **-ūpī**, **-uptum** vt to break off
praeruptus ppp of **praerumpō** ♦ adj steep, abrupt; headstrong
praes, **-aedis** m surety; property of a surety
praesaep- etc see **praesēp-**
praesāgiō, **-īre** vt to have a presentiment of, forebode
praesāgītiō, **-ōnis** f foreboding
praesāgium, **-ī** and **-iī** nt presentiment; prediction
praesāgus adj foreboding, prophetic
praesciō, **-īre**, **-iī** vt to know before
praescīscō, **-ere** vt to find out beforehand
praescius adj foreknowing
praescrībō, **-bere**, **-psī**, **-ptum** vt to write first; to direct, command; to dictate, describe; to put forward as a pretext
praescrīptiō, **-ōnis** f preface, heading; order, rule; pretext
praescrīptum, **-ī** nt order, rule
praescrīptus ppp of **praescrībō**
praesecō, **-āre**, **-uī**, **-tum** and **-ātum** vt to cut off, pare
praesēns, **-entis** adj present, in person; (things) immediate, ready, prompt; (mind) resolute; (gods) propitious ♦ ntpl present state of affairs; **in ~** for the present; **~ in rē praesentī** on the spot
praesēnsiō, **-ōnis** f foreboding; preconception
praesēnsus ppp of **praesentiō**
praesentārius adj instant, ready
praesentia, **-ae** f presence; effectiveness
praesentiō, **-entīre**, **-ēnsī**, **-ēnsum** vt to presage, have a foreboding of
praesēpe, **-is** nt, **praesēpēs**, **-is** f stable, fold, pen; hovel; hive
praesēpiō, **-īre**, **-sī**, **-tum** vt to barricade
praesēpis f = **praesēpe**
praesertim adv especially
praeserviō, **-īre** vi to serve as a slave
praeses, **-idis** m guardian, protector; chief, ruler
praesideō, **-idēre**, **-ēdī** vi to guard, defend; to preside over, direct
praesidiārius adj garrison-
praesidium, **-ī** and **-iī** nt defence, protection; support, assistance; guard, garrison, convoy; defended position, entrenchment
praesignificō, **-āre** vt to foreshadow
praesignis adj conspicuous
praesonō, **-āre**, **-uī** vi to sound before
praespargō, **-ere** vt to strew before
praestābilis adj outstanding; preferable
praestāns, **-antis** pres p of **praestō²** ♦ adj outstanding, pre-eminent
praestantia, **-ae** f pre-eminence
praestes, **-itis** adj presiding, guardian

praestīgiae, -ārum *fpl* illusion, sleight of hand

praestīgiātor, -ōris *m*, **praestīgiātrīx, -rīcis** *f* conjurer, cheat

praestinō, -āre *vt* to buy

praestitī *perf of* **praestō²**

praestituō, -uere, -uī, -ūtum *vt* to prearrange, prescribe

praestitus *ppp of* **praestō²**

praestō¹ *adv* at hand, ready

praestō², -āre, -itī, -itum *and* **-ātum** *vi* to be outstanding, be superior; (*impers*) it is better ♦ *vt* to excel; to be responsible for, answer for; (*duty*) to discharge, perform; (*quality*) to show, prove; (*things*) to give, offer, provide; **sē praestāre** behave, prove

praestōlor, -ārī, -ātus *vt, vi* to wait for, expect

praestrictus *ppp of* **praestringō**

praestringō, -ingere, -inxī, -ictum *vt* to squeeze; to blunt, dull; (*eyes*) to dazzle

praestruō, -ere, -xī, -ctum *vt* to block up; to build beforehand

praesul, -is *m/f* public dancer

praesultātor, -ōris *m* public dancer

praesultō, -āre *vi* to dance before

praesum, -esse, -fuī *vi* (*with dat*) to be at the head of, be in command of; to take the lead; to protect

praesūmō, -ere, -psī, -ptum *vt* to take first; to anticipate; to take for granted

praesūtus *adj* sewn over at the point

praetemptō, -āre *vt* to feel for, grope for; to test in advance

praetendō, -dere, -dī, -tum *vt* to hold out, put before, spread in front of; to give as an excuse, allege

praetentō *etc see* **praetemptō**

praetentus *ppp of* **praetendō** ♦ *adj* lying over against

praetepeō, -ēre, -uī *vi* to glow before

praeter *adv* beyond; excepting ♦ *prep* (*with acc*) past, along; except, besides; beyond, more than, in addition to, contrary to

praeteragō, -ere *vt* to drive past

praeterbītō, -ere *vt, vi* to pass by

praeterdūcō, -ere *vt* to lead past

praeterea *adv* besides; moreover; henceforth

praetereō, -īre, -iī, -itum *vi* to go past ♦ *vt* to pass, overtake; to escape, escape the notice of; to omit, leave out, forget, neglect; to reject, exclude; to surpass; to transgress

praeterequitāns, -antis *adj* riding past

praeterfluō, -ere *vt, vi* to flow past

praetergredior, -dī, -ssus *vt* to pass, march past; to surpass

praeterhāc *adv* further, more

praeteritus *ppp of* **praetereō** ♦ *adj* past, gone by ♦ *ntpl* the past

praeterlābor, -bī, -psus *vt* to flow past, move past ♦ *vi* to slip away

praeterlātus *adj* driving, flying past

praetermeō, -āre *vi* to pass by

praetermissiō, -ōnis *f* omission, passing over

praetermittō, -ittere, -īsī, -issum *vt* to let pass; to omit, neglect; to make no mention of; to overlook

praeterquam *adv* except, besides

praetervectiō, -ōnis *f* passing by

praetervehor, -hī, -ctus *vt, vi* to ride past, sail past; to march past; to pass by, pass over

praetervolō, -āre *vt, vi* to fly past; to escape

praetexō, -ere, -uī, -tum *vt* to border, fringe; to adorn; to pretend, disguise

praetextātus *adj* wearing the toga praetexta, under age

praetextus¹ *ppp of* **praetexō** ♦ *adj* wearing the toga praetexta ♦ *f* toga with a purple border; Roman tragedy ♦ *nt* pretext

praetextus², -ūs *m* splendour; pretence

praetimeō, -ēre *vi* to be afraid in advance

praetinctus *adj* dipped beforehand

praetor, -ōris *m* chief magistrate, commander; praetor; propraetor, governor

praetōriānus *adj* of the emperor's bodyguard

praetōrium, -ī *and* **-iī** *nt* general's tent, camp headquarters; governor's residence; council of war; palace, grand building; emperor's bodyguard

praetōrius *adj* praetor's, praetorian; of a propraetor; of the emperor's bodyguard ♦ *m* ex-praetor; **praetōria cohors** bodyguard of general *or* emperor; **porta praetōria** camp gate facing the enemy

praetorqueō, -ēre *vt* to strangle first

praetrepidāns, -antis *adj* very impatient

praetruncō, -āre *vt* to cut off

praetulī *perf of* **praeferō**

praetūra, -ae *f* praetorship

praeumbrāns, -antis *adj* obscuring

praeūstus *adj* hardened at the point; frostbitten

praeut *adv* compared with

praevaleō, -ēre, -uī *vi* to be very powerful, have most influence, prevail

praevalidus *adj* very strong, very powerful; too strong

praevāricātiō, -ōnis *f* collusion

praevāricātor, -ōris *m* advocate guilty of collusion

praevāricor, -ārī, -ātus *vi* (*with dat*) to favour by collusion

praevehor, -hī, -ctus *vi* to ride, fly in front, flow past

praeveniō, -enīre, -ēnī, -entum *vt, vi* to come before; to anticipate, prevent

praeverrō, -ere *vt* to sweep before

praevertō, -ere, -ī, praevertor, -ī *vt* to put first, prefer; to turn to first, attend first to; to outstrip; to anticipate, frustrate, prepossess

praevideō, -idēre, -īdī, -īsum *vt* to foresee

praevitiō, -āre *vt* to taint beforehand

praevius *adj* leading the way

praevolō, -āre *vi* to fly in front

pragmaticus *adj* of affairs ♦ *m* legal expert

prandeō, -ēre, -ī *vi* to take lunch ♦ *vt* to eat

prandium, -ī *and* **-iī** *nt* lunch

prānsor, -ōris *m* guest at lunch

prānsus *adj* having lunched, fed

prasinus *adj* green

prătēnsis *adj* meadow (*in cpds*)

prātulum, -ī *nt* small meadow

prātum, -ī *nt* meadow; grass

prāvē *adv* wrongly, badly

prāvitās, -ātis *f* irregularity; perverseness, depravity

prāvus *adj* crooked, deformed; perverse, bad, wicked

Prāxitelēs, -is *m famous Greek sculptor*

Prāxitelius *adj see* **Prāxitelēs**

precāriō *adv* by request

precārius *adj* obtained by entreaty

precātiō, -ōnis *f* prayer

precātor, -ōris *m* intercessor

preces *pl of* **prex**

preciae, -ārum *fpl kind of vine*

precor, -ārī, -ātus *vt, vi* to pray, beg, entreat; to wish (well); curse

prehendō, -endere, -endī, -ēnsum *vt* to take hold of, catch; to seize, detain; to surprise; (*eye*) to take in; (*mind*) to grasp

prehēnsō *etc see* **prēnsō**

prehēnsus *ppp of* **prehendō**

prēlum, -ī *nt* wine press, oil press

premō, -mere, -ssī, -ssum *vt* to press, squeeze; to press together, compress; (*eyes*) to close; (*reins*) to tighten; (*trees*) to prune; to press upon, lie, sit, stand on, cover, conceal, surpass; to press hard on, follow closely; (*coast*) to hug; to press down, lower, burden; (*fig*) to overcome, rule; (*words*) to disparage; to press in, sink, stamp, plant; to press back, repress, check, stop

prendō *etc see* **prehendō**

prēnsātiō, -ōnis *f* canvassing

prēnsō, prehēnsō, -āre, -āvī, -ātum *vt* to clutch at, take hold of, buttonhole

prēnsus *ppp of* **prehendō**

presbyter, -ī *m* (ECCL) elder

pressē *adv* concisely, accurately, simply

pressī *perf of* **premō**

pressiō, -ōnis *f* fulcrum

pressō, -āre *vt* to press

pressus¹ *ppp of* **premō** ♦ *adj* (*style*) concise, compressed; (*pace*) slow; (*voice*) subdued

pressus², -ūs *m* pressure

prēster, -ēris *m* waterspout

pretiōsē *adv* expensively

pretiōsus *adj* valuable, expensive; extravagant

pretium, -ī *and* **-iī** *nt* price, value; worth; money, fee, reward; **māgnī pretiī, in pretiō** valuable; **operae ~** worth while

prex, -ecis *f* request, entreaty; prayer; good wish; curse

Priamēis, -ēidis *f* Cassandra

Priamēius *adj see* **Priamus**

Priamidēs, -idae *m* son of Priam

Priamus, -ī *m* king of Troy

Priāpus, -ī *m god of fertility and of gardens*

prīdem *adv* long ago, long

prīdiē *adv* the day before

prīmaevus *adj* youthful

prīmānī, -ōrum *mpl* soldiers of the 1st legion

prīmārius *adj* principal, first-rate

prīmigenus *adj* original

prīmipīlāris, -is *m* chief centurion

prīmipīlus, -ī *m* chief centurion

prīmitiae, -ārum *fpl* first fruits

prīmitus *adv* originally

prīmō *adv* at first; firstly

prīmōrdium, -ī *and* **-iī** *nt* beginning; **prīmōrdia rērum** atoms

prīmōris *adj* first, foremost, tip of; principal ♦ *mpl* nobles; (MIL) front line

prīmulum *adv* first

prīmulus *adj* very first

prīmum *adv* first, to begin with, in the first place; for the first time; **cum ~, ubi ~, ut ~** as soon as; **quam ~** as soon as possible; **~ dum** in the first place

prīmus *adj* first, foremost, tip of; earliest; principal, most eminent; **~ veniō** I am the first to come; **prima lux** dawn, daylight; **prīmō mēnse** at the beginning of the month; **prīmīs digitīs** with the fingertips; **prīmās agere** play the leading part; **prīmās dare** give first place to; **in prīmīs** in the front line; especially

prīnceps, -ipis *adj* first, in front, chief, most eminent ♦ *m* leader, chief; first citizen, emperor; (MIL) company, captain, captaincy ♦ *pl* (MIL) the second line

prīncipālis *adj* original; chief; the emperor's

prīncipātus, -ūs *m* first place; post of commander-in-chief; emperorship

prīncipiālis *adj* from the beginning

prīncipium, -ī *and* **-iī** *nt* beginning, origin; first to vote ♦ *pl* first principles; (MIL) front line; camp headquarters

prior, -ōris (*nt* **-us**) *adj* former, previous, first; better, preferable ♦ *mpl* forefathers

prīscē *adv* strictly

prīscus *adj* former, ancient, old-fashioned

prīstinus *adj* former, original; of yesterday

prius *adv* previously, before; in former times; **~ quam** before, sooner than

prīvātim *adv* individually, privately; at home

prīvātiō, -ōnis *f* removal

prīvātus *adj* individual, private; not in public office ♦ *m* private citizen

Prīvernās, -ātis *adj see* **Prīvernum**

Prīvernum, -ī *nt old Latin town*

prīvīgna, -ae *f* stepdaughter

prīvīgnus, -ī *m* stepson; (*pl*) stepchildren

prīvilēgium, -ī *and* **-iī** *nt* law in favour of or against an individual

prīvō, -āre, -āvī, -ātum *vt* to deprive, rob; to free

prīvus *adj* single, one each; own, private

prō¹ *adv* (*with* **ut** *and* **quam**) in proportion (as) ♦ *prep* (*with abl*) in front of, on the front of; for, on behalf of, instead of, in return for; as, as good as; according to, in proportion to; by virtue of; **prō eō ac** just as; **prō eō quod** just because; **prō eō quantum, prō eō ut** in proportion as

prō² *interj* (*expressing wonder or sorrow*) O!, alas!

proăgorus, -ī m chief magistrate (*in Sicilian towns*)

proavītus adj ancestral

proavus, -ī m great-grandfather, ancestor

probābilis adj laudable; credible, probable

probābilitās, -ātis f credibility

probābiliter adv credibly

probātiō, -ōnis f approval; testing

probātor, -ōris m approver

probātus adj tried, excellent; acceptable

probē adv well, properly; thoroughly, well done!

probitās, -ātis f goodness, honesty

probō, -āre, -āvī, -ātum vt to approve, approve of; to appraise; to recommend; to prove, show

probrōsus adj abusive; disgraceful

probrum, -ī nt abuse, reproach; disgrace; infamy, unchastity

probus adj good, excellent; honest, upright

procācitās, -ātis f impudence

procāciter adv insolently

procāx, -ācis adj bold, forward, insolent

prōcēdō, -ēdere, -essī, -essum vi to go forward, advance; to go out, come forth; (*time*) to go on, continue; (*fig*) to make progress, get on; (*events*) to turn out, succeed

procella, -ae f hurricane, storm; (*MIL*) charge

procellōsus adj stormy

procer, -is m chief, noble, prince

prōcēritās, -ātis f height; length

prōcērus adj tall; long

prōcessiō, -ōnis f advance

prōcessus, -ūs m advance, progress

prōcidō, -ere, -ī vi to fall forwards, fall down

prōcinctus, -ūs m readiness (*for action*)

prōclāmātor, -ōris m bawler

prōclāmō, -āre vi to cry out

prōclīnātus adj tottering

prōclīnō, -āre vt to bend

prōclīvē adv downwards; easily

prōclīvis, prōclīvus adj downhill, steep; (*mind*) prone, willing; (*act*) easy; **in prōclīvī** easy

prōclīvitās, -ātis f descent; tendency

prōclīvus etc see **prōclīvis**

Procnē, -ēs f wife of Tereus (*changed to a swallow*); swallow

prōcōnsul, -is m proconsul, governor

prōcōnsulāris adj proconsular

prōcōnsulātus, -ūs m proconsulship

prōcrāstinātiō, -ōnis f procrastination

prōcrāstinō, -āre vt to put off from day to day

prōcreātiō, -ōnis f begetting

prōcreātor, -ōris m creator, parent

prōcreātrīx, -īcis f mother

prōcreō, -āre vt to beget, produce

prōcrēscō, -ere vi to be produced, grow up

Procrūstēs, -ae m Attic highwayman (*who tortured victims on a bed*)

prōcubō, -āre vi to lie on the ground

prōcūdō, -dere, -dī, -sum vt to forge; to produce

procul adv at a distance, far, from afar

prōculcō, -āre vt to trample down

prōcumbō, -mbere, -buī, -bitum vi to fall forwards, bend over; to sink down, be broken down

prōcūrātiō, -ōnis f management; (*religion*) expiation

prōcūrātor, -ōris m administrator, financial agent; (*province*) governor

prōcūrātrīx, -īcis f governess

prōcūrō, -āre, -āvī, -ātum vt to take care of, manage; to expiate ♦ vi to be a procurator

prōcurrō, -rrere, -currī and **-rrī, -rsum** vi to rush forward; to jut out

prōcursātiō, -ōnis f charge

prōcursātor, -ōris m skirmisher

prōcursō, -āre vi to make a sally

prōcursus, -ūs m charge

prōcurvus adj curving forwards

procus¹, -ī m nobleman

procus², -ī m wooer, suitor

Procyōn, -ōnis m Lesser Dog Star

prōdeambulō, -āre vi to go out for a walk

prōdeō, -īre, -iī, -itum vi to come out, come forward, appear; to go ahead, advance; to project

prōdesse infin of **prōsum**

prōdīcō, -īcere, -īxī, -ictum vt to appoint, adjourn

prōdictātor, -ōris m vice-dictator

prōdigē adv extravagantly

prōdigentia, -ae f profusion

prōdigiāliter adv unnaturally

prōdigiōsus adj unnatural, marvellous

prōdigium, -ī and **-iī** nt portent; unnatural deed; monster

prōdigō, -igere, -ēgī, -āctum vt to squander

prōdigus adj wasteful; lavish, generous

prōditiō, -ōnis f betrayal

prōditor, -ōris m traitor

prōditus ppp of **prōdō**

prōdō, -ere, -idī, -itum vt to bring forth, produce; to make known, publish; to betray, give up; (*tradition*) to hand down

prōdoceō, -ēre vt to preach

prodromus, -ī m forerunner

prōdūcō, -ūcere, -ūxī, -uctum vt to bring forward, bring out; to conduct; to drag in front; to draw out, extend; (*acting*) to perform; (*child*) to beget, bring up; (*fact*) to bring to light; (*innovation*) to introduce; (*rank*) to promote; (*slave*) to put up for sale; (*time*) to prolong, protract, put off; (*tree*) to cultivate; (*vowel*) to lengthen

prōductē adv long

prōductiō, -ōnis f lengthening

prōductō, -āre vt to spin out

prōductus ppp of **prōdūcō** ♦ adj lengthened, long

proēgmenon, -ī nt a preferred thing

proeliātor, -ōris m fighter

proelior, -ārī, -ātus vi to fight, join battle

proelium, -ī and **-iī** nt battle, conflict

profānō, -āre vt to desecrate

profānus adj unholy, common; impious; ill-omened

profātus ppa of **profor**

profectiō, **-ōnis** f departure; source
profectō adv really, certainly
profectus ppa of **proficīscor**
prŏfectus¹ ppp of **prŏficiō**
prŏfectus², **-ūs** m growth, progress, profit
prŏferō, **-ferre**, **-tulī**, **-lātum** vt to bring forward, forth or out; to extend, enlarge; (time) to prolong, defer; (instance) to mention, quote; (knowledge) to publish, reveal; **pedem prŏferre** proceed; **signa prŏferre** advance
professiō, **-ōnis** f declaration; public register; profession
professor, **-ōris** m teacher
professōrius adj authoritative
professus ppa of **profiteor**
profēstus adj not holiday, working
prŏficiō, **-icere**, **-ēcī**, **-ectum** vi to make progress, profit; to be of use
proficīscor, **-icīscī**, **-ectus** vi to set out, start; to originate, proceed
profiteor, **-itērī**, **-essus** vt to declare, profess; to make an official return of; to promise, volunteer
prōflīgātor, **-ōris** m spendthrift
prōflīgātus adj dissolute
prōflīgō, **-āre**, **-āvī**, **-ātum** vt to dash to the ground; to destroy, overthrow; to bring almost to an end; to degrade
prōflō, **-āre** vt to breathe out
prōfluēns, **-entis** pres p of **prōfluō** ♦ adj flowing; fluent ♦ f running water
prōfluenter adv easily
prōfluentia, **-ae** f fluency
prōfluō, **-ere**, **-xī** vi to flow on, flow out; (fig) to proceed
prōfluvium, **-ī** and **-iī** nt flowing
profor, **-ārī**, **-ātus** vi to speak, give utterance
profugiō, **-ugere**, **-ūgī** vi to flee, escape; to take refuge (with) ♦ vt to flee from
profugus adj fugitive; exiled; nomadic
prōfuī perf of **prōsum**
profundō, **-undere**, **-ūdī**, **-ūsum** vt to pour out, shed; to bring forth, produce; to prostrate; to squander; **sē profundere** burst forth, rush out
profundus adj deep, vast, high; infernal; (fig) profound, immoderate ♦ nt depths, abyss
profūsē adv in disorder, extravagantly
profūsus ppp of **profundō** ♦ adj lavish; excessive
prōgener, **-ī** m grandson-in-law
prōgenerō, **-āre** vt to beget
prōgeniēs, **-ēī** f descent; offspring, descendants
prōgenitor, **-ōris** m ancestor
prōgignō, **-ignere**, **-enuī**, **-enitum** vt to beget, produce
prōgnātus adj born, descended ♦ m son, descendant
Prognē see **Procnē**
prognōstica, **-ōrum** ntpl weather signs
prōgredior, **-dī**, **-ssus** vi to go forward, advance; to go out
prōgressiō, **-ōnis** f advancing, increase; (RHET) climax

prōgressus¹ ppa of **prōgredior**
prōgressus², **-ūs** m advance, progress; (events) march
prōh interj see **prō²**
prohibeō, **-ēre**, **-uī**, **-itum** vt to hinder, prevent; to keep away, protect; to forbid
prohibitiō, **-ōnis** f forbidding
prōiciō, **-icere**, **-iēcī**, **-iectum** vt to throw down, fling forwards; to banish; (building) to make project; (fig) to discard, renounce; to forsake; (words) to blurt out; (time) to defer; **sē prōicere** rush forward, run into danger; to fall prostrate
prōiectiō, **-ōnis** f forward stretch
prōiectus¹ ppp of **prōiciō** ♦ adj projecting, prominent; abject, useless; downcast; addicted (to)
prōiectus², **-ūs** m jutting out
proinde, **proin** adv consequently, therefore; just (as)
prōlābor, **-bī**, **-psus** vi to slide, move forward; to fall down; (fig) to go on, come to; to slip out; to fail, fall, sink into ruin
prōlāpsiō, **-ōnis** f falling
prōlāpsus ppa of **prōlābor**
prōlātiō, **-ōnis** f extension; postponement; adducing
prōlātō, **-āre** vt to extend; to postpone
prōlātus ppp of **prōferō**
prōlectō, **-āre** vt to entice
prōlēs, **-is** f offspring; child; descendants, race
prōlētārius, **-ī** and **-iī** m citizen of the lowest class
prōliciō, **-cere**, **-xī** vt to entice
prōlixē adv fully, copiously, willingly
prōlixus adj long, wide, spreading; (person) obliging; (circumstances) favourable
prōlogus, **-ī** m prologue
prōloquor, **-quī**, **-cūtus** vt to speak out
prōlubium, **-ī** and **-iī** nt inclination
prōlūdō, **-dere**, **-sī**, **-sum** vi to practise
prōluō, **-uere**, **-uī**, **-ūtum** vt to wash out, wash away
prōlūsiō, **-ōnis** f prelude
prōluviēs, **-ēī** f flood; excrement
prōmereō, **-ēre**, **-uī**, **prōmereor**, **-ērī**, **-itus** vt to deserve, earn
prōmeritum, **-ī** nt desert, merit, guilt
Promētheus, **-eī** and **-eos** m demigod who stole fire from the gods
Promēthēus adj see **Promētheus**
prōminēns, **-entis** pres p of **prōmineō** ♦ adj projecting ♦ nt headland, spur
prōmineō, **-ēre**, **-uī** vi to jut out, overhang; to extend
prōmiscam, **prōmiscamē**, **prōmiscuē** adv indiscriminately
prōmiscuus, **prōmiscus** adj indiscriminate, in common; ordinary; open to all
prōmīsī perf of **prōmittō**
prōmissiō, **-ōnis** f promise
prōmissor, **-ōris** m promiser
prōmissum, **-ī** nt promise
prōmissus ppp of **prōmittō** ♦ adj long

prōmittō, -ittere, -īsī, -issum vt to let grow; to promise, give promise of

prōmō, -ere, -psī, -ptum vt to bring out, produce; to disclose

prōmont- etc see **prōmunt-**

prōmontorium, -ī and **-iī** nt headland, promontory, ridge

prōmōtus ppp of **prōmoveō** ♦ ntpl preferable things

prōmoveō, -ovēre, -ōvī, -ōtum vt to move forward, advance; to enlarge; to postpone; to disclose

prōmpsī perf of **prōmō**

prōmptē adv readily; easily

prōmptō, -āre vt to distribute

prōmptū abl m: **in ~** at hand, in readiness; obvious, in evidence; easy

prōmptus ppp of **prōmō** ♦ adj at hand, ready; prompt, resolute; easy

prōmulgātiō, -ōnis f promulgating

prōmulgō, -āre, -āvī, -ātum vt to make public, publish

prōmulsis, -idis f hors d'oeuvre

prōmus, -ī m cellarer, butler

prōmūtuus adj as a loan in advance

prōnepōs, -ōtis m great-grandson

pronoea, -ae f providence

prōnōmen, -inis nt pronoun

prōnuba, -ae f matron attending a bride

prōnūntiātiō, -ōnis f declaration; (RHET) delivery; (LOGIC) proposition

prōnūntiātor, -ōris m narrator

prōnūntiātum, -ātī nt proposition

prōnūntiō, -āre, -āvī, -ātum vt to declare publicly, announce; to recite, deliver; to narrate; to nominate

prōnurus, -ūs f granddaughter-in-law

prōnus adj leaning forward; headlong, downwards; sloping, sinking; (fig) inclined, disposed, favourable; easy

prooemium, -ī and **-iī** nt prelude, preface

propāgātiō, -ōnis f propagating; extension

propāgātor, -ōris m enlarger

propāgō[1], -āre, -āvī, -ātum vt to propagate; to extend; to prolong

propāgō[2], -inis f (plant) layer, slip; (men) offspring, posterity

prōpalam adv openly, known

prōpatulum, -ī nt open space

prōpatulus adj open

prope adv (compar **propius**, superl **proximē**) near; nearly ♦ prep (with acc) near, not far from

propediem adv very soon

prōpellō, -ellere, -ulī, -ulsum vt to drive, push forward, impel; to drive away, keep off

propemodum, propemodo adv almost

prōpendeō, -endēre, -endī, -ēnsum vi to hang down; to preponderate; to be disposed (to)

prōpēnsē adv willingly

prōpēnsiō, -ōnis f inclination

prōpēnsus adj inclining; inclined, well-disposed; important

properanter adv hastily, quickly

properantia, -ae f haste

properātiō, -ōnis f haste

properātō adv quickly

properātus adj speedy

properē adv quickly

properipēs, -edis adj swiftfooted

properō, -āre, -āvī, -ātum vt to hasten, do with haste ♦ vi to make haste, hurry

Propertius, -ī m Latin elegiac poet

properus adj quick, hurrying

prōpexus adj combed forward

propīnō, -āre vt to drink as a toast; to pass on (a cup)

propinquitās, -ātis f nearness; relationship, friendship

propinquō, -āre vi to approach ♦ vt to hasten

propinquus adj near, neighbouring; related ♦ m/f relation ♦ nt neighbourhood

propior, -ōris adj nearer; more closely related, more like; (time) more recent

propitiō, -āre vt to appease

propitius adj favourable, gracious

propius adv nearer, more closely

prōpōla, -ae f retailer

prōpolluō, -ere vt to defile further

prōpōnō, -ōnere, -osuī, -ositum vt to set forth, display; to publish, declare; to propose, resolve; to imagine; to expose; (LOGIC) to state the first premise; **ante oculōs prōpōnere** picture to oneself

Propontiacus adj see **Propontis**

Propontis, -idis and **-idos** f Sea of Marmora

prōporrō adv furthermore; utterly

prōportiō, -ōnis f symmetry, analogy

prōpositiō, -ōnis f purpose; theme; (LOGIC) first premise

prōpositum, -ī nt plan, purpose; theme; (LOGIC) first premise

prōpositus ppp of **prōpōnō**

prōpraetor, -ōris m propraetor, governor; vice-praetor

propriē adv properly, strictly; particularly

proprietās, -ātis f peculiarity, property

proprītim adv properly

proprius adj one's own, peculiar; personal, characteristic; permanent; (words) literal, regular

propter adv near by ♦ prep (with acc) near, beside; on account of; by means of

proptereā adv therefore

prōpudium, -ī and **-iī** nt shameful act; villain

prōpugnāculum, -ī nt bulwark, tower; defence

prōpugnātiō, -ōnis f defence

prōpugnātor, -ōris m defender, champion

prōpugnō, -āre vi to make a sortie; to fight in defence

prōpulsātiō, -ōnis f repulse

prōpulsō, -āre, -āvī, -ātum vt to repel, avert

prōpulsus ppp of **prōpellō**

Propylaea, -ōrum ntpl gateway to the Acropolis of Athens

prō quaestōre m proquaestor

prōquam conj according as

prōra, -ae f prow, bows; ship

prōrēpō, -ere, -sī, -tum vi to crawl out

prōrēta, -ae *m* man at the prow

prōreus, -eī *m* man at the prow

prōripiō, -ipere, -ipuī, -eptum *vt* to drag out; to hurry away; **sē prōripere** rush out, run away

prōrogātiō, -ōnis *f* extension; deferring

prōrogō, -āre, -āvī, -ātum *vt* to extend, prolong, continue; to defer

prōrsum *adv* forwards; absolutely

prōrsus *adv* forwards; absolutely; in short

prōrumpō, -umpere, -ūpī, -uptum *vt* to fling out; (*pass*) to rush forth ♦ *vi* to break out, burst forth

prōruō, -ere, -ī, -tum *vt* to throw down, demolish ♦ *vi* to rush forth

prōruptus *ppp of* **prōrumpō**

prōsāpia, -ae *f* lineage

proscaenium, -ī *and* **-iī** *nt* stage

proscindō, -ndere, -dī, -ssum *vt* to plough up; (*fig*) to revile

prōscrībō, -bere, -psī, -ptum *vt* to publish in writing; to advertise; to confiscate; to proscribe, outlaw

prōscrīptiō, -ōnis *f* advertisement; proscription

prōscrīpturiō, -īre *vi* to want to have a proscription

prōscrīptus *ppp of* **prōscrībō** ♦ *m* outlaw

prōsecō, -āre, -uī, -tum *vt* to cut off (*for sacrifice*)

prōsēminō, -āre *vt* to scatter; to propagate

prōsentiō, -entīre, -ēnsī *vt* to see beforehand

prōsequor, -quī, -cūtus *vt* to attend, escort; to pursue, attack; to honour (with); (*words*) to proceed with, continue

Proserpina, -ae *f* Proserpine (*daughter of Ceres and wife of Pluto*)

proseucha, -ae *f* place of prayer

prōsiliō, -īre, -uī *vi* to jump up, spring forward; to burst out, spurt

prōsocer, -ī *m* wife's grandfather

prōspectō, -āre *vt* to look out at, view; to look forward to, await; (*place*) to look towards

prōspectus¹ *ppp of* **prōspiciō**

prōspectus², -ūs *m* sight, view, prospect; gaze

prōspeculor, -ārī *vi* to look out, reconnoitre ♦ *vt* to watch for

prosper, prosperus *adj* favourable, successful

prosperē *adv see* **prosper**

prosperitās, -ātis *f* good fortune

prosperō, -āre *vt* to make successful, prosper

prosperus *etc see* **prosper**

prōspicientia, -ae *f* foresight

prōspiciō, -icere, -exī, -ectum *vi* to look out, watch; to see to, take precautions ♦ *vt* to descry, watch for; to foresee; to provide; (*place*) to command a view of

prōsternō, -ernere, -rāvī, -rātum *vt* to throw in front, prostrate; to overthrow, ruin; **sē prōsternere** fall prostrate; to demean oneself

prōstibulum, -ī *nt* prostitute

prōstituō, -uere, -uī, -ūtum *vt* to put up for sale, prostitute

prōstō, -āre, -itī *vi* to project; to be on sale; to prostitute oneself

prōstrātus *ppp of* **prōsternō**

prōsubigō, -ere *vt* to dig up

prōsum, -desse, -fuī *vi* (*with dat*) to be useful to, benefit

Prōtagorās, -ae *m* Greek sophist (*native of Abdera*)

prōtēctus *ppp of* **prōtegō**

prōtegō, -egere, -ēxī, -ēctum *vt* to cover over, put a projecting roof on; (*fig*) to shield, protect

prōtēlō, -āre *vt* to drive off

prōtēlum, -ī *nt* team of oxen; (*fig*) succession

prōtendō, -dere, -dī, -tum *vt* to stretch out, extend

prōtentus *ppp of* **prōtendō**

prōterō, -erere, -rīvī, -rītum *vt* to trample down, crush; to overthrow

prōterreō, -ēre, -uī, -itum *vt* to scare away

protervē *adv* insolently; boldly

protervitās, -ātis *f* forwardness, insolence

protervus *adj* forward, insolent, violent

Prōtesilāēus *adj see* **Prōtesilāus**

Prōtesilāus, -ī *m* first Greek killed at Troy

Prōteus, -eī *and* **-eos** *m* seagod with power to assume many forms

prothymē *adv* gladly

prōtinam *adv* immediately

prōtinus *adv* forward, onward; continuously; right away, forthwith

prōtollō, -ere *vt* to stretch out; to put off

prōtractus *ppp of* **prōtrahō**

prōtrahō, -here, -xī, -ctum *vt* to draw on (to); to drag out; to bring to light, reveal

prōtrītus *ppp of* **prōterō**

prōtrūdō, -dere, -sī, -sum *vt* to thrust forward, push out; to postpone

prōtulī *perf of* **prōferō**

prōturbō, -āre, -āvī, -ātum *vt* to drive off; to overthrow

prout *conj* according as

prōvectus *ppp of* **prōvehō** ♦ *adj* advanced

prōvehō, -here, -xī, -ctum *vt* to carry along, transport; to promote, advance, bring to; (*speech*) to prolong; (*pass*) to drive, ride, sail on

prōveniō, -enīre, -ēnī, -entum *vi* to come out, appear; to arise, grow; to go on, prosper, succeed

prōventus, -ūs *m* increase; result, success

prōverbium, -ī *and* **-iī** *nt* saying, proverb

prōvidēns, -entis *pres p of* **prōvideō** ♦ *adj* prudent

prōvidenter *adv* with foresight

prōvidentia, -ae *f* foresight, forethought

prōvideō, -idēre, -īdī, -īsum *vi* to see ahead; to take care, make provision ♦ *vt* to foresee; to look after, provide for; to obviate

prōvidus *adj* foreseeing, cautious, prudent; provident

prōvincia, -ae *f* sphere of action, duty, province

prōvinciālis *adj* provincial ♦ *mpl* provincials

prōvīsiō, -ōnis *f* foresight; precaution

prōvīsō¹ *adv* with forethought

prōvīsō², -ere *vi* to go and see

prōvīsor, -ōris m foreseer; provider
prōvīsus¹ ppp of prōvideō
prōvīsus², -ūs m looking forward; foreseeing; providing, providence
prōvīvō, -vere, -xī vi to live on
prōvocātiō, -ōnis f challenge; appeal
prōvocātor, -ōris m kind of gladiator
prōvocō, -āre, -āvī, -ātum vt to challenge, call out; to provoke; to bring about ♦ vi to appeal
prōvolō, -āre vi to fly out, rush out
prōvolvō, -vere, -vī, -ūtum vt to roll forward, tumble over; (pass) to fall down, humble oneself, be ruined; sē prōvolvere wallow
prōvomō, -ere vt to belch forth
proximē adv next, nearest; (time) just before or after; (with acc) next to, very close to, very like
proximitās, -ātis f nearness; near relationship; similarity
proximus adj nearest, next; (time) previous, last, following, next; most akin, most like ♦ m next of kin ♦ nt next door
proxum- etc see proxim-
prūdēns, -entis adj foreseeing, aware; wise, prudent, circumspect; skilled, versed (in)
prūdenter adv prudently; skilfully
prūdentia, -ae f prudence, discretion; knowledge
pruīna, -ae f hoar frost
pruīnōsus adj frosty
prūna, -ae f live coal
prūnitius adj of plum tree wood
prūnum, -ī nt plum
prūnus, -ī f plum tree
prūriō, -īre vi to itch
prytanēum, -ī nt Greek town hall
prytanis, -is m Greek chief magistrate
psallō, -ere vi to play the lyre or lute
psaltērium, -ī and -iī nt kind of lute
psaltria, -ae f girl musician
psecas, -adis f slave who perfumed the ladies' hair
psēphisma, -tis nt decree of the people
Pseudocatō, -ōnis m sham Cato
pseudomenos, -ī m sophistical argument
pseudothyrum, -ī nt back door
psithius adj psithian (kind of Greek vine)
psittacus, -ī m parrot
psychomantēum, psychomantīum, -ī nt place of necromancy
-pte enclitic (to pronouns) self, own
ptisanārium, -ī and -iī nt gruel
Ptolemaeūs, Ptolemaeus adj see Ptolemaeus
Ptolemaeus, -ī m Ptolemy (name of Egyptian kings)
pūbēns, -entis adj full-grown; (plant) juicy
pūbertās, -ātis f manhood; signs of puberty
pūbēs¹, pūber, -eris adj grown up, adult; (plant) downy
pūbēs², -is f hair at age of puberty; groin; youth, men, people
pūbēscō, -ēscere, -uī vi to grow to manhood, become mature; to become clothed
pūblicānus adj of public revenue ♦ m tax farmer

pūblicātiō, -ōnis f confiscation
pūblicē adv by or for the State, at the public expense; all together
pūblicitus adv at the public expense; in public
pūblicō, -āre, -āvī, -ātum vt to confiscate; to make public
Pūblicola, -ae m P. Valerius (an early Roman consul)
pūblicum, -ī nt State revenue; State territory; public
pūblicus adj of the State, public, common ♦ m public official; pūblica causa criminal trial; rēs pūblica the State; dē pūblicō at the public expense; in pūblicō in public
Publius, -ī m Roman first name
pudendus adj shameful
pudēns, -entis adj bashful, modest
pudenter adv modestly
pudet, -ēre, -uit and -itum est vt impers to shame, be ashamed
pudibundus adj modest
pudīcē adv see pudīcus
pudīcitia, -ae f modesty, chastity
pudīcus adj modest, chaste
pudor, -ōris m shame, modesty, sense of honour; disgrace
puella, -ae f girl; sweetheart, young wife
puellāris adj girlish, youthful
puellula, -ae f little girl
puellus, -ī m little boy
puer, -ī m boy, child; son; slave
puerīlis adj boyish, child's; childish, trivial
puerīliter adv like a child; childishly
pueritia, -ae f childhood, youth
puerperium, -ī and -iī nt childbirth
puerperus adj to help childbirth ♦ f woman in labour
puertia etc see pueritia
puerulus, -ī m little boy, slave
pugil, -is m boxer
pugilātiō, -iōnis f, pugilātus, -ūs m boxing
pugillāris adj that can be held in the hand ♦ mpl, ntpl writing tablets
pugillātōrius adj: follis ~ punchball
pugiō, -ōnis m dirk, dagger
pugiunculus, -ī m small dagger
pugna, -ae f fight, battle
pugnācitās, -ātis f fondness for a fight
pugnāciter adv aggressively
pugnāculum, -ī nt fortress
pugnātor, -ōris m fighter
pugnāx, -ācis adj fond of a fight, aggressive; obstinate
pugneus adj with the fist
pugnō, -āre, -āvī, -ātum vi to fight; to disagree; to struggle; sēcum pugnāre be inconsistent; pugnātum est the battle was fought
pugnus, -ī m fist
pulchellus adj pretty little
pulcher, -rī adj beautiful, handsome; fine, glorious
pulchrē adv excellently; well done!
pulchritūdō, -inis f beauty, excellence
pūlēium, pūlegium, -ī and -iī nt pennyroyal

pūlex, -icis *m* flea
pullārius, -ī *and* **-iī** *m* keeper of the sacred chickens
pullātus *adj* dressed in black
pullulō, -āre *vi* to sprout
pullus¹, -ī *m* young (*of animals*), chicken
pullus² *adj* dark-grey; mournful ♦ *nt* dark grey clothes
pulmentārium, -ārī *and* **-āriī, pulmentum, -ī** *nt* relish; food
pulmō, -ōnis *m* lung
pulmōneus *adj* of the lungs
pulpa, -ae *f* fleshy part
pulpāmentum, -ī *nt* titbits
pulpitum, -ī *nt* platform, stage
puls, pultis *f* porridge
pulsātiō, -ōnis *f* beating
pulsō, -āre, -āvī, -ātum *vt* to batter, knock, strike
pulsus¹ *ppp of* **pellō**
pulsus², -ūs *m* push, beat, blow; impulse
pultiphagus, -ī *m* porridge eater
pultō, -āre *vt* to beat, knock at
pulvereus *adj* of dust, dusty, fine as dust; raising dust
pulverulentus *adj* dusty; laborious
pulvillus, -ī *m* small cushion
pulvīnar, -āris *nt* sacred couch; seat of honour
pulvīnus, -ī *m* cushion, pillow
pulvis, -eris *m* dust, powder; arena; effort
pulvisculus, -ī *m* fine dust
pūmex, -icis *m* pumice stone; stone, rock
pūmiceus *adj* of soft stone
pūmicō, -āre *vt* to smooth with pumice stone
pūmiliō, -ōnis *m/f* person of small stature
pūnctim *adv* with the point
pūnctum, -ī *nt* point, dot; vote; (*time*) moment; (*speech*) short section
pūnctus *ppp of* **pungō**
pungō, -ere, pupugī, pūnctum *vt* to prick, sting, pierce; (*fig*) to vex
Pūnicānus *adj* in the Carthaginian style
Pūnicē *adv* in Punic
pūniceus *adj* reddish, purple
Pūnicum, -ī *nt* pomegranate
Pūnicus *adj* Punic, Carthaginian; purple-red
pūniō, poeniō, -īre, pūnior, -īrī *vt* to punish; to avenge
pūnītor, -ōris *m* avenger
pūpa, -ae *f* doll
pūpilla, -ae *f* ward; (*eye*) pupil
pūpillāris *adj* of a ward, of an orphan
pūpillus, -ī *m* orphan, ward
puppis, -is *f* after part of a ship, stern; ship
pupugī *perf of* **pungō**
pūpula, -ae *f* (*eye*) pupil
pūpulus, -ī *m* little boy
pūrē *adv* cleanly, brightly; plainly, simply, purely, chastely
pūrgāmen, -inis *nt* sweepings, dirt; means of expiation
pūrgāmentum, -ī *nt* refuse, dirt

pūrgātiō, -ōnis *f* purging; justification
pūrgō, -āre, -āvī, -ātum *vt* to cleanse, purge, clear away; to exculpate, justify; to purify
pūriter *adv* cleanly, purely
purpura, -ae *f* purple-fish, purple; purple cloth; finery, royalty
purpurātus *adj* wearing purple ♦ *m* courtier
purpureus *adj* red, purple, black; wearing purple; bright, radiant
purpurissum, -ī *nt* kind of rouge
pūrus *adj* clear, unadulterated, free from obstruction or admixture; pure, clean; plain, unadorned; (*moral*) pure, chaste ♦ *nt* clear sky
pūs, pūris *nt* pus; (*fig*) malice
pusillus *adj* very little; petty, paltry
pūsiō, -ōnis *m* little boy
pūstula, -ae *f* pimple, blister
putāmen, -inis *nt* peeling, shell, husk
putātiō, -ōnis *f* pruning
putātor, -ōris *m* pruner
puteal, -ālis *nt* low wall round a well or sacred place
puteālis *adj* well- (*in cpds*)
pūteō, -ēre *vi* to stink
Puteolānus *adj see* **Puteolī**
Puteolī, -ōrum *mpl* town on the Campanian coast
puter, putris, -ris *adj* rotten, decaying; crumbling, flabby
putēscō, -ēscere, -uī *vi* to become rotten
puteus, -ī *m* well; pit
pūtidē *adv see* **pūtidus**
pūtidiusculus *adj* somewhat nauseating
pūtidus *adj* rotten, stinking; (*speech*) affected, nauseating
putō, -āre, -āvī, -ātum *vt* to think, suppose; to think over; to reckon, count; (*money*) to settle; (*tree*) to prune
pūtor, -ōris *m* stench
putrefaciō, -facere, -fēcī, -factum *vt* to make rotten; to make crumble
putrēscō, -ere *vi* to rot, moulder
putridus *adj* rotten, decayed; withered
putris *etc see* **puter**
putus¹ *adj* perfectly pure
putus², -ī *m* boy
pycta, pyctēs, -ae *m* boxer
Pydna, -ae *f* town in Macedonia
Pydnaeus *adj see* **Pydna**
pȳga, -ae *f* buttocks
Pygmaeus *adj* Pygmy
Pyladēs, -ae *and* **-is** *m* friend of Orestes
Pyladēus *adj see* **Pyladēs**
Pylae, -ārum *fpl* Thermopylae
Pylaicus *adj see* **Pylae**
Pylius *adj see* **Pylos**
Pylos, -ī *f* Pylus (*Peloponnesian town, home of Nestor*)
pyra, -ae *f* funeral pyre
Pȳramaeus *adj see* **Pȳramus**
pȳramis, -idis *f* pyramid
Pȳramus, -ī *m* lover of Thisbe
Pȳrēnē, -ēs *f* Pyrenees

pyrethrum, **-ī** *nt* Spanish camomile
Pyrgēnsis *adj see* **Pyrgī**
Pyrgī, **-ōrum** *mpl* ancient town in Etruria
pyrōpus, **-ī** *m* bronze
Pyrrha, **-ae**, **Pyrrhē**, **-ēs** *f* wife of Deucalion
Pyrrhaeus *adj see* **Pyrrha**
Pyrrhō, **-ōnis** *m* Greek philosopher (*founder of the Sceptics*)
Pyrrhōnēus *adj see* **Pyrrhō**
Pyrrhus, **-ī** *m* son of Achilles; king of Epirus, enemy of Rome

Pȳthagorās, **-ae** *m* Greek philosopher who founded a school in S. Italy
Pȳthagorēus, **-icus** *adj* Pythagorean
Pȳthius, **Pȳthicus** *adj* Pythian, Delphic ♦ *m* Apollo ♦ *f* priestess of Apollo ♦ *ntpl* Pythian Games
Pȳthō, **-ūs** *f* Delphi
Pȳthōn, **-ōnis** *m* serpent killed by Apollo
pȳtisma, **-tis** *nt* what is spat out
pȳtissō, **-āre** *vi* to spit out wine
pyxis, **-dis** *f* small box, toilet box

Qq

quā *adv* where, which way; whereby; as far as; partly ... partly

quācumque *adv* wherever; anyhow

quādam: ~ **tenus** *adv* only so far

quadra, -ae *f* square; morsel; table

quadrāgēnī, -ōrum *adj* forty each

quadrāgēsimus *adj* fortieth ♦ *f* 2.5 per cent tax

quadrāgiēns, quadrāgiēs *adv* forty times

quadrāgintā *num* forty

quadrāns, -antis *m* quarter; (*coin*) quarter as

quadrantārius *adj* of a quarter

quadrātum, -ī *nt* square; (*ASTR*) quadrature

quadrātus *ppp of* **quadrō** ♦ *adj* square; **quadrātō agmine** in battle order

quadrīduum, -ī *nt* four days

quadriennium, -ī *and* **-iī** *nt* four years

quadrifāriam *adv* in four parts

quadrifidus *adj* split in four

quadrīgae, -ārum *fpl* team of four; chariot

quadrīgārius, -ī *and* **-iī** *m* chariot racer

quadrīgātus *adj* stamped with a chariot

quadrīgulae, -ārum *fpl* little four horse team

quadriiugī, -ōrum *mpl* team of four

quadriiugis, quadriiugus *adj* of a team of four

quadrilībris *adj* weighing four pounds

quadrīmulus *adj* four years old

quadrīmus *adj* four years old

quadringēnārius *adj* of four hundred each

quadringēnī, -ōrum *adj* four hundred each

quadringentēsimus *adj* four-hundredth

quadringentī, -ōrum *num* four hundred

quadringentiēns, quadringentiēs *adv* four hundred times

quadripertītus *adj* fourfold

quadrirēmis, -is *f* quadrireme

quadrivium, -ī *and* **-iī** *nt* crossroads

quadrō, -āre *vt* to make square; to complete ♦ *vi* to square, fit, agree

quadrum, -ī *nt* square

quadrupedāns, -antis *adj* galloping

quadrupēs, -edis *adj* four-footed, on all fours ♦ *m/f* quadruped

quadruplātor, -ōris *m* informer, twister

quadruplex, -icis *adj* four-fold

quadruplum, -ī *nt* four times as much

quaeritō, -āre *vt* to search diligently for; to earn (*a living*); to keep on asking

quaerō, -rere, -sīvī *and* **-siī, -sītum** *vt* to look for, search for; to seek, try to get; to acquire, earn; (*plan*) to think out, work out; (*question*) to ask, make inquiries; (*LAW*) to investigate; (*with inf*) to

try, wish; **quid quaeris?** in short; **sī quaeris/ quaerimus** to tell the truth

quaesītiō, -ōnis *f* inquisition

quaesītor, -ōris *m* investigator, judge

quaesītus *ppp of* **quaerō** ♦ *adj* special; far-fetched ♦ *nt* question ♦ *ntpl* gains

quaesīvī *perf of* **quaerō**

quaesō, -ere *vt* to ask, beg

quaesticulus, -ī *m* slight profit

quaestiō, -ōnis *f* seeking, questioning; investigation, research; criminal trial; court; **servum in quaestiōnem ferre** take a slave for questioning by torture; **quaestiōnēs perpetuae** standing courts

quaestiuncula, -ae *f* trifling question

quaestor, -ōris *m* quaestor, treasury official

quaestōrius *adj* of a quaestor ♦ *m* ex-quaestor ♦ *nt* quaestor's tent or residence

quaestuōsus *adj* lucrative, productive; money-making; wealthy

quaestūra, -ae *f* quaestorship; public money

quaestus, -ūs *m* profit, advantage; money-making, occupation; **quaestuī habēre** make money out of; **quaestum facere** make a living

quālibet *adv* anywhere; anyhow

quālis *adj* (*interrog*) what kind of?; (*rel*) such as, even as

quāliscumque *adj* of whatever kind; any, whatever

qualiscunque *adj* = **quāliscumque**

quālitās, -ātis *f* quality, nature

quāliter *adv* just as

quālubet *adv* anywhere; anyhow

quālus, -ī *m* wicker basket

quam *adv* (*interrog, excl*) how?, how much?; (*comparison*) as, than; (*with superl*) as ... as possible; (*emphatic*) very; **dīmidium ~ quod** half of what; **quīntō diē ~** four days after

quamdiū *adv* how long?; as long as

quamlibet, quamlubet *adv* as much as you like, however

quamobrem *adv* (*interrog*) why?; (*rel*) why ♦ *conj* therefore

quamquam *conj* although; and yet

quamvīs *adv* however, ever so ♦ *conj* however much, although

quānam *adv* what way

quandō *adv* (*interrog*) when?; (*rel*) when; (*with sī, nē, num*) ever ♦ *conj* when; since

quandōcumque, quandocunque *adv* whenever, as often as; some day

quandōque *adv* whenever; some day ♦ *conj* seeing that

quandō quidem *conj* seeing that, since

quanquam *etc see* **quamquam**

quantillus *adj* how little, how much

quantopere *adv* how much; (*after* **tantopere**) as

quantulus *adj* how little, how small

quantuluscumque *adj* however small, however trifling

quantum *adv* how much; as much as; **quantumcumque** as much as ever; **quantumlibet** however much; **quantumvīs** as much as you like; although

quantus *adj* how great; so great as, such as; **quantī** how dear, how highly; **quantō** (*with comp*) how much; the; **in quantum** as far as

quantuscumque *adj* however great, whatever size

quantuslibet *adj* as great as you like

quantus quantus *adj* however great

quantusvīs *adj* however great

quāpropter *adv* why; and therefore

quāquā *adv* whatever way

quārē *adv* how, why; whereby; and therefore

quartadecumānī, -ōrum *mpl* men of the fourteenth legion

quartānus *adj* every four days ♦ *f* quartan fever ♦ *mpl* men of the fourth legion

quartārius, -ī *and* **-iī** *m* quarter pint

quartus *adj* fourth; **quartum/quartō** for the fourth time

quartusdecimus *adj* fourteenth

quasi *adv* as if; as it were; (*numbers*) about

quasillus, -ī *m*, **quasillum, -ī** *nt* wool basket

quassātiō, -ōnis *f* shaking

quassō, -āre, -āvī, -ātum *vt* to shake, toss; to shatter, damage

quassus *ppp of* **quatiō** ♦ *adj* broken

quatefaciō, -facere, -fēcī *vt* to shake, give a jolt to

quātenus *adv* (*interrog*) how far?; how long?; (*rel*) as far as; in so far as, since

quater *adv* four times; ~ **deciēs** fourteen times

quaternī, -ōrum *adj* four each, in fours

quatiō, -tere, -ssī, -ssum *vt* to shake, disturb, brandish; to strike, shatter; (*fig*) to agitate, harass

quattuor *num* four

quattuordecim *num* fourteen

quattuorvirātus, -ūs *m* membership of quattuorviri

quattuorvirī, -ōrum *mpl* board of four officials

-que *conj* and; both ... and; (*after neg*) but

quemadmodum *adv* (*interrog*) how?; (*rel*) just as

queō, -īre, -īvī *and* **-iī, -itum** *vi* to be able, can

quercētum, -ī *nt* oak forest

querceus *adj* of oak

quercus, -ūs *f* oak; garland of oak leaves; acorn

querēla, querella, -ae *f* complaint; plaintive sound

queribundus *adj* complaining

querimōnia, -ae *f* complaint; elegy

queritor, -ārī *vi* to complain much

quernus *adj* oak- (*in cpds*)

queror, -rī, -stus *vt, vi* to complain, lament; (*birds*) to sing

querquetulānus *adj* of oakwoods

querulus *adj* complaining; plaintive, warbling

questus¹ *ppa of* **queror**

questus², -ūs *m* complaint, lament

quī¹, quae, quod *pron* (*interrog*) what?, which?; (*rel*) who, which, that; what; and this, he *etc*; (*with* **sī, nisi, nē, num**) any

quī² *adv* (*interrog*) how?; (*rel*) with which, whereby; (*indef*) somehow; (*excl*) indeed

quia *conj* because; **quianam** why?

quicquam *nt see* **quisquam**

quicque *nt see* **quisque**

quicquid *nt see* **quisquis**

quīcum with whom, with which

quīcumque, quīcunque *pron* whoever, whatever, all that; every possible

quid *nt see* **quis** ♦ *adv* why?

quīdam, quaedam, quoddam *pron* a certain, a sort of, a ...

quiddam *nt* something

quidem *adv* (*emphatic*) in fact; (*qualifying*) at any rate; (*conceding*) it is true; (*alluding*) for instance; **nē ... ~** not even

quidlibet *nt* anything

quidnam *nt see* **quisnam**

quidnī *adv* why not?

quidpiam *nt see* **quispiam**

quidquam *nt see* **quisquam**

quidquid *nt see* **quisquis**

quiēs, -ētis *f* rest, peace, quiet; sleep, dream, death; neutrality; lair

quiēscō, -scere, -vī, -tum *vi* to rest, keep quiet; to be at peace, keep neutral; to sleep; (*with acc and infin*) to stand by and see; (*with inf*) to cease

quiētē *adv* peacefully, quietly

quiētus *ppa of* **quiēscō** ♦ *adj* at rest; peaceful, neutral; calm, quiet, asleep

quīlibet, quaelibet, quodlibet *pron* any, anyone at all

quīn *adv* (*interrog*) why not?; (*correcting*) indeed, rather ♦ *conj* who not; but that, but, without; (*preventing*) from; (*doubting*) that

quīnam, quaenam, quodnam *pron* which?, what?

Quīnct- *etc see* **Quīnt-**

quīncūnx, -ūncis *m* five-twelfths; number five on a dice; **in quīncūncem dispositī** arranged in oblique lines

quīndeciēns, quīndeciēs *adv* fifteen times

quīndecim *num* fifteen; ~ **prīmī** fifteen chief magistrates

quīndecimvirālis *adj* of the council of fifteen

quīndecimvirī, -ōrum *mpl* council of fifteen

quīngēnī, -ōrum *adj* five hundred each

quīngentēsimus *adj* five-hundredth

quīngentī, -ōrum *num* five hundred

quīngentiēns, quīngentiēs *adv* five hundred times

quīnī, -ōrum *adj* five each; five; ~ **dēnī** fifteen each; ~ **vīcēnī** twenty-five each

quīnquāgēnī, -ōrum *adj* fifty each

quīnquāgēsimus *adj* fiftieth ♦ *f* 2 per cent tax

quīnquāgintā *num* fifty

177

Quīnquātria, -iōrum and **-ium** ntpl festival of Minerva

Quīnquātrūs, -uum fpl festival of Minerva

quīnque num five

quīnquennālis adj quinquennial; lasting five years

quīnquennis adj five years old; quinquennial

quīnquennium, -ī and **-iī** nt five years

quīnquēpartītus adj fivefold

quīnqueprīmī, -ōrum mpl five leading men

quīnquerēmis adj five-banked ♦ f quinquereme

quīnquevirātus, -ūs m membership of the board of five

quīnquevirī, -ōrum mpl board of five

quīnquiēns, quīnquiēs adv five times

quīnquiplicō, -āre vt to multiply by five

quīntadecimānī, -ōrum mpl men of the fifteenth legion

quīntānus adj of the fifth ♦ f street in a camp between the 5th and 6th maniples ♦ mpl men of the fifth legion

Quīntiliānus, -ī m Quintilian (famous teacher of rhetoric in Rome)

Quīntīlis adj of July

quīntum, quīntō adv for the fifth time

Quīntus, -ī m Roman first name

quīntus adj fifth

quīntusdecimus adj fifteenth

quippe adv (affirming) certainly, of course ♦ conj (explaining) for in fact, because, since; ~ **quī** since I, he etc

quippiam etc see **quispiam**

quippinī adv certainly

Quirīnālis adj of Romulus; Quirinal (hill)

Quirīnus, -ī m Romulus ♦ adj of Romulus

Quirīs, -ītis m inhabitant of Cures; Roman citizen; citizen

quirītātiō, -ōnis f shriek

Quirītēs mpl inhabitants of Cures; Roman citizens

quirītō, -āre vi to cry out, wail

quis, quid pron who?, what?; (indef) anyone, anything

quīs poetic dat pl and abl pl of **quī**[1]

quisnam, quaenam, quidnam pron who?, what?

quispiam, quaepiam, quodpiam and **quidpiam** pron some, some one, something

quisquam, quaequam, quicquam and **quidquam** pron any, anyone, anything; **nec** ~ and no one

quisque, quaeque, quodque pron each, every, every one; **quidque, quicque** everything; **decimus** ~ every tenth; **optimus** ~ all the best; **prīmus** ~ the first possible

quisquiliae, -ārum fpl refuse, rubbish

quisquis, quaequae, quodquod, quidquid and **quicquid** pron whoever, whatever, all

quīvīs, quaevīs, quodvīs, quidvīs pron any you please, anyone, anything

quīvīscumque, quaevīscumque, quodvīscumque pron any whatsoever

quō adv (interrog) where?; whither?; for what purpose?, what for?; (rel) where, to which (place), to whom; (with comp) the (more); (with sī) anywhere ♦ conj (with subj) in order that; **nōn quō** not that

quoad adv how far?; how long? ♦ conj as far as, as long as; until

quōcircā conj therefore

quōcumque adv whithersoever

quod conj as for, in that, that; because; why; ~ **sī** but if

quōdam modo adv in a way

quoi old dat form of **quī**[1]

quōius old gen form of **quī**[1]

quōlibet adv anywhere, in any direction

quom etc conj see **cum**[2]

quōminus conj that not; (preventing) from

quōmodo adv (interrog) how?; (rel) just as; **quōmodocumque** howsoever; **quōmodonam** how?

quōnam adv where, where to?

quondam adv once, formerly; sometimes; (fut) one day

quōniam conj since, seeing that

quōpiam adv anywhere

quōquam adv anywhere

quoque adv also, too

quōquō adv to whatever place, wherever

quōquō modo adv howsoever

quōquō versus, quōquō versum adv in every direction

quōrsus, quōrsum adv where to?, in what direction?; what for?, to what end?

quot adj how many; as many as, every

quotannīs adv every year

quotcumque adj however many

quotēnī, -ōrum adj how many

quotīd- etc see **cottīd-**

quotiēns, quotiēs adv how often?; (rel) as often as

quotiēnscumque adv however often

quotquot adj however many

quotumus adj which number?, what date?

quotus adj what number, how many; ~ **quisque** how few; **quota hōra** what time

quotuscumque adj whatever number, however big

quōusque adv how long, till when; how far

quōvīs adv anywhere

quum etc conj see **cum**[2]

Rr

rabidē *adv* furiously
rabidus *adj* raving, mad; impetuous
rabiēs, (*acc* **-em**, *abl* **-ē**) *f* madness, rage, fury
rabiō, -ere *vi* to rave
rabiōsē *adv* wildly
rabiōsulus *adj* somewhat rabid
rabiōsus *adj* furious, mad
rabula, -ae *m* wrangling lawyer
racēmifer, -ī *adj* clustered
racēmus, -ī *m* stalk of a cluster; bunch of grapes; grape
radiātus *adj* radiant
rādīcitus *adv* by the roots; utterly
rādīcula, -ae *f* small root
radiō, -āre *vt* to irradiate ♦ *vi* to radiate, shine
radius, -i *and* **-iī** *m* stick, rod; (*light*) beam, ray; (*loom*) shuttle; (*MATH*) rod for drawing figures, radius of a circle; (*plant*) long olive; (*wheel*) spoke
rādīx, -īcis *f* root; radish; (*hill*) foot; (*fig*) foundation, origin
rādō, -dere, -sī, -sum *vt* to scrape, shave, scratch; to erase; to touch in passing, graze, pass along
raeda, -ae *f* four-wheeled carriage
raedārius, -ī *and* **-iī** *m* driver
Raetī, -ōrum *mpl Alpine people between Italy and Germany*
Raetia, -iae *f* country of the Raetī
Raeticus, Raetius, Raetus *adj see* **Raetia**
rāmālia, -ium *ntpl* twigs, brushwood
rāmentum, -ī *nt* shavings, chips
rāmeus *adj* of branches
rāmex, -icis *m* rupture, blood vessels of the lungs
Ramnēnsēs, Ramnēs, -ium *mpl one of the original Roman tribes; a century of equites*
rāmōsus *adj* branching
rāmulus, -ī *m* twig, sprig
rāmus, -ī *m* branch, bough
rāna, -ae *f* frog; frogfish
rancēns, -entis *adj* putrid
rancidulus *adj* rancid
rancidus *adj* rank, rancid; disgusting
rānunculus, -ī *m* tadpole
rapācida, -ae *m* son of a thief
rapācitās, -ātis *f* greed
rapāx, -ācis *adj* greedy, grasping, ravenous
raphanus, -ī *m* radish
rapidē *adv* swiftly, hurriedly
rapiditās, -ātis *f* rapidity

rapidus *adj* tearing, devouring; swift, rapid; hasty, impetuous
rapīna, -ae *f* pillage, robbery; booty, prey
rapiō, -ere, -uī, -tum *vt* to tear, snatch, carry off; to seize, plunder; to hurry, seize quickly
raptim *adv* hastily, violently
raptiō, -ōnis *f* abduction
raptō, -āre, -āvī, -ātum *vt* to seize and carry off, drag away, move quickly; to plunder, lay waste; (*passion*) to agitate
raptor, -ōris *m* plunderer, robber, ravisher
raptus¹ *ppp of* **rapiō** ♦ *nt* plunder
raptus², -ūs *m* carrying off, abduction; plundering
rāpulum, -ī *nt* small turnip
rāpum, -ī *nt* turnip
rārēfaciō, -facere, -fēcī, -factum (*pass* **-fīō**) *vt* to rarefy
rārēscō, -ere *vi* to become rarefied, grow thin; to open out
rāritās, -ātis *f* porousness, open texture; thinness, fewness
rārō, rārē *adv* seldom
rārus *adj* porous, open in texture; thin, scanty; scattered, straggling, here and there; (*MIL*) in open order; few, infrequent; uncommon, rare
rāsī *perf of* **rādō**
rāsilis *adj* smooth, polished
rāstrum, -ī *nt* hoe, mattock
rāsus *ppp of* **rādō**
ratiō, -ōnis *f* 1. (*reckoning of*) account, calculation; list, register; affair, business 2. (*relation*) respect, consideration; procedure, method, system, way, kind 3. (*reason*) reasoning, thought; cause, motive; science, knowledge, philosophy; ~ atque ūsus theory and practice; ~ est it is reasonable; Stōicōrum ~ Stoicism; ratiōnem dūcere, ratiōnem inīre calculate; ratiōnem habēre take account of, have to do with, consider; ratiōnem reddere give an account of; cum ratiōne reasonably; meae ratiōnēs my interests; ā ratiōnibus accountant
ratiōcinātiō, -ōnis *f* reasoning; syllogism
ratiōcinātīvus *adj* syllogistic
ratiōcinātor, -ōris *m* accountant
ratiōcinor, -ārī, -ātus *vt, vi* to calculate; to consider; to argue, infer
ratiōnālis *adj* rational; syllogistic
ratis, -is *f* raft; boat

179

ratiuncula, -ae f small calculation; slight reason; petty syllogism

ratus ppa of **reor ◆** adj fixed, settled, sure; valid; **prō ratā (parte)** proportionally; **ratum dūcere, ratum facere, ratum habēre** ratify

raucisonus adj hoarse

raucus adj hoarse; harsh, strident

raudus, -eris nt copper coin

raudusculum, -ī nt bit of money

Ravenna, -ae f port in N.E. Italy

Ravennās, -ātis adj see **Ravenna**

rāvis (acc **-im**) f hoarseness

rāvus adj grey, tawny

rea, -ae f defendant, culprit

reapse adv in fact, actually

Reāte, -is nt ancient Sabine town

Reātīnus adj see **Reāte**

rebellātiō, -ōnis f revolt

rebellātrīx, -īcis adj rebellious

rebelliō, -ōnis f revolt

rebellis adj rebellious **◆** mpl rebels

rebellium, -ī and -iī nt revolt

rebellō, -āre vi to revolt

rebītō, -ere vi to return

reboō, -āre vi to re-echo **◆** vt to make resound

recalcitrō, -āre vi to kick back

recaleō, -ēre vi to be warm again

recalēscō, -ere vi to grow warm again

recalfaciō, -facere, -fēcī vt to warm again

recalvus adj bald in front

recandēscō, -ēscere, -uī vi to whiten (in response); to glow

recantō, -āre, -āvī, -ātum vt to recant; to charm away

reccidī perf of **recidō**

recēdō, -ēdere, -essī, -essum vi to move back, withdraw, depart; (place) to recede; (head) to be severed

recellō, -ere vi to spring back

recēns, -entis adj fresh, young, recent; (writer) modern; (with ab) immediately after **◆** adv newly, just

recēnseō, -ēre, -uī, -um vt to count; to review

recēnsiō, -ōnis f revision

recēnsus ppp of **recēnseō**

recēpī perf of **recipiō**

receptāculum, -ī nt receptacle, reservoir; refuge, shelter

receptō, -āre vt to take back; to admit, harbour; to tug hard at

receptor, -ōris m (male) receiver, shelterer

receptrīx, -īcis f (female) receiver, shelterer

receptum, -ī nt obligation

receptus¹ ppp of **recipiō**

receptus², -ūs m withdrawal; retreat; return; refuge; **receptuī canere** sound the retreat

recessī perf of **recēdō**

recessim adv backwards

recessus, -ūs m retreat, departure; recess, secluded spot; (tide) ebb

recidīvus adj resurrected; recurring

recidō, -idere, -cidī, -āsum vi to fall back; to recoil, relapse; (fig) to fall, descend

recīdō, -dere, -dī, -sum vt to cut back, cut off

recingō, -gere, -ctum vt to ungird, loose

recinō, -ere vt, vi to re-echo, repeat; to sound a warning

reciper- etc see **recuper-**

recipiō, -ipere, -ēpī, -eptum vt to take back, retake; to get back, regain, rescue; to accept, admit; (MIL) to occupy; (duty) to undertake; (promise) to pledge, guarantee; **sē recipere** withdraw, retreat; **nōmen recipere** receive notice of a prosecution

reciprocō, -āre vt to move to and fro; (ship) to bring round to another tack; (proposition) to reverse **◆** vi (tide) to rise and fall

reciprocus adj ebbing

recīsus ppp of **recīdō**

recitātiō, -ōnis f reading aloud, recital

recitātor, -ōris m reader, reciter

recitō, -āre, -āvī, -ātum vt to read out, recite

reclāmātiō, -ōnis f outcry (of disapproval)

reclāmitō, -āre vi to cry out against

reclāmō, -āre vi to cry out, protest; to reverberate

reclīnis adj leaning back

reclīnō, -āre, -āvī, -ātum vt to lean back

reclūdō, -dere, -sī, -sum vt to open up; to disclose

reclūsus ppp of **reclūdō**

recoctus ppp of **recoquō**

recōgitō, -āre vi to think over, reflect

recognitiō, -ōnis f review

recognōscō, -ōscere, -ōvī, -itum vt to recollect; to examine, review

recolligō, -igere, -ēgī, -ēctum vt to gather up; (fig) to recover, reconcile

recolō, -olere, -oluī, -ultum vt to recultivate; to resume; to reflect on, contemplate; to revisit

recomminīscor, -ī vi to recollect

recompositus adj rearranged

reconciliātiō, -ōnis f restoration, reconciliation

reconciliō, -āre, -āvī, -ātum vt to win back again, restore, reconcile

reconcinnō, -āre vt to repair

reconditus ppp of **recondō ◆** adj hidden, secluded; abstruse, profound; (disposition) reserved

recondō, -ere, -idī, -itum vt to store away, stow; to hide away, bury

recōnflō, -āre vt to rekindle

recoquō, -quere, -xī, -ctum vt to cook again, boil again; to forge again, recast; (fig) to rejuvenate

recordātiō, -ōnis f recollection

recordor, -ārī, -ātus vt, vi to recall, remember; to ponder over

recreō, -āre, -āvī, -ātum vt to remake, reproduce; to revive, refresh

recrepō, -āre vt, vi to ring, re-echo

recrēscō, -scere, -vī vi to grow again

recrūdēscō, -ēscere, -uī vi (wound) to open again; (war) to break out again

rēctā adv straight forward, right on

rēctē *adv* straight; correctly, properly, well; quite; (*colloq*) good, all right, no thank you

rēctiō, -ōnis *f* government

rēctor, -ōris *m* guide, driver, helmsman; governor, master

rēctum, -ī *nt* right, virtue

rēctus *ppp of* **regō** ♦ *adj* straight; upright, steep; right, correct, proper; (*moral*) good, virtuous

recubō, -āre *vi* to lie, recline

recultus *ppp of* **recolō**

recumbō, -mbere, -buī *vi* to lie down, recline; to fall, sink down

recuperātiō, -ōnis *f* recovery

recuperātor, -ōris *m* recapturer; (*pl*) board of justices who tried civil cases requiring a quick decision, esp cases involving foreigners

recuperātōrius *adj* of the recuperatores

recuperō, -āre, -āvī, -ātum *vt* to get back, recover, recapture

recūrō, -āre *vt* to restore

recurrō, -ere, -ī *vi* to run back; to return, recur; to revert

recursō, -āre *vi* to keep coming back, keep recurring

recursus, -ūs *m* return, retreat

recurvō, -āre *vt* to bend back, curve

recurvus *adj* bent, curved

recūsātiō, -ōnis *f* refusal, declining; (*LAW*) objection, counterplea

recūsō, -āre, -āvī, -ātum *vt* to refuse, decline, be reluctant; (*LAW*) to object, plead in defence

recussus *adj* reverberating

redāctus *ppp of* **redigō**

redambulō, -āre *vi* to come back

redamō, -āre *vt* to love in return

redārdēscō, -ere *vi* to blaze up again

redarguō, -ere, -ī *vt* to refute, contradict

redauspicō, -āre *vi* to take auspices for going back

redditus *ppp of* **reddō**

reddō, -ere, -idī, -itum *vt* to give back, return, restore; to give in response, repay; to give up, deliver, pay; (*copy*) to represent, reproduce; (*speech*) to report, repeat, recite, reply; to translate; (*with adj*) to make; **iūdicium reddere** fix the date for a trial; **iūs reddere** administer justice

redēgī *perf of* **redigō**

redēmī *perf of* **redimō**

redemptiō, -ōnis *f* ransoming; bribing; (*revenue*) farming

redemptō, -āre *vt* to ransom

redemptor, -ōris *m* contractor

redemptūra, -ae *f* contracting

redemptus *ppp of* **redimō**

redeō, -īre, -iī, -itum *vi* to go back, come back, return; (*speech*) to revert; (*money*) to come in; (*circumstances*) to be reduced to, come to

redhālō, -āre *vt* to exhale

redhibeō, -ēre *vt* to take back

redigō, -igere, -ēgī, -āctum *vt* to drive back, bring back; (*money*) to collect, raise; (*to a condition*) to reduce, bring; (*number*) to reduce; **ad irritum redigere** make useless

rediī *perf of* **redeō**

redimīculum, -ī *nt* band

redimiō, -īre, -iī, -ītum *vt* to bind, crown, encircle

redimō, -imere, -ēmī, -emptum *vt* to buy back; to ransom, redeem; to release, rescue; (*good*) to procure; (*evil*) to avert; (*fault*) to make amends for; (*COMM*) to undertake by contract, hire

redintegrō, -āre, -āvī, -ātum *vt* to restore, renew, refresh

redipīscor, -ī *vt* to get back

reditiō, -ōnis *f* returning

reditus, -ūs *m* return, returning; (*money*) revenue

redivīvus *adj* renovated

redoleō, -ēre, -uī *vi* to give out a smell ♦ *vt* to smell of, smack of

redomitus *adj* broken in again

redōnō, -āre *vt* to restore; to give up

redūcō, -ūcere, -ūxī, -uctum *vt* to draw back; to lead back, bring back; to escort home; to marry again; (*troops*) to withdraw; (*fig*) to restore; (*to a condition*) to make into

reductiō, -ōnis *f* restoration

reductor, -ōris *m* man who brings back

reductus *ppp of* **redūcō** ♦ *adj* secluded, aloof

reduncus *adj* curved back

redundantia, -ae *f* extravagance

redundō, -āre, -āvī, -ātum *vi* to overflow; to abound, be in excess; (*fig*) to stream

reduvia, -ae *f* hangnail

redux, -cis *adj* (*gods*) who brings back; (*men*) brought back, returned

refectus *ppp of* **reficiō**

refellō, -ere, -ī *vt* to disprove, rebut

referciō, -cīre, -sī, -tum *vt* to stuff, cram, choke full

referiō, -īre *vt* to hit back; to reflect

referō, -ferre, -ttulī, -lātum *vt* to bring back, carry back; to give back, pay back, repay; to repeat, renew; (*authority*) to refer to, trace back to; (*blame, credit*) to ascribe; (*likeness*) to reproduce, resemble; (*memory*) to recall; (*news*) to report, mention; (*opinion*) to reckon amongst; (*record*) to enter; (*senate*) to lay before, move; (*speech*) to reply, say in answer; **grātiam referre** be grateful, requite; **pedem referre, gradum referre** return; retreat; **ratiōnēs referre** present an account; **sē referre** return

rēfert, -ferre, -tulit *vi* (*impers*) it is of importance, it matters, it concerns; **meā ~** it matters to me

refertus *ppp of* **referciō** ♦ *adj* crammed, full

referveō, -ēre *vi* to boil over

refervēscō, -ere *vi* to bubble up

reficiō, -icere, -ēcī, -ectum *vt* to repair, restore; (*body, mind*) to refresh, revive; (*money*) to get back, get in return; (*POL*) to re-elect

refīgō, -gere, -xī, -xum *vt* to unfasten, take down; (*fig*) to annul

refingō, -ere vt to remake
refīxus ppp of **refigō**
reflāgitō, -āre vt to demand back
reflātus, -ūs m contrary wind
reflectō, -ctere, -xī, -xum vt to bend back, turn back; (fig) to bring back ♦ vi to give way
reflexus ppp of **reflectō**
reflō, -āre, -āvī, -ātum vi to blow contrary ♦ vt to breathe out again
refluō, -ere vi to flow back, overflow
refluus adj ebbing
reformīdō, -āre vt to dread; to shun in fear
refōrmō, -āre vt to reshape
refōtus ppp of **refoveō**
refoveō, -ovēre, -ōvī, -ōtum vt to refresh, revive
refrāctāriolus adj rather stubborn
refrāctus ppp of **refringō**
refrāgor, -ārī, -ātus vi (with dat) to oppose, thwart
refrēgī perf of **refringō**
refrēnō, -āre vt to curb, restrain
refricō, -āre, -uī, -ātum vt to scratch open; to reopen, renew ♦ vi to break out again
refrīgerātiō, -ōnis f coolness
refrīgerō, -āre, -āvī, -ātum vi to cool, cool off; (fig) to flag
refrīgēscō, -gēscere, -xī vi to grow cold; (fig) to flag, grow stale
refringō, -ingere, -ēgī, -āctum vt to break open; to break off; (fig) to break, check
refrīxī perf of **refrīgēscō**
refugiō, -ugere, -ūgī vi to run back, flee, shrink ♦ vt to run away from, shun
refugium, -ī and **-iī** nt refuge
refugus adj fugitive, receding
refulgeō, -gēre, -sī vi to flash back, reflect light
refundō, -undere, -ūdī, -ūsum vt to pour back, pour out; (pass) to overflow
refūsus ppp of **refundō**
refūtātiō, -ōnis f refutation
refūtātus, -ūs m refutation
refūtō, -āre, -āvī, -ātum vt to check, repress; to refute, disprove
rēgālis adj king's, royal, regal
rēgāliter adv magnificently; tyrannically
regerō, -rere, -ssī, -stum vt to carry back, throw back
rēgia, -ae f palace; court; (camp) royal tent; (town) capital
rēgiē adv regally; imperiously
rēgificus adj magnificent
regignō, -ere vt to reproduce
Rēgillānus, Rēgillēnsis adj see **Rēgillus**
Rēgillus, -ī m Sabine town; lake in Latium (scene of a Roman victory over the Latins)
regimen, -inis nt guiding, steering; rudder; rule, command, government; ruler
rēgīna, -ae f queen, noblewoman
Rēgīnus adj see **Rēgium**
regiō, -ōnis f direction, line; boundary line; quarter, region; district, ward, territory; (fig)

sphere, province; **ē regiōne** in a straight line; (with gen) exactly opposite
regiōnātim adv by districts
Rēgium, -ī and **-iī** nt town in extreme S. of Italy (now Reggio)
rēgius adj king's, kingly, royal; princely, magnificent
reglūtinō, -āre vt to unstick
rēgnātor, -ōris m ruler
rēgnātrīx, -īcis adj imperial
rēgnō, -āre, -āvī, -ātum vi to be king, rule, reign; to be supreme, lord it; (things) to prevail, predominate ♦ vt to rule over
rēgnum, -ī nt kingship, monarchy; sovereignty, supremacy; despotism; kingdom; domain
regō, -ere, rēxī, rēctum vt to keep straight, guide, steer; to manage, direct; to control, rule, govern; **regere fīnēs** (law) mark out the limits
regredior, -dī, -ssus vi to go back, come back, return; (MIL) to retire
regressus ppa of **regredior**
regressus², -ūs m return; retreat
rēgula, -ae f rule, ruler; stick, board; (fig) rule, pattern, standard
rēgulus, -ī m petty king, chieftain; prince
Rēgulus, -ī m Roman consul taken prisoner by the Carthaginians
regustō, -āre vt to taste again
rēiciō, -icere, -iēcī, -iectum vt to throw back, throw over the shoulder, throw off; to drive back, repel; to cast off, reject; to reject with contempt, scorn; (jurymen) to challenge, refuse; (matter for discussion) to refer; (time) to postpone; **sē rēicere** fling oneself
rēiectāneus adj to be rejected
rēiectiō, -ōnis f rejection; (LAW) challenging
rēiectō, -āre vt to throw back
rēiectus ppp of **rēiciō**
relābor, -bī, -psus vi to glide back, sink back, fall back
relanguēscō, -ēscere, -ī vi to faint; to weaken
relātiō, -ōnis f (LAW) retorting; (pl) magistrate's report; (RHET) repetition
relātor, -ōris m proposer of a motion
relātus¹ ppp of **referō**
relātus², -ūs m official report; recital
relaxātiō, -ōnis f easing
relaxō, -āre, -āvī, -ātum vt to loosen, open out; (fig) to release, ease, relax, cheer
relēctus ppp of **relegō**
relēgātiō, -ōnis f banishment
relegō, -egere, -ēgī, -ēctum vt to gather up; (place) to traverse, sail over again; (speech) to go over again, reread
relēgō, -āre, -āvī, -ātum vt to send away, send out of the way; to banish; (fig) to reject; to refer, ascribe
relentēscō, -ere vi to slacken off
relēvī perf of **relinō**
relevō, -āre, -āvī, -ātum vt to lift up; to lighten; (fig) to relieve, ease, comfort
relictiō, -ōnis f abandoning

relictus *ppp of* **relinquō**
rēlicuus *etc see* **reliquus**
religātiō, -ōnis *f* tying up
rēligiō, -ōnis *f* religious scruple, reverence, awe; religion; superstition; scruples, conscientiousness; holiness, sanctity (*in anything*); object of veneration, sacred place; religious ceremony, observance
rēligiōsē *adv* devoutly; scrupulously, conscientiously
rēligiōsus *adj* devout, religious; superstitious; involving religious difficulty; scrupulous, conscientious; (*objects*) holy, sacred
religō, -āre, -āvī, -ātum *vt* to tie up, fasten behind; (*ship*) to make fast, moor; (*fig*) to bind
relinō, -inere, -ēvī *vt* to unseal
relinquō, -inquere, -īquī, -ictum *vt* to leave, leave behind; to bequeath; to abandon, forsake; (*argument*) to allow; (*pass*) to remain
rēliquiae, -ārum *fpl* leavings, remainder, relics
reliquus *adj* remaining, left; (*time*) subsequent, future; (*debt*) outstanding ♦ *nt* remainder, rest; arrears ♦ *mpl* the rest; **reliquum est** it remains, the next point is; **reliquī facere** leave behind, leave over, omit; **in reliquum** for the future
rell- *etc see* **rel-**
relūceō, -cēre, -xī *vi* to blaze
relūcēscō, -cēscere, -xī *vi* to become bright again
reluctor, -ārī, -ātus *vi* to struggle against, resist
remaneō, -anēre, -ānsī *vi* to remain behind; to remain, continue, endure
remānō, -āre *vi* to flow back
remānsiō, -ōnis *f* remaining behind
remedium, -ī *and* **-iī** *nt* cure, remedy, medicine
remēnsus *ppa of* **remētior**
remeō, -āre *vi* to come back, go back, return
remētior, -tīrī, -nsus *vt* to measure again; to go back over
rēmex, -igis *m* rower, oarsman
Rēmī, -ōrum *mpl* people of Gaul (*in region of what is now* Rheims)
rēmigātiō, -ōnis *f* rowing
rēmigium, -ī *and* **-iī** *nt* rowing; oars; oarsmen
rēmigō, -āre *vi* to row
remigrō, -āre *vi* to move back, return (home)
reminīscor, -ī *vt*, *vi* (*usu gen*) to remember, call to mind
remisceō, -scēre, -scuī, -xtum *vt* to mix up, mingle
remissē *adv* mildly, gently
remissiō, -ōnis *f* release; (*tension*) slackening, relaxing; (*payment*) remission; (*mind*) slackness, mildness, relaxation; (*illness*) abating
remissus *ppp of* **remittō** ♦ *adj* slack; negligent; mild, indulgent, cheerful
remittō, -ittere, -īsī, -issum *vt* to let go back, send back, release; to slacken, loosen, relax; to emit, produce; (*mind*) to relax, relieve; (*notion*) to discard, give up; (*offence, penalty*) to

let off, remit; (*right*) to resign, sacrifice; (*sound*) to give back ♦ *vi* to abate
remixtus *ppp of* **remisceō**
remōlior, -īrī, -ītus *vt* to heave back
remollēscō, -ere *vi* to become soft again, be softened
remolliō, -īre *vt* to weaken
remora, -ae *f* hindrance
remorāmina, -um *ntpl* hindrances
remordeō, -dēre, -dī, -sum *vt* (*fig*) to worry, torment
remoror, -ārī, -ātus *vi* to linger, stay behind ♦ *vt* to hinder, delay, defer
remorsus *ppp of* **remordeō**
remōtē *adv* far
remōtiō, -ōnis *f* removing
remōtus *ppp of* **removeō** ♦ *adj* distant, remote; secluded; (*fig*) far removed, free from
removeō, -ovēre, -ōvī, -ōtum *vt* to move back, withdraw, set aside; to subtract
remūgiō, -īre *vi* to bellow in answer, re-echo
remulceō, -cēre, -sī *vt* to stroke; (*tail*) to droop
remulcum, -ī *nt* towrope
remūnerātiō, -ōnis *f* recompense, reward
remūneror, -ārī, -ātus *vt* to repay, reward
remurmurō, -āre *vi* to murmur in answer
Remus, -ī *m* brother of Romulus
rēmus, -ī *m* oar
renārrō, -āre *vt* to tell over again
renāscor, -scī, -tus *vi* to be born again; to grow, spring up again
renātus *ppa of* **renāscor**
renāvigō, -āre *vi* to sail back
reneō, -ēre *vt* to unspin, undo
rēnēs, -um *mpl* kidneys
renīdeō, -ēre *vi* to shine back, be bright; to be cheerful, smile, laugh
renīdēscō, -ere *vi* to reflect the gleam of
renītor, -ī *vi* to struggle, resist
renō, -āre *vi* to swim back
rēnō, -ōnis *m* fur
renōdō, -āre *vt* to tie back in a knot
renovāmen, -inis *nt* new condition
renovātiō, -ōnis *f* renewal; compound interest
renovō, -āre, -āvī, -ātum *vt* to renew, restore; to repair, revive, refresh; (*speech*) to repeat; **faenus renovāre** take compound interest
renumerō, -āre *vt* to pay back
renūntiātiō, -ōnis *f* report, announcement
renūntiō, -āre, -āvī, -ātum *vt* to report, bring back word; to announce, make an official statement; (*election*) to declare elected, return; (*duty*) to refuse, call off, renounce
renūntius, -ī *and* **-iī** *m* reporter
renuō, -ere, -ī *vt*, *vi* to deny, decline, refuse
renūtō, -āre *vi* to refuse firmly
reor, rērī, ratus *vi* to think, suppose
repāgula, -ōrum *ntpl* (*door*) bolts, bars
repandus *adj* curving back, turned up
reparābilis *adj* retrievable
reparcō, -ere *vi* to be sparing with, refrain

reparō, -āre, -āvī, -ātum *vt* to retrieve, recover; to restore, repair; to purchase; (*mind, body*) to refresh; (*troops*) to recruit

repastinātiō, -ōnis *f* digging up again

repellō, -ellere, -pulī, -ulsum *vt* to push back, drive back, repulse; to remove, reject

rependō, -endere, -endī, -ēnsum *vt* to return by weight; to pay, repay; to requite, compensate

repēns, -entis *adj* sudden; new

repēnsus *ppp of* **rependō**

repentē *adv* suddenly

repentīnō *adv* suddenly

repentīnus *adj* sudden, hasty; upstart

repercō *etc see* **reparcō**

repercussus¹ *ppp of* **repercutiō**

repercussus², -ūs *m* reflection, echo

repercutiō, -tere, -ssī, -ssum *vt* to make rebound, reflect, echo

reperiō, -īre, repperī, -tum *vt* to find, find out; to get, procure; to discover, ascertain; to devise, invent

repertor, -ōris *m* discoverer, inventor, author

repertus *ppp of* **reperiō** ♦ *ntpl* discoveries

repetītiō, -ōnis *f* repetition; (RHET) anaphora

repetītor, -ōris *m* reclaimer

repetītus *ppp of* **repetō** ♦ *adj:* **altē/longē ~** far-fetched

repetō, -ere, -īvī *and* **-iī, -ītum** *vt* to go back to, revisit; to fetch back, take back; (MIL) to attack again; (*action, speech*) to resume, repeat; (*memory*) to recall, think over; (*origin*) to trace, derive; (*right*) to claim, demand back; **rēs repetere** demand satisfaction; reclaim one's property; **pecūniae repetundae** extortion

repetundae, -ārum *fpl* extortion (*by a provincial governor*)

repexus *adj* combed

repleō, -ēre, -ēvī, -ētum *vt* to fill up, refill; to replenish, make good, complete; to satiate, fill to overflowing

replētus *adj* full

replicātiō, -ōnis *f* rolling up

replicō, -āre *vt* to roll back, unroll, unfold

rēpō, -ere, -sī, -tum *vi* to creep, crawl

repōnō, -ōnere, -osuī, -ositum *vt* to put back, replace, restore; to bend back; to put (*in the proper place*); (*performance*) to repeat; (*something received*) to repay; (*store*) to lay up, put away; (*task*) to lay aside, put down; (*hope*) to place, rest; (*with* **prō**) substitute; **in numerō repōnere, in numerum repōnere** count, reckon among

reportō, -āre, -āvī, -ātum *vt* to bring back, carry back; (*prize*) to win, carry off; (*words*) to report

reposcō, -ere *vt* to demand back; to claim, require

repositus *ppp of* **repōnō** ♦ *adj* remote

repostor, -ōris *m* restorer

repostus *etc see* **repositus**

repōtia, -ōrum *ntpl* second drinking

repperī *perf of* **reperiō**

reppulī *perf of* **repellō**

repraesentātiō, -ōnis *f* vivid presentation; (COMM) cash payment

repraesentō, -āre, -āvī, -ātum *vt* to exhibit, reproduce; to do at once, hasten; (COMM) to pay cash

reprehendō, -endere, -endī, -ēnsum *vt* to hold back, catch, restrain; to hold fast, retain; to blame, rebuke, censure; to refute

reprehēnsiō, -ōnis *f* check; blame, reprimand, refutation

reprehēnsō, -āre *vt* to keep holding back

reprehēnsor, -ōris *m* censurer, critic, reviser

reprehēnsus *ppp of* **reprehendō**

reprendō *etc see* **reprehendō**

repressor, -ōris *m* restrainer

repressus *ppp of* **reprimō**

reprimō, -imere, -essī, -essum *vt* to keep back, force back; to check, restrain, suppress

reprōmissiō, -ōnis *f* counterpromise

reprōmittō, -ittere, -īsī, -issum *vt* to promise in return, engage oneself

rēptō, -āre *vi* to creep about, crawl along

repudiātiō, -ōnis *f* rejection

repudiō, -āre, -āvī, -ātum *vt* to reject, refuse, scorn; (*wife*) to divorce

repudium, -ī *and* **-iī** *nt* divorce; repudiation

repuerāscō, -ere *vi* to become a child again; to behave like a child

repugnanter *adv* reluctantly

repugnantia, -ium *ntpl* contradictions

repugnō, -āre, -āvī, -ātum *vi* to oppose, resist; to disagree, be inconsistent

repulsa, -ae *f* refusal, denial, repulse; (*election*) rebuff

repulsō, -āre *vi* to throb, reverberate

repulsus¹ *ppp of* **repellō**

repulsus², -ūs *m* (*light*) reflection; (*sound*) echoing

repungō, -ere *vt* to prod again

repūrgō, -āre, -āvī, -ātum *vt* to clear again, cleanse again; to purge away

reputātiō, -ōnis *f* pondering over

reputō, -āre, -āvī, -ātum *vt* to count back; to think over, consider

requiēs, -ētis *f* rest, relaxation, repose

requiēscō, -scere, -vī, -tum *vi* to rest, find rest; to cease ♦ *vt* to stay

requiētus *adj* rested, refreshed

requīritō, -āre *vt* to keep asking after

requīrō, -rere, -sīvī *and* **-siī, -sītum** *vt* to search for, look for; to ask, inquire after; (*with* **ex** *or* **ab**) to question; to need, want, call for; to miss, look in vain for

requīsītus *ppp of* **requīrō**

rēs, reī *f* thing, object; circumstance, case, matter, affair; business, transaction; fact, truth, reality; possessions, wealth, money; advantage, interest; (LAW) case; (MIL) campaign, operations; (POL) politics, power, the State; (*writing*) subject matter, story, history; **rēs mihi est tēcum** I have to do with you; **rēs dīvīna** sacrifice; **rēs mīlitāris** war; **rēs pūblica** public affairs, politics, the State, republic; **rēs rūstica** agriculture; **rem**

facere get rich; **rem gerere** wage war, fight; **ad rem** to the point, to the purpose; **in rem** usefully; **ob rem** to the purpose; **ob eam rem** therefore; **ī in malam rem** go to the devil!; **contrā rem pūblicam** unconstitutionally; **ē rē pūblicā** constitutionally; **rē vērā** in fact, actually; **eā rē** for that reason; **tuā rē**, **ex tuā rē** to your advantage; **ab rē** unhelpfully; **ē rē (nātā)** as things are; **prō rē** according to circumstances; **rēs adversae** failure, adversity; **rēs dubiae** danger; **rēs gestae** achievements, career; **rēs novae** revolution; **rēs prosperae**, **rēs secundae** success, prosperity; **rērum māximus** greatest in the world; **rērum scrīptor** historian

resacrō *etc see* **resecrō**

resaeviō, -īre *vi* to rage again

resalūtō, -āre *vt* to greet in return

resānēscō, -ēscere, -uī *vi* to heal up again

resarciō, -cīre, -tum *vt* to patch up, repair

rescindō, -ndere, -dī, -ssum *vt* to cut back, cut open, break down; to open up; *(law, agreement)* to repeal, annul

rescīscō, -īscere, -īvī *and* **-iī, -ītum** *vt* to find out, learn

rescissus *ppp of* **rescindō**

rescrībō, -bere, -psī, -ptum *vt* to write back, reply; to rewrite, revise; *(emperors)* to give a decision; *(MIL)* to transfer, re-enlist; *(money)* to place to one's credit, pay back

rescrīptus *ppp of* **rescrībō** ♦ *nt* imperial rescript

resecō, -āre, -uī, -tum *vt* to cut back, cut short; to curtail; **ad vīvum resecāre** cut to the quick

resecrō, -āre *vt* to pray again; to free from a curse

resectus *ppp of* **resecō**

resecūtus *ppa of* **resequor**

resēdī *perf of* **resideō**; **resīdō**

resēminō, -āre *vt* to reproduce

resequor, -quī, -cūtus *vt* to answer

reserō, -āre, -āvī, -ātum *vt* to unbar, unlock; to disclose

reservō, -āre, -āvī, -ātum *vt* to keep back, reserve; to preserve, save

reses, -idis *adj* remaining; inactive; idle; calm

resideō, -idēre, -ēdī *vi* to remain behind; to be idle, be listless; *(fig)* to remain, rest

resīdō, -īdere, -ēdī *vi* to sit down, sink down, settle; to subside; *(fig)* to abate, calm down

residuus *adj* remaining, left over; *(money)* outstanding

resignō, -āre *vt* to unseal, open; *(fig)* to reveal; *(COMM)* to cancel, pay back

resiliō, -īre, -uī *vi* to spring back; to recoil, rebound, shrink

resīmus *adj* turned up

rēsīna, -ae *f* resin

rēsīnātus *adj* smeared with resin

resipiō, -ere *vt* to savour of, smack of

resipīscō, -īscere, -iī *and* **-uī** *vi* to come to one's senses

resistō, -istere, -titī *vi* to stand still, stop, halt; to resist, oppose; to rise again

resolūtus *ppp of* **resolvō**

resolvō, -vere, -vī, -ūtum *vt* to unfasten, loosen, open, release; to melt, dissolve; to relax; *(debt)* to pay up; *(difficulty)* to banish, dispel; *(tax)* to abolish; *(words)* to explain

resonābilis *adj* answering

resonō, -āre *vi* to resound, re-echo ♦ *vt* to echo the sound of; to make resound

resonus *adj* echoing

resorbeō, -ēre *vt* to suck back, swallow again

respectō, -āre *vi* to look back; to gaze about, watch ♦ *vt* to look back at, look for; to have regard for

respectus¹ *ppp of* **respiciō**

respectus², -ūs *m* looking back; refuge; respect, regard

respergō, -gere, -sī, -sum *vt* to besprinkle, splash

respersiō, -ōnis *f* sprinkling

respersus *ppp of* **respergō**

respiciō, -icere, -exī, -ectum *vt* to look back at, see behind; *(help)* to look to; *(care)* to have regard for, consider, respect ♦ *vi* to look back, look

respīrāmen, -inis *nt* windpipe

respīrātiō, -ōnis *f* breathing; exhalation; taking breath, pause

respīrātus, -ūs *m* inhaling

respīrō, -āre, -āvī, -ātum *vt, vi* to breathe, blow back; to breathe again, revive; *(things)* to abate

resplendeō, -ēre *vi* to flash back, shine brightly

respondeō, -ondēre, -ondī, -ōnsum *vt* to answer, reply; *(lawyer, priest, oracle)* to advise, give a response; *(law court)* to appear; *(pledge)* to promise in return; *(things)* to correspond, agree, match; **pār parī respondēre** return like for like, give tit for tat

respōnsiō, -ōnis *f* answering; refutation

respōnsitō, -āre *vi* to give advice

respōnsō, -āre *vt, vi* to answer back; to defy

respōnsor, -ōris *m* answerer

respōnsum, -ī *nt* answer, reply; response, opinion, oracle

rēspūblica, reīpūblicae *f* public affairs, politics, the State, republic

respuō, -ere, -ī *vt* to spit out, eject; to reject, refuse

restagnō, -āre *vi* to overflow; to be flooded

restaurō, -āre *vt* to repair, rebuild

resticula, -ae *f* rope, cord

restinctiō, -ōnis *f* quenching

restinctus *ppp of* **restinguō**

restinguō, -guere, -xī, -ctum *vt* to extinguish, quench; *(fig)* to destroy

restiō, -ōnis *m* rope maker

restipulātiō, -ōnis *f* counterobligation

restipulor, -ārī *vt* to stipulate in return

restis, -is *f* rope

restitī *perf of* **resistō**; **restō**

restitō, -āre *vi* to stay behind, hesitate

restituō, -uere, -uī, -ūtum *vt* to replace, restore; to rebuild, renew; to give back, return; (*to a condition*) to reinstate; (*decision*) to quash, reverse; (*character*) to reform

restitūtiō, -ōnis *f* restoration; reinstating

restitūtor, -ōris *m* restorer

restitūtus *ppp of* **restituō**

restō, -āre, -itī *vi* to stand firm; to resist; to remain, be left; to be in store (for); **quod restat** for the future

restrictē *adv* sparingly; strictly

restrictus *ppp of* **restringō** ◆ *adj* tight, short; niggardly; severe

restringō, -ngere, -nxī, -ctum *vt* to draw back tightly, bind fast; (*teeth*) to bare; (*fig*) to check

resultō, -āre *vi* to rebound; to re-echo

resūmō, -ere, -psī, -ptum *vt* to take up again, get back, resume

resupīnō, -āre *vt* to turn back, throw on one's back

resupīnus *adj* lying back, face upwards

resurgō, -gere, -rēxī, -rēctum *vi* to rise again, revive

resuscitō, -āre *vt* to revive

retardātiō, -ōnis *f* hindering

retardō, -āre, -āvī, -ātum *vt* to retard, detain, check

rēte, -is *nt* net; (*fig*) snare

retēctus *ppp of* **retegō**

retegō, -egere, -ēxī, -ēctum *vt* to uncover, open; to reveal

retemptō, -āre *vt* to try again

retendō, -endere, -endī, -entum *and* **-ēnsum** *vt* to slacken, relax

retēnsus *ppp of* **retendō**

retentiō, -ōnis *f* holding back

retentō¹ *etc see* **retemptō**

retentō², -āre *vt* to keep back, hold fast

retentus *ppp of* **retendō**; **retineō**

retēxī *perf of* **retegō**

retexō, -ere, -uī, -tum *vt* to unravel; (*fig*) to break up, cancel; to renew

rētiārius, -ī *and* **-iī** *m* net-fighter

reticentia, -ae *f* saying nothing; pause

reticeō, -ēre, -uī *vi* to be silent, say nothing ◆ *vt* to keep secret

rēticulum, -ī *nt* small net, hairnet; network bag

retināculum, -ī *nt* tether, hawser

retinēns, -entis *pres p of* **retineō** ◆ *adj* tenacious, observant

retinentia, -ae *f* memory

retineō, -inēre, -inuī, -entum *vt* to hold back, detain, restrain; to keep, retain, preserve

retinniō, -īre *vi* to ring

retonō, -āre *vi* to thunder in answer

retorqueō, -quēre, -sī, -tum *vt* to turn back, twist

retorridus *adj* dried up, wizened

retortus *ppp of* **retorqueō**

retractātiō, -ōnis *f* hesitation

retractō, -āre, -āvī, -ātum *vt* to rehandle, take up again; to reconsider, revise; to withdraw ◆ *vi* to draw back, hesitate

retractus *ppp of* **retrahō** ◆ *adj* remote

retrahō, -here, -xī, -ctum *vt* to draw back, drag back; to withdraw, remove

retrectō *etc see* **retractō**

retribuō, -uere, -uī, -ūtum *vt* to restore, repay

retrō *adv* back, backwards, behind; (*time*) back, past

retrōrsum *adv* backwards, behind; in reverse order

retrūdō, -dere, -sum *vt* to push back; to withdraw

rettulī *perf of* **referō**

retundō, -undere, -udī *and* **-tudī, -ūsum** *and* **-ūnsum** *vt* to blunt; (*fig*) to check, weaken

retūnsus, retūsus *ppp of* **retundō** ◆ *adj* blunt, dull

reus, -ī *m* the accused, defendant; guarantor, debtor, one responsible; culprit, criminal; **vōtī ~** one who has had a prayer granted

revalēscō, -ēscere, -uī *vi* to recover

revehō, -here, -xī, -ctum *vt* to carry back, bring back; (*pass*) to ride, drive, sail back

revellō, -ellere, -ellī, -ulsum (-olsum) *vt* to pull out, tear off; to remove

revēlō, -āre *vt* to unveil, uncover

reveniō, -enīre, -ēnī, -entum *vi* to come back, return

rēvērā *adv* in fact, actually

reverendus *adj* venerable, awe-inspiring

reverēns, -entis *pres p of* **revereor** ◆ *adj* respectful, reverent

reverenter *adv* respectfully

reverentia, -ae *f* respect, reverence, awe

revereor, -ērī, -itus *vt* to stand in awe of; to respect, revere

reversiō, revorsiō, -ōnis *f* turning back; recurrence

reversus *ppa of* **revertor**

revertō, -ere, -ī, revertor, -tī, -sus *vi* to turn back, return; to revert

revexī *perf of* **revehō**

revictus *ppp of* **revincō**

revinciō, -cīre, -xī, -ctum *vt* to tie back, bind fast

revincō, -incere, -īcī, -ictum *vt* to conquer, repress; (*words*) to refute, convict

revinctus *ppp of* **revinciō**

revirēscō, -ēscere, -uī *vi* to grow green again; to be rejuvenated; to grow strong again, flourish again

revīsō, -ere *vt, vi* to come back to, revisit

revīvēscō, -vīscō, -vīscere, -xī *vi* to come to life again, revive

revocābilis *adj* revocable

revocāmen, -inis *nt* recall

revocātiō, -ōnis *f* recalling; (*word*) withdrawing

revocō, -āre, -āvī, -ātum *vt* to call back, recall; (*action*) to revoke; (*former state*) to recover, regain; (*growth*) to check; (*guest*) to invite in return; (*judgment*) to apply, refer; (*LAW*) to summon again; (*performer*) to encore; (*troops*) to withdraw

revolō, -āre *vi* to fly back

revolsus *etc see* **revulsus**

revolūbilis *adj* that may be rolled back

revolūtus *ppp of* **revolvō**

revolvō, -vere, -vī, -ūtum *vt* to roll back, unroll, unwind; (*speech*) to relate, repeat; (*thought*) to think over; (*writing*) to read over; (*pass*) to revolve, return, come round

revomō, -ere, -uī *vt* to disgorge

revor- *etc see* **rever-**

revulsus *ppp of* **revellō**

rēx, rēgis *m* king; tyrant, despot; leader; patron, rich man

rēxī *perf of* **regō**

Rhadamanthus, -ī *m* judge in the lower world

Rhaeti *etc see* **Raetī**

Rhamnūs, -ūntis *f* town in Attica (famous for its statue of Nemesis)

Rhamnūsis, -ūsidis *f* Nemesis

Rhamnūsius *adj see* **Rhamnūs**

rhapsōdia, -ae *f* a book of Homer

Rhea, -ae *f* Cybele

Rhea Silvia, Rheae Silviae *f* mother of Romulus and Remus

Rhēgium *etc see* **Rēgium**

Rhēnānus *adj* Rhenish

rhēnō *etc see* **rēnō**

Rhēnus, -ī *m* Rhine

Rhēsus, -ī *m* Thracian king (killed at Troy)

rhētor, -oris *m* teacher of rhetoric; orator

rhētorica, -ae, rhētoricē, -ēs *f* art of oratory, rhetoric

rhētoricē *adv* rhetorically, in an oratorical manner

rhētoricī, -ōrum *mpl* teachers of rhetoric

rhētoricus *adj* rhetorical, on rhetoric

rhīnocerōs, -ōtis *m* rhinoceros

rhō *nt indecl* (Greek letter) rho

Rhodanus, -ī *m* Rhone

Rhodius *adj see* **Rhodos**

Rhodopē, -ēs *f* mountain range in Thrace

Rhodopēius *adj* Thracian

Rhodos, Rhodus, -ī *f* (island) of Rhodes

Rhoetēum, -ī *nt* promontory on the Dardanelles (near Troy)

Rhoetēus *adj* Trojan

rhombus, -ī *m* magician's circle; (*fish*) turbot

rhomphaea, -ae *f* long barbarian javelin

rhythmicus, -ī *m* teacher of prose rhythm

rhythmos, rhythmus, -i *m* rhythm, symmetry

rīca, -ae *f* sacrificial veil

rīcinium, -ī *and* **-iī** *nt* small cloak with hood

rictum, -ī *nt*, **rictus, -ūs** *m* open mouth, gaping jaws

rīdeō, -dēre, -sī, -sum *vi* to laugh, smile ♦ *vt* to laugh at, smile at; to ridicule

rīdibundus *adj* laughing

rīdiculāria, -ium *ntpl* jokes

rīdiculē *adv* jokingly; absurdly

rīdiculus *adj* amusing, funny; ridiculous, silly ♦ *m* jester ♦ *nt* joke

rigēns, -entis *pres p of* **rigeō** ♦ *adj* stiff, rigid, frozen

rigeō, -ēre *vi* to be stiff

rigēscō, -ēscere, -uī *vi* to stiffen, harden; to bristle

rigidē *adv* rigorously

rigidus *adj* stiff, rigid, hard; (*fig*) hardy, strict, inflexible

rigō, -āre *vt* to water, moisten, bedew; to convey (*water*)

rigor, -ōris *m* stiffness, hardness; numbness, cold; strictness, severity

riguī *perf of* **rigēscō**

riguus *adj* irrigating; watered

rīma, -ae *f* crack, chink

rīmor, -ārī, -ātus *vt* to tear open; to search for, probe, examine; to find out

rīmōsus *adj* cracked, leaky

ringor, -ī *vi* to snarl

rīpa, -ae *f* river bank; shore

Rīphaeī, -ōrum *mpl* mountain range in N. Scythia

Rīphaeus *adj see* **Rīphaeī**

rīpula, -ae *f* riverbank

riscus, -ī *m* trunk, chest

rīsī *perf of* **rīdeō**

rīsor, -ōris *m* scoffer

rīsus, -ūs *m* laughter, laugh; laughing stock

rīte *adv* with the proper formality or ritual; duly, properly, rightly; in the usual manner; fortunately

rītus, -ūs *m* ritual, ceremony; custom, usage; **rītū** after the manner of

rīvālis, -is *m* rival in love

rīvālitās, -ātis *f* rivalry in love

rīvulus, -ī *m* brook

rīvus, -ī *m* stream, brook; **ē rīvō flūmina māgna facere** make a mountain of a molehill

rixa, -ae *f* quarrel, brawl, fight

rixor, -ārī, -ātus *vi* to quarrel, brawl, squabble

rōbīginōsus *adj* rusty

rōbīgō, -inis *f* rust; blight, mould, mildew

rōboreus *adj* of oak

rōborō, -āre *vt* to strengthen, invigorate

rōbur, -oris *nt* oak; hard wood; prison, dungeon (*at Rome*); (*fig*) strength, hardness, vigour; best part, élite, flower

rōbustus *adj* of oak; strong, hard; robust, mature

rōdō, -dere, -sī, -sum *vt* to gnaw; (*rust*) to corrode; (*words*) to slander

rogālis *adj* of a pyre

rogātiō, -ōnis *f* proposal, motion, bill; request; (RHET) question

rogātiuncula, -ae *f* unimportant bill; question

rogātor, -ōris *m* proposer; polling clerk

rogātus, -ūs *m* request

rogitō, -āre *vt* to ask for, inquire eagerly

rogō, -āre, -āvī, -ātum *vt* to ask, ask for; (*bill*) to propose, move; (*candidate*) to put up for election; **lēgem rogāre, populum rogāre** introduce a bill; **magistrātum populum rogāre** nominate for election to an office; **mīlitēs sacrāmentō rogāre** administer the oath to the troops; **mālō emere quam rogāre** I'd rather buy it than borrow it

rogus, -ī *m* funeral pyre

Rōma, -ae *f* Rome

Rōmānus *adj* Roman

Rōmuleus, Rōmulus *adj* of Romulus; Roman

Rōmulidae, -idārum *mpl* the Romans

Rōmulus, -ī *m founder and first king of Rome*

rōrāriī, -ōrum *mpl* skirmishers

rōridus *adj* dewy

rōrifer, -ī *adj* dew-bringing

rōrō, -āre *vi* to distil dew; to drip, trickle ♦ *vt* to bedew, wet

rōs, rōris *m* dew; moisture, water; (*plant*) rosemary; **rōs marīnus** rosemary

rosa, -ae *f* rose; rose bush

rosāria, -ōrum *ntpl* rose garden

rōscidus *adj* dewy; wet

Roscius¹, -ī *m*: L. ~ Othō *tribune in 67 BC, whose law reserved theatre seats for the equites*; Q. ~ Gallus *famous actor defended by Cicero*; Sex. ~ *of Ameria, defended by Cicero*

Roscius², -iānus *adj see* **Roscius¹**

rosētum, -ī *nt* rosebed

roseus *adj* rosy; of roses

rōsī *perf of* **rōdō**

rōstrātus *adj* beaked, curved; **columna rōstrāta** *column commemorating a naval victory*

rōstrum, -ī *nt* (*bird*) beak, bill; (*animal*) snout, muzzle; (*ship*) beak, end of prow; (*pl*) orators' platform in the Forum

rōsus *ppp of* **rōdō**

rota, -ae *f* wheel; potter's wheel, torture wheel; car, disc

rotō, -āre, -āvī, -ātum *vt* to turn, whirl, roll; (*pass*) to revolve

rotundē *adv* elegantly

rotundō, -āre *vt* to round off

rotundus *adj* round, circular, spherical; (*style*) well-turned, smooth

rubefaciō, -facere, -fēcī, -factum *vt* to redden

rubēns, -entis *pres p of* **rubeō** ♦ *adj* red; blushing

rubeō, -ēre *vi* to be red; to blush

ruber, -rī *adj* red; **mare rubrum** Red Sea; Persian Gulf; **ōceanus** ~ Indian Ocean; **Saxa rubra** *stone quarries between Rome and Veii*

rubēscō, -ēscere, -uī *vi* to redden, blush

rubēta¹, -ae *f* toad

rubēta², -ōrum *ntpl* bramble bushes

rubeus *adj* of bramble

Rubicō, -ōnis *m stream marking the frontier between Italy and Gaul*

rubicundulus *adj* reddish

rubicundus *adj* red, ruddy

rŭbīg- *etc see* **rōbīg-**

rubor, -ōris *m* redness; blush; bashfulness; shame

rubrīca, -ae *f* red earth, red ochre

rubuī *perf of* **rubēscō**

rubus, -ī *m* bramble bush; bramble, blackberry

ructō, -āre, ructor, -ārī *vt, vi* to belch

ructus, -us *m* belching

rudēns, -entis *pres p of* **rudō** ♦ *m* rope; (*pl*) rigging

Rudiae, -iārum *fpl town in E. Italy* (*birthplace of Ennius*)

rudiārius, -ī and -iī *m* retired gladiator

rudīmentum, -ī *nt* first attempt, beginning

Rudīnus *adj see* **Rudiae**

rudis¹ *adj* unwrought, unworked, raw; coarse, rough, badly-made; (*age*) new, young; (*person*) uncultured, unskilled, clumsy; ignorant (of), inexperienced (in)

rudis², -is *f* stick, rod; foil (*for fighting practice*); (*fig*) discharge

rudō, -ere, -īvī, -ītum *vi* to roar, bellow, bray; to creak

rŭdus¹, -eris *nt* rubble, rubbish; piece of copper

rŭdus², -eris *nt* copper coin

Rŭfulī, -ōrum *mpl* military tribunes (*chosen by the general*)

rŭfulus *adj* red-headed

rŭfus *adj* red, red-haired

rŭga, -ae *f* wrinkle, crease

rŭgō, -āre *vi* to become creased

rŭgōsus *adj* wrinkled, shrivelled, corrugated

ruī *perf of* **ruō**

ruīna, -ae *f* fall, downfall; collapse, falling in; debris, ruins; destruction, disaster, ruin (*fig*)

ruīnōsus *adj* collapsing; ruined

rumex, -icis *f* sorrel

rŭmificō, -āre *vt* to report

Rūmīna, -ae *f goddess of nursing mothers*; **fīcus Rūmīnālis** *the fig tree of Romulus and Remus* (*under which the she-wolf suckled them*)

rŭminātiō, -ōnis *f* chewing the cud; (*fig*) ruminating

rŭminō, -āre *vt, vi* to chew the cud

rūmor, -ōris *m* noise, cheering; rumour, hearsay; public opinion; reputation

rumpia *etc see* **rhomphaea**

rumpō, -ere, rūpī, ruptum *vt* to break, burst; tear; to break down, burst through; (*activity*) to interrupt; (*agreement*) to violate, annul; (*delay*) to put an end to; (*voice*) to give vent to; (*way*) to force through

rŭmusculī, -ōrum *mpl* gossip

rŭna, -ae *f* dart

runcō, -āre *vt* to weed

ruō, -ere, -ī, -tum *vi* to fall down, tumble; to rush, run, hurry; to come to ruin ♦ *vt* to dash down, hurl to the ground; to throw up, turn up

rŭpēs, -is *f* rock, cliff

rūpī *perf of* **rumpō**

ruptor, -ōris *m* violator

ruptus *ppp of* **rumpō**

rūricola, -ae *adj* rural, country- (*in cpds*)

rūrigena, -ae *m* countryman

rūrsus, rūrsum, rūsum *adv* back, backwards; on the contrary, in return; again

rūs, rūris *nt* the country, countryside; estate, farm; **rūs** to the country; **rūrī** in the country; **rūre** from the country

ruscum, -ī *nt* butcher's-broom

russus *adj* red

rūsticānus *adj* country- (*in cpds*), rustic
rūsticātiō, -ōnis *f* country life
rūsticē *adv* in a countrified manner, awkwardly
rūsticitās, -ātis *f* country manners, rusticity
rūsticor, -ārī *vi* to live in the country
rūsticulus, -ī *m* yokel
rūsticus *adj* country- (*in cpds*), rural, rough, clownish ♦ *m* countryman
rūsum *see* **rūrsus**
rūta, -ae *f* (*herb*) rue; (*fig*) unpleasantness

ruta caesa *ntpl* minerals and timber on an estate
rutilō, -āre *vt* to colour red ♦ *vi* to glow red
rutilus *adj* red, auburn
rutrum, -ī *nt* spade, shovel, trowel
rūtula, -ae *f* little piece of rue
Rutulī, -ōrum *mpl* ancient Latin people
Rutulus *adj* Rutulian
Rutupiae, -iārum *fpl* seaport in Kent (*now* Richborough)
Rutupīnus *adj see* **Rutupiae**
rutus *ppp of* **ruō**

Ss

Saba, -ae *f town in Arabia Felix*
Sabaeus *adj see* **Saba**
Sabāzia, -iōrum *ntpl festival of Bacchus*
Sabāzius, -ī *m* Bacchus
sabbata, -ōrum *ntpl* Sabbath, Jewish holiday
Sabellus¹, -ī *m* Sabine, Samnite
Sabellus², -icus *adj see* **Sabellus¹**
Sabīnī, -ōrum *mpl* Sabines (*a people of central Italy*)
Sabīnus *adj* Sabine ♦ *f* Sabine woman ♦ *nt*
  Sabine estate; Sabine wine; **herba Sabīna**
  savin (*a kind of juniper*)
Sabrīna, -ae *f* (*river*) Severn
saburra, -ae *f* sand, ballast
Sacae, -ārum *mpl tribe of Scythians*
saccipērium, -ī *and* **-iī** *nt* purse-pocket
saccō, -āre *vt* to strain, filter
sacculus, -ī *m* little bag, purse
saccus, -ī *m* bag, purse, wallet
sacellum, -ī *nt* chapel
sacer, -rī *adj* sacred, holy; devoted for sacrifice,
  forfeited; accursed, criminal, infamous; **Mōns**
  ~ *hill to which the Roman plebs seceded;* **Via sacra**
  street from the Forum to the Capitol
sacerdōs, -ōtis *m/f* priest, priestess
sacerdōtium, -ī *and* **-iī** *nt* priesthood
sacrāmentum, -ī *nt* deposit made by parties to a
  lawsuit; civil lawsuit, dispute; (MIL) oath of
  allegiance, engagement
sacrārium, -ī *and* **-iī** *nt* shrine, chapel
sacrātus *adj* holy, hallowed; **sacrāta lēx** *a law*
  whose violation was punished by devotion to the infernal
  gods
sacricola, -ae *m/f* sacrificing priest or priestess
sacrifer, -ī *adj* carrying holy things
sacrificālis *adj* sacrificial
sacrificātiō, -ōnis *f* sacrificing
sacrificium, -ī *and* **-iī** *nt* sacrifice
sacrificō, -āre *vt, vi* to sacrifice
sacrificulus, -ī *m* sacrificing priest; **rēx ~** high
  priest
sacrificus *adj* sacrificial
sacrilēgium, -ī *and* **-iī** *nt* sacrilege
sacrilegus *adj* sacrilegious; profane, wicked ♦ *m*
  temple-robber
sacrō, -āre, -āvī, -ātum *vt* to consecrate; to
  doom, curse; to devote, dedicate; to make
  inviolable; (*poetry*) to immortalize
sacrōsanctus *adj* inviolable, sacrosanct
sacruficō *etc see* **sacrificō**
sacrum, -rī *nt* holy thing, sacred vessel;
  shrine; offering, victim; rite; (*pl*) sacrifice,

worship, religion; **sacra facere** sacrifice;
  inter ~ saxumque with one's back to the wall;
  hērēditās sine sacrīs *a gift with no awkward*
  obligations
saeclum *etc see* **saeculum**
saeculāris *adj* centenary; (ECCL) secular, pagan
saeculum, -ī *nt* generation, lifetime, age; the
  age, the times; century; **in saecula** (ECCL) for
  ever
saepe *adv* often, frequently
saepe numerō *adv* very often
saepēs, -is *f* hedge, fence
saepīmentum, -ī *nt* enclosure
saepiō, -īre, -sī, -tum *vt* to hedge round, fence
  in, enclose; (*fig*) to shelter, protect
saeptus *ppp of* **saepiō** ♦ *nt* fence, wall; stake,
  pale; (*sheep*) fold; (*Rome*) voting area in the Campus
  Martius
saeta, -ae *f* hair, bristle
saetiger, -ī *adj* bristly
saetōsus *adj* bristly, hairy
saevē, saeviter *adv* fiercely, cruelly
saevidicus *adj* furious
saeviō, -īre, -iī, -ītum *vi* to rage, rave
saevitia, -ae *f* rage; ferocity, cruelty
saevus *adj* raging, fierce; cruel, barbarous
sāga, -ae *f* fortune teller
sagācitās, -ātis *f* (*dogs*) keen scent; (*mind*)
  shrewdness
sagāciter *adv* keenly; shrewdly
sagātus *adj* wearing a soldier's cloak
sagāx, -ācis *adj* (*senses*) keen, keen-scented;
  (*mind*) quick, shrewd
sagīna, -ae *f* stuffing, fattening; food, rich food;
  fatted animal
sagīnō, -āre *vt* to cram, fatten; to feed, feast
sāgiō, -īre *vi* to perceive keenly
sagitta, -ae *f* arrow
sagittārius, -ī *and* **-iī** *m* archer
sagittifer, -ī *adj* armed with arrows
sagmen, -inis *nt* tuft of sacred herbs (*used as a*
  mark of inviolability)
sagulum, -ī *nt* short military cloak
sagum, -ī *nt* military cloak; woollen mantle
Saguntīnus *adj see* **Saguntum**
Saguntum, -ī *nt*, **Saguntus, -ī**, **Saguntos, -ī** *f*
  town in E. Spain
sāgus *adj* prophetic
sāl, salis *m* salt; brine, sea; (*fig*) shrewdness, wit,
  humour, witticism; good taste
salacō, -ōnis *m* swaggerer

Salamīnius *adj see* **Salamīs**
Salamīs, -īnis *f Greek island near Athens; town in Cyprus*
salapūtium, -ī *and* **-iī** *nt* manikin
salārius *adj* salt- (*in cpds*) ♦ *nt* allowance, salary
salāx, -ācis *adj* lustful, salacious
salebra, -ae *f* roughness, rut
Saliāris *adj* of the Salii; sumptuous
salictum, -ī *nt* willow plantation
salientēs, -ium *fpl* springs
salignus *adj* of willow
Saliī, -ōrum *mpl* priests of Mars
salillum, -ī *nt* little saltcellar
salīnae, -ārum *fpl* saltworks
salīnum, -ī *nt* saltcellar
saliō, -īre, -uī, -tum *vi* to leap, spring; to throb
saliunca, -ae *f* Celtic nard
salīva, -ae *f* saliva, spittle; taste
salix, -icis *f* willow
Sallustiānus *adj see* **Sallustius**
Sallustius, -ī *m* Sallust (*Roman historian*); his wealthy grand-nephew
Salmōneus, -eos *m* son of Aeolus (*punished in Tartarus for imitating lightning*)
Salmōnis, -idis *f* his daughter Tyro
salsāmentum, -ī *nt* brine, pickle; salted fish
salsē *adv* wittily
salsus *adj* salted; salt, briny; (*fig*) witty
saltātiō, -ōnis *f* dancing, dance
saltātor, -ōris *m* dancer
saltātōrius *adj* dancing- (*in cpds*)
saltātrīx, -īcis *f* dancer
saltātus, -ūs *m* dance
saltem *adv* at least, at all events; **nōn ~** not even
saltō, -āre *vt, vi* to dance
saltuōsus *adj* wooded
saltus¹, -ūs *m* leap, bound
saltus², -ūs *m* woodland pasture, glade; pass, ravine
salūber *adj see* **salūbris**
salūbris *adj* health-giving, wholesome; healthy, sound
salūbritās, -ātis *f* healthiness; health
salūbriter *adv* wholesomely; beneficially
saluī *perf of* **saliō**
salum, -ī *nt* sea, high sea
salūs, -ūtis *f* health; welfare, life; safety; good wish, greeting; **salūtem dīcere** greet; bid farewell
salūtāris *adj* wholesome, healthy; beneficial; **~ littera** letter A (*for* **absolvō** = *acquittal*)
salūtāriter *adv* beneficially
salūtātiō, -ōnis *f* greeting; formal morning visit, levee
salūtātor, -ōris *m* morning caller; male courtier
salūtātrīx, -rīcis *f* morning caller; female courtier
salūtifer, -ī *adj* health-giving
salūtigerulus *adj* carrying greetings
salūtō, -āre, -āvī, -ātum *vt* to greet, salute, wish well; to call on, pay respects to
salvē¹ *adv* well, in good health; all right
salvē² *impv of* **salveō**

salveō, -ēre *vi* to be well, be in good health; **salvē, salvētō, salvēte** hail!, good day!, goodbye!; **salvēre iubeō** I bid good day
salvus, salvos *adj* safe, alive, intact, well; without violating; all right; **~ sīs** good day to you!; **salva rēs est** all is well; **salvā lēge** without breaking the law
Samaous *adj see* **Samē**
Samarobrīva, -ae *f Belgian town (now Amiens)*
sambūca, -ae *f* harp
sambūcistria, -ae *f* harpist
Samē, -ēs *f old name of the Greek island Cephalonia*
Samius *adj* Samian ♦ *ntpl* Samian pottery
Samnīs, -ītis *adj* Samnite
Samnium, -ī *and* **-iī** *nt* district of central Italy
Samos, Samus, -ī *f Aegean island off Asia Minor (famous for its pottery and as the birthplace of Pythagoras)*
Samothrāces, -um *mpl* Samothracians
Samothrācia, -iae, Samothrāca, -ae *f* Samothrace (*island in the N. Aegean*)
Samothrācius *adj see* **Samothrācia**
sānābilis *adj* curable
sānātiō, -ōnis *f* healing
sanciō, -īre, -xī, -ctum *vt* to make sacred or inviolable; to ordain, ratify; to enact a punishment against
sanctimōnia, -ae *f* sanctity; chastity
sanctiō, -ōnis *f* decree, penalty for violating a law
sanctitās, -ātis *f* sacredness; integrity, chastity
sanctitūdō, -inis *f* sacredness
sanctō *adv* solemnly, religiously
sanctor, -ōris *m* enacter
sanctus *ppp of* **sanciō** ♦ *adj* sacred, inviolable; holy, venerable; pious, virtuous, chaste
sandaligerula, -ae *f* sandalbearer
sandalium, -ī *and* **-iī** *nt* sandal, slipper
sandapila, -ae *f* common bier
sandyx, -ycis *f* scarlet
sānē *adv* sensibly; (*intensive*) very, doubtless; (*ironical*) to be sure, of course; (*concessive*) of course, indeed; (*in answer*) certainly, surely; (*with impv*) then, if you please; **~ quam** very much; **haud ~** not so very, not quite
sanguen *etc see* **sanguis**
sanguināns, -antis *adj* bloodthirsty
sanguinārius *adj* bloodthirsty
sanguineus *adj* bloody, of blood; blood-red
sanguinolentus *adj* bloody; blood-red; sanguinary
sanguis, -inis *m* blood, bloodshed; descent, family; offspring; (*fig*) strength, life; **sanguinem dare** shed one's blood; **sanguinem mittere** let blood
saniēs (*acc* **-em**, *abl* **-ē**) *f* diseased blood, matter; venom
sānitās, -ātis *f* (*body*) health, sound condition; (*mind*) sound sense, sanity; (*style*) correctness, purity
sanna, -ae *f* grimace, mocking
sanniō, -ōnis *m* clown
sānō, -āre, -āvī, -ātum *vt* to cure, heal; (*fig*) to remedy, relieve
Sanquālis avis *f* osprey

sānus *adj* (*body*) sound, healthy; (*mind*) sane, sensible; (*style*) correct; **male ~** mad, inspired; **sānun es?** are you in your senses?

sanxī *perf of* **sanciō**

sapa, -ae *f* new wine

sapiēns, -entis *pres p of* **sapiō** ♦ *adj* wise, discreet ♦ *m* wise man, philosopher; man of taste

sapienter *adv* wisely, sensibly

sapientia, -ae *f* wisdom, discernment; philosophy; knowledge

sapiō, -ere, -īvī *and* **-uī** *vi* to have a flavour or taste; to have sense, be wise ♦ *vt* to taste of, smell of, smack of; to understand

sapor, -ōris *m* taste, flavour; (*food*) delicacy; (*fig*) taste, refinement

Sapphicus *adj see* **Sapphō**

Sapphō, -ūs *f* famous Greek lyric poetess, native of Lesbos

sarcina, -ae *f* bundle, burden; (*MIL*) pack

sarcinārius *adj* baggage- (*in cpds*)

sarcinātor, -ōris *m* patcher

sarcinula, -ae *f* little pack

sarciō, -cīre, -sī, -tum *vt* to patch, mend, repair

sarcophagus, -ī *m* sepulchre

sarculum, -ī *nt* light hoe

Sardēs, Sardis, -ium *fpl* Sardis (*capital of Lydia*)

Sardiānus *adj see* **Sardēs**

Sardinia, -iniae *f* (*island of*) Sardinia

sardonyx, -chis *m* sardonyx

Sardus, Sardōus, Sardiniēnsis *adj see* **Sardinia**

sariō, -īre, -īvī *vt* to hoe, weed

sarīsa, -ae *f* Macedonian lance

sarīsophorus, -ī *m* Macedonian lancer

Sarmatae, -ārum *mpl* Sarmatians (*a people of S.E. Russia*)

Sarmaticus, -is *adj see* **Sarmatae**

sarmentum, -ī *nt* twigs, brushwood

Sarpēdōn, -onis *m* king of Lycia

Sarra, -ae *f* Tyre

sarrācum, -ī *nt* cart

Sarrānus *adj* Tyrian

sarriō *etc see* **sariō**

sarsī *perf of* **sarciō**

sartāgō, -inis *f* frying pan

sartor, -ōris *m* hoer, weeder

sartus *ppp of* **sarciō**

sat *etc see* **satis**

satagō, -ere *vi* to have one's hands full, be in trouble; to bustle about, fuss

satelles, -itis *m/f* attendant, follower; assistant, accomplice

satiās, -ātis *f* sufficiency; satiety

satietās, -ātis *f* sufficiency; satiety

satin, satine *see* **satisne**

satiō¹, -āre, -āvī, -ātum *vt* to satisfy, appease; to fill, saturate; to glut, cloy, disgust

satiō², -ōnis *f* sowing, planting; (*pl*) fields

satis, sat *adj* enough, sufficient ♦ *adv* enough, sufficiently; tolerably, fairly, quite; **~ accipiō** take sufficient bail; **~ agō, ~ agitō** have one's hands full, be harassed; **~ dō** offer sufficient bail; **~ faciō** satisfy; give satisfaction, make amends; (*creditor*) pay

satisdatiō, -ōnis *f* giving security

satisdō *see* **satis**

satisfaciō *see* **satis**

satisfactiō, -ōnis *f* amends, apology

satisne *adv* quite, really

satius *compar of* **satis**; better, preferable

sator, -ōris *m* sower, planter; father; promoter

satrapēs, -is *m* satrap (*Persian governor*)

satur, -ī *adj* filled, sated; (*fig*) rich

satura, -ae *f* mixed dish; medley; (*poem*) satire; **per saturam** confusingly

saturēia, -ōrum *ntpl* (*plant*) savory

saturitās, -ātis *f* repletion; fulness, plenty

Saturnālia, -ium *and* **-iōrum** *ntpl* festival of Saturn in December

Saturnia, -iae *f* Juno

Saturnīnus, -ī *m* revolutionary tribune in 103 and 100 B.C.

Saturnius *adj see* **Saturnus**

Saturnus, -ī *m* Saturn (*god of sowing, ruler of the Golden Age*); (the planet) Saturn

saturō, -āre, -āvī, -ātum *vt* to fill, glut, satisfy; to disgust

satus¹ *ppp of* **serō¹** ♦ *m* son ♦ *f* daughter ♦ *ntpl* crops

satus², -ūs *m* sowing, planting; begetting

satyriscus, -ī *m* little satyr

satyrus, -ī *m* satyr

sauciātiō, -ōnis *f* wounding

sauciō, -āre *vt* to wound, hurt

saucius *adj* wounded, hurt; ill, stricken

Sauromatae *etc see* **Sarmatae**

sāviātiō, -ōnis *f* kissing

sāviolum, -ī *nt* sweet kiss

sāvior, -ārī *vt* to kiss

sāvium, -ī *and* **-iī** *nt* kiss

saxātilis *adj* rock- (*in cpds*)

saxētum, -ī *nt* rocky place

saxeus *adj* of rock, rocky

saxificus *adj* petrifying

saxōsus *adj* rocky, stony

saxulum, -ī *nt* small rock

saxum, -ī *nt* rock, boulder; the Tarpeian Rock

scaber, -rī *adj* rough, scurfy; mangy, itchy

scabiēs (*acc* **-em**, *abl* **-ē**) *f* roughness; scurf; mange, itch

scabillum, -ī *nt* stool; a castanet played with the foot

scabō, -ere, scābī *vt* to scratch

Scaea porta, Scaeae portae *f* the west gate of Troy

scaena, -ae *f* stage, stage setting; (*fig*) limelight, public life; outward appearance, pretext

scaenālis *adj* theatrical

scaenicus *adj* stage- (*in cpds*), theatrical ♦ *m* actor

Scaevola, -ae *m* early Roman who burned his hand off before Porsenna; famous jurist of Cicero's day

scaevus *adj* on the left; perverse ♦ *f* omen

scālae, -ārum *fpl* steps, ladder, stairs

scalmus, -ī *m* tholepin

scalpellum, -ī *nt* scalpel, lancet

scalpō, -ere, -sī, -tum *vt* to carve, engrave; to scratch

scalprum, -ī *nt* knife, penknife; chisel

scalpurriō, -īre *vi* to scratch

Scamander, -rī *m* river of Troy (*also called Xanthus*)

scammōnea, -ae *f* (*plant*) scammony**

scamnum, -ī *nt* bench, stool; throne

scandō, -ere *vt, vi* to climb, mount

scapha, -ae *f* boat, skiff

scaphium, -ī *and* **-iī** *nt* a boat-shaped cup

scapulae, -ārum *fpl* shoulder blades; shoulders

scāpus, -ī *m* shaft; (*loom*) yarnbeam

scarus, -ī *m* (*fish*) scar

scatebra, -ae *f* gushing water

scateō, -ēre, scatō, -ere *vi* to bubble up, gush out; (*fig*) to abound, swarm

scatūrīginēs, -um *fpl* springs

scatūriō, -īre *vi* to gush out; (*fig*) to be full of

scaurus *adj* large-ankled

scelerātē *adv* wickedly

scelerātus *adj* desecrated; wicked, infamous, accursed; pernicious

scelerō, -āre *vt* to desecrate

scelerōsus *adj* vicious, accursed

scelestē *adv* wickedly

scelestus *adj* wicked, villainous, accursed; unlucky

scelus, -eris *nt* wickedness, crime, sin; (*person*) scoundrel; (*event*) calamity

scēn- *etc see* **scaen-**

scēptrifer, -ī *adj* sceptered

scēptrum, -ī *nt* staff, sceptre; kingship, power

scēptūchus, -ī *m* sceptre-bearer

scheda *etc see* **scida**

schēma, -ae *f* form, figure, style

Schoenēis, -ēidis *f* Atalanta

Schoenēius *adj see* **Schoenēis**

Schoeneus, -eī *m* father of Atalanta

schoenobatēs, -ae *m* rope dancer

schola, -ae *f* learned discussion, dissertation; school; sect, followers

scholasticus *adj* of a school ♦ *m* rhetorician

scida, -ae *f* sheet of paper

sciēns, -entis *pres p of* **sciō** ♦ *adj* knowing, purposely; versed in, acquainted with

scienter *adv* expertly

scientia, -ae *f* knowledge, skill

scīlicet *adv* evidently, of course; (*concessive*) no doubt; (*ironical*) I suppose, of course

scilla *etc see* **squilla**

scindō, -ndere, -dī, -ssum *vt* to cut open, tear apart, split, break down; to divide, part

scintilla, -ae *f* spark

scintillō, -āre *vi* to sparkle

scintillula, -ae *f* little spark

sciō, -īre, -īvī, -ītum *vt* to know; to have skill in; (*with inf*) to know how to; **quod sciam** as far as I know; **scītō** you may be sure

Scīpiadēs, -ae *m* Scipio

scīpiō, -ōnis *m* staff

Scīpiō, -ōnis *m* famous Roman family name (*esp the conqueror of Hannibal Africanus*); Aemilianus (*destroyer of Carthage and patron of literature*)

scirpeus *adj* rush (*in cpds*) ♦ *f* wickerwork frame

scirpiculus, -ī *m* rush basket

scirpus, -ī *m* bulrush

scīscitor, -ārī, -ātus, scīscitō, -āre *vt* to inquire; to question

scīscō, -scere, -vī, -tum *vt* to inquire, learn; (*POL*) to approve, decree, appoint

scissus *ppp of* **scindō** ♦ *adj* split; (*voice*) harsh

scītāmenta, -ōrum *ntpl* dainties

scītē *adv* cleverly, tastefully

scītor, -ārī, -ātus *vt, vi* to inquire; to consult

scītulus *adj* neat, smart

scītum, -ī *nt* decree, statute

scītus¹ *ppp of* **sciō; scīscō** ♦ *adj* clever, shrewd, skilled; (*words*) sensible, witty; (*appearance*) fine, smart

scītus², -ūs *m* decree

sciūrus, -ī *m* squirrel

scīvī *perf of* **sciō; scīscō**

scobis, -is *f* sawdust, filings

scomber, -rī *m* mackerel

scōpae, -ārum *fpl* broom

Scopās, -ae *m* famous Greek sculptor

scopulōsus *adj* rocky

scopulus, -ī *m* rock, crag, promontory; (*fig*) danger

scorpiō, -ōnis, scorpius, -ī, scorpios, -ī *m* scorpion; (MIL) a kind of catapult

scortātor, -ōris *m* fornicator

scorteus *adj* of leather

scortor, -ārī *vi* to associate with harlots

scortum, -ī *nt* harlot, prostitute

screātor, -ōris *m* one who clears his throat noisily

screātus, -ūs *m* clearing the throat

scrība, -ae *m* clerk, writer

scrībō, -bere, -psī, -ptum *vt* to write, draw; to write down, describe; (*document*) to draw up; (LAW) to designate; (MIL) to enlist

scrīnium, -ī *and* **-iī** *nt* book box, lettercase

scrīptiō, -ōnis *f* writing; composition; text

scrīptitō, -āre, -āvī, -ātum *vt* to write regularly, compose

scrīptor, -ōris *m* writer, author; secretary; **rērum ~** historian

scrīptula, -ōrum *ntpl* lines of a squared board

scrīptum, -ī *nt* writing, book, work; (LAW) ordinance; **duodecim scrīpta** Twelve Lines (*a game played on a squared board*)

scrīptūra, -ae *f* writing; composition; document; (POL) tax on public pastures; (*will*) provision

scrīptus¹ *ppp of* **scrībō**

scrīptus², -ūs *m* clerkship

scrīpulum, -ī *nt* small weight, scruple

scrobis, -is *f* ditch, trench; grave

scrōfa, -ae *f* breeding sow

scrōfipāscus, -ī *m* pig breeder

scrūpeus *adj* stony, rough

scrūpōsus *adj* rocky, jagged

scrūpulōsus *adj* stony, rough; (*fig*) precise

scrūpulum *etc see* **scrīpulum**

scrūpulus, -ī *m* small sharp stone; (*fig*) uneasiness, doubt, scruple

scrūpus, -ī *m* sharp stone; (*fig*) uneasiness

scrūta, -ōrum *ntpl* trash

scrūtor, -ārī, -ātus *vt* to search, probe into, examine, to find out

sculpō, -ere, -sī, -tum *vt* to carve, engrave

sculpōneae, -ārum *fpl* clogs

sculptilis *adj* carved

sculptor, -ōris *m* sculptor
sculptus *ppp of* **sculpō**
scurra, -ae *m* jester; dandy
scurrīlis *adj* jeering
scurrīlitās, -ātis *f* scurrility
scurror, -ārī *vi* to play the fool
scūtāle, -is *nt* sling strap
scūtātus *adj* carrying a shield
scutella, -ae *f* bowl
scutica, -ae *f* whip
scutra, -ae *f* flat dish
scutula¹, -ae *f* small dish
scutula² *f* wooden roller; secret letter
scutulāta, -ae *f* a checked garment
scūtulum, -ī *nt* small shield
scūtum, -ī *nt* shield
Scylla, -ae *f* dangerous rock or sea monster (in the Straits of Messina)
Scyllaeus *adj see* **Scylla**
scymnus, -ī *m* cub
scyphus, -ī *m* wine cup
Scyrius, -ias *adj see* **Scyros**
Scyros, Scyrus, -ī *f* Aegean island near Euboea
scytala *see* **scutula²**
Scytha, Scythēs, -ae *m* Scythian
Scythia, -iae *f* Scythia (country N.E. of the Black Sea)
Scythicus *adj* Scythian
Scythis, -idis *f* Scythian woman
sē *pron* himself, herself, itself, themselves; one another; **apud sē** at home; in his senses; **inter sē** mutually
sēbum, -ī *nt* tallow, suet, grease
sēcēdō, -ēdere, -essī, -essum *vi* to withdraw, retire; to revolt, secede
sēcernō, -ernere, -rēvī, -rētum *vt* to separate, set apart; to dissociate; to distinguish
sēcessiō, -ōnis *f* withdrawal; secession
sēcessus, -ūs *m* retirement, solitude; retreat, recess
sēclūdō, -dere, -sī, -sum *vt* to shut off, seclude; to separate, remove
sēclūsus *ppp of* **sēclūdō** ♦ *adj* remote
secō, -āre, -uī, -tum *vt* to cut; to injure; to divide; (*MED*) to operate on; (*motion*) to pass through; (*dispute*) to decide
sēcrētiō, -ōnis *f* separation
sēcrētō *adv* apart, in private, in secret
sēcrētum, -ī *nt* privacy, secrecy; retreat, remote place; secret, mystery
sēcrētus *ppp of* **sēcernō** ♦ *adj* separate; solitary, remote; secret, private
secta, -ae *f* path; method, way of life; (*POL*) party; (*PHILOS*) school
sectārius *adj* leading
sectātor, -ōris *m* follower, adherent
sectilis *adj* cut; for cutting
sectiō, -ōnis *f* auctioning of confiscated goods
sector¹, -ōris *m* cutter; buyer at a public sale
sector², -ārī, -ātus *vt* to follow regularly, attend; to chase, hunt
sectūra, -ae *f* digging
sectus *ppp of* **secō**
sēcubitus, -ūs *m* lying alone

sēcubō, -āre, -uī *vi* to sleep by oneself; to live alone
secuī *perf of* **secō**
sēcul- *etc see* **saecul-**
sēcum with himself *etc*
secundānī, -ōrum *mpl* men of the second legion
secundārius *adj* second-rate
secundō¹ *adv* secondly
secundō², -āre *vt* to favour, make prosper
secundum *prep* (*place*) behind, along; (*time*) after; (*rank*) next to; (*agreement*) according to, in favour of ♦ *adv* behind
secundus *adj* following, next, second; inferior; favourable, propitious, fortunate ♦ *fpl* (*play*) subsidiary part; (*fig*) second fiddle ♦ *ntpl* success, good fortune; **secundō flūmine** downstream; **rēs secundae** prosperity, success
secūricula, -ae *f* little axe
secūrifer, -ī *adj* armed with an axe
secūriger, -ī *adj* armed with an axe
secūris, -is *f* axe; (*fig*) death blow; (*POL*) authority, supreme power
sēcūritās, -ātis *f* freedom from anxiety, composure; negligence; safety, feeling of security
sēcūrus *adj* untroubled, unconcerned; carefree, cheerful; careless
secus¹ *nt* (*indecl*) sex
secus² *adv* otherwise, differently; badly; **nōn ~** even so
secūtor, -ōris *m* pursuer
sed *conj* but; but also, but in fact
sēdātē *adv* calmly
sēdātiō, -ōnis *f* calming
sēdātus *ppp of* **sēdō** ♦ *adj* calm, quiet, composed
sēdecim *num* sixteen
sēdēcula, -ae *f* low stool
sedentārius *adj* sitting
sedeō, -ēre, sēdī, sessum *vi* to sit; (*army*) to be encamped, blockade; (*magistrates*) to be in session; (*clothes*) to suit, fit; (*places*) to be low-lying; (*heavy things*) to settle, subside; (*weapons*) to stick fast; (*inactivity*) to be idle; (*thought*) to be firmly resolved
sēdēs, -is *f* seat, chair; abode, home; site, ground, foundation
sēdī *perf of* **sedeō**
sedīle, -is *nt* seat, chair
sēditiō, -ōnis *f* insurrection, mutiny
sēditiōsē *adv* seditiously
sēditiōsus *adj* mutinous, factious; quarrelsome; troubled
sēdō, -āre, -āvī, -ātum *vt* to calm, allay, lull
sēdūcō, -ūcere, -ūxī, -uctum *vt* to take away, withdraw; to divide
sēductiō, -ōnis *f* taking sides
sēductus *ppp of* **sēdūcō** ♦ *adj* remote
sēdulitās, -ātis *f* earnestness, assiduity; officiousness
sēdulō *adv* busily, diligently; purposely
sēdulus *adj* busy, diligent, assiduous; officious
seges, -itis *f* cornfield; crop
Segesta, -ae *f* town in N.W. Sicily

Segestānus *adj see* **Segesta**
segmentātus *adj* flounced
segmentum, -ī *nt* brocade
segne, segniter *adv* slowly, lazily
segnipēs, -edis *adj* slow of foot
segnis *adj* slow, sluggish, lazy
segnitia, -ae, segnitiēs (*acc* **-em**, *abl* **-ē**) *f* slowness, sluggishness, sloth
sēgregō, -āre, -āvī, -ātum *vt* to separate, put apart; to dissociate
sēiugātus *adj* separated
sēiugis, -is *m* chariot and six
sēiūnctim *adv* separately
sēiūnctiō, -ōnis *f* separation
sēiūnctus *ppp of* **sēiungō**
sēiungō, -gere, sēiūnxī, sēiūnctum *vt* to separate, part
sēlēctiō, -ōnis *f* choice
sēlēctus *ppp of* **sēligō**
Seleucus, -ī *m king of Syria*
sēlībra, -ae *f* half pound
sēligō, -igere, -ēgī, -ēctum *vt* to choose, select
sella, -ae *f* seat, chair, stool, sedan chair; **~ cūrūlis** *chair of office for higher magistrates*
sellisternia, -ōrum *ntpl sacred banquets to goddesses*
sellula, -ae *f* stool; sedan chair
sellulārius, -ī *and* **-iī** *m* mechanic
sēmanimus *etc see* **sēmianimis**
semel *adv* once; once for all; first; ever; **~ atque iterum** again and again; **~ aut iterum** once or twice
Semelē, -ēs *f mother of Bacchus*
Semelēius *adj see* **Semelē**
sēmen, -inis *nt* seed; (*plant*) seedling, slip; (*men*) race, child; (*physics*) particle; (*fig*) origin, instigator
sēmentifer, -ī *adj* fruitful
sēmentis, -is *f* sowing, planting; young corn
sēmentīvus *adj* of seed time
sēmermis *etc see* **sēmiermis**
sēmēstris *adj* half-yearly, for six months
sēmēsus *adj* half-eaten
sēmet *pron* self, selves
sēmiadapertus *adj* half-open
sēmianimis, -us *adj* half-dead
sēmiapertus *adj* half-open
sēmibōs, -ovis *adj* half-ox
sēmicaper, -rī *adj* half-goat
sēmicremātus, sēmicremus *adj* half-burned
sēmicubitālis *adj* half a cubit long
sēmideus *adj* half-divine ♦ *m* demigod
sēmidoctus *adj* half-taught
sēmiermis, -us *adj* half-armed
sēmiēsus *adj* half-eaten
sēmifactus *adj* half-finished
sēmifer, -ī *adj* half-beast; half-savage
sēmigermānus *adj* half-German
sēmigravis *adj* half-overcome
sēmigrō, -āre *vi* to go away
sēmihiāns, -antis *adj* half-opened
sēmihomō, -inis *m* half-man, half-human
sēmihōra, -ae *f* half an hour
sēmilacer, -ī *adj* half-mangled

sēmilautus *adj* half-washed
sēmilīber, -ī *adj* half-free
sēmilixa, -ae *m* not much better than a camp follower
sēmimarīnus *adj* half in the sea
sēmimās, -āris *m* hermaphrodite ♦ *adj* castrated
sēmimortuus *adj* half-dead
sēminārium, -ī *and* **-iī** *nt* nursery, seed plot
sēminātor, -ōris *m* originator
sēminecis *adj* half-dead
sēminium, -ī *and* **-iī** *nt* procreation; breed
sēminō, -āre *vt* to sow; to produce; to beget
sēminūdus *adj* half-naked; almost unarmed
sēmipāgānus *adj* half-rustic
sēmiplēnus *adj* half-full, half-manned
sēmiputātus *adj* half-pruned
Semīramis, -is *and* **-idis** *f queen of Assyria*
Semīramius *adj see* **Semiramis**
sēmirāsus *adj* half-shaven
sēmireductus *adj* half turned back
sēmirefectus *adj* half-repaired
sēmirutus *adj* half-demolished, half in ruins
sēmis, -issis *m* (*coin*) half an as; (*interest*) 1/2 per cent per month (*i.e. 6 per cent per annum*); (*area*) half an acre
sēmisepultus *adj* half-buried
sēmisomnus *adj* half-asleep
sēmisupīnus *adj* half lying back
sēmita, -ae *f* path, way
sēmitālis *adj* of byways
sēmitārius *adj* frequenting byways
sēmiūst- *etc see* **sēmūst-**
sēmivir, -ī *adj* half-man; emasculated; unmanly
sēmivīvus *adj* half-dead
sēmodius, -ī *and* **-iī** *m* half a peck
sēmōtus *ppp of* **sēmoveō** ♦ *adj* remote; distinct
sēmoveō, -ovēre, -ōvī, -ōtum *vt* to put aside, separate
semper *adv* always, ever, every time
sempiternus *adj* everlasting, lifelong
Semprōnius[1], -ī *m Roman family name* (*esp the Gracchi*)
Semprōnius[2], -iānus *adj see* **Semprōnius[1]**
sēmūncia, -ae *f* half an ounce; a twenty-fourth
sēmūnciārius *adj* (*interest*) at the rate of one twenty-fourth
sēmūstulātus *adj* half-burned
sēmūstus *adj* half-burned
senāculum, -ī *nt* open air meeting place (*of the Senate*)
sēnāriolus, -ī *m* little trimeter
sēnārius, -ī *and* **-iī** *m* (iambic) trimeter
senātor, -ōris *m* senator
senātōrius *adj* senatorial, in the Senate
senātus, -ūs *m* Senate; meeting of the Senate
senātūscōnsultum, -ī *nt* decree of the Senate
Seneca, -ae *m* Stoic philosopher, *tutor of Nero*
senecta, -ae *f* old age
senectus *adj* old, aged
senectūs, -ūtis *f* old age; old men
seneō, -ēre *vi* to be old
senēscō, -ēscere, -uī *vi* to grow old; (*fig*) to weaken, wane, pine away

195

senex, **-is** (*compar* **-ior**) *adj* old (*over* 45) ◆ *m/f* old man, old woman

sēnī, **-ōrum** *adj* six each, in sixes; six; ~ **dēnī** sixteen each

senīlis *adj* of an old person, senile

sēniō, **-ōnis** *m* number six on a dice

senior *compar of* **senex**

senium, **-ī** *and* **-ī** *nt* weakness of age, decline; affliction; peevishness

Senonēs, **-um** *mpl* tribe of S. Gaul

sēnsī *perf of* **sentiō**

sēnsifer, **-ī** *adj* sensory

sēnsilis *adj* having sensation

sēnsim *adv* tentatively, gradually

sēnsus¹ *ppp of* **sentiō** ◆ *ntpl* thoughts

sēnsus², **-ūs** *m* (*body*) feeling, sensation, sense; (*intellect*) understanding, judgment, thought; (*emotion*) sentiment, attitude, frame of mind; (*language*) meaning, purport, sentence; **commūnis** ~ universal human feelings, human sympathy, social instinct

sententia, **-ae** *f* opinion, judgment; purpose, will; (*LAW*) verdict, sentence; (*POL*) vote, decision; (*language*) meaning, sentence, maxim, epigram; **meā sententiā** in my opinion; **dē meā sententiā** in accordance with my wishes; **ex meā sententiā** to my liking; **ex animī meī sententiā** to the best of my knowledge and belief; **in sententiam pedibus īre** support a motion

sententiola, **-ae** *f* phrase

sententiōsē *adv* pointedly

sententiōsus *adj* pithy

senticētum, **-ī** *nt* thornbrake

sentīna, **-ae** *f* bilge water; (*fig*) dregs, scum

sentiō, **-īre**, **sēnsī**, **sēnsum** *vt* (*senses*) to feel, see, perceive; (*circumstances*) to experience, undergo; (*mind*) to observe, understand; (*opinion*) to think, judge; (*LAW*) to vote, decide

sentis, **-is** *m* thorn, brier

sentīscō, **-ere** *vt* to begin to perceive

sentus *adj* thorny; untidy

senuī *perf of* **senēscō**

seorsum, **seorsus** *adv* apart, differently

sēparābilis *adj* separable

sēparātim *adv* apart, separately

sēparātiō, **-ōnis** *f* separation, severing

sēparātius *adv* less closely

sēparātus *adj* separate, different

sēparō, **-āre**, **-āvī**, **-ātum** *vt* to part, separate, divide; to distinguish

sepeliō, **-elīre**, **-elīvī** *and* **-eliī**, **-ultum** *vt* to bury; (*fig*) to overwhelm, overcome

sēpia, **-ae** *f* cuttlefish

Sēplasia, **-ae** *f* street in Capua where perfumes were sold

sēpōnō, **-ōnere**, **-osuī**, **-ositum** *vt* to put aside, pick out; to reserve; to banish; to appropriate; to separate

sēpositus *ppp of* **sēpōnō** ◆ *adj* remote; distinct, choice

sēpse *pron* oneself

septem *num* seven

September, **-ris** *m* September ◆ *adj* of September

septemdecim *etc see* **septendecim**

septemfluus *adj* with seven streams

septemgeminus *adj* sevenfold

septemplex, **-icis** *adj* sevenfold

septemtriō *etc see* **septentriō**

septemvirālis *adj* of the septemviri ◆ *mpl* the septemviri

septemvirātus, **-ūs** *m* office of septemvir

septemvirī, **-ōrum** *mpl* board of seven officials

septēnārius, **-ī** *and* **-ī** *m* verse of seven feet

septendecim *num* seventeen

septēnī, **-ōrum** *adj* seven each, in sevens

septentriō, **-ōnis** *m*, **septentriōnēs**, **-ōnum** *mpl* Great Bear, Little Bear; north; north wind

septentriōnālis *adj* northern ◆ *ntpl* northern regions

septiēns, **septiēs** *adv* seven times

septimānī, **-ōrum** *mpl* men of the seventh legion

septimum *adv* for the seventh time

septimus *adj* seventh

septimus decimus seventeenth

septingentēsimus *adj* seven hundredth

septingentī, **-ōrum** *adj* seven hundred

septuāgēsimus *adj* seventieth

septuāgintā *adj* seventy

septuennis *adj* seven years old

septumus *adj see* **septimus**

septūnx, **-ūncis** *m* seven ounces, seven-twelfths

sepulcrālis *adj* funeral

sepulcrētum, **-ī** *nt* cemetery

sepulcrum, **-ī** *nt* grave, tomb

sepultūra, **-ae** *f* burial, funeral

sepultus *ppp of* **sepeliō**

Sequāna, **-ae** *f* (river) Seine

Sequānī, **-ōrum** *mpl* people of N. Gaul

sequāx, **-ācis** *adj* pursuing, following

sequēns, **-entis** *pres p of* **sequor** ◆ *adj* following, next

sequester, **-rī** *and* **-ris** *m* trustee; agent, mediator

sequestrum, **-rī** *nt* deposit

sēquius *compar of* **secus²**; otherwise; **nihilō** ~ nonetheless

sequor, **-quī**, **-cūtus** *vt*, *vi* to follow; to accompany, go with; (*time*) to come after, come next, ensue; (*enemy*) to pursue; (*objective*) to make for, aim at; (*pulling*) to come away easily; (*share, gift*) to go to, come to; (*words*) to come naturally

sera, **-ae** *f* door bolt, bar

Serāpēum, **-ēī** *nt* temple of Serapis

Serāpis, **-is** *and* **-idis** *m* chief Egyptian god

serēnitās, **-ātis** *f* fair weather

serēnō, **-āre** *vt* to clear up, brighten up

serēnus *adj* fair, clear; (*wind*) fair-weather; (*fig*) cheerful, happy ◆ *nt* clear sky, fair weather

Sērēs, **-um** *mpl* Chinese

serēscō, **-ere** *vi* to dry off

sēria, **-ae** *f* tall jar

sērica, **-ōrum** *ntpl* silks

Sēricus *adj* Chinese; silk

seriēs (*acc* **-em**, *abl* **-ē**) *f* row, sequence, succession

sēriō *adv* in earnest, seriously

sēriola, -ae *f* small jar

Serīphius *adj see* **Serīphus**

Serīphus, Serīphos, -ī *f* Aegean island

sērius¹ *adj* earnest, serious

sērius² *compar of* **sērō**

sermō, -ōnis *m* conversation, talk; learned discussion, discourse; common talk, rumour; language, style; everyday language, prose; (*pl*) Satires (*of Horace*)

sermōcinor, -ārī *vi* to converse

sermunculus, -ī *m* gossip, rumour

serō¹, -ere, sēvī, -satum *vt* to sow, plant; (*fig*) to produce, sow the seeds of

serō², -ere, -tum *vt* to sow, join, wreathe; (*fig*) to compose, devise, engage in

sērō (*compar* **-ius**) *adv* late; too late

serpēns, -entis *m/f* snake, serpent; (*constellation*) Draco

serpentigena, -ae *m* offspring of a serpent

serpentipēs, -edis *adj* serpent-footed

serperastra, -ōrum *ntpl* splints

serpō, -ere, -sī, -tum *vi* to creep, crawl; (*fig*) to spread slowly

serpyllum, -ī *nt* wild thyme

serra, -ae *f* saw

serrācum *etc see* **sarrācum**

serrātus *adj* serrated, notched

serrula, -ae *f* small saw

Sertōriānus *adj see* **Sertōrius**

Sertōrius, -ī *m* commander under Marius, who held out against Sulla in Spain

sertus *ppp of* **serō²** ✦ *ntpl* garlands

serum, -ī *nt* whey, serum

sērum, -ī *nt* late hour

sērus *adj* late; too late; **sērā nocte** late at night

serva, -ae *f* maidservant, slave

servābilis *adj* that can be saved

servātor, -ōris *m* deliverer; watcher

servātrīx, -īcis *f* deliverer

servīlis *adj* of slaves, servile

servīliter *adv* slavishly

Servīlius¹, -ī *m* Roman family name of many consuls

Servīlius², -ānus *adj see* **Servīlius¹**

serviō, -īre, -īvī *and* **-iī, -ītum** *vi* to be a slave; (*with dat*) to serve, be of use to, be good for; (*property*) to be mortgaged

servitium, -ī *and* **-iī** *nt* slavery, servitude; slaves

servitūdō, -inis *f* slavery

servitūs, -ūtis *f* slavery, service; slaves; (*property*) liability

Servius, -ī *m* sixth king of Rome; famous jurist of Cicero's day

servō, -āre, -āvī, -ātum *vt* to save, rescue; to keep, preserve, retain; to store, reserve; to watch, observe, guard; (*place*) to remain in

servolus, -ī *m* young slave

servos, -ī *m see* **servus**

servula, -ae *f* servant girl

servulus, -ī *m* young slave

servus, -ī *m* slave, servant ✦ *adj* slavish, serving; (*property*) liable to a burden

sescēnāris *adj* a year and a half old

sescēnī, -ōrum *adj* six hundred each

sescentēsimus *adj* six hundredth

sescentī, -ōrum *num* six hundred; an indefinitely large number

sescentiēns, sescentiēs *adv* six hundred times

sēsē *etc see* **sē**

seselis, -is *f* (*plant*) seseli

sesqui *adv* one and a half times

sesquialter, -ī *adj* one and a half

sesquimodius, -ī *and* **-iī** *m* a peck and a half

sesquioctāvus *adj* of nine to eight

sesquiopus, -eris *nt* a day and a half's work

sesquipedālis *adj* a foot and a half

sesquipēs, -edis *m* a foot and a half

sesquiplāga, -ae *f* a blow and a half

sesquiplex, -icis *adj* one and a half times

sesquitertius *adj* of four to three

sessilis *adj* for sitting on

sessiō, -ōnis *f* sitting; seat; session; loitering

sessitō, -āre, -āvī *vi* to sit regularly

sessiuncula, -ae *f* small meeting

sessor, -ōris *m* spectator; resident

sēstertium, -ī *nt* 1000 sesterces; **dēna sēstertia** 10,000 sesterces; **centēna mīlia** ~ 100,000 sesterces; **deciēns** ~ 1,000,000 sesterces

sēstertius, -ī *and* **-iī** *m* sesterce (a silver coin)

Sestius¹, -ī *m* tribune defended by Cicero

Sestius², -iānus *adj* of Sestius

Sestos, Sestus, -ī *f* town on Dardanelles (home of Hero)

Sestus *adj see* **Sestos**

sēt- *etc see* **saet-**

Sētia, -iae *f* town in S. Latium (famous for wine)

Sētiaīnus *adj see* **Sētia**

sētius *compar of* **secus²**

seu *etc see* **sīve**

sevērē *adv* sternly, severely

sevēritās, -ātis *f* strictness, austerity

sevērus *adj* strict, stern; severe, austere; grim, terrible

sēvī *perf of* **serō¹**

sēvocō, -āre *vt* to call aside; to withdraw, remove

sēvum *etc see* **sēbum**

sex *num* six

sexāgēnārius *adj* sixty years old

sexāgēnī, -ōrum *adj* sixty each

sexāgēsimus *adj* sixtieth

sexāgiēns, sexāgiēs *adv* sixty times

sexāgintā *num* sixty

sexangulus *adj* hexagonal

sexcēn- *etc see* **sescēn-**

sexcēnārius *adj* of six hundred

sexennis *adj* six years old, after six years

sexennium, -ī *and* **-iī** *nt* six years

sexiēns, sexiēs *adv* six times

sexprīmī, -ōrum *mpl* a provincial town council

sextadecimānī, -ōrum *mpl* men of the sixteenth legion

sextāns, -antis *m* a sixth; (*coin, weight*) a sixth of an as

sextārius, -ī *and* **-iī** *m* pint

Sextīlis, -is *m* August ✦ *adj* of August

sextula, -ae f a sixth of an ounce
sextum adv for the sixth time
sextus adj sixth; ~ **decimus** sixteenth
sexus, -ūs m sex
sī conj if; if only; to see if; **sī forte** in the hope that; **sī iam** assuming for the moment; **sī minus** if not; **sī quandō** whenever; **sī quidem** if indeed; since; **sī quis** if anyone, whoever; **mīrum sī** surprising that; **quod sī** and if, but if
sībila, -ōrum ntpl whistle, hissing
sībilō, -āre vi to hiss, whistle ♦ vt to hiss at
sībilus¹, -ī m whistle, hissing
sībilus² adj hissing
Sibulla, Sibylla, -ae f prophetess, Sibyl
Sibyllīnus adj see **Sibulla**
sīc adv so, thus, this way, as follows; as one is, as things are; on this condition; yes
sīca, -ae f dagger
Sicānī, -ōrum mpl ancient people of Italy (later of Sicily)
Sicānia, -iae f Sicily
Sicānus, -ius adj Sicanian, Sicilian
sīcārius, -ī and -iī m assassin, murderer
siccē adv (speech) firmly
siccitās, -ātis f dryness, drought; (body) firmness; (style) dullness
siccō, -āre, -āvī, -ātum vt to dry; to drain, exhaust; (sore) to heal up
siccoculus adj dry-eyed
siccus adj dry; thirsty, sober; (body) firm, healthy; (argument) solid, sound; (style) flat, dull ♦ nt dry land
Sicilia, -ae f Sicily
sicilicula, -ae f little sickle
Siciliēnsis, Sicilis, -dis adj Sicilian
sīcine is this how?
sīcubi adv if anywhere, wheresoever
Siculus adj Sicilian
sīcunde adv if from anywhere
sīcut, sīcutī adv just as, as in fact; (comparison) like, as; (example) as for instance; (with subj) as if
Sicyōn, -ōnis f town in N. Peloponnese
Sicyōnius adj see **Sicyōn**
sīdereus adj starry; (fig) radiant
Sidicīnī, -ōrum mpl people of Campania
Sidicīnus adj see **Sidicīnī**
sīdō, -ere, -ī vi to sit down, settle; to sink, subside; to stick fast
Sīdōn, -ōnis f famous Phoenician town
Sīdōnis, -ōnidis adj Phoenician ♦ f Europa; Dido
Sīdōnius adj Sidonian, Phoenician
sīdus, -eris nt constellation; heavenly body, star; season, climate, weather; destiny; (pl) sky; (fig) fame, glory
siem archaic subj of **sum**
Sigambrī etc see **Sugambrī**
Sīgēum, -ī nt promontory near Troy
Sīgēus, -ius adj Sigean
sigilla, -ōrum ntpl little figures; seal
sigillātus adj decorated with little figures
signātor, -ōris m witness (to a document)
signifer, -ī adj with constellations; ~ **orbis** Zodiac ♦ m (MIL) standard-bearer
significanter adv pointedly, tellingly

significātiō, -ōnis f indication, signal, token; sign of approval; (RHET) emphasis; (word) meaning
significō, -āre, -āvī, -ātum vt to indicate, show; to betoken, portend; (word) to mean
signō, -āre, -āvī, -ātum vt to mark, stamp, print; (document) to seal; (money) to coin, mint; (fig) to impress, designate, note
signum, -ī nt mark, sign, token; (MIL) standard; signal, password; (art) design, statue; (document) seal; (ASTR) constellation; **signa cōnferre** join battle; **signa cōnstituere** halt; **signa convertere** wheel about; **signa ferre** move camp; attack; **signa inferre** attack; **signa prōferre** advance; **signa sequī** march in order; **ab signīs discēdere** leave the ranks; **sub signīs īre** march in order
Sīla, -ae f forest in extreme S. Italy
sīlānus, -ī m fountain, jet of water
silēns, -entis pres p of **sileō** ♦ adj still, silent ♦ mpl the dead
silentium, -ī and -iī nt stillness, silence; (fig) standstill, inaction
Sīlēnus, -ī m old and drunken companion of Bacchus
sileō, -ēre, -uī vi to be still, be silent; to cease ♦ vt to say nothing about
siler, -is nt willow
silēscō, -ere vi to calm down, fall silent
silex, -icis m flint, hard stone; rock
silicernium, -ī and -iī nt funeral feast
silīgō, -inis f winter wheat; fine flour
siliqua, -ae f pod, husk; (pl) pulse
sillybus, -ī m label bearing a book's title
Silurēs, -um mpl British tribe in S. Wales
silūrus, -ī m sheatfish
sīlus adj snub-nosed
silva, -ae f wood, forest; plantation, shrubbery; (plant) flowering stem; (fig) material
Silvānus, -ī m god of uncultivated land
silvēscō, -ere vi to run to wood
silvestris adj wooded, forest- (in cpds), pastoral
silvicola, -ae m/f sylvan
silvicultrīx, -īcis adj living in the woods
silvifragus adj tree-breaking
silvōsus adj woody
sīmia, -ae f ape
simile, -is nt comparison, parallel
similis adj like, similar; ~ **atque** like what; **vērī** ~ probable
similiter adv similarly
similitūdō, -inis f likeness, resemblance; imitation; analogy; monotony; (RHET) simile
sīmiolus, -ī m monkey
sīmītū adv at the same time, together
sīmius, -ī and -iī m ape
Simoīs, -entis m river of Troy
Simōnidēs, -is m Greek lyric poet of Ceos (famous for dirges)
Simōnidēus adj see **Simōnidēs**
simplex, -icis adj single, simple; natural, straightforward; (character) frank, sincere
simplicitās, -ātis f singleness; frankness, innocence
simpliciter adv simply, naturally; frankly
simplum, -ī nt simple sum

simpulum, **-ī** *nt* small ladle; **excitāre fluctūs in simpulō** raise a storm in a teacup

simpuvium, **-ī** *and* **-iī** *nt* libation bowl

simul *adv* at the same time, together, at once; likewise, also; both ... and; **~ ac**, **~ atque**, **~ ut** as soon as ◆ *conj* as soon as

simulācrum, **-ī** *nt* likeness, image, portrait, statue; phantom, ghost; (*writing*) symbol; (*fig*) semblance, shadow

simulāmen, **-inis** *nt* copy

simulāns, **-antis** *pres p of* **simulō** ◆ *adj* imitative

simulātē *adv* deceitfully

simulātiō, **-ōnis** *f* pretence, shamming, hypocrisy

simulātor, **-ōris** *m* imitator; pretender, hypocrite

simulatque *conj* as soon as

simulō, **-āre**, **-āvī**, **-ātum** *vt* to imitate, represent; to impersonate; to pretend, counterfeit

simultās, **-ātis** *f* feud, quarrel

sīmulus *adj* snub-nosed

sīmus *adj* snub-nosed

sīn *conj* but if; **sīn aliter**, **sīn minus** but if not

sināpī, **-is** *nt*, **sinapis**, **-is** *f* mustard

sincērē *adv* honestly

sincēritās, **-ātis** *f* integrity

sincērus *adj* clean, whole, genuine; (*fig*) pure, sound, honest

sincipitāmentum, **-ī** *nt* half a head

sinciput, **-itis** *nt* half a head; brain

sine *prep* (with abl) without, -less (*in cpds*)

singillātim *adv* singly, one by one

singulāris *adj* one at a time, single, sole; unique, extraordinary

singulāriter *adv* separately; extremely

singulārius *adj* single

singulī, **-ōrum** *adj* one each, single, one

singultim *adv* in sobs

singultō, **-āre** *vi* to sob, gasp, gurgle ◆ *vt* to gasp out

singultus, **-ūs** *m* sob, gasp, death rattle

singulus *etc see* **singulī**

sinister, **-rī** *adj* left; (*fig*) perverse, unfavourable; (*Roman auspices*) lucky; (*Greek auspices*) unlucky

sinistra, **-rae** *f* left hand, left-hand side

sinistrē *adv* badly

sinistrōrsus, **-um** *adv* to the left

sinō, **-ere**, **sīvī**, **situm** *vt* to let, allow; to let be; **nē dī sīrint** God forbid!

Sinōpē, **-ēs** *f* Greek colony on the Black Sea

Sinōpēnsis, **-eus** *adj see* **Sinōpē**

Sinuessa, **-ae** *f town on the borders of Latium and Campania*

Sinuessānus *adj see* **Sinuessa**

sīnum *etc see* **sīnus**

sinuō, **-āre**, **-āvī**, **-ātum** *vt* to wind, curve

sinuōsus *adj* winding, curved

sinus, **-ūs** *m* curve, fold; (*fishing*) net; (GEOG) bay, gulf, valley; (*hair*) curl; (*ship*) sail; (*toga*) fold, pocket, purse; (*person*) bosom; (*fig*) protection, love, heart, hiding place; **in sinū gaudēre** be secretly glad

sīnus, **-ī** *m* large cup

sīparium, **-ī** *and* **-iī** *nt* act curtain

sīphō, **-ōnis** *m* siphon; fire engine

sīquandō *adv* if ever

sīquī, **sīquis** *pron* if any, if anyone, whoever

sīquidem *adv* if in fact ◆ *conj* since

sirempse *adj* the same

Sīrēn, **-ēnis** *f* Siren

sīris, **sīrit** *perf subj of* **sinō**

Sīrius, **-ī** *m* Dog Star ◆ *adj* of Sirius

sirpe, **-is** *nt* silphium

sīrus, **-ī** *m* corn pit

sīs *adv* (for **sī vīs**) please

sistō, **-ere**, **stitī**, **statum** *vt* to place, set, plant; (LAW) to produce in court; (*monument*) to set up; (*movement*) to stop, arrest, check ◆ *vi* to stand, rest; (LAW) to appear in court; (*movement*) to stand still, stop, stand firm; **sē sistere** appear, present oneself; **tūtum sistere** see safe; **vadimōnium sistere** duly appear in court; **sistī nōn potest** the situation is desperate

sistrum, **-ī** *nt* Egyptian rattle, cymbal

sisymbrium, **-ī** *and* **-iī** *nt* fragrant herb (*perhaps mint*)

Sīsyphidēs, **-idae** *m* Ulysses

Sīsyphius *adj see* **Sīsyphus**

Sīsyphus, **-ī** *m criminal condemned in Hades to roll a rock repeatedly up a hill*

sitella, **-ae** *f* lottery urn

Sīthonis, **-idis** *adj* Thracian

Sīthonius *adj* Thracian

sitīculōsus *adj* thirsty, dry

sitiēns, **-entis** *pres p of* **sitiō** ◆ *adj* thirsty, dry; parching; (*fig*) eager

sitienter *adv* eagerly

sitiō, **-īre** *vi* to be thirsty; to be parched ◆ *vt* to thirst for, covet

sitis, **-is** *f* thirst; drought

sittybus *etc see* **sillybus**

situla, **-ae** *f* bucket

situs¹ *ppp of* **sinō** ◆ *adj* situated, lying; founded; (*fig*) dependent

situs², **-ūs** *m* situation, site; structure; neglect, squalor, mould; (*mind*) dullness

sīve *conj* or if, or; whether ... or

sīvī *perf of* **sinō**

smaragdus, **-ī** *m/f* emerald

smīlax, **-acis** *f* bindweed

Smintheus, **-eī** *m* Apollo

Smyrna, **-ae** *f Ionian town in Asia Minor*

Smyrnaeus *adj see* **Smyrna**

sobol- *etc see* **subol-**

sobriē *adv* temperately; sensibly

sobrīna, **-ae** *f* cousin (*on the mother's side*)

sobrīnus, **-ī** *m* cousin (*on the mother's side*)

sobrius *adj* sober; temperate, moderate; (*mind*) sane, sensible

soccus, **-ī** *m* slipper (*esp the sock worn by actors in comedy*)

socer, **-ī** *m* father-in-law

sociābilis *adj* compatible

sociālis *adj* of allies, confederate; conjugal

sociāliter *adv* sociably

sociennus, **-ī** *m* friend

societās, **-ātis** *f* fellowship, association; alliance

sociō, -āre, -āvī, -ātum vt to unite, associate, share

sociofraudus, -ī m deceiver of friends

socius adj associated, allied ♦ m friend, companion; partner, ally

sōcordia, -ae f indolence, apathy; folly

sōcordius adv more carelessly, lazily

sōcors, -dis adj lazy, apathetic; stupid

Sōcratēs, -is m famous Athenian philosopher

Sōcraticus adj of Socrates, Socratic ♦ mpl the followers of Socrates

socrus, -ūs f mother-in-law

sodālicium, -ī and **-iī** nt fellowship; secret society

sodālicius adj of fellowship

sodālis, -is m/f companion, friend; member of a society, accomplice

sodālitās, -ātis f companionship, friendship; society, club; secret society

sodālitius etc see **sodālicius**

sodēs adv please

sōl, sōlis m sun; sunlight, sun's heat; (poetry) day; (myth) Sun god; **sōl oriēns, sōlis ortus** east; **sōl occidēns, sōlis occāsus** west

sōlāciolum, -ī nt a grain of comfort

sōlācium, -ī and **-iī** nt comfort, consolation, relief

sōlāmen, -inis nt solace, relief

sōlāris adj of the sun

sōlārium, -ī and **-iī** nt sundial; clock; balcony, terrace

sōlātium etc see **sōlācium**

sōlātor, -ōris m consoler

soldūriī, -ōrum mpl retainers

soldus etc see **solidus**

solea, -ae f sandal, shoe; fetter; (fish) sole

soleārius, -ī and **-iī** m sandal maker

soleātus adj wearing sandals

soleō, -ēre, -itus vi to be accustomed, be in the habit, usually do; **ut solēre** as usual

solidē adv for certain

soliditās, -ātis f solidity

solidō, -āre vt to make firm, strengthen

solidus adj solid, firm, dense; whole, complete; (fig) sound, genuine, substantial ♦ nt solid matter, firm ground

sōliferreum, -ī nt an all-iron javelin

sōlistimus adj (AUG) most favourable

sōlitārius adj solitary, lonely

sōlitūdō, -inis f solitariness, loneliness; destitution; (place) desert

solitus ppa of **soleō** ♦ adj usual, customary ♦ nt custom; **plūs solitō** more than usual

solium, -ī and **-iī** nt seat, throne; tub; (fig) rule

sōlivagus adj going by oneself; single

sollemne, -is nt religious rite, festival; usage, practice

sollemnis adj annual, regular; religious, solemn; usual, ordinary

sollemniter adv solemnly

sollers, -tis adj skilled, clever, expert; ingenious

sollerter adv cleverly

sollertia, -ae f skill, ingenuity

sollicitātiō, -ōnis f inciting

sollicitō, -āre, -āvī, -ātum vt to stir up, disturb; to trouble, distress, molest; to rouse, urge, incite, tempt, tamper with

sollicitūdō, -inis f uneasiness, anxiety

sollicitus adj agitated, disturbed; (mind) troubled, worried, alarmed; (things) anxious, careful; (cause) disquieting

solliferreum etc see **sōliferreum**

sollistimus etc see **sōlistimus**

soloecismus, -ī m grammatical mistake

Solōn, -ōnis m famous Athenian lawgiver

sōlor, -ārī, -ātus vt to comfort, console; to relieve, ease

sōlstitiālis adj of the summer solstice; midsummer

sōlstitium, -ī and **-iī** nt summer solstice; midsummer, summer heat

solum, -ī nt ground, floor, bottom; soil, land, country; (foot) sole; (fig) basis; **solō aequāre** raze to the ground

sōlum adv only, merely

sōlus (gen **-īus**, dat **-ī**) see **vicis** ♦ adj only, alone; lonely, forsaken; (place) lonely, deserted

solūtē adv loosely, freely, carelessly, weakly, fluently

solūtiō, -ōnis f loosening; payment

solūtus ppp of **solvō** ♦ adj loose, free; (from distraction) at ease, at leisure, merry; (from obligation) exempt; (from restraint) free, independent, unprejudiced; (moral) lax, weak, insolent; (language) prose, unrhythmical; (speaker) fluent; **ōrātiō solūta, verba solūta** prose

solvō, -vere, -vī, -ūtum vt to loosen, undo; to free, release, acquit, exempt; to dissolve, break up, separate; to relax, slacken, weaken; to cancel, remove, destroy; to solve, explain; to pay, fulfil; (argument) to refute; (discipline) to undermine; (feelings) to get rid of; (hair) to let down; (letter) to open; (sail) to unfurl; (siege) to raise; (troops) to dismiss ♦ vi to set sail; to pay; **nāvem solvere** set sail; **poenās solvere** be punished; **praesēns solvere** pay cash; **rem solvere** pay; **sacrāmentō solvere** discharge; **solvendō esse** be solvent

Solyma, -ōrum ntpl Jerusalem

Solymus adj of the Jews

somniculōsē adv sleepily

somniculōsus adj sleepy

somnifer, -ī adj soporific; fatal

somniō, -āre vt to dream, dream about; to talk nonsense

somnium, -ī and **-iī** nt dream; nonsense, fancy

somnus, -ī m sleep; sloth

sonābilis adj noisy

sonipēs, -edis m steed

sonitus, -ūs m sound, noise

sonivius adj noisy

sonō, -āre, -uī, -itum vi to sound, make a noise ♦ vt to utter, speak, celebrate; to sound like

sonor, -ōris m sound, noise

sonōrus adj noisy, loud

sōns, sontis adj guilty

sonticus adj critical; important

sonus, -ī m sound, noise; (fig) tone

sophistēs, -ae *m* sophist
Sophoclēs, -is *m* famous Greek tragic poet
Sophoclēus *adj* of Sophocles, Sophoclean
sophus *adj* wise
sōpiō, -īre, -īvī, -ītum *vt* to put to sleep; *(fig)* to calm, lull
sopor, -ōris *m* sleep; apathy
sopōrifer, -ī *adj* soporific, drowsy
sopōrō, -āre *vt* to lull to sleep; to make soporific
sopōrus *adj* drowsy
Sōracte, -is *nt* mountain in S. Etruria
sorbeō, -ēre, -uī *vt* to suck, swallow; *(fig)* to endure
sorbillō, -āre *vt* to sip
sorbitiō, -ōnis *f* drink, broth
sorbum, -ī *nt* service berry
sorbus, -ī *f* service tree
sordeō, -ēre *vi* to be dirty, be sordid; to seem shabby; to be of no account
sordēs, -is *f* dirt, squalor, shabbiness; mourning; meanness; vulgarity; *(people)* rabble
sordēscō, -ere *vi* to become dirty
sordidātus *adj* shabbily dressed, in mourning
sordidē *adv* meanly, vulgarly
sordidulus *adj* soiled, shabby
sordidus *adj* dirty, squalid, shabby; in mourning; poor, mean; base, vile
sōrex, -icis *m* shrewmouse
sōricīnus *adj* of the shrewmouse
sōrītēs, -ae *m* chain syllogism
soror, -ōris *f* sister
sorōricīda, -ae *m* murderer of a sister
sorōrius *adj* of a sister
sors, sortis *f* lot; allotted duty; oracle, prophecy; fate, fortune; *(money)* capital, principal
sōrsum *etc see* **seorsum**
sortilegus *adj* prophetic ♦ *m* soothsayer
sortior, -īrī, -ītus *vi* to draw or cast lots ♦ *vt* to draw lots for, allot, obtain by lot; to distribute, share; to choose; to receive
sortītiō, -ōnis *f* drawing lots, choosing by lot
sortītus¹ *ppa of* **sortior** ♦ *adj* assigned, allotted; **sortītō** by lot
sortītus², -ūs *m* drawing lots
Sosius, -ī *m* Roman family name *(esp two brothers Sosii, famous booksellers in Rome)*
sōspes, -itis *adj* safe and sound, unhurt; favourable, lucky
sōspita, -ae *f* saviour
sōspitālis *adj* beneficial
sōspitō, -āre *vt* to preserve, prosper
sōtēr, -ēris *m* saviour
spādīx, -īcis *adj* chestnut-brown
spadō, -ōnis *m* eunuch
spargō, -gere, -sī, -sum *vt* to throw, scatter, sprinkle; to strew, spot, moisten; to disperse, spread abroad
sparsus *ppp of* **spargō** ♦ *adj* freckled
Sparta, -ae, Spartē, -ēs *f* famous Greek city
Spartacus, -ī *m* gladiator who led a revolt against Rome
Spartānus, -icus *adj* Spartan
Spartiātēs, -iātae *m* Spartan
spartum, -ī *nt* Spanish broom

sparulus, -ī *m* bream
sparus, -ī *m* hunting spear
spatha, -ae *f* broadsword
spatior, -ārī, -ātus *vi* to walk; to spread
spatiōsē *adv* greatly; after a time
spatiōsus *adj* roomy, ample, large; *(time)* prolonged
spatium, -ī *and* **-iī** *nt* space, room, extent; *(between points)* distance; *(open space)* square, walk, promenade; *(race)* lap, track, course; *(time)* period, interval; *(opportunity)* time, leisure; *(metre)* quantity
speciēs, -ēī *f* seeing, sight; appearance, form, outline; *(thing seen)* sight; *(mind)* idea; *(in sleep)* vision, apparition; *(fair show)* beauty, splendour; *(false show)* pretence, pretext; *(classification)* species; **in speciem** for the sake of appearances; like; **per speciem** under the pretence; **sub speciē** under the cloak
specillum, -ī *nt* probe
specimen, -inis *nt* sign, evidence, proof; pattern, ideal
speciōsē *adv* handsomely
speciōsus *adj* showy, beautiful; specious, plausible
spectābilis *adj* visible; notable, remarkable
spectāclum, spectāculum, -ī *nt* sight, spectacle; public show, play; theatre, seats
spectāmen, -inis *nt* proof
spectātiō, -ōnis *f* looking; testing
spectātor, -ōris *m* onlooker, observer, spectator; critic
spectātrīx, -īcis *f* observer
spectātus *ppp of* **spectō** ♦ *adj* tried, proved; worthy, excellent
spectiō, -ōnis *f* the right to take auspices
spectō, -āre, -āvī, -ātum *vt* to look at, observe, watch; *(place)* to face; *(aim)* to look to, bear in mind, contemplate, tend towards; *(judging)* to examine, test
spectrum, -ī *nt* spectre
specula, -ae *f* watchtower, lookout; height
spēcula, -ae *f* slight hope
speculābundus *adj* on the lookout
speculāris *adj* transparent ♦ *ntpl* window
speculātor, -ōris *m* explorer, investigator; *(MIL)* spy, scout
speculātōrius *adj* for spying, scouting ♦ *f* spy boat
speculātrīx, -īcis *f* watcher
speculor, -ārī, -ātus *vt* to spy out, watch for, observe
speculum, -ī *nt* mirror
specus, -ūs *m, nt* cave; hollow, chasm
spēlaeum, -ī *nt* cave, den
spēlunca, -ae *f* cave, den
spērābilis *adj* to be hoped for
spērāta, -ātae *f* bride
Sperchēis, -idis *adj see* **Sperchēus**
Sperchēus, Sperchēos, -ī *m* river in Thessaly
spernō, -ere, sprēvī, sprētum *vt* to remove, reject, scorn
spērō, -āre, -āvī, -ātum *vt* to hope, hope for, expect; to trust; to look forward to

spēs – stagnum

spēs, **speī** f hope, expectation; **praeter spem** unexpectedly; **spē dēiectus** disappointed

Speusippus, **-ī** m successor of Plato in the Academy

sphaera, **-ae** f ball, globe, sphere

Sphinx, **-ingis** f fabulous monster near Thebes

spīca, **-ae** f (grain) ear; (plant) tuft; (ASTR) brightest star in Virgo

spīceus adj of ears of corn

spīculum, **-ī** nt point, sting; dart, arrow

spīna, **-ae** f thorn; prickle; fish bone; spine, back; (pl) difficulties, subtleties

spīnētum, **-ī** nt thorn hedge

spīneus adj of thorns

spīnifer, **-ī** adj prickly

spīnōsus adj thorny, prickly; (style) difficult

spinter, **-ēris** nt elastic bracelet

spīnus, **-ī** f blackthorn, sloe

spīra, **-ae** f coil; twisted band

spīrābilis adj breathable, life-giving

spīrāculum, **-ī** nt vent

spīrāmentum, **-ī** nt vent, pore; breathing space

spīritus, **-ūs** m breath, breathing; breeze, air; inspiration; character, spirit, courage, arrogance

spīrō, **-āre**, **-āvī**, **-ātum** vi to breathe, blow; to be alive; to be inspired ♦ vt to emit, exhale; (fig) to breathe, express

spissātus adj condensed

spissē adv closely; slowly

spissēscō, **-ere** vi to thicken

spissus adj thick, compact, crowded; slow; (fig) difficult

splendeō, **-ēre** vi to be bright, shine; to be illustrious

splendēscō, **-ere** vi to become bright

splendidē adv brilliantly, magnificently, nobly

splendidus adj bright, brilliant, glittering; (sound) clear; (dress, house) magnificent; (person) illustrious; (appearance) showy

splendor, **-ōris** m brightness, lustre; magnificence; clearness; nobility

spoliātiō, **-ōnis** f plundering

spoliātor, **-ōris** m robber

spoliātrīx, **-īcis** f robber

spoliō, **-āre**, **-āvī**, **-ātum** vt to strip; to rob, plunder

spolium, **-ī** and **-iī** nt (beast) skin; (enemy) spoils, booty

sponda, **-ae** f bed frame; bed, couch

spondālium, **-ī** and **-iī** nt hymn accompanied by the flute

spondeō, **-ēre**, **spopondī**, **spōnsum** vt to promise, pledge, vow; (LAW) to go bail for; (marriage) to betroth

spondēus, **-ī** m spondee

spongia, **-ae** f sponge; coat of mail

spōnsa, **-ae** f fiancée, bride

spōnsālia, **-ium** ntpl engagement

spōnsiō, **-ōnis** f promise, guarantee; (LAW) agreement that the loser in a suit pays the winner a sum; bet

spōnsor, **-ōris** m guarantor, surety

spōnsus[1] ppp of **spondeō** ♦ m fiancé, bridegroom ♦ nt agreement, covenant

spōnsus[2], **-ūs** m contract, surety

sponte f (abl) voluntarily, of one's own accord; unaided, by oneself; spontaneously

spopondī perf of **spondeō**

sportella, **-ae** f fruit basket

sportula, **-ae** f small basket; gift to clients, dole

sprētiō, **-ōnis** f contempt

sprētor, **-ōris** m despiser

sprētus ppp of **spernō**

sprēvī perf of **spernō**

spūma, **-ae** f foam, froth

spūmēscō, **-ere** vi to become frothy

spūmeus adj foaming, frothy

spūmifer, **-ī** adj foaming

spūmiger, **-ī** adj foaming

spūmō, **-āre** vi to foam, froth

spūmōsus adj foaming

spuō, **-uere**, **-uī**, **-ūtum** vi to spit ♦ vt to spit out

spurcē adv obscenely

spurcidicus adj obscene

spurcificus adj obscene

spurcitia, **-ae**, **spurcitiēs**, **-ēī** f filth, smut

spurcō, **-āre** vt to befoul

spurcus adj filthy, nasty, foul

spūtātilicus adj despicable

spūtātor, **-ōris** m spitter

spūtō, **-āre** vt to spit out

spūtum, **-ī** nt spit, spittle

squāleō, **-ēre**, **-uī** vi to be rough, stiff, clotted; to be parched; to be neglected, squalid, filthy; to be in mourning

squālidē adv rudely

squālidus adj rough, scaly; neglected, squalid, filthy; (speech) unpolished

squālor, **-ōris** m roughness; filth, squalor

squāma, **-ae** f scale; scale armour

squāmeus adj scaly

squāmifer, **-ī** adj scaly

squāmiger, **-ī** adj scaly ♦ mpl fishes

squāmōsus adj scaly

squilla, **-ae** f prawn, shrimp

st interj sh!

stabilīmentum, **-ī** nt support

stabiliō, **-īre** vt to make stable; to establish

stabilis adj firm, steady; (fig) steadfast, unfailing

stabilitās, **-ātis** f firmness, steadiness, reliability

stabulō, **-āre** vt to house, stable ♦ vi to have a stall

stabulum, **-ī** nt stall, stable, steading; lodging, cottage; brothel

stacta, **-ae** f myrrh oil

stadium, **-ī** and **-iī** nt stade, furlong; racetrack

Stagīra, **-ōrum** ntpl town in Macedonia (birthplace of Aristotle)

Stagīrītēs, **-ītae** m Aristotle

stagnō, **-āre** vi to form pools; to be inundated ♦ vt to flood

stagnum, **-ī** nt standing water, pool, swamp; waters

stāmen, -inis *nt* warp; thread; (*instrument*) string; (*priest*) fillet

stāmineus *adj* full of threads

stata *adj*: **Stata māter** Vesta

statārius *adj* standing, stationary, steady; calm ◆ *f* refined comedy ◆ *mpl* actors in this comedy

statēra, -ae *f* scales

statim *adv* steadily; at once, immediately; ~ **ut** as soon as

statiŏ, -ōnis *f* standing still; station, post, residence; (*pl*) sentries; (NAUT) anchorage

Statius, -ī *m* Caecilius (*early writer of comedy*), Papinius (*epic and lyric poet of the Silver Age*)

statīvus *adj* stationary ◆ *ntpl* standing camp

Stator, -ōris *m* the Stayer (*epithet of Jupiter*)

stator, -ōris *m* attendant, orderly

statua, -ae *f* statue

statūmen, -inis *nt* (*ship*) rib

statuŏ, -uere, -uī, -ūtum *vt* to set up, place; to bring to a stop; to establish, constitute; to determine, appoint; to decide, settle; to decree, prescribe; (*with inf*) to resolve, propose; (*with acc and infin*) to judge, consider, conclude; (*army*) to draw up; (*monument*) to erect; (*price*) to fix; (*sentence*) to pass; (*tent*) to pitch; (*town*) to build; **condiciōnem statuere** dictate (to); **fīnem statuere** put an end (to); **iūs statuere** lay down a principle; **modum statuere** impose restrictions; **apud animum statuere** make up one's mind; **dē sē statuere** commit suicide; **gravius statuere in** deal severely with

statūra, -ae *f* height, stature

status¹ *ppp of* **sistŏ** ◆ *adj* appointed, due

status², -ūs *m* posture, attitude; position; (*social*) standing, status, circumstances; (POL) situation, state, form of government; (*nature*) condition; **reī pūblicae ~** the political situation; constitution; **dē statū movēre** dislodge

statūtus *ppp of* **statuŏ**

stega, -ae *f* deck

stēliŏ *see* **stēlliŏ**

stēlla, -ae *f* star; ~ **errāns** planet

stēllāns, -antis *adj* starry

stēllātus *adj* starred; set in the sky

stēllifer, -ī *adj* starry

stēlliger, -ī *adj* starry

stēlliŏ, -ōnis *m* newt

stemma, -tis *nt* pedigree

stercoreus, -ī *adj* filthy

stercorŏ, -āre *vt* to manure

stercus, -oris *nt* dung

sterilis *adj* barren, sterile; bare, empty; unprofitable, fruitless

sterilitās, -ātis *f* barrenness

sternāx, -ācis *adj* bucking

sternŏ, -ere, strāvī, strātum *vt* to spread, cover, strew; to smooth, level; to stretch out, extend; to throw to the ground, prostrate; to overthrow; (*bed*) to make; (*horse*) to saddle; (*road*) to pave

sternūmentum, -ī *nt* sneezing

sternuŏ, -ere, -ī *vt, vi* to sneeze

Steropē, -ēs *f* a Pleiad

sterquilīnium, -ī *and* **-iī, sterquilīnum, -ī** *nt* dung heap

stertŏ, -ere, -uī *vi* to snore

Stēsichorus, -ī *m* Greek lyric poet

stetī *perf of* **stŏ**

Sthenelēius, Sthenelēis, ēidis *adj see* **Sthenelus**

Sthenelus, -ī *m* father of Eurystheus; father of Cycnus

stigma, -tis *nt* brand

stigmatiās, -ae *m* branded slave

stilla, -ae *f* drop

stillicidium, -ī *and* **-iī** *nt* dripping water, rainwater from the eaves

stillŏ, -āre, -āvī, -ātum *vi* to drip, trickle ◆ *vt* to let fall in drops, distil

stilus, -ī *m* stake; pen; (*fig*) writing, composition, style; **stilum vertere** erase

stimulātiŏ, -ōnis *f* incentive

stimulātrīx, -īcis *f* provocative woman

stimuleus *adj* smarting

stimulŏ, -āre, -āvī, -ātum *vt* to goad; to trouble, torment; to rouse, spur on, excite

stimulus, -ī *m* goad; (MIL) stake; (*pain*) sting, pang; (*incentive*) spur, stimulus

stinguŏ, -ere *vt* to extinguish

stīpātiŏ, -ōnis *f* crowd, retinue

stīpātor, -ōris *m* attendant; (*pl*) retinue, bodyguard

stīpendiārius *adj* tributary, liable to a money tax; (MIL) receiving pay ◆ *mpl* tributary peoples

stīpendium, -ī *and* **-iī** *nt* tax, tribute; soldier's pay; military service, campaign; ~ **merēre**, ~ **merērī** serve; ~ **ēmerērī** complete one's period of service

stīpes, -itis *m* log, trunk; tree; (*insult*) blockhead

stīpŏ, -āre, -āvī, -ātum *vt* to press, pack together; to cram, stuff full; to crowd round, accompany in a body

stips, stipis *f* donation, contribution

stipula, -ae *f* stalk, blade, stubble; reed

stipulātiŏ, -ōnis *f* promise, bargain

stipulātiuncula, -ae *f* slight stipulation

stipulātus *adj* promised

stipulor, -ārī *vt, vi* to demand a formal promise, bargain, stipulate

stīria, -ae *f* icicle

stirpēs *etc see* **stirps**

stirpitus *adv* thoroughly

stirps, -is *f* lower trunk and roots, stock; plant, shoot; family, lineage, progeny; origin; **ab stirpe** utterly

stīva, -ae *f* plough handle

stlattārius *adj* seaborne

stŏ, stāre, stetī, statum *vi* to stand; to remain in position, stand firm; to be conspicuous; (*fig*) to persist, continue; (*battle*) to go on; (*hair*) to stand on end; (NAUT) to ride at anchor; (*play*) to be successful; (*price*) to cost; (*with* **ab, cum, prō**) to be on the side of, support; (*with* **in**) to rest, depend on; (*with* **per**) to be the fault of; **stat sententia** one's mind is made up; **per**

Āfrānium stetit quōminus dīmicārētur thanks to Afranius there was no battle

Stōicē *adv* like a Stoic

Stōicus *adj* Stoic ♦ *m* Stoic philosopher ♦ *ntpl* Stoicism

stola, -ae *f* long robe (*esp worn by matrons*)

stolidē *adv* stupidly

stolidus *adj* dull, stupid

stomachor, -ārī, -ātus *vi* to be vexed, be annoyed

stomachōsē *adv see* **stomachōsus**

stomachōsus *adj* angry, irritable

stomachus, -ī *m* gullet; stomach; taste, liking; dislike, irritation, chagrin

stōrea, storia, -ae *f* rush mat, rope mat

strabō, -ōnis *m* squinter

strāgēs, -is *f* heap, confused mass; havoc, massacre

strāgulus *adj* covering ♦ *nt* bedspread, rug

strāmen, -inis *nt* straw, litter

strāmentum, -ī *nt* straw, thatch; straw bed; covering, rug

strāmineus *adj* straw-thatched

strangulō, -āre, -āvī, -ātum *vt* to throttle, choke

strangūria, -ae *f* difficult discharge of urine

stratēgēma, -tis *nt* a piece of generalship, stratagem

stratēgus, -ī *m* commander, president

stratiōticus *adj* military

strātum, -ī *nt* coverlet, blanket; bed, couch; horsecloth, saddle; pavement

strātus *ppp of* **sternō** ♦ *adj* prostrate

strāvī *perf of* **sternō**

strēnuē *adv* energetically, quickly

strēnuitās, -ātis *f* energy, briskness

strēnuus *adj* brisk, energetic, busy; restless

strepitō, -āre *vi* to make a noise, rattle, rustle

strepitus, -ūs *m* din, clatter, crashing, rumbling; sound

strepō, -ere, -uī *vi* to make a noise, clang, roar, rumble, rustle *etc* ♦ *vt* to bawl out

striāta, -ae *f* scallop

strictim *adv* superficially, cursorily

strictūra, -ae *f* mass of metal

strictus *ppp of* **stringō** ♦ *adj* close, tight

strīdeō, -ēre, -ī, strīdō, -ere, -ī *vi* to creak, hiss, shriek, whistle

strīdor, -ōris *m* creaking, hissing, grating

strīdulus *adj* creaking, hissing, whistling

strigilis *f* scraper, strigil

strigō, -āre *vi* to stop, jib

strigōsus *adj* thin, scraggy; (*style*) insipid

stringō, -ngere, -nxī, -ctum *vt* to draw together, draw tight; to touch, graze; to cut off, prune, trim; (*sword*) to draw; (*mind*) to affect, pain

stringor, -ōris *m* twinge

strix, -igis *f* screech owl

stropha, -ae *f* trick

Strophades, -um *fpl* islands off S. Greece

strophiārius, -ī *and* **-iī** *m* maker of breastbands

strophium, -ī *and* **-iī** *nt* breastband; headband

structor, -ōris *m* mason, carpenter; (*at table*) server, carver

structūra, -ae *f* construction, structure; works

structus *ppp of* **struō**

struēs, -is *f* heap, pile

struix, -icis *f* heap, pile

strūma, -ae *f* tumour

strūmōsus *adj* scrofulous

struō, -ere, -xī, -ctum *vt* to pile up; to build, erect; to arrange in order; to make, prepare; to cause, contrive, plot

strūtheus *adj* sparrow- (*in cpds*)

strūthiocamēlus, -ī *m* ostrich

Strȳmōn, -onis *m* river between Macedonia and Thrace (*now Struma*)

Strȳmonius *adj* Strymonian, Thracian

studeō, -ēre, -uī *vi* (*usu with dat*) to be keen, be diligent, apply oneself to; to study; (*person*) to be a supporter of

studiōsē *adv* eagerly, diligently

studiōsus *adj* (*usu with gen*) keen on, fond of, partial to; studious ♦ *m* student

studium, -ī *and* **-iī** *nt* enthusiasm, application, inclination; fondness, affection; party spirit, partisanship; study, literary work

stultē *adv* foolishly

stultiloquentia, -ae *f* foolish talk

stultiloquium, -ī *and* **-iī** *nt* foolish talk

stultitia, -ae *f* folly, silliness

stultividus *adj* simple-sighted

stultus *adj* foolish, silly ♦ *m* fool

stupefaciō, -facere, -fēcī, -factum (*pass* **-fīō**) *vt* to stun, astound

stupeō, -ēre, -uī *vi* to be stunned, be astonished; to be brought to a standstill ♦ *vt* to marvel at

stupēscō, -ere *vi* to become amazed

stūpeus *etc see* **stuppeus**

stupiditās, -ātis *f* senselessness

stupidus *adj* senseless, astounded; dull, stupid

stupor, -ōris *m* numbness, bewilderment; dullness, stupidity

stuppa, -ae *f* tow

stuppeus *adj* of tow

stuprō, -āre, -āvī, -ātum *vt* to defile; to ravish

stuprum, -ī *nt* debauchery, unchastity

sturnus, -ī *m* starling

Stygius *adj* of the lower world, Stygian

stylus *etc see* **stilus**

Stymphalicus, Stymphalicius, Stymphalicis *adj* Stymphalian

Stymphalum, -ī *nt*, **Stymphalus, -ī** *m* district of Arcadia (*famous for birds of prey killed by Hercules*)

Styx, -ygis *and* **-ygos** *f* river of Hades

Styxius *adj see* **Styx**

suādēla, -ae *f* persuasion

suādeō, -dēre, -sī, -sum *vi* (*with dat*) to advise, urge, recommend

suāsiō, -ōnis *f* speaking in favour (*of a proposal*), *persuasive type of oratory*

suāsor, -ōris *m* adviser; advocate

suāsus¹ *ppp of* **suādeō**

suāsus², -ūs *m* advice

suāveolēns, -entis *adj* fragrant

suāviātiō *etc see* **sāviātiō**

suāvidicus *adj* charming
suāviloquēns, -entis *adj* charming
suāviloquentia, -ae *f* charm of speech
suāvior *etc see* **sāvior**
suāvis *adj* sweet, pleasant, delightful
suāvitās, -ātis *f* sweetness, pleasantness, charm
suāviter *adv see* **suāvis**
suāvium *etc see* **sāvium**
sub *prep* 1. (*with abl*) (*place*) under, beneath; (*hills, walls*) at the foot of, close to; (*time*) during, at; (*order*) next to; (*rule*) under, in the reign of 2. (*with acc*) (*place*) under, along under; (*hills, walls*) up to, to; (*time*) up to, just before, just after; **sub ictum venīre** come within range; **sub manum** to hand
subabsurdē *adv see* **subabsurdus**
subabsurdus *adj* somewhat absurd
subaccūsō, -āre *vt* to find some fault with
subāctiō, -ōnis *f* working (*the soil*)
subāctus *ppp of* **subigō**
subadroganter *adv* a little conceitedly
subagrestis *adj* rather boorish
subalāris *adj* carried under the arms
subamārus *adj* rather bitter
subaquilus *adj* brownish
subauscultō, -āre *vt, vi* to listen secretly, eavesdrop
subbasilicānus, -ī *m* lounger
subblandior, -īrī *vi* (*with dat*) to flirt with
subc- *etc see* **succ-**
subdidī *perf of* **subdō**
subdifficilis *adj* rather difficult
subdiffīdō, -ere *vi* to be a little doubtful
subditīcius *adj* sham
subditīvus *adj* sham
subditus *ppp of* **subdō** ♦ *adj* spurious
subdō, -ere, -idī, -itum *vt* to put under, plunge into; to subdue; to substitute, forge
subdoceō, -ēre *vt* to teach as an assistant
subdolē *adv* slily
subdolus *adj* sly, crafty, underhand
subdubitō, -āre *vi* to be a little undecided
subdūcō, -ūcere, -ūxī, -uctum *vt* to pull up, raise; to withdraw, remove; to take away secretly, steal; (*account*) to balance; (*ship*) to haul up, beach; **sē subdūcere** steal away, disappear
subductiō, -ōnis *f* (*ship*) hauling up; (*thought*) reckoning
subductus *ppp of* **subdūcō**
subedō, -esse, -ēdī *vt* to wear away underneath
subēgī *perf of* **subigō**
subeō, -īre, -iī, -itum *vi* to go under, go in; to come up to, climb, advance; to come immediately after; to come to the assistance; to come as a substitute, succeed; to come secretly, steal in; to come to mind, suggest itself ♦ *vt* to enter, plunge into; to climb; to approach, attack; to take the place of; to steal into; to submit to, undergo, suffer; (*mind*) to occur to
sūber, -is *nt* cork tree; cork
subesse *infin of* **subsum**

subf- *etc see* **suff-**
subg- *etc see* **sugg-**
subhorridus *adj* somewhat uncouth
subiaceō, -ēre, -uī *vi* to lie under, be close (to); to be connected (with)
subiciō, -icere, -iēcī, -iectum *vt* to put under, bring under; to bring up, throw up; to bring near; to submit, subject, expose; to subordinate, deal with under; to append, add on, answer; to adduce, suggest; to substitute; to forge; to suborn; **sē subicere** grow up
subiectē *adv* submissively
subiectiō, -ōnis *f* laying under; forging
subiectō, -āre *vt* to lay under, put to; to throw up
subiector, -ōris *m* forger
subiectus *ppp of* **subiciō** ♦ *adj* neighbouring, bordering; subject, exposed
subigitātiō, -ōnis *f* lewdness
subigitō, -āre *vt* to behave improperly to
subigō, -igere, -ēgī, -āctum *vt* to bring up to; to impel, compel; to subdue, conquer; (*animal*) to tame, break in; (*blade*) to sharpen; (*boat*) to row, propel; (*cooking*) to knead; (*earth*) to turn up, dig; (*mind*) to train
subiī *perf of* **subeō**
subimpudēns, -entis *adj* rather impertinent
subinānis *adj* rather empty
subinde *adv* immediately after; repeatedly
subīnsulsus *adj* rather insipid
subinvideō, -ēre *vi* to be a little envious of
subinvīsus *adj* somewhat odious
subinvītō, -āre *vt* to invite vaguely
subīrāscor, -scī, -tus *vi* to be rather angry
subīrātus *adj* rather angry
subitārius *adj* sudden, emergency (*in cpds*)
subitō *adv* suddenly
subitus *ppp of* **subeō** ♦ *adj* sudden, unexpected; (*man*) rash; (*troops*) hastily raised ♦ *nt* surprise, emergency
subiūnctus *ppp of* **subiungō**
subiungō, -ungere, -ūnxī, -ūnctum *vt* to harness; to add, affix; to subordinate, subdue
sublābor, -bī, -psus *vi* to sink down; to glide away
sublāpsus *ppa of* **sublābor**
sublātē *adv* loftily
sublātiō, -ōnis *f* elevation
sublātus *ppp of* **tollō** ♦ *adj* elated
sublectō, -āre *vt* to coax
sublēctus *ppp of* **sublegō**
sublegō, -egere, -ēgī, -ēctum *vt* to gather up; to substitute; (*child*) to kidnap; (*talk*) to overhear
sublestus *adj* slight
sublevātiō, -ōnis *f* alleviation
sublevō, -āre, -āvī, -ātum *vt* to lift up, hold up; to support, encourage; to lighten, alleviate
sublica, -ae *f* pile, palisade
sublicius *adj* on piles
subligāculum, -ī, subligar, -āris *nt* loincloth
subligō, -āre *vt* to fasten on
sublīmē *adv* aloft, in the air

sublīmis *adj* high, raised high, lifted up; (*character*) eminent, aspiring; (*language*) lofty, elevated

sublīmitās, -ātis *f* loftiness

sublīmus *etc see* **sublīmis**

sublingiō, -ōnis *m* scullion

sublinō, -inere, -ēvī, -itum *vt*: ōs sublinere to fool, bamboozle

sublitus *ppp of* **sublinō**

sublūceō, -ēre *vi* to glimmer

subluō, -ere *vt* (*river*) to flow past the foot of

sublūstris *adj* faintly luminous

sublūtus *ppp of* **subluō**

subm- *etc see* **summ-**

subnātus *adj* growing up underneath

subnectō, -ctere, -xuī, -xum *vt* to tie under, fasten to

subnegō, -āre *vt* to half refuse

subnexus *ppp of* **subnectō**

subniger, -rī *adj* darkish

subnīxus, subnīsus *adj* supported, resting (on); relying (on)

subnuba, -ae *f* rival

subnūbilus *adj* overcast

subō, -āre *vi* to be in heat

subobscēnus *adj* rather indecent

subobscūrus *adj* somewhat obscure

subodiōsus *adj* rather odious

suboffendō, -ere *vi* to give some offence

subolēs, -is *f* offspring, children

subolēscō, -ere *vi* to grow up

subolet, -ēre *vi* (*impers*) there is a faint scent; ~ mihi I detect, have an inkling

suborior, -īrī *vi* to spring up in succession

subōrnō, -āre, -āvī, -ātum *vt* to fit out, equip; to instigate secretly, suborn

subortus, -ūs *m* rising up repeatedly

subp- *etc see* **supp-**

subrancidus *adj* slightly tainted

subraucus *adj* rather hoarse

subrēctus *ppp of* **subrigō**

subrēmigō, -āre *vi* to paddle under (*water*)

subrēpō, -ere, -sī, -tum *vi* to creep along, steal up to

subreptus *ppp of* **subripiō**

subrīdeō, -dēre, -sī *vi* to smile

subrīdiculē *adv* rather funnily

subrigō, -igere, -ēxī, -ēctum *vt* to lift, raise

subringor, -ī *vi* to make a wry face, be rather vexed

subripiō, -ipere, -ipuī *and* **-upuī, -eptum** *vt* to take away secretly, steal

subrogō, -āre *vt* to propose as successor

subrōstrānī, -ōrum *mpl* idlers

subrubeō, -ēre *vi* to blush slightly

subrūfus *adj* ginger-haired

subruō, -ere, -ī, -tum *vt* to undermine, demolish

subrūsticus *adj* rather countrified

subrutus *ppp of* **subruō**

subscrībō, -bere, -psī, -ptum *vt* to write underneath; (*document*) to sign, subscribe; (*censor*) to set down; (*LAW*) to add to an indictment, prosecute; (*fig*) to record; (*with dat*) to assent to, approve

subscrīptiō, -ōnis *f* inscription underneath; signature; (*censor*) noting down; (*LAW*) subscription (*to an indictment*); register

subscrīptor, -ōris *m* subscriber (*to an indictment*)

subscrīptus *ppp of* **subscrībō**

subsecīvus *etc see* **subsicīvus**

subsecō, -āre, -uī, -ctum *vt* to cut off, clip

subsēdī *perf of* **subsīdō**

subsellium, -ī *and* **-iī** *nt* bench, seat; (*LAW*) the bench, the court

subsentiō, -entīre, -ēnsī *vt* to have an inkling of

subsequor, -quī, -cūtus *vt*, *vi* to follow closely; to support; to imitate

subserviō, -īre *vi* to be a slave; (*fig*) to comply (with)

subsicīvus *adj* left over; (*time*) spare; (*work*) overtime

subsidiārius *adj* in reserve ◆ *mpl* reserves

subsidium, -ī *and* **-iī** *nt* reserve ranks, reserve troops; relief, aid, assistance

subsīdō, -īdere, -ēdī, -essum *vi* to sit down, crouch, squat; to sink down, settle, subside; (*ambush*) to lie in wait; (*residence*) to stay, settle ◆ *vt* to lie in wait for

subsignānus *adj* special reserve (troops)

subsignō, -āre *vt* to register; to guarantee

subsiliō, -īre, -uī *vi* to leap up

subsistō, -istere, -titī *vi* to stand still, make a stand; to stop, halt; to remain, continue, hold out; (*with dat*) to resist ◆ *vt* to withstand

subsortior, -īrī, -ītus *vt* to choose as a substitute by lot

subsortītiō, -ōnis *f* choosing of substitutes by lot

substantia, -ae *f* means, wealth

substernō, -ernere, -rāvī, -rātum *vt* to scatter under, spread under; (*fig*) to put at one's service

substitī *perf of* **subsistō**

substituō, -uere, -uī, -ūtum *vt* to put next; to substitute; (*idea*) to present, imagine

substitūtus *ppp of* **substituō**

substō, -āre *vi* to hold out

substrātus *ppp of* **substernō**

substrictus *ppp of* **substringō** ◆ *adj* narrow, tight

substringō, -ngere, -nxī, -ctum *vt* to bind up; to draw close; to check

substructiō, -ōnis *f* foundation

substruō, -ere, -xī, -ctum *vt* to lay, pave

subsultō, -āre *vi* to jump up

subsum, -esse *vi* to be underneath; to be close to, be at hand; (*fig*) to underlie, be latent in

subsūtus *adj* fringed at the bottom

subtēmen, -inis *nt* woof; thread

subter *adv* below, underneath ◆ *prep* (*with acc and abl*) beneath; close up to

subterdūcō, -cere, -xī *vt* to withdraw secretly

subterfugiō, -ugere, -ūgī *vt* to escape from, evade

subterlābor, **-ī** vt, vi to flow past under; to slip away

subterrāneus adj underground

subtexō, **-ere**, **-uī**, **-tum** vt to weave in; to veil, obscure

subtīlis adj slender, fine; (senses) delicate, nice; (judgment) discriminating, precise; (style) plain, direct

subtīlitās, **-ātis** f fineness; (judgment) acuteness, exactness; (style) plainness, directness

subtīliter adv finely; accurately; simply

subtimeō, **-ēre** vt to be a little afraid of

subtractus ppp of **subtrahō**

subtrahō, **-here**, **-xī**, **-ctum** vt to draw away from underneath; to take away secretly; to withdraw, remove

subtristis adj rather sad

subturpiculus adj a little bit mean

subturpis adj rather mean

subtus adv below, underneath

subtūsus adj slightly bruised

subūcula, **-ae** f shirt, vest

sūbula, **-ae** f awl

subulcus, **-ī** m swineherd

Subūra, **-ae** f a disreputable quarter of Rome

Subūrānus adj see **Subūra**

suburbānitās, **-ātis** f nearness to Rome

suburbānus adj near Rome ♦ nt villa near Rome ♦ mpl inhabitants of the towns near Rome

suburbium, **-ī** and **-iī** nt suburb

suburgeō, **-ēre** vt to drive close (to)

subvectiō, **-ōnis** f transport

subvectō, **-āre** vt to carry up regularly

subvectus¹ ppp of **subvehō**

subvectus², **-ūs** m transport

subvehō, **-here**, **-xī**, **-ctum** vt to carry up, transport upstream

subveniō, **-enīre**, **-ēnī**, **-entum** vi (with dat) to come to the assistance of, relieve, reinforce

subventō, **-āre** vi (with dat) to come quickly to help

subvereor, **-ērī** vi to be a little afraid

subversor, **-ōris** m subverter

subversus ppp of **subvertō**

subvertō, **-tere**, **-tī**, **-sum** vt to turn upside down, upset; to overthrow, subvert

subvexī perf of **subvehō**

subvexus adj sloping upwards

subvolō, **-āre** vi to fly upwards

subvolvō, **-ere** vt to roll uphill

subvortō etc see **subvertō**

succavus adj hollow underneath

succēdō, **-ēdere**, **-essī**, **-essum** vt, vi (with dat) to go under, pass into, take on; (with dat, acc, in) to go up, climb; (with dat, acc, ad, sub) to march on, advance to; (with dat, in) to come to take the place of, relieve; (with dat, in, ad) to follow after, succeed, succeed to; (result) to turn out, be successful

succendō, **-endere**, **-endī**, **-ēnsum** vt to set fire to, kindle; (fig) to fire, inflame

succēnseō etc see **suscēnseō**

succēnsus ppp of **succendō**

succenturiātus adj in reserve

succenturiō, **-ōnis** m under-centurion

successī perf of **succēdō**

successiō, **-ōnis** f succession

successor, **-ōris** m successor

successus¹ ppp of **succēdō**

successus², **-ūs** m advance uphill; result, success

succīdia, **-ae** f leg or side of meat, flitch

succidō, **-ere**, **-ī** vi to sink, give way

succīdō, **-dere**, **-dī**, **-sum** vt to cut off, mow down

succiduus adj sinking, failing

succinctus ppp of **succingō**

succingō, **-gere**, **-xī**, **-ctum** vt to gird up, tuck up; to equip, arm

succingulum, **-ī** nt girdle

succinō, **-ere** vi to chime in

succīsus ppp of **succīdō**

succlāmātiō, **-ōnis** f shouting, barracking

succlāmō, **-āre**, **-āvī**, **-ātum** vt to shout after, interrupt with shouting

succontumēliōsē adv somewhat insolently

succrēscō, **-ere** vi to grow up from or to

succrispus adj rather curly

succumbō, **-mbere**, **-buī**, **-bitum** vi to fall, sink under; to submit, surrender

succurrō, **-rere**, **-rī**, **-sum** vi to come quickly up; to run to the help of, succour; (idea) to occur

succus etc see **sūcus**

succussus, **-ūs** m shaking

succustōs, **-ōdis** m assistant keeper

succutiō, **-tere**, **-ssī**, **-ssum** vt to toss up

sūcidus adj juicy, fresh, plump

sūcinum, **-ī** nt amber

sūctus ppp of **sūgō**

sucula¹, **-ae** f winch, windlass

sucula², **-ae** f piglet; (pl) the Hyads

sūcus, **-ī** m juice, sap; medicine, potion; taste, flavour; (fig) strength, vigour, life

sūdārium, **-ī** and **-iī** nt handkerchief

sūdātōrius adj for sweating ♦ nt sweating bath

sudis, **-is** f stake, pile, pike, spike

sūdō, **-āre**, **-āvī**, **-ātum** vi to sweat, perspire; to be drenched with; to work hard ♦ vt to exude

sūdor, **-ōris** m sweat, perspiration; moisture; hard work, exertion

sudus adj cloudless, clear ♦ nt fine weather

sueō, **-ēre** vi to be accustomed

suēscō, **-scere**, **-vī**, **-tum** vi to be accustomed ♦ vt to accustom

Suessa, **-ae** f town in Latium

Suessiōnēs, **-um** mpl people of Gaul (near what is now Soissons)

suētus ppp of **suēscō** ♦ adj accustomed; usual

Suēvī, **-ōrum** mpl people of N.E. Germany

sūfes, **-etis** m chief magistrate of Carthage

suffarcinātus adj stuffed full

suffectus ppp of **sufficiō** ♦ adj (consul) appointed to fill a vacancy during the regular term of office

sufferō, **-re** vt to support, undergo, endure

suffes etc see **sūfes**

sufficiō, -icere, -ēcī, -ectum *vt* to dye, tinge; to supply, provide; to appoint in place (of another), substitute ♦ *vi* to be adequate, suffice

suffīgō, -gere, -xī, -xum *vt* to fasten underneath, nail on

suffīmen, -inis, suffīmentum, -ī *nt* incense

suffiō, -īre *vt* to fumigate, perfume

suffīxus *ppp of* **suffīgō**

sufflāmen, -inis *nt* brake

sufflō, -āre *vt* to blow up; to puff up

suffōcō, -āre *vt* to choke, stifle

suffodiō, -odere, -ōdī, -ossum *vt* to stab; to dig under, undermine

suffossus *ppp of* **suffodiō**

suffrāgātiō, -ōnis *f* voting for, support

suffrāgātor, -ōris *m* voter, supporter

suffrāgātōrius *adj* supporting a candidate

suffrāgium, -ī *and* **-iī** *nt* vote, ballot; right of suffrage; (*fig*) judgment, approval; **~ ferre** vote

suffrāgor, -ārī, -ātus *vi* to vote for; to support, favour

suffringō, -ere *vt* to break

suffugiō, -ugere, -ūgī *vi* to run for shelter ♦ *vt* to elude

suffugium, -ī *and* **-iī** *nt* shelter, refuge

suffulciō, -cīre, -sī, -tum *vt* to prop up, support

suffundō, -undere, -ūdī, -ūsum *vt* to pour in; to suffuse, fill; to tinge, colour; (*blush*) to overspread

suffūror, -ārī *vi* to filch

suffuscus *adj* darkish

suffūsus *ppp of* **suffundō**

Sugambrī, -ōrum *mpl* people of N.W. Germany

suggerō, -rere, -ssī, -stum *vt* to bring up to, supply; to add on, put next

suggestum, -ī *nt* platform

suggestus¹ *ppp of* **suggerō**

suggestus², -ūs *m* platform, stage

suggrandis *adj* rather large

suggredior, -dī, -ssus *vi* to come up close, approach ♦ *vt* to attack

sūgillātiō, -ōnis *f* affronting

sūgillātus *adj* bruised; insulted

sūgō, -gere, -xī, -ctum *vt* to suck

suī¹ *gen of* **sē**

suī² *perf of* **suō**

suillus *adj* of pigs

sulcō, -āre *vt* to furrow, plough

sulcus, -ī *m* furrow; trench; track

sulfur, -uris *n* sulphur

Sulla, -ae *m* famous Roman dictator

Sullānus *adj see* **Sulla**

sullāturiō, -īre *vi* to hanker after being a Sulla

Sulmō, -ōnis *m* town in E. Italy (*birthplace of Ovid*)

Sulmōnēnsis *adj see* **Sulmō**

sultis *adv* please

sum, esse, fuī *vi* to be, exist; **sum ab** belong to; **sum ad** be designed for; **sum ex** consist of; **est, sunt** there is, are; **est mihi** I have; **mihi tēcum nīl est** I have nothing to do with you; **est quod** something; there is a reason for; **est ubi** sometimes; **est ut** it is possible that;

est (*with gen*) to belong to, be the duty of, be characteristic of; (*with inf*) it is possible, it is permissible; **sunt quī** some; **fuit Ilium** Troy is no more

sūmen, -inis *nt* udder, teat; sow

summa, -ae *f* main part, chief point, main issue; gist, summary; sum, amount, the whole; supreme power; **~ rērum** the general interest, the whole responsibility; **~ summārum** the universe; **ad summam** in short, in fact; in conclusion; **in summā** in all; after all

Summānus, -ī *m* god of nocturnal thunderbolts

summās, -ātis *adj* high-born, eminent

summātim *adv* cursorily, summarily

summātus, -ūs *m* sovereignty

summē *adv* in the highest degree, extremely

summergō, -gere, -sī, -sum *vt* to plunge under, sink

summersus *ppp of* **summergō**

sumministrō, -āre, -āvī, -ātum *vt* to provide, furnish

summissē *adv* softly; humbly, modestly

summissiō, -ōnis *f* lowering

summissus *ppp of* **summittō** ♦ *adj* low; (*voice*) low, calm; (*character*) mean, grovelling, submissive, humble

summittō, -ittere, -īsī, -issum *vt* (*growth*) to send up, raise, rear; to despatch, supply; to let down, lower, reduce, moderate; to supersede; to send secretly; **animum summittere** submit; **sē summittere** condescend

summolestē *adv* with some annoyance

summolestus *adj* a little annoying

summoneō, -ēre, -uī *vt* to drop a hint to

summōrōsus *adj* rather peevish

summōtor, -ōris *m* clearer

summōtus *ppp of* **summoveō**

summoveō, -ovēre, -ōvī, -ōtum *vt* to move away, drive off; to clear away (*to make room*), withdraw, remove, banish; (*fig*) to dispel

summum¹, -ī *nt* top, surface

summum² *adv* at the most

summus *adj* highest, the top of, the surface of; last, the end of; (*fig*) utmost, greatest, most important; (*person*) distinguished, excellent ♦ *m* head of the table

summūtō, -āre *vt* to substitute

sūmō, -ere, -psī, -ptum *vt* to take, take up; to assume, arrogate; (*action*) to undertake; (*argument*) to assume, take for granted; (*dress*) to put on; (*punishment*) to exact; (*for a purpose*) to use, spend

sūmptiō, -ōnis *f* assumption

sūmptuārius *adj* sumptuary

sūmptuōsē *adv see* **sūmptuōsus**

sūmptuōsus *adj* expensive, lavish, extravagant

sūmptus¹ *ppp of* **sūmō**

sūmptus², -ūs *m* expense, cost

Sūnium, -ī *and* **-iī** *nt* S.E. promontory of Attica

suō, suere, suī, sūtum *vt* to sew, stitch, join together

suōmet, suōpte *abl of* **suus**

suovetaurīlia, -ium *ntpl* sacrifice of a pig, sheep and bull

supellex, -ectilis *f* furniture, goods, outfit

super[1] *etc adj see* **superus**

super[2] *adv* above, on the top; besides, moreover; left, remaining ◆ *prep (with abl)* upon, above; concerning; besides; (*time*) at; (*with acc*) over, above, on; beyond; besides, over and above

superā *etc see* **suprā**

superābilis *adj* surmountable, conquerable

superaddō, -ere, -itum *vt* to add over and above

superāns, -antis *pres p of* **superō** ◆ *adj* predominant

superātor, -ōris *m* conqueror

superbē *adv* arrogantly, despotically

superbia, -ae *f* arrogance, insolence, tyranny; pride, lofty spirit

superbiloquentia, -ae *f* arrogant speech

superbiō, -īre *vi* to be arrogant, take a pride in; to be superb

superbus *adj* arrogant, insolent, overbearing; fastidious; superb, magnificent

supercilium, -ī *and* **-iī** *nt* eyebrow; (*hill*) brow, ridge; (*fig*) arrogance

superēmineō, -ēre *vt* to overtop

superesse *infin of* **supersum**

superficiēs, -ēī *f* surface; (*LAW*) a building (*esp on another's land*)

superfiō, -ierī *vi* to be left over

superfīxus *adj* fixed on top

superfluō, -ere *vi* to overflow

superfuī *perf of* **supersum**

superfundō, -undere, -ūdī, -ūsum *vt, vi* to pour over, shower; (*pass*) to overflow, spread out

superfūsus *ppp of* **superfundō**

supergredior, -dī, -ssus *vt* to surpass

superiaciō, -iacere, -iēcī, -iectum *and* **-iactum** *vt* to throw over, overspread; to overtop; (*fig*) to exaggerate

superiectus *ppp of* **superiaciō**

superimmineō, -ēre *vi* to overhang

superimpendēns, -entis *adj* overhanging

superimpōnō, -ōnere, -osuī, -ositum *vt* to place on top

superimpositus *ppp of* **superimpōnō**

superincidēns, -entis *adj* falling from above

superincubāns, -antis *adj* lying upon

superincumbō, -ere *vi* to fling oneself down upon

superingerō, -ere *vt* to pour down

superiniciō, -icere, -iēcī, -iectum *vt* to throw upon, put on top

superiniectus *ppp of* **superiniciō**

superīnsternō, -ere *vt* to lay over

superior, -ōris *adj* higher, upper; (*time, order*) preceding, previous, former; (*age*) older; (*battle*) victorious, stronger; (*quality*) superior, greater

superlātiō, -ōnis *f* exaggeration

superlātus *adj* exaggerated

supernē *adv* at the top, from above

supernus *adj* upper; celestial

superō, -āre, -āvī, -ātum *vi* to rise above, overtop; to have the upper hand; to be in excess, be abundant; to be left over, survive ◆ *vt* to pass over, surmount, go beyond; to surpass, outdo; (*MIL*) to overcome, conquer; (*NAUT*) to sail past, double

superobruō, -ere *vt* to overwhelm

superpendēns, -entis *adj* overhanging

superpōnō, -ōnere, -osuī, -ositum *vt* to place upon; to put in charge of

superpositus *ppp of* **superpōnō**

superscandō, -ere *vt* to climb over

supersedeō, -edēre, -ēdī, -essum *vi* to forbear, desist from

superstes, -itis *adj* standing over; surviving

superstitiō, -ōnis *f* awful fear, superstition

superstitiōsē *adv* superstitiously; scrupulously

superstitiōsus *adj* superstitious; prophetic

superstō, -āre *vt, vi* to stand over, stand on

superstrātus *adj* spread over

superstruō, -ere, -xī, -ctum *vt* to build on top

supersum, -esse, -fuī *vi* to be left, remain; to survive; to be in abundance, be sufficient; to be in excess

supertegō, -ere *vt* to cover over

superurgēns, -entis *adj* pressing from above

superus (*compar* **-ior**, *superl* **suprēmus** *and* **summus**) *adj* upper, above ◆ *mpl* the gods above; the living ◆ *ntpl* the heavenly bodies; higher places; **mare superum** Adriatic Sea

supervacāneus *adj* extra, superfluous

supervacuus *adj* superfluous, pointless

supervādō, -ere *vt* to climb over, surmount

supervehor, -hī, -ctus *vt* to ride past, sail past

superveniō, -enīre, -ēnī, -entum *vt* to overtake, come on top of ◆ *vi* to come on the scene, arrive unexpectedly

superventus, -ūs *m* arrival

supervolitō, -āre *vt* to fly over

supervolō, -āre *vt, vi* to fly over

supīnō, -āre, -āvī, -ātum *vt* to upturn, lay on its back

supīnus *adj* lying back, face up; sloping, on a slope; backwards; (*mind*) indolent, careless

suppāctus *ppp of* **suppingō**

suppaenitet, -ēre *vt impers* to be a little sorry

suppalpor, -ārī *vi* to coax gently

suppār, -aris *adj* nearly equal

supparasītor, -ārī *vi* to flatter gently

supparus, -ī *m*, **supparum, -ī** *nt* woman's linen garment; topsail

suppeditātiō, -ōnis *f* abundance

suppeditō, -āre, -āvī, -ātum *vi* to be at hand, be in full supply, be sufficient; to be rich in ◆ *vt* to supply, furnish

suppēdō, -ere *vi* to break wind quietly

suppetiae, -ārum *fpl* assistance

suppetior, -ārī, -ātus *vi* to come to the assistance of

suppetō, -ere, -īvī *and* **-iī, -ītum** *vi* to be available, be in store; to be equal to, suffice for

suppīlō, -āre *vt* to steal

suppingō, -ingere, -āctum vt to fasten underneath

supplantō, -āre vt to trip up

supplēmentum, -ī nt full complement; reinforcements

suppleō, -ēre vt to fill up, make good, make up to the full complement

supplex, -icis adj suppliant, in entreaty

supplicātiō, -ōnis f day of prayer, public thanksgiving

suppliciter adv in supplication

supplicium, -ī and -iī nt prayer, entreaty; sacrifice; punishment, execution, suffering; **suppliciō afficere** execute

supplicō, -āre, -āvī, -ātum vi (with dat) to entreat, pray to, worship

supplōdō, -dere, -sī vt to stamp

supplōsiō, -ōnis f stamping

suppōnō, -ōnere, -osuī, -ositum vt to put under, apply; to subject; to add on; to substitute, falsify

supportō, -āre vt to bring up, transport

suppositīcius adj spurious

suppositiō, -ōnis f substitution

suppositus ppp of **suppōnō**

supposuī perf of **suppōnō**

suppressiō, -ōnis f embezzlement

suppressus ppp of **supprimō** ♦ adj (voice) low

supprimō, -imere, -essī, -essum vt to sink; to restrain, detain, put a stop to; to keep secret, suppress

supprōmus, -ī m underbutler

suppudet, -ēre vt impers to be a little ashamed

suppūrō, -āre vi to fester

suppus adj head downwards

supputō, -āre vt to count up

suprā adv above, up on top; (time) earlier, previously; (amount) more; **~ quam** beyond what ♦ prep (with acc) over, above; beyond; (time) before; (amount) more than, over

suprāscandō, -ere vt to surmount

suprēmum adv for the last time

suprēmus adj highest; last, latest; greatest, supreme ♦ ntpl moment of death; funeral rites; testament

sūra, -ae f calf (of the leg)

sūrculus, -ī m twig, shoot; graft, slip

surdaster, -rī adj rather deaf

surditās, -ātis f deafness

surdus adj deaf; silent

surēna, -ae m grand vizier (of the Parthians)

surgō, -ere, surrēxī, surrēctum vi to rise, get up, stand up; to arise, spring up, grow

surpere etc = **surripere**

surr- etc see **subr-**

surrēxī perf of **surgō**

surruptīcius adj stolen

surrupuī perf of **subripiō**

sūrsum, sūrsus adv upwards, up, high up; **~ deōrsum** up and down

sūs, suis m/f pig, boar, hog, sow

Sūsa, -ōrum ntpl ancient Persian capital

suscēnseō, -ēre, -uī vi to be angry, be irritated

susceptiō, -ōnis f undertaking

susceptus ppp of **suscipiō**

suscipiō, -ipere, -ēpī, -eptum vt to take up, undertake; to receive, catch; (child) to acknowledge; to beget; to take under one's protection

suscitō, -āre, -āvī, -ātum vt to lift, raise; to stir, rouse, awaken; to encourage, excite

suspectō, -āre vt, vi to look up at, watch; to suspect, mistrust

suspectus[1] ppp of **suspiciō** ♦ adj suspected, suspicious

suspectus[2] **-ūs** m looking up; esteem

suspendium, -ī and -iī nt hanging

suspendō, -endere, -endī, -ēnsum vt to hang, hang up; (death) to hang; (building) to support; (mind) to keep in suspense; (movement) to check, interrupt; (pass) to depend

suspēnsus ppp of **suspendō** ♦ adj raised, hanging, poised; with a light touch; (fig) in suspense, uncertain, anxious; dependent; **suspēnsō gradū** on tiptoe

suspicāx, -ācis adj suspicious

suspiciō, -icere, -exī, -ectum vt to look up at, look up to; to admire, respect; to mistrust

suspiciō, -ōnis f mistrust, suspicion

suspīciōsē adv suspiciously

suspīciōsus adj suspicious

suspicor, -ārī, -ātus vt to suspect; to surmise, suppose

suspīrātus, -ūs m sigh

suspīritus, -ūs m deep breath, difficult breathing; sigh

suspīrium, -ī and -iī nt deep breath, sigh

suspīrō, -āre, -āvī, -ātum vi to sigh ♦ vt to sigh for; to exclaim with a sigh

susque dēque adv up and down

sustentāculum, -ī nt prop

sustentātiō, -ōnis f forbearance

sustentō, -āre, -āvī, -ātum vt to hold up, support; (fig) to uphold, uplift; (food, means) to sustain, support; (enemy) to check, hold; (trouble) to suffer; (event) to hold back, postpone

sustineō, -inēre, -inuī, -entum vt to hold up, support; to check, control; (fig) to uphold, maintain; (food, means) to sustain, support; (trouble) to bear, suffer, withstand; (event) to put off

sustollō, -ere vt to lift up, raise; to destroy

sustulī perf of **tollō**

susurrātor, -ōris m whisperer

susurrō, -āre vt, vi to murmur, buzz, whisper

susurrus[1], **-ī** m murmuring, whispering

susurrus[2] adj whispering

sūtēla, -ae f trick

sūtilis adj sewn

sūtor, -ōris m shoemaker; **~ nē suprā crepidam** let the cobbler stick to his last

sūtōrius adj shoemaker's; ex-cobbler

sūtrīnus adj shoemaker's

sūtūra, -ae f seam

sūtus ppp of **suō**

suus adj his, her, its, their; one's own, proper, due, right ♦ mpl one's own troops, friends, followers etc ♦ nt one's own property

Sybaris, -is f town in E. Italy (noted for its debauchery)

Sybarīta, -ītae *m* Sybarite
Sychaeus, -ī *m husband of Dido*
sycophanta, -ae *m* slanderer, cheat, sycophant
sycophantia, -ae *f* deceit
sycophantiōsē *adv* deceitfully
sycophantor, -ārī *vi* to cheat
Syēnē, -ēs *f town in S. Egypt (now Aswan)*
syllaba, -ae *f* syllable
syllabātim *adv* syllable by syllable
symbola, -ae *f* contribution
symbolus, -ī *m* token, symbol
symphōnia, -ae *f* concord, harmony
symphōniacus *adj* choir *(in cpds)*
Symplēgades, -um *fpl* clashing rocks in the Black Sea
synedrus, -ī *m* senator *(in Macedonia)*
Synephēbī, -ōrum *mpl* Youths Together *(comedy by Caecilius)*

syngrapha, -ae *f* promissory note
syngraphus, -ī *m* written contract; passport, pass
Synnada, -ōrum *ntpl town in Phrygia (famous for marble)*
Synnadēnsis *adj see* **Synnada**
synodūs, -ontis *m* bream
synthesis, -is *f* dinner service; suit of clothes; dressing gown
Syphāx, -ācis *m king of Numidia*
Syrācūsae, -ārum *fpl* Syracuse
Syrācūsānus, Syrācūsānius, Syrācosius *adj* Syracusan
Syria, -iae *f country at the E. end of the Mediterranean*
Syrius, Syriacus, Syriscus *adj* Syrian
syrma, -ae *f* robe with a train; *(fig)* tragedy
Syrtis, -is *f Gulf of Sidra in N. Africa;* sandbank

Tt

tabella, -ae f small board, sill; writing tablet, voting tablet, votive tablet; picture; (pl) writing, records, dispatches

tabellārius adj about voting ♦ m courier

tābeō, -ēre vi to waste away; to be wet

taberna, -ae f cottage; shop; inn; (circus) stalls

tabernāculum, -ī nt tent; ~ **capere** choose a site (for auspices)

tabernāriī, -ōrum mpl shopkeepers

tābēs, -is f wasting away, decaying, melting; putrefaction; plague, disease

tābēscō, -ēscere, -uī vi to waste away, melt, decay; (fig) to pine, languish

tābidulus adj consuming

tābidus adj melting, decaying; pining; corrupting, infectious

tābificus adj melting, wasting

tabula, -ae f board, plank; writing tablet; votive tablet; map; picture; auction; (pl) account books, records, lists, will; ~ **Sullae** Sulla's proscriptions; **XII tabulae** Twelve Tables of Roman laws; **tabulae novae** cancellation of debts

tabulārium, -ī and -iī nt archives

tabulātiō, -ōnis f flooring, storey

tabulātum, -ī nt flooring, storey; (trees) layer, row

tābum, -ī nt decaying matter; disease, plague

taceō, -ēre, -uī, -itum vi to be silent, say nothing; to be still, be hushed ♦ vt to say nothing about, not speak of

tacitē adv silently; secretly

taciturnitās, -ātis f silence, taciturnity

taciturnus adj silent, quiet

Tacitus, -ī m famous Roman historian

tacitus ppp of **taceō** ♦ adj silent, mute, quiet; secret, unmentioned; tacit, implied; **per tacitum** quietly

tāctilis adj tangible

tāctiō, -ōnis f touching; sense of touch

tāctus¹ ppp of **tangō**

tāctus², -ūs m touch, handling, sense of touch; influence

taeda, -ae f pitch pine, pinewood; torch; plank; (fig) wedding

taedet, -ēre, -uit and -taesum est vt (impers) to be weary (of), loathe

taedifer, -ī adj torch-bearing

taedium, -ī and -iī nt weariness, loathing

Taenaridēs, -idae m Spartan (esp Hyacinthus)

Taenarius, -is adj of Taenarus; Spartan

Taenarum, -ī nt, **Taenaron, -ī** nt, **Taenarus, -ī** m/f, **Taenaros, -ī** m/f town and promontory in S. Greece (now Matapan), lower world

taenia, -ae f hairband, ribbon

taesum est perf of **taedet**

taeter, -rī adj foul, hideous, repulsive

taetrē adv hideously

taetricus see **tetricus**

tagāx, -ācis adj light-fingered

Tagus, -ī m river of Lusitania (now Tagus)

tālāris adj reaching to the ankles ♦ ntpl winged sandals; a garment reaching to the ankles

tālārius adj of dice

Talāsius, -ī and -iī m god of weddings; wedding cry

tālea, -ae f rod, stake

talentum, -ī nt talent, a Greek weight about 25.4kg; a large sum of money (esp the Attic talent of 60 minae)

tāliō, -ōnis f retaliation in kind

tālis adj such; the following

talpa, -ae f mole

tālus, -ī m ankle; heel; (pl) knuckle bones, oblong dice

tam adv so, so much, so very

tamdiū adv so long, as long

tamen adv however, nevertheless, all the same

Tāmesis, -is, Tāmesa, -ae m Thames

tametsī conj although

Tanagra, -ae f town in Boeotia

Tanais, -is m river in Sarmatia (now Don)

Tanaquil, -ilis f wife of the elder Tarquin

tandem adv at last, at length, finally; (question) just

tangō, -ere, tetigī, tāctum vt to touch, handle; (food) to taste; (with force) to hit, strike; (with liquid) to sprinkle; (mind) to affect, move; (place) to reach; to border on; (task) to take in hand; (by trick) to take in, fool; (in words) to touch on, mention; **dē caelō tāctus** struck by lightning

tanquam see **tamquam**

Tantaleus adj see **Tantalus**

Tantalidēs, -idae m Pelops, Atreus, Thyestes or Agamemnon

Tantalis, -idis f Niobe or Hermione

Tantalus, -ī m father of Pelops (condemned to hunger and thirst in Tartarus, or to the threat of an overhanging rock)

tantillus adj so little, so small

tantisper adv so long, just for a moment

tantopere *adv* so much
tantulus *adj* so little, so small
tantum *adv* so much, so, as; only, merely;
~ **modo** only; ~ **nōn** all but, almost; ~ **quod**
only just
tantummodo *adv* only
tantundem *adv* just as much, just so much
tantus *adj* so great; so little ♦ *nt* so much; so
little; **tantī esse** be worth so much, be so dear,
be so important; **tantō** so much, so far; *(with
comp)* so much the; **tantō opere** so much; **in
tantum** to such an extent; **tria tanta** three
times as much
tantusdem *adj* just so great
tapēta, -ae *m*, **tapētia, -ium** *ntpl* carpet,
tapestry, hangings
Taprobanē, -ēs *f* Ceylon
tardē *adv* slowly, tardily
tardēscō, -ere *vi* to become slow, falter
tardipēs, -edis *adj* limping
tarditās, -ātis *f* slowness, tardiness; *(mind)*
dullness
tardiusculus *adj* rather slow
tardō, -āre, -āvī, -ātum *vt* to retard, impede ♦ *vi*
to delay, go slow
tardus *adj* slow, tardy, late; *(mind)* dull; *(speech)*
deliberate
Tarentīnus *adj* Tarentine
Tarentum, -ī *nt* town in S. Italy (now Taranto)
tarmes, -itis *m* woodworm
Tarpēius *adj* Tarpeian; **mōns** ~ *the Tarpeian Rock
on the Capitoline Hill from which criminals were thrown*
tarpezīta, -ae *m* banker
Tarquiniēnsis *adj* of Tarquinii
Tarquiniī, -iōrum *mpl* ancient town in Etruria
Tarquinius[1] *adj* of Tarquin
Tarquinius[2]**, -ī** *m* Tarquin (*esp Priscus, the fifth king
of Rome, and Superbus, the last king*)
Tarracīna, -ae *f*, **Tarracīnae, -ārum** *fpl town
in Latium*
Tarracō, -ōnis *f town in Spain* (now Tarragona)
Tarracōnēnsis *adj see* **Tarracō**
Tarsēnsis *adj see* **Tarsus**
Tarsus, -ī *f capital of Cilicia*
Tartareus *adj* infernal
Tartarus, -ī *m*, **Tartaros, -ī** *m*, **Tartara, -ōrum**
ntpl Tartarus, the lower world (*esp the part
reserved for criminals*)
tat *interj* hallo there!
Tatius[1]**, -ī** *m* Sabine king (*who ruled jointly with
Romulus*)
Tatius[2] *adj see* **Tatius**[1]
Taum, -ī *nt* Firth of Tay
taureus *adj* bull's ♦ *f* whip of bull's hide
Taurī, -ōrum *mpl Thracians of the Crimea*
tauriförmis *adj* bull-shaped
Taurīnī, -ōrum *mpl people of N. Italy (near what is
now Turin)*
taurīnus *adj* bull's
Tauromenītānus *adj see* **Tauromenium**
Tauromenium, -ī and -iī *nt town in E. Sicily*
taurus, -ī *m* bull
Taurus, -ī *m mountain range in S.E. Asia Minor*
taxātiō, -ōnis *f* valuing
taxeus *adj* of yews

taxillus, -ī *m* small dice
taxō, -āre *vt* to value, estimate
taxus, -ī *f* yew
Tāygeta, -ōrum *ntpl*, **Tāygetus, -ī** *m mountain
range in S. Greece*
Tāygetē, -ēs *f a Pleiad*
tē *acc and abl of* **tū**
-te *suffix for* **tū**
Teānēnsis *adj see* **Teānum**
Teānum, -ī *nt town in Apulia; town in Campania*
techina, -ae *f* trick
Tecmessa, -ae *f wife of Ajax*
tēctor, -ōris *m* plasterer
tēctōriolum, -ī *nt* a little plaster
tēctōrium, -ī and -iī *nt* plaster, stucco
tēctōrius *adj* of a plasterer
tēctum, -ī *nt* roof, ceiling, canopy; house,
dwelling, shelter
tēctus *ppp of* **tegō** ♦ *adj* hidden; secret, reserved,
close
tēcum with you
Tegea, -ae *f town in Arcadia*
Tegeaeus *adj* Arcadian ♦ *m the god Pan* ♦ *f
Atalanta*
Tegeātae, -ātārum *mpl* Tegeans
teges, -etis *f* mat
tegillum, -ī *nt* hood, cowl
tegimen, -inis *nt* covering
tegimentum, -ī *nt* covering
tegmen- *etc see* **tegim-**
tegō, -ere, tēxī, -tēctum *vt* to cover; to hide,
conceal; to protect, defend; to bury; **latus
tegere** walk by the side of
tēgula, -ae *f* tile; (*pl*) tiled roof
tegum- *etc see* **tegim-**
Tēius *adj* of Teos
tēla, -ae *f* web; warp; yarnbeam, loom; (*fig*) plan
Telamōn, -ōnis *m father of Ajax*
Tēlegonus, -ī *m son of Ulysses and Circe*
Tēlemachus, -ī *m son of Ulysses and Penelope*
Tēlephus, -ī *m king of Mysia (wounded by Achilles'
spear)*
tellūs, -ūris *f* the earth; earth, ground; land,
country
tēlum, -ī *nt* weapon, missile; javelin, sword; (*fig*)
shaft, dart
temerārius *adj* accidental; rash, thoughtless
temerē *adv* by chance, at random; rashly,
thoughtlessly; **nōn** ~ not for nothing; not
easily; hardly ever
temeritās, -ātis *f* chance, rashness,
thoughtlessness
temerō, -āre, -āvī, -ātum *vt* to desecrate,
disgrace
tēmētum, -ī *nt* wine, alcohol
temnō, -ere *vt* to slight, despise
tēmō, -ōnis *m* beam (*of plough or carriage*); (ASTR)
the Plough
Tempē *ntpl famous valley in Thessaly*
temperāmentum, -ī *nt* moderation,
compromise
temperāns, -antis *pres p of* **temperō** ♦ *adj*
moderate, temperate
temperanter *adv* with moderation
temperantia, -ae *f* moderation, self-control

temperātē *adv* with moderation
temperātiō, -ōnis *f* proper mixture, composition, constitution; organizing power
temperātor, -ōris *m* organizer
temperātus *ppp of* **temperō** ♦ *adj* moderate, sober
temperī *adv* in time, at the right time
temperiēs, -ēī *f* due proportion; temperature, mildness
temperō, -āre, -āvī, -ātum *vt* to mix in due proportion, blend, temper; to regulate, moderate, tune; to govern, rule ♦ *vi* to be moderate, forbear, abstain; *(with dat)* to spare, be lenient to
tempestās, -ātis *f* time, season, period; weather; storm; *(fig)* storm, shower
tempestīvē *adv* at the right time, appropriately
tempestīvitās, -ātis *f* seasonableness
tempestīvus *adj* timely, seasonable, appropriate; ripe, mature; early
templum, -ī *nt* space marked off for taking auspices; open space, region, quarter; sanctuary; temple
temporārius *adj* for the time, temporary
temptābundus *adj* making repeated attempts
temptāmentum, -ī *nt* trial, attempt, proof
temptāmina, -um *ntpl* attempts, essays
temptātiō, -ōnis *f* trial, proof; attack
temptātor, -ōris *m* assailant
temptō, -āre, -āvī, -ātum *vt* to feel, test by touching; to make an attempt on, attack; to try, essay, attempt; to try to influence, tamper with, tempt, incite; **vēnās temptāre** feel the pulse
tempus, -oris *nt* time; right time, opportunity; danger, emergency, circumstance; *(head)* temple; *(verse)* unit of metre; *(verb)* tense; **tempore** at the right time, in time; **ad ~** at the right time; for the moment; **ante ~** too soon; **ex tempore** on the spur of the moment; to suit the circumstances; **in tempore** in time; **in ~** temporarily; **per ~** just in time; **prō tempore** to suit the occasion
tēmulentus *adj* intoxicated
tenācitās, -ātis *f* firm grip; stinginess
tenāciter *adv* tightly, firmly
tenāx, -ācis *adj* gripping, tenacious; sticky; *(fig)* firm, persistent; stubborn; stingy
tendicula, -ae *f* little snare
tendō, -ere, tetendī, tentum *and* **tēnsum** *vt* to stretch, spread; to strain; *(arrow)* to aim, shoot; *(bow)* to bend; *(course)* to direct; *(lyre)* to tune; *(tent)* to pitch; *(time)* to prolong; *(trap)* to lay ♦ *vi* to encamp; to go, proceed; to aim, tend; *(with inf)* to endeavour, exert oneself
tenebrae, -ārum *fpl* darkness, night; unconsciousness, death, blindness; *(place)* dungeon, haunt, the lower world; *(fig)* ignorance, obscurity
tenebricōsus *adj* gloomy
tenebrōsus *adj* dark, gloomy
Tenedius *adj see* **Tenedos**
Tenedos, Tenedus, -ī *f* Aegean island near Troy
tenellulus *adj* dainty little

teneō, -ēre, -uī *vt* to hold, keep; to possess, occupy, be master of; to attain, acquire; *(argument)* to maintain, insist; *(category)* to comprise; *(goal)* to make for; *(interest)* to fascinate; *(LAW)* to bind, be binding on; *(mind)* to grasp, understand, remember; *(movement)* to hold back, restrain ♦ *vi* to hold on, last, persist; *(rumour)* to prevail; **cursum tenēre** keep on one's course; **sē tenēre** remain; to refrain
tener, -ī *adj* tender, delicate; young, weak; effeminate; *(poet)* erotic
tenerāscō, -ere *vi* to grow weak
tenerē *adv* softly
teneritās, -ātis *f* weakness
tenor, -ōris *m* steady course; **ūnō tenōre** without a break, uniformly
tēnsa, -ae *f* carriage bearing the images of the gods in procession
tēnsus *ppp of* **tendō** ♦ *adj* strained
tentā- *etc see* **temptā-**
tentīgō, -inis *f* lust
tentō *etc see* **temptō**
tentōrium, -ī *and* **-iī** *nt* tent
tentus *ppp of* **tendō**
tenuiculus *adj* paltry
tenuis *adj* thin, fine; small, shallow; *(air)* rarefied; *(water)* clear; *(condition)* poor, mean, insignificant; *(style)* refined, direct, precise
tenuitās, -ātis *f* thinness, fineness; poverty, insignificance; *(style)* precision
tenuiter *adv* thinly; poorly; with precision; superficially
tenuō, -āre, -āvī, -ātum *vt* to make thin, attenuate, rarefy; to lessen, reduce
tenus *prep (with gen or abl)* as far as, up to, down to; **verbō ~** in name, nominally
Teos, -ī *f* town on coast of Asia Minor (birthplace of Anacreon)
tepefaciō, -facere, -fēcī, -factum *vt* to warm
tepeō, -ēre *vi* to be warm, be lukewarm; *(fig)* to be in love
tepēscō, -ēscere, -uī *vi* to grow warm; to become lukewarm, cool off
tepidus *adj* warm, lukewarm
tepor, -ōris *m* warmth; coolness
ter *adv* three times, thrice
terdeciēns, terdeciēs *adv* thirteen times
terebinthus, -ī *f* turpentine tree
terebra, -ae *f* gimlet
terebrō, -āre *vt* to bore
teredō, -inis *f* grub
Terentia, -iae *f* Cicero's wife
Terentius¹, -ī *m* Roman family name (esp the comic poet Terence)
Terentius², -iānus *adj see* **Terentius¹**
teres, -etis *adj* rounded (esp cylindrical), smooth, shapely; *(fig)* polished, elegant
Tēreus, -eī *and* **-eos** *m* king of Thrace (husband of Procne, father of Itys)
tergeminus *adj* threefold, triple
tergeō, -gēre, -sī, -sum *vt* to wipe off, scour, clean; to rub up, burnish
tergīnum, -ī *nt* rawhide
tergiversātiō, -ōnis *f* refusal, subterfuge

tergiversor, -ārī, -ātus *vi* to hedge, boggle, be evasive

tergō *etc see* **tergeō**

tergum, -ī *nt* back; rear; (*land*) ridge; (*water*) surface; (*meat*) chine; (*skin*) hide, leather, *anything made of leather;* **terga vertere** take to flight; **ā tergō** behind, in the rear

tergus, -oris *see* **tergum**

termes, -itis *m* branch

Terminália, -ium *ntpl Festival of the god of Boundaries*

terminātiō, -ōnis *f* decision; (*words*) clausula

terminō, -āre, -āvī, -ātum *vt* to set bounds to, limit; to define, determine; to end

terminus, -ī *m* boundary line, limit, bound; god of boundaries

ternī, -ōrum *adj* three each; three

terō, -ere, -trīvī, trītum *vt* to rub, crush, grind; to smooth, sharpen; to wear away, use up; (*road*) to frequent; (*time*) to waste; (*word*) to make commonplace

Terpsichorē, -ēs *f Muse of dancing*

terra, -ae *f* dry land, earth, ground, soil; land, country; **orbis terrārum** the world; **ubi terrārum** where in the world

terrēnus *adj* of earth; terrestrial, land- (*in cpds*) ♦ *nt* land

terreō, -ēre, -uī, -itum *vt* to frighten, terrify; to scare away; to deter

terrestris *adj* earthly, on earth, land- (*in cpds*)

terribilis *adj* terrifying, dreadful

terricula, -ōrum *ntpl* scare, bogy

terrificō, -āre *vt* to terrify

terrificus *adj* alarming, formidable

terrigena, -ae *m* earth-born

terriloquus *adj* alarming

territō, -āre *vt* to frighten, intimidate

territōrium, -ī *and* **-iī** *nt* territory

territus *adj* terrified

terror, -ōris *m* fright, alarm, terror; a terror

tersī *perf of* **tergeō**

tersus *ppp of* **tergeō** ♦ *adj* clean; neat, terse

tertiadecimānī, -ōrum *mpl* men of the thirteenth legion

tertiānus *adj* recurring every second day ♦ *f* a fever ♦ *mpl* men of the third legion

tertiō *adv* for the third time; thirdly

tertium *adv* for the third time

tertius *adj* third; ~ **decimus (decumus)** thirteenth

terūncius, -ī *and* **-iī** *m* quarter-as; a fourth; (*fig*) farthing

tesqua, tesca, -ōrum *ntpl* waste ground, desert

tessella, -ae *f* cube of mosaic stone

tessera, -ae *f* cube, dice; (MIL) password; token (*for mutual recognition of friends*); ticket (*for doles*)

tesserārius, -ī *and* **-iī** *m* officer of the watch

testa, -ae *f* brick, tile; (*earthenware*) pot, jug, sherd; (*fish*) shell, shellfish

testāmentārius *adj* testamentary ♦ *m* forger of wills

testāmentum, -ī *nt* will, testament

testātiō, -ōnis *f* calling to witness

testātus *ppa of* **testor** ♦ *adj* public

testiculus, -ī *m* testicle

testificātiō, -ōnis *f* giving evidence, evidence

testificor, -ārī, -ātus *vt* to give evidence, vouch for; to make public, bring to light; to call to witness

testimōnium, -ī *and* **-iī** *nt* evidence, testimony; proof

testis¹, -is *m/f* witness; eyewitness

testis², -is *m* testicle

testor, -ārī, -ātus *vt* to give evidence, testify; to prove, vouch for; to call to witness, appeal to ♦ *vi* to make a will

testū (*abl* **-ū**) *nt* earthenware lid, pot

testūdineus *adj* of tortoiseshell, tortoise- (*in cpds*)

testūdō, -inis *f* tortoise; tortoiseshell; lyre, lute; (MIL) shelter for besiegers, covering of shields; (*building*) vault

testum, -i *nt* earthenware lid, pot

tēte *emphatic acc of* **tū**

tetendī *perf of* **tendō**

tēter *etc see* **taeter**

Tēthys, -os *f sea goddess;* the sea

tetigī *perf of* **tangō**

tetrachmum, tetradrachmum, -ī *nt* four drachmas

tetraō, -ōnis *m* blackcock, grouse or capercaillie

tetrarchēs, -ae *m* tetrarch, ruler

tetrarchia, -ae *f* tetrarchy

tetricus *adj* gloomy, sour

tetulī *archaic perf of* **ferō**

Teucer, -rī *m* son of Telamon of Salamis; son-in-law of Dardanus

Teucrī, -rōrum *mpl* Trojans

Teucria, -riae *f* Troy

Teutonī, -ōrum, Teutones, -um *mpl* Teutons (*a German people*)

Teutonicus *adj* Teutonic, German

tēxī *perf of* **tegō**

texō, -ere, -uī, -tum *vt* to weave; to plait; to build, make; (*fig*) to compose, contrive

textilis *adj* woven ♦ *nt* fabric

textor, -ōris *m* weaver

textrīnum, -ī *nt* weaving; shipyard

textūra, -ae *f* web, fabric

textus¹ *ppp of* **texō** ♦ *nt* web, fabric

textus², -ūs *m* texture

texuī *perf of* **texō**

Thāis, -idis *f an Athenian courtesan*

thalamus, -ī *m* room, bedroom; marriage bed; marriage

thalassicus *adj* sea-green

thalassinus *adj* sea-green

Thalēs, -is *and* **-ētis** *m early Greek philosopher (one of the seven wise men)*

Thalia, -ae *f Muse of comedy*

thallus, -ī *m* green bough

Thamyrās, -ae *m blinded Thracian poet*

Thapsitānus *adj see* **Thapsus**

Thapsus, Thapsos, -ī *f town in N. Africa (scene of Caesar's victory)*

Thasius *adj see* **Thasus**

Thasus, Thasos, -ī *f Greek island in N. Aegean*

Thaumantias, -dis *f* Iris

theãtrãlis *adj* of the theatre, in the theatre

theātrum, **-ī** *nt* theatre; audience; *(fig)* theatre, stage

Thēbae, **-ārum** *fpl* Thebes *(capital of Boeotia)*; *town in Upper Egypt*

Thēbais, **-aidis** *f* Theban woman; *epic poem by Statius*

Thēbānus *adj* Theban

thēca, **-ae** *f* case, envelope

Themis, **-dis** *f goddess of justice*

Themistoclēs, **-ī** *and* **-is** *m famous Athenian statesman*

Themistoclēus *adj see* **Themistoclēs**

thēnsaurārius *adj* of treasure

thēnsaurus *see* **thēsaurus**

theologus, **-ī** *m* theologian

Theophrastus, **-ī** *m Greek philosopher (successor to Aristotle)*

Theopompēus, **-īnus** *adj see* **Theopompus**

Theopompus, **-ī** *m Greek historian*

thermae, **-ārum** *fpl* warm baths

Thermōdōn, **-ontis** *m river of Pontus (where the Amazons lived)*

Thermōdontēus, **-ontiacus** *adj* Amazonian

thermopōlium *nt* restaurant serving warm drinks

thermōpotō, **-āre** *vt* to refresh with warm drinks

Thermopylae, **-ārum** *fpl famous Greek pass defended by Leonidas*

thēsaurus, **-ī** *m* treasure, store; storehouse, treasury

Thēseus, **-eī** *and* **-eos** *m Greek hero (king of Athens)*

Thēsēus, **-ēius** *adj* of Theseus, Athenian

Thēsīdēs, **-īdae** *m* Hippolytus; *(pl)* Athenians

Thespiae, **-ārum** *fpl Boeotian town near Helicon*

Thespiēnsis, **Thespias**, **-adis** *adj* Thespian

Thespis, **-is** *m traditional founder of Greek tragedy*

Thessalia, **-iae** *f Thessaly (district of N. Greece)*

Thessalicus, **Thessalus**, **Thessalis**, **-idis** *adj* Thessalian

Thetis, **-idis** *and* **-idos** *f sea nymph (mother of Achilles)*; the sea

thiasus, **-ī** *m* Bacchic dance

Thoantēus *adj see* **Thoās**

Thoās, **-antis** *m king of Crimea (killed by Orestes), king of Lemnos (father of Hypsipyle)*

tholus, **-ī** *m* rotunda

thōrāx, **-ācis** *m* breastplate

Thrāca, **-ae**, **Thrācē**, **-ēs**, **Thrācia**, **-iae** *f* Thrace

Thracius, **Thrēicius** *adj* Thracian

Thrasea, **-ae** *m Stoic philosopher under Nero*

Thrasymachus, **-ī** *m Greek sophist*

Thrāx, **-ācis** *m* Thracian; *kind of gladiator*

Thrēssa, **-ae**, **Thrēissa**, **-ae** *f* Thracian woman

Thrēx, **-ēcis** *m kind of gladiator*

Thūcydidēs, **-is** *m famous Greek historian*

Thūcydidius *adj* Thucydidean

Thūlē, **-ēs** *f island in the extreme N. (perhaps Shetland)*

thunnus *see* **thynnus**

thūr, **-is** *nt* = **tūs**

Thūriī, **-iōrum** *mpl town in S. Italy*

Thūrīnus *adj see* **Thūriī**

thūs *see* **tūs**

thȳa, **thȳia**, **-ae** *f* citrus tree

Thybris, **-is** *and* **-idis** *m* (river) Tiber

Thyestēs, **-ae** *m brother of Atreus (whose son's flesh he served up to him to eat)*

Thyestēus *adj see* **Thyestēs**

Thyestiadēs, **-iadae** *m* Aegisthus

Thyias, **Thȳas**, **-adis** *f* Bacchante

Thȳlē *see* **Thūlē**

thymbra, **-ae** *f* savory

thymum, **-ī** *nt* garden thyme

Thȳnia, **-iae** *f* Bithynia

thynnus, **-ī** *m* tuna

Thȳnus, **Thȳniacus**, **Thȳnias** *adj* Bithynian

Thyōneus, **-eī** *m* Bacchus

thyrsus, **-ī** *m* Bacchic wand

tiāra, **-ae** *f*, **tiārās**, **-ae** *m* turban

Tiberiānus *adj see* **Tiberius**

Tiberīnus¹, **Tiberīnis** *adj see* **Tiberis**

Tiberīnus², **-īnī** *m* Tiber

Tiberis, **Tibris**, **-is** *m* (river) Tiber

Tiberius, **-ī** *m Roman praenomen (esp the second emperor)*

tibi *dat of* **tū**

tībia, **-ae** *f* shinbone; pipe, flute

tībīcen, **-inis** *m* flute player; pillar

tībīcina, **-ae** *f* flute player

tībīcinium, **-ī** *and* **-iī** *nt* flute playing

Tibullus, **-ī** *m Latin elegiac poet*

Tībur, **-is** *nt town on the river Anio (now Tivoli)*

Tīburs, **-tis**, **Tīburtīnus**, **Tīburnus** *adj* Tiburtine

Tīcīnus, **-ī** *m tributary of the river Po*

Tigellīnus, **-ī** *m favourite of Nero*

tigillum, **-ī** *nt* small log, small beam

tignārius *adj* working in wood; **faber ~** carpenter

tignum, **-ī** *nt* timber, trunk, log

Tigrānēs, **-is** *m king of Armenia*

tigris, **-is** *and* **-idis** *f* tiger

tīlia, **-ae** *f* lime tree

Tīmaeus, **-ī** *m Sicilian historian; Pythagorean philosopher; a dialogue of Plato*

timefactus *adj* frightened

timeō, **-ēre**, **-uī** *vt, vi* to fear, be afraid

timidē *adv* timidly

timiditās, **-ātis** *f* timidity, cowardice

timidus *adj* timid, cowardly

timor, **-ōris** *m* fear, alarm; a terror

tinctilis *adj* dipped in

tinctus *ppp of* **tingō**

tinea, **-ae** *f* moth, bookworm

tingō, **-gere**, **-xī**, **-ctum** *vt* to dip, soak; to dye, colour; *(fig)* to imbue

tinnīmentum, **-ī** *nt* ringing noise

tinniō, **-īre** *vt, vi* to ring, tinkle

tinnītus, **-ūs** *m* ringing, jingle

tinnulus *adj* ringing, jingling

tintinnābulum, **-ī** *nt* bell

tintinō, **-āre** *vi* to ring

tīnus, **-ī** *m a shrub, laurustinus*

tinxī *perf of* **tingō**

Tīphys, **-os** *m helmsman of the Argo*

tippula, **-ae** *f* water spider

Tīresiās, -ae *m* blind soothsayer of Thebes

Tīridātēs, -ae *m* king of Armenia

tīrō, -ōnis *m* recruit, beginner

Tīrō, -ōnis *m* Cicero's freedman secretary

tīrōcinium, -ī and **-iī** *nt* first campaign; recruits; (fig) first attempt, inexperience

Tīrōniānus *adj see* **Tīrō**

tīrunculus, -ī *m* young beginner

Tīryns, -this *f* ancient town in S.E. Greece (home of Hercules)

Tīrynthius *adj* of Tiryns, of Hercules ◆ *m* Hercules

tis archaic gen of **tū**

Tīsiphonē, -ēs *f* a Fury

Tīsiphonēus *adj* guilty

Tītān, -ānis, Tītānus, -ānī *m* Titan (an ancient race of gods); the sun

Tītānius, Tītāniacus, Tītānis *adj see* **Tītān**

Tīthōnius *adj see* **Tīthōnus**

Tīthōnus, -ī *m* consort of Aurora (granted immortality without youth)

tītillātiō, -ōnis *f* tickling

tītillō, -āre *vt* to tickle

titubanter *adv* falteringly

titubātiō, -ōnis *f* staggering

titubō, -āre *vi* to stagger, totter; to stammer; to waver, falter

titulus, -ī *m* inscription, label, notice; title of honour; fame; pretext

Tityos, -ī *m* giant punished in Tartarus

Tmōlus, -ī *m* mountain in Lydia

toculiō, -ōnis *m* usurer

tōfus, -ī *m* tufa

toga, -ae *f* toga (dress of the Roman citizen); (fig) peace; ~ **candida** dress of election candidates; ~ **picta** ceremonial dress of a victor in triumph; ~ **praetexta** purple-edged toga of magistrates and children; ~ **pūra**, ~ **virīlis** plain toga of manhood

togātus *adj* wearing the toga ◆ *m* Roman citizen; client ◆ *f* drama on a Roman theme

togula, -ae *f* small toga

tolerābilis *adj* bearable, tolerable; patient

tolerābiliter *adv* patiently

tolerāns, -antis pres p of **tolerō** ◆ *adj* patient

toleranter *adv* patiently

tolerantia, -ae *f* endurance

tolerātiō, -ōnis *f* enduring

tolerātus *adj* tolerable

tolerō, -āre, -āvī, -ātum *vt* to bear, endure; to support, sustain

tollēnō, -ōnis *m* crane, derrick, lift

tollō, -ere, sustulī, sublātum *vt* to lift, raise; to take away, remove; to do away with, abolish, destroy; (anchor) to weigh; (child) to acknowledge, bring up; (mind) to elevate, excite, cheer; (passenger) to take on board; **signa tollere** decamp

Tolōsa, -ae *f* Toulouse

Tolōsānus *adj see* **Tolōsa**

tolūtim *adv* at a trot

tomāculum, -ī *nt* sausage

tōmentum, -ī *nt* stuffing, padding

Tomis, -is *f* town on the Black Sea (to which Ovid was exiled)

Tomītānus *adj see* **Tomis**

Tonāns, -antis *m* Thunderer (epithet of Jupiter)

tondeō, -ēre, totondī, tōnsum *vt* to shear, clip, shave; to crop, reap, mow; to graze, browse on; (fig) to fleece, rob

tonitrālis *adj* thunderous

tonitrus, -ūs *m*, **tonitrua, -uōrum** *ntpl* thunder

tonō, -āre, -uī *vi* to thunder ◆ *vt* to thunder out

tōnsa, -ae *f* oar

tōnsillae, -ārum *fpl* tonsils

tōnsor, -ōris *m* barber

tōnsōrius *adj* for shaving

tōnstrīcula, -ae *f* barber girl

tōnstrīna, -ae *f* barber's shop

tōnstrīx, -īcis *f* woman barber

tōnsūra, -ae *f* shearing, clipping

tōnsus¹ ppp of **tondeō**

tōnsus², -ūs *m* coiffure

tōphus see **tōfus**

topiārius *adj* of ornamental gardening ◆ *m* topiarist ◆ *f* topiary

topicē, -ēs *f* the art of finding topics

toral, -ālis *nt* valance

torcular, -āris, torcularium, -ī *nt* press

toreuma, -tis *nt* embossed work, relief

tormentum, -ī *nt* windlass, torsion catapult, artillery; shot; rack, torture; (fig) torment, anguish

tormina, -um *ntpl* colic

torminōsus *adj* subject to colic

tornō, -āre, -āvī, -ātum *vt* to turn (in a lathe), round off

tornus, -ī *m* lathe

torōsus *adj* muscular

torpēdō, -inis *f* numbness, lethargy; (fish) electric ray

torpeō, -ēre *vi* to be stiff, be numb; to be stupefied

torpēscō, -ēscere, -uī *vi* to grow stiff, numb, listless

torpidus *adj* benumbed

torpor, -ōris *m* numbness, torpor, listlessness

torquātus *adj* wearing a neckchain

Torquātus, -ī *m* surname of Manlius

torqueō, -quēre, -sī, -tum *vt* to turn, twist, bend, wind; (missile) to whirl, hurl, brandish; (body) to rack, torture; (mind) to torment

torquēs, torquis, -is *m/f* neckchain, necklace, collar

torrēns, -entis pres p of **torreō** ◆ *adj* scorching, hot; rushing, rapid ◆ *m* torrent

torreō, -ēre, -uī, tostum *vt* to parch, scorch, roast

torrēscō, -ere *vi* to become parched

torridus *adj* parched, dried up; frostbitten

torris, -is *m* brand, firebrand

torsī perf of **torqueō**

tortē *adv* awry

tortilis *adj* twisted, winding

tortor¹, -ārī *vi* to writhe

tortor², -ōris *m* torturer, executioner

tortuōsus *adj* winding; (fig) complicated

tortus¹ ppp of **torqueō** ◆ *adj* crooked; complicated

tortus², -ūs *m* twisting, writhing

torulus, -ī m tuft (of hair)

torus, -ī m knot, bulge; muscle, brawn; couch, bed; (earth) bank, mound; (language) ornament

torvitās, -ātis f wildness, grimness

torvus adj wild, grim, fierce

tostus ppp of **torreō**

tot adj (indecl) so many, as many

totidem adj (indecl) just as many, the same number of

totiēns, totiēs adv so often, as often

totondī perf of **tondeō**

tōtus (gen **-īus**, dat **-ī**) adj entire, the whole, all; entirely, completely taken up with; **ex tōtō** totally; **in tōtō** on the whole

toxicum, -ī nt poison

trabālis adj for beams; **clāvus ~** large nail

trabea, -ae f ceremonial robe

trabeātus adj wearing a ceremonial robe

trabs, -abis f beam, timber; tree; ship; roof

Trāchīn, -īnis f town in Thessaly (where Hercules cremated himself)

Trāchīnius adj see **Trāchīn**

tractābilis adj manageable, tractable

tractātiō, -ōnis f handling, treatment

tractātus, -ūs m handling

tractim adv slowly, little by little

tractō, -āre, -āvī, -ātum vt to maul; to handle, deal with, manage; (activity) to conduct, perform; (person) to treat; (subject) to discuss, consider

tractus¹ ppp of **trahō ♦** adj fluent

tractus², -ūs m dragging, pulling, drawing; train, track; (place) extent, region, district; (movement) course; (time) lapse; (word) drawling

trādidī perf of **trādō**

trāditiō, -ōnis f surrender; handing down

trāditor, -ōris m traitor

trāditus ppp of **trādō**

trādō, -ere, -idī, -itum vt to hand over, deliver, surrender; to commit, entrust; to betray; to bequeath, hand down; (narrative) to relate, record; (teaching) to propound; **sē trādere** surrender, devote oneself

trādūcō, trānsdūcō, -ūcere, -ūxī, -uctum vt to bring across, lead over, transport across; to transfer; to parade, make an exhibition of (in public); (time) to pass, spend

trāductiō, -ōnis f transference; (time) passage; (word) metonymy

trāductor, -ōris m transferrer

trāductus ppp of **trādūcō**

trādux, -ucis m vine layer

tragicē adv dramatically

tragicocōmoedia, -ae f tragicomedy

tragicus adj of tragedy, tragic; in the tragic manner, lofty; terrible, tragic **♦** m writer of tragedy

tragoedia, -ae f tragedy; (fig) bombast

tragoedus, -ī m tragic actor

trāgula, -ae f kind of javelin

trahea, -ae f sledge

trahō, -here, -xī, -ctum vt to draw, drag, pull, take with one; to pull out, lengthen; to draw together, contract; to carry off, plunder; (liquid) to drink, draw; (money) to squander; (wool) to

spin; (fig) to attract; (appearance) to take on; (consequence) to derive, get; (praise, blame) to ascribe, refer; (thought) to ponder; (time) to spin out

trāiciō, -icere, -iēcī, -iectum vt to throw across, shoot across; (troops) to get across, transport; (with weapon) to pierce, stab; (river, etc) to cross; (fig) to transfer **♦** vi to cross

trāiectiō, -ōnis f crossing, passage; (fig) transferring; (RHET) exaggeration; (words) transposition

trāiectus¹ ppp of **trāiciō**

trāiectus², -ūs m crossing, passage

trālāt- etc see **trānslāt-**

Trallēs, -ium fpl town in Lydia

Tralliānus adj see **Trallēs**

trālūceō etc see **trānslūceō**

trāma, -ae f woof, web

trāmes, -itis m footpath, path

trāmittō etc see **trānsmittō**

trānatō etc see **trānsnatō**

trānō, -āre, -āvī, -ātum vt, vi to swim across; (air) to fly through

tranquillē adv quietly

tranquillitās, -ātis f quietness, calm; (fig) peace, quiet

tranquillō, -āre vt to calm

tranquillus adj quiet, calm **♦** nt calm sea

trāns prep (with acc) across, over, beyond

trānsabeō, -īre, -iī vt to pierce

trānsāctor, -ōris m manager

trānsāctus ppp of **trānsigō**

trānsadigō, -ere vt to drive through, pierce

Trānsalpīnus adj Transalpine

trānscendō, trānsscendō, -endere, -endī, -ēnsum vt, vi to pass over, surmount; to overstep, surpass, transgress

trānscrībō, transscrībō, -bere, -psī, -ptum vt to copy out; (fig) to make over, transfer

trānscurrō, -rere, -rī, -sum vt, vi to run across, run past, traverse

trānscursus, -ūs m running through; (speech) cursory remark

trānsd- etc see **trād-**

trānsēgī perf of **trānsigō**

trānsenna, -ae f net, snare; trellis, latticework

trānseō, -īre, -iī, -itum vt, vi to pass over, cross over; to pass along or through; to pass by; to outstrip, surpass, overstep; (change) to turn into; (speech) to mention briefly, leave out, pass on; (time) to pass, pass away

trānsferō, -ferre, -tulī, -lātum vt to bring across, transport, transfer; (change) to transform; (language) to translate; (RHET) to use figuratively; (time) to postpone; (writing) to copy

trānsfīgō, -gere, -xī, -xum vt to pierce; to thrust through

trānsfīxus ppp of **trānsfīgō**

trānsfodiō, -odere, -ōdī, -ossum vt to run through, stab

trānsfōrmis adj changed in shape

trānsfōrmō, -āre vt to change in shape

trānsfossus ppp of **trānsfodiō**

trānsfuga, -ae m/f deserter

trānsfugiō, -ugere, -ūgī vi to desert, come over

trānsfugium, -ī *and* -iī *nt* desertion

trānsfundō, -undere, -ūdī, -ūsum *vt* to decant, transfuse

trānsfūsiō, -ōnis *f* transmigration

trānsfūsus *ppp of* **trānsfundō**

trānsgredior, -dī, -ssus *vt, vi* to step across, cross over, cross; to pass on; to exceed

trānsgressiō, -ōnis *f* passage; (*words*) transposition

trānsgressus[1] *ppa of* **trānsgredior**

trānsgressus[2], -ūs *m* crossing

trānsiciō *etc see* **trāiciō**

trānsigō, -igere, -ēgī, -āctum *vt* to carry through, complete, finish; (*difference*) to settle; (*time*) to pass, spend; (*with* **cum**) to put an end to; (*with weapon*) to stab

trānsiī *perf of* **trānseō**

trānsiliō, **trānssiliō**, -īre, -uī *vi* to jump across ♦ *vt* to leap over; (*fig*) to skip, disregard; to exceed

trānsitiō, -ōnis *f* passage; desertion; (*disease*) infection

trānsitō, -āre *vi* to pass through

trānsitus[1] *ppp of* **trānseō**

trānsitus[2], -ūs *m* passing over, passage; desertion; passing by; transition

trānslātīcius, **trālātīcius** *adj* traditional, customary, common

trānslātiō, **trālātiō**, -ōnis *f* transporting, transferring; (*language*) metaphor

trānslātīvus *adj* transferable

trānslātor, -ōris *m* transferrer

trānslātus *ppp of* **trānsferō**

trānslegō, -ere *vt* to read through

trānslūceō, -ēre *vi* to be reflected; to shine through

trānsmarīnus *adj* overseas

trānsmeō, -āre *vi* to cross

trānsmigrō, -āre *vi* to emigrate

trānsmissiō, -ōnis *f* crossing

trānsmissus[1] *ppp of* **trānsmittō**

trānsmissus[2], -ūs *m* crossing

trānsmittō, -ittere, -īsī, -issum *vt* to send across, put across; to let pass through; to transfer, entrust, devote; to give up, pass over; (*place*) to cross over, go through, pass ♦ *vi* to cross

trānsmontānus *adj* beyond the mountains

trānsmoveō, -ovēre, -ōvī, -ōtum *vt* to move, transfer

trānsmūtō, -āre *vt* to shift

trānsnatō, **trānatō**, -āre *vi* to swim across ♦ *vt* to swim

trānsnō *etc see* **trānō**

Trānspadānus *adj* north of the Po

trānspectus, -ūs *m* view

trānspiciō, -ere *vt* to look through

trānspōnō, -ōnere, -osuī, -ositum *vt* to transfer

trānsportō, -āre *vt* to carry across, transport, remove

trānspositus *ppp of* **trānspōnō**

Trānsrhēnānus *adj* east of the Rhine

trānss- *etc see* **trāns-**

Trānstiberīnus *adj across the* Tiber

trānstineō, -ēre *vi* to get through

trānstrum, -ī *nt* thwart

trānstulī *perf of* **trānsferō**

trānsultō, -āre *vi* to jump across

trānsūtus *adj* pierced

trānsvectiō, -ōnis *f* crossing

trānsvectus *ppp of* **trānsvehō**

trānsvehō, -here, -xī, -ctum *vt* to carry across, transport

trānsvehor, -hī, -ctus *vi* to cross, pass over; (*parade*) to ride past; (*time*) to elapse

trānsverberō, -āre *vt* to pierce through, wound

trānsversus, **trāversus** *adj* lying across, crosswise, transverse; **digitum trānsversum** a finger's breadth; **dē trānsversō** unexpectedly; **ex trānsversō** sideways

trānsvolitō, -āre *vt* to fly through

trānsvolō, -āre *vt, vi* to fly across, fly through; to move rapidly across; to fly past, disregard

trānsvorsus *etc see* **trānsversus**

trapētus, -ī *m* olive mill, oil mill

trapezīta *etc see* **tarpezīta**

Trapezūs, -ūntis *f* Black Sea town (*now* Trabzon)

Trasumennus, **Trasimēnus**, -ī *m lake in* Etruria (*where Hannibal defeated the Romans*)

trāv- *see* **trānsv-**

trāvectiō *etc see* **trānsvectiō**

traxī *perf of* **trahō**

trecēnī, -ōrum *adj* three hundred each

trecentēsimus *adj* three-hundredth

trecentī, -ōrum *num* three hundred

trecentiēns, **trecentiēs** *adv* three hundred times

trechedīpna, -ōrum *ntpl* dinner shoes (*of parasites*)

tredecim *num* thirteen

tremebundus *adj* trembling

tremefaciō, -facere, -fēcī, -factum *vt* to shake

tremendus *adj* formidable, terrible

tremēscō, **tremīscō**, -ere *vi* to begin to shake ♦ *vt* to be afraid of

tremō, -ere, -uī *vi* to tremble, quake, quiver ♦ *vt* to tremble at, dread

tremor, -ōris *m* shaking, quiver, tremor; earthquake

tremulus *adj* trembling, shivering

trepidanter *adv* with agitation

trepidātiō, -ōnis *f* agitation, alarm, consternation

trepidē *adv* hastily, in confusion

trepidō, -āre, -āvī, -ātum *vi* to be agitated, bustle about, hurry; to be alarmed; to flicker, quiver ♦ *vt* to start at

trepidus *adj* restless, anxious, alarmed; alarming, perilous

trēs, **trium** *num* three

trēssis, -is *m* three asses

trēsvirī, **triumvirōrum** *mpl* three commissioners, triumvirs

Trēverī, -ōrum *mpl* people of E. Gaul (*about what is now* Trier)

Trēvericus *adj see* **Trēverī**

triangulum, -ī *nt* triangle

triangulus *adj* triangular

triāriī, -ōrum *mpl* the third line (*in Roman battle order*), the reserves
tribuārius *adj* of the tribes
tribūlis, -is *m* fellow tribesman
tribulum, -ī *nt* threshing sledge
tribulus, -ī *m* star thistle
tribūnal, -ālis *nt* platform; judgment seat; camp platform, cenotaph
tribūnātus, -ūs *m* tribuneship, rank of tribune
tribūnicius *adj* of a tribune ♦ *m* ex-tribune
tribūnus, -ī *m* tribune; ~ **plēbis** tribune of the people, *a magistrate who defended the rights of the plebeians;* ~ **mīlitum** *or* **militāris** military tribune, *an officer under the legatus;* **tribūnī aerāriī** paymasters
tribuō, -uere, -uī, -ūtum *vt* to assign, allot; to give, bestow, pay; to concede, allow; to ascribe, attribute; (*subject*) to divide; (*time*) to devote
tribus, -ūs *m* tribe
tribūtārius *adj*: **tribūtāriae tabellae** letters of credit
tribūtim *adv* by tribes
tribūtiō, -ōnis *f* distribution
tribūtum, -ī *nt* contribution, tribute, tax
tribūtus¹ *ppp of* **tribuō**
tribūtus² *adj* arranged by tribes
trīcae, -ārum *fpl* nonsense; tricks, vexations
trīcēnī, -ōrum *adj* thirty each, in thirties
triceps, -ipitis *adj* three-headed
trīcēsimus *adj* thirtieth
trichila, -ae *f* arbour, summerhouse
trīciēns, trīciēs *adv* thirty times
trīclīnium, -ī *and* **-iī** *nt* dining couch; dining room
trīcō, -ōnis *m* mischief-maker
trīcor, -ārī *vi* to make mischief, play tricks
tricorpor, -is *adj* three-bodied
tricuspis, -idis *adj* three-pointed
tridēns, -entis *adj* three-pronged ♦ *m* trident
tridentifer, -ī *adj* trident-wielding
tridentiger, -ī *adj* trident-wielding
triduum, -ī *nt* three days
triennia, -ium *ntpl* a triennial festival
triennium, -ī *and* **-iī** *nt* three years
triēns, -entis *m* a third; (*coin*) a third of an as; (*measure*) a third of a pint
trientābulum, -ī *nt* land given by the State as a third of a debt
trientius *adj* sold for a third
triērarchus, -ī *m* captain of a trireme
triēris, -is *f* trireme
trietēricus *adj* triennial ♦ *ntpl* festival of Bacchus
trietēris, -idis *f* three years; a triennial festival
trifāriam *adv* in three parts, in three places
trifaux, -aucis *adj* three-throated
trifidus *adj* three-forked
trifōrmis *adj* triple
trifūr, -ūris *m* archthief
trifurcifer, -ī *m* hardened criminal
trigeminus *adj* threefold, triple ♦ *mpl* triplets
trīgintā *num* thirty
trigōn, -ōnis *m* a ball game
trilībris *adj* three-pound

trilinguis *adj* three-tongued
trilīx, -īcis *adj* three-ply, three-stranded
trimēstris *adj* of three months
trimetrus, -ī *m* trimeter
trīmus *adj* three years old
Trīnacria, -iae *f* Sicily
Trīnacrius, Trīnacris, -idis *adj* Sicilian
trīnī, -ōrum *adj* three each, in threes; triple
Trinobantēs, -um *mpl* British tribe in East Anglia
trinōdis *adj* three-knotted
triōbolus, -ī *m* half-a-drachma
Triōnēs, -um *mpl* the Plough; the Little Bear
tripartītō *adv* in *or* into three parts
tripartītus, tripertītus *adj* divided into three parts
tripectorus *adj* three-bodied
tripedālis *adj* three-foot
tripert- *etc see* **tripart-**
tripēs, -edis *adj* three-legged
triplex, -icis *adj* triple, threefold ♦ *nt* three times as much ♦ *mpl* three-leaved writing tablet
triplus *adj* triple
Triptolemus, -ī *m* inventor of agriculture, judge in Hades
tripudiō, -āre *vi* to dance
tripudium, -ī *and* **-iī** *nt* ceremonial dance, dance; a favourable omen (*when the sacred chickens ate greedily*)
tripūs, -odis *f* tripod; the Delphic oracle
triquetrus *adj* triangular; Sicilian
trirēmis *adj* with three banks of oars ♦ *f* trireme
trīs *etc see* **trēs**
triscurria, -ōrum *ntpl* sheer fooling
tristē *adv* sadly; severely
tristiculus *adj* rather sad
tristificus *adj* ominous
tristimōnia, -ae *f* sadness
tristis *adj* sad, glum, melancholy; gloomy, sombre, dismal; (*taste*) bitter; (*smell*) offensive; (*temper*) severe, sullen, ill-humoured
tristitia, -ae *f* sadness, sorrow, melancholy; moroseness, severity
tristitiēs, -ēī *f* sorrow
trisulcus *adj* three-forked
tritavus, -ī *m* great-great-great-grandfather
trīticeus *adj* of wheat, wheaten
trīticum, -ī *nt* wheat
Trītōn, -ōnis *m* sea god (*son of Neptune*); African lake (*where Minerva was born*)
Trītōnius, -ōniacus, -ōnis *adj* of Lake Triton, of Minerva ♦ *f* Minerva
trītūra, -ae *f* threshing
trītus¹ *ppp of* **terō** ♦ *adj* well-worn; (*judgment*) expert; (*language*) commonplace, trite
trītus², -ūs *m* rubbing, friction
triumphālis *adj* triumphal ♦ *ntpl* insignia of a triumph
triumphō, -āre, -āvī, -ātum *vi* to celebrate a triumph; to triumph, exult ♦ *vt* to triumph over, win by conquest
triumphus, -ī *m* triumphal procession, victory parade; triumph, victory
triumvir, -ī *m* commissioner, triumvir; mayor (*of a provincial town*)
triumvirālis *adj* triumviral

triumvirātus, **-ūs** *m* office of triumvir, triumvirate

triumvirī, **-ōrum** *mpl* three commissioners, triumvirs

trivenēfica, **-ae** *f* old witch

trīvī *perf of* **terō**

Trivia, **-ae** *f* Diana

triviālis *adj* common, popular

trivium, **-ī** *and* **-iī** *nt* crossroads; public street

trivius *adj* of the crossroads

Trōas, **-adis** *f the district of Troy*, Troad; Trojan woman ♦ *adj* Trojan

trochaeus, **-ī** *m* trochee; tribrach

trochlea, **-ae** *f* block and tackle

trochus, **-ī** *m* hoop

Trōglodytae, **-ārum** *mpl cave dwellers of Ethiopia*

Trōia, **-ae** *f* Troy

Trōilus, **-ī** *m son of Priam*

Trōiugena, **-ae** *m/f* Trojan; Roman

Trōius, **Trōiānus**, **Trōicus** *adj* Trojan

tropaeum, **-ī** *nt* victory memorial, trophy; victory; memorial, token

Trōs, **-ōis** *m king of Phrygia*; Trojan

trucīdātiō, **-ōnis** *f* butchery

trucīdō, **-āre**, **-āvī**, **-ātum** *vt* to slaughter, massacre

truculentē *adv see* **truculentus**

truculentia, **-ae** *f* ferocity, inclemency

truculentus *adj* ferocious, grim, wild

trudis, **-is** *f* pike

trūdō, **-dere**, **-sī**, **-sum** *vt* to push, thrust, drive; *(buds)* to put forth

trulla, **-ae** *f* ladle, scoop; washbasin

truncō, **-āre**, **-āvī**, **-ātum** *vt* to lop off, maim, mutilate

truncus, **-ī** *m (tree)* trunk, bole; *(human)* trunk, body; *(abuse)* blockhead ♦ *adj* maimed, broken, stripped (of); defective

trūsī *perf of* **trūdō**

trūsitō, **-āre** *vt* to keep pushing

trūsus *ppp of* **trūdō**

trutina, **-ae** *f* balance, scales

trux, **-ucis** *adj* savage, grim, wild

trȳgōnus, **-ī** *m* stingray

tū *pron* you, thou

tuātim *adv* in your usual fashion

tuba, **-ae** *f* trumpet, war trumpet

tuber, **-is** *f kind of apple tree*

tūber, **-is** *nt* swelling, lump; *(food)* truffle

tubicen, **-inis** *m* trumpeter

tubilūstria, **-ōrum** *ntpl* festival of trumpets

tuburcinor, **-ārī** *vi* to gobble up, guzzle

tubus, **-ī** *m* pipe

tuditō, **-āre** *vt* to strike repeatedly

tueor, **-ērī**, **-itus** *and* **-tūtus** *vt* to see, watch, look; to guard, protect, keep

tugurium, **-ī** *and* **-iī** *nt* hut, cottage

tuitiō, **-ōnis** *f* defence

tuitus *ppa of* **tueor**

tulī *perf of* **ferō**

Tulliānum, **-ī** *nt* State dungeon of Rome

Tulliānus *adj see* **Tullius**

Tulliola, **-ae** *f* little Tullia (Cicero's daughter)

Tullius, **-ī** *and* **-iī** *m Roman family name (esp the sixth king)*, *the orator Cicero*

Tullus, **-ī** *m third king of Rome*

tum *adv (time)* then, at that time; *(sequence)* then, next ♦ *conj* moreover, besides; **tum … tum** at one time … at another; **tum … cum** at the time when, whenever; **cum … tum** not only … but; **tum dēmum** only then; **tum ipsum** even then; **tum māximē** just then; **tum vērō** then more than ever

tumefaciō, **-facere**, **-fēcī**, **-factum** *vt* to make swell; *(fig)* to puff up

tumeō, **-ēre** *vi* to swell, be swollen; *(emotion)* to be excited; *(pride)* to be puffed up; *(language)* to be turgid

tumēscō, **-ēscere**, **-uī** *vi* to begin to swell, swell up

tumidus *adj* swollen, swelling; *(emotion)* excited, enraged; *(pride)* puffed up; *(language)* bombastic

tumor, **-ōris** *m* swelling, bulge; hillock; *(fig)* commotion, excitement

tumulō, **-āre** *vt* to bury

tumulōsus *adj* hilly

tumultuārius *adj* hasty; *(troops)* emergency

tumultuātiō, **-ōnis** *f* commotion

tumultuō, **-āre**, **tumultuor**, **-ārī** *vi* to make a commotion, be in an uproar

tumultuōsē *adv see* **tumultuōsus**

tumultuōsus *adj* uproarious, excited, turbulent

tumultus, **-ūs** *m* commotion, uproar, disturbance; *(MIL)* rising, revolt, civil war; *(weather)* storm; *(mind)* disorder

tumulus, **-ī** *m* mound, hill; burial mound, barrow

tunc *adv (time)* then, at that time; *(sequence)* then, next; **~ dēmum** only then; **~ quoque** then too; even so

tundō, **-ere**, **tutudī**, **tūnsum** *and* **tūsum** *vt* to beat, thump, hammer; *(grain)* to pound; *(speech)* to din, importune

Tūnēs, **-ētis** *m* Tunis

tunica, **-ae** *f* tunic; *(fig)* skin, husk

tunicātus *adj* wearing a tunic

tunicula, **-ae** *f* little tunic

tūnsus *ppp of* **tundō**

tuor *etc see* **tueor**

turba, **-ae** *f* disorder, riot, disturbance; brawl, quarrel; crowd, mob, troop, number

turbāmenta, **-ōrum** *ntpl* propaganda

turbātē *adv* in confusion

turbātiō, **-ōnis** *f* confusion

turbātor, **-ōris** *m* agitator

turbātus *ppp of* **turbō**[1] ♦ *adj* troubled, disorderly

turbellae, **-ārum** *fpl* stir, row

turben *etc see* **turbō**[2]

turbidē *adv* in disorder

turbidus *adj* confused, wild, boisterous; *(water)* troubled, muddy; *(fig)* disorderly, troubled, alarmed, dangerous

turbineus *adj* conical

turbō[1], **-āre**, **-āvī**, **-ātum** *vt* to disturb, throw into confusion; *(water)* to trouble, make muddy

turbō², **-inis** *m* whirl, spiral, rotation; reel, whorl, spindle; (*toy*) top; (*wind*) tornado, whirlwind; (*fig*) storm

turbulentē, **turbulenter** *adv* wildly

turbulentus *adj* agitated, confused, boisterous, stormy; troublemaking, seditious

turdus, **-ī** *m* thrush

tūreus *adj* of incense

turgeō, **-gēre**, **-sī** *vi* to swell, be swollen; (*speech*) to be bombastic

turgēscō, **-ere** *vi* to swell up, begin to swell; (*fig*) to become enraged

turgidulus *adj* poor swollen

turgidus *adj* swollen, distended; bombastic

tūribulum, **-ī** *nt* censer

tūricremus *adj* incense-burning

tūrifer, **-ī** *adj* incense-producing

tūrilegus *adj* incense-gathering

turma, **-ae** *f* troop, squadron (*of cavalry*); crowd

turmālis *adj* of a troop; equestrian

turmātim *adv* troop by troop

Turnus, **-ī** *m* Rutulian king (*chief opponent of Aeneas*)

turpiculus *adj* ugly little; slightly indecent

turpificātus *adj* debased

turpilucricupidus *adj* fond of filthy lucre

turpis *adj* ugly, deformed, unsightly; base, disgraceful ♦ *nt* disgrace

turpiter *adv* repulsively; shamefully

turpitūdō, **-inis** *f* deformity; disgrace, infamy

turpō, **-āre** *vt* to disfigure, soil

turriger, **-ī** *adj* turreted

turris, **-is** *f* tower, turret; siege tower; (*elephant*) howdah; (*fig*) mansion

turrītus *adj* turreted; castellated; towering

tursī *perf of* **turgeō**

turtur, **-is** *m* turtledove

tūs, **tūris** *nt* incense, frankincense

Tusculānēnsis *adj* at Tusculum

Tusculānum, **-ānī** *nt* villa at Tusculum (*esp Cicero's*)

Tusculānus *adj* Tusculan

Tusculum, **-ī** *nt* Latin town near Rome

tūsculum, **-ī** *nt* a little incense

Tusculus *adj* Tusculan

Tuscus *adj* Etruscan

tussiō, **-īre** *vi* to cough, have a cough

tussis, **-is** *f* cough

tūsus *ppp of* **tundō**

tūtāmen, **-inis** *nt* defence

tūtāmentum, **-ī** *nt* protection

tūte *emphatic form of* **tū**

tūtē *adv* safely, in safety

tūtēla, **-ae** *f* keeping, charge, protection; (*of minors*) guardianship, wardship; (*person*) watcher, guardian; ward, charge

tūtor¹, **-ārī**, **-ātus**, **tūtō**, **-āre** *vt* to watch, guard, protect; to guard against

tūtor², **-ōris** *m* protector; (LAW) guardian

tutudī *perf of* **tundō**

tūtus *ppp of* **tueor** ♦ *adj* safe, secure; cautious ♦ *nt* safety

tuus *adj* your, yours, thy, thine; your own, your proper; of you

Tȳdeus, **-eī** *and* **-eos** *m* father of Diomedes

Tȳdīdēs, **-īdae** *m* Diomedes

tympanotrība, **-ae** *m* timbrel player

tympanum, **typanum**, **-ī** *nt* drum, timbrel (*esp of the priests of Cybele*); (*mechanism*) wheel

Tyndareus, **-eī** *m* king of Sparta (*husband of Leda*)

Tyndaridae, **-idārum** *mpl* Castor and Pollux

Tyndaris, **-idis** *f* Helen; Clytemnestra

Typhōeus, **-eos** *m* giant under Etna

Typhōius, **-is** *adj see* **Typhōeus**

typus, **-ī** *m* figure

tyrannicē *adv see* **tyrannicus**

tyrannicīda, **-ae** *m* tyrannicide

tyrannicus *adj* tyrannical

tyrannis, **-idis** *f* despotism, tyranny

tyrannoctonus, **-ī** *m* tyrannicide

tyrannus, **-ī** *m* ruler, king; despot, tyrant

Tyrās, **-ae** *m* (*river*) Dniester

Tyrius *adj* Tyrian, Phoenician, Carthaginian; purple

tȳrotarīchos, **-ī** *m* dish of salt fish and cheese

Tyrrhēnia, **-iae** *f* Etruria

Tyrrhēnus *adj* Etruscan, Tyrrhenian

Tyrtaeus, **-ī** *m* Spartan war poet

Tyrus, **Tyros**, **-ī** *f* Tyre (*famous Phoenician seaport*)

Uu

über¹, -is *nt* breast, teat; (*fig*) richness

über², -is *adj* fertile, plentiful, rich (in); (*language*) full, copious

überius (*superl* **-rime**) *compar* more fully, more copiously

übertās, -ātis *f* richness, plenty, fertility

übertim *adv* copiously

ubī *adv* (*interrog*) where; (*rel*) where, in which, with whom; when

ubīcumque *adv* wherever; everywhere

Ubiī, -ōrum *mpl* German tribe on the lower Rhine

ubīnam *adv* where (in fact)?

ubīquāque *adv* everywhere

ubīque *adv* everywhere, anywhere

ubiubī *adv* wherever

ubīvīs *adv* anywhere

ūdus *adj* wet, damp

ulcerō, -āre *vt* to make sore, wound

ulcerōsus *adj* full of sores; wounded

ulcīscor, -ī, ultus *vt* to take vengeance on, punish; to take vengeance for, avenge

ulcus, -eris *nt* sore, ulcer; ~ **tangere** touch on a delicate subject

ūlīgō, -inis *f* moisture, marshiness

Ulixēs, -is *m* Ulysses, Odysseus (*king of Ithaca, hero of Homer's Odyssey*)

ullus (*gen* **-īus**, *dat* **-ī**) *adj* any

ulmeus *adj* of elm

ulmus, -ī *f* elm; (*pl*) elm rods

ulna, -ae *f* elbow; arm; (*measure*) ell

ulterior, -ōris *compar* farther, beyond, more remote

ulterius *compar of* **ultrā**

ultimus *superl* farthest, most remote, the end of; (*time*) earliest, latest, last; (*degree*) extreme, greatest, lowest ♦ *ntpl* the end; **ultimum** for the last time; **ad ultimum** finally

ultiō, -ōnis *f* vengeance, revenge

ultor, -ōris *m* avenger, punisher

ultrā *adv* beyond, farther, besides ♦ *prep* (*with acc*) beyond, on the far side of; (*time*) past; (*degree*) over and above

ultrīx, -īcis *adj* avenging

ultrō *adv* on the other side, away; besides; of one's own accord, unasked, voluntarily

ultrō tribūta *ntpl* State expenditure for public works

ultus *ppa of* **ulcīscor**

ulula, -ae *f* screech owl

ululātus, -ūs *m* wailing, shrieking, yells, whoops

ululō, -āre, -āvī, -ātum *vi* to shriek, yell, howl ♦ *vt* to cry out to

ulva, -ae *f* sedge

umbella, -ae *f* parasol

Umber, -rī *adj* Umbrian ♦ *m* Umbrian dog

umbilīcus, -ī *m* navel; (*fig*) centre; (*book*) roller end; (*sea*) cockle or pebble

umbō, -ōnis *m* boss (*of a shield*); elbow

umbra, -ae *f* shadow, shade; (*dead*) ghost; (*diner*) uninvited guest; (*fish*) grayling; (*painting*) shade; (*place*) shelter, school, study; (*unreality*) semblance, mere shadow

umbrāculum, -ī *nt* arbour; school; parasol

umbrāticola, -ae *m* lounger

umbrāticus *adj* fond of idling; in retirement

umbrātilis *adj* in retirement, private, academic

Umbria, -riae *f* Umbria (*district of central Italy*)

umbrifer, -ī *adj* shady

umbrō, -āre *vt* to shade

umbrōsus *adj* shady

ūmectō, -āre *vt* to wet, water

ūmectus *adj* damp, wet

ūmeō, -ēre *vi* to be damp, be wet

umerus, -ī *m* upper arm, shoulder

ūmēscō, -ere *vi* to become damp, get wet

ūmidē *adv* with damp

ūmidulus *adj* dampish

ūmidus *adj* wet, damp, dank, moist

ūmor, -ōris *m* liquid, fluid, moisture

umquam, unquam *adv* ever, at any time

ūnā *adv* together

ūnanimāns, -antis *adj* in full agreement

ūnanimitās, -ātis *f* concord

ūnanimus *adj* of one accord, harmonious

ūncia, -ae *f* a twelfth; (*weight*) ounce; (*length*) inch

ūnciārius *adj* of a twelfth; (*interest*) 8 1/3 per cent

ūnciātim *adv* little by little

uncīnātus *adj* barbed

ūnciola, -ae *f* a mere twelfth

ūnctiō, -ōnis *f* anointing

ūnctitō, -āre *vt* to anoint regularly

ūnctiusculus *adj* rather too unctuous

ūnctor, -ōris *m* anointer

ūnctūra, -ae *f* anointing (*of the dead*)

ūnctus *ppp of* **ungō** ♦ *adj* oiled; greasy, resinous; (*fig*) rich, sumptuous ♦ *nt* sumptuous dinner

uncus¹, -ī *m* hook, grappling-iron

uncus² *adj* hooked, crooked, barbed

unda, -ae *f* wave, water; (*fig*) stream, surge

223

unde *adv* from where, whence; from whom, from which; ~ **petitur** the defendant; ~ **unde** from wherever; somehow or other

ūndeciēns, ūndeciēs *adv* eleven times

ūndecim *num* eleven

ūndecimus *adj* eleventh

undecumque *adv* from wherever

ūndēnī, -ōrum *adj* eleven each, eleven

ūndēnōnāgintā *num* eighty-nine

ūndeoctōgintā *num* seventy-nine

ūndēquadrāgintā *num* thirty-nine

ūndēquīnquāgēsimus *adj* forty-ninth

ūndēquīnquāgintā *num* forty-nine

ūndēsexāgintā *num* fifty-nine

ūndētrīcēsimus *adj* twenty-ninth

ūndēvīcēsimānī, -ōrum *mpl* men of the nineteenth legion

ūndēvīcēsimus *adj* nineteenth

ūndēvīgintī *num* nineteen

undique *adv* from every side, on all sides, everywhere; completely

undisonus *adj* sea-roaring

undō, -āre *vi* to surge; *(fig)* to roll, undulate

undōsus *adj* billowy

ūnetvīcēsimānī, -ōrum *mpl* men of the twenty-first legion

ūnetvīcēsimus *adj* twenty-first

ungō, unguō, -gere, ūnxī, ūnctum *vt* to anoint, smear, grease

unguen, -inis *nt* fat, grease, ointment

unguentārius, -ī and -iī *m* perfumer

unguentātus *adj* perfumed

unguentum, -ī *nt* ointment, perfume

unguiculus, -ī *m* fingernail

unguis, -is *m* nail *(of finger or toe)*; claw, talon, hoof; **ad unguem** with perfect finish; **trānsversum unguem** a hair's breadth; **dē tenerō unguī** from earliest childhood

ungula, -ae *f* hoof, talon, claw

unguō *etc see* **ungō**

ūnicē *adv* solely, extraordinarily

ūnicolor, -ōris *adj* all one colour

ūnicus *adj* one and only, sole; unparalleled, unique

ūnifōrmis *adj* simple

ūnigena, -ae *adj* only-begotten; of the same parentage

ūnimanus *adj* with only one hand

ūniō, -ōnis *m* a single large pearl

ūniter *adv* together in one

ūniversālis *adj* general

ūniversē *adv* in general

ūniversitās, -ātis *f* the whole; the universe

ūniversus *adj* all taken together, entire, general ♦ *mpl* the community as a whole ♦ *nt* the universe; **in ūniversum** in general

unquam *etc see* **umquam**

ūnus *num* one ♦ *adj* sole, single, only; one and the same; the outstanding one; an individual; ~ **et alter** one or two; ~ **quisque** every single one; **nēmō** ~ not a single one; **ad ūnum** to a man

ūnxī *perf of* **ungō**

ūpiliō, -ōnis *m* shepherd

upupa, -ae *f* hoopoe; crowbar

Ūrania, -ae, Ūraniē, -ēs *f Muse of astronomy*

urbānē *adv* politely; wittily, elegantly

urbānitās, -ātis *f* city life; refinement, politeness; wit

urbānus *adj* town *(in cpds)*, city *(in cpds)*; refined, polite; witty, humorous; impertinent ♦ *m* townsman

urbicapus, -ī *m* taker of cities

urbs, urbis *f* city; Rome

urceolus, -ī *m* jug

urceus, -ī *m* pitcher, ewer

ūrēdō, -inis *f* blight

urgeō, -gēre, -sī *vt, vi* to force on, push forward; to press hard on, pursue closely; to crowd, hem in; to burden, oppress; *(argument)* to press, urge; *(work, etc)* to urge on, ply hard, follow up

ūrīna, -ae *f* urine

ūrīnātor, -ōris *m* diver

urna, -ae *f* water jar, urn; voting urn, lottery urn, cinerary urn, money jar

urnula, -ae *f* small urn

ūrō, -ere, ūssī, ūstum *vt* to burn; to scorch, parch; *(cold)* to nip; *(MED)* to cauterize; *(rubbing)* to chafe, hurt; *(passion)* to fire, inflame; *(vexation)* to annoy, oppress

ursa, -ae *f* she-bear, bear; *(ASTR)* Great Bear, Lesser Bear

ursī *perf of* **urgeō**

ursīnus *adj* bear's

ursus, -ī *m* bear

urtīca, -ae *f* nettle

ūrus, -ī *m* wild ox

Usipetēs, -etum, Usipetiī, -iōrum *mpl German tribe on the Rhine*

ūsitātē *adv* in the usual manner

ūsitātus *adj* usual, familiar

uspiam *adv* anywhere, somewhere

usquam *adv* anywhere; in any way, at all

usque *adv* all the way (to, from), right on, right up to; *(time)* all the time, as long as, continuously; *(degree)* even, as much as; ~ **quāque** everywhere; every moment, on every occasion

ūssī *perf of* **ūrō**

ūstor, -ōris *m* cremator

ūstulō, -āre *vt* to burn

ūstus *ppp of* **ūrō**

ūsūcapiō[1], -apere, -ēpī, -aptum *vt* to acquire ownership of, take over

ūsūcapiō[2], -ōnis *f* ownership by use or possession

ūsūra, -ae *f* use, enjoyment; interest, usury

ūsūrārius *adj* for use and enjoyment; paying interest

ūsurpātiō, -ōnis *f* making use (of)

ūsurpō, -āre, -āvī, -ātum *vt* to make use of, employ, exercise; *(LAW)* to take possession of, enter upon; *(senses)* to perceive, make contact with; *(word)* to call by, speak of

ūsus[1] *ppa of* **ūtor**

ūsus[2], -ūs *m* use, enjoyment, practice; experience, skill; usage, custom; intercourse, familiarity; usefulness, benefit, advantage; need, necessity; ~ **est,** ~ **venit** there is need (of);

ūsuī esse, **ex ūsū esse** be of use, be of service; **ūsū venīre** happen; **~ et frūctus** use and enjoyment, usufruct

ut, **utī** *adv* how; (*rel*) as; (*explaining*) considering how, according as; (*place*) where; **ut in ōrātōre** for an orator ♦ *conj* **1**. (*with indic*: *manner*) as; (: *concessive*) while, though; (: *time*) when, as soon as **2**. (*with subj*: *expressing the idea of a verb*) that, to; (: *purpose*) so that, to; (: *causal*) seeing that; (: *concessive*) granted that, although; (: *result*) that, so that; (: *fear*) that not; **ut ... ita** while ... nevertheless; **ut nōn** without; **ut quī** seeing that I, he *etc*; **ut quisque māximē** the more one way or another

utcumque, **utcunque** *adv* however; whenever; one way or another

ūtēnsilis *adj* of use ♦ *ntpl* necessaries

uter (*gen* **-rius**, *dat* **-rī**), **-ra**, **-rum** *pron* which (*of two*), the one that; one or the other

ūter, **-ris** *m* bag, skin, bottle

utercumque, **utracumque**, **utrumcumque** *pron* whichever (of two)

uterlibet, **utralibet**, **utrumlibet** *pron* whichever (of the two) you please, either one

uterque, **utraque**, **utrumque** *pron* each (*of two*), either, both

uterum, **-ī** *nt*, **uterus**, **-ī** *m* womb; child; belly

utervīs, **utravīs**, **utrumvīs** *pron* whichever (of two) you please; either

utī *etc see* **ut**

ūtī *infin of* **ūtor**

ūtibilis *adj* useful, serviceable

Utica, **-ae** *f* town near Carthage (where Cato committed suicide)

Uticēnsis *adj see* **Utica**

ūtilis *adj* useful, expedient, profitable; fit (for)

ūtilitās, **-ātis** *f* usefulness, expediency, advantage

ūtiliter *adv* usefully, advantageously

utinam *adv* I wish!, would that!, if only!

utique *adv* at least, by all means, especially

ūtor, **ūtī**, **ūsus** *vi* (*with abl*) to use, employ; to possess, enjoy; to practise, experience; (*person*) to be on intimate terms with, find; **ūtendum rogāre** borrow

utpote *adv* inasmuch as, as being

ūtrārius, **-ī** *and* **-iī** *m* watercarrier

ūtriculārius, **-ī** *and* **-iī** *m* bagpiper

utrimque, **utrinque** *adv* on both sides, on either side

utrō *adv* in which direction

utrobīque *see* **utrubīque**

utrōque *adv* in both directions, both ways

utrubī *adv* on which side

utrubīque *adv* on both sides, on either side

utrum *adv* whether

utut *adv* however

ūva, **-ae** *f* grape, bunch of grapes; vine; cluster

ūvēscō, **-ere** *vi* to become wet

ūvidulus *adj* moist

ūvidus *adj* wet, damp; drunken

uxor, **-ōris** *f* wife

uxorcula, **-ae** *f* little wife

uxōrius *adj* of a wife; fond of his wife

Vv

vacāns, -antis *pres p of* **vacō** ♦ *adj* unoccupied; (*woman*) single

vacātiō, -ōnis *f* freedom, exemption; exemption from military service; payment for exemption from service

vacca, -ae *f* cow

vaccīnium, -ī *and* **-iī** *nt* hyacinth

vaccula, -ae *f* heifer

vacēfīō, -ierī *vi* to become empty

vacillō, -āre *vi* to stagger, totter; to waver, be unreliable

vacīvē *adv* at leisure

vacīvitās, -ātis *f* want

vacīvus *adj* empty, free

vacō, -āre, -āvī, -ātum *vi* to be empty, vacant, unoccupied; to be free, aloof (from); to have time for, devote one's time to; **vacat** there is time

vacuātus *adj* empty

vacuēfaciō, -facere, -fēcī, -factum *vt* to empty, clear

vacuitās, -ātis *f* freedom, exemption; vacancy

vacuus *adj* empty, void, wanting; vacant; free (from), clear; disengaged, at leisure; (*value*) worthless; (*woman*) single ♦ *nt* void, space

vadimōnium, -ī *and* **-iī** *nt* bail, security; **~ sistere** appear in court; **~ dēserere** default

vādō, -ere *vi* to go, go on, make one's way

vador, -ārī, -ātus *vt* to bind over by bail

vadōsus *adj* shallow

vadum, -ī *nt* shoal, shallow, ford; water, sea; bottom

vae *interj* woe!, alas!

vafer, -rī *adj* crafty, subtle

vafrē *adv* artfully

vagē *adv* far afield

vāgīna, -ae *f* sheath, scabbard; (*grain*) husk

vāgiō, -īre *vi* to cry

vāgītus, -ūs *m* crying, bleating

vagor, -ārī, -ātus *vi* to wander, rove, go far afield; (*fig*) to spread

vāgor, -ōris *m* cry

vagus *adj* wandering, unsettled; (*fig*) fickle, wavering, vague

vah *interj* (*expressing surprise, joy, anger*) oh!, ah!

valdē *adv* greatly, intensely; very

valē, valēte *interj* goodbye, farewell

valēns, -entis *pres p of* **valeō** ♦ *adj* strong, powerful, vigorous; well, healthy

valenter *adv* strongly

valentulus *adj* strong

valeō, -ēre, -uī, -itum *vi* to be strong; to be able, have the power (to); to be well, fit, healthy; (*fig*) to be powerful, effective, valid; (*force*) to prevail; (*money*) to be worth; (*word*) to mean; **valēre apud** have influence over, carry weight with; **valēre iubeō** say goodbye to; **valē dīcō** say goodbye; **valeās** away with you!

valēscō, -ere *vi* to grow strong, thrive

valētūdinārium, -ī *and* **-iī** *nt* hospital

valētūdō, -inis *f* state of health, health; illness

valgus *adj* bow-legged

validē *adv* powerfully, very

validus *adj* strong, powerful, able; sound, healthy; effective

vallāris *adj* (*decoration*) for scaling a rampart

vallēs, vallis, -is *f* valley

vallō, -āre, -āvī, -ātum *vt* to palisade, entrench, fortify

vallum, -ī *nt* rampart, palisade, entrenchment

vallus, -ī *m* stake; palisade, rampart; (*comb*) tooth

valvae, -ārum *fpl* folding door

vānēscō, -ere *vi* to disappear, pass away

vānidicus, -ī *m* liar

vāniloquentia, -ae *f* idle talk

vāniloquus *adj* untruthful; boastful

vānitās, -ātis *f* emptiness; falsehood, worthlessness, fickleness; vanity

vānitūdō, -inis *f* falsehood

vannus, -ī *f* winnowing fan

vānus *adj* empty; idle, useless, groundless; false, untruthful, unreliable; conceited

vapidus *adj* spoilt, corrupt

vapor, -ōris *m* steam, vapour; heat

vapōrārium, -ī *and* **-iī** *nt* steam pipe

vapōrō, -āre *vt* to steam, fumigate, heat ♦ *vi* to burn

vappa, -ae *f* wine that has gone flat; (*person*) good-for-nothing

vāpulō, -āre *vi* to be flogged, beaten; to be defeated

variantia, -ae *f* diversity

variātiō, -ōnis *f* difference

vāricō, -āre *vi* to straddle

vāricōsus *adj* varicose

vāricus *adj* with feet wide apart

variē *adv* diversely, with varying success

varietās, -ātis *f* difference, diversity

variō, -āre, -āvī, -ātum *vt* to diversify, variegate; to make different, change, vary ♦ *vi* to change colour; to differ, vary

varius *adj* coloured, spotted, variegated; diverse, changeable, various; *(ability)* versatile; *(character)* fickle

Varius, -ī *m* epic poet *(friend of Vergil and Horace)*

varix, -icis *f* varicose vein

Varrō, -ōnis *m* consul defeated at Cannae; antiquarian writer of Cicero's day

Varrōniānus *adj see* **Varrō**

vārus *adj* knock-kneed; crooked; contrary

vas, vadis *m* surety, bail

vās, vāsis *nt*, **vāsa, -ōrum** *ntpl* vessel, dish; utensil, implement; *(MIL)* baggage

vāsārium, -ī *and* **-iī** *nt* furnishing allowance *(of a governor)*

vāsculārius, -ī *and* **-iī** *m* metalworker

vāsculum, -ī *nt* small dish

vastātiō, -ōnis *f* ravaging

vastātor, -ōris *m* ravager

vastē *adv (size)* enormously; *(speech)* coarsely

vastificus *adj* ravaging

vastitās, -ātis *f* desolation, desert; devastation, destruction

vastitiēs, -ēī *f* ruin

vastō, -āre, -āvī, -ātum *vt* to make desolate, denude; to lay waste, ravage

vastus *adj* empty, desolate, uncultivated; ravaged, devastated; *(appearance)* uncouth, rude; *(size)* enormous, vast

vāsum *etc see* **vās**

vātēs, -is *m/f* prophet, prophetess; poet, bard

Vāticānus *adj* Vatican *(hill on right bank of Tiber)*

vāticinātiō, -ōnis *f* prophesying, prediction

vāticinātor, -ōris *m* prophet

vāticinor, -ārī, -ātus *vt, vi* to prophesy; to celebrate in verse; to rave, rant

vāticinus *adj* prophetic

-ve *conj* or; either ... or

vēcordia, -ae *f* senselessness; insanity

vēcors, -dis *adj* senseless, foolish, mad

vectīgal, -ālis *nt* tax, honorarium *(to a magistrate)*; income

vectiō, -ōnis *f* transport

vectis, -is *m* lever, crowbar; *(door)* bolt, bar

Vectis, -is *f* Isle of Wight

vectō, -āre *vt* to carry; *(pass)* to ride

vector, -ōris *m* carrier; passenger, rider

vectōrius *adj* transport *(in cpds)*

vectūra, -ae *f* transport; *(payment)* carriage, fare

vectus *ppp of* **vehō**

Vediovis, -is = **Vēiovis**

vegetus *adj* lively, sprightly

vēgrandis *adj* small

vehemēns, -entis *adj* impetuous, violent; powerful, strong

vehementer *adv* violently, eagerly; powerfully, very much

vehementia, -ae *f* vehemence

vehiculum, -ī *nt* carriage, cart; *(sea)* vessel

vehō, -here, -xī, -ctum *vt* to carry, convey; *(pass)* to ride, sail, drive

Vēiēns, -entis, Vēientānus, Vēius *adj see* **Vēiī**

Vēiī, -ōrum *mpl* ancient town in S. Etruria

Vēiovis, -is *m* ancient Roman god *(anti-Jupiter)*

vel *conj* or, or perhaps; or rather; or else; either ... or ◆ *adv* even, if you like; perhaps; for instance; **vel māximus** the very greatest

Vēlābrum, -ī *nt* low ground between Capitol and Palatine hills

vēlāmen, -inis *nt* covering, garment

vēlāmentum, -ī *nt* curtain; *(pl)* draped olive branches carried by suppliants

vēlārium, -ī *and* **-iī** *nt* awning

vēlātī, -ōrum *mpl* supernumerary troops

vēles, -itis *m* light-armed soldier, skirmisher

vēlifer, -ī *adj* carrying sail

vēlificātiō, -ōnis *f* sailing

vēlificō, -āre *vi* to sail ◆ *vt* to sail through

vēlificor, -ārī *vi* to sail; *(with dat)* to make an effort to obtain

Velīnus, -ī *m* a Sabine lake

vēlitāris *adj* of the light-armed troops

vēlitātiō, -ōnis *f* skirmishing

vēlitēs *pl of* **vēles**

vēlitor, -ārī *vi* to skirmish

vēlivolus *adj* sail-winged

velle *infin of* **volō**

vellicō, -āre *vt* to pinch, pluck, twitch; *(speech)* to taunt, disparage

vellō, -ere, vellī *and* **vulsī, vulsum** *vt* to pluck, pull, pick; to pluck out, tear up

vellus, -eris *nt* fleece, pelt; wool; fleecy clouds

vēlō, -āre, -āvī, -ātum *vt* to cover up, clothe, veil; *(fig)* to conceal

vēlōcitās, -ātis *f* speed, rapidity

vēlōciter *adv* rapidly

vēlōx, -ōcis *adj* fast, quick, rapid

vēlum, -ī *nt* sail; curtain, awning; **rēmis vēlisque** with might and main; **vēla dare** set sail

velut, velutī *adv* as, just as; for instance; just as if

vemēns *etc see* **vehemēns**

vēna, -ae *f* vein, artery; vein of metal; water course; *(fig)* innermost nature of feelings, talent, strength; **vēnās temptāre** feel the pulse; **vēnās tenēre** have one's finger on the pulse *(of)*

vēnābulum, -ī *nt* hunting spear

Venāfrānus *adj see* **Venāfrum**

Venāfrum, -ī *nt* Samnite town famous for olive oil

vēnālicius *adj* for sale ◆ *m* slave dealer

vēnālis *adj* for sale; bribable ◆ *m* slave offered for sale

vēnāticus *adj* hunting- *(in cpds)*

vēnātiō, -ōnis *f* hunting; a hunt; public show of fighting wild beasts; game

vēnātor, -ōris *m* hunter

vēnātōrius *adj* hunter's

vēnātrīx, -īcis *f* huntress

vēnātūra, -ae *f* hunting

vēnātus, -ūs *m* hunting

vēndibilis *adj* saleable; *(fig)* popular

vēnditātiō, -ōnis *f* showing off, advertising

vēnditātor, -ōris *m* braggart

vēnditiō, -ōnis *f* sale

vēnditō, -āre *vt* to try to sell; to praise up, advertise; **sē vēnditāre** ingratiate oneself *(with)*

vēnditor, -ōris *m* seller

vēndō (*pass* **vēneō**), **-ere**, **-idī**, **-itum** *vt* to sell; to betray; to praise up

venēficium, -ī *and* **-iī** *nt* poisoning; sorcery

venēficus *adj* poisonous; magic ◆ *m* sorcerer ◆ *f* sorceress

venēnātus *adj* poisonous; magic

venēnifer, -ī *adj* poisonous

venēnō, -āre *vt* to poison

venēnum, -ī *nt* drug, potion; dye; poison; magic charm; (*fig*) mischief; charm

vēneō, -īre, -iī, -itum *vi* to be sold

venerābilis *adj* honoured, venerable

venerābundus *adj* reverent

venerātiō, -ōnis *f* respect, reverence

venerātor, -ōris *m* reverencer

Venereus, Venerius *adj* of Venus ◆ *m* highest throw (*at dice*)

veneror, -ārī, -ātus *vt* to worship, revere, pray to; to honour, respect; to ask for, entreat

Venetia, -iae *f* district of the Veneti

Veneticus *adj see* **Venetia**

Venetus *adj* Venetian; (*colour*) blue

vēnī *perf of* **veniō**

venia, -ae *f* indulgence, favour, kindness; permission, leave; pardon, forgiveness; **bonā tuā veniā** by your leave; **bonā veniā audīre** give a fair hearing

vēniī *perf of* **vēneō**

veniō, -īre, vēnī, ventum *vi* to come; (*fig*) to fall into, incur, go as far as; **in amīcitiam venīre** make friends (with); **in spem venīre** entertain hopes

vēnor, -ārī, -ātus *vt, vi* to hunt, chase

venter, -ris *m* stomach, belly; womb, unborn child

ventilātor, -ōris *m* juggler

ventilō, -āre *vt* to fan, wave, agitate

ventiō, -ōnis *f* coming

ventitō, -āre *vi* to keep coming, come regularly

ventōsus *adj* windy; like the wind; fickle; conceited

ventriculus, -ī *m* belly; (*heart*) ventricle

ventriōsus *adj* pot-bellied

ventulus, -ī *m* breeze

ventus, -ī *m* wind

vēnūcula, -ae *f kind of grape*

vēnum, vēnō for sale

vēnumdō, vēnundō, -āre, -edī, -atum *vt* to sell, put up for sale

Venus, -eris *f* goddess of love; planet Venus; highest throw (*at dice*)

venus, -eris *f* charm, beauty; love, mating

Venusia, -iae *f town in Apulia (birthplace of Horace)*

Venusīnus *adj see* **Venusia**

venustās, -ātis *f* charm, beauty

venustē *adv* charmingly

venustulus *adj* charming little

venustus *adj* charming, attractive, beautiful

vēpallidus *adj* very pale

veprēcula, -ae *f* little brier bush

veprēs, -is *m* thornbush, bramblebush

vēr, vēris *nt* spring; **vēr sacrum** offerings of firstlings

vērātrum, -ī *nt* hellebore

vērāx, -ācis *adj* truthful

verbēna, -ae *f* vervain; (*pl*) sacred boughs carried by heralds or priests

verber, -is *nt* lash, scourge; (*missile*) strap; (*pl*) flogging, strokes

verberābilis *adj* deserving a flogging

verberātiō, -ōnis *f* punishment

verbereus *adj* deserving a flogging

verberō¹, -āre, -āvī, -ātum *vt* to flog, beat, lash

verberō², -ōnis *m* scoundrel

verbōsē *adv* verbosely

verbōsus *adj* wordy

verbum, -ī *nt* word; saying, expression; (*GRAM*) verb; (*pl*) language, talk; **~ ē verbō, ~ dē verbō, ~ prō verbō** literally; **ad ~** word for word; **verbī causā (grātiā)** for instance; **verbō** orally; briefly; **verba dare** cheat, fool; **verba facere** talk; **meīs verbīs** in my name

vērē *adv* really, truly, correctly

verēcundē *adv see* **verēcundus**

verēcundia, -ae *f* modesty, shyness; reverence, dread; shame

verēcundor, -ārī *vi* to be bashful, feel shy

verēcundus *adj* modest, shy, bashful

verendus *adj* venerable

vereor, -ērī, -itus *vt, vi* to fear, be afraid; to revere, respect

verētrum, -ī *nt* the private parts

Vergiliae, -ārum *fpl* the Pleiads

Vergilius, -ī *m* Vergil, Virgil (*famous epic poet*)

vergō, -ere *vt* to turn, incline ◆ *vi* to turn, incline, decline; (*place*) to face

vēridicus *adj* truthful

vērī similis *adj* probable

vērī similitūdō, -inis *f* probability

vēritās, -ātis *f* truth, truthfulness; reality, real life; (*character*) integrity; (*language*) etymology

veritus *ppa of* **vereor**

vermiculātus *adj* inlaid with wavy lines, mosaic

vermiculus, -ī *m* grub

vermina, -um *ntpl* stomach pains

vermis, -is *m* worm

verna, -ae *f* slave born in his master's home

vernāculus *adj* of home-born slaves; native

vernīlis *adj* slavish; (*remark*) smart

vernīliter *adv* slavishly

vernō, -āre *vi* to bloom, be spring-like; to be young

vernula, -ae *f* young home-born slave; native

vērnus *adj* of spring

vērō *adv* in fact, assuredly; (*confirming*) certainly, yes; (*climax*) indeed; (*adversative*) but in fact; **minimē ~** certainly not

Vērōna, -ae *f town in N. Italy (birthplace of Catullus)*

Vērōnēnsis *adj see* **Vērōna**

verpus, -ī *m* circumcised man

Verrēs, -is *m* praetor prosecuted by Cicero

verrēs, -is *m* boar

verrīnus *adj* boar's, pork (*in cpds*)

Verrius, Verrīnus *adj see* **Verrēs**

verrō, -rere, -rī, -sum *vt* to sweep, scour; to sweep away, carry off

verrūca, -ae *f* wart; (*fig*) slight blemish

verrūcōsus *adj* warty

verruncō, -āre vi to turn out successfully

versābundus adj rotating

versātilis adj revolving; versatile

versicolor, -ōris adj of changing or various colours

versiculus, -ī m short line; (pl) unpretentious verses

versificātor, -ōris m versifier

versipellis adj of changed appearance; crafty ◆ m werewolf

versō, -āre, -āvī, -ātum vt to keep turning, wind, twist; (fig) to upset, disturb, ruin; (mind) to ponder, consider

versor, -ārī, -ātus vi to live, be, be situated; to be engaged (in), be busy (with)

versum adv turned, in the direction

versūra, -ae f borrowing to pay a debt; loan

versus¹ ppp of **vertō** ◆ adv turned, in the direction

versus², -ūs m line, row; verse; (dance) step

versūtē adv craftily

versūtiae, -ārum fpl tricks

versūtiloquus adj sly

versūtus adj clever; crafty, deceitful

vertex, -icis m whirlpool, eddy; whirlwind; crown of the head, head; top, summit; (sky) pole

verticōsus adj eddying, swirling

vertīgō, -inis f turning round; dizziness

vertō, -tere, -tī, -sum vt to turn; to turn over, invert; to turn round; to turn into, change, exchange; (cause) to ascribe, impute; (language) to translate; (war) to overthrow, destroy; (pass) to be (in), be engaged (in) ◆ vi to turn; to change; to turn out; **in fugam vertere** put to flight; **terga vertere** flee; **solum vertere** emigrate; **vitiō vertere** blame; **annō vertente** in the course of a year

Vertumnus, -ī m god of seasons

verū, -ūs nt spit; javelin

vērum¹ adv truly, yes; but actually; but, yet; **~ tamen** nevertheless

vērum², -ī nt truth, reality; right; **vērī similis** probable

vērus adj true, real, actual; truthful; right, reasonable

verūtum, -ī nt javelin

verūtus adj armed with the javelin

vervēx, -ēcis m wether

vēsānia, -ae f madness

vēsāniēns, -entis adj raging

vēsānus adj mad, insane; furious, raging

vescor, -ī vi (with abl) to feed, eat; to enjoy

vescus adj little, feeble; corroding

vēsīca, -ae f bladder; purse; football

vēsīcula, -ae f small bladder, blister

vespa, -ae f wasp

Vespasiānus, -ī m Roman emperor

vesper, -is and **-ī** m evening; supper; evening star; west; **vespere, vesperī** in the evening

vespera, -ae f evening

vesperāscō, -ere vi to become evening, get late

vespertiliō, -ōnis m bat

vespertīnus adj evening (in cpds), in the evening; western

vesperūgō, -inis f evening star

Vesta, -ae f Roman goddess of the hearth

Vestālis adj Vestal ◆ f virgin priestess of Vesta

vester, -rī adj your, yours

vestibulum, -ī nt forecourt, entrance

vestīgium, -ī and **-iī** nt footstep, footprint, track; (fig) trace, sign, vestige; (time) moment, instant; **ē vestīgiō** instantly

vestīgō, -āre, -āvī, -ātum vt to track, trace, search for, discover

vestīmentum, -ī nt clothes

vestiō, -īre, -iī, -ītum vt to clothe, dress; to cover, adorn

vestipica, -ae f wardrobe woman

vestis, -is f clothes, dress; coverlet, tapestry, blanket; (snake) slough; **vestem mūtāre** change one's clothes; go into mourning

vestispica etc see **vestipica**

vestītus, -ūs m clothes, dress; covering; **mūtāre vestītum** go into mourning; **redīre ad suum vestītum** come out of mourning

Vesuvius, -ī m (the volcano) Vesuvius

veterānus adj veteran

veterāscō, -scere, -vī vi to grow old

veterātor, -ōris m expert, old hand; sly fox

veterātōriē adv see **veterātōrius**

veterātōrius adj crafty

veterīnus adj of burden ◆ f and ntpl beasts of burden

veternōsus adj lethargic, drowsy

veternus, -ī m lethargy, drowsiness

vetitus ppp of **vetō** ◆ nt prohibition

vetō, -āre, -uī, -itum vt to forbid, prohibit, oppose; (tribune) to protest

vetulus adj little old, poor old

vetus, -eris adj old, former ◆ mpl the ancients ◆ fpl the old shops (in the Forum) ◆ ntpl antiquity, tradition

vetustās, -ātis f age, long standing; antiquity; great age, future age

vetustus adj old, ancient; old-fashioned

vexāmen, -inis nt shaking

vexātiō, -ōnis f shaking; trouble, distress

vexātor, -ōris m troubler, opponent

vexī perf of **vehō**

vexillārius, -ī and **-iī** m standard-bearer, ensign; (pl) special reserve of veterans

vexillum, -ī nt standard, flag; company, troop; **~ prōpōnere** hoist the signal for battle

vexō, -āre, -āvī, -ātum vt to shake, toss, trouble, distress, injure, attack

via, -ae f road, street, way; journey, march; passage; (fig) way, method, fashion; the right way; **viā** properly; **inter viās** on the way

viālis adj of the highways

viārius adj for the upkeep of roads

viāticātus adj provided with travelling money

viāticus adj for a journey ◆ nt travelling allowance; (MIL) prizemoney, savings

viātor, -ōris m traveller; (LAW) summoner

vībix, -īcis f weal

vibrō, -āre, -āvī, -ātum vt to wave, shake, brandish, hurl, launch ◆ vi to shake, quiver, vibrate; to shimmer, sparkle

vīburnum, -ī nt wayfaring-tree or guelder rose

vīcānus *adj* village (*in cpds*) ◆ *mpl* villagers
Vīca Pota, **Vīcae Potae** *f goddess of victory*
vicārius *adj* substituted ◆ *m* substitute, proxy; underslave
vīcātim *adv* from street to street; in villages
vice (*with gen*) on account of; like
vicem in turn; (*with gen*) instead of; on account of; like; **tuam ~** on your account
vīcēnārius *adj* of twenty
vīcēnī, **-ōrum** *adj* twenty each, in twenties
vicēs *pl of* **vicis**
vīcēsimānī, **-ōrum** *mpl* men of the twentieth legion
vīcēsimārius *adj* derived from the 5 per cent tax
vīcēsimus *adj* twentieth ◆ *f* a 5 per cent tax
vīcī *perf of* **vincō**
vicia, **-ae** *f* vetch
vīciēns, **vīciēs** *adv* twenty times
vīcīnālis *adj* neighbouring
vīcīnia, **-ae** *f* neighbourhood, nearness
vīcīnitās, **-ātis** *f* neighbourhood, nearness
vīcīnus *adj* neighbouring, nearby; similar, kindred ◆ *m/f* neighbour ◆ *nt* neighbourhood
vicis *gen* (*acc* **-em**, *abl* **-e**) *f* interchange, alternation, succession; recompense, retaliation; fortune, changing conditions; duty, function, place; **in vicem** in turn, mutually
vicissim *adv* in turn, again
vicissitūdō, **-inis** *f* interchange, alternation
victima, **-ae** *f* victim, sacrifice
victimārius, **-ī** and **-iī** *m* assistant at sacrifices
victitō, **-āre** *vi* to live, subsist
victor, **-ōris** *m* conqueror, victor, winner ◆ *adj* victorious
victōria, **-ae** *f* victory
victōriātus, **-ūs** *m* silver coin stamped with Victory
Victōriola, **-ae** *f* little statue of Victory
victrīx, **-īcis** *f* conqueror ◆ *adj* victorious
victus *ppp of* **vincō**
vīctus, **-ūs** *m* sustenance, livelihood; way of life
vīculus, **-ī** *m* hamlet
vīcus, **-ī** *m* (*city*) quarter, street; (*country*) village, estate
vidēlicet *adv* clearly, evidently; (*ironical*) of course; (*explaining*) namely
videō, **-ēre**, **vīdī**, **vīsum** *vt* to see, look at; (*mind*) to observe, be aware, know; to consider, think over; to see to, look out for; to live to see; (*pass*) to seem, appear; to seem right, be thought proper; **mē vidē** rely on me; **vīderit** let him see to it; **mihi videor esse** I think I am; **sī (tibi) vidētur** if you like
viduāta *adj* widowed
viduitās, **-ātis** *f* bereavement, want; widowhood
vīdulus, **-ī** *m* trunk, box
viduō, **-āre** *vt* to bereave
viduus *adj* bereft, bereaved; unmarried; (*with abl*) without ◆ *f* widow; spinster
Vienna, **-ae** *f* town in Gaul on the Rhone (now Vienne)
viētus *adj* shrivelled
vigeō, **-ēre**, **-uī** *vi* to thrive, flourish

vigēscō, **-ere** *vi* to begin to flourish, become lively
vigēsimus *etc see* **vīcēsimus**
vigil, **-is** *adj* awake, watching, alert ◆ *m* watchman, sentinel; (*pl*) the watch, police
vigilāns, **-antis** *pres p of* **vigilō** ◆ *adj* watchful
vigilanter *adv* vigilantly
vigilantia, **-ae** *f* wakefulness; vigilance
vigilāx, **-ācis** *adj* watchful
vigilia, **-ae** *f* lying awake, sleeplessness; keeping watch, guard; a watch; the watch, sentries; vigil; vigilance
vigilō, **-āre**, **-āvī**, **-ātum** *vi* to remain awake; to keep watch; to be vigilant ◆ *vt* to spend awake, make while awake at night
vīgintī *num* twenty
vīgintivirātus, **-ūs** *m* membership of a board of twenty
vīgintivirī, **-ōrum** *mpl* a board or commission of twenty men
vigor, **-ōris** *m* energy, vigour
vīlica, **-ae** *f* wife of a steward
vīlicō, **-āre** *vi* to be an overseer
vīlicus, **-ī** *m* overseer, manager of an estate, steward
vīlis *adj* cheap; worthless, poor, mean, common
vīlitās, **-ātis** *f* cheapness, low price; worthlessness
vīliter *adv* cheaply
vīlla, **-ae** *f* country house, villa
vīllic- *etc see* **vīlic-**
vīllōsus *adj* hairy, shaggy
vīllula, **-ae** *f* small villa
vīllum, **-ī** *nt* a drop of wine
villus, **-ī** *m* hair, fleece; (*cloth*) nap
vīmen, **-inis** *nt* osier; basket
vīmentum, **-ī** *nt* osier
Vīminālis *adj* Viminal (hill of Rome)
vīmineus *adj* of osiers, wicker
vīnāceus *adj* grape- (*in cpds*)
Vīnālia, **-ium** *ntpl* Wine festival
vīnārius *adj* of wine, wine (*in cpds*) ◆ *m* vintner ◆ *nt* wine flask
vincibilis *adj* easily won
vinciō, **-īre**, **-xī**, **-ctum** *vt* to bind, fetter; to encircle; (*fig*) to confine, restrain, envelop, attach
vinclum *nt see* **vinculum**
vincō, **-ere**, **vīcī**, **victum** *vt* to conquer, defeat, subdue; to win, prevail, be successful; (*fig*) to surpass, excel; (*argument*) to convince, refute, prove conclusively; (*life*) to outlive
vinctus *ppp of* **vinciō**
vinculum, **-ī** *nt* bond, fetter, chain; (*pl*) prison
vīndēmia, **-ae** *f* vintage, grape harvest
vīndēmiātor, **-ōris** *m* vintager
vīndēmiola, **-ae** *f* small vintage
Vīndēmitor, **-ōris** *m* the Vintager (a star in Virgo)
vindex, **-icis** *m* champion, protector; liberator; avenger ◆ *adj* avenging
vindicātiō, **-ōnis** *f* punishment of offences
vindiciae, **-ārum** *fpl* legal claim; **vindiciās ab lībertāte in servitūtem dare** condemn a free person to slavery

vindicō, -āre, -āvī, -ātum vt to lay claim to; to claim, appropriate; to liberate, protect, champion; to avenge, punish; **in lībertātem vindicāre** emancipate

vindicta, -ae f rod used in manumitting a slave; defence, deliverance; revenge, punishment

vīnea, -ae f vineyard; vine; (MIL) penthouse (for besiegers)

vīnētum, -ī nt vineyard

vīnitor, -ōris m vine-dresser

vinnulus adj delightful

vīnolentia, -ae f wine drinking

vīnolentus adj drunk

vīnōsus adj fond of wine, drunken

vīnum, -ī nt wine

vinxī perf of **vinciō**

viola, -ae f violet; stock

violābilis adj vulnerable

violāceus adj violet

violārium, -ī and **-iī** nt violet bed

violārius, -ī and **-iī** m dyer of violet

violātiō, -ōnis f desecration

violātor, -ōris m violator, desecrator

violēns, -entis adj raging, vehement

violenter adv violently, furiously

violentia, -ae f violence, impetuosity

violentus adj violent, impetuous, boisterous

violō, -āre, -āvī, -ātum vt to do violence to, outrage, violate; (agreement) to break

vīpera, -ae f viper, adder, snake

vīpereus adj snake's, serpent's

vīperīnus adj snake's, serpent's

vir, virī m man; grown man; brave man, hero; husband; (MIL) footsoldier

virāgō, -inis f heroine, warrior maid

virecta, -ōrum ntpl grassy sward

vireō, -ēre, -uī vi to be green; (fig) to be fresh, flourish

vīrēs pl of **vīs¹**

virēscō, -ere vi to grow green

virga, -ae f twig; graft; rod, staff, walking stick, wand; (colour) stripe

virgātor, -ōris m flogger

virgātus adj made of osiers; striped

virgētum, -ī nt thicket of osiers

virgeus adj of brushwood

virgidēmia, -ae f crop of flogging

virginālis adj maidenly, of maids

virginārius adj of maids

virgineus adj maidenly, virgin, of virgins

virginitās, -ātis f maidenhood

virgō, -inis f maid, virgin; young woman, girl; (constellation) Virgo; a Roman aqueduct

virgula, -ae f wand

virgulta, -ōrum ntpl thicket, shrubbery; cuttings, slips

virguncula, -ae f little girl

viridāns, -antis adj green

viridārium, -ī and **-iī** nt plantation, garden

viridis adj green; fresh, young, youthful ♦ ntpl greenery

viriditās, -ātis f verdure, greenness; freshness

viridor, -ārī vi to become green

virīlis adj male, masculine; man's, adult; manly, brave, bold; ~ **pars** one's individual part or duty; **prō virīlī parte, prō virīlī portiōne** to the best of one's ability

virīlitās, -ātis f manhood

virīliter adv manfully

virītim adv individually, separately

vīrōsus adj slimy; rank

virtūs, -ūtis f manhood, full powers; strength, courage, ability, worth; (MIL) valour, prowess, heroism; (moral) virtue; (things) excellence, worth

vīrus, -ī nt slime; poison; offensive smell; salt taste

vīs¹ (acc **vim**, abl **vī**, pl **vīrēs**) f power, force, strength; violence, assault; quantity, amount; (mind) energy, vigour; (word) meaning, import; (pl) strength; (MIL) troops; **per vim** forcibly; **dē vī damnārī** be convicted of assault; **prō vīribus** with all one's might

vīs² 2nd pers of **volō²**

viscātus adj limed

viscerātiō, -ōnis f public distribution of meat

viscō, -āre vt to make sticky

viscum, -ī nt mistletoe; bird lime

viscus, -eris (pl **-era, -erum**) nt internal organs; flesh; womb, child; (fig) heart, bowels

vīsendus adj worth seeing

vīsiō, -ōnis f apparition; idea

vīsitō, -āre vt to see often; to visit

vīsō, -ere, -ī, -um vt to look at, survey; to see to; to go and see, visit

Visurgis, -is m (river) Weser

vīsus¹ ppp of **videō** ♦ nt vision

vīsus², -ūs m sight, the faculty of seeing; a sight, vision

vīta, -ae f life, livelihood; way of life; career, biography

vītābilis adj undesirable

vītābundus adj avoiding, taking evasive action

vītālis adj of life, vital ♦ nt subsistence ♦ ntpl vitals

vītāliter adv with life

vītātiō, -ōnis f avoidance

Vitellius¹, -ī m Roman emperor in AD 69

Vitellius², -iānus adj see **Vitellius¹**

vitellus, -ī m little calf; (egg) yolk

vīteus adj of the vine

vīticula, -ae f little vine

vītigenus adj produced from the vine

vitilēna, -ae f procuress

vitiō, -āre, -āvī, -ātum vt to spoil, corrupt, violate; to falsify

vitiōsē adv badly, defectively

vitiōsitās, -ātis f vice

vitiōsus adj faulty, corrupt; wicked, depraved; ~ **cōnsul** a consul whose election had a religious flaw in it

vītis, -is f vine; vine branch, centurion's staff, centurionship

vītisator, -ōris m vine planter

vitium, -ī and **-iī** nt fault, flaw, defect; (moral) failing, offence, vice; (religion) flaw in the auspices

vītō, -āre, -āvī, -ātum vt to avoid, evade, shun

vītor, -ōris *m* basket maker, cooper
vitreus *adj* of glass; glassy ♦ *ntpl* glassware
vītricus, -ī *m* stepfather
vitrum, -ī *nt* glass; woad
vitta, -ae *f* headband, sacrificial fillet
vittātus *adj* wearing a fillet
vitula, -ae *f (of cow)* calf
vitulīnus *adj* of veal ♦ *f* veal
vītulor, -ārī *vi* to hold a celebration
vitulus, -ī *m* calf; foal; ~ **marīnus** seal
vituperābilis *adj* blameworthy
vituperātiō, -ōnis *f* blame, censure; scandalous conduct
vituperātor, -ōris *m* critic
vituperō, -āre *vt* to find fault with, disparage; *(omen)* to spoil
vīvārium, -ī *and* **-iī** *nt* fishpond, game preserve
vīvātus *adj* animated
vīvāx, -ācis *adj* long-lived; lasting; *(sulphur)* inflammable
vīvēscō, -ere *vi* to grow, become active
vīvidus *adj* full of life; *(art)* true to life, vivid; *(mind)* lively
vīvirādīx, -īcis *f* a rooted cutting, layer
vīvīscō *etc see* **vīvēscō**
vīvō, -vere, -xī, -ctum *vi* to live, be alive; to enjoy life; *(fame)* to last, be remembered; *(with abl)* to live on; **vīve** farewell!; **vīxērunt** they are dead
vīvus *adj* alive, living; *(light)* burning; *(rock)* natural; *(water)* running; **vīvō videntīque** before his very eyes; **mē vīvō** as long as I live, in my lifetime; **ad vīvum resecāre** cut to the quick; **dē vīvō dētrahere** take out of capital
vix *adv* with difficulty, hardly, scarcely
vixdum *adv* hardly, as yet
vīxī *perf of* **vīvō**
vocābulum, -ī *nt* name, designation; *(GRAM)* noun
vōcālis *adj* speaking, singing, tuneful ♦ *f* vowel
vocāmen, -inis *nt* name
vocātiō, -ōnis *f* invitation; *(LAW)* summons
vocātus, -ūs *m* summons, call
vōciferātiō, -ōnis *f* loud cry, outcry
vōciferor, -ārī *vt* to cry out loud, shout
vocitō, -āre, -āvī, -ātum *vt* to usually call; to shout
vocīvus *etc see* **vacīvus**
vocō, -āre, -āvī, -ātum *vt* to call, summon; to call, name; *(gods)* to call upon; *(guest)* to invite; *(MIL)* to challenge; *(fig)* to bring *(into some condition or plight)*; **vocāre dē** name after; **in dubium vocāre** call in question; **in iūdicium vocāre** call to account
vōcula, -ae *f* weak voice; soft tone; gossip
volaema *ntpl* kind of large pear
Volaterrae, -ārum *fpl* old Etruscan town *(now* Volterra)
Volaterrānus *adj see* **Volaterrae**
volāticus *adj* winged; fleeting, inconstant
volātilis *adj* winged; swift; fleeting
volātus, -ūs *m* flight
Volcānius *adj see* **Volcānus**
Volcānus, -ī *m* Vulcan *(god of fire)*, fire

volēns, -entis *pres p of* **volō²** ♦ *adj* willing, glad, favourable; **mihi volentī est** it is acceptable to me
volg- *etc see* **vulg-**
volitō, -āre *vi* to fly about, flutter; to hurry, move quickly; *(fig)* to hover, soar; to get excited
voln- *etc see* **vuln-**
volō¹, -āre, -āvī, -ātum *vi* to fly; to speed
volō², velle, voluī *vt* to wish, want; to be willing; to will, purpose, determine; *(opinion)* to hold, maintain; *(word, action)* to mean; ~ **dīcere** I mean; **bene velle** like; **male velle** dislike; **ōrātum tē** ~ I beg you; **paucīs tē** ~ a word with you!; **numquid vīs** *(before leaving)* is there anything else?; **quid sibi vult?** what does he mean?; what is he driving at?; **velim faciās** please do it; **vellem fēcissēs** I wish you had done it
volōnēs, -um *mpl* volunteers
volpēs *etc see* **vulpēs**
Volscī, -ōrum *mpl* people in S. Latium
Volscus *adj* Volscian
volsella, -ae *f* tweezers
volsus *ppp of* **vellō**
volt *old 3rd pers sg of* **volō²**
voltis *old 2nd pers pl of* **volō²**
Voltumna, -ae *f* patron goddess of Etruria
voltus *etc see* **vultus**
volūbilis *adj* spinning, revolving; *(fortune)* fickle; *(speech)* fluent
volubilitās, -ātis *f* whirling motion; roundness; fluency; inconstancy
volūbiliter *adv* fluently
volucer, -ris *adj* winged; flying, swift; fleeting
volucris, -is *f* bird; insect
volūmen, -inis *nt* roll, book; coil, eddy, fold
voluntārius *adj voluntary* ♦ *mpl* volunteers
voluntās, -ātis *f* will, wish, inclination; attitude, goodwill; last will, testament; **suā voluntāte** of one's own accord; **ad voluntātem** with the consent (of)
volup *adv* agreeably, to one's satisfaction
voluptābilis *adj* agreeable
voluptās, -ātis *f* pleasure, enjoyment; *(pl)* entertainments, sports
voluptuārius *adj* pleasureable, agreeable; voluptuous
volūtābrum, -ī *nt* wallowing place
volūtātiō, -ōnis *f* wallowing
volūtō, -āre *vt* to roll about, turn over; *(mind)* to occupy, engross; *(thought)* to ponder, think over; *(pass)* to wallow, flounder
volūtus *ppp of* **volvō**
volva, -ae *f* womb; *(dish)* sow's womb
volvō, -vere, -vī, -ūtum *vt* to roll, turn round; to roll along; *(air)* to breathe; *(book)* to open; *(circle)* to form; *(thought)* to ponder, reflect on; *(time)* to roll on; *(trouble)* to undergo; *(pass)* to roll, revolve ♦ *vi* to revolve, elapse
vōmer, -eris *m* ploughshare
vomica, -ae *f* sore, ulcer, abscess, boil
vōmis *etc see* **vōmer**
vomitiō, -ōnis *f* vomiting
vomitus, -ūs *m* vomiting, vomit

vomō, **-ere**, **-uī**, **-itum** *vt* to vomit, throw up; to emit, discharge

vorāgō, **-inis** *f* abyss, chasm, depth

vorāx, **-ācis** *adj* greedy, ravenous; consuming

vorō, **-āre**, **-āvī**, **-ātum** *vt* to swallow, devour; (*sea*) to swallow up; (*reading*) to devour

vors-, **vort-** *see* **vers-**, **vert-** *etc*

vōs *pron* you

Vosegus, **-ī** *m* Vosges (mountains)

voster *etc see* **vester**

vōtīvus *adj* votive, promised in a vow

votō *etc see* **vetō**

vōtum, **-ī** *nt* vow, prayer; votive offering; wish, longing; **vōtī damnārī** have one's prayer granted

vōtus *ppp of* **voveō**

voveō, **-ēre**, **vōvī**, **vōtum** *vt* to vow, promise solemnly; to dedicate; to wish

vōx, **vōcis** *f* voice; sound, cry, call; word, saying, expression; accent; **unā vōce** unanimously

Vulcānus *see* **Volcānus**

vulgāris *adj* common, general

vulgāriter *adv* in the common fashion

vulgātor, **-ōris** *m* betrayer

vulgātus *adj* common; generally known, notorious

vulgivagus *adj* roving; inconstant

vulgō¹ *adv* publicly, commonly, usually, everywhere

vulgō², **-āre**, **-āvī**, **-ātum** *vt* to make common, spread; to publish, divulge, broadcast; to prostitute; to level down

vulgus, **-ī** *nt* (*occ m*) the mass of the people, the public; crowd, herd; rabble, populace

vulnerātiō, **-ōnis** *f* wounding, injury

vulnerō, **-āre**, **-āvī**, **-ātum** *vt* to wound, hurt; to damage

vulnificus *adj* wounding, dangerous

vulnus, **-eris** *nt* wound, injury; (*things*) damage, hole; (*fig*) blow, misfortune, pain

vulpēcula, **-ae** *f* little fox

vulpēs, **-is** *f* fox; (*fig*) cunning

vulsī *perf of* **vellō**

vulsus *ppp of* **vellō**

vulticulus, **-ī** *m* a mere look (from)

vultum *etc see* **vultus**

vultuōsus *adj* affected

vultur, **-is** *m* vulture

vulturius, **-ī** *and* **-iī** *m* vulture, bird of prey; (*dice*) an unlucky throw

Vulturnus, **-ī** *m* river in Campania

vultus, **-ūs** *m* look, expression (*esp in the eyes*); face; (*things*) appearance

vulva *etc see* **volva**

Xx

Xanthippē, **-ēs** *f wife of Socrates*

Xanthus, **-ī** *m river of Troy (identified with Scamander); river of Lycia*

xenium, **-ī** *and* **-iī** *nt* present

Xenocratēs, **-is** *m disciple of Plato*

Xenophanēs, **-is** *m early Greek philosopher*

Xenophōn, **-ontis** *m famous Greek historian*

Xenophontēus *adj see* **Xenophōn**

xērampelinae, **-ārum** *fpl* dark-coloured clothes

Xerxēs, **-is** *m Persian king defeated at Salamis*

xiphiās, **-ae** *m* swordfish

xystum, **-ī** *nt*, **xystus**, **-ī** *m* open colonnade, walk, avenue

Zz

Zacynthius *adj see* **Zacynthus**
Zacynthus, Zacynthos, -ī *f island off W. Greece (now* Zante*)*
Zama, -ae *f town in Numidia (where Scipio defeated Hannibal)*
Zamēnsis *adj see* **Zama**
zămia, -ae *f* harm
Zanclaeus, Zanclēius *adj see* **Zanclē**
Zanclē, -ēs *f old name of Messana*
zēlotypus *adj* jealous
Zēnō, Zēnōn, -ōnis *m founder of Stoicism; a philosopher of Elea; an Epicurean teacher of Cicero*
Zephyrītis, -idis *f* Arsinoe (*queen of Egypt*)

Zephyrus, -ī *m* west wind, zephyr; wind
Zēthus, -ī *m brother of Amphion*
Zeuxis, -is *and* **-idis** *m famous Greek painter*
zmaragdus *etc see* **smaragdus**
Zmyrna *etc see* **Smyrna**
zŏdiacus, -ī *m* zodiac
zōna, -ae *f* belt, girdle; (GEOG) zone; (ASTR) Orion's Belt
zōnārius *adj* of belts; **sector** ~ cutpurse ♦ *m* belt maker
zōnula, -ae *f* little belt
zōthēca, -ae *f* private room
zōthēcula, -ae *f* cubicle

ROMAN LIFE AND CULTURE

KEY EVENTS IN ROMAN HISTORY

B.C.

753	Foundation of Rome. Romulus became first king.
600-510	Rome ruled by Etruscan kings.
510	Expulsion of Tarquin and republic established.
507	Consecration of Temple of Jupiter on Capitol.
451	Code of Twelve Tables laid basis of Roman law.
390	Gauls sacked Rome.
367	Lex Liciniae Sextiae; plebeians allowed to be consul.
354	Treaty with Samnites.
343-341	First Samnite war; Romans occupied northern Campania.
340-338	Latin War; separate treaties made with Latins.
327-304	Second Samnite war; Rome increased influence in southern Italy.
321	Samnites defeated Romans at Caudine Forks; truce.
312	Appian Way, first Roman road, built.
298-290	Third Samnite war; Rome now all-powerful in southern Italy.
287	Hortensian Law; People's Assembly became a law-making body.
282-272	Wars with Tarentum and King Pyrrhus of Epirus.
270	Whole peninsula under Roman power.
264-241	First Punic war; Rome defended Greek cities in Sicily.
260	Fleet built; first naval victory at Mylae against Carthaginians.
241	Roman victory over Carthage secured Sicily, source of corn supply.
226	River Ebro treaty; Carthage should not cross into northern Spain.
218-201	Second Punic war against Hannibal.
216	Rome defeated at Battle of Cannae.
214-205	First Macedonian war with Philip V.
202	Scipio defeated Hannibal at Zama.
201	Peace concluded with Carthage; Rome now controlled the western Mediterranean.
200-196	Second Macedonian war; freedom of Greece proclaimed.
172-168	Third Macedonian war; Perseus crushed at Pydna.
148	Macedonia became a Roman province.
146	Carthage destroyed; Corinth destroyed.
133	Tiberius Gracchus became tribune; his assassination caused class conflict.
123-122	Gaius Gracchus carried out political/economic reforms.
121	Gaius was killed.
111-105	Marius and Sulla conducted war against Jugurtha of Numidia.
91-89	Social war between Rome and allies.
89-85	War with Mithridates VI of Pontus.
83-82	Civil war between Sulla and Marius; Sulla captured Rome.
81-79	Sulla, dictator, restored constitution, introduced reforms.
78	Death of Sulla.

1

77-72	Pompey fought Sertorius in Spain.
73-71	Spartacus' slave revolt.
70	Pompey and Crassus joint consuls; tribunes restored.
67	End of war against Mithridates; pirates controlled by Pompey.
63	Cicero suppressed Catiline's conspiracy.
60	First Triumvirate (Caesar, Pompey, Crassus) was formed.
58-51	Caesar conquered Gaul.
53	Battle of Carrhae; Rome defeated by Parthians; Crassus killed.
49	Caesar crossed Rubicon; civil war with Pompey began.
48	Pompey defeated by Caesar at Pharsalus; Caesar became dictator.
44	Caesar assassinated; Antony sought revenge against conspirators.
43	Second Triumvirate (Antony, Octavian, Lepidus).
42	Battle of Philippi; Triumvirate defeated Brutus and Cassius.
41-40	Antony and Octavian divided territory.
33-32	Rupture between Antony and Octavian.
31	Battle of Actium; Octavian defeated Antony and Cleopatra at sea.
27	Octavian returned powers to Senate; received name Augustus.
18	Julian laws promoted morality, condemned adultery, regulated divorce.
12	Augustus became Pontifex Maximus, head of state religion.
2	Augustus became 'pater patriae', father of his country; apex of his power.

A.D.

4	Tiberius adopted as Augustus' heir.
6	Annexation of Judaea.
9	Varus' three legions destroyed in Germany.
14	Death of Augustus.
14-37	Tiberius emperor; efficient administrator but unpopular.
14-16	Germanicus' successful campaign in Germany.
19	Germanicus died mysteriously; funeral at Antioch.
21-22	Sejanus organized Praetorian Guard.
26-31	Sejanus powerful in Rome; executed in 31.
37-41	Caligula emperor; cruel and tyrannical, was murdered by a tribune.
41-54	Claudius emperor; conquered Britain; showed political judgement.
57-68	Nero emperor; great fire (64); Christians persecuted.
68-69	Year of four emperors - Galba, Otho, Vitellius, Vespasian.
69-79	Vespasian began Flavian dynasty. Colosseum built.
70	Titus, Vespasian's son, captured Jerusalem, destroyed the Temple.
79-81	Titus emperor. Vesuvius erupted (79), Pompeii destroyed.
81-96	Domitian emperor. Border built in Germany; period ended in terror.
96-98	Nerva emperor after Domitian's assassination.
98-117	Trajan emperor - conqueror of Dacia and Parthian empire.
117-138	Hadrian, cultured traveller, soldier and administrator of empire.
122	Hadrian's Wall built between Solway and Tyne.
138-161	Antoninus Pius emperor; orderly, peaceful rule.
141-143	Antonine's Wall built between Forth and Clyde.
161-180	Marcus Aurelius emperor; Commodus, his son, shared power (177-180).

162	War with Parthia.
175-180	War against Germans on the Danube.
180-192	Commodus emperor.
193-211	Septimius Severus became emperor after crisis; died in Britain.
	Authorized special benefits for army.
211-217	Deterioration under criminal rule of Caracalla.
212	All free men of the empire became citizens.
284-305	Diocletian and Maximian co-emperors, empire divided into 12 dioceses.
	Prices imposed throughout empire.
303	Christians persecuted by Diocletian.
312	Constantine's victory at Milvian Bridge gave him Rome.
313	Edict of Milan ended persecution of Christians.
324	Constantine became sole emperor.
325	Council of Nicaea made Christianity religion of the empire.
330	Constantine made Byzantium seat of government; renamed it Constantinople.
337	Constantine died a Christian, trying to reorganize the empire.
379-395	Emperor Theodosius kept empire formally intact.
410	Alaric and Goths captured and destroyed Rome.

GOVERNMENT AND ADMINISTRATION

Republic

There was no written constitution. The Republic evolved from the struggle between the Senate and the People - Senatus Populusque Romanus - SPQR.

The Senate (Senatus)

This was the governing body, largely in the hands of the nobles (nobiles) or patricians (patricii).

- it prepared proposals to bring before the people
- it passed decrees (senatus consulta)
- it dealt with emergencies
- it controlled finances and building contracts
- it appointed magistrates to provinces
- it directed foreign relations
- it supervised state religion

The People (Populus)

The resolutions of the people, plebiscita, could have the force of law, but the Senate was allowed greater control. There were four assemblies:

- comitia curiata   formal duties
- comitia centuriata   elected magistrates
- comitia tributa   elected lesser magistrates
- comitia plebis   passed plebiscita

The Knights (Equites)

A third element, or class, emerged (originally from Rome's cavalry) to engage in trade and finance. These businessmen acquired more political influence and became wealthy. By the time of Cicero, they could enter the Senate. Cicero tried to reconcile the three classes, **senatores**, **equites** and **plebs** by his **concordia ordinum** (harmony of the classes).

Magistrates (Magistratus)

A magistrate was an official elected annually by the people. Offices were held in a strict order - cursus honorum. After ten years' military service, a young man could begin on the lowest rung of the ladder as follows:

Age	Office	Number	Duties
28	**Quaestor**	(8)	• administered finance maintained public records
30	**Aedile**	(4)	• maintained roads, water supply organized games and festivals
33(39)	**Praetor**	(6)	• civil judge could introduce laws
39(43)	**Consul**	(2)	• commanded army conducted elections presided over Senate carried out its decrees

Other magistrates:

Tribune (10) (tribunus plebis)	•	defended plebs' rights had right of veto
Censor (2)	•	conducted census (every 5 years) conducted purification revised roll of senators
Dictator (1)	•	ruled in crisis (maximum of 6 months) conducted military and domestic matters

Imperium (supreme power) was held by consuls and praetors and dictators.

Potestas (power to enforce laws) was held by all magistrates.

Lictores (lictors *or* officials) carried **fasces** (bundles of rods) in front of consuls, praetors and dictators as a sign of their authority.

ORGANIZATION OF THE ARMY

Empire

At the time of Augustus there were 28 **legions** (later 25), each legion consisting of approximately 5000 infantrymen, trained for close combat. It was organized as follows:

Legio	Legion	5000 men
10 Cohortes	Cohorts	500 men
6 Centuriae	Centuries	80/100 men

Officers		
Legatus	legionary commander	
6 **Tribuni Militum**	tribunes	
60 **Centuriones**	centurions (from ranks), in charge of centuries	

Recruitment	Citizens
Length of service	20/25 years
Duties	Offensive in important battles, repelling invasion *etc*
Pay	250/300 denarii per day
On retirement	Land or cash bounty

Additional **auxiliary forces** were recruited to help the legions. Particularly necessary were cavalry, drawn from all parts of the Empire, slingers, bowmen, etc. Infantrymen were often recruited locally and formed cohorts of about 500 men.

Auxilia	Auxiliaries	
Ala	Cavalry unit	500 men approx.
16 Turmae	turmae	32 men
Cohors	Infantry unit	500 men

Officers	
Decurio	Decurion (cavalry officer)
Recruitment	Non-citizens
Length of service	25 years
Duties	Frontier skirmishes, occupation, assisting legions
Pay	100 denarii per day
On retirement	Citizenship for self/family

The **Praetorian Guard** was the Emperor's special bodyguard. Three cohorts were based in Rome, six more in nearby towns.

Praetorium	Praetorian Guard	4500 men
9 Cohortes	cohorts	500 men

Officers	
2 Praefecti Praetorio	praetorian prefects
Recruitment	Citizens (Italy)
Length of service	16 years
Duties	Preserving emperor's power and safety
Pay	1000 denarii per day
On retirement	5000 denarii

FAMILY TREE

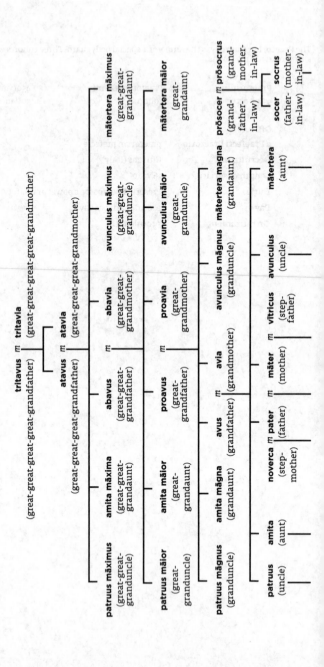

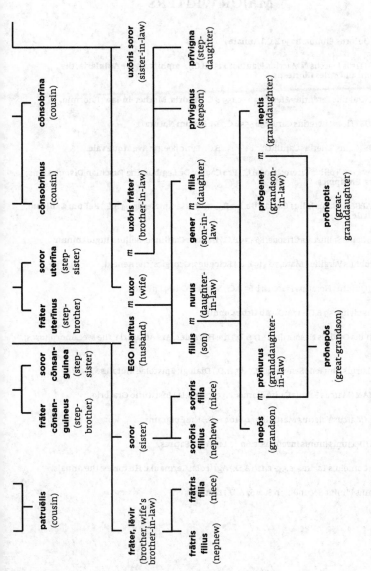

patruēlis (cousin)

cōnsobrīnus (cousin) **cōnsobrīna** (cousin)

uxōris soror (sister-in-law)

frāter cōnsanguineus (step-brother) **soror cōnsanguinea** (step-sister)

frāter uterīnus (step-brother) **soror uterīna** (step-sister)

uxōris frāter (brother-in-law)

prīvignus (stepson) **prīvigna** (step-daughter)

frāter, lēvir (brother, wife's brother-in-law)

EGO marītus (husband) m *uxor* (wife)

soror (sister)

frātris fīlius (nephew) **frātris fīlia** (niece)

sorōris fīlius (nephew) **sorōris fīlia** (niece)

fīlius (son) m **nurus** (daughter-in-law)

gener (son-in-law) m **fīlia** (daughter)

prīvignus (stepson)

nepōs (grandson) **prōnurus** (granddaughter-in-law) m

prōnepōs (great-grandson)

prōgener (grandson-in-law) m **neptis** (granddaughter)

prōneptis (great-granddaughter)

Note: This is the Family Tree of the man designated EGO in the fourth generation from the end.

9

MAJOR WRITERS

ENNIUS (Quintus Ennius: b 239 B.C.) **Annales**.

PLAUTUS (Titus Maccus *or* Maccius Plautus: b 254 B.C.) **Amphitruo**; the **Aulularia**; the **Menaechmi** and **Miles Gloriosus**.

TERENCE (Publius Terentius Afer: c.190 - c.159 B.C.) **Andria; Mother-in-law; Phormio**.

LUCRETIUS (Titus Lucretius Carus: 94 - 55B.C.) **De Rerum Natura**.

CATULLUS (Gaius Valerius Catullus: c.84 - c.54 B.C.) Lyric poetry; **Ave atque vale**.

CICERO (Marcus Tullius Cicero: b 106 B.C.) **Pro Caelio; De Legibus**; the **Tusculan Disputations; De Officiis; Philippics**.

JULIUS CAESAR (Gaius Julius Caesar: b c.102 B.C. and assassinated in 44 B.C.) **Bellum Gallicum; Bellum Civile**.

SALLUST (Gaius Sallustius Crispus: 86 - 35 B.C.) **Bellum Catilinae; Bellum Iugurthinum**.

VIRGIL (Publius Vergilius Maro: 70 - 19 B.C.) **Eclogues; Georgics**; the **Aeneid**.

HORACE (Quintus Horatius Flaccus: b 65 B.C.) **Satires; Odes; Epistles**.

LIVY (Titus Livius: 59 B.C. - 17A.D.) **Ab Urbe Condita**.

OVID (Publius Ovidius Naso: 43B.C. - 17 A.D.) the **Heroides, Ars Amatoria**; the **Metamorphoses; Tristia**.

SENECA (Lucius Annaeus Seneca: 4 B.C. - 65 A.D.) **Dialogi; Epistolae Morales**.

QUINTILIAN (Marcus Fabius Quintilianus: c.35 - c.95 A.D.) **Institutio Oratorio**.

MARTIAL (Marcus Valerius Martialis: 40 - 104 A.D.) the **Epigrams**.

JUVENAL (Decimus Iunius Iuvenalis: c.60 - c.140 A.D.) **Satires**.

TACITUS (Cornelius Tacitus: c.55 - c.120 A.D.) **Agricola; Germania; Histories**; the **Annals**.

PLINY (Gaius Plinius Secundus: b 61 *or* 62 A.D.) **Letters**.

GEOGRAPHICAL NAMES

The following list of geographical names and their adjectives includes both ancient and medieval Latin forms. The former are printed in Roman type, the latter in Italics. Medieval place names tend to have a variety of Latin forms, but only one has been selected in each case; occasionally both the ancient and the medieval forms have been given. Modern names which have a ready made Latin form (e.g. America) have been omitted, and many names not included in this selection can be easily Latinized on the analogy of those which do appear.

Aachen	Aquīsgrānum nt	adj Aquīsgrānēnsis
Aberdeen	Aberdōnia f	adj Aberdōnēnsis
Abergavenny	Gobannium nt	
Aberystwith	Aberistyvium nt	
Adige, River	Athesis m	
Adriatic	Mare superum nt	adj Hadriāticus
Aegean	Mare Aegaeum nt	adj Aegaeus
Afghanistan	Ariāna f	adj Ariānus
Africa	Libya f,	adj Libycus,
	Africa f	Africānus
Agrigento	Agrigentum nt	adj Agrigentīnus
Aisne, River	Axona m	
Aix-en-Provence	Aquae Sextiae fpl	adj Aquēnsis
Aix-la-Chapelle	Aquīsgrānum nt	adj Aquisgrānēnsis
Aix-les-Bains	Aquae Grātiānae fpl	
Ajaccio	Adiacium nt	adj Adiacēnsis
Aldborough	Isurium (nt)	
	Brigantum	
Alexandria	Alexandrēa,	adj Alexandrīnus
	Alexandrīa f	
Algiers	Algerium nt	adj Algerīnus
Alps	Alpēs fpl	adj Alpīnus
Alsace	Alsatia f	
Amalfi	Amalphis f	adj Amalphītānus
Ambleside	Galava f	
Amiens	Ambiānum nt	adj Ambiānēnsis
Amsterdam	Amstelodamum nt	adj Amstelodamēnsis
Ancaster	Causennae fpl	
Angers	Andegāvum nt	adj Andegāvēnsis
Anglesey	Mona f	
Aniene, River	Aniō m	adj Aniēnus
Anjou	Andegāvēnsis ager m	
Ankara	Ancyra f	adj Ancyrānus
Antibes	Antipolis f	adj Antipolītānus
Antioch	Antiochīa f	adj Antiochēnus
Antwerp	Antwerpium nt	adj Antwerpiēnsis
Anzio	Antium nt	adj Antīas, Antiānus
Aosta	Augusta Praetōria f	
Apennines	Mōns Apennīnus m	

Aragon	*Aragōnia f*	
Archangel	*Archangelopolis f*	
Ardennes	*Arduenna f*	
Arezzo	*Ārētium nt*	*adj* Ārētinus
Argenteuil	*Argentōlium nt*	
Argyll	*Argadia f*	
Aries	Arelās *f*	*adj* Arelātēnsis
Armagh	Armācha *f*	*adj* Armāchānus
Arno, *River*	Arnus *m*	*adj* Arniēnsis
Arras	Atrebatēs *mpl*	*adj* Atrebatēnsis
Artois	Atrebatēs *mpl*	
Assisi	Assīsium *nt*	*adj* Assīsiēnsis
Athens	Athēnae *fpl*	*adj* Athēniēnsis
Atlantic	Mare Atlanticum *nt*	
Augsburg	Augusta (*f*) Vindelicōrum	*adj* Augustānus
Autun	Augustodūnum *nt*	*adj* Augustodūnēnsis
Auvergne	Arvernī *mpl*	*adj* Arvernus
Aventine	Aventīnus *m*	
Avignon	Aveniō *f*	*adj* Aveniōnēnsis
Avon, *River*	Auvona *m*	
Babylon	Babylōn *f*	*adj* Babylōnius
Baden-Baden	Aquae Aurēliae *fpl*	
Balearic Islands	Baliārēs Insulae *fpl*	*adj* Baliāricus
Balkh	Bactra *ntpl*	*adj* Bactriānus
Baltic	*Balticum Mare nt*	
Bangor	*Bangertium nt*	*adj* Bangertiēnsis
Barcelona	Barcinō *f*	*adj* Barcinōnēnsis
Bari	Bārium *nt*	*adj* Bārēnsis
Basle	Basilēa *f*	*adj* Basilēēnsis
Basques	Vasconēs *mpl*	*adj* Vasconicus
Bath	Aquae (*fpl*) Sulis	
Bayeux	*Augustodūrum nt*	
Bayreuth	*Barūthum nt*	
Beauvais	Bellovacī *mpl*	*adj* Bellovacēnsis
Beirut	Bērȳtus *f*	*adj* Bērȳtius
Belgium	Belgae *mpl*	*adj* Belgicus
Bergen	Bergae *fpl*	
Berlin	*Berolīnum nt*	*adj* Berolīnēnsis
Berne	Vērona *f*	
Berwick	*Barvīcum nt*	
Besancon	Vesontiō *m*	*adj* Bisuntīnus
Black Sea	Pontus (Euxīnus) *m*	*adj* Ponticus
Bobbio	*Bobbium nt*	*adj* Bobbiēnsis
Bohemia	Boiohaemī *mpl*	
Bologna	Bonōnia *f*	*adj* Bonōniēnsis
Bonn	Bonna *f*	
Bordeaux	Burdigala *f*	*adj* Burdigalēnsis
Boulogne	Bonōnia *f*	*adj* Bononiēnsis
Bourges	Avāricum *nt*	*adj* Avāricensis

Brabant	*Brabantia f*	
Braganza	Brigantia *f*	*adj* Brigantiēnsis
Brancaster	Branodūnum *nt*	
Brandenburg	*Brandenburgia f*	*adj* Brandenburgēnsis
Bremen	*Brēma f*	*adj* Brēmēnsis
Breslau	*Bratislavia f*	*adj* Bratislaviēnsis
Brindisi	*Brundisium nt*	*adj* Brundisīnus
Bristol	*Bristolium nt*	*adj* Bristoliēnsis
Britain	Britannia *f*	*adj* Britannicus
Brittany	Armoricae *fpl*	
Bruges	*Brugae fpl*	*adj* Brugēnsis
Brunswick	*Brunsvīcum nt*	*adj* Brunsvīcēnsis
Brussels	*Bruxellae fpl*	*adj* Bruxellēnsis
Bucharest	*Bucarestum nt*	*adj* Bucarestiēnsis
Burgos	*Burgī mpl*	*adj* Burgitānus
Burgundy	Burgundiōnēs *mpl*	
Cadiz	Gādēs *fpl*	*adj* Gāditānus
Caen	*Cadomum nt*	*adj* Cadomēnsis
Caerleon	Isca *f*	
Caermarthen	Maridūnum *nt*	
Caernarvon	Segontium *nt*	
Caerwent	Venta (*f*) Silurum	
Cagliari	Caralis *f*	*adj* Caralītānus
Cairo	Cairus *f*	
Calais	*Calētum nt*	*adj* Calētanus
Cambrai	*Camerācum nt*	*adj* Camerācēnsis
Cambridge	*Cantabrigia f*	*adj* Cantabrigiēnsis
Campagna	Campānia *f*	*adj* Campānus
Cannes	*Canoē f*	
Canterbury	Durovernum *nt*,	*adj* Cantuāriēnsis
	Cantuāria *f*	
Capri	Capreae *fpl*	*adj* Capreēnsis
Cardigan	Ceretica *f*	
Carlisle	Luguvallium *nt*	
Cartagena	Carthāgō Nova *f*	
Carthage	Carthāgō *f*	*adj* Carthāginiēnsis
Caspian Sea	Mare Caspium *nt*	
Cevennes	Gebenna *f*	*adj* Gebennicus
Ceylon	Tāprobanē *f*	
Champagne	*Campānia f*	*adj* Campānicus
Chartres	Carnūtēs *mpl*	*adj* Carnōtēnus
Chelmsford	Caesaromagus *m*	
Cherbourg	Caesaris burgus *m*	
Chester	Deva *f*	
Chichester	Rēgnum *nt*	
China	Sēres *mpl*	
Cirencester	Corinium (*nt*)	*adj* Sēricus
	Dobunōrum	
Clairvaux	*Clāra Vallis f*	*adj* Clāravallēnsis
Clermont	Nemossus *f*	

Cluny	*Clīniacum nt*	*adj Clīniacēnsis*
Clyde, *River*	Clōta *f*	
Colchester	Camulodūnum *nt*	
Cologne	Colōnia Agrippīna *f*	*adj Colōniēnsis*
Como, *Lake*	Lārius *m*	*adj Lārius*
Constance, *Lake*	Lacus Brigantīnus *m*	
Copenhagen	*Hafnia f*	
Corbridge	Corstopitum *nt*	
Cordoba	Corduba *f*	*adj Cordubēnsis*
Corfu	Corcȳra *f*	*adj Corcȳraeus*
Corinth	Corinthus *f*	*adj Corinthius*
Cork	Corcagia *f*	*adj Corcagiēnsis*
Cornwall	Cornubia *f*	
Cracow	Cracovia *f*	*adj Cracoviēnsis*
Crete	Crēta *f*	*adj Crētēnsis, Crēticus*
Cumberland	*Cumbria f*	
Cyprus	Cyprus *f*	*adj Cyprius*
Cyrene	Cȳrēnae *fpl*	*adj Cȳrēnaicus*
Damascus	Damascus *f*	*adj Damascēnus*
Danube, *River*	(*lower*) Ister *m*, (*upper*) Dānuvius *m*	
Dardanelles	Hellēspontus *m*	*adj Hellespontius*
Dee, *River*	Deva *f*	
Denmark	Dānia *f*	*adj Dānicus*
Derby	*Derventiō m*	
Devon	*Devōnia f*	
Dijon	Diviō *f*	*adj Diviōnēnsis*
Dneiper, *River*	Borysthenēs *m*	
Dneister, *River*	Danaster *m*	
Don, *River* (Russian)	Tanais *m*	
Doncaster	Dānum *nt*	
Dorchester	Durnovāria *f*	
Douro, *River*	Durius *m*	
Dover	Dubrī *mpl*	
Dover, *Straits of*	Fretum Gallicum *nt*	
Dresden	Dresda *f*	*adj Dresdēnsis*
Dublin	Dublīnum *nt*	*adj Dublīnēnsis*
Dumbarton	Britannodūnum *nt*	
Dundee	Taodūnum *nt*	
Dunstable	Durocobrīvae *fpl*	
Durham	Dunelmum *nt*	*adj Dunelmēnsis*
Ebro, *River*	Hibērus *m*	
Eden, *River*	Itūna *f*	
Edinburgh	Edinburgum *nt*	*adj Edinburgēnsis*
Egypt	Aegyptus *f*	*adj Aegyptius*
Elba	Ilva *f*	
Elbe, *River*	Albis *m*	
England	Anglia *f*	*adj Anglicus*
Etna	Aetna *f*	*adj Aetnaeus*
Europe	Eurōpa	*adj Eurōpaeus*

Exeter	Isca (f) Dumnoniōrum	
Fiesole	Faesulae *fpl*	*adj* Faesulānus
Flanders	Menapiī *mpl*	
Florence	Flōrentia *f*	*adj* Flōrentīnus
Fontainebleau	Bellofontānum *nt*	
Forth, *River*	Bodotria *f*	
France	Gallia *f*	*adj* Gallicus
Frankfurt	Francofurtum *nt*	
Frejus	Forum (*nt*) Iūliī	*adj* Foroiūliēnsis
Friesland	Frīsiī *mpl*	*adj* Frīsius
Gallipoli	Callipolis *f*	*adj* Callipolitānus
Galloway	Gallovidia *f*	
Ganges	Gangēs *m*	*adj* Gangēticus
Garda, *Lake*	Bēnācus *m*	
Garonne, *River*	Carumna *f*	
Gaul	Gallia *f*	*adj* Gallicus
Gdansk	Gedānum *m*	
Geneva	Genāva *f*	*adj* Genāvēnsis
Geneva, *Lake*	Lemannus lacus *m*	
Genoa	Genua *f*	*adj* Genuēnsis
Germany	Germānia *f*	*adj* Germānicus
Ghent	Gandavum *nt*	*adj* Gandavēnsis
Gibraltar	Calpē *f*	*adj* Calpētānus
Gibraltar, *Straits of*	Fretum Gāditānum *nt*	
Glasgow	Glasgua *f*	*adj* Glasguēnsis
Gloucester	Glēvum *nt*	
Gothenburg	Gothoburgum *nt*	
Graz	Graecium *nt*	
Greece	Graecia *f*	*adj* Graecus
Greenwich	Grenovicum *nt*	
Grenoble	Grātiānopolis *f*	
Groningen	Groninga *f*	
Guadalquivir, *River*	Baetis *m*	
Guadiana, *River*	Anas *m*	
Guernsey	Sarnia *f*	
Hague, *The*	Haga (f) Comitis	
Halle	Halla *f*	*adj* Hallēnsis
Hamadān	Ecbatana *ntpl*	
Hamburg	Hamburgum *nt*	*adj* Hamburgēnsis
Hanover	Hannovera *f*	
Harwich	Harvīcum *nt*	
Havre	Grātiae Portus *m*	
Hebrides	Ebūdae Insulae *fpl*	
Hexham	Axelodūnum *nt*	
Holland	Batāvī *mpl*	*adj* Batāvus
Ibiza	Ebusus *f*	*adj* Ebusitānus
Ilkley	Olicāna *f*	
Inn, *River*	Aenus *m*	
Ipswich	Gippevīcum *nt*	
Ireland	Hibernia *f*	*adj* Hibernicus

Isar, *River*	Isara *f*	
Istanbul	Bȳzantium *nt*	*adj* Bȳzantīnus
Italy	Italia *f*	*adj* Italicus
Jersey	Caesarea *f*	
Jerusalem	Hierosolyma *ntpl*	*adj* Hierosolymītānus
Jutland	Chersonnēsus Cimbrica *f*	
Karlsbad	*Aquae Carolīnae fpl*	
Kent	Cantium *nt*	
Kiel	*Chilonium nt*	
Koblenz	Cōnfluentēs *mpl*	
Lancaster	*Lancastria f*	
Lanchester	Longovicium *nt*	
Land's End	Bolerium Prōmunturium *nt*	
Lausanne	Lausonium *nt*	*adj* Lausoniēnsis
Lebanon	Libanus *m*	
Leeds	*Ledesia f*	
Leicester	Ratae (*fpl*) Coritānōrum	
Leiden	Lugdūnum (*nt*) Batāvōrum	
Leipsig	Lipsia *f*	*adj* Lipsiēnsis
Lérida	Ilerda *f*	*adj* Ilerdēnsis
Lichfield	Etocētum *nt*	
Limoges	Augustorītum *nt*	
Lincoln	Lindum *nt*	
Lisbon	Olisīpō *m*	*adj* Olisīpōnēnsis
Lizard Point	Damnonium Prōmunturium *nt*	
Loire, *River*	Liger *m*	*adj* Ligericus
Lombardy	*Langobardia f*	
London	Londinium *nt*	*adj* Londiniēnsis
Lorraine	*Lōthāringia f*	
Lucerne	*Lūceria f*	*adj* Lūcernēnsis
Lund	Londinium (*nt*) Gothōrum	
Lyons	Lugdūnum *nt*	*adj* Lugdūnēnsis
Madrid	*Matrītum nt*	*adj* Matrītēnsis
Maggiore, *Lake*	Verbannus *m*	
Main, *River*	Moenus *m*	
Mainz	Mogontiacum *nt*	
Majorca	Baliāris Māior *f*	
Malta	Melita *f*	
Man, *Isle of*	Monapi *f*	
Manchester	Mancunium *nt*	
Marmara, *Sea of*	Propontis *f*	
Marne, *River*	*Māterna f*	
Marseilles	Massilia *f*	*adj* Massiliēnsis
Matapan	Taenarum *nt*	*adj* Taenarius

Mediterranean	Mare internum *nt*	
Melun	Melodūnum *nt*	
Mérida	Ēmerita *f*	*adj* Ēmeritēnsis
Messina	Messāna *f*	*adj* Messānius
Metz	Dīvodūrum *nt*	
Meuse, *River*	Mosa *f*	
Milan	Mediōlānum *nt*	*adj* Mediōlānēnsis
Minorca	Baliāris Minor *f*	
Modena	Mutina *f*	*adj* Mutinensis
Mons	Montēs *mpl*	
Monte Cassino	Casīnum *nt*	*adj* Casīnās
Moray	Moravia *f*	
Morocco	Maurētānia *f*	*adj* Maurus
Moscow	Moscovia *f*	
Moselle, *River*	Mosella *f*	
Munich	Monacum *nt*	*adj* Monacēnsis
Nantes	Namnētēs *mpl*	
Naples	Neāpolis *f*	*adj* Neāpolītānus
Neckar, *River*	Nīcer *m*	
Newcastle	Pōns (*m*) Aeliī,	*adj* Novocastrēnsis
	Novum Castrum *nt*	
Nice	Nīcaea *f*	*adj* Nicaeēnsis
Nile, *River*	Nīlus *m*	*adj* Nīlōticus
Nîmes	Nemausus *f*	*adj* Nemausēnsis
Norway	Norvēgia *f*	*adj* Norvēgiānus
Norwich	Nordovīcum *nt*	
Oder, *River*	Viadrus *m*	
Oporto	Portus Calēnsis *m*	
Orange	Arausiō *f*	
Orkneys	Orcades *fpl*	
Orléans	Aurēliānum *nt*	*adj* Aurēliānēnsis
Oudenarde	Aldenarda *f*	
Oxford	Oxonia *f*	*adj* Oxoniēnsis
Padua	Patavium *nt*	*adj* Patavīnus
Palermo	Panormus *m*	*adj* Panormitānus
Paris	Lutetia *f*, Parīsiī *mpl*	*adj* Parīsiēnsis
Patras	Patrae *fpl*	*adj* Patrēnsis
Persian Gulf	Mare Rubrum *nt*	
Piacenza	Placentia *f*	*adj* Placentīnus
Po, *River*	Padus *m*	*adj* Padānus
Poitiers	Limōnum *nt*	
Poland	Polōnia *f*	
Portsmouth	Māgnus Portus *m*	
Portugal	Lūsitānia *f*	
Pozzuoli	Puteolī *mpl*	*adj* Puteolānus
Prague	Prāga *f*	*adj* Prāgēnsis
Provence	Prōvincia *f*	
Pyrenees	Pȳrēnaeī montēs *mpl*	

17

Red Sea	Sinus Arābicus *m*	
Rheims	Dūrocortorum *nt*	
Rhine, *River*	Rhēnus *m*	*adj* Rhēnānus
Rhodes	Rhodos *f*	*adj* Rhodius
Rhône, *River*	Rhodanus *m*	
Richborough	Rutupiae *fpl*	*adj* Rutupīnus
Rimini	Arīminum	*adj* Arīminēnsis
Rochester	Dūrobrīvae *fpl*	
Rome	Rōma *f*	*adj* Rōmānus
Rotterdam	Roterodamum *nt*	*adj* Roterodamēnsis
Rouen	Rothomagus *f*	*adj* Rothomagēnsis
Saar, *River*	Sangona *f*	
Salisbury	Sarisberia *f*	
Salzburg	Iuvāvum *nt*	*adj* Salisburgēnsis
Saône, *River*	Arar *m*	
Savoy	Sabaudia *f*	
Scheidt, *River*	Scaldis *m*	
Schleswig	Slesvīcum *nt*	
Scilly Isles	Cassiterides *fpl*	
Scotland	Calēdonia *f*	*adj* Calēdonius
Seine, *River*	Sēquana *f*	
Severn, *River*	Sabrīna *f*	
Seville	Hīspalis *f*	*adj* Hispalēnsis
Shrewsbury	Salōpia *f*	
Sicily	Sicilia *f*	*adj* Siculus
Sidra, *Gulf of*	Syrtis (māior) *f*	
Silchester	Callēva (*f*) Atrebatum	
Soissons	Augusta (*f*) Suessiōnum	
Solway Firth	Itūna (*f*) aestuarium	
Somme, *River*	Samara *f*	
Spain	Hispānia *f*	*adj* Hispānus
St.Albans	Verulamium *nt*	
St.Andrews	Andreopolis *f*	
St. Bernard	(*Great*) Mōns Pennīnus *m*, (*Little*) Alpis Grāia *f*	
St. Gallen	Sangallanēse coenobium *nt*	*adj* Sangallēnsis
St. Gotthard	Alpēs summae *fpl*	
St.Moritz	Agaunum *nt*	*adj* Agaunēnsis
Strasbourg	Argentorātus *f*	*adj* Argentorātēnsis
Swabia	Suēvia *f*	*adj* Suēvicus
Sweden	Suēcia *f*	*adj* Suēcicus
Switzerland	Helvētia *f*	*adj* Helvēticus
Syracuse	Syrācūsae *fpl*	*adj* Syrācūsānus
Tangier	Tingī *f*	*adj* Tingitānus
Taranto	Tarentum *nt*	*adj* Tarentīnus
Tarragona	Tarracō *f*	*adj* Tarracōnēnsis
Tay, *River*	Taus *m*	
Thames, *River*	Tamesis *m*	

Thebes	Thēbae *fpl*	*adj* Thēbānus
Tiber, *River*	Tiberis *m*	*adj* Tiberīnus
Tivoli	Tībur *nt*	*adj* Tīburtīnus
Toledo	Tolētum *nt*	*adj* Tolētanus
Toulon	Tolōna *f*	*adj* Tolōnēnsis
Toulouse	Tolōsa *f*	*adj* Tolōsānus
Tours	Caesarodūnum *nt*	
Trèves, Trier	Augusta (*f*) Treverōrum	
Trieste	Tergeste *nt*	*adj* Tergestīnus
Tripoli	Tripolis *f*	*adj* Tripolitānus
Tunis	Tūnēs *f*	*adj* Tūnētānus
Turin	Augusta (*f*) Taurīnōrum	*adj* Taurīnus
Tuscany	Etrūria *f*	*adj* Etrūscus
Tyrrhenian Sea	Mare īnferum *nt*	
Utrecht	*Ultrāiectum nt*	*adj* Ultrāiēctensis
Vardar, *River*	Axius *m*	
Venice	Venetī *mpl*, *Venetiae fpl*	*adj* Venetus
Verdun	*Virodūnum nt*	*adj* Virodūnēnsis
Versailles	*Versāliae fpl*	*adj* Versāliēnsis
Vichy	Aquae (*fpl*) Sōlis	
Vienna	*Vindobona f*	*adj* Vindobonēnsis
Vosges	Vosegus *m*	
Wales	*Cambria f*	
Wallsend	Segedūnum *nt*	
Warsaw	*Varsavia f*	*adj* Varsaviēnsis
Wash, *The*	Metaris (*m*) aestuārium	
Wear, *River*	Vedra *f*	
Weser, *River*	Visurgis *m*	
Westminster	*Westmonastērium nt*	*adj* Westmonastēriēnsis
Wiesbaden	Mattiacum *nt*	*adj* Mattiacus
Wight, *Isle of*	Vectis *f*	
Winchester	Venta (*f*) Belgārum	
Worcester	Vigornia *f*	
Worms	*Vormatia f*	
Wroxeter	Viroconium *nt*	
York	Eborācum *nt*	*adj* Eborācēnsis
Zuider Zee	Flēvō *m*	
Zurich	*Turicum nt*	*adj* Tigurīnus

NUMERALS

	Cardinal		Ordinal	
1	ūnus	I	prīmus	1st
2	duo	II	secundus, alter	2nd
3	trēs	III	tertius	3rd
4	quattuor	IV	quārtus	4th
5	quīque	V	quīntus	5th
6	sex	VI	sextus	6th
7	septem	VII	septimus	7th
8	octō	VIII	octāvus	8th
9	novem	IX	nōnus	9th
10	decem	X	decimus	10th
11	undecim	XI	undecimus	11th
12	duodecim	XII	duodecimus	12th
13	tredecim	XIII	tertius decimus	13th
14	quattuordecim	XIV	quārtus decimus	14th
15	quīndecim	XV	quīntus decimus	15th
16	sēdecim	XVI	sextus decimus	16th
17	septendecim	XVII	septimus decimus	17th
18	duodēvīgintī	XVIII	duodēvīcēsimus	18th
19	ūndēvīgintī	XIX	ūndēvīcēsimus	19th
20	vīgintī	XX	vīcēsimus	20th
21	vīgintī ūnus	XXI	vīcēsimus prīmus	21st
28	duodētrīgintā	XXVIII	duodētrīcēsimus	28th
29	ūndētrīgintā	XXIX	ūndētrīcēsimus	29th
30	trīgintā	XXX	trīcēsimus	30th
40	quadrāgintā	XL	quadrāgēsimus	40th
50	quīnquāgintā	L	quīnquāgēsimus	50th
60	sexāgintā	LX	sexāgēsimus	60th
70	septuāgintā	LXX	septuāgēsimus	70th
80	octōgintā	LXXX	octōgēsimus	80th
90	nōnāgintā	XC	nōnāgēsimus	90th
100	centum	C	centēsimus	100th
101	centum et ūnus	CI	centēsimus prīmus	101st
122	centum vīgintī duo	CXXII	centēsimus vīcēsimus alter	122nd
200	ducentī	CC	ducentēsimus	200th
300	trecentī	CCC	trecentēsimus	300th
400	quadringentī	CCCC	quadringentēsimus	400th
500	quīngentī	D	quīngentēsimus	500th
600	sēscentī	DC	sēscentēsimus	600th
700	septingentī	DCC	septingentēsimus	700th
800	octingentī	DCCC	octingentēsimus	800th
900	nōngentī	DCCCC	nōngentēsimus	900th
1000	mīlle	M	mīllēsimus	1000th
1001	mīlle et ūnus	MI	mīllēsimus prīmus	1001st
1102	mīlle centum duo	MCII	mīllēsimus centēsimus alter	1102nd
3000	tria mīlia	MMM	ter mīllēsimus	3000th
5000	quīnque mīlia	IↃↃ	quīnquiēs mīllēsimus	5000th
10,000	decem mīlia	CCIↃↃ	deciēs mīllēsimus	10,000th
100,000	centum mīlia	CCCIↃↃↃ	centiēs mīllēsimus	100,000th
1,000,000	deciēs centēna mīlia	CCCCIↃↃↃↃ	deciēs centiēs mīllēsimus	1,000,000th

NUMERALS

	Distributive		Adverb	
1	singulī	I	semel	1st
2	bīnī	II	bis	2nd
3	ternī (trīnī)	III	ter	3rd
4	quaternī	IV	quater	4th
5	quīnī	V	quīnquiēs	5th
6	sēnī	VI	sexiēs	6th
7	septēnī	VII	septiēs	7th
8	octōnī	VIII	octiēs	8th
9	novēnī	IX	noviēs	9th
10	dēnī	X	deciēs	10th
11	undēnī	XI	undeciēs	11th
12	duodēnī	XII	duodeciēs	12th
13	ternī dēnī	XIII	ter deciēs	13th
14	quaternī dēnī	XIV	quattuordeciēs	14th
15	quīnī dēnī	XV	quīndeciēs	15th
16	sēnī dēnī	XVI	sēdeciēs	16th
17	septēni dēnī	XVII	septiēs deciēs	17th
18	duodēvīcēnī	XVIII	duodēviciēs	18th
19	undēvīcēnī	XIX	ūndēvīciēs	19th
20	vīcēnī	XX	vīciēs	20th
21	vīcēnī singulī	XXI	semel et vīciēs	21st
28	duodētrīcēnī	XXVIII	duodētrīciēs	28th
29	ūndētrīcēnī	XXIX	ūndētrīciēs	29th
30	trīcēnī	XXX	trīciēs	30th
40	quadrāgēnī	XL	quadrāgiēs	40th
50	quīnquāgēnī	L	quīnquāgiēs	50th
60	sexāgēnī	LX	sexāgiēs	60th
70	septuāgēnī	LXX	septuāgiēs	70th
80	octōgēnī	LXXX	octōgiēs	80th
90	nōnagēnī	XC	nōnāgiēs	90th
100	centēnī	C	centiēs	100th
101	centēnī singulī	CI	semel et centiēs	101st
122	centēnī vīcēnī bīnī	CXXII	centiēs vīciēs bis	122nd
200	ducēnī	CC	ducentiēs	200th
300	trecēnī	CCC	trecentiēs	300th
400	quadringēnī	CCCC	quadringentiēs	400th
500	quīngēnī	D	quīngentiēs	500th
600	sexcēnī	DC	sexcentiēs	600th
700	septingēnī	DCC	septingentiēs	700th
800	octingēnī	DCCC	octingentiēs	800th
900	nōngēnī	DCCCC	nōngentiēs	900th
1000	singula mīlia	M	mīlliēs	1000th
1001	singula mīlia singulī	MI	semel et mīlliēs	1001st
1102	singula mīlia centēnī bīnī	MCII	mīlliēs centiēs bis	1102nd
3000	trīna mīlia	MMM	ter mīlliēs	3000th
5000	quīna mīlia	IↃↃ	quīnquiēs mīlliēs	5000th
10,000	dēna mīlia	CCIↃↃ	deciēs mīlliēs	10,000th
100,000	centēna mīlia	CCCIↃↃↃ	centiēs mīlliēs	100,000th
1,000,000	deciēs centēna mīlia	CCCCIↃↃↃↃ	mīlliēs mīlliēs	1,000,000th

DATES

MONTHS

Three days of the month have special names:

Kalendae the 1st.

Nōnae the 5th of most months, but the 7th of March, May, July and October.

> "In March, July, October, May,
> The Nones are on the 7th day."

Idūs the 13thof most months, but the 15th of March, May, July and October.

If the date is one of these three days, it is expressed in the ablative, with the adjective of the month in agreement, *e.g.*

1stJanuary, **Kalendīs Iānuāriīs**, usually abbreviated **Kal. Ian.**

The day immediately before any of these three is expressed by **prīdiē** with the accusative, *e.g.*

4th February, **prīdiē Nōnās Februāriās**, usually abbreviated **prid. Non. Feb.**

All other dates are expressed as so many days before the next named day, and in reckoning the interval both the date and the named day are counted, *e.g.* the 11th is the 5th day before the 15th.

The formula is all in the accusative, beginning with the words **ante diem**, *e.g.* 11th March, **ante diem quintum Idūs Martiās**, usually abbreviated **a.d. V Id. Mar.**

The following selection of dates for April and May should be a sufficient guide to the dates of any month in the year:-

APRIL		MAY
Kal. Apr.	1	Kal. Mai.
a.d. IV Non. Apr.	2	a.d. VI Non. Mai.
a.d. III Non. Apr.	3	a.d. V Non. Mai.
prid. Non. Apr.	4	a.d. IV Non. Mai.
Non. Apr.	5	a.d. III Non. Mai.
a.d. VIII Id. Apr.	6	prid. Non. Mai.
a.d. VII ld. Apr.	7	Non. Mai.
a.d. VI Id. Apr.	8	a.d. VIII Id. Mai.
a.d. V ld. Apr.	9	a.d. VII Id. Mai.
a.d. IV Id. Apr.	10	a.d. VI ld. Mai.
a.d. III Id. Apr.	11	a.d. V Id. Mai.
prid. Id. Apr.	12	a.d. IV Id. Mai.
ld. Apr.	13	a.d. III Id. Mai.
a.d. XVIII Kal. Mai.	14	prid. Id. Mai.
a.d. XVII Kal. Mai.	15	Id. Mai.
a.d. XVI Kal. Mai.	16	a.d. XVII Kal. Iun.

a.d. XV Kal. Mai.	**17**	a.d. XVI Kal. Iun.
a.d. XII Kal. Mai.	**20**	a.d. XIII Kal. Iun.
a.d. VII Kal. Mai.	**25**	a.d. VIII Kal. Iun.
prid. Kal. Mai.	**30**	a.d. III Kal. Iun.
-	**31**	prid. Kal. Iun.

YEARS

A year is denoted either by giving the names of the consuls or by reckoning the number of years from the traditional date of the foundation of Rome, 753 B.C. (A date B.C. should be subtracted from 754, a date A.D. should be added to 753.)

E.g. "In the year 218 B.C.," *either* P. Cornelio Scipione Ti. Sempronio Longo coss. *or* a. u. c. DXXXVI.

MEASURES

Length

12 ūnciae	=	1 pēs
5 pedēs	=	1 passus
125 passūs	=	1 stadium
8 stadia	=	mīlle passūs

The Roman mile was about 1.48km.

Area

100 pedēs quadrātī	=	1 scrīpulum
144 scrīpula	=	1 āctus quadrātus
2 āctūs quadrātī	=	1 iugerum
2 iugera	=	1 hērēdium
100 hērēdia	=	1 centuria

The **iugerum** was about 2529.28 square metres.

Capacity

	4 cochleāria	=	1 cyathus
	12 cyathī	=	1 sextārius
(liquid)	6 sextāriī	=	1 congius
	8 congiī	=	1 amphora
	20 amphorae	=	1 culleus
(dry)	8 sextāriī	=	1 sēmodius
	2 sēmodiī	=	1 modius

The **sextārius** was about half a litre, the **modius** about 9 litres.

Weight

4 scrīpula	=	1 sextula
6 sextulae	=	1 ūncia
12 ūnciae	=	1 lībra

The Roman lb. was about 326 g, and the **ūncia** was therefore about 27 g. The twelfths of the **lībra** have the following names, which are also used to denote fractions generally, *e.g.* **hērēs ex triente**, heir to a third of an estate.

$\frac{1}{12}$ ūncia	$\frac{5}{12}$ quīncūnx	$\frac{3}{4}$ dōdrāns
$\frac{1}{6}$ sextāns	$\frac{1}{2}$ sēmis	$\frac{5}{6}$ dextāns
$\frac{1}{4}$ quadrāns	$\frac{7}{12}$ septūnx	$\frac{11}{12}$ deūnx
$\frac{1}{3}$ triēns	$\frac{2}{3}$ bēs	

MONEY

Roman

2½ assēs	=	1 sēstertius (or nummus)
4 sēstertii	=	1 dēnārius
25 dēnārii	=	1 aureus

The sesterce is represented by a symbol for $2\frac{1}{2}$, properly **II S(ēmis)**, usually standardized in the form HS. The *ntpl* **sēstertia** with the distributive numeral denotes thousands of sesterces, and the numeral adverb with the *gen pl* **sēstertium** (understanding **centena milia**) means hundred thousands, *e.g.*

10,000 sesterces	=	dēna sēstertia	=	HS $\bar{\mathrm{X}}$
1,000,000 sesterces	=	deciēs sēstertium	=	HS I$\bar{\mathrm{X}}$I

Greek

100 drachumae	=	1 mina
60 minae	=	1 talentum

LATIN VERSE

QUANTITY

Both vowels and syllables in Latin may be described as long or short. A long vowel or syllable is one on which the voice dwells for a longer time than on a short one, in much the same way as a minim is long compared with a crotchet in musical notation.

A syllable is long if the vowel in it is either long in itself or followed by two or more consonants. The letter **x** counts as a double consonant, the letter **h** not at all, and the following pairs of consonants occurring in the same word after a short vowel do not necessarily make the syllable long:

br, cr, dr, fr, gr, pr, tr; fl, gl, pl.

A syllable is short if its vowel is a short one and not followed by two or more consonants (except for the groups noted in the preceding paragraph).

Examples: In **dūcō** both the vowels are long ("by nature") and therefore the two syllables are long.

In **deus** both the vowels are short, neither is followed by more than one consonant, and therefore the two syllables are short; but if a word beginning with a consonant follows, then the syllable **-us** will become long.

In **adsunt** both the vowels are short, but they are both followed by two consonants, and the two syllables are therefore "long by position".

This long or short characteristic of Latin vowels and syllables is called "quantity." To determine the quantities of vowels no general rules can be given, and some of them are now not known for certain. The vowel quantities of words will have to be learned when the words are learned, or else looked up when the need arises. In final syllables, however, there is a certain regularity to be found, and the following table shows the commonest of these:

ENDING

	Long	Short
-a	1st decl abl sing	1st decl nom and voc sing
	1st conj impv sing	all nom and acc ntpl
	numerals and most adverbs	**ita, quia**
-e	5th decl abl sing	all other noun and verb endings
	2nd conj impv sing	
	most adverbs	**bene, male**
	Greek nouns	enclitics

-i	all endings, except	**quasi, nisi**: and sometimes **mihi, tibi, sibi, ibi, ubi**
-o	all endings, except	sometimes iambic words, esp **cito, duo, ego, homo, modo, puto, rogo, scio**
-u	all endings	
-as	all endings, except	Greek nouns
-es	all endings, except	3rd decl/ nom sing with short **-e-** in stem **es** (be) and compounds **penes**
-is	1st and 2nd decl dat and abl pl 3rd decl acc pl 4th conj 2nd pers sing **vīs, sīs, velīs**	all others
-os	all endings, except	2nd decl/ nom sing **os** (bone) **compos, impos**
-us	3rd decl/ nom sing with long **-u-** in stem 4th decl/ gen sing and nom and acc pl	all others

METRES

Latin Verse is a pattern of long and short syllables, grouped together in "feet" or in lyric lines.

FEET

The commonest Feet employed in Latin metres are:

Anapaest	(short-short-long)	˘˘—
Dactyl	(long-short-short)	—˘˘
Iambus	(short-long)	˘—
Proceleusmatic	(short-short-short-short)	˘˘˘˘
Spondee	(long-long)	——
Tribrach	(short-short-short)	˘˘˘
Trochee	(long-short)	—˘

CAESURA AND DIAERESIS

The longer lines usually have a regular break near the middle, occurring either in the middle of a foot (**Caesura**) or at the end of a foot (**Diaeresis**). This break need not imply a pause in the sense of the words, but merely the end of a word, provided that it does not go too closely with the word following, as in the case of a preposition before a noun. See examples on pages 30-35 where the caesura is marked †, and the diaeresis //.

ELISION

A vowel or a vowel followed by **m** at the end of a word ("open vowel") is regularly elided before a vowel at the beginning of the next word in the same line. In reciting, the elided syllable should not be dropped entirely, but slurred into the following vowel. An open vowel at the end of a line does not elide before a vowel at the beginning of the next line.

FINAL SYLLABLES

Where the metre requires the final syllable in a line to be long, this syllable may in fact be a short one. This position in the line is commonly called a **syllaba anceps**,and marked down as being either long or short. It is perhaps better to regard this syllable, when the vowel is short, as long by position, since metrical length is a matter of duration, and the end of a line calls naturally for a slight pause in reading, even if the sense runs on to the next line. In the metrical schemes which follow, a long final syllable should be understood in this sense: it may in itself be a short one.

Latin metres fall into three fairly distinct categories, associated with three different genres of verse:

1. *Dactylic*
2. *Iambic and Trochaic*
3. *Lyric*

DACTYLIC VERSE

The Dactylic metres are the **Hexameter** and the **Pentameter**. The Hexameter is the medium of epic, didactic and pastoral poetry, of satires and epistles, and other examples of occasional verse. In conjunction with the Pentameter it forms the **Elegiac Couplet**, the metre most commonly used for love poetry, occasional pieces, and the epigram.

Dactylic Hexameter

The first four feet may be either **dactyls** or **spondees**, the 5th is regularly a dactyl, the 6th always a spondee. In Virgil and later poets the last word is either disyllabic or trisyllabic. A **Caesura** normally occurs in either the 3rd or the 4th foot, and pastoral poetry often has the "**Bucolic Diaeresis**" at the end of the 4th foot. In Virgilian and later usage there is a tendency for words and feet to overlap in the first four feet and to coincide in the last two. Similarly in the first part of the line the metrical ictus and the normal accent of the spoken word tend to fall on different syllables, whereas they regularly coincide in the last two feet.

Example:

> Clāss(em) āp|tēnt tăcĭ|tī ꞌ sŏcĭ|ōsqu(e) ād |lītŏră| tōrquēnt
>
> (*Virgil, Aen.* 4, 289)

Occasional lines will be found in the poets, which deliberately violate the above rules for the sake of obtaining some special effect,

> pēr cō|nūbĭă| nōstrā,ꞌ pěr| īncēp|tōs hўmě|nāeōs
>
> (*Aen.* 4, 316)

The above echoes Greek hexameter, where the final word is Greek and has four syllables, and the caesura comes between the two short syllables of the dactyl in the 3rd foot:

> cūm sŏcĭ|īs nā|tōqŭe ꞌ pě|nātĭ bŭs| ēt māg|nīs dīs
>
> (*Aen.* 3, 12)

Note the solemn, archaic touch, suggesting a line of Ennius, where the 5th foot is a spondee, and the last word is monosyllabic.

pārtŭrĭ|ēnt mōn|tēs, ⁺nā| sēctūr| rīdĭcŭ|lŭs mūs

(Hor, A. P. 139)

The monosyllabic ending, above, creates a comic effect.

Dactylic Pentameter

This line has two equal parts of 2½ feet each. The two feet in the first part may be either **dactyls** or **spondees**, those in the second part are always dactylic. The two half-feet are long (though the final syllable may be a short one), and there is always a diaeresis between the two parts of the line. In Ovid and later poets the last word in the line is regularly disyllabic.

Example:

Aēnē|ān ănĭ|mō // nōxquĕ dĭ|ēsquĕ rĕ|fērt

(Ovid, Her. 7, 26)

SCANSION

The following procedure may assist beginners to scan a normal hexameter or pentameter correctly :-

> 1. Mark off elisions.
> 2. Mark the first syllable long, and (Hexameter) the last five dactyl and spondee, or (Pentameter) the last seven syllables, two dactyls and a long syllable.
> 3. Mark all diphthongs long.
> 4. Mark all syllables that are long by position, omitting any doubtful cases.
> 5. Mark any other syllables known to be long.
> 6. Mark any syllables known to be short.
> 7. Fill in the few (if any) remaining syllables, and identify the principal caesura.
> 8. Read the line aloud.

IAMBIC AND TROCHAIC VERSE

The Iambic and Trochaic metres occur mainly in dramatic verse, but some are found elsewhere, as in the lyrics of Catullus and Horace. The principal Iambic metres are the **Senarius**, the **Septenarius**, and the **Octonarius**; the principal Trochaic metres are the Septenarius and Octonarius.

Iambic Senarius

Basically this line consists of six iambic feet, but in practice such a line is very rare.
Example:

Phăsēl|lŭs īl|lĕ quēm| vĭdē|tĭs, hōs|pĭtēs

(Cat. 4,1)

In drama the last foot is always iambic, and the 5th regularly a spondee. The **spondee** is also very common in the first four feet, the **dactyl** and the **tribrach** are frequent, occasionally the **anapaest** is found, and, more rarely, the **proceleusmatic**. There is usually a **caesura** in either the third or the fourth foot.

Example:

Ĭn hāc| hăbĭtās|sĕ plătĕ|ā dīc|tūmst Chrŷ|sĭdēm

(Ter, And. 796)

Iambic Septenarius

This line consists of seven and a half feet, basically iambic, but allowing the same variations as in the Senarius. The 4th foot is regularly an Iambus, and is usually followed by a diaeresis: this is an aid to identifying the line.

Example:

N(am) īdcīr|c(o) āccēr|sōr nūp|tĭās| quōd m(i) ād|părā|rī sēn|sīt

(Ter, And.690)

Iambic Octonarius

This line has eight iambic feet, with the same variations as in the other iambic lines. The 4th and 8th feet are regularly iambic, and a diaeresis follows the 4th foot.

Example:

Cūrā|bĭtūr.| sēd pătĕr| ădēst.| căvĕt(e) ēs|sĕ trīs|tēm sēn|tĭăt

(Ter, And.403)

Trochaic Septenarius

Apart from drama, this line is common in popular verses, and comes into its own in later Latin poetry. It consists of seven and a half **trochees**, but in practice only the seventh foot is regularly trochaic, while the others may be **spondee**, **dactyl**, **tribrach**, or (more rarely) **anapaest**. There is usually a diaeresis after the 4th foot.

Example:

Crās ă|mēt qūī| nūnqu(am) ă|māvīt,| quīqu(e) ă|māvīt| crās ă|mēt

(Pervigilium Veneris)

Trochaic Octonarius

This is a line of eight trochees, allowing the same variations as above. There is a diaeresis after the 4th foot.

Example:

Prōin tū| sōllĭcĭ|tūdĭn|(em) īstām| fālsām| quāe t(e) ēx|crŭcĭăt| mīttās

(Ter, Heaut. 177)

LYRIC VERSE

In most lyric metres the line is not to be subdivided into feet, but is itself the unit of scansion, and has a fixed number of syllables. The commonest, which are those used by Catullus and Horace, are the **Hendecasyllabic**, the **Asclepiads**, the **Glyconic** and the **Pherecratic**, which occur either singly or in combinations to form either couplets or stanzas of four lines. Beside these groupings there are the **Alcaic** and **Sapphic** stanzas. Elisions occur much more rarely than in the other metres.

Hendecasyllabic

This is Catullus's favourite line. It consists of eleven syllables in the following pattern:

_ _ _ ˘ ˘ _ ˘ _ ˘ _ _

Either the first or the second syllable may occasionally be short, and there is usually a caesura after the 5th syllable.

Example:

Vīvāmūs, mĕă Lēsbĭ(a), ātqu(e) ămēmūs

(Cat. 5, 1)

Asclepiads

There are two Asclepiad lines, of which the **Lesser** is by far the commoner. It has twelve syllables, in the following pattern with a caesura after the 6th syllable:

$$- - - \;\, \breve{} \breve{} - | - \breve{} \breve{} - \breve{} -$$

Māecēnās, ătăvīs⁺ ēdĭtĕ rēgĭbūs

(*Hor, Od.* I, 1, 1)

The **Greater Asclepiad** is formed by adding a **choriambus** $- \breve{} \breve{} -$ after the 6th syllable with a **diaeresis** both before and after it.

Example:

Nūllām, Vārĕ, săcrā vītĕ prĭŭs sēvĕrĭs ārbŏrēm

(*Hor, Od.* I, 18, 1)

Glyconic

The **Glyconic** occurs by itself in Catullus, but more usually it is found in combination with the **Lesser Asclepiad** or the **Pherecratic**. It consists of eight syllables ($- - - \breve{} \breve{} - \breve{} -$), so that it is like a Lesser Asclepiad minus the choriambus. It has no regular caesura.

Example:

Dōnēc grātŭs ĕrām tĭbī

(*Hor, Od.* III, 9, 1)

Pherecratic

The **Pherecratic** is a Glyconic minus the second last (short) syllable. It is found only in combination with other lines.

Example:

Sūspēndīssĕ pŏtēntī

(*Hor, Od.* I, 5, 11)

Alcaic Stanza

The **Alcaic stanza** has four lines, of which the first two have the same pattern $--\breve{}---\breve{}-\breve{}-$. In these there is a regular caesura after the 5th syllable. The third line is $--\breve{}---\breve{}--$ and the 4th $-\breve{}-\breve{}-\breve{}-\breve{}--$. Neither of the last two lines has a regular break in it.

Example:

Nūnc ēst bĭbēndūm,† nūnc pĕdĕ lībĕrō
pūlsāndă tēllūs, † nūnc Sălĭārĭbūs
ōrnārĕ pūlvīnār dĕōrūm
tēmpŭs ĕrāt dăpĭbūs, sŏdālēs.

(*Hor, Od.* I.37, 1-4)

Sapphic Stanza

The **Sapphic stanza** also has four lines, of which the first three are the same: $-\breve{}---\breve{}\ \breve{}-\breve{}-\ -$. As in the Alcaic there is a **caesura** after the 5th syllable. The last line is a short **Adonic** $-\breve{}\ \breve{}--$

Example:

Īntĕgēr vītāe † scĕlĕrīsquĕ pūrūs
nōn ĕgēt Maurīs † iăcūlīs nĕqu(e) ārcū
nēc vĕnēnātīs † grăvĭdā săgīttīs,
Fūscĕ, phărētrā.

(*Hor, Od.* I. 22, 1-4)

LATIN PHRASES USED IN ENGLISH

What follows is a list of some of the Latin phrases used in English today.

ab initio	from the beginning.
ab ovo	(lit: from the egg) from the beginning.
absit omen	(lit: may the (evil) omen be absent) may the presentiment not become real or take place.
ab urbe condita	(used in dates) from the foundation of the city (*i.e. from the foundation of Rome in 753 B.C.*).
A.D.	abbr for **anno Domini**.
ad hoc	(lit: for this) for a particular purpose only: **an ad hoc committee; an ad hoc decision**.
ad hominem	(lit: according to the person) **1** directed against a person rather than against his or her arguments. **2** based on or appealing to emotion rather than reason.
ad infinitum	without end; endlessly; to infinity.
ad interim	for the meantime; for the present: **ad interim measures**.
ad-lib	(abbr for **ad libitum**) • *adj* improvised; impromptu • *adv* without restraint; freely; as one pleases • *vb* to improvise and deliver without preparation.
ad libitum	(lit: according to pleasure) as one pleases.
ad majorem Dei gloriam	for the greater glory of God (*the Jesuit motto*).
ad nauseam	(lit: to (the point of) nausea) to a disgusting extent.
ad rem	(lit: to the matter) to the point; without digression: **to reply ad rem; an ad rem discussion**.
advocatus diaboli	devil's advocate.
ad valorem	(lit: according to value) in proportion to the estimated value of the goods taxed.
aet.	(abbr for **aetatis**) at the age of.
Agnus Dei	Lamb of God.
alma mater	(lit: nurturing mother) one's former university, college or school.
alter ego	(lit: other self) **1** a second self. **2** a very close and intimate friend.
a.m.	abbr for **ante meridiem**.
AMDG	abbr for **ad majorem Dei gloriam**.
amor patriae	love of one's country; patriotism.
an.	(abbr for **anno**) in the year.
anno Domini	in the year of our Lord.
anno urbis conditae	in the year of the foundation of the city (*i.e. of Rome in 753 B.C., used in dates*)
anno regni	in the year of the reign (of).

annus mirabilis	(lit: wonderful year) a year of wonders.
antebellum	(lit: before the war) of or during the period before a war, especially the American Civil War.
ante meridiem	before noon.
ante-mortem	before death (*esp in legal or medical contexts*).
a.p.	(abbr for **ante prandium**) before a meal (*in prescriptions*).
apparatus criticus	(lit: critical apparatus) textual notes (*list of variant readings, etc., relating to a document, especially in a scholarly edition of a text*).
aq.	abbr for **aqua**.
aqua vitae	(lit: water of life) brandy.
a.r.	abbr for **anno regni**.
arbiter elegantiae *or* elegantiarum	judge in a matter of taste.
arcus senilis	(lit: senile bow) opaque circle around the cornea of the eye (*often seen in elderly people*).
argumentum ad hominem	(lit:argument according to the person: *Logic*) **1** fallacious argument that attacks not an opponent's beliefs but his motives or character. **2** argument that shows an opponent's statement to be inconsistent with his other beliefs.
ars longa vita brevis	art is long, life is short.
AUC	abbr for: **1 ab urbe condita. 2 anno urbis conditae.**
aut vincere aut mori	death or victory.
aurora australis	the southern lights.
aurora borealis	the northern lights.
ave	**1** hail! **2** farewell!
ave atque vale	hail and farewell!
Ave Maria	Hail Mary.
beatae memoriae	of blessed memory.
Beata Virgo	the Blessed Virgin.
Beata Virgo Maria	the Blessed Virgin Mary.
b.i.d	(abbr for **bis in die**) twice a day (*in prescriptions*).
bis dat, qui cito dat	the person who gives promptly gives twice.
BV	abbr for **Beata Virgo**.
c,ca	abbr for **circa**.
camera obscura	(lit: dark chamber) camera obscura.
carpe diem	(lit: seize the day) enjoy the pleasures of the moment, without concern for the future.
casus belli	(lit: occasion of war) **1** an event or act used to justify a war. **2** the immediate cause of a quarrel.
caveat emptor	let the buyer beware.
cetera desunt	the rest is missing.

ceteris paribus	other things being equal.
circa	around.
Codex Juris Canonici	(lit: book of canon law) the official code of canon law (*in the Roman Catholic Church*).
cogito, ergo sum	I think, therefore I am (*the basis of Descartes' philosophy*).
compos mentis	of sound mind; sane.
coram populo	in the presence of the people; openly.
corpus delicti	(lit: the body of the crime: LAW) the body of facts that constitute an offence.
Corpus Juris Canonici	(lit: body of canon law) the official compilation of canon law (*in the Roman Catholic Church*).
Corpus Juris Civilis	(lit: body of civil law) the body of Roman or civil law.
corrigenda	things to be corrected.
corpus vile	(lit: worthless body) person or thing fit only to be the object of an experiment.
culpa	1 (*LAW*) an act of neglect. 2 (*gen*) a fault; sin; guilt.
cum grano salis	with a grain of salt; not too literally.
cum laude	(*chiefly US*) with praise (*the lowest of three designations for above-average achievement in examinations*).
curriculum vitae	(lit: the course of one's life) curriculum vitae.
de facto	*adv* in fact • *adj* existing in fact.
de gustibus non est disputandum there is no arguing about tastes.	
de jure	according to law; by right; legally.
de mortuis nil nisi bonum	say nothing but good of the dead.
de novo	anew.
Deo gratias	thanks be to God.
Deo Optimo Maximo	to God, the best, the Greatest.
Deo volente	God willing.
de profundis	out of the depths of misery or dejection.
deus ex machina	(lit: the god from the machine) 1(in ancient Greek and Roman drama) a god introduced into a play to resolve the plot. 2 any unlikely or artificial device serving this purpose.
Dies Irae	(lit: the day of wrath) 1 a famous Latin hymn of the 13th century, describing the Last Judgment. It is used in the Mass for the dead. 2 a musical setting of this hymn, usually part of a setting of the Requiem.
disjecta membra	the scattered remains.
DOM	abbr for **Deo Optimo Maximo**.
dramatis personae	(lit: the persons of the drama) the list of characters in a drama.

Ecce Homo	behold the man (*the words of Pontius Pilate to Christ's accusers [John 19:5]*).
editio princeps	(lit: the first edition) the first printed edition of a work.
e.g., eg	abbr for **exempli gratia**.
emeritus	retired from office.
e pluribus unum	one out of many (*motto of USA*).
ER	**1** (abbr for **Elizabeth Regina**) Queen Elizabeth; **2** (abbr for **Eduardus Rex**) King Edward.
errare est humanum	to err is human.
erratum (*pl* **errata**)	error.
et seq.	(abbr for **et sequens**) and the following.
et seqq.	(abbr for **et sequentia**) and those that follow.
ex	(lit: out of, from) **1** (FINANCE) not participating in; excluding; without: **ex bonus; ex dividend; ex rights. 2** (COMMERCE) without charge to the buyer until removed from: **ex quay; ex ship; ex works**.
ex cathedra	(lit: from the chair) **1** with authority. **2** defined by the pope as infallibly true, to be accepted by all Roman Catholics.
exeat	(lit: let him or her go out) formal leave of absence.
exempli gratia	for example.
exeunt	they go out (*used as a stage direction*).
exeunt omnes	they all go out (*used as a stage direction*).
exit	he or she goes out (*used as a stage direction*).
ex libris	(lit: from the books (of)) from the collection or library of.
ex officio	by right of position or office.
ex parte	(LAW) on behalf of one side or party only (*of an application in a judicial proceeding*): **an ex parte injunction**.
ex post facto	having retrospective effect: **an ex post facto law**.
ex silentio	(lit: from silence) based on a lack of evidence to the contrary (*of a theory, assumption etc*).
extempore	(lit: instantaneously) without planning or preparation; impromptu.
ex voto	*adv, adj* in accordance with a vow • *n* offering made in fulfilment of a vow.
facile princeps	(lit: easily first) an obvious leader.
fecit (*abbr* **fec**)	(he or she) made it (*used formerly on works of art next to the artist's name*).
felo de se	suicide.
festina lente	more haste, less speed.
fiat lux	let there be light.
Fidei Defensor	defender of the faith.

fidus Achates	(lit: faithful Achates) faithful friend or companion (*the name of the faithful companion of Aeneas in Virgil's Aeneid*).
floruit	(he or she) flourished (*used to indicate the period when a historical figure, whose birth and death dates are unknown, was most active*).
fons et origo	the source and origin.
genius loci	(lit: genius of the place) **1** the guardian spirit of a place. **2** the special atmosphere of a particular place.
Gloria in Excelsis Deo	(lit: glory to God in the highest) **1** the Greater Doxology, beginning in Latin with these words. **2** a musical setting of this.
Gloria Patri	(lit: glory to the father) **1** the Lesser Doxology, beginning in Latin with these words. **2** a musical setting of this.
hinc illae lacrimae	hence those tears.
HJ	(abbr for **hic jacet**) here lies (*on gravestones*).
HJS	(abbr for **hic jacet sepultus**) here lies buried (*on gravestones*).
horrible dictu	horrible to relate.
ibid.	abbr for **ibidem**.
ibidem	in the same place (*in annotations, bibliographies, etc., when referring to a book, article, chapter, or page previously cited*).
id est	that is (to say); in other words.
idem	the same (*used to refer to an article, chapter, etc., previously cited*).
i.e.	abbr for **id est**.
ign.	abbr for **ignotus**.
ignoratio elenchi	(lit: an ignorance of proof: *Logic*) **1** a purported refutation of a proposition that does not in fact prove it false but merely establishes a related but strictly irrelevant proposition. **2** the fallacy of arguing in this way.
ignotum per ignotius	(lit: the unknown by means of the more unknown) an explanation that is obscurer than the thing to be explained.
ignotus	unknown.
ignis fatuus	will o' the wisp.
Imp.	**1** (abbr for **Imperator**) Emperor; **2** (abbr for **Imperatrix**) Empress.
in absentia	in one's absence; in the absence of: **he was condemned in absentia**.
in aeternum	forever; eternally.
in articulo mortis	at the point of death.

in camera	(lit: in the chamber) in private.
in extenso	at full length.
in extremis	(lit: in the furthest reaches) **1** in extremity; in dire straits. **2** at the point of death.
infra	below.
infra dig	(abbr for **infra dignitatem**) beneath one's dignity.
in loco parentis	in place of a parent (*said of a person acting in a parental capacity*).
in medias res	(lit: into the midst of things) in or into the middle of events or a narrative.
in memoriam	in memory of; as a memorial to (*used in obituaries, epitaphs etc*).
in perpetuum	forever
in personam	(lit: against the person) directed against a specific person or persons (*LAW: of a judicial act*).
in propria persona	in person; personally.
in rem	(lit: against the matter) directed against property rather than against a specific person (*LAW: of a judicial act*).
in rerum natura	in the nature of things.
INRI	(lit: Jesus of Nazareth, King of the Jews) abbr for **Iesus Nazarenus Rex Iudaeorum** (*the inscription placed over Christ's head during the Crucifixion*).
in situ	(lit: in position) in the natural, original, or appropriate position.
inter alia	among other things.
inter alios	among other people.
inter vivos	(*LAW*) between living people: **an inter vivos gift**.
in toto	totally; entirely; completely.
in utero	within the womb.
in vacuo	in a vacuum.
in vino veritas	in wine there is truth.
in vitro	(lit: in glass) made to occur outside the body of the organism in an artificial environment (*of biological processes or reactions*): **in vitro fertilization**.
in vivo	(lit: in a living (thing)) occurring or carried out in the living organism (*of biological processes or experiments*).
ipse dixit	(lit: he himself said it) an arbitrary and unsupported assertion.
ipsissima verba	the very words.
ipso facto	by the fact itself.
i.q.	(lit: the same as) abbr for **idem quod**.
lapsus linguae	a slip of the tongue
lc	(abbr for (**in**) **loco citato**) in the place cited.

lex loci	the law of the place.
lex non scripta	the unwritten law; common law.
lex scripta	the written law; statute law.
lex talionis	the law of revenge or retaliation.
loc. cit.	(abbr for (**in**) **loco citato**) in the place cited (*in textual annotation*).
magna cum laude	(chiefly *u.s.*) with great praise (*the second of three designations for above-average achievement in examinations*).
magnum opus	a great work of art or literature (*especially the greatest single work of an artist*).
mala fide	undertaken in bad faith.
mare clausum	(lit: closed sea: LAW) a sea coming under the jurisdiction of one nation and closed to all others.
mare liberum	(lit: free sea: LAW) a sea open to navigation by shipping of all nations.
mare nostrum	(lit: our sea) the Mediterranean.
mater	mother (*often used facetiously*).
mater dolorosa	(lit: sorrowful mother) the Virgin Mary sorrowing for the dead Christ (*especially as depicted in art*).
materfamilias	(lit:mother of family) the mother of a family or the female head of a family.
materia medica	(lit: medical matter) **1** the branch of medical science concerned with the study of drugs used in the treatment of disease. **2** the drugs used in the treatment of disease.
mea culpa	(lit: my fault) an acknowledgement of guilt.
memento mori	(lit: remember you must die) an object, such as a skull, intended to remind people of the inevitability of death.
mens sana in corpore sano	a healthy mind in a healthy body.
mens rea	(lit: guilty mind: LAW) a criminal intention or knowledge that an act is wrong.
miles gloriosus	a braggart soldier (*especially as a stock figure in comedy*).
mirabile dictu	wonderful to relate.
mittimus	(lit: we send) a warrant of commitment to prison or a command to a jailer directing him to hold someone in prison.
modus operandi	procedure; method of operating; manner of working.
modus ponens	(lit: mood that affirms) the principle that whenever a conditional statement and its antecedent are given to be true its consequent may be validly inferred.

modus tollens	(lit: mood that denies) the principle that whenever a conditional statement and the negation of its consequent are given to be true, the negation of its antecedent may be validly inferred.
modus vivendi	(lit: way of living) a working arrangement between conflicting interests; practical compromise.
motu proprio	(lit: of his own accord) an administrative papal bull.
multum in parvo	much in a small space.
mutatis mutandis	with the necessary changes.
NB, N.B., nb, n.b.	(abbr for **nota bene**) note well.
nem. con.	(abbr for **nemine contradicente**) no-one contradicting; unanimously.
nemo me impune lacessit	no-one provokes me with impunity.
ne plus ultra	(lit: not more beyond) the extreme or perfect point or state.
nihil	nil; nothing.
nihil obstat	there is no obstacle.
nil desperandum	(lit: nothing to be despaired of) never despair.
nisi prius	(lit: unless previously) **1** *in England* (a) a direction that a case be brought up to Westminster for trial before a single judge and jury. (b) the writ giving this direction. **2** *in the US* a court where civil actions are tried by a single judge sitting with a jury as distinguished from an appellate court.
nolens volens	whether willing or unwilling.
noli me tangere	(lit: do not touch me) a warning against interfering with or against touching a person or thing.
nolle prosequi	(lit: do not pursue) an entry made on the court record when the plaintiff in a civil suit or prosecutor in a criminal prosecution undertakes not to continue the action or prosecution.
nolo contendere	(lit: I do not wish to contend) a plea made by a defendant to a criminal charge having the same effect in those proceedings as a plea of guilty but not precluding him from denying the charge in a subsequent action.
non compos mentis	(lit: not in control of one's mind) mentally incapable of managing one's own affairs; of unsound mind; insane.
non prosequitur	(lit: he does not proceed) a judgment in favour of a defendant when the plaintiff failed to take the necessary steps in an action within the time allowed.
non sequitur	(lit: it does not follow) **1** (*gen*) a statement having little or no relevance to what preceded it. **2** (*Logic*) a conclusion that does not follow from the premises.
nulli secundus	second to none

numen	(lit: divine power) **1** (*especially in ancient Roman religion*) a deity or spirit presiding over a thing or place. **2** a guiding principle, force, or spirit.
Nunc Dimittis	(lit: now let depart) **1** the Canticle of Simeon (*Luke 2:29-32*). **2** a musical setting of this.
ob.	**1** abbr for **obiit**. **2** (abbr for **obiter**) incidentally; in passing.
obiit	he or she died (*on gravestones*).
obiter dictum	(lit: something said in passing) **1** (*LAW*) an observation by a judge on some point of law not directly in issue in the case before him and thus neither requiring his decision nor serving as a precedent, but nevertheless of persuasive authority. **2** any comment, remark, or observation made in passing.
obscurum per obscurius	(lit: the obscure by means of the more obscure) an explanation that is obscurer than the thing to be explained.
omnium-gatherum	(often facetious) a miscellaneous collection; assortment.
onus probandi	(*LAW*) the burden of proof.
op. cit.	(abbr of **opere citato**) in the work cited.
opus anglicanum	(lit: English work) fine embroidery (*especially of church vestments*).
ora pro nobis	pray for us.
o tempora! o mores!	oh the times! oh the customs!
p.a.	abbr of **per annum**.
pace	by leave of; with due deference to (*used to acknowledge politely someone who disagrees with the speaker or writer*).
pari passu	with equal speed or progress; equably (*often used to refer to the right of creditors to receive assets from the same source without one taking precedence*).
passim	here and there; throughout (*used to indicate that what is referred to occurs frequently in the work cited*).
paterfamilias	(lit: father of the family) **1** the male head of a household. **2** the head of a household having authority over its members.
pax vobiscum	peace be with you.
peccavi	(lit: I have sinned) a confession of guilt.
peculium	(lit: property) property that a father or master allowed his child or slave to hold as his own.
per annum	every year; year by year.
per ardua ad astra	through difficulties to the stars (*motto of the RAF*).
per capita	(lit: according to heads) of or for each person.
per contra	on the contrary

per diem	(lit: for the day) **1** every day; by the day. **2** an allowance for daily expenses, usually those incurred while working.
per mensem	every month; by the month.
per pro	(abbr for **per procurationem**) by delegation to; through the agency of (*used when signing documents on behalf of someone else*).
persona grata	an acceptable person (*especially a diplomat acceptable to the government of the country to which he is sent*).
persona non grata	unacceptable or unwelcome person.
petitio principii	(lit: an assumption at the beginning: *Logic*) a form of fallacious reasoning in which the conclusion has been assumed in the premises; begging the question.
pia mater	(lit: pious mother) the innermost of the three membranes that cover the brain and spinal cord.
pinxit	(he or she) painted this (*used formerly on works of art next to the artist's name*).
p.m., P.M., pm, PM	abbr for **1** post meridiem **2** postmortem.
post-bellum	(lit: after war) of or during the period after a war, especially the American Civil War.
post hoc	(lit: after this: *Logic*) the fallacy of assuming that temporal succession is evidence of causal relation.
post hoc, ergo propter hoc	after this, therefore because of this (*a fallacy of reasoning*).
post meridiem	afternoon.
postmortem	(lit: after death) *n* **1** dissection and examination of a dead body to determine the cause of death. **2** analysis or study of a recently completed event • *adj* occurring after death.
pp	abbr for **1** per pro. **2** post prandium after a meal (*in prescriptions*).
PPS	(lit: after postscript; abbr for **post postscriptum**) additional postscript.
pr	(abbr for: **per rectum**) through the rectum (*in prescriptions*).
prima facie	at a first view
primum mobile	(lit: first moving (thing)) prime mover.
primus inter pares	first among equals.
prn	(abbr for **pro re nata**) as the situation demands, as needed (*in prescriptions*).
pro forma	(lit: for form's sake) **1** prescribing a set form or procedure. **2** performed in a set manner.
pro patria	for one's country
pro rata	in proportion.
pro tempore	for the time being.
proxime accessit	(lit: he or she came next) the runner-up.

q.e.	(abbr for **quod est**) which is.
QED	abbr for **quod erat demonstrandum**.
QEF	abbr for **quod erat faciendum**.
quid pro quo	(lit: something for something) **1** a reciprocal exchange. **2** something given in compensation, especially an advantage or object given in exchange for another.
quis custodiet ipsos custodes?	who will guard the guards?
q.l.	(abbr for **quantum libet**) as much as you please (*in prescriptions*).
qm	(abbr for **quaque mane**) every morning (*in prescriptions*).
qn	(abbr for **quaque nocte**) every night (*in prescriptions*).
quod erat demonstrandum	which was to be proved.
quod erat faciendum	which was to be done.
quot homines, tot sententiae	there are as many opinions as there are people.
quo vadis?	whither goest thou?
qqv	abbr for **quae vide**) which (words, items etc) see (*denoting a cross reference to more than one item*).
qs	(abbr for **quantum sufficit**) as much as will suffice (*in prescriptions*).
qv	(abbr for **quod vide**) which (word, item etc) see (*denoting a cross reference*).
rara avis	(lit: rare bird) an unusual, uncommon or exceptional person or thing.
reductio ad absurdum	(lit: reduction to the absurd) **1** a method of disproving a proposition by showing that its inevitable consequences would be absurd. **2** a method of indirectly proving a proposition by assuming its negation to be true and showing that this leads to an absurdity. **3** application of a principle or a proposed principle to an instance in which it is absurd.
requiescat	(lit: may he or she rest) a prayer for the repose of the souls of the dead.
requiescat in pace	may he or she rest in peace.
res gestae	(lit: things done) **1** things done or accomplished; achievements. **2** (*LAW*) incidental facts and circumstances that are admissible in evidence because they introduce or explain the matter in issue.
res ipsa loquitur	(*LAW*) the thing or matter speaks for itself.
res judicata	(*LAW*) a matter already adjudicated upon that cannot be raised again.
res publica	(lit: the public thing) the state, republic, or commonwealth.

resurgam	I shall rise again.
RI	**1** (abbr for **Regina et Imperatrix**) Queen and Empress. **2** (abbr for **Rex et Imperator**) King and Emperor.
rigor mortis	(lit: rigidity of death) the stiffness of joints and muscular rigidity of a dead body.
RIP	abbr for **requiescat** or **requiescant in pace**.
risus sardonicus	(lit: sardonic laugh) fixed contraction of the facial muscles resulting in a peculiar distorted grin, caused especially by tetanus.
sanctum sanctorum	(lit: holy of holies) **1** (*Bible*) the holy of holies. **2** (*often facetious*) an especially private place.
sartor resartus	the tailor patched.
schola cantorum	(lit: school of singers) a choir or choir school maintained by a church.
scire facias	(lit: cause (him) to know) **1** (*LAW, rare*) a judicial writ founded upon some record, such as a judgement, letters patent, etc., requiring the person against whom it is brought to show cause why the record should not be enforced or annulled. **2** a proceeding begun by the issue of such a writ.
semper fidelis	always faithful.
semper idem	always the same.
seq.	(abbr for **sequens**) the following (one).
seqq.	(abbr for **sequentia**) the following (ones).
seriatim	in order.
sic	thus (*often used to call attention to some quoted mistake*).
sic itur ad astra	such is the way to the stars.
sic transit gloria mundi	so passes the glory of the world.
si monumentum requiris, circumspice	if you seek (his) monument, look around you (*inscription on the architect Sir Christopher Wren's tomb in St Paul's Cathedral*).
sine die	without a day.
sine prole	(*LAW*) without issue.
sine qua non	(lit: without which not) an indispensable condition or requirement.
sl	(abbr for **sine loco**) without place (*of publication*).
sp	abbr for **sine prole**.
spiritus asper	rough breathing.
spiritus lenis	smooth breathing.
SPQR	(abbr for **Senatus Populusque Romanus**) the Senate and People of Rome.
sq.	(abbr for **sequens**) the following (one).
sqq.	(abbr for **sequentia**) the following (ones).

Stabat Mater	(lit: the mother was standing) **1** a Latin hymn, probably of the 13th century, commemorating the sorrows of the Virgin Mary at the crucifixion and used in the Mass and various other services. **2** a musical setting of this hymn.
status quo	(lit: the state in which) the existing state of affairs.
stet	let it stand.
sub judice	before a court of law or a judge; under judicial consideration.
sub rosa	(lit: under the rose) secretly.
sub voce	under the word.
sui generis	(lit: of its own kind) unique.
sui juris	(lit: of one's own right) (*LAW*) of full age and not under disability; legally competent to manage one's own affairs; independent.
summa cum laude	(*chiefly U.S.*) with the utmost praise (*the highest of three designations for above-average achievement in examinations. In Britain it is sometimes used to designate a first-class honours degree*).
summum bonum	the principle of goodness in which all moral values are included or from which they are derived; highest or supreme good.
suo jure	(*chiefly LAW*) in one's own right.
suo loco	(*chiefly LAW*) in a person or thing's own or rightful place.
supra	above.
sursum corda	lift up your hearts (to God).
sv	abbr for **sub voce**.
tabula rasa	(lit: a scraped tablet) **1** the mind in its uninformed original state. **2** an opportunity for a fresh start; clean slate.
taedium vitae	(lit: weariness of life) the feeling that life is boring and dull.
Te Deum	(lit: Thee, God) **1** an ancient Latin hymn in rhythmic prose, sung or recited at matins in the Roman Catholic Church and in English translation at morning prayer in the Church of England and used by both churches as an expression of thanksgiving on special occasions. **2** a musical setting of this hymn. **3** a service of thanksgiving in which the recital of this hymn forms a central part.
te igitur	(lit: Thee, therefore: *Roman Catholic Church*) the first prayer of the canon of the Mass.
tempore	in the time of.
tempus fugit	time flies.
terminus ad quem	(lit: the end to which) the aim or terminal point.
terminus a quo	(lit: the end from which) the starting point; beginning.

terra firma	the solid earth; firm ground.
terra incognita	an unexplored or unknown land, region or area for study.
tertium quid	a third something.
t.i.d.	(abbr for **ter in die**) three times a day (*in prescriptions*).
tu quoque	you likewise (*a retort made by a person accused of a crime implying that the accuser is also guilty of the same crime*).
uberrima fides	utmost good faith.
ubique	everywhere.
ubi supra	where (mentioned or cited) above.
ultima Thule	(lit: the most distant Thule) **1** the utmost boundary or limit. **2** a remote goal or aim.
ultra vires	beyond one's powers.
una voce	with one voice.
urbi et orbi	(*Roman Catholic Church*) to the city and the world (*a phrase qualifying the solemn papal blessing*).
ut dict.	(abbr for **ut dictum**) as directed.
ut infra	as below.
ut supra	as above.
v.	abbr for **1 verso. 2 versus. 3 vide**.
vade in pace	go in peace.
vade mecum	(lit: go with me) a handbook or other aid carried on the person for immediate use when needed.
vae victis	woe to the conquered!
vale	farewell!
veni, vidi, vici	I came, I saw, I conquered.
venire facias	(lit: you must make come: *LAW*) a writ directing a sheriff to summon suitable persons to form a jury.
verbatim et litteratim	word for word and letter for letter.
verb. sap.	(abbr for **verbum sapienti sat est**) a word is enough to the wise.
verso	**1** the back of a sheet of printed paper. **2** the side of a coin opposite to the obverse; reverse.
versus	**1** against; in opposition to. **2** as opposed to; in contrast with.
via	by way of.
via media	a middle course.
vice	in the place of; instead of; as a substitute for.
vice versa	the other way round.
vide	see.
videlicet	namely; to wit.

vi et armis   (lit: by force and arms) a kind of trespass accompanied by force and violence.

VIR   (abbr for **Victoria Imperatrix Regina**) Victoria, Empress and Queen.

virginibus puerisque   for maidens and youths.

vis inertiae   the power of inertia.

viva voce   (lit: with living voice) *adv, adj* by word of mouth • *n* an oral examination.

viz.   abbr for **videlicet**.

vl   (abbr for **varia lecto**) variant reading.

volente Deo   God willing.

vox populi   the voice of the people; popular or public opinion.

vox populi, vox Dei   the voice of the people is the voice of God.

VR   (abbr for **Victoria Regina**) Queen Victoria.

VRI   (abbr for **Victoria Regina et Imperatrix**) Victoria, Queen and Empress.

ENGLISH – LATIN

Aa

a, an *art not translated; (a certain)* quīdam; **twice a day** bis in diē; **four acres a man** quaterna in singulōs iūgera

aback *adv:* **taken ~** dēprehēnsus

abaft *adv* in puppī ♦ *prep* post, pōne

abandon *vt* relinquere; *(wilfully)* dērelinquere, dēserere; *(to danger)* ōbicere; *(to pleasure)* dēdere; *(plan)* abicere; **~ hope** spem abicere

abandoned *adj* perditus

abase *vt* dēprimere; **~ oneself** sē prōsternere

abash *vt* perturbāre; rubōrem incutere *(dat)*

abate *vt* minuere, imminuere; *(a portion)* remittere ♦ *vi (fever)* dēcēdere; *(passion)* dēfervēscere; *(price)* laxāre; *(storm)* cadere

abatement *n* remissiō *f*, dēminūtiō *f*

abbess *n* abbātissa *f*

abbey *n* abbātia *f*

abbot *n* abbās *m*

abbreviate *vt* imminuere

abbreviation *n (writing)* nota *f*

abdicate *vt* sē abdicāre *(abl)*

abdication *n* abdicātiō *f*

abduct *vt* abripere

abduction *n* raptus *m*

aberration *n* error *m*

abet *vt* adiuvāre, adesse *(dat)*, favēre *(dat)*

abettor *n* adiūtor *m*, minister *m*, fautor *m*, socius *m*

abeyance *n:* **in ~** intermissus; **be in ~** iacēre

abhor *vt* ōdisse, invīsum habēre

abhorrence *n* odium *nt*

abhorrent *adj:* **~ to** aliēnus ab

abide *vi (dwell)* habitāre; *(tarry)* commorārī; *(last)* dūrāre; **~ by** *vt fus* stāre *(abl)*, perstāre in *(abl)*

abiding *adj* perpetuus, diūturnus

ability *n (to do)* facultās *f*, potestās *f*; *(physical)* vīrēs *fpl*; *(mental)* ingenium *nt*; **to the best of my ~** prō meā parte, prō virīlī parte

abject *adj* abiectus, contemptus; *(downcast)* dēmissus

abjectly *adv* humiliter, dēmissē

abjure *vt* ēiūrāre

ablative *n* ablātīvus *m*

ablaze *adj* flāgrāns, ārdēns

able *adj* perītus, doctus; **be ~** posse, valēre

able-bodied *adj* rōbustus

ablution *n* lavātiō *f*

ably *adv* perītē, doctē

abnegation *n* abstinentia *f*

abnormal *adj* inūsitātus; *(excess)* immodicus

abnormally *adv* inūsitātē, praeter mōrem

aboard *adv* in nāvī; **go ~** nāvem cōnscendere; **put ~** impōnere

abode *n* domicilium *nt*, sēdes *f*

abolish *vt* tollere, ē mediō tollere, abolēre; *(LAW)* abrogāre

abolition *n* dissolūtiō *f*; *(LAW)* abrogātiō *f*

abominable *adj* dētestābilis, nefārius

abominably *adv* nefāriē, foedē

abominate *vt* dētestārī

abomination *n* odium *nt*; *(thing)* nefas *nt*

aboriginal *adj* prīscus

aborigines *n* aborīginēs *mpl*

abortion *n* abortus *m*

abortive *adj* abortīvus; *(fig)* inritus; **be ~** ad inritum redigī

abound *vi* abundāre, superesse; **~ in** abundāre *(abl)*, adfluere *(abl)*

abounding *adj* abundāns, adfluēns; cōpiōsus ab

about *adv (place) usu expressed by compound verbs*; *(number)* circiter, ferē, fermē ♦ *prep (place)* circā, circum *(acc)*; *(number)* circā, ad *(acc)*; *(time)* sub *(acc)*; *(concerning)* dē *(abl)*; **~ to die** moritūrus; **I am ~ to go** in eō est ut eam

above *adv* suprā; **from ~** dēsuper; **over and ~** īnsuper ♦ *prep* suprā *(acc)*; *(motion)* super *(acc)*; *(rest)* super *(abl)*; **be ~** *(conduct)* indignārī

abreast *adv (ships)* aequātīs prōrīs; **walk ~ of** latus tegere *(dat)*

abridge *vt* contrahere, compendī facere

abridgement *n* epitomē *f*

abroad *adv* peregrē; *(out of doors)* forīs; **be ~** peregrīnārī; **from ~** peregrē

abrogate *vt* dissolvere; *(LAW)* abrogāre

abrupt *adj* subitus, repentīnus; *(speech)* concīsus

abscess *n* vomica *f*

abscond *vi* aufugere

absence *n* absentia *f*; **in my ~** mē absente; **leave of ~** commeātus *m*

absent *adj* absēns; **be ~** abesse; **~ oneself** *vi* deesse, nōn adesse

absent-minded *adj* immemor, parum attentus

absolute *adj* absolūtus, perfectus; *(not limited)* īnfīnītus; *(not relative)* simplex; **~ power** rēgnum *nt*, dominātus *m*; **~ ruler** rēx

absolutely *adv* absolūtē, omnīnō

absolution *n* venia *f*

absolve *vt* absolvere, exsolvere; *(from punishment)* condōnāre

absorb *vt* bibere, absorbēre; *(fig)* distringere; **I am absorbed in** tōtus sum in *(abl)*

absorbent *adj* bibulus

abstain vi abstinēre, sē abstinēre; (*from violence*) temperāre

abstemious adj sobrius

abstinence n abstinentia f, continentia f

abstinent adj abstinēns, sobrius

abstract adj mente perceptus, cōgitātiōne comprehēnsus ♦ n epitomē f ♦ vt abstrahere, dēmere

abstraction n (*idea*) nōtiō f; (*inattention*) animus parum attentus

abstruse adj reconditus, obscūrus, abstrūsus

absurd adj ineptus, absurdus

absurdity n ineptiae fpl, insulsitās f

absurdly adv ineptē, absurdē

abundance n cōpia f, abundantia f; **there is ~ of** abundē est (*gen*)

abundant adj cōpiōsus, abundāns, largus; **be ~** abundāre

abundantly adv abundē, abundanter, adfātim

abuse vt abūtī (*abl*); (*words*) maledīcere (*dat*) ♦ n probra ntpl, maledicta ntpl, convīcium nt, contumēlia f

abusive adj maledicus, contumēliōsus

abut vi adiacēre; **abutting on** cōnfīnis (*dat*), fīnitimus (*dat*)

abysmal adj profundus

abyss n profundum nt, vorāgō f; (*water*) gurges m; (*fig*) barathrum nt

academic adj scholasticus; (*style*) umbrātilis; (*sect*) Acadēmicus

academy n schola f; (*Plato's*) Acadēmīa f

accede vi adsentīrī; **~ to** accipere

accelerate vt, vi adcelerāre, festīnāre; (*process*) mātūrāre

accent n vōx f; (*intonation*) sonus m; (*mark*) apex m ♦ vt (*syllable*) acuere; (*word*) sonum admovēre (*dat*)

accentuate vt exprimere

accept vt accipere

acceptable adj acceptus, grātus, probābilis; **be ~** placēre

acceptation n significātiō f

access n aditus m; (*addition*) accessiō f; (*illness*) impetus m

accessary n socius m, particeps m

accessible adj (*person*) adfābilis, facilis; **be ~** (*place*) patēre; (*person*) facilem sē praebēre

accession n (*addition*) accessiō f; (*king's*) initium rēgnī

accident n cāsus m, calamitās f

accidental adj fortuītus

accidentally adv cāsū, fortuītō

acclaim vt adclāmāre

acclamation n clāmor m, studium nt

acclimatize vt aliēnō caelō adsuēfacere

accommodate vt accommodāre, aptāre; (*lodging*) hospitium parāre (*dat*); **~ oneself to** mōrigerārī (*dat*)

accommodating adj facilis

accommodation n hospitium nt

accompany vt comitārī; (*courtesy*) prōsequī; (*to Forum*) dēdūcere; (*music*) concinere (*dat*)

accomplice n socius m, particeps m, cōnscius m

accomplish vt efficere, perficere, patrāre

accomplished adj doctus, perītus

accomplishment n effectus m, perfectiō f, fīnis m; **accomplishments** pl artēs fpl

accord vi inter sē congruere, cōnsentīre ♦ vt dare, praebēre, praestāre ♦ n cōnsēnsus m, concordia f; (*music*) concentus m; **of one's own ~** suā sponte, ultrō; **with one ~** ūnā vōce

accordance n: **in ~ with** ex, ē (*abl*), secundum (*acc*)

according adv: **~ to** ex, ē (*abl*), secundum (*acc*); (*proportion*) prō (*abl*); **~ as** prōut

accordingly adv itaque, igitur, ergō

accost vt appellāre, adloquī, compellāre

account n ratiō f; (*story*) nārrātiō f, expositiō f; **on ~ of** ob (*acc*); propter (*acc*), causā (*gen*); **be of no ~** (*person*) nihilī aestimārī, nēquam esse; **on that ~** idcircō, ideō; **on your ~** tuā grātiā, tuō nōmine; **give an ~** ratiōnem reddere; **present an ~** ratiōnem referre; **take ~ of** ratiōnem habēre (*gen*); **put down to my ~** mihi expēnsum ferre; **the accounts balance** ratiō cōnstat/convenit ♦ vi: **~ for** ratiōnēs reddere, adferre (*cūr*); **that accounts for it** haec causa est, (*proverb*)hinc illae lacrimae

accountable adj reus; **I am ~ for** mihi ratiō reddenda est (*gen*)

accountant n ā ratiōnibus, ratiōcinātor m

account book n tabulae fpl; cōdex acceptī et expēnsī

accoutred adj īnstructus, ōrnātus

accoutrements n ōrnāmenta ntpl, arma ntpl

accredited adj pūblicā auctōritate missus

accretion n accessiō f

accrue vi (*addition*) cēdere; (*advantage*) redundāre

accumulate vt cumulāre, congerere, coacervāre ♦ vi crēscere, cumulārī

accumulation n cumulus m, acervus m

accuracy n cūra f; (*writing*) subtīlitās f

accurate adj (*work*) exāctus, subtīlis; (*worker*) dīligēns

accurately adv subtīliter, ad amussim, dīligenter

accursed adj sacer; (*fig*) exsecrātus, scelestus

accusation n (*act*) accūsātiō f; (*charge*) crīmen nt; (*unfair*) īnsimulātiō f; (*false*) calumnia f; **bring an ~ against** accūsāre; (*to a magistrate*) nōmen dēferre (*gen*)

accusative n (*case*) accūsātīvus m

accuse vt accūsāre, crīminārī, reum facere; (*falsely*) īnsimulāre; **the accused** reus; (*said by prosecutor*) iste

accuser n accūsātor m; (*civil suit*) petītor m; (*informer*) dēlātor m

accustom vt adsuēfacere; **~ oneself** adsuēscere, cōnsuēscere

accustomed adj adsuētus; **be ~** solēre; **become ~** adsuēscere, cōnsuēscere

ace n ūniō f; **I was within an ace of going** minimum āfuit quīn īrem

acerbity n acerbitās f

ache n dolor m ♦ vi dolēre

achieve vt cōnficere, patrāre; (*win*) cōnsequī, adsequī

achievement n factum nt, rēs gesta

acid adj acidus

acknowledge vt (*fact*) agnōscere; (*fault*) fatērī, cōnfitērī; (*child*) tollere; (*service*) grātiās agere prō *(abl)*; **I have to ~ your letter of 1st March** accēpī litterās tuās Kal. Mart. datās

acknowledgement *n* cōnfessiō *f*; grātia *f*

acme *n* fastīgium *nt*, flōs *m*

aconite *n* aconītum *nt*

acorn *n* glāns *f*

acoustics *n* rēs audītōria *f*

acquaint *vt* certiōrem facere, docēre; **~ oneself with** cognōscere; **acquainted with** gnārus *(gen)*, perītus *(gen)*

acquaintance *n (with fact)* cognitiō *f*, scientia *f*; *(with person)* familiāritās *f*, ūsus *m*; *(person)* nōtus *m*, familiāris *m*

acquiesce *vi (assent)* adquiēscere; *(submit)* aequō animō patī

acquiescence *n*: **with your ~** tē nōn adversante, pāce tuā

acquire *vt* adquīrere, adipīscī, cōnsequī; nancīscī

acquirements *n* artēs *fpl*

acquisition *n (act)* comparātiō *f*, quaestus *m*; *(thing)* quaesītum *nt*

acquisitive *adj* quaestuōsus

acquit *vt* absolvere; **~ oneself** sē praestāre, officiō fungī

acquittal *n* absolūtiō *f*

acre *n* iūgerum *nt*

acrid *adj* asper, ācer

acrimonious *adj* acerbus, truculentus

acrimony *n* acerbitās *f*

acrobat *n* fūnambulus *m*

acropolis *n* arx *f*

across *adv* trānsversus ♦ *prep* trāns *(acc)*

act *n* factum *nt*, facinus *nt*; *(play)* āctus *m*; *(POL)* āctum *nt*, senātus cōnsultum *nt*, dēcrētum *nt*; **I was in the act of saying** in eō erat ut dīcerem; **caught in the act** dēprehēnsus ♦ *vi* facere, agere; *(conduct)* sē gerere; *(stage)* histriōnem esse, partēs agere; *(pretence)* simulāre ♦ *vt*: **act a part** partēs agere, persōnam sustinēre; **act the part of** agere; **act as** esse, munere fungī *(gen)*; **act upon** *(instructions)* exsequī

action *n (doing)* āctiō *f*; *(deed)* factum *nt*, facinus *nt*; *(legal)* āctiō *f*, līs *f*; *(of play)* āctiō *f*; *(of speaker)* gestus *m*; **bring an ~ against** lītem intendere, āctiōnem īnstituere *(dat)*; **be in ~** agere, rem gerere; *(MIL)* pugnāre, in aciē dīmicāre; **man of ~** vir strēnuus

active *adj* impiger, strēnuus, sēdulus, nāvus

actively *adv* impigrē, strēnuē, nāviter

activity *n (motion)* mōtus *m*; *(energy)* industria *f*, sēdulitās *f*

actor *n* histriō *m*; *(in comedy)* cōmoedus *m*; *(in tragedy)* tragoedus *m*

actress *n* mīma *f*

actual *adj* vērus, ipse

actually *adv* rē vērā

actuate *vt* movēre, incitāre

acumen *n* acūmen *nt*, ingenī aciēs, argūtiae *fpl*

acute *adj* acūtus, ācer; *(pain)* ācer; *(speech)* argūtus, subtīlis

acutely *adv* acūtē, ācriter, argūtē

acuteness *n (mind)* acūmen *nt*, aciēs *f*, subtīlitas *f*

adage *n* prōverbium *nt*

adamant *n* adamās *m* ♦ *adj* obstinātus

adamantine *adj* adamantinus

adapt *vt* accommodāre

adaptable *adj* flexibilis, facile accommodandus

adaptation *n* accommodātiō *f*

add *vt* addere, adicere, adiungere; **be added** accēdere

adder *n* vīpera *f*

addicted *adj* dēditus

addition *n* adiūnctiō *f*, accessiō *f*; additāmentum *nt*, incrēmentum *nt*; **in ~** īnsuper, praetereā; **in ~ to** praeter *(acc)*

additional *adj* novus, adiūnctus

addled *adj (egg)* inritus; *(brain)* inānis

address *vt* compellāre, alloquī; *(crowd)* cōntiōnem habēre apud *(acc)*; *(letter)* īnscrībere; **~ oneself** *(to action)* accingī ♦ *n* adloquium *nt*; *(public)* cōntiō *f*, ōratiō *f*; *(letter)* īnscrīptiō *f*

adduce *vt (argument)* adferre; *(witness)* prōdūcere

adept *adj* perītus

adequate *adj* idōneus, dignus, pār; **be ~** sufficere

adequately *adv* satis, ut pār est

adhere *vi* haerēre, adhaerēre; **~ to** inhaerēre *(dat)*, inhaerēscere in *(abl)*; *(agreement)* manēre, stāre in *(abl)*

adherent *n* adsectātor *m*; *(of party)* fautor *m*; *(of person)* cliēns *m*

adhesive *adj* tenax

adieu *interj* valē, valēte; **bid ~ to** valēre iubēre

adjacent *adj* fīnitimus, vīcīnus; **be ~ to** adiacēre *(dat)*

adjoin *vi* adiacēre *(dat)*

adjoining *adj* fīnitimus, adiūnctus; proximus

adjourn *vt (short time)* differre; *(longer time)* prōferre; *(case)* ampliāre ♦ *vi* rem differre, prōferre

adjournment *n* dīlātiō *f*, prōlātiō *f*

adjudge *vt* addīcere, adiūdicāre

adjudicate *vi* dēcernere

adjudicator *n* arbiter *m*

adjunct *n* appendix *f*, accessiō *f*

adjure *vt* obtestārī, obsecrāre

adjust *vt (adapt)* accommodāre; *(put in order)* compōnere

adjutant *n (MIL)* optiō *m*; *(civil)* adiūtor *m*

administer *vt* administrāre, gerere; *(justice)* reddere; *(oath to)* iūreiūrandō adigere; *(medicine)* dare, adhibēre

administration *n* administrātiō *f*

administrator *n* administrātor *m*, prōcūrātor *m*

admirable *adj* admīrābilis, ēgregius

admirably *adv* ēgregiē

admiral *n* praefectus classis; **admiral's ship** nāvis praetōria

admiralty *n* praefectī classium

admiration *n* admīrātiō *f*, laus *f*

admire *vt* admīrārī; mīrārī

admirer *n* laudātor *m*; amātor *m*

admissible *adj* aequus

admission *n (entrance)* aditus *m*; *(of guilt etc)* cōnfessiō *f*

admit *vt (let in)* admittere, recipere, accipere; *(to membership)* adscīscere; *(argument)* concēdere; *(fault)* fatērī; **~ of** patī, recipere

admittedly *adv* sānē

admonish *vt* admonēre, commonēre, hortārī

admonition n admonitiō f
ado n negōtium nt; **make much ado about nothing** fluctūs in simpulō excitāre; **without more ado** prōtinus, sine morā
adolescence n prīma adulēscentia f
adolescent adj adulēscēns ◆ n adulēscentulus m
adopt vt (person) adoptāre; (custom) adscīscere; **~ a plan** consilium capere
adoption n (person) adoptiō f; (custom) adsūmptiō f; **by ~** adoptīvus
adoptive adj adoptīvus
adorable adj amābilis, venustus
adorably adv venustē
adoration n (of gods) cultus m; (of kings) venerātiō f; (love) amor m
adore vt (worship) venerārī; (love) adamāre
adorn vt ōrnāre, exōrnāre, decorāre
adornment n ōrnāmentum nt, decus nt; ōrnātus m
adrift adj fluctuāns; **be ~** fluctuāre
adroit adj sollers, callidus
adroitly adv callidē, scītē
adroitness n sollertia f, calliditās f
adulation n adūlātiō f, adsentātiō f
adulatory adj blandus
adult adj adultus
adulterate vt corrumpere, adulterāre
adulterer n adulter m
adulteress n adultera f
adulterous adj incestus
adultery n adulterium nt; **commit ~** adulterāre
adults npl pūberēs mpl
adumbrate vt adumbrāre
advance vt prōmovēre; (a cause) fovēre; (money) crēdere; (opinion) dīcere; (to honours) prōvehere; (time) mātūrāre ◆ vi prōcēdere, prōgredī, adventāre; (MIL) signa prōferre, pedem īnferre; (progress) prōficere; (walk) incēdere; **~ to the attack** signa īnferre ◆ n prōgressus m, prōcessus m; (attack) impetus m; (money) mūtuae pecūniae; **in ~** mātūrius; **fix in ~** praefīnīre; **get in ~** praecipere
advanced adj prōvectus; **well ~** (task) adfectus
advancement n (POL) honōs m
advantage n (benefit) commodum nt, bonum nt, ūsus m; (of place or time) opportūnitās f; (profit) fructus m; (superiority) praestantia f; **it is an ~ bono est; be of ~** prōdesse (dat), ūsuī esse (dat); **to your ~** in rem tuam; **it is to your ~** tibi expedit, tuā interest; **take ~ of** (circumstances) ūtī; (person) dēcipere, fallere; **have an ~ over** praestāre (dat); **be seen to ~** māximē placēre
advantageous adj ūtilis, opportūnus
advantageously adv ūtiliter, opportūnē
advent n adventus m
adventitious adj fortuītus
adventure n (exploit) facinus memorābile nt; (hazard) perīculum nt
adventurer n vir audāx m; (social) parasītus m
adventurous adj audāx
adversary n adversārius m, hostis m
adverse adj adversus, contrārius, inimīcus
adversely adv contrāriē, inimīcē, male
adversity n rēs adversae fpl, calamitās f
advert vi: **~ to** attingere
advertise vt prōscrībere; vēnditāre

advertisement n prōscrīptiō f, libellus m
advice n cōnsilium nt; (POL) auctōritās f; (legal) respōnsum nt; **ask ~ of** cōnsulere; **on the ~ of** Sulla auctōre Sullā
advisable adj ūtilis, operae pretium
advise vt monēre, suādēre (dat), cēnsēre (dat); **~ against** dissuādēre
advisedly adv cōnsultō
adviser n auctor m, suāsor m
advocacy n patrōcinium nt
advocate n patrōnus m, causidicus m; (supporter) auctor m; **be an ~** causam dīcere ◆ vt suādēre, cēnsēre
adze n ascia f
aedile n aedīlis m
aedile's adj aedīlicius
aedileship n aedīlitās f
aegis n aegis f; (fig) praesidium nt
Aeneid n Aenēis f
aerial adj āerius
aesthetic adj pulchritūdinis amāns, artificiōsus
afar adv procul; **from ~** procul
affability n cōmitās f, facilitās f, bonitās f
affable adj cōmis, facilis, commodus
affably adv cōmiter
affair n negōtium nt, rēs f
affect vt afficere, movēre, commovēre; (concern) attingere; (pretence) simulāre
affectation n simulātiō f; (RHET) adfectātiō f; (in diction) īnsolentia f; quaesīta ntpl
affected adj (style) molestus, pūtidus
affectedly adv pūtidē
affecting adj miserābilis
affection n amor m, cāritās f, studium nt; (family) pietās f
affectionate adj amāns, pius
affectionately adv amanter, piē
affiance vt spondēre
affidavit n testimōnium nt
affinity n affīnitās f, cognātiō f
affirm vt adfirmāre, adsevērāre
affirmation n adfirmātiō f
affirmative adj: **I reply in the ~** āiō
affix vt adfīgere, adiungere
afflict vt adflīctāre, angere, vexāre; afflīgere
affliction n miseria f, dolor m, rēs adversae fpl
affluence n cōpia f, opēs fpl
affluent adj dīves, opulentus, loculēs
afford vt praebēre, dare; **I cannot ~** rēs mihi nōn suppetit ad
affray n rixa f, pugna f
affright vt terrēre ◆ n terror m, pavor m
affront vt offendere, contumēliam dīcere (dat) ◆ n iniūria f, contumēlia f
afield adv forīs; **far ~** peregrē
afloat adj natāns; **be ~** natāre
afoot adv pedibus; **be ~** gerī
aforesaid adj suprā dictus
afraid adj timidus; **be ~ of** timēre, metuere; verērī
afresh adv dēnuō, dē integrō
Africa n Africa f
aft adv in puppī, puppim versus
after adj posterior ◆ adv posthāc, posteā; **the day ~** postrīdiē ◆ conj postquam; **the day ~** postrīdiē

quam ♦ *prep* post (*acc*); (*in rank*) secundum (*acc*); (*in imitation*) ad (*acc*), dē (*abl*); **~ all** tamen, dēnique; **~ reading the book** librō lēctō; **one thing ~ another** aliud ex aliō; **immediately ~** statim ab

aftermath *n* ēventus *m*

afternoon *n*: **in the ~** post merīdiem ♦ *adj* postmerīdiānus

afterthought *n* posterior cōgitātiō *f*

afterwards *adv* post, posteā, deinde

again *adv* rūrsus, iterum; **~ and ~** etiam atque etiam, identidem; **once ~** dēnuō; (*new point in a speech*) quid?

against *prep* contrā (*acc*), adversus (*acc*), in (*acc*); **~ the stream** adversō flūmine; **~ one's will** invitus

agape *adj* hiāns

age *n* (*life*) aetās *f*; (*epoch*) aetās *f*, saeculum *nt*; **old age** senectūs *f*; **he is of age** suī iūris est; **he is eight years of age** octō annōs nātus est, nōnum annum agit; **of the same age** aequālis

aged *adj* senex, aetāte prōvectus; (*things*) antīquus

agency *n* opera *f*; **through the ~ of** per (*acc*)

agent *n* āctor *m*, prōcūrātor *m*; (*in crime*) minister *m*

aggrandize *vt* augēre, amplificāre

aggrandizement *n* amplificātiō *f*

aggravate *vt* (*wound*) exulcerāre; (*distress*) augēre; **become aggravated** ingravēscere

aggravating *adj* molestus

aggregate *n* summa *f*

aggression *n* incursiō *f*, iniūria *f*

aggressive *adj* ferōx

aggressiveness *n* ferōcitās *f*

aggressor *n* oppugnātor *m*

aggrieved *adj* īrātus; **be ~** indignārī

aghast *adj* attonitus, stupefactus; **stand ~** obstupēscere

agile *adj* pernix, vēlōx

agility *n* pernīcitās *f*

agitate *vt* agitāre; (*mind*) commovēre, perturbāre

agitation *n* commōtiō *f*, perturbātiō *f*, trepidātiō *f*; (*POL*) tumultus *m*

agitator *n* turbātor *m*, concitātor *m*

aglow *adj* fervidus ♦ *adv*: **be ~** fervēre

ago *adv* abhinc (*acc*); **three days ago** abhinc trēs diēs; **long ago** antīquitus, iamprīdem, iamdūdum; **a short time ago** dūdum

agog *adj* sollicitus, ērēctus

agonize *vt* cruciāre, torquēre

agonizing *adj* horribilis

agony *n* cruciātus *m*, dolor *m*

agrarian *adj* agrārius; **~ party** agrāriī *mpl*

agree *vi* (*together*) cōnsentīre, congruere; (*with*) adsentīrī (*dat*), sentīre cum; (*bargain*) pacīscī; (*facts*) cōnstāre, convenīre; (*food*) facilem esse ad concoquendum; **~ upon** cōnstituere, compōnere; **it is agreed** constat (inter omnes)

agreeable *adj* grātus, commodus, acceptus

agreeableness *n* dulcēdō *f*, iūcunditās *f*

agreeably *adv* iūcundē

agreement *n* (*together*) cōnsēnsus *m*, concordia *f*; (*with*) adsēnsus *m*; (*pact*) pactiō *f*, conventum

nt, foedus *nt*; **according to ~** compāctō, ex compositō; **be in ~** cōnsentīre, congruere

agricultural *adj* rūsticus, agrestis

agriculture *n* rēs rūstica *f*, agrī cultūra *f*

aground *adv*: **be ~** sīdere; **run ~** in lītus ēicī, offendere

ague *n* horror *m*, febris *f*

ahead *adv* ante; **go ~** anteīre, praeīre; **go-ahead** *adj* impiger; **ships in line ~** agmen nāvium

aid *vt* adiuvāre, succurrere (*dat*), subvenīre (*dat*) ♦ *n* auxilium *nt*, subsidium *nt*

aide-de-camp *n* optiō *m*

ail *vt* dolēre ♦ *vi* aegrōtāre, labōrāre, languēre

ailing *adj* aeger, īnfirmus

ailment *n* morbus *m*, valētūdō *f*

aim *vt* intendere; **aim at** petere; (*fig*) adfectāre, spectāre, sequī; (*with verb*) id agere ut ♦ *n* fīnis *m*, prōpositum *nt*

aimless *adj* inānis, vānus

aimlessly *adv* sine ratiōne

aimlessness *n* vānitās *f*

air *n* āēr *m*; (*breeze*) aura *f*; (*look*) vultus *m*, speciēs *f*; (*tune*) modus *m*; **in the open air** sub dīvō; **airs** fastus *m*; **give oneself airs** sē iactāre

airily *adv* hilarē

airy *adj* (*of air*) āerius; (*light*) tenuis; (*place*) apertus; (*manner*) hilaris

aisle *n* āla *f*

ajar *adj* sēmiapertus

akin *adj* cōnsanguineus, cognātus

alacrity *n* alacritās *f*

alarm *n* terror *m*, formīdō *f*, trepidātiō *f*; (*sound*) clāmor *m*; **sound an ~** ad arma conclāmāre; **give the ~** increpāre; **be in a state of ~** trepidāre ♦ *vt* terrēre, perterrēre, perturbāre

alarming *adj* formīdolōsus

alas *interj* heu

albeit *conj* etsī, etiamsī

alcove *n* zōthēca *f*

alder *n* alnus *f*

alderman *n* decuriō *m*

ale *n* cervīsia *f*

alehouse *n* caupōna *f*, taberna *f*

alert *adj* prōmptus, alacer, vegetus

alertness *n* alacritās *f*

alien *adj* externus; **~ to** abhorrēns ab ♦ *n* peregrīnus *m*

alienate *vt* aliēnāre, abaliēnāre, āvertere, āvocāre

alienation *n* aliēnātiō *f*

alight *adj*: **be ~** ārdēre; **set ~** accendere ♦ *vi* (*from horse*) dēscendere, dēsilīre; (*bird*) īnsīdere

alike *adj* pār, similis ♦ *adv* aequē, pariter

alive *adj* vīvus; **be ~** vīvere

all *adj* omnis; (*together*) ūniversus, cūnctus; (*whole*) tōtus; **all but** paene; **all for** studiōsus (*gen*); **all in** cōnfectus; **all of** tōtus; **all over with** āctum dē (*abl*); **all the best men** optimus quisque; **all the more** eō plūs, tantō plūs; **at all** ullō modō, quid; **it is all up with** actum est de (*abl*); **not at all** haudquāquam ♦ *n* fortūnae *fpl*

allay *vt* sēdāre, mītigāre, lēnīre

allegation *n* adfirmātiō *f*; (*charge*) īnsimulātiō *f*

allege *vt* adfirmāre, praetendere; (*in excuse*) excūsāre

allegiance n fidēs f; **owe ~ to** in fidē esse (gen); **swear ~ to** in verba iūrāre (gen)
allegory n allēgoria f, immūtāta ōrātiō f
alleviate vt mītigāre, adlevāre, sublevāre
alleviation n levātiō f, levāmentum nt
alley n (garden) xystus m; (town) angiportus m
alliance n societās f, foedus nt
allied adj foederātus, socius; (friends) coniūnctus
alligator n crocodīlus m
allocate vt adsignāre, impertīre
allot vt adsignāre, distribuere; **be allotted** obtingere
allotment n (land) adsignātiō f
allow vt sinere, permittere (dat), concēdere (dat), patī; (admit) fatērī, concēdere; (approve) comprobāre; **it is allowed** licet (dat+infin); **for** vt ratiōnem habēre (gen)
allowance n venia f, indulgentia f; (pay) stīpendium nt; (food) cibāria ntpl; (for travel) viāticum nt; **make ~ for** indulgēre (dat), ignōscere (dat), excusāre
alloy n admixtum nt
all right adj rēctē; **it is all right** bene est
allude vi: **~ to** dēsignāre, attingere, significāre
allure vt adlicere, pellicere
allurement n blanditia f, blandīmentum nt, illecebra f
alluring adj blandus
alluringly adv blandē
allusion n mentiō f, indicium nt
alluvial adj: **~ land** adluviō f
ally n socius m ♦ vt sociāre, coniungere
almanac n fāstī mpl
almighty adj omnipotēns
almond n (nut) amygdalum nt; (tree) amygdala f
almost adv paene, ferē, fermē, propemodum
alms n stipem (no nom) f
aloe n aloē f
aloft adj sublīmis ♦ adv sublīmē
alone adj sōlus, sōlitārius, ūnus ♦ adv sōlum
along prep secundum (acc), praeter (acc) ♦ adv porrō; **all ~** iamdūdum, ab initiō; **~ with** unā cum (abl)
alongside adv: **bring ~** adpellere; **come ~** ad crepīdinem accēdere
aloof adv procul; **stand ~** sē removēre ♦ adj sēmōtus
aloofness n sōlitūdō f, sēcessus m
aloud adv clārē, māgnā vōce
alphabet n elementa ntpl
Alps n Alpēs fpl
already adv iam
also adv etiam, et, quoque; īdem
altar n āra f
alter vt mūtāre, commūtāre; (order) invertere
alteration n mūtātiō f, commūtātiō f
altercation n altercātiō f, iūrgium nt
alternate adj alternus ♦ vt variāre
alternately adv invicem
alternation n vicem (no nom) f vicissitūdō f
alternative adj alter, alius ♦ n optiō f
although conj quamquam (+indic), etsī/etiamsī (+cond clause); quamvīs (subj)
altitude n altitūdō f
altogether adv omnīnō; (emphasis) plānē, prōrsus

altruism n beneficentia f
alum n alūmen nt
always adv semper
amalgamate vt miscēre, coniungere
amalgamation n coniūnctiō f, temperātiō f
amanuensis n librārius m
amass vt cumulāre, coacervāre
amateur n idiōta m
amatory adj amātōrius
amaze vt obstupefacere; attonāre; **be amazed** obstupēscere
amazement n stupor m; **in ~** attonitus, stupefactus
ambassador n lēgātus m
amber n sūcinum nt
ambidextrous adj utrīusque manūs compos
ambiguity n ambiguitās f; (RHET) amphibolia f
ambiguous adj ambiguus, anceps, dubius
ambiguously adv ambiguē
ambition n glōria f, laudis studium
ambitious adj glōriae cupidus, laudis avidus
amble vi ambulāre
ambrosia n ambrosia f
ambrosial adj ambrosius
ambuscade n īnsidiae fpl
ambush n īnsidiae fpl ♦ vt īnsidiārī (dat)
ameliorate vt corrigere, meliōrem reddere
amelioration n prōfectus m
amenable adj facilis, docilis
amend vt corrigere, ēmendāre
amendment n ēmendātiō f
amends n (apology) satisfactiō f; **make ~ for** expiāre; **make ~ to** satisfacere (dat)
amenity n (scenery) amoenitās f; (comfort) commodum nt
amethyst n amethystus f
amiability n benignitās f, suāvitās f
amiable adj benignus, suāvis
amiably adv benignē, suāviter
amicable adj amīcus, cōmis
amicably adv amīcē, cōmiter
amid, amidst prep inter (acc)
amiss adv perperam, secus, incommodē; **take ~ aegrē ferre
amity n amīcitia f
ammunition n tēla ntpl
amnesty n venia f
among, amongst prep inter (acc), apud (acc)
amorous adj amātōrius, amāns
amorously adv cum amōre
amount vi: **~ to** efficere; (fig) esse ♦ n summa f
amours n amōrēs mpl
amphibious adj anceps
amphitheatre n amphitheātrum nt
ample adj amplus, satis
amplification n amplificātiō f
amplify vt amplificāre
amplitude n amplitūdō f, cōpia f
amputate vt secāre, amputāre
amuck adv: **run ~** bacchārī
amulet n amulētum nt
amuse vt dēlectāre, oblectāre
amusement n oblectāmentum nt, dēlectātiō f; **for ~** animī causā
amusing adj rīdiculus, facētus
an indef art see **a**

anaemic *adj* exsanguis
analogous *adj* similis
analogy *n* prōportiō *f*, comparātiō *f*
analyse *vt* excutere, perscrūtārī
analysis *n* explicātiō *f*
anapaest *n* anapaestus *m*
anarchical *adj* sēditiōsus
anarchy *n* reī pūblicae perturbātiō, lēgēs nullae
fpl, licentia *f*
anathema *n* exsecrātiō *f*; (*object*) pestis *f*
ancestor *n* proavus *m*; **ancestors** *pl* māiōrēs *mpl*
ancestral *adj* patrius
ancestry *n* genus *nt*, orīgō *f*
anchor *n* ancora *f*; **lie at ~** in ancorīs stāre;
weigh ~ ancoram tollere ◆ *vi* ancoram iacere
anchorage *n* statiō *f*
ancient *adj* antīquus, prīscus, vetustus;
~ history, **~ world** antīquitās *f*; **from/in**
~ times antīquitus; **the ancients** veterēs
and *conj* et, atque, ac, -que; **and ... not** nec,
neque; **and so** itaque
anecdote *n* fābella *f*
anent *prep* dē (*abl*)
anew *adv* dēnuō, ab integrō
angel *n* angelus *m*
angelic *adj* angelicus; (*fig*) dīvīnus, eximius
anger *n* īra *f* ◆ *vt* inrītāre
angle *n* angulus *m* ◆ *vi* hāmō piscārī
angler *n* piscātor *m*
Anglesey *n* Mona *f*
angrily *adv* īrātē
angry *adj* īrātus; **be ~** īrāscī (*dat*)
anguish *n* cruciātus *m*, dolor *m*; (*mind*) angor *m*
angular *adj* angulātus
animal *n* animal *nt*; (*domestic*) pecus *f*; (*wild*) fera *f*
animate *vt* animāre
animated *adj* excitātus, vegetus
animation *n* ārdor *m*, alacritās *f*
animosity *n* invidia *f*, inimīcitia *f*
ankle *n* tālus *m*
annalist *n* annālium scrīptor
annals *n* annālēs *mpl*
annex *vt* addere
annexation *n* adiectiō *f*
annihilate *vt* dēlēre, exstinguere, perimere
annihilation *n* exstinctiō *f*, interneciō *f*
anniversary *n* diēs anniversārius; (*public*)
sollemne *nt*
annotate *vt* adnotāre
annotation *n* adnotātiō *f*
announce *vt* nūntiāre; (*officially*) dēnūntiāre,
prōnūntiāre; (*election result*) renūntiāre
announcement *n* (*official*) dēnūntiātiō *f*; (*news*)
nūntius *m*
announcer *n* nūntius *m*
annoy *vt* inrītāre, vexāre; **be annoyed with**
aegrē ferre
annoyance *n* molestia *f*, vexātiō *f*; (*felt*) dolor *m*
annoying *adj* molestus
annual *adj* annuus, anniversārius
annually *adv* quotannīs
annuity *n* annua *ntpl*
annul *vt* abrogāre, dissolvere, tollere
annulment *n* abrogātiō *f*
anoint *vt* ungere, illinere
anomalous *adj* novus

anomaly *n* novitās *f*
anon *adv* mox
anonymous *adj* incertī auctōris
anonymously *adv* sine nōmine
another *adj* alius; (*second*) alter; **of ~** aliēnus; **one**
after ~ alius ex aliō; **one ~** inter sē, alius alium;
in ~ place alibī; **to ~ place** aliō; **in ~ way** aliter;
at ~ time aliās
answer *vt* respondēre (*dat*); (*by letter*) rescrībere
(*dat*); (*agree*) respondēre, congruere; **~ a charge**
crīmen dēfendere; **~ for** *vt* (*surety*) praestāre;
(*account*) ratiōnem referre; (*substitute*) instar
esse (*gen*) ◆ *n* respōnsum *nt*; (*to a charge*) dēfēnsiō
f; **~ to the name of** vocārī; **give an ~** respondēre
answerable *adj* reus; **I am ~ for ...** ratiō mihī
reddenda est ... (*gen*)
ant *n* formīca *f*
antagonism *n* simultās *f*, inimīcitia *f*
antagonist *n* adversārius *m*, hostis *m*
antarctic *adj* antarcticus
antecedent *adj* antecēdēns, prior
antediluvian *adj* prīscus, horridus,
Deucaliōnēus
antelope *n* dorcas *f*
anterior *adj* prior
anteroom *n* vestibulum *nt*
anthology *n* excerpta *ntpl*; **make an ~** excerpere
anthropology *n* rēs hūmānae *fpl*
anticipate *vt* (*expect*) exspectāre; (*forestall*)
antevenīre, occupāre; (*in thought*) animō
praecipere
anticipation *n* exspectātiō *f*, spēs *f*;
praesūmptiō *f*
antics *n* gestus *m*, ineptiae *fpl*
anticyclone *n* serēnitās *f*
antidote *n* remedium *nt*, medicāmen *nt*
antipathy *n* fastīdium *nt*, odium *nt*; (*things*)
repugnantia *f*
antiphonal *adj* alternus
antiphony *n* alterna *ntpl*
antipodes *n* contrāria pars terrae
antiquarian *adj* historicus
antiquary *n* antīquārius *m*
antiquated *adj* prīscus, obsolētus
antique *adj* antīquus, prīscus
antiquity *n* antīquitās *f*, vetustas *f*, veterēs *mpl*
antithesis *n* contentiō *f*, contrārium *nt*
antlers *n* cornua *ntpl*
anvil *n* incūs *f*
anxiety *n* sollicitūdō *f*, metus *m*, cūra *f*; anxietās
f
anxious *adj* sollicitus, anxius; avidus; cupidus
any *adj* ullus; (*interrog*) ecquī; (*after* **sī, nisī, num,**
nē) quī; (*indef*) quīvīs, quīlibet; **hardly any**
nullus ferē; **any further** longius; **any longer**
(*of time*) diutius
anybody *pron* aliquis; (*indef*) quīvīs, quīlibet;
(*after* **sī, nisī, num, nē**) quis; (*interrog*) ecquis,
numquis; (*after neg*) quisquam; **hardly ~** nēmō
ferē
anyhow *adv* ullō modō, quōquō modō
anyone *pron see* **anybody**
anything *pron* aliquid; quidvīs, quidlibet;
(*interrog*) ecquid, numquid; (*after neg*) quicquam;
(*after* **sī, nisī, num, nē**) quid; **hardly ~** nihil
ferē

anywhere adv usquam, ubīvīs
apace adv citō, celeriter
apart adv seōrsum, sēparātim ✦ adj dīversus; **be six feet** ~ sex pedēs distāre; **set** ~ sēpōnere; **stand** ~ distāre; **joking** ~ remōtō iocō; ~ **from** praeter (acc)
apartment n cubiculum nt, conclāve nt
apathetic adj lentus, languidus, ignāvus
apathy n lentitūdō f, languor m, ignāvia f
ape n sīmia f ✦ vt imitārī
aperture n hiātus m, forāmen nt, rīma f
apex n fastīgium nt
aphorism n sententia f
apiary n alveārium nt
apiece adv in singulōs; **two** ~ bīnī
aplomb n cōnfīdentia f
apocryphal adj commentīcius
apologetic adj cōnfitēns, veniam petēns
apologize vi veniam petere, sē excūsāre
apology n excūsātiō f
apoplectic adj apoplēcticus
apoplexy n apoplēxis f
apostle n apostolus m
apothecary n medicāmentārius m
appal vt perterrēre, cōnsternere
appalling adj dīrus
apparatus n īnstrūmenta ntpl, ōrnāmenta ntpl
apparel n vestis f, vestīmenta ntpl
apparent adj manifestus, apertus, ēvidēns
apparently adv speciē, ut vidētur
apparition n vīsum nt, speciēs f
appeal vi (to magistrate) appellāre; (to people) prōvocāre ad; (to gods) invocāre, testārī; (to senses) placēre (dat) ✦ n appellātiō f, prōvocātiō f, testātiō f
appear vi (in sight) appārēre; (in court) sistī; (in public) prōdīre; (at a place) adesse, advenīre; (seem) vidērī
appearance n (coming) adventus m; (look) aspectus m, faciēs f; (semblance) speciēs f; (thing) vīsum nt; **for the sake of appearances** in speciem; (formula) dicis causā; **make one's** ~ prōcēdere, prōdīre
appeasable adj plācābilis
appease vt plācāre, lēnīre, mītigāre, sēdāre
appeasement n plācātiō f; (of enemy) pācificātiō f
appellant n appellātor m
appellation n nōmen nt
append vt adiungere, subicere
appendage n appendix f, adiūnctum nt
appertain vi pertinēre
appetite n adpetītus m; (for food) famēs f
applaud vt plaudere; (fig) laudāre
applause n plausus m; (fig) adsēnsiō f, adprobātiō f
apple n pōmum nt; mālum nt; ~ **tree** mālus f; ~ **of my eye** ocellus meus; **upset the** ~ **cart** plaustrum percellere
appliance n māchina f, īnstrūmentum nt
applicable adj aptus, commodus; **be** ~ pertinēre
applicant n petītor m
application n (work) industria f; (mental) intentiō f; (asking) petītiō f; (MED) fōmentum nt
apply vt adhibēre, admovēre; (use) ūtī (abl); ~ **oneself to** sē adplicāre, incumbere in (acc)

✦ vi pertinēre; (to a person) adīre (acc); (for office) petere
appoint vt (magistrate) creāre, facere, cōnstituere; (commander) praeficere; (guardian, heir) īnstituere; (time) dīcere, statuere; (for a purpose) dēstināre; (to office) creāre
appointment n cōnstitūtum nt; (duty) mandātum nt; (office) magistrātus m; **have an** ~ **with** cōnstitūtum habēre cum; **keep an** ~ ad cōnstitūtum venīre
apportion vt dispertīre, dīvidere; (land) adsignāre
apposite adj aptus, appositus
appraisal n aestimātiō f
appraise vt aestimāre
appreciable adj haud exiguus
appreciate vt aestimāre
appreciation n aestimātiō f
apprehend vt (person) comprehendere; (idea) intellegere, mente comprehendere; (fear) metuere, timēre
apprehension n comprehēnsiō f; metus m, formīdō f
apprehensive adj anxius, sollicitus; **be** ~ **of** metuere
apprentice n discipulus m, tīrō m
apprenticeship n tīrōcinium nt
apprise vt docēre, certiōrem facere
approach vt appropinquāre ad (acc), accēdere ad; (person) adīre ✦ vi (time) adpropinquāre; (season) appetere ✦ n (act) accessus m, aditus m; (time) adpropinquātiō f; (way) aditus m; **make approaches to** adīre ad, ambīre, petere
approachable adj (place) patēns; (person) facilis
approbation n adprobātiō f, adsēnsiō f
appropriate adj aptus, idōneus, proprius ✦ vt adscīscere, adsūmere
appropriately adv aptē, commodē
approval n adprobātiō f, adsēnsus m, favor m
approve vt, vi adprobāre, comprobāre, adsentīrī (dat); (LAW) scīscere
approved adj probātus, spectātus
approximate adj propinquus ✦ vi: ~ **to** accēdere ad
approximately adv prope, propemodum; (number) ad (acc)
appurtenances n īnstrūmenta ntpl, apparātus m
apricot n armēniacum nt; ~ **tree** n armēniaca f
April n mēnsis Aprīlis m; **of** ~ Aprīlis
apron n operīmentum nt
apropos of prep quod attinet ad
apse n apsis f
apt adj aptus, idōneus; (pupil) docilis, prōmptus; **apt to** prōnus, prōclīvis ad; **be apt to** solēre
aptitude n ingenium nt, facultās f
aptly adv aptē
aquarium n piscīna f
aquatic adj aquātilis
aqueduct n aquae ductus m
aquiline adj (nose) aduncus
arable land n arvum nt
arbiter n arbiter m
arbitrarily adv ad libīdinem, licenter
arbitrary adj libīdinōsus (act); (ruler) superbus
arbitrate vi dīiūdicāre, disceptāre

arbitration n arbitrium nt, diiūdicātiō f
arbitrator n arbiter m, disceptātor m
arbour n umbrāculum nt
arbutus n arbutus f
arc n arcus m
arcade n porticus f
arch n fornix m, arcus m ♦ vt arcuāre ♦ adj lascīvus, vafer
archaeologist n antīquitātis investīgātor m
archaeology n antīquitātis investīgātiō f
archaic adj prīscus
archaism n verbum obsolētum nt
archbishop n archiepiscopus m
arched adj fornicātus
archer n sagittārius m
archery n sagittāriōrum ars f
architect n architectus m
architecture n architectūra f
architrave n epistylium nt
archives n tabulae (pūblicae) fpl
arctic adj arcticus, septentriōnālis ♦ n septentriōnēs mpl
ardent adj ārdēns, fervidus, vehemēns
ardently adv ārdenter, ācriter, vehementer
ardour n ārdor m, fervor m
arduous adj difficilis, arduus
area n regiō f; (MATH) superficiēs f
arena n harēna f
argonaut n argonauta m
argosy n onerāria f
argue vi (discuss) disserere, disceptāre; (dispute) ambigere; disputāre; (reason) argūmentārī ♦ vt (prove) arguere
argument n (discussion) contrōversia f, disputātiō f; (reason) ratiō f; (proof, theme) argūmentum nt
argumentation n argūmentātiō f
argumentative adj lītigiōsus
aria n canticum nt
arid adj āridus, siccus
aright adv rectē, vērē
arise vi orīrī, coorīrī, exsistere; ~ from nāscī ex, proficīscī ab
aristocracy n optimātēs mpl, nōbilēs mpl; (govt) optimātium dominātus m
aristocrat n optimās m
aristocratic adj patricius, generōsus
arithmetic n numerī mpl, arithmētica ntpl
ark n arca f
arm n bracchium nt; (upper) lacertus m; (sea) sinus m; (weapon) tēlum nt ♦ vt armāre ♦ vi arma capere
armament n bellī apparātus m; cōpiae fpl
armed adj (men) armātus; **light-armed troops** levis armātūra f, vēlitēs mpl
armistice n indutiae fpl
armlet n armilla f
armour n arma ntpl; (kind of) armātūra f
armourer n (armōrum) faber m
armoury n armāmentārium nt
armpit n āla f
arms npl (MIL) arma ntpl; **by force of ~** vī et armīs; **under ~** in armīs
army n exercitus m; (in battle) aciēs f; (on march) agmen nt
aroma n odor m

aromatic adj frāgrāns
around adv circum, circā ♦ prep circum (acc)
arouse vt suscitāre, ērigere, excitāre
arraign vt accūsāre
arrange vt (in order) compōnere, ōrdināre, dīgerere, dispōnere; (agree) pacīscī; ~ **a truce** indūtiās compōnere
arrangement n ōrdō m, collocātiō f, dispositiō f; pactum nt, cōnstitūtum nt
arrant adj summus
array n vestis f, habitus m; (MIL) aciēs f ♦ vt vestīre, exōrnāre; (MIL) īnstruere
arrears n residuae pecūniae fpl, reliqua ntpl
arrest vt comprehendere, adripere; (attention) in sē convertere; (movement) morārī, tardāre ♦ n comprehēnsiō f
arrival n adventus m
arrive vi advenīre ('ad'+acc), pervenīre ('ad'+acc)
arrogance n superbia f, adrogantia f, fastus m
arrogant adj superbus, adrogāns
arrogantly adv superbē, adroganter
arrogate vt adrogāre
arrow n sagitta f
arsenal n armāmentārium nt
arson n incēnsiōnis crīmen nt
art n ars f, artificium nt; **fine arts** ingenuae artēs
artery n artēria f
artful adj callidus, vafer, astūtus
artfully adv callidē, astūtē
artfulness n astūtia f, dolus m
artichoke n cinara f
article n rēs f, merx f; (clause) caput nt; (term) condiciō f
articulate adj explānātus, distinctus ♦ vt explānāre, exprimere
articulately adv explānātē, clārē
articulation n prōnūntiātiō f
artifice n ars f, artificium nt, dolus m
artificer n artifex m, opifex m, faber m
artificial adj (work) artificiōsus; (appearance) fūcātus
artificially adv arte, manū
artillery n tormenta ntpl
artisan n faber m, opifex m
artist n artifex m; pictor m
artistic adj artificiōsus, ēlegāns
artistically adv artificiōsē, ēleganter
artless adj (work) inconditus; (person) simplex
artlessly adv inconditē; simpliciter, sine dolō
artlessness n simplicitās f
as adv (before adj, adv) tam; (after **aequus, īdem, similis**) ac, atque; (correlative) quam, quālis, quantus ♦ conj (compar) ut (+indic), sīcut, velut, quemadmodum; (cause) cum (+indic), quōniam, quippe quī; (time) dum, ut ♦ relat pron quī, quae, quod (subj); **as being** utpote; **as follows** ita; **as for** quod attinet ad; **as if** quasī, tamquam si, velut; (while) usu expressed by pres part; **as it were** ut ita dīcam; **as yet** adhūc; **as soon as** simul ac/atque (+perf indic); **as ... as possible** quam (+ superl) ♦ n (coin) as m
ascend vt, vi ascendere
ascendancy n praestantia f, auctōritās f
ascendant adj surgēns, potēns; **be in the ~** praestāre

ascent n ascēnsus m; (slope) clīvus m
ascertain vt comperīre, cognōscere
ascetic adj nimis abstinēns, austērus
asceticism n dūritia f
ascribe vt adscrībere, attribuere, adsignāre
ash n (tree) fraxinus f ♦ adj fraxineus
ashamed adj: **I am** ~ pudet mē; ~ **of** pudet (+ acc of
person, + gen of thing)
ashen adj pallidus
ashes n cinis m
ashore adv (motion) in lītus; (rest) in lītore; **go**
~ ēgredī
Asia n Asia f
aside adv sēparatim, sē- (in cpd)
ask vt (question) rogāre, quaerere; (request) petere,
poscere; (beg, entreat) orāre; **ask for** vt petere;
rogāre; scīscitārī; percontārī
askance adv oblīquē; **look** ~ **at** līmīs oculīs
aspicere, invidēre (dat)
askew adv prāvē
aslant adv oblīquē
asleep adj sōpītus; **be** ~ dormīre; **fall**
~ obdormīre, somnum inīre
asp n aspis f
asparagus n asparagus m
aspect n (place) aspectus m; (person) vultus m;
(circumstances) status m; **have a southern** ~ ad
merīdiem spectāre; **there is another** ~ **to the**
matter aliter sē rēs habet
aspen n pōpulus f
asperity n acerbitās f
asperse vt maledīcere (dat), calumniārī
aspersion n calumnia f; **cast aspersions on**
calumniārī, īnfamiā aspergere
asphalt n bitūmen nt
asphyxia n strangulātiō f
asphyxiate vt strangulāre
aspirant n petītor m
aspirate n (GRAM) aspīrātiō f
aspiration n spēs f; (POL) ambitiō f
aspire vi: ~ **to** adfectāre, petere, spērāre,
contendere
ass n asinus m, asellus m; (fig) stultus
assail vt oppugnāre, adorīrī, aggredī
assailable adj expugnābilis
assailant n oppugnātor m
assassin n sīcārius m, percussor m
assassinate vt interficere, occīdere, iugulāre
assassination n caedēs f, parricīdium nt
assault vt oppugnāre, adorīrī, aggredī; (speech)
invehī in (acc) ♦ n impetus m, oppugnātiō f;
(personal) vīs f
assay vt (metal) spectāre; temptāre, cōnārī
assemble vt convocāre, congregāre, cōgere ♦ vi
convenīre, congregārī
assembly n coetus m, conventus m; (plebs)
concilium nt; (Roman people) comitia ntpl; (troops)
cōntiō f; (things) congeriēs f
assent vi adsentīrī, adnuere ♦ n adsēnsus m
assert vt adfirmāre, adsevērāre, dīcere
assertion n adfirmātiō f, adsevērātiō f, dictum
nt, sententia f
assess vt cēnsēre, aestimāre; ~ **damages** lītem
aestimāre
assessment n cēnsus m, aestimātiō f
assessor n cēnsor m; (assistant) cōnsessor m

assets n bona ntpl
assiduity n dīligentia f, sēdulitās f, industria f
assiduous adj dīligēns, sēdulus, industrius
assign vt tribuere, attribuere; (land) adsignāre;
(in writing) perscrībere; (task) dēlēgāre; (reason)
adferre
assignation n cōnstitūtum nt
assignment n adsignātiō f, perscrīptiō f; (task)
mūnus nt, pēnsum nt
assimilate vt aequāre; (food) concoquere;
(knowledge) concipere
assist vt adiuvāre, succurrere (dat), adesse (dat)
assistance n auxilium nt, opem (no nom) f; **come**
to the ~ **of** subvenīre (dat); **be of** ~ **to** auxiliō
esse (dat)
assistant n adiūtor m, minister m
assize n conventus m; **hold assizes** conventūs
agere
associate vt cōnsociāre, coniungere ♦ vi rem
inter sē cōnsociāre; ~ **with** familiāriter ūtī (abl)
♦ n socius m, sodālis m
association n societās f; (club) sodālitās f
assort vt dīgerere, dispōnere ♦ vi congruere
assortment n (of goods) variae mercēs fpl
assuage vt lēnīre, mītigāre, sēdāre
assume vt (for oneself) adsūmere, adrogāre;
(hypothesis) pōnere; (office) inīre
assumption n (hypothesis) sūmptiō f, positum nt
assurance n (given) fidēs f, pignus nt; (felt)
fidūcia f; (boldness) cōnfīdentia f
assure vt cōnfirmāre, prōmittere (dat)
assured adj (person) fidēns; (fact) explōrātus,
certus
assuredly adv certō, certē, profectō, sānē
astern adv ā puppī; (movement) retrō; ~ **of** post
asthma n anhēlitus m
astonish vt obstupefacere; attonāre
astonished adj attonitus, stupefactus; **be** ~ **at**
admīrārī
astonishing adj mīrificus, mīrus
astonishment n stupor m, admīrātiō f
astound vt obstupefacere
astray adj vagus; **go** ~ errāre, aberrāre, deerrāre
astride adj vāricus
astrologer n Chaldaeus m, mathēmaticus m
astrology n Chaldaeōrum dīvīnātiō f
astronomer n astrologus m
astronomy n astrologia f
astute adj callidus, vafer
astuteness n calliditās f
asunder adv sēparātim, dis- (in cpd)
asylum n asȳlum nt
at prep in (abl), ad (acc); (time) usu expressed by abl;
(towns, small islands) locative; **at the house of**
apud (acc); **at all events** saltem; see also **dawn**,
hand, **house** etc
atheism n deōs esse negāre
atheist n atheos m; **be an** ~ deōs esse negāre
Athenian adj Atheniensis
Athens n Athenae fpl; **at/from** ~ Athenīs; **to**
~ Athenās
athirst adj sitiēns; (fig) avidus
athlete n athlēta m
athletic adj rōbustus, lacertōsus
athletics n athlētica ntpl
athwart prep trāns (acc)

atlas *n* orbis terrārum dēscrīptiō *f*
atmosphere *n* āēr *m*
atom *n* atomus *f*, corpus indīviduum *nt*
atone *vi*: ~ **for** expiāre
atonement *n* expiātiō *f*, piāculum *nt*
atrocious *adj* immānis, nefārius, scelestus
atrociously *adv* nefāriē, scelestē
atrociousness *n* immānitās *f*
atrocity *n* nefas *nt*, scelus *nt*, flāgitium *nt*
atrophy *vi* marcēscere
attach *vt* adiungere, adfīgere, illigāre; (*word*)
  subicere; **attached to** amāns (*gen*)
attachment *n* vinculum *nt*; amor *m*, studium *nt*
attack *vt* oppugnāre, adorīrī, aggredī; impetum
  facere in (*acc*); (*speech*) īnsequī, invehī in
  (*acc*); (*disease*) ingruere in (*acc*) ♦ *n* impetus *m*,
  oppugnātiō *f*, incursus *m*
attacker *n* oppugnātor *m*
attain *vt* adsequī, adipīscī, cōnsequī; ~ **to**
  pervenīre ad
attainable *adj* impetrābilis, in prōmptū
attainder *n*: **bill of** ~ prīvilēgium *nt*
attainment *n* adeptiō *f*
attainments *npl* doctrīna *f*, ērudītiō *f*
attaint *vt* māiestātis condemnāre
attempt *vt* cōnārī, temptāre; (*with effort*) mōlīrī
  ♦ *n* cōnātus *m*, inceptum *nt*; (*risk*) perīculum *nt*;
  first attempts rudīmenta *ntpl*
attend *vt* (*meeting*) adesse (*dat*), interesse (*dat*);
  (*person*) prōsequī, comitārī; (*master*) appārēre
  (*dat*); (*invalid*) cūrāre ♦ *vi* animum advertere,
  animum attendere; ~ **to** (*task*) adcūrāre; ~ **upon**
  prōsequī, adsectārī; ~ **the lectures of** audīre;
  not ~ aliud agere; ~ **first to** praevertere (*dat*);
  well attended frequēns; **thinly attended**
  īnfrequēns
attendance *n* (*courtesy*) adsectātiō *f*; (*MED*)
  cūrātiō *f*; (*service*) appāritiō *f*; **constant**
  ~ adsiduitās *f*; **full** ~ frequentia *f*; **poor**
  ~ īnfrequentia *f*; **dance** ~ **on** haerēre (*dat*)
attendant *n* famulus *m*, minister *m*; (*on*
  candidate) sectātor *m*; (*on nobleman*) adsectātor *m*;
  (*on magistrate*) apparitor *m*
attention *n* animadversiō *f*, animī attentiō *f*;
  (*to work*) cūra *f*; (*respect*) observantia *f*; **attract**
  ~ digitō mōnstrārī; **call** ~ **to** indicāre; **pay** ~ **to**
  animadvertere, observāre; ratiōnem habēre
  (*gen*); **attention!** hōc age!
attentive *adj* intentus; (*to work*) dīligēns
attentively *adv* intentē, dīligenter
attenuate *vt* attenuāre
attest *vt* cōnfirmāre, testārī
attestation *n* testificātiō *f*
attestor *n* testis *m*
attic *n* cēnāculum *nt*
attire *vt* vestīre ♦ *n* vestis *f*, habitus *m*
attitude *n* (*body*) gestus *m*, status *m*, habitus *m*;
  (*mind*) ratiō *f*
attorney *n* āctor *m*; advocātus *m*
attract *vt* trahere, attrahere, adlicere
attraction *n* vīs attrahendī; illecebra *f*,
  invītāmentum *nt*
attractive *adj* suāvis, venustus, lepidus
attractively *adv* suāviter, vēnustē, lepidē
attractiveness *n* venustās *f*, lepōs *m*

attribute *vt* tribuere, attribuere, adsignāre ♦ *n*
  proprium *nt*
attrition *n* attrītus *m*
attune *vt* modulārī
auburn *adj* flāvus
auction *n* auctiō *f*; (*public*) hasta *f*; **hold an**
  ~ auctiōnem facere; **sell by** ~ sub hastā
  vēndere
auctioneer *n* praecō *m*
audacious *adj* audāx; protervus
audaciously *adv* audācter, protervē
audacity *n* audācia *f*, temeritās *f*
audible *adj*: **be** ~ exaudīrī posse
audibly *adv* clārā vōce
audience *n* audītōrēs *mpl*; (*interview*) aditus *m*;
  give an ~ **to** admittere
audit *vt* īnspicere ♦ *n* ratiōnum īnspectiō *f*
auditorium *n* cavea *f*
auditory *adj* audītōrius
auger *n* terebra *f*
augment *vt* augēre, adaugēre ♦ *vi* crēscere,
  augērī
augmentation *n* incrēmentum *nt*
augur *n* augur *m*; **augur's staff** lituus *m* ♦ *vi*
  augurārī; (*fig*) portendere
augural *adj* augurālis
augurship *n* augurātus *m*
augury *n* augurium *nt*, auspicium *nt*; ōmen
  nt; **take auguries** augurārī; **after taking**
  auguries augurātō
August *n* mēnsis Augustus, Sextīlis; **of**
  ~ Sextīlis
august *adj* augustus
aunt *n* (*paternal*) amita *f*; (*maternal*) mātertera *f*
auspices *n* auspicium *nt*; **take** ~ auspicārī;
  after taking ~ auspicātō; **without taking**
  ~ inauspicātō
auspicious *adj* faustus, fēlīx
auspiciously *adv* fēlīciter, prosperē
austere *adj* austērus, sevērus, dūrus
austerely *adv* sevērē
austerity *n* sevērītās *f*, dūritia *f*
authentic *adj* vērus, certus
authenticate *vt* recognōscere
authenticity *n* auctōritās *f*, fidēs *f*
author *n* auctor *m*, inventor *m*; scrīptor *m*
authoress *n* auctor *f*
authoritative *adj* fīdus; imperiōsus
authority *n* auctōritās *f*, potestās *f*, iūs *nt*; (*MIL*)
  imperium *nt*; (*LIT*) auctor *m*, scrīptor *m*; **enforce**
  ~ iūs suum exsequī; **have great** ~ multum
  pollēre; **on Caesar's** ~ auctōre Caesare; **an** ~ **on**
  perītus (*gen*)
authorize *vt* potestātem facere (*dat*), mandāre;
  (*LAW*) sancīre
autobiography *n* dē vītā suā scrīptus liber *m*
autocracy *n* imperium singulāre *nt*, tyrannis *f*
autocrat *n* tyrannus *m*, dominus *m*
autocratic *adj* imperiōsus
autograph *n* manus *f*, chīrographum *nt*
automatic *adj* necessārius
automatically *adv* necessāriō
autonomous *adj* līber
autonomy *n* lībertās *f*
autumn *n* auctumnus *m*
autumnal *adj* auctumnālis

auxiliaries *npl* auxilia *ntpl*, auxiliāriī *mpl*
auxiliary *adj* auxiliāris ◆ *n* adiūtor *m*; ~ **forces**
  auxilia *ntpl*; novae copiae *fpl*
avail *vi* valēre ◆ *vt* prōdesse (*dat*); ~ **oneself of** ūtī
  (*abl*) ◆ *n* ūsus *m*; **of no** ~ frustrā
available *adj* ad manum, in prōmptū
avalanche *n* montis ruīna *f*
avarice *n* avāritia *f*, cupīditās *f*
avaricious *adj* avārus, cupidus
avariciously *adv* avārē
avenge *vt* ulcīscī (*abl*), vindicāre
avenger *n* ultor *m*, vindex *m*
avenue *n* xystus *m*; (*fig*) aditus *m*, iānua *f*
aver *vt* adfirmāre, adsevērāre
average *n* medium *nt*; **on the** ~ ferē
averse *adj* āversus (*abl*); **be** ~ **to** abhorrēre ab
aversion *n* odium *nt*, fastīdium *nt*
avert *vt* arcēre, dēpellere; (*by prayer*) dēprecārī
aviary *n* aviārium *nt*
avid *adj* avidus
avidity *n* aviditās *f*
avidly *adv* avidē
avoid *vt* vītāre, fugere, dēclīnāre; (*battle*)
  dētrectāre
avoidance *n* fuga *f*, dēclīnātiō *f*
avow *vt* fatērī, cōnfitērī
avowal *n* cōnfessiō *f*
avowed *adj* apertus
avowedly *adv* apertē, palam
await *vt* exspectāre; (*future*) manēre

awake *vt* suscitāre, exsuscitare ◆ *vi* expergīscī
  ◆ *adj* vigil
awaken *vt* exsuscitāre
award *vt* tribuere; (LAW) adiūdicāre ◆ *n* (*decision*)
  arbitrium *nt*, iūdicium *nt*; (*thing*) praemium *nt*
aware *adj* gnārus; conscius (*gen*); **be** ~ scīre;
  become ~ **of** percipere
away *adv* ā-, ab- (*in cpd*); **be** ~ abesse ab (*abl*); **far**
  ~ procul, longē; **make** ~ **with** dē mediō tollere
awe *n* formīdō *f*, reverentia *f*, rēligiō *f*; **stand in**
  awe of verērī; (*gods*) venerārī
awe-struck *adj* stupidus
awful *adj* terribilis, formīdolōsus, dīrus
awfully *adv* formīdolōsē
awhile *adv* aliquamdiū, aliquantisper,
  parumper
awkward *adj* incallidus, inconcinnus; (*to handle*)
  inhabilis; (*fig*) molestus
awkwardly *adv* incallidē, imperītē
awkwardness *n* imperītia *f*, īnscītia *f*
awl *n* sūbula *f*
awning *n* vēlum *nt*
awry *adj* prāvus, dissidēns
axe *n* secūris *f*
axiom *n* prōnūntiātum *nt*, sententia *f*
axiomatic *adj* ēvidēns, manifestus
axis *n* axis *m*
axle *n* axis *m*
aye *adv* semper; **for aye** in aeternum
azure *adj* caeruleus

Bb

baa *vi* bālāre ♦ *n* bālātus *m*
babble *vi* garrīre, blaterāre
babbler *n* garrulus *m*
babbling *adj* garrulus
babe *n* īnfāns *m/f*
babel *n* dissonae vōcēs *fpl*
baboon *n* sīmia *f*
baby *n* īnfāns *m/f*
Bacchanalian *adj* Bacchicus
Bacchante *n* Baccha *f*
bachelor *n* caelebs *m*; (*degree*) baccalaureus *m*
back *n* tergum *nt*; (*animal*) dorsum *nt*; (*head*) occipitium *nt*; **at one's ~** ā tergō; **behind one's ~** (*fig*) clam (*acc*); **put one's ~ up** stomachum movēre (*dat*); **turn one's ~ on** sē āvertere ab ♦ *adj* āversus, postīcus ♦ *adv* retrō, retrōrsum, re- (*in cpd*) ♦ *vt* obsecundāre (*dat*), adesse (*dat*); **~ water** inhibēre rēmīs, inhibēre nāvem ♦ *vi*: **~ out of** dētrectāre, dēfugere
backbite *vt* obtrectāre (*dat*), maledīcere (*dat*)
backbone *n* spīna *f*
backdoor *n* postīcum *nt*
backer *n* fautor *m*
background *n* recessus *m*, umbra *f*
backing *n* fidēs *f*, favor *m*
backslide *vi* dēscīscere
backward *adj* āversus; (*slow*) tardus; (*late*) sērus
backwardness *n* tardītās *f*, pigritia *f*
backwards *adv* retrō, retrōrsum
bacon *n* lārdum *nt*
bad *adj* malus, prāvus, improbus, turpis; **go bad** corrumpī; **be bad for** obesse (*dat*), nocēre (*dat*)
badge *n* īnsigne *nt*, īnfula *f*
badger *n* mēles *f* ♦ *vt* sollicitāre
badly *adv* male, prāvē, improbē, turpiter
badness *n* prāvītās *f*, nēquitia *f*, improbitās *f*
baffle *vt* ēlūdere, fallere, frustrārī
bag *n* saccus *m*, folliculus *m*; **handbag** mantica *f*
bagatelle *n* nūgae *fpl*, floccus *m*
baggage *n* impedīmenta *ntpl*, vāsa *ntpl*, sarcinae *fpl*; **~ train** impedīmenta *ntpl*; **without ~** expedītus
bail *n* vadimōnium *nt*; (*person*) vas *m*; **become ~ for** spondēre prō (*abl*); **accept ~ for** vadārī; **keep one's ~** vadimōnium obīre ♦ *vt* spondēre prō (*abl*)
bailiff *n* (POL) apparitor *m*; (*private*) vīlicus *m*
bait *n* esca *f*, illecebra *f* ♦ *vt* lacessere
bake *vt* coquere, torrēre
bakehouse *n* pistrīna *f*
baker *n* pistor *m*
bakery *n* pistrīna *f*

balance *n* (*scales*) lībra *f*, trutina *f*; (*equilibrium*) lībrāmentum *nt*; (*money*) reliqua *ntpl* ♦ *vt* lībrāre; (*fig*) compēnsāre; **the account balances** ratiō cōnstat
balance sheet *n* ratiō acceptī et expēnsī
balcony *n* podium *nt*, Maeniānum *nt*
bald *adj* calvus; (*style*) āridus, iēiūnus
baldness *n* calvitium *nt*; (*style*) iēiūnitās *f*
bale *n* fascis *m*; **~ out** *vt* exhaurīre
baleful *adj* fūnestus, perniciōsus, tristis
balk *n* tignum *nt* ♦ *vt* frustrārī, dēcipere
ball *n* globus *m*; (*play*) pila *f*; (*wool*) glomus *nt*; (*dance*) saltātiō *f*
ballad *n* carmen *nt*
ballast *n* saburra *f*
ballet *n* saltātiō *f*
ballot *n* suffrāgium *nt*
ballot box urna *f*
balm *n* unguentum *nt*; (*fig*) sōlātium *nt*
balmy *adj* lēnis, suāvis
balsam *n* balsamum *nt*
balustrade *n* cancellī *mpl*
bamboozle *vt* cōnfundere
ban *vt* interdīcere (*dat*), vetāre ♦ *n* interdictum *nt*
banal *adj* trītus
banana *n* ariēna *f*; (*tree*) pāla *f*
band *n* vinculum *nt*, redimīculum *nt*; (*head*) īnfula *f*; (*men*) caterva *f*, manus *f*, grex *m* ♦ *vi*: **~ together** cōnsociārī
bandage *n* fascia *f*, īnfula *f* ♦ *vt* obligāre, adligāre
bandbox *n*: **out of a ~** (*fig*) dē capsulā
bandeau *n* redimīculum *nt*
bandit *n* latrō *m*
bandy *vt* iactāre; **~ words** altercārī ♦ *adj* vārus
bane *n* venēnum *nt*, pestis *f*, perniciēs *f*
baneful *adj* perniciōsus, pestifer
bang *vt* pulsāre ♦ *n* fragor *m*
bangle *n* armilla *f*
banish *vt* pellere, expellere, ēicere; (LAW) aquā et ignī interdīcere (*dat*); (*temporarily*) relēgāre; (*feeling*) abstergēre
banishment *n* (*act*) aquae et ignis interdictiō *f*; relēgātiō *f*; (*state*) exsilium *nt*, fuga *f*
bank *n* (*earth*) agger *m*; (*river*) rīpa *f*; (*money*) argentāria *f*
banker *n* argentārius *m*; (*public*) mēnsārius *m*
bankrupt *adj*: **be ~** solvendō nōn esse; **declare oneself ~** bonam cōpiam ēiūrāre; **go ~** dēcoquere ♦ *n* dēcoctor *m*
banner *n* vexillum *nt*

banquet n cēna f, epulae fpl; convīvium nt; (religious) daps f ♦ vi epulārī
banter n cavillātiō f ♦ vi cavillārī
baptism n baptisma nt
baptize vt baptizāre
bar n (door) sera f; (gate) claustrum nt; (metal) later m; (wood) asser m; (lever) vectis m; (obstacle) impedīmentum nt; (law-court) cancellī mpl; (barristers) advocātī mpl; (profession) forum nt; **of the bar** forēnsis; **practise at the bar** causās agere ♦ vt (door) obserāre; (way) obstāre (dat), interclūdere, prohibēre; (exception) excipere, exclūdere
barb n aculeus m, dēns m, hāmus m
barbarian n barbarus m ♦ adj barbarus
barbarism n barbaria f
barbarity n saevitia f, ferōcia f, immānitās f, inhūmānitās f
barbarous adj barbarus, saevus, immānis, inhūmānus
barbarously adv barbarē, inhūmānē
barbed adj hāmātus
barber n tōnsor m; **barber's shop** tōnstrīna f
bard n vātēs m/f; (Gallic) bardus m
bare adj nūdus; (mere) merus; **lay ~** nūdāre, aperīre, dētegere ♦ vt nūdāre
barefaced adj impudēns
barefoot adj nūdis pedibus
bare-headed adj capite aperto
barely adv vix
bargain n pactum nt, foedus nt; **make a ~** pacīscī; **make a bad ~** male emere; **into the ~** grātiīs ♦ vi pacīscī
barge n linter f
bark n cortex m; (dog) lātrātus m; (ship) nāvis f, ratis f ♦ vi lātrāre
barking n latratus m
barley n hordeum f; **of ~** hordeāceus
barn n horreum nt
barrack vt obstrepere (dat)
barracks n castra ntpl
barrel n cūpa f; ligneum vās nt
barren adj sterilis
barrenness n sterilitās f
barricade n claustrum nt, mūnīmentum nt ♦ vt obsaepīre, obstruere; **~ off** intersaepīre
barrier n impedīmentum nt, claustra ntpl; (racecourse) carcer nt
barrister n advocātus m, patrōnus m, causidicus m
barrow n ferculum nt; (mound) tumulus m
barter vt mūtāre ♦ vi mercēs mūtāre ♦ n mūtātiō f, commercium nt
base adj turpis, vīlis; (birth) humilis, ignōbilis; (coin) adulterīnus ♦ n fundāmentum nt; (statue) basis f; (hill) rādīcēs fpl; (MIL) castra ntpl
baseless adj falsus, inānis
basely adv turpiter
basement n basis f; (storey) īmum tabulātum nt
baseness n turpitūdō f
bashful adj pudīcus, verēcundus
bashfully adv verēcundē
bashfulness n pudor m, verēcundia f
basic adj prīmus
basin n alveolus m, pelvis f; **washbasin** aquālis m

basis n fundāmentum nt
bask vi aprīcārī
basket n corbis f, fiscus m; (for bread) canistrum nt; (for wool) quasillum nt
basking n aprīcātiō f
bas-relief n toreuma nt
bass adj (voice) gravis
bastard adj nothus
bastion n prōpugnāculum nt
bat n vespertīliō m; (games) clāva f
batch n numerus m
Bath n Aquae Sulis fpl
bath n balneum nt; (utensil) lābrum nt, lavātiō f; **Turkish ~** Lacōnicum nt; **cold ~** frīgidārium nt; **hot ~** calidārium nt; **~ superintendent** balneātor m ♦ vt lavāre
bathe vt lavāre ♦ vi lavārī, perluī
bathroom n balneāria ntpl
baths n (public baths) balneae fpl
batman n cālō m
baton n virga f, scīpiō m
battalion n cohors f
batter vt quassāre, pulsāre, verberāre
battering ram n ariēs m
battery n (assault) vīs f
battle n pugna f, proelium nt, certāmen nt; **a ~ was fought** pugnatum est; **pitched ~** iūstum proelium; **line of ~** aciēs f; **drawn ~** anceps proelium ♦ vi pugnāre, contendere; **~ order** aciēs f
battle-axe n bipennis f
battlefield, battle-line n aciēs f
battlement n pinna f
bawl vt vōciferārī, clāmitāre
bay n (sea) sinus m; (tree) laurus f, laurea f; **of bay** laureus; **at bay** interclūsus ♦ adj (colour) spādīx ♦ vi (dog) lātrāre
be vi esse; (circumstances) versārī; (condition) sē habēre; **be at** adesse (dat); **be amongst** interesse (dat); **be in** inesse (dat); **consul-to-be** cōnsul dēsignātus; **how are you?** quid agis?; **so be it** estō; see also **absent, here** etc
beach n lītus nt, acta f ♦ vt (ship) subdūcere
beacon n ignis m
bead n pilula f
beadle n apparitor m
beak n rōstrum nt
beaked adj rōstrātus
beaker n cantharus m, scyphus m
beam n (wood) trabs f, tignum nt; (balance) iugum nt; (light) radius m; (ship) latus nt; **on the ~** ā latere ♦ vi fulgēre; (person) adrīdēre
beaming adj hilaris
bean n faba f
bear n ursus m, ursa f; **Great Bear** septentriōnēs mpl, Arctos f; **Little Bear** septentriō minor m, Cynosūra f; **bear's** ursīnus ♦ vt (carry) ferre, portāre; (endure) ferre, tolerāre, patī; (produce) ferre, fundere; (child) parere; **~ down upon** appropinquāre; **~ off** ferre; **~ out** vt arguere; **~ up** vi: **~ up under** obsistere (dat), sustinēre; **~ upon** innītī (dat); (refer) pertinēre ad; **~ with** vt indulgēre (dat); **~ oneself** sē gerere; **I cannot ~ to** addūcī nōn possum ut
bearable adj tolerābilis
beard n barba f ♦ vt ultrō lacessere

bearded *adj* barbātus
beardless *adj* imberbis
bearer *n* bāiulus *m*; (*letter*) tabellārius *m*; (*litter*) lectīcārius *m*; (*news*) nūntius *m*
bearing *n* (*person*) gestus *m*, vultus *m*; (*direction*) regiō *f*; **have no ~ on** nihil pertinēre ad; **I have lost my bearings** ubi sim nesciō
beast *n* bestia *f*; (*large*) bēlua *f*; (*wild*) fera *f*; (*domestic*) pecus *f*
beastliness *n* foedītās *f*, stuprum *nt*
beastly *adj* foedus
beast of burden *n* iūmentum *nt*
beat *n* ictus *m*; (*heart*) palpitātiō *f*; (*music*) percussiō *f*; (*oars, pulse*) pulsus *m* ♦ *vt* ferīre, percutere, pulsāre; (*the body in grief*) plangere; (*punish*) caedere; (*whip*) verberāre; (*conquer*) vincere, superāre ♦ *vi* palpitāre, micāre; **~ back** repellere; **~ in** perfringere; **~ out** excutere; (*metal*) extundere; **~ a retreat** receptui canere; **~ about the bush** circuitiōne ūtī; **be beaten** vāpulāre; **dead ~** cōnfectus
beating *n* verbera *ntpl*; (*defeat*) clādes *f*; (*time*) percussiō *f*; **get a ~** vāpulāre
beatitude *n* beātitūdō *f*, fēlīcitās *f*
beau *n* nitidus homō *m*; (*lover*) amāns *m*
beauteous *adj* pulcher, fōrmōsus
beautiful *adj* pulcher, formōsus; (*looks*) decōrus; (*scenery*) amoenus
beautifully *adv* pulchrē
beautify *vt* exōrnāre, decorāre
beauty *n* fōrma *f*, pulchritūdō *f*, amoenitās *f*
beaver *n* castor *m*, fiber *m*; (*helmet*) buccula *f*
becalmed *adj* ventō dēstitūtus
because *conj* quod, quia, quōniam (+ *indic*), quippe quī; **~ of** propter (*acc*)
beck *n* nūtus *m*
beckon *vt* innuere, vocāre
become *vi* fierī; **what will ~ of me?** quid me fīet? ♦ *vt* decēre, convenīre in (*acc*)
becoming *adj* decēns, decōrus
becomingly *adv* decōrē, convenienter
bed *n* cubīle *nt*, lectus *m*, lectulus *m*; **go to bed** cubitum īre; **make a bed** lectum sternere; **be bedridden** lectō tenērī; **camp bed** grabātus *m*; **flowerbed** pulvīnus *m*; **marriage bed** lectus geniālis *m*; **riverbed** alveus *m*
bedaub *vt* illinere, oblinere
bedclothes *n* strāgula *ntpl*
bedding *n* strāgula *ntpl*
bedeck *vt* ōrnāre, exōrnāre
bedew *vt* inrōrāre
bedim *vt* obscūrāre
bedpost *n* fulcrum *nt*
bedraggled *adj* sordidus, madidus
bedroom *n* cubiculum *nt*
bedstead *n* sponda *f*
bee *n* apis *f*; **queen bee** rēx *m*
beech *n* fāgus *f* ♦ *adj* fāginus
beef *n* būbula *f*
beehive *n* alvus *f*
beekeeper *n* apiārius *m*
beer *n* cervīsia *f*, fermentum *nt*
beet *n* bēta *f*
beetle *n* (*insect*) scarabaeus *m*; (*implement*) fistūca *f*
beetling *adj* imminēns, mināx

befall *vi, vt* accidere, ēvenīre (*dat*); (*good*) contingere (*dat*)
befit *vt* decēre, convenīre in (*acc*)
before *adv* ante, anteā, antehāc ♦ *prep* ante (*acc*); (*place*) prō (*abl*); (*presence*) apud (*acc*), cōram (*abl*) ♦ *conj* antequam, priusquam
beforehand *adv* ante, anteā; prae (*in cpd*)
befoul *vt* inquināre, foedāre
befriend *vt* favēre (*dat*), adiuvāre; (*in trouble*) adesse (*dat*)
beg *vt* ōrāre, obsecrāre, precārī, poscere ab, petere ab; **beg for** petere ♦ *vi* mendīcāre
beget *vt* gignere, prōcreāre, generāre
begetter *n* generātor *m*, creātor *m*
beggar *n* mendīcus *m*
beggarly *adj* mendīcus, indigēns
beggary *n* mendīcitās *f*, indigentia *f*
begin *vt, vi* incipere, coepisse; (*speech*) exōrdīrī; (*plan*) īnstituere, incohāre; (*time*) inīre; **~ with** incipere ab
beginning *n* initium *nt*, prīncipium *nt*, exōrdium *nt*, inceptiō *f*; (*learning*) rudīmenta *ntpl*, elementa *ntpl*; (*origin*) orīgō *f*, fōns *m*; **at the ~ of spring** ineunte vēre
begone *interj* apage, tē āmovē
begotten *adj* genitus, nātus
begrudge *vt* invidēre (*dat*)
beguile *vt* dēcipere, fallere
behalf *n*: **on ~ of** prō (*abl*); **on my ~** meō nōmine
behave *vi* sē gerere, sē praebēre (*with adj*); **well behaved** bene mōrātus
behaviour *n* mōrēs *mpl*
behead *vt* dētruncāre, secūrī percutere
behest *n* iūssum *nt*
behind *adv* pōne, post, ā tergō ♦ *prep* post (*acc*), pōne (*acc*)
behindhand *adv* sērō; **be ~** parum prōficere
behold *vt* aspicere, cōnspicere, intuērī ♦ *interj* ecce, ēn
beholden *adj* obnoxius, obstrictus, obligātus
behoof *n* ūsus *m*
behove *vt* oportēre
being *n* (*life*) animātiō *f*; (*nature*) nātūra *f*; (*person*) homō *m/f*
bejewelled *adj* gemmeus, gemmātus
belabour *vt* verberāre, caedere
belated *adj* sērus
belch *vi* ructāre, ēructāre
beldam *n* anus *f*
beleaguer *vt* obsidēre, circumsedēre
belie *vt* abhorrēre ab, repugnāre
belief *n* fidēs *f*, opīniō *f*; (*opinion*) sententia *f*; **to the best of my ~** ex animī meī sententiā; **past ~** incrēdibilis
believe *vt, vi* (*thing*) crēdere; (*person*) crēdere (*dat*); (*suppose*) crēdere, putāre, arbitrārī, opīnārī; **~ in gods** deōs esse crēdere; **make ~** simulāre
believer *n* deōrum cultor *m*; Christiānus *m*
belike *adv* fortasse
belittle *vt* obtrectāre
bell *n* tintinnābulum *nt*; (*public*) campāna *f*
belle *n* fōrmōsa *f*, pulchra *f*
belles-lettres *n* litterae *fpl*
bellicose *adj* ferōx
belligerent *adj* bellī particeps
bellow *vi* rūdere, mūgīre ♦ *n* mūgītus *m*

bellows n follis m
belly n abdōmen nt, venter m; (sail) sinus m ♦ vi tumēre
belong vi esse (gen), proprium esse (gen), inesse (dat); (concern) attinēre, pertinēre
belongings n bona ntpl
beloved adj cārus, dīlectus, grātus
below adv īnfrā, subter ♦ adj īnferus ♦ prep īnfrā (acc), sub (abl, acc)
belt n zōna f; (sword) balteus m
bemoan vt dēplōrāre, lāmentārī
bemused adj stupefactus, stupidus
bench n subsellium nt; (rowing) trānstrum nt; (LAW) iūdicēs mpl; **seat on the ~** iūdicātus m
bend vt flectere, curvāre, inclīnāre; (bow) intendere; (course) tendere, flectere; (mind) intendere ♦ vi sē īnflectere; (person) sē dēmittere; **~ back** reflectere; **~ down** vi dēflectere; sē dēmittere ♦ n flexus m, ānfrāctus m
beneath adv subter ♦ prep sub (acc or abl)
benediction n bonae precēs fpl
benedictory adj faustus
benefaction n beneficium nt, dōnum nt
benefactor n patrōnus m; **be a ~** bene merērī (dē)
beneficence n beneficentia f, līberālitās f
beneficent adj beneficus
beneficial adj ūtilis, salūbris
benefit n beneficium nt; (derived) fructus m; **have the ~ of** fruī (abl) ♦ vt prōdesse (dat), usuī esse (dat)
benevolence n benevolentia f, benignitās f
benevolent adj benevolus, benignus
benevolently adv benevolē, benignē
benighted adj nocte oppressus; (fig) ignārus, indoctus
benign adj benignus, cōmis
bent n (mind) inclīnātiō f, ingenium nt ♦ adj curvus, flexus; (mind) attentus; **be ~ on** studēre (dat)
benumb vt stupefacere
benumbed adj stupefactus, torpidus; **be ~** torpēre
bequeath vt lēgāre
bequest n lēgātum nt
bereave vt orbāre, prīvāre
bereavement n damnum nt
bereft adj orbus, orbātus, prīvātus
berry n bāca f
berth n statiō f; **give a wide ~ to** dēvītāre
beryl n bēryllus m
beseech vt implōrāre, ōrāre, obsecrāre
beset vt obsidēre, circumsedēre
beside prep ad (acc), apud (acc); (close) iuxtā (acc); **~ the point** nihil ad rem; **be ~ oneself** nōn esse apud sē
besides adv praetereā, accēdit quod; (in addition) īnsuper ♦ prep praeter (acc)
besiege vt obsidēre, circumsedēre
besieger n obsessor m
besmear vt illinere
besmirch vt maculāre
besom n scōpae fpl
besotted adj stupidus
bespatter vt aspergere

bespeak vt (order) imperāre; (denote) significāre
besprinkle vt aspergere
best adj optimus; **the ~ part** māior pars ♦ n flōs m, rōbur nt; **do one's ~** prō virīlī parte agere; **do one's ~ to** operam dare ut; **have the ~ of it** vincere; **make the ~ of** (a situation) aequō animō accipere; **to the ~ of one's ability** prō virīlī parte; **to the ~ of my knowledge** quod sciam ♦ adv optimē
bestial adj foedus
bestir vt movēre; **~ oneself** expergīscī
bestow vt dōnāre, tribuere, dare, cōnferre
bestride vt (horse) sedēre in (abl)
bet n pignus nt ♦ vt oppōnere ♦ vi pignore contendere
betake vt cōnferre, recipere; **~ oneself** sē cōnferre
bethink vt: **~ oneself** sē colligere; **~ oneself of** respicere
betide vi accidere, ēvenīre
betoken vt significāre; (foretell) portendere
betray vt prōdere, trādere; (feelings) arguere; **without betraying one's trust** salvā fidē
betrayal n prōditiō f
betrayer n prōditor m; (informer) index m
betroth vt spondēre, dēspondēre
betrothal n spōnsālia ntpl
better adj melior; **it is ~ to** praestat (inf); **get the ~ of** vincere, superāre; **I am ~** (in health) melius est mihī; **I had ~ go** praestat īre; **get ~** convalēscere; **think ~ of** sententiam mūtāre dē ♦ adv melius ♦ vt corrigere; **~ oneself** prōficere
betterment n prōfectus m
between prep inter (acc)
beverage n pōtiō f
bevy n manus f, grex f
bewail vt dēflēre, lāmentārī, dēplōrāre
beware vt cavēre
bewilder vt cōnfundere, perturbāre
bewildered adj attonitus
bewilderment n perturbātiō f, admīrātiō f
bewitch vt fascināre; (fig) dēlēnīre
beyond adv ultrā, suprā ♦ prep ultrā (acc), extrā (acc); (motion) trāns (acc); (amount) ultrā, suprā (acc); **go/pass ~** excēdere, ēgredī
bezel n pāla f
bias n inclīnātiō f; (party) favor m ♦ vt inclīnāre
biassed adj prōpēnsior
bibber n pōtor m, pōtātor m
Bible n litterae sacrae fpl
bibulous adj bibulus
bicephalous adj biceps
bicker vi altercārī, iūrgāre
bid vt iubēre; (guest) vocāre, invītāre ♦ vi (at auction) licērī; **bid for** licērī; **bid good day** salvēre iubēre; **he bids fair to make progress** spēs est eum prōfecturum esse
biddable adj docilis
bidding n iussum nt; (auction) licitātiō f
bide vt manēre, opperīrī
biennial adj biennālis
bier n ferculum nt
bifurcate vi sē scindere
bifurcation n (road) trivium nt

big *adj* mägnus, grandis, amplus; *(with child)*
gravida; **very big** permägnus; **talk big** glöriärī
bight *n* sinus *m*
bigness *n* mägnitüdö *f*, amplitüdö *f*
bigot *n* nimis obstinätus fautor *m*
bigoted *adj* contumäx
bigotry *n* contumäcia *f*, nimia obstinätio *f*
bile *n* bīlis *f*, fel *nt*
bilgewater *n* sentina *f*
bilk *vt* fraudäre
bill *n* *(bird)* röstrum *nt*; *(implement)* falx *f*; *(LAW)*
rogätiö *f*, lēx *f*; *(money)* syngrapha *f*; *(notice)*
libellus *m*, titulus *m*; **introduce a ~** populum
rogäre, lēgem ferre; **carry a ~** lēgem perferre
billet *n* hospitium *nt* ♦ *vt* in hospitia dīvidere
billhook *n* falx *f*
billow *n* fluctus *m*
billowy *adj* undösus
billy goat *n* caper *m*
bin *n* lacus *m*
bind *vt* adligäre, dēligäre, vincīre; *(by oath)*
adigere; *(by obligation)* obligäre, obstringere;
(wound) obligäre; **~ fast** dēvincīre; **~ together**
conligäre; **~ over** *vt* vadärī
binding *n* compägēs *f* ♦ *adj* *(LAW)* ratus; **it is ~ on**
oportet
bindweed *n* convolvulus *m*
biographer *n* vītae närrätor *m*
biography *n* vīta *f*
bipartite *adj* bipartītus
biped *n* bipēs *m*
birch *n* bētula *f*; *(flogging)* virgae ulmeae *fpl*
bird *n* avis *f*; **birds of a feather** parēs cum
paribus facillimē congregantur; **kill two birds
with one stone** ūnö saltū duös aprös capere,
dē eädem fidēliä duös parietēs dealbäre;
bird's-eye view of dēspectus in *(acc)*
birdcatcher *n* auceps *m*
birdlime *n* viscum *nt*
birth *n* *(act)* partus *m*; *(origin)* genus *nt*; **low
~** ignöbilitäs *f*; **high ~** nöbilitäs *f*; **by ~** nätü,
ortü
birthday *n* nätälis *m*
birthday party *n* nätälicia *ntpl*
birthplace *n* locus nätälis *m*; *(fig)* incünäbula
ntpl
birthright *n* patrimönium *nt*
bisect *vt* dīvidere
bishop *n* epīscopus *m*
bison *n* ürus *m*
bit *n* pars *f*; *(food)* frustum *nt*; *(broken off)*
fragmentum *nt*; *(horse)* frēnum *nt*; **bit by bit**
minütätim; **a bit** *adv* aliquantulum; **a bit sad**
tristior
bitch *n* *(dog)* canis *f*
bite *vt* mordēre; *(frost)* ürere ♦ *n* morsus *m*; **with
a ~** mordicus
biting *adj* mordäx
bitter *adj* *(taste)* acerbus, amärus; *(words)* asper
bitterly *adv* acerbē, asperē
bittern *n* bütiö *m*, ardea *f*
bitterness *n* acerbitäs *f*
bitumen *n* bitümen *nt*
bivouac *n* excubiae *fpl* ♦ *vi* excubäre
bizarre *adj* īnsolēns
blab *vt*, *vi* garrīre, effütīre

black *adj* *(dull)* äter; *(glossy)* niger; *(dirt)* sordidus;
(eye) līvidus; *(looks)* trux; **~ and blue** līvidus ♦ *n*
ätrum *nt*, nigrum *nt*; **dressed in ~** äträtus; *(in
mourning)* sordidätus
blackberry *n* mörum *nt*
blackbird *n* merula *f*
blacken *vt* nigräre, nigrum reddere; *(character)*
īnfämäre, obtrectäre *(dat)*
blackguard *n* scelestus, scelerätus *m*
blacking *n* äträmentum *nt*
blacklist *n* pröscrīptiö *f*
black magic *n* magicae artēs *fpl*
blackmail *n* minae *fpl* ♦ *vt* minīs cögere
black mark *n* nota *f*
blacksmith *n* faber *m*
bladder *n* vēsīca *f*
blade *n* *(grass)* herba *f*; *(oar)* palma *f*; *(sword)*
lämina *f*
blame *vt* reprehendere, culpäre; **I am to ~** reus
sum ♦ *n* reprehēnsiö *f*, culpa *f*
blameless *adj* innocēns
blamelessly *adv* innocenter
blamelessness *n* innocentia *f*, integritäs *f*
blameworthy *adj* accüsäbilis, nocēns
blanch *vi* exalbēscere, pallēscere
bland *adj* mītis, lēnis
blandishment *n* blanditiae *fpl*
blank *adj* vacuus, pürus; *(look)* stolidus
blanket *n* lödīx *f*; **wet ~** nimium sevērus
blare *vi* canere, strīdere ♦ *n* clangor *m*, strīdor *m*
blarney *n* lēnöcinium *nt*
blaspheme *vi* maledīcere
blasphemous *adj* maledicus, impius
blasphemy *n* maledicta *ntpl*, impietäs *f*
blast *n* flätus *m*, īnflätus *m* ♦ *vt* disicere,
discutere; *(crops)* röbīgine adficere
blatant *adj* raucus
blaze *n* flamma *f*, ignis *m*, fulgor *m* ♦ *vi* flägräre,
ärdēre, fulgēre; **~ up** exärdēscere ♦ *vt*: **~ abroad**
pervulgäre
blazon *vt* promulgäre
bleach *vt* candidum reddere
bleak *adj* dēsertus, tristis, inamoenus
bleary-eyed *adj* lippus
bleat *vi* bäläre ♦ *n* bälätus *m*
bleed *vi* sanguinem fundere ♦ *vt* sanguinem
mittere *(dat)*; **my heart bleeds** animus mihī
dolet
bleeding *adj* crüdus, sanguineus ♦ *n* sanguinis
missiö *f*
blemish *n* macula *f*, vitium *nt* ♦ *vt* maculäre,
foedäre
blend *vt* miscēre, immiscēre, admiscēre ♦ *n*
coniünctiö *f*
bless *vt* beäre; laudäre; *(ECCL)* benedīcere; **~ with**
augēre *(abl)*; **~ my soul!** ita mē dī ament!
blessed *adj* beätus, fortünätus; *(emperors)* dīvus
blessing *n* *(thing)* commodum *nt*, bonum *nt*;
(ECCL) benedīctiö *f*
blight *n* röbīgö *f*, ürēdö *f* ♦ *vt* röbīgine adficere;
(fig) nocēre *(dat)*
blind *adj* caecus; *(in one eye)* luscus; *(fig)* ignärus,
stultus; *(alley)* nön pervius; *(forces)* necessärius;
turn a ~ eye to cönīvēre in *(abl)* ♦ *vt* excaecäre,
caecäre; *(fig)* occaecäre; *(with light)* praestringere
blindfold *adj* capite obvolütö

blindly *adv* temerē

blindness *n* caecitās *f*; (*fig*) temeritās *f*, īnsipientia *f*

blink *vi* nictāre

bliss *n* fēlīcitās *f*, laetitia *f*

blissful *adj* fēlīx, beātus, laetus

blissfully *adv* fēlīciter, beātē

blister *n* pustula *f*

blithe *adj* hilaris, laetus

blithely *adv* hilare, laetē

blizzard *n* hiems *f*

bloated *adj* tumidus, turgidus

blob *n* gutta *f*, particula *f*

block *n* (*wood*) stīpes *m*, caudex *m*; (*stone*) massa *f*; (*houses*) īnsula *f*; ~ **letter** quadrāta littera; **stumbling** ~ offēnsiō *f* ♦ *vt* claudere, obstruere, interclūdere; ~ **the way** obstāre

blockade *n* obsidiō *f*; **raise a** ~ obsidiōnem solvere ♦ *vt* obsidēre, interclūdere

blockhead *n* caudex *m*, bārō *m*, truncus *m*

blockhouse *n* castellum *nt*

blond *adj* flāvus

blood *n* sanguis *m*; (*shed*) cruor *m*; (*murder*) caedēs *f*; (*kin*) genus *nt*; **let** ~ sanguinem mittere; **staunch** ~ sanguinem supprimere; **bad** ~ simultās *f*; **in cold** ~ cōnsultō; **own flesh and** ~ cōnsanguineus

bloodless *adj* exsanguis; (*victory*) incruentus

bloodshed *n* caedēs *f*

bloodshot *adj* sanguineus

bloodstained *adj* cruentus

bloodsucker *n* hirūdō *f*

bloodthirsty *adj* sanguinārius

blood vessel *n* vēna *f*

bloody *adj* cruentus

bloom *n* flōs *m*; **in** ~ flōrēns ♦ *vi* flōrēre, flōrēscere, vigēre

blooming *adj* flōrēns, flōridus

blossom *n* flōs *m* ♦ *vi* efflōrēscere, flōrēre

blot *n* macula *f*; (*erasure*) litūra *f* ♦ *vt* maculāre; ~ **out** dēlēre, oblitterāre

blotch *n* macula *f*

blotched *adj* maculōsus

blow *vt*, *vi* (*wind*) flāre; (*breath*) adflāre, anhēlāre; (*instrument*) canere; (*flower*) efflōrēscere; (*nose*) ēmungere; ~ **out** *vi* exstinguere; ~ **over** *vi* (*storm*) cadere; (*fig*) abīre; ~ **up** *vt* īnflāre; (*destroy*) discutere, disturbāre ♦ *n* ictus *m*; (*on the cheek*) alapa *f*; (*fig*) plāga *f*; (*misfortune*) calamitās *f*; **aim a** ~ **at** petere; **come to blows** ad manūs venīre

blowy *adj* ventōsus

bludgeon *n* fustis *m*

blue *adj* caeruleus; **black and** ~ līvidus; **true** ~ fīdissimus; ~ **blood** nōbilitās *f*

bluff *n* rūpēs *f*, prōmontōrium *nt* ♦ *adj* inurbānus ♦ *vt* fallere, dēcipere, verba dare (*dat*), impōnere (*dat*)

blunder *vi* errāre, offendere ♦ *n* error *m*, errātum *nt*; (*in writing*) mendum *nt*

blunt *adj* hebes; (*manners*) horridus, rūsticus, inurbānus; **be** ~ hebēre ♦ *vt* hebetāre, obtundere, retundere

bluntly *adv* līberius, plānē et apertē

blur *n* macula *f* ♦ *vt* obscūrāre

blurt *vt*: ~ **out** ēmittere

blush *vi* rubēre, ērubēscere ♦ *n* rubor *m*

bluster *vi* dēclāmitāre, lātrāre

boa *n* boa *f*

Boadicea *n* Boudicca *f*

boar *n* verrēs *m*; (*wild*) aper *m*

board *n* tabula *f*; (*table*) mēnsa *f*; (*food*) vīctus *m*; (*committee*) concilium *nt*; (*judicial*) quaestiō *f*; (*of ten men*) decemvirī *mpl*; (*gaming*) abacus *m*, alveus *m*; **on** ~ in nāvī; **go on** ~ in nāvem cōnscendere; **go by the** ~ intercidere, perīre; **above** ~ sine fraude ♦ *vt* (*building*) contabulāre; (*ship*) cōnscendere; (*person*) vīctum praebēre (*dat*) ♦ *vi*: ~ **with** dēvertere ad

boarder *n* hospes *m*

boast *vi* glōriārī, sē iactāre; ~ **of** glōriārī dē (*abl*) ♦ *n* glōria *f*, glōriātiō *f*, iactātiō *f*

boastful *adj* glōriōsus

boastfully *adv* glōriōsē

boasting *n* glōriātiō *f* ♦ *adj* glōriōsus

boat *n* linter *f*, scapha *f*, cymba *f*; (*ship*) nāvis *f*; **be in the same** ~ (*fig*) in eādem nāvī esse

boatman *n* nauta *m*

boatswain *n* hortātor *m*

bobbin *n* fūsus *m*

bode *vt* portendere, praesāgīre

bodiless *adj* sine corpore

bodily *adj* corporeus

bodkin *n* acus *f*

body *n* corpus *nt*; (*dead*) cadāver *nt*; (*small*) corpusculum *nt*; (*person*) homō *m/f*; (*of people*) globus *m*, numerus *m*; (*of troops*) manus *f*, caterva *f*; (*of cavalry*) turma *f*; (*of officials*) collēgium *nt*; (*heavenly*) astrum *nt*; **in a** ~ ūniversī, frequentēs

bodyguard *n* custōs *m*, stīpātōrēs *mpl*; (*emperor's*) praetōriānī *mpl*

bog *n* palūs *f*

bogey *n* mōnstrum *nt*

boggle *vi* tergiversārī, haesitāre

boggy *adj* palūster

bogus *adj* falsus, fictus

Bohemian *adj* līberior, solūtior, libīdinōsus

boil *vt* coquere; (*liquid*) fervefacere; ~ **down** dēcoquere ♦ *vi* fervēre, effervēscere; (*sea*) exaestuāre; (*passion*) exārdēscere, aestuāre; ~ **over** effervēscere ♦ *n* (MED) fūrunculus *m*

boiler *n* cortīna *f*

boiling *adj* (*hot*) fervēns

boisterous *adj* (*person*) turbulentus, vehemēns; (*sea*) turbidus, agitātus; (*weather*) procellōsus, violentus

boisterously *adv* turbidē, turbulentē

boisterousness *n* tumultus *m*, violentia *f*

bold *adj* audāx, fortis, intrepidus; (*impudent*) impudēns, protervus; (*language*) līber; (*headland*) prōminēns; **make** ~ audēre

boldly *adv* audācter, fortiter, intrepidē; impudenter

boldness *n* audācia *f*, cōnfīdentia *f*; impudentia *f*, petulantia *f*; (*speech*) lībertās *f*

bolster *n* pulvīnus *m* ♦ *vt*: ~ **up** sustinēre, cōnfirmāre

bolt *n* (*door*) claustrum *nt*, pessulus *m*, sera *f*; (*missile*) tēlum *nt*, sagitta *f*; (*lightning*) fulmen *nt*; **make a** ~ **for it** sē prōripere, aufugere; **a** ~ **from the blue** rēs subita, rēs inopīnāta ♦ *vt* (*door*) obserāre, obdere

bombard vt tormentīs verberāre; (fig) lacessere
bombast n ampullae fpl
bombastic adj tumidus, īnflātus; **be ~** ampullārī
bond n vinculum nt, catēna f, compes f; (of union) cōpula f, iugum nt, nōdus m; (document) syngrapha f; (agreement) foedus nt ♦ adj servus, addictus
bondage n servitūs f, famulātus m
bone n os nt; (fish) spīna f ♦ vt exossāre
boneless adj exos
bonfire n ignis festus m
bonhomie n festīvitās f
bon mot n dictum nt, sententia f
bonny adj pulcher, bellus
bony adj osseus
boo vt explōdere
book n liber m; (small) libellus m; (scroll) volūmen nt; (modern form) cōdex m; **books** (COMM) rationēs fpl, tabulae fpl; **bring to ~** in iūdicium vocāre
bookbinder n glūtinātor m
bookcase n librārium nt, pēgma nt
bookish adj litterārum studiōsus
book-keeper n āctuārius m
bookseller n librārius m, bibliopōla m
bookshop n bibliothēca f, librāria taberna f
bookworm n tinea f
boom n (spar) longurius m; (harbour) ōbex m/f ♦ vi resonāre
boon n bonum nt, beneficium nt, dōnum nt ♦ adj festīvus; **~ companion** sodālis m, compōtor m
boor n agrestis m, rūsticus m
boorish adj agrestis, rūsticus, inurbānus
boorishly adv rūsticē
boost vt efferre; (wares) vēnditāre
boot n calceus m; (MIL) caliga f; (rustic) pērō m; (tragic) cothurnus m ♦ vi prōdesse; **to ~** īnsuper, praetereā
booted adj calceātus, caligātus
booth n taberna f
bootless adj inūtilis, vānus
bootlessly adv frustrā
booty n praeda f, spolia ntpl
border n ōra f, margō f; (country) fīnis m; (dress) limbus m ♦ vt praetexere, margināre; fīnīre ♦ vi: **~ on** adiacēre (dat), imminēre (dat), attingere; (fig) fīnitimum esse (dat)
bordering adj fīnitimus
bore vt perforāre, perterebrāre; (person) obtundere, fatīgāre; **~ out** exterebrāre ♦ n terebra f; (hole) forāmen nt; (person) homō importūnus m, ineptus m
boredom n lassitūdō f
borer n terebra f
born adj nātus; **be ~** nāscī
borough n mūnicipium nt
borrow vt mūtuārī
borrowed adj mūtuus; (fig) aliēnus
borrowing n mūtuātiō f; (to pay a debt) versūra f
bosky adj nemorōsus
bosom n sinus m; (fig) gremium nt; **~ friend** familiāris m/f, sodālis m; **be a ~ friend of** ab latere esse (gen)
boss n bulla f; (shield) umbō m
botanist n herbārius m
botany n herbāria f

botch vt male sarcīre, male gerere
both pron ambō, uterque (gen **utriusque** each of two) ♦ adv: **~ ... and** et ... et, cum ... tum
bother n negōtium nt ♦ vt vexāre, molestus esse (dat) ♦ vi operam dare
bothersome adj molestus
bottle n lagoena f, amphora f ♦ vt (wine) diffundere
bottom n fundus m; (ground) solum nt; (ship) carīna f; **the ~ of** īmus; **be at the ~ of** (cause) auctōrem esse; **go to the ~** pessum īre, perīre; **send to the ~** pessum dare; **from the ~** funditus, ab īnfimō
bottomless adj profundus, fundō carēns
bottommost adj īnfimus
bough n rāmus m
boulder n saxum nt
boulevard n platea f
bounce vi salīre, resultāre
bound n fīnis m, modus m, terminus m; (leap) saltus m; **set bounds to** modum facere (dat) ♦ vt fīnīre, dēfīnīre, termināre ♦ vi salīre, saltāre ♦ adj adligātus, obligātus, obstrictus; **be ~ to** (duty) dēbēre; **it is ~ to happen** necesse est ēveniat; **be ~ for** tendere in (acc); **be stormbound** tempestāte tenērī
boundaries npl fīnes mpl
boundary n fīnis m; (of fields) terminus m; (fortified) līmes m; **~ stone** terminus m
boundless adj immēnsus, īnfīnītus
boundlessness n īnfīnitās f, immēnsum nt
bounteous adj see bountiful
bounteously adv largē, līberāliter, cōpiōsē
bountiful adj largus, līberālis, benignus
bounty n largitās f, līberālitās f; (store) cōpia f
bouquet n corollārium nt; (of wine) flōs m
bourn n fīnis m
bout n certāmen nt; (drinking) cōmissātiō f
bovine adj būbulus; (fig) stolidus
bow n arcus m; (ship) prōra f; (courtesy) salūtātiō f; **have two strings to one's bow** duplicī spē ūtī; **rainbow** arcus m ♦ vt flectere, inclīnāre ♦ vi caput dēmittere
bowels n alvus f; (fig) viscera ntpl
bower n umbrāculum nt, trichila f
bowl n (cooking) catīnus m; (drinking) calix m; (mixing wine) crātēra f; (ball) pila f ♦ vt volvere; **~ over** prōruere
bow-legged adj valgus
bowler n (game) dator m
bowstring n nervus m
box n arca f, capsa f; (for clothes) cista f; (for medicine) pyxis f; (for perfume) alabaster m; (tree) buxus f; (wood) buxum nt; (blow on ears) alapa f ♦ vt inclūdere; **box the ears of** alapam dūcere (dat), colaphōs īnfringere (dat) ♦ vi (fight) pugnīs certāre
boxer n pugil m
boxing n pugilātiō f
boxing glove n caestus m
boy n puer m; **become a boy again** repuerāscere
boycott vt repudiāre
boyhood n pueritia f; **from ~** ā puerō
boyish adj puerīlis
boyishly adv puerīliter

brace n (building) fībula f; (strap) fascia f; (pair) pār
nt ♦ vt adligāre; (strengthen) firmāre
bracelet n armilla f
bracing adj (air) salūbris
bracken n filix f
bracket n uncus m
brackish adj amārus
bradawl n terebra f
brag vi glōriārī, sē iactāre
braggart n glōriōsus m
braid vt nectere
brain n cerebrum nt; ingenium nt
brainless adj sōcors, stultus
brainy adj ingeniōsus
brake n (wood) dūmētum nt; (on wheel) sufflāmen
nt
bramble n rubus m
bran n furfur nt
branch n rāmus m; (kind) genus nt ♦ vi: ~ out
rāmōs porrigere
branching adj rāmōsus
brand n (fire) torris m, fax f; (mark) nota f; (sword)
ēnsis m; (variety) genus nt ♦ vt (mark) inūrere;
(stigma) notāre; ~ new recēns
brandish vt vibrāre
brass n orichalcum nt
bravado n ferōcitās f; out of ~ per speciem
ferōcitātis
brave adj fortis, ācer ♦ vt adīre, patī
bravely adv fortiter, ācriter
bravery n fortitūdō f, virtūs f
bravo interj bene, euge, macte
brawl n rixa f, iūrgium nt ♦ vi rixārī
brawn n lacertī mpl
brawny adj lacertōsus, rōbūstus
bray vi rūdere
brazen adj aēneus; (fig) impudēns
brazier n foculus m
breach n (in wall) ruīna f; (of friendship) dissēnsiō f
♦ vt perfringere; ~ of trust mala fidēs; commit
a ~ of promise prōmissīs nōn stāre
breach of the peace n iūrgium nt, tumultus m
bread n pānis m
breadth n lātitūdō f; in ~ in lātitūdinem (acc)
break vt frangere, perfringere; ~ down vt
īnfringere, dīruere; ~ in vt (animal) domāre;
~ into pieces dīrumpere; ~ off vt abrumpere,
dēfringere; (action) dīrimere; ~ open effringere,
solvere; ~ through vt interrumpere; ~ up
vt dissolvere, interrumpere; ~ one's word
fidem fallere, violāre; without breaking
the law salvīs lēgibus ♦ vi rumpī, frangī;
(day) illūcēscere; (strength) dēficere; ~ off vi
dēsinere; ~ into intrāre; ~ out vi ērumpere;
(sore) recrūdēscere; (trouble) exārdēscere; ~ up vi
dīlābī, dissolvī; (meeting) dīmittī; ~ through vi
inrumpere; ~ with dissidēre ab ♦ n intermissiō
f, intervallum nt
breakable adj fragilis
breakage n frāctum nt
breakdown n (activity) mora f; (health) dēbilitās f
breaker n fluctus m
breakfast n iēntāculum nt, prandium nt ♦ vi
ientāre, prandēre
breakwater n mōlēs f
bream n sparulus m

breast n pectus nt; (woman's) mamma f; make a
clean ~ of cōnfitērī
breastplate n lōrīca f
breastwork n lōrīca f, pluteus m
breath n spīritus m, anima f; (bad) hālitus m;
(quick) anhēlitus m; (of wind) aura f, adflātus
m; below one's ~ mussitāns; catch one's
~ obstipēscere; hold one's ~ animam
comprimere, continēre; take a ~ spīritum
dūcere; take one's ~ away exanimāre; waste
one's ~ operam perdere; out of ~ exanimātus
breathable adj spīrābilis
breathe vt, vi spīrāre, respīrāre; (quickly)
anhēlāre; ~ again respīrāre; ~ in vi spīritum
dūcere; ~ out vt, vi exspīrāre, exhālāre; ~ upon
īnspīrāre (dat), adflāre (dat); ~ one's last
animam agere, efflāre
breathing n hālitus m, respīrātiō f
breathing space n respīrātiō f
breathless adj exanimātus
breeches n brācae fpl
breed n genus nt ♦ vt generāre, prōcreāre; (raise)
ēducāre, alere; (fig) adferre, efficere; well-bred
generōsus
breeder n (animal) mātrix f; (man) generātor m;
(fig) nūtrix f
breeding n (act) fētūra f; (manners) mōrēs mpl;
good ~ hūmānitās f
breeze n aura f, flātus m
breezy adj ventōsus; (manner) hilaris
brevity n brevitās f
brew vt coquere ♦ vi (fig) parārī, imminēre
bribe vt corrumpere ♦ vi largīrī ♦ n pecūnia f,
mercēs f
briber n corruptor m, largītor m
bribery n ambitus m, largītiō f
brick n later m ♦ adj latericius
brickwork n latericium nt
bridal adj nūptiālis; (bed) geniālis ♦ n nūptiae fpl
bride n nūpta f
bridegroom n marītus m
bridge n pōns m ♦ vt pontem impōnere (dat)
bridle n frēnum nt ♦ vt frēnāre, īnfrēnāre
brief adj brevis; to be ~ nē longum sit, nē multa
briefly adv breviter, paucīs verbīs
briefness n brevitās f
brier n veprēs m, sentis m
brig n līburna f
brigade n legiō f; (cavalry) turma f
brigadier n lēgātus m
brigand n latrō m, praedō m
brigandage n latrōcinium nt
bright adj clārus, lūculentus; (sky) serēnus;
(intellect) ingeniōsus; (manner) hilaris, laetus; be
~ lūcēre, splendēre
brighten vt illūstrāre; laetificāre ♦ vi lūcēscere;
(person) hilarem fierī
brightly adv clārē
brightness n fulgor m, candor m; (sky) serēnitās f
brilliance n splendor m, fulgor m; (style) nitor m,
lūmen nt, īnsignia ntpl
brilliant adj clārus, illūstris, splendidus; (fig)
īnsignis, praeclārus, lūculentus
brilliantly adv splendidē, praeclārē, lūculentē
brim n lābrum nt, margō f; fill to the ~ explēre
brimstone n sulfur nt

brindled *adj* varius
brine *n* salsāmentum *nt*
bring *vt* ferre; (*person*) dūcere; (*charge*) intendere; (*to a place*) adferre, addūcere, advehere, dēferre; (*to a destination*) perdūcere; (*to a worse state*) redigere; ~ **about** *vt* efficere; ~ **before** dēferre ad, referre ad; ~ **back** *vt* (*thing*) referre; (*person*) redūcere; ~ **down** *vt* dēdūcere, dēferre; ~ **forth** (*from store*) dēprōmere; (*child*) parere; (*crops*) ferre, ēdere, ~ **forward** *vt* (*for discussion*) iactāre, iacere; (*reason*) adferre; ~ **home** (*bride*) dēdūcere; (*in triumph*) dēportāre; ~ **home to** pervincere; ~ **in** *vt* invehere, indūcere, intrōdūcere; (*import*) importāre; (*revenue*) reddere; ~ **off** *vt* (*success*) reportāre; ~ **on** īnferre, importāre; (*stage*) indūcere; ~ **out** *vt* efferre; (*book*) ēdere; (*play*) dare; (*talent*) ēlicere; ~ **over** perdūcere, trādūcere; ~ **to bear** adferre; ~ **to light** nūdāre, dētegere; ~ **to pass** perficere, peragere; ~ **to shore** ad litus appellere; ~ **together** contrahere, cōgere; (*enemies*) conciliāre; ~ **up** *vt* (*child*) ēducāre, tollere; (*troops*) admovēre; (*topic*) prōferre; ~ **upon oneself** sibī cōnscīscere, sibī contrahere
brink *n* ōra *f*, margō *f*
briny *adj* salsus
brisk *adj* alacer, vegetus, ācer
briskly *adv* ācriter
briskness *n* alacritās *f*
bristle *n* sēta *f* ♦ *vi* horrēre, horrēscere
bristly *adj* horridus, hirsūtus
Britain *n* Britannia *f*
Britons *n* Britannī *mpl*
brittle *adj* fragilis
broach *vt* (*topic*) in medium prōferre
broad *adj* lātus; (*accent*) lātus; (*joke*) inurbānus; (*daylight*) multus
broadcast *vt* dissēmināre
broaden *vt* dīlātāre
broadly *adv* lātē
broadsword *n* gladius *m*
brocade *n* Attalica *ntpl*
brochure *n* libellus *m*
brogue *n* pērō *m*
broil *n* rixa *f*, iūrgium *nt* ♦ *vt* torrēre
broiling *adj* torridus
broken *adj* frāctus; (*fig*) cōnfectus; (*speech*) īnfrāctus
broken-hearted *adj* dolōre cōnfectus
broker *n* īnstitor *m*
bronze *n* aes *nt* ♦ *adj* aēneus, aerātus
brooch *n* fībula *f*
brood *n* fētus *m*; (*fig*) gēns *f* ♦ *vi* incubāre (*dat*); (*fig*) incubāre (*dat*); ~ **over** meditārī
brook *n* rīvus *m* ♦ *vt* ferre, patī
brooklet *n* rīvulus *m*
broom *n* (*plant*) genista *f*; (*brush*) scōpae *fpl*
broth *n* iūs *nt*
brother *n* frāter *m*; (*full*) germānus *m*
brotherhood *n* frāternitās *f*
brother-in-law *n* lēvir *m*, uxōris frāter *m*, sorōris marītus *m*
brotherly *adj* frāternus
brow *n* frōns *f*; (*eye*) supercilium *nt*; (*hill*) dorsum *nt*
browbeat *vt* obiūrgāre, exagitāre

brown *adj* fulvus, spādīx; (*skin*) adūstus
browse *vi* pāscī, dēpāscī
bruise *vt* atterere, frangere, contundere ♦ *n* vulnus *nt*
bruit *vt* pervulgāre
brunt *n* vīs *f*; **bear the ~ of** exhaurīre
brush *n* pēniculus *m*; (*artist's*) pēnicillus *m*; (*quarrel*) rixa *f* ♦ *vt* verrere, dētergēre; (*teeth*) dēfricāre; ~ **aside** *vt* aspernārī, neglegere; ~ **up** *vt* (*fig*) excolere
brushwood *n* virgulta *ntpl*; (*for cutting*) sarmenta *ntpl*
brusque *adj* parum cōmis
brutal *adj* atrōx, saevus, inhūmānus
brutality *n* atrōcitās *f*, saevitia *f*
brutally *adv* atrōciter, inhūmānē
brute *n* bēlua *f*, bestia *f*
brutish *adj* stolidus
bubble *n* bulla *f* ♦ *vi* bullāre; ~ **over** effervēscere; ~ **up** scatēre
buccaneer *n* praedō *m*, pīrāta *m*
buck *n* cervus *m* ♦ *vi* exsultāre
bucket *n* situla *f*, fidēlia *f*
buckle *n* fībula *f* ♦ *vt* fībulā nectere; ~ **to** accingī
buckler *n* parma *f*
buckram *n* carbasus *m*
bucolic *adj* agrestis
bucolics *n* būcolica *ntpl*
bud *n* gemma *f*, flōsculus *m* ♦ *vi* gemmāre
budge *vi* movērī, cēdere
budget *n* pūblicae pecūniae ratiō *f* ♦ *vi*: ~ **for** prōvidēre (*dat*)
buff *adj* lūteus
buffalo *n* ūrus *m*
buffet *n* (*blow*) alapa *f*; (*fig*) plāga *f*; (*sideboard*) abacus *m* ♦ *vt* iactāre, tundere
buffoon *n* scurra *m*, balatrō *m*
buffoonery *n* scurrilitās *f*
bug *n* cīmex *m*
bugbear *n* terricula *ntpl*, terror *m*
bugle *n* būcina *f*
bugler *n* būcinātor *m*
build *vt* aedificāre, struere; (*bridge*) facere; (*road*) mūnīre; ~ **on** *vt* (*add*) adstruere; (*hopes*) pōnere; ~ **on sand** in aquā fundāmenta pōnere; ~ **up** *vt* exstruere; (*to block*) inaedificāre; (*knowledge*) īnstruere; ~ **castles in the air** spem inānem pāscere ♦ *n* statūra *f*
builder *n* aedificātor *m*, structor *m*
building *n* (*act*) aedificātiō *f*; (*structure*) aedificium *nt*
bulb *n* bulbus *m*
bulge *vi* tumēre, tumēscere, prōminēre ♦ *n* tuberculum *nt*; (*of land*) locus prōminēns *m*
bulk *n* māgnitūdō *f*, amplitūdō *f*; (*mass*) mōlēs *f*; (*most*) plērīque, māior pars
bulky *adj* amplus, grandis
bull *n* taurus *m*; **bull's** taurīnus; **take the ~ by the horns** rem fortiter adgredī
bulldog *n* Molossus *m*
bullet *n* glāns *f*
bulletin *n* libellus *m*
bullion *n* aurum īnfectum *nt*, argentum īnfectum *nt*
bullock *n* iuvencus *m*

bully n obiūrgātor m, patruus m ◆ vt obiūrgāre, exagitāre
bulrush n scirpus m
bulwark n prōpugnāculum nt; (fig) arx f
bump n (swelling) tuber nt, tuberculum nt; (knock) ictus m ◆ vi: ~ **against** offendere
bumper n plēnum pōculum nt ◆ adj plēnus, māximus
bumpkin n rūsticus m
bumptious adj adrogāns
bunch n fasciculus m; (of berries) racēmus m
bundle n fascis m; (of hay) manipulus m ◆ vt obligāre
bung n obtūrāmentum nt ◆ vt obtūrāre
bungle vt male gerere
bunk n lectus m, lectulus m
buoy n cortex m ◆ vt sublevāre
buoyancy n levitās f
buoyant adj levis; (fig) hilaris
bur n lappa f
burden n onus nt; beast of ~ iūmentum nt ◆ vt onerāre; **be a** ~ oneri esse
burdensome adj gravis, molestus
bureau n scrīnium nt
burgeon vi gemmāre
burgess n mūniceps m
burgh n mūnicipium nt
burgher n mūniceps m
burglar n fūr m
burglary n fūrtum nt
burial n fūnes nt, humātiō f, sepultūra f
burin n caelum nt
burlesque n imitātiō f ◆ vt per iocum imitārī
burly adj crassus
burn vt incendere, ūrere; (to ashes) cremāre ◆ vi ārdēre, flāgrāre; ~ **up** ambūrere, combūrere, exūrere; **be burned down** dēflāgrāre; ~ **out** vi exstinguī; ~ **the midnight oil** lūcubrāre ◆ n (MED) ambūstum nt
burning adj igneus
burnish vt polīre
burrow n cunīculus m ◆ vi dēfodere
burst vt rumpere, dīrumpere ◆ vi rumpī, dīrumpī; ~ **in** inrumpere; ~ **into tears** in lacrimās effundī; ~ **open** refringere; ~ **out** ērumpere, prōrumpere; ~ **out laughing** cachinnum tollere; ~ **through** perrumpere per (acc); ~ **upon** offerrī (dat), invādere ◆ n ēruptiō f; (noise) fragor m; ~ **of applause** clāmōrēs mpl; **with a** ~ **of speed** citātō gradū, citātō equō
bury vt sepelīre, humāre; (ceremony) efferre; (hiding) condere; (things) dēfodere; (fig) obruere; ~ **the hatchet** amīcitiam reconciliāre
bush n frutex m; dūmus m; **beat about the** ~ circuitiōne ūtī

bushel n medimnus m
bushy adj fruticōsus; (thick) dēnsus; (hair) hirsūtus
busily adv strēnuē, impigrē
business n negōtium nt; (occupation) ars f, quaestus m; (public life) forum nt; (matter) rēs f; **it is your** ~ tuum est; **make it one's** ~ **to** id agere ut; **you have no** ~ **to** nōn tē decet (inf); **mind one's own** ~ suum negōtium agere; ~ **days** diēs fāstī mpl
businessman negōtiātor m
buskin n cothurnus m
bust n imāgō f
bustle vi trepidāre, festīnāre; ~ **about** discurrere
busy adj negōtiōsus, occupātus; (active) operōsus, impiger, strēnuus; ~ **in** occupātus (abl); ~ **on** intentus (dat); **keep** ~ vt exercēre; ~ **oneself with** pertractāre, studēre (dat)
busybody n: **be a** ~ alienīs negōtīs sē immiscēre
but conj sed, at; (2nd place) autem, tamen ◆ adv modo ◆ prep praeter (acc); **nothing but** nihil nisī; **but that, but what** quīn; **not but what** nihilōminus
butcher n lanius m ◆ vt trucīdāre
butcher's shop n laniēna f
butchery n strāgēs f, occīdiō f
butler n prōmus m
butt n (cask) cadus m; (of ridicule) lūdibrium nt ◆ vi arietāre; ~ **in** interpellāre
butter n būtyrum nt
butterfly n pāpiliō m
buttock n clūnis m/f
button n bulla f
buttonhole vt (fig) dētinēre, prēnsāre
buttress n antērides fpl ◆ vt fulcīre
buxom adj nitidus
buy vt emere; **buy provisions** obsōnāre; **buy back** vt redimere; **buy off** vt redimere; **buy up** vt coemere
buyer n emptor m; (at auctions) manceps m
buzz n strīdor m, susurrus m ◆ vi strīdere, susurrāre
buzzard n būteō m
by prep (near) ad (acc), apud (acc); prope (acc); (along) secundum (acc); (past) praeter (acc); (agent) ā, ab (abl); (instrument) abl; (time) ante (acc); (oath) per (acc) ◆ adv prope, iuxtā; **by and by** mox; **be by** adesse, adstāre; **by force of arms** vī et armīs; **by land and sea** terrā marique
bygone adj praeteritus
bystander n arbiter m ◆ pl circumstantēs mpl
byway n dēverticulum nt, trāmes m, sēmita f
byword n prōverbium nt

Cc

cabal *n* factiō *f*
cabbage *n* brassica *f*, caulis *m*
cabin *n* casa *f*; (*ship*) cubiculum *nt*
cabinet *n* armārium *nt*
cable *n* fūnis *m*; (*anchor*) ancorāle *nt*
cache *n* thēsaurus *m*
cachet *n* nota *f*
cackle *vi* strepere *n*, strepitus *m*, clangor *m*
cacophonous *adj* dissonus
cacophony *n* vōcēs dissonae *fpl*
cadaverous *adj* cadāverōsus
cadence *n* clausula numerōsa *f*, numerus *m*
cadet *n* (*son*) nātū minor; (*MIL*) contubernālis *m*
cage *n* cavea *f* ♦ *vt* inclūdere
caitiff *n* ignāvus *m*
cajole *vt* blandīrī, dēlēnīre
cake *n* placenta *f*
calamitous *adj* exitiōsus, calamitōsus
calamity *n* calamitās *f*, malum *nt*; (*MIL*) clādēs *f*
calculate *vt* ratiōnem dūcere, inīre
calculation *n* ratiō *f*
calculator *n* ratiōcinātor *m*
calendar *n* fāstī *mpl*
calends *n* Kalendae *fpl*
calf *n* (*animal*) vitulus *m*, vitula *f*; (*leg*) sūra *f*
calibre *n* (*fig*) ingenium *nt*, auctōritās *f*
call *vt* vocāre; (*name*) appellāre, nōmināre; (*aloud*) clāmāre; (*to a place*) advocāre, convocāre; **~ aside** sēvocāre; **~ down** (*curse*) dētestārī; **~ for** *vt* postulāre, requīrere; **~ forth** ēvocāre, excīre, ēlicere; **~ in** *vt* advocāre; **~ together** convocāre; **~ on** *vt* (*for help*) implōrāre; (*visit*) salūtāre; **~ off** *vt* āvocāre, revocāre; **~ out** *vi* exclāmāre; **~ up** *vt* (*dead*) excitāre, ēlicere; (*MIL*) ēvocāre ♦ *n* vōx *f*, clāmor *m*; (*summons*) invītātiō *f*; (*visit*) salūtātiō *f*
caller *n* salūtātor *m*
calling *n* ars *f*, quaestus *m*
callous *adj* dūrus; **become ~** obdūrēscere
callow *adj* rudis
calm *adj* tranquillus, placidus; (*mind*) aequus ♦ *vi*: **~ down** (*fig*) dēfervēscere ♦ *vt* sēdāre, tranquillāre ♦ *n* tranquillitās *f*; **dead ~** (*at sea*) malacia *f*
calmly *adv* tranquillē, placidē; aequō animō
calumniate *vt* obtrectāre, crīminārī; (*falsely*) calumniārī
calumniator *n* obtrectātor *m*
calumny *n* opprobria *ntpl*, obtrectātiō *f*
calve *vi* parere

cambric *n* linteum *nt*
camel *n* camēlus *m*
camouflage *n* dissimulātiō ♦ *vt* dissimulāre
camp *n* castra *ntpl*; **summer ~** aestīva *ntpl*; **winter ~** hīberna *ntpl*; **in ~** sub pellibus; **pitch ~** castra pōnere; **strike ~** castra movēre ♦ *adj* castrēnsis ♦ *vi* tendere
campaign *n* stīpendium *nt*, bellum *nt*; (*rapid*) expedītiō *f* ♦ *vi* bellum gerere, stīpendium merēre
campaigner *n* mīles *m*; **old ~** veterānus *m*; (*fig*) veterātor *m*
campbed *n* grabātus *m*
camp followers *n* lixae *mpl*
can¹ *n* hirnea *f*
can² *vi* posse (*inf*); (*know how*) scīre
canaille *n* vulgus *nt*, plebs *f*
canal *n* fossa nāvigābilis *f*, eurīpus *m*
cancel *vt* indūcere, abrogāre
cancellation *n* (*writing*) litūra *f*; (*LAW*) abrogātiō *f*
cancer *n* cancer *m*; (*fig*) carcinōma *nt*, ulcus *nt*
cancerous *adj* (*fig*) ulcerōsus
candelabrum *n* candēlābrum *nt*
candid *adj* ingenuus, apertus, līber, simplex
candidate *n* petītor *m*; **be a ~ for** petere
candidature *n* petītiō *f*
candidly *adv* ingenuē
candle *n* candēla *f*
candlestick *n* candēlābrum *nt*
candour *n* ingenuitās *f*, simplicitās *f*, lībertās *f*
cane *n* (*reed*) harundō *f*; (*for walking, punishing*) virga *f* ♦ *vt* verberāre
canine *adj* canīnus
canister *n* capsula *f*
canker *n* (*plants*) rōbigō *f*; (*fig*) aerūgō *f*, carcinōma *nt* ♦ *vt* corrumpere
Cannae *n* Cannae *fpl*
cannibal *n* anthrōpophagus *m*
cannon *n* tormentum *nt*
cannot *vi* nōn posse, nequīre; **I ~ help but ...** facere nōn possum quīn ... (*subj*), nōn possum nōn ... (*inf*)
canny *adj* prūdens, prōvidus, cautus, circumspectus
canoe *n* linter *f*
canon *n* nōrma *f*, rēgula *f*; (*ECCL*) canonicus *m*
canopy *n* aulaeum *nt*
cant *n* fūcus *m*, fūcāta verba *ntpl* ♦ *vt* oblīquāre
cantankerous *adj* importūnus

23

cantankerousness n importūnitās f
canter n lēnis cursus m ♦ vi lēniter currere
canticle n canticum nt
canto n carmen nt
canton n pāgus m
canvas n carbasus m, linteum nt ♦ adj carbaseus; **under ~** sub pellibus
canvass vi ambīre ♦ vt prēnsāre, circumīre
canvassing n ambitus m, ambitiō f
cap n pilleus m; (priest's) galērus m, apex m
capability n facultās f, potestās f
capable adj capāx, doctus, perītus
capably adv bene, doctē
capacious adj capāx, amplus
capacity n capācitās f, amplitūdō f; (mind) ingenium nt
caparison n ephippium nt
cape n (GEOG) prōmontōrium nt; (dress) chlamys f
caper vi saltāre; (animal) lascīvīre ♦ n saltus m
capering n lascivia f
capital adj (chief) praecipuus, prīnceps; (excellent) ēgregius; (LAW) capitālis; **convict of a ~ offence** capitis damnāre ♦ n (town) caput nt; (money) sors f; (class) negōtiātorēs mpl; **make ~ out of** ūtī (abl)
capitalist n faenerātor m
capital punishment n capitis supplicum nt
Capitol n Capitolium nt
capitulate vi sē dēdere; **troops who have capitulated** dēditiciī mpl
capitulation n dēditiō f
capon n capō m
caprice n libīdō f, incōnstantia f
capricious adj incōnstāns, levis
capriciously adv incōnstanter, leviter
capriciousness n incōnstantia f, libīdō f
capsize vt ēvertere ♦ vi ēvertī
captain n dux m, praefectus m, prīnceps m; (MIL) centuriō m; (naval) nāvarchus m; (of merchant ship) magister m ♦ vt praeesse (dat), dūcere
captaincy n centuriātus m
caption n caput nt
captious adj mōrōsus; (question) captiōsus
captiously adv mōrōsē
captiousness n mōrōsitās f
captivate vt capere, dēlēnīre, adlicere
captive n captīvus m
captivity n captīvitās f, vincula ntpl
captor n (by storm) expugnātor m; victor m
capture n (by storm) expugnātiō f ♦ vt capere
car n currus m
caravan n commeātus m
carbuncle n (MED) fūrunculus m; (stone) acaustus m
carcass n cadāver nt
card n charta f; (ticket) tessera f; (wool) pecten nt ♦ vt pectere
cardamom n amōmum nt
cardinal adj praecipuus; **~ point** cardō m ♦ n (ECCL) cardinālis
care n cūra f; (anxiety) sollicitūdō f; (attention) dīligentia f; (charge) custōdia f; **take ~** cavēre; **take ~ of** cūrāre ♦ vi cūrāre; **~ for** vt (look after) cūrāre; (like) amāre; **I don't ~** nīl moror; **I couldn't ~ less about ...** floccī nōn faciō ...,

pendō; **I don't ~ about** mittō, nihil moror; **for all I ~** per mē
career n curriculum nt; (POL) cursus honōrum; (completed) rēs gestae fpl ♦ vi ruere, volāre
carefree adj sēcūrus
careful adj (cautious) cautus; (attentive) dīligēns, attentus; (work) accūrātus
carefully adv cautē; dīligenter, attentē; accūrātē
careless adj incautus, neglegēns
carelessly adv incautē, neglegenter
carelessness n incūria f, neglegentia f
caress vt fovēre, blandīrī ♦ n blandīmentum nt, amplexus m
cargo n onus nt
caricature n (picture) gryllus m; (fig) imāgō dētorta f ♦ vt dētorquēre
carmine n coccum nt ♦ adj coccineus
carnage n strāgēs f, caedēs f
carnal adj corporeus; (pleasure) libīdinōsus
carnival n fēriae fpl
carol n carmen nt ♦ vi cantāre
carouse vi perpōtāre, cōmissārī ♦ n cōmissātiō f
carp vi obtrectāre; **~ at** carpere, rōdere
carpenter n faber m, lignārius m
carpet n tapēte nt
carriage n (conveying) vectūra f; (vehicle) vehiculum nt; (for journeys) raeda f, petorritum nt; (for town) carpentum nt, pīlentum nt; (deportment) gestus m, incessus m; **~ and pair** bīgae fpl; **~ and four** quadrīgae fpl
carrier n vector m; (porter) bāiulus m; **letter ~** tabellārius m
carrion n cadāver nt
carrot n carōta f
carry vt portāre, vehere, ferre, gerere; (LAW) perferre; (by assault) expugnāre; **~ away** auferre, āvehere; (by force) rapere; (with emotion) efferre; **~ all before one** ēvincere; **~ along** (building) dūcere; **~ back** reportāre; revehere, referre; **~ down** dēportāre, dēvehere; **~ in** invehere, intrōferre; **~ off** auferre, asportāre, āvehere; (by force) abripere, ēripere; (prize) ferre, reportāre; (success) bene gerere; **~ on** vt gerere; (profession) exercēre; **~ out** vi efferre, ēgerere, ēvehere; (task) exsequī; **~ out an undertaking** rem suscipere; **~ over** trānsportāre, trānsferre; **~ the day** vincere; **~ one's point** pervincere; **~ through** perferre; **~ to** adferre, advehere; **~ up** subvehere ♦ vi (sound) audīrī; **~ on** vi pergere; (flirt) lascīvīre
cart n plaustrum nt; carrus nt; **put the ~ before the horse** praeposterum dīcere ♦ vt plaustrō vehere
Carthage n Carthāgō, Carthāginis f
Carthaginian adj Carthāginiēnsis; Pūnicus; **the Carthaginians** Poenī mpl
carthorse n iūmentum nt
carve vt sculpere; (on surface) caelāre; (meat) secāre; **~ out** exsculpere
carver n caelātor m
carving n caelātūra f
cascade n cataracta m
case n (instance) exemplum nt, rēs f; (legal) āctiō f, līs f, causa f; (plight) tempus nt; (GRAM) cāsus m; (receptacle) thēca f, involucrum nt; **in ~** sī; (to prevent) nē; **in any ~** utut est rēs; **in that ~** ergō; **such is the ~** sic sē rēs habet; **civil**

~ causa prīvāta; **criminal** ~ causa pūblica; **win a** ~ causam, lītem obtinēre; **lose a** ~ causam, lītem āmittere

casement *n* fenestra *f*

cash *n* nummī *mpl*; (*ready*) numerātum *nt*, praesēns pecūnia *f*; **pay** ~ ex arcā absolvere, repraesentāre

cash box *n* arca *f*

cashier *n* dispēnsātor *m* ♦ *vt* (*MIL*) exauctōrāre

cash payment *n* repraesentātiō *f*

cask *n* cūpa *f*

casket *n* arcula *f*, pyxis *f*

casque *n* galea *f*, cassis *f*

cast *vt* iacere; (*account*) inīre; (*eyes*) conicere; (*lots*) conicere; (*covering*) exuere; (*metal*) fundere; ~ **ashore** ēicere; ~ **away** prōicere; ~ **down** dēicere; (*humble*) abicere; ~ **in one's teeth** exprobrāre; ~ **lots** sortīrī; ~ **off** *vi* abicere, exuere; ~ **out** prōicere, ēicere, pellere ♦ *n* iactus *m*; (*moulding*) typus *m*, fōrma *f*; **with a** ~ **in the eye** paetus

castanet *n* crotalum *nt*

castaway *n* ēiectus *m*

caste *n* ōrdō *m*

castigate *vt* animadvertere, castīgāre

castigation *n* animadversiō *f*, castīgātiō *f*

castle *n* arx *f*, castellum *nt*

castrate *vt* castrāre

casual *adj* fortuītus; (*person*) neglegēns

casually *adv* temerē

casualty *n* īnfortūnium *nt* ♦ *pl*: **casualties** occīsī *mpl*

casuist *n* sophistēs *m*

cat *n* fēlēs *f*

cataclysm *n* dīluvium *nt*, ruīna *f*

catalogue *n* index *m*

catapult *n* catapulta *f*, ballista *f*

cataract *n* cataracta *f*

catarrh *n* gravēdō *f*; **liable to** ~ gravēdinōsus

catastrophe *n* calamitās *f*, ruīna *f*

catastrophic *adj* calamitōsus, exitiōsus

catch *vt* capere, dēprehendere, excipere; (*disease*) contrahere, nancīscī; (*fire*) concipere, comprehendere; (*meaning*) intellegere; ~ **at** captāre; ~ **out** *vi* dēprehendere; ~ **up with** adsequī; ~ **birds** aucupārī; ~ **fish** piscārī ♦ *n* bolus *m*

categorical *adj* (*statement*) plānus

categorically *adv* sine exceptiōne

category *n* numerus *m*, genus *nt*

cater *vi* obsōnāre

cateran *n* praedātor *m*

caterer *n* obsōnātor *m*

caterpillar *n* ērūca *f*

caterwaul *vi* ululāre

catgut *n* chorda *f*

catharsis *n* pūrgātiō *f*

cathedral *n* aedēs *f*

catholic *adj* generālis

catkin *n* iūlus *m*

cattle *n* (*collectively*) pecus *nt*; (*singly*) pecus *f*; (*for plough*) armenta *ntpl*

cattle breeder *n* pecuārius *m*

cattle market *n* forum boārium *nt*

cattle thief *n* abāctor *m*

cauldron *n* cortīna *f*

cause *n* causa *f*; (*person*) auctor *m*; (*LAW*) causa *f*; (*party*) partēs *fpl*; **give** ~ **for** māteriam dare (*gen*); **make common** ~ **with** facere cum, stāre ab; **plead a** ~ causam dīcere; **in the** ~ **of** prō (*abl*); **without** ~ iniūriā ♦ *vt* efficere ut (*subj*), facere, facessere (*with 'ut'*), cūrāre (*with gerundive*); (*feelings*) movēre, inicere, ciēre

causeless *adj* vānus, sine causā

causeway *n* agger *m*

caustic *adj* (*fig*) mordāx

cauterize *vt* adūrere

caution *n* (*wariness*) cautiō *f*, prūdentia *f*; (*warning*) monitum *nt* ♦ *vt* monēre, admonēre

cautious *adj* cautus, prōvidus, prūdens

cautiously *adv* cautē, prūdenter

cavalcade *n* pompa *f*

cavalier *n* eques *m* ♦ *adj* adrogāns

cavalierly *adv* adroganter

cavalry *n* equitēs *mpl*, equitātus *m* ♦ *adj* equester; **troop of** ~ turma *f*

cavalryman *n* eques *m*

cave *n* spēlunca *f*, caverna *f*; antrum *nt*; ~ **in** *vi* concidere, conlābī

cavern *n* spēlunca *f*, caverna *f*

cavil *vi* cavillārī; ~ **at** carpere, cavillārī ♦ *n* captiō *f*, cavillātiō *f*

cavity *n* caverna *f*, cavum *nt*

cavort *vi* saltāre

caw *vi* cornīcārī

cease *vi* dēsinere, dēsistere

ceaseless *adj* adsiduus, perpetuus

ceaselessly *adv* adsiduē, perpetuō

cedar *n* cedrus *f* ♦ *adj* cedrinus

cede *vt* cēdere, concēdere

ceiling *n* tēctum *nt*; (*panelled*) lacūnar *nt*, laqueārium *nt*

celebrate *vt* (*rite*) celebrāre, agitāre; (*in crowds*) frequentāre; (*person, theme*) laudāre, celebrāre, dīcere

celebrated *adj* praeclārus, illūstris, nōtus; **the** ~ ille

celebration *n* celebrātiō *f*; (*rite*) sollemne *nt*

celebrity *n* celebritās *f*, fāma *f*; (*person*) vir illūstris

celerity *n* celeritās *f*, vēlōcitās *f*

celery *n* apium *nt*

celestial *adj* caelestis; dīvīnus

celibacy *n* caelibātus *m*

celibate *n* caelebs *m*

cell *n* cella *f*

cellar *n* cella *f*

cement *n* ferrūmen *nt* ♦ *vt* coagmentāre

cemetery *n* sepulchrētum *nt*

cenotaph *n* tumulus honōrārius, tumulus inānis *m*

censer *n* tūribulum *nt*, acerra *f*

censor *n* cēnsor *m* ♦ *vt* cēnsēre

censorious *adj* cēnsōrius, obtrectātor

censorship *n* cēnsūra *f*

censure *n* reprehēnsiō *f*, animadversiō *f*; (*censor's*) nota *f* ♦ *vt* reprehendere, animadvertere, increpāre; notāre

census *n* cēnsus *m*

cent *n*: **one per** ~ centēsima *f*; **12 per** ~ **per annum** centēsima *f* (*ie monthly*)

centaur *n* centaurus *m*

centaury n (*plant*) centaurēum nt
centenarian n centum annōs nātus m, nāta f
centenary n centēsimus annus m
centesimal adj centēsimus
central adj medius
centralize vt in ūnum locum cōnferre; (*power*) ad ūnum dēferre
centre n centrum nt, media pars f; **the ~ of** medius
centuple adj centuplex
centurion n centuriō m
century n (MIL) centuria f; (*time*) saeculum nt
ceramic adj fictilis
cereal n frūmentum nt
ceremonial adj sollemnis ♦ n rītus m
ceremonious adj (*rite*) sollemnis; (*person*) officiōsus
ceremoniously adv sollemniter; officiōsē
ceremony n caerimōnia f, rītus m; (*politeness*) officium nt; (*pomp*) apparātus m; **master of ceremonies** dēsignātor m
cerise n coccum nt ♦ adj coccineus
certain adj (*sure*) certus; (*future*) explōrātus; **a ~** quīdam, quaedam, quoddam; **be ~** (*know*) prō certō scīre/habēre
certainly adv certē, certō, sine dubiō; (*yes*) ita, māximē; (*concessive*) quidem
certainty n (*thing*) certum nt; (*belief*) fidēs f; **for a ~** prō certō, explōrātē; **regard as a ~** prō explōrātō habēre
certificate n testimōnium nt
certify vt (*writing*) recognōscere; (*fact*) adfirmāre, testificārī
cessation n fīnis m; (*from labour*) quiēs f; (*temporary*) intermissiō f; (*of hostilities*) indutiae fpl
chafe vt ūrere; (*fig*) inrītāre ♦ vi stomachārī
chaff n palea f ♦ vt lūdere
chaffinch n fringilla f
chagrin n dolor m, stomachus m ♦ vt stomachum facere (*dat*), sollicitāre
chain n catēna f; (*for neck*) torquis m; (*sequence*) seriēs f; **chains** pl vincula ntpl ♦ vt vincīre
chair n sella f; (*of office*) sella curūlis f; (*sedan*) sella gestātōria f, lectīca f; (*teacher's*) cathedra f
chairman n (*at meeting*) magister m; (*of debate*) disceptātor m
chalet n casa f
chalice n calix m
chalk n crēta f
chalky adj crētōsus
challenge n prōvocātiō f ♦ vt prōvocāre, lacessere; (*statement*) in dubium vocāre; (*fig*) invītāre, dēposcere
challenger n prōvocātor m
chamber n conclāve nt; (*bed*) cubiculum nt; (*bridal*) thalamus m; (*parliament*) cūria f
chamberlain n cubiculārius m
chambermaid n serva f, ancilla f
chameleon n chamaeleōn f
chamois n rūpicapra f
champ vt mandere
champion n prōpugnātor m, patrōnus m; (*winner*) victor m ♦ vt favēre (*dat*), adesse (*dat*)
chance n fors f, fortūna f, cāsus m; (*opportunity*) occāsiō f; potestās f, facultās f; (*prospect*) spēs f;
game of ~ ālea f; **by ~** cāsū, fortuītō; **have an eye to the main ~** forō ūtī; **on the ~ of** sī forte ♦ adj fortuītus ♦ vi accidere, ēvenīre; **it chanced that** ... accidit ut ... (*subj*); **~ upon** incidere in, invenīre ♦ vt periclitārī
chancel n absis f
chancellor n cancellārius m
chancy adj dubius, perīculōsus
chandelier n candēlābrum nt
chandler n candēlārum prōpōla m
change n mūtātiō f, commūtātiō f, permūtātiō f; (POL) rēs novae fpl; (*alternation*) vicēs fpl; vicissitūdō f; (*money*) nummī minōrēs mpl ♦ vt mūtāre, commūtāre, permūtāre ♦ vi mūtārī; **~ hands** abaliēnarī; **~ places** ōrdinem permūtāre, inter sē loca permūtāre
changeable adj incōnstāns, mūtābilis
changeableness n incōnstantia f, mūtābilitās f
changeful adj varius
changeless adj cōnstāns, immūtābilis
changeling adj subditus m
channel n canālis m; (*sea*) fretum nt; (*irrigation*) rīvus m; (*groove*) sulcus m
chant vt cantāre, canere ♦ n cantus m
chaos n chaos nt; (*fig*) perturbātiō f
chaotic adj perturbātus
chap n rīma f; (*man*) homō m
chapel n sacellum nt, aedicula f
chaplain n diāconus m
chaplet n corōna f, sertum nt
chaps n (*animal*) mālae fpl
chapter n caput nt
char vt ambūrere
character n (*inborn*) indolēs f, ingenium nt, nātūra f; (*moral*) mōrēs mpl; (*reputation*) existimātiō f; (*kind*) genus nt; (*mark*) signum nt, littera f; (THEAT) persōna f, partēs fpl; **sustain a ~** persōnam gerere; **I know his ~** sciō quālis sit
characteristic adj proprius ♦ n proprium nt
characteristically adv suō mōre
characterize vt dēscrībere; proprium esse (*gen*)
charcoal n carbō m
charge n (LAW) accūsātiō f, crīmen nt; (MIL) impetus m, dēcursus m; (*cost*) impēnsa f; (*task*) mandātum nt, onus nt; (*trust*) cūra f, tūtēla f; **bring a ~ against** lītem intendere (*dat*); **entertain a ~ against** nōmen recipere (*gen*); **give in ~** in custōdiam trādere; **put in ~ of** praeficere (*acc, dat*); **be in ~ of** praeesse (*dat*) ♦ vt (LAW) accūsāre; (*falsely*) īnsimulāre; (MIL) incurrere in (*acc*), signa īnferre in (*acc*), impetum facere in (*acc*); (*duty*) mandāre; (*cost*) ferre, īnferre; (*empty space*) complēre; (*trust*) committere; (*speech*) hortārī; **~ to the account of** expēnsum ferre (*dat*)
chargeable adj obnoxius
charger n (*dish*) lānx f; (*horse*) equus m
charily adv cautē, parcē
chariot n currus m; (*races*) quadrīgae fpl; (*war*) essedum nt
charioteer n aurīga m; (*war*) essedārius m
charitable adj benevolus, benignus
charitably adv benevolē, benignē
charity n amor m, benignitās f; līberālitās f
charlatan n plānus m

charm n (spell) carmen nt; (amulet) bulla f; (fig)
  blanditiae fpl, dulcēdō f, illecebra f; (beauty)
  venus f, lepōs m ♦ vt (magic) fascināre; (delight)
  dēlectāre, dēlēnīre
charming adj venustus, lepidus; (speech)
  blandus; (scenery) amoenus
charmingly adv venustē, blandē
chart n tabula f
charter n diplōma nt ♦ vt condūcere
chary adj (cautious) cautus; (sparing) parcus
chase vt fugāre; (hunt) vēnārī; (pursue) persequī,
  īnsequī; (engrave) caelāre; ~ away pellere,
  abigere ♦ n vēnātus m, vēnātiō f; (pursuit)
  īnsectātiō f
chaser n (in metal) caelātor m
chasm n hiātus m
chaste adj castus, pudīcus; (style) pūrus
chasten vt castīgāre, corrigere
chastener n castīgātor m, corrēctor m
chastise vt castīgāre, animadvertere
chastisement n castīgātiō f, poena f
chastity n castitās f, pudīcitia f
chat vi colloquī, sermōcinārī ♦ n sermō m,
  colloquium nt
chatelaine n domina f
chattels n bona ntpl, rēs mancipī
chatter vi garrīre; (teeth) crepitāre ♦ n garrulitās
  f, loquācitās f
chatterbox n lingulāca m/f
chatterer n garrulus m, loquāx m
chattering adj garrulus, loquāx ♦ n garrulitās f,
  loquācitās f; (teeth) crepitus m
cheap adj vīlis; **hold ~** parvī aestimāre; **buy**
  ~ bene emere
cheapen vt pretium minuere (gen)
cheaply adv vīliter, parvō pretiō
cheapness n vīlitās f
cheat vt dēcipere, fraudāre, dēfraudāre,
  frustrārī ♦ n fraudātor m
check vt cohibēre, coercēre; (movement) impedīre,
  inhibēre; (rebuke) reprehendere; (test) probāre
  ♦ n impedīmentum nt, mora f; (MIL) offēnsiō
  f; (rebuke) reprehēnsiō f; (test) probātiō f; (ticket)
  tessera f
checkmate n incitae calcēs fpl ♦ vt ad incitās
  redigere
cheek n gena f; (impudence) ōs nt; **cheeks** pl mālae
  fpl; **how have you the ~ to say?** quō ōre dīcis?
cheekbone n maxilla f
cheeky adj impudēns
cheep vi pīpilāre
cheer vt hilarāre, exhilarāre; hortārī; (in sorrow)
  cōnsōlārī ♦ vi clāmāre, adclāmāre; ~ **up!** bonō
  animō es! ♦ n (shout) clāmor m, plausus m; (food)
  hospitium nt; (mind) animus m
cheerful adj alacer, hilaris, laetus
cheerfully adv hilare, laetē
cheerfulness n hilaritās f
cheerily adv hilare
cheerless adj tristis, maestus
cheerlessly adv triste
cheery adj hilaris
cheese n cāseus m
chef n coquus m
cheque n perscrīptiō f, syngrapha f
chequer vt variāre

chequered adj varius; (mosaic) tessellātus
cherish vt fovēre, colere
cherry n (fruit) cerasum nt; (tree) cerasus f
chess n latrunculī mpl
chessboard n abacus m
chest n (box) arca f, arcula f; (body) pectus nt; ~ **of**
  drawers armārium nt
chestnut n castanea f ♦ adj (colour) spādīx
chevalier n eques m
chevaux-de-frise n ēricius m
chew vt mandere
chic adj expolītus, concinnus
chicanery n (LAW) calumnia f; (fig) dolus m
chick n pullus m
chicken n pullus m; **don't count your chickens**
  before they're hatched adhūc tua messis in
  herbā est
chicken-hearted adj timidus, ignāvus
chick-pea n cicer nt
chide vt reprehendere, increpāre, obiūrgāre
chief n prīnceps m, dux m ♦ adj praecipuus,
  prīmus; ~ **point** caput nt
chief command n summa imperiī
chiefly adv in prīmīs, praesertim, potissimum
chieftain n prīnceps m, rēgulus m
chilblain n perniō m
child n īnfāns m/f; puer m, puerulus m, puella f;
  fīlius m, fīlia f; **child's play** lūdus m
childbed n puerperium nt
childbirth n partus m
childhood n pueritia f; **from** ~ ā puerō
childish adj puerīlis
childishly adv puerīliter
childless adj orbus
childlessness n orbitās f
childlike adj puerīlis
children npl līberī mpl
chill n frīgus nt ♦ adj frīgidus ♦ vt refrīgerāre
chilly adj frīgidus, frīgidior
chime vi sonāre, canere; ~ **in** interpellāre; (fig)
  cōnsonāre ♦ n sonus m
chimera n chimaera f; (fig) somnium nt
chimerical adj commentīcius
chimney n camīnus m
chin n mentum nt
china n fictilia ntpl
chink n rīma f; (sound) tinnītus m ♦ vi crepāre,
  tinnīre
chip n assula f, fragmentum nt ♦ vt dolāre
chirp vi pīpilāre
chirpy adj hilaris
chisel n scalprum nt, scalpellum nt ♦ vt sculpere
chit n (child) pūsiō m, puerulus m
chitchat n sermunculī mpl
chitterlings n hillae fpl
chivalrous adj generōsus
chivalry n virtūs f; (men) iuventūs f; (class)
  equitēs mpl
chive n caepe nt
chock n cuneus m
chock-full adj refertus
choice n dēlēctus m, ēlēctiō f; (of alternatives) optiō
  f ♦ adj lēctus, eximius, exquīsītus
choiceness n ēlegantia f, praestantia f
choir n chorus m

choke vt suffocāre; (emotion) reprimere; (passage) obstruere

choler n bīlis f; (anger) īra f, stomachus m

choleric adj īrācundus

choose vt legere, ēligere, dēligere; (alternative) optāre; (for office) dēsignāre; (with infin) velle, mālle

chop vt concīdere; ~ **off** praecīdere ♦ n (meat) offa f

chopper n secūris f

choppy adj (sea) asper

choral adj symphōniacus

chord n (string) nervus m, chorda f

chortle vi cachinnāre

chorus n (singers) chorus m; (song) concentus m, symphōnia f; **in** ~ unā vōce

christen vt baptizāre

Christian adj Christiānus

Christianity n Christiānismus m

chronic adj inveterātus; **become** ~ inveterāscere

chronicle n annālēs mpl, ācta pūblica ntpl ♦ vt in annālēs referre

chronicler n annālium scrīptor m

chronological adj: **in** ~ **order** servātō temporum ōrdine; **make a** ~ **error** temporibus errāre

chronology n temporum ratiō f, temporum ōrdō m

chronometer n hōrologium nt

chubby adj pinguis

chuck vt conicere; ~ **out** extrūdere

chuckle vi rīdēre ♦ n rīsus m

chum n sodālis m

church n ecclēsia f

churl n rūsticus m

churlish adj difficilis, importūnus; avārus

churlishly adv rūsticē, avārē

churlishness n mōrōsitās f, avāritia f

chute n (motion) lāpsus m; (place) dēclīve nt

cicada n cicāda f

cincture n cingulum nt

cinder n cinis m

cipher n numerus m, nihil nt; (code) notae fpl; **in** ~ per notās

circle n orbis m, circulus m, gȳrus m; **form a** ~ **in** orbem cōnsistere ♦ vi sē circumagere, circumīre

circlet n īnfula f

circuit n ambitus m, circuitus m; (assizes) conventus m

circuitous adj longus; **a** ~ **route** circuitus m; (speech) ambāgēs fpl

circular adj rotundus

circulate vt (news) pervulgāre ♦ vi circumagī; (news) circumferrī, percrēbrēscere

circulation n ambitus m; **be in** ~ in manibus esse; **go out of** ~ obsolēscere

circumcise vt circumcīdere

circumference n ambitus m

circumlocution n ambāgēs fpl, circuitiō f

circumnavigate vt circumvehī

circumscribe vt circumscrībere; (restrict) coercēre, fīnīre

circumspect adj cautus, prūdēns

circumspection n cautiō f, prūdentia f, circumspectiō f

circumspectly adv cautē, prūdenter

circumstance n rēs f; **circumstances** rērum status m; (wealth) rēs f; **as circumstances arise** ē rē nātā; **under the circumstances** cum haec ita sint, essent; **under no circumstances** nēquāquam

circumstantial adj adventīcius; (detailed) accūrātus; ~ **evidence** coniectūra f

circumstantially adv accūrātē, subtīliter

circumvallation n circummūnītiō f

circumvent vt circumvenīre, fallere

circus n circus m

cistern n lacus m, cisterna f

citadel n arx f

citation n (LAW) vocātiō f; (mention) commemorātiō f

cite vt in iūs vocāre; (quote) commemorāre, prōferre

citizen n cīvis m/f; (of provincial town) mūniceps m; **fellow** ~ cīvis m/f; **Roman citizens** Quirītes mpl ♦ adj cīvīlis, cīvicus

citizenship n cīvitās f; **deprived of** ~ capite dēminūtus; **loss of** ~ capitis dēminūtiō f

citron n (fruit) citrum nt; (tree) citrus f

city n urbs f, oppidum nt

civic adj cīvīlis, cīvicus

civil adj (of citizens) cīvīlis; (war) cīvīlis, intestīnus, domesticus; (manners) urbānus, cōmis, officiōsus; (lawsuit) prīvātus

civilian n togātus m

civility n urbānitās f, cōmitās f; (act) officium nt

civilization n exculta hominum vīta f, cultus atque hūmānitās

civilize vt excolere, expolīre, ad hūmānum cultum dēdūcere

civil war n bellum cīvīle, bellum domesticum, bellum intestīnum

clad adj vestītus

claim vt (for oneself) adrogāre, adserere; (something due) poscere, postulāre, vindicāre; (at law) petere; (statement) adfirmāre ♦ n postulātiō f, postulātum nt; (at law) petītiō f, vindiciae fpl

claimant n petītor m

clam n chāma f

clamber vi scandere

clammy adj ūmidus, lentus

clamorous adj vōciferāns

clamour n strepitus m, clāmōrēs mpl ♦ vi: ~ **against** obstrepere (dat)

clamp n cōnfībula f

clan n gēns f

clandestine adj fūrtīvus

clandestinely adv clam, fūrtim

clang n clangor m, crepitus m ♦ vi increpāre

clangour n clangor m

clank n crepitus m ♦ vi crepitāre

clansman n gentīlis m

clap vi plaudere, applaudere; ~ **eyes on** cōnspicere; ~ **in prison** in vincula conicere ♦ n plausus m; (thunder) fragor m

clapper n plausor m

claptrap n iactātiō f

claque n plausōrēs mpl, operae fpl

clarify vt pūrgāre; (knowledge) illūstrāre ♦ vi liquēre

clarinet n tībia f

clarion n lituus m, cornū nt
clarity n perspicuitās f
clash n concursus m; (sound) strepitus m, crepitus m; (fig) discrepantia f ♦ vi concurrere; (sound) increpāre; (fig) discrepāre ♦ vt conflīgere
clasp n fībula f; (embrace) amplexus m ♦ vt implicāre; amplectī, complectī; ~ **together** interiungere
class n (POL) ōrdō m, classis f; (kind) genus nt; (school) classis f ♦ vt dēscrībere; ~ **as** in numerō (gen pl) referre, repōnere, habēre
classic n scrīptor classicus m
classical adj classicus; ~ **literature** litterae Graecae et Rōmānae
classics npl scrīptōrēs Graecī et Rōmānī
classify vt dēscrībere, in ōrdinem redigere
class-mate n condiscipulus m
clatter n crepitus m ♦ vi increpāre
clause n (GRAM) incīsum nt, membrum nt; (LAW) caput nt; (will) ēlogium nt; **in short clauses** incīsim
claw n unguis m, ungula f ♦ vt unguibus lacerāre
clay n argilla f; **made of** ~ fictilis
clayey adj argillāceus
claymore n gladius m
clean adj mundus; (fig) pūrus, castus; ~ **slate** novae tabulae fpl; **make a** ~ **sweep of** omnia tollere; **show a** ~ **pair of heels** sē in pedēs conicere; **my hands are** ~ innocēns sum ♦ adv prōrsus, tōtus ♦ vt pūrgāre
cleanliness n munditia f
cleanly adj mundus, nitidus ♦ adv mundē, pūrē
cleanse vt pūrgāre, abluere, dētergēre
clear adj clārus; (liquid) limpidus; (sound) pūrus; (sound) clārus; (weather) serēnus; (fact) manifestus, perspicuus; (language) illūstris, dīlūcidus; (conscience) rēctus, innocēns; **it is** ~ **liquet**; ~ **of** līber (abl), expers (gen); **be** ~ **about** rēctē intellegere; **keep** ~ **of** ēvītāre; **the coast is** ~ arbitrī absunt ♦ vt (of obstacles) expedīre, pūrgāre; (of a charge) absolvere; (self) pūrgāre; (profit) lucrārī; ~ **away** āmovēre, tollere; ~ **off** vt (debt) solvere, exsolvere ♦ vi facessere; ~ **out** ēluere, dētergēre; ~ **up** vt (difficulty) illūstrāre, ēnōdāre, explicāre ♦ vi (weather) disserēnāscere
clearance n pūrgātiō f; (space) intervallum nt
clearing n (in forest) lūcus m
clearly adv clārē; manifestē, apertē, perspicuē; (with clause) vidēlicet
clearness n clāritās f; (weather) serēnitās f; (mind) acūmen nt; (style) perspicuitās f
clear-sighted adj sagāx, perspicāx
cleavage n discidium nt
cleave vt (cut) findere, discindere ♦ vi (cling): ~ **to** haerēre (dat), adhaerēre (dat)
cleaver n dolabra f
cleft n rīma f, hiātus m ♦ adj fissus, discissus
clemency n clēmentia f, indulgentia f; **with** ~ clēmenter
clement adj clēmēns, misericors
clench vt (nail) retundere; (hand) comprimere
clerk n scrība m; (of court) lēctor m
clever adj callidus, ingeniōsus, doctus, astūtus
cleverly adv doctē, callidē, ingeniōsē
cleverness n calliditās f, sollertia f
clew n glomus nt

cliché n verbum trītum nt
client n cliēns m/f; (lawyer's) cōnsultor m; **body of clients** clientēla f
clientele n clientēla f
cliff n rūpēs f, scopulus m
climate n caelum nt
climax n (RHET) gradātiō f; (fig) culmen nt
climb vt, vi scandere, ascendere; ~ **down** dēscendere ♦ n ascēnsus m
climber n scandēns m
clime n caelum nt, plāga f
clinch vt cōnfirmāre
cling vi adhaerēre; ~ **together** cohaerere
clink vi tinnīre ♦ n tinnītus m
clip vt tondēre; praecīdere
clippers n forfex f
clique n factiō f
cloak n (rain) lacerna f; (travel) paenula f; (MIL) sagum nt; palūdāmentum nt; (Greek) pallium nt; (fig) involūcrum nt; (pretext) speciēs f ♦ vt tegere, dissimulāre
clock n hōrologium nt; (sun) sōlārium nt; (water) clepsydra f; **ten o'clock** quarta hōra
clockwise adv dextrōvorsum, dextrōrsum
clod n glaeba f
clog n (shoe) sculpōnea f; (fig) impedīmentum nt ♦ vt impedīre
cloister n porticus f
cloistered adj (fig) umbrātilis
close¹ adj (shut) clausus; (tight) artus; (narrow) angustus; (near) propinquus; (compact) refertus, dēnsus; (stingy) parcus; (secret) obscūrus; (weather) crassus; ~ **together** dēnsus, refertus; **at** ~ **quarters** comminus; **be** ~ **at hand** (deal) pacīscī; (offer) accipere ♦ n fīnis m, terminus m; (action) exitus m; (sentence) conclūsiō f; **at the** ~ **of summer** aestāte exeunte
closely adv prope; (attending) attentē; (associating) coniūnctē; **follow** ~ īnstāre (dat)
closeness n propinquitās f; (weather) gravitās f, crassitūdō f; (with money) parsimōnia f; (friends) coniūnctiō f; (manner) cautiō f
closet n cubiculum nt, cella f ♦ vt inclūdere
clot n (blood) concrētus sanguis m ♦ vi concrēscere
cloth n textile nt; (piece) pannus m; (linen) linteum nt; (covering) strāgulum nt
clothe vt vestīre
clothes n vestis f, vestītus m, vestīmenta ntpl
clothier n vestiārius m
clothing n vestis f, vestītus m, vestīmenta ntpl
clotted adj concrētus
cloud n nūbēs f; (storm) nimbus m; (dust) globus m; (disfavour) invidia f ♦ vt nūbibus obdūcere; (fig) obscūrāre
clouded adj obnūbilus
cloudiness n nūbilum nt
cloudless adj pūrus, serēnus
cloudy adj obnūbilus

clout *n* pannus *m*
cloven *adj* (hoof) bifidus
clover *n* trifolium *nt*
clown *n* (boor) rūsticus *m*; (comic) scurra *m*
clownish *adj* rūsticus, inurbānus
clownishness *n* rūsticitās *f*
cloy *vt* satiāre
cloying *adj* pūtidus
club *n* (stick) fustis *m*, clāva *f*; (society) sodālitās *f*;
~ **together** *vi* in commūne cōnsulere, pecūniās
cōnferre
club-footed *adj* scaurus
cluck *vi* singultīre ♦ *n* singultus *m*
clue *n* indicium *nt*, vestīgium *nt*
clump *n* massa *f*; (earth) glaeba *f*; (trees) arbustum
nt; (willows) salictum *nt*
clumsily *adv* ineptē, inēleganter; incondītē,
īnfabrē
clumsiness *n* īnscītia *f*
clumsy *adj* (person) inconcinnus, ineptus; (thing)
inhabilis; (work) inconditus
cluster *n* cumulus *m*; (grapes) racēmus *m*; (people)
corōna *f* ♦ *vi* congregārī
clutch *vt* prehendere, adripere; ~ **at** captāre
nt, comprehēnsiō *f*; **from one's clutches** ē
manibus; **in one's clutches** in potestāte
clutter *n* turba *f* ♦ *vt* impedīre, obstruere
coach *n* currus *m*, raeda *f*, pīlentum *nt*; (trainer)
magister *m* ♦ *vt* ēdocēre, praecipere (dat)
coachman *n* aurīga *m*, raedārius *m*
coagulate *vt* cōgere ♦ *vi* concrēscere
coagulation *n* concrētiō *f*
coal *n* carbō *m*; **carry coals to Newcastle** in
silvam ligna ferre
coalesce *vi* coīre, coalēscere
coalition *n* coitiō *f*, cōnspīrātiō *f*
coarse *adj* (quality) crassus; (manners) rūsticus,
inurbānus; (speech) īnfacētus
coarsely *adv* inurbānē, inēleganter
coarseness *n* crassitūdō *f*; rūsticitās *f*
coast *n* lītus *nt*, ōra maritima *f* ♦ *vi*: ~ **along**
legere, praetervehī
coastal *adj* lītorālis, maritimus
coastline *n* lītus *nt*
coat *n* pallium *nt*; (animals) pellis *f* ♦ *vt* indūcere,
inlinere
coating *n* corium *nt*
coax *vt* blandīrī, dēlēnīre
coaxing *adj* blandus ♦ *n* blanditiae *fpl*
cob *n* (horse) mannus *m*; (swan) cygnus *m*
cobble *n* lapis *m* ♦ *vt* sarcīre
cobbler *n* sūtor *m*
cobweb *n* arāneum *nt*
cock *n* gallus *m*, gallus gallīnāceus *m*; (other birds)
mās *m*; (tap) epitonium *nt*; (hay) acervus *m*
cockatrice *n* basiliscus *m*
cockchafer *n* scarabaeus *m*
cockcrow *n* gallī cantus *m* ♦ *vt* ērigere
cockerel *n* pullus *m*
cockroach *n* blatta *f*
cocksure *adj* cōnfīdēns
cod *n* callarias *m*
coddle *vt* indulgēre (dat), permulcēre
code *n* fōrmula *f*; (secret) notae *fpl*
codicil *n* cōdicillī *mpl*
codify *vt* in ōrdinem redigere

coequal *adj* aequālis
coerce *vt* cōgere
coercion *n* vīs *f*
coffer *n* arca *f*, cista *f*; (public) fiscus *m*
coffin *n* arca *f*
cog *n* dēns *m*
cogency *n* vīs *f*, pondus *nt*
cogent *adj* gravis, validus
cogitate *vi* cōgitāre, meditārī
cogitation *n* cōgitātiō *f*; meditātiō *f*
cognate *adj* cognātus
cognition *n* cognitiō *f*
cognizance *n* cognitiō *f*; **take ~ of** cognōscere
cognizant *adj* gnārus
cohabit *vi* cōnsuēscere
cohabitation *n* cōnsuētūdō *f*
coheir *n* cohērēs *m/f*
cohere *vi* cohaerēre; (statement) congruere
coherence *n* coniūnctiō *f*; (fig) convenientia *f*
coherent *adj* congruēns
cohesion *n* coagmentātiō *f*
cohesive *adj* tenāx
cohort *n* cohors *f*
coil *n* spīra *f* ♦ *vt* glomerāre
coin *n* nummus *m* ♦ *vt* cūdere; (fig) fingere
coinage *n* monēta *f*; (fig) fictum *nt*
coincide *vi* concurrere; (opinion) cōnsentīre
coincidence *n* concursus *m*; cōnsēnsus *m*; **by
a ~** cāsū
coincidental *adj* fortuītus
coiner *n* (of money) signātor *m*
col *n* iugum *nt*
colander *n* cōlum *nt*
cold *adj* frīgidus; (icy) gelidus; **very ~** perfrīgidus;
be ~, feel ~ algēre, frīgēre; **get ~** algēscere,
frīgēscere ♦ *n* frīgus *nt*; (felt) algor *m*; (malady)
gravēdō *f*; **catch ~** algēscere, frīgus colligere;
catch a ~ gravēdinem contrahere; **have a
~** gravēdine labōrāre
coldish *adj* frīgidulus, frīgidior
coldly *adv* (manner) sine studiō
coldness *n* frīgus *nt*, algor *m*
cold water *n* frīgida *f*
colic *n* tormina *ntpl*
collar *n* collāre *nt*
collarbone *n* iugulum *nt*
collate *vt* cōnferre, comparāre
collateral *adj* adiūnctus; (evidence)
cōnsentāneus
collation *n* collātiō *f*; (meal) prandium *nt*,
merenda *f*
colleague *n* collēga *m*
collect *vt* colligere, cōgere, congerere; (persons)
congregāre, convocāre; (taxes) exigere;
(something due) recipere; ~ **oneself** animum
colligere; **cool and collected** aequō animō ♦ *vi*
convenīre, congregārī
collection *n* (persons) coetus *m*, conventus *m*;
(things) congeriēs *f*; (money) exāctiō *f*
collective *adj* commūnis
collectively *adv* commūniter
collector *n* (of taxes) exāctor *m*
college *n* collēgium *nt*
collide *vi* concurrere, cōnflīctārī
collier *n* carbōnārius *m*
collision *n* concursus *m*

collocation n collocātiō f
collop n offa f
colloquial adj cottīdiānus
colloquy n sermō m, colloquium nt
collude vi praevāricārī
collusion n praevāricātiō f
collusive adj praevāricātor
colonel n lēgātus m
colonial adj colōnicus ♦ n colōnus m
colonist n colōnus m
colonization n dēductiō f
colonize vt colōniam dēdūcere, cōnstituere in (acc)
colonnade n porticus f
colony n colōnia f
colossal adj ingēns, vastus
colossus n colossus m
colour n color m; (paint) pigmentum nt; (artificial) fūcus m; (complexion) color m; (pretext) speciēs f; **take on a ~** colōrem dūcere; **under ~ of** per speciem (gen); **local ~** māteria dē regiōne sūmpta ♦ vt colōrāre; (dye) īnficere, fūcāre; (fig) praetendere (dat) ♦ vi rubēre, ērubēscere
colourable adj speciōsus
coloured adj (naturally) colōrātus; (artificially) fūcātus
colourful adj fūcōsus, varius
colouring n pigmentum nt; (dye) fūcus m
colourless adj perlūcidus; (person) pallidus; (fig) īnsulsus
colours n (MIL) signum nt, vexillum nt; (POL) partēs fpl; **sail under false ~** aliēnō nōmine ūtī; **with flying ~** māximā cum glōriā
colour sergeant n signifer m
colt n equuleus m, equulus m
coltsfoot n farfarus m
column n columna f; (MIL) agmen nt
coma n sopor m
comb n pecten m; (bird) crista f; (loom) pecten m; (honey) favus m ♦ vt pectere
combat n pugna f, proelium nt, certāmen nt ♦ vi pugnāre, dīmicāre, certāre ♦ vt pugnāre cum (abl), obsistere (dat)
combatant n pugnātor m ♦ adj pugnāns; **non-combatant** imbellis
combative adj ferōx, pugnāx
combination n coniūnctiō f, cōnfūsiō f; (persons) cōnspīrātiō f; (illegal) coniūrātiō f
combine vt coniungere, iungere ♦ vi coīre, coniungī ♦ n societās f
combustible adj ignī obnoxius
combustion n dēflāgrātiō f, incendium nt
come vi venīre, advenīre; (after a journey) dēvenīre; (interj) age!; **how comes it that …?** quī fit ut …?; **~ across** vi invenīre, offendere; **~ after** sequī, excipere, succēdere (dat); **~ again** revenīre, redīre; **~ away** vi abscēdere; (when pulled) sequī; **~ back** vi revenīre, redīre; regredī; **~ between** intervenīre, intercēdere; **~ down** vi dēvenīre, dēscendere; (from the past) trādī, prōdī; **~ forward** vi prōcēdere, prōdīre; **~ from** vi (origin) dēfluere; **~ in** vi inīre, introīre; ingredī; (revenue) redīre; **~ near** accēdere ad (acc), appropinquāre (dat); **~ nearer and nearer** adventāre; **~ of** vi (family) ortum esse ab, ex (abl); **~ off** vi ēvādere, discēdere; **~ on** vi prōcēdere; (progress) prōficere;

(interj) age, agite; **~ on the scene** intervenīre, supervenīre, adesse; **~ out** vi exīre, ēgredī; (hair, teeth) cadere; (flower) flōrēscere; (book) ēdī; **~ over** vi trānsīre; (feeling) subīre, occupāre; **~ to** vi advenīre ad, in (acc); (person) adīre; (amount) efficere; **~ to the help of** subvenīre (dat); succurrere (dat); **~ to nought** ad nihilum recidere; **~ to pass** ēvenīre, fierī; **~ together** convenīre, coīre; **~ up** vi subīre, succēdere; (growth) prōvenīre; **~ upon** vt invenīre; **he is coming to** animus eī redit
comedian n (actor) cōmoedus m; (writer) cōmicus m
comedienne n mīma f
comedy n cōmoedia f
comeliness n decor m, decōrum nt
comely adj decōrus, pulcher
comestibles n vīctus m
comet n comētēs m
comfort vt sōlārī, cōnsōlārī, adlevāre ♦ n sōlācium nt, cōnsōlātiō f
comfortable adj commodus; **make oneself ~** corpus cūrāre
comfortably adv commodē
comforter n cōnsōlātor m
comfortless adj incommodus; **be ~** sōlātiō carēre
comforts npl commoda ntpl
comic adj cōmicus; facētus ♦ n scurra m
comical adj facētus, rīdiculus
coming adj futūrus ♦ n adventus m
comity n cōmitās f
command vt iubēre (+ acc and infin), imperāre (dat and ut + subj); dūcere; (feelings) regere; (resources) fruī (abl); (view) prōspectāre ♦ n (MIL) imperium nt; (sphere) prōvincia f; (order) imperium nt, iussum nt, mandātum nt; **be in ~ of** praeesse (dat); **put in ~ of** praeficere (dat); **~ of language** fācundia f
commandant n praefectus m
commandeer vt pūblicāre
commander n dux m, praefectus m
commander in chief n imperātor m
commandment n mandātum nt
commemorate vt celebrāre, memoriae trādere
commemoration n celebrātiō f
commence vt incipere, exōrdīrī, initium facere (gen)
commencement n initium nt, exōrdium nt, prīncipium nt
commend vt laudāre; (recommend) commendāre; (entrust) mandāre; **~ oneself** sē probāre
commendable adj laudābilis, probābilis
commendation n laus f, commendātiō f
commendatory adj commendātīcius
commensurable adj pār
commensurate adj congruēns, conveniēns
comment vi dīcere, scrībere; **~ on** interpretārī; (with notes) adnotāre ♦ n dictum nt, sententia f
commentary n commentāriī mpl
commentator n interpres m
commerce n mercātūra f, commercium nt; **engage in ~** mercātūrās facere, negōtiārī
commercial dealings n commercium nt
commercial traveller n īnstitor m
commination n minae fpl

comminatory *adj* mināx
commingle *vt* intermiscēre
commiserate *vt* miserērī (*gen*)
commiseration *n* misericordia *f*; (RHET) commiserātiō *f*
commissariat *n* rēs frūmentāria *f*, commeātus *m*; (*staff*) frūmentāriī *mpl*
commissary *n* lēgātus *m*; reī frūmentāriae praefectus *m*
commission *n* (*charge*) mandātum *nt*; (*persons*) triumvirī *mpl*, decemvirī *mpl*; (*abroad*) lēgātiō *f*; **get a ~** (MIL) tribūnum fierī; **standing ~** (LAW) quaestiō perpetua *f* ♦ *vt* mandāre, adlēgāre
commissioner *n* lēgātus *m*; **three commissioners** triumvirī *mpl*; **ten commissioners** decemvirī *mpl*
commit *vt* (*charge*) committere, mandāre; (*crime*) admittere; (*to prison*) conicere; (*to an undertaking*) obligāre, obstringere; **~ to memory** memoriae trādere; **~ to writing** litterīs mandāre; **~ an error** errāre; **~ a theft** fūrtum facere; *see also* **suicide**
commitment *n* mūnus *nt*, officium *nt*
committee *n* dēlēctī *mpl*
commodious *adj* capāx
commodity *n* merx *f*, rēs *f*
commodore *n* praefectus classis *m*
common *adj* (*for all*) commūnis; (*ordinary*) vulgāris, cottīdiānus; (*repeated*) frequēns, crēber; (*inferior*) nēquam ♦ *n* compāscuus ager *m*, prātum *nt*; **~ man** homō plēbēius *m*; **~ soldier** gregārius mīles *m*
commonalty *n* plēbs *f*
commoner *n* homō plēbēius *m*
common law *n* mōs māiōrum *m*
commonly *adv* ferē, vulgō
common people *n* plēbs *f*, vulgus *nt*
commonplace *n* trītum prōverbium *nt*; (RHET) locus commūnis *m* ♦ *adj* vulgāris, trītus
commons *n* plēbs *f*; (*food*) diāria *ntpl*
common sense *n* prūdentia *f*
commonwealth *n* cīvitās *f*, rēs pūblica *f*
commotion *n* perturbātiō *f*, tumultus *m*; **cause a ~** tumultuārī
communal *adj* commūnis
commune *n* pāgus *m* ♦ *vi* colloquī, sermōnēs cōnferre
communicate *vt* commūnicāre; (*information*) nūntiāre, patefacere ♦ *vi*: **~ with** commūnicāre (*dat*), commercium habēre (*gen*), agere cum (*abl*)
communication *n* (*dealings*) commercium *nt*; (*information*) litterae *fpl*, nūntius *m*; (*passage*) commeātus *m*; **cut off the communications of** interclūdere
communicative *adj* loquāx
communion *n* societās *f*
communiqué *n* litterae *fpl*, praedicātiō *f*
communism *n* bonōrum aequātiō *f*
community *n* cīvitās *f*, commūne *nt*; (*participation*) commūniō *f*
commutation *n* mūtātiō *f*
commute *vt* mūtāre, commūtāre
compact *n* foedus *nt*, conventum *nt* ♦ *adj* dēnsus ♦ *vt* dēnsāre

companion *n* socius *m*, comes *m/f*; (*intimate*) sodālis *m*; (*at school*) condiscipulus *m*; (*in army*) commīlitō *m*, contubernālis *m*
companionable *adj* facilis, commodus
companionship *n* sodālitās *f*, cōnsuētūdō *f*; (MIL) contubernium *nt*
company *n* societās *f*, cōnsuētūdō *f*; (*gathering*) coetus *m*, conventus *m*; (*guests*) cēnantēs *mpl*; (*commercial*) societās *f*; (*magistrates*) collēgium *nt*; (MIL) manipulus *m*; (THEAT) grex *m*, caterva *f*; **~ of ten** decuria *f*
comparable *adj* comparābilis, similis
comparative *adj* māgnus, sī cum aliīs cōnfertur
comparatively *adv* ut in tālī tempore, ut in eā regiōne, ut est captus hominum; **~ few** perpaucī, nullus ferē
compare *vt* comparāre, cōnferre; **compared with** ad (*acc*)
comparison *n* comparātiō *f*, collātiō *f*; (RHET) similitūdō *f*; **in ~ with** prō (*abl*)
compartment *n* cella *f*, pars *f*
compass *n* ambitus *m*, spatium *nt*, modus *m*; **pair of compasses** circinus *m* ♦ *vt* circumdare, cingere; (*attain*) cōnsequī
compassion *n* misericordia *f*
compassionate *adj* misericors, clēmēns
compassionately *adv* clēmenter
compatibility *n* convenientia *f*
compatible *adj* congruēns, conveniēns; **be ~** congruere
compatibly *adv* congruenter, convenienter
compatriot *n* cīvis *m*, populāris *m*
compeer *n* pār *m*; aequālis *m*
compel *vt* cōgere
compendious *adj* brevis
compendiously *adv* summātim
compendium *n* epitomē *f*
compensate *vt* compēnsāre, satisfacere (*dat*)
compensation *n* compēnsātiō *f*; pretium *nt*, poena *f*
compete *vi* certāre, contendere
competence *n* facultās *f*; (LAW) iūs *nt*; (*money*) quod sufficit
competent *adj* perītus, satis doctus, capāx; (*witness*) locuplēs; **it is ~** licet
competition *n* certāmen *nt*, contentiō *f*
competitor *n* competītor *m*, aemulus *m*
compilation *n* collectānea *ntpl*, liber *m*
compile *vt* compōnere
compiler *n* scrīptor *m*
complacency *n* amor suī *m*
complacent *adj* suī contentus
complain *vi* querī, conquerī; **~ of** (*person*) nōmen dēferre (*gen*)
complainant *n* accūsātor *m*, petītor *m*
complaint *n* questus *m*, querimōnia *f*; (LAW) crīmen *nt*; (MED) morbus *m*, valētūdō *f*
complaisance *n* cōmitās *f*, obsequium *nt*, indulgentia *f*
complaisant *adj* cōmis, officiōsus, facilis
complement *n* complēmentum *nt*; numerus suus *m*; **make up the ~ of** complēre
complete *vt* (*amount, time*) complēre, explēre; (*work*) cōnficere, perficere, absolvere, peragere

♦ *adj* perfectus, absolūtus, integer; (*victory*) iūstus; (*amount*) explētus

completely *adv* funditus, omnīnō, absolūtē, plānē; penitus

completeness *n* integritās *f*; (*perfection*) perfectiō *f*

completion *n* (*process*) absolūtiō *f*, cōnfectiō *f*; (*end*) fīnis *m*; **bring to ~** absolvere

complex *adj* implicātus, multiplex

complexion *n* color *m*

complexity *n* implicātiō *f*

compliance *n* accommodātiō *f*, obsequium *nt*, obtemperātiō *f*

compliant *adj* obsequēns, facilis

complicate *vt* implicāre, impedīre

complicated *adj* implicātus, involūtus, impedītus

complication *n* implicātiō *f*

complicity *n* cōnscientia *f*

compliment *n* blandīmentum *nt*, honōs *m* ♦ *vt* blandīrī, laudāre; **~ on** grātulārī (*dat*) dē (*abl*)

complimentary *adj* honōrificus, blandus

compliments *npl* (*as greeting*) salūs *f*

comply *vi* obsequī (*dat*), obtemperāre (*dat*); mōrem gerere (*dat*), mōrigerārī (*dat*)

component *n* elementum *nt*, pars *f*

comport *vt* gerere

compose *vt* (*art*) compōnere, condere, pangere; (*whole*) efficere, cōnflāre; (*quarrel*) compōnere, dīrimere; (*disturbance*) sēdāre; **be composed of** cōnsistere ex (*abl*), cōnstāre ex (*abl*)

composed *adj* tranquillus, placidus

composer *n* auctor *m*, scrīptor *m*

composite *adj* multiplex

composition *n* (*process*) compositiō *f*, scrīptūra *f*; (*product*) opus *nt*, poēma *nt*, carmen *nt*; (*quality*) structūra *f*

composure *n* sēcūritās *f*, aequus animus *m*; (*face*) tranquillitās *f*

compound *vt* miscēre; (*words*) duplicāre, iungere ♦ *vi* (*agree*) pacīscī ♦ *adj* compositus ♦ *n* (*word*) iūnctum verbum *nt*; (*area*) saeptum *nt*

compound interest *n* anatocismus *m*

comprehend *vt* intellegere, comprehendere; (*include*) continēre, complectī

comprehensible *adj* perspicuus

comprehension *n* intellegentia *f*, comprehēnsiō *f*

comprehensive *adj* capāx; **be ~** lātē patēre, multa complectī

compress *vt* comprimere, coartāre ♦ *n* fōmentum *nt*

compression *n* compressus *m*

comprise *vt* continēre, complectī, comprehendere

compromise *n* (*by one side*) accommodātiō *f*; (*by both sides*) comprōmissum *nt* ♦ *vi* comprōmittere ♦ *vt* implicāre, in suspiciōnem vocāre; **be compromised** in suspiciōnem venīre

comptroller *n* moderātor *m*

compulsion *n* necessitās *f*, vīs *f*; **under ~** coāctus

compulsory *adj* necesse, lēge imperātus; **use ~ measures** vim adhibēre

compunction *n* paenitentia *f*

computation *n* ratiō *f*

compute *vt* computāre, ratiōnem dūcere

comrade *n* socius *m*, contubernālis *m*

comradeship *n* contubernium *nt*

concatenation *n* seriēs *f*

concave *adj* concavus

conceal *vt* cēlāre, abdere, abscondere; (*fact*) dissimulāre

concealment *n* occultātiō *f*; (*place*) latebrae *fpl*; (*of facts*) dissimulātiō *f*; **in ~** abditus, occultus; **be in ~** latēre, latitāre; **go into ~** dēlitēscere

concede *vt* concēdere

conceit *n* (*idea*) nōtiō *f*; (*wit*) facētiae *fpl*; (*pride*) superbia *f*, adrogantia *f*, vānitās *f*

conceited *adj* glōriōsus, adrogāns

conceitedness *n* adrogantia *f*, vānitās *f*

conceive *vt* concipere, comprehendere, intellegere

concentrate *vt* (*in one place*) cōgere, congregāre; (*attention*) intendere, dēfīgere

concentrated *adj* dēnsus

concentration *n* animī intentiō *f*

concept *n* nōtiō *f*

conception *n* conceptus *m*; (*mind*) intellegentia *f*, īnfōrmātiō *f*; (*idea*) nōtiō *f*, cōgitātiō *f*, cōnsilium *nt*

concern *vt* (*refer*) attinēre ad (*acc*), interesse (*gen*); (*worry*) sollicitāre; **it concerns me** meā rēfert, meā interest; **as far as I am concerned** per mē ♦ *n* rēs *f*, negōtium *nt*; (*importance*) mōmentum *nt*; (*worry*) sollicitūdō *f*, cūra *f*; (*regret*) dolor *m*

concerned *adj* sollicitus, anxius; **be ~** dolēre; **be ~ about** molestē ferre

concerning *prep* dē (*abl*)

concernment *n* sollicitūdō *f*

concert *n* (*music*) concentus *m*; (*agreement*) cōnsēnsus *m*; **in ~** ex compositō, ūnō animō ♦ *vt* compōnere; (*plan*) inīre

concession *n* concessiō *f*; **by the ~ of** concessū (*gen*); **make a ~** concēdere, tribuere

conciliate *vt* conciliāre

conciliation *n* conciliātiō *f*

conciliator *n* arbiter *m*

conciliatory *adj* pācificus

concise *adj* brevis; (*style*) dēnsus

concisely *adv* breviter

conciseness *n* brevitās *f*

conclave *n* sēcrētus cōnsessus *m*

conclude *vt* (*end*) termināre, fīnīre, cōnficere; (*settle*) facere, compōnere, pangere; (*infer*) īnferre, colligere

conclusion *n* (*end*) fīnis *m*; (*of action*) exitus *m*; (*of speech*) perōrātiō *f*; (*inference*) coniectūra *f*; (*decision*) placitum *nt*, sententia *f*; **in ~** dēnique; **try conclusions with** contendere cum

conclusive *adj* certus, manifestus, gravis

conclusively *adv* sine dubiō

concoct *vt* coquere; (*fig*) cōnflāre

concoction *n* (*fig*) māchinātiō *f*

concomitant *adj* adiūnctus

concord *n* concordia *f*; (*music*) harmonia *f*

concordant *adj* concors

concordat *n* pactum *nt*, foedus *nt*

concourse *n* frequentia *f*, celebrātiō *f*; (*moving*) concursus *m*

concrete *adj* concrētus; **in the ~** rē

concretion *n* concrētiō *f*

concubine n concubīna f
concupiscence n libīdō f
concur vi (time) concurrere; (opinion) cōnsentīre, adsentīre
concurrence n (time) concursus m; (opinion) cōnsēnsus m
concurrent adj (time) aequālis; (opinion) cōnsentāneus; **be ~** concurrere, cōnsentīre
concurrently adv simul, ūnā
concussion n ictus m
condemn vt damnāre, condemnāre; (disapprove) improbāre; **~ to death** capitis damnāre; **~ for treason** dē māiestāte damnāre
condemnation n damnātiō f; condemnātiō f
condemnatory adj damnātōrius
condense vt dēnsāre; (words) premere
condescend vi dēscendere, sē submittere
condescending adj cōmis
condescension n cōmitās f
condiment n condīmentum nt
condition n (of body) habitus m; (external) status m, condiciō f, rēs f; (in society) locus m, fortūna f; (of agreement) condiciō f, lēx f; **conditions of sale** mancipī lēx f; **on ~ that** eā condicione ut (subj); **in ~** (animals) nitidus ♦ vt fōrmāre, regere
conditional adj: **the assistance is ~ on** eā condiciōne succurritur ut (subj)
conditionally adv sub condiciōne
conditioned adj (character) mōrātus
condole vi: **~ with** cōnsōlārī
condolence n cōnsōlātiō f
condonation n venia f
condone vt condōnāre, ignōscere (dat)
conduce vi condūcere (ad), prōficere (ad)
conducive adj ūtilis, accommodātus
conduct vt dūcere; (escort) dēdūcere; (to a place) addūcere, perdūcere; (business) gerere, administrāre; (self) gerere ♦ n mōrēs mpl; (past) vīta f, facta ntpl; (business) administrātiō f; **safe ~** praesidium nt
conductor n dux m, ductor m
conduit n canālis m, aquae ductus m
cone n cōnus m
coney n cunīculus m
confabulate vi colloquī
confection n cuppēdō f
confectioner n cuppēdinārius m
confectionery n dulcia ntpl
confederacy n foederātae cīvitātēs fpl, societās f
confederate adj foederātus ♦ n socius m ♦ vi coniūrāre, foedus facere
confederation n societās f
confer vt cōnferre, tribuere ♦ vi colloquī, sermōnem cōnferre; **~ about** agere dē (abl)
conference n colloquium nt, congressus m
conferment n dōnātiō f
confess vt fatērī, cōnfitērī
confessedly adv manifestō
confession n cōnfessiō f
confidant n cōnscius m
confide vi fīdere (dat), cōnfīdere (dat) ♦ vt crēdere, committere
confidence n fidēs f, fidūcia f; **have ~ in** fīdere (dat), cōnfīdere (dat); **inspire ~ in** fidem facere (dat); **tell in ~** tūtīs auribus dēpōnere

confident adj fīdēns; **~ in** frētus (abl); **be ~ that** certō scīre, prō certō habēre
confidential adj arcānus, intimus
confidentially adv inter nōs
confidently adv fīdenter
confiding adj crēdulus
configuration n figūra f, fōrma f
confine vt (prison) inclūdere, in vincula conicere; (limit) termināre, circumscrībere; (restrain) coercēre, cohibēre; (to bed) dētinēre; **be confined** (women) parturīre
confinement n custōdia f, vincula ntpl, inclūsiō f; (women) puerperium nt
confines n fīnēs mpl
confirm vt (strength) corrōborāre, firmāre; (decision) sancīre, ratum facere; (fact) adfirmāre, comprobāre
confirmation n cōnfirmātiō f, adfirmātiō f
confirmed adj ratus
confiscate vt pūblicāre
confiscation n pūblicātiō f
conflagration n incendium nt, dēflāgrātiō f
conflict n (physical) concursus m; (hostile) certāmen nt, proelium nt; (verbal) contentiō f, contrōversia f; (contradiction) repugnantia f, discrepantia f ♦ vi inter sē repugnāre
conflicting adj contrārius
confluence n cōnfluēns m
confluent adj cōnfluēns
conform vt accommodāre ♦ vi sē cōnfōrmāre (ad), obsequī (dat), mōrem gerere (dat)
conformable adj accommodātus, conveniēns
conformably adv convenienter
conformation n structūra f, cōnfōrmātiō f
conformity n convenientia f, cōnsēnsus m
confound vt (mix) cōnfundere, permiscēre; (amaze) obstupefacere; (thwart) frustrārī; (suppress) opprimere, obruere; **~ you!** dī tē perduint
confounded adj miser, sacer, nefandus
confoundedly adv mīrum quantum nefāriē
confraternity n frāternitās f
confront vt sē oppōnere (dat), obviam īre (dat), sē cōram offerre
confuse vt permiscēre, perturbāre
confused adj perturbātus
confusedly adv perturbātē, prōmiscuē
confusion n perturbātiō f; (shame) rubor m
confutation n refūtātiō f
confute vt refūtāre, redarguere, convincere
congé n commeātus m
congeal vt congelāre, dūrāre ♦ vi concrēscere
congealed adj concrētus
congenial adj concors, congruēns, iūcundus
congeniality n concordia f, mōrum similitūdō f
congenital adj nātīvus
conger n conger m
congested adj refertus, dēnsus; (with people) frequentissimus
congestion n congeriēs f; frequentia f
conglomerate vt glomerāre
conglomeration n congeriēs f, cumulus m
congratulate vt grātulārī (dat)
congratulation n grātulātiō f
congratulatory adj grātulābundus

congregate *vt* congregāre, cōgere ♦ *vi* convenīre, congregārī

congregation *n* conventus *m*, coetus *m*

congress *n* conventus *m*, cōnsessus *m*, concilium *nt*; senātus *m*

congruence *n* convenientia *f*

congruent *adj* conveniēns, congruēns

congruently *adv* convenienter, congruenter

congruous *adj see* **congruent**

conical *adj* turbinātus

coniferous *adj* cōnifer

conjectural *adj* opīnābilis

conjecturally *adv* coniectūrā

conjecture *n* coniectūra *f* ♦ *vt* conicere, augurārī

conjoin *vt* coniungere

conjoint *adj* coniūnctus

conjointly *adv* coniūnctē, ūnā

conjugal *adj* coniugālis

conjugate *vt* dēclīnāre

conjugation *n* (GRAM) dēclīnātiō *f*

conjunct *adj* coniūnctus

conjunction *n* coniūnctiō *f*, concursus *m*

conjure *vt* (*entreat*) obtestārī, obsecrāre; (*spirits*) ēlicere, ciēre ♦ *vi* praestigiīs ūtī

conjurer *n* praestigiātor *m*

conjuring *n* praestigiae *fpl*

connate *adj* innātus, nātūrā īnsitus

connect *vt* iungere, coniungere, cōpulāre, connectere

connected *adj* coniūnctus; (*unbroken*) continēns; (*by marriage*) adfīnis; **be ~ with** contingere; **be closely ~ with** inhaerēre (*dat*), cohaerēre cum (*abl*)

connectedly *adv* coniūnctē, continenter

connection *n* coniūnctiō *f*, contextus *m*, seriēs *f*; (*kin*) necessitūdō *f*; (*by marriage*) adfīnitās *f*; **~ between ... and ...** ratiō (*gen*) ... cum ... (*abl*); **I have no ~ with you** nīl mihī tēcum est

connivance *n* venia *f*, dissimulātiō *f*

connive *vi* conīvēre in (*abl*), dissimulāre

connoisseur *n* intellegēns *m*

connotation *n* vīs *f*, significātiō *f*

connote *vt* significāre

connubial *adj* coniugālis

conquer *vt* vincere, superāre

conquerable *adj* superābilis, expugnābilis

conqueror *n* victor *m*

conquest *n* victōria *f*; (*town*) expugnātiō *f*; (*prize*) praemium *nt*, praeda *f*; **the ~ of Greece** Graecia capta

conscience *n* cōnscientia *f*; **guilty ~** mala cōnscientia; **have a clear ~** nullīus culpae sibi cōnscium esse; **have no ~** nullam rēligiōnem habēre

conscientious *adj* probus, rēligiōsus

conscientiously *adv* bonā fidē, rēligiōsē

conscientiousness *n* fidēs *f*, rēligiō *f*

conscious *adj* sibī cōnscius; (*aware*) gnārus; (*physically*) mentis compos; **be ~** sentīre

consciously *adv* sciēns

consciousness *n* animus *m*; (*of action*) cōnscientia *f*; **he lost ~** animus eum relīquit

conscript *n* tīrō *m* ♦ *vt* cōnscrībere

conscription *n* dēlēctus *m*; (*of wealth*) pūblicātiō *f*

consecrate *vt* dēdicāre, cōnsecrāre; (*self*) dēvovēre

consecrated *adj* sacer

consecration *n* dēdicātiō *f*, cōnsecrātiō *f*; (*self*) dēvōtiō *f*

consecutive *adj* dēinceps, continuus

consecutively *adv* dēinceps, ōrdine

consensus *n* cōnsēnsus *m*

consent *vi* adsentīre (*dat*), adnuere (*inf*); (*together*) cōnsentīre ♦ *n* (*one side*) adsēnsus *m*; (*all*) cōnsēnsus *m*; **by common ~** omnium cōnsēnsū

consequence *n* ēventus *m*, exitus *m*; (LOGIC) conclūsiō *f*; (*importance*) mōmentum *nt*, auctōritās *f*; **it is of ~** interest; **what will be the ~ of?** quō ēvādet?

consequent *adj* cōnsequēns

consequential *adj* cōnsentāneus; (*person*) adrogāns

consequently *adv* itaque, igitur, proptereā

conservation *n* cōnservātiō *f*

conservative *adj* reī pūblicae cōnservandae studiōsus; (*estimate*) mediōcris; **~ party** optimātēs *mpl*

conservator *n* custōs *m*, cōnservātor *m*

conserve *vt* cōnservāre, servāre

consider *vt* cōnsīderāre, contemplārī; (*reflect*) sēcum volūtāre, meditari, dēlīberāre, cōgitāre; (*deem*) habēre, dūcere; (*respect*) respicere, observāre

considerable *adj* aliquantus, nōnnullus; (*person*) illūstris

considerably *adv* aliquantum; (*with compar*) aliquantō, multō

considerate *adj* hūmānus, benignus

considerately *adv* hūmānē, benignē

consideration *n* cōnsīderātiō *f*, contemplātiō *f*, dēlīberātiō *f*; (*respect*) respectus *m*, ratiō *f*; (*importance*) mōmentum *nt*; (*reason*) ratiō *f*; (*pay*) pretium *nt*; **for a ~** mercēde, datā mercēde; **in ~ of** propter (*acc*), prō (*abl*); **on no ~** nēquāquam; **with ~** cōnsultō; **without ~** temerē; **take into ~** ad cōnsilium dēferre; **show ~ for** respectum habēre (*gen*)

considered *adj* (*reasons*) exquīsītus

considering *prep* prō (*abl*), propter (*acc*) ♦ *conj* ut, quōniam

consign *vt* mandāre, committere

consist *vi* cōnstāre; **~ in** cōnstāre ex (*abl*), continērī (*abl*), positum esse in (*abl*); **~ with** congruere (*dat*), convenīre (*dat*)

consistence *n* firmitās *f*

consistency *n* cōnstantia *f*

consistent *adj* cōnstāns; (*with*) cōnsentāneus, cōngruens; (*of movement*) aequābilis; **be ~** cohaerēre

consistently *adv* constanter

consolable *adj* cōnsōlābilis

consolation *n* cōnsōlātiō *f*; (*thing*) sōlācium *nt*

consolatory *adj* cōnsōlātōrius

console *vt* cōnsōlārī

consoler *n* cōnsōlātor *m*

consolidate *vt* (*liquid*) cōgere; (*strength*) corrōborāre; (*gains*) obtinēre ♦ *vi* concrēscere

consolidation *n* concrētiō *f*; cōnfirmātiō *f*

consonance *n* concentus *m*

consonant *adj* cōnsonus, haud absonus ♦ *n* cōnsonāns *f*

consort *n* cōnsors *m/f*, socius *m*; (*married*) coniunx *m/f* ♦ *vi*: ~ **with** familiāriter ūtī (*abl*), coniūnctissimē vīvere cum (*abl*)

conspectus *n* summārium *nt*

conspicuous *adj* ēminēns, īnsignis, manifestus; **be** ~ ēminēre

conspicuously *adv* manifestō, palam, ante oculōs

conspiracy *n* coniūrātiō *f*

conspirator *n* coniūrātus *m*

conspire *vi* coniūrāre; (*for good*) cōnspīrāre

constable *n* lictor *m*

constancy *n* cōnstantia *f*, firmitās *f*; **with** ~ cōnstanter

constant *adj* cōnstāns; (*faithful*) fīdus, fidēlis; (*continuous*) adsiduus

constantly *adv* adsiduē, saepe, crēbrō

constellation *n* sīdus *nt*

consternation *n* trepidātiō *f*, pavor *m*; **throw into** ~ perterrēre, cōnsternere

constituency *n* suffrāgātōrēs *mpl*

constituent *adj*: ~ **part** elementum *nt* ♦ *n* (*voter*) suffrāgātor *m*

constitute *vt* creāre, cōnstituere; esse

constitution *n* nātūra *f*, status *m*; (*body*) habitus *m*; (POL) cīvitātis fōrma *f*, reī pūblicae status *m*, lēgēs *fpl*

constitutional *adj* lēgitimus, iūstus

constitutionally *adv* ē rē pūblicā

constrain *vt* cōgere

constraint *n* vīs *f*; **under** ~ coāctus; **without** ~ suā sponte

constrict *vt* comprimere, cōnstringere

constriction *n* contractiō *f*

construct *vt* aedificāre, exstruere

construction *n* aedificātiō *f*; (*method*) structūra *f*; (*meaning*) interpretātiō *f*; **put a wrong** ~ **on** in malam partem interpretārī

construe *vt* interpretārī

consul *n* cōnsul *m*; ~ **elect** cōnsul dēsignātus; **ex-consul** cōnsulāris *m*

consular *adj* cōnsulāris

consulship *n* cōnsulātus *m*; **stand for the** ~ cōnsulātum petere; **hold the** ~ cōnsulātum gerere; **in my** ~ mē cōnsule

consult *vt* cōnsulere; ~ **the interests of** cōnsulere (*dat*) ♦ *vi* dēlīberāre, cōnsiliārī

consultation *n* (*asking*) cōnsultātiō *f*; (*discussion*) dēlīberātiō *f*

consume *vt* cōnsūmere, absūmere; (*food*) edere

consumer *n* cōnsūmptor *m*

consummate *adj* summus, perfectus ♦ *vt* perficere, absolvere

consummation *n* absolūtiō *f*; fīnis *m*, ēventus *m*

consumption *n* cōnsūmptiō *f*; (*disease*) tābēs *f*, phthisis *f*

consumptive *adj* pulmōnārius

contact *n* tāctus *m*, contāgiō *f*; **come in** ~ **with** contingere

contagion *n* contāgiō *f*

contagious *adj* tābificus; **be** ~ contāgiīs vulgārī

contain *vt* capere, continēre; (*self*) cohibēre

container *n* vās *nt*

contaminate *vt* contāmināre, īnficere

contamination *n* contāgiō *f*, lābēs *f*

contemplate *vt* contemplārī, intuērī; (*action*) in animō habēre; (*prospect*) spectāre

contemplation *n* contemplātiō *f*; (*thought*) cōgitātiō *f*

contemplative *adj* cōgitāns, meditāns; **in a** ~ **mood** cōgitātiōnī dēditus

contemporaneous *adj* aequālis

contemporaneously *adv* simul

contemporary *adj* aequālis

contempt *n* contemptiō *f*; **be an object of** ~ contemptuī esse; **treat with** ~ contemptum habēre, conculcāre

contemptible *adj* contemnendus, abiectus, vīlis

contemptuous *adj* fastīdiōsus

contemptuously *adv* contemptim, fastīdiōsē

contend *vi* certāre, contendere; (*in battle*) dīmicāre, pugnāre; (*in words*) adfirmāre, adsevērāre

contending *adj* contrārius

content *adj* contentus ♦ *n* aequus animus *m* ♦ *vt* placēre (*dat*), satisfacere (*dat*); **be contented** satis habēre

contentedly *adv* aequō animō

contention *n* certāmen *nt*; contrōversia *f*; (*opinion*) sententia *f*

contentious *adj* pugnāx, lītigiōsus

contentiously *adv* pugnāciter

contentiousness *n* contrōversiae studium *nt*

contentment *n* aequus animus *m*

contents *n* quod inest, quae insunt; (*of speech*) argūmentum *nt*

conterminous *adj* adfīnis

contest *n* certāmen *nt*, contentiō *f* ♦ *vt* (LAW) lēge agere dē (*abl*); (*office*) petere; (*dispute*) repugnāre (*dat*), resistere (*dat*)

contestable *adj* contrōversus

contestant *n* petītor *m*, aemulus *m*

context *n* contextus *m*

contiguity *n* vīcīnia *f*, propinquitās *f*

contiguous *adj* vīcīnus, adiacēns; **be** ~ **to** adiacēre (*dat*), contingere

continence *n* continentia *f*, abstinentia *f*

continent *adj* continēns, abstinēns ♦ *n* continēns *f*

continently *adv* continenter, abstinenter

contingency *n* cāsus *m*, rēs *f*

contingent *adj* fortuītus ♦ *n* (MIL) numerus *m*

continual *adj* adsiduus, perpetuus

continually *adv* adsiduē, semper

continuance *n* perpetuitās *f*, adsiduitās *f*

continuation *n* continuātiō *f*; (*of a command*) prōrogātiō *f*; (*of a story*) reliqua pars *f*

continue *vt* continuāre; (*time*) prōdūcere; (*command*) prōrogāre ♦ *vi* (*action*) pergere; (*time*) manēre; (*endurance*) perstāre, dūrāre; ~ **to** *imperf indic*

continuity *n* continuātiō *f*; (*of speech*) perpetuitās *f*

continuous *adj* continuus, continēns, perpetuus

continuously *adv* perpetuō, continenter

contort *vt* contorquēre, dētorquēre

contortion *n* distortiō *f*

contour *n* fōrma *f*

contraband *adj* interdictus, vetitus
contract *n* pactum *nt*, mandātum *nt*, conventum *nt*; (POL) foedus *nt*; **trial for a breach of** ~ mandātī iūdicium *nt* ♦ *vt* (*narrow*) contrahere, addūcere; (*short*) dēminuere; (*illness*) contrahere; (*agreement*) pacīscī; (*for work*) locāre; (*to do work*) condūcere ♦ *vi* pacīscī
contraction *n* contractiō *f*; (*word*) compendium *nt*
contractor *n* redemptor *m*, conductor *m*
contradict *vt* (*person*) contrādīcere (*dat*), refrāgārī (*dat*); (*statement*) īnfitiās īre (*dat*); (*self*) repugnāre (*dat*)
contradiction *n* repugnantia *f*, īnfitiae *fpl*
contradictory *adj* repugnāns, contrārius; **be** ~ inter sē repugnāre
contradistinction *n* oppositiō *f*
contraption *n* māchina *f*
contrariety *n* repugnantia *f*
contrariwise *adv* ē contrāriō
contrary *adj* contrārius, adversus; (*person*) difficilis, mōrōsus; ~ **to** contrā (*acc*), praeter (*acc*); ~ **to expectations** praeter opīniōnem ♦ *n* contrārium *nt*; **on the** ~ ē contrāriō, contrā; (*retort*) immo
contrast *n* discrepantia *f* ♦ *vt* comparāre, oppōnere ♦ *vi* discrepāre
contravene *vt* (LAW) violāre; (*statement*) contrādīcere (*dat*)
contravention *n* violātiō *f*
contribute *vt* cōnferre, adferre, contribuere ♦ *vi*: ~ **towards** cōnferre ad (*acc*), adiuvāre; ~ **to the cost** impēnsās cōnferre
contribution *n* conlātiō *f*; (*money*) stipem (*no nom*) *f*
contributor *n* quī cōnfert
contributory *adj* adiūnctus
contrite *adj* paenitēns
contrition *n* paenitentia *f*
contrivance *n* māchinātiō *f*, excōgitātiō *f*; (*thing*) māchina *f*; (*idea*) cōnsilium *nt*; (*deceit*) dolus *m*
contrive *vt* māchinārī, excōgitāre, struere; (*to do*) efficere ut
contriver *n* māchinātor *m*, artifex *m*, auctor *m*
control *n* (*restraint*) frēnum *nt*; (*power*) moderātiō *f*, potestās *f*, imperium *nt*; **have** ~ **of** praeesse (*dat*); **out of** ~ impotēns ♦ *vt* moderārī (*dat*), imperāre (*dat*)
controller *n* moderātor *m*
controversial *adj* concertātōrius
controversy *n* contrōversia *f*, disceptātiō *f*
controvert *vt* redarguere, impugnāre, in dubium vocāre
contumacious *adj* contumāx, pervicāx
contumaciously *adv* contumāciter, pervicāciter
contumacy *n* contumācia *f*, pervicācia *f*
contusion *n* sūgillātiō *f*
conundrum *n* aenigma *nt*
convalesce *vi* convalēscere
convalescence *n* melior valētūdō *f*
convalescent *adj* convalēscēns
convene *vt* convocāre
convenience *n* opportūnitās *f*, commoditās *f*; (*thing*) commodum *nt*; **at your** ~ commodō tuō

convenient *adj* idōneus, commodus, opportūnus; **be** ~ convenīre; **very** ~ percommodus
conveniently *adv* opportūnē, commodē
convention *n* (*meeting*) conventus *m*; (*agreement*) conventum *nt*; (*custom*) mōs *m*, iūsta *ntpl*
conventional *adj* iūstus, solitus
conventionality *n* mōs *m*, cōnsuētūdō *f*
converge *vi* in medium vergere, in eundem locum tendere
conversant *adj* perītus, doctus, exercitātus; **be** ~ **with** versārī in (*abl*)
conversation *n* sermō *m*, colloquium *nt*
converse *n* sermō *m*, colloquium *nt*; (*opposite*) contrārium *nt* ♦ *vi* colloquī, sermōnem cōnferre ♦ *adj* contrārius
conversely *adv* ē contrāriō, contrā
conversion *n* mūtātiō *f*; (*moral*) mōrum ēmendātiō *f*
convert *vt* mūtāre, convertere; (*to an opinion*) dēdūcere ♦ *n* discipulus *m*
convertible *adj* commūtābilis
convex *adj* convexus
convexity *n* convexum *nt*
convey *vt* vehere, portāre, convehere; (*property*) abaliēnāre; (*knowledge*) commūnicāre; (*meaning*) significāre; ~ **across** trānsmittere, trādūcere, trānsvehere; ~ **away** auferre, āvehere; ~ **down** dēvehere, dēportāre; ~ **into** importāre, invehere; ~ **to** advehere, adferre; ~ **up** subvehere
conveyance *n* vehiculum *nt*; (*property*) abaliēnātiō *f*
convict *vt* (*prove guilty*) convincere; (*sentence*) damnāre ♦ *n* reus *m*
conviction *n* (LAW) damnātiō *f*; (*argument*) persuāsiō *f*; (*belief*) fidēs *f*; **carry** ~ fidem facere; **have a** ~ persuāsum habēre
convince *vt* persuādēre (*dat*); **I am firmly convinced** mihi persuāsum habeō
convincing *adj* (*argument*) gravis; (*evidence*) manifestus
convincingly *adv* manifestō
convivial *adj* convīvālis, festīvus
conviviality *n* festīvitās *f*
convocation *n* conventus *m*
convoke *vt* convocāre
convolution *n* spīra *f*
convoy *n* praesidium *nt* ♦ *vt* prōsequī
convulse *vt* agitāre; **be convulsed with laughter** sē in cachinnōs effundere
convulsion *n* (MED) convulsiō *f*; (POL) tumultus *m*
convulsive *adj* spasticus
coo *vi* gemere
cook *vt* coquere ♦ *n* coquus *m*
cookery *n* ars coquīnāria *f*
cool *adj* frīgidus; (*conduct*) impudens; (*mind*) impavidus, lentus ♦ *n* frīgus *nt* ♦ *vt* refrīgerāre; (*passion*) restinguere, sēdāre ♦ *vi* refrīgēscere, refrīgerārī, dēfervēscere
coolly *adv* aequō animō; impudenter
coolness *n* frīgus *nt*; (*mind*) aequus animus *m*; impudentia *f*
coop *n* hara *f*; (*barrel*) cūpa *f* ♦ *vt* inclūdere
co-operate *vi* operam cōnferre; ~ **with** adiuvāre, socius esse (*gen*)

co-operation n cōnsociātiō f; auxilium nt, opera f
co-operative adj (person) officiōsus
co-operator n socius m
co-opt vt cooptāre
coot n fulica f
copartner n socius m
copartnership n societās f
cope vi: ~ **with** contendere cum (abl); **able to** ~ **with** pār (dat); **unable to** ~ **with** impār (dat)
copier n librārius m
coping n fastīgium nt
copious adj cōpiōsus, largus, plēnus, abundāns
copiously adv cōpiōsē, abundanter
copiousness n cōpia f, ūbertās f
copper n aes nt ♦ adj aēneus
coppersmith n faber aerārius m
coppice, copse n dūmētum nt, virgultum nt
copy n exemplar nt ♦ vt imitārī; (writing) exscrībere, trānscrībere
copyist n librārius m
coracle n linter f
coral n cūrālium nt
cord n fūniculus m
cordage n fūnēs mpl
cordial adj cōmis, festīvus, amīcus; (greetings) multus
cordiality n cōmitās f, studium nt
cordially adv cōmiter, libenter, ex animō
cordon n corōna f
core n (fig) nucleus m
cork n sūber nt; (bark) cortex m
corn n frūmentum nt ♦ adj frūmentārius; (on the foot) clāvus m; **price of** ~ annōna f
corndealer n frūmentārius m
cornel n (tree) cornus f
corner n angulus m
cornet n cornū nt
cornfield n seges f
cornice n corōna f
coronet n diadēma nt
corporal adj corporeus
corporal punishment n verbera ntpl
corporation n collēgium nt; (civic) magistrātūs mpl
corporeal adj corporeus
corps n manus f
corpse n cadāver nt
corpulence n obēsum corpus nt
corpulent adj obēsus, pinguis
corpuscle n corpusculum nt
corral n praesēpe nt
correct vt corrigere, ēmendāre; (person) castīgāre ♦ adj vērus; (language) ēmendātus
correction n ēmendātiō f; (moral) corrēctiō f; (punishment) castīgātiō f
correctly adv bene, vērē
correctness n (fact) vēritās f; (language) integritās f; (moral) probitās f
corrector n ēmendātor m, corrēctor m
correspond vi (agree) respondēre (dat), congruere (dat); (by letter) inter sē scrībere
correspondence n similitūdō f; epistulae fpl
correspondent n epistulārum scrīptor m
corresponding adj pār
correspondingly adv pariter

corridor n porticus f
corrigible adj ēmendābilis
corroborate vt cōnfirmāre
corroboration n cōnfirmātiō f
corrode vt ēdere, edere
corrosive adj edāx
corrugate vt rūgāre
corrugated adj rūgōsus
corrupt vt corrumpere, dēprāvāre; (text) vitiāre ♦ adj corruptus, vitiātus; (person) prāvus, vēnālis; (text) vitiātus
corrupter n corruptor m
corruptible adj (matter) dissolūbilis; (person) vēnālis
corruption n (of matter) corruptiō f; (moral) corruptēla f, dēprāvātiō f; (bribery) ambitus m
corsair n pīrāta m
cortège n pompa f
coruscate vi fulgēre
coruscation n fulgor m
Corybant n Corybas m
Corybantic adj Corybantius
cosmetic n medicāmen nt
cosmic adj mundānus
cosmopolitan adj mundānus
cosmos n mundus m
cost vt emī, stāre (dat); **it ~ me dear** māgnō mihi stetit, male ēmī; **it ~ me a talent** talentō mihi stetit, talentō ēmī; **it ~ me my freedom** lībertātem perdidī ♦ n pretium nt, impēnsa f; **~ of living** annōna f; **to your ~** incommodō tuō, dētrīmentō tuō; **at the ~ of one's reputation** violātā fāmā, nōn salvā existimātiōne; **I sell at ~ price** quantī ēmī vēndō
costliness n sūmptus m; cāritās f
costly adj cārus; (furnishings) lautus, sūmptuōsus
costume n habitus m
cosy adj commodus
cot n lectulus m
cote n columbārium nt
cottage n casa f, tugurium nt
cottager n rūsticus m
cotton n (tree) gossympinus f; (cloth) xylinum nt
couch n lectus m ♦ vi recumbere ♦ vt (lance) intendere; (words) exprimere, reddere
cough n tussis f ♦ vi tussīre
council n concilium nt; (small) cōnsilium nt
councillor n (town) decuriō m
counsel n (debate) cōnsultātiō f; (advice) cōnsilium nt, (law) advocātus m, patrōnus m; **take ~** cōnsiliārī, dēlīberāre; **take ~ of** cōnsulere ♦ vt suādēre (dat), monēre
counsellor n cōnsiliārius m
count vt numerāre, computāre; ~ **as** dūcere, habēre; ~ **amongst** pōnere in (abl); ~ **up** vt ēnumerāre; ~ **upon** cōnfidere (dat); **be counted among** in numerō esse (gen) ♦ vi aestimārī, habērī ♦ n ratiō f; (in indictment) caput nt; (title) comes m
countenance n faciēs f, vultus m, ōs nt; (fig) favor m; **put out of** ~ conturbāre ♦ vt favēre (dat), indulgēre (dat)
counter n (for counting) calculus m; (for play) tessera f; (shop) mēnsa f ♦ adj contrārius ♦ adv contrā, obviam ♦ vt obsistere (dat), respondēre (dat)

counteract vt obsistere (dat), adversārī (dat); (malady) medērī (dat)

counterattack vt in vicem oppugnāre, adgredī

counterattraction n altera illecebra f

counterbalance vt compēnsāre, exaequāre

counterclockwise adv sinistrōrsus

counterfeit adj falsus, fūcātus, adsimulātus, fictus ♦ vt fingere, simulāre, imitārī

countermand vt renūntiāre

counterpane n lōdīx f, strāgulum nt

counterpart n pār m/f/nt

counterpoise n aequum pondus nt ♦ vt compēnsāre, exaequāre

countersign n (MIL) tessera f

counting table n abacus m

countless adj innumerābilis

countrified adj agrestis, rūsticus

country n (region) regiō f, terra f; (territory) fīnēs mpl; (native) patria f; (not town) rūs nt; (open) agrī mpl; **of our ~** nostrās; **live in the ~** rūsticārī; **living in the ~** rūsticātiō f

country house n vīlla f

countryman n agricola m; **fellow ~** populāris m, cīvis m

countryside n agrī mpl, rus nt

couple n pār nt; **a ~ of** duo ♦ vt cōpulāre, coniungere

couplet n distichon nt

courage n fortitūdō f, animus m; (MIL) virtūs f; **have the ~ to** audēre; **lose ~** animōs dēmittere; **take ~** bonō animō esse

courageous adj fortis, ācer; audāx

courageously adv fortiter, ācriter

courier n tabellārius m

course n (movement) cursus m; (route) iter nt; (sequence) seriēs f; (career) dēcursus; (for races) stadium nt, circus m; (of dinner) ferculum nt; (of stones) ōrdō m; (of water) lāpsus m; **of ~** certē, sānē, scīlicet; **as a matter of ~** continuō; **in due ~** mox; **in the ~ of** inter (acc), in (abl); **keep on one's ~** cursum tenēre; **be driven off one's ~** dēicī; **second ~** secunda mēnsa

court n (space) ārea f; (of house) ātrium nt; (of king) aula f; (suite) cohors f, comitēs mpl; (LAW) iūdicium nt, iūdicēs mpl; **pay ~ to** ambīre, īnservīre (dat); **hold a ~** forum agere; **bring into ~** in iūs vocāre ♦ vt colere, ambīre; (danger) sē offerre (dat); (woman) petere

courteous adj cōmis, urbānus, hūmānus

courteously adv cōmiter, urbānē

courtesan n meretrīx f

courtesy n (quality) cōmitās f, hūmānitās f; (act) officium nt

courtier n aulicus m; **courtiers** pl aula f

courtly adj officiōsus

cousin n cōnsobrīnus m, cōnsobrīna f

cove n sinus m

covenant n foedus nt, pactum nt ♦ vi pacīscī

cover vt tegere, operīre; (hide) vēlāre; (march) claudere; **~ over** obdūcere; **~ up** vi obtegere ♦ n integumentum nt, operculum nt; (shelter) latebrae fpl, suffugium nt; (pretence) speciēs f; **under ~ of** sub (abl), sub speciē (gen); **take ~** dēlitēscere

covering n integumentum nt, involucrum nt, operculum nt; (of couch) strāgulum nt

coverlet n lōdīx f

covert adj occultus; (language) oblīquus ♦ n latebra f, perfugium nt; (thicket) dūmētum nt

covertly adv occultē, sēcrētō

covet vt concupīscere, expetere

covetous adj avidus, cupidus

covetously adv avidē, cupidē

covetousness n aviditās f, cupiditās f

covey n grex f

cow n vacca f ♦ vt terrēre

coward n ignāvus m

cowardice n ignāvia f

cowardly adj ignāvus

cower vi subsīdere

cowherd n bubulcus m

cowl n cucullus m

coxswain n rēctor m

coy adj pudens, verēcundus

coyly adv pudenter, modestē

coyness n pudor m, verēcundia f

cozen vt fallere, dēcipere

crab n cancer m

crabbed adj mōrōsus, difficilis

crack n (chink) rīma f; (sound) crepitus m ♦ vt findere, frangere; (whip) crepitāre (abl) ♦ vi (open) fatīscere; (sound) crepāre, crepitāre

crackle vi crepitāre

crackling n crepitus m

cradle n cūnae fpl; (fig) incūnābula ntpl

craft n ars f; (deceit) dolus m; (boat) nāvigium nt

craftily adv callidē, sollerter; dolōsē

craftsman n artifex m, faber m

craftsmanship n ars f, artificium nt

crafty adj callidus, sollers; dolōsus

crag n rūpēs f, scopulus m

cram vt farcīre, refercīre; (with food) sagīnāre

cramp n convulsiō f; (tool) cōnfībula f ♦ vt coercēre, coartāre

crane n (bird) grus f; (machine) māchina f, trochlea f

crank n uncus m; (person) ineptus m

crannied adj rīmōsus

cranny n rīma f

crash n (fall) ruīna f; (noise) fragor m ♦ vi ruere; strepere

crass adj crassus; **~ stupidity** mera stultitia

crate n crātēs fpl

crater n crātēr m

cravat n focāle nt

crave vt (desire) concupīscere, adpetere, exoptāre; (request) ōrāre, obsecrāre

craven adj ignāvus

craving n cupīdō f, dēsīderium nt, adpetītiō f

crawl vi (animal) serpere; (person) rēpere

crayfish n commarus m

craze n libīdō f ♦ vt mentem aliēnāre

craziness n dēmentia f

crazy adj dēmēns, fatuus

creak vi crepāre

creaking n crepitus m

cream n spūma lactis f; (fig) flōs m

crease n rūga f ♦ vt rūgāre

create vt creāre, facere, gignere

creation n (process) fabricātiō f; (result) opus nt; (human) hominēs mpl

creative *adj* (*nature*) creātrīx; (*mind*) inventor, inventrīx

creator *n* creātor *m*, auctor *m*, opifex *m*

creature *n* animal *nt*; (*person*) homō *m/f*

credence *n* fidēs *f*

credentials *n* litterae commendātīciae *fpl*; (*fig*) auctōritās *f*

credibility *n* fidēs *f*; (*source*) auctōritās *f*

credible *adj* crēdibilis; (*witness*) locuplēs

credit *n* (*belief*) fidēs *f*; (*repute*) existimātiō *f*; (*character*) auctōritās *f*, grātia *f*; (COMM) fidēs *f*; be a ~ to decus esse (*gen*); it is to your ~ tibī laudī est; give ~ for laudem tribuere (*gen*); have ~ fidē stāre ◆ *vt* crēdere (*dat*); (*with money*) acceptum referre (*dat*)

creditable *adj* honestus, laudābilis

creditably *adv* honestē, cum laude

creditor *n* crēditor *m*

credulity *n* crēdulitās *f*

credulous *adj* crēdulus

creed *n* dogma *nt*

creek *n* sinus *m*

creel *n* vīdulus *m*

creep *vi* (*animal*) serpere; (*person*) rēpere; (*flesh*) horrēre

cremate *vt* cremāre

crescent *n* lūna *f*

crescent-shaped *adj* lūnātus

cress *n* nasturtium *nt*

crest *n* crista *f*

crested *adj* cristātus

crestfallen *adj* dēmissus

crevasse *n* hiātus *m*

crevice *n* rīma *f*

crew *n* nautae *mpl*, rēmigēs *mpl*, grex *f*, turba *f*

crib *n* (*cot*) lectulus *m*; (*manger*) praesēpe *nt*

cricket *n* gryllus *m*

crier *n* praecō *m*

crime *n* scelus *nt*, facinus *nt*, flāgitium *nt*

criminal *adj* scelestus, facinorōsus, flāgitiōsus ◆ *n* reus *m*

criminality *n* scelus *nt*

criminally *adv* scelestē, flāgitiōsē

crimson *n* coccum *nt* ◆ *adj* coccineus

cringe *vi* adūlārī, adsentārī

crinkle *n* rūga *f*

cripple *vt* dēbilitāre, mūtilāre; (*fig*) frangere

crisis *n* discrīmen *nt*

crisp *adj* fragilis; (*manner*) alacer; (*hair*) crispus

crisscross *adj* in quīncūncem dispositus

criterion *n* index *m*, indicium *nt*; take as a ~ referre ad (*acc*)

critic *n* iūdex *m*; (*literary*) criticus, grammaticus *m*; (*adverse*) castīgātor *m*

critical *adj* (*mind*) accūrātus, ēlegāns; (*blame*) cēnsōrius, sevērus; (*danger*) perīculōsus, dubius; ~ moment discrīmen *nt*

critically *adv* accūrātē, ēleganter; sevērē; cum perīculō

criticism *n* iūdicium *nt*; (*adverse*) reprehēnsiō *f*

criticize *vt* iūdicāre; reprehendere, castīgāre

croak *vi* (*raven*) crōcīre; (*frog*) coaxāre

croaking *n* cantus *m* ◆ *adj* raucus

crock *n* olla *f*

crockery *n* fictilia *ntpl*

crocodile *n* crocodīlus *m*; weep ~ tears lacrimās cōnfingere

crocus *n* crocus *m*

croft *n* agellus *m*

crone *n* anus *f*

crony *n* sodālis *m*

crook *n* pedum *nt* ◆ *vt* incurvāre

crooked *adj* incurvus, aduncus; (*deformed*) prāvus; (*winding*) flexuōsus; (*morally*) perversus

crookedly *adv* perversē, prāvē

crookedness *n* prāvitās *f*

croon *vt*, *vi* cantāre

crop *n* (*grain*) segēs *f*, messis *f*; (*tree*) fructus *m*; (*bird*) ingluviēs *f* ◆ *vt* (*reap*) metere; (*graze*) carpere, tondēre; ~ up *vi* intervenīre

cross *n* (*mark*) decussis *m*; (*torture*) crux *f* ◆ *adj* trānsversus, oblīquus; (*person*) acerbus, īrātus ◆ *vt* trānsīre; (*water*) trāicere; (*mountain*) trānscendere; superāre; (*enemy*) obstāre (*dat*), frustrārī; ~ out *vt* (*writing*) expungere ◆ *vi* trānsīre; ~ over (*on foot*) trānsgredī; (*by sea*) trānsmittere

crossbar *n* iugum *nt*

crossbow *n* scorpiō *m*

cross-examination *n* interrogātiō *f*

cross-examine *vt* interrogāre, percontārī

cross-grained *adj* (*fig*) mōrōsus

crossing *n* trānsitus *m*; (*on water*) trāiectus *m*

cross purpose *n*: be at cross purposes dīversa spectāre

cross-question *vt* interrogāre

crossroads *n* quadrivium *nt*

crosswise *adv* ex trānsversō; divide ~ decussāre

crotchety *adj* mōrōsus, difficilis

crouch *vi* subsīdere, sē submittere

crow *n* cornīx *f*; as the ~ flies rēctā regiōne ◆ *vi* cantāre; (*fig*) exsultāre, gestīre

crowbar *n* vectis *m*

crowd *n* turba *f*, concursus *m*, frequentia *f*; (*small*) grex *m*; multitūdō *f*; in crowds gregātim ◆ *vi* frequentāre, celebrāre ◆ *vt* (*place*) complēre; (*person*) stīpāre

crowded *adj* frequēns

crown *n* corōna *f*; (*royal*) diadēma *nt*; (*of head*) vertex *m*; (*fig*) apex *m*, flōs *m*; the ~ of summus ◆ *vt* corōnāre; (*fig*) cumulāre, fastīgium impōnere (*dat*)

crucial *adj* gravissimus, māximī mōmentī; ~ moment discrīmen *nt*

crucifixion *n* crucis supplicium *nt*

crucify *vt* crucī suffīgere

crude *adj* crūdus; (*style*) dūrus, inconcinnus

crudely *adv* dūrē, asperē

crudity *n* asperitās *f*

cruel *adj* crūdēlis, saevus, atrōx

cruelly *adv* crūdēliter, atrōciter

cruelty *n* crūdēlitās *f*, saevitia *f*, atrōcitās *f*

cruise *n* nāvigātiō *f* ◆ *vi* nāvigāre

cruiser *n* speculātōria nāvis *f*

crumb *n* mīca *f*

crumble *vi* corruere, putrem fierī ◆ *vt* putrefacere, friāre

crumbling *adj* putris

crumple vt rūgāre
crunch vt dentibus frangere
crupper n postilēna f
crush vt frangere, contundere, obterere; (fig)
adflīgere, opprimere, obruere ♦ n turba f,
frequentia f
crust n crusta f; (bread) frustum nt
crusty adj (fig) stomachōsus
crutch n baculum nt
cry vt, vi clāmāre, clāmitāre; (weep) flēre;
(infant) vāgīre; **cry down** dētrectāre; **cry
out** exclāmāre, vōciferārī; **cry out against**
adclāmāre, reclāmāre; **cry up** laudāre,
vēnditāre ♦ n clāmor m, vōx f; (child's) vāgītus m;
(of grief) plōrātus m
cryptic adj arcānus
crystal n crystallum nt ♦ adj crystallinus
cub n catulus m
cube n cubus m
cubit n cubitum nt
cuckoo n coccyx m
cucumber n cucumis m
cud n: **chew the cud** rūminārī
cudgel n fustis m ♦ vt verberāre
cue n signum nt, indicium nt
cuff n (blow) alapa f
cuirass n lōrīca f
culinary adj coquīnārius
cull vt legere, carpere, dēlībāre
culminate vi ad summum fastīgium venīre
culmination n fastīgium nt
culpability n culpa f, noxa f
culpable adj nocēns
culprit n reus m
cultivate vt (land) colere, subigere; (mind)
excolere; (interest) fovēre, studēre (dat)
cultivation n cultus m, cultūra f
cultivator n cultor m, agricola m
cultural adj hūmānior
culture n hūmānitās f, bonae artēs fpl
cultured adj doctus, litterātus
culvert n cloāca f
cumber vt impedīre, obesse (dat); (load) onerāre
cumbersome adj molestus, gravis
cumulative adj alius ex aliō; **be** ~ cumulārī
cuneiform adj cuneātus
cunning adj callidus, astūtus ♦ n ars f, astūtia f,
calliditās f
cunningly adv callidē, astūtē
cup n pōculum nt; **drink the cup of** (fig)
exanclāre, exhaurīre; **in one's cups** ēbrius,
pōtus
cupboard n armārium nt
Cupid n Cupīdō m, Amor m
cupidity n avāritia f
cupola n tholus m
cupping glass n cucurbita f
cur n canis m
curable adj sānābilis
curative adj salūbris
curator n custōs m
curb vt frēnāre, īnfrēnāre; (fig) coercēre,
cohibēre ♦ n frēnum nt
curdle vt cōgere ♦ vi concrēscere

curds n concrētum lac nt
cure vt sānāre, medērī (dat) ♦ n remedium nt;
(process) sānātiō f
curio n dēliciae fpl
curiosity n studium nt; (thing) mīrāculum nt
curious adj (inquisitive) cūriōsus, cupidus; (artistic)
ēlābōrātus; (strange) mīrus, novus
curiously adv cūriōsē; summā arte; mīrum in
modum
curl n (natural) cirrus m; (artificial) cincinnus m ♦ vt
(hair) crispāre ♦ vi (smoke) volvī
curling irons n calamistrī mpl
curly adj crispus
currency n (coin) monēta f; (use) ūsus m; **gain
~** (rumour) percrēbrēscere
current adj vulgātus, ūsitātus; (time) hīc ♦ n
flūmen nt; **with the ~** secundō flūmine;
against the ~ adversō flūmine
currently adv vulgō
curriculum n īnstitūtiō f
curry vt (favour) aucupārī
curse n exsecrātiō f, maledictum nt; (formula)
exsecrābile carmen nt; (fig) pestis f; **curses** interj
malum! ♦ vt exsecrārī, maledīcere (dat)
cursed adj exsecrātus, sacer; scelestus
cursorily adv breviter, strictim
cursory adj brevis
curt adj brevis
curtail vt minuere, contrahere
curtailment n dēminūtiō f, contractiō f
curtain n aulaeum nt ♦ vt vēlāre
curule adj curūlis
curve n flexus m, arcus m ♦ vt flectere, incurvāre,
arcuāre
cushion n pulvīnus m
custodian n custōs m
custody n custōdia f, tūtēla f; (prison) carcer m;
hold in ~ custōdīre
custom n mōs m, cōnsuētūdō f; (national)
īnstitūtum nt; **customs** pl portōria ntpl
customarily adv plērumque, dē mōre, vulgō
customary adj solitus, ūsitātus; (rite) sollemnis;
it is ~ mōs est
customer n emptor m
customs officer n portitor m
cut vt secāre, caedere, scindere; (corn) metere;
(branch) amputāre; (acquaintance) āversārī;
(hair) dētondēre; **cut away** abscindere,
resecāre; **cut down** rescindere, caedere,
succīdere; **cut into** incīdere; **cut off** vt
abscīdere, praecīdere; (exclude) exclūdere;
(intercept) interclūdere, intercipere; (head)
abscindere; **cut out** vt excīdere, exsecāre;
(omit) ōmittere; **cut out for** aptus ad, nātus
ad (acc); **cut round** circumcīdere; **cut short**
praecīdere; (speech) incīdere, interrumpere;
cut through intercīdere; **cut up** vt concīdere
♦ n vulnus nt
cutlass n gladius m
cutlery n cultrī mpl
cutter n sector m; (boat) lembus m
cutthroat n sīcārius m
cutting n (plant) propāgō f ♦ adj acūtus; (fig)
acerbus, mordāx

cuttlefish *n* sēpia *f*
cyclamen *n* baccar *nt*
cycle *n* orbis *m*
cyclone *n* turbō *f*
cylinder *n* cylindrus *m*
cymbal *n* cymbalum *nt*

cynic *n* (PHILOS) cynicus *m*
cynical *adj* mordāx, acerbus
cynically *adv* mordāciter, acerbē
cynicism *n* acerbitās *f*
cynosure *n* cynosūra *f*
cypress *n* cypressus *f*

Dd

dabble *vi:* ~ **in** gustāre, leviter attingere
dactyl *n* dactylus *m*
dactylic *adj* dactylicus
dagger *n* sīca *f*, pugiō *f*
daily *adj* diūrnus, cottīdiānus ♦ *adv* cottīdiē, in diēs
daintily *adv* molliter, concinnē; fastīdiōsē
daintiness *n* munditia *f*, concinnitās *f*; (*squeamish*) fastīdium *nt*
dainty *adj* mundus, concinnus, mollis; fastīdiōsus; **dainties** *npl* cuppēdia *ntpl*
dais *n* suggestus *m*
daisy *n* bellis *f*
dale *n* vallis *f*
dalliance *n* lascīvia *f*
dally *vi* lūdere; morārī
dam *n* mōlēs *f*, agger *m*; (*animal*) māter *f* ♦ *vt* obstruere, exaggerāre
damage *n* damnum *nt*, dētrīmentum *nt*, malum *nt*; (*inflicted*) iniūria *f*; (LAW) damnum *nt*; **assess damages** lītem aestimāre ♦ *vt* laedere, nocēre (*dat*); (*by evidence*) laedere; (*reputation*) violāre
damageable *adj* fragilis
dame *n* mātrōna *f*, domina *f*
damn *vt* damnāre, exsecrārī
damnable *adj* dētestābilis, improbus
damnably *adv* improbē
damnation *n* malum *nt*
damp *adj* ūmidus ♦ *n* ūmor *m* ♦ *vt* madefacere; (*enthusiasm*) restinguere, dēmittere
damsel *n* puella *f*, virgō *f*
damson *n* Damascēnum *nt*
dance *vi* saltāre ♦ *n* saltātiō *f*; (*religious*) tripudium *nt*
dancer *n* saltātor *m*, saltātrīx *f*
dandruff *n* porrīgō *f*
dandy *n* dēlicātus *m*
danger *n* perīculum *nt*, discrīmen *nt*
dangerous *adj* perīculōsus, dubius; (*in attack*) īnfestus
dangerously *adv* perīculōsē
dangle *vt* suspendere ♦ *vi* pendēre
dank *adj* ūmidus
dapper *adj* concinnus, nitidus
dapple *vt* variāre, distinguere
dappled *adj* maculōsus, distinctus
dare *vt* audēre; (*challenge*) prōvocāre; **I ~ say** haud sciō an
daring *n* audācia *f* ♦ *adj* audāx
daringly *adv* audācter

dark *adj* obscūrus, opācus; (*colour*) fuscus, āter; (*fig*) obscūrus; **it is getting** ~ advesperāscit; **keep** ~ silēre ♦ *n* tenebrae *fpl*; (*mist*) cālīgō *f*; **keep in the** ~ cēlāre
darken *vt* obscūrāre, occaecāre
darkish *adj* subobscūrus
darkling *adj* obscūrus
darkness *n* tenebrae *fpl*; (*mist*) cālīgō *f*
darksome *adj* obscūrus
darling *adj* cārus, dīlēctus ♦ *n* dēliciae *fpl*, voluptās *f*
darn *vt* resarcīre
darnel *n* lolium *nt*
dart *n* tēlum *nt*; iaculum *nt* ♦ *vi* ēmicāre, sē conicere ♦ *vt* iaculārī, iacere
dash *vt* adflīgere; (*hope*) frangere; ~ **against** illīdere, incutere; ~ **down** dēturbāre; ~ **out** ēlīdere; ~ **to pieces** discutere; ~ **to the ground** prōsternere ♦ *vi* currere, sē incitāre, ruere ♦ *n* impetus *m*; (*quality*) ferōcia *f*
dashing *adj* ferōx, animōsus
dastardly *adj* ignāvus
date *n* (*fruit*) palmula *f*; (*time*) tempus *nt*, diēs *m*; **out of** ~ obsolētus; **become out of** ~ exolēscere; **to** ~ adhūc; **be up to** ~ praesentī mōre ūtī ♦ *vt* (*letter*) diem adscrībere; (*past event*) repetere ♦ *vi* initium capere
dative *n* datīvus *m*
daub *vt* inlinere
daughter *n* fīlia *f*; (*little*) fīliola *f*
daughter-in-law *n* nurus *f*
daunt *vt* terrēre, perterrēre
dauntless *adj* impavidus, intrepidus
dauntlessly *adv* impavidē, intrepidē
dawdle *vi* cessāre, cunctārī
dawdler *n* cunctātor *m*
dawn *n* aurōra *f*, dīlūculum *nt*; (*fig*) orīgō *f*, prima lux *f*; **at** ~ prīmā lūce ♦ *vi* dīlūcēscere; **day dawns** diēs illūcēscit; **it dawns upon me** mente concipiō
day *n* diēs *m/f*; (*period*) aetās *f*; **day about** alternīs diēbus; **day by day** in diēs; cottīdiē; **by day** (*adj*) diūrnus; (*adv*) interdiū; **during the day** interdiū; **every day** cottīdiē; **from day to day** in diēs, diem dē diē; **late in the day** multō diē; **next day** postrīdiē; **one day/some day** ōlim; **the day after** (*adv*) postrīdiē; (*conj*) postrīdiē quam; **the day after tomorrow** perendiē; **the day before** (*adv*) prīdiē; (*conj*) prīdiē quam; **the day before yesterday** nūdius tertius; **the present day** haec aetās; **time of day** hōra; **twice a day** bis (in) diē; **days of old**

43

praeteritum tempus; **days to come** posteritās; **better days** rēs prosperae; **evil days** rēs adversae; **three days** trīduum *nt*; **two days** biduum *nt*; **win the day** vincere
daybook *n* adversāria *ntpl*
daybreak *n* aurōra *f*, prīma lūx *f*
daylight *n* diēs *m*; **become ~** illūcēscere
daystar *n* lūcifer *m*
daytime *n* diēs *m*; **in the ~** interdiū
daze *vt* obstupefacere ♦ *n* stupor *m*
dazzle *vt* praestringere
dazzling *adj* splendidus, nitēns
deacon *n* diāconus *m*
deaconess *n* diāconissa *f*
dead *adj* mortuus; (*in battle*) occīsus; (*LIT*) frīgidus; (*place*) iners, sōlitarius; (*senses*) hebes; **~ of night** nox intempesta *f*; **be ~ to** nōn sentīre; **in ~ earnest** sēriō ac vērō; **rise from the ~** revīvīscere ♦ *adv* prōrsus, omnīnō
dead beat *adj* cōnfectus
dead body *n* cadāver *m*
dead calm *n* malacia *f*
dead certainty *n* rēs certissima
deaden *vt* (*senses*) hebetāre, obtundere; (*pain*) restinguere
deadlock *n* incitae *fpl*; **reach a ~** ad incitās redigī
dead loss *n* mera iactūra
deadly *adj* fūnestus, exitiōsus, exitiābilis; (*enmity*) implācābilis; (*pain*) acerbissimus
dead weight *n* mōlēs *f*
deaf *adj* surdus; **become ~** obsurdēscere; **be ~ to** nōn audīre, obdūrēscere contrā
deafen *vt* (*with noise*) obtundere
deafness *n* surditās *f*
deal *n* (*amount*) cōpia *f*; **a good ~** aliquantum *nt*, bona pars *f*; (*wood*) abiēs *f* ♦ *adj* abiēgnus ♦ *vt* (*blow*) dare, īnflīgere; (*share*) dīvidere, partīrī ♦ *vi* agere, negōtiārī; **~ with** (*person*) agere cum (*abl*); (*matter*) tractāre
dealer *n* (*wholesale*) negōtiātor *m*, mercātor *m*; (*retail*) caupō *m*
dealings *n* commercium *nt*, negōtium *nt*, rēs *f*
dean *n* decānus *m*
dear *adj* (*love*) cārus, grātus; (*cost*) cārus, pretiōsus; **my ~ Quintus** mī Quīnte; (*beginning of letter from Marcus*) Marcus Quīntō salūtem; **~ me!** (*sorrow*) heī!; (*surprise*) ehem!; **buy ~** male emere; **sell ~** bene vēndere
dearly *adv* (*love*) valdē, ārdenter; (*value*) magnī
dearness *n* cāritās *f*
dearth *n* inopia *f*, pēnūria *f*
death *n* mors *f*; (*natural*) obitus *m*; (*violent*) nex *f*, interitus *m*; **condemn to ~** capitis damnāre; **put to ~** interficere; **give the ~ blow to** interimere
deathbed *n*: **on one's ~** moriēns, moribundus
deathless *adj* immortālis
deathly *adj* pallidus
debar *vt* prohibēre, exclūdere
debase *vt* dēprāvāre, corrumpere; (*coin*) adulterāre; (*self*) prōsternere, dēmittere
debasement *n* dēdecus *nt*; (*coin*) adulterium *nt*
debatable *adj* ambiguus, dubius
debate *vt* disputāre, disceptāre ♦ *n* contrōversia *f*, disceptātiō *f*, altercātiō *f*
debater *n* disputātor *m*

debauch *vt* corrumpere, pellicere ♦ *n* cōmissātiō *f*
debauched *adj* perditus, prāvus
debauchee *n* cōmissātor *m*
debaucher *n* corruptor *m*
debauchery *n* luxuria *f*, stuprum *nt*
debilitate *vt* dēbilitāre
debility *n* īnfirmitās *f*
debit *n* expēnsum *nt* ♦ *vt* in expēnsum referre
debonair *adj* urbānus, cōmis
debouch *vi* exīre
debris *n* rūdus *nt*
debt *n* aes aliēnum *nt*; (*booked*) nōmen *nt*; (*fig*) dēbitum *nt*; **be in ~** in aere aliēnō esse; **pay off ~** aes aliēnum persolvere; **run up ~** aes aliēnum contrahere; **collect debts** nōmina exigere; **abolition of debts** novae tabulae *fpl*
debtor *n* dēbitor *m*
decade *n* decem annī *mpl*
decadence *n* occāsus *m*
decadent *adj* dēgener, dēterior
decamp *vi* (*MIL*) castra movēre; (*fig*) discēdere, aufugere
decant *vt* dēfundere, diffundere
decanter *n* lagoena *f*
decapitate *vt* dētruncāre
decay *vi* dīlābī, perīre, putrēscere; (*fig*) tābēscere, senēscere ♦ *n* ruīna *f*, lāpsus *m*; (*fig*) occāsus *m*, dēfectiō *f*
deceased *adj* mortuus
deceit *n* fraus *f*, fallācia *f*, dolus *m*
deceitful *adj* fallāx, fraudulentus, dolōsus
deceitfully *adv* fallāciter, dolōsē
deceive *vt* dēcipere, fallere, circumvenīre, fraudāre
deceiver *n* fraudātor *m*
December *n* mēnsis December *m*; **of ~** December
decemvir *n* decemvir *m*; **of the decemvirs** decemvirālis
decemvirate *n* decemvirātus *m*
decency *n* honestum *nt*, decōrum *nt*, pudor *m*
decent *adj* honestus, pudēns
decently *adv* honestē, pudenter
deception *n* fraus *f*, fallācia *f*
deceptive *adj* fallāx, fraudulentus
decide *vt*, *vi* (*dispute*) diiūdicāre, dēcernere, dīrimere; **~ to do** statuere, cōnstituere (*inf*); **I have decided** mihī certum est; **~ the issue** dēcernere
decided *adj* certus, firmus
decidedly *adv* certē, plānē
deciduous *adj* cadūcus
decimate *vt* decimum quemque occīdere
decipher *vt* expedīre, ēnōdāre
decision *n* (*of judge*) iūdicium *nt*; (*of council*) dēcrētum *nt*; (*of senate*) auctōritās *f*; (*of referee*) arbitrium *nt*; (*personal*) sententia *f*; (*quality*) cōnstantia *f*
decisive *adj* certus; **~ moment** discrīmen *nt*
decisively *adv* sine dubiō
deck *vt* ōrnāre, exōrnāre ♦ *n* (*ship*) pōns *m*; **with a ~** cōnstrātus
decked *adj* ōrnātus; (*ship*) cōnstrātus
declaim *vt*, *vi* dēclāmāre, prōnūntiāre
declamation *n* dēclāmātiō *f*

declamatory *adj* dēclāmātōrius
declaration *n* adfirmātiō *f*, adsevērātiō *f*;
 (*formal*) prōfessiō *f*; (*of war*) dēnūntiātiō *f*
declare *vt* affirmāre, adsevērāre; (*secret*) aperīre,
 expōnere; (*proclamation*) dēnūntiāre, ēdīcere;
 (*property in census*) dēdicāre; (*war*) indīcere
declension *n* dēclīnātiō *f*
declination *n* dēclīnātiō *f*
decline *n* (*slope*) dēclīve *nt*, dēiectus *m*; (*of age*)
 senium *nt*; (*of power*) dēfectiō *f*; (*of nation*)
 occāsus *m* ◆ *vi* inclīnāre, occidere; (*fig*) ruere,
 dēlābī, dēgenerāre ◆ *vt* dētrectāre, recūsare;
 (GRAM) dēclīnāre
decode *vt* expedīre, ēnōdāre
decompose *vt* dissolvere ◆ *vi* putrēscere
decomposed *adj* putridus
decomposition *n* dissolūtiō *f*
decorate *vt* ōrnāre, decorāre
decoration *n* ōrnāmentum *nt*; (*medal*) īnsigne *nt*
decorous *adj* pudēns, modestus, decōrus
decorously *adv* pudenter, modestē
decorum *n* pudor *m*, honestum *nt*
decoy *n* illecebra *f* ◆ *vt* adlicere, inescāre
decrease *n* dēminūtiō *f*, dēcessiō *f* ◆ *vt*
 dēminuere, extenuāre ◆ *vi* dēcrēscere
decree *n* (*of magistrate*) dēcrētum *nt*, ēdictum
 nt; (*of senate*) cōnsultum *nt*, auctōritās *f*; (*of
 people*) scītum *nt* ◆ *vt* ēdīcere, dēcernere; (*people*)
 scīscere, iubēre; **the senate decrees** placet
 senātuī
decrepit *adj* īnfirmus, dēbilis, dēcrepitus
decrepitude *n* īnfirmitās *f*, dēbilitās *f*
decry *vt* obtrectāre, reprehendere
decurion *n* decuriō *m*
dedicate *vt* dēdicāre, cōnsecrāre; (*life*) dēvovēre
dedication *n* dēdicātiō *f*; dēvōtiō *f*
dedicatory *adj* commendātīcius
deduce *vt* colligere, conclūdere
deduct *vt* dēmere, dētrahere
deduction *n* (*inference*) conclūsiō *f*, cōnsequēns
 nt; (*subtraction*) dēductiō *f*, dēminūtiō *f*
deed factum *nt*, facinus *nt*; gestum *nt*; (*legal*)
 tabulae *fpl*; **deeds** *pl* rēs gestae *fpl*
deem *vt* dūcere, cēnsēre, habēre
deep *adj* altus, profundus; (*discussion*) abstrūsus;
 (*sleep*) artus; (*sound*) gravis; (*width*) lātus; **three
 ~** (MIL) ternī in lātitūdinem ◆ *n* altum *nt*
deepen *vt* dēfodere, altiōrem reddere; (*fig*)
 augēre ◆ *vi* altiōrem fierī; (*fig*) crēscere
deepest *adj* īmus
deeply *adv* altē, graviter; (*inside*) penitus; **very
 ~** valdē, vehementer
deep-seated *adj* (*fig*) inveterātus
deer *n* cervus *m*, cerva *f*; (*fallow*) dāma *f*
deface *vt* dēfōrmāre, foedāre
defaced *adj* dēfōrmis
defacement *n* dēfōrmitās *f*
defalcation *n* peculātus *m*
defamation *n* calumnia *f*, opprobrium *nt*
defamatory *adj* contumēliōsus, probrōsus
defame *vt* īnfāmāre, obtrectāre, calumniārī
default *vi* dēesse; (*money*) nōn solvere ◆ *n*
 dēfectiō *f*, culpa *f*; **let judgment go by
 ~** vadimōnium dēserere, nōn respondēre
defaulter *n* reus *m*

defeat *vt* vincere, superāre; (*completely*)
 dēvincere; (*plan*) frustrārī, disicere ◆ *n* clādēs
 f; (*at election*) repulsa *f*, offēnsiō *f*; (*of plan*)
 frustrātiō *f*
defeatism *n* patientia *f*
defeatist *n* imbellis *m*
defect *n* vitium *nt*
defection *n* dēfectiō *f*, sēditiō *f*
defective *adj* mancus, vitiōsus
defence *n* praesidium *nt*, tūtēla *f*; patrōcinium
 nt; (*speech*) dēfēnsiō *f*; **speak in ~** dēfendere
defenceless *adj* inermis, indēfēnsus; **leave
 ~** nūdāre
defences *npl* mūnīmenta *ntpl*, mūnītiōnēs *fpl*
defend *vt* dēfendere, tuērī, custōdīre
defendant *n* reus *m*
defender *n* dēfēnsor *m*, prōpugnātor *m*; (LAW)
 patrōnus *m*
defensible *adj* iūstus
defensive *adj* dēfēnsiōnis causā; **be on the ~** sē
 dēfendere
defensively *adv* dēfendendō
defer *vt* differre, prōlātāre ◆ *vi* mōrem gerere
 (*dat*); **I ~ to you** in this hōc tibī tribuō
deference *n* obsequium *nt*, observantia *f*; **show
 ~ to** observāre, īnservīre (*dat*)
deferential *adj* observāns, officiōsus
deferment *n* dīlatiō *f*, prōlātiō *f*
defiance *n* ferōcia *f*, minae *fpl*
defiant *adj* ferōx, mināx
defiantly *adv* ferōciter, mināciter
deficiency *n* vitium *nt*; (*lack*) pēnūria *f*, inopia *f*
deficient *adj* vitiōsus, inops; **be ~** dēesse,
 dēficere
deficit *n* lacūna *f*
defile *n* faucēs *fpl*, angustiae *fpl* ◆ *vt* inquināre,
 contāmināre
defilement *n* sordēs *f*, foeditās *f*
define *vt* (*limits*) fīnīre, dēfīnīre, termināre;
 (*meaning*) explicāre
definite *adj* certus, dēfīnītus
definitely *adv* dēfīnītē; prōrsus
definition *n* dēfīnītiō *f*, explicātiō *f*
definitive *adj* dēfīnītīvus
deflate *vt* laxāre
deflect *vt* dēdūcere, dēclīnāre ◆ *vi* dēflectere,
 dēgredī
deflection *n* dēclīnātiō *f*, flexus *m*
deform *vt* dēfōrmāre
deformed *adj* dēfōrmis, distortus
deformity *n* dēfōrmitās *f*, prāvitās *f*
defraud *vt* fraudāre, dēfraudāre
defrauder *n* fraudātor *m*
defray *vt* solvere, suppeditāre
deft *adj* habilis
deftly *adv* habiliter
defunct *adj* mortuus
defy *vt* contemnere, spernere, adversārī (*dat*);
 (*challenge*) prōvocāre, lacessere
degeneracy *n* dēprāvātiō *f*
degenerate *adj* dēgener ◆ *vi* dēgenerāre,
 dēscīscere
degradation *n* īnfāmia *f*, ignōminia *f*, nota *f*
degrade *vt* notāre, abicere; (*from office*) movēre
degrading *adj* turpis, indignus

degree n gradus; (social) locus m; **in some ~** aliquā ex parte; **by degrees** gradātim, sēnsim
deification n apotheōsis f
deified adj (emperor) dīvus
deify vt cōnsecrāre, inter deōs referre
deign vi dignārī
deity n deus m
dejected adj adflīctus, dēmissus
dejectedly adv animō dēmissō
dejection n maestitia f
delay vt dēmorārī, dētinēre, retardāre ♦ vi cunctārī, cessāre ♦ n mora f, cunctātiō f
delayer n morātor m, cunctātor m
delectable adj iūcundus, amoenus
delegate vt lēgāre, mandāre, committere ♦ n lēgātus m
delegation n lēgātiō f, lēgātī mpl
delete vt dēlēre
deleterious adj perniciōsus, noxius
deletion n (writing) litūra f
deliberate vi dēlīberāre, cōnsulere ♦ adj (act) cōnsīderātus; (intention) certus; (manner) cōnsīderātus; (speech) lentus
deliberately adv dē industriā
deliberation n dēlīberātiō f
deliberative adj dēlīberātīvus
delicacy n (judgment) subtīlitās f, ēlegantia f; (manners) mollitia f, luxus m; (health) valētūdō f; (food) cuppēdia ntpl
delicate adj mollis; (health) īnfirmus; (shape) gracilis; (feelings) hūmānus
delicately adv molliter; hūmānē
delicious adj suāvis, lautus
delight n voluptās f, gaudium nt, dēlectātiō f ♦ vt dēlectāre, oblectāre, iuvāre ♦ vi gaudēre, dēlectārī
delightful adj iūcundus, dulcis, festīvus; (scenery) amoenus
delightfully adv iūcundē, suāviter
delimitation n dēfīnītiō f
delineate vt dēscrībere, dēpingere
delineation n dēscrīptiō f
delinquency n culpa f, dēlictum nt, noxa f
delinquent n nocēns m/f, reus m
delirious adj dēlīrus, āmēns, furiōsus; **be ~** furere, dēlīrāre
delirium n furor m, āmentia f
deliver vt (from) līberāre, exsolvere, ēripere; (blow) intendere; (message) referre; (speech) habēre; ~ **to** dēferre, trādere, dare; ~ **up** dēdere, trādere; **be delivered of** parere
deliverance n līberātiō f
deliverer n līberātor m
delivery n (of things due) trāditiō f; (of speech) āctiō f, prōnūntiātiō f; (of child) partus m
dell n convallis f
Delphi n Delphī mpl
delude vt dēcipere, frustrārī, dēlūdere
deluge n ēluviō f ♦ vt inundāre
delusion n error m, fraus f
delusive adj fallāx, inānis
delve vt fodere
demagogue n plēbicola m
demand vt poscere, postulāre, imperāre; (urgently) flāgitāre, poscere; (thing due) exigere;

(answer) quaerere; ~ **back** repetere ♦ n postulātiō f, postulātum nt
demarcation n līmes m
demean vt (self) dēmittere
demeanour n gestus m, mōs m, habitus m
demented adj dēmēns, furiōsus
demerit n culpa f, vitium nt
demesne n fundus m
demigod n hērōs m
demise n obitus m ♦ vt lēgāre
democracy n cīvitās populāris f
democrat n homō populāris m/f
democratic adj populāris
demolish vt dēmōlīrī, dīruere, dēstruere; (argument) discutere
demolition n ruīna f, ēversiō f
demon n daemōn m
demonstrate vt (show) mōnstrāre, ostendere, indicāre; (prove) dēmōnstrāre
demonstration n exemplum nt; (proof) dēmōnstrātiō f
demonstrative adj (manner) vehemēns; (RHET) dēmōnstrātīvus
demoralization n corruptiō f, dēprāvātiō f
demoralize vt corrumpere, dēprāvāre, labefactāre
demote vt locō movēre
demur vi gravārī, recūsāre ♦ n mora f, dubitātiō f
demure adj modestus, verēcundus
demurely adv modestē, verēcundē
demureness n modestia f, verēcundia f, pudor m
demurrer n (LAW) exceptiō f
den n latibulum nt, latebra f; (of vice) lustrum nt
denarius n dēnārius m
denial n īnfitiātiō f, negātiō f
denigrate vt obtrectāre, calumniārī
denizen n incola m/f
denominate vt nōmināre, appellāre
denomination n nōmen nt; (religious) secta f
denote vt notāre, significāre
denouement n exitus m
denounce vt dēferre, incūsāre
denouncer n dēlātor m
dense adj dēnsus; (crowd) frequēns; (person) stolidus
density n crassitūdō f; (crowd) frequentia f
dent n nota f
dentate adj dentātus
denture n dentēs mpl
denudation n spoliātiō f
denude vt spoliāre, nūdāre
denunciation n (report) indicium nt, dēlātiō f; (threat) minae fpl
deny vt īnfitiārī, īnfitiās īre, negāre, abnuere; (on oath) abiūrāre; ~ **oneself** genium dēfraudāre
depart vi discēdere (abl), abīre, exīre, ēgredī
department n (district) regiō f, pars f; (duty) prōvincia f, mūnus nt
departure n discessus m, abitus m, dīgressus m, exitus m; (change) mūtātiō f; (death) obitus m
depend vi pendēre; (be dependent) pendēre ex (abl), nītī (abl); (rely) fīdere, cōnfīdere; **depending on** frētus (abl)
dependable adj fīdus

dependant n cliēns m/f
dependence n clientēla f; (reliance) fīdūcia f
dependency n prōvincia f
dependent adj subiectus, obnoxius
depict vt dēscrībere, dēpingere; (to the life) expingere
deplete vt dēminuere
depletion n dēminūtiō f
deplorable adj turpis, nefandus, pessimus
deplorably adv turpiter, pessimē, miserē
deplore vt dēplōrāre, dēflēre, conquerī
deploy vt explicāre; instruere, dispōnere
depopulate vt vastāre, nūdāre
depopulation n vastātiō f, sōlitūdō f
deport vt (banish) dēportāre; (self) gerere
deportation n exsilium nt
deportment n gestus m, habitus m
depose vt dēmovēre, dēpellere; (evidence) testārī
deposit n fīdūcia f, dēpositum nt ♦ vt dēpōnere, mandāre
depositary n sequester m
deposition n (LAW) testimōnium nt, indicium nt
depository n apothēca f
depot n (for arms) armāmentārium nt; (for trade) emporium nt
deprave vt dēprāvāre, corrumpere
depraved adj prāvus
depravity n dēprāvātiō f, turpitūdō f
deprecate vt abōminārī, dēprecārī
deprecation n dēprecātiō f
depreciate vt obtrectāre, dētrectāre
depreciation n obtrectātiō f; (price) vīlitās f
depredation n praedātiō f, dīreptiō f
depress vt dēprimere; (mind) adflīgere, frangere; **be depressed** iacēre, animum dēspondēre
depressing adj maestus, tristis
depression n (place) cavum nt; (mind) tristitia f, sollicitūdō f
deprivation n prīvātiō f, spoliātiō f
deprive vt prīvāre, spoliāre
depth n altitūdō f; (place) profundum nt, gurges m
deputation n lēgātiō f, lēgātī mpl
depute vt lēgāre, mandāre
deputy n lēgātus m; (substitute) vicārius m
derange vt conturbāre
deranged adj īnsānus, mente captus
derangement n perturbātiō f; (mind) īnsānia f, dēmentia f
derelict adj dēsertus
dereliction n (of duty) neglegentia f
deride vt dērīdēre, inlūdere
derision n rīsus m, irrīsiō f
derisive adj mordāx
derivation n orīgō f
derive vt dūcere, trahere; (advantage) capere, parāre; (pleasure) dēcerpere, percipere; **be derived** dēfluere
derogate vi dērogāre, dētrahere; ~ **from** imminuere, obtrectāre
derogation n imminūtiō f, obtrectātiō f
derogatory adj indignus; ~ **remarks** obtrectātiō f
derrick n trochlea f
descant vt disserere ♦ n cantus m

descend vi dēscendere; (water) dēlābī; (from heaven) dēlābī; (by inheritance) pervenīre, prōdī; (morally) dēlābī, sē dēmittere; **be descended from** orīrī ex (abl)
descendant n prōgeniēs f; **descendants** pl minōrēs mpl, posterī mpl
descent n dēscensus m; (slope) clīvus m, dēiectus m; (birth) genus nt; (hostile) dēcursus m, incursiō f; **make a ~ upon** inrumpere in (acc), incursāre in (acc)
describe vt dēscrībere; (tell) nārrāre; (portray) dēpingere, exprimere
description n dēscrīptiō f; (tale) nārrātiō f; (kind) genus nt
descry vt cernere, cōnspicere, prōspectāre
desecrate vt prōfānāre, exaugurāre
desecration n exaugurātiō f, violātiō f
desert vt dēserere, dērelinquere, dēstituere ♦ vi dēscīscere, dēficere ♦ adj dēsertus, sōlitārius ♦ n (place) sōlitūdō f, loca dēserta ntpl; (merit) meritum nt
deserted adj dēsertus
deserter n dēsertor m; (MIL) trānsfuga m
desertion n dēfectiō f, trānsfugium nt
deserve vt merērī; dignus esse quī (subj); ~ **well of** bene merērī dē (abl)
deserved adj meritus
deservedly adv meritō
deserving adj dignus
desiccate vt siccāre
design n (drawing) adumbrātiō f; (plan) cōnsilium nt, prōpositum nt; **by** ~ cōnsultō ♦ vt adumbrāre, in animō habēre
designate vt dēsignāre, mōnstrāre; (as heir) scrībere; (as official) dēsignāre ♦ adj dēsignātus
designation n nōmen nt, titulus m
designedly adv dē industriā, cōnsultō
designer n auctor m, inventor m
designing adj vafer, dolōsus
desirable adj optābilis, expetendus, grātus
desire n cupīditās f; studium nt; (uncontrolled) libīdō f; (natural) adpetītiō f ♦ vt cupere; (much) exoptāre, expetere; (command) iubēre
desirous adj cupidus, avidus, studiōsus
desist vi dēsistere
desk n scrīnium nt
desolate adj dēsertus, sōlitārius; (place) vastus ♦ vt vastāre
desolation n sōlitūdō f, vastitās f; (process) vastātiō f
despair vi dēspērāre dē (abl), animum dēspondēre ♦ n dēspērātiō f
despairingly adv dēspēranter
despatch see dispatch
desperado n homō dēspērātus m
desperate adj (hopeless) dēspērātus; (wicked) perditus; (dangerous) perīculōsus
desperately adv dēspēranter
desperation n dēspērātiō f
despicable adj dēspectus, abiectus, turpis
despicably adv turpiter
despise vt contemnere, dēspicere, spernere
despiser n contemptor m
despite n malevolentia f, odium nt
despoil vt spoliāre, nūdāre
despoiler n spoliātor m, praedātor m

despond vi animum dēspondēre, dēspērāre
despondency n dēspērātiō f
despondent adj abiectus, adflīctus, dēmissus; **be ~** animum dēspondēre
despondently adv animō dēmissō
despot n dominus m, rēx m
despotic adj imperiōsus, superbus
despotically adv superbē
despotism n dominātiō f, superbia f, rēgnum nt
dessert n secunda mēnsa f
destination n fīnis m
destine vt dēstināre, dēsignāre; **destined to be** futūrus
destiny n fātum nt; **of ~** fātālis
destitute adj inops, pauper, prīvātus; **~ of** expers (gen)
destitution n inopia f, egestās f
destroy vt dēlēre, ēvertere, dīrimere, perdere
destroyer n ēversor m
destructible adj fragilis
destruction n exitium nt, ēversiō f, excidium nt
destructive adj exitiābilis, perniciōsus
destructively adv perniciōsē
desuetude n dēsuētūdō f
desultorily adv carptim
desultory adj varius, incōnstāns
detach vt abiungere, sēiungere, āmovēre, sēparāre
detachment n (MIL) manus f, cohors f; (mind) integer animus m, līber animus
detail n: **in ~** singillātim ♦ vt exsequī; **details** pl singula ntpl
detain vt dēmorārī, dētinēre, distinēre, morārī
detect vt dēprehendere, patefacere
detection n dēprehēnsiō f
detective n inquīsītor m
detention n retentiō f; (prison) vincula ntpl
deter vt dēterrēre, absterrēre, impedīre
deteriorate vi dēgenerāre
deterioration n dēprāvātiō f, lāpsus m
determinate adj certus, fīnītus
determination n obstinātiō f, cōnstantia f; (intention) prōpositum nt, sententia f
determine vt (fix) fīnīre; (decide) statuere, cōnstituere
determined adj obstinātus; (thing) certus; **I am ~ to** mihi certum est (inf)
determinedly adv cōnstanter
deterrent n: **act as a ~ to** dēterrēre
detest vt ōdisse, dētestārī
detestable adj dētestābilis, odiōsus
detestation n odium nt, invidia f
dethrone vt rēgnō dēpellere
detour n circuitus m; **make a ~** iter flectere; (MIL) agmen circumdūcere
detract vi: **~ from** dērogāre, dētrahere
detraction n obtrectātiō f
detractor n obtrectātor m, invidus m
detriment n damnum nt, dētrīmentum nt
detrimental adj damnōsus; **be ~ to** dētrīmentō esse (dat)
devastate vt vastāre, populārī
devastation n vastātiō f, populātiō f; (state) vastitās f
develop vt ēvolvere, explicāre; (person) ēducāre, alere ♦ vi crēscere; **~ into** ēvādere in (acc)

development n explicātiō f; (of men) ēducātiō f; (of resources) cultus m; (of events) exitus m
deviate vi dēcēdere dē viā, aberrāre, dēclīnāre; (speech) dēgredī
deviation n dēclīnātiō f; (from truth) error m; (in speech) dīgressus m
device n (plan) cōnsilium nt; (machine) māchina f; (emblem) īnsigne nt
devil n diabolus m; **go to the ~** abī in malam crucem!; **talk of the ~** lupus in fābulā!
devilish adj scelestus, impius
devil-may-care adj praeceps, lascīvus
devilment n malitia f
devilry n magicae artēs fpl
devious adj dēvius, errābundus
devise vt excōgitāre, commentārī, fingere
devoid adj vacuus, expers; **be ~ of** carēre (abl)
devolve vi obtingere, obvenīre ♦ vt dēferre, committere
devote vt dēdicāre; (attention) dēdere, trādere; (life) dēvovēre
devoted adj dēditus, studiōsus; (victim) dēvōtus, sacer; **be ~ to** studēre (dat), incumbere (dat)
devotee n cultor m
devotion n amor m, studium nt; rēligiō f
devour vt dēvorāre, cōnsūmere; (fig) haurīre
devout adj pius, rēligiōsus
devoutly adv piē, rēligiōsē
dew n rōs m
dewy adj rōscidus
dexterity n ars f, sollertia f
dexterous adj sollers, habilis
dexterously adv sollerter, habiliter
diabolical adj scelestus, nefārius
diadem n diadēma nt
diagnose vt discernere, diiūdicāre
diagnosis n iūdicium nt
diagonal adj oblīquus
diagram n fōrma f
dial n sōlārium nt
dialect n dialectus f, sermō m
dialectic n ars disserendī f, dialecticē f ♦ adj dialecticus
dialectician n dialecticus m
dialogue n dialogus m, colloquium nt
diameter n diametros f
diamond n adamās m
diaphanous adj perlūcidus
diaphragm n praecordia ntpl
diary n ephēmeris f
diatribe n convīcium nt
dice n tālus m, tessera f; **game of ~** ālea f
dictate vt dictāre ♦ n praeceptum nt; **dictates of nature** nātūrae iūdicia ntpl
dictation n dictāta ntpl; (fig) arbitrium nt
dictator n dictātor m; **dictator's** dictātōrius
dictatorial adj imperiōsus, superbus
dictatorship n dictātūra f
diction n (enunciation) ēlocūtiō f; (words) ōrātiō f
dictionary n verbōrum thēsaurus m
die n signum nt; **the die is cast** iacta ālea est ♦ vi morī, perīre, obīre; (in battle) cadere, occumbere; **die off** dēmorī; **die out** ēmorī; **be dying to** exoptāre
diet n (food) diaeta f; (meeting) conventus m
differ vi differre, discrepāre, dissentīre

difference n discrepantia f, dissimilitūdō f; (of opinion) dissēnsiō f; **there is a ~** interest
different adj dīversus, varius, dissimilis; **~ from** alius … ac; **in ~ directions** dīversī; **they say ~ things** alius aliud dīcit
differentiate vt discernere
differently adv dīversē, variē, alius aliter; **~ from** aliter … ac
difficult adj difficilis, arduus; **very ~** perdifficilis, perarduus
difficulty n difficultās f, labor m, negōtium nt; **with ~** difficulter, aegrē, vix; **be in ~** labōrāre
diffidence n diffīdentia f; (shyness) pudor m; **with ~** modestē
diffident adj diffīdēns; (shy) modestus, verēcundus
diffidently adv modestē
diffuse vt diffundere, dispergere; **be diffused** diffluere ♦ adj fūsus, diffūsus, cōpiōsus
diffusely adv diffūsē, cōpiōsē
diffuseness n cōpia f
dig vt fodere, dūcere; (nudge) fodicāre; **dig up** vt effodere, ēruere
digest vt coquere, concoquere ♦ n summārium nt
digestion n concoctiō f; **with a bad ~** crūdus
digger n fossor m
dignified adj gravis, augustus
dignify vt honōrāre, honestāre
dignity n gravitās f, māiestās f, amplitūdō f
digress vi dēvertere, dīgredī, dēclīnāre
digression n dēclīnātiō f, dīgressus m
dike n (ditch) fossa f; (mound) agger m
dilapidated adj ruīnōsus
dilapidation n ruīna f
dilate vt dīlātāre; (speech) plūra dīcere
dilatorily adv tardē, cunctanter
dilatoriness n mora f, cunctātiō f
dilatory adj tardus, lentus, segnis
dilemma n nōdus m, angustiae fpl; **be in a ~** haerēre; **be on the horns of a ~** auribus tenēre lupum
diligence n dīligentia f, industria f, cūra f
diligent adj dīligēns, industrius, sēdulus
diligently adv dīligenter, sēdulō
dill n anēthum nt
dilly-dally vi cessāre
dilute vt dīluere, temperāre
dim adj obscūrus; (fig) hebes ♦ vt obscūrāre; hebetāre
dimension n modus m; **dimensions** pl amplitūdō f, māgnitūdō f
diminish vt minuere, imminuere, extenuāre, īnfringere ♦ vi dēcrēscere
diminution n imminūtiō f, dēminūtiō f
diminutive adj parvulus, exiguus ♦ n (word) dēminūtum nt
diminutiveness n exiguitās f
dimly adv obscūrē
dimness n tenebrae fpl, cālīgō f
dimple n gelasīnus m
din n fragor m, strepitus m; **make a din** strepere ♦ vt obtundere
dine vi cēnāre
diner n convīva m
dinghy n scapha f

dingy adj sordidus; (colour) fuscus
dining room n cēnātiō f
dinner n cēna f
dinner party convīvium nt
dint n ictus m; **by ~ of** per (acc)
dip vt imbuere, mergere ♦ vi mergī; **dip into** (study) perstringere
diploma n diplōma nt
diplomacy n (embassy) lēgātiō f; (tact) iūdicium nt, sagācitās f
diplomat n lēgātus m
diplomatic adj sagāx, circumspectus
diptych n tabellae fpl
dire adj dīrus, horridus
direct vt regere, dīrigere; (attention) attendere, admovēre, advertere; (course) tendere; (business) administrāre, moderārī; (letter) īnscrībere; (order) imperāre (dat), iubēre; (to a place) viam mōnstrāre (dat); (weapon) intendere ♦ adj rēctus, dīrēctus; (person) simplex; (language) apertus ♦ adv rēctā
direction n (of going) cursus m, iter nt; (of looking) pars f, regiō f; (control) administrātiō f, regimen nt; (order) praeceptum nt, iussum nt; **in the ~ of Rome** Rōmam versus; **in all directions** passim, undique; **in both directions** utrōque
directly adv (place) rēctā; (time) prōtinus, continuō, statim; (language) apertē ♦ conj simulac
directness n (fig) simplicitās f
director n dux m, gubernātor m, moderātor m
dirge n nēnia f
dirk n pūgiō m
dirt n sordēs f; (mud) lūtum nt
dirty adj sordidus, foedus; (speech) inquinātus ♦ vt foedāre, inquināre
disability n vitium nt
disable vt dēbilitāre, imminuere
disabled adj mutilus, dēbilis
disabuse vt errōrem dēmere (dat)
disaccustom vt dēsuēfacere
disadvantage n incommodum nt, dētrīmentum nt; **it is a ~** dētrīmentō est
disadvantageous adj incommodus, inīquus
disadvantageously adv incommodē
disaffected adj aliēnātus, sēditiōsus
disaffection n aliēnātiō f, sēditiō f
disagree vi discrepāre, dissentīre, dissidēre
disagreeable adj molestus, incommodus, iniūcundus
disagreeably adv molestē, incommodē
disagreement n discordia f, dissēnsiō f, discrepantia f
disallow vt improbāre, abnuere, vetāre
disappear vi dēperīre, perīre, abīre, diffugere, ēvānēscere
disappearance n dēcessiō f, fuga f
disappoint vt dēcipere, spē dēicere, frustrārī; **be disappointed in a hope** ā spē dēcidere, dē spē dēicī
disappointment n frustrātiō f, malum nt
disapprobation n reprehēnsiō f, improbātiō f
disapproval n improbātiō f
disapprove vt, vi improbāre, reprehendere
disarm vt exarmāre, dearmāre; (fig) mītigāre
disarrange vt turbāre, cōnfundere

49

disarranged *adj* incompositus
disarrangement *n* turbātiō *f*
disarray *n* perturbātiō *f* ♦ *vt* perturbāre
disaster *n* calamitās *f*, cāsus *m*; (MIL) clādēs *f*
disastrous *adj* īnfēlīx, exitiōsus, calamitōsus
disavow *vt* diffitērī, īnfitiārī
disavowal *n* īnfitiātiō *f*
disband *vt* dīmittere
disbelief *n* diffīdentia *f*, suspiciō *f*
disbelieve *vt* diffīdere (*dat*)
disburden *vt* exonerāre
disburse *vt* ērogāre, expendere
disbursement *n* impēnsa *f*
disc *n* orbis *m*
discard *vt* mittere, pōnere, prōicere
discern *vt* cōnspicere, dīspicere, cernere; (*fig*) intellegere
discernment *n* iūdicium *nt*, intellegentia *f*, sagācitās *f*
discharge *vt* (*load*) exonerāre; (*debt*) exsolvere; (*duty*) fungī (*abl*), exsequī; (*officer*) exauctōrāre; (*troops*) missōs facere, dīmittere; (*weapon*) iacere, iaculārī; (*prisoner*) absolvere; (*from body*) ēdere, reddere ♦ *vi* (*river*) effundī, īnfluere ♦ *n* (*bodily*) dēfluxiō *f*; (MIL) missiō *f*, dīmissiō *f*; (*of a duty*) perfūnctiō *f*
disciple *n* discipulus *m*
discipline *n* (MIL) modestia *f*; (*punishment*) castīgātiō *f*; (*study*) disciplīna *f* ♦ *vt* coercēre, castīgāre
disciplined *adj* modestus
disclaim *vt* renūntiāre, repudiāre, rēicere
disclaimer *n* repudiātiō *f*
disclose *vt* aperīre, patefacere, indicāre
disclosure *n* indicium *nt*
discoloration *n* dēcolōrātiō *f*
discolour *vt* dēcolōrāre
discoloured *adj* dēcolor
discomfit *vt* vincere, conturbāre, dēprehendere
discomfiture *n* clādēs *f*; (POL) repulsa *f*
discomfort *n* molestia *f*, incommodum *nt*
disconcert *vt* conturbāre, percellere
disconcerting *adj* molestus
disconnect *vt* abiungere, sēiungere
disconnected *adj* dissolūtus, abruptus
disconnectedly *adv* dissolūtē
disconsolate *adj* maestus, dēmissus
disconsolately *adv* animō dēmissō
discontent *n* offēnsiō *f*, fastīdium *nt*, taedium *nt*
discontented *adj* invidus, fastīdiōsus, parum contentus
discontentedly *adv* invītus, inīquō animō
discontinuance *n* intermissiō *f*
discontinue *vt* intermittere ♦ *vi* dēsistere, dēsinere
discord *n* discordia *f*; (*music*) dissonum *nt*
discordance *n* discrepantia *f*, dissēnsiō *f*
discordant *adj* discors, discrepāns; (*music*) dissonus, absonus
discount *vt* dētrahere; (*fig*) praetermittere ♦ *n* dēcessiō *f*; **be at a ~** iacēre
discountenance *vt* improbāre
discourage *vt* dēhortārī, dēterrēre; **be discouraged** animum dēmittere, animō dēficere

discouragement *n* animī abiectiō *f*; (*cause*) incommodum *nt*
discourse *n* sermō *m*; (*lecture*) ōrātiō *f* ♦ *vi* conloquī, disserere, disputāre
discourteous *adj* inurbānus, asper, inhūmānus
discourteously *adv* inhūmānē, rūsticē
discourtesy *n* inhūmānitās *f*, acerbitās *f*
discover *vt* (*find*) invenīre, reperīre; (*detect*) dēprehendere; (*reveal*) aperīre, patefacere; (*learn*) cognōscere
discoverer *n* inventor *m*
discovery *n* inventum *nt*
discredit *vt* notāre, fidem imminuere (*gen*) ♦ *n* invidia *f*, lābēs *f*; **be in ~** iacēre
discreditable *adj* inhonestus, turpis
discreditably *adv* inhonestē, turpiter
discreet *adj* prūdēns, sagāx, cautus
discreetly *adv* prūdenter, sagāciter, cautē
discrepancy *n* discrepantia *f*, dissēnsiō *f*
discretion *n* prūdentia *f*; (*tact*) iūdicium *nt*; (*power*) arbitrium *nt*, arbitrātus *m*; **at your ~** arbitrātū tuō; **surrender at ~** in dēditiōnem venīre, sine ullā pactiōne sē tradere; **years of ~** adulta aetās *f*
discretionary *adj* līber
discriminate *vt*, *vi* discernere, internōscere, distinguere
discriminating *adj* perspicāx, sagāx
discrimination *n* discrīmen *nt*, iūdicium *nt*
discursive *adj* vagus, loquāx; **be ~** excurrere
discuss *vt* agere, disputāre, disceptāre dē (*abl*); **~ terms of peace** dē pāce agere
discussion *n* disceptātiō *f*, disputātiō *f*
disdain *vt* contemnere, aspernārī, fastīdīre ♦ *n* contemptiō *f*, fastīdium *nt*
disdainful *adj* fastīdiōsus, superbus
disdainfully *adv* fastīdiōsē, superbē
disease *n* morbus *m*; pestilentia *f*
diseased *adj* aeger, aegrōtus
disembark *vi* ē nāve ēgredī ♦ *vt* mīlitēs *etc* ē nāve expōnere
disembarkation *n* ēgressus *m*
disembodied *adj* sine corpore
disembowel *vt* exenterāre
disencumber *vt* exonerāre
disengage *vt* expedīre, līberāre; (*mind*) abstrahere, abdūcere
disengaged *adj* vacuus, ōtiōsus
disentangle *vt* expedīre, explicāre, exsolvere
disfavour *n* invidia *f*
disfigure *vt* dēfōrmāre, foedāre
disfigured *adj* dēfōrmis
disfigurement *n* dēfōrmātiō *f*
disfranchise *vt* cīvitātem adimere (*dat*)
disfranchised *adj* capite dēminūtus
disfranchisement *n* capitis dēminūtiō *f*
disgorge *vt* ēvomere
disgrace *n* dēdecus *nt*, ignōminia *f*, īnfāmia *f* ♦ *vt* dēdecorāre, dēdecorī esse (*dat*)
disgraceful *adj* ignōminiōsus, flāgitiōsus, turpis; **~ thing** flāgitium *nt*
disgracefully *adv* turpiter, flāgitiōsē
disgruntled *adj* mōrōsus, invidus
disguise *n* integumentum *nt*; (*fig*) speciēs *f*, simulātiō *f*; **in ~** mūtātā veste ♦ *vt* obtegere,

involvere; *(fact)* dissimulāre; ~ **oneself** vestem mūtāre

disgust *vt* displicēre *(dat)*, fastīdium movēre *(dat)*; **be disgusted** stomachārī; **I am disgusted** mē taedet, mē piget ♦ *n* fastīdium *nt*, taedium *nt*

disgusting *adj* taeter, foedus, dēfōrmis

disgustingly *adv* foedē

dish *n* lanx *f*; *(course)* ferculum *nt*

dishearten *vt* percellere; **be disheartened** animō dēficere, animum dēmittere

dishevelled *adj* solūtus, passus

dishonest *adj* perfidus, inīquus, improbus

dishonestly *adv* improbē, dolō malō

dishonesty *n* mala fidēs *f*, perfidia *f*, fraus *f*

dishonour *n* dēdecus *nt*, ignōminia *f*, turpitūdō *f* ♦ *vt* dēdecorāre

dishonourable *adj* ignōminiōsus, indecōrus, turpis

dishonourably *adv* turpiter, inhonestē

disillusion *vt* errōrem adimere *(dat)*

disinclination *n* odium *nt*

disinclined *adj* invītus, āversus

disinfect *vt* pūrgāre

disingenuous *adj* dolōsus, fallāx

disingenuously *adv* dolōsē

disinherit *vt* abdicāre, exhērēdāre

disinherited *adj* exhērēs

disintegrate *vt* dissolvere ♦ *vi* dīlābī, dissolvī

disinter *vt* effodere, ēruere

disinterested *adj* grātuītus, favōris expers

disinterestedly *adv* sine favōre

disinterestedness *n* innocentia *f*, integritās *f*

disjoin *vt* sēiungere

disjointed *adj* parum cohaerēns

disk *n* orbis *m*

dislike *n* odium *nt*, offēnsiō *f*, invidia *f* ♦ *vt* ōdisse; **I ~** mihī displicet, mē piget *(gen)*

dislocate *vt* extorquēre

dislocated *adj* luxus

dislodge *vt* dēmovēre, dēicere, dēpellere, dētrūdere

disloyal *adj* īnfīdus, īnfidēlis; *(to gods, kin, country)* impius

disloyally *adv* īnfidēliter

disloyalty *n* perfidia *f*, īnfidēlitās *f*; impietās *f*

dismal *adj* fūnestus, maestus

dismally *adv* miserē

dismantle *vt* nūdāre; *(building)* dīruere

dismay *n* pavor *m*, formīdō *f* ♦ *vt* terrēre, perturbāre

dismember *vt* discerpere

dismiss *vt* dīmittere; *(troops)* missōs facere; *(from service)* exauctōrāre; *(fear)* mittere, pōnere

dismissal *n* missiō *f*, dīmissiō *f*

dismount *vi* dēgredī, (ex equō) dēscendere

disobedience *n* contumācia *f*

disobedient *adj* contumāx

disobediently *adv* contrā iūssa

disobey *vt* nōn pārēre *(dat)*, aspernārī

disoblige *vt* displicēre *(dat)*, offendere

disobliging *adj* inofficiōsus, difficilis

disobligingly *adv* contrā officium

disorder *n* turba *f*, cōnfūsiō *f*; *(MED)* morbus *m*; *(POL)* mōtus *m*, tumultus *m* ♦ *vt* turbāre, miscēre, sollicitāre

disorderly *adj* immodestus, inōrdinātus, incompositus; *(POL)* turbulentus, sēditiōsus; **in a ~ manner** nūllō ōrdine, temerē

disorganize *vt* dissolvere, perturbāre

disown *vt* *(statement)* īnfitiārī; *(thing)* abnuere, repudiāre; *(heir)* abdicāre

disparage *vt* obtrectāre, dētrectāre

disparagement *n* obtrectātiō *f*, probrum *nt*

disparager *n* obtrectātor *m*, dētrectātor *m*

disparate *adj* dispār

disparity *n* discrepantia *f*, dissimilitūdō *f*

dispassionate *adj* studiī expers

dispassionately *adv* sine īrā et studiō

dispatch *vt* mittere, dīmittere; *(finish)* absolvere, perficere; *(kill)* interficere ♦ *n* *(letter)* litterae *fpl*; *(speed)* celeritās *f*

dispel *vt* dispellere, discutere

dispensation *n* *(distribution)* partītiō *f*; *(exemption)* venia *f*; *(of heaven)* sors *f*; **by divine ~** dīvīnitus

dispense *vt* dispertīrī, dīvidere ♦ *vi*: **~ with** ōmittere, praetermittere, repudiāre

dispersal *n* dīmissiō *f*, diffugium *nt*

disperse *vt* dispergere, dissipāre, dīsicere ♦ *vi* diffugere, dīlābī

dispirited *adj* dēmissō animō; **be ~** animō dēficere, animum dēmittere

displace *vt* locō movēre

display *n* ostentātiō *f*, iactātiō *f*; **for ~** per speciem ♦ *vt* exhibēre, ostendere, praestāre, sē ferre

displease *vt* displicēre *(dat)*, offendere; **be displeased** aegrē ferre, stomachārī, indignārī

displeasing *adj* ingrātus, odiōsus

displeasure *n* invidia *f*, offēnsiō *f*, odium *nt*

disport *vt*: **~ oneself** lūdere

disposal *n* *(sale)* vēnditiō *f*; *(power)* arbitrium *nt*

dispose *vt* *(troops)* dispōnere; *(mind)* inclīnāre, addūcere ♦ *vi*: **~ of** abaliēnāre, vēndere; *(get rid)* tollere; *(argument)* refellere

disposed *adj* adfectus, inclīnātus, prōnus; **well ~** benevolus, bonō animō

disposition *n* animus *m*, adfectiō *f*, ingenium *nt*, nātūra *f*; *(of troops)* dispositiō *f*

dispossess *vt* dētrūdere, spoliāre

disproportion *n* inconcinnitās *f*

disproportionate *adj* impār, inconcinnus

disproportionately *adv* inaequāliter

disprove *vt* refūtāre, redarguere, refellere

disputable *adj* dubius, ambiguus

disputation *n* disputātiō *f*

dispute *n* altercātiō *f*, contrōversia *f*; *(violent)* iūrgium *nt*; **beyond ~** certissimus ♦ *vi* altercārī, certāre, rixārī ♦ *vt* negāre, in dubium vocāre

disqualification *n* impedīmentum *nt*

disqualify *vt* impedīre

disquiet *n* sollicitūdō *f* ♦ *vt* sollicitāre

disquisition *n* disputātiō *f*

disregard *n* neglegentia *f*, contemptiō *f* ♦ *vt* neglegere, contemnere, ōmittere

disrepair *n* vitium *nt*; **in ~** male sartus

disreputable *adj* inhonestus, īnfāmis

disrepute *n* īnfāmia *f*

disrespect *n* neglegentia *f*, contumācia *f*

disrespectful *adj* contumāx, īnsolēns

disrespectfully *adv* īnsolenter

disrobe vt nūdāre, vestem exuere (dat) ♦ vi vestem exuere
disrupt vt dīrumpere, dīvellere
disruption n discidium nt
dissatisfaction n molestia f, aegritūdō f, dolor m
dissatisfied adj parum contentus; **I am ~ with** ... mē taedet (gen) ...
dissect vt incīdere; (fig) investīgāre
dissemble vt, vi dissimulāre; mentīrī
dissembler n simulātor m
disseminate vt dīvulgāre, dissēmināre
dissension n discordia f, dissēnsiō f; (violent) iūrgium nt
dissent vi dissentīre, dissidēre ♦ n dissēnsiō f
dissertation n disputātiō f
disservice n iniūria f, incommodum nt
dissident adj discors
dissimilar adj dispār, dissimilis
dissimilarity n discrepantia f, dissimilitūdō f
dissimulation n dissimulātiō f
dissipate vt dissipāre, diffundere, disperdere
dissipated adj dissolūtus, lascīvus, luxuriōsus
dissipation n dissipātiō f; (vice) luxuria f, licentia f
dissociate vt dissociāre, sēiungere
dissociation n sēparātiō f, discidium nt
dissoluble adj dissolūbilis
dissolute adj dissolūtus, perditus, libīdinōsus
dissolutely adv libīdinōsē, luxuriōsē
dissoluteness n luxuria f
dissolution n dissolūtiō f, discidium nt
dissolve vt dissolvere; (ice) liquefacere; (meeting) dīmittere; (contract) dīrimere ♦ vi liquēscere; (fig) solvī
dissonance n dissonum nt
dissonant adj dissonus
dissuade vt dissuādēre (dat), dēhortārī
dissuasion n dissuāsiō f
distaff n colus f
distance n intervallum nt, spatium nt; (long way) longinquitās f; **at a ~** (far) longē; (within sight) procul; (fight) ēminus; **at a ~ of ...** spatiō (gen) ...; **within striking ~** intrā iactum tēlī
distant adj longinquus; (measure) distāns; (person) parum familiāris; **be ~** abesse (abl)
distaste n fastīdium nt
distasteful adj molestus, iniūcundus
distemper n morbus m
distend vt distendere
distil vt, vi stillāre
distinct adj (different) dīversus; (separate) distinctus; (clear) clārus, argūtus; (marked) distinctus; (sure) certus; (well-drawn) expressus
distinction n discrīmen nt; (dissimilarity) discrepantia f; (public status) amplitūdō f; (honour) honōs m, decus nt; (mark) īnsigne nt; **there is a ~** interest; **without ~** prōmiscuē
distinctive adj proprius, īnsignītus
distinctively adv propriē, īnsignītē
distinctly adv clārē, distinctē, certē, expressē
distinguish vt distinguere, internōscere, dīiūdicāre, discernere; (honour) decorāre, ōrnāre; **~ oneself** ēminēre
distinguished adj īnsignis, praeclārus, ēgregius, amplissimus

distort vt dētorquēre; (fig) dēprāvāre
distorted adj distortus
distortion n distortiō f; dēprāvātiō f
distract vt distrahere, distinēre, āvocāre; (mind) aliēnāre
distracted adj āmēns, īnsānus
distraction n (state) indīligentia f; (cause) invītāmentum nt; (madness) furor m, dēmentia f; **to ~** efflīctim
distraught adj āmēns, dēmēns
distress n labor m, dolor m, aegrimōnia f, aerumna f; **be in ~** labōrāre ♦ vt adflīgere, sollicitāre
distressed adj adflīctus, sollicitus; **be ~ at** rem etc aegrē ferre
distressing adj tristis, miser, acerbus
distribute vt distribuere, dīvidere, dispertīre
distribution n partītiō f, distribūtiō f
district n regiō f, pars f
distrust n diffīdentia f ♦ vt diffīdere (dat), nōn crēdere (dat)
distrustful adj diffīdēns
distrustfully adv diffīdenter
disturb vt perturbāre, conturbāre; commovēre; (mind) sollicitāre
disturbance n turba f, perturbātiō f; (POL) mōtus m, tumultus m
disturber n turbātor m
disunion n discordia f, discidium nt
disunite vt dissociāre, sēiungere
disuse n dēsuētūdō f; **fall into ~** obsolēscere
disused adj dēsuētus, obsolētus
disyllabic adj disyllabus
ditch n fossa f, scrobis m
dithyrambic adj dithyrambicus
dittany n dictamnum nt
ditty n carmen nt, cantilēna f
diurnal adj diūrnus
divan n lectus m, lectulus m
dive vi dēmergī
diver n ūrīnātor m
diverge vi dēvertere, dīgredī; (road) sē scindere; (opinions) discrepāre
divergence n dīgressiō f; discrepantia f
divers adj complūrēs
diverse adj varius, dīversus
diversify vt variāre
diversion n (of water) dērīvātiō f; (of thought) āvocātiō f; (to amuse) oblectāmentum nt; **create a ~** (MIL) hostēs dīstringere; **for a ~** animī causā
diversity n varietās f, discrepantia f
divert vt dēflectere, āvertere; (attention) āvocāre, abstrahere; (water) dērīvāre; (to amuse) oblectāre, placēre (dat)
diverting adj iūcundus; (remark) facētus
divest vt exuere, nūdāre; **~ oneself of** (fig) pōnere, mittere
divide vt dīvidere; (troops) dīdūcere; **~ among** partīrī, distribuere; **~ from** sēparāre ab, sēiungere ab; **~ out** dispertīrī, dīvidere ♦ vi discēdere, sē scindere; (senate) in sententiam īre; **be divided** (opinions) discrepāre
divination n dīvīnātiō f; (from birds) augurium nt; (from entrails) haruspicium nt
divine adj dīvīnus ♦ vt dīvīnāre, augurārī, hariolārī; **by ~ intervention** dīvīnitus

divinely *adv* dīvīnē
diviner *n* dīvīnus *m*, augur *m*, haruspex *m*
divinity *n* (*status*) dīvīnitās *f*; (*god*) deus *m*, dea *f*
divisible *adj* dīviduus
division *n* (*process*) dīvīsiō *f*, partītiō *f*; (*variance*)
    discordia *f*, dissēnsiō *f*; (*section*) pars *f*; (*grade*)
    classis *f*; (*of army*) legiō *f*; (*of time*) discrīmen *nt*;
    (*in senate*) discessiō *f*
divorce *n* dīvortium *nt*, repudium *nt* ♦ *vt* (*wife*)
    nūntium mittere (*dat*); (*things*) dīvellere,
    sēparāre
divulge *vt* aperīre, patefacere, ēvulgāre, ēdere
dizziness *n* vertīgō *f*
dizzy *adj* vertīginōsus; (*fig*) attonitus
do *vt* facere, agere; (*duty*) fungī (*abl*); (*wrong*)
    admittere; **do away with** *vt* tollere; (*kill*)
    interimere; **do one's best to** id agere ut
    (*subj*); **do without** repudiāre; **do not ...** nolī/
    nolīte (*inf*); **how do you do?** quid agis?; **I have**
    nothing to do with you mihī tēcum nihil est
    commercī; **it has nothing to do with me** nihil
    est ad mē; **that will do** iam satis est; **be done**
    fierī; **have done with** dēfungī (*abl*)
docile *adj* docilis
docility *n* docilitās *f*
dock *n* (*ships*) nāvāle *nt*; (*LAW*) cancellī *mpl* ♦ *vt*
    praecīdere
dockyard *n* nāvālia *ntpl*
doctor *n* medicus *m*; (*univ*) doctor *m* ♦ *vt* cūrāre
doctrine *n* dogma *nt*, dēcrētum *nt*; (*system*) ratiō *f*
document *n* litterae *fpl*, tabula *f*
dodge *vt* dēclīnāre, ēvādere ♦ *n* dolus *m*
doe *n* cerva *f*
doer *n* āctor *m*, auctor *m*
doff *vt* exuere
dog *n* canis *m/f*; **dog star** Canīcula *f*; **dog's**
    canīnus ♦ *vt* īnsequī, īnstāre (*dat*)
dogged *adj* pertināx
doggedly *adv* pertināciter
dogma *n* dogma *nt*, praeceptum *nt*
dogmatic *adj* adrogāns
dogmatically *adv* adroganter
doing *n* factum *nt*
dole *n* sportula *f* ♦ *vt*: ~ **out** dispertīrī, dīvidere
doleful *adj* lūgubris, flēbilis, maestus
dolefully *adv* flēbiliter
dolefulness *n* maestitia *f*, miseria *f*
doll *n* pūpa *f*
dolorous *adj* lūgubris, maestus
dolour *n* maestitia *f*, dolor *m*
dolphin *n* delphīnus *m*
dolt *n* stīpes *m*, caudex *m*
domain *n* ager *m*; (*king's*) rēgnum *nt*
dome *n* tholus *m*, testūdō *f*
domestic *adj* domesticus, familiāris; (*animal*)
    mānsuētus ♦ *n* famulus *m*, servus *m*, famula *f*,
    ancilla *f*; **domestics** *pl* familia *f*
domesticate *vt* mānsuēfacere
domesticated *adj* mānsuētus
domesticity *n* larēs suī *mpl*
domicile *n* domicilium *nt*, domus *f*
dominant *adj* superior, praepotēns
dominate *vt* dominārī in (*acc*), imperāre (*dat*);
    (*view*) dēspectāre
domination *n* dominātiō *f*, dominātus *m*
domineer *vi* dominārī, rēgnāre

dominion *n* imperium *nt*, rēgnum *nt*
don *vt* induere ♦ *n* scholasticus *m*
donate *vt* dōnāre
donation *n* dōnum *nt*
donkey *n* asellus *m*
donor *n* dōnātor *m*
doom *n* fātum *nt* ♦ *vt* damnāre
door *n* (*front*) iānua *f*; (*back*) postīcum *nt*; (*double*)
    forēs *fpl*; **folding doors** valvae *fpl*; **out of doors**
    forīs; (*to*) forās; **next** ~ **to** iuxtā (*acc*)
doorkeeper *n* iānitor *m*
doorpost *n* postis *m*
doorway *n* ōstium *nt*
dormant *adj* sōpītus; **lie** ~ iacēre
dormitory *n* cubiculum *nt*
dormouse *n* glīs *m*
dose *n* pōculum *nt*
dot *n* pūnctum *nt*
dotage *n* senium *nt*
dotard *n* senex dēlīrus *m*
dote *vi* dēsipere; ~ **upon** dēamāre
doting *adj* dēsipiēns, peramāns
dotingly *adv* perditē
double *adj* duplex; (*amount*) duplus; (*meaning*)
    ambiguus ♦ *n* duplum *nt* ♦ *vt* duplicāre;
    (*promontory*) superāre; (*fold*) complicāre ♦ *vi*
    duplicārī; (*MIL*) currere
double-dealer *n* fraudātor *m*
double-dealing *adj* fallāx, dolōsus ♦ *n* fraus *f*,
    dolus *m*
doublet *n* tunica *f*
doubly *adv* bis, dupliciter
doubt *n* dubium *nt*; (*hesitancy*) dubitātiō *f*;
    (*distrust*) suspiciō *f*; **give one the benefit of the**
    ~ innocentem habēre; **no** ~ sānē; **I do not** ~ **that**
    ... nōn dubito quīn ... (*subj*); **there is no** ~ **that**
    ... nōn dubium est quīn ... (*subj*) ♦ *vt* dubitāre;
    (*distrust*) diffīdere (*dat*), suspicārī
doubtful *adj* dubius, incertus; (*result*) anceps;
    (*word*) ambiguus
doubtfully *adv* dubiē; (*hesitation*) dubitanter
doubtless *adv* scīlicet, nīmīrum
doughty *adj* fortis, strēnuus
dove *n* columba *f*
dovecote *n* columbārium *nt*
dowdy *adj* inconcinnus
dower *n* dōs *f* ♦ *vt* dōtāre
dowerless *adj* indōtātus
down *n* plūmae *fpl*, lānūgō *f*; (*thistle*) pappus *m*
    ♦ *adv* deōrsum; **be** ~ iacēre; ~ **with!** perea(n)t;
    up and ~ sūrsum deōrsum ♦ *prep* dē (*abl*);
    ~ **from** dē (*abl*)
downcast *adj* dēmissus, maestus
downfall *n* ruīna *f*; (*fig*) occāsus *m*
downhearted *adj* dēmissus, frāctus animī
downhill *adj* dēclīvis; (*fig*) prōclīvis ♦ *adv* in
    praeceps
downpour *n* imber *m*
downright *adj* dīrēctus; (*intensive*) merus
downstream *adv* secundō flūmine
downtrodden *adj* subiectus, oppressus
downward *adj* dēclīvis, prōclīvis
downwards *adv* deōrsum
downy *adj* plūmeus
dowry *n* dōs *f*
doyen *n* pater *m*

doze vi dormītāre
dozen n duodecim
drab adj sordidior
drachma n drachma f
draft n (writing) exemplum nt; (MIL) dīlēctus m; (money) syngrapha f; (literary) silva f ♦ vt scrībere; (MIL) mittere
drag vt trahere ♦ vi (time) trahī; ~ **on** vi (war) prōdūcere ♦ n harpagō m; (fig) impedīmentum nt
dragnet n ēverriculum nt
dragon n drācō m
dragoon n eques m
drain n cloāca f ♦ vt (water) dērīvāre; (land) siccāre; (drink) exhaurīre; (resources) exhaurīre
drainage n dērīvātiō f
drake n anas m
drama n fābula f; **the** ~ scaena f
dramatic adj scaenicus
dramatist n fābulārum scrīptor m
dramatize vt ad scaenam compōnere
drape vt vēlāre
drapery n vestīmenta ntpl
drastic adj vehemēns, efficāx
draught n (air) aura f; (drink) haustus m; (net) bolus m
draughts n latrunculī mpl
draw vt dūcere, trahere; (bow) addūcere; (inference) colligere; (picture) scrībere, pingere; (sword) stringere, dēstringere; (tooth) eximere; (water) haurīre; ~ **aside** sēdūcere; ~ **away** āvocāre; ~ **back** vt retrahere ♦ vi recēdere; ~ **near** adpropinquāre; ~ **off** dētrahere; (water) dērīvāre; ~ **out** vt ēdūcere; (lengthen) prōdūcere; ~ **over** obdūcere; ~ **taut** addūcere; ~ **together** contrahere; ~ **up** vt (MIL) īnstruere; (document) scrībere
drawback n scrūpulus m; **this was the only** ~ hōc ūnum dēfuit
drawing n dēscrīptiō f; (art) graphicē f
drawing room n sellāria f
drawings npl līneāmenta ntpl
drawl vi lentē dīcere
drawling adj lentus in dīcendō
dray n plaustrum nt
dread n formīdō f, pavor m, horror m ♦ adj dīrus ♦ vt expavēscere, extimēscere, formīdāre
dreadful adj terribilis, horribilis, formīdolōsus, dīrus
dreadfully adv vehementer, atrōciter
dream n somnium nt ♦ vt, vi somniāre
dreamy adj somniculōsus
dreariness n (place) vastitās f; (mind) tristitia f
dreary adj (place) vastus; (person) tristis
dregs n faex f; (of oil) amurca f; **drain to the** ~ exhaurīre
drench vt perfundere
dress n vestis f, vestītus m, vestīmenta ntpl; (style) habitus m ♦ vt vestīre; (wound) cūrāre; (tree) amputāre ♦ vi induī; ~ **up** vi vestum induere
dressing n (MED) fōmentum nt
drift n (motion) mōtus m; (snow) agger m; (language) vīs f; **I see the** ~ **of your speech** videō quōrsum ōrātiō tua tendat ♦ vi fluitāre; (fig) lābī, ferrī
drill n terebra f; (MIL) exercitātiō f ♦ vt (hole) terebrāre; (MIL) exercēre; (pupil) īnstruere

drink vt, vi bibere, pōtāre; ~ **a health** propīnāre, Graecō mōre bibere; ~ **deep of** exhaurīre; ~ **in** haurīre; ~ **up** ēpōtāre ♦ n pōtiō f
drinkable adj pōtulentus
drinker n pōtor m
drinking bout n pōtātiō f
drip vi stillāre, dēstillāre
drive vt agere; (force) cōgere; ~ **away** abigere; (fig) pellere, prōpulsāre; ~ **back** repellere; ~ **home** dēfīgere; ~ **in/into** īnfīgere in (acc); (flock) cōgere in (acc); ~ **off** dēpellere; ~ **out** exigere, expellere, exturbāre; ~ **through** trānsfīgere ♦ vi vehī; ~ **away** āvehī; ~ **back** revehī; ~ **in** invehī; ~ **on** vt impellere; ~ **round** circumvehī; ~ **past** praetervehī; **what are you driving at?** quōrsum tua spectat ōrātiō? ♦ n gestātiō f
drivel vi dēlīrāre
drivelling adj dēlīrus, ineptus ♦ n ineptiae fpl
driver n aurīga m; rēctor m
drizzle vi rōrāre
droll adj facētus, ioculāris
drollery n facētiae fpl
dromedary n dromas m
drone n (bee) fūcus m; (sound) bombus m ♦ vi fremere
droop vi dēmittī; (flower) languēscere; (mind) animum dēmittere
drooping adj languidus
drop n gutta f ♦ vi cadere; (liquid) stillāre ♦ vt mittere; (anchor) iacere; (hint) ēmittere; (liquid) īnstillāre; (work) dēsistere ab (abl) ♦ vi: ~ **behind** cessāre; ~ **in** vi vīsere, supervenīre; ~ **out** excidere
dross n scōria f; (fig) faex f
drought n siccitās f
drouth n sitis f
drove n grex f
drover n bubulcus m
drown vt mergere, obruere; (noise) obscūrāre ♦ vi aquā perīre
drowse vi dormītāre
drowsily adv somniculōsē
drowsiness n sopor m
drowsy adj sēmisomnus, somniculōsus
drub vt pulsāre, verberāre
drudge n mediastīnus m ♦ vi labōrāre
drudgery n labor m
drug n medicāmentum nt ♦ vt medicāre
Druids n Druidae, Druidēs mpl
drum n tympanum nt; (container) urna f
drummer n tympanista m
drunk adj pōtus, ēbrius, tēmulentus
drunkard n ēbriōsus m
drunken adj ēbriōsus, tēmulentus
drunkenness n ēbrietās f
dry adj siccus, āridus; (thirst) sitiēns; (speech) āridus, frīgidus; (joke) facētus; **be dry** ārēre ♦ vt siccāre ♦ vi ārēscere; **dry up** exārēscere
dryad n dryas f
dry rot n rōbīgō f
dual adj duplex
duality n duplex nātūra f
dubiety n dubium nt
dubious adj dubius, incertus; (meaning) ambiguus
dubiously adv dubiē; ambiguē

duck *n* anas *f* ◆ *vt* dēmergere ◆ *vi* dēmergī, sē dēmittere
duckling *n* anaticula *f*
duct *n* ductus *m*
dudgeon *n* dolor *m*, stomachus *m*
due *adj* dēbitus, meritus, iūstus; **be due** dēbērī; **it is due to me that … not** per mē stat quōminus *(subj)*; **be due to** orīrī ex, fierī *(abl)* ◆ *n* iūs *nt*, dēbitum *nt*; *(tax)* vectīgal *nt*; *(harbour)* portōrium *nt*; **give every man his due** suum cuīque tribuere ◆ *adv* rēctā; **due to** ob *(acc)*, propter *(acc)*
duel *n* certāmen *nt*
dug *n* ūber *nt*
duke *n* dux *m*
dulcet *adj* dulcis
dull *adj* hebes; *(weather)* subnūbilus; *(language)* frīgidus; *(mind)* tardus; **be ~** hebēre; **become ~** hebēscere ◆ *vt* hebetāre, obtundere, retundere
dullard *n* stolidus *m*
dulness *n* *(mind)* tarditās *f*, stultitia *f*
duly *adv* rītē, ut pār est
dumb *adj* mūtus; **be struck ~** obmūtēscere
dun *n* flāgitātor *m* ◆ *vt* flāgitāre ◆ *adj* fuscus
dunce *n* bārō *m*
dune *n* tumulus *m*
dung *n* fimus *m*
dungeon *n* carcer *m*, rōbur *nt*
dupe *vt* dēlūdere, fallere ◆ *n* crēdulus *m*
duplicate *n* exemplar *nt* ◆ *vt* duplicāre
duplicity *n* fraus *f*, perfidia *f*
durability *n* firmitās *f*, firmitūdō *f*
durable *adj* firmus, perpetuus

durably *adv* firmē
duration *n* spatium *nt*; *(long)* diūturnitās *f*
duress *n* vīs *f*
during *prep* inter *(acc)*, per *(acc)*
dusk *n* crepusculum *nt*, vesper *m*; **at ~** primā nocte, primīs tenebrīs
dust *n* pulvis *m*; **throw ~ in the eyes of** tenebrās offundere *(dat)* ◆ *vt* dētergēre
dusty *adj* pulverulentus
dutiful *adj* pius, officiōsus
dutifully *adv* piē, officiōsē
dutifulness *n* pietās *f*
duty *n* *(moral)* officium *nt*; *(task)* mūnus *nt*; *(tax)* vectīgal *nt*; **be on ~** *(MIL)* statiōnem agere, excubāre; **do one's ~** officiō fungī; **do ~ for** *(person)* in locum sufficī *(gen)*; *(thing)* adhibērī prō *(abl)*; **it is my ~** dēbeō, mē oportet, meum est; **it is the ~ of a commander** ducis est; **sense of ~** pietās *f*
duty call *n* salūtātiō *f*
duty-free *adj* immūnis
dwarf *n* *(of plant)* nānus *m*
dwell *vi* habitāre; **~ in** incolere; **~ upon** *(theme)* commorārī in *(abl)*
dweller *n* incola *m*
dwelling *n* domus *f*, domicilium *nt*; *(place)* sēdēs *f*
dwindle *vi* dēcrēscere, extenuārī
dye *n* fūcus *m*, color *m* ◆ *vt* īnficere, fūcāre
dyer *n* īnfector *m*
dying *adj* moribundus, moriēns
dynasty *n* domus *(rēgia) f*
dyspepsia *n* crūditās *f*

Ee

each *adj, pron* quisque; (*of two*) uterque; **~ other** inter sē; **one ~** singulī; **~ year** quotannīs
eager *adj* avidus, cupidus, alācer; **~ for** avidus (*gen*)
eagerly *adv* avidē, cupidē, ācriter
eagerness *n* cupīdō *f*, ārdor *m*, studium *nt*; alacritās *f*
eagle *n* aquila *f*
ear *n* auris *f*; (*of corn*) spīca *f*; **give ear** aurem praebēre, auscultāre; **go in at one ear and out at the other** surdīs auribus nārrārī; **prick up one's ears** aurēs ērigere; **with long ears** aurītus
earl *n* comes *m*
earlier *adv* ante; anteā
early *adj* (*in season*) mātūrus; (*in day*) mātūtīnus; (*at beginning*) prīmus; (*in history*) antīquus ♦ *adv* (*in day*) māne; (*before time*) mātūrē, temperī; **~ in life** ab ineunte aetāte
earn *vt* merērī, cōnsequī; **~ a living** vīctum quaerere, quaestum facere
earnest *adj* (*serious*) sērius; (*eager*) ācer, sēdulus ♦ *n* pignus *nt*; (*money*) arrabō *m*; **in ~** sēdulō, ēnīxē
earnestly *adv* sēriō, graviter, sēdulō
earnestness *n* gravitās *f*, studium *nt*
earnings *n* quaestus *m*
earring *n* elenchus *m*
earth *n* (*planet*) tellūs *f*; (*inhabited*) orbis terrārum *m*; (*land*) terra *f*; (*soil*) solum *nt*, humus *f*; (*fox's*) latibulum *nt*; **where on earth?** ubī gentium?; **of the ~** terrestris
earthen *adj* (*ware*) fictilis; (*mound*) terrēnus
earthenware *n* fictilia *ntpl* ♦ *adj* fictilis
earthly *adj* terrestris
earthquake *n* terrae mōtus *m*
earthwork *n* agger *m*
earthy *adj* terrēnus
ease *n* facilitās *f*; (*leisure*) ōtium *nt*; **at ~** ōtiōsus; (*in mind*) sēcūrus; **ill at ~** sollicitus ♦ *vt* laxāre, relevāre; (*pain*) mītigāre
easily *adv* facile; (*gladly*) libenter; (*at leisure*) ōtiōsē; **not ~** nōn temerē
easiness *n* facilitās *f*
east *n* Oriēns *m*, sōlis ortus *m*; **~ wind** eurus *m*
Easter *n* Pascha *f*
easterly, eastern *adj* orientālis
eastward *adv* ad orientem
easy *adj* facilis; (*manner*) adfābilis, facilis; (*mind*) sēcūrus; (*speech*) expedītus; (*discipline*) remissus; **~ circumstances** dīvitiae *fpl*, abundantia *f*

eat *vt* edere; cōnsūmere; vescī (*abl*); **eat away** rōdere; **eat up** exedere
eatable *adj* esculentus
eating *n* cibus *m*
eaves *n* suggrunda *f*
eavesdropper *n* sermōnis auceps *m*
ebb *n* dēcessus *m*, recessus *m*; **at ebbtide** minuente aestū; **be at a low ebb** (*fig*) iacēre ♦ *vi* recēdere
ebony *n* ebenus *f*
ebullient *adj* fervēns
ebullition *n* fervor *m*
eccentric *adj* īnsolēns
eccentricity *n* īnsolentia *f*
echo *n* imāgō *f* ♦ *vt, vi* resonāre
eclipse *n* dēfectus *m*, dēfectiō *f* ♦ *vt* obscūrāre; **be eclipsed** dēficere, labōrāre
eclogue *n* ecloga *f*
economic *adj* quaestuōsus, sine iactūrā
economical *adj* (*person*) frūgī, parcus
economically *adv* nullā iactūrā factā
economics *n* reī familiāris dispēnsātiō *f*
economize *vi* parcere
economy *n* frūgālitās *f*
ecstasy *n* alacritās *f*, furor *m*
ecstatic *adj* gaudiō ēlātus
eddy *n* vertex *m* ♦ *vi* volūtārī
edge *n* ōra *f*, margō *f*; (*of dish*) labrum *nt*; (*of blade*) aciēs *f*; **take the ~ off** obtundere; **on ~** (*fig*) suspēnsō animō ♦ *vt* (*garment*) praetexere; (*blade*) acuere ♦ *vi*: **~ in** sē īnsinuāre
edging *n* limbus *m*
edible *adj* esculentus
edict *n* ēdictum *nt*, dēcrētum *nt*
edification *n* ērudītiō *f*
edifice *n* aedificium *nt*
edify *vt* ērudīre
edit *vt* recognōscere, recēnsēre
edition *n* ēditiō *f*
educate *vt* ērudīre, īnfōrmāre; **~ in** īnstituere ad (*acc*)
education *n* doctrīna *f*; (*process*) īnstitūtiō *f*
eel *n* anguilla *f*
eerie *adj* mōnstruōsus
efface *vt* dēlēre, tollere
effect *n* (*result*) ēventus *m*; (*impression*) vīs *f*, effectus *m*; (*show*) iactātiō *f*; **effects** *pl* bona *ntpl*; **for ~** iactātiōnis causā; **in ~** rē vērā; **to this ~** in hanc sententiam; **without ~** inritus ♦ *vt* efficere, facere, patrāre
effective *adj* valēns, validus; (RHET) gravis, ōrnātus

effectively *adv* validē, graviter, ōrnātē
effectiveness *n* vīs *f*
effectual *adj* efficāx, idōneus
effectually *adv* efficāciter
effectuate *vt* efficere, cōnsequī
effeminacy *n* mollitiēs *f*
effeminate *adj* mollis, effēminātus
effeminately *adv* molliter, effēminātē
effervesce *vi* effervēscere
effete *adj* effētus
efficacious *adj* efficāx
efficaciously *adv* efficāciter
efficacy *n* vīs *f*
efficiency *n* virtūs *f*, perītia *f*
efficient *adj* capāx, perītus; (LOGIC) efficiēns
efficiently *adv* perītē, bene
effigy *n* simulācrum *nt*, effigiēs *f*
effloresce *vi* flōrēscere
efflorescence *n* (*fig*) flōs *m*
effluvium *n* hālitus *m*
effort *n* opera *f*, cōnātus *m*; (*of mind*) intentiō *f*; **make an** ~ ēnītī
effrontery *n* audācia *f*, impudentia *f*
effusive *adj* officiōsus
egg *n* ōvum *nt*; **lay an egg** ōvum parere ♦ *vt* impellere, īnstīgāre
egoism *n* amor suī *m*
egoist *n* suī amāns *m*
egotism *n* iactātiō *f*
egotist *n* glōriōsus *m*
egregious *adj* singulāris
egress *n* exitus *m*
eight *num* octō; ~ **each** octōnī; ~ **times** octiēns
eighteen *num* duodēvīgintī
eighteenth *adj* duodēvīcēsimus
eighth *adj* octāvus
eight hundred *num* octingentī
eight hundredth *adj* octingentēsimus
eightieth *adj* octōgēsimus
eighty *num* octōgintā; ~ **each** octōgēnī; ~ **times** octōgiēns
either *pron* alteruter, uterlibet, utervīs ♦ *conj* aut, vel; ~ ... **or** aut ... aut, vel ... vel
ejaculation *n* clāmor *m*
eject *vt* ēicere, expellere
ejection *n* expulsiō *f*
eke *vt*: **eke out** parcendō prōdūcere
elaborate *vt* ēlabōrāre ♦ *adj* ēlabōrātus, exquīsītus
elaborately *adv* summō labōre, exquīsītē
elan *n* ferōcia *f*
elapse *vi* abīre, intercēdere; **allow to** ~ intermittere; **a year has elapsed since** annus est cum (+ *indic*)
elated *adj* ēlātus; **be** ~ efferrī
elation *n* laetitia *f*
elbow *n* cubitum *nt*
elder *adj* nātū māior, senior ♦ *n* (*tree*) sambūcus *f*
elderly *adj* aetāte prōvectus
elders *npl* patrēs *mpl*
eldest *adj* nātū māximus
elecampane *n* inula *f*
elect *vt* ēligere, dēligere; (*magistrate*) creāre; (*colleague*) cooptāre ♦ *adj* dēsignātus; (*special*) lēctus
election *n* (POL) comitia *ntpl*

electioneering *n* ambitiō *f*
elector *n* suffrāgātor *m*
elegance *n* ēlegantia *f*, lepōs *m*, munditia *f*, concinnitās *f*
elegant *adj* ēlegāns, concinnus, nitidus
elegantly *adv* ēleganter, concinnē
elegiac *adj*: ~ **verse** elegī *mpl*, versūs alternī *mpl*
elegy *n* elegīa *f*
element *n* elementum *nt*; **elements** *pl* initia *ntpl*, prīncipia *ntpl*; **out of one's** ~ peregrīnus
elementary *adj* prīmus
elephant *n* elephantus *m*, elephas *m*
elevate *vt* efferre, ērigere
elevated *adj* ēditus, altus
elevation *n* altitūdō *f*; (*style*) ēlātiō *f*
eleven *num* ūndecim; ~ **each** ūndēnī; ~ **times** ūndeciēns
eleventh *adj* ūndecimus
elf *n* deus *m*
elicit *vt* ēlicere; (*with effort*) ēruere
elide *vt* ēlīdere
eligible *adj* idōneus, aptus
eliminate *vt* tollere, āmovēre
elite *n* flōs *m*, rōbur *nt*
elk *n* alcēs *f*
ell *n* ulna *f*
ellipse *n* (RHET) dētractiō *f*; (*oval*) ōvum *nt*
elm *n* ulmus *f* ♦ *adj* ulmeus
elocution *n* prōnūntiātiō *f*
elongate *vt* prōdūcere
elope *vi* aufugere
eloquence *n* ēloquentia *f*; (*natural*) fācundia *f*, dīcendī vīs *f*
eloquent *adj* ēloquēns; (*natural*) fācundus; (*fluent*) disertus
eloquently *adv* fācundē, disertē
else *adv* aliōquī, aliter ♦ *adj* alius; **or** ~ aliōquī; **who** ~ quis alius
elsewhere *adv* alibī; ~ **to** aliō
elucidate *vt* ēnōdāre, illūstrāre
elucidation *n* ēnōdātiō *f*, explicātiō *f*
elude *vt* ēvītāre, frustrārī, fallere
elusive *adj* fallāx
emaciated *adj* macer
emaciation *n* maciēs *f*
emanate *vi* mānāre; (*fig*) ēmānāre, orīrī
emanation *n* exhālātiō *f*
emancipate *vt* ēmancipāre, manū mittere, līberāre
emancipation *n* lībertās *f*
emasculate *vt* ēnervāre, dēlumbāre
embalm *vt* condīre
embankment *n* agger *m*, mōlēs *f*
embargo *n* interdictum *nt*
embark *vi* cōnscendere, nāvem cōnscendere; ~ **upon** (*fig*) ingredī ♦ *vt* impōnere
embarkation *n* cōnscēnsiō *f*
embarrass *vt* (*by confusing*) perturbāre; (*by obstructing*) impedīre; (*by revealing*) dēprehendere; **be embarrassed** haerēre
embarrassing *adj* incommodus, intempestīvus
embarrassment *n* (*in speech*) haesitātiō *f*; (*in mind*) sollicitūdō *f*; (*in business*) angustiae *fpl*, difficultās *f*; (*cause*) molestia *f*, impedīmentum *nt*
embassy *n* lēgātiō *f*

embedded *adj* dēfixus
embellish *vt* adōrnāre, exōrnāre, decorāre
embellishment *n* decus *nt*, exōrnātiō *f*,
ōrnāmentum *nt*
embers *n* cinis *m*, favilla *f*
embezzle *vt* pecularī, dēpecularī
embezzlement *n* peculātus *m*
embezzler *n* peculātor *m*
embitter *vt* exacerbāre
emblazon *vt* īnsignīre
emblem *n* īnsigne *nt*
embodiment *n* exemplar *nt*
embody *vt* repraesentāre; (MIL) cōnscrībere
embolden *vt* cōnfirmāre; ~ **the hearts of**
animōs cōnfirmāre
emboss *vt* imprimere, caelāre
embrace *vt* amplectī, complectī; (*items*)
continēre, comprehendere; (*party*) sequī;
(*opportunity*) adripere ◆ *n* amplexus *m*,
complexus *m*
embroider *vt* acū pingere
embroidery *n* vestis picta *f*
embroil *vt* miscēre, implicāre
emend *vt* ēmendāre, corrigere
emendation *n* ēmendātiō *f*, corrēctiō *f*
emerald *n* smaragdus *m*
emerge *vi* ēmergere, exsistere; ēgredī
emergency *n* tempus *nt*, discrīmen *nt* ◆ *adj*
subitārius
emigrate *vi* migrāre, ēmigrāre
emigration *n* migrātiō *f*
eminence *n* (*ground*) tumulus *m*, locus ēditus *m*;
(*rank*) praestantia *f*, amplitūdō *f*
eminent *adj* ēgregius, ēminēns, īnsignis,
amplus
eminently *adv* ēgregiē, prae cēterīs, in prīmīs
emissary *n* lēgātus *m*
emit *vt* ēmittere
emolument *n* lucrum *nt*, ēmolumentum *nt*
emotion *n* animī mōtus *m*, commōtiō *f*,
adfectus *m*
emotional *adj* (*person*) mōbilis; (*speech*)
flexanimus
emperor *n* prīnceps *m*, imperātor *m*
emphasis *n* pondus *nt*; (*words*) impressiō *f*
emphasize *vt* exprimere
emphatic *adj* gravis
emphatically *adv* adsevēranter, vehementer
empire *n* imperium *nt*
employ *vt* ūtī (*abl*); (*for purpose*) adhibēre; (*person*)
exercēre
employed *adj* occupātus
employees *npl* operae *fpl*
employer *n* redemptor *m*
employment *n* (*act*) ūsus *m*; (*work*) quaestus *m*
empower *vt* permittere (*dat*), potestātem facere
(*dat*)
emptiness *n* inānitās *f*
empty *adj* inānis, vacuus; (*fig*) vānus, inritus ◆ *vt*
exhaurīre, exinānīre ◆ *vi* (*river*) īnfluere
emulate *vt* aemulārī
emulation *n* aemulātiō *f*
emulous *adj* aemulus
emulously *adv* certātim
enable *vt* potestātem facere (*dat*); efficere ut
(*subj*)

enact *vt* dēcernere, ēdīcere, scīscere; (*part*) agere
enactment *n* dēcrētum *nt*, lēx *f*
enamoured *adj* amāns; **be ~ of** dēamāre
encamp *vi* castra pōnere, tendere
encampment *n* castra *ntpl*
encase *vt* inclūdere
enchant *vt* fascināre; (*fig*) dēlectāre
enchantment *n* fascinātiō *f*; blandīmentum *nt*
enchantress *n* sāga *f*
encircle *vt* cingere, circumdare, amplectī
enclose *vt* inclūdere, saepīre
enclosure *n* saeptum *nt*, māceria *f*
encompass *vt* cingere, circumdare, amplectī
encounter *vt* obviam īre (*dat*), occurrere (*dat*); (*in
battle*) concurrere cum (*abl*), congredī cum ◆ *n*
occursus *m*, concursus *m*
encourage *vt* cōnfirmāre, (co)hortārī,
sublevāre, favēre (*dat*)
encouragement *n* hortātiō *f*, favor *m*, auxilium
nt
encroach *vi* invādere; ~ **upon** occupāre; (*fig*)
imminuere
encrust *vt* incrustāre
encumber *vt* impedīre, onerāre
encumbrance *n* impedīmentum *nt*, onus *nt*
end *n* fīnis *m*; (*aim*) prōpositum *nt*; (*of action*)
ēventus *m*, exitus *m*; (*of speech*) perōrātiō *f*;
end to end continuī; **at a loose end** vacuus,
ōtiōsus; **for two days on end** biduum
continenter; **in the end** dēnique; **the end of**
extrēmus; (*time*) exāctus; **put an end to** fīnem
facere (*dat*), fīnem impōnere (*dat*); **to the end
that** eō cōnsiliō ut (*subj*); **to what end?** quō?,
quōrsum? ◆ *vt* fīnīre, cōnficere; (*mutual dealings*)
dīrimere ◆ *vi* dēsinere; (*event*) ēvādere; (*sentence*)
cadere; (*speech*) perōrāre; (*time*) exīre; **end up as**
ēvādere; **end with** dēsinere in (*acc*)
endanger *vt* perīclitārī, in discrīmen addūcere
endear *vt* dēvincīre
endearing *adj* blandus
endearment *n* blanditiae *fpl*
endeavour *vt* cōnārī, ēnītī ◆ *n* cōnātus *m*
ending *n* fīnis *m*, exitus *m*
endive *n* intubum *nt*
endless *adj* īnfīnītus; (*time*) aeternus, perpetuus
endlessly *adv* sine fīne, īnfīnītē
endorse *vt* ratum facere
endow *vt* dōnāre, īnstruere
endowed *adj* praeditus (*abl*)
endowment *n* dōnum *nt*
endurance *n* patientia *f*
endure *vi* dūrāre, permanēre ◆ *vt* ferre, tolerāre,
patī
enemy *n* (*public*) hostis *m*, hostēs *mpl*; (*private*)
inimīcus *m*; **greatest ~** inimīcissimus *m*;
~ **territory** hosticum *nt*
energetic *adj* impiger, nāvus, strēnuus; (*style*)
nervōsus
energetically *adv* impigrē, nāviter, strēnuē
energy *n* impigritās *f*, vigor *m*, incitātiō *f*; (*mind*)
contentiō *f*; (*style*) nervī *mpl*
enervate *vt* ēnervāre, ēmollīre
enervation *n* languor *m*
enfeeble *vt* īnfirmāre, dēbilitāre
enfold *vt* involvere, complectī
enforce *vt* (LAW) exsequī; (*argument*) cōnfirmāre

enfranchise vt cīvitāte dōnāre; (slave) manū mittere

engage vt (affection) dēvincīre; (attention) distinēre, occupāre; (enemy) manum cōnserere cum (abl); (hire) condūcere; (promise) spondēre, recipere; ~ **the enemy** proelium cum hostibus committere; **be engaged in** versārī in (abl) ♦ vi: ~ **in** ingredī, suscipere

engagement n (COMM) occupātiō f; (MIL) pugna f, certāmen nt; (agreement) spōnsiō f; **keep an** ~ fidem praestāre; **break an** ~ fidem fallere; **I have an** ~ **at your house** prōmīsī ad tē

engaging adj blandus

engender vt ingenerāre, ingignere

engine n māchina f

engineer n māchinātor m ♦ vt mōlīrī

engraft vt īnserere

engrave vt īnsculpere, incīdere, caelāre

engraver n sculptor m, caelātor m

engraving n sculptūra f, caelātūra f

engross vt dīstringere, occupāre; **engrossed in** tōtus in (abl)

engulf vt dēvorāre, obruere

enhance vt amplificāre, augēre, exaggerāre

enigma n aenigma nt, ambāgēs fpl

enigmatic adj ambiguus, obscūrus

enigmatically adv per ambāgēs, ambiguē

enjoin vt imperāre (dat), iniungere (dat)

enjoy vt fruī (abl); (advantage) ūtī (abl); (pleasure) percipere, dēcerpere; ~ **oneself** dēlectārī, geniō indulgēre

enjoyable adj iūcundus

enjoyment n frūctus m; dēlectātiō f, voluptās f

enlarge vt augēre, amplificāre, dīlātāre; (territory) prōpāgāre; ~ **upon** amplificāre

enlargement n amplificātiō f, prōlātiō f

enlighten vt inlūstrāre; docēre, ērudīre

enlightenment n ērudītiō f, hūmānitās f

enlist vt scrībere, cōnscrībere; (sympathy) conciliāre ♦ vi nōmen dare

enliven vt excitāre

enmesh vt impedīre, implicāre

enmity n inimīcitia f, simultās f

ennoble vt honestāre, excolere

ennui n taedium nt

enormity n immānitās f; (deed) scelus nt, nefās nt

enormous adj immānis, ingēns

enormously adv immēnsum

enough adj satis (indecl, gen) ♦ adv satis; **more than** ~ satis superque; **I have had** ~ **of ...** mē taedet (gen) ...

enquire vi quaerere, percontārī; ~ **into** cognōscere, inquīrere in (acc)

enquiry n percontātiō f; (legal) quaestiō f

enrage vt inrītāre, incendere

enrapture vt dēlectāre

enrich vt dītāre, locuplētāre; ~ **with** augēre (abl)

enrol vt adscrībere, cōnscrībere ♦ vi nōmen dare

enshrine vt dēdicāre; (fig) sacrāre

enshroud vt involvere

ensign n signum nt, īnsigne nt; (officer) signifer m

enslave vt in servitūtem redigere

enslavement n servitūs f

ensnare vt dēcipere, inlaqueāre, inrētīre

ensue vi īnsequī

ensure vt praestāre; ~ **that** efficere ut (subj)

entail vt adferre

entangle vt impedīre, implicāre, inrētīre

entanglement n implicātiō f

enter vi inīre, ingredī, intrāre; (riding) invehī; ~ **into** introīre in (acc); ~ **upon** inīre, ingredī ♦ vt (place) intrāre; (account) ferre, indūcere; (mind) subīre

enterprise n inceptum nt; (character) prōmptus animus m

enterprising adj prōmptus, strēnuus

entertain vt (guest) invītāre, excipere; (state of mind) habēre, concipere; (to amuse) oblectāre

entertainer n acroāma nt

entertainment n hospitium nt; oblectāmentum nt; acroāma nt

enthral vt capere

enthusiasm n studium nt, fervor m; ~ **for** studium nt (gen)

enthusiastic adj studiōsus, fervidus

enthusiastically adv summō studiō

entice vt inlicere, ēlicere, invītāre

enticement n illecebra f, lēnōcinium nt

entire adj integer, tōtus, ūniversus

entirely adv omnīnō, funditus, penitus

entitle vt (book) īnscrībere; **be entitled to** merērī, dignum esse quī (subj), iūs habēre (gen)

entity n rēs f

entomb vt humāre, sepelīre

entrails n intestīna ntpl, exta ntpl

entrance n aditus m, introitus m; (act) ingressiō f; (of house) vestibulum nt; (of harbour) ōstium nt ♦ vt fascināre, cōnsōpīre, capere

entreat vt implōrāre, obsecrāre; (successfully) exōrāre

entreaty n precēs fpl

entrenchment n mūnītiō f

entrust vt committere, crēdere, mandāre; (for keeping) dēpōnere

entry n introitus m, aditus m; **make an** ~ (book) in tabulās referre

entwine vt implicāre, involvere

enumerate vt numerāre, dīnumerāre

enunciate vt ēdīcere; (word) exprimere

envelop vt implicāre, involvere

envelope n involucrum nt

enviable adj beātus

envious adj invidus, invidiōsus

enviously adv invidiōsē

environment n vīcīnia f; **our** ~ ea in quibus versāmur

envoy n lēgātus m

envy n invidia f ♦ vt invidēre (dat)

enwrap vt involvere

ephemeral adj brevis

ephor n ephorus m

epic adj epicus ♦ n epos nt

epicure n dēlicātus m

epigram n sententia f; (poem) epigramma nt

epilepsy n morbus comitiālis m

epilogue n epilogus m

episode n ēventum nt

epistle n epistula f, litterae fpl

epitaph n epigramma nt, titulus m

epithet n adsūmptum nt

epitome *n* epitomē *f*
epoch *n* saeculum *nt*
equable *adj* aequālis; (*temper*) aequus
equal *adj* aequus, pār; **be ~ to** aequāre; (*task*) sufficere (*dat*) ♦ *n* pār *m/f* ♦ *vt* aequāre, adaequāre
equality *n* aequālitās *f*
equalize *vt* adaequāre, exaequāre
equally *adv* aequē, pariter
equanimity *n* aequus animus *m*
equate *vt* aequāre
equator *n* aequinoctiālis circulus *m*
equestrian *adj* equester
equidistant *adj*: **be ~** aequō spatiō abesse, idem distāre
equilibrium *n* lībrāmentum *nt*
equine *adj* equīnus
equinoctial *adj* aequinoctiālis
equinox *n* aequinoctium *nt*
equip *vt* armāre, īnstruere, ōrnāre
equipment *n* arma *ntpl*, īnstrūmenta *ntpl*, adparātus *m*
equipoise *n* lībrāmentum *nt*
equitable *adj* aequus, iūstus
equitably *adv* iūstē, aequē
equity *n* aequum *nt*, aequitās *f*
equivalent *adj* pār, īdem īnstar (*gen*)
equivocal *adj* anceps, ambiguus
equivocally *adv* ambiguē
equivocate *vi* tergiversārī
era *n* saeculum *nt*
eradicate *vt* ēvellere, exstirpāre
erase *vt* dēlēre, indūcere
erasure *n* litūra *f*
ere *conj* priusquam
erect *vt* ērigere; (*building*) exstruere; (*statute*) pōnere ♦ *adj* ērēctus
erection *n* (*process*) exstructiō *f*; (*product*) aedificium *nt*
erode *vt* rōdere
erotic *adj* amātōrius
err *vi* errāre, peccāre
errand *n* mandātum *nt*
errant *adj* vagus
erratic *adj* incōnstāns
erroneous *adj* falsus
erroneously *adv* falsō, perperam
error *n* error *m*; (*moral*) peccātum *nt*; (*writing*) mendum *nt*
erudite *adj* doctus
erudition *n* doctrīna *f*, ērudītiō *f*
erupt *vi* ērumpere
eruption *n* ēruptiō *f*
escapade *n* ausum *nt*
escape *vi* effugere, ēvādere ♦ *vt* fugere, ēvītāre; (*memory*) excidere ex (*abl*); **~ the notice of** fallere, praeterīre ♦ *n* effugium *nt*, fuga *f*; **way of ~** effugium *nt*
eschew *vt* vītāre
escort *n* praesidium *nt*; (*private*) dēductor *m* ♦ *vt* comitārī, prōsequī; (*out of respect*) dēdūcere
especial *adj* praecipuus
especially *adv* praecipuē, praesertim, māximē, in prīmīs
espionage *n* inquīsītiō *f*
espouse *vt* (*wife*) dūcere; (*cause*) fovēre

espy *vt* cōnspicere, cōnspicārī
essay *n* cōnātus *m*; (*test*) perīculum *nt*; (LIT) libellus *m* ♦ *vt* cōnārī, incipere
essence *n* vīs *f*, nātūra *f*
essential *adj* necesse, necessārius
essentially *adv* necessāriō
establish *vt* īnstituere, condere; (*firmly*) stabilīre
established *adj* firmus, certus; **be ~** cōnstāre; **become ~** (*custom*) inveterāscere
establishment *n* (*act*) cōnstitūtiō *f*; (*domestic*) familia *f*
estate *n* fundus *m*, rūs *nt*; (*in money*) rēs *f*; (*rank*) ōrdō *m*
esteem *vt* aestimāre, respicere ♦ *n* grātia *f*, opīniō *f*
estimable *adj* optimus
estimate *vt* aestimāre, ratiōnem inīre (*gen*) ♦ *n* aestimātiō *f*, iūdicium *nt*
estimation *n* opīniō *f*, sententia *f*
estrange *vt* aliēnāre, abaliēnāre
estrangement *n* aliēnātiō *f*, discidium *nt*
estuary *n* aestuārium *nt*
eternal *adj* aeternus, perennis
eternally *adv* semper, aeternum
eternity *n* aeternitās *f*
etesian winds *n* etēsiae *fpl*
ether *n* (*sky*) aethēr *m*
ethereal *adj* aetherius, caelestis
ethic, ethical *adj* mōrālis
ethics *n* mōrēs *mpl*, officia *ntpl*
Etruscan *n* Etruscus *m* ♦ *adj* Etruscus
etymology *n* verbōrum notātiō *f*
eulogist *n* laudātor *m*
eulogize *vt* laudāre, conlaudāre
eulogy *n* laudātiō *f*
eunuch *n* eunūchus *m*
euphony *n* sonus *m*
evacuate *vt* (*place*) exinānīre; (*people*) dēdūcere
evacuation *n* discessiō *f*
evade *vt* dēclīnāre, dēvītāre, ēlūdere
evaporate *vt* exhālāre ♦ *vi* exhālārī
evaporation *n* exhālātiō *f*
evasion *n* tergiversātiō *f*
evasive *adj* ambiguus
eve *n* vesper *m*; (*before festival*) pervigilium *nt*; **on the eve of** prīdiē (*gen*)
even *adj* aequus, aequālis; (*number*) pār ♦ *adv* et, etiam; (*tentative*) vel; **~ if** etsī, etiamsī; tametsī; **~ more** etiam magis; **~ so** nihilōminus; **~ yet** etiamnum; **not ~ ...** nē quidem ♦ *vt* aequāre
evening *n* vesper *m* ♦ *adj* vespertīnus; **~ is drawing on** invesperāscit; **in the ~** vesperī
evening star *n* Vesper *m*, Hesperus *m*
evenly *adv* aequāliter, aequābiliter
evenness *n* aequālitās *f*, aequābilitās *f*
event *n* ēventum *nt*; (*outcome*) ēventus *m*
eventide *n* vespertīnum tempus *nt*
eventuality *n* cāsus *m*
eventually *adv* mox, aliquandō, tandem
ever *adv* unquam; (*after* **sī, nisi, num, nē**) quandō; (*always*) semper; (*after interrog*) -nam, tandem; **ever so** nimium, nimium quantum; **best ~** omnium optimus; **for ~** in aeternum
everlasting *adj* aeternus, perpetuus, immortālis
evermore *adv* semper, in aeternum

every *adj* quisque, omnis; ~ **four years** quīntō quōque annō; ~ **now and then** interdum; **in** ~ **direction** passim, undique; ~ **other day** alternīs diēbus; ~ **day** cottīdiē ♦ *adj* cottīdiānus

everybody *pron* quisque, omnēs *mpl*; ~ **agrees** inter omnēs constat; ~ **knows** nēmō est quīn sciat

everyday *adj* cottīdiānus

everyone *pron see* **everybody**

everything omnia *ntpl*; **your health is** ~ **to me** meā māximē interest tē valēre

everywhere *adv* ubīque, passim

evict *vt* dēicere, dētrūdere

eviction *n* dēiectiō *f*

evidence *n* testimōnium *nt*, indicium *nt*; (*person*) testis *m/f*; (*proof*) argūmentum *nt*; **on the** ~ **of** fidē (*gen*); **collect** ~ **against** inquīrere in (*acc*); **turn King's** ~ indicium profitērī

evident *adj* manifestus, ēvidēns, clārus; **it is** ~ appāret

evidently *adv* manifestō, clārē

evil *adj* malus, improbus, scelerātus

evildoer *n* scelerātus *m*, maleficus *m*

evil eye *n* fascinum *nt*, malum *nt*, improbitās *f*

evil-minded *adj* malevolus

evince *vt* praestāre

evoke *vt* ēvocāre, ēlicere

evolution *n* seriēs *f*, prōgressus *m*; (MIL) dēcursus *m*, dēcursiō *f*

evolve *vt* explicāre, ēvolvere ♦ *vi* crēscere

ewe *n* ovis *f*

ewer *n* hydria *f*

exacerbate *vt* exacerbāre, exasperāre

exact *vt* exigere ♦ *adj* accūrātus; (*person*) dīligēns; (*number*) exāctus

exaction *n* exāctiō *f*

exactly *adv* accūrātē; (*reply*) ita prōrsus; ~ **as** perinde que

exactness *n* cūra *f*, dīligentia *f*

exaggerate *vt* augēre, in māius extollere

exalt *vt* efferre, extollere; laudāre

exaltation *n* ēlātiō *f*

examination *n* inquīsītiō *f*, scrūtātiō *f*; (*of witness*) interrogātiō *f*; (*test*) probātiō *f*

examine *vt* investīgāre, scrūtārī; īnspicere; (*witness*) interrogāre; (*case*) quaerere dē (*abl*); (*candidate*) probāre

examiner *n* scrūtātor *m*

example *n* exemplum *nt*, documentum *nt*; **for** ~ exemplī grātiā; **make an** ~ **of** animadvertere in (*acc*); **I am an** ~ exemplō sum

exasperate *vt* exacerbāre, inrītāre

exasperation *n* inrītātiō *f*

excavate *vt* fodere

excavation *n* fossiō *f*

excavator *n* fossor *m*

exceed *vt* excēdere, superāre

exceedingly *adv* nimis, valdē, nimium quantum

excel *vt* praestāre (*dat*), exsuperāre ♦ *vi* excellere

excellence *n* praestantia *f*, virtūs *f*

excellent *adj* ēgregius, praestāns, optimus

excellently *adv* ēgregiē, praeclārē

except *vt* excipere ♦ *prep* praeter (*acc*) ♦ *adv* nisī ♦ *conj* praeterquam, nisī quod

exception *n* exceptiō *f*; **make an** ~ **of** excipere; **take** ~ **to** gravārī quod; **with the** ~ **of** praeter (*acc*)

exceptional *adj* ēgregius, eximius

exceptionally *adv* ēgregiē, eximiē

excerpt *vt* excerpere ♦ *n* excerptum *nt*

excess *n* immoderātiō *f*, intemperantia *f* ♦ *adj* supervacāneus; **be in** ~ superesse

excessive *adj* immoderātus, immodestus, nimius

excessively *adv* immodicē, nimis

exchange *vt* mūtāre, permūtāre ♦ *n* permūtātiō *f*; (*of currencies*) collybus *m*

exchequer *n* aerārium *nt*; (*emperor's*) fiscus *m*

excise *n* vectīgālia *ntpl* ♦ *vt* excīdere

excision *n* excīsiō *f*

excitable *adj* mōbilis

excite *vt* excitāre, concitāre; (*to action*) incitāre, incendere; (*to hope*) ērigere, exacuere; (*emotion*) movēre, commovēre

excitement *n* commōtiō *f*

exclaim *vt* exclāmāre; ~ **against** adclāmāre (*dat*)

exclamation *n* clāmor *m*, exclāmātiō *f*

exclude *vt* exclūdere

exclusion *n* exclūsiō *f*

exclusive *adj* proprius

exclusively *adv* sōlum

excogitate *vt* excōgitāre

excrescence *n* tūber *nt*

excruciating *adj* acerbissimus

exculpate *vt* pūrgāre, absolvere

excursion *n* iter *nt*; (MIL) excursiō *f*

excuse *n* excūsātiō *f*; (*false*) speciēs *f* ♦ *vt* excūsāre, ignōscere (*dat*); (*something due*) remittere; **plead in** ~ excūsāre; **put forward as an** ~ praetendere

execrable *adj* dētestābilis, sacer, nefārius

execrate *vt* dētestārī, exsecrārī

execration *n* dētestātiō *f*, exsecrātiō *f*

execute *vt* efficere, patrāre, exsequī; suppliciō afficere; (*behead*) secūrī percutere

execution *n* effectus *m*; (*penalty*) supplicium *nt*, mors *f*

executioner *n* carnifex *m*

exemplar *n* exemplum *nt*

exempt *adj* immūnis, līber ♦ *vt* līberāre

exemption *n* (*from tax*) immūnitās *f*; (*from service*) vacātiō *f*

exercise *n* exercitātiō *f*, ūsus *m*; (*school*) dictāta *ntpl* ♦ *vt* exercēre, ūtī (*abl*); (*mind*) acuere

exert *vt* extendere, intendere, ūtī (*abl*); ~ **oneself** mōlīrī, ēnītī, sē intendere

exertion *n* mōlīmentum *nt*; (*mind*) intentiō *f*

exhalation *n* exhālātiō *f*, vapor *m*

exhale *vt* exhālāre, exspīrāre

exhaust *vt* exhaurīre; (*tire*) dēfatīgāre, cōnficere

exhaustion *n* dēfatīgātiō *f*

exhaustive *adj* plēnus

exhibit *vt* exhibēre, ostendere, expōnere; (*on stage*) ēdere

exhibition *n* expositiō *f*, ostentātiō *f*

exhilarate *vt* exhilarāre

exhort *vt* hortārī, cohortārī

exhortation *n* hortātiō *f*, hortāmen *nt*

exhume *vt* ēruere

exigency *n* necessitās *f*

exile n exsilium nt, fuga f; (temporary) relēgātiō f; (person) exsul m; **live in** ~ exsulāre ♦ vt in exsilium pellere, dēportāre; (temporarily) relēgāre

exist vi esse

existence n vīta f

exit n exitus m, ēgressus m

exodus n discessus m

exonerate vt absolvere

exorbitant adj nimius, immoderātus

exotic adj peregrīnus

expand vt extendere, dīlātāre

expanse n spatium nt, lātitūdō f

expatiate vi: ~ upon amplificāre

expatriate vt extermināre ♦ n extorris m

expect vt exspectāre, spērāre

expectancy, expectation n spēs f, exspectātiō f; opīniō f

expediency n ūtile nt, ūtilitās f

expedient adj ūtilis, commodus; **it is** ~ expedit ♦ n modus m, ratiō f

expediently adv commodē

expedite vt mātūrāre

expedition n (MIL) expedītiō f

expeditious adj prōmptus, celer

expeditiously adv celeriter

expel vt pellere, expellere, ēicere

expend vt impendere, expendere

expenditure n impēnsae fpl, sūmptus m

expense n impēnsae fpl, impendia ntpl; **at my** ~ meō sūmptū; **at the public** ~ dē pūblicō

expensive adj cārus, pretiōsus; (furnishings) lautus

expensively adv sūmptuōsē, māgnō pretiō

experience n ūsus m, experientia f ♦ vt experīrī, patī

experienced adj perītus, expertus (gen)

experiment n experīmentum nt ♦ vi: ~ with experīrī

expert adj perītus, sciēns

expertly adv perītē, scienter

expertness n perītia f

expiate vt expiāre, lūere

expiation n (act) expiātiō f; (penalty) piāculum nt

expiatory adj piāculāris

expiration n (breath) exspīrātiō f; (time) exitus m

expire vi exspīrāre; (die) animam agere, animam efflāre; (time) exīre

expiry n exitus m, fīnis m

explain vt explicāre, expōnere, explānāre, interpretārī; (lucidly) ēnōdāre; (in detail) ēdisserere

explanation n explicātiō f, ēnōdātiō f, interpretātiō f

explicit adj expressus, apertus

explicitly adv apertē

explode vt discutere ♦ vi dīrumpī

exploit n factum nt, ausum nt; **exploits** pl rēs gestae fpl ♦ vt ūtī (abl), fruī (abl)

explore vt, vi explōrāre, scrūtārī

explorer n explōrātor m

explosion n fragor m

exponent n interpres m, auctor m

export vt exportāre ♦ n exportātiō f

exportation n exportātiō f

expose vt dētegere, dēnūdāre, patefacere; (child) expōnere; (to danger) obicere; (MIL) nūdāre; (for sale) prōpōnere; ~ **oneself** se obicere

exposed adj apertus, obnoxius

exposition n explicātiō f, interpretātiō f

expostulate vi expostulāre, conquerī

expostulation n expostulātiō f

exposure n (of child) expositiō f; (of guilt) dēprehēnsiō f; (to hardship) patientia f

expound vt expōnere, interpretārī

expounder n interpres m

express vt (in words) exprimere, dēclārāre, ēloquī; (in art) effingere ♦ adj expressus; (speed) celerrimus

expression n significātiō f; (word) vōx f, verbum nt; (face) vultus m

expressive adj significāns; ~ **of** index (gen); **be very** ~ māximam vim habēre

expressively adv significanter

expressiveness n vīs f

expressly adv plānē

expulsion n expulsiō f, ēiectiō f

expurgate vt pūrgāre

exquisite adj ēlegāns, exquīsītus, eximius; (judgment) subtīlis

exquisitely adv ēleganter, exquīsītē

ex-service adj ēmeritus

extant adj superstes; **be** ~ exstāre

extempore adv ex tempore, subitō ♦ adj extemporālis

extemporize vi subita dīcere

extend vt extendere, dīlātāre; (hand) porrigere; (line) dūcere; (office) prōrogāre; (territory) propāgāre ♦ vi patēre, porrigī; ~ **into** incurrere in (acc)

extension n prōductiō f, prōlātiō f; (of office) prōrogātiō f; (of territory) propāgātiō f; (extra) incrēmentum nt

extensive adj effūsus, amplus, lātus

extensively adv lātē

extent n spatium nt, amplitūdō f; **to a large** ~ māgnā ex parte; **to some** ~ aliquā ex parte; **to this** ~ hāctenus; **to such an** ~ adeō

extenuate vt levāre, mītigāre

exterior adj externus, exterior ♦ n speciēs f

exterminate vt occīdiōne occīdere, interimere

extermination n occīdiō f, interneciō f

external adj externus

externally adv extrīnsecus

extinct adj mortuus; (custom) obsolētus

extinction n exstinctiō f, interitus m

extinguish vt exstinguere, restinguere

extinguisher n exstinctor m

extirpate vt exstirpāre, excīdere

extol vt laudāre, laudibus efferre

extort vt extorquēre, exprimere

extortion n (offence) rēs repetundae fpl

extortionate adj inīquus, rapāx

extra adv īnsuper, praetereā ♦ adj additus

extract vt excerpere, extrahere ♦ n: **make extracts** excerpere

extraction n ēvulsiō f; (descent) genus nt

extraneous adj adventīcius, aliēnus

extraordinarily adv mīrificē, eximiē

extraordinary adj extraōrdinārius; (strange) mīrus, novus; (outstanding) eximius, īnsignis

extravagance n intemperantia f; (*language*) immoderātiō f, luxuria f; (*spending*) sūmptus m
extravagant adj immoderātus, immodestus; (*spending*) sūmptuōsus, prōdigus
extreme adj extrēmus, ultimus
extremely adv valdē, vehementer
extremity n extrēmum nt, fīnis m; (*distress*) angustiae fpl; **the ~ of** extrēmus
extricate vt expedīre, absolvere; **~ oneself** ēmergere
exuberance n ūbertās f, luxuria f
exuberant adj ūber, laetus, luxuriōsus
exuberantly adv ūbertim
exude vt exsūdāre ♦ vi mānāre
exult vi exsultārī, laetārī, gestīre
exultant adj laetus
exultantly adv laetē
exultation n laetitia f
eye n oculus m; (*needle*) forāmen nt; **cast eyes on** oculōs conicere in (*acc*); **have an eye to** spectāre; **in your eyes** iūdice tē; **keep one's eyes on** oculōs dēfigere in (*abl*); **lose an eye** alterō oculō capī; **see eye to eye** cōnsentīre; **set eyes on** cōnspicere; **shut one's eyes to** cōnīvēre in (*abl*); **take one's eyes off** oculōs dēicere ab (*abl*); **up to the eyes in** tōtus in (*abl*); **with a cast in the eye** paetus; **with sore eyes** lippus; **sore eyes** lippitūdō f; **with one's own eyes** cōram; **with one's eyes open** sciēns ♦ vt intuērī, aspicere
eyeball n pūpula f
eyebrow n supercilium nt
eyelash n palpebrae pilus m
eyelid n palpebra f
eyeshot n oculōrum coniectus m
eyesight n aciēs f, oculī mpl
eyesore n turpe nt; **it is an ~ to me** oculī meī dolent
eye tooth n dēns canīnus m
eyewash n sycophantia f
eyewitness n arbiter m; **be an ~ of** interesse (*dat*)

Ff

fable *n* fābula *f*, apologus *m*
fabled *adj* fābulōsus
fabric *n* (*built*) structūra *f*; (*woven*) textile *nt*
fabricate *vt* fabricārī; (*fig*) comminīscī, fingere
fabricated *adj* commentīcius
fabrication *n* (*process*) fabricātiō *f*; (*thing*) commentum *nt*
fabricator *n* auctor *m*
fabulous *adj* commentīcius, fictus
fabulously *adv* incrēdibiliter
facade *n* frōns *f*
face *n* faciēs *f*, ōs *nt*; (*aspect*) aspectus *m*; (*impudence*) ōs *nt*; ~ **to** ~ cōram; **how shall I have the** ~ **to go back?** quō ōre redībō?; **on the** ~ **of it** ad speciem, prīmō aspectū; **put a bold** ~ **on** fortēm sē praebēre; **save** ~ factum pūrgāre; **set one's** ~ **against** adversārī (*dat*) ◆ *vt* spectāre ad (*acc*); (*danger*) obviam īre (*dat*), sē oppōnere (*dat*) ◆ *vi* (*place*) spectāre, vergere; ~ **about** (*MIL*) signa convertere
facetious *adj* facētus, salsus
facetiously *adv* facētē, salsē
facetiousness *n* facētiae *fpl*, salēs *mpl*
facile *adj* facilis
facilitate *vt* expedīre
facilities *npl* opportūnitās *f*
facility *n* facilitās *f*
facing *adj* adversus ◆ *prep* exadversus (*acc*)
facsimile *n* exemplār *nt*
fact *n* rēs *f*, vērum *nt*; **as a matter of** ~ enimvērō; **the** ~ **that** quod; **in** ~ rē vērā ◆ *conj* etenim; (*climax*) dēnique
faction *n* factiō *f*
factious *adj* factiōsus, sēditiōsus
factiously *adv* sēditiōsē
factor *n* prōcūrātor *m*
factory *n* officīna *f*
faculty *n* facultās *f*, vīs *f*
fad *n* libīdō *f*
fade *vi* dēflōrēscere, marcēscere
faded *adj* marcidus
faggot *n* (*twigs*) sarmentum *nt*
fail *vi* dēficere, dēesse; (*fig*) cadere, dēcidere; (*in business*) forō cēdere; ~ **to** nōn posse; ~ **to come** nōn venīre ◆ *vt* dēficere, dēstituere
failing *n* culpa *f*, vitium *nt*
failure *n* (*of supply*) dēfectiō *f*; (*in action*) offēnsiō *f*; (*at election*) repulsa *f*
fain *adv* libenter
faint *adj* (*body*) languidus, dēfessus; (*impression*) hebes, levis; (*courage*) timidus; (*colour*) pallidus;

be ~ languēre; hebēre ◆ *vi* intermorī, animō linquī; **I feel** ~ animō male est
faint-hearted *adj* animo dēmissus; timidus
faintly *adv* languidē; leviter
faintness *n* dēfectiō *f*, languor *m*; levitās *f*
fair *adj* (*appearance*) pulcher, fōrmōsus; (*hair*) flāvus; (*skin*) candidus; (*weather*) serēnus; (*wind*) secundus; (*copy*) pūrus; (*dealings*) aequus; (*speech*) speciōsus, blandus; (*ability*) mediocris; (*reputation*) bonus ◆ *n* nūndinae *fpl*; ~ **and square** sine fūcō ac fallāciīs
fairly *adv* iūre, iūstē; mediocriter
fairness *n* aequitās *f*
fair play *n* aequum et bonum *nt*
fairy *n* nympha *f*
faith *n* fidēs *f*; **in good** ~ bonā fidē
faithful *adj* fidēlis, fīdus
faithfully *adv* fidēliter
faithfulness *n* fidēlitās *f*
faithless *adj* īnfidēlis, īnfidus, perfidus
faithlessly *adv* īnfidēliter
faithlessness *n* īnfidēlitās *f*
fake *vt* simulāre
falchion *n* falx *f*
falcon *n* falcō *m*
fall *vi* cadere; (*gently*) lābī; (*morally*) prōlābī; (*dead*) concidere, occidere; (*fortress*) expugnārī, capī; ~ **at** accidere; ~ **away** dēficere, dēscīscere; ~ **back** recidere; (*MIL*) pedem referre; ~ **between** intercidere; ~ **behind** cessāre; ~ **by the way** intercidere; ~ **down** dēcidere, dēlābī; (*building*) ruere, corruere; ~ **due** cadere; ~ **flat** sē prōsternere; (*speech*) frīgēre; ~ **forward** prōlābī; ~ **foul of** incurrere in (*acc*); ~ **headlong** sē praecipitāre; ~ **in, ~ into** incidere; ~ **in with** occurrere (*dat*); ~ **off** dēcidere; (*fig*) dēscīscere; ~ **on** incumbere in (*acc*), incidere in (*acc*); ~ **out** excidere; (*event*) ēvenīre; (*hair*) dēfluere; ~ **short of** deesse ab; ~ **to** (*by lot*) obtingere, obvenīre (*dat*); ~ **to the ground** (*case*) iacēre; ~ **upon** invādere, ingruere in (*acc*); (*one's neck*) in collum invādere ◆ *n* cāsus *m*; (*building*) ruīna *f*; (*moral*) lāpsus *m*; (*season*) autumnus *m*; **the** ~ **of Capua** Capua capta
fallacious *adj* captiōsus, fallāx
fallaciously *adv* fallāciter
fallacy *n* captiō *f*
fallible *adj*: **be** ~ errāre solēre
fallow *adj* (*land*) novālis ◆ *n* novāle *nt*; **lie** ~ cessāre
false *adj* falsus, fictus

falsehood n falsum nt, mendācium nt; **tell a ~** mentīrī
falsely adv falsō
falsify vt vitiāre, interlinere
falter vi (speech) haesitāre; (gait) titubāre
faltering adj (speech) īnfrāctus; (gait) titubāns ♦ n haesitātiō f
fame n fāma f, glōria f, nōmen nt
famed adj illūstris, praeclārus
familiar adj (friend) intimus; (fact) nōtus; (manner) cōmis; **~ spirit** genius m; **be ~ with** nōvisse; **be on ~ terms with** familiāriter ūtī (abl)
familiarity n ūsus m, cōnsuētūdō f
familiarize vt adsuēfacere
familiarly adv familiāriter
family n domus f, gēns f ♦ adj domesticus, familiāris; **~ property** rēs familiāris f
famine n famēs f
famished adj famēlicus
famous adj illūstris, praeclārus, nōbilis; **make ~** nōbilitāre; **the ~** ille
fan n flābellum nt; (winnowing) vannus f ♦ vt ventilāre; **fan the flames of** (fig) īnflammāre
fanatic n (religious) fānāticus m
fanciful adj (person) incōnstāns; (idea) commentīcius
fancy n (faculty) mēns f; (idea) opīnātiō f; (caprice) libīdō f; **take a ~ to** amāre incipere; **~oneself** sē amāre ♦ vt animō fingere, imāginārī, sibi prōpōnere; **~ you thinking …!** tē crēdere …! ♦ adj dēlicātus
fancy-free adj sēcūrus, vacuus
fang n dēns m
fantastic adj commentīcius, mōnstruōsus
fantasy n imāginātiō f; (contemptuous) somnium nt
far adj longinquus ♦ adv longē, procul; (with compar) multō; **be far from** longē abesse ab; **be not far from doing** haud multum abest quin (subj); **by far** longē; **how far?** quātenus?, quoūsque?; **so far** hāctenus, eātenus; (limited) quādam tenus; **thus far** hāctenus; **far and wide** lātē; **far be it from me to say** equidem dīcere nōlim; **far from thinking …** I adeō nōn crēdō … ut; **as far as** prep tenus (abl) ♦ adv ūsque ♦ conj quātenus; (know) quod
farce n mīmus m
farcical adj rīdiculus
fare vi sē habēre, agere ♦ n vectūra f; (boat) naulum nt; (food) cibus m
farewell interj valē, valēte; **say ~ to** valēre iubēre
far-fetched adj quaesītus, arcessītus, altē repetītus
farm n fundus m, praedium nt ♦ vt (soil) colere; (taxes) redimere; **~out** locāre
farmer n agricola m; (of taxes) pūblicānus m
farming n agrīcultūra f
farrow vt parere ♦ n fētus m
far-sighted adj prōvidus, prūdēns
farther adv longius, ultrā ♦ adj ulterior
farthest adj ultimus, extrēmus ♦ adv longissimē
fasces n fascēs mpl
fascinate vt dēlēnīre, capere
fascination n dulcēdō f, dēlēnīmenta ntpl, lēnōcinia ntpl

fashion n mōs m, ūsus m; (manner) modus m, ratiō f; (shape) fōrma f ♦ vt fingere, fōrmāre; **after the ~ of** rītū (gen); **come into ~** in mōrem venīre; **go out of ~** obsolēscere
fashionable adj ēlegāns; **it is ~** mōris est
fashionably adv ēleganter
fast adj (firm) firmus; (quick) celer; **make ~** dēligāre ♦ adv firmē; celeriter; **be ~ asleep** artē dormīre ♦ vi iēiūnus esse, cibō abstinēre ♦ n iēiūnium nt
fasten vt fīgere, ligāre; **~ down** dēfīgere; **~ on** inligāre; **~ to** adligāre; **~ together** conligāre, cōnfīgere
fastening n iūnctūra f
fastidious adj dēlicātus, ēlegāns
fastidiously adv fastīdiōsē
fastidiousness n fastīdium nt
fasting n iēiūnium nt, inedia f ♦ adj iēiūnus
fastness n arx f, castellum nt
fat adj pinguis, opīmus, obēsus; **grow fat** pinguēscere ♦ n adeps m/f
fatal adj (deadly) fūnestus, exitiābilis; (fated) fātālis
fatality n fātum nt, cāsus m
fatally adv: **be ~ wounded** vulnere perīre
fate n fātum nt, fortūna f, sors f
fated adj fātālis
fateful adj fātālis; fūnestus
Fates npl (goddesses) Parcae fpl
father n pater m; (fig) auctor m ♦ vt gignere; **~ upon** addīcere, tribuere
father-in-law n socer m
fatherland n patria f
fatherless adj orbus
fatherly adj paternus
fathom n sex pedēs mpl ♦ vt (fig) exputāre
fathomless adj profundus
fatigue n fatīgātiō f, dēfatīgātiō f ♦ vt fatīgāre, dēfatīgāre
fatness n pinguitūdō f
fatten vt sagīnāre
fatty adj pinguis
fatuity n īnsulsitās f, ineptiae fpl
fatuous adj fatuus, īnsulsus, ineptus
fault n culpa f, vitium nt; (written) mendum nt; **count as a ~** vitiō vertere; **find ~ with** incūsāre; **it is not your ~ that …** nōn per tē stat quōminus (subj)
faultily adv vitiōsē, mendōsē
faultiness n vitium nt
faultless adj ēmendātus, integer
faultlessly adv ēmendātē
faulty adj vitiōsus, mendōsus
faun n faunus m
fauna n animālia ntpl
favour n grātia f, favor m; (done) beneficium nt; **win ~ with** grātiam inīre apud; **by your ~** bonā veniā tuā ♦ vt favēre (dat), indulgēre (dat)
favourable adj faustus, prosperus, secundus
favourably adv faustē, fēlīciter, benignē
favourite adj dīlectus, grātissimus ♦ n dēliciae fpl
favouritism n indulgentia f, studium nt
fawn n hinnuleus m ♦ adj (colour) gilvus ♦ vi: **~ upon** adūlārī
fawning adj blandus ♦ n adūlātiō f

fear n timor m, metus m, formīdō f ✦ vt timēre,
metuere, formīdāre, verērī; **fearing that**
veritus ne (+imperf subj)
fearful adj timidus; horrendus, terribilis,
formīdolōsus
fearfully adv timidē; formīdolōsē
fearless adj impavidus, intrepidus
fearlessly adv impavidē, intrepidē
fearlessness n fīdentia f, audācia f
fearsome adj formīdolōsus
feasible adj: **it is** ~ fierī potest
feast n epulae fpl; (private) convīvium nt; (public)
epulum nt; (religious) daps f; (festival) festus diēs
m ✦ vi epulārī, convīvārī; (fig) pāscī ✦ vt: ~ **one's
eyes on** oculōs pāscere (abl)
feat n factum nt, facinus nt
feather n penna f; (downy) plūma f; **birds of a**
~ **flock together** parēs cum paribus facillimē
congregantur
feathered adj pennātus
feathery adj plūmeus
feature n līneāmentum nt; (fig) proprium nt
February n mēnsis Februārius m; **of**
~ Februārius
federal adj sociālis, foederātus
federate vi societātem facere
federated adj foederātus
federation n societās f, foederātae cīvitātēs fpl
fee n honōs m, mercēs f
feeble adj imbēcillus, īnfirmus, dēbilis
feebleness n imbēcillitās f, īnfirmitās f
feebly adv īnfirmē
feed vt alere, pāscere ✦ vi pāscī; ~ **on** vescī (abl) ✦ n
pābulum nt
feel vt sentīre; (with hand) tractāre, tangere;
(emotion) capere, adficī (abl); (opinion) cēnsēre,
sentīre; ~ **one's way** pedetemptim prōgredī ✦ vi
sentīre; **I** ~ **glad** gaudeō; ~ **sure** pro certō habēre
feeling n sēnsus m, tāctus m; (mind) animus
m, adfectus m; (pity) misericordia f; **good**
~ voluntās f; **bad** ~ invidia f
feign vt simulāre, fingere
feignedly adv simulātē, fictē
feint n simulātiō f
felicitate vt grātulārī (dat)
felicitation n grātulātiō f
felicitous adj fēlīx, aptus
felicity n fēlīcitās f
feline adj fēlīnus
fell vt (tree) succīdere; (enemy) sternere, caedere
✦ adj dīrus, crūdēlis, atrōx ✦ n mōns m; (skin)
pellis f
fellow n socius m, aequālis m; (contemptuous)
homō m
fellow citizen n cīvis m/f
fellow countryman n cīvis m/f, populāris m/f
fellow feeling n misericordia f
fellowship n societās f, sodālitās f
fellow slave n cōnservus m
fellow soldier n commīlitō m
fellow student n condiscipulus m
felon n nocēns m
felonious adj scelestus, scelerātus
felony n scelus nt, noxa f
felt n coāctum nt
female adj muliebris ✦ n fēmina f

feminine adj muliebris
fen n palūs f
fence n saepēs f; **sit on the** ~ quiēscere, medium
sē gerere ✦ vt saepīre; ~ **off** intersaepīre ✦ vi
bātuere, rudibus lūdere
fencing n rudium lūdus m; ~ **master** lānista m
fend vt arcēre ✦ vi prōvidēre
fennel n ferula f
fenny adj palūster
ferment n fermentum nt; (fig) aestus m ✦ vt
fermentāre; (fig) excitāre, accendere ✦ vi fervēre
fermentation n fervor m
fern n filix f
ferocious adj ferōx, saevus, truculentus
ferociously adv truculentē
ferocity n ferōcitās f, saevitia f
ferret n viverra m ✦ vt: ~ **out** rīmārī, ēruere
ferry n trāiectus m; (boat) cymba f, pontō m ✦ vt
trānsvehere
ferryman n portitor m
fertile adj fertīlis, fēcundus
fertility n fertīlitās f, fēcunditās f
fertilize vt fēcundāre, laetificāre
fervent adj fervidus, ārdēns
fervently adv ārdenter
fervid adj fervidus
fervour n ārdor m, fervor m
festal adj festus
fester vi exulcerārī
festival n diēs festus m, sollemne nt
festive adj (time) festus; (person) festīvus
festivity n hilaritās f; (event) sollemne nt
festoon n sertum nt ✦ vt corōnāre
fetch vt arcessere, addūcere; (price) vēnīre (gen);
~ **out** dēprōmere; ~ **water** aquārī
fetching adj lepidus, blandus
fetid adj foetidus, pūtidus
fetter n compēs f, vinculum nt ✦ vt compedēs
inicere (dat), vincīre; (fig) impedīre
fettle n habitus m, animus m
feud n simultās f, inimīcitia f
fever n febris f
feverish adj febrīculōsus; (fig) sollicitus
few adj paucī; **very few** perpaucī; **how few?**
quotus quisque?
fewness n paucitās f
fiancé n spōnsus m
fiasco n calamitās f; **be a** ~ frīgēre
fiat n ēdictum nt
fibre n fibra f
fickle adj incōnstāns, levis, mōbilis
fickleness n incōnstantia f, levitās f, mōbilitās f
fiction n fābula f, commentum nt
fictitious adj fictus, falsus, commentīcius;
(character) persōnātus
fictitiously adv fictē
fidelity n fidēlitās f, fidēs f
fidget vi sollicitārī
field n ager m; (ploughed) arvum nt; (of grain) seges
f; (MIL) campus m, aciēs f; (scope) campus m, locus
m; **in the** ~ (MIL) mīlitiae; **hold the** ~ vincere,
praevalēre; ~ **of vision** cōnspectus m
fiend n diabolus m
fiendish adj nefārius, improbus
fierce adj saevus, ācer, atrōx; (look) torvus
fiercely adv ācriter, atrōciter, saevē

fierceness *n* saevitia *f*, atrōcitās *f*
fieriness *n* ārdor *m*, fervor *m*
fiery *adj* igneus, flammeus; (*fig*) ārdēns, fervidus
fife *n* tībia *f*
fifteen *num* quīndecim; ~ **each** quīndēnī;
~ **times** quīndeciēns
fifteenth *adj* quīntus decimus
fifth *adj* quīntus ♦ *n* quīnta pars *f*
fiftieth *adj* quīnquāgēsimus
fifty *num* quīnquāgintā
fig *n* fīcus *f*; (*tree*) ficus *f*; **of fig** fīculnus; **not care
a fig for** floccī nōn facere
fight *n* pugna *f*, proelium *nt* ♦ *vi* pugnāre,
dīmicāre; ~ **it out** dēcernere, dēcertāre; ~ **to the
end** dēpugnāre ♦ *vt* (*battle*) committere; (*enemy*)
pugnāre cum (*abl*)
fighter *n* pugnātor *m*
fighting *n* dīmicātiō *f*
figment *n* commentum *nt*
figurative *adj* trānslātus; **in ~ language**
trānslātīs per similitūdinem verbīs; **use
figuratively** trānsferre
figure *n* figūra *f*, fōrma *f*; (*in art*) signum *nt*;
(*of speech*) figūra *f*, trānslātiō *f*; (*pl, on pottery*)
sigilla *ntpl* ♦ *vt* figūrāre, fōrmāre; (*art*) fingere,
effingere; ~ **to oneself** sibi prōpōnere
figured *adj* sigillātus
figurehead *n* (*of ship*) īnsigne *nt*
filament *n* fibra *f*
filch *vt* fūrārī, surripere
file *n* (*tool*) līma *f*; (*line*) ōrdō *m*, agmen *nt*; (*of
papers*) fasciculus *m*; **files** *pl* tabulae *fpl*; **in single
~** simplicī ōrdine; **the rank and ~** gregāriī
mīlitēs ♦ *vt* līmāre
filial *adj* pius
filigree *n* diatrēta *ntpl*
fill *vt* implēre, explēre, complēre; (*office*) fungī
(*abl*); ~ **up** supplēre
fillet *n* īnfula *f*, vitta *f* ♦ *vt* (*fish*) exossāre
fillip *n* stimulus *m*
filly *n* equula *f*
film *n* membrāna *f*
filter *n* cōlum *nt* ♦ *vt* dēliquāre ♦ *vi* percōlārī
filth *n* sordēs *f*, caenum *nt*
filthily *adv* foedē, inquinātē
filthiness *n* foeditās *f*, impūritās *f*
filthy *adj* foedus, impūrus; (*speech*) inquinātus
fin *n* pinna *f*
final *adj* ultimus, postrēmus, extrēmus
finally *adv* dēnique, tandem, postrēmō
finance *n* rēs nummāria *f*; (*state*) vectīgālia *ntpl*
financial *adj* aerārius
financier *n* faenerātor *m*
finch *n* fringilla *f*
find *vt* invenīre, reperīre; (*supplies*) parāre;
(*verdict*) iūdicāre; (*pleasure*) capere; ~ **fault with**
incūsāre; ~ **guilty** damnāre; ~ **out** comperīre,
cognōscere
finder *n* inventor *m*
finding *n* iūdicium *nt*, sententia *f*
fine *n* (LAW) multa *f*, damnum *nt*; **in ~** dēnique
♦ *vt* multāre ♦ *adj* (*thin*) tenuis, subtīlis; (*refined*)
ēlegāns, mundus, decōrus; (*beautiful*) pulcher,
venustus; (*showy*) speciōsus; (*of weather*) serēnus
finely *adv* pulchrē, ēleganter, subtīliter

fineness *n* tenuitās *f*; ēlegantia *f*; pulchritūdō *f*;
speciēs *f*; serēnitās *f*
finery *n* ōrnātus *m*, munditiae *fpl*
finesse *n* astūtia *f*, ars *f*, argūtiae *fpl*
finger *n* digitus *m*; **a finger's breadth**
trānsversus digitus; **not lift a ~** (*in effort*) nē
manum quidem vertere ♦ *vt* pertractāre
fingertips *npl* extrēmī digitī
finish *n* fīnis *m*; (*art*) perfectiō *f* ♦ *vt* fīnīre,
perficere; cōnficere; (*with art*) perficere, expolīre
♦ *vi* dēsinere; ~ **off** transigere, peragere,
absolvere
finishing post *n* mēta *f*
finishing touch *n* manus extrēma
finite *adj* circumscrīptus
fir *n* abiēs *f*; **of fir** abiēgnus
fire *n* ignis *m*; (*conflagration*) incendium *nt*; (*in
hearth*) focus *m*; (*fig*) ārdor *m*, calor *m*, impetus
m; **be on ~** ārdēre, flagrāre; **catch ~** flammam
concipere, ignem comprehendere; **set on
~** accendere, incendere ♦ *vt* incendere; (*fig*)
īnflammāre; (*missile*) iaculārī
firebrand *n* fax *f*
fire brigade *n* vigilēs *mpl*
fireplace *n* focus *m*
fireside *n* focus *m*
firewood *n* lignum *nt*
firm *n* societās *f* ♦ *adj* firmus, stabilis; (*mind*)
cōnstāns; **stand ~** perstāre
firmament *n* caelum *nt*
firmly *adv* firmē, cōnstanter
firmness *n* firmitās *f*, firmitūdō *f*; cōnstantia *f*
first *adj* prīmus, prīnceps; (*of two*) prior ♦ *adv*
prīmum; **at ~** prīmō, prīncipiō; **at ~ hand** ipse,
ab ipsō; **come in ~** vincere; **give ~ aid to** ad
tempus medērī (*dat*); **I was the ~ to see** prīmus
vīdī
first-class *adj* classicus
first fruits *npl* prīmitiae *fpl*
firstly *adv* prīmum
first-rate *adj* eximius, lūculentus
firth *n* aestuārium *nt*, fretum *nt*
fiscal *adj* vectīgālis, aerārius
fish *n* piscis *m* ♦ *vi* piscārī; (*fig*) expiscārī
fisher, fisherman *n* piscātor *m*
fishing *n* piscātus *m* ♦ *adj* piscātōrius
fishing-rod *n* harundō *f*
fish market *n* forum piscārium *nt*
fishmonger *n* piscārius *m*
fish pond *n* piscīna *f*
fissile *adj* fissilis
fissure *n* rīma *f*
fist *n* pugnus *m*
fit *n* (MED) convulsiō *f*; (*of anger, illness*) impetus *m*;
by fits and starts temerē, carptim ♦ *vt* aptāre,
accommodāre; (*dress*) sedēre (*dat*); **fit out**
armāre, īnstruere ♦ *adj* aptus, idōneus, dignus;
I see fit to mihi vidētur; **fit for** aptus ad (*acc*)
fitful *adj* dubius, incōnstāns
fitfully *adv* incōnstanter
fitly *adv* dignē, aptē
fitness *n* convenientia *f*
fitting *n* adparātus *m*, īnstrūmentum *nt* ♦ *adj*
idōneus, dignus; **it is ~** convenit, decet
fittingly *adv* dignē, convenienter

five *num* quīnque; ~ **each** quīnī; ~ **times** quīnquiēns; ~ **years** quīnquennium *nt*, lūstrum *nt*; ~ **sixths** quīnque partēs
five hundred *num* quīngentī; **five hundred each** quīngēnī; **five hundred times** quīngentiēns
five hundredth *adj* quīngentēsimus
fix *vt* fīgere; *(time)* dīcere, cōnstituere; *(decision)* statuere ♦ *n* angustiae *fpl*; **put in a fix** dēprehendere
fixed *adj* fixus; *(attention)* intentus; *(decision)* certus; *(star)* inerrāns; **be firmly ~ in** īnsidēre *(dat)*
fixedly *adv* intentē
fixity *n* stabilitās *f*; *(of purpose)* cōnstantia *f*
fixtures *npl* adfixa *ntpl*
flabbergast *vt* obstupefacere
flabbiness *n* mollitia *f*
flabby *adj* flaccidus, mollis
flag *n* vexillum *nt*; ~ **officer** praefectus classis *m* ♦ *vi* flaccēre, flaccēscere, languēscere
flagellate *vt* verberāre
flagon *n* lagoena *f*
flagrant *adj* manifestus; flāgitiōsus
flagrantly *adv* flāgitiōsē
flagship *n* nāvis imperātōria *f*
flail *n* fūstis *m*
flair *n* iūdicium *nt*
flake *n* squāma *f*; **flakes** *pl* *(snow)* nix *f*
flame *n* flamma *f* ♦ *vi* flagrāre, exārdēscere
flaming *adj* flammeus
flamingo *n* phoenīcopterus *m*
flank *n* latus *nt*; cornū *nt*; **on the ~** ab latere, ad latus ♦ *vt* latus tegere *(gen)*
flap *n* flābellum *nt*; *(dress)* lacinia *f* ♦ *vt* plaudere *(abl)*
flare *n* flamma *f*, fulgor *m* ♦ *vi* exārdēscere, flagrāre
flash *n* fulgor *m*; *(lightning)* fulgur *nt*; *(time)* mōmentum *nt* ♦ *vi* fulgēre; *(motion)* micāre
flashy *adj* speciōsus
flask *n* ampulla *f*
flat *adj* plānus; *(ground)* aequus; *(on back)* supīnus; *(on face)* prōnus; *(music)* gravis; *(style)* āridus, frīgidus; **fall ~** *(fig)* frīgēre ♦ *n* *(land)* plānitiēs *f*; *(sea)* vadum *nt*; *(house)* tabulātum *nt*
flatly *adv* prōrsus
flatness *n* plānitiēs *f*
flatten *vt* aequāre, complānāre
flatter *vt* adūlārī *(dat)*, adsentārī *(dat)*, blandīrī *(dat)*
flatterer *n* adsentātor *m*
flattering *adj* blandus
flatteringly *adv* blandē
flattery *n* adūlātiō *f*, adsentātiō *f*, blanditiae *fpl*
flatulence *n* īnflātiō *f*
flatulent *adj* īnflātus
flaunt *vt* iactāre ♦ *vi* iactāre, glōriārī
flaunting *n* iactātiō *f* ♦ *adj* glōriōsus
flauntingly *adv* glōriōsē
flautist *n* tībīcen *m*
flavour *n* gustātus *m*, sapor *m* ♦ *vt* imbuere, condīre
flavouring *n* condītiō *f*
flavourless *adj* īnsulsus
flaw *n* vitium *nt*

flawless *adj* ēmendātus
flax *n* līnum *nt*
flaxen *adj* flāvus
flay *vt* dēglūbere
flea *n* pūlex *m*
fleck *n* macula *f* ♦ *vt* variāre
fledged *adj* pennātus
flee *vi* fugere, effugere; *(for refuge)* cōnfugere
fleece *n* vellus *nt* ♦ *vt* tondēre; *(fig)* spoliāre
fleecy *adj* lāneus
fleet *n* classis *f* ♦ *adj* vēlōx, celer
fleeting *adj* fugāx
fleetness *n* vēlōcitās *f*, celeritās *f*
flesh *n* cārō *f*; *(fig)* corpus *nt*; **in the ~** vīvus; **one's own ~ and blood** cōnsanguineus; **put on ~** pinguēscere
fleshiness *n* corpus *nt*
fleshliness *n* libīdō *f*
fleshly *adj* libīdinōsus
fleshy *adj* pinguis
flexibility *n* lentitia *f*
flexible *adj* flexibilis, lentus
flicker *vi* coruscāre
flickering *adj* tremulus
flight *n* *(flying)* volātus *m*; *(fleeing)* fuga *f*; *(steps)* scāla *f*; **put to ~** fugāre, in fugam conicere; **take to ~** sē in fugam dare, terga vertere
flightiness *n* mōbilitās *f*
flighty *adj* mōbilis, incōnstāns
flimsy *adj* tenuis, pertenuis
flinch *vi* recēdere
fling *vt* iacere, conicere; *(missile)* intorquēre; ~ **away** abicere, prōicere; ~ **open** patefacere; ~ **in one's teeth** obicere *(dat)*; ~ **to the ground** prōsternere ♦ *vi* sē incitāre ♦ *n* iactus *m*
flint *n* silex *m*
flinty *adj* siliceus
flippancy *n* lascīvia *f*
flippant *adj* lascīvus, protervus
flippantly *adv* petulanter
flirt *vi* lūdere, lascīvīre ♦ *n* lascīvus *m*, lascīva *f*
flit *vi* volitāre
flitch *n* succīdia *f*
float *vi* innāre, fluitāre; *(in air)* volitāre; ~ **down** dēfluere
flock *n* grex *m*; *(wool)* floccus *m* ♦ *vi* concurrere, congregārī, cōnfluere; ~ **in** adfluere
flog *vt* verberāre, virgīs caedere
flogging *n* verbera *ntpl*
flood *n* *(deluge)* ēluviō *f*; *(river)* torrēns *m*; *(tide)* accessus *m*; *(fig)* flūmen *nt* ♦ *vt* inundāre
floodgate *n* cataracta *f*
floor *n* solum *nt*; *(paved)* pavīmentum *nt*; *(storey)* tabulātum *nt*; *(threshing)* ārea *f* ♦ *vt* contabulāre; **be floored** *(in argument)* iacēre
flora *n* herbae *fpl*
floral *adj* flōreus
florid *adj* flōridus
flotilla *n* classicula *f*
flounce *vi* sē conicere ♦ *n* īnstita *f*
flounder *vi* volutāre; *(in speech)* haesitāre
flour *n* fārīna *f*
flourish *vi* flōrēre, vigēre ♦ *vt* vibrāre, iactāre ♦ *n* (RHET) calamistrī *mpl*; *(music)* clangor *m*
flout *vt* aspernārī, inlūdere *(dat)*

flow vi fluere, mānāre; (tide) accēdere; ~ **back** recēdere; ~ **between** interfluere; ~ **down** dēfluere; ~ **into** īnfluere in (acc); ~ **out** prōfluere, ēmānāre; ~ **past** praeterfluere; ~ **through** permānāre; ~ **together** cōnfluere; ~ **towards** adfluere ♦ n flūmen nt, cursus m; (tide) accessus m; (words) flūmen nt
flower n flōs m, flōsculus m ♦ vi flōrēre, flōrēscere
floweret n flōsculus m
flowery adj flōridus
flowing adj prōfluēns; ~ **with** abundāns (abl)
flowingly adv prōfluenter
flown adj īnflātus
fluctuate vi aestuāre, fluctuāre
fluctuating adj incōnstāns, incertus
fluctuation n aestus m, dubitātiō f
fluency n fācundia f, verbōrum cōpia f
fluent adj disertus, prōfluēns
fluently adv disertē, prōfluenter
fluid adj liquidus ♦ n liquor m
fluidity n liquor m
fluke n (anchor) dēns m; (luck) fortuītum nt
flurry n trepidātiō f ♦ vt sollicitāre, turbāre
flush n rubor m; **in the first ~ of victory** victōriā ēlātus ♦ vi ērubēscere ♦ adj (full) abundāns; (level) aequus
fluster n trepidātiō f ♦ vt turbāre, sollicitāre
flute n tībia f; **play the ~** tībiā canere
fluted adj striātus
flutter n tremor m; (fig) trepidātiō f ♦ vi (heart) palpitāre; (mind) trepidāre; (bird) volitāre
fluvial adj fluviātilis
flux n fluxus m; **be in a state of ~** fluere
fly n musca f ♦ vi volāre; (flee) fugere; **fly apart** dissilīre; **fly at** involāre in (acc); **fly away** āvolāre; **fly from** fugere; **fly in the face of** obviam īre (dat); **fly out** ēvolāre; **fly to** advolāre ad (acc); **fly up** ēvolāre, subvolāre; **let fly at** immittere in (acc)
flying adj volucer, volātilis; (time) fugāx
foal n equuleus m, equulus m ♦ vt parere
foam n spūma f ♦ vi spūmāre; (with rage) saevīre
foaming adj spūmeus
focus vt (mind) intendere
fodder n pābulum nt
foe n hostis m; (private) inimīcus m
fog n cālīgō f, nebula f
foggy adj cālīginōsus, nebulōsus
foible n vitium nt
foil n (metal) lāmina f; (sword) rudis f ♦ vt ēlūdere, ad inritum redigere
foist vt inculcāre, interpōnere
fold n sinus m; (sheep) ovīle nt ♦ vt plicāre, complicāre; (hands) comprimere; (sheep) inclūdere; ~ **back** replicāre; ~ **over** plicāre; ~ **together** complicāre; ~ **up in** involvere in (abl)
folding doors npl valvae fpl
foliage n frondēs fpl
folk n hominēs mpl ♦ adj patrius
follow vt sequī; (calling) facere; (candidate) adsectārī; (enemy) īnsequī; (example) imitārī; (instructions) pārēre (dat); (predecessor) succēdere (dat); (road) pergere; (speaker) intellegere; ~ **closely** īnsequī; ~ **hard on the heels of** īnsequī, īnsistere (dat), īnstāre (dat); ~ **out**

exsequī; ~ **to the grave** exsequī; ~ **up** subsequī, īnsistere (dat) ♦ vi (time) īnsequī; (inference) sequī; **as follows** ita, in hunc modum
follower n comes m; (of candidate) adsectātor m; (of model) imitātor m; (of teacher) audītor m
following adj tālis; īnsequēns, proximus, posterus; **on the ~ day** postrīdiē, postero diē, proximo diē ♦ n adsectātōrēs mpl
folly n stultitia f, dēmentia f, īnsipientia f
foment vt fovēre, (fig) augēre
fond adj amāns, studiōsus; ineptus; **be ~ of** amāre
fondle vt fovēre, mulcēre
fondly adv amanter; ineptē
food n cibus m; (fig) pābulum nt
fool n stultus m, ineptus m; (jester) scurra m; **make a ~ of** ludibriō habēre; **play the ~** dēsipere ♦ vt dēcipere, lūdere; ~ **away** disperdere ♦ vi dēsipere
foolery n ineptiae fpl, nūgae fpl
foolhardy adj temerārius
foolish adj stultus, ineptus, īnsipiēns
foolishly adv stultē, ineptē
foolishness n stultitia f, īnsipientia f
foot n pēs m; (MIL) peditātus m; **a ~ long** pedālis; **on ~** pedes; **set ~ on** īnsistere (dat); **set on ~** īnstituere; **the ~ of** īmus ♦ vt (bill) solvere
football n follis m
footing n locus m, status m; **keep one's ~** īnsistere; **on an equal ~** ex aequō
footman n pedisequus m
footpad n grassātor m
footpath n sēmita f, trāmes m
footprint n vestīgium nt
foot soldier n pedes m
footstep n vestīgium nt; **follow in the footsteps of** vestīgiīs ingredī (gen)
foppish adj dēlicātus
for prep (advantage) dat; (duration) acc; (after noun) gen; (price) abl; (behalf) prō (abl); (cause) propter (acc), causā (gen); (after neg) prae (abl); (feelings) erga (acc); (lieu) prō (abl); (purpose) ad, in (acc); (time fixed) in (acc) ♦ conj namque; nam (1st word), enim (2nd word); (with pron) quippe quī; **for a long time** diū; **for some time** aliquamdiū
forage n pābulum nt ♦ vi pābulārī, frūmentārī
forager n pābulātor m, frūmentātor m
foraging n pābulātiō f, frūmentātiō f
forasmuch as conj quoniam
foray n incursiō f
forbear vi parcere (dat), supersedēre (inf)
forbearance n venia f, indulgentia f
forbears n māiōrēs mpl
forbid vt vetāre (+ acc and infin), interdīcere (dat and 'quominus' and subj); **Heaven ~ !**, dī meliōra!
forbidding adj tristis
force n vīs f; (band of men) manus m; **by ~ of arms** vī et armis ♦ vt cōgere, impellere; (way) rumpere, mōlīrī; (growth) festīnāre; ~ **an engagement** hostes proeliārī cogere; ~ **down** dētrūdere; ~ **out** extrūdere, expellere, exturbāre; ~ **upon** inculcāre; ~ **a way in** intrōrumpere, inrumpere
forced adj (march) māgnus; (style) quaesītus; ~ **march** māgnum iter
forceful adj validus

forceps n forceps m/f
forces npl (MIL) cōpiae fpl
forcible adj validus; (fig) gravis
forcibly adv vī, violenter; (fig) graviter
ford n vadum nt ♦ vt vadō trānsīre
fore adj prior; **to the ~** praestō ♦ adv: **~ and aft** in longitūdinem
forearm n bracchium nt ♦ vt: **be forearmed** praecavēre
forebode vt ōminārī, portendere; praesentīre
foreboding n praesēnsiō f; ōmen nt
forecast n praedictiō f ♦ vt praedīcere, prōvidēre
forecourt n vestibulum nt
forefathers n māiōrēs mpl
forefinger n index m
foreground n ēminentia ntpl
forehead n frōns f
foreign adj peregrīnus, externus; (goods) adventīcius; **~ to** aliēnus ab; **~ ways** peregrīnitās f
foreigner n peregrīnus m, advena m
foreknow vt praenōscere
foreknowledge n prōvidentia f
foreland n prōmontōrium nt
foremost adj prīmus, prīnceps
forenoon n antemerīdiānum tempus nt
forensic adj forēnsis
forerunner n praenūntius m
foresee vt praevidēre
foreshadow vt praemonēre
foresight n prōvidentia f
forest n silva f
forestall vt occupāre, antevenīre
forester n silvicola m
foretaste vt praegustāre
foretell vt praedīcere, vāticinārī
forethought n prōvidentia f
forewarn vt praemonēre
foreword n praefātiō f
forfeit n multa f, damnum nt ♦ vt āmittere, perdere, multārī (abl); (bail) dēserere
forfeiture n damnum nt
forgather vi congregārī, convenīre
forge n fornāx f ♦ vt fabricārī, excūdere; (document) subicere; (will) suppōnere; (signature) imitārī; (money) adulterīnōs nummōs percutere
forged adj falsus, adulterīnus, commentīcius
forger n (of will) subiector m
forgery n falsum nt, commentum nt
forget vt oblīvīscī (gen); (thing learnt) dēdiscere; **be forgotten** memoriā cadere, ex animō effluere
forgetful adj immemor; (by habit) oblīviōsus
forgetfulness n oblīviō f
forgive vt ignōscere (dat), veniam dare (dat)
forgiveness n venia f
forgo vt dīmittere, renūntiāre; (rights) dēcēdere dē iūre
fork n furca f; (small) furcula f; (road) trivium nt
forlorn adj inops, dēstitūtus, exspēs
form n fōrma f, figūra f; (of procedure) fōrmula f; (condition) vigor m; (etiquette) mōs m; (seat) scamnum nt; (school) schola f; (hare's) latibulum nt ♦ vt fōrmāre, fingere, efficere; (MIL) īnstruere; (plan) inīre, capere
formal adj iūstus; (rite) sollemnis

formality n iūsta ntpl, rītus m; **as a ~** dicis causā; **with due ~** rītē
formally adv rītē
formation n fōrma f, figūra f; (process) cōnfōrmātiō f; **in ~** (MIL) īnstructus
former adj prior, prīstinus, vetus; **the ~** ille
formerly adv anteā, ōlim, quondam
formidable adj formīdolōsus
formidably adv formīdolōsē
formula n fōrmula f; (dictated) praefātiō f
formulate vt compōnere
forsake vt dērelinquere, dēstituere, dēserere
forswear vt pēierāre, abiūrāre
fort n castellum nt
forth adv forās; (time) posthāc
forthwith adv extemplō, statim, prōtinus
fortieth adj quadrāgēsimus
fortification n (process) mūnītiō f; (place) mūnīmentum nt, arx f
fortify vt mūnīre, ēmūnīre, commūnīre; (fig) cōnfirmāre
fortitude n fortitūdō f
fortnight n quīndecim diēs mpl
fortnightly adv quīntō decimō quōque diē
fortress n arx f, castellum nt
fortuitous adj fortuītus
fortuitously adv fortuītō, cāsū
fortunate adj fēlīx, fortūnātus
fortunately adv fēlīciter, bene
fortune n fortūna f, fors f; (wealth) rēs f, dīvitiae fpl; **good ~** fēlīcitās f, secundae rēs fpl; **bad ~** adversae rēs fpl; **make one's ~** rem facere, rem quaerere; **tell fortunes** hariolārī
fortune-hunter n captātor m
fortune-teller n hariolus m, sāga f
forty num quadrāgintā; **~ each** quadrāgēnī; **~ times** quadrāgiēns
forum n forum nt
forward adj (person) protervus, audāx; (fruit) praecox ♦ adv porrō, ante; **bring ~** prōferre; **come ~** prōdīre ♦ vt (letter) perferre; (cause) adiuvāre, favēre (dat)
forwardness n audācia f, alacritās f
forwards adv porrō, prōrsus; **backwards and ~** rursum prōrsum, hūc illūc
fosse n fossa f
foster vt alere, nūtrīre; (fig) fovēre
foster child n alumnus m, alumna f
foster father n altor m, ēducātor m
foster mother n altrīx f, nūtrīx f
foul adj foedus; (speech) inquinātus; **fall ~ of** inruere in (acc)
foully adv foedē, inquinātē
foul-mouthed adj maledicus
foulness n foeditās f
found vt condere, fundāre, īnstituere; (metal) fundere
foundation n fundāmenta ntpl
founder n fundātor m, conditor m ♦ vi submergī, naufragium facere
foundling n expositīcius m, expositīcia f
fount n fōns m
fountain n fōns m
fountainhead n fōns m, orīgō f

four *num* quattuor *(indecl)*; ~ **each** quaternī;
~ **times** quater; ~ **days** quadriduum *nt*; ~ **years**
quadriennium *nt*
fourfold *adj* quadruplex ♦ *adv* quadrifāriam
four hundred *num* quadringentī; **four hundred
each** quadringēnī; **four hundred times**
quadringentiēns
four hundredth *adj* quadringentēsimus
fourteen *num* quattuordecim; ~ **each** quaternī
dēnī; ~ **times** quater deciēns
fourteenth *adj* quartus decimus
fourth *adj* quartus ♦ *n* quadrāns *m*; **three
fourths** dōdrāns *m*, trēs partēs *fpl*
fowl *n* avis *f*; gallīna *f*
fowler *n* auceps *m*
fox *n* vulpes *f*; **fox's** vulpīnus
foxy *adj* astūtus, vafer
fracas *n* rīxa *f*
fraction *n* pars *f*
fractious *adj* difficilis
fracture *n* frāctum os *nt* ♦ *vt* frangere
fragile *adj* fragilis
fragility *n* fragilitās *f*
fragment *n* fragmentum *nt*
fragrance *n* odor *m*
fragrant *adj* suāvis
fragrantly *adv* suāviter
frail *adj* fragilis, īnfirmus, dēbilis
frailty *n* dēbilitās *f*; *(moral)* error *m*
frame *vt* fabricārī, fingere, effingere; *(document)*
compōnere ♦ *n* fōrma *f*; *(of mind)* adfectiō *f*,
habitus *m*; **in a ~ of mind** animātus
framer *n* fabricātor *m*, opifex *m*; *(of law)* lātor *m*
framework *n* compāgēs *f*
franchise *n* suffrāgium *nt*, cīvitās *f*
frank *adj* ingenuus, apertus; *(speech)* līber
frankincense *n* tūs *nt*
frankly *adv* ingenuē, apertē; līberē
frankness *n* ingenuitās *f*; *(speech)* lībertās *f*
frantic *adj* furēns, furiōsus, dēlīrus
frantically *adv* furenter
fraternal *adj* frāternus
fraternally *adv* frāternē
fraternity *n* frāternitās *f*; *(society)* sodālitās *f*;
(guild) collēgium *nt*
fraternize *vi* amīcitiam iungere
fratricide *n* frātricīda *m*; *(act)* frātris
parricīdium *nt*
fraud *n* fraus *f*, dolus *m*, falsum *nt*; *(criminal)*
dolus malus *m*
fraudulence *n* fraus *f*
fraudulent *adj* fraudulentus, dolōsus
fraudulently *adv* dolōsē, dolō malō
fraught *adj* plēnus
fray *n* pugna *f*, rīxa *f* ♦ *vt* terere
freak *n* mōnstrum *nt*; *(caprice)* libīdō *f*
freckle *n* lentīgō *f*
freckly *adj* lentīginōsus
free *adj* līber; *(disengaged)* vacuus; *(generous)*
līberālis; *(from cost)* grātuītus; *(from duty)*
immūnis; *(from encumbrance)* expedītus; **be
~ from** vacāre *(abl)*; **I am still ~ to** integrum est
mihī *(inf)*; **set ~** absolvere, līberāre; *(slave)* manū
mittere ♦ *adv* grātīs, grātuītō ♦ *vt* līberāre,
expedīre, exsolvere
freebooter *n* praedō *m*

freeborn *adj* ingenuus
freedman *n* lībertus *m*
freedom *n* lībertās *f*; *(from duty)* immūnitās *f*
freehold *n* praedium līberum *nt* ♦ *adj* immūnis
freely *adv* līberē; *(lavishly)* cōpiōsē, largē; *(frankly)*
apertē; *(voluntarily)* ultrō, suā sponte
freeman *n* cīvis *m*
free will *n* voluntās *f*; **of one's own free will** suā
sponte
freeze *vt* gelāre, glaciāre ♦ *vi* concrēscere
freezing *adj* gelidus; **it is ~** gelat
freight *n* vectūra *f*; *(cargo)* onus *nt* ♦ *vt* onerāre
freighter *n* nāvis onerāria *f*
frenzied *adj* furēns, furiōsus, fānāticus
frenzy *n* furor *m*, īnsania *f*
frequency *n* adsiduitās *f*
frequent *adj* frequēns, crēber ♦ *vt* frequentāre,
commeāre in *(acc)*
frequently *adv* saepe, saepenumerō, frequenter
fresh *adj* *(new)* recēns, novus; *(vigorous)* integer;
(water) dulcis; *(wind)* ācer
freshen *vt* renovāre ♦ *vi* *(wind)* incrēbrēscere
freshly *adv* recenter
freshman *n* tīrō *m*
freshness *n* novitās *f*, viriditās *f*
fret *vi* maerēre, angī ♦ *vt* sollicitāre
fretful *adj* mōrōsus, querulus
fretfulness *n* mōrōsitās *f*
fretted *adj* laqueātus
friable *adj* puter
friction *n* trītus *m*
friend *n* amīcus *m*, familiāris *m/f*, hospes *m*,
sodālis *m*; **make friends with** sē cōnferre ad
amīcitiam *(gen)*
friendless *adj* sine amīcīs
friendliness *n* cōmitās *f*, officium *nt*
friendly *adj* cōmis, facilis, benīgnus; **on ~ terms**
familiāriter
friendship *n* amīcitia *f*, familiāritās *f*
frigate *n* liburna *f*
fright *n* horror *m*, pavor *m*, terror *m*; **take
~** extimēscere, expavēscere
frighten *vt* terrēre, exterrēre, perterrēre; ~ **away**
absterrēre; ~ **off** dēterrēre; ~ **the life out of**
exanimāre
frightful *adj* horribilis, immānis; *(look)* taeter
frightfully *adv* foedē
frigid *adj* frīgidus
frigidity *n* frīgus *nt*
frill *n* fimbriae *fpl*; (RHET) calamistrī *mpl*
fringe *n* fimbriae *fpl*
frisk *vi* lascīvīre, exsultāre
frisky *adj* lascīvus
fritter *vt*: ~ **away** dissipāre; *(time)* extrahere
frivolity *n* levitās *f*
frivolous *adj* levis, inānis
frivolously *adv* ināniter
fro *adv*: **to and fro** hūc illūc
frock *n* stola *f*
frog *n* rāna *f*
frolic *n* lūdus *m* ♦ *vi* lūdere, lascīvīre
frolicsome *adj* lascīvus, hilaris
from *prep* ab *(abl)*, ā *before consonants*; *(out)* ē, ex
(abl); *(cause)* propter *(acc)*; *(prevention)* quōminus,
quīn; ~ **all directions** undique

front n frōns f; **in ~ ā** fronte, adversus; **in ~ of** pro (abl)
frontier n līmes m, cōnfīnia ntpl; **frontiers** fīnes mpl
front line n prima aciēs
frost n gelū nt
frostbitten adj: **be ~** vī frīgoris ambūrī
frosty adj gelidus, glaciālis
froth n spūma f ♦ vi spūmās agere
frothy adj spūmeus
froward adj contumāx
frown n frontis contractiō f ♦ vi frontem contrahere
frozen adj glaciālis
fructify vt fēcundāre
frugal adj parcus, frūgī
frugality n frūgālitās f, parsimōnia f
frugally adv parcē, frūgāliter
fruit n frūctus m; (tree) māla ntpl; (berry) bāca f; (fig) frūctus m; **fruits** pl (of earth) frūgēs fpl
fruiterer n pōmārius m
fruitful adj fēcundus, frūctuōsus
fruitfully adv ferāciter
fruitfulness n fēcunditās f, ūbertās f
fruition n frūctus m
fruitless adj inūtilis, vānus
fruitlessly adv nēquīquam, frustrā
fruit tree n pōmum nt
frustrate vt frustrārī, ad inritum redigere
frustration n frustrātiō f
fry vt frīgere
frying pan n sartāgō f; **out of the frying pan into the fire** incidit in Scyllam quī vult vītāre Charybdim
fuel n fōmes m
fugitive adj fugitīvus ♦ n fugitīvus m, trānsfuga m; (from abroad) extorris m
fulfil vt (duty) explēre, implēre; (promise) praestāre; (order) exsequī, perficere
fulfilment n absolūtiō f
full adj plēnus (abl), refertus, explētus; (entire) integer; (amount) solidus; (brother) germānus; (measure) iūstus; (meeting) frequēns; (style) cōpiōsus; **at ~ length** porrēctus; **at ~ speed** citātō gradū, citātō equō
fuller n fullō m
full-grown adj adultus
full moon n lūna plēna
fullness n (style) cōpia f; (time) mātūritās f
fully adv plēnē, penitus, funditus
fulminate vi intonāre
fulsome adj fastīdiōsus, pūtidus
fumble vi haesitāre

fume n fūmus m, hālitus m ♦ vi stomachārī
fumigate vt suffīre
fun n iocus m, lūdus m; **for fun** animī causā; **make fun of** inlūdere, dēlūdere, lūdibriō habēre
function n officium nt, mūnus nt
fund n cōpia f
fundamental adj prīmus ♦ n prīncipium nt, elementum nt
funds npl sors f, pecūniae fpl
funeral n fūnus nt, exsequiae fpl ♦ adj fūnebris
funeral pile n rogus m
funeral pyre n rogus m
funeral rites npl exsequiae fpl, īnferiae fpl
funereal adj fūnebria, lūgubris
funnel n īnfundibulum nt
funny adj ioculāris, rīdiculus
fur n pellis m
furbelow n īnstita f
furbish vt expolīre; **~ up** interpolāre
Furies npl Furiae fpl
furious adj saevus, vehemēns, perīrātus
furiously adv furenter, saevē, vehementer
furl vt (sail) legere
furlong n stadium nt
furlough n commeātus m
furnace n fornāx f
furnish vt praebēre, suppeditāre; (equip) īnstruere, ōrnāre
furniture n supellex f
furrow n sulcus m ♦ vt sulcāre
furry adj villōsus
further adj ulterior ♦ adv ultrā, porrō; amplius ♦ vt adiuvāre, cōnsulere (dat)
furtherance n prōgressus m; (means) īnstrūmentum nt
furthermore adv praetereā, porrō
furthest adj ultimus ♦ adv longissimē
furtive adj fūrtīvus, clandestīnus
furtively adv clam, fūrtim
fury n furor m, saevitia f; īra f
fuse vt fundere; (together) coniungere
fusion n coniūnctiō f
fuss n importūnitās f, querimōnia f ♦ vi conquerī, sollicitārī
fussy adj importūnus, incommodus
fusty adj mūcidus
futile adj inānis, inūtilis, futilis
futility n vānitās f, futilitās f
future adj futūrus, posterus ♦ n posterum nt, reliquum nt; **in ~** posthāc; **for the ~** in posterum
futurity n posterum tempus nt, posteritās f

Gg

gabble vi garrīre
gable n fastīgium nt
gadfly n tabānus m
gag vt ōs praeligāre (dat), ōs obvolvere (dat)
gage n pignus nt
gaiety n laetitia f, hilaritās f, festīvitās f
gaily adv hilare, festīve
gain n lucrum nt, quaestus m ♦ vt comparāre;
  adipīscī; (profit) lucrārī; (thing) parāre, cōnsequī,
  capere; (case) vincere; (place) pervenīre ad;
  (possession of) potīrī (gen); (victory) reportāre;
  ~ **over** conciliāre; ~ **ground** incrēbrēscere;
  ~ **possession of** potior (abl); ~ **the upper hand**
  rem obtinēre
gainful adj quaestuōsus
gainsay vt contrādīcere (dat)
gait n incessus m, ingressiō f
gaiters n ocreae fpl
gala n diēs festus m
galaxy n circulus lacteus m
gale n ventus m
gall n fel nt, bīlis m ♦ vt ūrere
gallant adj fortis, audāx; (courteous) officiōsus
gallantly adv fortiter; officiōsē
gallantry n virtūs f; urbānitās f
gall bladder n fel nt
gallery n porticus f
galley n nāvis āctuāria f; (cook's) culīna f
galling adj amārus, mordāx
gallon n congius m
gallop n cursus m; **at the ~** citātō equō, admissō
  equō ♦ vi admissō equō currere
gallows n īnfēlīx arbor m, furca f
gallows bird n furcifer m
galore adv adfatim
gamble n ālea f ♦ vi āleā lūdere
gambler n āleātor m
gambling n ālea f
gambol n lūsus m ♦ vi lūdere, lascīvīre, exsultāre
game n lūdus m; (with dice) ālea f; (hunt) praeda f;
  play the ~ rēctē facere; **public games** lūdī mpl;
  Olympic games Olympia ntpl; **the game's up**
  āctum est ♦ adj animōsus
gamester n āleātor m
gammon n perna f
gander n ānser m
gang n grex m, caterva f
gangster n grassātor m
gangway n forus m
gaol n carcer m
gaoler n custōs m
gap n hiātus m, lacūna f

gape vi hiāre, inhiāre; (opening) dēhiscere
garb n habitus m, amictus m ♦ vt amicīre
garbage n quisquiliae fpl
garden n hortus m; (public) hortī mpl
gardener n hortulānus m; (ornamental) topiārius
  m
gardening n hortī cultūra f; (ornamental) topiāria
  f
gargle vi gargarissāre
garish adj speciōsus, fūcātus
garland n sertum nt, corōna f ♦ vt corōnāre
garlic n ālium nt
garment n vestis f, vestīmentum nt
garnish vt ōrnāre, decorāre
garret n cēnāculum nt
garrison n praesidium nt, dēfēnsōrēs mpl ♦ vt
  praesidiō mūnīre, praesidium collocāre in (abl)
garrotte vt laqueō gulam frangere (dat)
garrulity n garrulitās f
garrulous adj garrulus, loquāx
gas n vapor m
gash n vulnus nt ♦ vt caedere, lacerāre
gasp n anhēlitus m, singultus m ♦ vi anhēlāre
gastronomy n gula f
gate n porta f
gather vt colligere, cōgere; (fruit) legere;
  (inference) colligere, conicere ♦ vi congregārī
gathering n conventus m, coetus m
gauche adj inconcinnus, illepidus
gaudily adv splendidē, speciōsē
gaudy adj speciōsus, fūcātus, lautus
gauge n modulus m ♦ vt mētīrī
Gaul n Gallia f; (person) Gallus m
gaunt adj macer
gauntlet n manica f
gauze n Coa ntpl
gay adj hilaris, festīvus, laetus
gaze vi intuērī; ~ **at** intuērī, adspectāre,
  contemplārī
gazelle n oryx m
gazette n ācta diūrna ntpl, ācta pūblica ntpl
gear n īnstrūmenta ntpl; (ship's) armāmenta ntpl
gelding n cantērius m
gelid adj gelidus
gem n gemma f
gender n genus nt
genealogical adj dē stirpe
genealogical table n stemma nt
genealogist n geneālogus m
genealogy n geneālogia f

general *adj* generālis, ūniversus; (*usual*) vulgāris, commūnis; **in** ~ omnīnō ♦ *n* dux *m*, imperātor *m*; **general's tent** praetorium *nt*
generalissimo *n* imperātor *m*
generality *n* vulgus *nt*, plērīque *mpl*
generalize *vi* ūniversē loquī
generally *adv* ferē, plērumque; (*discuss*) īnfīnītē
generalship *n* ductus *m*
generate *vt* gignere, generāre
generation *n* aetās *f*, saeculum *nt*
generic *adj* generālis
generically *adv* genere
generosity *n* līberālitās *f*, largitās *f*
generous *adj* līberālis, largus, benīgnus
generously *adv* līberāliter, largē, benīgnē
genesis *n* orīgō *f*, prīncipium *nt*
genial *adj* cōmis, hilaris
geniality *n* cōmitās *f*, hilaritās *f*
genially *adv* cōmiter, hilare
genitive *n* genitīvus *m*
genius *n* (*deity*) genius *m*; (*talent*) ingenium *nt*, indolēs *f*; **of** ~ ingeniōsus
genre *n* genus *nt*
genteel *adj* urbānus, polītus
gentility *n* urbānitās *f*, ēlegantia *f*
gentle *adj* (*birth*) ingenuus; (*manner*) hūmānus, indulgēns, mītis; (*slope*) lēnis, mollis; (*thing*) placidus, lēnis
gentleman *n* vir *m*, ingenuus *m*, vir honestus *m*
gentlemanly *adj* ingenuus, līberālis, honestus
gentleness *n* hūmānitās *f*, indulgentia *f*, lēnitās *f*
gentlewoman *n* ingenua *f*, mulier honesta *f*
gently *adv* lēniter, molliter, placidē
gentry *n* ingenuī *mpl*, optimātēs *mpl*; (*contempt*) hominēs *mpl*
genuine *adj* vērus, germānus, sincērus
genuinely *adv* germānē, sincērē
genuineness *n* fidēs *f*
geographical *adj* geōgraphicus; ~ **position** situs *m*
geography *n* geōgraphia *f*
geometrical *adj* geōmetricus
geometry *n* geōmetria *f*
Georgics *n* Geōrgica *ntpl*
germ *n* germen *nt*, sēmen *nt*
germane *adj* adfīnis
germinate *vi* gemmāre
gesticulate *vi* sē iactāre, gestū ūtī
gesticulation *n* gestus *m*
gesture *n* gestus *m*, mōtus *m*
get *vt* adipīscī, nancīscī, parāre; (*malady*) contrahere; (*request*) impetrāre; (*return*) capere; (*reward*) ferre; **get sth done** cūrāre (*with gerundive*); **get sb to do** persuādēre (*dat*), addūcere; **get by heart** ēdiscere; **get in** repōnere; **get the better of** superāre; **go and get** arcessere ♦ *vi* fierī; **get about** (*rumour*) palam fierī, percrēbrēscere; **get away** effugere; **get at** (*intent*) spectāre; **get behind** cessāre; **get off** absolvī; **get on** prōficere; **get out** effugere, ēvādere; **get out of hand** lascīvīre; **get out of the way** dē viā dēcēdere; **get ready** parāre; **get rid of** abicere, tollere; **get to** pervenīre ad; **get to know** cognōscere; **get together** congregārī; **get up** exsurgere

get-up *n* ōrnātus *m*
ghastliness *n* pallor *m*
ghastly *adj* pallidus; (*sight*) taeter
ghost *n* larva *f*, īdōlon *nt*; **ghosts** *pl* mānēs *mpl*; **give up the** ~ animam agere, efflāre
giant *n* Gigas *m*
gibberish *n* barbaricus sermō *m*
gibbet *n* furca *f*
gibe *vi* inrīdēre
giddiness *n* vertīgō *f*
giddy *adj* vertīginōsus; (*fig*) levis
gift *n* dōnum *nt*; (*small*) mūnusculum *nt*; **gifts** *pl* (*mind*) ingenium *nt*
gifted *adj* ingeniōsus
gig *n* cisium *nt*
gigantic *adj* ingēns, immānis
gild *vt* inaurāre
gill *n* (*measure*) quartārius *m*; (*fish*) branchia *f*
gilt *adj* aurātus
gimlet *n* terebra *f*
gin *n* pedica *f*, laqueus *m*
ginger *n* zingiberī *nt*
gingerly *adv* pedetemptim
giraffe *n* camēlopardālis *f*
gird *vt* circumdāre; ~ **on** accingere; ~ **oneself** cingī; ~ **up** succingere
girder *n* tignum *nt*
girdle *n* cingulus *m* ♦ *vt* cingere
girl *n* puella *f*, virgō *f*
girlhood *n* aetās puellāris *f*
girlish *adj* puellāris
girth *n* ambitus *m*, amplitūdō *f*
gist *n* firmāmentum *nt*
give *vt* dare, dōnāre, tribuere; (*thing due*) reddere; ~ **away** largīrī; (*bride*) in matrimōnium collocāre; (*secret*) prōdere; ~ **back** reddere, restituere; ~ **birth (to)** parere; ~ **in** (*name*) profiterī; ~ **off** ēmittere; ~ **out** (*orders*) ēdere; (*sound*) ēmittere; ~ **thanks** gratias agere; ~ **up** dēdere, trādere; (*hope of*) dēspērāre; (*rights*) dēcēdere dē, renūntiāre; ~ **way** cēdere; (*MIL*) inclīnāre ♦ *vi* labāre; ~ **in** sē victum fatērī; (*MIL*) manūs dare; ~ **out** (*fail*) dēficere; (*pretend*) ferre; ~ **up** dēsistere; ~ **way** cēdere
giver *n* dator *m*
glacial *adj* glaciālis
glad *adj* laetus, alacer, hilaris; **be** ~ gaudēre
gladden *vt* exhilarāre, oblectāre
glade *n* saltus *m*
gladiator *n* gladiātor *m*
gladiatorial *adj* gladiātōrius; **present a** ~ **show** gladiātōrēs dare
gladly *adv* laetē, libenter
gladness *n* laetitia *f*, alacritās *f*, gaudium *nt*
glamorous *adj* venustus
glamour *n* venustās *f*
glance *n* aspectus *m* ♦ *vi* oculōs conicere; ~ **at** aspicere; (*fig*) attingere, perstringere; ~ **off** stringere
glare *n* fulgor *m* ♦ *vi* fulgēre; ~ **at** torvīs oculīs intuērī
glaring *adj* (*look*) torvus; (*fault*) manifestus; **be** ~ ante pedēs positum esse
glass *n* vitrum *nt*; (*mirror*) speculum *nt*
glassy *adj* vitreus
glaze *vt* vitrō obdūcere

gleam n fulgor m, lūx f ♦ vi fulgēre, lūcēre
gleaming adj splendidus, nitidus
glean vi spīcās legere
gleaning n spīcilegium nt
glebe n fundus m
glee n hilaritās f, gaudium nt
gleeful adj hilaris, festīvus, laetus
gleefully adv hilare, laetē
glen n vallis f
glib adj prōfluēns, fācundus
glibly adv prōfluenter
glide n lāpsus m ♦ vi lābī; ~ **away** ēlābī
glimmer vi sublūcēre ♦ n: **a ~ of** hope spēcula f
glimpse n aspectus m ♦ vt cōnspicārī
glint vi renīdēre
glisten vi fulgēre, nitēre
glitter vi micāre
gloaming n crepusculum nt
gloat vi: ~ **over** inhiāre, animō haurīre, oculōs pāscere (abl)
globe n globus m, sphaera f; (inhabited) orbis terrārum m
globular adj globōsus
globule n globulus m, pilula f
gloom n tenebrae fpl; tristitia f
gloomy adj tenebricōsus; tristis, dēmissus
glorify vt illūstrāre, extollere, laudāre
glorious adj illūstris, praeclārus, splendidus
gloriously adv praeclārē, splendidē
glory n laus f, glōria f, decus nt ♦ vi glōriārī, sē iactāre
gloss n nitor m ♦ vt: ~ **over** (fig) dissimulāre
glossy adj nitidus
glove n manica f
glow n (light) lūmen nt; (heat) ārdor m; (passion) calor m ♦ vi lūcēre, ārdēre, calēre, candēre
glowing adj candēns, ārdēns, calidus
glue n glūten nt ♦ vt glūtināre
glum adj tristis, maestus
glut vt explēre, saturāre ♦ n satietās f, abundantia f
glutton n gāneō m, helluō m
gluttonous adj edāx, vorāx, avidus
gluttony n gula f, edācitās f
gnarled adj nōdōsus
gnash vt, vi frendere; ~ **one's teeth** dentibus frendere
gnat n culex m
gnaw vt rōdere; ~ **away** ērōdere
gnawing adj mordāx
go vi īre, vādere; (depart) abīre, discēdere; (event) ēvādere; (mechanism) movērī; **go about** incipere, adgredī; **go after** īnsequī; **go away** abīre, discēdere; **go back** redīre, regredī; **go before** anteīre, praeīre; **go by** praeterīre; (rule) sequī, ūtī (abl); **go down** dēscendere; (storm) cadere; (star) occidere; **go for** petere; **go forward** prōgredī; **go in** intrāre, ingredī; **go in for** (profession) facere, exercēre; **go off** abīre; **go on** pergere; (event) agī; **go out** exīre, ēgredī; (fire) extinguī; **go over** trānsīre; (to enemy) dēscīscere; (preparation) meditārī; (reading) legere; (work done) retractāre; **go round** circumīre, ambīre; **go through** percurrere; penetrāre; (suffer) perferre; **go to** adīre, petere; **go up** ascendere; **go to the help of** subvenīre (dat); **go to meet** obviam īre;

go with comitārī; **go without** carēre (abl), sē abstinēre (abl) ♦ n vīs f, ācrimōnia f
goad n stimulus m ♦ vt irrītāre; pungere; (fig) stimulāre
go-ahead adj impiger
goal n fīnis m, mēta f
goat n caper m, capra f
gobble vt dēvorāre
go-between n internūntius m, internūntia f; (bribery) sequester m
goblet n pōculum nt, scyphus m
god n deus m
goddess n dea f
godhead n dīvīnitās f, nūmen nt
godless adj impius
godlike adj dīvīnus
godliness n pietās f, rēligiō f
godly adj pius
godsend n quasi caelō dēmissus
going n itiō f; (way) iter nt; (departure) profectiō f, discessus m
goitre n strūma nt
gold n aurum nt ♦ adj aureus
golden adj aureus; (hair) flāvus
gold leaf n bractea f
goldmine n aurāria f
goldsmith n aurārius m, aurifex m
good adj bonus, probus; (fit) idōneus, aptus; (considerable) magnus; ~ **day!** salvē, salvēte!; ~ **looks** fōrma f, pulchritūdō f; ~ **nature** facilitās f, cōmitās f ♦ n bonum nt, commodum nt; **do ~ to** prōdesse (dat); **make ~** supplēre, praestāre; **seem ~** vidērī ♦ interj bene
goodbye interj valē, valēte; **say ~ to** valēre iubēre
good-for-nothing adj nēquam
good-humoured adj cōmis
good-looking adj pulcher
goodly adj pulcher; (size) amplus
good nature n facilitās f, cōmitās f
good-natured adj facilis, benīgnus, benevolus
goodness n bonitās f; (character) virtūs f, probitās f, pietās f
goods npl bona ntpl, rēs f; (for sale) merx f
good-tempered adj mītis, lēnis
goodwill n benevolentia f, favor m, grātia f
goose n ānser m/f
goose flesh n horror m
gore n cruor m ♦ vt cornibus cōnfodere
gorge n faucēs fpl, gula f; (GEOG) angustiae fpl ♦ vt: ~ **oneself** sē ingurgitāre
gorgeous adj lautus, splendidus
gorgeously adv lautē, splendidē
gorgeousness n lautitia f
gormandize vi helluārī
gory adj cruentus
gospel n ēvangelium nt
gossip n (talk) sermunculus m, rūmusculus m, fāma f; (person) lingulāca f ♦ vi garrīre
gouge vt ēruere
gourd n cucurbita f
gourmand n helluō m, gāneō m
gout n podagra f, articulāris morbus m
gouty adj arthrīticus
govern vt (subjects) regere; (state) administrāre, gubernāre; (emotion) moderārī (dat), cohibēre
governess n ēducātrīx f

government n gubernātiō f, administrātiō f;
(*men*) magistrātūs mpl
governor n gubernātor m, moderātor m;
(*province*) prōcōnsul m, prōcūrātor m
gown n (*men*) toga f; (*women*) stola f
grab vt adripere, corripere
grace n grātia f, lepōs m, decor m; (*favour*) grātia f,
venia f; (*of gods*) pāx f; **be in the good graces of**
in grātiā esse apud (*acc*); **with a bad ~** invītus
♦ vt decorāre, ōrnāre
graceful adj decōrus, venustus, lepidus
gracefully adv venustē, lepidē
graceless adj illepidus, impudēns
gracious adj benīgnus, prōpitius, misericors
graciously adv benīgnē, līberāliter
graciousness n benīgnitās f, līberālitās f
gradation n gradus m
grade n gradus m
gradient n clīvus m
gradual adj lēnis
gradually adv gradātim, sēnsim, paulātim
graft n surculus m; (*POL*) ambitus m ♦ vt īnserere
grafting n īnsitiō f
grain n frūmentum nt; (*seed*) grānum nt; **against
the ~** invītā Minervā
grammar n grammatica f
grammarian n grammaticus m
granary n horreum nt
grand adj (*person*) amplus, illūstris, ēgregius;
(*way of life*) lautus, māgnificus; (*language*)
grandis, sublīmis
granddaughter n neptis f; **great ~** prōneptis f
grandeur n māiestās f, māgnificentia f; (*style*)
granditās f
grandfather n avus m; **great ~** proavus m; **great-
great-grandfather** abavus m; **of a ~** avītus
grandiloquence n māgniloquentia f
grandiloquent adj grandiloquus, tumidus
grandiose adj māgnificus
grandmother n avia f; **great ~** proavia f
grandson n nepōs m; **great ~** prōnepōs m
grant vt dare, concēdere, tribuere; (*admit*) fatērī
♦ n concessiō f
grape n ūva f
graphic adj expressus; **give a ~ account of** ante
oculōs ponere, oculīs subicere
grapnel n manus ferrea f, harpagō f
grapple vi luctārī
grappling iron n manus ferrea f
grasp vt prēnsāre, comprehendere; (*with mind*)
complectī, adsequī, percipere, intellegere; **~ at**
captāre, adpetere ♦ n manus f, comprehēnsiō f;
(*mind*) captus m
grasping adj avārus, rapāx
grass n herba f
grasshopper n gryllus m
grassy adj herbōsus; herbidus
grate n focus m ♦ vt atterere; **~ upon** offendere
grateful adj grātus; **feel ~** grātiam habēre
gratefully adv grātē
gratification n voluptās f
gratify vt mōrem gerere (*dat*), mōrigerārī (*dat*),
grātificārī (*dat*)
gratifying adj iūcundus
gratis adv grātuītō, grātīs
gratitude n grātia f; **show ~** grātiam referre

gratuitous adj grātuītus
gratuitously adv grātuītō
gratuity n stips f; (*MIL*) dōnātīvum nt
grave n sepulchrum nt ♦ adj gravis, austērus ♦ vt
scalpere
gravel n glārea f
gravely adv graviter, sevērē
gravitate vi vergere
gravity n (*person*) sevēritās f, tristitia f;
(*circumstances*) gravitās f, mōmentum nt; (*physics*)
nūtus m; **by force of ~** nūtū suō
gray adj rāvus; (*hair*) cānus
graze vi pāscī ♦ vt (*cattle*) pāscere; (*by touch*)
stringere
grazing n pāstus m
grease n arvīna f ♦ vt ungere
greasy adj pinguis, ūnctus
great adj māgnus, grandis, ingēns, amplus;
(*fame*) īnsignis, praeclārus; **as ~ as ... tantus ...
quantus; ~ deal** plūrimum; **~ many** plūrimī;
how ~ quantus; **very ~** permāgnus
greatcoat n lacerna f
greatest adj māximus
greatly adv multum, māgnopere
greave n ocrea f
greed n avāritia f
greedily adv avārē, cupidē
greedy adj avārus, cupidus; avidus
Greek adj Graecus
green adj viridis; (*unripe*) crūdus; **be ~** virēre
greenness n viriditās f
greens n olus nt
greet vt salūtāre
greeting n salūs f, salūtātiō f
grey adj rāvus; (*hair*) cānus
greyhound n vertagus m
grief n dolor m, maeror m, lūctus m; **come to
~** perīre
grievance n querimōnia f; iniūria f
grieve vi dolēre, maerēre, lūgēre
grievous adj tristis, lūctuōsus; molestus, gravis,
acerbus
grievously adv graviter, valdē
grim adj trux, truculentus; atrōx
grimace n ōris dēprāvātiō f; **make a ~ ōs dūcere**
grime n sordēs f, lutum nt
grimy adj sordidus, lutulentus
grin n rīsus m ♦ vi adrīdēre
grind vt contundere; (*corn*) molere; (*blade*) acuere;
~ down (*fig*) opprimere
grindstone n cōs f
grip vt comprehendere, arripere ♦ n
comprehēnsiō f; **come to grips with** in
complexum venīre (*gen*)
gripe n tormina ntpl
grisly adj horridus, dīrus
grist n (*fig*) ēmolumentum nt
grit n harēna f
groan n gemitus m ♦ vi gemere, ingemere
groin n inguen nt
groom n agāsō m
groove n canālis m, stria f
grope vi praetentāre
gross adj crassus, pinguis; (*morally*) turpis,
foedus
grossly adv foedē, turpiter; (*very*) valdē

grossness n crassitūdō f; turpitūdō f
grotto n spēlunca f, antrum nt
ground n (bottom) solum nt; (earth) terra f, humus f; (cause) ratiō f, causa f; (sediment) faex f; **on the ~** humī; **on the grounds that** quod (subj); **to the ~** humum; **gain ~** prōficere; (rumour) incrēbrēscere; **lose ~** cēdere; (MIL) inclīnāre ◆ vt īnstituere ◆ vi (ship) sīdere
grounding n īnstitūtiō f
groundless adj vānus, inānis
groundlessly adv frustrā, temerē
grounds n faex f; (property) praedium nt; (reason) causa f; **I have good ~ for doing** nōn sine causā faciō, iūstīs dē causīs faciō
groundwork n fundāmentum nt
group n globus m, circulus m ◆ vt dispōnere
grouse n (bird) tetraō m; (complaint) querēla f ◆ vi querī
grove n nemus nt, lūcus m
grovel vi serpere, sē prōsternere, sē advolvere
grovelling adj humilis, abiectus
grow vi crēscere, glīscere; (spread) percrēbrēscere; (become) fierī; **~ old** (con)senēscere; **~ up** adolēscere, pūbēscere; **let ~** (hair) prōmittere ◆ vt (crops) colere; (beard) dēmittere
growl n fremitus m ◆ vi fremere
grown-up adj adultus, grandis
growth n incrēmentum nt, auctus m
grub n vermiculus m
grudge n invidia f ◆ vt invidēre (dat); (thing) gravārī
grudgingly adv invītus, gravātē
gruesome adj taeter
gruff adj acerbus, asper
grumble vi querī, mussāre ◆ n querēla f
grumpy adj mōrōsus, querulus
grunt n grunnītus m ◆ vi grunnīre
guarantee n (money) spōnsiō f; (promise) fidēs f; (person) praes m ◆ vt spondēre, praestāre
guarantor n spōnsor m
guard n custōdia f, praesidium nt; (person) custōs m; **on ~** in statiōne; **be on one's ~** cavēre; **keep ~** statiōnem agere; **off one's ~** imprūdēns, inopīnāns; **be taken off one's ~** dē gradū dēicī ◆ vt custōdīre, dēfendere; (keep) cōnservāre; **~ against** cavēre
guarded adj cautus
guardedly adv cautē

guardhouse n custōdia f
guardian n custōs m; (of minors) tūtor m
guardianship n custōdia f, tūtēla f
guardian spirit n genius m
gudgeon n gōbius m
guerdon n praemium nt, mercēs f
guess n coniectūra f ◆ vt dīvīnāre, conicere
guest n hospes m, hospita f; (at dinner) convīva m; **uninvited ~** umbra f; **guest's** hospitālis
guffaw n cachinnus m ◆ vi cachinnāre
guidance n moderātiō f; **under the ~ of God** dūcente deō
guide n dux m, ductor m; (in policy) auctor m ◆ vt dūcere; (steer) regere; (control) moderārī
guild n collēgium nt
guile n dolus m, fraus f
guileful adj dolōsus, fraudulentus
guilefully adv dolōsē
guileless adj simplex, innocēns
guilelessly adv sine fraude
guilt n culpa f, scelus nt
guiltless adj innocēns, īnsōns
guiltlessly adv integrē
guilty adj nocēns, sōns; **find ~** damnāre
guise n speciēs f
guitar n fidēs fpl; **play the ~** fidibus canere
gulf n sinus m; (chasm) hiātus m
gull n mergus m ◆ vt dēcipere
gullet n gula f, guttur nt
gullible adj crēdulus
gulp vt dēvorāre, haurīre
gum n gummī nt; (mouth) gingīva f
gumption n prūdentia f
gurgle vi singultāre
gush vi sē prōfundere, ēmicāre ◆ n scatūrīginēs fpl
gust n flāmen nt, impetus m
gusto n studium nt
gusty adj ventōsus
gut n intestīnum nt ◆ vt exenterāre; (fig) extergēre
gutter n canālis m
guzzle vi sē ingurgitāre
gymnasium n gymnasium nt, palaestra f; **head of a ~** gymnasiarchus m
gymnastic adj gymnicus; **gymnastics** pl palaestra f
gyrate vi volvī

Hh

habit n mōs m, cōnsuētūdō f; (dress) habitus m, vestītus m; **be in the ~ of** solēre

habitable adj habitābilis

habitation n domus f, domicilium nt; (place) sēdēs f

habitual adj ūsitātus

habitually adv ex mōre, persaepe

habituate vt adsuēfacere, īnsuēscere

hack vt caedere, concīdere ♦ n (horse) caballus m

hackneyed adj trītus

Hades n īnferī mpl

haft n manubrium nt

hag n anus f

haggard adj ferus

haggle vi altercārī

hail n grandō f ♦ vi: **it hails** grandinat ♦ vt salūtāre, adclāmāre ♦ interj avē, avēte; salvē, salvēte; **I ~ from Rome** Rōma mihi patria est

hair n capillus m; crīnis m; (single) pīlus m; (animals) sēta f, villus nt; **deviate a hair's breadth from** trānsversum digitum discēdere ab; **split hairs** cavillārī

hairdresser n tōnsor m

hairless adj (head) calvus; (body) glaber

hairpin n crīnāle nt

hairsplitting adj captiōsus ♦ n cavillātiō f

hairy adj pīlōsus

halberd n bipennis f

halcyon n alcēdō f; **~ days** alcēdōnia ntpl

hale adj validus, rōbustus ♦ vt trahere, rapere

half n dīmidium nt, dīmidia pars f ♦ adj dīmidius, dīmidiātus; **~ as much again** sesquī; **well begun is ~ done** dīmidium factī quī coepit habet

half-asleep adj sēmisomnus

half-baked adj (fig) rudis

half-dead adj sēmianimis, sēmivīvus

half-full adj sēmiplēnus

half-hearted adj incūriōsus, sōcors

half-heartedly adv sine studiō

half-hour n sēmihōra f

half-moon n lūna dīmidiāta f

half-open adj sēmiapertus

half pound n sēlībra f

half-way adj medius; **~ up the hill** in mediō colle

half-yearly adj sēmestris

hall n ātrium nt; (public) exedra f

hallo interj heus

hallow vt sacrāre

hallucination n error m, somnium nt

halo n corōna f

halt vi īnsistere, cōnsistere ♦ vt sistere ♦ n: **come to a ~** cōnsistere, agmen cōnstituere ♦ adj claudus

halter n capistrum nt; (fig) laqueus m

halve vt bipartīre

ham n perna f

hamlet n vīcus m

hammer n malleus m ♦ vt tundere; **~ out** excūdere

hamper n corbis f ♦ vt impedīre; (with debt) obstringere

hamstring vt poplitem succīdere (dat)

hand n manus f; **left ~** laeva f, sinistra f; **right ~** dextra f; **an old ~** veterātor m; **at ~** praestō, ad manum; **be at ~** adesse; **at first ~** ipse; **at second ~** ab aliō; **on the one ~ ... on the other** et ... et, quidem ... at; **near at ~** in expedītō, inibī; **the matter in ~** quod nunc īnstat, quae in manibus sunt; **get out of ~** lascīvīre; **have a ~ in** interesse (dat); **have one's hands full** satis agere; **lay hands on** manum adferre, inicere (dat); **live from ~ to mouth** ad hōram vīvere; **pass from ~ to ~** per manūs trādere; **take in ~** suscipere; **hands** pl (workmen) operae fpl ♦ vt trādere, porrigere; **~ down** trādere, prōdere; **~ over** dēferre, reddere

handbill n libellus m

handbook n ars f

handcuffs n manicae fpl

handful n manipulus m

handicap n impedīmentum nt

handicraft n artificium nt, ars operōsa f

handily adv habiliter

handiness n habilitās f; commoditās f

handiwork n opus nt, manus f

handkerchief n sūdārium nt

handle n (cup) ānsa f; (knife) manubrium nt; (fig) ānsa f, occāsiō f ♦ vt tractāre

handling n tractātiō f

handmaid n famula f

handsome adj fōrmōsus, pulcher; (gift) līberālis

handsomely adv pulchrē; līberāliter

handsomeness n pulchritūdō f, fōrma f

hand-to-hand adv: **fight ~** manum cōnserere, comminus pugnāre

handwriting n manus f

handy adj (to use) habilis; (near) praestō

hang vt suspendere; (head) dēmittere; (wall) vestīre ♦ vi pendēre; **~ back** gravārī, dubitāre; **~ down** dēpendēre; **~ on to** haerēre (dat); **~ over** imminēre (dat), impendēre (dat); **go and be hanged** abī in malam crucem!

hanger-on n cliēns m/f, assecla m/f
hanging n (death) suspendium nt; **hangings** pl
aulaea ntpl ♦ adj pendulus
hangman n carnifex m
hanker vi: ~ **after** appetere, exoptāre
hap n fors f
haphazard adj fortuītus
hapless adj miser, īnfēlīx
haply adv fortasse
happen vi accidere, ēvenīre, contingere; (become)
fierī; **as usually happens** ut fit; ~ **upon**
incidere in (acc); **it happens that** accidit ut
(subj)
happily adv fēlīciter, beātē, bene
happiness n fēlīcitās f
happy adj fēlīx, beātus; laetus; (in some respect)
fortūnātus
harangue n cōntiō f ♦ vt cōntiōnārī apud (acc),
hortārī
harass vt vexāre, lacessere, exagitāre, sollicitāre
harassing adj molestus
harbinger n praenūntius m
harbour n portus m ♦ vt recipere
harbour dues n portōria ntpl
hard adj dūrus; (circumstances) asper, inīquus;
(task) difficilis, arduus; ~ **of hearing** surdaster;
grow ~ dūrēscere ♦ adv sēdulō, valdē; ~ **by**
prope, iuxtā; **I am** ~ **put to it to do** aegerrimē
faciō
hard cash n praesēns pecūnia f
harden vt dūrāre ♦ vi dūrēscere; (fig)
obdūrēscere; **become hardened** obdūrēscere
hard-fought adj atrōx
hard-hearted adj crūdēlis, dūrus, inhūmānus
hardihood n audācia f
hardily adv sevērē
hardiness n rōbur nt; dūritia f
hardly adv vix, aegrē; (severely) dūriter, acerbē;
~ **any** nullus ferē
hardness n dūritia f; (fig) asperitās f, inīquitās f;
(difficulty) difficultās f; ~ **of hearing** surditās f
hard-pressed adj: **be** ~ labōrāre
hardship n labor m, malum nt, iniūria f
hard-working adj industrius, nāvus, sēdulus
hardy adj dūrus, rōbustus, sevērus
hare n lepus m
hark interj auscultā, auscultāte ♦ vi: ~ **back to**
repetere
harm n iniūria f, damnum nt, malum nt,
dētrīmentum nt; **come to** ~ dētrīmentum
capere, accipere ♦ vt laedere, nocēre (dat)
harmful adj damnōsus, noxius
harmfully adv male
harmless adj innocēns
harmlessly adv innocenter; (escape) salvus,
incolumis, inviolātus
harmonious adj cōnsonus, canōrus; (fig)
concors; (things) congruēns
harmoniously adv modulātē; concorditer;
convenienter
harmonize vi concinere, cōnsentīre, congruere
harmony n concentus m; (fig) concordia f,
cōnsēnsus m
harness n arma ntpl ♦ vt īnfrēnāre, iungere
harp n fidēs fpl; **play the** ~ fidibus canere ♦ vi:
~ **on** (fig) cantāre, dictitāre; **be always harping**

on the same thing cantilēnam eandem
canere
harpist n fidicen m, fidicina f
harpoon n iaculum nt
harpy n Harpyia f
harrow n rāstrum nt ♦ vt occāre
harrower n occātor m
harrowing adj horrendus
harry vt vexāre, dīripere
harsh adj dūrus, acerbus, asper; (person)
inclēmēns, sevērus
harshly adv acerbē, asperē; sevērē
harshness n acerbitās f, asperitās f; crūdēlitās f
hart n cervus m
harvest n messis f ♦ vt metere, dēmetere
harvester n messor m
hash n farrāgō f ♦ vt comminuere
haste n festīnātiō f, properātiō f; **in**
~ festīnanter; **in hot** ~ incitātus; **make**
~ festīnāre
hasten vt mātūrāre, adcelerāre ♦ vi festīnāre,
properāre, mātūrāre
hastily adv properē, raptim; temerē, incōnsulte;
īrācundē
hastiness n temeritās f; (temper) īrācundia f
hasty adj properus, celer; (action) incōnsultus,
temerārius; (temper) īrācundus, ācer; **over**
~ praeproperus
hat n petasus m
hatch vt exclūdere, parere
hatchet n dolābra f
hate n odium nt, invidia f ♦ vt ōdisse
hated adj: **to be** ~ (by sb) odiō esse (dat)
hateful adj odiōsus, invīsus
hatefully adv odiōsē
hatred n odium nt
haughtily adv adroganter, superbē, insolenter
haughtiness n fastus m, adrogantia f, superbia f
haughty adj adrogāns, superbus, īnsolēns
haul vt trahere ♦ n bolus m
haulage n vectūra f
haulm n culmus m
haunch n femur nt
haunt vt frequentāre ♦ n locus m; (animals)
lustrum nt
have vt habēre, tenēre; (get done) cūrāre (with
gerundive); **I** ~ **a house** est mihī domus; **I** ~ **to**
go mihī abeundum est; ~ **it out with** rem
dēcernere cum; ~ **on** gerere, gestāre, induī; **I**
had better go melius est īre, praestat īre; **I had**
rather mālim, māllem
haven n portus m; (fig) perfugium nt
havoc n exitium nt, vastātiō f, ruīna f
hawk n accipiter m ♦ vt (wares) circumferre
hawker n īnstitor m
hay n faenum nt; **make hay while the sun**
shines forō ūtī
hazard n perīculum nt, discrīmen nt, ālea f ♦ vt
perīclitārī, in āleam dare
hazardous adj perīculōsus
haze n nebula f
hazel n corylus f
hazy adj nebulōsus; (fig) incertus
he pron hic, ille, is
head n caput nt; (person) dux m, prīnceps
m; (composition) caput nt; (mind) animus m,

79

ingenium *nt*; ~ **over heels** cernuus; **off one's ~ dēmēns**; **be at the ~ of** dūcere, praeesse (*dat*); **come to a ~** caput facere; (*fig*) in discrīmen addūcī; **give one his ~** indulgēre (*dat*), habēnās immittere (*dat*); **keep one's ~** praesentī animō ūtī; **lose one's ~** suī compotem nōn esse; **shake one's ~** abnuere ◆ *vt* dūcere, praeesse (*dat*); ~ **off** intercipere ◆ *vi* (*in a direction*) tendere

headache *n* capitis dolor *m*

headfirst *adj* praeceps

heading *n* caput *nt*

headland *n* prōmontōrium *nt*

headlong *adj* praeceps ◆ *adv* in praeceps; **rush ~** sē praecipitāre

headquarters *n* (MIL) praetōrium *nt*

headship *n* prīncipātus *m*

headsman *n* carnifex *m*

headstrong *adj* impotēns, pervicāx

headway *n* prōfectus *m*

heady *adj* incōnsultus; (*wine*) vehemēns

heal *vt* sānāre, medērī (*dat*) ◆ *vi* sānēscere; ~ **over** obdūcī

healer *n* medicus *m*

healing *adj* salūbris

health *n* valētūdō *f*, salūs *f*; **state of ~** valētūdō *f*; **ill ~** valētūdō *f*; **be in good ~** valēre; **drink the ~ of** propīnāre (*dat*)

healthful *adj* salūbris

healthiness *n* sānitās *f*

healthy *adj* sānus, integer; (*conditions*) salūber

heap *n* acervus *m*, cumulus *m*; **in heaps** acervātim ◆ *vt* acervāre; ~ **together** congerere; ~ **up** adcumulāre, coacervāre, congerere

hear *vt* audīre, (*case*) cognōscere; ~ **clearly** exaudīre; ~ **in secret** inaudīre

hearer *n* audītor *m*

hearing *n* (*sense*) audītus *m*; (*act*) audītiō *f*; (*of case*) cognitiō *f*; **get a ~** sibī audientiam facere; **hard of ~** surdaster; **without a ~** indictā causā

hearken *vi* auscultāre

hearsay *n* fāma *f*, rūmor *m*

heart *n* cor *nt*; (*emotion*) animus *m*, pectus *nt*; (*courage*) animus *m*; (*interior*) viscera *ntpl*; **by ~** memoriā, memoriter; **learn by ~** ēdiscere; **the ~ of the matter** rēs ipsa; **lose ~** animum dēspondēre; **take to ~** graviter ferre

heartache *n* dolor *m*, angor *m*

heartbroken *adj* animī frāctus, aeger; **be ~** animō labōrāre

heartburning *n* invidia *f*

heartfelt *adj* sincērus

hearth *n* focus *m*; ~ **and home** ārae et focī

heartily *adv* vehementer, valdē

heartiness *n* studium *nt*, vigor *m*

heartless *adj* dūrus, inhūmānus, crūdēlis

heartlessly *adv* inhūmānē

heartlessness *n* inhūmānitās *f*, crūdēlitās *f*

hearty *adj* studiōsus, vehemēns; (*health*) rōbustus; (*feeling*) sincērus

heat *n* ārdor *m*, calor *m*; (*emotion*) ārdor *m*, aestus *m*; (*race*) missus *m* ◆ *vt* calefacere, fervefacere; (*fig*) accendere; **become heated** incalēscere

heatedly *adv* ferventer, ārdenter

heath *n* inculta loca *ntpl*

heathcock *n* attagēn *m*

heathen *n* pāgānus *m*

heather *n* erīcē *f*

heave *vt* tollere; (*missile*) conicere; (*sigh*) dūcere ◆ *vi* tumēre, fluctuāre

heaven *n* caelum *nt*, dī *mpl*; ~ **forbid!** dī meliōra; **from ~** dīvīnitus; **in heaven's name** prō deum fidem!; **be in seventh ~** digitō caelum attingere

heavenly *adj* caelestis, dīvīnus

heavily *adv* graviter

heaviness *n* gravitās *f*, pondus *nt*; (*of spirit*) maestitia *f*

heavy *adj* gravis; (*air*) crassus; (*spirit*) maestus; (*shower*) māgnus, dēnsus

heckle *vt* interpellāre

heckler *n* interpellātor *m*

hectic *adj* violēns, ācer, fervidus

hector *vt* obstrepere (*dat*)

hedge *n* saepēs *f* ◆ *vt* saepīre; ~ **off** intersaepīre ◆ *vi* tergiversārī

hedgehog *n* echīnus *m*, ēricius *m*

heed *vt* cūrāre, respicere ◆ *n* cūra *f*, opera *f*; **pay ~** animum attendere; **take ~** cavēre

heedful *adj* attentus, cautus, dīligēns

heedfully *adv* attentē, cautē

heedfulness *n* cūra *f*, dīligentia *f*

heedless *adj* incautus, immemor, neglegēns

heedlessly *adv* incautē, neglegenter, temerē

heedlessness *n* neglegentia *f*

heel *n* calx *f*; **take to one's heels** sē in pedēs conicere ◆ *vi* sē inclīnāre

hegemony *n* prīncipātus *m*

heifer *n* būcula *f*

height *n* altitūdō *f*; (*person*) prōcēritās *f*; (*hill*) collis *m*, iugum *nt*; (*fig*) fastīgium *nt*; **the ~ of** summus

heighten *vt* augēre, exaggerāre

heinous *adj* atrōx, nefārius

heinously *adv* atrōciter, nefāriē

heinousness *n* atrōcitās *f*

heir *n* hērēs *m*; **sole ~** hērēs ex asse

heiress *n* hērēs *f*

heirship *n* hērēditās *f*

hell *n* Tartarus *m*, īnfernī *mpl*

hellish *adj* īnfernus, scelestus

helm *n* gubernāculum *nt*, clāvus *m*

helmet *n* galea *f*

helmsman *n* gubernātor *m*

helots *n* Hīlōtae *mpl*

help *n* auxilium *nt*, subsidium *nt*; **I am a ~** auxiliō sum ◆ *vt* iuvāre (*acc*), auxiliārī, subvenīre (*dat*), succurrere (*dat*) ◆ *vi* prōdesse; **I cannot ~** facere nōn possum quīn (*subj*); **it can't be helped** fierī nōn potest aliter; **so ~ me God** ita mē dī ament

helper *n* adiūtor *m*, adiūtrix *f*

helpful *adj* ūtilis; **be ~ to** auxiliō esse (*dat*)

helpless *adj* inops

helplessness *n* inopia *f*

hem *n* ōra *f*, limbus *m* ◆ *vt*: **hem in** interclūdere, circumsedēre

hemlock *n* cicūta *f*

hemp *n* cannabis *f*

hen *n* gallīna *f*

hence *adv* hinc; (*consequence*) igitur, ideō

henceforth, **henceforward** *adv* dehinc, posthāc, ex hōc tempore

her *adj* suus, ēius
herald *n* praecō *m*; (POL) fētiālis *m* ♦ *vt* praenūntiāre
herb *n* herba *f*, olus *nt*
herbage *n* herbae *fpl*
herd *n* pecus *nt*; grex *f*, armentum *nt* ♦ *vi* congregārī
herdsman *n* pāstor *m*
here *adv* hīc; **be ~** adesse; **~ and there** passim; **~ ... there** alibī ... alibī; **from ~** hinc; **~ is ...** ecce (*acc*) ...
hereabouts *adv* hīc ferē
hereafter *adv* posthāc, posteā
hereat *adv* hīc
hereby *adv* ex hōc, hinc
hereditary *adj* hērēditārius, patrius
heredity *n* genus *nt*
herein *adv* hīc
hereinafter *adv* īnfrā
hereof *adv* ēius reī
hereupon *adv* hīc, quō factō
herewith *adv* cum hōc, ūnā
heritable *adj* hērēditārius
heritage *n* hērēditās *f*
hermaphrodite *n* androgynus *m*
hermit *n* homō sōlitārius *m*
hero *n* vir fortissimus *m*; (*demigod*) hērōs *m*
heroic *adj* fortissimus, māgnanimus; (*epic*) hērōicus; (*verse*) hērōus
heroically *adv* fortissimē, audācissimē
heroism *n* virtūs *f*, fortitūdō *f*
heron *n* ardea *f*
hers *pron* suus, ēius
herself *pron* ipsa *f*; (*reflexive*) sē
hesitancy *n* dubitātiō *f*
hesitant *adj* incertus, dubius
hesitate *vi* dubitāre, haesitāre
hesitating *adj* dubius
hesitatingly *adv* cunctanter
hesitation *n* dubitātiō *f*; **with ~** dubitanter
heterogeneous *adj* dīversus, aliēnigenus
hew *vt* dolāre, caedere; **hew down** excīdere, interscindere
hexameter *n* hexameter *m*
heyday *n* flōs *m*
hiatus *n* hiātus *m*
hiccup *n* singultus *m* ♦ *vi* singultīre
hide *vt* cēlāre, abdere, abscondere, occultāre; **~ away** abstrūdere; **~ from** cēlāre (*acc*) ♦ *vi* sē abdere, latēre; **~ away** dēlitēscere ♦ *n* pellis *f*, corium *nt*
hideous *adj* foedus, dēfōrmis, turpis
hideously *adv* foedē
hideousness *n* foeditās *f*, dēfōrmitās *f*
hiding *n* (*place*) latebra *f*
hierarchy *n* ōrdinēs *mpl*
high *adj* altus, excelsus; (*ground*) ēditus; (*pitch*) acūtus; (*rank*) amplus; (*price*) cārus; (*tide*) māximus; (*wind*) māgnus; **~ living** luxuria *f*; **~ treason** māiestās *f*; **~ and mighty** superbus; **on ~** sublīmis ♦ *adv* altē
highborn *adj* nōbilis, generōsus
high-class *adj* (*goods*) lautus
high-flown *adj* īnflātus, tumidus
high-handed *adj* superbus, īnsolēns
high-handedly *adv* superbē, licenter

high-handedness *n* licentia *f*, superbia *f*
highland *adj* montānus
highlander *n* montānus *m*
highlands *npl* montāna *ntpl*
highly *adv* (*value*) māgnī; (*intensity*) valdē
highly-strung *adj* trepidus
high-minded *adj* generōsus
high-spirited *adj* ferōx, animōsus
highway *n* via *f*
highwayman *n* grassātor *m*, latrō *m*
hilarious *adj* festīvus, hilaris
hilariously *adv* festīvē, hilare
hilarity *n* festīvitās *f*, hilaritās *f*
hill *n* collis *m*, mōns *m*; (*slope*) clīvus *m*
hillock *n* tumulus *m*
hilly *adj* montuōsus, clīvōsus
hilt *n* manubrium *nt*, capulus *m*
himself *pron* ipse; (*reflexive*) sē
hind *n* cerva *f*
hinder *vt* impedīre, obstāre (*dat*), morārī
hindmost *adj* postrēmus; (*in column*) novissimus
hindrance *n* impedīmentum *nt*, mora *f*
hinge *n* cardō *f*
hint *n* indicium *nt*, suspiciō *f*; **throw out a ~** inicere ♦ *vt* subicere, significāre
hip *n* coxendīx *f*
hippodrome *n* spatium *nt*
hire *vt* condūcere; **~ out** locāre ♦ *n* conductiō *f*, locātiō *f*; (*wages*) mercēs *f*
hired *adj* mercennārius, conductus
hireling *n* mercennārius *m*
hirsute *adj* hirsūtus
his *adj* suus, ēius
hiss *vi* sībilāre ♦ *vt*: **~ off stage** explōdere, exsībilāre ♦ *n* sībilus *m*
historian *n* historicus *m*, rērum scrīptor *m*
historical *adj* historicus
history *n* historia *f*; **the ~ of Rome** rēs Rōmānae *fpl*; **since the beginning of ~** post hominum memoriam; **ancient ~** antīquitās *f*
histrionic *adj* scaenicus
hit *n* ictus *m*, plāga *f*; **a hit!** (*in duel*) habet! ♦ *vt* ferīre, icere, percutere; **hit against** offendere; **hit upon** invenīre
hitch *n* mora *f* ♦ *vt* implicāre; **~ up** succingere
hither *adv* hūc; **~ and thither** hūc illūc ♦ *adj* citerior
hitherto *adv* adhūc, hāctenus, hūcusque
hive *n* alveārium *nt*
hoar *adj* cānus ♦ *n* pruīna *f*
hoard *n* thēsaurus *m*, acervus *m* ♦ *vt* condere, recondere
hoarfrost *n* pruīna *f*
hoarse *adj* raucus, fuscus
hoarsely *adv* raucā vōce
hoary *adj* cānus
hoax *n* fraus *f*, fallācia *f*, lūdus *m* ♦ *vt* dēcipere, fallere
hobble *vi* claudicāre
hobby *n* studium *nt*
hob-nob *vi* familiāriter ūtī (*abl*)
hocus-pocus *n* trīcae *fpl*
hoe *n* sarculum *nt* ♦ *vt* sarrīre
hog *n* sūs *m*, porcus *m*; **hog's** porcīnus
hogshead *n* dōlium *nt*
hoist *vt* tollere; (*sail*) vēla dare

hold n (*grasp*) comprehēnsiō f; (*power*) potestās f; (*ship*) alveus m; **gain a ~ over** obstringere, sibi dēvincīre; **get ~ of** potīrī (*abl*); **keep ~ of** retinēre; **lose ~ of** ōmittere; **take ~ of** prehendere, comprehendere ◆ vt tenēre, habēre; (*possession*) obtinēre, possidēre; (*office*) gerere, fungī (*abl*); (*capacity*) capere; (*meeting*) habēre; **~ a meeting** concilium habēre; **~ one's own with** parem esse (*dat*); **~ over** differre, prōlātāre; **~ water** (*fig*) stāre ◆ vi manēre, dūrāre; (*opinion*) dūcere, existimāre, adfirmāre; **~ back** vt retinēre, inhibēre ◆ vi gravārī, dubitāre; **~ cheap** parvī facere; **~ fast** vt retinēre, amplectī ◆ vi haerēre; **~ good** valēre; **~ out** vt porrigere, extendere; (*hope*) ostendere ◆ vi dūrāre, perstāre; **~ together** cohaerēre; **~ up** tollere; (*falling*) sustinēre; (*movement*) obstāre (*dat*), morārī; **~ with** adsentīre (*dat*)
holdfast n fībula f
holding n (*land*) agellus m
hole n forāmen nt, cavum nt; **make a ~ in** pertundere, perforāre
holiday n ōtium nt; festus diēs m; **on ~** fēriātus; **holidays** pl fēriae fpl
holily adv sanctē
holiness n sanctitās f
hollow adj cavus, concavus; (*fig*) inānis, vānus ◆ n cavum nt, caverna f ◆ vt excavāre
hollowness n (*fig*) vānitās f
holly n aquifolium nt
holy adj sanctus
homage n observantia f, venerātiō f; **pay ~ to** venerārī, colere
home n domus f; (*town, country*) patria f; **at ~** domī; **from ~** domō ◆ adj domesticus ◆ adv domum
homeless adj profugus
homely adj simplex, rūsticus; (*speech*) plēbēius
homestead n fundus m
homewards adv domum
homicide n (*act*) homicīdium nt, caedēs f; (*person*) homicīda m
homily n sermō m
homogeneous adj aequābilis
homologous adj cōnsimilis
hone n cōs f ◆ vt acuere
honest adj probus, frūgī, integer
honestly adv probē, integrē
honesty n probitās f, fidēs f
honey n mel nt
honeycomb n favus m
honeyed adj mellītus, mulsus
honorarium n stips f
honorary adj honōrārius
honour n honōs m; (*repute*) honestās f; existimātiō f; (*chastity*) pudor m; (*trust*) fidēs f; (*rank*) dignitās f; (*award*) decus nt, īnsigne nt; (*respect*) observantia f ◆ vt honōrāre, decorāre; (*respect*) observāre, colere; **do ~ to** honestāre
honourable adj honestus, probus; (*rank*) illūstris, praeclārus
honourably adv honestē
hood n cucullus m
hoodwink vt verba dare (*dat*)
hoof n ungula f
hook n uncus m, hāmus m ◆ vt hāmō capere

hooked adj aduncus, hāmātus
hoop n circulus m; (*toy*) trochus m
hoot vi obstrepere; **~ off** (*stage*) explōdere
hop n saltus m; **catch on the hop** in ipsō articulō opprimere ◆ vi salīre
hope n spēs f; **in the ~ that** sī forte; **give up ~** spem dēpōnere, dēspērāre; **past ~** dēspērātus; **entertain hopes** spem habēre ◆ vt spērāre
hopeful adj bonae speī; **be ~** aliquam spem habēre
hopefully adv nōn sine spē
hopeless adj dēspērātus
hopelessly adv dēspēranter
hopelessness n dēspērātiō f
horde n multitūdō f
horizon n fīniēns m
horizontal adj aequus, lībrātus
horizontally adv ad lībram
horn n cornū nt; (*shepherd's*) būcina f
horned adj corniger
hornet n crabrō m; **stir up a hornet's nest** crabrōnēs inrītāre
horny adj corneus
horoscope n sīdus nātālicium nt
horrible adj horrendus, horribilis, dīrus, foedus
horribly adv foedē
horrid adj horribilis
horrify vt terrēre, perterrēre
horror n horror m, terror m; odium nt
horse n equus m; (*cavalry*) equitēs mpl; **flog a dead ~** asellum currere docēre; **spur a willing ~** currentem incitāre; **horse's** equīnus
horseback n: **ride on ~** in equō vehī; **fight on ~** ex equō pugnāre
horseman n eques m
horseradish n armoracia f
horse soldier n eques m
horticulture n hortōrum cultus m
hospitable adj hospitālis
hospitably adv hospitāliter
hospital n valētūdinārium nt
hospitality n hospitālitās f, hospitium nt
host n hospes m; (*inn*) caupō m; (*number*) multitūdō f; (*MIL*) exercitus m
hostage n obses m/f
hostelry n taberna f, dēversōrium nt
hostile adj hostīlis, īnfēnsus, inimīcus; īnfestus; **in a ~ manner** īnfēnsē, hostīliter, inimīcē
hostility n inimīcitia f; **hostilities** pl bellum nt
hot adj calidus, fervidus, aestuōsus; (*boiling*) fervēns; (*fig*) ārdēns; **be hot** calēre, fervēre, ārdēre; **get hot** calēscere
hotch-potch n farrāgō f
hotel n dēversōrium nt
hot-headed adj ārdēns, temerārius, praeceps
hotly adv ārdenter, ācriter
hot-tempered adj īrācundus
hot water n calida f
hound n canis m ◆ vt īnstāre (*dat*)
hour n hōra f
hourly adv in hōrās
house n domus f, aedēs fpl; (*country*) vīlla f; (*family*) domus f, gēns f; **at the ~ of** apud (*acc*); **full ~** frequēns senātus, frequēns theātrum ◆ vt hospitiō accipere, recipere; (*things*) condere

household n familia f, domus f ◆ adj familiāris, domesticus

householder n paterfamiliās m, dominus m

housekeeping n reī familiāris cūra f

housemaid n ancilla f

housetop n fastīgium nt

housewife n māterfamiliās f, domina f

housing n hospitium nt; (horse) ōrnāmenta ntpl

hovel n gurgustium nt

hover vi pendēre; (fig) impendēre

how adv (interrog) quemadmodum; quōmodō, quō pactō; (excl) quam; **how great/big/large** quantus; **how long** (time) quamdiū; **how many** quot; **how much** quantum; **how often** quotiēns

howbeit adv tamen

however adv tamen; autem, nihilōminus; utcumque, quōquō modō; ~ **much** quamvīs, quantumvīs; ~ **great** quantuscumque

howl n ululātus m ◆ vi ululāre; (wind) fremere

howsoever adv utcumque

hub n axis m

hubbub n tumultus m

huckster n īnstitor m, propōla m

huddle n turba f ◆ vi congregārī

hue n color m; **hue and cry** clāmor m

huff n offēnsiō f ◆ vt offendere

hug n complexus m ◆ vt complectī

huge adj ingēns, immānis, immēnsus, vastus

hugely adv vehementer

hugeness n immānitās f

hulk n alveus m

hull n alveus m

hum n murmur nt, fremitus m ◆ vi murmurāre, fremere

human adj hūmānus

human being n homō m/f

humane adj hūmānus, misericors

humanely adv hūmānē, hūmāniter

humanism n litterae fpl

humanist n homō litterātus m

humanity n hūmānitās f; misericordia f

humanize vt excolere

humanly adv hūmānitus

human nature n hūmānitās f

humble adj humilis, modestus ◆ vt dēprimere; (oneself) summittere

humbleness n humilitās f

humbly adv summissē, modestē

humbug n trīcae fpl

humdrum adj vulgāris; (style) pedester

humid adj ūmidus, madidus; **be** ~ madēre

humidity n ūmor m

humiliate vt dēprimere, dēdecorāre

humiliation n dēdecus nt

humility n modestia f, animus summissus m

humorist n homō facētus m

humorous adj facētus, ioculāris, rīdiculus

humorously adv facētē

humour n facētiae fpl; (disposition) ingenium nt; (mood) libīdō f; **be in a bad** ~ sibī displicēre ◆ vt indulgēre (dat), mōrem gerere (dat), mōrigerārī (dat)

hump n gibbus m

hunchback n gibber m

hundred num centum; ~ **each** centēnī; ~ **times** centiēns

hundredth adj centēsimus

hundredweight n centumpondium nt

hunger n famēs f ◆ vi ēsurīre

hungrily adv avidē

hungry adj ēsuriēns, iēiūnus, avidus; **be** ~ ēsurīre

hunt n vēnātiō f, vēnātus m ◆ vt vēnārī, indāgāre, exagitāre

hunter n vēnātor m

hunting n vēnātiō f; (fig) aucupium nt

hunting spear n vēnābulum nt

huntress n vēnātrix f

huntsman n vēnātor m

hurdle n crātēs f; (obstacle) obex m/f

hurl vt conicere, ingerere, iaculārī, iācere

hurly-burly n turba f, tumultus m

hurrah interj euax, iō

hurricane n procella f

hurried adj praeproperus, praeceps, trepidus

hurriedly adv properātō, cursim, festīnanter

hurry vt adcelerāre, mātūrāre ◆ vi festīnāre, properāre; ~ **along** vt rapere; ~ **away** vi discēdere, properāre; ~ **about** vi discurrere; ~ **on** vt mātūrāre; ~ **up** vi properāre ◆ n festīnātiō f; **in a** ~ festīnanter, raptim

hurt n iniūria f, damnum nt; vulnus nt ◆ vt laedere, nocēre (dat); **it hurts** dolet

hurtful adj nocēns, damnōsus

hurtfully adv nocenter, damnōsē

hurtle vi volāre; sē praecipitāre

husband n vir m, marītus m ◆ vt parcere (dat)

husbandry n agrī cultūra f; (economy) parsimōnia f

hush n silentium nt ◆ vt silentium facere (dat), lēnīre ◆ vi tacēre, silēre; ~ **up** comprimere, cēlāre ◆ interj st!

hushed adj tacitus

husk n folliculus m, siliqua f ◆ vt dēglūbāre

husky adj fuscus, raucus

hustle vt trūdere, īnstāre (dat)

hut n casa f, tugurium nt

hutch n cavea f

hyacinth n hyacinthus m

hybrid n hibrida m/f

hydra n hydra f

hyena n hyaena f

hygiene n salūbritās f

hygienic adj salūbris

hymeneal adj nūptiālis

hymn n carmen nt ◆ vt canere

hyperbole n superlātiō f

hypercritical adj Aristarchus m

hypocaust n hypocaustum nt

hypocrisy n simulātiō f, dissimulātiō f

hypocrite n simulātor m, dissimulātor m

hypocritical adj simulātus, fictus

hypothesis n positum nt, sūmptiō f, coniectūra f

hypothetical adj sūmptus

I i

I *pron* ego
iambic *adj* iambēus
iambus *n* iambus *m*
ice *n* glaciēs *f*
icicle *n* stīria *f*
icon *n* simulacrum *nt*
icy *adj* glaciālis, gelidus
idea *n* nōtiō *f*, nōtitia *f*, imāgō *f*; (*Platonic*) fōrma *f*; (*expressed*) sententia *f*; **conceive the ~ of** īnfōrmāre; **with the ~ that** eō consiliō ut (*subj*)
ideal *adj* animō comprehēnsus; (*perfect*) perfectus, optimus ◆ *n* specimen *nt*, speciēs *f*, exemplar *nt*
identical *adj* īdem, cōnsimilis
identify *vt* agnōscere
identity *n*: **establish the ~ of** cognōscere quis sit
Ides *n* Idūs *fpl*
idiocy *n* animī imbēcillitās *f*
idiom *n* proprium *nt*, sermō *m*
idiomatic *adj* proprius
idiomatically *adv* sermōne suō, sermōne propriō
idiosyncrasy *n* proprium *nt*, libīdō *f*
idiot *n* excors *m*
idiotic *adj* fatuus, stultus
idiotically *adv* stultē, ineptē
idle *adj* ignāvus, dēses, iners; (*unoccupied*) ōtiōsus, vacuus; (*useless*) inānis, vānus; **be ~** cessāre, dēsidēre; **lie ~** (*money*) iacēre ◆ *vi* cessāre
idleness *n* ignāvia *f*, dēsidia *f*, inertia *f*; ōtium *nt*
idler *n* cessātor *m*
idly *adv* ignāvē; ōtiōsē; frustrā, nēquīquam
idol *n* simulacrum *nt*; (*person*) dēliciae *fpl*
idolater *n* falsōrum deōrum cultor *m*
idolatry *n* falsōrum deōrum cultus *m*
idolize *vt* venerārī
idyll *n* carmen Theocrītēum *nt*
if *conj* sī; (*interrog*) num, utrum; **if anyone** sī quis; **if ever** sī quandō; **if not** nisī; **if only** dum, dummodo; **if … or** sīve … sīve; **as if** quasi, velut; **but if** sīn, quodsī; **even if** etiamsī
igneous *adj* igneus
ignite *vt* accendere, incendere ◆ *vi* ignem concipere
ignoble *adj* (*birth*) ignōbilis; (*repute*) illīberālis, turpis
ignominious *adj* ignōminiōsus, īnfāmis, turpis
ignominiously *adv* turpiter
ignominy *n* ignōminia *f*, īnfāmia *f*, dēdecus *nt*
ignoramus *n* idiōta *m*, indoctus *m*
ignorance *n* īnscītia *f*, ignōrātiō *f*

ignorant *adj* ignārus, indoctus; (*of something*) īnscītus, rudis; (*unaware*) īnscius; **be ~ of** nescīre, ignōrāre
ignorantly *adv* īnscienter, īnscītē, indoctē
ignore *vt* praetermittere
ilex *n* īlex *f*
Iliad *n* Ilias *f*
ill *adj* aeger, aegrōtus, invalidus; (*evil*) malus; **be ill** aegrōtāre; **fall ill** in morbum incidere; **ill at ease** sollicitus ◆ *adv* male, improbē ◆ *n* malum *nt*, incommodum *nt*, aerumna *f*, damnum *nt*
ill-advised *adj* incōnsultus
ill-bred *adj* agrestis, inurbānus
ill-disposed *adj* malevolus, invidus
illegal *adj* illicitus, vetitus
illegally *adv* contrā lēgēs
ill-fated *adj* īnfēlīx
ill-favoured *adj* turpis
ill-gotten *adj* male partus
ill-health *n* valētūdō *f*
illicit *adj* vetitus
illimitable *adj* īnfīnītus
illiteracy *n* litterārum īnscītia *f*
illiterate *adj* illitterātus, inērudītus
ill-natured *adj* malevolus, malignus
illness *n* morbus *m*, valētūdō *f*
illogical *adj* absurdus
ill-omened *adj* dīrus, īnfaustus
ill-starred *adj* īnfēlīx
ill-tempered *adj* īrācundus, amārus, stomachōsus
ill-timed *adj* immātūrus, intempestīvus
ill-treat *vt* malefacere (*dat*)
illuminate *vt* illūmināre, illūstrāre
illumination *n* lūmina *ntpl*
illusion *n* error *m*, somnium *nt*
illusive, illusory *adj* fallāx
illustrate *vt* illūstrāre; (*with instances*) exemplō cōnfīrmāre
illustration *n* exemplum *nt*
illustrious *adj* illūstris, īnsignis, praeclārus
illustriously *adv* praeclārē
ill will *n* invidia *f*
image *n* imāgō *f*, effigiēs *f*; (*idol*) simulacrum *nt*; (*verbal*) figūra *f*, similitūdō *f*
imagery *n* figūrae *fpl*
imaginary *adj* commentīcius, fictus
imagination *n* cōgitātiō *f*, opīnātiō *f*
imaginative *adj* ingeniōsus
imagine *vt* animō fingere, animum indūcere, ante oculōs pōnere; (*think*) opīnārī, arbitrārī

imbecile *adj* animō imbēcillus, fatuus, mente captus

imbecility *n* animī imbēcillitās *f*

imbibe *vt* adbibere; *(fig)* imbuī *(abl)*

imbrue *vt* īnficere

imbue *vt* imbuere, īnficere, tingere

imitable *adj* imitābilis

imitate *vt* imitārī

imitation *n* imitātiō *f*; *(copy)* imāgō *f*

imitator *n* imitātor *m*, imitātrix *f*, aemulātor *m*

immaculate *adj* integer, ēmendātus

immaculately *adv* integrē, sine vitiō

immaterial *adj* indifferēns

immature *adj* immātūrus

immeasurable *adj* immēnsus, īnfīnītus

immediate *adj* īnstāns, praesēns; *(neighbour)* proximus

immediately *adv* statim, extemplō, cōnfestim

immemorial *adj* antīquissimus; **from time ~** post hominum memoriam

immense *adj* immēnsus, immānis, ingēns, vastus

immensely *adv* vehementer

immensity *n* immēnsum *nt*, māgnitūdō *f*

immerse *vt* immergere, mergere

immigrant *n* advena *m*

immigrate *vi* migrāre

imminent *adj* īnstāns, praesēns; **be ~** imminēre, impendēre

immobile *adj* fīxus, immōbilis

immoderate *adj* immoderātus, immodestus

immoderately *adv* immoderātē, immodestē

immodest *adj* impudīcus, inverēcundus

immolate *vt* immolāre

immoral *adj* prāvus, corruptus, turpis

immorality *n* corruptī mōrēs *mpl*, turpitūdō *f*

immorally *adv* prāvē, turpiter

immortal *adj* immortālis, aeternus

immortality *n* immortālitās *f*

immortalize *vt* in astra tollere

immortally *adv* aeternum

immovable *adj* fīxus, immōbilis

immune *adj* immūnis, vacuus

immunity *n* immūnitās *f*, vacātiō *f*

immure *vt* inclūdere

immutability *n* immūtābilitās *f*

immutable *adj* immūtābilis

imp *n* puer improbus *m*

impact *n* ictus *m*, incussus *m*

impair *vt* imminuere, corrumpere

impale *vt* induere, īnfīgere

impalpable *adj* tenuissimus

impart *vt* impertīre, commūnicāre; *(courage)* addere

impartial *adj* aequus, medius

impartiality *n* aequābilitās *f*

impartially *adv* sine favōre

impassable *adj* invius; *(mountains)* inexsuperābilis; *(fig)* inexplicābilis

impasse *n* mora *f*, incitae *fpl*

impassioned *adj* ārdēns, fervidus

impassive *adj* rigidus, sēnsū carēns

impatience *n* aviditās *f*; *(of anything)* impatientia *f*

impatient *adj* trepidus, avidus; impatiēns

impatiently *adv* aegrē

impeach *vt* diem dīcere *(dat)*, accūsāre

impeachment *n* accūsātiō *f*, crīmen *nt*

impeccable *adj* ēmendātus

impecunious *adj* pauper

impede *vt* impedīre, obstāre *(dat)*

impediment *n* impedīmentum *nt*

impel *vt* impellere, incitāre

impend *vi* impendēre, imminēre, īnstāre

impenetrable *adj* impenetrābilis; *(country)* invius, impervius

impenitent *adj*: **I am ~** nīl mē paenitet

imperative *adj* necessārius

imperceptible *adj* tenuissimus, obscūrus

imperceptibly *adv* sēnsim

imperfect *adj* imperfectus, vitiōsus

imperfection *n* vitium *nt*

imperfectly *adv* vitiōsē

imperial *adj* imperātōrius, rēgius

imperil *vt* in discrīmen addūcere, labefactāre

imperious *adj* imperiōsus, superbus

imperiously *adv* superbē

imperishable *adj* immortālis, aeternus

impersonate *vt* partēs agere *(gen)*

impertinence *n* importūnitās *f*, protervitās *f*

impertinent *adj* importūnus, protervus, ineptus

impertinently *adv* importūnē, ineptē, protervē

imperturbable *adj* immōtus, gravis

impervious *adj* impervius, impenetrābilis

impetuosity *n* ārdor *m*, violentia *f*, vīs *f*

impetuous *adj* violēns, fervidus, effrēnātus

impetuously *adv* effrēnātē

impetus *n* impetus *m*

impiety *n* impietās *f*

impinge *vi* incidere

impious *adj* impius, profānus; **it is ~** nefas est

impiously *adv* impiē

impish *adj* improbus

implacable *adj* implācābilis, inexōrābilis, dūrus

implacably *adv* dūrē

implant *vt* īnserere, ingignere

implement *n* īnstrūmentum *nt* ♦ *vt* implēre, exsequī

implicate *vt* implicāre, impedīre

implication *n* indicium *nt*

implicit *adj* tacitus; absolūtus

implicitly *adv* absconditē; *(trust)* omnīnō, summā fidē

implore *vt* implōrāre, obsecrāre

imply *vt* significāre, continēre; **be implied** inesse

impolite *adj* inurbānus, illepidus

impolitely *adv* inurbānē

impolitic *adj* incōnsultus, imprūdēns

imponderable *adj* levissimus

import *vt* importāre, invehere; *(mean)* velle ♦ *n* significātiō *f*

importance *n* gravitās *f*, mōmentum *nt*; *(rank)* dignitās *f*, amplitūdō *f*, auctōritās *f*; **it is of great ~ to me** meā māgnī rēfert

important *adj* gravis, magnī mōmentī; **it is ~** interest *(gen)*, rēfert; **more ~**, **most ~** antīquior, antīquissimus

importation *n* invectiō *f*

imports *npl* importātīcia *ntpl*

importunate *adj* molestus
importune *vt* flāgitāre, īnstāre (*dat*)
impose *vt* impōnere; (*by order*) indīcere, iniungere; ~ **upon** illūdere, fraudāre, abūtī (*abl*)
imposing *adj* māgnificus, lautus
imposition *n* fraus *f*; (*tax*) tribūtum *nt*
impossible *adj*: **it is ~** fierī nōn potest
impost *n* tribūtum *nt*, vectīgal *nt*
impostor *n* planus *m*, fraudātor *m*
imposture *n* fraus *f*, fallācia *f*
impotence *n* īnfirmitās *f*
impotent *adj* īnfirmus, dēbilis; (*with rage*) impotēns
impotently *adv* frustrā; (*rage*) impotenter
impound *vt* inclūdere; (*confiscate*) pūblicāre
impoverish *vt* in inopiam redigere
impracticable *adj*: **be ~** fierī nōn posse
imprecate *vt* exsecrārī
imprecation *n* exsecrātiō *f*
impregnable *adj* inexpugnābilis
impregnate *vt* imbuere, īnficere
impress *vt* imprimere; (*on mind*) īnfigere; (*person*) permovēre; (MIL) invītum scrībere
impression *n* (*copy*) exemplar *nt*; (*mark*) signum *nt*; (*feeling*) impulsiō *f*; (*belief*) opīniātiō *f*; **make an ~ of** exprimere; **make an ~ on** commovēre; **have the ~** opīnārī
impressionable *adj* crēdulus
impressive *adj* gravis
impressively *adv* graviter
impressiveness *n* gravitās *f*
imprint *n* impressiō *f*, signum *nt* ◆ *vt* imprimere; (*on mind*) īnfigere, inūrere
imprison *vt* inclūdere, in vincula conicere
imprisonment *n* custōdia *f*, vincula *ntpl*
improbable *adj* incrēdibilis, haud vērīsimilis
impromptu *adv* ex tempore
improper *adj* indecōrus, ineptus
improperly *adv* prāvē, perperam
impropriety *n* culpa *f*, offēnsa *f*
improve *vt* ēmendāre, corrigere; (*mind*) excolere ◆ *vi* prōficere, meliōrem fierī
improvement *n* ēmendātiō *f*, prōfectus *m*
improvident *adj* imprōvidus; (*with money*) prōdigus
improvidently *adv* imprōvidē; prōdigē
improvise *vt* ex tempore compōnere, excōgitāre
imprudence *n* imprūdentia *f*
imprudent *adj* imprūdēns
imprudently *adv* imprūdenter
impudence *n* impudentia *f*, audācia *f*
impudent *adj* impudēns, audāx
impudently *adv* impudenter, protervē
impugn *vt* impugnāre, in dubium vocāre
impulse *n* impetus *m*, impulsus *m*
impulsive *adj* praeceps, violentus
impulsively *adv* impetū quōdam animī
impulsiveness *n* impetus *m*, violentia *f*
impunity *n* impūnitās *f*; **with ~** impūne
impure *adj* impūrus, incestus, inquinātus
impurely *adv* impūrē, incestē, inquinātē
impurity *n* impūritās *f*, sordēs *fpl*
imputation *n* crīmen *nt*
impute *vt* attribuere, adsignāre; ~ **as a fault** vitiō vertere

in *prep* (*abl*); (*with motion*) in (*acc*); (*authors*) apud (*acc*); (*time*) *abl*; **in doing this** dum hoc faciō; **in my youth** adulēscēns; **in that** quod ◆ *adv* (*rest*) intrā; (*motion*) intrō
inaccessible *adj* inaccessus
inaccuracy *n* neglegentia *f*, incūria *f*; (*error*) mendum *nt*
inaccurate *adj* parum dīligēns, neglegēns
inaccurately *adv* neglegenter
inaction *n* inertia *f*
inactive *adj* iners, quiētus; **be ~** cessāre
inactivity *n* inertia *f*, ōtium *nt*
inadequate *adj* impār, parum idōneus
inadequately *adv* parum
inadvertency *n* imprūdentia *f*
inadvertent *adj* imprūdēns
inadvertently *adv* imprūdenter
inane *adj* inānis, vānus; ineptus, stultus
inanely *adv* ineptē
inanimate *adj* inanimus
inanity *n* ineptiae *fpl*, stultitia *f*
inapplicable *adj*: **be ~** nōn valēre
inappropriate *adj* aliēnus, parum aptus
inarticulate *adj* īnfāns
inartistic *adj* sine arte, dūrus, inēlegāns
inasmuch as *conj* quōniam, cum (*subj*)
inattention *n* incūria *f*, neglegentia *f*
inattentive *adj* neglegēns
inattentively *adv* neglegenter
inaudible *adj*: **be ~** audīrī nōn posse
inaugurate *vt* inaugurāre, cōnsecrāre
inauguration *n* cōnsecrātiō *f*
inauspicious *adj* īnfaustus, īnfēlix
inauspiciously *adv* malīs ōminibus
inborn *adj* innātus
incalculable *adj* inaestimābilis
incantation *n* carmen *nt*
incapable *adj* inhabilis, indocilis; **be ~** nōn posse
incapacitate *vt* dēbilitāre
incapacity *n* inertia *f*, īnscītia *f*
incarcerate *vt* inclūdere, in vincula conicere
incarnate *adj* hūmānā speciē indūtus
incautious *adj* incautus, temerārius
incautiously *adv* incautē
incendiary *adj* incendiārius
incense *n* tūs *nt* ◆ *vt* inrītāre, stomachum movēre (*dat*); **be incensed** stomachārī
incentive *n* incitāmentum *nt*, stimulus *m*
inception *n* initium *nt*, exōrdium *nt*
incessant *adj* adsiduus
incessantly *adv* adsiduē
incest *n* incestus *m*
inch *n* digitus *m*, ūncia *f*
incident *n* ēventum *nt*, cāsus *m*, rēs *f*
incidental *adj* fortuïtus
incidentally *adv* cāsū
incipient *adj* prīmus
incisive *adj* ācer
incite *vt* īnstīgāre, impellere, hortārī, incitāre
incitement *n* invītāmentum *nt*, stimulus *m*
inciter *n* īnstimulātor *m*
incivility *n* importūnitās *f*, inhūmānitās *f*
inclemency *n* (*weather*) intemperiēs *f*
inclement *adj* asper, tristis

inclination *n* inclīnātiō *f*, animus *m*, libīdō *f*;
(*slope*) clīvus *m*
incline *vt* inclīnāre; (*person*) indūcere ✦ *vi*
inclīnāre, incumbere; **~ towards** sē adclīnāre
✦ *n* adclīvitās *f*, clīvus *m*
inclined *adj* inclīnātus, prōpēnsus; **I am ~ to**
think haud sciō an
include *vt* inclūdere, continēre, complectī
incognito *adv* clam
incoherent *adj* interruptus; **be ~** nōn cohaerēre
income *n* fructus *m*, mercēs *f*
incommensurate *adj* dispār
incommode *vt* molestiam adferre (*dat*)
incomparable *adj* singulāris, eximius
incompatibility *n* discrepantia *f*, repugnantia *f*
incompatible *adj* īnsociābilis, repugnāns; **be**
~ with dissidēre ab, repugnāre (*dat*)
incompetence *n* inertia *f*, īnscītia *f*
incompetent *adj* iners, īnscītus
incomplete *adj* imperfectus
incomprehensible *adj* incrēdibilis
inconceivable *adj* incrēdibilis
inconclusive *adj* inānis
incongruous *adj* absonus, aliēnus
inconsiderable *adj* exiguus
inconsiderate *adj* imprōvidus, incōnsultus
inconsistency *n* discrepantia *f*, incōnstantia *f*
inconsistent *adj* incōnstāns; **be ~** discrepāre; **be**
~ with abhorrēre ab, repugnāre (*dat*)
inconsistently *adv* incōnstanter
inconsolable *adj* nōn cōnsōlābilis
inconspicuous *adj* obscūrus; **be ~** latēre
inconstancy *n* incōnstantia *f*, levitās *f*
inconstant *adj* incōnstāns, levis, mōbilis
inconstantly *adv* incōnstanter
incontestable *adj* certus
incontinence *n* incontinentia *f*
incontinent *adj* intemperāns
inconvenience *n* incommodum *nt* ✦ *vt*
incommodāre
inconvenient *adj* incommodus
inconveniently *adv* incommodē
incorporate *vt* īnserere, adiungere
incorrect *adj* falsus; **be ~** nōn cōnstāre
incorrectly *adv* falsō, perperam
incorrigible *adj* improbus, perditus
incorruptibility *n* integritās *f*
incorruptible *adj* incorruptus
increase *n* incrēmentum *nt*, additāmentum *nt*,
auctus *m* ✦ *vt* augēre, amplificāre ✦ *vi* crēscere,
incrēscere
increasingly *adv* magis magisque
incredible *adj* incrēdibilis
incredibly *adv* incrēdibiliter
incredulous *adj* incrēdulus
increment *n* incrēmentum *nt*
incriminate *vt* crīminārī
inculcate *vt* inculcāre, īnfīgere
incumbent *adj*: **it is ~ on** oportet
incur *vt* subīre; (*guilt*) admittere
incurable *adj* īnsānābilis
incursion *n* incursiō *f*
indebted *adj* obnoxius; **be ~** dēbēre
indecency *n* obscēnitās *f*
indecent *adj* obscēnus, impudīcus
indecently *adv* obscēnē

indecision *n* dubitātiō *f*
indecisive *adj* anceps, dubius; **the battle is**
~ ancipitī Marte pugnātur
indecisively *adv* incertō ēventū
indecorous *adj* indecōrus
indeed *adv* profectō, sānē; (*concessive*) quidem;
(*interrog*) itane vērō?; (*reply*) certē, vērō; (*with pron*)
dēmum; (*with adj, adv, conj*) adeō
indefatigable *adj* impiger
indefensible *adj*: **be ~** dēfendī nōn posse; (*belief*)
tenērī nōn posse; (*offence*) excūsārī nōn posse
indefinite *adj* incertus, ambiguus, īnfīnītus
indefinitely *adv* ambiguē; (*time*) in incertum
indelicate *adj* pūtidus, indecōrus
independence *n* lībertās *f*
independent *adj* līber, suī iūris
indescribable *adj* inēnārrābilis
indestructible *adj* perennis
indeterminate *adj* incertus
index *n* index *m*
indicate *vt* indicāre, significāre
indication *n* indicium *nt*, signum *nt*
indict *vt* diem dīcere (*dat*), accūsāre, nōmen
dēferre (*gen*)
indictment *n* accūsātiō *f*
indifference *n* neglegentia *f*, languor *m*
indifferent *adj* (*manner*) neglegēns, frīgidus,
sēcūrus; (*quality*) mediocris
indifferently *adv* neglegenter; mediocriter;
(*without distinction*) promiscuē, sine discrīmine
indigence *n* indigentia *f*, egestās *f*
indigenous *adj* indigena
indigent *adj* indigēns, egēnus
indigestible *adj* crūdus
indigestion *n* crūditās *f*
indignant *adj* indignābundus, īrātus; **be**
~ indignārī
indignantly *adv* īrātē
indignation *n* indignātiō *f*, dolor *m*
indignity *n* contumēlia *f*, indignitās *f*
indigo *n* Indicum *nt*
indirect *adj* oblīquus
indirectly *adv* oblīquē, per ambāgēs
indirectness *n* ambāgēs *fpl*
indiscipline *n* lascīvia *f*, licentia *f*
indiscreet *adj* incōnsultus, imprūdēns
indiscreetly *adv* incōnsultē, imprūdenter
indiscretion *n* imprūdentia *f*; (*act*) culpa *f*
indiscriminate *adj* prōmiscuus
indiscriminately *adv* prōmiscuē, sine
discrīmine
indispensable *adj* necesse, necessārius
indisposed *adj* īnfirmus, aegrōtus; (*will*)
āversus, aliēnātus; **be ~** aegrōtāre; abhorrēre,
aliēnārī
indisposition *n* īnfirmitās *f*, valētūdō *f*
indisputable *adj* certus, manifestus
indisputably *adv* certē, sine dubiō
indissoluble *adj* indissolūbilis
indistinct *adj* obscūrus, obtūsus; (*speaker*) balbus
indistinctly *adv* obscūrē; **pronounce**
~ opprimere; **speak ~** balbutīre
individual *adj* proprius ✦ *n* homō *m/f*, prīvātus
m; **individuals** *pl* singulī *mpl*
individuality *n* proprium *nt*
individually *adv* singulātim, prīvātim

indivisible *adj* indīviduus
indolence *n* dēsidia *f*, ignāvia *f*, inertia *f*
indolent *adj* dēses, ignāvus, iners
indolently *adv* ignāvē
indomitable *adj* indomitus
indoor *adj* umbrātilis
indoors *adv* intus; *(motion)* intrā
indubitable *adj* certus
indubitably *adv* sine dubiō
induce *vt* indūcere, addūcere, persuādēre *(dat)*
inducement *n* illecebra *f*, praemium *nt*
induction *n* (LOGIC) inductiō *f*
indulge *vt* indulgēre *(dat)*
indulgence *n* indulgentia *f*, venia *f*; *(favour)*
    grātia *f*
indulgent *adj* indulgēns, lēnis
indulgently *adv* indulgenter
industrious *adj* industrius, impiger, dīligēns
industriously *adv* industriē
industry *n* industria *f*, dīligentia *f*, labor *m*
inebriated *adj* ēbrius
inebriation *n* ēbrietās *f*
ineffable *adj* eximius
ineffective *adj* inūtilis, invalidus
ineffectively *adv* ināniter
ineffectual *adj* inritus
inefficient *adj* īnscītus, parum strēnuus
inelegant *adj* inēlegāns, inconcinnus
inelegantly *adv* inēleganter
inept *adj* ineptus
ineptly *adv* ineptē
inequality *n* dissimilitūdō *f*, inīquitās *f*
inert *adj* iners, sōcors, immōbilis
inertia *n* inertia *f*
inertly *adv* tardē, lentē
inestimable *adj* inaestimābilis
inevitable *adj* necessārius
inevitably *adv* necessāriō
inexact *adj* parum subtīlis
inexhaustible *adj* perennis
inexorable *adj* inexōrābilis
inexpediency *n* inūtilitās *f*, incommodum *nt*
inexpedient *adj* inūtilis; **it is ~** nōn expedit
inexpensive *adj* vīlis
inexperience *n* imperītia *f*, īnscītia *f*
inexperienced *adj* imperītus, rudis, īnscītus
inexpert *adj* imperītus
inexpiable *adj* inexpiābilis
inexplicable *adj* inexplicābilis, inēnōdābilis
inexpressible *adj* inēnārrābilis
inextricable *adj* inexplicābilis
infallible *adj* certus, errōris expers
infamous *adj* īnfāmis, flāgitiōsus
infamously *adv* flāgitiōsē
infamy *n* īnfāmia *f*, flāgitium *nt*, dēdecus *nt*
infancy *n* īnfantia *f*; *(fig)* incūnābula *ntpl*
infant *n* īnfāns *m/f*
infantile *adj* puerīlis
infantry *n* peditēs *mpl*, peditātus *m*
infantryman *n* pedes *m*
infatuate *vt* īnfatuāre
infatuated *adj* dēmēns
infatuation *n* dēmentia *f*
infect *vt* īnficere
infection *n* contāgiō *f*
infer *vt* īnferre, colligere

inference *n* conclūsiō *f*
inferior *adj* *(position)* īnferior; *(quality)* dēterior
infernal *adj* īnfernus
infest *vt* frequentāre
infidel *adj* impius
infidelity *n* perfidia *f*, īnfidēlitās *f*
infiltrate *vi* sē īnsinuāre
infinite *adj* īnfinītus, immēnsus
infinitely *adv* longē, immēnsum
infinitesimal *adj* minimus
infinity *n* īnfinītās *f*
infirm *adj* īnfirmus, invalidus
infirmary *n* valētūdinārium *nt*
infirmity *n* morbus *m*
inflame *vt* accendere, incendere, īnflammāre;
    be inflamed exārdēscere
inflammation *n* (MED) īnflātiō *f*
inflate *vt* īnflāre
inflated *adj* *(fig)* īnflātus, tumidus
inflexible *adj* rigidus
inflexion *n* (GRAM) flexūra *f*; *(voice)* flexiō *f*
inflict *vt* īnflīgere, incutere; *(burden)* impōnere;
    (penalty) sūmere; **be inflicted with** labōrāre ex
infliction *n* poena *f*; malum *nt*
influence *n* *(physical)* impulsiō *f*, mōmentum
    nt; *(moral)* auctōritās *f*; *(partial)* grātia *f*; **have**
    ~ valēre; **have great ~ with** plūrimum posse
    apud; **under the ~ of** īnstinctus *(abl)* ♦ *vt*
    impellere, movēre, addūcere
influential *adj* gravis, potēns; grātiōsus
influenza *n* gravēdō *f*
inform *vt* docēre, certiōrem facere; **~ against**
    nōmen dēferre *(gen)*
informant *n* index *m*, auctor *m*
information *n* indicium *nt*, nūntius *m*
informer *n* index *m*, dēlātor *m*; **turn ~** indicium
    profitērī
infrequent *adj* rārus
infrequently *adv* rārō
infringe *vt* violāre, imminuere
infringement *n* violātiō *f*
infuriate *vt* efferāre
infuriated *adj* furibundus
infuse *vt* īnfundere; *(fig)* inicere
ingenious *adj* ingeniōsus, callidus; *(thing)*
    artificiōsus
ingeniously *adv* callidē, summā arte
ingenuity *n* ars *f*, artificium *nt*, acūmen *nt*
ingenuous *adj* ingenuus, simplex
ingenuously *adv* ingenuē, simpliciter
ingenuousness *n* ingenuitās *f*
ingle *n* focus *m*
inglorious *adj* inglōrius, ignōbilis, inhonestus
ingloriously *adv* sine glōriā, inhonestē
ingot *n* later *m*
ingrained *adj* īnsitus
ingratiate *vt*: **~ oneself with** grātiam inīre ab,
    sē īnsinuāre in familiāritātem *(gen)*; **~ oneself**
    into sē īnsinuāre in *(acc)*
ingratitude *n* ingrātus animus *m*
ingredient *n* pars *f*
inhabit *vt* incolere, habitāre in *(abl)*
inhabitable *adj* habitābilis
inhabitant *n* incola *m/f*
inhale *vt* haurīre
inharmonious *adj* dissonus

inherent *adj* īnsitus; **be ~ in** inhaerēre (*dat*), inesse (*dat*)
inherently *adv* nātūrā
inherit *vt* excipere
inheritance *n* hērēditās *f*, patrimōnium *nt*; **divide an ~** herctum ciēre; **come into an ~** hērēditātem adīre
inheritor *n* hērēs *m/f*
inhibit *vt* prohibēre, inhibēre
inhospitable *adj* inhospitālis
inhuman *adj* inhūmānus, immānis, crūdēlis
inhumanity *n* inhūmānitās *f*, crūdēlitās *f*
inhumanly *adv* inhūmānē, crūdēliter
inimical *adj* inimīcus
inimitable *adj* singulāris, eximius
iniquitous *adj* inīquus, improbus, nefārius
iniquity *n* scelus *nt*, flāgitium *nt*
initial *adj* prīmus
initiate *vt* initiāre; (*with knowledge*) imbuere
initiative *n* initium *nt*; **take the ~** initium capere, facere; occupāre (*inf*)
inject *vt* inicere
injudicious *adj* incōnsultus, imprūdēns
injunction *n* iussum *nt*, praeceptum *nt*
injure *vt* laedere, nocēre (*dat*)
injurious *adj* damnōsus, nocēns
injury *n* iniūria *f*, damnum *nt*; (*bodily*) vulnus *nt*
injustice *n* iniūria *f*, inīquitās *f*
ink *n* ātrāmentum *nt*
inkling *n* audītiō *f*, suspiciō *f*
inland *adj* mediterrāneus; **further ~** interior
inlay *vt* īnserere
inlet *n* sinus *m*, aestuārium *nt*
inly *adv* penitus
inmate *n* inquilīnus *m*
inmost *adj* intimus
inn *n* dēversōrium *nt*; caupōna *f*, taberna *f*
innate *adj* innātus, īnsitus
inner *adj* interior
innermost *adj* intimus
innkeeper *n* caupō *m*
innocence *n* innocentia *f*
innocent *adj* innocēns, īnsōns; (*character*) integer, castus
innocently *adv* innocenter, integrē, castē
innocuous *adj* innoxius
innovate *vt* novāre
innovation *n* novum *nt*, nova rēs *f*
innovator *n* novārum rērum auctor *m*
innuendo *n* verbum inversum *nt*
innumerable *adj* innumerābilis
inoffensive *adj* innocēns
inoffensively *adv* innocenter
inopportune *adj* intempestīvus
inopportunely *adv* intempestīvē
inordinate *adj* immodicus, immoderātus
inordinately *adv* immoderātē
inquest *n* quaestiō *f*; **hold an ~ on** quaerere dē
inquire *vi* exquīrere, rogāre; **~ into** inquīrere in (*acc*), investīgāre
inquiry *n* quaestiō *f*, investīgātiō *f*; (*asking*) interrogātiō *f*; **make ~** exquīrere; **make inquiries about** inquīrere in (*acc*); **hold an ~ on** quaerere dē, quaestiōnem īnstituere dē
inquisition *n* inquīsītiō *f*
inquisitive *adj* cūriōsus

inquisitiveness *n* cūriōsitās *f*
inquisitor *n* inquīsītor *m*
inroad *n* incursiō *f*, impressiō *f*; **make an ~** incursāre
insane *adj* īnsānus, mente captus; **be ~** īnsānīre
insanity *n* īnsānia *f*, dēmentia *f*
insatiable *adj* īnsatiābilis, inexplēbilis, īnsaturābilis
insatiably *adv* īnsaturābiliter
inscribe *vt* īnscrībere
inscription *n* epigramma *nt*; (*written*) īnscrīptiō *f*
inscrutable *adj* obscūrus
insect *n* bestiola *f*
insecure *adj* īnstabilis, intūtus
insecurity *n* perīcula *ntpl*
insensate *adj* ineptus, stultus
insensible *adj* torpidus; (*fig*) dūrus
insensitive *adj* dūrus
inseparable *adj* coniūnctus; **be the ~ companion of** ab latere esse (*gen*)
inseparably *adv* coniūnctē
insert *vt* īnserere, immittere, interpōnere
insertion *n* interpositiō *f*
inshore *adv* prope lītus
inside *adv* intus; (*motion*) intrō ♦ *adj* interior ♦ *n* pars *f* interior ♦ *prep* intrā (*acc*); **get right ~ sē** īnsinuāre in (*acc*); **turn ~ out** excutere; **on the ~** interior
insidious *adj* īnsidiōsus, subdolus
insidiously *adv* īnsidiōsē
insight *n* intellegentia *f*, cognitiō *f*
insignia *n* īnsignia *ntpl*
insignificance *n* levitās *f*
insignificant *adj* levis, exiguus, nullīus mōmentī; (*position*) humilis
insincere *adj* simulātus, fūcōsus
insincerely *adv* simulātē
insincerity *n* simulātiō *f*, fraus *f*
insinuate *vt* īnsinuāre; (*hint*) significāre ♦ *vi* sē īnsinuāre
insinuating *adj* blandus
insinuation *n* ambigua verba *ntpl*
insipid *adj* īnsulsus, frīgidus
insipidity *n* īnsulsitās *f*
insist *vi* īnstāre; **~ on** postulāre
insistence *n* pertinācia *f*
insistent *adj* pertināx
insolence *n* īnsolentia *f*, contumācia *f*, superbia *f*
insolent *adj* īnsolēns, contumāx, superbus
insolently *adv* īnsolenter
insoluble *adj* inexplicābilis
insolvency *n* reī familiāris naufragium *nt*
insolvent *adj*: **be ~** solvendō nōn esse
inspect *vt* īnspicere; (MIL) recēnsēre
inspection *n* cognitiō *f*; (MIL) recēnsiō *f*
inspector *n* cūrātor *m*
inspiration *n* adflātus *m*, īnstinctus *m*
inspire *vt* īnstinguere, incendere
instability *n* mōbilitās *f*
install *vt* inaugurāre
instalment *n* pēnsiō *f*
instance *n* exemplum *nt*; **for ~** exemplī causā, grātiā; **at the ~** admonitū; **at my ~** mē auctōre ♦ *vt* memorāre

instant *adj* īnstāns, praesēns ◆ *n* temporis pūnctum *nt*, mōmentum *nt*
instantaneous *adj* praesēns
instantaneously *adv* continuō, īlicō
instantly *adv* īlicō, extemplō
instead of *prep* prō (*abl*), locō (*gen*); (*with verb*) nōn … sed
instigate *vt* īnstigāre, impellere
instigation *n* impulsus *m*, stimulus *m*; auctōritās *f*; **at my ~** mē auctōre
instigator *n* īnstimulātor *m*, auctor *m*
instil *vt* imbuere, adspīrāre, inicere
instinct *n* nātūra *f*, ingenium *nt*, sēnsus *m*
instinctive *adj* nātūrālis
instinctively *adv* nātūrā, ingeniō suō
institute *vt* īnstituere, inaugurāre
institution *n* īnstitūtum *nt*; societās *f*
instruct *vt* docēre, īnstituere, īnstruere; ērudīre; (*order*) praecipere (*dat*)
instruction *n* doctrīna *f*, disciplīna *f*; praeceptum *nt*; **give instructions** dēnūntiāre, praecipere
instructor *n* doctor *m*, praeceptor *m*
instructress *n* magistra *f*
instrument *n* īnstrūmentum *nt*; (*music*) fidēs *fpl*; (*legal*) tabulae *fpl*
instrumental *adj* ūtilis
instrumentalist *n* fidicen *m*, fidicina *f*
instrumentality *n* opera *f*
insubordinate *adj* turbulentus, sēditiōsus
insubordination *n* intemperantia *f*, licentia *f*
insufferable *adj* intolerandus, intolerābilis
insufficiency *n* inopia *f*
insufficient *adj* minor; **be ~** nōn sufficere
insufficiently *adv* parum
insulate *vt* sēgregāre
insult *n* iniūria *f*, contumēlia *f*, probrum *nt* ◆ *vt* maledīcere (*dat*), contumēliam impōnere (*dat*)
insulting *adj* contumēliōsus
insultingly *adv* contumēliōsē
insuperable *adj* inexsuperābilis
insupportable *adj* intolerandus, intolerābilis
insurance *n* cautiō *f*
insure *vi* cavēre
insurgent *n* rebellis *m*
insurmountable *adj* inexsuperābilis
insurrection *n* mōtus *m*, sēditiō *f*
intact *adj* integer, intāctus, incolumis
integrity *n* integritās *f*, innocentia *f*, fidēs *f*
intellect *n* ingenium *nt*, mēns *f*, animus *m*
intellectual *adj* ingeniōsus
intelligence *n* intellegentia *f*, acūmen *nt*; (MIL) nūntius *m*
intelligent *adj* ingeniōsus, sapiēns, argūtus
intelligently *adv* ingeniōsē, sapienter, satis acūtē
intelligible *adj* perspicuus, apertus
intemperance *n* intemperantia *f*, licentia *f*
intemperate *adj* intemperāns, intemperātus
intemperately *adv* intemperanter
intend *vt* (*with inf*) in animō habēre, velle; (*with object*) dēstināre
intense *adj* ācer, nimius
intensely *adv* valdē, nimium
intensify *vt* augēre, amplificāre; **be intensified** ingravēscere

intensity *n* vīs *f*
intensive *adj* ācer, multus, adsiduus
intensively *adv* summō studiō
intent *adj* ērēctus, intentus; **be ~ on** animum intendere in (*acc*) ◆ *n* cōnsilium *nt*; **with ~** cōnsultō
intention *n* cōnsilium *nt*, prōpositum *nt*; **it is my ~** mihī in animō est; **with the ~ of** eā mente, eō cōnsiliō ut (*subj*)
intentionally *adv* cōnsultō, dē industriā
inter *vt* humāre
intercalary *adj* intercalāris
intercalate *vt* intercalāre
intercede *vi* intercēdere, dēprecārī
intercept *vt* excipere, intercipere; (*cut off*) interclūdere
intercession *n* dēprecātiō *f*; (*tribune's*) intercessiō *f*
intercessor *n* dēprecātor *m*
interchange *vt* permūtāre ◆ *n* permūtātiō *f*, vicissitūdō *f*
intercourse *n* commercium *nt*, ūsus *m*, cōnsuētūdō *f*
interdict *n* interdictum *nt* ◆ *vt* interdīcere (*dat*), vetāre
interest *n* (*advantage*) commodum *nt*; (*study*) studium *nt*; (*money*) faenus *nt*, ūsūra *f*; **compound ~** anatocismus *m*; **rate of ~** faenus *nt*; **~ at 12 per cent (per annum)** centēsimae *fpl*; **it is of ~** interest; **it is in my interests** meā interest; **consult the interests of** cōnsulere (*dat*); **take an ~ in** animum intendere (*dat*) ◆ *vt* dēlectāre, capere; (*audience*) tenēre; **~ oneself in** studēre (*dat*)
interested *adj* attentus; (*for gain*) ambitiōsus
interesting *adj* iūcundus, novus
interfere *vi* intervenīre; (*with*) sē interpōnere (*dat*), sē admiscēre ad; (*hinder*) officere (*dat*)
interference *n* interventus *m*, intercessiō *f*
interim *n*: **in the ~** interim, intereā
interior *adj* interior ◆ *n* pars interior *f*; (*country*) interiōra *ntpl*
interject *vt* exclāmāre
interjection *n* interiectiō *f*
interlace *vt* intexere
interlard *vt* variāre
interlock *vt* implicāre
interloper *n* interpellātor *m*
interlude *n* embolium *nt*
intermarriage *n* cōnūbium *nt*
intermediary *adj* medius ◆ *n* internūntius *m*
intermediate *adj* medius
interment *n* humātiō *f*
interminable *adj* sempiternus, longus
intermingle *vt* intermiscēre ◆ *vi* sē immiscēre
intermission *n* intercapēdō *f*, intermissiō *f*
intermittent *adj* interruptus
intermittently *adv* interdum
intern *vt* inclūdere
internal *adj* internus; (POL) domesticus
internally *adv* intus, domī
international *adj*: **~ law** iūs gentium
internecine *adj* internecīvus
interplay *n* vicēs *fpl*
interpolate *vt* interpolāre
interpose *vt* interpōnere ◆ *vi* intercēdere

interposition *n* intercessiō *f*
interpret *vt* interpretārī
interpretation *n* interpretātiō *f*
interpreter *n* interpres *m/f*
interrogate *vt* interrogāre, percontārī
interrogation *n* interrogātiō *f*, percontātiō *f*
interrupt *vt* (*action*) intercipere; (*speaker*) interpellāre; (*talk*) dirimere; (*continuity*) intermittere
interrupter *n* interpellātor *m*
interruption *n* interpellātiō *f*; intermissiō *f*
intersect *vt* dīvidere, secāre
intersperse *vt* distinguere
interstice *n* rīma *f*
intertwine *vt* intexere, implicāre
interval *n* intervallum *nt*, spatium *nt*; **after an ~** spatiō interpositō; **after an ~ of a year** annō interiectō; **at intervals** interdum; **at frequent intervals** identidem; **leave an ~** intermittere
intervene *vt* intercēdere, intervenīre
intervention *n* intercessiō *f*, interventus *m*; **by the ~ of** intercursū (*gen*)
interview *n* colloquium *nt*, aditus *m* ♦ *vt* convenīre
interweave *vt* implicāre, intexere
intestate *adj* intestātus ♦ *adv* intestātō
intestine *adj* intestīnus; (*POL*) domesticus ♦ *npl* intestīna *ntpl*; (*victim's*) exta *ntpl*
intimacy *n* familiāritās *f*
intimate *adj* familiāris; **be an ~ friend of** ab latere esse (*gen*); **a very ~ friend** perfamiliāris *m/f* ♦ *vt* dēnūntiāre
intimately *adv* familiāriter
intimation *n* dēnūntiātiō *f*; (*hint*) indicium *nt*
intimidate *vt* minārī (*dat*), terrōrem inicere (*dat*)
intimidation *n* metus *m*, minae *fpl*
into *prep* in (*acc*), intrā (*acc*)
intolerable *adj* intolerandus, intolerābilis
intolerably *adv* intoleranter
intolerance *n* impatientia *f*
intolerant *adj* impatiēns, intolerāns
intonation *n* sonus *m*, flexiō *f*
intone *vt* cantāre
intoxicate *vt* ēbrium reddere
intoxicated *adj* ēbrius
intoxication *n* ēbrietās *f*
intractable *adj* indocilis, difficilis
intransigent *adj* obstinātus
intrepid *adj* intrepidus, impavidus
intrepidity *n* audācia *f*, fortitūdō *f*
intricacy *n* implicātiō *f*
intricate *adj* implicātus, involūtus
intricately *adv* implicitē
intrigue *n* factiō *f*, artēs *fpl*, fallācia *f* ♦ *vi* māchinārī, fallāciīs ūtī
intriguing *adj* factiōsus; blandus
intrinsic *adj* vērus, innātus
intrinsically *adv* per sē
introduce *vt* indūcere, īnferre, importāre; (*acquaintance*) commendāre; (*custom*) īnstituere
introduction *n* exōrdium *nt*, prooemium *nt*; (*of person*) commendātiō *f*; **letter of ~** litterae commendātīciae *fpl*
intrude *vi* sē interpōnere, intervenīre
intruder *n* interpellātor *m*, advena *m*; (*fig*) aliēnus *m*

intrusion *n* interpellātiō *f*
intuition *n* sēnsus *m*, cognitiō *f*
inundate *vt* inundāre
inundation *n* ēluviō *f*
inure *vt* dūrāre, adsuēfacere
invade *vt* invādere
invalid *adj* aeger, dēbilis; (*null*) inritus
invalidate *vt* īnfirmāre
invaluable *adj* inaestimābilis
invariable *adj* cōnstāns, immūtābilis
invariably *adv* semper
invasion *n* incursiō *f*
invective *n* convīcium *nt*
inveigh *vi*: **~ against** invehī in (*acc*), īnsectārī
inveigle *vt* illicere, pellicere
invent *vt* fingere, comminīscī, invenīre
invention *n* inventum *nt*; (*faculty*) inventiō *f*
inventor *n* inventor *m*, auctor *m*
inverse *adj* inversus
inversely *adv* inversō ōrdine
invert *vt* invertere
invest *vt* (*in office*) inaugurāre; (*MIL*) obsidēre, circumsedēre; (*money*) locāre
investigate *vt* investīgāre, indāgāre; (*case*) cognōscere
investigation *n* investīgātiō *f*, indāgātiō *f*; (*case*) cognitiō *f*
investment *n* (*MIL*) obsessiō *f*; (*money*) locāta pecūnia *f*
inveterate *adj* inveterātus, vetus; **become ~** inveterāscere
invidious *adj* invidiōsus
invidiously *adv* invidiōsē
invigorate *vt* recreāre, reficere
invincible *adj* invictus
inviolable *adj* inviolātus; (*person*) sacrōsanctus
inviolably *adv* inviolātē
inviolate *adj* integer
invisible *adj* caecus; **be ~** vidērī nōn posse
invitation *n* invītātiō *f*; **at the ~ of** invītātū (*gen*)
invite *vt* invītāre, vocāre
inviting *adj* suāvis, blandus
invitingly *adv* blandē, suāviter
invocation *n* testātiō *f*
invoke *vt* invocāre, testārī
involuntarily *adv* īnscienter, invītus
involuntary *adj* coāctus
involve *vt* implicāre, involvere; **be involved in** inligārī (*abl*)
invulnerable *adj* inviolābilis; **be ~** vulnerārī nōn posse
inward *adj* interior
inwardly *adv* intus
inwards *adv* intrōrsus
inweave *vt* intexere
inwrought *adj* intextus
irascibility *n* īrācundia *f*
irascible *adj* īrācundus
irate *adj* īrātus
ire *n* īra *f*
iris *n* hyacinthus *m*
irk *vt* incommodāre; **I am irked** mē piget
irksome *adj* molestus
irksomeness *n* molestia *f*
iron *n* ferrum *nt*; **of ~** ferreus ♦ *adj* ferreus

ironical *adj* inversus
ironically *adv* inversīs verbīs
iron mine *n* ferrāria *f*
ironmonger *n* negōtiātor ferrārius *m*
ironmongery *n* ferrāmenta *ntpl*
iron ore *n* ferrum īnfectum *nt*
iron-tipped *adj* ferrātus
irony *n* illūsiō *f*, verbōrum inversiō *f*,
 dissimulātiō *f*
irradiate *vt* illūstrāre
irrational *adj* absurdus, ratiōnis expers; (*animal*)
 brūtus
irrationally *adv* absurdē, sine ratiōne
irreconcilable *adj* repugnāns, īnsociābilis
irrefutable *adj* certus, invictus
irregular *adj* incompositus; (*ground*) inaequālis;
 (*meeting*) extraōrdinārius; (*troops*) tumultuārius
irregularity *n* inaequālitās *f*; (*conduct*) prāvitās *f*,
 licentia *f*; (*election*) vitium *nt*
irregularly *adv* nullō ōrdine; (*elected*) vitiō
irrelevant *adj* aliēnus
irreligion *n* impietās *f*
irreligious *adj* impius
irremediable *adj* īnsānābilis
irreparable *adj* inrevocābilis
irreproachable *adj* integer, innocēns
irresistible *adj* invictus
irresolute *adj* dubius, anceps
irresolutely *adv* dubitanter
irresolution *n* dubitātiō *f*
irresponsibility *n* licentia *f*
irresponsible *adj* lascīvus, levis
irretrievable *adj* inrevocābilis

irreverence *n* impietās *f*
irreverent *adj* impius
irreverently *adv* impiē
irrevocable *adj* inrevocābilis
irrigate *vt* inrigāre
irrigation *n* inrigātiō *f*
irritability *n* īrācundia *f*
irritable *adj* īrācundus
irritate *vt* inrītāre, stomachum movēre (*dat*)
irritation *n* īrācundia *f*, stomachus *m*
island *n* īnsula *f*
islander *n* īnsulānus *m*
isle *n* īnsula *f*
isolate *vt* sēgregāre, sēparāre
isolation *n* sōlitūdō *f*
issue *n* (*result*) ēventus *m*, exitus *m*; (*children*)
 prōlēs *f*; (*question*) rēs *f*; (*book*) ēditiō *f*; **decide
 the ~** dēcernere, dēcertāre; **the point at ~** quā
 dē rē agitur ♦ *vt* distribuere; (*book*) ēdere;
 (*announcement*) prōmulgāre; (*coin*) ērogāre ♦ *vi*
 ēgredī, ēmānāre; (*result*) ēvādere, ēvenīre
isthmus *n* isthmus *m*
it *pron* hōc, id
itch *n* (*disease*) scabiēs *f*; (*fig*) cacoēthes *nt* ♦ *vi*
 prūrīre
item *n* nōmen *nt*, rēs *f*
iterate *vt* iterāre
itinerant *adj* vāgus, circumforāneus
itinerary *n* iter *nt*
its *adj* suus, ēius
itself *pron* ipse, ipsa, ipsum
ivory *n* ebur *nt* ♦ *adj* eburneus
ivy *n* hedera *f*

Jj

jabber *vi* blaterāre
jackdaw *n* grāculus *m*
jaded *adj* dēfessus, fatīgātus
jagged *adj* serrātus
jail *n* carcer *m*
jailer *n* custōs *m*, carcerārius *m*
jam *vt* comprimere; (*way*) obstruere
jamb *n* postis *m*
jangle *vi* crepitāre; rixārī
janitor *n* iānitor *m*
January *n* mēnsis Iānuārius *m*; **of ~** Iānuārius
jar *n* urna *f*; (*for wine*) amphora *f*; (*for water*) hydria *f*; (*sound*) offēnsa *f*; (*quarrel*) rixa *f* ◆ *vi* offendere
jasper *n* iaspis *f*
jaundice *n* morbus arquātus
jaundiced *adj* ictericus
jaunt *n*: **take a ~** excurrere
jauntily *adv* hilare, festīvē
jauntiness *n* hilaritās *f*
jaunty *adj* hilaris, festīvus
javelin *n* iaculum *nt*, pīlum *nt*; **throw the ~** iaculārī
jaw *n* māla *f*; **jaws** *pl* faucēs *fpl*
jay *n* grāculus *m*
jealous *adj* invidus; **be ~ of** invidēre (*dat*)
jealousy *n* invidia *f*
jeer *n* irrīsiō *f* ◆ *vi* irrīdēre; **~ at** illūdere
jejune *adj* iēiūnus, exīlis
jeopardize *vt* in perīculum addūcere
jeopardy *n* perīculum *nt*
jerk *n* subitus mōtus *m*
jest *n* iocus *m*
jester *n* scurra *m*
jet *n* (*mineral*) gagātēs *m*; (*of water*) saltus *m* ◆ *vi* salīre
jetsam *n* ēiectāmenta *ntpl*
jettison *vt* ēicere
jetty *n* mōlēs *f*
Jew *n* Iūdaeus *m*
jewel *n* gemma *f*
Jewish *adj* Iūdaicus
jig *n* tripudium *nt*
jilt *vt* repudiāre
jingle *n* nēnia *f* ◆ *vi* crepitāre, tinnīre
job *n* opus *nt*
jocose *adj see* **jocular**
jocular *adj* facētus, ioculāris
jocularity *n* facētiae *fpl*
jocularly *adv* facētē, per iocum
jocund *adj* hilaris, festīvus
jog *vt* fodicāre; (*fig*) stimulāre ◆ *vi* ambulāre

join *vt* iungere, coniungere, cōpulāre ◆ *vi* coniungī, sē coniungere; **~ in** interesse (*dat*), sē immiscēre (*dat*); **~ battle with** proelium committere (*abl*)
joiner *n* faber *m*
joint *adj* commūnis ◆ *n* commissūra *f*; (*of body*) articulus *m*, nōdus *m*; **~ by ~** articulātim
jointed *adj* geniculātus
joint-heir *n* cohērēs *m/f*
jointly *adv* ūnā, coniūnctē
joist *n* tignum *nt*
joke *n* iocus *m* ◆ *vi* iocārī, lūdere
joking *n* iocus *m*; **~ apart** remōtō iocō
jokingly *adv* per iocum
jollity *n* hilaritās *f*, festīvitās *f*
jolly *adj* hilaris, festīvus
jolt *vt* iactāre
jolting *n* iactātiō *f*
jostle *vt* agitāre, offendere
jot *n* minimum *nt*; **not a jot** nihil; **not care a jot** nōn floccī facere
journal *n* ācta diūrna *ntpl*
journey *n* iter *nt*
journeyman *n* opifex *m*
Jove *n* Iuppiter *m*
jovial *adj* hilaris
joviality *n* hilaritās *f*
jovially *adv* hilare
jowl *n* māla *f*; **cheek by ~** iuxtā
joy *n* gaudium *nt*, laetitia *f*, alacritās *f*
joyful *adj* laetus, hilaris
joyfully *adv* laetē, hilare
joyfulness *n* gaudium *nt*, laetitia *f*
joyless *adj* tristis, maestus
joyous *adj see* **joyful**
joyously *adv see* **joyfully**
jubilant *adj* laetus, gaudiō exsultāns
judge *n* iūdex *m*, arbiter *m* ◆ *vt* iūdicāre; (*think*) exīstimāre, cēnsēre; **~ between** diiūdicāre
judgeship *n* iūdicātus *m*
judgment *n* iūdicium *nt*, arbitrium *nt*; (*opinion*) sententia *f*; (*punishment*) poena *f*; (*wisdom*) iūdicium *nt*; **in my ~** meō animō, meō arbitrātū; **pass ~ on** statuere dē; **sit in ~** iūdicium exercēre
judgment seat *n* tribūnal *nt*
judicature *n* iūrisdictiō *f*; (*men*) iūdicēs *mpl*
judicial *adj* iūdiciālis; (*LAW*) iūdiciārius
judiciary *n* iūdicēs *mpl*
judicious *adj* prūdēns, cōnsīderātus
judiciously *adv* prūdenter

jug *n* hydria *f*, urceus *m*
juggler *n* praestīgiātor *m*
juggling *n* praestīgiae *fpl*
juice *n* liquor *m*, sūcus *m*
juicy *adj* sūcī plēnus
July *n* mēnsis Quīnctīlis, Iūlius *m*; **of**
~ Quīnctīlis, Iūlius
jumble *n* congeriēs *f* ♦ *vt* cōnfundere
jump *n* saltus *m* ♦ *vi* salīre; ~ **across** transilīre;
~ **at** (*opportunity*) captāre, adripere, amplectī;
~ **down** dēsilīre; ~ **on to** īnsilīre in (*acc*)
junction *n* coniūnctiō *f*
juncture *n* tempus *nt*
June *n* mēnsis Iūnius; **of** ~ Iūnius
junior *adj* iūnior, nātū minor
juniper *n* iūniperus *f*
Juno *n* Iūnō, Iūnōnis *f*
Jupiter *n* Iuppiter, Iovis *m*
juridical *adj* iūdiciārius
jurisconsult *n* iūriscōnsultus *m*
jurisdiction *n* iūrisdictiō *f*, diciō *f*; **exercise** ~ iūs
dīcere

jurisprudence *n* iūrisprūdentia *f*
jurist *n* iūriscōnsultus *m*
juror *n* iūdex *m*
jury *n* iūdicēs *mpl*
just *adj* iūstus, aequus ♦ *adv* (*exactly*) prōrsus;
(*only*) modo; (*time*) commodum, modo; (*with
adv*) dēmum, dēnique; (*with pron*) adeō dēmum,
ipse; ~ **as** (*comparison*) aequē ac, perinde ac,
quemadmodum; sīcut; ~ **before** (*time*) cum
māximē, sub (*acc*); ~ **now** modo, nunc; ~ **so** ita
prōrsus, sānē; **only** ~ vix
justice *n* iūstitia *f*, aequitās *f*, iūs *nt*; (*person*)
praetor *m*; **administer** ~ iūs reddere
justiciary *n* praetor *m*
justifiable *adj* iūstus
justifiably *adv* iūre
justification *n* pūrgātiō *f*, excūsātiō *f*
justify *vt* excūsāre, pūrgāre
justly *adv* iūstē, aequē; iūre, meritō
jut *vi* prōminēre, excurrere
jutting *adj* prōiectus
juvenile *adj* iuvenīlis, puerīlis

Kk

keel *n* carīna *f*

keen *adj* ācer; (*mind*) acūtus, argūtus; (*sense*) sagāx; (*pain*) acerbus; **I am ~ on** studeō

keenly *adv* ācriter, sagāciter, acūtē, acerbē

keenness *n* (*scent*) sagācitās *f*; (*sight*) aciēs *f*; (*pain*) acerbitās *f*; (*eagerness*) studium *nt*, ārdor *m*

keep *vt* servāre, tenēre, habēre; (*celebrate*) agere, celebrāre; (*guard*) custōdīre; (*obey*) observāre; (*preserve*) cōnservāre; (*rear*) alere, pāscere; (*store*) condere; **~ apart** distinēre; **~ away** arcēre; **~ back** dētinēre, reservāre; **~ down** comprimere; (*exuberance*) dēpāscere; **~ in** cohibēre, claudere; **~ in with** grātiam sequī (*gen*); **~ off** arcēre, dēfendere; **~ one's word** fidem praestāre; **~ one's hands off** manūs abstinēre; **~ house** domī sē retinēre; **~ secret** cēlāre; **~ together** continēre; **~ up** sustinēre, cōnservāre; **~ up with** subsequī; **~ waiting** dēmorārī ◆ *vi* dūrāre, manēre ◆ *n* arx *f*

keeper *n* custōs *m*

keeping *n* custōdia *f*; **in ~ with** prō (*abl*); **be in ~ with** convenīre (*dat*)

keg *n* cadus *m*

ken *n* cōnspectus *m*

kennel *n* stabulum *nt*

kerb *n* crepīdō *f*

kernel *n* grānum *nt*, nucleus *m*

kettle *n* lebēs *f*

key *n* clāvis *f*; (*fig*) claustra *ntpl*, iānua *f*; **key position** cardō *m*

kick *vi* calcitrāre ◆ *vt* calce ferīre

kid *n* haedus *m*

kidnap *vt* surripere

kidnapper *n* plagiārius *m*

kidney *n* rēn *m*

kidney bean *n* phasēlus *m*

kid's *adj* haedīnus

kill *vt* interficere, interimere; (*in battle*) occīdere; (*murder*) necāre, iugulāre; (*time*) perdere

killer *n* interfector *m*

kiln *n* fornāx *f*

kin *n* cognātī *mpl*, propinquī *mpl*; **next of kin** proximī *mpl*

kind *adj* bonus, benīgnus, benevolus, cōmis ◆ *n* genus *nt*; **of such a ~** tālis; **what ~ of** quālis

kindle *vt* incendere, succendere, īnflammāre

kindliness *n* cōmitās *f*, hūmānitās *f*

kindling *n* (*fuel*) fōmes *m*

kindly *adv* benīgnē

kindness *n* benīgnitās *f*, benevolentia *f*; (*act*) beneficium *nt*, officium *nt*, grātia *f*

kindred *n* necessitūdō *f*, cognātiō *f*; propinquī *mpl*, cognātī *mpl* ◆ *adj* cognātus, adfīnis

king *n* rēx *m*

kingdom *n* rēgnum *nt*

kingfisher *n* alcēdō *f*

kingly *adj* rēgius, rēgālis

kingship *n* rēgnum *nt*

kink *n* vitium *nt*

kinsfolk *n* cognātī *mpl*, necessāriī *mpl*

kinsman *n* cognātus *m*, propinquus *m*, necessārius *m*

kinswoman *n* cognāta *f*, propinqua *f*, necessāria *f*

kismet *n* fātum *nt*

kiss *n* ōsculum *nt* ◆ *vt* ōsculārī

kit *n* (*MIL*) sarcina *f*

kitchen *n* culīna *f*

kitchen garden *n* hortus *m*

kite *n* mīluus *m*

kite's *adj* mīluīnus

knack *n* calliditās *f*, artificium *nt*; **have the ~ of** callēre

knapsack *n* sarcina *f*

knave *n* veterātor *m*

knavish *adj* improbus

knavishly *adv* improbē

knead *vt* depsere, subigere

knee *n* genū *nt*

kneel *vi* genibus nītī

knife *n* culter *m*; (*surgeon's*) scalprum *nt*

knight *n* eques *m* ◆ *vt* in ōrdinem equestrem recipere

knighthood *n* ōrdō equester *m*

knightly *adj* equester

knit *vt* texere; (*brow*) contrahere

knob *n* bulla *f*

knock *vt* ferīre, percutere; **~ at** pulsāre; **~ against** offendere; **~ down** dēicere, adflīgere; (*at auction*) addīcere; **~ off** dēcutere; (*work*) dēsistere ab; **~ out** ēlīdere, excutere; (*unconscious*) exanimāre; (*fig*) dēvincere; **~ up** suscitāre ◆ *n* pulsus *m*, ictus *m*

knock-kneed *adj* vārus

knoll *n* tumulus *m*

knot *n* nōdus *m* ◆ *vt* nectere

knotty *adj* nōdōsus; **~ point** nōdus *m*

know *vt* scīre; (*person*) nōvisse; **~ all about** explōrātum habēre; **~ again** agnōscere; **~ how to** scīre; **not ~** ignōrāre, nescīre; **let me ~** fac sciam, fac mē certiōrem; **get to ~** cognōscere ◆ *n*: **in the ~** cōnscius

95

knowing *adj* prūdēns, callidus
knowingly *adv* cōnsultō, sciēns
knowledge *n* scientia *f*, doctrīna *f*; *(practical)* experientia *f*; *(of something)* cognitiō *f*
knowledgeable *adj* gnārus, doctus

known *adj* nōtus; **make ~** dēclārāre
knuckle *n* articulus *m*
knuckle bone *n* tālus *m*
kowtow *vi* adulārī
kudos *n* glōria *f*, laus *f*

LI

label n titulus m ✦ vt titulō īnscrībere
laboratory n officīna f
laborious adj labōriōsus, operōsus
laboriously adv operōsē
laboriousness n labor m
labour n labor m, opera f; (work done) opus nt; (work allotted) pēnsum nt; (workmen) operae fpl; **be in ~** parturīre ✦ vi labōrāre, ēnītī; **~ at** ēlabōrāre; **~ under a delusion** errōre fallī
laboured adj adfectātus
labourer n operārius m; **labourers** pl operae fpl
labyrinth n labyrinthus m
lace n texta rēticulāta ntpl; (shoe) ligula f ✦ vt nectere
lacerate vt lacerāre
laceration n lacerātiō f
lack n inopia f, dēfectiō f ✦ vt egēre (abl), carēre (abl)
lackey n pedisequus m
laconic adj brevis
laconically adv ūnō verbō, paucīs verbīs
lacuna n lacūna f
lad n puer m
ladder n scāla f
lade vt onerāre
laden adj onustus, onerātus
lading n onus nt
ladle n trulla f
lady n domina f, mātrōna f, mulier f
ladylike adj līberālis, honestus
lag vi cessāre
lagoon n stagnum nt
lair n latibulum nt
lake n lacus m
lamb n agnus m; (flesh) agnīna f; **ewe ~** agna f
lame adj claudus; (argument) inānis; **be ~** claudicāre
lameness n claudicātiō f
lament n lāmentātiō f, lāmentum nt ✦ vt lūgēre, lāmentārī; (regret) dēplōrāre
lamentable adj lāmentābilis, miserābilis
lamentably adv miserābiliter
lamentation n lāmentātiō f
lamp n lucerna f, lychnus m
lampoon n satura f ✦ vt carmine dēstringere
lance n hasta f, lancea f
lancer n hastātus m
lancet n scalpellum nt
land n terra f; (country) terra f, regiō f; (territory) fīnēs mpl; (native) patria f; (property) praedium nt, ager m; (soil) solum nt ✦ vt expōnere ✦ vi ē nāve ēgredī ✦ adj terrēnus, terrestris
landfall n adpulsus m
landing place n ēgressus m
landlady n caupōna f
landlord n dominus m; (inn) caupō m
landmark n lapis m; **be a ~** ēminēre
landscape n agrōrum prōspectus m
landslide n terrae lābēs f, lāpsus m
landwards adv terram versus
lane n (country) sēmita f; (town) angiportus m
language n lingua f; (style) ōrātiō f, sermō m; (diction) verba ntpl; **bad ~** maledicta ntpl
languid adj languidus, remissus
languidly adv languidē
languish vi languēre, languēscere; (with disease) tābēscere
languor n languor m
lank, lanky adj exīlis, gracilis
lantern n lanterna f, lucerna f
lap n gremium nt, sinus m ✦ vt lambere; (cover) involvere
lapse n (time) lāpsus m; (mistake) errātum nt; **after the ~ of a year** interiectō annō ✦ vi lābī; (agreement) inritum fierī; (property) revertī
larceny n fūrtum nt
larch n larix f ✦ adj larignus
lard n adeps m/f
larder n cella pēnāria f
large adj māgnus, grandis, amplus; **at ~** solūtus; **very ~** permāgnus; **as ~ as ...** tantus ... quantus
largely adv plērumque
largesse n largitiō f; (MIL) dōnātivum nt; (civil) congiārium nt; **give ~** largīrī
lark n alauda f
lascivious adj libīdinōsus
lasciviously adv libīdinōsē
lasciviousness n libīdō f
lash n flagellum nt, lōrum nt; (eye) cilium nt ✦ vt verberāre; (tie) adligāre; (with words) castīgāre
lashing n verbera ntpl
lass n puella f
lassitude n languor m
last adj ultimus, postrēmus, suprēmus; (in line) novissimus; (preceding) proximus; **at ~** tandem, dēmum, dēnique; **for the ~ time** postrēmum ✦ n fōrma f; **let the cobbler stick to his ~** nē sūtor suprā crepidam ✦ vi dūrāre, permanēre
lasting adj diūtinus, diūturnus
lastly adv postrēmō, dēnique
latch n pessulus m
latchet n corrigia f
late adj sērus; (date) recēns; (dead) dēmortuus; (emperor) dīvus; **~ at night** multā nocte; **till ~ in**

the day ad multum diem ♦ *adv* sērō; **too** ~ sērō; **too** ~ **to** sērius quam quī (*subj*); **of** ~ nūper

lately *adv* nūper

latent *adj* occultus, latitāns

later *adj* posterior ♦ *adv* posteā, posthāc, mox

latest *adj* novissimus

lath *n* tigillum *nt*

lathe *n* tornus *m*

lather *n* spūma *f*

Latin *adj* Latīnus; **speak** ~ Latīnē loquī; **understand** ~ Latīnē scīre; **translate into** ~ Latīnē reddere; **in** ~ Latīnē

Latinity *n* Latīnitās *f*

latitude *n* (GEOG) caelum *nt*; (*scope*) lībertās *f*, licentia *f*

latter *adj* posterior; **the** ~ hīc

latterly *adv* nūper

lattice *n* trānsenna *f*

laud *n* laus *f* ♦ *vt* laudāre

laudable *adj* laudābilis, laude dignus

laudatory *adj* honōrificus

laugh *n* rīsus *m*; (*loud*) cachinnus *m* ♦ *vi* rīdēre, cachinnāre; ~ **at** (*joke*) rīdēre; (*person*) dērīdēre; ~ **up one's sleeve** in sinū gaudēre

laughable *adj* rīdiculus

laughing stock *n* lūdibrium *nt*

laughter *n* rīsus *m*

launch *vt* (*missile*) contorquēre; (*ship*) dēdūcere; ~ **an attack** impetum dare ♦ *vi*: ~ **out into** ingredī in (*acc*) ♦ *n* celōx *f*, lembus *m*

laureate *adj* laureātus

laurel *n* laurus *m* ♦ *adj* laureus

lave *vt* lavāre

lavish *adj* prōdigus, largus ♦ *vt* largīrī, profundere

lavishly *adv* prōdigē, effūsē

lavishness *n* largitās *f*

law *n* lēx *f*; (*system*) iūs *nt*; (*divine*) fās *nt*; **civil law** iūs cīvīle; **constitutional law** iūs pūblicum; **international law** iūs gentium; **go to law** lēge agere, lītigāre; **break the law** lēges violāre; **pass a law** (*magistrate*) lēgem perferre; (*people*) lēgem iubēre

law-abiding *adj* bene mōrātus

law court *n* iūdicium *nt*; (*building*) basilica *f*

lawful *adj* lēgitimus; (*morally*) fās

lawfully *adv* lēgitimē, lēge

lawgiver *n* lēgum scrīptor *m*

lawless *adj* exlēx

lawlessly *adv* licenter

lawlessness *n* licentia *f*

lawn *n* prātulum *nt*

law-suit *n* līs *f*, āctiō *f*

lawyer *n* iūriscōnsultus *m*, causidicus *m*

lax *adj* dissolūtus, remissus

laxity *n* dissolūtiō *f*

lay *adj* (ECCL) lāicus ♦ *vt* pōnere, locāre; (*ambush*) collocāre, tendere; (*disorder*) sēdāre; (*egg*) parere; (*foundation*) iacere; (*hands*) inicere; (*plan*) capere, inīre; (*trap*) tendere; (*wager*) facere; **lay aside** pōnere; (*in store*) repōnere; **lay by** repōnere; **lay down** dēpōnere; (*rule*) statuere; **lay hold of** prehendere, adripere; **lay in** condere; **lay a motion before** referre ad; **lay on** impōnere; **lay open** patefacere; (*to attack*) nūdāre; **lay out** (*money*) impendere, ērogāre; (*camp*)

mētārī; **lay siege to** obsidēre; **lay to heart** in pectus dēmittere; **lay up** recondere; **lay upon** iniungere, impōnere; **lay violent hands on** vim adferre, adhibēre (*dat*); **whatever they could lay hands on** quod cuīque in manum vēnisset; **lay waste** vastāre ♦ *n* carmen *nt*, melos *nt*

layer *n* corium *nt*; (*stones*) ōrdō *m*; (*plant*) propāgō *f*

layout *n* dēsignātiō *f*

laze *vi* ōtiārī

lazily *adv* ignāvē, ōtiōsē

laziness *n* ignāvia *f*, dēsidia *f*, pigritia *f*

lazy *adj* ignāvus, dēsidiōsus, piger

lea *n* prātum *nt*

lead[1] *vt* dūcere; (*life*) agere; (*wall*) perdūcere; (*water*) dērīvāre; ~ **across** trādūcere; ~ **around** circumdūcere; ~ **astray** in errōrem indūcere; ~ **away** abdūcere; ~ **back** redūcere; ~ **down** dēdūcere; ~ **in** intrōdūcere; ~ **on** addūcere; ~ **out** ēdūcere; ~ **over** trādūcere; ~ **the way** dūcere, praeīre; ~ **up to** tendere ad, spectare ad; **the road leads ...** via fert ...

lead[2] *n* plumbum *nt* ♦ *adj* plumbeus

leaden *adj* (*colour*) līvidus

leader *n* dux *m*, ductor *m*

leadership *n* ductus *m*

leading *adj* prīmus, prīnceps, praecipuus

leaf *n* folium *nt*, frōns *f*; (*paper*) scheda *f*; **put forth leaves** frondēscere

leaflet *n* libellus *m*

leafy *adj* frondōsus

league *n* foedus *nt*, societās *f*; (*distance*) tria mīlia passuum ♦ *vi* coniūrāre, foedus facere

leagued *adj* foederātus

leak *n* rīma *f* ♦ *vi* mānāre, rīmās agere

leaky *adj* rīmōsus

lean *adj* macer, exīlis, gracilis ♦ *vi* nītī; ~ **back** sē reclīnāre; ~ **on** innītī in (*abl*), incumbere (*dat*); ~ **over** inclīnāre

leaning *n* prōpēnsiō *f* ♦ *adj* inclīnātus

leanness *n* gracilitās *f*, maciēs *f*

leap *n* saltus *m* ♦ *vi* salīre; (*for joy*) exsultāre; ~ **down** dēsilīre; ~ **on to** īnsilīre in (*acc*)

leap year *n* annus bissextilis *m*

learn *vt* discere; (*news*) accipere, audīre; (*by heart*) ēdiscere; (*discover*) cognōscere

learned *adj* doctus, ērudītus, litterātus

learnedly *adv* doctē

learner *n* tīrō *m*, discipulus *m*

learning *n* doctrīna *f*, ērudītiō *f*, litterae *fpl*

lease *n* (*taken*) conductiō *f*; (*given*) locātiō *f* ♦ *vt* condūcere; locāre

leash *n* cōpula *f*

least *adj* minimus ♦ *adv* minimē; **at** ~ saltem; **to say the** ~ ut levissimē dīcam; **not in the** ~ haudquāquam

leather *n* corium *nt*, alūta *f*

leathery *adj* lentus

leave *n* (*of absence*) commeātus *m*; (*permission*) potestās *f*, venia *f*; **ask** ~ veniam petere; **give** ~ potestātem facere; **obtain** ~ impetrāre; **by your** ~ pace tuā, bonā tuā veniā ♦ *vt* relinquere, dēserere; (*legacy*) lēgāre; ~ **alone** nōn tangere, manum abstinēre ab; ~ **behind** relinquere; ~ **in the lurch** dēstituere, dērelinquere; ~ **off** dēsinere, dēsistere ab; (*temporarily*)

intermittere; (*garment*) pōnere; ~ out
praetermittere, ōmittere ♦ *vi* discēdere ab (*abl*),
abīre
leaven *n* fermentum *nt*
leavings *n* rēliquiae *fpl*
lecherous *adj* salāx
lecture *n* acroāsis *f*, audītiō *f* ♦ *vi* docēre,
scholam habēre
lecturer *n* doctor *m*
lecture room *n* audītōrium *nt*
ledge *n* līmen *nt*
ledger *n* cōdex acceptī et expēnsī
lee *n* pars ā ventō tūta
leech *n* hirūdō *f*
leek *n* porrum *nt*
leer *vi* līmīs oculīs intuērī
lees *n* faex *f*; (*of oil*) amurca *f*
left *adj* sinister, laevus ♦ *n* sinistra *f*, laeva *f*; on
the ~ ā laevā, ad laevam, ā sinistrā
leg *n* crūs *nt*; (*of table*) pēs *m*
legacy *n* lēgātum *nt*; ~ hunter captātor *m*
legal *adj* lēgitimus
legalize *vt* sancīre
legally *adv* secundum lēgēs, lēge
legate *n* lēgātus *m*
legation *n* lēgātiō *f*
legend *n* fābula *f*; (*inscription*) titulus *m*
legendary *adj* fābulōsus
legerdemain *n* praestīgiae *fpl*
legging *n* ocrea *f*
legible *adj* clārus
legion *n* legiō *f*; men of the 10th ~ decumānī *mpl*
legionary *n* legiōnārius *m*
legislate *vi* lēgēs scrībere, lēgēs facere
legislation *n* lēgēs *fpl*, lēgēs scrībendae
legislator *n* lēgum scrīptor *m*
legitimate *adj* lēgitimus
legitimately *adv* lēgitimē
leisure *n* ōtium *nt*; at ~ ōtiōsus, vacuus; have
~ for vacāre (*dat*)
leisured *adj* ōtiōsus
leisurely *adj* lentus
lend *vt* commodāre, mūtuum dare; (*at interest*)
faenerārī; (*ear*) aurēs praebēre, admovēre; ~ a
ready ear aurēs patefacere; ~ assistance opem
ferre
length *n* longitūdō *f*; (*time*) diūturnitās *f*; at
~ tandem, dēmum, dēnique; (*speech*) cōpiōsē
lengthen *vt* extendere; (*time*) prōtrahere; (*sound*)
prōdūcere
lengthwise *adv* in longitūdinem
lengthy *adj* longus, prōlixus
leniency *n* clēmentia *f*
lenient *adj* clēmēns, mītis
leniently *adv* clēmenter
lentil *n* lēns *f*
leonine *adj* leōnīnus
leopard *n* pardus *m*
less *adj* minor ♦ *adv* minus; ~ than (*num*) intrā
(*acc*); much ~, still ~ nēdum
lessee *n* conductor *m*
lessen *vt* minuere, imminuere, dēminuere ♦ *vi*
dēcrēscere
lesson *n* documentum *nt*; be a ~ to documentō
esse (*dat*); **lessons** *pl* dictāta *ntpl*; give lessons
scholās habēre; give lessons in docēre

lessor *n* locātor *m*
lest *conj* nē (*subj*)
let *vt* (*allow*) sinere; (*lease*) locāre; (*imper*) fac; let
alone ōmittere; (*mention*) nē dīcam; let blood
sanguinem mittere; let down dēmittere; let
fall ā manibus mittere; (*word*) ēmittere; let
fly ēmittere; let go mittere, āmittere; (*ship*)
solvere; let in admittere; let loose solvere;
let off absolvere, ignōscere (*dat*); let oneself
go geniō indulgēre; let out ēmittere; let slip
āmittere, ōmittere
lethal *adj* mortifer
lethargic *adj* veternōsus
lethargy *n* veternus *m*
letter *n* epistula *f*, litterae *fpl*; (*of alphabet*) littera
f; the ~ of the law scrīptum *nt*; to the ~ ad
praescrīptum; by ~ per litterās; **letters** (*learning*)
litterae *fpl*; man of letters scrīptor *m*
lettered *adj* litterātus
lettuce *n* lactūca *f*
levee *n* salūtātiō *f*
level *adj* aequus, plānus ♦ *n* plānitiēs *f*;
(*instrument*) lībra *f*; do one's ~ best prō virīlī
parte agere; put on a ~ with exaequāre
cum ♦ *vt* aequāre, adaequāre, inaequāre; (*to
the ground*) solō aequāre, sternere; (*weapon*)
intendere
level-headed *adj* prūdēns
levelled *adj* (*weapon*) īnfestus
lever *n* vectis *m*
levity *n* levitās *f*; (*fun*) iocī *mpl*, facētiae *fpl*
levy *vt* (*troops*) scrībere; (*tax*) exigere ♦ *n* dīlectus
m
lewd *adj* impudīcus
lewdness *n* impudīcitia *f*
liable *adj* obnoxius; render ~ obligāre
liaison *n* cōnsuētūdō *f*
liar *n* mendāx *m*
libel *n* probrum *nt*, calumnia *f* ♦ *vt* calumniārī
libellous *adj* probrōsus, fāmōsus
liberal *adj* līberālis; (*in giving*) largus, benīgnus;
~ education bonae artēs *fpl*
liberality *n* līberālitās *f*, largitās *f*
liberally *adv* līberāliter, largē, benīgnē
liberate *vt* līberāre; (*slave*) manū mittere
liberation *n* līberātiō *f*
liberator *n* līberātor *m*
libertine *n* libīdinōsus *m*
liberty *n* lībertās *f*; (*excess*) licentia *f*; I am at
~ to mihī licet (*inf*); I am still at ~ to integrum
est mihī (*inf*); take a ~ with licentius ūtī (*abl*),
familiārius sē gerere in (*acc*)
libidinous *adj* libīdinōsus
librarian *n* librārius *m*
library *n* bibliothēca *f*
licence *n* (*permission*) potestās *f*; (*excess*) licentia *f*
license *vt* potestātem dare (*dat*)
licentious *adj* dissolūtus
licentiousness *n* libīdō *f*, licentia *f*
lick *vt* lambere; mulcēre
lictor *n* lictor *m*
lid *n* operculum *nt*
lie *n* mendācium *nt*; give the lie to redarguere;
tell a lie mentīrī ♦ *vi* mentīrī; lie down iacēre;
(*place*) situm esse; (*consist*) continērī; as far as
in me lies quantum in mē est; lie at anchor

stāre; **lie between** interiacēre; **lie down**
cubāre, discumbere; **lie heavy on** premere;
lie hid latēre; **lie in wait** īnsidiārī; **lie low**
dissimulāre; **lie on** incumbere (*dat*); **lie open**
patēre; hiāre
lien *n* nexus *m*
lieu *n*: **in ~ of** locō (*gen*)
lieutenant *n* decuriō *m*; legātus *m*
life *n* vīta *f*; (*in danger*) salūs *f*, caput *nt*; (*biography*)
vīta *f*; (*breath*) anima *f*; (RHET) sanguis *m*; (*time*)
aetās *f*; **come to ~ again** revīvīscere; **draw to
the ~** exprimere; **for ~** aetātem; **matter of
~ and death** capitāle *nt*; **prime of ~** flōs aetātis;
way of ~ mōrēs *mpl*
lifeblood *n* sanguis *m*
life-giving *adj* almus, vītalis
lifeguard *n* custōs *m*; (*emperor's*) praetōriānus *m*
lifeless *adj* exanimis; (*style*) exsanguis
lifelike *adj* expressus
lifelong *adj* perpetuus
lifetime *n* aetās *f*
lift *vt* tollere, sublevāre; **~ up** efferre, attollere
light *n* lūx *f*, lūmen *nt*; (*painting*) lūmen *nt*; **bring
to ~** in lūcem prōferre; **see in a favourable ~** in
meliōrem partem interpretārī; **throw ~ on**
lūmen adhibēre (*dat*) ♦ *vt* accendere, incendere;
(*illuminate*) illūstrāre, illūmināre; **be lit up**
collūcēre ♦ *vi*: **~ upon** invenīre, offendere ♦ *adj*
illūstris; (*movement*) agilis; (*weight*) levis; **grow
~** illūcēscere, dīlūcēscere; **make ~ of** parvī
pendere
light-armed *adj* expedītus
lighten *vi* fulgurāre ♦ *vt* levāre
lighter *n* linter *f*
light-fingered *adj* tagāx
light-footed *adj* celer, pernīx
light-headed *adj* levis, volāticus
light-hearted *adj* hilaris, laetus
lightly *adv* leviter; pernīciter
lightness *n* levitās *f*
lightning *n* fulgur *nt*; (*striking*) fulmen *nt*; **be hit
by ~** dē caelō percutī; **of ~** fulgurālis
like *adj* similis, pār; **~ this** ad hunc modum ♦ *adv*
similiter, sīcut, rītū (*gen*) ♦ *vt* amāre; **I ~** mihī
placet, mē iuvat; **I ~ to** libet (*inf*); **I don't ~** nīl
moror, mihī displicet; **look ~** similem esse,
referre
likelihood *n* vērī similitūdō *f*
likely *adj* vērī similis ♦ *adv* sānē
liken *vt* comparāre, aequiperāre
likeness *n* imāgō *f*, īnstar *nt*, similitūdō *f*
likewise *adv* item; (*also*) etiam
liking *n* libīdō *f*, grātia *f*; **to one's ~** ex sententiā
lily *n* līlium *nt*
limb *n* membrum *nt*, artus *m*
lime *n* calx *f*; (*tree*) tilia *f*
limelight *n* celebritās *f*; **enjoy the ~** mōnstrārī
digitō
limestone *n* calx *f*
limit *n* fīnis *m*, terminus *m*, modus *m*; **mark
the limits of** dētermināre ♦ *vt* fīnīre, dēfinīre,
termināre; (*restrict*) circumscrībere
limitation *n* modus *m*
limp *adj* mollis, flaccidus ♦ *vi* claudicāre
limpid *adj* limpidus
linden *n* tilia *f*

line *n* līnea *f*; (*battle*) aciēs *f*; (*limit*) modus *m*;
(*outline*) līneāmentum *nt*; (*writing*) versus *m*; **in
a straight ~** ē regiōne; **~ of march** agmen *nt*;
read between the lines dissimulāta dispicere;
ship of the ~ nāvis longa; **write a ~** pauca
scrībere ♦ *vt* (*street*) saepīre
lineage *n* genus *nt*, stirps *f*
lineal *adj* (*descent*) gentīlis
lineaments *n* līneāmenta *ntpl*, ōris ductūs *mpl*
linen *n* linteum *nt* ♦ *adj* linteus
liner *n* nāvis *f*
linger *vi* cunctārī, cessāre, dēmorārī
lingering *adj* tardus ♦ *n* cunctātiō *f*
linguist *n*: **be a ~** complūrēs linguās callēre
link *n* ānulus *m*; (*fig*) nexus *m*, vinculum *nt* ♦ *vt*
coniungere
lintel *n* līmen superum *nt*
lion *n* leō *m*; **lion's** leōnīnus; **lion's share** māior
pars
lioness *n* leaena *f*
lip *n* lābrum *nt*; **be on everyone's lips** in ōre
omnium hominum esse, per omnium ōra ferrī
lip service *n*: **pay lip service to** verbō tenus
obsequī (*dat*)
liquefy *vt* liquefacere
liquid *adj* liquidus ♦ *n* liquor *m*
liquidate *vt* persolvere
liquor *n* liquor *m*; vīnum *nt*
lisp *vi* balbūtīre
lisping *adj* blaesus
lissom *adj* agilis
list *n* index *m*, tabula *f*; (*ship*) inclīnātiō *f*
♦ *vt* scrībere ♦ *vi* (*lean*) sē inclīnāre; (*listen*)
auscultāre; (*wish*) cupere
listen *vi* auscultāre; **~ to** auscultāre, audīre
listener *n* audītor *m*, auscultātor *m*
listless *adj* languidus
listlessness *n* languor *m*
literally *adv* ad verbum
literary *adj* (*man*) litterātus; **~ pursuits** litterae
fpl, studia *ntpl*
literature *n* litterae *fpl*
lithe *adj* mollis, agilis
litigant *n* lītigātor *m*
litigate *vi* lītigāre
litigation *n* līs *f*
litigious *adj* lītigiōsus
litter *n* (*carriage*) lectīca *f*; (*brood*) fētus *m*; (*straw*)
strāmentum *nt*; (*mess*) strāgēs *f* ♦ *vt* sternere;
(*young*) parere
little *adj* parvus, exiguus; (*time*) brevis; **very
~** perexiguus, minimus; **~ boy** puerulus *m* ♦ *n*
paulum *nt*, aliquantulum *nt*; **for a ~** paulisper,
parumper; **~ or nothing** vix quicquam ♦ *adv*
paulum, nōnnihil; (*with comp*) paulō; **~ by
~** paulātim, sēnsim, gradātim; **think ~ of** parvī
aestimāre; **too ~** parum (*gen*)
littleness *n* exiguitās *f*
littoral *n* lītus *nt*
live *vi* vīvere, vītam agere; (*dwell*) habitāre;
~ down (*reproach*) ēluere; **~ on** (*food*) vescī (*abl*)
♦ *adj* vīvus
livelihood *n* vīctus *m*
liveliness *n* alacritās *f*, hilaritās *f*
livelong *adj* tōtus
lively *adj* alacer, hilaris

liven vt exhilarāre

liver n iecur nt

livery n vestis famulāris f

livid adj līvidus; **be ~** līvēre

living adj vīvus ♦ n vīctus m; (earning) quaestus m

lizard n lacerta f

lo interj ecce

load n onus nt ♦ vt onerāre

loaf n pānis m ♦ vi grassārī

loafer n grassātor m

loam n lutum nt

loan n mūtuum nt, mūtua pecūnia f

loathe vt fastīdīre, ōdisse

loathing n fastīdium nt

loathsome adj odiōsus, taeter

lobby n vestibulum nt

lobe n fibra f

lobster n astacus m

local adj indigena, locī

locality n locus m

locate vt reperīre; **be located** situm esse

location n situs m

loch n lacus m

lock n (door) sera f; (hair) coma f ♦ vt obserāre

locomotion n mōtus m

locust n locusta f

lodge n casa f ♦ vi dēversārī ♦ vt īnfīgere; (complaint) dēferre

lodger n inquilīnus m

lodging n hospitium nt, dēversōrium nt

loft n cēnāculum nt

loftiness n altitūdō f, sublīmitās f

lofty adj excelsus, sublīmis

log n stīpes m; (fuel) lignum nt

loggerhead n: **be at loggerheads** rixārī

logic n dialecticē f

logical adj dialecticus, ratiōne frētus

logically adv ex ratiōne

logician n dialecticus m

loin n lumbus m

loiter vi grassārī, cessāre

loiterer n grassātor m, cessātor m

loll vi recumbere

lone adj sōlus, sōlitārius

loneliness n sōlitūdō f

lonely, lonesome adj sōlitārius

long adj longus; (hair) prōmissus; (syllable) prōductus; (time) longus, diūturnus; **in the ~ run** aliquandō; **for a ~ time** diū; **to make a ~ story short** nē longum sit, nē longum faciam ♦ adv diū; **~ ago** iampnīdem, iamdūdum; **as ~ as** (conj) dum; **before ~** mox; **for ~** diū; **how ~** quamdiū, quousque; **I have ~ been wishing** iam prīdem cupiō; **not ~ after** haud multō post; **any longer** (time) diūtius; (distance) longius; **no longer** nōn iam ♦ vi: **~ for** dēsīderāre, exoptāre, expetere; **~ to** gestīre

longevity n vīvācitās f

longing n dēsīderium nt, cupīdō f ♦ adj avidus

longingly adv avidē

longitudinally adv in longitūdinem

long-lived adj vīvāx

long-suffering adj patiēns

long-winded adj verbōsus, longus

longwise adv in longitūdinem

look n aspectus m; (expression) vultus m ♦ vi aspicere; (seem) vidērī, speciem praebēre; **~ about** circumspicere; **~ after** prōvidēre (dat), cūrāre; **~ at** spectāre ad (acc), aspicere, intuērī; (with mind) contemplārī; **~ back** respicere; **~ down on** dēspectāre; (fig) dēspicere; **~ for** quaerere, petere; **~ forward to** exspectāre; **~ here** heus tu, ehodum; **~ into** īnspicere, intrōspicere; **~ out** prōspicere; (beware) cavēre; **~ round** circumspicere; **~ through** perspicere; **~ to** ratiōnem habēre (gen); (leader) spem pōnere in (abl); **~ towards** spectāre ad; **~ up** suspicere; **~ up to** suspicere; **~ upon** habēre

looker-on n arbiter m

lookout n (place) specula f; (man) vigil m, excubiae fpl

looks npl speciēs f; **good ~** fōrma f, pulchritūdō f

loom n tēla f ♦ vi in cōnspectum sē dare

loop n orbis m, sinus m

loophole n fenestra f

loose adj laxus, solūtus, remissus; (morally) dissolūtus; **let ~ on** immittere in (acc) ♦ vt (undo) solvere; (slacken) laxāre

loosely adv solūtē, remissē

loosen vt (re)solvere; (structure) labefacere

looseness n dissolūtiō f, dissolūtī mōrēs mpl

loot n praeda f, rapīna f

lop vt amputāre

lopsided adj inaequālis

loquacious adj loquāx

loquacity n loquācitās f

lord n dominus m ♦ vi: **~ it** dominārī

lordliness n superbia f

lordly adj superbus; (rank) nōbilis

lordship n dominātiō f, imperium nt

lore n litterae fpl, doctrīna f

lose vt āmittere, perdere; **~ an eye** alterō oculō capī; **~ heart** animum dēspondēre; **~ one's way** deerrāre ♦ vi (in contest) vincī

loss n damnum nt, dētrīmentum nt; **be at a ~** haerēre, haesitāre; **suffer ~** damnum accipere, facere; **losses** (in battle) caesī mpl

lost adj āmissus, absēns; **be ~** perīre, interīre; **give up for ~** dēplōrāre

lot n sors f; **be assigned by lot** sorte obvenīre; **draw a lot** sortem dūcere; **draw lots for** sortīrī; **a lot of** multus, plūrimus

loth adj invītus

lottery n sortēs fpl; (fig) ālea f

lotus n lōtos f

loud adj clārus, māgnus

loudly adv māgnā vōce

loudness n māgna vōx f

lounge vi ōtiārī

louse n pedis m/f

lout n agrestis m

lovable adj amābilis

love n amor m; **be hopelessly in ~** dēperīre; **fall in ~ with** adamāre ♦ vt amāre, dīligere; **I ~ to** mē iuvat (inf)

love affair n amor m

loveless adj amōre carēns

loveliness n grātia f, venustās f

lovely adj pulcher, amābilis, venustus

love poem n carmen amātōrium nt

lover n amāns m, amātor m

lovesick adj amōre aeger
loving adj amāns
lovingly adv amanter
low adj humilis; (birth) ignōbilis; (price) vīlis; (sound) gravis; (spirits) dēmissus; (voice) dēmissus; **at low water** aestūs dēcessū; **be low** iacēre; **lay low** interficere ♦ vi mūgīre
lower adj īnferior; **the ~ world** īnferī mpl; **of the ~ world** īnfernus ♦ adv īnferius ♦ vt dēmittere, dēprimere ♦ vi (cloud) obscūrārī, minārī
lowering adj mināx
lowest adj īnfimus, īmus
lowing n mūgītus m
lowland adj campestris
lowlands n campī mpl
lowliness n humilitās f
lowly adj humilis, obscūrus
low-lying adj dēmisssus; **be ~** sedēre
lowness n humilitās f; (spirit) tristitia f
loyal adj fidēlis, fīdus; (citizen) bonus
loyally adv fidēliter
loyalty n fidēs f, fidēlitās f
lubricate vt ungere
lucid adj clārus, perspicuus
lucidity n perspicuitās f
lucidly adv clārē, perspicuē
luck n fortūna f, fors f; **good ~** fēlicitās f; **bad ~** īnfortūnium nt
luckily adv fēliciter, faustē, prosperē
luckless adj īnfēlīx
lucky adj fēlīx, fortūnātus; (omen) faustus
lucrative adj quaestuōsus
lucre n lucrum nt, quaestus m
lucubration n lūcubrātiō f
ludicrous adj rīdiculus
ludicrously adv rīdiculē
lug vt trahere
luggage n impedīmenta ntpl, sarcina f
lugubrious adj lūgubris, maestus
lukewarm adj tepidus; (fig) segnis, neglegēns; **be ~** tepēre
lukewarmly adv segniter, neglegenter

lukewarmness n tepor m; (fig) neglegentia f, incūria f
lull vt sōpīre; (storm) sēdāre ♦ n intermissiō f
lumber n scrūta ntpl
luminary n lūmen nt, astrum nt
luminous adj lūcidus, illūstris
lump n massa f; (on body) tuber nt
lumpish adj hebes, crassus, stolidus
lunacy n īnsānia f
lunar adj lūnāris
lunatic n īnsānus m
lunch n prandium nt ♦ vi prandēre
lung n pulmō m; (pl, RHET) latera ntpl
lunge n ictus m ♦ vi prōsilīre
lurch n: **leave in the ~** dērelinquere, dēstituere ♦ vi titubāre
lure n esca f ♦ vt allicere, illicere, ēlicere
lurid adj lūridus
lurk vi latēre, latitāre, dēlitēscere
luscious adj praedulcis
lush adj luxuriōsus
lust n libīdō f ♦ vi libīdine flagrāre, concupīscere
lustful adj libīdinōsus
lustily adv validē, strēnuē
lustiness n vigor m, nervī mpl
lustration n lūstrum nt
lustre n fulgor m, splendor m
lustrous adj illūstris
lusty adj validus, lacertōsus
lute n cithara f, fidēs fpl
lute player n citharista m, citharistria f, fidicen m, fidicina f
luxuriance n luxuria f
luxuriant adj luxuriōsus
luxuriate vi luxuriārī
luxuries npl lautitiae fpl
luxurious adj luxuriōsus, sūmptuōsus, lautus
luxuriously adv sūmptuōsē, lautē
luxury n luxuria f, luxus m
lynx n lynx m/f; **lynx-eyed** lyncēus
lyre n lyra f, fidēs fpl; **play the ~** fidibus canere
lyric adj lyricus ♦ n carmen nt
lyrist n fidicen m, fidicina f

Mm

mace n scīpiō m
machination n dolus m
machine n māchina f
mackerel n scomber m
mad adj īnsānus, furiōsus, vēcors, dēmēns; **be mad** īnsānīre, furere
madam n domina f
madden vt furiāre, mentem aliēnāre (dat)
madly adv īnsānē, furiōsē, dēmenter
madness n īnsānia f, furor m, dēmentia f; (animals) rabiēs f
maelstrom n vertex m
magazine n horreum nt, apothēca f
maggot n vermiculus m
magic adj magicus ♦ n magicae artēs fpl
magician n magus m, veneficus m
magistracy n magistrātus m
magistrate n magistrātus m
magnanimity n māgnanimitās f, līberalitās f
magnanimous adj generōsus, līberālis, māgnanimus
magnet n magnēs m
magnificence n māgnificentia f, adparātus m
magnificent adj māgnificus, amplus, splendidus
magnificently adv māgnificē, amplē, splendidē
magnify vt amplificāre, exaggerāre
magnitude n māgnitūdō f
magpie n pīca f
maid n virgō f; (servant) ancilla f
maiden n virgō f
maidenhood n virginitās f
maidenly adj virginālis
mail n (armour) lōrīca f; (letters) epistulae fpl
maim vt mutilāre
maimed adj mancus
main adj prīnceps, prīmus; ~ **point** caput nt ♦ n (sea) altum nt, pelagus nt; **with might and** ~ manibus pedibusque, omnibus nervīs
mainland n continēns f
mainly adv praecipuē, plērumque
maintain vt (keep) tenēre, servāre; (keep up) sustinēre; (keep alive) alere, sustentāre; (argue) adfirmāre, dēfendere
maintenance n (food) alimentum nt
majestic adj augustus, māgnificus
majestically adv augustē
majesty n māiestās f
major adj māior
majority n māior pars f, plērīque; **have attained one's** ~ suī iūris esse

make vt facere, fingere; (appointment) creāre; (bed) sternere; (cope) superāre; (compulsion) cōgere; (consequence) efficere; (craft) fabricārī; (harbour) capere; (living) quaerere; (sum) efficere; (with adj) reddere; (with verb) cōgere; ~ **away with** tollere, interimere; ~ **good** supplēre, resarcīre; ~ **light of** parvī facere; ~ **one's way** iter facere; ~ **much of** māgnī aestimāre, multum tribuere (dat); ~ **for** petere; ~ **out** arguere; ~ **over** dēlēgāre, trānsferre; ~ **ready** pārāre; ~ **a speech** ōrātiōnem habēre; ~ **a truce** indutias compōnere; ~ **war on** bellum inferre; ~ **up** (loss) supplēre; (total) efficere; (story) fingere; **be made** fierī
make-believe n simulātiō f
maker n fabricātor m, auctor m
make-up n medicāmina ntpl
maladministration n (charge) repetundae fpl
malady n morbus m
malcontent adj novārum rērum cupidus
male adj mās, masculus
malefactor n nocēns m, reus m
malevolence n malevolentia f
malevolent adj malevolus, malignus
malevolently adv malignē
malformation n dēprāvātiō f
malice n invidia f, malevolentia f; **bear** ~ **towards** invidēre (dat)
malicious adj invidiōsus, malevolus, malignus
maliciously adv malignē
malign adj malignus, invidiōsus ♦ vt obtrectāre
malignant adj malevolus
maligner n obtrectātor m
malignity n malevolentia f
malleable adj ductilis
mallet n malleus m
mallow n malva f
malpractices n dēlicta ntpl
maltreat vt laedere, vexāre
malversation n peculātus m
man n (human being) homō m/f; (male) vir m; (MIL) mīles m; (chess) latrunculus m; **to a man** omnēs ad ūnum; **man who** is qui; **old man** senex m; **young man** adulēscēns m; **man of war** nāvis longa f ♦ vt (ship) complēre; (walls) praesidiō firmāre
manacle n manicae fpl ♦ vt manicās inicere (dat)
manage vt efficere, gerere, gubernāre, administrāre; (horse) moderārī; (with verb) posse
manageable adj tractābilis, habilis
management n administrātiō f, cūra f; (finance) dispēnsātiō f

manager n administrātor m, moderātor m; dispēnsātor m
mandate n mandātum nt
mane n iuba f
manful adj virīlis, fortis
manfully adv virīliter, fortiter
manger n praesēpe nt
mangle vt dīlaniāre, lacerāre
mangy adj scaber
manhood n pūbertās f, toga virīlis f
mania n īnsānia f
maniac n furiōsus m
manifest adj manifestus, apertus, clārus ♦ vt dēclārāre, aperīre
manifestation n speciēs f
manifestly adv manifestō, apertē
manifesto n ēdictum nt
manifold adj multiplex, varius
manikin n homunciō m, homunculus m
manipulate vt tractāre
manipulation n tractātiō f
mankind n hominēs mpl, genus hūmānum nt
manliness n virtūs f
manly adj fortis, virīlis
manner n modus m, ratiō f; (custom) mōs m, ūsus m; **manners** pl mōrēs mpl; **after the ~ of** rītū, mōre (gen); **good manners** hūmānitās f, modestia f
mannered adj mōrātus
mannerism n mōs m
mannerly adj bene mōrātus, urbānus
manoeuvre n (MIL) dēcursus m, dēcursiō f; (fig) dolus m ♦ vi dēcurrere; (fig) māchinārī
manor n praedium nt
mansion n domus f
manslaughter n homicīdium nt
mantle n pallium nt; (women's) palla f
manual adj: ~ **labour** opera f ♦ n libellus m, ars f
manufacture n fabrica f ♦ vt fabricārī
manumission n manūmissiō f
manumit vt manū mittere, ēmancipāre
manure n fimus m, stercus nt ♦ vt stercorāre
manuscript n liber m, cōdex m
many adj multī, ā ... quot; **how many?** quot?; **so ~** tot; **in ~ places** multifāriam; **a good ~** complūrēs; **too ~** nimis multī; **the ~** vulgus nt; **very ~** permultī, plūrimī
map n tabula f ♦ vt: **map out** dēscrībere, dēsignāre
maple n acer nt ♦ adj acernus
mar vt corrumpere, dēfōrmāre
marauder n praedātor m, dēpopulātor m
marble n marmor nt ♦ adj marmoreus
March n mēnsis Martius m; **of ~** Martius
march n iter nt; **line of ~** agmen nt; **by forced marches** māgnīs itineribus; **on the ~** ex itinere, in itinere; **quick ~** plēnō gradū; **a regular day's ~** iter iūstum nt ♦ vi contendere, iter facere, incēdere, īre; ~ **out** exīre; ~ **on** signa prōferre, prōgredī ♦ vt dūcere; ~ **out** ēdūcere; ~ **in** intrōdūcere
mare n equa f
margin n margō f; (fig) discrīmen nt
marigold n caltha f
marine adj marīnus ♦ n mīles classicus m
mariner n nauta m

marital adj marītus
maritime adj maritimus
marjoram n amāracus m
mark n nota f; (of distinction) īnsigne nt; (target) scopos m; (trace) vestīgium nt; **beside the ~** nihil ad rem; **it is the ~ of a wise man to** sapientis est (inf); **be wide of the ~** errāre ♦ vt notāre, dēsignāre; (observe) animadvertere, animum attendere; ~ **out** (site) mētārī, dēsignāre; (for purpose) dēnotāre
marked adj īnsignis, manifestus
markedly adv manifestō
marker n index m
market n macellum nt; ~ **day** nūndinae fpl; ~ **town** emporium nt; **cattle ~** forum boārium nt; **fish ~** forum piscārium nt
marketable adj vēndibilis
marketplace n forum nt
market prices npl annōna f
market town n emporium nt
marking n macula f
maroon vt dērelinquere
marriage n mātrimōnium nt, coniugium nt; (ceremony) nūptiae fpl; **give in ~** collocāre; ~ **bed** lectus geniālis m
marriageable adj nūbilis
marrow n medulla f
marry vt (a wife) dūcere, in mātrimōnium dūcere; (a husband) nūbere (dat)
marsh n palūs f
marshal n imperātor m ♦ vt īnstruere
marshy adj palūster
mart n forum nt
marten n mēlēs f
martial adj bellicōsus, ferōx
martyr n dēvōtus m; (ECCL) martyr m/f
marvel n mīrāculum nt, portentum nt ♦ vi mīrārī; ~ **at** admīrārī
marvellous adj mīrus, mīrificus, mīrābilis
marvellously adv mīrē, mīrum quantum
masculine adj mās, virīlis
mash n farrāgō f ♦ vt commiscēre, contundere
mask n persōna f ♦ vt persōnam induere (dat); (fig) dissimulāre
mason n structor m
masonry n lapidēs mpl, caementum nt
masquerade n simulātiō f ♦ vi vestem mūtāre; ~ **as** speciem sibi induere (gen), persōnam ferre (gen)
mass n mōlēs f; (of small things) congeriēs f; (of people) multitūdō f; (ECCL) missa f; **the masses** vulgus nt, plēbs f ♦ vt congerere, coacervāre
massacre n strāgēs f, caedēs f, interneciō f ♦ vt trucīdāre
massive adj ingēns, solidus
massiveness n mōlēs f, soliditās f
mast n mālus m
master n dominus m; (school) magister m; **be ~ of** dominārī in (abl); (skill) perītum esse (gen); **become ~ of** potīrī (abl); **be one's own ~** suī iūris esse; **not ~ of** impotēns (gen); **a past ~** veterātor m ♦ vt dēvincere; (skill) ēdiscere; (passion) continēre
masterful adj imperiōsus
masterly adj doctus, perītus
masterpiece n praeclārum opus nt

mastery *n* dominātiō *f*, imperium *nt*, arbitrium *nt*
masticate *vt* mandere
mastiff *n* Molossus *m*
mat *n* storea *f*
match *n* (*person*) pār *m/f*; (*marriage*) nūptiae *fpl*; (*contest*) certāmen *nt*; **a ~ for** pār (*dat*); **no ~ for** impār (*dat*) ♦ *vt* exaequāre, adaequāre ♦ *vi* congruere
matchless *adj* singulāris, ūnicus
mate *n* socius *m*; (*married*) coniunx *m/f* ♦ *vi* coniungī
material *adj* corporeus; (*significant*) haud levis ♦ *n* māteriēs *f*; (*literary*) silva *f*
materialize *vi* ēvenīre
materially *adv* māgnopere
maternal *adj* māternus
mathematical *adj* mathēmaticus
mathematician *n* mathēmaticus *m*, geōmetrēs *m*
mathematics *n* ars mathēmatica *f*, numerī *mpl*
matin *adj* mātūtīnus
matricide *n* (*act*) mātricīdium *nt*; (*person*) mātricīda *m*
matrimony *n* mātrimōnium *nt*
matrix *n* fōrma *f*
matron *n* mātrōna *f*
matter *n* māteria *f*, corpus *nt*; (*affair*) rēs *f*; (*MED*) pūs *nt*; **what is the ~ with you?** quid tibī est? ♦ *vi*: **it matters** interest, rēfert
matting *n* storea *f*
mattock *n* dolābra *f*
mattress *n* culcita *f*
mature *adj* mātūrus; (*age*) adultus ♦ *vi* mātūrēscere
maturity *n* mātūritās *f*; (*age*) adulta aetās *f*
maul *n* fistūca *f* ♦ *vt* contundere, dīlaniāre
maw *n* ingluviēs *f*
mawkish *adj* pūtidus
mawkishly *adv* pūtidē
maxim *n* dictum *nt*, praeceptum *nt*, sententia *f*
maximum *adj* quam māximus, quam plūrimus
May *n* mēnsis Māius *m*; **of May** Māius
may *vi* posse; **I may** licet mihī
mayor *n* praefectus *m*
maze *n* labyrinthus *m*
mead *n* (*drink*) mulsum *nt*; (*land*) prātum *nt*
meagre *adj* exīlis, iēiūnus
meagrely *adv* exīliter, iēiūnē
meagreness *n* exīlitās *f*
meal *n* (*flour*) farīna *f*; (*repast*) cibus *m*
mealy-mouthed *adj* blandiloquus
mean *adj* humilis, abiectus; (*birth*) ignōbilis; (*average*) medius, mediocris ♦ *n* modus *m*, mediocritās *f* ♦ *vt* dīcere, significāre; (*word*) valēre; (*intent*) velle, in animō habēre
meander *vi* sinuōsō cursū fluere
meaning *n* significātiō *f*, vīs *f*, sententia *f*; **what is the ~ of?** quid sibī vult?, quōrsum spectat?
meanly *adv* abiectē, humiliter
meanness *n* humilitās *f*; (*conduct*) illīberālitās *f*, avāritia *f*
means *n* īnstrūmentum *nt*; (*of doing*) facultās *f*; (*wealth*) opēs *fpl*; **by ~ of** per (*acc*); **by all ~** māximē; **by no ~** nūllō modō, haudquāquam; **of small ~** pauper

meantime, meanwhile *adv* intereā, interim
measles *n* boa *f*
measure *n* modus *m*, mēnsūra *f*; (*rhythm*) numerī *mpl*; (*plan*) cōnsilium *nt*; (*LAW*) rogātiō *f*, lēx *f*; **beyond ~** nimium; **in some ~** aliquā ex parte; **take measures** cōnsulere; **take the ~ of** quālis sit cognōscere; **without ~** immoderātē ♦ *vt* mētīrī; **~ out** dīmētīrī; (*land*) mētārī
measured *adj* moderātus
measureless *adj* īnfīnītus, immēnsus
measurement *n* mēnsūra *f*
meat *n* carō *f*
mechanic *n* opifex *m*, faber *m*
mechanical *adj* mēchanicus
mechanical device māchinātiō *f*
mechanics *n* māchinālis scientia *f*
mechanism *n* māchinātiō *f*
medal *n* īnsigne *nt*
meddle *vi* sē interpōnere
meddlesome *adj* cūriōsus
Medes *n* Mēdī *mpl*
mediate *vi* intercēdere; **~ between** compōnere, conciliāre
mediator *n* intercessor *m*, dēprecātor *m*
medical *adj* medicus
medicate *vt* medicāre
medicinal *adj* medicus, salūbris
medicine *n* (*art*) medicīna *f*; (*drug*) medicāmentum *nt*
medicine chest *n* narthēcium *nt*
mediocre *adj* mediocris
mediocrity *n* mediocritās *f*
meditate *vi* meditārī, cōgitāre, sēcum volūtāre
meditation *n* cōgitātiō *f*, meditātiō *f*
medium *n* internūntius *m*; (*means*) modus *m* ♦ *adj* mediocris
medley *n* farrāgō *f*
meek *adj* mītis, placidus
meekly *adv* summissō animō
meet *adj* idōneus, aptus ♦ *n* conventus *m* ♦ *vi* convenīre ♦ *vt* obviam īre (*dat*), occurrere (*dat*); (*fig*) obīre; **~ with** invenīre, excipere
meeting *n* cōnsilium *nt*, conventus *m*
melancholic *adj* melancholicus
melancholy *n* ātra bīlis *f*; tristitia *f*, maestitia *f* ♦ *adj* tristis, maestus
mêlée *n* turba *f*, concursus *m*
mellow *adj* mītis; (*wine*) lēnis; **become ~** mītēscere; **make ~** mītigāre
mellowness *n* mātūritās *f*
melodious *adj* canōrus, numerōsus
melodiously *adv* numerōsē
melody *n* melos *nt*, modī *mpl*
melt *vt* liquefacere, dissolvere; (*fig*) movēre ♦ *vi* liquēscere, dissolvī; (*fig*) commovērī; **~ away** dēliquēscere
member *n* membrum *nt*; (*person*) socius *m*
membrane *n* membrāna *f*
memento *n* monumentum *nt*
memoir *n* commentārius *m*
memorable *adj* memorābilis, commemorābilis
memorandum *n* hypomnēma *nt*
memorial *n* monumentum *nt*
memorize *vt* ēdiscere
memory *n* memoria *f*; **from ~** memoriter

menace n minae fpl ♦ vt minārī, minitārī; (things) imminēre (dat)
menacing adj mināx
menacingly adv mināciter
menage n familia f
mend vt sarcīre, reficere ♦ vi meliōrem fierī; (health) convalēscere
mendacious adj mendāx
mendacity n mendācium nt
mendicant n mendīcus m
mendicity n mendīcitās f
menial adj servīlis, famulāris ♦ n servus m, famulus m
menstrual adj mēnstruus
mensuration n mētiendī ratiō f
mental adj cōgitātiōnis, mentis
mentality n animī adfectus m, mēns f
mentally adv cōgitātiōne, mente
mention n mentiō f ♦ vt memorāre, mentiōnem facere (gen); (casually) inicere; (briefly) attingere; omit to ~ praetermittere
mentor n auctor m, praeceptor m
mercantile adj mercātōrius
mercenary adj mercennārius, vēnālis ♦ n mercennārius mīles m
merchandise n mercēs fpl
merchant n mercātor m
merchantman n nāvis onerāria f
merchant ship n nāvis onerāria f
merciful adj misericors, clēmens
mercifully adv clēmenter
merciless adj immisericors, inclēmens, inhūmānus
mercilessly adv inhūmānē
mercurial adj hilaris
mercy n misericordia f, clēmentia f, venia f; at the ~ of obnoxius (dat), in manū (gen)
mere n lacus m ♦ adj merus m
merely adv sōlum, tantum, dumtaxat
meretricious adj meretricius; ~ attractions lēnōcinia ntpl
merge vt cōnfundere ♦ vi cōnfundī
meridian n merīdiēs m ♦ adj merīdiānus
merit n meritum nt, virtūs f ♦ vt merērī
meritorious adj laudābilis
meritoriously adv optimē
mermaid n nympha f
merrily adv hilare, festīvē
merriment n hilaritās f, festīvitās f
merry adj hilaris, festīvus; make ~ lūdere
merrymaking n lūdus m, festīvitās f
mesh n macula f
mess n (dirt) sordēs f, squālor m; (trouble) turba f; (food) cibus m; (MIL) contubernālēs mpl
message n nūntius m
messenger n nūntius m
messmate n contubernālis m
metal n metallum nt ♦ adj ferreus, aereus
metamorphose vt mūtāre, trānsfōrmāre
metamorphosis n mūtātiō f
metaphor n trānslātiō f
metaphorical adj trānslātus
metaphorically adv per trānslātiōnem
metaphysics n dialectica ntpl
mete vt mētīrī
meteor n fax caelestis f

meteorology n prognōstica ntpl
methinks vi: ~ I am mihī videor esse
method n ratiō f, modus m
methodical adj dispositus; (person) dīligēns
methodically adv dispositē
meticulous adj accūrātus
meticulously adv accūrātē
meticulousness n cūra f
metonymy n immūtātiō f
metre n numerī mpl, modī mpl
metropolis n urbs f
mettle n ferōcitās f, virtūs f
mettlesome adj ferōx, animōsus
mew n (bird) larus m; **mews** pl stabula ntpl ♦ vi vāgīre
miasma n hālitus m
mid adj medius ♦ prep inter (acc)
midday n merīdiēs m ♦ adj merīdiānus
middle adj medius ♦ n medium nt; in the ~ medius, in mediō; ~ of medius
middling adj mediocris
midge n culex m
midget n (offensive) pūmiliō m/f
midland adj mediterrāneus
midnight n media nox f
midriff n praecordia ntpl
midst n medium nt; in the ~ medius; in the ~ of inter (acc); through the ~ of per medium
midsummer n sōlstitium nt ♦ adj sōlstitiālis
midway adv medius
midwife n obstetrix f
midwinter n brūma f ♦ adj brūmālis
mien n aspectus m, vultus m
might n vīs f, potentia f; with ~ and main omnibus nervīs, manibus pedibusque
mightily adv valdē, magnopere
mighty adj ingēns, validus
migrate vi abīre, migrāre
migration n peregrīnātiō f
migratory adj advena
mild adj mītis, lēnis, clēmēns
mildew n rōbīgō f
mildly adv lēniter, clēmenter
mildness n clēmentia f, mānsuētūdō f; (weather) caelī indulgentia f
mile n mīlle passūs mpl; **miles** pl mīlia passuum
milestone n lapis m, mīliārium nt
militant adj ferōx
military adj mīlitāris ♦ n mīlitēs mpl
military service n mīlitia f
militate vi: ~ against repugnāre (dat), facere contrā (acc)
militia n mīlitēs mpl
milk n lac nt ♦ vt mulgēre
milk pail n mulctra f
milky adj lacteus
mill n pistrīnum nt
milled adj (coin) serrātus
millennium n mīlle annī mpl
miller n pistor m
millet n mīlium nt
million num deciēs centēna mīlia ntpl
millionaire n rēx m
millstone n mola f, molāris m
mime n mīmus m
mimic n imitātor m, imitātrīx f ♦ vt imitārī

mimicry n imitātiō f
minatory adj mināx
mince vt concīdere; **not ~ words** plānē apertēque dīcere ♦ n minūtal nt
mind n mēns f, animus m, ingenium nt; (opinion) sententia f; (memory) memoria f; **be in one's right ~** mentis suae esse; **be of the same ~** eadem sentīre; **be out of one's ~** īnsānīre; **bear in ~** meminisse (gen), memorem esse (gen); **call to ~** memoriā repetere, recordārī; **have a ~ to** libet; **have in ~** in animō habēre; **put one's ~ to** animum applicāre ad (acc); **make up one's ~** animum indūcere, animō obstināre, statuere; **put in ~ of** admonēre (gen); **speak one's ~** sententiam suam aperīre; **to one's ~** ex sententiā ♦ vt cūrāre, attendere; **~ one's own business** suum negōtium agere ♦ vi gravārī; **I don't ~** nīl moror; **never ~** mitte
minded adj animātus
mindful adj memor
mine n metallum nt; (MIL) cuniculus m; (fig) thēsaurus m ♦ vi fodere; (MIL) cuniculum agere ♦ pron meus
miner n fossor m
mineral n metallum nt
mingle vt miscēre, commiscēre ♦ vi sē immiscēre
miniature n minima pictūra f
minimize vt dētrectāre
minimum n minimum nt ♦ adj quam minimus
minion n cliēns m/f, dēlicātus m
minister n administer m ♦ vi ministrāre, servīre
ministry n mūnus nt, officium nt
minor adj minor ♦ n pupillus m, pupilla f
minority n minor pars f; **in one's ~** nōndum suī iūris
Minotaur n Mīnōtaurus m
minstrel n fidicen m
minstrelsy n cantus m
mint n (plant) menta f; (money) Monēta f ♦ vt cūdere
minute¹ n temporis mōmentum nt
minute² adj minūtus, exiguus, subtīlis
minutely adv subtīliter
minuteness n exiguitās f, subtīlitas f
minutiae n singula ntpl
minx n lascīva f
miracle n mīrāculum nt, mōnstrum nt
miraculous adj mīrus, mīrābilis
miraculously adv dīvīnitus
mirage n falsa speciēs f
mire n lutum nt
mirror n speculum nt ♦ vt reddere
mirth n hilaritās f, laetitia f
mirthful adj hilaris, laetus
mirthfully adv hilare, laetē
miry adj lutulentus
misadventure n īnfortūnium nt, cāsus m
misapply vt abūtī (abl); (words) invertere
misapprehend vt male intellegere
misapprehension n error m
misappropriate vt intervertere
misbegotten adj nothus
misbehave vi male sē gerere
miscalculate vi errāre, fallī
miscalculation n error m

miscall vt maledīcere (dat)
miscarriage n abortus m; (fig) error m
miscarry vi aborīrī; (fig) cadere, inritum esse
miscellaneous adj prōmiscuus, varius
miscellany n farrāgō f
mischance n īnfortūnium nt
mischief n malum nt, facinus nt, maleficium nt; (children) lascīvia f
mischievous adj improbus, maleficus; lascīvus
misconceive vt male intellegere
misconception n error m
misconduct n dēlictum nt, culpa f
misconstruction n prāva interpretātiō f
misconstrue vt male interpretārī
miscreant n scelerātus m
misdeed n maleficium nt, dēlictum nt
misdemeanour n peccātum nt, culpa f
miser n avārus m
miserable adj miser, īnfēlīx; **make oneself ~** sē cruciāre
miserably adv miserē
miserliness n avāritia f
miserly adj avārus
misery n miseria f, aerumna f
misfortune n malum nt, īnfortūnium nt, incommodum nt, rēs adversae fpl
misgiving n suspiciō f, cūra f; **have misgivings** parum cōnfīdere
misgovern vt male regere
misgovernment n prāva administrātiō f
misguide vt fallere, dēcipere
misguided adj dēmēns
mishap n īnfortūnium nt
misinform vt falsa docēre
misinterpret vt male interpretārī
misinterpretation n prāva interpretātiō f
misjudge vt male iūdicāre
mislay vt āmittere
mislead vt dēcipere, indūcere, auferre
mismanage vt male gerere
misnomer n falsum nōmen nt
misogyny n mulierum odium nt
misplace vt in aliēnō locō collocāre
misplaced adj (fig) vānus
misprint n mendum nt
mispronounce vt prāvē appellāre
misquote vt perperam prōferre
misrepresent vt dētorquēre, invertere; (person) calumniārī
misrepresentation n calumnia f
misrule n prāva administrātiō f
miss vt (aim) aberrāre (abl); (loss) requīrere, dēsīderāre; (notice) praetermittere ♦ n error m; (girl) virgō f
misshapen adj distortus, dēfōrmis
missile n tēlum nt
missing adj absēns; **be ~** dēesse, dēsīderārī
mission n lēgātiō f
missive n litterae fpl
misspend vt perdere, dissipāre
misstatement n falsum nt, mendācium nt
mist n nebula f, cālīgō f
mistake n error m; (writing) mendum nt; **full of mistakes** mendōsus ♦ vt: **~ for** habēre prō (abl); **be mistaken** errāre, fallī
mistletoe n viscum nt

mistranslate vt prāvē reddere
mistress n domina f; (school) magistra f; (lover) amīca f
mistrust n diffidentia f, suspiciō f ♦ vt diffīdere (dat)
mistrustful adj diffīdēns
mistrustfully adv diffīdenter
misty adj nebulōsus
misunderstand vt male intellegere ♦ vi errāre
misunderstanding n error m; (quarrel) discidium nt
misuse n malus ūsus m ♦ vt abūtī (abl)
mite n parvulus m; (insect) vermiculus m
mitigate vt mītigāre, lēnīre
mitigation n mītigātiō f
mix vt miscēre; **mix in** admiscēre; **mix together** commiscēre; **get mixed up with** admiscērī cum, sē interpōnere (dat)
mixed adj prōmiscuus
mixture n (act) temperātiō f; (state) dīversitās f
mnemonic n artificium memoriae nt
moan n gemitus m ♦ vi gemere
moat n fossa f
mob n vulgus nt, turba f ♦ vt circumfundī in (acc)
mobile adj mōbilis, agilis
mobility n mōbilitās f, agilitās f
mobilize vt (MIL) ēvocāre
mock vt irrīdēre, lūdibriō habēre, lūdificārī; (ape) imitārī; **~ at** inlūdere ♦ n lūdibrium nt ♦ adj simulātus, fictus
mocker n dērīsor m
mockery n lūdibrium nt, irrīsus m
mode n modus m, ratiō f
model n exemplar nt, exemplum nt ♦ vt fingere
modeller n fictor m
moderate adj (size) modicus; (conduct) moderātus ♦ vt temperāre; (emotion) temperāre (dat) ♦ vi mītigārī
moderately adv modicē, moderātē, mediocriter
moderation n moderātiō f, modus m; (mean) mediocritās f
moderator n praefectus m
modern adj recēns
modernity n haec aetās f
modest adj pudīcus, verēcundus
modestly adv verēcundē, pudenter
modesty n pudor m, verēcundia f
modicum n paullulum nt, aliquantulum nt
modification n mūtātiō f
modify vt immūtāre; (LAW) derogāre aliquid dē
modulate vt (voice) īnflectere
modulation n flexiō f, inclīnātiō f
moiety n dīmidia pars f
moist adj ūmidus
moisten vt ūmectāre, rigāre
moisture n ūmor m
molar n genuīnus m
mole n (animal) talpa f; (on skin) naevus m; (pier) mōlēs f
molecule n corpusculum nt
molehill n: **make a mountain out of a ~** ē rīvō flūmina māgna facere, arcem facere ē cloācā
molest vt sollicitāre, vexāre
molestation n vexātiō f
mollify vt mollīre, lēnīre
molten adj liquefactus

moment n temporis mōmentum nt, temporis pūnctum nt; **for a ~** parumper; **in a ~** iam; **without a moment's delay** nūllā interpositā morā; **be of great ~** māgnō mōmentō esse; **it is of ~** interest
momentary adj brevis
momentous adj gravis, māgnī mōmentī
momentum n impetus m
monarch n rēx m, tyrannus m
monarchical adj rēgius
monarchy n rēgnum nt
monastery n monastērium nt
monetary adj pecūniārius
money n pecūnia f; (cash) nummī mpl; **for ~** mercēde; **ready ~** nummī, praesēns pecūnia; **make ~** rem facere, quaestum facere
moneybag n fiscus m
moneyed adj nummātus, pecūniōsus
moneylender n faenerātor m
moneymaking n quaestus m
mongoose n ichneumōn m
mongrel n (dog) hibrida m
monitor n admonitor m
monk n monachus m
monkey n sīmia f
monograph n libellus m
monologue n ōrātiō f
monopolize vt absorbēre, sibī vindicāre
monopoly n arbitrium nt
monosyllabic adj monosyllabus
monosyllable n monosyllabum nt
monotonous adj aequābilis
monotony n taedium nt
monster n mōnstrum nt, portentum nt, bēlua f
monstrosity n mōnstrum nt
monstrous adj immānis, mōnstruōsus; improbus
month n mēnsis m
monthly adj mēnstruus
monument n monumentum nt
monumental adj ingēns
mood n adfectiō f, adfectus m, animus m; (GRAM) modus m; **I am in the ~ for** libet (inf)
moody adj mōrōsus, tristis
moon n lūna f; **new ~** interlūnium nt
moonlight n: **by ~** ad lūnam
moonshine n somnia ntpl
moonstruck adj lūnāticus
moor vt religāre ♦ n tesqua ntpl
moorings n ancorae fpl
moot n conventus m; **it is a ~ point** discrepat ♦ vt iactāre
mop n pēniculus m ♦ vt dētergēre
mope vi maerēre
moral adj honestus, probus; (opposed to physical) animī; (PHILOS) mōrālis ♦ n documentum nt
morale n animus m; **~ is low** iacet animus
morality n bonī mōrēs mpl, virtūs f
moralize vi dē officiīs disserere
morally adv honestē
morals npl mōrēs mpl
morass n palūs f
moratorium n mora f
morbid adj aeger
mordant adj mordāx

more *adj* plūs, pluris *(in sg + gen, in pl + adj)* ♦ *adv* plūs, magis, amplius; *(extra)* ultrā; ~ **than** amplius quam; ~ **than three feet** amplius trēs pedēs; ~ **and** ~ magis magisque; **never** ~ immo; ~ **or less** ferē; **no** ~ *(time)* nōn diūtius, nunquam posteā

moreover *adv* tamen, autem, praetereā

moribund *adj* moribundus

morning *n* māne *nt*; **early in the** ~ bene māne; **this** ~ hodiē māne; **good** ~ salvē ♦ *adj* mātūtīnus

morning call *n* salūtātiō *f*

morning watch *n* (NAUT) tertia vigilia *f*

moron *n* (*offensive*) sōcors *m*

morose *adj* acerbus, tristis

moroseness *n* acerbitās *f*, tristitia *f*

morrow *n* posterus diēs *m*; **on the** ~ posterō diē, postrīdiē

morsel *n* offa *f*

mortal *adj* mortālis, hūmānus; *(wound)* mortifer ♦ *n* mortālis *m/f*, homō *m/f*; **poor** ~ homunculus *m*

mortality *n* mortālitās *f*; *(death)* mors *f*; **the** ~ **was high** plūrimī periērunt

mortally *adv*: **be** ~ **wounded** mortiferum vulnus accipere

mortar *n* mortārium *nt*

mortgage *n* pignus *nt*, fīdūcia *f* ♦ *vt* obligāre

mortification *n* dolor *m*, angor *m*

mortified *adj*: **be** ~ **at** aegrē ferre

mortify *vt* mordēre, vexāre; *(lust)* coercēre ♦ *vi* putrēscere

mortise *vt* immittere

mosaic *n* emblēma *nt*, lapillī *mpl* ♦ *adj* tessellātus

mosquito *n* culex *m*

mosquito net *n* cōnōpēum *nt*

moss *n* muscus *m*

mossy *adj* muscōsus

most *adj* plūrimus, plērusque; **for the** ~ **part** māximam partem ♦ *adv* māximē, plūrimum

mostly *adv* plērumque, ferē

mote *n* corpusculum *nt*

moth *n* tinea *f*

mother *n* māter *f*; **of a** ~ māternus

mother-in-law *n* socrus *f*

motherless *adj* mātre orbus

motherly *adj* māternus

mother tongue *n* patrius sermō *m*

mother wit *n* Minerva *f*

motif *n* argūmentum *nt*

motion *n* mōtus *m*; *(for law)* rogātiō *f*; *(in debate)* sententia *f*; **propose a** ~ ferre; **set in** ~ movēre ♦ *vt* innuere

motionless *adj* immōbilis

motive *n* causa *f*, ratiō *f*; **I know your** ~ **in asking** sciō cūr rogēs

motley *adj* versicolor, varius

mottled *adj* maculōsus

motto *n* sententia *f*

mould *n* fōrma *f*; *(soil)* humus *f*; *(fungus)* mūcor *m* ♦ *vt* fingere, fōrmāre

moulder *vi* putrēscere ♦ *n* fictor *m*

mouldering *adj* puter

mouldiness *n* situs *m*

mouldy *adj* mūcidus

moult *vi* pennas exuere

mound *n* agger *m*, tumulus *m*

mount *n* mōns *m*; *(horse)* equus *m* ♦ *vt* scandere, cōnscendere, ascendere ♦ *vi* ascendere; ~ **up** ēscendere

mountain *n* mōns *m*

mountaineer *n* montānus *m*

mountainous *adj* montuōsus

mourn *vi* maerēre, lūgēre ♦ *vt* dēflēre, lūgēre

mourner *n* plōrātor *m*; *(hired)* praefica *f*

mournful *adj* *(cause)* lūctuōsus, acerbus; *(sound)* lūgubris, maestus

mournfully *adv* maestē

mourning *n* maeror *nt*, lūctus *m*; *(dress)* sordēs *fpl*; **in** ~ fūnestus; **be in** ~ lūgere; **put on** ~ vestem mūtāre, sordēs suscipere; **wearing** ~ ātrātus

mouse *n* mūs *m*

mousetrap *n* mūscipulum *nt*

mouth *n* ōs *nt*; *(river)* ōstium *nt*

mouthful *n* bucca *f*

mouthpiece *n* interpres *m*

movable *adj* mōbilis; **movables** *npl* rēs *fpl*, supellex *f*

move *vt* movēre; *(emotion)* commovēre; ~ **backwards and forwards** reciprocāre; ~ **out of the way** dēmovēre; ~ **up** admovēre ♦ *vi* movērī; *(residence)* dēmigrāre; *(proposal)* ferre, cēnsēre; ~ **into** immigrāre in *(acc)*; ~ **on** prōgredī

movement *n* mōtus *m*; *(process)* cursus *m*; *(society)* societās *f*

mover *n* auctor *m*

moving *adj* flēbilis, flexanimus

mow *vt* secāre, dēmetere

mower *n* faenisex *m*

much *adj* multus ♦ *adv* multum; *(with compar)* multō; **as** ~ **as** tantum quantum; **so** ~ tantum; *(with verbs)* adeo; ~ **less** nēdum; **too** ~ nimis ♦ *n* multum *nt*

muck *n* stercus *nt*

mud *n* lutum *nt*

muddle *n* turba *f* ♦ *vt* turbāre

muffle *vt* involvere; ~ **up** obvolvere

muffled *adj* surdus

mug *n* pōculum *nt*

mulberry *n* mōrum *nt*; *(tree)* mōrus *f*

mule *n* mūlus *m*

muleteer *n* mūliō *m*

mulish *adj* obstinātus

mullet *n* mullus *m*

multifarious *adj* multiplex, varius

multiform *adj* multifōrmis

multiply *vt* multiplicāre ♦ *vi* crēscere

multitude *n* multitūdō *f*

multitudinous *adj* crēberrimus

mumble *vt* *(words)* opprimere ♦ *vi* murmurāre

munch *vt* mandūcāre

mundane *adj* terrestris

municipal *adj* mūnicipālis

municipality *n* mūnicipium *nt*

munificence *n* largitās *f*

munificent *adj* largus, mūnificus

munificently *adv* mūnificē

munitions *n* bellī adparātus *m*

mural *adj* mūrālis

murder n parricīdium nt, caedēs f; **charge with ~** inter sīcāriōs accūsāre; **trial for ~** quaestiō inter sīcāriōs ◆ vt interficere, iūgulāre, necāre
murderer n sīcārius m, homicīda m, parricīda m, percussor m
murderess n interfectrīx f
murderous adj cruentus
murky adj tenebrōsus
murmur n murmur nt; (angry) fremitus m ◆ vi murmurāre; fremere
murmuring n admurmurātiō f
muscle n torus m
muscular adj lacertōsus
muse vi meditārī ◆ n Mūsa f
mushroom n fungus m, bōlētus m
music n (art) mūsica f; (sound) cantus m, modī mpl
musical adj (person) mūsicus; (sound) canōrus
musician n mūsicus m; (strings) fidicen m; (wind) tībīcen m
muslin n sindōn f
must n (wine) mustum nt ◆ vi dēbēre; **I ~ go** mē oportet īre, mihī eundum est
mustard n sināpi nt
muster vt convocāre, cōgere; (review) recēnsēre ◆ vi convenīre, coīre ◆ n conventus m; (review) recēnsiō f
muster roll n album nt
mustiness n situs m
musty adj mūcidus
mutability n incōnstantia f
mutable adj incōnstāns, mūtābilis

mute adj mūtus
mutilate vt mūtilāre, truncāre
mutilated adj mūtilus, truncus
mutilation n lacerātiō f
mutineer n sēditiōsus m
mutinous adj sēditiōsus
mutiny n sēditiō f ◆ vi sēditiōnem facere
mutter vi mussitāre
mutton n carō ovilla f
mutual adj mūtuus
mutually adv mūtuō, inter sē
muzzle n ōs nt, rōstrum nt; (guard) fiscella f ◆ vt fiscellā capistrāre
my adj meus
myriad n decem mīlia; (any large no.) sēscentī
myrmidon n satelles m
myrrh n murra f
myrtle n myrtus f ◆ adj myrteus
myrtle grove n myrtētum nt
myself pron ipse, egomet; (reflexive) mē
mysterious adj arcānus, occultus
mysteriously adv occultē
mystery n arcānum nt; (rites) mystēria ntpl; (fig) latebra f
mystic adj mysticus
mystical adj mysticus
mystification n fraus f, ambāgēs fpl
mystify vt fraudāre, cōnfundere
myth n fābula f
mythical adj fābulōsus
mythology n fābulae fpl

Nn

nabob n rēx m

nadir n fundus m

nag n caballus m ♦ vt obiūrgītāre

naiad n nāias f

nail n clāvus m; (finger) unguis m; **hit the ~ on the head** rem acū tangere ♦ vt clāvīs adfīgere

naive adj simplex

naively adv simpliciter

naiveté n simplicitās f

naked adj nūdus

nakedly adv apertē

name n nōmen nt; (repute) existimātiō f; (term) vocābulum nt; **by ~** nōmine; **have a bad ~** male audīre; **have a good ~** bene audīre; **in the ~ of** verbīs (gen); (oath) per ♦ vt appellāre, vocāre, nōmināre; (appoint) dīcere

nameless adj nōminis expers, sine nōmine

namely adv nempe, dīcō

namesake n gentīlis m/f

nanny goat n capra f

nap n brevis somnus m; (cloth) villus nt

napkin n linteum nt

narcissus n narcissus m

narcotic adj somnifer

nard n nardus f

narrate vt nārrāre, ēnārrāre

narration n nārrātiō f

narrative n fābula f

narrator n nārrātor m

narrow adj angustus ♦ vt coartāre ♦ vi coartārī

narrowly adv aegrē, vix

narrowness n angustiae fpl

narrows n angustiae fpl

nasal adj nārium

nascent adj nāscēns

nastily adv foedē

nastiness n foedītās f

nasty adj foedus, taeter, impūrus

natal adj nātālis

nation n populus m; (foreign) gēns f

national adj pūblicus, cīvīlis; (affairs) domesticus

nationality n cīvitās f

native adj indigena; (speech) patrius ♦ n incola m, indigena m/f

native land n patria f

nativity n ortus m

natural adj nātūrālis; (innate) nātīvus, genuīnus, īnsitus

naturalization n cīvitās f

naturalize vt cīvitāte dōnāre

naturalized adj (person) cīvitāte dōnātus; (thing) īnsitus

naturally adv nātūrāliter, secundum nātūram; (of course) scīlicet, certē

nature n nātūra f; rērum nātūra f; (character) indolēs f, ingenium nt; (species) genus nt; **course of ~** nātūra f; **I know the ~ of** sciō quālis sit

naught n nihil nt; **set at ~** parvī facere

naughty adj improbus

nausea n nausea f; (fig) fastīdium nt

nauseate vt fastīdium movēre (dat); **be nauseated with** fastīdīre

nauseous adj taeter

nautical adj nauticus, maritimus

naval adj nāvālis

navel n umbilīcus m

navigable adj nāvigābilis

navigate vt, vi nāvigāre

navigation n rēs nautica f; (sailing) nāvigātiō f

navigator n nauta m, gubernātor m

navy n classis f, cōpiae nāvālēs fpl

nay adv nōn; **nay more** immo

near adv prope ♦ adj propinquus ♦ prep prope (acc), ad (acc); **lie ~** adiacēre (dat) ♦ vt adpropinquāre (dat)

nearby adj iuxtā

nearer adj propior

nearest adj proximus

nearly adv paene, prope, fermē

neat adj nitidus, mundus, concinnus; (wine) pūrus

neatly adv mundē, concinnē

neatness n munditia f

nebulous adj nebulōsus; (fig) incertus

necessaries n rēs ad vīvendum necessāriae fpl

necessarily adv necessāriō, necesse

necessary adj necessārius, necesse; **it is ~** oportet (+ acc and infin or gerundive of vt)

necessitate vt cōgere (inf), efficere ut (subj)

necessitous adj egēnus, pauper

necessity n necessitās f; (thing) rēs necessāria f; (want) paupertās f, egestās f

neck n collum nt

neckcloth n fōcāle nt

necklace n monīle nt, torquis m

nectar n nectar nt

need n (necessity) necessitās f; (want) egestās f, inopia f, indigentia f; **there is ~ of** opus est (abl); **there is no ~ to** nihil est quod, cūr (subj) ♦ vt egēre (abl), carēre, indigēre (abl); **I ~** opus est mihī (abl)

needful adj necessārius

111

needle n acus f
needless adj vānus, inūtilis
needlessly adv frustrā, sine causā
needs adv necesse ♦ npl necessitātēs fpl
needy adj egēns, inops, pauper
nefarious adj nefārius, scelestus
negation n negātiō f, īnfitiātiō f
negative adj negāns ♦ n negātiō f; **answer in the** ~ negāre ♦ vt vetāre, contrādīcere (dat)
neglect n neglegentia f, incūria f; (of duty) dērelictiō f ♦ vt neglegere, ōmittere
neglectful adj neglegēns, immemor
negligence n neglegentia f, incūria f
negligent adj neglegēns, indīligēns
negligently adv neglegenter, indīligenter
negligible adj levissimus, minimī mōmentī
negotiate vi agere dē ♦ vt (deal) peragere; (difficulty) superāre
negotiation n āctiō f, pactum nt
negotiator n lēgātus m, conciliātor m
negro n (offensive) Aethiops m
neigh vi hinnīre
neighbour n vīcīnus m, fīnitimus m
neighbourhood n vīcīnia f, vīcīnitās f
neighbouring adj vīcīnus, fīnitimus, propinquus
neighbourly adj hūmānus, amīcus
neighing n hinnītus m
neither adv neque, nec; nēve, neu ♦ pron neuter ♦ adj neuter, neutra, neutrum (like **alter**); **neither... nor** nec/neque ... nec/neque
neophyte n tīrō m
nephew n frātris fīlius m, sorōris fīlius m
Nereid n Nērēis f
nerve n nervus m; (fig) audācia f; **nerves** pl pavor m, trepidātiō f; **have the** ~ **to** audēre ♦ vt cōnfirmāre
nervous adj diffīdēns, sollicitus, trepidus
nervously adv trepidē
nervousness n sollicitūdō f, diffīdentia f
nest n nīdus m ♦ vi nīdificāre
nestle vi recubāre
nestling n pullus m
net n rēte nt ♦ vt inrētīre
nether adj īnferior
nethermost adj īnfimus, īmus
netting n rēticulum nt
nettle n urtīca f ♦ vt inrītāre, ūrere
neuter adj neuter
neutral adj medius; **be** ~ neutrī partī sē adiungere, medium sē gerere
neutralize vt compēnsāre
never adv nunquam
nevertheless adv nihilōminus, at tamen
new adj novus, integer, recēns
newcomer n advena m/f
newfangled adj novus, inaudītus
newly adv nūper, modo
newness n novitās f
news n nūntius m; **what news?** quid novī?; ~ **was brought that** nūntiātum est (+ acc and infin)
newspaper n ācta diūrna/pūblica ntpl
newt n lacerta f

next adj proximus; (time) īnsequēns ♦ adv dēinde, dēinceps; ~ **day** postrīdiē; ~ **to** iuxtā; **come** ~ **to** excipere
nibble vi rōdere
nice adj bellus, dulcis; (exact) accūrātus; (particular) fastīdiōsus
nicely adv bellē, probē
nicety n subtīlitās f
niche n aedicula f
nick n: **in the** ~ **of time** in ipsō articulō temporis
nickname n cognōmen nt
niece n frātris fīlia f, sorōris fīlia f
niggardliness n illīberālitās f, avāritia f
niggardly adj illīberālis, parcus, avārus
nigh adv prope
night n nox f; **by** ~ noctū; **all** ~ pernox; **spend the** ~ pernoctāre; **be awake all** ~ pervigilāre ♦ adj nocturnus
night bird n noctua f
nightfall n prīmae tenebrae fpl; **at** ~ sub noctem
nightingale n luscinia f
nightly adj nocturnus ♦ adv noctū
nightmare n incubus m
night work n lūcubrātiō f
nimble adj agilis, pernīx
nimbleness n agilitās f, pernīcitās f; (mind) argūtiae fpl
nimbly adv pernīciter
nine num novem; ~ **each** novēnī; ~ **times** noviēns; ~ **days'** novendiālis
nine hundred num nōngentī
nine hundredth adj nōngentēsimus
nineteen num ūndēvigintī; ~ **each** ūndēvīcēnī; ~ **times** deciēns et noviēns
nineteenth adj ūndēvīcēsimus
ninetieth adj nōnāgēsimus
ninety num nōnāgintā; ~ **each** nōnāgēnī; ~ **times** nōnāgiēns
ninth adj nōnus
nip vt vellicāre; (frost) ūrere
nippers n forceps m
nipple n papilla f
no adv nōn; (correcting) immo; **say no** negāre ♦ adj nullus
nobility n nōbilitās f; (persons) optimātēs mpl, nōbilēs mpl
noble adj nōbilis; (birth) generōsus; (appearance) decōrus
nobleman n prīnceps m, optimās m
nobly adv nōbiliter, praeclārē
nobody n nēmō m
nocturnal adj nocturnus
nod n nūtus m ♦ vi nūtāre; (sign) adnuere; (sleep) dormītāre
noddle n caput nt
node n nōdus m
noise n strepitus m, sonitus m; (loud) fragor m; **make a** ~ increpāre, strepere ♦ vt: ~ **abroad** ēvulgāre; **be noised abroad** percrēbrēscere
noiseless adj tacitus
noiselessly adv tacitē
noisily adv cum strepitū
noisome adj taeter, gravis
noisy adj clāmōsus
nomadic adj vagus
nomenclature n vocābula ntpl

nominally *adv* nōmine, verbō
nominate *vt* nōmināre, dīcere; (*in writing*) scrībere
nomination *n* nōminātiō *f*
nominative *adj* nōminātīvus
nominee *n* nōminātus *m*
nonappearance *n* absentia *f*
nonce *n*: for the ~ semel
nonchalance *n* aequus animus *m*
nonchalantly *adv* aequō animō
noncombatant *adj* imbellis
noncommittal *adj* circumspectus
nondescript *adj* īnsolitus
none *adj* nullus ♦ *pron* nēmō *m*
nonentity *n* nihil *nt*, nullus *m*
nones *n* Nōnae *fpl*
nonexistent *adj* quī nōn est
nonplus *vt* ad incitās redigere
nonresistance *n* patientia *f*
nonsense *n* nūgae *fpl*, ineptiae *fpl*
nonsensical *adj* ineptus, absurdus
nook *n* angulus *m*
noon *n* merīdiēs *m* ♦ *adj* merīdiānus
no one *pron* nēmō *m*
noose *n* laqueus *m*
nor *adv* neque, nec; nēve, neu
norm *n* nōrma *f*
normal *adj* solitus
normally *adv* plērumque
north *n* septentriōnēs *mpl* ♦ *adj* septentriōnālis
northeast *adv* inter septentriōnēs et orientem
northerly *adj* septentriōnālis
northern *adj* septentriōnālis
North Pole *n* arctos *f*
northwards *adv* ad septentriōnēs versus
northwest *adv* inter septentriōnēs et occidentem ♦ *adj*: ~ **wind** Cōrus *m*
north wind *n* aquilō *m*
nose *n* nāsus *m*, nārēs *fpl*; **blow the ~** ēmungere; **lead by the ~** labiīs ductāre ♦ *vi* scrūtārī
nostril *n* nāris *f*
not *adv* nōn, haud; **not at all** haudquāquam; **not as if** nōn quod, nōn quō; **not but what** nōn quīn; **not even** nē ... quidem; **not so very** nōn ita; **not that** nōn quō; **and not** neque; **does not, did not** (*interrog*) nonne; **if ... not** nisi; **that not** (*purpose*) nē; (*fear*) nē nōn; **not long after** haud multō post; **not only ... but also** non modo/ solum ... sed etiam; **not yet** nōndum
notability *n* vir praeclārus *m*
notable *adj* insignis, īnsignītus, memorābilis
notably *adv* insignītē
notary *n* scrība *m*
notation *n* notae *fpl*
notch *n* incīsūra *f* ♦ *vt* incīdere
note *n* (*mark*) nota *f*; (*comment*) adnotātiō *f*; (*letter*) litterulae *fpl*; (*sound*) vōx *f*; **make a ~ of** in commentāriōs referre ♦ *vt* notāre; (*observe*) animadvertere
notebook *n* pugillārēs *mpl*
noted *adj* īnsignis, praeclārus, nōtus
noteworthy *adj* memorābilis
nothing *n* nihil, nīl *nt*; ~ **but** merus, nīl nisi; **come to ~** in inritum cadere; **for ~** frustrā; (*gift*) grātīs, grātuītō; **good for ~** nēquam; **think ~ of** nihilī facere

notice *n* (*official*) prōscrīptiō *f*; (*private*) libellus *m*; **attract ~** cōnspicī; **escape ~** latēre; **escape the ~ of** fallere; **give ~ of** dēnūntiāre; **take ~ of** animadvertere ♦ *vt* animadvertere, cōnspicere
noticeable *adj* cōnspicuus, īnsignis
noticeably *adv* īnsignītē
notification *n* dēnūntiātiō *f*
notify *vt* (*event*) dēnūntiāre, indicāre; (*person*) renūntiāre (*dat*), certiōrem facere
notion *n* nōtiō *f*, īnfōrmātiō *f*; suspiciō *f*
notoriety *n* īnfāmia *f*
notorious *adj* fāmōsus, īnfāmis; (*thing*) manifestus
notoriously *adv* manifestō
notwithstanding *adv* nihilōminus, tamen ♦ *prep*: ~ **the danger** in tantō discrīmine
nought *n* nihil, nīl *nt*
noun *n* nōmen *nt*
nourish *vt* alere, nūtrīre
nourisher *n* altor *m*, altrīx *f*
nourishment *n* cibus *m*, alimenta *ntpl*
novel *adj* novus, inaudītus ♦ *n* fābella *f*
novelty *n* rēs nova *f*; novitās *f*, īnsolentia *f*
November *n* mēnsis November *m*; **of** ~ November
novice *n* tīrō *m*
now *adv* nunc; (*past*) iam; **now and then** interdum; **just now** nunc; (*lately*) dūdum, modo; **now ... now** modo ... modo ♦ *conj* at, autem
nowadays *adv* nunc, hodiē
nowhere *adv* nusquam
nowise *adv* nullō modō, haudquāquam
noxious *adj* nocēns, noxius
nuance *n* color *m*
nucleus *n* sēmen *nt*
nude *adj* nūdus
nudge *vt* fodicāre
nudity *n* nūdātum corpus *nt*
nugget *n* massa *f*
nuisance *n* malum *nt*, incommodum *nt*
null *adj* inritus
nullify *vt* inritum facere; (*LAW*) abrogāre
numb *adj* torpēns, torpidus; **be ~** torpēre; **become ~** torpēscere
number *n* numerus *m*; **a ~ of** complūrēs, aliquot; **a great ~** multitūdō *f*, frequentia *f*; **a small ~** īnfrequentia *f*; **in large numbers** frequentēs ♦ *vt* numerāre, ēnumerāre
numberless *adj* innumerābilis
numbness *n* torpor *m*
numerous *adj* frequēns, crēber, plūrimī
nun *n* monacha *f*
nuptial *adj* nūptiālis
nuptials *n* nūptiae *fpl*
nurse *n* nūtrīx *f* ♦ *vt* (*child*) nūtrīre; (*sick*) cūrāre; (*fig*) fovēre
nursery *n* (*children*) cubiculum *nt*; (*plants*) sēminārium *nt*
nursling *n* alumnus *m*, alumna *f*
nurture *n* ēducātiō *f*
nut *n* nux *f*
nutrition *n* alimenta *ntpl*
nutritious *adj* salūbris
nutshell *n* putāmen *nt*
nut tree *n* nux *f*
nymph *n* nympha *f*

Oo

O *interj* ō!
oaf *n* agrestis *m*
oak *n* quercus *f*; (*evergreen*) īlex *f*; (*timber*) rōbur *nt* ♦ *adj* quernus, īlignus, rōboreus; **oak forest** quercētum *nt*
oakum *n* stuppa *f*
oar *n* rēmus *m*
oarsman *n* rēmex *m*
oaten *adj* avēnāceus
oath *n* iūsiūrandum *nt*; (MIL) sacrāmentum *nt*; (*imprecation*) exsecrātiō *f*; **false ~** periūrium *nt*; **take an ~** iūrāre; **take an ~ of allegiance to** in verba iūrāre (*gen*)
oats *n* avēna *f*
obduracy *n* obstinātus animus *m*
obdurate *adj* obstinātus, pervicāx
obdurately *adv* obstinātē
obedience *n* oboedientia *f*, obsequium *nt*
obedient *adj* oboediēns, obsequēns; **be ~ to** pārēre (*dat*), obtemperāre (*dat*), obsequī (*dat*)
obediently *adv* oboedienter
obeisance *n* obsequium *nt*; **make ~ to** adōrāre
obelisk *n* obeliscus *m*
obese *adj* obēsus, pinguis
obesity *n* obēsitās *f*, pinguitūdō *f*
obey *vt* pārēre (*dat*), obtemperāre (*dat*), oboedīre (*dat*); **~ orders** dictō pārēre
obituary *n* mortēs *fpl*
object *n* rēs *f*; (*aim*) fīnis *m*, prōpositum *nt*; **be an ~ of hate** odiō esse; **with what ~** quō cōnsiliō ♦ *vi* recūsāre, gravārī; **but, it is objected** at enim; **~ to** improbāre
objection *n* recūsātiō *f*, mora *f*; **I have no ~** nīl moror
objectionable *adj* invīsus, iniūcundus
objective *adj* externus ♦ *n* prōpositum *nt*, fīnis *m*
objurgate *vt* obiūrgāre, culpāre
oblation *n* dōnum *nt*
obligation *n* (*legal*) dēbitum *nt*; (*moral*) officium *nt*; **lay under an ~** obligāre, obstringere
obligatory *adj* dēbitus, necessārius
oblige *vt* (*force*) cōgere; (*contract*) obligāre, obstringere; (*compliance*) mōrem gerere (*dat*), mōrigerārī (*dat*); **I am obliged to** (*action*) dēbeō (*inf*); (*person*) amāre, grātiam habēre (*dat*)
obliging *adj* cōmis, officiōsus
obligingly *adv* cōmiter, officiōsē
oblique *adj* oblīquus
obliquely *adv* oblīquē
obliquity *n* (*moral*) prāvitās *f*
obliterate *vt* dēlēre, oblitterāre
obliteration *n* litūra *f*

oblivion *n* oblīviō *f*
oblivious *adj* oblīviōsus, immemor
oblong *adj* oblongus
obloquy *n* vītuperātiō *f*, opprobrium *nt*
obnoxious *adj* invīsus
obscene *adj* obscaenus, impūrus
obscenity *n* obscaenitās *f*, impūritās *f*
obscure *adj* obscūrus, caecus ♦ *vt* obscūrāre, officere (*dat*)
obscurely *adv* obscūrē; (*speech*) per ambāgēs
obscurity *n* obscūritās *f*; (*speech*) ambāgēs *fpl*
obsequies *n* exsequiae *fpl*
obsequious *adj* officiōsus, ambitiōsus
obsequiously *adv* officiōsē
obsequiousness *n* adsentātiō *f*
observance *n* observantia *f*; (*rite*) rītus *m*
observant *adj* attentus, dīligēns
observation *n* observātiō *f*, animadversiō *f*; (*remark*) dictum *nt*
observe *vt* animadvertere, contemplārī; (*see*) cernere, cōnspicere; (*remark*) dīcere; (*adhere to*) cōnservāre, observāre
observer *n* spectātor *m*, contemplātor *m*
obsess *vt* occupāre; **I am obsessed by** tōtus sum in (*abl*)
obsession *n* studium *nt*
obsolescent *adj*: **be ~** obsolēscere
obsolete *adj* obsolētus; **become ~** exolēscere
obstacle *n* impedīmentum *nt*, mora *f*
obstinacy *n* pertinācia *f*, obstinātus animus *m*
obstinate *adj* pertināx, obstinātus
obstinately *adv* obstinātō animō
obstreperous *adj* clāmōsus, ferus
obstruct *vt* impedīre, obstruere, obstāre (*dat*); (POL) intercēdere (*dat*); (*fig*) officere (*dat*)
obstruction *n* impedīmentum *nt*; (POL) intercessiō *f*
obstructionist *n* intercessor *m*
obtain *vt* adipīscī, nancīscī, cōnsequī; comparāre; (*by request*) impetrāre ♦ *vi* tenēre, obtinēre
obtrude *vi* sē inculcāre ♦ *vt* ingerere
obtrusive *adj* importūnus, molestus
obtuse *adj* hebes, stolidus
obtusely *adv* stolidē
obtuseness *n* stupor *m*
obverse *adj* obversus
obviate *vt* tollere, praevertere
obvious *adj* ēvidēns, manifestus, apertus; **it is ~** appāret
obviously *adv* ēvidenter, apertē, manifestō

occasion n occāsiō f, locus m; (reason) causa f ✦ vt movēre, facessere, auctōrem esse (gen)
occasional adj fortuītus
occasionally adv interdum, nōnnunquam
occidental adj occidentālis
occult adj arcānus
occupancy n possessiō f
occupant n habitātor m, possessor m
occupation n quaestus m, occupātiō f
occupier n possessor m
occupy vt possidēre; (MIL) occupāre; (space) complēre; (attention) distinēre, occupāre
occur vi ēvenīre, accidere; (to mind) occurrere, in mentem venīre
occurrence n ēventum nt; rēs f
ocean n mare nt, ōceanus m
October n mēnsis Octōber m; of ~ Octōber
ocular adj oculōrum; give ~ proof of ante oculōs pōnere, videntī dēmōnstrāre
odd adj (number) impār; (moment) subsecīvus; (appearance) novus, īnsolitus
oddity n novitās f; (person) homō rīdiculus m
oddly adv mīrum in modum
odds n praestantia f; be at ~ with dissidēre cum; the ~ are against us imparēs sumus; the ~ are in our favour superiōrēs sumus
ode n carmen nt
odious adj invīsus, odiōsus
odium n invidia f
odorous adj odōrātus
odour n odor m
of prep gen; (origin) ex, dē; (cause) abl; all of us nōs omnēs; the city of Rome urbs Rōma
off adv procul; (prefix) ab-; off and on interdum; off with you aufer tē; come off ēvādere; well off beātus; well off for abundāns (abl)
offal n quisquiliae fpl
offence n offēnsiō f; (legal) dēlictum nt; commit an ~ dēlinquere
offend vt laedere, offendere; be offended aegrē ferre ✦ vi delinquere; ~ against peccāre in (acc), violāre
offender n reus m
offensive adj odiōsus; (smell) gravis; (language) contumēliōsus; take the ~ bellum īnferre
offensively adv odiōsē; graviter
offer vt offerre, dare, praebēre; (hand) porrigere; (violence) adferre; (honour) dēferre; (with verb) profitērī, pollicērī ✦ n condiciō f; ~ for sale venditāre
offering n dōnum nt; (to the dead) īnferiae fpl
off-hand adj neglegēns, incūriōsus
office n (POL) magistrātus m, mūnus nt, honōs m; (kindness) officium nt; (place) mēnsa f
officer n praefectus m; lēgātus m
official adj pūblicus ✦ n adiūtor m, minister m
officially adv pūblicē
officiate vi operārī, officiō fungī
officious adj molestus
officiously adv molestē
officiousness n occursātiō f
offing n: in the ~ procul
offset vt compēnsāre
offspring n prōgeniēs f, līberī mpl; (animal) fētus m

often adv saepe, saepenumerō; as ~ as quotiēns; totiēs ... quotiēs; how often? quotiēns?; so ~ totiēns; very ~ persaepe
ogle vi: ~ at līmīs oculīs intuērī
ogre n mōnstrum nt
oh interj (joy, surprise) ōh!; (sorrow) prō!
oil n oleum nt ✦ vt ungere
oily adj oleōsus
ointment n unguentum nt
old adj (person) senex; (thing) vetus; (ancient) antīquus, prīscus; old age senectūs f; be ten years old decem annōs habēre; ten years old decem annōs nātus; two years old bīmus; good old antīquus; good old days antīquitās f; grow old senēscere; of old quondam
olden adj prīscus, prīstinus
older adj nātū māior, senior
oldest adj nātū māximus
old-fashioned adj antīquus, obsolētus
old man n senex m
oldness n vetustās f
old woman n anus f
oligarchy n paucōrum dominātiō f, optimātium factiō f
olive n olea f; ~ orchard olīvētum nt
Olympiad n Olympias f
Olympic adj Olympicus; win an ~ victory Olympia vincere
Olympic Games n Olympia ntpl
omen n ōmen nt, auspicium nt; announce a bad ~ obnūntiāre; obtain favourable omens litāre
ominous adj īnfaustus, mināx
omission n praetermissiō f, neglegentia f
omit vt ōmittere, praetermittere
omnipotence n īnfīnīta potestās f
omnipotent adj omnipotēns
on prep (place) in (abl), in- (prefix); (time) abl; (coast of) ad (acc); (subject) dē (abl); (side) ab (abl) ✦ adv porrō, usque; and so on ac deinceps; on hearing the news nūntiō acceptō; on equal terms (in battle) aequō Marte; on the following day posterō/proximō diē, postrīdiē; on this side of citrā (acc)
once adv semel; (past) ōlim, quondam; at ~ extemplō, statim; (together) simul; for ~ aliquandō; ~ and for all semel; ~ more dēnuō, iterum; ~ upon a time ōlim, quondam
one num ūnus ✦ pron quīdam; (of two) alter, altera, alterum; one and the same ūnus; one another inter sē, alius alium; one or the other alteruter; one day ōlim; one each singulī; one would have thought crēderēs; be one of in numerō esse (gen); be at one idem sentīre; it is all one nihil interest; the one alter, hic; this is the one hōc illud est
one-eyed adj luscus
oneness n ūnitās f
onerous adj gravis
oneself pron ipse; (reflexive) sē
one-sided adj inaequālis, inīquus
onion n caepe nt
onlooker n spectātor m
only adj ūnus, sōlus; (son) ūnicus ✦ adv sōlum, tantum, modo; (with clause) nōn nisi, nīl nisi, nihil aliud quam; (time) dēmum; if ~ sī modo; (wish) utinam

onrush – orphan

onrush n incursus m
onset n impetus m
onslaught n incursus m; **make an ~ on** (words) invehī in (acc)
onto prep in (acc)
onus n officium nt
onward, onwards adv porrō
onyx n onyx m
ooze vi mānāre, stillāre
opaque adj haud perlūcidus
open adj apertus; (wide) patēns, hiāns; (ground) pūrus, apertus; (question) integer; **lie ~** patēre; **stand ~** hiāre; **throw ~** adaperīre, patefacere; **it is ~ to me to** mihī integrum est (inf); **while the question is still ~** rē integrā ♦ vt aperīre, patefacere; (book) ēvolvere; (letter) resolvere; (speech) exōrdīrī; (with ceremony) inaugurāre; (will) resignāre ♦ vi aperīrī, hiscere; (sore) recrūdēscere; **~ out** extendere, pandere; **~ up** (country) aperīre
open air n: **in the open air** sub dīvō
open-handed adj largus, mūnificus
open-handedness n largitās f
open-hearted adj ingenuus
opening n forāmen nt, hiātus m; (ceremony) cōnsecrātiō f; (opportunity) occāsiō f, ānsa f ♦ adj prīmus
openly adv palam, apertē
open-mouthed adj: **stand ~ at** inhiāre
operate vi rem gerere ♦ vt movēre
operation n opus nt, āctiō f; (MED) sectiō f
operative adj efficāx
ophthalmia n lippitūdō f
opiate adj somnifer
opine vi opīnārī, existimāre
opinion n sententia f; (of person) existimātiō f; **public ~** fāma f; **in my ~** meō iūdiciō, meō animō
opponent n adversārius m, hostis m
opportune adj opportūnus, tempestīvus
opportunely adv opportūnē
opportunity n occāsiō f; (to act) facultās f; potestās f
oppose vt (barrier) obicere; (contrast) oppōnere ♦ vi adversārī (dat), resistere (dat), obstāre (dat); **be opposed to** adversārī (dat); (opinion) dīversum esse ab
opposite adj (facing) adversus; (contrary) contrārius, dīversus ♦ prep contrā (acc), adversus (acc); **directly ~** ē regiōne (gen) ♦ adv ex adversō
opposition n repugnantia f; (party) factiō adversa f
oppress vt opprimere, adflīgere; (burden) premere, onerāre
oppression n iniūria f, servitūs f
oppressive adj gravis, inīquus; **become more ~** ingravēscere
oppressor n tyrannus m
opprobrious adj turpis
opprobriously adv turpiter
opprobrium n dēdecus nt, ignōminia f
optical adj oculōrum
optical illusion n oculōrum lūdibrium nt
optimism n spēs f

option n optiō f, arbitrium nt; **I have no ~** nōn est arbitriī meī
optional adj: **it is ~ for you** optiō tua est
opulence n opēs fpl, cōpia f
opulent adj dīves, cōpiōsus
or conj aut, vel, -ve; (after utrum) an; **or else** aliōquīn; **or not** (direct) annōn; (indirect) necne
oracle n ōrāculum nt
oracular adj fātidicus; (fig) obscūrus
oral adj: **give an ~ message** vōce nūntiāre
orally adv vōce, verbīs
oration n ōrātiō f
orator n ōrātor m
oratorical adj ōrātōrius
oratory n ēloquentia f, rhētoricē f; (for prayer) sacellum nt; **of ~** dīcendī, ōrātōrius
orb n orbis m
orbit n orbis m, ambitus m
orchard n pōmārium nt
ordain vt ēdīcere, sancīre
ordeal n labor m
order n (arrangement) ōrdō m; (class) ōrdō m; (battle) aciēs f; (command) iussum nt, imperium nt; (money) perscrīptiō f; **in ~** dispositus; (succession) deinceps; **in ~ that/to** ut (subj); **in ~ that not** nē (subj); **put in ~** dispōnere, ōrdināre; **by ~ of** iussū (gen); **out of ~** incompositus; **without orders from** iniussū (gen) ♦ vt (arrange) dispōnere, ōrdināre; (command) iubēre (+ acc and infin), imperāre (dat and 'ut' +subj or 'nē' +subj)
orderly adj ōrdinātus; (conduct) modestus ♦ n accēnsus m
ordinance n ēdictum nt, institūtum nt
ordinarily adv plērumque, ferē
ordinary adj ūsitātus, solitus, cottīdiānus
ordnance n tormenta ntpl
ordure n stercus m
ore n aes nt; **iron ore** ferrum īnfectum nt
Oread n (myth) Oreas f
organ n (bodily) membrum nt; (musical) organum nt, hydraulus m
organic adj nātūrālis
organically adv nātūrā
organization n ōrdinātiō f, structūra f
organize vt ōrdināre, īnstituere, adparāre
orgies n orgia ntpl
orgy n cōmissātiō f
orient n oriēns m
oriental adj Asiāticus
orifice n ōstium nt
origin n orīgō f, prīncipium nt; (source) fōns m; (birth) genus nt
original adj prīmus, prīstinus; (LIT) proprius ♦ n exemplar nt
originally adv prīncipiō, antīquitus
originate vt īnstituere, auctōrem esse (gen) ♦ vi exorīrī; **~ in** innāscī in (abl), initium dūcere ab
originator n auctor m
orisons n precēs fpl
ornament n ōrnāmentum nt; (fig) decus nt ♦ vt ōrnāre, decorāre; **I am ~** ornamentō sum
ornamental adj decōrus; **be ~** decorī esse
ornamentally adv ōrnātē
ornate adj ōrnātus
ornately adv ōrnātē
orphan n orbus m, orba f

orphaned *adj* orbātus
orthodox *adj* antīquus
orthography *n* orthographia *f*
oscillate *vi* reciprocāre
osculate *vt* ōsculārī
osier *n* vīmen *nt* ♦ *adj* vīmineus
osprey *n* haliaeetos *m*
ostensible *adj* speciōsus
ostensibly *adv* per speciem
ostentation *n* iactātiō *f*, ostentātiō *f*
ostentatious *adj* glōriōsus, ambitiōsus
ostentatiously *adv* glōriōsē
ostler *n* agāsō *m*
ostrich *n* strūthiocamēlus *m*
other *adj* alius; (*of two*) alter; **one or the
~** alteruter; **every ~ year** tertiō quōque annō; **on
the ~ side of** ultrā (*acc*); **of others** aliēnus
otherwise *adv* aliter; (*if not*) aliōquī
otter *n* lutra *f*
ought *vi* dēbēre (+ *infin or gerundive of vt*); **I ~ mē**
oportet; **I ~ to have said** dēbuī dīcere
ounce *n* ūncia *f*; **two ounces** sextāns *m*; **three
ounces** quadrāns *m*; **four ounces** triēns *m*;
five ounces quīncūnx *m*; **six ounces** sēmis *m*;
seven ounces septūnx *m*; **eight ounces** bēs *m*;
nine ounces dōdrāns *m*; **ten ounces** dextāns
m; **eleven ounces** deūnx *m*
our *adj* noster
ourselves *pron* ipsī; (*reflexive*) nōs
oust *vt* extrūdere, ēicere
out *adv* (*rest*) forīs; (*motion*) forās; **out of** dē, ē/ex
(*abl*); (*cause*) propter (*acc*); (*beyond*) extrā, ultrā
(*acc*); **be out** (*book*) in manibus esse; (*calculation*)
errāre; (*fire*) exstinctum esse; (*secret*) palam esse
outbreak *n* initium *nt*, ēruptiō *f*
outburst *n* ēruptiō *f*
outcast *n* profugus *m*
outcome *n* ēventus *m*, exitus *m*
outcry *n* clāmor *m*, adclāmātiō *f*; **raise an
~ against** obstrepere (*dat*)
outdistance *vt* praevertere
outdo *vt* superāre
outdoor *adj* sub dīvō
outer *adj* exterior
outermost *adj* extrēmus
outfit *n* īnstrūmenta *ntpl*; vestīmenta *ntpl*
outflank *vt* circumīre
outgrow *vt* excēdere ex
outing *n* excursiō *f*
outlandish *adj* barbarus
outlaw *n* prōscrīptus *m* ♦ *vt* prōscrībere, aquā et
ignī interdīcere (*dat*)
outlawry *n* aquae et ignis interdictiō *f*
outlay *n* impēnsa *f*, sūmptus *m*
outlet *n* ēmissārium *nt*, exitus *m*
outline *n* ductus *m*, adumbrātiō *f* ♦ *vt*
adumbrāre
outlive *vt* superesse (*dat*)
outlook *n* prōspectus *m*
outlying *adj* longinquus, exterior
outnumber *vt* numerō superiōrēs esse,
multitūdine superāre
out-of-doors *adv* forīs
outpost *n* statiō *f*
outpouring *n* effūsiō *f*
output *n* fructus *m*

outrage *n* flāgitium *nt*, iniūria *f* ♦ *vt* laedere,
violāre
outrageous *adj* flāgitiōsus, indignus
outrageously *adv* flāgitiōsē
outrider *n* praecursor *m*
outright *adv* penitus, prōrsus; semel
outrun *vt* praevertere
outset *n* initium *nt*
outshine *vt* praelūcēre (*dat*)
outside *adj* externus ♦ *adv* extrā, forīs; (*motion
to*) forās; **~ in** inversus; **from ~** extrīnsecus
♦ *n* exterior pars *f*; (*show*) speciēs *f*; **at
the ~** summum, ad summum; **on the
~** extrīnsecus ♦ *prep* extrā (*acc*)
outsider *n* aliēnus *m*; (*POL*) novus homō *m*
outskirts *n* suburbānus ager *m*; **on the
~** suburbānus
outspoken *adj* līber
outspokenness *n* lībertās *f*
outspread *adj* patulus
outstanding *adj* ēgregius, īnsignis, singulāris;
(*debt*) residuus
outstep *vt* excēdere
outstretched *adj* passus, porrēctus, extentus
outstrip *vt* praevertere
outvote *vt* suffrāgiīs superāre
outward *adj* externus; **~ form** speciēs *f* ♦ *adv*
domō, forās
outweigh *vt* praeponderāre
outwit *vt* dēcipere, circumvenīre
outwork *n* prōpugnāculum *nt*, bracchium *nt*
outworn *adj* exolētus
oval *adj* ōvātus ♦ *n* ōvum *nt*
ovation *n* (*triumph*) ovātiō *f*; **receive an ~ cum**
laudibus excipī
oven *n* furnus *m*, fornāx *f*
over *prep* (*above*) super (*abl*), suprā (*acc*); (*across*)
super (*acc*); (*extent*) per (*acc*); (*time*) inter (*acc*);
~ and above super (*acc*), praeter (*acc*); **all ~** per;
~ against adversus (*acc*) ♦ *adv* suprā; (*excess*)
nimis; (*done*) cōnfectus; **~ again** dēnuō; **~ and
above** īnsuper; **~ and ~** identidem; **be left
~** superesse, restāre; **it is all ~ with** āctum est
dē
overall *adj* tōtus ♦ *adv* ubīque, passim
overawe *vt* formīdinem inicere (*dat*)
overbalance *vi* titubāre
overbearing *adj* superbus
overboard *adv* ē nāvī, in mare; **throw
~** excutere, iactāre
overbold *adj* importūnus
overburden *vt* praegravāre
overcast *adj* nūbilus
overcoat *n* paenula *f*, lacerna *f*
overcome *vt* superāre, vincere
overconfidence *n* cōnfidentia *f*
overconfident *adj* cōnfidēns
overdo *vt* modum excēdere in (*abl*)
overdone *adj* (*style*) pūtidus
overdraw *vt* (*style*) exaggerāre
overdue *adj* (*money*) residuus
overestimate *vt* māiōris aestimāre
overflow *n* ēluviō *f* ♦ *vi* abundāre, redundāre ♦ *vt*
inundāre
overgrown *adj* obsitus; **be ~** luxuriāre
overhang *vt*, *vi* impendēre, imminēre (*dat*)

overhaul vt reficere
overhead adv īnsuper
overhear vt excipere, auscultāre
overjoyed adj nimiō gaudiō ēlātus
overladen adj praegravātus
overland adv terrā
overlap vt implicāre
overlay vt indūcere
overload vt (fig) obruere
overlook vt (place) dēspectāre, imminēre
(dat); (knowledge) ignōrāre; (notice) neglegere,
praetermittere; (fault) ignōscere (dat)
overlord n dominus m
overmaster vt dēvincere
overmuch adv nimis, plūs aequō
overnight adj nocturnus ♦ adv noctū
overpower vt superāre, domāre, obruere,
opprimere
overpraise vt in māius extollere
overrate vt māiōris aestimāre
overreach vt circumvenīre
overriding adj praecipuus
overrule vt rescindere
overrun vt pervagārī; (fig) obsidēre
oversea adj trānsmarīnus
oversee vt praeesse (dat)
overseer n cūrātor m, custōs m
overset vt ēvertere
overshadow vt officere (dat)
overshoot vt excēdere
oversight n neglegentia f
overspread vt offendere (dat), obdūcere

overstep vt excēdere
overt adj apertus
overtake vt cōnsequī; (surprise) opprimere,
dēprehendere
overtax vt (fig) abūtī (abl)
overthrow vt ēvertere; (destroy) prōflīgāre,
dēbellāre ♦ n ēversiō f, ruīna f
overtly adv palam
overtop vt superāre
overture n exōrdium nt; **make overtures to**
temptāre, agere cum, lēgātōs mittere ad
overturn vt ēvertere
overweening adj superbus, adrogāns, īnsolēns
overwhelm vt obruere, dēmergere, opprimere
overwhelming adj īnsignis, vehementissimus
overwhelmingly adv mīrum quantum
overwork vi plūs aequō labōrāre ♦ vt cōnficere
♦ n immodicus labor m
overwrought adj (emotion) ēlātus; (style)
ēlabōrātus
owing adj: **be ~** dēbērī; **~ to** (person) per; (cause) ob/
propter (acc)
owl n būbō m; ulula f
own adj proprius; **my own** meus; **have of one's
own** domī habēre; **hold one's own** parem esse
♦ vt possidēre, habēre; (admit) fatērī, cōnfitērī
owner n dominus m, possessor m
ownership n possessiō f, mancipium nt
ox n bōs m
ox herd n bubulcus m
oyster n ostrea f

Pp

pace n passus m; (speed) gradus m; **keep ~** gradum cōnferre ♦ vi incēdere; **~ up and down** spatiārī, inambulāre
pacific adj pācificus; (quiet) placidus
pacification n pācificātiō f
pacifist n imbellis m
pacify vt (anger) plācāre; (rising) sēdāre
pack n (MIL) sarcina f; (animals) grex m; (people) turba f ♦ vt (kit) colligere; (crowd) stīpāre; **~ together** coartāre; **~ up** colligere, compōnere ♦ vi vāsa colligere; **send packing** missum facere ♦ adj (animal) clītellārius
package n fasciculus m, sarcina f
packet n fasciculus m; (ship) nāvis āctuāria f
packhorse n iūmentum nt
packsaddle n clītellae fpl
pact n foedus nt, pactum nt
pad n pulvillus m
padding n tōmentum nt
paddle n rēmus m ♦ vi rēmigāre
paddock n saeptum nt
paean n paeān m
pagan adj pāgānus
page n (book) pāgina f; (boy) puer m
pageant n pompa f, spectāculum nt
pageantry n adparātus m
pail n situla f
pain n dolor m; **be in ~** dolēre ♦ vt dolōre adficere
painful adj acerbus; (work) labōriōsus
painfully adv acerbē, labōriōsē
painless adj dolōris expers
painlessly adv sine dolōre
painlessness n indolentia f
pains npl opera f; **take ~** operam dare; **take ~ with** (art) ēlabōrāre
painstaking adj dīligēns, operōsus
painstakingly adv dīligenter, summā cūrā
paint n pigmentum nt; (cosmetic) fūcus m ♦ vt pingere; (red) fūcāre; (in words) dēpingere; (portrait) dēpingere
paintbrush n pēnicillus m
painter n pictor m
painting n pictūra f
pair n pār nt ♦ vt coniungere, compōnere
palace n rēgia f
palatable adj suāvis, iūcundus
palate n palātum nt
palatial adj rēgius
palaver n colloquium nt, sermunculī mpl
pale n pālus m, vallus m; **beyond the ~** extrāneus ♦ adj pallidus; **look ~** pallēre; **grow ~** pallēscere;

~ brown subfuscus; **~ green** subviridis ♦ vi pallēscere
paleness n pallor m
palimpsest n palimpsēstus m
paling n saepēs f
palisade n (MIL) vallum nt
palish adj pallidulus
pall n (funeral) pallium nt ♦ vi taedēre
pallet n grabātus m
palliasse n strāmentum nt
palliate vt extenuāre, excūsāre
palliation n excūsātiō f
palliative n lēnīmentum nt
pallid adj pallidus
pallor n pallor m
palm n (hand) palma f; (tree) palma f ♦ vt: **~ off** impōnere
palmy adj flōrēns
palpable adj tractābilis; (fig) manifestus
palpably adv manifestō, propalam
palpitate vi palpitāre, micāre
palpitation n palpitātiō f
palsied adj membrīs captus
palsy n paralysis f
paltry adj vīlis, frīvolus
pamper vt indulgēre (dat)
pampered adj dēlicātus
pamphlet n libellus m
pan n patina f, patella f; (frying) sartāgō f; (of balance) lanx f
pancake n laganum nt
pander n lēnō m ♦ vi: **~ to** lēnōcinārī (dat)
panegyric n laudātiō f
panegyrist n laudātor m
panel n (wall) abacus m; (ceiling) lacūnār nt; (judges) decuria f
panelled adj laqueātus
pang n dolor m
panic n pavor m ♦ vi trepidāre
panic-stricken adj pavidus
panniers n clītellae fpl
panoply n arma ntpl
panorama n prōspectus m
panpipe n fistula f
pant vi anhēlāre
panther n panthēra f
panting n anhēlitus m
pantomime n mīmus m
pantry n cella penāria f
pap n mamma f
paper n charta f
papyrus n papyrus f

par *n*: on a par with pār *(dat)*
parable *n* parabolē *f*
parade *n* pompa *f*; *(show)* adparātus *m* ◆ *vt* trādūcere, iactāre ◆ *vi* pompam dūcere, incēdere
paradox *n* verba sēcum repugnantia; **paradoxes** *pl* paradoxa *ntpl*
paragon *n* exemplar *nt*, specimen *nt*
paragraph *n* caput *nt*
parallel *adj* parallēlus; *(fig)* cōnsimilis
paralyse *vt* dēbilitāre; *(with fear)* percellere; **be paralysed** torpēre
paralysis *n* dēbilitās *f*; *(fig)* torpēdō *f*
paramount *adj* prīnceps, summus
paramour *n* adulter *m*
parapet *n* lōrīca *f*
paraphernalia *n* adparātus *m*
paraphrase *vt* vertere
parasite *n* parasītus *m*
parasol *n* umbella *f*
parboiled *adj* subcrūdus
parcel *n* fasciculus *m* ◆ *vt*: ~ **out** distribuere, dispertīre
parch *vt* torrēre
parched *adj* torridus, āridus; **be** ~ ārēre
parchment *n* membrāna *f*
pardon *n* venia *f* ◆ *vt* ignōscere *(dat)*; *(offence)* condōnāre
pardonable *adj* ignōscendus
pare *vt* dēglūbere; *(nails)* resecāre
parent *n* parēns *m/f*, genitor *m*, genetrīx *f*
parentage *n* stirps *f*, genus *nt*
parental *adj* patrius
parenthesis *n* interclūsiō *f*
parings *n* praesegmina *ntpl*
parish *n* (ECCL) paroecia *f*
parity *n* aequālitās *f*
park *n* hortī *mpl*
parlance *n* sermō *m*
parley *n* colloquium *nt* ◆ *vi* colloquī, agere
parliament *n* senātus *m*; **house of** ~ cūria *f*
parliamentary *adj* senātōrius
parlour *n* exedrium *nt*
parlous *adj* difficilis, perīculōsus
parochial *adj* mūnicipālis
parody *n* carmen ioculāre *nt* ◆ *vt* calumniārī
parole *n* fidēs *f*
paronomasia *n* agnōminātiō *f*
paroxysm *n* accessus *m*
parricide *n* *(doer)* parricīda *m*; *(deed)* parricīdium *nt*
parrot *n* psittacus *m*
parry *vt* ēlūdere, prōpulsāre
parsimonious *adj* parcus
parsimoniously *adv* parcē
parsimony *n* parsimōnia *f*, frūgālitās *f*
part *n* pars *f*; *(play)* partēs *fpl*, persōna *f*; *(duty)* officium *nt*; **parts** loca *ntpl*; *(ability)* ingenium *nt*; **for my** ~ equidem; **for the most** ~ māximam partem; **on the** ~ **of** ab; **act the** ~ **of** persōnam sustinēre, partēs agere; **have no** ~ **in** expers esse *(gen)*; **in** ~ partim; **it is the** ~ **of a wise man** sapientis est; **play one's** ~ officiō satisfacere; **take** ~ **in** interesse *(dat)*, particeps esse *(gen)*; **take in good** ~ in bonam partem accipere; **take someone's** ~ adesse alicuī, dēfendere aliquem;

from all parts undique; **in foreign parts** peregrē; **in two parts** bifāriam; (MIL) bipartītō; **in three parts** trifāriam; (MIL) tripartītō; **of parts** ingeniōsus ◆ *vt* dīvidere, sēparāre, dirimere; ~ **company** dīversōs discēdere ◆ *vi* dīgredī, discēdere; *(things)* dissilīre; ~ **with** renūntiāre
partake *vi* interesse, particeps esse; ~ **of** gustāre
partial *adj* *(biased)* inīquus, studiōsus; *(incomplete)* mancus; **be** ~ **to** favēre *(dat)*, studēre *(dat)*; **win a** ~ **victory** aliquā ex parte vincere
partiality *n* favor *m*, studium *nt*
partially *adv* partim, aliquā ex parte
participant *n* particeps *m/f*
participate *vi* interesse, particeps esse
participation *n* societās *f*
particle *n* particula *f*
parti-coloured *adj* versicolor, varius
particular *adj* *(own)* proprius; *(special)* praecipuus; *(exact)* dīligēns, accūrātus; *(fastidious)* fastīdiōsus; **a** ~ **person** quīdam ◆ *n* rēs *f*; **with full particulars** subtīliter; **give all the particulars** omnia exsequī; **in** ~ praesertim
particularity *n* subtīlitās *f*
particularize *vt* singula exsequī
particularly *adv* praecipuē, praesertim, in prīmīs, māximē
parting *n* dīgressus *m*, discessus *m* ◆ *adj* ultimus
partisan *n* fautor *m*, studiōsus *m*
partisanship *n* studium *nt*
partition *n* *(act)* partītiō *f*; *(wall)* pariēs *m*; *(compartment)* loculāmentum *nt* ◆ *vt* dīvidere
partly *adv* partim, ex parte
partner *n* socius *m*; *(in office)* collēga *m*
partnership *n* societās *f*; **form a** ~ societātem inīre
partridge *n* perdīx *m/f*
parturition *n* partus *m*
party *n* (POL) factiō *f*, partēs *fpl*; *(entertainment)* convīvium *nt*; (MIL) manus *f*; *(individual)* homō *m/f*; *(associate)* socius *m*, cōnscius *m*
party spirit *n* studium *nt*
parvenu *n* novus homō *m*
pass *n* *(hill)* saltus *m*; *(narrow)* angustiae *fpl*, faucēs *fpl*; *(crisis)* discrīmen *nt*; *(document)* diplōma *nt*; *(fighting)* petītiō *f*; **things have come to such a** ~ in eum locum ventum est, adeō rēs rediit ◆ *vi* īre, praeterīre; *(time)* trānsīre; *(property)* pervenīre; ~ **away** abīre; *(die)* morī, perīre; *(fig)* dēfluere; ~ **by** praeterīre; ~ **for** habērī prō *(abl)*; ~ **off** abīre; ~ **on** pergere; ~ **over** trānsīre; **come to** ~ fierī, ēvenīre; **let** ~ intermittere, praetermittere ◆ *vt* praeterīre; *(riding)* praetervehī; *(by hand)* trādere; (LAW) iubēre; *(limit)* excēdere; *(sentence)* interpōnere, dīcere; *(test)* satisfacere *(dat)*; *(time)* dēgere, agere; ~ **accounts** ratiōnēs ratās habēre; ~ **the day** diem cōnsūmere; ~ **a law** lēgem ferre; ~ **a decree** dēcernere; ~ **off** ferre; ~ **over** praeterīre, mittere; *(fault)* ignōscere *(dat)*; ~ **round** trādere; ~ **through** trānsīre
passable *adj* *(place)* pervius; *(standard)* mediocris
passably *adv* mediocriter

passage n iter nt, cursus m; (land) trānsitus m; (sea) trānsmissiō f; (book) locus m; **of ~** (bird) advena

passenger n vector m

passer-by n praeteriēns m

passing n obitus m ♦ adj admodum

passion n animī mōtus m, permōtiō f, ārdor m; (anger) īra f; (lust) libīdō f

passionate adj ārdēns, impotēns, ācer; īrācundus

passionately adv vehementer, ārdenter; īrācundē; **be ~ in love** amōre ārdēre

passive adj iners

passiveness n inertia f, patientia f

passport n diplōma nt

password n tessera f

past adj praeteritus; (recent) proximus ♦ n praeterita ntpl ♦ prep praeter (acc); (beyond) ultrā (acc)

paste n glūten nt ♦ vt glūtināre

pastime n lūdus m, oblectāmentum nt

pastoral adj pastōrālis; (poem) būcolicus

pastry n crustum nt

pasture n pāstus m, pāscuum nt ♦ vt pāscere

pat vt dēmulcēre ♦ adj opportūnus

patch n pannus m ♦ vt resarcīre

patchwork n centō m

pate n caput nt

patent adj apertus, manifestus ♦ n prīvilēgium nt

patently adv manifestō

paternal adj paternus

path n sēmita f, trāmes m

pathetic adj miserābilis

pathetically adv miserābiliter

pathfinder n explorātor m

pathless adj āvius

pathos n misericordia f; (RHET) dolor m

pathway n sēmita f

patience n patientia f

patient adj patiēns ♦ n aeger m

patiently adv patienter, aequō animō

patois n sermō m

patrician adj patricius ♦ n patricius m

patrimony n patrimōnium nt

patriot n amāns patriae m

patriotic adj pius, amāns patriae

patriotically adv prō patriā

patriotism n amor patriae m

patrol n excubiae fpl ♦ vi circumīre

patron n patrōnus m, fautor m

patronage n patrōcinium nt

patroness n patrōna f, fautrīx f

patronize vt favēre (dat), fovēre

patronymic n nōmen nt

patter vi crepitāre ♦ n crepitus m

pattern n exemplar nt, exemplum nt, nōrma f; (ideal) specimen nt; (design) figūra f

paucity n paucitās f

paunch n abdōmen nt, venter m

pauper n pauper m

pause n mora f, intervallum nt ♦ vi īnsistere, intermittere

pave vt sternere; **~ the way** (fig) viam mūnīre

pavement n pavīmentum nt

pavilion n tentōrium nt

paw n pēs m ♦ vt pede pulsāre

pawn n (chess) latrunculus m; (COMM) pignus nt, fīdūcia f ♦ vt oppignerāre

pawnbroker n pignerātor m

pay n mercēs f; (MIL) stīpendium nt; (workman) manupretium nt ♦ vt solvere, pendere; (debt) exsolvere; (in full) persolvere; (honour) persolvere; (MIL) stīpendium numerāre (dat); (penalty) dare, luere; **pay down** numerāre; **pay for** condūcere; **pay off** dissolvere, exsolvere; **pay out** expendere; (publicly) ērogāre; **pay up** dēpendere; **pay a compliment to** laudāre; **pay respects to** salūtāre ♦ vi respondēre; **it pays** expedit

payable adj solvendus

paymaster n (MIL) tribūnus aerārius m

payment n solūtiō f; (money) pēnsiō f

pea n pīsum nt; **like as two peas** tam similis quam lac lactī est

peace n pāx f; **~ and quiet** ōtium nt; **breach of the ~** vīs f; **establish ~** pācem conciliāre; **hold one's ~** reticēre; **sue for ~** pācem petere

peaceable adj imbellis, placidus

peaceably adv placidē

peaceful adj tranquillus, placidus, pācātus

peacefully adv tranquillē

peacemaker n pācificus m

peace-offering n piāculum nt

peach n Persicum nt

peacock n pāvō m

peak n apex m, vertex m

peal n (bell) sonitus m; (thunder) fragor m ♦ vi sonāre

pear n pirum nt; (tree) pirus f

pearl n margarīta f

pearly adj gemmeus; (colour) candidus

peasant n agricola m, colōnus m

peasantry n agricolae mpl

pebble n calculus m

pebbly adj lapidōsus

peccadillo n culpa f

peck n (measure) modius m ♦ vt vellicāre

peculate vi pecūlārī

peculation n pecūlātus m

peculiar adj (to one) proprius; (strange) singulāris

peculiarity n proprietās f, nota f

peculiarly adv praecipuē, praesertim

pecuniary adj pecūniārius

pedagogue n magister m

pedant n scholasticus m

pedantic adj nimis dīligens

pedantically adv dīligentius

pedantry n nimia dīligentia f

peddle vt circumferre

pedestal n basis f

pedestrian adj pedester ♦ n pedes m

pedigree n stirps f, stemma nt ♦ adj generōsus

pediment n fastīgium nt

pedlar n īnstitor m, circumforāneus m

peel n cortex m ♦ vt glūbere

peep vi dīspicere ♦ n aspectus m; **at ~ of day** prīmā lūce

peer vi: **~ at** intuērī ♦ n pār m; (rank) patricius m

peerless adj ūnicus, ēgregius

peevish adj stomachōsus, mōrōsus

peevishly adv stomachōsē, mōrōsē

peevishness n stomachus m, mōrōsitās f

peg n clāvus m; **put a round peg in a square hole** bovī clītellās impōnere ♦ vt clāvīs dēfīgere
pelf n lucrum nt
pellet n globulus m
pell-mell adv prōmiscuē, turbātē
pellucid adj perlūcidus
pelt n pellis f ♦ vt petere ♦ vi violenter cadere
pen n calamus m, stilus m; (cattle) saeptum nt ♦ vt scrībere
penal adj poenālis
penalize vt poenā adficere, multāre
penalty n poena f, damnum nt; (fine) multa f; **pay the ~** poenās dare
penance n supplicium nt
pencil n graphis f
pending adj sub iūdice ♦ prep inter (acc)
penetrable adj pervius
penetrate vt penetrāre
penetrating adj ācer, acūtus; (mind) perspicāx
penetration n (mind) acūmen nt
peninsula n paenīnsula f
penitence n paenitentia f
penitent adj: **I am ~** mē paenitet
penknife n scalpellum nt
penmanship n scrīptiō f, manus f
pennant n vexillum nt
penny n dēnārius m
pension n annua ntpl
pensioner n ēmeritus m
pensive adj attentus
pensiveness n cōgitātiō f
pent adj inclūsus
penthouse n (MIL) vīnea f
penurious adj parcus, avārus, tenāx
penuriousness n parsimōnia f, tenācitās f
penury n egestās f, inopia f
people n hominēs mpl; (nation) populus m, gēns f; **common ~** plēbs f ♦ vt frequentāre
peopled adj frequēns
pepper n piper nt
peradventure adv fortasse
perambulate vi spatiārī, inambulāre
perceive vt sentīre, percipere, intellegere
perceptible adj: **be ~** sentīrī posse, audīrī posse
perception n sēnsus m
perch n (bird's) pertica f; (fish) perca f ♦ vi īnsidēre
perchance adv fortasse, forsitan (subj)
percolate vi permānāre
percussion n ictus m
perdition n exitium nt
peregrinate vi peregrīnārī
peregrination n peregrīnātiō f
peremptorily adv praecīsē, prō imperiō
peremptory adj imperiōsus
perennial adj perennis
perfect adj perfectus, absolūtus; (entire) integer; (faultless) ēmendātus ♦ vt perficere, absolvere
perfection n perfectiō f, absolūtiō f
perfectly adv perfectē, ēmendātē; (quite) plānē
perfidious adj perfidus, perfidiōsus
perfidiously adv perfidiōsē
perfidy n perfidia f
perforate vt perforāre, terebrāre
perforation n forāmen nt
perforce adv per vim, necessāriō

perform vt perficere, peragere; (duty) exsequī, fungī (abl); (play) agere
performance n (process) execūtiō f, fūnctiō f; (deed) factum nt; (stage) fābula f
performer n āctor m; (music) tībīcen m, fidicen m; (stage) histriō m
perfume n odor m, unguentum nt ♦ vt odōrāre
perfumer n unguentārius m
perfumery n unguenta ntpl
perfunctorily adv neglegenter
perfunctory adj neglegēns
perhaps adv fortasse, forsitan (subj), nesciō an (subj); (tentative) vel; (interrog) an
peril n perīculum m, discrīmen nt
perilous adj perīculōsus
perilously adv perīculōsē
perimeter n ambitus m
period n tempus nt, spatium nt; (history) aetās f; (end) terminus m; (sentence) complexiō f, ambitus m
periodic adj (style) circumscrīptus
periodical adj status
periodically adv certīs temporibus, identidem
peripatetic adj vagus; (sect) peripatēticus
periphery n ambitus m
periphrasis n circuitus m
perish vi perīre, interīre
perishable adj cadūcus, fragilis, mortālis
peristyle n peristȳlium nt
perjure vi: **~ oneself** pēierāre
perjured adj periūrus
perjurer n periūrus m
perjury n periūrium nt; **commit ~** pēierāre
permanence n cōnstantia f, stabilitās f
permanent adj stabilis, diūturnus, perpetuus
permanently adv perpetuō
permeable adj penetrābilis
permeate vt penetrāre ♦ vi permānāre
permissible adj licitus, concessus; **it is ~** licet
permission n potestās f; **ask ~** veniam petere; **give ~** veniam dare, potestātem facere; **by ~ of** permissū (gen); **with your kind ~** bonā tuā veniā; **without your ~** tē invītō
permit vt sinere, permittere (dat); **I am permitted** licet mihī
pernicious adj perniciōsus, exitiōsus
perorate vi perōrāre
peroration n perōrātiō f, epilogus m
perpendicular adj dīrēctus
perpendicularly adv ad perpendiculum, ad līneam
perpetrate vt facere, admittere
perpetual adj perpetuus, perennis, sempiternus
perpetually adv perpetuō
perpetuate vt continuāre, perpetuāre
perpetuity n perpetuitās f
perplex vt sollicitāre, cōnfundere
perplexing adj ambiguus, perplexus
perplexity n haesitātiō f
perquisite n pecūlium nt
persecute vt īnsectārī, exagitāre; persequī
persecution n īnsectātiō f
persecutor n īnsectātor m
perseverance n persevērantia f, cōnstantia f
persevere vi persevērāre, perstāre; **~ in** tenēre

Persian n Persa m
persist vt īnstāre, perstāre, persevērāre
persistence, persistency n pertinācia f,
  persevērantia f
persistent adj pertināx
persistently adv pertināciter, persevēranter
person n homō m/f; (counted) caput nt; (character)
  persōna f; (body) corpus nt; in ~ ipse praesēns
personage n vir m
personal adj prīvātus, suus
personality n nātūra f; (person) vir ēgregius m
personally adv ipse, cōram
personal property n pecūlium nt
personate vt persōnam gerere (gen)
personification n prosōpopoeia f
personify vt hūmānam nātūram tribuere (dat)
personnel n membra ntpl, sociī mpl
perspective n scaenographia f
perspicacious adj perspicāx, acūtus
perspicacity n perspicācitās f, acūmen nt
perspicuity n perspicuitās f
perspicuous adj perspicuus
perspiration n sūdor m
perspire vi sūdāre
persuade vt persuādēre (dat); (by entreaty)
  exōrāre
persuasion n persuāsiō f
persuasive adj blandus
persuasively adv blandē
pert adj procāx, protervus
pertain vi pertinēre, attinēre
pertinacious adj pertināx
pertinaciously adv pertināciter
pertinacity n pertinācia f
pertinent adj appositus; be ~ ad rem pertinēre
pertinently adv appositē
pertly adv procāciter, protervē
perturb vt perturbāre
perturbation n animī perturbātiō f, trepidātiō f
peruke n capillāmentum nt
perusal n perlēctiō f
peruse vt perlegere; (book) ēvolvere
pervade vt permānāre per, complēre; (emotion)
  perfundere
pervasive adj crēber
perverse adj perversus, prāvus
perversely adv perversē
perversion n dēprāvātiō f
perversity n perversitās f
pervert vt dēprāvāre; (words) dētorquēre; (person)
  corrumpere
perverter n corruptor m
pessimism n dēspērātiō f
pest n pestis f
pester vt sollicitāre
pestilence n pestilentia f, pestis f
pestilential adj pestilēns, nocēns
pestle n pistillum nt
pet n dēliciae fpl ♦ vt in dēliciīs habēre, dēlēnīre
petard n: be hoist with his own ~ suō sibī
  gladiō iugulārī
petition n precēs fpl; (POL) libellus m ♦ vt ōrāre
petrify vt (fig) dēfigere; be petrified stupēre,
  obstupēscere
pettifogger n lēgulēius m
pettiness n levitās f

pettish adj stomachōsus
petty adj levis, minūtus
petulance n protervitās f
petulant adj protervus, petulāns
petulantly adv petulanter
pew n subsellium nt
phalanx n phalanx f
phantasy n commentīcia ntpl
phantom n simulacrum nt, īdōlon nt
phases npl vicēs fpl
pheasant n phāsiānus m
phenomenal adj eximius, singulāris
phenomenon n rēs f, novum nt, spectāculum nt
philander vi lascīvīre
philanthropic adj hūmānus, beneficus
philanthropically adv hūmānē
philanthropy n hūmānitās f, beneficia ntpl
Philippic n Philippica f
philologist n grammaticus m
philology n grammatica ntpl
philosopher n philosophus m, sapiēns m
philosophical adj philosophus; (temperament)
  aequābilis
philosophize vi philosophārī
philosophy n philosophia f, sapientia f
philtre n philtrum nt
phlegm n pituīta f; (temper) lentitūdō f
phlegmatic adj lentus
phoenix n phoenīx m
phrase n locūtiō f; (GRAM) incīsum nt
phraseology n verba ntpl, ōrātiō f
physic n medicāmentum nt; **physics** pl physica
  ntpl
physical adj physicus; (of body) corporis
physician n medicus m
physicist n physicus m
physique n corpus nt, vīrēs fpl
piazza n forum nt
pick n (tool) dolabra f; (best part) lēctī mpl, flōs
  m ♦ vt (choose) legere, dēligere; (pluck) carpere;
  ~ out ēligere, excerpere; ~ up colligere
pickaxe n dolabra f
picked adj ēlēctus, dēlēctus
picket n (MIL) statiō f
pickle n muria f ♦ vt condīre
picture n pictūra f, tabula f ♦ vt dēpingere; (to
  oneself) ante oculōs pōnere
picturesque adj (scenery) amoenus
pie n crustum nt
piebald adj bicolor, varius
piece n pars f; (broken off) fragmentum nt; (food)
  frustum nt; (coin) nummus m; (play) fābula f;
  break in pieces comminuere; fall to pieces
  dīlābī; take to pieces dissolvere; tear in pieces
  dīlaniāre
piecemeal adv membrātim, minūtātim
pied adj maculōsus
pier n mōlēs f
pierce vt perfodere, trānsfīgere; (bore) perforāre;
  (fig) pungere
piercing adj acūtus
piety n pietās f, religiō f
pig n porcus m, sūs m/f; buy a pig in a poke spem
  pretiō emere; pig's suillus
pigeon n columba f; wood ~ palumbēs f
pig-headed adj pervicāx

pigment *n* pigmentum *nt*
pigsty *n* hara *f*
pike *n* dolō *m*, hasta *f*
pikeman *n* hastātus *m*
pile *n* acervus *m*, cumulus *m*; (*funeral*) rogus *m*; (*building*) mōlēs *f*; (*post*) sublica *f* ◆ *vt* cumulāre, congerere; ~ **up** exstruere, adcumulāre, coacervāre
pile-driver *n* fistūca *f*
pilfer *vt* fūrārī, surripere
pilferer *n* fūr *m*, fūrunculus *m*
pilgrim *n* peregrīnātor *m*
pilgrimage *n* peregrīnātio *f*
pill *n* pilula *f*
pillage *n* rapīna *f*, dēpopulātiō *f*, expīlātiō *f* ◆ *vt* dīripere, dēpopulārī, expīlāre
pillager *n* expīlātor *m*, praedātor *m*
pillar *n* columen *nt*, columna *f*
pillory *n* furca *f*
pillow *n* pulvīnus *nt*, culcita *f*
pilot *n* gubernātor *m*, ductor *m* ◆ *vt* regere, gubernāre
pimp *n* lēnō *m*
pimple *n* pustula *f*
pin *n* acus *f* ◆ *vt* adfīgere
pincers *n* forceps *m/f*
pinch *vt* pervellere, vellicāre; (*shoe*) ūrere; (*for room*) coartāre
pine *n* pīnus *f* ◆ *vi* tābēscere; ~ **away** intābēscere; ~ **for** dēsīderāre
pinion *n* penna *f*
pink *adj* rubicundus
pinnace *n* lembus *m*
pinnacle *n* fastīgium *nt*
pint *n* sextārius *m*
pioneer *n* antecursor *m*
pious *adj* pius, religiōsus
piously *adv* piē, religiōsē
pip *n* grānum *nt*
pipe *n* (*music*) fistula *f*, tībia *f*; (*water*) canālis *m* ◆ *vi* fistulā canere
piper *n* tībīcen *m*
pipkin *n* olla *f*
piquancy *n* sāl *m*, vīs *f*
piquant *adj* salsus, argūtus
pique *n* offēnsio *f*, dolor *m* ◆ *vt* offendere
piracy *n* latrōcinium *nt*
pirate *n* pīrāta *m*, praedō *m*
piratical *adj* pīrāticus
piscatorial *adj* piscātōrius
piston *n* embolus *m*
pit *n* fovea *f*, fossa *f*; (THEAT) cavea *f*
pitch *n* pix *f*; (*sound*) sonus *m* ◆ *vt* (*camp*) pōnere; (*tent*) tendere; (*missile*) conicere
pitch-black *adj* piceus
pitched battle *n* proelium iustum *nt*
pitcher *n* hydria *f*
pitchfork *n* furca *f*
pitch pine *n* picea *f*
piteous *adj* miserābilis, flēbilis
piteously *adv* miserābiliter
pitfall *n* fovea *f*
pith *n* medulla *f*
pithy *adj* (*style*) dēnsus; ~ **saying** sententia *f*
pitiable *adj* miserandus
pitiful *adj* miser, miserābilis; misericors

pitifully *adv* miserē, miserābiliter
pitiless *adj* immisericors, immītis
pitilessly *adv* crūdēliter
pittance *n* (*food*) dēmēnsum *nt*; (*money*) stips *f*
pity *n* misericordia *f*; **take ~ on** miserērī (+*acc of person, gen of things*); **it is a ~ that** male accidit quod ◆ *vt* miserērī (*gen*); **I ~ mē** miseret (*gen*)
pivot *n* cardō *m*
placability *n* plācābilitās *f*
placable *adj* plācābilis
placard *n* libellus *m*
placate *vt* plācāre
place *n* locus *m*; **in another ~** alibī; **in the first ~** prīmum; **in ~ of** locō (*gen*), pro (*abl*); **to this ~** hūc; **out of ~** intempestīvus; **give ~ to** cēdere (*dat*); **take ~** fierī, accidere; **take the ~ of** in locum (*gen*) succēdere ◆ *vt* pōnere, locāre, collocāre; ~ **beside** adpōnere; ~ **over** (*in charge*) praepōnere; ~ **round** circumdare; ~ **upon** impōnere
placid *adj* placidus, tranquillus, quiētus
placidity *n* tranquillitās *f*, sedātus animus *m*
placidly *adv* placidē, quiētē
plagiarism *n* fūrtum *nt*
plagiarize *vt* fūrārī
plague *n* pestilentia *f*, pestis *f*
plain *adj* (*lucid*) clārus, perspicuus; (*unadorned*) subtīlis, simplex; (*frank*) sincērus; (*ugly*) invenustus ◆ *n* campus *m*, plānitiēs *f*; **of the ~** campester
plainly *adv* perspicuē; simpliciter, sincērē
plainness *n* perspicuitās *f*; simplicitās *f*
plaint *n* querella *f*
plaintiff *n* petītor *m*
plaintive *adj* flēbilis, queribundus
plaintively *adv* flēbiliter
plait *vt* implicāre, nectere
plan *n* cōnsilium *nt*; (*of a work*) fōrma *f*, dēsignātiō *f*; (*of living*) ratiō *f*; (*intent*) prōpositum *nt*; (*drawing*) dēscrīptiō *f* ◆ *vt* (*a work*) dēsignāre, dēscrībere; (*intent*) cōgitāre, meditārī; cōnsilium capere *or* inīre; (*with verb*) in animō habēre (*inf*)
plane *n* (*surface*) plānitiēs *f*; (*tree*) platanus *f*; (*tool*) runcīna *f* ◆ *adj* aequus, plānus ◆ *vt* runcīnāre
planet *n* stēlla errāns *f*
plank *n* tabula *f*
plant *n* herba *f*, planta *f* ◆ *vt* (*tree*) serere; (*field*) cōnserere; (*colony*) dēdūcere; (*feet*) pōnere; ~ **firmly** īnfīgere
plantation *n* arbustum *nt*
planter *n* sator *m*, colōnus *m*
plaque *n* tabula *f*
plaster *n* albārium *nt*, tectōrium *nt*; (MED) emplastrum *nt*; ~ **of Paris** gypsum *nt* ◆ *vt* dealbāre
plasterer *n* albārius *m*
plastic *adj* ductilis, fūsilis
plate *n* (*dish*) catillus *m*; (*silver*) argentum *nt*; (*layer*) lāmina *f* ◆ *vt* indūcere
platform *n* suggestus *m*; rōstrum *nt*, tribūnal *nt*
platitude *n* trīta sententia *f*
platter *n* patella *f*, lanx *f*
plaudit *n* plausus *m*
plausibility *n* vērīsimilitūdō *f*
plausible *adj* speciōsus, vērī similis

play n lūdus m; (THEAT) fābula f; (voice) inclīnātiō f; (scope) campus m; (hands) gestus m; ~ **on words** agnōminātiō f; **fair** ~ aequum et bonum ♦ vi lūdere; (fountain) scatēre ♦ vt (music) canere; (instrument) canere (abl); (game) lūdere (abl); (part) agere; ~ **the part of** agere; ~ **a trick on** lūdificārī, impōnere (dat)
playbill n ēdictum nt
player n lūsor m; (at dice) āleātor m; (on flute) tībīcen m; (on lyre) fidicen m; (on stage) histriō m
playful adj lascīvus; (words) facētus
playfully adv per lūdum, per iocum
playfulness n lascīvia f; facētiae fpl
playground n ārea f
playmate n collūsor m
playwright n fābulārum scrīptor m
plea n causa f; (in defence) dēfēnsiō f, excūsātiō f
plead vi causam agere, causam ōrāre, causam dīcere; (in excuse) dēprecārī, excūsāre; ~ **with** obsecrāre
pleader n āctor m, causidicus m
pleasant adj iūcundus, dulcis, grātus; (place) amoenus
pleasantly adv iūcundē, suāviter
pleasantry n facētiae fpl, iocus m
please vt placēre (dat), dēlectāre; **try to** ~ īnservīre (dat); **just as you** ~ quod commodum est; **if you** ~ sīs; **pleased with** contentus (abl); **be pleased with oneself** sibī placēre ♦ adv amābō
pleasing adj grātus, iūcundus, amoenus; **be** ~ **to** cordī esse (dat)
pleasurable adj iūcundus
pleasure n voluptās f; (decision) arbitrium nt; **it is my** ~ libet; **derive** ~ voluptātem capere ♦ vt grātificārī (dat)
pleasure grounds n hortī mpl
pleasure-loving adj dēlicātus
plebeian adj plēbēius ♦ n: **the plebeians** plēbs f
plebiscite n suffrāgium nt
plectrum n plēctrum nt
pledge n pignus nt ♦ vt obligāre; ~ **oneself** prōmittere, spondēre; ~ **one's word** fidem obligāre, fidem interpōnere
Pleiads n Plēiadēs fpl
plenary adj īnfīnītus
plenipotentiary n lēgātus m
plenitude n cōpia f, mātūritās f
plentiful adj cōpiōsus, largus
plentifully adv cōpiōsē, largē
plenty n cōpia f, abundantia f; (enough) satis
pleonasm n redundantia f
pleurisy n lateris dolor m
pliable adj flexibilis, mollis, lentus
pliant adj flexibilis, mollis, lentus
pliers n forceps m/f
plight n habitus m, discrīmen nt ♦ vt spondēre
plod vi labōrāre, operam īnsūmere
plot n coniūrātiō f, īnsidiae fpl; (land) agellus m; (play) argūmentum nt ♦ vi coniūrāre, mōlīrī
plotter n coniūrātus m
plough n arātrum nt ♦ vt arāre; (sea) sulcāre; ~ **up** exarāre
ploughing n arātiō f
ploughman n arātor m
ploughshare n vōmer m

pluck n fortitūdō f ♦ vt carpere, legere; ~ **out** ēvellere; ~ **up courage** animum recipere, animō adesse
plucky adj fortis
plug n obtūrāmentum nt ♦ vt obtūrāre
plum n prūnum nt; (tree) prūnus f
plumage n plūmae fpl
plumb n perpendiculum nt ♦ adj dīrēctus ♦ adv ad perpendiculum ♦ vt (building) ad perpendiculum exigere; (depth) scrūtārī
plumber n artifex plumbārius m
plumb line n līnea f, perpendiculum nt
plume n crista f ♦ vt: ~ **oneself on** iactāre, prae sē ferre
plummet n perpendiculum nt
plump adj pinguis
plumpness n nitor m
plunder n (act) rapīna f; (booty) praeda f ♦ vi praedārī ♦ vt dīripere, expīlāre
plunderer n praedātor m, spoliātor m
plundering n rapīna f ♦ adj praedābundus
plunge vt mergere, dēmergere; (weapon) dēmittere ♦ vi mergī, sē dēmergere
plural adj plūrālis
plurality n multitūdō f, plūrēs pl
ply vt exercēre
poach vt surripere
pocket n sinus m
pocket money n pecūlium nt
pod n siliqua f
poem n poēma nt, carmen nt
poesy n poēsis f
poet n poēta m
poetess n poētria f
poetic adj poēticus
poetical adj = **poetic**
poetically adv poēticē
poetry n (art) poētica f; (poems) poēmata ntpl, carmina ntpl
poignancy n acerbitās f
poignant adj acerbus, acūtus
poignantly adv acerbē, acūtē
point n (dot) pūnctum nt; (place) locus m; (item) caput nt; (sharp end) aciēs f; (of sword) mucrō m; (of epigram) acūleī mpl; ~ **of honour** officium nt; **beside the** ~ ab rē; **to the** ~ ad rem; **from this** ~ hinc; **to that** ~ eō; **up to this** ~ hāctenus, adhūc; **without** ~ īnsulsus; **in** ~ **of fact** nempe; **make a** ~ **of doing** consultō facere; **on the** ~ **of death** moritūrus; **on the** ~ **of happening** inibī; **I was on the** ~ **of saying** in eō erat ut dīcerem; **matters have reached such a** ~ eō rēs recidit; **come to the** ~ ad rem redīre; **the** ~ **at issue is** illud quaeritur; **the main** ~ cardō m, caput nt; **turning** ~ articulus temporis m ♦ vt acuere, exacuere; (aim) intendere; (punctuate) distinguere; ~ **out** indicāre, dēmōnstrāre, ostendere
point-blank adj simplex ♦ adv praecīsē
pointed adj acūtus; (criticism) acūleātus; (wit) salsus
pointedly adv apertē, dīlūcidē
pointer n index m
pointless adj īnsulsus, frīgidus
pointlessly adv īnsulsē
point of view n iūdicium nt, sententia f

poise n lībrāmen nt; (fig) urbānitās f ♦ vt lībrāre
poison n venēnum nt ♦ vt venēnō necāre; (fig) īnficere
poisoned adj venēnātus
poisoner n venēficus m
poisoning n venēficium nt
poisonous adj noxius
poke vt trūdere, fodicāre
polar adj septentriōnālis
pole n asser m, contus m; (ASTR) polus m
poleaxe n bipennis f
polemic n contrōversia f
police n lictōrēs mpl; (night) vigilēs mpl
policy n ratiō f, cōnsilium nt; **honesty is the best ~** ea māximē condūcunt quae sunt rēctissima
polish n (appearance) nitor m; (character) urbānitās f; (LIT) līma f ♦ vt polīre; (fig) expolīre
polished adj polītus, mundus; (person) excultus, urbānus; (style) līmātus
polite adj urbānus, hūmānus, cōmis
politely adv urbānē, cōmiter
politeness n urbānitās f, hūmānitās f, cōmitās f
politic adj prūdēns, circumspectus
political adj cīvīlis, pūblicus; **~ life** rēs pūblica f
politician n magistrātus m
politics n rēs pūblica f; **take up ~** ad rem pūblicam accēdere
polity n reī pūblicae fōrma f
poll n caput nt; (voting) comitia ntpl ♦ vi suffrāgia inīre
poll tax n tribūtum nt in singula capita impositum
pollute vt inquināre, contāmināre
pollution n corruptēla f
poltroon n ignāvus m
pomegranate n mālum Pūnicum nt
pomp n adparātus m
pomposity n māgnificentia f, glōria f
pompous adj māgnificus, glōriōsus
pompously adv māgnificē, glōriōsē
pompousness n māgnificentia f
pond n stagnum nt, lacūna f
ponder vi sēcum reputāre ♦ vt animō volūtāre, in mente agitāre
ponderous adj gravis, ponderōsus
ponderously adv graviter
poniard n pugiō m
pontiff n pontifex m
pontifical adj pontificālis, pontificius
pontoon n pontō m
pony n mannus m
pooh-pooh vt dērīdēre
pool n lacūna f, stagnum nt ♦ vt cōnferre
poop n puppis f
poor adj pauper, inops; (meagre) exīlis; (inferior) improbus; (pitiable) miser; **~ little** misellus
poorly adj aeger, aegrōtus ♦ adv parum, tenuiter
pop n crepitus m ♦ vi ēmicāre
pope n pāpa m
poplar n pōpulus f
poppy n papāver nt
populace n vulgus nt, plēbs f
popular adj grātus, grātiōsus; (party) populāris
popularity n populī favor m, studium nt
popularly adv vulgō

populate vt frequentāre
population n populus m, cīvēs mpl
populous adj frequēns
porcelain n fictilia ntpl
porch n vestibulum nt
porcupine n hystrīx f
pore n forāmen nt ♦ vi: **~ over** scrūtārī, incumbere in (acc)
pork n porcīna f
porous adj rārus
porridge n puls f
port n portus m ♦ adj (side) laevus, sinister
portage n vectūra f
portal n porta f
portcullis n cataracta f
portend vt portendere
portent n mōnstrum nt, portentum nt
portentous adj mōnstruōsus
porter n iānitor m; (carrier) bāiulus m
portico n porticus f
portion n pars f; (marriage) dōs f; (lot) sors f
portliness n amplitūdō f
portly adj amplus, opīmus
portrait n imāgō f, effigiēs f
portray vt dēpingere, exprimere, effingere
pose n status m, habitus m ♦ vt pōnere ♦ vi habitum sūmere
poser n nōdus m
posit vt pōnere
position n (GEOG) situs m; (body) status m, gestus m; (rank) dignitās f; (office) honōs m; (MIL) locus m; **be in a ~ to** habēre (inf); **take up a ~** (MIL) locum capere
positive adj certus; **be ~ about** adfirmāre
positively adv certō, adfirmātē, rē vērā
posse n manus f
possess vt possidēre, habēre; (take) occupāre, potīrī (abl)
possession n possessiō f; **possessions** pl bona ntpl, fortūnae fpl; **take ~ of** potīrī (abl), occupāre, manum inicere (dat); (inheritance) obīre; (emotion) invādere, incēdere (dat); **gain ~ of** potior (abl)
possessor n possessor m, dominus m
possibility n facultās f; **there is a ~** fierī potest
possible adj: **it is ~** fierī potest; **as big as ~** quam māximus
possibly adv fortasse
post n pālus m; (MIL) statiō f; (office) mūnus nt; (courier) tabellārius m; **leave one's ~** locō cēdere, signa relinquere ♦ vt (troops) locāre, collocāre; (at intervals) dispōnere; (letter) dare, tabellāriō dare; (entry) in cōdicem referre; **be posted** (MIL) in statiōne esse
postage n vectūra f
poster n libellus m
posterior adj posterior
posterity n posterī mpl; (time) posteritās f
postern n postīcum nt
posthaste adv summā celeritāte
posthumous adj postumus
posthumously adv (born) patre mortuō; (published) auctōre mortuō
postpone vt differre, prōferre
postponement n dīlātiō f
postscript n: **add a ~** adscrībere, subicere

postulate *vt* sūmere ♦ *n* sūmptiō *f*
posture *n* gestus *m*, status *m*
pot *n* olla *f*, matella *f*
pot-bellied *adj* ventriōsus
potency *n* vīs *f*
potent *adj* efficāx, valēns
potentate *n* dynastēs *m*, tyrannus *m*
potential *adj* futūrus
potentiality *n* facultās *f*
potentially *adv* ut fierī posse vidētur; ~ **an emperor** capāx imperiī
potently *adv* efficienter
potion *n* pōtiō *f*
pot-pourri *n* farrāgō *f*
potsherd *n* testa *f*
pottage *n* iūs *nt*
potter *n* figulus *m*; **potter's** figulāris
pottery *n* fictilia *ntpl*
pouch *n* pēra *f*, sacculus *m*
poultice *n* fōmentum *nt*, emplastrum *nt*
poultry *n* gallīnae *fpl*
pounce *vi* involāre, īnsilīre
pound *n* lībra *f*; **five pounds** (*weight*) **of gold** aurī quīnque pondo ♦ *vt* conterere; pulsāre
pour *vt* fundere; ~ **forth** effundere; ~ **in** īnfundere; ~ **on** superfundere; ~ **out** effundere ♦ *vi* fundī, fluere; ~ **down** ruere, sē praecipitāre
pouring *adj* (*rain*) effūsus
poverty *n* paupertās *f*, egestās *f*, inopia *f*; (*style*) iēiūnitās *f*
powder *n* pulvis *m*
powdery *adj* pulvereus
power *n* potestās *f*; (*strength*) vīrēs *fpl*; (*excessive*) potentia *f*; (*supreme*) imperium *nt*; (*divine*) nūmen *nt*; (*legal*) auctōritās *f*; (*of father*) manus *f*; **as far as is in my** ~ quantum in mē est; **have great** ~ multum valēre, posse; **have** ~ **of attorney** cognitōrem esse; **it is still in my** ~ **to** integrum est mihī (*inf*)
powerful *adj* validus, potēns
powerfully *adv* valdē
powerless *adj* impotēns, imbēcillus; **be** ~ nihil valēre
powerlessness *n* imbēcillitas *f*
practicable *adj* in apertō; **be** ~ fierī posse
practical *adj* (*person*) habilis
practical joke *n* lūdus *m*
practical knowledge *n* ūsus *m*
practically *adv* ferē, paene
practice *n* ūsus *m*, exercitātiō *f*; (*RHET*) meditātiō *f*; (*habit*) consuētūdō *f*, mōs *m*; **corrupt practices** malae artēs
practise *vt* (*occupation*) exercēre, facere; (*custom*) factitāre; (*RHET*) meditārī ♦ *vi* (*MED*) medicīnam exercēre; (*LAW*) causās agere
practised *adj* exercitātus, perītus
practitioner *n* (*MED*) medicus *m*
praetor *n* praetor *nt*; **praetor's** praetōrius
praetorian *adj* praetōrius
praetorian guards *npl* praetōriānī *mpl*
praetorship *n* praetūra *f*
praise *n* laus *f* ♦ *vt* laudāre
praiser *n* laudātor *m*
praiseworthy *adj* laudābilis, laude dignus
prance *vi* exsultāre
prank *n* lūdus *m*

prate *vi* garrīre
prating *adj* garrulus
pray *vi* deōs precārī, deōs venerārī ♦ *vt* precārī, ōrāre; ~ **for** petere, precārī; ~ **to** adōrāre
prayer, **prayers** *n* precēs *fpl*
prayerful *adj* supplex
preach *vt*, *vi* docēre, praedicāre
preacher *n* ōrātor *m*
preamble *n* exōrdium *nt*
prearranged *adj* cōnstitūtus
precarious *adj* dubius, perīculōsus
precariousness *n* discrīmen *nt*
precaution *n* cautiō *f*, prōvidentia *f*; **take precautions** cavēre, praecavēre
precede *vt* praeīre (*dat*), anteīre (*dat*), antecēdere
precedence *n* prīmārius locus *m*; **give** ~ **to** cēdere (*dat*); **take** ~ (*thing*) antīquius esse; (*person*) prīmās agere
precedent *n* exemplum *nt*; (*LAW*) praeiūdicium *nt*; **breach of** ~ īnsolentia *f*; **in defiance of** ~ īnsolenter
preceding *adj* prior, superior
precept *n* praeceptum *nt*
preceptor *n* doctor *m*, magister *m*
precinct *n* terminus *m*, templum *nt*
precious *adj* cārus; pretiōsus; (*style*) pūtidus
precious stone *n* gemma *f*
precipice *n* locus praeceps *m*, rūpēs *f*
precipitancy *n* festīnātiō *f*
precipitate *vt* praecipitāre ♦ *adj* praeceps; praeproperus
precipitation *n* festīnātiō *f*
precipitous *adj* dēruptus, praeceps, praeruptus
precise *adj* certus, subtīlis; (*person*) accūrātus
precisely *adv* dēmum
precision *n* cūra *f*
preclude *vt* exclūdere, prohibēre
precocious *adj* praecox
precocity *n* festīnāta mātūritās *f*
preconceive *vt* praecipere; **preconceived idea** praeiūdicāta opīniō *f*
preconception *n* praeceptiō *f*
preconcerted *adj* ex compositō factus
precursor *n* praenūntius *m*
predatory *adj* praedātōrius
predecessor *n* dēcessor *m*; **my** ~ **cui** succēdō
predestination *n* fātum *nt*, necessitās *f*
predestine *vt* dēvovēre
predetermine *vt* praefinīre
predicament *n* angustiae *fpl*, discrīmen *nt*
predicate *n* attribūtum *nt*
predict *vt* praedīcere, augurārī
prediction *n* praedictiō *f*
predilection *n* amor *m*, studium *nt*
predispose *vt* inclīnāre, praeparāre
predisposition *n* inclīnātiō *f*
predominance *n* potentia *f*, praestantia *f*
predominant *adj* praepotēns, praecipuus
predominantly *adv* plērumque
predominate *vi* pollēre, dominārī
pre-eminence *n* praestantia *f*
pre-eminent *adj* ēgregius, praecipuus, excellēns
pre-eminently *adv* ēgregiē, praecipuē, excellenter
preface *n* prooemium *nt*, praefātiō *f* ♦ *vi* praefārī

prefect n praefectus m
prefecture n praefectūra f
prefer vt (charge) dēferre; (to office) anteferre; (choice) antepōnere (acc and dat), posthabēre (dat and acc); (with verb) mālle
preferable adj potior
preferably adv potius
preference n favor m; **give ~ to** antepōnere, praeoptāre; **in ~ to** potius quam
preferment n honōs m, dignitās f
prefix vt praetendere ♦ n praepositiō f
pregnancy n graviditās f
pregnant adj gravida
prejudge vt praeiūdicāre
prejudice n praeiūdicāta opīniō f; (harmful) invidia f, incommodum nt; **without ~** cum bonā veniā ♦ vt obesse (dat); **be prejudiced against** invidēre (dat), male opīnārī dē (abl)
prejudicial adj damnōsus; **be ~ to** obesse (dat), nocēre (dat), officere (dat), dētrīmentō esse (dat)
preliminaries npl praecurrentia ntpl
preliminary adj prīmus ♦ n prōlūsiō f
prelude n prooemium nt
premature adj immātūrus; (birth) abortīvus
prematurely adv ante tempus
premeditate vt praecōgitāre, praemeditārī
premeditated adj praemeditātus
premier adj prīnceps, praecipuus
premise n (major) prōpositiō f; (minor) adsūmptiō f; **premises** pl aedēs fpl, domus f
premium n praemium nt; **be at a ~** male emī
premonition n monitus m
preoccupation n sollicitūdō f
preoccupied adj sollicitus, districtus
preordain vt praefīnīre
preparation n (process) adparātiō f, comparātiō f; (product) adparātus m; (of speech) meditātiō f; **make preparations for** īnstruere, exōrnāre, comparāre
prepare vt parāre, adparāre, comparāre; (speech) meditārī; (with verb) parāre; **prepared for** parātus ad (acc)
preponderance n praestantia f
preponderate vi praepollēre, vincere
preposition n praepositiō f
prepossess vt commendāre (dat and acc), praeoccupāre
prepossessing adj suāvis, iūcundus
prepossession n favor m
preposterous adj absurdus
prerogative n iūs nt
presage n ōmen nt ♦ vt ōminārī, portendere
prescience n prōvidentia f
prescient adj prōvidus
prescribe vt imperāre; (MED) praescrībere; (limit) fīnīre
prescription n (MED) compositiō f; (right) ūsus m
presence n praesentia f; (appearance) aspectus m; **~ of mind** praesēns animus m; **in the ~ of** cōram (abl); apud (abl); **in my ~** mē praesente
present adj praesēns, īnstāns; **be ~** adesse; **be ~ at** interesse (dat) ♦ n praesēns tempus nt; (gift) dōnum nt; **at ~** in praesentī, nunc; **for the ~** in praesēns ♦ vt dōnāre, offerre; (on stage) indūcere; (in court) sistere; **~ itself** occurrere
presentable adj spectābilis

presentation n dōnātiō f
presentiment n augurium nt
presently adv mox
preservation n cōnservātiō f
preserve vt cōnservāre, tuērī; (food) condīre
preside vi praesidēre (dat)
presidency n praefectūra f
president n praefectus m
press n prēlum nt ♦ vt premere; (crowd) stīpāre; (urge) īnstāre (dat); **~ for** flāgitāre; **~ hard** (pursuit) īnsequī, īnstāre (dat), īnsistere (dat); **~ out** exprimere; **~ together** comprimere
pressing adj īnstāns, gravis
pressure n pressiō f, nīsus m
prestige n auctōritās f, opīniō f
presumably adv sānē
presume vt sūmere, conicere ♦ vi audēre, cōnfīdere; **I ~** opīnor, crēdō
presuming adj adrogāns
presumption n coniectūra f; (arrogance) adrogantia f, licentia f
presumptuous adj adrogāns, audāx
presumptuously adv adroganter, audacter
presuppose vt praesūmere
pretence n simulātiō f, speciēs f; **under ~ of** per speciem (gen); **under false pretences** dolō malō
pretend vt simulāre, fingere; **~ that ... not** dissimulāre
pretender n captātor m
pretension n postulātum nt; **make pretensions to** adfectāre, sibī adrogāre
pretentious adj adrogāns, glōriōsus
pretext n speciēs f; **under ~ of** per speciem (gen); **on the ~ that** quod (subj)
prettily adv pulchrē, bellē
prettiness n pulchritūdō f, lepōs m
pretty adj fōrmōsus, pulcher, bellus ♦ adv admodum, satis
prevail vi vincere; (custom) tenēre, obtinēre; **~ upon** persuādēre (dat); (by entreaty) exōrāre
prevailing adj vulgātus
prevalent adj vulgātus; **be ~** obtinēre; **become ~** incrēbrēscere
prevaricate vi tergiversārī
prevarication n tergiversātiō f
prevaricator n veterātor m
prevent vt impedīre (+ quōminus/quīn + subj), prohibēre (+ acc and infin)
prevention n impedītiō f
previous adj prior, superior
previously adv anteā, antehāc
prevision n prōvidentia f
prey n praeda f ♦ vi: **~ upon** īnsectārī; (fig) vexāre, carpere
price n pretium nt; (of corn) annōna f; **at a high ~** māgnī; **at a low ~** parvī ♦ vt pretium cōnstituere (gen)
priceless adj inaestimābilis
prick vt pungere; (goad) stimulāre; **~ up the ears** aurēs adrigere
prickle n acūleus m
prickly adj aculeātus, horridus
pride n superbia f, fastus m; (boasting) glōria f; (object) decus nt; (best part) flōs m ♦ vt: **~ oneself on** iactāre, prae sē ferre

priest *n* sacerdōs *m*; *(especial)* flāmen *m*; **high ~** pontifex *m*, antistēs *m*

priestess *n* sacerdōs *f*; **high ~** antistita *f*

priesthood *n* sacerdōtium *nt*, flāminium *nt*

prig *n* homō fastīdiōsus *m*

priggish *adj* fastīdiōsus

prim *adj* modestior

primarily *adv* prīncipiō, praecipuē

primary *adj* prīmus, praecipuus

prime *adj* prīmus, ēgregius; **~ mover** auctor *m* ♦ *n* flōs *m*; **in one's ~** flōrēns ♦ *vt* īnstruere, ērudīre

primeval *adj* prīscus

primitive *adj* prīstinus, incultus

primordial *adj* prīscus

prince *n* rēgulus *m*; rēgis fīlius *m*; prīnceps *m*

princely *adj* rēgālis

princess *n* rēgis fīlia *f*

principal *adj* praecipuus, prīnceps, māximus ♦ *n* *(person)* prīnceps *m/f*; *(money)* sors *f*

principally *adv* in prīmīs, māximē, māximam partem

principle *n* prīncipium *nt*; *(rule)* fōrmula *f*, ratiō *f*; *(character)* fidēs *f*; **principles** *pl* īnstitūta *ntpl*, disciplīna *f*; **first principles** elementa *ntpl*, initia *ntpl*

print *n* nota *f*, signum *nt*; *(foot)* vestīgium *nt* ♦ *vt* imprimere

prior *adj* prior, potior

priority *n*: **give ~ to** praevertere *(dat)*

prise *vt* sublevāre; **~ open** vectī refringere

prison *n* carcer *m*, vincula *ntpl*; **put in ~** in vincula conicere

prisoner *n* reus *m*; *(for debt)* nexus *m*; *(of war)* captīvus *m*; **~ at the bar** reus *m*, rea *f*; **take ~ capere**

pristine *adj* prīscus, prīstinus, vetus

privacy *n* sēcrētum *nt*

private *adj* *(individual)* prīvātus; *(home)* domesticus; *(secluded)* sēcrētus ♦ *n* (MIL) gregārius mīles *m*

privately *adv* clam, sēcrētō

private property *n* res familiāris *f*

privation *n* inopia *f*, egestās *f*

privet *n* ligustrum *nt*

privilege *n* iūs *nt*, immūnitās *f*

privileged *adj* immūnis

privy *adj* sēcrētus; **~ to** cōnscius *(gen)*

prize *n* praemium *nt*; *(captured)* praeda *f*; **~ money** manubiae *fpl* ♦ *vt* māgnī aestimāre

pro-Athenian *adj* rērum Athēniēnsium studiōsus

probability *n* vērī similitūdō *f*

probable *adj* vērī similis; **more ~** vērō propior

probably *adv* fortasse

probation *n* probātiō *f*

probationer *n* tīrō *m*

probe *vt* īnspicere, scrūtārī

probity *n* honestās *f*, integritās *f*

problem *n* quaestiō *f*; **the ~ is** illud quaeritur

problematical *adj* dubius, anceps

procedure *n* ratiō *f*, modus *m*; (LAW) fōrmula *f*

proceed *vi* pergere, prōcēdere, prōgredī; *(narrative)* īnsequī; **~ against** persequī, lītem intendere *(dat)*; **~ from** orīrī, proficīscī ex

proceedings *n* ācta *ntpl*

proceeds *n* fructus *m*, reditus *m*

process *n* ratiō *f*; (LAW) āctiō *f*; **in the ~ of time** post aliquod tempus

procession *n* pompa *f*; *(fig)* agmen *nt*

proclaim *vt* ēdīcere, prōnūntiāre, praedicāre, dēclārāre; **~ war upon** bellum indīcere *(dat)*

proclamation *n* ēdictum *nt*

proclivity *n* prōpēnsiō *f*

proconsul *n* prōcōnsul *m*

proconsular *adj* prōcōnsulāris

proconsulship *n* prōcōnsulātus *m*

procrastinate *vt* differre, prōferre ♦ *vi* cunctārī

procrastination *n* prōcrāstinātiō *f*, mora *f*

procreate *vt* generāre, prōcreāre

procreation *n* prōcreātiō *f*

procreator *n* generātor *m*

procumbent *adj* prōnus

procurator *n* prōcūrātor *m*

procure *vt* parāre, adipīscī, adquīrere; *(by request)* impetrāre

procurer *n* lēnō *m*

prod *vt* stimulāre

prodigal *adj* prōdigus ♦ *n* nepōs *m*

prodigality *n* effūsiō *f*

prodigally *adv* effūsē

prodigious *adj* ingēns, immānis

prodigy *n* prōdigium *nt*, portentum *nt*; *(fig)* mīrāculum *nt*

produce *vt* ēdere; *(young)* parere; *(crops)* ferre; *(play)* dare, docēre; *(line)* prōdūcere; *(in court)* sistere; *(into view)* prōferre; *(from store)* prōmere, dēprōmere ♦ *n* fructus *m*; *(of earth)* frūgēs *fpl*; *(in money)* reditus *m*

product *n* opus *nt*; **~ of** fructus *(gen)*

production *n* opus *nt*

productive *adj* fēcundus, ferāx, fructuōsus

productivity *n* fēcunditās *f*, ūbertās *f*

profanation *n* violātiō *f*

profane *adj* profānus, impius ♦ *vt* violāre, polluere

profanely *adv* impiē

profanity *n* impietās *f*

profess *vt* profitērī, prae sē ferre; **~ to be** profitērī sē

profession *n* professiō *f*; *(occupation)* ars *f*, haeresis *f*

professor *n* doctor *m*

proffer *vt* offerre, pollicērī

proficiency *n* prōgressus *m*, perītia *f*; **attain ~** prōficere

proficient *adj* perītus

profile *n* ōris līneāmenta *ntpl*; *(portrait)* oblīqua imāgō *f*

profit *n* lucrum *nt*, ēmolumentum *nt*, fructus *m*; **make a ~ out of** quaestuī habēre ♦ *vt* prōdesse *(dat)* ♦ *vi*: **~ by** fruī *(abl)*, ūtī *(abl)*; *(opportunity)* arripere

profitable *adj* fructuōsus, ūtilis

profitably *adv* ūtiliter

profligacy *n* flāgitium *nt*, perditī mōrēs *mpl*

profligate *adj* perditus, dissolūtus ♦ *n* nepōs *m*

profound *adj* altus; *(discussion)* abstrūsus

profoundly *adv* penitus

profundity *n* altitūdō *f*

profuse *adj* prōdigus, effūsus

profusely *adv* effūsē

profusion n abundantia f, adfluentia f; **in ~ abundē**
progenitor n auctor m
progeny n prōgeniēs f, prōlēs f
prognostic n signum nt
prognosticate vt ōminārī, augurārī, praedīcere
prognostication n ōmen nt, praedictiō f
programme n libellus m
progress n prōgressus m; **make ~** prōficere ♦ vi prōgredī
progression n prōgressus m
progressively adv gradātim
prohibit vt vetāre, interdīcere (dat)
prohibition n interdictum nt
project n prōpositum nt ♦ vi ēminēre, exstāre; (land) excurrere ♦ vt prōicere
projectile n tēlum nt
projecting adj ēminēns
projection n ēminentia f
proletarian adj plēbēius
proletariat n plēbs f
prolific adj fēcundus
prolix adj verbōsus, longus
prolixity n redundantia f
prologue n prologus m
prolong vt dūcere, prōdūcere; (office) prōrogāre
prolongation n (time) propāgātiō f; (office) prōrogātiō f
promenade n ambulātiō f ♦ vi inambulāre, spatiārī
prominence n ēminentia f
prominent adj ēminēns, īnsignis; **be ~** ēminēre
promiscuous adj prōmiscuus
promiscuously adv prōmiscuē
promise n prōmissum nt; **break a ~** fidem fallere; **keep a ~** fidem praestāre; **make a ~** fidem dare; **a youth of great ~** summae speī adulēscēns ♦ vt prōmittere, pollicērī; (in marriage) dēspondēre; **~ in return** reprōmittere ♦ vi: **~ well** bonam spem ostendere
promising adj bonae speī
promissory note n syngrapha f
promontory n prōmunturium nt
promote vt favēre (dat); (growth) alere; (in rank) prōdūcere
promoter n auctor m, fautor m
promotion n dignitās f
prompt adj alacer, prōmptus ♦ vt incitāre, commovēre; (speaker) subicere
prompter n monitor m
promptitude n alacritās f, celeritās f
promptly adv extemplō, citō
promulgate vt prōmulgāre, palam facere
promulgation n prōmulgātiō f
prone adj prōnus; (mind) inclīnātus
prong n dēns m
pronounce vt ēloquī, appellāre; (oath) interpōnere; (sentence) dīcere, prōnūntiāre
pronounced adj manifestus, īnsignis
pronouncement n ōrātiō f, adfirmātiō f
pronunciation n appellātiō f
proof n documentum nt, argūmentum nt; (test) probātiō f ♦ adj immōtus, impenetrābilis
prop n adminiculum nt, firmāmentum nt ♦ vt fulcīre
propaganda n documenta ntpl

propagate vt propāgāre
propagation n propāgātiō f
propel vt incitāre, prōpellere
propensity n inclīnātiō f
proper adj idōneus, decēns, decōrus; rēctus; **it is ~** decet
properly adv decōrē; rēctē
property n rēs f, rēs mancipī, bona ntpl; (estate) praedium nt; (attribute) proprium nt; (slave's) pecūlium nt
prophecy n vāticinium nt, praedictiō f
prophesy vt vāticinārī, praedīcere
prophet n vātēs m, fātidicus m
prophetess n vātēs f
prophetic adj dīvīnus, fātidicus
prophetically adv dīvīnitus
propinquity n (place) vīcīnitās f; (kin) propinquitās f
propitiate vt plācāre
propitiation n plācātiō f, litātiō f
propitious adj fēlīx, faustus; (god) praesēns
proportion n mēnsūra f; **in ~** prō portiōne, prō ratā parte; **in ~ to** prō (abl)
proportionately adv prō portiōne, prō ratā parte
proposal n condiciō f
propose vt prōpōnere; (motion) ferre, rogāre; (penalty) inrogāre; (candidate) rogāre magistrātum
proposer n auctor m, lātor m
proposition n (offer) condiciō f; (plan) cōnsilium nt, prōpositum nt; (LOGIC) prōnūntiātum nt
propound vt expōnere, in medium prōferre
propraetor n prōpraetor m
proprietor n dominus m
propriety n decōrum nt; (conduct) modestia f; **with ~** decenter
propulsion n impulsus m
prorogation n prōrogātiō f
prorogue vt prōrogāre
prosaic adj pedester
proscribe vt prōscrībere
proscription n prōscrīptiō f
prose n ōrātiō f, ōrātiō solūta f
prosecute vt (task) exsequī, gerere; (at law) accūsāre, lītem intendere (dat)
prosecution n exsecūtiō f; (at law) accūsātiō f; (party) accūsātor m
prosecutor n accūsātor m
prosody n numerī mpl
prospect n prōspectus m; (fig) spēs f ♦ vi explōrāre
prospective adj futūrus, spērātus
prosper vi flōrēre, bonā fortūnā ūtī ♦ vt fortūnāre
prosperity n fortūna f, rēs secundae fpl, fēlīcitās f
prosperous adj fēlīx, fortūnātus, secundus
prosperously adv prosperē
prostrate adj prōstrātus, adflīctus; **lie ~** iacēre ♦ vt prōsternere, dēicere; **~ oneself** prōcumbere, sē prōicere
prostration n frāctus animus m
prosy adj longus
protagonist n prīmārum partium āctor m

protect vt tuērī, dēfendere, custōdīre, prōtegere
protection n tūtēla f, praesidium nt; (LAW) patrōcinium nt; (POL) fidēs f; **put oneself under the ~ of** in fidem venīre (gen); **take under one's ~** in fidem recipere
protector n patrōnus m, dēfēnsor m, custōs m
protectress n patrōna f
protégé n clⁱēns m
protest n obtestātiō f; (POL) intercessiō f ♦ vi obtestārī, reclāmāre; (POL) intercēdere
protestation n adsevērātiō f
prototype n archetypum nt
protract vt dūcere, prōdūcere
protrude vi prōminēre
protruding adj exsertus
protuberance n ēminentia f, tūber nt
protuberant adj ēminēns, turgidus
proud adj superbus, adrogāns, īnsolēns; **be ~** superbīre; **be ~ of** iactāre
proudly adv superbē
prove vt dēmōnstrāre, arguere, probāre; (test) experīrī ♦ vi (person) sē praebēre; (event) ēvādere; **~ oneself** sē praebēre, sē praestāre; **not proven** nōn liquet
proved adj expertus
provenance n orīgō f
provender n pābulum nt
proverb n prōverbium nt
proverbial adj trītus; **become ~** in prōverbium venīre
provide vt parāre, praebēre; **~ for** prōvidēre (dat); **the law provides** lēx iubet; **~ against** praecavēre
provided that conj dum, dummodo (subj)
providence n prōvidentia f; Deus m
provident adj prōvidus, cautus
providential adj dīvīnus; secundus
providentially adv dīvīnitus
providently adv cautē
providing conj dum, dummodo
province n prōvincia f
provincial adj prōvinciālis; (contemptuous) oppidānus, mūnicipālis
provision n parātus m; **make ~ for** prōvidēre (dat); **make ~** cavēre
provisionally adv ad tempus
provisions n cibus m, commeātus m, rēs frūmentāria f
proviso n condiciō f; **with this ~** hāc lēge
provocation n inrītāmentum nt, offēnsiō f
provocative adj (language) molestus, invidiōsus
provoke vt inrītāre, lacessere; (to action) excitāre
provoking adj odiōsus, molestus
provost n praefectus m
prow n prōra f
prowess n virtūs f
prowl vi grassārī, vagārī
proximate adj proximus
proximity n propinquitās f, vīcīnia f
proxy n vicārius m
prude n fastīdiōsa f
prudence n prūdentia f
prudent adj prūdēns, cautus, sagāx
prudently adv prūdenter, cautē
prudery n fastīdiōsa quaedam pudīcitia f

prudish adj fastīdiōsus
prune vt amputāre
pruner n putātor m
pruning hook n falx f
pry vi inquīrere; **pry into** scrūtārī
pseudonym n falsum nōmen nt
psychology n animī ratiō f
Ptolemy n Ptolemaeus m
puberty n pūbertās f
public adj pūblicus; (speech) forēnsis; **~ life** rēs pūblica f, forum nt; **in ~** forīs; **appear in ~** in medium prōdīre; **make ~** in mediō pōnere, forās perferre; **make a ~ case of** in medium vocāre; **act for the ~ good** in medium cōnsulere; **be a ~ figure** in lūce versārī, digitō mōnstrārī ♦ n vulgus nt, hominēs mpl
publican n (taxes) pūblicānus m; (inn) caupō m
publication n ēditiō f, prōmulgātiō f; (book) liber m
publicity n lūx f, celebritās f
publicly adv palam; (by the state) pūblicē
public opinion n fāma f
publish vt vulgāre, dīvulgāre; (book) ēdere
pucker vt corrūgāre
puerile adj puerīlis
puerility n ineptiae fpl
puff n aura f ♦ vt īnflāre ♦ vi anhēlāre
puffed up adj īnflātus, tumidus
pugilism n pugilātus m
pugilist n pugil m
pugnacious adj pugnāx
pugnacity n ferōcitās f
puissance n potentia f, vīrēs fpl
puissant adj potēns
pull n tractus m; (of gravity) contentiō f ♦ vt trahere, tractāre; **~ apart** distrahere; **~ at** vellicāre; **~ away** āvellere; **~ back** retrahere; **~ down** dēripere, dētrahere; (building) dēmōlīrī; **~ off** āvellere; **~ out** ēvellere, extrahere; **~ through** vi pervincere; (illness) convalēscere; **~ up** (plant) ēruere; (movement) coercēre; **~ to pieces** dīlaniāre
pullet n pullus gallīnāceus m
pulley n trochlea f
pulmonary adj pulmōneus
pulp n carō f
pulpit n suggestus m
pulsate vi palpitāre, micāre
pulse n (plant) legūmen nt; (of blood) vēnae fpl; **feel the ~** vēnās temptāre
pulverize vt contundere
pumice stone n pūmex m
pummel vt verberāre
pump n antlia f ♦ vt haurīre; **~ out** exhaurīre
pumpkin n cucurbita f
pun n agnōminātiō f
punch n ictus m ♦ vt pertundere, percutere
punctilious adj religiōsus
punctiliousness n religiō f
punctual adj accūrātus, dīligēns
punctuality n dīligentia f
punctually adv ad hōram, ad tempus
punctuate vt distinguere
punctuation n interpūnctiō f
puncture n pūnctiō f ♦ vt pungere

pundit – python

pundit *n* scholasticus *m*
pungency *n* ācrimōnia *f*; (*in debate*) acūleī *mpl*
pungent *adj* ācer, mordāx
punish *vt* pūnīre, animadvertere in (*acc*); poenam sūmere dē (*abl*); **be punished** poenās dare
punishable *adj* poenā dignus
punisher *n* vindex *m*, ultor *m*
punishment *n* poena *f*, supplicium *nt*; (*censors'*) animadversiō *f*; **capital** ~ capitis supplicium *nt*; **corporal** ~ verbera *ntpl*; **inflict** ~ **on** poenā adficere, poenam capere dē (*abl*), supplicium sūmere dē (*abl*); **submit to** ~ poenam subīre; **undergo** ~ poenās dare, pendere, solvere
punitive *adj* ulcīscendī causā
punt *n* pontō *m*
puny *adj* pusillus
pup *n* catulus *m* ♦ *vi* parere
pupil *n* discipulus *m*, discipula *f*; (*eye*) aciēs *f*, pūpula *f*
pupillage *n* tūtēla *f*
puppet *n* pūpa *f*
puppy *n* catulus *m*
purblind *adj* luscus
purchase *n* emptiō *f*; (*formal*) mancipium *nt* ♦ *vt* emere
purchaser *n* emptor *m*; (*at auction*) manceps *m*
pure *adj* pūrus, integer; (*morally*) castus; (*mere*) merus
purely *adv* pūrē, integrē; (*solely*) sōlum, nīl nisi; (*quite*) omnīnō, plānē
purgation *n* pūrgātiō *f*
purge *vt* pūrgāre, expūrgāre
purification *n* lūstrātiō *f*, pūrgātiō *f*
purify *vt* pūrgāre, expūrgāre
purist *n* fastīdiōsus *m*
purity *n* integritās *f*, castitās *f*
purloin *vt* surripere, fūrārī
purple *n* purpura *f* ♦ *adj* purpureus
purport *n* sententia *f*; (*of words*) vīs *f*; **what is the** ~ **of?** quō spectat?, quid vult? ♦ *vt* velle spectāre ad
purpose *n* prōpositum *nt*, cōnsilium *nt*, mēns *f*; **for that** ~ eō; **for the** ~ **of** ad (*acc*), ut (*subj*), eā mente ut, eō cōnsiliō ut (*subj*); **on** ~ cōnsultō, dē industriā; **to the** ~ ad rem; **to what purpose?** quō?, quōrsum?; **to no** ~ frustrā, nēquīquam; **without achieving one's** ~ rē īnfectā ♦ *vt* in animō habēre, velle
purposeful *adj* intentus
purposeless *adj* inānis
purposely *adv* cōnsultō, dē industriā
purr *n* murmur *nt* ♦ *vi* murmurāre
purse *n* marsupium *nt*, crumēna *f*; **privy** ~ fiscus *m* ♦ *vt* adstringere
pursuance *n* exsecūtiō *f*; **in** ~ **of** secundum (*acc*)

pursue *vt* īnsequī, īnsectārī, persequī; (*closely*) īnstāre (*dat*), īnsistere (*dat*); (*aim*) petere; (*course*) īnsistere
pursuer *n* īnsequēns *m*; (*LAW*) accūsātor *m*
pursuit *n* īnsectātiō *f*; (*hunt*) vēnātiō *f*; (*ambition*) studium *nt*
purvey *vt* parāre; (*food*) obsōnāre
purveyance *n* prōcūrātiō *f*
purveyor *n* obsōnātor *m*
purview *n* prōvincia *f*
pus *n* pūs *nt*
push *n* pulsus *m*, impetus *m* ♦ *vt* impellere, trūdere, urgēre; ~ **away** āmovēre; ~ **back** repellere; ~ **down** dēprimere, dētrūdere; ~ **forward** prōpellere; ~ **in** intrūdere; ~ **on** incitāre; ~ **through** perrumpere
pushing *adj* cōnfidēns
pusillanimity *n* ignāvia *f*, timor *m*
pusillanimous *adj* ignāvus, timidus
pustule *n* pustula *f*
put *vt* (*in a state*) dare; (*in a position*) pōnere; (*in words*) reddere; (*argument*) pōnere; (*spur*) subdere; (*to some use*) adhibēre; **put an end to fīnem** facere (*dat*); **put a question to** interrogāre; **put against** adpōnere; **put among** intericere; **put aside** sēpōnere; **put away** pōnere, dēmovēre; (*store*) repōnere; **put back** repōnere; repellere; **put beside** adpōnere; **put between** interpōnere; **put by** condere; **put down** dēpōnere; (*revolt*) opprimere; **put forth** extendere; (*growth*) mittere; **put forward** ostentāre; (*plea*) adferre; **put in** immittere, īnserere; (*ship*) adpellere; **put off** differre; **put on** impōnere; (*clothes*) induere; (*play*) dare; **put out** ēicere; (*eye*) effodere; (*fire*) exstinguere; (*money*) pōnere; (*tongue*) exserere; **put out of the way** dēmovēre; **put out to sea** in altum ēvehi, solvere; **put over** superimpōnere; **put to** adpōnere; (*flight*) dare in (*acc*), fugāre, prōflīgāre; in fugam conicere; (*sea*) solvere; **put together** cōnferre; **put under** subicere; **put up** (*for sale*) prōpōnere; (*lodge*) dēvertere, dēversārī apud; **put up with** ferre, patī; **put upon** impōnere
putrefaction *n* pūtor *m*
putrefy *vi* putrēscere
putrid *adj* putridus
puzzle *n* nōdus *m* ♦ *vt* impedīre, sollicitāre; **be puzzled** haerēre
puzzling *adj* ambiguus, perplexus
pygmy *n* pygmaeus *m*
pyramid *n* pȳramis *f*
pyramidal *adj* pȳramidātus
pyre *n* rogus *m*
Pyrenees *npl* Pyrenaeī (montēs) *mpl*
python *n* pȳthōn *m*

Qq

quack n (*doctor*) circulātor m ♦ vi tetrinnīre
quadrangle n ārea f
quadruped n quadrupēs m/f
quadruple adj quadruplex
quaestor n quaestor m; **quaestor's** quaestōrius
quaestorship n quaestūra f
quaff vt ēpōtāre, haurīre
quagmire n palūs f
quail n (*bird*) coturnīx f ♦ vi pāvēscere, trepidāre
quaint adj novus, īnsolitus
quaintness n īnsolentia f
quake vi horrēre, horrēscere ♦ n (*earth*) mōtus m
quaking n horror m, tremor m ♦ adj tremulus
qualification n condiciō f; (*limitation*) exceptiō f
qualified adj (*for*) aptus, idōneus, dignus; (*in*) perītus, doctus
qualify vi prōficere ♦ vt temperāre, mītigāre
qualities npl ingenium nt
quality n nātūra f, vīs f; indolēs f; (*rank*) locus m, genus nt; **I know the ~ of** sciō quālis sit
qualm n religiō f, scrūpulus m
quandary n angustiae fpl; **be in a ~** haerēre
quantity n cōpia f, numerus m; (*metre*) vōcum mēnsiō f; **a large ~** multum nt, plūrimum nt; **a small ~** aliquantulum nt
quarrel n dissēnsiō f, contrōversia f; (*violent*) rixa f, iūrgium nt ♦ vi rixārī, altercārī
quarrelsome adj pugnāx, lītigiōsus
quarry n lapicīdinae fpl, metallum nt; (*prey*) praeda f ♦ vt excīdere
quart n duō sextāriī mpl
quartan n (*fever*) quartāna f
quarter n quarta pars f, quadrāns m; (*sector*) regiō f; (*direction*) pars f, regiō f; (*respite*) missiō f; **quarters** castra ntpl; (*billet*) hospitium nt; **come to close quarters** manum cōnserere; (*armies*) signa cōnferre; **winter quarters** hīberna ntpl ♦ vt quadrifidam dīvidere; (*troops*) in hospitia dīvidere
quarterdeck n puppis f
quarterly adj trimestris ♦ adv quartō quōque mēnse
quartermaster n (*navy*) gubernātor m; (*army*) castrōrum praefectus m
quarterstaff n rudis f
quash vt comprimere; (*decision*) rescindere
quatrain n tetrastichon nt
quaver n tremor m ♦ vi tremere
quavering adj tremebundus
quay n crepīdō f
queasy adj fastīdiōsus
queen n rēgīna f; (*bee*) rēx m

queer adj īnsolēns, rīdiculus
quell vt opprimere, domāre, dēbellāre
quench vt exstinguere, restinguere; (*thirst*) sēdāre, explēre
querulous adj querulus, queribundus
query n interrogātiō f ♦ vt in dubium vocāre ♦ vi rogāre
quest n investīgātiō f; **go in ~ of** investīgāre, anquīrere
question n interrogātiō f; (*at issue*) quaestiō f, rēs f; (*in doubt*) dubium nt; **ask a ~** rogāre, quaerere, scīscitārī, percontārī; **call in ~** in dubium vocāre, addubitāre; **out of the ~** indignus; **be out of the ~** improbārī, fierī nōn posse; **the ~ is** illud quaeritur; **there is no ~ that** nōn dubium est quīn (*subj*); **without ~** sine dubiō ♦ vt interrogāre; (*closely*) percontārī; (*doubt*) in dubium vocāre ♦ vi dubitāre
questionable adj incertus, dubius
questioner n percontātor m
questioning n interrogātiō f
queue n agmen nt
quibble n captiō f ♦ vi cavillārī
quibbler n cavillātor m
quibbling adj captiōsus
quick adj (*speed*) celer, vēlōx, citus; (*to act*) alacer, impiger; (*to perceive*) sagāx; (*with hands*) facilis; (*living*) vīvus; **be ~** properāre, festīnāre; **cut to the ~** ad vīvum resecāre; (*fig*) mordēre
quicken vt adcelerāre; (*with life*) animāre
quickening adj vītālis
quickly adv celeriter, citō; (*haste*) properē; (*mind*) acūtē; **as ~ as possible** quam celerrimē
quickness n celeritās f, vēlōcitās f; (*to act*) alacritās f; (*to perceive*) sagācitās f, sollertia f
quicksand n syrtis f
quick-tempered adj īrācundus
quick-witted adj acūtus, sagāx, perspicāx
quiescence n inertia f, ōtium nt
quiescent adj iners, ōtiōsus
quiet adj tranquillus, quiētus, placidus; (*silent*) tacitus; **be ~** quiēscere; silēre ♦ n quiēs f, tranquillitās f; silentium nt; (*peace*) pāx f ♦ vt pācāre, compōnere
quietly adv tranquillē, quiētē; tacitē, per silentium; aequō animō
quietness n tranquillitās f; silentium nt
quill n penna f
quince n cydōnium nt
quinquennial adj quinquennālis
quinquereme n quinquerēmis f
quintessence n flōs m, vīs f

133

quip n sāl m, facētiae fpl
quirk n captiuncula f; **quirks** pl trīcae fpl
quit vt relinquere ♦ adj līber, solūtus
quite adv admodum, plānē, prōrsus; **not ~** minus, parum; (time) nōndum
quits n parēs mpl
quiver n pharetra f ♦ vi tremere, contremere

quivering adj tremebundus, tremulus
quoit n discus m
quota n pars f, rata pars f
quotation n (act) commemorātiō f; (passage) locus m
quote vt prōferre, commemorāre
quoth vt inquit

Rr

rabbit *n* cunīculus *m*
rabble *n* turba *f*; (*class*) vulgus *nt*, plēbēcula *f*
rabid *adj* rabidus
rabidly *adv* rabidē
race *n* (*descent*) genus *nt*, stirps *f*; (*people*) gēns *f*,
   nōmen *nt*; (*contest*) certāmen *nt*; (*fig*) cursus *m*,
   curriculum *nt*; (*water*) flūmen *nt*; **run a ~** cursū
   certāre; **run the ~** (*fig*) spatium dēcurrere ◆ *vi*
   certāre, contendere
racecourse *n* (*foot*) stadium *nt*; (*horse*) spatium *nt*
racer *n* cursor *m*
racial *adj* gentīlis
rack *n* (*torture*) tormentum *nt*; (*shelf*) pluteus *m*;
   be on the ~ (*fig*) cruciāri ◆ *vt* torquēre, cruciāre;
   ~ off (*wine*) diffundere
racket *n* (*noise*) strepitus *m*
racy *adj* (*style*) salsus
radiance *n* splendor *m*, fulgor *m*
radiant *adj* splendidus, nitidus
radiantly *adv* splendidē
radiate *vi* fulgēre; (*direction*) dīversōs tendere ◆ *vt*
   ēmittere
radical *adj* īnsitus, innātus; (*thorough*) tōtus ◆ *n*
   novārum rērum cupidus *m*
radically *adv* omnīnō, penitus, funditus
radish *n* rādīx *f*
radius *n* radius *m*
raffish *adj* dissolūtus
raffle *n* ālea *f* ◆ *vt* āleā vēndere
raft *n* ratis *f*
rafter *n* trabs *f*, tignum *nt*
rag *n* pannus *m*
rage *n* īra *f*, furor *m*; **be all the ~** in ōre omnium
   esse; **spend one's ~** exsaevīre ◆ *vi* furere,
   saevīre; (*furiously*) dēbacchārī
ragged *adj* pannōsus
raid *n* excursiō *f*, incursiō *f*, impressiō *f*; **make a
   ~** excurrere ◆ *vt* incursiōnem facere in (*acc*)
rail *n* longurius *m* ◆ *vt* saepīre ◆ *vi*: **~ at**
   maledīcere (*dat*), convīcia facere (*dat*)
railing *n* saepēs *f*, cancellī *mpl*
raillery *n* cavillātiō *f*
raiment *n* vestis *f*
rain *n* pluvia *f*, imber *m* ◆ *vi* pluere; **it is raining**
   pluit
rainbow *n* arcus *m*
rainstorm *n* imber *m*
rainy *adj* pluvius
raise *vt* tollere, ēlevāre; (*army*) cōgere,
   cōnscrībere; (*children*) ēducāre; (*cry*) tollere; (*from
   dead*) excitāre; (*laugh*) movēre; (*money*) cōnflāre;
   (*price*) augēre; (*siege*) exsolvere; (*structure*)

exstruere; (*to higher rank*) ēvehere; **~ up** ērigere,
sublevāre
raisin *n* astaphis *f*
rajah *n* dynastēs *m*
rake *n* rastrum *nt*; (*person*) nepōs *m* ◆ *vt* rādere;
   ~ in conrādere; **~ up** (*fig*) ēruere
rakish *adj* dissolūtus
rally *n* conventus *m* ◆ *vt* (*troops*) in ōrdinem
   revocāre; (*with words*) hortārī; (*banter*) cavillārī
   ◆ *vi* sē colligere
ram *n* ariēs *m*; (*battering*) ariēs *m* ◆ *vt*: **ram down**
   fistūcāre; **ram home** (*fact*) inculcāre
ramble *n* errātiō *f* ◆ *vi* vagārī, errāre
rambling *adj* vagus; (*plant*) errāticus; (*speech*)
   fluēns
ramification *n* rāmus *m*
rammer *n* fistūca *f*
rampage *vi* saevīre
rampant *adj* ferōx
rampart *n* agger *m*, vallum *nt*
ranch *n* lātifundium *nt*
rancid *adj* pūtidus
rancour *n* odium *nt*, acerbitās *f*, invidia *f*
random *adj* fortuītus; **at ~** temerē
range *n* ōrdō *m*, seriēs *f*; (*mountain*) iugum *nt*; (*of
   weapon*) iactus *m*; **within ~** intrā tēlī iactum;
   come within ~ sub ictum venīre ◆ *vt* ōrdināre
   ◆ *vi* ēvagārī, pervagārī; (*in speech*) excurrere
rank *n* (*line*) ōrdō *m*; (*class*) ōrdō *m*; (*position*) locus
   m, dignitās *f*; **~ and file** gregāriī mīlitēs *mpl*;
   keep the ranks ōrdinēs observāre; **the ranks**
   (MIL) aciēs, acieī *f*; **leave the ranks** ōrdine
   ēgredī, ab signīs discēdere; **reduce to the
   ranks** in ōrdinem redigere ◆ *adj* luxuriōsus;
   (*smell*) gravis, foetidus ◆ *vt* numerāre ◆ *vi* in
   numerō habērī
rankle *vi* exulcerāre
rankness *n* luxuriēs *f*
ransack *vt* dīripere, spoliāre
ransom *n* redemptiō *f*, pretium *nt* ◆ *vt* redimere
rant *vi* latrāre
ranter *n* rabula *m*, latrātor *m*
rap *n* ictus *m* ◆ *vt* ferīre
rapacious *adj* rapāx, avidus
rapaciously *adv* avidē
rapacity *n* rapācitās *f*, aviditās *f*
rape *n* raptus *m*
rapid *adj* rapidus, vēlōx, citus, incitātus
rapidity *n* celeritās *f*, vēlōcitās *f*, incitātiō *f*
rapidly *adv* rapidē, vēlōciter, citō
rapine *n* rapīna *f*
rapt *adj* intentus

rapture n laetitia f, alacritās f
rare adj rārus; (occurrence) īnfrequēns; (quality) singulāris
rarefy vt extenuāre
rarely adv rārō
rarity n rāritās f; (thing) rēs īnsolita f
rascal n furcifer m, scelestus m
rascally adj improbus
rash adj temerārius, audāx, incōnsultus; praeceps
rashly adv temerē, incōnsultē
rashness n temeritās f, audācia f
rat n mūs m/f
rate n (cost) pretium nt; (standard) nōrma f; (tax) vectīgal nt; (speed) celeritās f; **at any ~** (concessive) utique, saltem; (adversative) quamquam, tamen ♦ vt (value) aestimāre; (scold) increpāre, obiūrgāre
rather adv potius, satius; (somewhat) aliquantum; (with comp) aliquantō; (with verbs) mālō; (correcting) immo; **~ sad** tristior; **I would ~** mālō; **I ~ think** haud sciō an; **~ than** magis quam, potius quam
ratification n (formal) sanctiō f
ratify vt ratum facere, sancīre; (LAW) iubēre
rating n taxātiō f, aestimātiō f; (navy) nauta m; (scolding) obiūrgātiō f
ratiocinate vi ratiōcinārī
ratiocination n ratiōcinātiō f
ration n dēmēnsum nt
rational adj animō praeditus; **be ~** sapere
rationality n ratiō f
rationally adv ratiōne
rations npl cibāria ntpl, diāria ntpl
rattle n crepitus m; (toy) crotalum nt ♦ vi crepitāre, increpāre
raucous adj raucus
ravage vt dēpopulārī, vastāre, dīripere
rave vi furere, īnsānīre; (fig) bacchārī, saevīre
raven n cornīx f
ravenous adj rapāx, vorāx
ravenously adv avidē
ravine n faucēs fpl, hiātus m
raving adj furiōsus, īnsānus ♦ n furor m
ravish vt rapere; (joy) efferre
raw adj crūdus; (person) rudis, agrestis
ray n radius m; **the first ray of hope appeared** prīma spēs adfulsit
raze vt excīdere, solō aequāre
razor n novācula f
reach n (space) spatium nt; (mind) captus m; (weapon) ictus m; **out of ~ of** extrā (acc); **within ~** ad manum ♦ vt advenīre ad (acc); (space) pertinēre ad; (journey) pervenīre ad
react vi adficī; **~ to** ferre
reaction n: **what was his ~ to?** quō animō tulit?
read vt legere; (a book) ēvolvere; (aloud) recitāre; **~ over** perlegere
reader n lēctor m
readily adv facile, libenter, ultrō
readiness n facilitās f; **in ~** ad manum, in prōmptū, in expedītō
reading n lēctiō f
readjust vt dēnuō accommodāre

ready adj parātus, prōmptus; (manner) facilis; (money) praesēns; **get ~, make ~** parāre, expedīre, adōrnāre
reaffirm vt iterum adfirmāre
real adj vērus, germānus
real estate n fundus m, solum nt
realism n vēritās f
realistic adj vērī similis
reality n rēs f, rēs ipsa f, vērum nt; **in ~** rēvērā
realize vt intellegere, animadvertere; (aim) efficere, peragere; (money) redigere
really adv vērē, rēvērā, profectō; **really?** itane vērō?
realm n rēgnum nt
reap vt metere; **~ the reward of** fructum percipere ex
reaper n messor m
reappear vi revenīre
rear vt alere, ēdūcāre; (structure) exstruere ♦ vi sē ērigere ♦ n tergum nt; (MIL) novissima aciēs f, novissimum agmen nt; **in the ~** ā tergō; **bring up the ~** agmen claudere, agmen cōgere ♦ adj postrēmus, novissimus
rearguard n novissimum agmen nt, novissimī mpl
rearrange vt ōrdinem mūtāre (gen)
reason n (faculty) mēns f, animus m, ratiō f; (sanity) sānitās f; (argument) ratiō f; (cause) causa f; (moderation) modus m; **by ~ of** propter (acc); **for this ~** idcircō, ideō, proptereā; **in ~** aequus, modicus; **with good ~** iūre; **without ~** temerē, sine causā; **without good ~** frustrā, iniūriā; **give a ~ for** ratiōnem adferre (gen); **I know the ~ for** sciō cūr, quamobrem (subj); **there is no ~ for** nōn est cūr, nihil est quod (subj); **lose one's ~** īnsānīre ♦ vi ratiōcinārī, disserere
reasonable adj aequus, iūstus; (person) modestus; (amount) modicus
reasonably adv ratiōne, iūstē; modicē
reasoning n ratiō f, ratiōcinātiō f
reassemble vt colligere, cōgere
reassert vt iterāre
reassume vt recipere
reassure vt firmāre, cōnfirmāre
rebate vt dēdūcere
rebel n rebellis m ♦ adj sēditiōsus ♦ vi rebelliōnem facere, rebellāre, dēscīscere
rebellion n sēditiō f, mōtus m
rebellious adj sēditiōsus
rebound vi resilīre
rebuff n repulsa f ♦ vt repellere, āversārī
rebuild vt renovāre, restaurāre
rebuke n reprehēnsiō f, obiūrgātiō f ♦ vt reprehendere, obiūrgāre, increpāre
rebut vt refūtāre, redarguere
recalcitrant adj invītus
recall n revocātiō f, reditus m ♦ vt revocāre; (from exile) redūcere; (to mind) reminīscī (gen), recordārī (gen)
recant vt retractāre
recantation n receptus m
recapitulate vt repetere, summātim dīcere
recapitulation n ēnumerātiō f
recapture n recipere
recast vt reficere, retractāre
recede vi recēdere

receipt n (act) acceptiō f; (money) acceptum nt; (written) apocha f
receive vt accipere, capere; (in turn) excipere
receiver n receptor m
recent adj recēns
recently adv nūper, recēns
receptacle n receptāculum nt
reception n aditus m, hospitium nt
receptive adj docilis
recess n recessus m, angulus m; (holiday) fēriae fpl
recharge vt replēre
recipe n compositiō f
recipient n quī accipit
reciprocal adj mūtuus
reciprocally adv mūtuō, inter sē
reciprocate vt referre, reddere
reciprocity n mūtuum nt
recital n nārrātiō f, ēnumerātiō f; (LIT) recitātiō f
recitation n recitātiō f
recite vt recitāre; (details) ēnumerāre
reciter n recitātor m
reck vt ratiōnem habēre (gen)
reckless adj temerārius, incautus, praeceps
recklessly adv incautē, temerē
recklessness n temeritās f, neglegentia f
reckon vt (count) computāre, numerāre; (think) cēnsēre, dūcere; (estimate) aestimāre; ~ on cōnfidere (dat); ~ up dīnumerāre; (cost) aestimāre; ~ with contendere cum
reckoning n ratiō f
reclaim vt repetere; (from error) revocāre
recline vi recumbere; (at table) accumbere; (pl) discumbere
recluse n homō sōlitārius m
recognition n cognitiō f
recognizance n vadimōnium nt
recognize vt agnōscere; (approve) accipere; (admit) fatērī
recoil vi resilīre; ~ from refugere; ~ upon recidere in (acc)
recollect vt reminīscī (gen)
recollection n memoria f, recordātiō f
recommence vt renovāre, redintegrāre
recommend vt commendāre; (advise) suādēre (dat)
recommendation n commendātiō f; (advice) cōnsilium nt; **letter of ~** litterae commendātīciae
recompense vt remūnerārī, grātiam referre (dat) ♦ n praemium nt, remūnerātiō f
reconcile vt compōnere, reconciliāre; **be reconciled** in grātiam redīre
reconciliation n reconciliātiō f, grātia f
recondite adj reconditus, abstrūsus
recondition vt reficere
reconnaissance n explōrātiō f
reconnoitre vt, vi explōrāre; **without reconnoitring** inexplōrātō
reconquer vt recipere
reconsider vt reputāre, retractāre
reconstruct vt restituere, renovāre
reconstruction n renovātiō f
record n monumentum nt; (LIT) commentārius m; **records** pl tabulae fpl, fāstī mpl, ācta ntpl; **break the ~** priōrēs omnēs superāre ♦ vt in commentārium referre; (history) perscrībere, nārrāre
recount vt nārrāre, commemorāre
recourse n: **have ~ to** (for safety) cōnfugere ad; (as expedient) dēcurrere ad
recover vt recipere, recuperāre; (loss) reparāre; **~ oneself** sē colligere; **~ one's senses** ad sānitātem revertī ♦ vi convalēscere
recovery n recuperātiō f; (from illness) salūs f
recreate vt recreāre
recreation n requiēs f, remissiō f, lūdus m
recriminate vi in vicem accūsāre
recrimination n mūtua accūsātiō f
recruit n tīrō m ♦ vt (MIL) cōnscrībere; (strength) reficere
recruiting officer n conquīsītor m
rectify vt corrigere, ēmendāre
rectitude n probitās f
recumbent adj supīnus
recuperate vi convalēscere
recur vi recurrere, redīre
recurrence n reditus m, reversiō f
recurrent adj adsiduus
red adj ruber
redden vi ērubēscere ♦ vt rutilāre
reddish adj subrūfus
redeem vt redimere, līberāre
redeemer n līberātor m
redemption n redemptiō f
red-haired adj rūfus
red-handed adj: **catch ~** in manifestō scelere dēprehendere
red-hot adj fervēns
red lead n minium nt
redness n rubor m
redolent adj: **be ~ of** redolēre
redouble vt ingemināre
redoubt n prōpugnāculum nt
redoubtable adj īnfestus, formīdolōsus
redound vi redundāre; **it redounds to my credit** mihī honōrī est
redress n remedium nt; **demand ~** rēs repetere ♦ vt restituere
reduce vt minuere, attenuāre; (to a condition) redigere, dēdūcere; (MIL) expugnāre; **~ to the ranks** in ōrdinem cōgere
reduction n imminūtiō f; (MIL) expugnātiō f
redundancy n redundantia f
redundant adj redundāns; **be ~** redundāre
reduplication n gem;inātiō f
re-echo vt reddere, referre ♦ vi resonāre
reed n harundō f
reedy adj harundineus
reef n saxa ntpl ♦ vt (sail) subnectere
reek n fūmus m ♦ vi fūmāre
reel vi vacillāre, titubāre
re-enlist vt rescrībere
re-establish vt restituere
refashion vt reficere
refer vt (person) dēlēgāre; (matter) rēicere, remittere ♦ vi: ~ to spectāre ad; (in speech) attingere, perstringere
referee n arbiter m
reference n ratiō f; (in book) locus m
refine vt excolere, expolīre; (metal) excoquere
refined adj hūmānus, urbānus, polītus

refinement n hūmānitās f, cultus m, ēlegantia f
refit vt reficere
reflect vt reddere, repercutere ◆ vi meditārī;
~ **upon** cōnsīderāre, sēcum reputāre; (blame)
reprehendere
reflection n (of light) repercussus m; (image)
imāgō f; (thought) meditātiō f, cōgitātiō f;
(blame) reprehēnsiō f; **cast reflections on**
maculīs aspergere, vitiō vertere; **with due**
~ cōnsīderātē; **without ~** incōnsultē
reflux n recessus m
reform n ēmendātiō f ◆ vt (lines) restituere; (error)
corrigere, ēmendāre, meliōrem facere ◆ vi sē
corrigere
reformation n corrēctiō f
reformer n corrēctor m, ēmendātor m
refract vt īnfringere
refractory adj contumāx
refrain vi temperāre, abstinēre (dat),
supersedēre (inf)
refresh vt recreāre, renovāre, reficere; (mind)
integrāre
refreshed adj requiētus
refreshing adj dulcis, iūcundus
refreshment n cibus m
refuge n perfugium nt; (secret) latebra f; **take**
~ **with** perfugere ad (acc); **take ~ in** confugere
refugee n profugus m
refulgence n splendor m
refulgent adj splendidus
refund vt reddere
refusal n recūsātiō f, dētrectātiō f
refuse n pūrgāmenta ntpl; (fig) faex f ◆ vt (request)
dēnegāre; (offer) dētrectāre, recūsāre; (with verb)
nōlle
refutation n refūtātiō f, reprehēnsiō f
refute vt refellere, redarguere, revincere
regain vt recipere
regal adj rēgius, rēgālis
regale vt excipere, dēlectāre; ~ **oneself** epulārī
regalia n īnsignia ntpl
regally adv rēgāliter
regard n respectus m, ratiō f; (esteem) grātia f;
with ~ to ad (acc), quod attinet ad ◆ vt (look)
intuērī, spectāre; (deem) habēre, dūcere; **send**
regards to salūtem dīcere (dat)
regarding prep dē (abl)
regardless adj neglegēns, immemor
regency n interrēgnum nt
regent n interrēx m
regicide n (person) rēgis interfector m; (act) rēgis
caedēs f
regime n administrātiō f
regimen n vīctus m
regiment n legiō f
region n regiō f, tractus m
register n tabulae fpl, album nt ◆ vt in tabulās
referre, perscrībere; (emotion) ostendere,
sūmere
registrar n tabulārius m
registry n tabulārium nt
regret n dolor m; (for past) dēsīderium nt; (for fault)
paenitentia f ◆ vt dolēre; **I ~** mē paenitet, mē
piget (gen)
regretful adj maestus
regretfully adv dolenter

regrettable adj īnfēlīx, īnfortūnātus
regular adj (consistent) cōnstāns; (orderly)
ōrdinātus; (habitual) solitus, adsiduus; (proper)
iūstus, rēctus
regularity n moderātiō f, ōrdō m; (consistency)
cōnstantia f
regularly adv ōrdine; cōnstanter; iūstē, rēctē
regulate vt ōrdināre, dīrigere; (control) moderārī
regulation n lēx f, dēcrētum nt
rehabilitate vt restituere
rehearsal n meditātiō f
rehearse vt meditārī
reign n rēgnum nt; (emperor's) prīncipātus m; **in**
the ~ of Numa rēgnante Numā ◆ vi rēgnāre;
(fig) dominārī
reimburse vt rependere
rein n habēna f; **give full ~ to** habēnās
immittere ◆ vt īnfrēnāre
reindeer n rēnō m
reinforce vt firmāre, cōnfirmāre
reinforcement n subsidium nt; **reinforcements**
pl novae cōpiae fpl
reinstate vt restituere, redūcere
reinstatement n restitūtiō f, reductiō f; (to legal
privileges) postlīminium nt
reinvigorate vt recreāre
reiterate vt dictitāre, iterāre
reiteration n iterātiō f
reject vt rēicere; (with scorn) respuere, aspernārī,
repudiāre
rejection n rēiectiō f, repulsa f
rejoice vi gaudēre, laetārī ◆ vt dēlectāre
rejoicing n gaudium nt
rejoin vt redīre ad ◆ vi respondēre
rejoinder n respōnsum nt
rejuvenate vt: **be rejuvenated** repuerāscere
rekindle vt suscitāre
relapse vi recidere
relate vt (tell) nārrāre, commemorāre, expōnere;
(compare) cōnferre ◆ vi pertinēre
related adj propinquus; (by birth) cognātus; (by
marriage) adfīnis; (fig) fīnitimus
relation n (tale) nārrātiō f; (connection) ratiō f; (kin)
necessārius m, cognātus m, adfīnis m
relationship n necessitūdō f; (by birth) cognātiō f;
(by marriage) adfīnitās f; (connection) vīcīnitās f
relative adj cum cēterīs comparātus ◆ n
propinquus m, cognātus m, adfīnis m,
necessārius m
relatively adv ex comparātiōne
relax vt laxāre, remittere ◆ vi languēscere
relaxation n remissiō f, requiēs f, lūdus m
relay n: **relays of horses** dispositī equī mpl
release vt solvere, exsolvere, līberāre, expedīre;
(LAW) absolvere ◆ n missiō f, līberātiō f
relegate vt relēgāre
relent vi concēdere, plācārī, flectī
relentless adj immisericors, inexōrābilis;
(things) improbus
relevant adj ad rem
reliability n fīdūcia f
reliable adj fīdus
reliance n fīdūcia f, fidēs f
reliant adj frētus
relic n rēliquiae fpl

relief n levātiō f, levāmen nt, adlevāmentum nt; (aid) subsidium nt; (turn of duty) vicēs fpl; (art) ēminentia f; (sculpture) toreuma nt; **bas ~** anaglypta ntpl; **in ~** ēminēns, expressus; **throw into ~** exprimere, distinguere
relieve vt levāre, sublevāre; (aid) subvenīre (dat); (duty) succēdere (dat), excipere; (art) distinguere
religion n religiō f, deōrum cultus m
religious adj religiōsus, pius; **~ feeling** religiō f
religiously adv religiōsē
relinquish vt relinquere; (office) sē abdicāre (abl)
relish n sapor m; (sauce) condīmentum nt; (zest) studium nt ♦ vt dēlectārī (abl)
reluctance n: **with ~** invītus
reluctant adj invītus
reluctantly adv invītus, gravātē
rely vi fīdere (dat), cōnfīdere (dat)
relying adj frētus (abl)
remain vi manēre, morārī; (left over) restāre, superesse
remainder n reliquum nt
remaining adj reliquus; **the ~** cēterī pl
remains n rēliquiae fpl
remand vt (LAW) ampliāre
remark n dictum nt ♦ vt dīcere; (note) observāre
remarkable adj īnsignis, ēgregius, memorābilis
remarkably adv īnsignītē, ēgregiē
remediable adj sānābilis
remedy n remedium nt ♦ vt medērī (dat), sānāre
remember vt meminisse (gen); (recall) recordārī (gen), reminīscī (gen)
remembrance n memoria f, recordātiō f
remind vt admonēre, commonefacere
reminder n admonitiō f, admonitum nt
reminiscence n recordātiō f
remiss adj dissolūtus, neglegēns
remission n venia f
remissness n neglegentia f
remit vt remittere; (fault) ignōscere (dat); (debt) dōnāre; (punishment) condōnāre; (question) referre
remittance n pecūnia f
remnant n fragmentum nt; **remnants** pl rēliquiae fpl
remonstrance n obtestātiō f, obiūrgātiō f
remonstrate vi reclāmāre; **~ with** obiūrgāre; **~ about** expostulāre
remorse n paenitentia f, cōnscientia f
remorseless adj immisericors
remote adj remōtus, reconditus
remotely adv procul
remoteness n longinquitās f
removal n āmōtiō f; (going) migrātiō f
remove vt āmovēre, dēmere, eximere, removēre; (out of the way) dēmovēre ♦ vi migrāre, dēmigrāre
remunerate vt remūnerārī
remuneration n mercēs f, praemium nt
rend vt scindere, dīvellere
render vt reddere; (music) interpretārī; (translation) vertere; (thanks) referre
rendering n interpretātiō f
rendez-vous n cōnstitūtum nt
renegade n dēsertor m
renew vt renovāre, integrāre, īnstaurāre, redintegrāre

renewal n renovātiō f; (ceremony) īnstaurātiō f
renounce vt renūntiāre, mittere, repudiāre
renovate vt renovāre, reficere
renown n fāma f, glōria f
renowned adj praeclārus, īnsignis, nōtus
rent n (tear) fissum nt; (pay) mercēs f ♦ vt (hire) condūcere; (lease) locāre
renunciation n cessiō f, repudiātiō f
repair vt reficere, sarcīre ♦ vi sē recipere ♦ n: **keep in good ~** tuērī; **in bad ~** ruīnōsus
reparable adj ēmendābilis
reparation n satisfactiō f
repartee n facētiae fpl, salēs mpl
repast n cēna f, cibus m
repay vt remūnerārī, grātiam referre (dat); (money) repōnere
repayment n solūtiō f
repeal vt abrogāre ♦ n abrogātiō f
repeat vt iterāre; (lesson) reddere; (ceremony) īnstaurāre; (performance) referre
repeatedly adv identidem, etiam atque etiam
repel vt repellere, dēfendere
repellent adj iniūcundus
repent vi: **I ~** mē paenitet (+gen of thing)
repentance n paenitentia f
repentant adj paenitēns
repercussion n ēventus m
repertory n thēsaurus m
repetition n iterātiō f
repine vi conquerī
replace vt repōnere, restituere; **~ by** substituere
replacement n supplēmentum nt
replenish vt replēre, supplēre
replete adj plēnus
repletion n satietās f
replica n apographon nt
reply vi respondēre ♦ n respōnsum nt
report n (talk) fāma f, rūmor m; (repute) opīniō f; (account) renūntiātiō f, litterae fpl; (noise) fragor m; **make a ~** renūntiāre ♦ vt referre, dēferre, renūntiāre
repose n quiēs f, requiēs f ♦ vt repōnere, pōnere ♦ vi quiēscere
repository n horreum nt
reprehend vt reprehendere, culpāre
reprehensible adj accūsābilis, improbus
reprehension n reprehēnsiō f, culpa f
represent vt dēscrībere, effingere, exprimere, imitārī; (character) partēs agere (gen), persōnam gerere (gen); (case) prōpōnere; (substitute for) vicārium esse (gen)
representation n imāgō f, imitātiō f; **make representations to** admonēre
representative n lēgātus m
repress vt reprimere, cohibēre
repression n coercitiō f
reprieve n mora f, venia f ♦ vt veniam dare (dat)
reprimand vt reprehendere, increpāre ♦ n reprehēnsiō f
reprisals n ultiō f
reproach vt exprobāre, obicere (dat) ♦ n exprobrātiō f, probrum nt; (cause) opprobrium nt
reproachful adj contumēliōsus
reprobate adj perditus
reproduce vt propāgāre; (likeness) referre

reproduction n prōcreātiō f; (*likeness*) imāgō f
reproductive adj genitālis
reproof n reprehēnsiō f, obiūrgātiō f
reprove vt reprehendere, increpāre, obiūrgāre
reptile n serpēns f
republic n lībera rēspūblica f, cīvitās populāris f
republican adj populāris
repudiate vt repudiāre
repudiation n repudiātiō f
repugnance n fastīdium nt, odium nt
repugnant adj invīsus, adversus
repulse n dēpulsiō f; (*at election*) repulsa f ♦ vt
repellere, āversārī, prōpulsāre
repulsion n repugnantia f
repulsive adj odiōsus, foedus
reputable adj honestus
reputation n fāma f, existimātiō f; (*for something*)
opīniō f (*gen*); **have a ~** nōmen habēre
repute n fāma f, existimātiō f; **bad ~** īnfāmia f
reputed adj: **I am ~ to be** dīcor esse
request n rogātiō f, postulātum nt; **obtain
a ~** impetrāre ♦ vt rogāre, petere; (*urgently*)
dēposcere
require vt (*demand*) imperāre, postulāre; (*need*)
egēre (*abl*); (*call for*) requīrere
requirement n postulātum nt, necessārium nt
requisite adj necessārius
requisition n postulātiō f ♦ vt imperāre
requital n grātia f, vicēs fpl
requite vt grātiam referre (*dat*), remūnerārī
rescind vt rescindere, abrogāre
rescript n rescrīptum nt
rescue vt ēripere, expedīre, servāre ♦ n salūs f;
come to the ~ of subvenīre (*dat*)
research n investīgātiō f
resemblance n similitūdō f, imāgō f, īnstar nt
resemble vt similem esse (*dat*), referre
resent vt aegrē ferre, indignārī
resentful adj īrācundus
resentment n dolor m, indignātiō f
reservation n (*proviso*) exceptiō f
reserve vt servāre; (*store*) recondere; (*in a deal*)
excipere ♦ n (MIL) subsidium nt; (*disposition*)
pudor m, reticentia f; (*caution*) cautiō f; **in ~** in
succenturiātus; **without ~** palam
reserved adj (*place*) adsignātus; (*disposition*)
taciturnus, tēctus
reservedly adv circumspectē
reserves npl subsidia ntpl
reservoir n lacus m
reside vi habitāre; **~ in** incolere
residence n domicilium nt, domus f
resident n incola m/f
residual adj reliquus
residue, residuum n reliqua pars f
resign vt cēdere; (*office*) abdicāre mē, tē *etc* dē
(*abl*); **~ oneself** acquiēscere ♦ vi sē abdicāre
resignation n abdicātiō f; (*state of mind*) patientia
f, aequus animus m
resigned adj patiēns; **be ~ to** aequō animō ferre
resilience n mollitia f
resilient adj mollis
resist vt resistere (*dat*), adversārī (*dat*),
repugnāre (*dat*)
resistance n repugnantia f; **offer ~** obsistere
(*dat*)

resistless adj invictus
resolute adj fortis, cōnstāns
resolutely adv fortiter, cōnstanter
resolution n (*conduct*) fortitūdō f, cōnstantia
f; (*decision*) dēcrētum nt, sententia f; (*into parts*)
sēcrētiō f
resolve n fortitūdō f, cōnstantia f ♦ vt dēcernere,
cōnstituere; (*into parts*) dissolvere; **the senate
resolves** placet senātuī
resonance n sonus m
resonant adj canōrus
resort n locus celeber m; **last ~** ultimum
auxilium nt ♦ vi frequentāre, ventitāre; (*have
recourse*) dēcurrere, dēscendere, cōnfugere
resound vi resonāre, personāre
resource n subsidium nt; (*means*) modus m;
resources pl opēs fpl, cōpiae fpl
resourceful adj versūtus, callidus
resourcefulness n calliditās f, versūtus animus
m
respect n (*esteem*) honōs m, observantia f;
(*reference*) ratiō f; **out of ~** honōris causā;
pay one's respects to salūtāre; **show ~ for**
observāre; **in every ~** ex omnī parte, in omnī
genere; **in ~ of** ad (*acc*), ab (*abl*) ♦ vt honōrāre,
observāre, verērī
respectability n honestās f
respectable adj honestus, līberālis, frūgī
respectably adv honestē
respectful adj observāns
respectfully adv reverenter
respectfulness n observantia f
respective adj suus (*with quisque*)
respectively adv alius ... alius
respiration n respīrātiō f, spīritus m
respire vi respīrāre
respite n requiēs f, intercapēdō f, intermissiō f
resplendence n splendor m
resplendent adj splendidus, illūstris
resplendently adv splendidē
respond vi respondēre
response n respōnsum nt
responsibility n auctōritās f, cūra f
responsible adj reus; (*witness*) locuplēs; **be ~ for**
praestāre
responsive adj (*pupil*) docilis; (*character*) facilis
rest n quiēs f, ōtium nt; (*after toil*) requiēs f;
(*remainder*) reliqua pars f; **be at ~** requiēscere; **set
at ~** tranquillāre; **the ~** (*others*) cēterī mpl; **the
~ of** reliquī ♦ vi requiēscere, acquiēscere; **~ on**
nītī (*abl*), innītī in (*abl*) ♦ vt (*hope*) pōnere in (*abl*)
resting place n cubīle nt, sēdēs f
restitution n satisfactiō f; **make ~** restituere;
demand ~ rēs repetere
restive adj contumāx
restless adj inquiētus, sollicitus; **be ~** fluctuārī
restlessness n sollicitūdō f
restoration n renovātiō f; (*of king*) reductiō f
restore vt reddere, restituere; (*to health*)
recreāre; (*to power*) redūcere; (*damage*) reficere,
redintegrāre
restorer n restitūtor m
restrain vt coercēre, comprimere, cohibēre
restraint n moderātiō f, temperantia f, frēnī mpl;
with ~ abstinenter
restrict vt continēre, circumscrībere

restricted *adj* artus; ~ **to** proprius *(gen)*
restriction *n* modus *m*, fīnis *m*; *(limitation)*
exceptiō *f*
result *n* ēventus *m*, ēventum *nt*, exitus *m*; **the ~ is
that** quō fit ut ♦ *vi* ēvenīre, ēvādere
resultant *adj* cōnsequēns
resume *vt* repetere
resuscitate *vt* excitāre, suscitāre
retail *vt* dīvēndere, vēndere
retailer *n* caupō *m*
retain *vt* retinēre, tenēre, cōnservāre
retainer *n* satelles *m*
retake *vt* recipere
retaliate *vi* ulcīscī
retaliation *n* ultiō *f*
retard *vt* retardāre, remorārī
retention *n* cōnservātiō *f*
retentive *adj* tenāx
reticence *n* taciturnitās *f*
reticent *adj* taciturnus
reticulated *adj* rēticulātus
retinue *n* satellitēs *mpl*, comitātus *m*
retire *vi* recēdere, abscēdere; *(from office)* abīre;
(from province) dēcēdere; *(MIL)* pedem referre, sē
recipere
retired *adj* ēmeritus; *(place)* remōtus
retirement *n* *(act)* recessus *m*, dēcessus *m*; *(state)*
sōlitūdō *f*, ōtium *nt*; **life of ~** vīta prīvāta
retiring *adj* modestus, verēcundus
retort *vt* respondēre, referre ♦ *n* respōnsum *nt*
retouch *vt* retractāre
retrace *vt* repetere, iterāre
retract *vt* revocāre, renūntiāre
retreat *n* *(MIL)* receptus *m*; *(place)* recessus *m*,
sēcessus *m*; **sound the ~** receptuī canere ♦ *vi* sē
recipere, pedem referre; regredī
retrench *vt* minuere, recīdere
retrenchment *n* parsimōnia *f*
retribution *n* poena *f*
retributive *adj* ultor, ultrīx
retrieve *vt* reparāre, recipere
retrograde *adj* *(fig)* dēterior
retrogression *n* regressus *m*
retrospect *n*: **in ~** respicientī
retrospective *adj*: **be ~** retrōrsum sē referre
retrospectively *adv* retrō
return *n* reditus *m*; *(pay)* remūnerātiō *f*; *(profit)*
fructus *m*, pretium *nt*; *(statement)* professiō *f*;
make a ~ of profitērī; **in ~ for** prō *(abl)*; **in ~ in**
vicem, vicissim ♦ *vt* reddere, restituere, referre
♦ *vi* redīre, revenīre, revertī; *(from province)*
dēcēdere
reunion *n* convīvium *nt*
reunite *vt* reconciliāre
reveal *vt* aperīre, patefacere
revel *n* cōmissātiō *f*, bacchātiō *f*; **revels** *pl* orgia
ntpl ♦ *vi* cōmissārī, bacchārī; ~ **in** luxuriārī
revelation *n* patefactiō *f*
reveller *n* cōmissātor *m*
revelry *n* cōmissātiō *f*
revenge *n* ultiō *f*; **take ~ on** vindicāre in *(acc)*
♦ *vt* ulcīscī
revengeful *adj* ulcīscendī cupidus
revenue *n* fructus *m*, reditus *m*, vectīgālia *ntpl*
reverberate *vi* resonāre
reverberation *n* repercussus *m*

revere *vt* venerārī, colere
reverence *n* venerātiō *f*; *(feeling)* religiō *f*;
reverentia *f*
reverent *adj* religiōsus, pius
reverently *adv* religiōsē
reverie *n* meditātiō *f*, somnium *nt*
reversal *n* abrogātiō *f*
reverse *adj* contrārius ♦ *n* contrārium *nt*; *(MIL)*
clādēs *f* ♦ *vt* invertere; *(decision)* rescindere
reversion *n* reditus *m*
revert *vi* redīre, revertī
review *n* recognitiō *f*, recēnsiō *f* ♦ *vt* *(MIL)*
recēnsēre
revile *vt* maledīcere *(dat)*
revise *vt* recognōscere, corrigere; *(LIT)* līmāre
revision *n* ēmendātiō *f*; *(LIT)* līma *f*
revisit *vt* revīsere
revival *n* renovātiō *f*
revive *vt* recreāre, excitāre ♦ *vi* revīvīscere,
renāscī
revocation *n* revocātiō *f*
revoke *vt* renūntiāre, īnfectum reddere
revolt *n* sēditiō *f*, dēfectiō *f* ♦ *vi* dēficere, rebellāre
revolting *adj* taeter, obscēnus
revolution *n* *(movement)* conversiō *f*; *(change)* rēs
novae *fpl*; *(revolt)* mōtus *m*; **effect a ~** rēs novāre
revolutionary *adj* sēditiōsus, novārum rērum
cupidus
revolve *vi* volvī, versārī, convertī ♦ *vt* *(in mind)*
volūtāre
revulsion *n* mūtātiō *f*
reward *n* praemium *nt*, mercēs *f* ♦ *vt*
remūnerārī, compēnsāre
rhapsody *n* carmen *nt*; *(epic)* rhapsōdia *f*
rhetoric *n* rhētorica *f*; **of ~** rhētoricus; **exercise
in ~** dēclāmātiō *f*; **practise ~** dēclāmāre;
teacher of ~ rhētor *m*
rhetorical *adj* rhētoricus, dēclāmātōrius
rhetorically *adv* rhētoricē
rhetorician *n* rhētor *m*, dēclāmātor *m*
rhinoceros *n* rhīnocerōs *m*
rhyme *n* homoeoteleuton *nt*; **without ~ or
reason** temerē
rhythm *n* numerus *m*, modus *m*
rhythmical *adj* numerōsus
rib *n* costa *f*
ribald *adj* obscēnus
ribaldry *n* obscēnitās *f*
ribbon *n* īnfula *f*
rice *n* oryza *f*
rich *adj* dīves, locuplēs, opulentus; *(fertile)* ūber,
opīmus; *(food)* pinguis
riches *n* dīvitiae *fpl*, opēs *fpl*
richly *adv* opulentē, largē, lautē
richness *n* ūbertās *f*, cōpia *f*
rid *vt* līberāre; **get rid of** dēpōnere, dēmovēre,
exuere
riddle *n* aenigma *nt*; *(sieve)* cribrum *nt* ♦ *vt* *(with
wounds)* cōnfodere
ride *vi* equitāre, vehī; ~ **a horse** equō vehī; ~ **at
anchor** stāre; ~ **away** abequitāre, āvehī; ~ **back**
revehī; ~ **between** interequitāre; ~ **down**
dēvehī; ~ **into** invehī; ~ **off** āvehī; ~ **out** ēvehī;
~ **past** praetervehī; ~ **round** circumvehī *(dat)*,
circumequitāre; ~ **up and down** perequitāre;
~ **up to** adequitāre ad, advehī ad

rider n eques m
ridge n iugum nt
ridicule n lūdibrium nt, irrīsus m ♦ vt irrīdēre, illūdere, lūdibriō habēre
ridiculous adj rīdiculus, dērīdiculus
ridiculously adv rīdiculē
riding n equitātiō f
rife adj frequēns
riff-raff n faex populī f
rifle vt expīlāre, spoliāre
rift n rīma f
rig vt (ship) armāre, ōrnāre ♦ n habitus m
rigging n rudentēs mpl
right adj rēctus; (just) aequus, iūstus; (true) rēctus, vērus; (proper) lēgitimus, fās; (hand) dexter; **it is ~** decet (+acc and infin); **it is not ~** dēdecet (+acc and infin); **you are ~** vēra dīcis; **if I am ~** nisi fallor; **in the ~ place** in locō; **at the ~ time** ad tempus; **at ~ angles** ad parēs angulōs; **on the ~ā** dextrā ♦ adv rēctē, bene, probē; (justifiably) iūre; **~ up** to usque ad (acc); **~ on** rēctā ♦ n (legal) iūs nt; (moral) fās nt ♦ vt (replace) restituere; (correct) corrigere; (avenge) ulcīscī
righteous adj iūstus, sanctus, pius
righteously adv iūstē, sanctē, piē
righteousness n sanctitās f, pietās f
rightful adj iūstus, lēgitimus
rightfully adv iūstē, lēgitimē
right hand n dextra f
right-hand adj dexter; **~ man** comes m
rightly adv rēctē, bene; iūre
right-minded adj sānus
rigid adj rigidus
rigidity n rigor m; (strictness) sevēritās f
rigidly adv rigidē, sevērē
rigmarole n ambāgēs fpl
rigorous adj dūrus; (strict) sevērus
rigorously adv dūriter, sevērē
rigour n dūritia f; sevēritās f
rile vt inrītāre, stomachum movēre (dat)
rill n rīvulus m
rim n labrum nt
rime n pruīna f
rind n cortex m
ring n ānulus m; (circle) orbis m; (of people) corōna f; (motion) gȳrus m ♦ vt circumdare; (bell) movēre ♦ vi tinnīre, sonāre
ringing n tinnītus m ♦ adj canōrus
ringleader n caput nt, dux m
ringlet n cincinnus m
rinse vt colluere
riot n tumultus m, rixa f; **run ~** exsultāre, luxuriārī, tumultuārī, turbās efficere; (revel) bacchārī
rioter n cōmissātor m
riotous adj tumultuōsus, sēditiōsus; (debauched) dissolūtus; **~ living** cōmissātiō f, luxuria f
riotously adv tumultuōsē; luxuriōsē
rip vt scindere
ripe adj mātūrus; **of ~ judgment** animī mātūrus
ripen vt mātūrāre ♦ vi mātūrēscere
ripeness n mātūritās f
ripple n unda f ♦ vi trepidāre
rise vi orīrī, surgere; (hill) ascendere; (wind) cōnsurgere; (passion) tumēscere; (voice) tollī; (in size) crēscere; (in rank) ascendere;

(in revolt) coorīrī, arma capere; **~ and fall** (tide) reciprocāre; **~ above** superāre; **~ again** resurgere; **~ in** (river) orīrī ex (abl); **~ out** ēmergere; **~ up** exsurgere ♦ n ascēnsus m; (slope) clīvus m; (increase) incrēmentum nt; (start) ortus m; **give ~ to** parere
rising n (sun) ortus m; (revolt) mōtus m ♦ adj (ground) ēditus
risk n perīculum nt; **run a ~** perīculum subīre, ingredī ♦ vt perīclitārī, in āleam dare
risky adj perīculōsus
rite n rītus m
ritual n caerimōnia f
rival adj aemulus ♦ n aemulus m, rīvālis m ♦ vt aemulārī
rivalry n aemulātiō f
river n flūmen nt, fluvius m ♦ adj fluviātilis
riverbed n alveus m
riverside n rīpa f
rivet n clāvus m ♦ vt (attention) dēfīgere
rivulet n rīvulus m, rīvus m
road n via f, iter nt; **on the ~** in itinere, ex itinere; **off the ~** dēvius; **make a ~** viam mūnīre
roadstead n statiō f
roam vi errāre, vagārī; **~ at large** ēvagārī
roar n fremitus m ♦ vi fremere
roast vt torrēre ♦ adj āssus ♦ n āssum nt
rob vt spoliāre, exspoliāre, expīlāre; (of hope) dēicere dē
robber n latrō m, fūr m; (highway) grassātor m
robbery n latrōcinium nt
robe n vestis f; (woman's) stola f; (of state) trabea f ♦ vt vestīre
robust adj rōbustus, fortis
robustness n rōbur nt, firmitās f
rock n saxum nt; (steep) rūpēs f, scopulus m ♦ vt agitāre ♦ vi agitārī, vacillāre
rocky adj saxōsus, scopulōsus
rod n virga f; (fishing) harundō f
roe n (deer) capreolus m, caprea f; (fish) ōva ntpl
rogue n veterātor m
roguery n nēquitia f, scelus nt
roguish adj improbus, malus
role n partēs fpl
roll n (book) volūmen nt; (movement) gȳrus m; (register) album nt; **call the ~ of** legere; **answer the ~ call** ad nōmen respondēre ♦ vt volvere ♦ vi volvī, volūtārī; **~ down** vt dēvolvere ♦ vi dēfluere; **~ over** vt prōvolvere ♦ vi prōlābī; **~ up** vt convolvere
roller n (AGR) cylindrus m; (for moving) phalangae fpl; (in book) umbilīcus m
rollicking adj hilaris
rolling adj volūbilis
Roman adj Rōmānus ♦ n: **the Romans** Rōmānī mpl
romance n fābula f; amor m
romantic adj fābulōsus; amātōrius
Rome n Rōma f; **at ~** Rōmae; **from ~** Rōmā; **to ~** Rōmam
romp vi lūdere
roof n tēctum nt; (of mouth) palātum nt ♦ vt tegere, integere
rook n corvus m
room n conclāve nt, camera f; (small) cella f; (bed) cubiculum nt; (dining) cēnāculum nt; (dressing)

apodytērium *nt*; *(space)* locus *m*; **make ~ for** locum dare *(dat)*, cēdere *(dat)*

roominess *n* laxitās *f*

roomy *adj* capāx

roost *vi* stabulārī

rooster *n* gallus gallīnāceus *m*

root *n* rādīx *f*; **take ~** coalēscere ♦ *vt*: **~ out** ērādīcāre

rooted *adj* *(fig)* dēfixus; **deeply ~** *(custom)* inveterātus; **be ~ in** īnsidēre *(dat)*; **become deeply ~** inveterāscere

rope *n* fūnis *m*; *(thin)* restis *f*; *(ship's)* rudēns *m*; **know the ropes** perītum esse

rose *n* rosa *f*

rosemary *n* rōs marīnus *m*

rostrum *n* rōstra *ntpl*, suggestus *m*

rosy *adj* roseus, purpureus

rot *n* tābēs *f* ♦ *vi* putrēscere, pūtēscere ♦ *vt* putrefacere

rotate *vi* volvī, sē convertere

rotation *n* conversiō *f*; *(succession)* ōrdō *m*, vicissitūdō *f*; **in ~** ōrdine; **move in ~** in orbem īre

rote *n*: **by ~** memoriter

rotten *adj* putridus

rotund *adj* rotundus

rotundity *n* rotunditās *f*

rouge *n* fūcus *m* ♦ *vt* fūcāre

rough *adj* asper; *(art)* incultus, rudis; *(manners)* agrestis, inurbānus; *(stone)* impolītus; *(treatment)* dūrus, sevērus; *(weather)* atrōx, procellōsus ♦ *vi*: **~ it** dūram vītam vīvere

rough-and-ready *adj* fortuītus

rough draft *n* *(LIT)* silva *f*

roughen *vt* asperāre, exasperāre

rough-hew *vt* dolāre

roughly *adv* asperē, dūriter; *(with numbers)* circiter

roughness *n* asperitās *f*

round *adj* rotundus; *(spherical)* globōsus; *(cylindrical)* teres ♦ *n* *(circle)* orbis *m*; *(motion)* gȳrus *m*; *(series)* ambitus *m*; **go the rounds** *(MIL)* vigiliās circumīre ♦ *vt* *(cape)* superāre; **~ off** rotundāre; *(sentence)* conclūdere; **~ up** compellere ♦ *adv* circum, circā; **go ~** ambīre ♦ *prep* circum *(acc)*, circā *(acc)*

roundabout *adj*: **~ story** ambāgēs *fpl*; **~ route** circuitus *m*, ānfrāctus *m*

roundly *adv* *(speak)* apertē, līberē

rouse *vt* excīre, excitāre; *(courage)* adrigere

rousing *adj* vehemēns

rout *n* fuga *f*; *(crowd)* turba *f* ♦ *vt* fugāre, fundere; in fugam conicere, prōflīgāre

route *n* cursus *m*, iter *nt*

routine *n* ūsus *m*, ōrdō *m*

rove *vi* errāre, vagārī

rover *n* vagus *m*; *(sea)* pīrāta *m*

row *n* *(line)* ōrdō *m*; *(noise)* turba *f*, rixa *f* ♦ *vi* *(boat)* rēmigāre ♦ *vt* rēmīs incitāre

rowdy *adj* turbulentus

rower *n* rēmex *m*

rowing *n* rēmigium *nt*

royal *adj* rēgius, rēgālis

royally *adv* rēgiē, rēgāliter

royalty *n* *(power)* rēgnum *nt*; *(persons)* rēgēs *mpl*, domus rēgia *f*

rub *vt* fricāre, terere; **rub away** conterere; **rub hard** dēfricāre; **rub off** dētergēre; **rub out** dēlēre; **rub up** expolīre

rubbing *n* trītus *m*

rubbish *n* quisquiliae *fpl*; *(talk)* nūgae *fpl*

rubble *n* rūdus *nt*

rubicund *adj* rubicundus

rudder *n* gubernāculum *nt*, clāvus *m*

ruddy *adj* rubicundus, rutilus

rude *adj* *(uncivilized)* barbarus, dūrus, inurbānus; *(insolent)* asper, importūnus

rudely *adv* horridē, rusticē; petulanter

rudeness *n* barbariēs *f*; petulantia *f*, importūnitās *f*

rudiment *n* elementum *nt*, initium *nt*

rudimentary *adj* prīmus, incohātus

rue *n* *(herb)* rūta *f* ♦ *vt*: **I rue** mē paenitet *(gen)*

rueful *adj* maestus

ruffian *n* grassātor *m*

ruffle *vt* agitāre; *(temper)* sollicitāre, commovēre

rug *n* strāgulum *nt*

rugged *adj* horridus, asper

ruggedness *n* asperitās *f*

ruin *n* ruīna *f*; *(fig)* exitium *nt*, perniciēs *f*; **go to ~** pessum īre, dīlābī ♦ *vt* perdere, dēperdere, pessum dare; *(moral)* corrumpere, dēprāvāre; **be ruined** perīre

ruined *adj* ruīnōsus

ruinous *adj* exitiōsus, damnōsus

rule *n* *(instrument)* rēgula *f*, amussis *f*; *(principle)* nōrma *f*, lēx *f*, praeceptum *nt*; *(government)* dominātiō *f*, imperium *nt*; **ten-foot ~** decempeda *f*; **as a ~** ferē; **lay down rules** praecipere; **make it a ~ to** īnstituere *(inf)*; **~ of thumb** ūsus *m* ♦ *vt* regere, moderārī ♦ *vi* rēgnāre, dominārī; *(judge)* ēdīcere; *(custom)* obtinēre; **~ over** imperāre *(dat)*

ruler *n* *(instrument)* rēgula *f*; *(person)* dominus *m*, rēctor *m*

ruling *n* ēdictum *nt*

rumble *vi* mūgīre

rumbling *n* mūgītus *m*

ruminate *vi* rūminārī

rummage *vi*: **~ through** rīmārī

rumour *n* fāma *f*, rūmor *m*

rump *n* clūnis *f*

run *vi* currere; *(fluid)* fluere, mānāre; *(road)* ferre; *(time)* lābī ♦ *n* cursus *m*; **run about** discurrere, cursāre; **run across** incidere in *(acc)*; **run after** sectārī; **run aground** offendere; **run away** aufugere, terga vertere; *(from)* fugere, dēfugere; **run down** dēcurrere, dēfluere ♦ *vt* *(in words)* obtrectāre; **run high** *(fig)* glīscere; **run into** incurrere in *(acc)*, īnfluere in *(acc)*; **run off with** abripere, abdūcere; **run on** pergere; **run out** *(land)* excurrere; *(time)* exīre; *(supplies)* dēficere; **run over** *vt* *(with car)* obterere; *(details)* percurrere; **run riot** luxuriārī; **run through** *(course)* dēcurrere; *(money)* disperdere; **run short** dēficere; **run up to** adcurrere ad; **run up against** incurrere in *(acc)*; **run wild** lascīvīre ♦ *vt* gerere, administrāre

runaway *adj* fugitīvus
rung *n* gradus *m*
runner *n* cursor *m*
running *n* cursus *m* ✦ *adj (water)* vīvus
rupture *n (fig)* dissidium *nt* ✦ *vt* dīrumpere
rural *adj* rūsticus, agrestis
ruse *n* fraus *f*, dolus *m*
rush *n (plant)* cārex *f*, iuncus *m*; *(movement)*
  impetus *m* ✦ *vi* currere, sē incitāre, ruere;
  ~ **forward** sē prōripere; prōruere; ~ **in** inruere,
  incurrere; ~ **out** ēvolāre, sē effundere ✦ *adj*
  iunceus

russet *adj* flāvus
rust *n (iron)* ferrūgō *f*; *(copper)* aerūgō *f* ✦ *vi*
  rōbīginem trahere
rustic *adj* rūsticus, agrestis
rusticate *vi* rūsticārī ✦ *vt* relēgāre
rusticity *n* mōrēs rūsticī *mpl*
rustle *vi* increpāre, crepitāre ✦ *n* crepitus *m*
rusty *adj* rōbīginōsus
rut *n* orbita *f*
ruthless *adj* inexōrābilis, crūdēlis
ruthlessly *adv* crūdēliter
rye *n* secāle *nt*

Ss

sabbath n sabbata ntpl
sable adj āter, niger
sabre n acīnacēs m
sacerdotal adj sacerdōtālis
sack n saccus m; (MIL) dīreptiō f ♦ vt dīripere,
  expīlāre; spoliāre
sackcloth n cilicium nt
sacred adj sacer, sanctus
sacredly adv sanctē
sacredness n sanctitās f
sacrifice n sacrificium nt, sacrum nt; (act)
  immolātiō f; (victim) hostia f; (fig) iactūra f ♦ vt
  immolāre, sacrificāre, mactāre; (fig) dēvovēre,
  addīcere ♦ vi sacra facere; (give up) prōicere
sacrificer n immolātor m
sacrilege n sacrilegium nt
sacrilegious adj sacrilegus
sacristan n aedituus m
sacrosanct adj sacrōsanctus
sad adj maestus, tristis; (thing) tristis
sadden vt dolōre adficere
saddle n strātum nt ♦ vt sternere; (fig) impōnere
saddlebags n clītellae fpl
sadly adv maestē
sadness n tristitia f, maestitia f
safe adj tūtus; (out of danger) incolumis, salvus; (to
  trust) fīdus; ~ and sound salvus ♦ n armārium
  nt
safe-conduct n fidēs pūblica f
safeguard n cautiō f, prōpugnāculum nt ♦ vt
  dēfendere
safely adv tūtō, impūne
safety n salūs f, incolumitās f; seek ~ in flight
  salutem fugā petere
saffron n crocus m ♦ adj croceus
sag vi dēmittī
sagacious adj prūdēns, sagāx, acūtus
sagaciously adv prūdenter, sagāciter
sagacity n prūdentia f, sagācitās f
sage n sapiēns m; (herb) salvia f ♦ adj sapiēns
sagely adv sapienter
sail n vēlum nt; set ~ vēla dare, nāvem solvere;
  shorten ~ vēla contrahere ♦ vi nāvigāre; ~ past
  legere, praetervehī
sailing n nāvigātiō f
sailor n nauta m
sail yard n antenna f
saint n vir sanctus m
sainted adj beātus
saintly adj sanctus
sake n: for the ~ of grātiā (gen), causā (gen),
  propter (acc); (behalf) prō (abl)

salacious adj salāx
salad n morētum nt
salamander n salamandra f
salary n mercēs f
sale n vēnditiō f; (formal) mancipium nt; (auction)
  hasta f; for ~ vēnālis; be for ~ prōstāre; offer for
  ~ vēnum dare
saleable adj vēndibilis
salient adj ēminēns; ~ points capita ntpl
saline adj salsus
saliva n salīva f
sallow adj pallidus
sally n ēruptiō f; (wit) facētiae fpl ♦ vi ērumpere,
  excurrere
salmon n salmō m
salon n ātrium nt
salt n sal m ♦ adj salsus
saltcellar n salīnum nt
saltpetre n nitrum nt
salt-pits n salīnae fpl
salty adj salsus
salubrious adj salūbris
salubriously adv salūbriter
salubriousness n salūbritās f
salutary adj salūtāris, ūtilis
salutation n salūs f
salute vt salūtāre
salvage vt servāre, ēripere
salvation n salūs f
salve n unguentum nt
salver n scutella f
same adj īdem; ~ as īdem ac; all the
  ~ nihilōminus; one and the ~ ūnus et īdem;
  from the ~ place indidem; in the ~ place
  ibīdem; to the ~ place eōdem; at the ~ time
  simul, eōdem tempore; (adversative) tamen; it is
  all the ~ to me meā nōn interest
Samnites n Samnītēs, Samnītium mpl
sample n exemplum nt, specimen nt ♦ vt gustāre
sanctify vt cōnsecrāre
sanctimony n falsa rēligiō f
sanction n comprobātiō f, auctōritās f ♦ vt
  ratum facere
sanctity n sanctitās f
sanctuary n fānum nt, dēlubrum nt; (for men)
  asȳlum nt
sand n harēna f
sandal n (outdoors) crepida f; (indoors) solea f
sandalled adj crepidātus, soleātus
sandpit n harēnāria f
sandstone n tōfus m
sandy adj harēnōsus; (colour) flāvus

145

sane *adj* sānus
sangfroid *n* aequus animus *m*
sanguinary *adj* cruentus
sanguine *adj* laetus
sanitary *adj* salūbris
sanity *n* mēns sāna *f*
sap *n* sūcus *m* ◆ *vt* subruere
sapience *n* sapientia *f*
sapient *adj* sapiēns
sapling *n* surculus *m*
sapper *n* cunīculārius *m*
sapphire *n* sapphīrus *f*
sarcasm *n* aculeī *mpl*, dicācitās *f*
sarcastic *adj* dicāx, acūleātus
sardonic *adj* amārus
sash *n* cingulum *nt*
satchel *n* loculus *m*
sate *vt* explēre, satiāre
satellite *n* satelles *m*
satiate *vt* explēre, satiāre, saturāre
satiety *n* satietās *f*
satire *n* satura *f*; (*pl, of Horace*) sermōnēs *mpl*
satirical *adj* acerbus
satirist *n* saturārum scrīptor *m*
satirize *vt* perstringere, notāre
satisfaction *n* (*act*) explētiō *f*; (*feeling*) voluptās *f*; (*penalty*) poena *f*; **demand ~** rēs repetere
satisfactorily *adv* ex sententiā
satisfactory *adj* idōneus, grātus
satisfied *adj*: **be ~** satis habēre, contentum esse
satisfy *vt* satisfacere (*dat*); (*desire*) explēre
satrap *n* satrapēs *m*
saturate *vt* imbuere
satyr *n* satyrus *m*
sauce *n* condīmentum *nt*; (*fish*) garum *nt*
saucer *n* patella *f*
saucily *adv* petulanter
saucy *adj* petulāns
saunter *vi* ambulāre
sausage *n* tomāculum *nt*, hīllae *fpl*
savage *adj* ferus, efferātus; (*cruel*) atrōx, inhūmānus; saevus
savagely *adv* ferōciter, inhūmānē
savagery *n* ferōcitās *f*, inhūmānitās *f*
savant *n* vir doctus *m*
save *vt* servāre; **~ up** reservāre ◆ *prep* praeter (*acc*)
saving *adj* parcus; **~ clause** exceptiō *f* ◆ *n* compendium *nt*; **savings** *pl* peculium *nt*
saviour *n* līberātor *m*
savory *n* thymbra *f*
savour *n* sapor *m*; (*of cooking*) nīdor *m* ◆ *vi* sapere; **~ of** olēre, redolēre
savoury *adj* condītus
saw *n* (*tool*) serra *f*; (*saying*) prōverbium *nt* ◆ *vt* serrā secāre
sawdust *n* scobis *f*
say *vt* dīcere; **say that ... not** negāre; **say no** negāre; **he says** (*quoting*) inquit; **he says yes** āit; **they say** ferunt (*+ acc and infin*)
saying *n* dictum *nt*
scab *n* (*disease*) scabiēs *f*; (*over wound*) crusta *f*
scabbard *n* vāgīna *f*
scabby *adj* scaber
scaffold, **scaffolding** *n* fala *f*
scald *vt* ūrere

scale *n* (*balance*) lanx *f*; (*fish, etc*) squāma *f*; (*gradation*) gradūs *mpl*; (*music*) diagramma *nt* ◆ *vt* scālīs ascendere
scallop *n* pecten *m*
scalp *n* capitis cutis *f*
scalpel *n* scalpellum *nt*
scamp *n* verberō *m*
scamper *vi* currere
scan *vt* contemplārī; (*verse*) mētīrī
scandal *n* īnfāmia *f*, opprobrium *nt*; (*talk*) calumnia *f*
scandalize *vt* offendere
scandalous *adj* flāgitiōsus, turpis
scansion *n* syllabārum ēnārrātiō *f*
scant *adj* exiguus, parvus
scantily *adv* exiguē, tenuiter
scantiness *n* exiguitās *f*
scanty *adj* exiguus, tenuis, exīlis; (*number*) paucus
scapegoat *n* piāculum *nt*
scar *n* cicātrīx *f*
scarce *adj* rārus; **make oneself ~** sē āmovēre, dē mediō recēdere ◆ *adv* vix, aegrē
scarcely *adv* vix, aegrē; **~ anyone** nēmō ferē
scarcity *n* inopia *f*, angustiae *fpl*
scare *n* formīdō *f* ◆ *vt* terrēre; **~ away** absterrēre
scarecrow *n* formīdō *f*
scarf *n* fōcāle *nt*
scarlet *n* coccum *nt* ◆ *adj* coccinus
scarp *n* rūpēs *f*
scathe *n* damnum *nt*
scatter *vt* spargere; dispergere, dissipāre; (*violently*) disicere ◆ *vi* diffugere
scatterbrained *adj* dēsipiēns
scattered *adj* rārus
scene *n* spectāculum *nt*; (*place*) theātrum *nt*
scenery *n* locī faciēs *f*, speciēs *f*; (*beautiful*) amoenitās *f*
scent *n* odor *m*; (*sense*) odōrātus *m*; **keen ~** sagācitās *f* ◆ *vt* odōrārī; (*perfume*) odōribus perfundere
scented *adj* odōrātus
sceptic *n* Pyrrhōnēus *m*
sceptical *adj* incrēdulus
sceptre *n* scēptrum *nt*
schedule *n* tabulae *fpl*, ratiō *f*
scheme *n* cōnsilium *nt*, ratiō *f* ◆ *vt* māchinārī, mōlīrī
schemer *n* māchinātor *m*
schism *n* discidium *nt*, sēcessiō *f*
scholar *n* vir doctus *m*, litterātus *m*; (*pupil*) discipulus *m*
scholarly *adj* doctus, litterātus
scholarship *n* litterae *fpl*, doctrīna *f*
scholastic *adj* umbrātilis
school *n* (*elementary*) lūdus *m*; (*advanced*) schola *f*; (*high*) gymnasium *nt*; (*sect*) secta *f*, domus *f* ◆ *vt* īnstituere
schoolboy *n* discipulus *m*
schoolmaster *n* magister *m*
schoolmistress *n* magistra *f*
science *n* doctrīna *f*, disciplīna *f*, ars *f*
scimitar *n* acīnacēs *m*
scintillate *vi* scintillāre
scion *n* prōgeniēs *f*
Scipio *n* Scīpiō, Scīpiōnis *m*

scissors *n* forfex *f*
scoff *vi* irrīdēre; ~ at dērīdēre
scoffer *n* irrīsor *m*
scold *vt* increpāre, obiūrgāre
scolding *n* obiūrgātiō *f*
scoop *n* trulla *f* ♦ *vt*: ~ out excavāre
scope *n* (*aim*) fīnis *m*; (*room*) locus *m*, campus *m*; ample ~ laxus locus
scorch *vt* exūrere, torrēre
scorched *adj* torridus
score *n* (*mark*) nota *f*; (*total*) summa *f*; (*reckoning*) ratiō *f*; (*number*) vīgintī ♦ *vt* notāre ♦ *vi* vincere
scorn *n* contemptiō *f* ♦ *vt* contemnere, spernere
scorner *n* contemptor *m*
scornful *adj* fastīdiōsus
scornfully *adv* contemptim
scorpion *n* scorpiō *m*, nepa *f*
scot-free *adj* immūnis, impūnītus
scoundrel *n* furcifer *m*
scour *vt* (*clean*) tergēre; (*range*) percurrere
scourge *n* flagellum *nt*; (*fig*) pestis *f* ♦ *vt* verberāre, virgīs caedere
scout *n* explōrātor *m*, speculātor *m* ♦ *vi* explōrāre, speculārī ♦ *vt* spernere, repudiāre
scowl *n* frontis contractiō *f* ♦ *vi* frontem contrahere
scraggy *adj* strigōsus
scramble *vi*: ~ for certātim captāre; ~ up scandere
scrap *n* frūstum *nt*
scrape *vt* rādere, scabere; ~ off abrādere
scraper *n* strigilis *f*
scratch *vt* rādere; (*head*) perfricāre; ~ out exsculpere, ērādere
scream *n* clāmor *m*, ululātus *m* ♦ *vi* clāmāre, ululāre
screech *n* ululātus *m* ♦ *vi* ululāre
screen *n* obex *m/f*; (*from sun*) umbra *f*; (*fig*) vēlāmentum *nt* ♦ *vt* tegere
screw *n* clāvus *m*; (*of winepress*) cochlea *f*
scribble *vt* properē scrībere
scribe *n* scrība *m*
script *n* scrīptum *nt*; (*handwriting*) manus *f*
scroll *n* volūmen *nt*
scrub *vt* dētergēre, dēfricāre
scruple *n* religiō *f*, scrūpulus *m*
scrupulous *adj* religiōsus; (*careful*) dīligēns
scrupulously *adv* religiōsē, dīligenter
scrupulousness *n* religiō *f*; dīligentia *f*
scrutinize *vt* scrūtārī, intrōspicere in (*acc*), excutere
scrutiny *n* scrūtātiō *f*
scud *vi* volāre
scuffle *n* rixa *f*
scull *n* calvāria *f*; (*oar*) rēmus *m*
scullery *n* culīna *f*
sculptor *n* fictor *m*, sculptor *m*
sculpture *n* ars fingendī *f*; (*product*) statuae *fpl* ♦ *vt* sculpere
scum *n* spūma *f*
scurf *n* porrīgō *f*
scurrility *n* maledicta *ntpl*
scurrilous *adj* maledicus
scurvy *adj* (*fig*) turpis, improbus
scythe *n* falx *f*

sea *n* mare *nt*; aequor *nt*; open sea altum *nt*; put to sea solvere; be at sea nāvigāre; (*fig*) in errōre versārī ♦ *adj* marīnus; (*coast*) maritimus
seaboard *n* lītus *nt*
seafaring *adj* maritimus, nauticus
seafight *n* nāvāle proelium *nt*
seagull *n* larus *m*
seal *n* (*animal*) phōca *f*; (*stamp*) signum *nt* ♦ *vt* signāre; ~ up obsignāre
seam *n* sūtūra *f*
seaman *n* nauta *m*
seamanship *n* scientia et ūsus nauticārum rērum
seaport *n* portus *m*
sear *vt* adūrere, torrēre
search *n* investigātiō *f* ♦ *vi* investīgāre, explōrāre ♦ *vt* excutere, scrūtārī; in ~ of causa (*gen*); ~ for quaerere, exquīrere, investīgāre; ~ into inquīrere, anquīrere; ~ out explōrāre, indāgāre
searcher *n* inquīsītor *m*
searching *adj* acūtus, dīligēns
seashore *n* lītus *nt*
seasick *adj*: be ~ nauseāre
seasickness *n* nausea *f*
seaside *n* mare *nt*
season *n* annī tempus *nt*, tempestās *f*; (*right time*) tempus *nt*, opportūnitās *f*; in ~ tempestīvē ♦ *vt* condīre
seasonable *adj* tempestīvus
seasonably *adv* tempestīvē
seasoned *adj* (*food*) condītus; (*wood*) dūrātus
seasoning *n* condīmentum *nt*
seat *n* sēdēs *f*; (*chair*) sedīle *nt*; (*home*) domus *f*, domicilium *nt*; keep one's ~ (*riding*) in equō haerēre ♦ *vt* collocāre; ~ oneself īnsīdēre
seated *adj*: be ~ sedēre
seaweed *n* alga *f*
seaworthy *adj* ad nāvigandum ūtilis
secede *vi* sēcēdere
secession *n* sēcessiō *f*
seclude *vt* sēclūdere, abstrūdere
secluded *adj* sēcrētus, remōtus
seclusion *n* sōlitūdō *f*, sēcrētum *nt*
second *adj* secundus, alter; a ~ time iterum ♦ *n* temporis pūnctum *nt*; (*person*) fautor *m*; ~ sight hariolātiō *f* ♦ *vt* favēre (*dat*), adesse (*dat*)
secondary *adj* īnferior, dēterior
seconder *n* fautor *m*
second-hand *adj* aliēnus, trītus
secondly *adv* deinde
secrecy *n* sēcrētum *nt*, silentium *nt*
secret *adj* secretus; occultus, arcānus; (*stealth*) fūrtīvus ♦ *n* arcānum *nt*; keep ~ dissimulāre, cēlāre; in ~ clam; be ~ latēre
secretary *n* scrība *m*, ab epistolīs, ā manū
secrete *vt* cēlāre, abdere
secretive *adj* tēctus
secretly *adv* clam, occultē, sēcrētō
sect *n* secta *f*, schola *f*, domus *f*
section *n* pars *f*
sector *n* regiō *f*
secular *adj* profānus
secure *adj* tūtus ♦ *vt* (*MIL*) firmāre, ēmūnīre; (*fasten*) religāre; (*obtain*) parāre, nancīscī
securely *adv* tūtō

security n salūs f, impūnitās f; (money) cautiō f,
pignus nt, spōnsiō f; **sense of** ~ sēcūritās f; **give
good** ~ satis dare; **on good** ~ (loan) nōminibus
rēctis cautus; **stand** ~ **for** praedem esse prō (abl)
sedan n lectīca f
sedate adj placidus, temperātus, gravis
sedately adv placidē
sedateness n gravitās f
sedge n ulva f
sediment n faex f, mōtus m
sedition n sēditiō f, mōtus m
seditious adj sēditiōsus
seditiously adv sēditiōsē
seduce vt illicere, pellicere
seducer n corruptor m
seduction n corruptēla f
seductive adj blandus
seductively adv blandē
sedulity n dīligentia f
sedulous adj dīligēns, sēdulus
sedulously adv dīligenter, sēdulō
see vt vidēre, cernere; (suddenly) cōnspicārī;
(performance) spectāre; (with mind) intellegere;
go and see vīsere, invīsere; **see to** vidēre,
cōnsulere (dat); curare (+acc and gerundive); **see
through** dīspicere; **see that you are** vidē ut sīs,
fac sīs; **see that you are not** vidē nē sīs, cavē sīs
seed n sēmen nt; (in a plant) grānum nt; (in fruit)
acinum nt; (fig) stirps f, prōgeniēs f
seedling n surculus m
seed-time n sēmentis f
seeing that conj quōniam, siquidem
seek vt petere, quaerere
seeker n indāgātor m
seem vi vidērī
seeming adj speciōsus ♦ n speciēs f
seemingly adv ut vidētur
seemly adj decēns, decōrus; **it is** ~ decet
seep vi mānāre, percōlārī
seer n vātēs m/f
seethe vi fervēre
segregate vt sēcernere, sēgregāre
segregation n sēparātiō f
seize vt rapere, corripere, adripere, prehendere;
(MIL) occupāre; (illness) adficere; (emotion)
invādere, occupāre
seizure n ēreptiō f, occupātiō f
seldom adv rārō
select vt ēligere, excerpere, dēligere ♦ adj lēctus,
ēlēctus
selection n ēlēctiō f, dēlēctus m; (lit) ecloga f
self n ipse; (reflexive) sē; **a second** ~ alter īdem
self-centred adj glōriōsus
self-confidence n cōnfidentia f, fidūcia f
self-confident adj cōnfidēns
self-conscious adj pudibundus
self-control n temperantia f
self-denial n abstinentia f
self-evident adj manifestus; **it is** ~ ante pedēs
positum est
self-governing adj līber
self-government n lībertās f
self-important adj adrogāns
self-interest n ambitiō f
selfish adj inhūmānus, avārus; **be** ~ suā causā
facere

selfishly adv inhūmānē, avārē
selfishness n inhūmānitās f, incontinentia f,
avāritia f
self-made adj (man) novus
self-possessed adj aequō animō
self-possession n aequus animus m
self-reliant adj cōnfidēns
self-respect n pudor m
self-restraint n modestia f
self-sacrifice n dēvōtiō f
selfsame adj ūnus et īdem
sell vt vēndere; (in lots) dīvēndere; **be sold** vēnīre
seller n vēnditor m
selvage n limbus m
semblance n speciēs f, imāgō f
semicircle n hēmicyclium nt
senate n senātus m; **hold a meeting of the**
~ senātum habēre; **decree of the** ~ senātus
cōnsultum nt
senate house n cūria f
senator n senātor m; (provincial) decuriō m;
senators pl patrēs mpl
senatorial adj senātōrius
send vt mittere; ~ **across** trānsmittere; ~ **ahead**
praemittere; ~ **away** dīmittere; ~ **back**
remittere; ~ **for** accersere; (doctor) adhibēre;
~ **forth** ēmittere; ~ **forward** praemittere; ~ **in**
immittere, intrōmittere; ~ **out** ēmittere; (in
different directions) dīmittere; ~ **out of the way**
ablēgāre; ~ **up** submittere
senile adj senīlis
senility n senium nt
senior adj nātū māior; (thing) prior
sensation n sēnsus m; (event) rēs nova f;
lose ~ obtorpēscere; **create a** ~ hominēs
obstupefacere
sensational adj novus, prōdigiōsus
sense n (faculty) sēnsus m; (wisdom) prūdentia
f; (meaning) vis f, sententia f; **common**
~ prūdentia f; **be in one's senses** apud sē esse,
mentis suae esse; **out of one's senses** dēmēns;
recover one's senses resipīscere; **what is the**
~ **of** quid sibī vult? ♦ vt sentīre
senseless adj absurdus, ineptus, īnsipiēns
senselessly adv īnsipienter
senselessness n īnsipientia f
sensibility n sēnsus m
sensible adj prūdēns, sapiēns
sensibly adv prūdenter, sapienter
sensitive adj mollis, inrītābilis, patibilis
sensitiveness n mollitia f
sensual adj libīdinōsus
sensuality n libīdō f, voluptās f
sensually adv libīdinōsē
sentence n (judge) iūdicium nt, sententia f;
(GRAM) sententia f; **pass** ~ iūdicāre; **execute**
~ lēge agere ♦ vt damnāre; ~ **to death** capitis
damnāre
sententious adj sententiōsus
sententiously adv sententiōsē
sentient adj patibilis
sentiment n (feeling) sēnsus m; (opinion)
sententia f; (emotion) mollitia f
sentimental adj mollis, flēbilis
sentimentality n mollitia f
sentimentally adv molliter

sentries *npl* statiōnēs *fpl*, excubiae *fpl*
sentry *n* custōs *m*, vigil *m*; **be on ~ duty** in
statiōne esse
separable *adj* dīviduus, sēparābilis
separate *vt* sēparāre, dīvidere, disiungere;
(*forcibly*) dīrimere, dīvellere ♦ *vi* dīgredī ♦ *adj*
sēparātus, sēcrētus
separately *adv* sēparātim, seōrsum
separation *n* sēparātiō *f*; (*violent*) discidium *nt*
September *n* mēnsis September *m*; **of**
~ September
sepulchral *adj* fūnebris
sepulchre *n* sepulcrum *nt*
sepulture *n* sepultūra *f*
sequel *n* exitus *m*, quae sequuntur
sequence *n* seriēs *f*, ōrdō *m*
sequestered *adj* sēcrētus
serenade *vt* occentāre
serene *adj* tranquillus, sēcūrus
serenely *adv* tranquillē
serenity *n* sēcūritās *f*
serf *n* servus *m*
serfdom *n* servitūs *f*
sergeant *n* signifer *m*
series *n* seriēs *f*, ōrdō *m*
serious *adj* gravis, sērius, sevērus
seriously *adv* graviter, sēriō, sevērē
seriousness *n* gravitās *f*
sermon *n* ōrātiō *f*
serpent *n* serpēns *f*
serpentine *adj* tortuōsus
serrated *adj* serrātus
serried *adj* cōnfertus
servant *n* (*domestic*) famulus *m*, famula *f*; (*public*)
minister *m*, ministra *f*; **family servants**
familia *f*
servant maid *n* ancilla *f*
serve *vt* servīre (*dat*); (*food*) ministrāre, adpōnere;
(*interest*) condūcere (*dat*) ♦ *vi* (MIL) stīpendia
merēre, mīlitāre; (*suffice*) sufficere; **~ as** esse
prō (*abl*); **~ in the cavalry** equō merēre; **~ in the**
infantry pedibus merēre; **having served one's**
time ēmeritus; **~ a sentence** poenam subīre;
~ well bene merērī dē (*abl*)
service *n* (*status*) servitium *nt*, famulātus *m*;
(*work*) ministerium *nt*; (*help*) opera *f*; (*by an*
equal) meritum *nt*, beneficium *nt*; (MIL) mīlitia
f, stīpendia *ntpl*; **be of ~ to** prōdesse (*dat*), bene
merērī dē; **I am at your ~** adsum tibī; **complete**
one's ~ stīpendia ēmerērī
serviceable *adj* ūtilis
servile *adj* servīlis; (*fig*) abiectus, humilis
servility *n* adūlātiō *f*
servitude *n* servitūs *f*
session *n* conventus *m*; **be in ~** sedēre
sesterce *n* sēstertius *m*; **10 sesterces** decem
sēstertiī; **10,000 sesterces** dēna sēstertia *ntpl*;
1,000,000 sesterces deciēs sēstertium
set *vt* pōnere, locāre, statuere, sistere; (*bone*)
condere; (*course*) dīrigere; (*example*) dare; (*limit*)
impōnere; (*mind*) intendere; (*music*) modulārī;
(*sail*) dare; (*sentries*) dispōnere; (*table*) īnstruere;
(*trap*) parāre ♦ *vi* (ASTR) occidere; **set about**
incipere; **set against** oppōnere; **set apart**
sēpōnere; **set aside** sēpōnere; **set down**
(*writing*) perscrībere; **set eyes on** cōnspicere;

set foot on ingredī; **set forth** expōnere, ēdere;
set free līberāre; **set in motion** movēre; **set in**
order compōnere, dispōnere; **set off** (*decoration*)
distinguere; (*art*) illūmināre; **set on** (*to attack*)
immittere; **set on foot** īnstituere; **set on fire**
incendere; **set one's heart on** exoptāre; **set out**
vi profīcīscī; **set over** praeficere, impōnere; **set**
up statuere; (*fig*) cōnstituere ♦ *adj* (*arrangement*)
status; (*purpose*) certus; (*rule*) praescrīptus;
(*speech*) compositus; **of set purpose** cōnsultō
♦ *n* (*persons*) numerus *m*; (*things*) congeriēs *f*;
(*current*) cursus *m*
setback *n* repulsa *f*
settee *n* lectulus *m*
setting *n* (ASTR) occāsus *m*; (*event*) locus *m*
settle *n* sella *f* ♦ *vt* statuere; (*annuity*) praestāre;
(*business*) trānsigere; (*colony*) dēdūcere; (*debt*)
exsolvere; (*decision*) cōnstituere; (*dispute*)
dēcīdere, compōnere ♦ *vi* (*abode*) cōnsīdere;
(*agreement*) cōnstituere, convenīre; (*sediment*)
dēsīdere; **~ in** īnsidēre (*dat*)
settled *adj* certus, explōrātus
settlement *n* (*of a colony*) dēductiō *f*; (*colony*)
colōnia *f*; (*of dispute*) dēcīsiō *f*, compositiō *f*; (*to*
wife) dōs *f*
settler *n* colōnus *m*
set to *n* pugna *f*
seven *num* septem; **~ each** septēnī; **~ times**
septiēns
seven hundred *num* septingentī
seven hundredth *adj* septingentēsimus
seventeen *num* septendecim
seventeenth *adj* septimus decimus
seventh *adj* septimus; **for the ~ time** septimum
seventieth *adj* septuāgēsimus
seventy *num* septuāgintā; **~ each** septuāgēnī;
~ times septuāgiēns
sever *vt* incīdere, sēparāre, dīvidere
several *adj* complūrēs, aliquot
severally *adv* singulī
severe *adj* gravis, sevērus, dūrus; (*style*) austērus;
(*weather*) asper; (*pain*) ācer, gravis
severely *adv* graviter, sevērē
severity *n* gravitās *f*; asperitās *f*; sevēritās *f*
sew *vt* suere; **sew up** cōnsuere; **sew up in**
īnsuere in (*acc*)
sewer *n* cloāca *f*
sex *n* sexus *m*
shabbily *adv* sordidē
shabbiness *n* sordēs *fpl*
shabby *adj* sordidus
shackle *n* compēs *f*, vinculum *nt* ♦ *vt* impedīre,
vincīre
shade *n* umbra *f*; (*colour*) color *m*; **shades** *pl*
mānēs *mpl*; **put in the ~** officere (*dat*) ♦ *vt*
opācāre, umbram adferre (*dat*)
shadow *n* umbra *f*
shadowy *adj* obscūrus; (*fig*) inānis
shady *adj* umbrōsus, opācus
shaft *n* (*missile*) tēlum *nt*, sagitta *f*; (*of spear*)
hastīle *nt*; (*of cart*) tēmō *m*; (*of light*) radius *m*;
(*excavation*) puteus *m*
shaggy *adj* hirsūtus
shake *vt* quatere, agitāre; (*structure*) labefacere,
labefactāre; (*belief*) īnfirmāre; (*resolution*)
labefactāre, commovēre; **~ hands with**

dextram dare (*dat*) ♦ *vi* quatī, agitārī, tremere, horrēscere; **~ off** dēcutere, excutere; **~ out** excutere

shaking *n* tremor *m*

shaky *adj* īnstābilis, tremebundus

shall *aux vb use fut indic*

shallot *n* caepa Ascalōnia *f*

shallow *adj* brevis, vadōsus; (*fig*) levis

shallowness *n* vada *ntpl*; (*fig*) levitās *f*

shallows *n* brevia *ntpl*, vada *ntpl*

sham *adj* fictus, falsus, fūcōsus ♦ *n* simulātiō *f*, speciēs *f* ♦ *vt* simulāre

shambles *n* laniēna *f*

shame *n* (*feeling*) pudor *m*; (*cause*) dēdecus *nt*, ignōminia *f*; **it shames** pudet (+*acc of person, gen of thing*); **it is a ~** flāgitium est ♦ *vt* rubōrem incutere (*dat*) ♦ *interj* prō pudor!

shamefaced *adj* verēcundus

shameful *adj* ignōminiōsus, turpis

shamefully *adv* turpiter

shameless *adj* impudēns

shamelessly *adv* impudenter

shamelessness *n* impudentia *f*

shank *n* crūs *nt*

shape *n* fōrma *f*, figūra *f* ♦ *vt* fōrmāre, fingere; (*fig*) īnfōrmāre ♦ *vi*: **~ well** prōficere

shapeless *adj* īnfōrmis, dēfōrmis

shapelessness *n* dēfōrmitās *f*

shapeliness *n* fōrma *f*

shapely *adj* fōrmōsus

shard *n* testa *f*

share *n* pars *f*; (*plough*) vōmer *m*; **go shares with** inter sē partīrī ♦ *vt* (*give*) partīrī, impertīre; (*have*) commūnicāre, participem esse (*gen*)

sharer *n* particeps *m/f*, socius *m*

shark *n* volpēs marīna *f*

sharp *adj* acūtus; (*fig*) ācer, acūtus; (*bitter*) amārus

sharpen *vt* acuere; (*fig*) exacuere

sharply *adv* ācriter, acūtē

sharpness *n* aciēs *f*; (*mind*) acūmen *nt*, argūtiae *fpl*; (*temper*) acerbitās *f*

shatter *vt* quassāre, perfringere, adflīgere; (*fig*) frangere

shave *vt* rādere; **~ off** abrādere

shavings *n* rāmenta *ntpl*

she *pron* haec, ea, illa

sheaf *n* manipulus *m*

shear *vt* tondēre, dētondēre

shears *n* forficēs *fpl*

sheath *n* vāgīna *f*

sheathe *vt* recondere

shed *vt* fundere; (*blood*) effundere; (*one's own*) profundere; (*tears*) effundere; (*covering*) exuere; **~ light on** (*fig*) lūmen adhibēre (*dat*)

sheen *n* nitor *m*

sheep *n* ovis *f*; (*flock*) pecus *nt*

sheepfold *n* ovīle *nt*

sheepish *adj* pudibundus

sheepishly *adv* pudenter

sheer *adj* (*absolute*) merus; (*steep*) praeruptus

sheet *n* (*cloth*) linteum *nt*; (*metal*) lāmina *f*; (*paper*) carta *f*, scheda *f*; (*sail*) pēs *m*; (*water*) aequor *nt*

shelf *n* pluteus *m*, pēgma *nt*

shell *n* concha *f*; (*egg*) putāmen *nt*; (*tortoise*) testa *f*

shellfish *n* conchӯlium *nt*

shelter *n* suffugium *nt*, tegmen *nt*; (*refuge*) perfugium *nt*, asӯlum *nt*; (*lodging*) hospitium *nt*; (*fig*) umbra *f* ♦ *vt* tegere, dēfendere; (*refugee*) excipere ♦ *vi* latēre; **~ behind** (*fig*) dēlitēscere in (*abl*)

sheltered *adj* (*life*) umbrātilis

shelve *vt* differre ♦ *vi* sē dēmittere

shelving *adj* dēclīvis

shepherd *n* pastor *m*

shield *n* scūtum *nt*; clipeus *m*; (*small*) parma *f*; (*fig*) praesidium *nt* ♦ *vt* prōtegere, dēfendere

shift *n* (*change*) mūtātiō *f*; (*expedient*) ars *f*, dolus *m*; **make ~ to** efficere ut; **in shifts** per vicēs ♦ *vt* mūtāre; (*move*) movēre ♦ *vi* mūtārī; discēdere

shiftless *adj* iners, inops

shifty *adj* vafer, versūtus

shilling *n* solidus *m*

shimmer *vi* micāre ♦ *n* tremulum lūmen *nt*

shin *n* tībia *f*

shine *vi* lūcēre, fulgēre; (*reflecting*) nitēre; (*fig*) ēminēre; **~ forth** ēlūcēre, ēnitēre; effulgēre; **~ upon** adfulgēre (*dat*) ♦ *n* nitor *m*

shingle *n* lapillī *mpl*, glārea *f*

shining *adj* lūcidus, splendidus; (*fig*) illūstris

shiny *adj* nitidus

ship *n* nāvis *f*; **admiral's ~** nāvis praetōria; **decked ~** nāvis tēcta, nāvis cōnstrāta ♦ *vt* (*cargo*) impōnere; (*to a place*) nāvī invehere

shipowner *n* nāviculārius *m*

shipping *n* nāvēs *fpl*

shipwreck *n* naufragium *nt*; **suffer ~** naufragium facere

shipwrecked *adj* naufragus

shirk *vt* dēfugere, dētrectāre

shirt *n* subūcula *f*

shiver *n* horror *m* ♦ *vi* horrēre, tremere ♦ *vt* perfringere, comminuere

shivering *n* horror *m*

shoal *n* (*fish*) exāmen *nt*; (*water*) vadum *nt*; **shoals** *pl* brevia *ntpl*

shock *n* impulsus *m*; (*battle*) concursus *m*, cōnflictus *m*; (*hair*) caesariēs *f*; (*mind*) offēnsiō *f* ♦ *vt* percutere, offendere

shocking *adj* atrōx, dētestābilis, flāgitiōsus

shoddy *adj* vīlis

shoe *n* calceus *m*

shoemaker *n* sūtor *m*

shoot *n* surculus *m*; (*vine*) pampinus *m* ♦ *vi* frondēscere; (*movement*) volāre; **~ up** ēmicāre ♦ *vt* (*missile*) conicere, iaculārī; (*person*) iaculārī, trānsfīgere

shop *n* taberna *f*

shore *n* lītus *nt*, ōra *f* ♦ *vt* fulcīre

short *adj* brevis; (*broken*) curtus; (*amount*) exiguus; **for a ~ time** parumper, paulisper; **~ of** (*number*) intrā (*acc*); **be ~ of** indigēre (*abl*); **cut ~** interpellāre; **in ~** ad summam, dēnique; **very ~** perbrevis; **fall ~ of** nōn pervenīre ad, abesse ab; **run ~** dēficere; **to cut a long story ~** nē multīs morer, nē multa

shortage *n* inopia *f*

shortcoming *n* dēlictum *nt*, culpa *f*

short cut *n* via compendiāria *f*

shorten *vt* curtāre, imminuere, contrahere; (*sail*) legere

shorthand *n* notae *fpl*

shorthand writer n āctuārius m
short-lived adj brevis
shortly adv (time) brevī; (speak) breviter; ~ **after** paulō post, nec multō post
shortness n brevitās f, exiguitās f; (difficulty) angustiae fpl
short-sighted adj (fig) imprōvidus, imprūdēns
short-sightedness n imprūdentia f
short-tempered adj īrācundus
shot n ictus m; (range) iactus m
should vi (duty) dēbēre
shoulder n umerus m; (animal) armus m ♦ vt (burden) suscipere
shout n clāmor m, adclāmātiō f ♦ vt, vi clāmāre, vōciferārī; ~ **down** obstrepere (dat); ~ **out** exclāmāre
shove vt trūdere, impellere
shovel n rutrum nt
show n speciēs f; (entertainment) lūdī mpl, spectāculum nt; (stage) lūdicrum nt; **for** ~ in speciem; **put on a** ~ spectācula dare ♦ vt mōnstrāre, indicāre, ostendere, ostentāre; (point out) dēmōnstrāre; (qualities) praestāre; ~ **off** vi sē iactāre ♦ vt ostentāre
shower n imber m ♦ vt fundere, conicere
showery adj pluvius
showiness n ostentātiō f
showing off n iactātiō f
showy adj speciōsus
shred n fragmentum nt; **in shreds** minūtātim; **tear to shreds** dīlaniāre ♦ vt concīdere
shrew n virāgō f
shrewd adj acūtus, ācer, sagāx
shrewdly adv acūtē, sagāciter
shrewdness n acūmen nt, sagācitās f
shriek n ululātus m ♦ vi ululāre
shrill adj acūtus, argūtus
shrine n fānum nt, dēlubrum nt
shrink vt contrahere ♦ vi contrahī; ~ **from** abhorrēre ab, refugere ab, dētrectāre
shrivel vt corrūgāre ♦ vi exārēscere
shroud n integumentum nt; **shrouds** pl rudentēs mpl ♦ vt involvere
shrub n frutex m
shrubbery n fruticētum nt
shudder n horror m ♦ vi exhorrēscere; ~ **at** horrēre
shuffle vt miscēre ♦ vi claudicāre; (fig) tergiversārī
shun vt vītāre, ēvītāre, dēfugere
shut vt claudere; (with cover) operīre; (hand) comprimere; ~ **in** inclūdere; ~ **off** interclūdere; ~ **out** exclūdere; ~ **up** inclūdere
shutter n foricula f, lūmināre nt
shuttle n radius m
shy adj timidus, pudibundus, verēcundus
shyly adv timidē, verēcundē
shyness n verēcundia f
sibyl n sibylla f
sick adj aeger, aegrōtus; **be** ~ aegrōtāre; **feel** ~ nauseāre; **I am** ~ **of** mē taedet (gen)
sicken vt fastīdium movēre (dat) ♦ vi nauseāre, aegrōtāre
sickle n falx f
sickly adj invalidus

sickness n nausea f; (illness) morbus m, aegritūdō f
side n latus nt; (direction) pars f; (faction) partēs fpl; (kin) genus nt; **on all sides** undique; **on both sides** utrimque; **on one** ~ unā ex parte; **on our** ~ ā nōbis; **be on the** ~ **of** stāre ab, sentīre cum; **on the far** ~ **of** ultrā (acc); **on this** ~ hīnc; **on this** ~ **of** cis (acc), citrā (acc) ♦ vi: ~ **with** stāre ab, facere cum
sideboard n abacus m
sidelong adj oblīquus
sideways adv oblīquē, in oblīquum
sidle vi oblīquō corpore incēdere
siege n obsidiō f, oppugnātiō f; **lay** ~ **to** obsidēre
siege works n opera ntpl
siesta n merīdiātiō f; **take a** ~ merīdiāre
sieve n crībrum nt
sigh n suspīrium nt; (loud) gemitus m ♦ vi suspīrāre, gemere
sight n (sense) vīsus m; (process) aspectus m; (range) cōnspectus m; (thing seen) spectāculum nt, speciēs f; **at** ~ ex tempore; **at first** ~ prīmō aspectū; **in** ~ in cōnspectū; **come into** ~ in cōnspectum sē dare; **in the** ~ **of** in oculīs (gen); **catch** ~ **of** cōnspicere; **lose** ~ **of** ē cōnspectū āmittere; (fig) oblīvīscī (gen) ♦ vt cōnspicārī
sightless adj caecus
sightly adj decōrus
sign n signum nt, indicium nt; (distinction) īnsigne nt; (mark) nota f; (trace) vestīgium nt; (proof) documentum nt; (portent) ōmen nt; (Zodiac) signum nt; **give a** ~ innuere ♦ vi signum dare, innuere ♦ vt subscrībere (dat); (as witness) obsignāre
signal n signum nt; **give the** ~ **for retreat** receptuī canere ♦ vi signum dare ♦ adj īnsignis, ēgregius
signalize vt nōbilitāre
signally adv ēgregiē
signature n nōmen nt, manus f, chīrographum nt
signet n signum nt
signet ring n anulus m
significance n interpretātiō f, significātiō f, vīs f; (importance) pondus nt
significant adj gravis, clārus
signification n significātiō f
signify vt significāre, velle; (omen) portendere; **it does not** ~ nōn interest
silence n silentium nt; **in** ~ per silentium ♦ vt comprimere; (argument) refūtāre
silent adj tacitus; (habit) taciturnus; **be** ~ silēre, tacēre; **be** ~ **about** silēre, tacēre; **become** ~ conticēscere
silently adv tacitē
silhouette n adumbrātiō f
silk n bombyx m; (clothes) sērica ntpl ♦ adj bombȳcinus, sēricus
silken adj bombȳcinus
sill n līmen nt
silliness n stultitia f, ineptiae fpl
silly adj fatuus, ineptus; stultus; **be** ~ dēsipere
silt n līmus m
silver n argentum nt ♦ adj argenteus
silver mine n argentāria f
silver plate n argentum nt

silver-plated adj argentātus
silvery adj argenteus
similar adj similis
similarity n similitūdō f
similarly adv similiter
simile n similitūdō f
simmer vi lēniter fervēre
simper vi molliter subrīdēre
simple adj simplex; (mind) fatuus; (task) facilis
simpleton n homō ineptus m
simplicity n simplicitās f; (mind) stultitia f
simplify vt faciliōrem reddere
simply adv simpliciter; (merely) sōlum, tantum
simulate vt simulāre
simulation n simulātiō f
simultaneously adv simul, ūnā, eōdem
  tempore
sin n peccātum nt, nefās nt, dēlictum nt ♦ vi
  peccāre
since adv abhinc; long ~ iamdūdum ♦ conj (time)
  ex quō tempore, postquam; (reason) cum (subj),
  quōniam; ~ he quippe quī ♦ prep ab (abl), ex (abl),
  post (acc); ever ~ usque ab
sincere adj sincērus, simplex, apertus
sincerely adv sincērē, ex animō
sincerity n fidēs f, simplicitās f
sinew n nervus m
sinewy adj nervōsus
sinful adj improbus, impius, incestus
sinfully adv improbē, impiē
sing vt canere, cantāre; ~ of canere
singe vt adūrere
singer n cantor m
singing n cantus m ♦ adj canōrus
single adj ūnus, sōlus, ūnicus; (unmarried) caelebs
  ♦ vt: ~ out ēligere, excerpere
single-handed adj ūnus
singly adv singillātim, singulī
singular adj singulāris; (strange) novus
singularly adv singulāriter, praecipuē
sinister adj īnfaustus, malevolus
sink vi dēsīdere; (in water) dēmergī; ~ in inlābī,
  īnsīdere ♦ vt dēprimere, mergere; (well) fodere;
  (fig) dēmergere
sinless adj integer, innocēns, castus
sinner n peccātor m
sinuous adj sinuōsus
sip vt gustāre, lībāre
siphon n siphō m
sir n (to master) ere; (to equal) vir optime; (title)
  eques m
sire n pater m
siren n sīrēn f
sirocco n Auster m
sister n soror f; **sister's** sorōrius
sisterhood n germānitās f; (society) sorōrum
  societās f
sister-in-law n glōs f
sisterly adj sorōrius
sit vi sedēre; **sit beside** adsidēre (dat); **sit down**
  cōnsīdere; **sit on** īnsīdere (dat); (eggs) incubāre;
  sit at table accumbere; **sit up** (at night) vigilāre
site n situs m, locus m; (for building) ārea f
sitting n sessiō f
situated adj situs

situation n situs m; (circumstances) status m,
  condiciō f
six num sex; **six each** sēnī; **six or seven** sex
  septem; **six times** sexiēns
six hundred num sēscentī; **six hundred each**
  sēscēnī; **six hundred times** sēscentiēns
six hundredth adj sēscentēsimus
sixteen num sēdecim; ~ **each** sēnī dēnī; ~ **times**
  sēdeciēns
sixteenth adj sextus decimus
sixth adj sextus; **for the ~ time** sextum
sixtieth adj sexāgēsimus
sixty num sexāgintā; ~ **each** sexāgēnī; ~ **times**
  sexāgiēns
size n māgnitūdō f, amplitūdō f; (measure)
  mēnsūra f, fōrma f
skate vi per glaciem lābī; ~ **on thin ice** (fig)
  incēdere per ignēs suppositōs cinerī dolōsō
skein n glomus nt
skeleton n ossa ntpl
sketch n adumbrātiō f, dēscrīptiō f ♦ vt
  adumbrāre, īnfōrmāre
skewer n verū nt
skiff n scapha f, lēnunculus m
skilful adj perītus, doctus, scītus; (with hands)
  habilis
skilfully adv perītē, doctē, habiliter
skill n ars f, perītia f, sollertia f
skilled adj perītus, doctus; ~ **in** perītus (gen)
skim vt dēspūmāre; ~ **over** (fig) legere,
  perstringere
skin n cutis f; (animal) pellis f ♦ vt pellem
  dētrahere (dat)
skinflint n avārus m
skinny adj macer
skip vi exsultāre ♦ vt praeterīre
skipper n magister m
skirmish n leve proelium nt ♦ vi vēlitārī
skirmisher n vēles m, excursor m
skirt n īnstita f; (border) limbus m ♦ vt contingere
  (dat); (motion) legere
skittish adj lascīvus
skulk vi latēre, dēlitēscere
skull n caput nt
sky n caelum nt; **of the sky** caelestis
skylark n alauda f
slab n tabula f
slack adj remissus, laxus; (work) piger, neglegēns
slacken vt remittere, dētendere ♦ vi laxārī
slackness n remissiō f; pigritia f
slag n scōria f
slake vt restinguere, sēdāre
slam vt adflīgere
slander n maledicta ntpl, obtrectātiō f; (LAW)
  calumnia f ♦ vt maledīcere (dat), īnfāmāre,
  obtrectāre (dat)
slanderer n obtrectātor m
slanderous adj maledicus
slang n vulgāria verba ntpl
slant vi in trānsversum īre
slanting adj oblīquus, trānsversus
slantingly adv oblīquē, ex trānsversō
slap n alapa f ♦ vt palmā ferīre
slapdash adj praeceps, temerārius
slash vt caedere ♦ n ictus m

slate n (*roof*) tēgula f; (*writing*) tabula f ♦ vt
increpāre
slatternly adj sordidus, incōmptus
slaughter n caedēs f, strāgēs f ♦ vt trucīdāre
slaughterhouse n laniēna f
slave n servus m; (*domestic*) famulus m;
(*home-born*) verna m; **be a ~ to** īnservīre (*dat*);
household slaves familia f
slave girl n ancilla f
slavery n servitūs f
slavish adj servīlis
slavishly adv servīliter
slay vt interficere, occīdere
slayer n interfector m
sleek adj nitidus, pinguis
sleep n somnus m; **go to ~** obdormīscere ♦ vi
dormīre; **~ off** vt ēdormīre
sleeper n dormītor m
sleepiness n sopor m
sleepless adj īnsomnis, vigil
sleeplessness n īnsomnia f
sleepy adj somniculōsus; **be ~** dormītāre
sleeve n manica f
sleight of hand n praestīgiae fpl
slender adj gracilis, exīlis
slenderness n gracilitās f
slice n frūstum nt ♦ vt secāre
slide n lāpsus m ♦ vi lābī
slight adj levis, exiguus, parvus ♦ n neglegentia f
♦ vt neglegere, offendere
slightingly adv contemptim
slightly adv leviter, paululum
slightness n levitās f
slim adj gracilis
slime n līmus m
sliminess n gracilitās f
slimy adj līmōsus, mūcōsus
sling n funda f ♦ vt mittere, iaculārī
slinger n funditor m
slink vi sē subdūcere
slip n lāpsus m; (*mistake*) offēnsiuncula f; (*plant*)
surculus m ♦ vi lābī; **~ away** ēlābī, dīlābī; **~ out**
ēlābī; (*word*) excidere; **give the ~ to** ēlūdere;
let ~ āmittere, ēmittere; (*opportunity*) ōmittere;
there's many a ~ twixt the cup and the lip
inter ōs et offam multa interveniunt
slipper n solea f
slippery adj lūbricus
slipshod adj neglegēns
slit n rīma f ♦ vt findere, incīdere
sloe n spīnus m
slope n dēclīve nt, clīvus m; (*steep*) dēiectus m ♦ vi
sē dēmittere, vergere
sloping adj dēclīvis, dēvexus; (*up*) adclīvis
slot n rīma f
sloth n inertia f, segnitia f, dēsidia f, ignāvia f
slothful adj ignāvus, iners, segnis
slothfully adv ignāvē, segniter
slouch vi languidē incēdere
slough n (*skin*) exuviae fpl; (*bog*) palūs f
slovenliness n ignāvia f, sordēs fpl
slovenly adj ignāvus, sordidus
slow adj tardus, lentus; (*mind*) hebes
slowly adv tardē, lentē
slowness n tarditās f
sludge n līmus m

slug n līmāx f
sluggard n homō ignāvus m
sluggish adj piger, segnis; (*mind*) hebes
sluggishly adv pigrē, segniter
sluggishness n pigritia f, inertia f
sluice n cataracta f
slumber n somnus m, sopor m ♦ vi dormīre
slump n vīlis annōna f
slur n nota f; **cast ~ on** dētrectāre ♦ vt: **~ words**
balbūtīre
sly adj astūtus, vafer, callidus; **on the sly** ex
opīnātō
slyly adv astūtē, callidē
slyness n astūtia f
smack n (*blow*) ictus m; (*with hand*) alapa f; (*boat*)
lēnunculus m; (*taste*) sapor m ♦ vt ferīre ♦ vi: **~ of**
olēre, redolēre
small adj parvus, exiguus; **how ~** quantulus,
quantillus; **so ~** tantulus; **very ~** perexiguus,
minimus; **a ~ meeting of** īnfrequēns
smaller adj minor
smallest adj minimus
smallness n exiguitās f, brevitās f
small talk n sermunculus m
smart adj (*action*) ācer, alacer; (*dress*) concinnus,
nitidus; (*pace*) vēlōx; (*wit*) facētus, salsus ♦ n
dolor m ♦ vi dolēre; (*fig*) ūrī, mordērī
smartly adv ācriter; nitidē; vēlōciter; facētē
smartness n alacritās f; (*dress*) nitor m; (*wit*)
facētiae fpl, sollertia f
smash n ruīna f ♦ vt frangere, comminuere
smattering n: **get a ~ of** odōrārī, prīmīs labrīs
attingere; **with a ~ of** imbūtus (*abl*)
smear vt oblinere, ungere
smell n (*sense*) odōrātus m; (*odour*) odor m; (*of
cooking*) nīdor m ♦ vt olfacere, odōrārī ♦ vi olēre
smelly adj olidus
smelt vt fundere
smile n rīsus m ♦ vi subrīdēre; **~ at** adrīdēre (*dat*);
~ upon rīdēre ad; (*fig*) secundum esse (*dat*)
smiling adj laetus
smirk vi subrīdēre
smith n faber m
smithy n fabrica f
smock n tunica f
smoke n fūmus m ♦ vi fūmāre
smoky adj fūmōsus
smooth adj lēvis; (*skin*) glaber; (*talk*) blandus;
(*sea*) placidus; (*temper*) aequus; (*voice*) lēvis, teres
♦ vt sternere, līmāre
smoothly adv lēviter, lēniter
smoothness n lēvitās f, lēnitās f
smother vt opprimere, suffocāre
smoulder vi fūmāre
smudge n macula f
smug adj suī contentus
smuggle vt fūrtim importāre
smugness n amor suī m
smut n fūlīgō f
snack n cēnula f; **take a ~** gustāre
snag n impedīmentum nt, scrūpulus m
snail n cochlea f
snake n anguis m, serpēns f
snaky adj vīpereus

snap vt rumpere, praerumpere; ~ **the fingers** digitīs concrepāre ♦ vi rumpī, dissilīre; ~ **at** mordēre; ~ **up** corripere

snare n laqueus m, plaga f, pedica f ♦ vt inrētīre

snarl n gannītus m ♦ vi gannīre

snatch vt rapere, ēripere, adripere, corripere; ~ **at** captāre

sneak n perfidus m ♦ vi conrēpere; ~ **in** sē īnsinuāre; ~ **out** ēlābī

sneaking adj humilis, fūrtīvus

sneer n irrīsiō f ♦ vi irrīdēre, dērīdēre

sneeze n sternūtāmentum nt ♦ vi sternuere

sniff vt odōrārī

snip vt praecīdere, secāre

snob n homō ambitiōsus m

snood n mitra f

snooze vi dormītāre

snore vi stertere

snoring n rhoncus m

snort n fremitus m ♦ vi fremere

snout n rōstrum nt

snow n nix f ♦ vi ningere; **snowed under** nive obrutus; **it is snowing** ningit

snowy adj nivālis; (colour) niveus

snub vt neglegere, praeterīre

snub-nosed adj sīmus

snuff n (candle) fungus m

snug adj commodus

snugly adv commodē

so adv (referring back) sīc; (referring forward) ita; (with adj and adv) tam; (with verb) adeō; (consequence) ergō, itaque, igitur; **and so** itaque; **so great** tantus; **so-so** sīc; **so as to** ut; **so be it** estō; **so big** tantus; **so far** usque adeō, adhūc; **so far as** quod; **so far from** adeō nōn; **so little** tantillus; **so long as** dum; **so many** tot; **so much** adj tantus ♦ adv tantum; (with compar) tantō; **so often** totiēns; **so that** ut (subj); **so that ... not** (purpose) nē; (result) ut nōn; **and so on** deinceps; **not so very** haud ita; **say so** id dīcere

soak vt imbuere, madefacere

soaking adj madidus

soap n sapō m

soar vi in sublīme ferrī, subvolāre; ~ **above** superāre

sob n singultus m ♦ vi singultāre

sober adj sobrius; (conduct) modestus; (mind) sānus

soberly adv sobriē, modestē

sobriety n modestia f, continentia f

so-called adj quī dīcitur

sociability n facilitās f

sociable adj facilis, cōmis

sociably adv faciliter, cōmiter

social adj sociālis, commūnis

socialism n populāris ratiō f

socialist n homō populāris m/f

society n societās f; (class) optimātēs mpl; (being with) convīctus m; **cultivate the ~ of** adsectārī; **secret ~** sodālitās f

sod n caespes m, glaeba f

soda n nitrum nt

sodden adj madidus

soever adv -cumque

sofa n lectus m

soft adj mollis; (fruit) mītis; (voice) submissus; (character) dēlicātus; (words) blandus

soften vt mollīre; (body) ēnervāre; (emotion) lēnīre, mītigāre ♦ vi mollēscere, mītēscere

soft-hearted adj misericors

softly adv molliter, lēniter; blandē

softness n mollitia f, mollitiēs f

soil n sōlum nt, humus f ♦ vt inquināre, foedāre

sojourn n commorātiō f, mānsiō f ♦ vi commorārī

sojourner n hospes m, hospita f

solace n sōlātium nt, levātiō f ♦ vt sōlārī, cōnsōlārī

solar adj sōlis

solder n ferrūmen nt ♦ vt ferrūmināre

soldier n mīles m; **be a ~** mīlitāre; **common ~** manipulāris m, gregārius mīles m; **fellow ~** commīlitō m; **foot ~** pedes m; **old ~** veterānus m ♦ vi mīlitāre

soldierly adj mīlitāris

soldiery n mīles m

sole adj sōlus, ūnus, ūnicus ♦ n (foot) planta f; (fish) solea f

solecism n soloecismus m

solely adv sōlum, tantum, modō

solemn adj gravis; (religion) sanctus

solemnity n gravitās f; sanctitās f

solemnize vt agere

solemnly adv graviter; rītē

solicit vt flāgitāre, obsecrāre

solicitation n flāgitātiō f

solicitor n advocātus m

solicitous adj anxius, trepidus

solicitously adv anxiē, trepidē

solicitude n cūra f, anxietās f

solid adj solidus; (metal) pūrus; (food) firmus; (argument) firmus; (character) cōnstāns, spectātus; **become ~** concrēscere; **make ~** cōgere

solidarity n societās f

solidify vt cōgere ♦ vi concrēscere

solidity n solidītās f

solidly adv firmē, cōnstanter

soliloquize vi sēcum loquī

soliloquy n ūnīus ōrātiō f

solitary adj sōlus, sōlitārius; (instance) ūnicus; (place) dēsertus

solitude n sōlitūdō f

solo n canticum nt

solstice n (summer) sōlstitium nt; (winter) brūma f

solstitial adj sōlstitiālis, brūmālis

soluble adj dissolūbilis

solution n (of puzzle) ēnōdātiō f

solve vt ēnōdāre, explicāre

solvency n solvendī facultās f

solvent adj: **be ~** solvendō esse

sombre adj obscūrus; (fig) tristis

some adj aliquī; (pl) nonnullī, aliquot; ~ **people** sunt quī (subj); ~ **... other** alius ... alius; **for ~ time** aliquamdiū; **with ~ reason** nōn sine causā ♦ pron aliquis; (pl) nonnullī, sunt quī (subj), erant quī (subj)

somebody pron aliquis; ~ **or other** nescioquis

somehow adv quōdammodō, nescio quōmodō

someone pron aliquis; (negative) quisquam; ~ **or other** nescioquis; ~ **else** alius

something *pron* aliquid; ~ **or other** nescioquid; ~ **else** aliud

sometime *adv* aliquandō; (*past*) quondam

sometimes *adv* interdum, nonnumquam; ~ ... ~ modo ... modo

somewhat *adv* aliquantum, nōnnihil, paulum; (*with compar*) paulō, aliquantō

somewhere *adv* alicubi; (*to*) aliquō; ~ **else** alibī; (*to*) aliō; **from** ~ alicunde; **from** ~ **else** aliunde

somnolence *n* somnus *m*

somnolent *adj* sēmisomnus

son *n* fīlius *m*; **small son** fīliolus *m*

song *n* carmen *nt*, cantus *m*

son-in-law *n* gener *m*

sonorous *adj* sonōrus, canōrus

soon *adv* mox, brevī, citō; **as ~ as** ut prīmum, cum prīmum (+*fut perf*), simul āc/atque (+ *perf indic*); **as possible** quam prīmum; **too** ~ praemātūrē, ante tempus

sooner *adv* prius, mātūrius; (*preference*) libentius, potius; ~ **or later** sērius ōcius; **no ~ said than done** dictum factum

soonest *adv* mātūrissimē

soot *n* fūlīgō *f*

soothe *vt* dēlēnīre, permulcēre

soothing *adj* lēnis, blandus

soothingly *adv* blandē

soothsayer *n* hariolus *m*, vātēs *m/f*, haruspex *m*

sooty *adj* fūmōsus

sop *n* offa *f*; (*fig*) dēlēnīmentum *nt*

sophism *n* captiō *f*

sophist *n* sophistēs *m*

sophistical *adj* acūleātus, captiōsus

sophisticated *adj* lepidus, urbānus

sophistry *n* captiō *f*

soporific *adj* sopōrifer, somnifer

soprano *adj* acūtus

sorcerer *n* veneficus *m*

sorceress *n* venefica *f*, saga *f*

sorcery *n* venēficium *nt*; (*means*) venēna *ntpl*, carmina *ntpl*

sordid *adj* sordidus; (*conduct*) illīberālis

sordidly *adv* sordidē

sordidness *n* sordēs *fpl*; illīberālitās *f*

sore *adj* molestus, gravis, acerbus; **feel** ~ dolēre ♦ *n* ulcus *nt*

sorely *adv* graviter, vehementer

sorrel *n* lapathus *f*, lapathum *nt*

sorrow *n* dolor *m*, aegritūdō *f*; (*outward*) maeror *m*; (*for death*) lūctus *m* ♦ *vi* dolēre, maerere, lūgēre

sorrowful *adj* maestus, tristis

sorrowfully *adv* maestē

sorry *adj* paenitēns; (*poor*) miser; **I am ~ for** (*remorse*) mē paenitet, mē piget (*gen*); (*pity*) mē miseret (*gen*)

sort *n* genus *nt*; **a ~ of** quīdam; **all sorts of** omnēs; **the ~ of** tālis; **this ~ of** huiusmodī; **the common** ~ plēbs *f*; **I am not the ~ of man to** nōn is sum quī (*subj*); **I am out of sorts** mihī displiceō ♦ *vt* dīgerere, compōnere; (*votes*) dīribēre

sortie *n* excursiō *f*, excursus *m*, ēruptiō *f*; **make a** ~ ērumpere, excurrere

sot *n* ēbriōsus *m*

sottish *adj* ēbriōsus, tēmulentus

sottishness *n* vīnolentia *f*

soul *n* anima *f*, animus *m*; (*essence*) vīs *f*; (*person*) caput *nt*; **not a** ~ nēmō ūnus; **the ~ of** (*fig*) medulla *f*

soulless *adj* caecus, dūrus

sound *n* sonitus *m*, sonus *m*; (*articulate*) vōx *f*; (*confused*) strepitus *m*; (*loud*) fragor *m*; (*strait*) fretum *nt* ♦ *vt* (*signal*) canere; (*instrument*) īnflāre; (*depth*) scrūtārī, temptāre; (*person*) animum temptāre (*gen*) ♦ *vi* canere, sonāre; (*seem*) vidērī; ~ **a retreat** receptuī canere ♦ *adj* sānus, salūbris; (*health*) firmus; (*sleep*) artus; (*judgment*) exquīsītus; (*argument*) vērus; **safe and** ~ salvus, incolumis

soundly *adv* (*beat*) vehementer; (*sleep*) artē; (*study*) penitus, dīligenter

soundness *n* sānitās *f*, integritās *f*

soup *n* iūs *nt*

sour *adj* acerbus, amārus, acidus; **turn** ~ acēscere; (*fig*) coacēscere ♦ *vt* (*fig*) exacerbāre

source *n* fōns *m*; (*river*) caput *nt*; (*fig*) fōns *m*, orīgō *f*; **have its ~ in** orīrī ex; (*fig*) proficīscī ex

sourness *n* acerbitās *f*; (*temper*) mōrōsitās *f*

souse *vt* immergere

south *n* merīdiēs *f* ♦ *adj* austrālis ♦ *adv* ad merīdiem

south-east *adv* inter sōlis ortum et merīdiem

southerly *adj* ad merīdiem versus

southern *adj* austrālis

south-west *adv* inter occāsum sōlis et merīdiem

south wind *n* auster *m*

souvenir *n* monumentum *nt*

sovereign *n* rēx *m*, rēgīna *f* ♦ *adj* prīnceps, summus

sovereignty *n* rēgnum *nt*, imperium *nt*, prīncipātus *m*; (*of the people*) māiestās *f*

sow[1] *n* scrōfa *f*, sūs *f*

sow[2] *vt* serere; (*field*) cōnserere ♦ *vi* sementem facere

sower *n* sator *m*

sowing *n* sēmentis *f*

spa *n* aquae *fpl*

space *n* (*extension*) spatium *nt*; (*not matter*) ināne *nt*; (*room*) locus *m*; (*distance*) intervallum *nt*; (*time*) spatium *nt*; **open** ~ āarea *f*; **leave a ~ of** intermittere ♦ *vt*: ~ **out** dispōnere

spacious *adj* amplus, capāx

spaciousness *n* amplitūdō *f*

spade *n* pāla *f*, rūtrum *nt*

span *n* (*measure*) palmus *m*; (*extent*) spatium *nt* ♦ *vt* iungere

spangle *n* bractea *f*

spangled *adj* distinctus

spar *n* tignum *nt*

spare *vt* parcere (*dat*); (*to give*) suppeditāre; ~ **time for** vacāre (*dat*) ♦ *adj* exīlis; (*extra*) subsecīvus

sparing *adj* parcus

sparingly *adv* parcē

spark *n* scintilla *f*; (*fig*) igniculus *m*

sparkle *vi* scintillāre, nitēre, micāre

sparrow *n* passer *m*

sparse *adj* rārus

spasm *n* convulsiō *f*

spasmodically *adv* interdum

spatter *vt* aspergere

spawn *n* ōva *ntpl*

speak *vt, vi* loquī; *(make speech)* dīcere, contiōnārī, ōrātiōnem habēre; ~ **out** ēloquī; ~ **to** adloquī; *(converse)* colloquī cum; ~ **well of** bene dīcere *(dat)*; **it speaks for itself** rēs ipsa loquitur

speaker *n* ōrātor *m*

speaking *n*: **art of** ~ dīcendī ars *f*; **practise public** ~ dēclāmāre ◆ *adj*: **likeness** ~ vīvida imāgō

spear *n* hasta *f*

spearman *n* hastātus *m*

special *adj* praecipuus, proprius

speciality *n* proprium *nt*

specially *adv* praecipuē, praesertim

species *n* genus *nt*

specific *adj* certus

specification *n* dēsignātiō *f*

specify *vt* dēnotāre, dēsignāre

specimen *n* exemplar *nt*, exemplum *nt*

specious *adj* speciōsus

speciously *adv* speciōsē

speciousness *n* speciēs *f*

speck *n* macula *f*

speckled *adj* maculīs distinctus

spectacle *n* spectāculum *nt*

spectacular *adj* spectābilis

spectator *n* spectātor *m*

spectral *adj* larvālis

spectre *n* larva *f*

speculate *vi* cōgitāre, coniectūrās facere; (COMM) forō ūtī

speculation *n* cōgitātiō *f*, coniectūra *f*; (COMM) ālea *f*

speculator *n* contemplātor *m*; (COMM) āleātor *m*

speech *n* ōrātiō *f*; *(language)* sermō *m*, lingua *f*; *(to people or troops)* cōntiō *f*; **make a** ~ ōrātiōnem/cōntiōnem habēre

speechless *adj* ēlinguis, mūtus

speed *n* celeritās *f*, cursus *m*, vēlōcitās *f*; **with all** ~ summā celeritāte; **at full** ~ māgnō cursū, incitātus; *(riding)* citātō equō ◆ *vt* adcelerāre, mātūrāre ◆ *vi* properāre, festīnāre

speedily *adv* celeriter, citō

speedy *adj* celer, vēlōx, citus

spell *n* carmen *nt*

spellbound *adj*: **be** ~ obstipēscere

spelt *n* far *nt*

spend *vt* impendere, īnsūmere; *(public money)* ērogāre; *(time)* agere, cōnsūmere, terere; *(strength)* effundere; ~ **itself** *(storm)* dēsaevīre; ~ **on** īnsūmere *(acc & dat)*

spendthrift *n* nepōs *m*, prōdigus *m*

sphere *n* globus *m*; *(of action)* prōvincia *f*

spherical *adj* globōsus

sphinx *n* sphinx *f*

spice *n* condīmentum *nt*; **spices** *pl* odōrēs *mpl* ◆ *vt* condīre

spicy *adj* odōrātus; *(wit)* salsus

spider *n* arānea *f*; **spider's web** arāneum *nt*

spike *n* dēns *m*, clāvus *m*

spikenard *n* nardus *m*

spill *vt* fundere, profundere ◆ *vi* redundāre

spin *vt* *(thread)* nēre, dēdūcere; *(top)* versāre; ~ **out** *(story)* prōdūcere ◆ *vi* circumagī, versārī

spindle *n* fūsus *m*

spine *n* spīna *f*

spineless *adj* ēnervātus

spinster *n* virgō *f*

spiral *adj* intortus ◆ *n* spīra *f*

spire *n* cōnus *m*

spirit *n* *(life)* anima *f*; *(intelligence)* mēns *f*; *(soul)* animus *m*; *(vivacity)* spīritus *m*, vigor *m*, vīs *f*; *(character)* ingenium *nt*; *(intention)* voluntās *f*; *(of an age)* mōrēs *mpl*; *(ghost)* anima *f*; **spirits** *pl* mānēs *mpl*; **full of** ~ alacer, animōsus

spirited *adj* animōsus, ācer

spiritless *adj* iners, frāctus, timidus

spiritual *adj* animī

spit *n* verū *nt* ◆ *vi* spuere, spūtāre; ~ **on** cōnspūtāre; ~ **out** exspuere

spite *n* invidia *f*, malevolentia *f*, līvor *m*; **in** ~ **of me** mē invītō; **in** ~ **of the difficulties** in his angustiīs ◆ *vt* incommodāre, offendere

spiteful *adj* malevolus, malignus, invidus

spitefully *adv* malevolē, malignē

spitefulness *n* malevolentia *f*

spittle *n* spūtum *nt*

splash *n* fragor *m* ◆ *vt* aspergere

spleen *n* splēn *m*; *(fig)* stomachus *m*

splendid *adj* splendidus, lūculentus; īnsignis; *(person)* amplus

splendidly *adv* splendidē, optimē

splendour *n* splendor *m*, fulgor *m*; *(fig)* lautitia *f*, adparātus *m*

splenetic *adj* stomachōsus

splice *vt* iungere

splint *n* ferula *f*

splinter *n* fragmentum *nt*, assula *f* ◆ *vt* findere

split *vt* findere ◆ *vi* dissilīre ◆ *adj* fissus ◆ *n* fissum *nt*; *(fig)* dissidium *nt*

splutter *vi* balbūtīre

spoil *n* praeda *f* ◆ *vt* *(rob)* spoliāre; *(mar)* corrumpere ◆ *vi* corrumpī

spoiler *n* spoliātor *m*; corruptor *m*

spoils *npl* spolia *ntpl*, exuviae *fpl*

spoke *n* radius *m*; **put a** ~ **in one's wheel** inicere scrūpulum *(dat)*

spokesman *n* interpres *m*, ōrātor *m*

spoliation *n* spoliātiō *f*, dīreptiō *f*

spondee *n* spondēus *m*

sponge *n* spongia *f*

sponsor *n* spōnsor *m*; *(fig)* auctor *m*

spontaneity *n* impulsus *m*, voluntās *f*

spontaneous *adj* voluntārius

spontaneously *adv* suā sponte, ultrō

spoon *n* cochlear *nt*

sporadic *adj* rārus

sporadically *adv* passim

sport *n* lūdus *m*; *(in Rome)* campus *m*; *(fun)* iocus *m*; *(ridicule)* lūdibrium *nt*; **make** ~ **of** illūdere *(dat)* ◆ *vi* lūdere

sportive *adj* lascīvus

sportiveness *n* lascīvia *f*

sportsman *n* vēnātor *m*

sportsmanlike *adj* honestus, generōsus

spot *n* macula *f*; *(place)* locus *m*; *(dice)* pūnctum *nt*; **on the** ~ īlicō ◆ *vt* maculāre; *(see)* animadvertere

spotless *adj* integer, pūrus; *(character)* castus

spotted *adj* maculōsus

spouse *n* coniunx *m/f*

spout n (of jug) ōs nt; (pipe) canālis m ♦ vi ēmicāre
sprain vt intorquēre
sprawl vi sē fundere
sprawling adj fūsus
spray n aspergō f ♦ vt aspergere
spread vt pandere, extendere; (news) dīvulgāre; (infection) vulgāre ♦ vi patēre; (rumour) mānāre, incrēbrēscere; (feeling) glīscere
spreadeagle vt dispandere
spreading adj (tree) patulus
spree n cōmissātiō f
sprig n virga f
sprightliness n alacritās f
sprightly adj alacer, hilaris
spring n (season) vēr nt; (water) fōns m; (leap) saltus m ♦ vi (grow) crēscere, ēnāscī; (leap) salīre; ~ **from** orīrī ex, proficīscī ex; ~ **on to** īnsilīre in (acc); ~ **up** exorīrī, exsilīre ♦ vt: ~ **a leak** rīmās agere; ~ **a surprise on** admīrātiōnēm movēre (dat) ♦ adj vērnus
springe n laqueus m
sprinkle vt aspergere; ~ **on** īnspergere (dat)
sprint vi currere
sprout n surculus m ♦ vi fruticārī
spruce adj nitidus, concinnus
sprung adj ortus, oriundus
spume n spūma f
spur n calcar nt; ~ **of a hill** prōminēns collis; **on the ~ of the moment** ex tempore ♦ vt incitāre; ~ **the willing horse** currentem incitāre; ~ **on** concitāre
spurious adj falsus, fūcōsus, fictus
spurn vt spernere, aspernārī, respuere
spurt vi ēmicāre; (run) sē incitāre ♦ n impetus m
spy n speculātor m, explōrātor m ♦ vi speculārī ♦ vt cōnspicere; **spy out** explōrāre
squabble n iūrgium nt ♦ vi rixārī
squad n (MIL) decuria f
squadron n (cavalry) āla f, turma f; (ships) classis f
squalid adj sordidus, dēfōrmis
squall n procella f
squally adj procellōsus
squalor n sordēs fpl, squālor m
squander vt dissipāre, disperdere, effundere
squanderer n prōdigus m
square n quadrātum nt; (town) ārea f ♦ vt quadrāre; (account) subdūcere ♦ vi cōnstāre, congruere ♦ adj quadrātus
squash vt conterere, contundere
squat vi subsīdere ♦ adj brevis atque obēsus
squatter n (on land) agripeta m
squawk vi crōcīre
squeak n strīdor m ♦ vi strīdēre
squeal n vāgītus m ♦ vi vāgīre
squeamish adj fastīdiōsus; **feel ~** nauseāre, fastīdīre
squeamishness n fastīdium nt, nausea f
squeeze vt premere, comprimere; ~ **out** exprimere
squint adj perversus ♦ n: **person with a ~** strabō m ♦ vi strabō esse
squinter n strabō m
squinting adj paetus
squire n armiger m; (landed) dominus m
squirm vi volūtārī
squirrel n sciūrus m

squirt vt ēicere, effundere ♦ vi ēmicāre
stab n ictus m, vulnus nt ♦ vt fodere, ferīre, percutere
stability n stabilitās f, firmitās f, cōnstantia f
stabilize vt stabilīre, firmāre
stable adj firmus, stabilis ♦ n stabulum nt, equīle nt; **shut the ~ door after the horse is stolen** clipeum post vulnera sūmere
stack n acervus m ♦ vt congerere, cumulāre
stadium n spatium nt
staff n scīpiō m, virga f; (augur's) lituus m; (officers) contubernālēs mpl
stag n cervus m
stage n pulpitum nt, proscēnium nt; (theatre) scēna f, theātrum nt; (scene of action) campus m; (of journey) iter nt; (of progress) gradus m ♦ adj scēnicus ♦ vt (play) dare, docēre
stage fright n horror m
stagger vi titubāre ♦ vt obstupefacere
stagnant adj iners
stagnate vi (fig) cessāre, refrīgēscere
stagnation n cessātiō f, torpor m
stagy adj scēnicus
staid adj sevērus, gravis
stain n macula f, lābēs f; (fig) dēdecus nt, ignōminia f ♦ vt maculāre, foedāre, contāmināre; ~ **with** īnficere (abl)
stainless adj pūrus, integer
stair n scālae fpl, gradus mpl
staircase n scālae fpl
stake n pālus m, stīpes m; (pledge) pignus nt; **be at ~** agī, in discrīmine esse ♦ vt (wager) dēpōnere
stale adj obsolētus, effētus; (wine) vapidus
stalemate n: **reach a ~** ad incitās redigī
stalk n (corn) calamus m; (plant) stīpes m ♦ vi incēdere ♦ vt vēnārī, īnsidiārī (dat)
stall n (animal) stabulum nt; (seat) subsellium nt; (shop) taberna f ♦ vt stabulāre
stallion n equus m
stalwart adj ingēns, rōbustus, fortis
stamina n patientia f
stammer n haesitātiō f ♦ vi balbūtīre
stammering adj balbus
stamp n fōrma f; (mark) nota f, signum nt; (of feet) supplōsiō f ♦ vt imprimere; (coin) ferīre, signāre; (fig) inūrere; ~ **one's feet** pedem supplōdere; ~ **out** exstinguere
stampede n discursus m; (fig) pavor m ♦ vi discurrere; (fig) expavēscere
stance n status m
stanchion n columna f
stand n (position) statiō f; (platform) suggestus m; **make a ~** resistere, restāre ♦ vi stāre; (remain) manēre; (matters) sē habēre ♦ vt statuere; (tolerate) ferre, tolerāre; ~ **against** resistere (dat); ~ **aloof** abstāre; ~ **by** adsistere (dat); (friend) adesse (dat); (promise) praestāre; ~ **convicted** manifestum tenērī; ~ **down** concēdere; ~ **fast** cōnsistere; ~ **one's ground** in locō perstāre; ~ **for** (office) petere; (meaning) significāre; (policy) postulāre; ~ **in awe of** in metū habēre; ~ **in need of** indigēre (abl); ~ **on** īnsistere in (abl); ~ **on end** horrēre; ~ **on one's dignity** gravitātem suam tuērī; ~ **out** ēminēre, exstāre; (against) resistere (dat); (to sea) in altum prōvehī; ~ **out of the way of** dēcēdere (dat); ~ **over** (case)

ampliāre; ~ **still** cōnsistere, īnsistere; ~ **to reason** sequī; ~ **trial** reum fierī; ~ **up** surgere, cōnsurgere; ~ **up for** dēfendere, adesse *(dat)*; ~ **up to** respōnsāre *(dat)*

standard *n* (MIL) signum *nt*; *(measure)* nōrma *f*; ~ **author** scrīptor classicus *m*; **up to** ~ iūstus; **judge by the** ~ **of** referre ad

standard-bearer *n* signifer *m*

standing *adj* perpetuus ♦ *n* status *m*; *(social)* locus *m*, ōrdō *m*; **of long** ~ inveterātus; **be of long** ~ inveterāscere

stand-offish *adj* tēctus

standstill *n*: **be at a** ~ haerēre, frīgēre; **bring to a** ~ ad incitās redigere; **come to a** ~ īnsistere

stanza *n* tetrastichon *nt*

staple *n* uncus *m* ♦ *adj* praecipuus

star *n* stēlla *f*, astrum *nt*; sīdus *nt*; **shooting stars** acontiae *fpl*

starboard *adj* dexter

starch *n* amylum *nt*

stare *n* obtūtus *m* ♦ *vi* intentīs oculīs intuērī, stupēre; ~ **at** contemplārī

stark *adj* rigidus; simplex ♦ *adv* plānē, omnīnō

starling *n* sturnus *m*

starry *adj* stēllātus

start *n* initium *nt*; *(movement)* saltus *m*; *(journey)* profectiō *f*; **by fits and starts** carptim; **have a day's** ~ **on** diē antecēdere ♦ *vt* incipere, īnstituere; *(game)* excitāre; *(process)* movēre ♦ *vi (with fright)* resilīre; *(journey)* proficīscī; ~ **up** exsilīre

starting place *n* carcerēs *mpl*

startle *vt* excitāre, terrēre

starvation *n* famēs *f*

starve *vi* fāme cōnficī; *(cold)* frīgēre ♦ *vt* fāme ēnecāre

starveling *n* famēlicus *m*

state *n (condition)* status *m*, condiciō *f*; *(pomp)* adparātus *m*; (POL) cīvitās *f*, rēs pūblica *f*; **the ~ of affairs is** ita sē rēs habet; **I know the ~ of affairs** quō in locō rēs sit sciō; **of the** ~ pūblicus ♦ *adj* pūblicus ♦ *vt* adfirmāre, expōnere, profitērī; ~ **one's case** causam dīcere

stateliness *n* māiestās *f*, gravitās *f*

stately *adj* gravis, grandis, nōbilis

statement *n* adfirmātiō *f*, dictum *nt*; *(witness)* testimōnium *nt*

state of health *n* valētūdō *f*

state of mind *n* adfectiō *f*

statesman *n* vir reī pūblicae gerendae perītus *m*, cōnsilī pūblicī auctor *m*

statesmanlike *adj* prūdēns

statesmanship *n* cīvīlis prūdentia *f*

static *adj* stabilis

station *n* locus *m*; (MIL) statiō *f*; *(social)* locus *m*, ōrdō *m* ♦ *vt* collocāre, pōnere; *(in different places)* dispōnere

stationary *adj* immōtus, statārius, stabilis

statistics *n* cēnsus *m*

statuary *n* fictor *m*

statue *n* statua *f*, signum *nt*, imāgō *f*

statuette *n* sigillum *nt*

stature *n* fōrma *f*, statūra *f*

status *n* locus *m*

status quo *n*: **restore the** ~ ad integrum restituere

statutable *adj* lēgitimus

statute *n* lēx *f*

staunch *vt (blood)* sistere ♦ *adj* fīdus, cōnstāns

stave *vt* perrumpere, perfringere; ~ **off** arcēre

stay *n* firmāmentum *nt*; *(fig)* columen *nt*; *(sojourn)* mānsiō *f*, commorātiō *f* ♦ *vt (prop)* fulcīre; *(stop)* dētinēre, dēmorārī ♦ *vi* manēre, commorārī

stead *n* locus *m*; **stand one in good** ~ prōdesse *(dat)*

steadfast *adj* firmus, stabilis, cōnstāns; ~ **at home** tenēre sē domī

steadfastly *adv* cōnstanter

steadfastness *n* firmitās *f*, cōnstantia *f*

steadily *adv* firmē, cōnstanter

steadiness *n* stabilitās *f*; *(fig)* cōnstantia *f*

steady *adj* stabilis, firmus; *(fig)* gravis, cōnstāns

steak *n* offa *f*

steal *vt* surripere, fūrārī ♦ *vi*: ~ **away** sē subdūcere; ~ **over** subrēpere *(dat)*; ~ **into** sē īnsinuāre in *(acc)*; ~ **a march on** occupāre

stealing *n* fūrtum *nt*

stealth *n* fūrtum *nt*; **by** ~ fūrtim, clam

stealthily *adv* fūrtim, clam

stealthy *adj* fūrtīvus, clandestīnus

steam *n* aquae vapor *m*, fūmus *m* ♦ *vi* fūmāre

steed *n* equus *m*

steel *n* ferrum *nt*, chalybs *m* ♦ *adj* ferreus ♦ *vt* dūrāre; ~ **oneself** obdūrēscere

steely *adj* ferreus

steelyard *n* statēra *f*

steep *adj* arduus, praeceps, praeruptus; *(slope)* dēclīvis ♦ *vt* imbuere

steeple *n* turris *f*

steepness *n* arduum *nt*

steer *vi*, *vt* gubernāre, regere, dīrigere ♦ *n* iuvencus *m*

steering *n* gubernātiō *f*

steersman *n* gubernātor *m*; rector *m*

stellar *adj* stēllārum

stem *n* stīpes *m*, truncus *m*; *(ship)* prōra *f* ♦ *vt* adversārī *(dat)*; ~ **the tide of** *(fig)* obsistere *(dat)*

stench *n* foetor *m*

stenographer *n* exceptor *m*, āctuārius *m*

stenography *n* notae *fpl*

stentorian *adj (voice)* ingēns

step *n* gradus *m*; *(track)* vestīgium *nt*; *(of stair)* gradus *m*; ~ **by** ~ gradātim; **flight of steps** gradus *mpl*; **take a** ~ gradum facere; **take steps to** ratiōnem inīre ut, vidēre ut; **march in** ~ in numerum īre; **out of** ~ extrā numerum ♦ *vi* gradī, incēdere; ~ **aside** dēcēdere; ~ **back** regredī; ~ **forward** prōdīre; ~ **on** insistere *(dat)*

stepdaughter *n* prīvīgna *f*

stepfather *n* vītricus *m*

stepmother *n* noverca *f*

stepson *n* prīvīgnus *m*

stereotyped *adj* trītus

sterile *adj* sterilis

sterility *n* sterilitās *f*

sterling *adj* integer, probus, gravis

stern *adj* dūrus, sevērus; *(look)* torvus ♦ *n* puppis *f*

sternly *adv* sevērē, dūriter

sternness *n* sevēritās *f*

stew *vt* coquere

steward *n* prōcūrātor *m*; *(of estate)* vīlicus *m*

stewardship n prōcūrātiō f
stick n (for beating) fūstis m; (for walking)
baculum nt ♦ vi haerēre; ~ **at nothing** ad
omnia dēscendere; ~ **fast in** inhaerēre
(dat), inhaerēscere in (abl); ~ **out** ēminēre;
~ **to** adhaerēre (dat); ~ **up** ēminēre; ~ **up for**
dēfendere ♦ vt (with glue) conglūtināre; (with
point) fīgere; ~ **into** īnfīgere; ~ **top on** praefigere
stickler n dīligēns (gen)
sticky adj lentus, tenāx
stiff adj rigidus; (difficult) difficilis; **be** ~ rigēre
stiffen vt rigidum facere ♦ vi rigēre
stiffly adv rigidē
stiff-necked adj obstinātus
stiffness n rigor m
stifle vt suffocāre; (fig) opprimere, restinguere
stigma n nota f
stigmatize vt notāre
stile n saepēs f
still adj immōtus, tranquillus, quiētus;
tacitus ♦ vt lēnīre, sēdāre ♦ adv etiam, adhūc,
etiamnum; (past) etiam tum; (with compar)
etiam; (adversative) tamen, nihilōminus
stillness n quiēs f, silentium nt
stilly adj tacitus
stilted adj (language) īnflātus
stilts n grallae fpl
stimulant n stimulus m
stimulate vt stimulāre, acuere, exacuere,
excitāre
stimulus n stimulus m
sting n aculeus m; (wound) ictus m; (fig) aculeus m,
morsus m ♦ vt pungere, mordēre
stingily adv sordidē
stinginess n avāritia f, sordēs fpl, tenācitās f
stinging adj (words) aculeātus, mordāx
stingy adj sordidus, tenāx
stink n foetor m ♦ vi foetere; ~ **of** olēre
stinking adj foetidus
stint n modus m; **without** ~ abundē ♦ vt
circumscrībere
stipend n mercēs f
stipulate vt pacīscī, stipulārī
stipulation n condiciō f, pactum nt
stir n tumultus m ♦ vt movēre, agitāre; (fig)
commovēre; ~ **up** excitāre, incitāre ♦ vi movērī
stirring adj impiger, tumultuōsus; (speech)
ārdēns
stitch vt suere ♦ n sūtūra f; (in side) dolor m
stock n stirps f, genus nt, gēns f; (equipment)
īnstrūmenta ntpl; (supply) cōpia f; (investment)
pecūniae fpl; **livestock** rēs pecuāria f ♦ vt
īnstruere ♦ adj commūnis, trītus
stockade n vallum nt
stock dove n palumbēs m/f
stock in trade n īnstrūmenta ntpl
stocks n (ship) nāvālia ntpl; (torture) compedēs fpl
stock-still adj plānē immōtus
stocky adj brevis atque obēsus
stodgy adj crūdus, īnsulsus
stoic n Stōicus m ♦ adj Stōicus
stoical adj dūrus, patiēns
stoically adv patienter
stoicism n Stōicōrum ratiō f, Stōicōrum
disciplīna f
stoke vt agitāre

stole n stola f
stolid adj stolidus
stolidity n īnsulsitās f
stolidly adv stolidē
stomach n stomachus m; venter m ♦ vt patī,
tolerāre
stone n lapis m, saxum nt; (precious) gemma
f, lapillus m; (of fruit) acinum nt; **leave no**
~ **unturned** omnia experīrī; **kill two birds
with one** ~ ūnō saltū duōs aprōs capere; **hewn**
~ saxum quadrātum; **unhewn** ~ caementum nt
♦ vt lapidibus percutere ♦ adj lapideus; ~ **blind**
plānē caecus; ~ **deaf** plānē surdus
stonecutter n lapicīda m
stony adj (soil) lapidōsus; (path) scrūpōsus;
(feeling) dūrus, ferreus
stool n sēdēcula f
stoop vi sē dēmittere; ~ **to** dēscendere in (acc)
stop n mora f; (punctuation) pūnctum nt; **come to
a** ~ īnsistere; **put a** ~ **to** comprimere, dirimere
♦ vt sistere, inhibēre, fīnīre; (restrain) cohibēre;
(hole) obtūrāre; ~ **up** occlūdere, interclūdere ♦ vi
dēsinere, dēsistere; (motion) īnsistere
stopgap n tībīcen m
stoppage n interclūsiō f, impedīmentum nt
stopper n obtūrāmentum nt
store n cōpia f; (place) horreum nt; (for wine)
apothēca f; **be in** ~ **for** manēre; **set great** ~ **by**
māgnī aestimāre ♦ vt condere, repōnere;
~ **away** recondere; ~ **up** repōnere, congerere
storehouse n (fig) thēsaurus m
storekeeper n cellārius m
storeship n nāvis frūmentāria f
storey n tabulātum nt
stork n cicōnia f
storm n tempestās f, procella f; **take by**
~ expugnāre ♦ vt (MIL) expugnāre ♦ vi saevīre;
~ **at** īnsectārī, invehī in (acc)
stormbound adj tempestāte dētentus
stormer n expugnātor m
storming n expugnātiō f
stormy adj turbidus, procellōsus; (fig)
turbulentus
story n fābula f, nārrātiō f; (short) fābella f;
(untrue) mendācium nt
storyteller n nārrātor m; (liar) mendāx m
stout adj pinguis; (brave) fortis; (strong) validus,
rōbustus; (material) firmus
stouthearted adj māgnanimus
stoutly adv fortiter
stove n camīnus m, fornāx f
stow vt repōnere, condere; ~ **away** vi in nāvī
dēlitēscere
straddle vi vāricāre
straggle vi deerrāre, pālārī
straggler n pālāns m
straggling adj dispersus, rārus
straight adj rēctus, dīrēctus; (fig) apertus, vērāx;
in a ~ **line** rēctā, ē regiōne; **set** ~ dīrigere ♦ adv
dīrēctō, rēctā
straighten vt corrigere, extendere
straightforward adj simplex, dīrēctus; (easy)
facilis
straightforwardness n simplicitās f
straightness n (fig) integritās f
straightway adv statim, extemplō

strain n contentiō f; (effort) labor m; (music) modī
mpl; (breed) genus nt ♦ vt intendere, contendere;
(injure) nimiā contentiōne dēbilitāre; (liquid)
dēliquāre, percōlāre ♦ vi ēnītī, vīrēs contendere
strained adj (language) accessītus
strainer n cōlum nt
strait adj angustus ♦ n fretum nt; **straits** pl
angustiae fpl
straiten vt coartāre, contrahere; **straitened
circumstances** angustiae fpl
strait-laced adj tristis, sevērus
strand n lītus nt; (of rope) fīlum nt ♦ vt (ship) ēicere
strange adj novus, īnsolitus; (foreign) peregrīnus;
(another's) aliēnus; (ignorant) rudis, expers
strangely adv mīrē, mīrum in modum
strangeness n novitās f, īnsolentia f
stranger n (from abroad) advena f; peregrīnus
m; (visiting) hospes m, hospita f; (not of the family)
externus m; (unknown) ignōtus m
strangle vt strangulāre, laqueō gulam frangere
strap n lōrum nt, habēna f
strapping adj grandis
stratagem n cōnsilium nt, fallācia f
strategic adj (action) prūdēns; (position) idōneus
strategist n artis bellicae perītus m
strategy n ars imperātōria f; cōnsilia ntpl
straw n (stalk) culmus m; (collective) strāmentum
nt; **not care a ~ for** floccī nōn facere ♦ adj
strāmenticius
strawberry n frāgum nt
strawberry tree n arbutus m
stray vt aberrāre, deerrāre; vagārī ♦ adj
errābundus
streak n līnea f, macula f; (light) radius m;
(character) vēna f ♦ vt maculāre
stream n flūmen nt, fluvius m; **down ~** secundō
flūmine; **up ~** adversō flūmine ♦ vi fluere, sē
effundere; **~ into** īnfluere in (acc)
streamlet n rīvus m, rīvulus m
street n via f, platea f
strength n vīrēs fpl; (of material) firmitās f; (fig)
rōbur nt, nervī mpl; (MIL) numerus m; **know the
enemy's ~** quot sint hostēs scīre; **on the ~ of**
frētus (abl)
strengthen vt firmāre, corrōborāre; (position)
mūnīre
strenuous adj impiger, strēnuus, sēdulus
strenuously adv impigrē, strēnuē
strenuousness n industria f
stress n (words) ictus m; (meaning) vīs f; (importance)
mōmentum nt; (difficulty) labor m; **lay great ~ on**
in māgnō discrīmine pōnere ♦ vt exprimere
stretch n spatium nt, tractus m; **at a ~** sine ullā
intermissiōne ♦ vt tendere, intendere; (length)
prōdūcere, extendere; (facts) in māius crēdere;
~ a point indulgēre; **~ before** obtendere;
~ forth porrigere; **~ oneself** (on ground) sternī;
~ out porrigere, extendere ♦ vi extendī,
patēscere
strew vt (things) sternere; (place) cōnsternere
stricken adj saucius
strict adj (defined) ipse, certus; (severe) sevērus,
rigidus; (accurate) dīligēns
strictly adv sevērē; dīligenter; **~ speaking**
scīlicet, immo
strictness n sevēritās f; dīligentia f

stricture n vītuperātiō f
stride n passus m; **make great strides** (fig)
multum prōficere ♦ vi incēdere, ingentēs
gradūs ferre
strident adj asper
strife n discordia f, pugna f
strike vt ferīre, percutere; (instrument) pellere,
pulsāre; (sail) subdūcere; (tent) dētendere; (mind)
venīre in (acc); (camp) movēre; (fear into) incutere
in (acc); **~ against** offendere; **~ out** dēlēre; **~ up**
(music) incipere; **~ a bargain** pacīscī; **be struck**
vāpulāre ♦ vi (work) cessāre
striking adj īnsignis, īnsignītus, ēgregius
strikingly adv īnsignītē
string n (cord) resticula f; (succession) seriēs f;
(instrument) nervus m; (bow) nervus m; **have two
strings to one's bow** duplicī spē ūtī ♦ vt (bow)
intendere; (together) coniungere
stringency n sevēritās f
stringent adj sevērus
strip vt nūdāre, spoliāre, dēnūdāre; **~ off** exuere;
(leaves) stringere, dēstringere ♦ n lacinia f
stripe n virga f; (on tunic) clāvus m; **stripes** pl
verbera ntpl
striped adj virgātus
stripling n adulescentulus m
strive vi nītī, ēnītī, contendere; (contend) certāre
stroke n ictus m; (lightning) fulmen nt; (oar)
pulsus m; (pen) līnea f; **~ of luck** fortūna
secunda f ♦ vt mulcēre, dēmulcēre
stroll vi deambulāre, spatiārī
strong adj fortis, validus; (health) rōbustus,
firmus; (material) firmus; (smell) gravis;
(resources) pollēns, potēns; (feeling) ācer, māgnus;
(language) vehemēns, probrōsus; **be ~** valēre; **be
twenty ~** vīgintī esse numerō
strongbox n arca f
stronghold n arx f
strongly adv validē, vehementer, fortiter,
ācriter, graviter
strong-minded adj pertināx, cōnstans
strophe n stropha f
structure n aedificium nt; (form) structūra f;
(arrangement) compositiō f
struggle n (effort) cōnātus m; (fight) pugna f,
certāmen nt ♦ vi nītī; certāre, contendere; (fight)
luctārī; **~ upwards** ēnītī
strut vi māgnificē incēdere
stubble n stipula f
stubborn adj pertināx, pervicāx
stubbornly adv pertināciter, pervicāciter
stubbornness n pertinācia f, pervicācia f
stucco n gypsum nt
stud n clāvus m; (horses) equī mpl
studded adj distinctus
student n discipulus m; **be a ~ of** studēre (dat)
studied adj meditātus, accūrātus; (language)
exquīsītus
studio n officīna f
studious adj litterīs dēditus, litterārum
studiōsus; (careful) attentus
studiously adv dē industriā
study vt studēre (dat); (prepare) meditārī; **~ under**
audīre ♦ n studium nt; (room) bibliothēca f
stuff n māteria f; (cloth) textile nt ♦ vt farcīre,
refercīre; (with food) sagīnāre

stuffing n sagina f; (of cushion) tōmentum nt
stultify vt ad inritum redigere
stumble vi offendere; ~ **upon** incidere in (acc), offendere
stumbling block n offēnsiō f
stump n stīpes m
stun vt stupefacere; (fig) obstupefacere, cōnfundere
stunned adj attonitus
stunt vt corporis auctum inhibēre
stunted adj curtus
stupefaction n stupor m
stupefied adj: **be** ~ stupēre, obstupefierī
stupefy vt obstupefacere
stupendous adj mīrus, mīrificus
stupid adj stultus, hebes, ineptus
stupidity n stultitia f
stupidly adv stultē, ineptē
stupor n stupor m
sturdily adv fortiter
sturdiness n rōbur nt, firmitās f
sturdy adj fortis, rōbustus
sturgeon n acipēnser m
stutter vi balbūtire
stuttering adj balbus
sty n hara f
style n (kind) genus nt, ratiō f; (of dress) habitus m; (of prose) ēlocūtiō f, ōrātiō f; (pen) stilus m ♦ vt appellāre
stylish adj ēlegāns, lautus, expolītus
stylishly adv ēleganter
suasion n suāsiō f
suave adj blandus, urbānus
suavity n urbānitās f
subaltern n succenturiō m
subdivide vt dīvidere
subdivision n pars f, mōmentum nt
subdue vt subigere, dēvincere, redigere, domāre; (fig) cohibēre
subdued adj dēmissus, summissus
subject n (person) cīvis m/f; (matter) rēs f; (theme) locus m, argūmentum nt ♦ adj subiectus; ~ **to** obnoxius (dat) ♦ vt subicere; obnoxium reddere
subjection n servitūs f
subjective adj proprius
subject matter n māteria f
subjoin vt subicere, subiungere
subjugate vt subigere, dēbellāre, domāre
sublime adj sublīmis, ēlātus, excelsus
sublimely adv excelsē
sublimity n altitūdō f, ēlātiō f
submarine adj submersus
submerge vt dēmergere; (flood) inundāre ♦ vi sē dēmergere
submersed adj submersus
submission n obsequium nt, servitium nt; (fig) patientia f
submissive adj submissus, docilis, obtemperāns
submissively adv submissē, oboedienter, patienter
submit vi sē dēdere; ~ **to** pārēre (dat), obtemperāre (dat), patī, subīre ♦ vt (proposal) referre
subordinate adj subiectus, secundus ♦ vt subiungere, subicere

suborn vt subicere, subōrnāre
subpoena vt testimōnium dēnūntiāre (dat)
subscribe vt (name) subscrībere; (money) cōnferre
subscription n collātiō f
subsequent adj sequēns, posterior
subsequently adv posteā, mox
subserve vt subvenīre (dat), commodāre
subservience n obsequium nt
subservient adj obsequēns; (thing) ūtilis, commodus
subside vi dēsīdere, resīdere; (fever) dēcēdere; (wind) cadere; (passion) dēfervēscere
subsidence n lābēs f
subsidiary adj subiectus, secundus
subsidize vt pecūniās suppeditāre (dat)
subsidy n pecūniae fpl, vectīgal nt
subsist vi cōnstāre, sustentārī
subsistence n vīctus m
substance n (matter) rēs f, corpus nt; (essence) nātūra f; (gist) summa f; (reality) rēs f; (wealth) opēs fpl
substantial adj solidus; (real) vērus; (important) gravis; (rich) opulentus, dīves
substantially adv rē; māgnā ex parte
substantiate vt cōnfirmāre
substitute vt subicere, repōnere, substituere ♦ n vicārius m
substratum n fundāmentum nt
subterfuge n latebra f, perfugium nt
subterranean adj subterrāneus
subtle adj (fine) subtīlis; (shrewd) acūtus, astūtus
subtlety n subtīlitās f; acūmen nt, astūtia f
subtly adv subtīliter; acūtē, astūte
subtract vt dētrahere, dēmere; (money) dēdūcere
subtraction n dētractiō f, dēductiō f
suburb n suburbium nt
suburban adj suburbānus
subvention n pecūniae fpl
subversion n ēversiō f, ruīna f
subversive adj sēditiōsus
subvert vt ēvertere, subruere
subverter n ēversor m
succeed vi (person) rem bene gerere; (activity) prosperē ēvenīre; ~ **in obtaining** impetrāre ♦ vt īnsequī, excipere, succēdere (dat)
success n bonus ēventus m, rēs bene gesta f
successful adj fēlīx; (thing) secundus; **be** ~ rem bene gerere; (play) stāre
successfully adv fēlīciter, prosperē, bene
succession n (coming next) successiō f; (line) seriēs f, ōrdō m; **alternate** ~ vicissitūdō f; **in** ~ deinceps, ex ōrdine
successive adj continuus, perpetuus
successively adv deinceps, ex ōrdine; (alternately) vicissim
successor n successor m
succinct adj brevis, pressus
succinctly adv breviter, pressē
succour n auxilium nt, subsidium nt ♦ vt subvenīre (dat), succurrere (dat), opem ferre (dat)
succulence n sūcus m
succulent adj sūcidus
succumb vi succumbere, dēficere
such adj tālis, ēiusmodī, hūiusmodī; (size) tantus; **at** ~ **a time** id temporis; ~ **great** tantus

suchlike *adj* hūiusmodī, ēiusdem generis
suck *vt* sūgere; ~ **in** sorbēre; ~ **up** exsorbēre, ēbibere
sucker *n* surculus *m*
sucking *adj* (*child*) lactēns
suckle *vt* nūtrīcārī, mammam dare (*dat*)
suckling *n* lactēns *m/f*
sudden *adj* subitus, repentīnus
suddenly *adv* subitō, repente
sue *vt* in iūs vocāre, lītem intendere (*dat*); **sue for** rogāre, petere, ōrāre
suffer *vt* patī, ferre, tolerāre; (*injury*) accipere; (*loss*) facere; (*permit*) patī, sinere ♦ *vi* dolōre adficī; ~ **defeat** clādem accipere; ~ **from** labōrāre ex, adficī (*abl*); ~ **for** poenās dare (*gen*)
sufferable *adj* tolerābilis
sufferance *n* patientia *f*, tolerantia *f*
suffering *n* dolor *m*
suffice *vi* sufficere, suppetere
sufficiency *n* satis
sufficient *adj* idōneus, satis (*gen*)
sufficiently *adv* satis
suffocate *vt* suffocāre
suffrage *n* suffrāgium *nt*
suffuse *vt* suffundere
sugar *n* saccharon *nt*
suggest *vt* admonēre, inicere, subicere; ~ **itself** occurrere
suggestion *n* admonitiō *f*; **at the ~ of** admonitū (*gen*); **at my ~** mē auctōre
suicidal *adj* fūnestus
suicide *n* mors voluntāria *f*; **commit ~** mortem sibī cōnscīscere
suit *n* (LAW) līs *f*, āctiō *f*; (*clothes*) vestītus *m* ♦ *vt* convenīre (*dat*), congruere (*dat*); (*dress*) sedēre (*dat*), decēre; **it suits** decet; **to ~ me** dē meā sententiā
suitability *n* convenientia *f*
suitable *adj* aptus (+ *dat or* 'ad' + *acc*), idōneus (+ *dat or* 'ad' + *acc*)
suitably *adv* aptē, decenter
suite *n* comitēs *mpl*, comitātus *m*
suitor *n* procus *m*, amāns *m*
sulk *vi* aegrē ferre, mōrōsum esse
sulky *adj* mōrōsus, tristis
sullen *adj* tristis, mōrōsus
sullenness *n* mōrōsitās *f*
sully *vt* īnfuscāre, contāmināre
sulphur *n* sulfur *nt*
sultriness *n* aestus *m*
sultry *adj* aestuōsus
sum *n* summa *f*; **sum of money** pecūnia *f* ♦ *vt* subdūcere, computāre; **sum up** summātim dēscrībere; **to sum up** ūnō verbō, quid plūra?
summarily *adv* strictim, summātim; sine morā
summarize *vt* summātim dēscrībere
summary *n* summārium *nt*, epitomē *f* ♦ *adj* subitus, praesēns
summer *n* aestās *f* ♦ *adj* aestīvus; **of ~** aestīvus
summit *n* vertex *m*, culmen *nt*; (*fig*) fastīgium *nt*; **the ~ of** summus
summon *vt* arcessere; (*meeting*) convocāre; (*witness*) citāre; ~ **up courage** animum sūmere
summons *n* (LAW) vocātiō *f* ♦ *vt* in iūs vocāre, diem dīcere (*dat*)
sumptuary *adj* sūmptuārius

sumptuous *adj* sūmptuōsus, adparātus, māgnificus, lautus
sumptuously *adv* sūmptuōsē, māgnificē
sun *n* sōl *m* ♦ *vt*: **sun oneself** aprīcārī
sunbeam *n* radius *m*
sunburnt *adj* adūstus
sunder *vt* sēparāre, dīvidere
sundial *n* sōlārium *nt*
sundry *adj* dīversī, complūrēs
sunlight *n* sōl *m*
sunlit *adj* aprīcus
sunny *adj* aprīcus, serēnus
sunrise *n* sōlis ortus *m*
sunset *n* sōlis occāsus *m*
sunshade *n* umbella *f*
sunshine *n* sōl *m*
sup *vi* cēnāre
superabundance *n* abundantia *f*
superabundant *adj* nimius
superabundantly *adv* satis superque
superannuated *adj* ēmeritus
superb *adj* māgnificus
superbly *adv* māgnificē
supercilious *adj* adrogāns, superbus
superciliously *adv* adroganter, superbē
superciliousness *n* adrogantia *f*, fastus *m*
supererogation *n*: **of ~** ultrō factus
superficial *adj* levis; **acquire a ~ knowledge of** prīmīs labrīs gustāre
superficiality *n* levitās *f*
superficially *adv* leviter, strictim
superfluity *n* abundantia *f*
superfluous *adj* supervacāneus, nimius; **be ~** redundāre
superhuman *adj* dīvīnus, hūmānō māior
superimpose *vt* superimpōnere
superintend *vt* prōcūrāre, praeesse (*dat*)
superintendence *n* cūra *f*
superintendent *n* cūrātor *m*, praefectus *m*
superior *adj* melior, amplior; **be ~** praestāre, superāre ♦ *n* prīnceps *m*, praefectus *m*
superiority *n* praestantia *f*; **have the ~** superāre; (*in numbers*) plūrēs esse
superlative *adj* ēgregius, optimus
supernatural *adj* dīvīnus
supernaturally *adv* dīvīnitus
supernumerary *adj* adscrīptīcius; ~ **soldiers** accēnsī *mpl*
superscription *n* titulus *m*
supersede *vt* succēdere (*dat*), in locum succēdere (*gen*); ~ **gold with silver** prō aurō argentum suppōnere
superstition *n* rēligiō *f*, superstitiō *f*
superstitious *adj* rēligiōsus, superstitiōsus
supervene *vi* īnsequī, succēdere
supervise *vt* prōcūrāre
supervision *n* cūra *f*
supervisor *n* cūrātor *m*
supine *adj* supīnus; (*fig*) neglegēns, segnis
supinely *adv* segniter
supper *n* cēna *f*; **after ~** cēnātus
supperless *adj* iēiūnus
supplant *vt* praevertere
supple *adj* flexibilis, mollis
supplement *n* appendix *f* ♦ *vt* amplificāre
supplementary *adj* additus

suppleness n mollitia f
suppliant n supplex m/f
supplicate vt supplicāre, obsecrāre
supplication n precēs fpl
supplies npl commeātus m
supply n cōpia f ♦ vt suppeditāre, praebēre; (loss) supplēre
support n firmāmentum nt; (help) subsidium nt, adiūmentum nt; (food) alimenta ntpl; (of party) favor m; (of needy) patrōcinium nt; **I ~** subsidio sum (dat); **lend ~ to rumours** alimenta rūmōribus addere ♦ vt fulcīre; (living) sustinēre, sustentāre; (with help) adiuvāre, opem ferre (dat); (at law) adesse (dat)
supportable adj tolerābilis
supporter n fautor m; (at trial) advocātus m; (of proposal) auctor m
supporting cast n adiūtōrēs mpl
suppose vi (assume) pōnere; (think) existimāre, opīnārī, crēdere; **~ it is true** fac vērum esse
supposedly adv ut fāma est
supposing conj sī; (for the sake of argument) sī iam
supposition n opīniō f; **on this ~** hōc positō
supposititious adj subditus, subditīvus
suppress vt opprimere, comprimere; (knowledge) cēlāre, reticēre; (feelings) coercēre, reprimere
suppression n (of fact) reticentia f
supremacy n imperium nt, dominātus m, prīncipātus m
supreme adj summus; **be ~** dominārī; **~ command** imperium nt
supremely adv ūnicē, plānē
sure adj certus; (fact) explōrātus; (friend) fīdus; **be ~ of** compertum habēre; **feel ~** persuāsum habēre, haud scīre an; pro certō habēre; **make ~ of** (fact) comperīre; (action) efficere ut; **to be ~** quidem; **~ enough** rē vērā
surely adv certō, certē, nonne; (tentative) scīlicet, sānē; **~ you do not think?** num putās?; **~ not** num
surety n (person) vās m, praes m, spōnsor m; (deposit) fīdūcia f; **be ~ for** spondēre prō
surf n fluctus m
surface n superficiēs f; **~ of the water** summa aqua
surfeit n satietās f ♦ vt satiāre, explēre
surge n aestus m, fluctus m ♦ vi tumēscere
surgeon n chīrūrgus m
surgery n chīrūrgia f
surlily adv mōrōsē
surliness n mōrōsitās f
surly adj mōrōsus, difficilis
surmise n coniectūra f ♦ vi suspicārī, conicere, augurārī
surmount vt superāre
surmountable adj superābilis
surname n cognōmen nt
surpass vt excellere, exsuperāre, antecēdere
surpassing adj excellēns
surplus n reliquum nt; (money) pecūniae residuae fpl
surprise n admīrātiō f; (cause) rēs inopīnāta f; **take by ~** dēprehendere ♦ adj subitus ♦ vt dēprehendere; (MIL) opprimere; **be surprised** dēmīrārī; **be surprised at** admīrārī
surprising adj mīrus, mīrābilis

surprisingly adv mīrē, mīrābiliter
surrender vt dēdere, trādere, concēdere ♦ vi sē dēdere; **~ unconditionally to** sē suaque omnia potestāti permittere (gen) ♦ n dēditiō f; (legal) cessiō f; **unconditional ~** permissiō f
surreptitious adj fūrtīvus
surreptitiously adv fūrtim, clam; **get in ~** inrēpere in (acc)
surround vt circumdare, cingere, circumvenīre, circumfundere
surrounding adj circumiectus; **surroundings** n vīcīnia f
survey vt contemplārī, cōnsīderāre; (land) mētārī ♦ n contemplātiō f; (land) mēnsūra f
surveyor n fīnītor m, agrīmēnsor m, mētātor m
survival n salūs f
survive vt superāre; superesse (dat)
survivor n superstes m/f
susceptibility n mollitia f
susceptible adj mollis
suspect vt suspicārī; **be suspected in** suspīciōnem venīre
suspend vt suspendere; (activity) differre; (person) locō movēre; **be suspended** pendēre
suspense n dubitātiō f; **be in ~** animī pendēre, haerēre
suspicion n suspīciō f; **direct ~ to** suspīciōnem adiungere ad
suspicious adj (suspecting) suspīciōsus; (suspected) dubius, anceps
sustain vt (weight) sustinēre; (life) alere, sustentāre; (hardship) ferre, sustinēre; (the part of) agere
sustenance n alimentum nt, vīctus m
sutler n lixa m
suzerain n dominus m
swaddling clothes n incūnābula ntpl
swagger vi sē iactāre
swaggerer n homō glōriōsus m
swallow n hirundō f ♦ vt dēvorāre; **~ up** absorbēre
swamp n palūs f ♦ vt opprimere
swampy adj ūlīginōsus
swan n cycnus m; **swan's** cycnēus
swank vi sē iactāre
sward n caespes m
swarm n exāmen nt; (fig) nūbēs f ♦ vi: **~ round** circumfundī
swarthy adj fuscus, aquilus
swathe vt conligāre
sway n diciō f, imperium nt; **bring under one's ~** suae diciōnis facere ♦ vt regere ♦ vi vacillāre
swear vi iūrāre; **~ allegiance to** iūrāre in verba (gen)
sweat n sūdor m ♦ vi sūdāre
sweep vt verrere; **~ away** rapere; **~ out** ēverrere
sweet adj dulcis, suāvis
sweeten vt dulcem reddere
sweetheart n dēliciae fpl
sweetly adv dulciter, suāviter
sweetness n dulcitūdō f, suāvitās f
sweet-tempered adj suāvis, cōmis
swell n tumor m ♦ vi tumēre, tumēscere; (fig) glīscere ♦ vt īnflāre
swelling adj tumidus ♦ n tumor m
swelter vi aestū labōrāre

swerve vi dēclīnāre, dēvertere ♦ n dēclīnātiō f
swift adj celer, vēlōx, incitātus
swiftly adv celeriter, vēlōciter
swiftness n celeritās f, vēlōcitās f
swill vt (rinse) colluere; (drink) ēpōtāre
swim vi nāre, innāre; (place) natāre; ~ across
trānāre; ~ ashore ēnāre; ~ to adnāre
swimming n natātiō f
swindle vt circumvenīre, verba dare (dat) ♦ n
fraus f
swine n sūs m/f
swineherd n subulcus m
swing n (motion) oscillātiō f ♦ vi oscillāre ♦ vt
lībrāre
swinish adj obscēnus
swirl n vertex m ♦ vi volūtārī
switch n virga f ♦ vt flectere, torquēre
swivel n cardō f
swollen adj tumidus, turgidus, īnflātus
swoon n dēfectiō f ♦ vi intermorī
swoop n impetus m ♦ vi lābī; ~ down on involāre
in (acc)
sword n gladius m; put to the ~ occīdere; with
fire and ~ ferrō ignīque
swordsman n gladiātor m
sworn adj iūrātus

sybarite n dēlicātus m
sycophancy n adsentātiō f, adūlātiō f
sycophant n adsentātor m, adūlātor m
syllable n syllaba f
syllogism n ratiōcinātiō f
sylvan adj silvestris
symbol n signum nt, īnsigne nt
symmetrical adj concinnus, aequus
symmetry n concinnitās f, aequitās f
sympathetic adj concors, misericors
sympathetically adv misericorditer
sympathize vi cōnsentīre; ~ with miserērī
(gen)
sympathy n concordia f, cōnsēnsus m;
misericordia f
symphony n concentus m
symptom n signum nt, indicium nt
syndicate n societās f
synonym n verbum idem dēclārāns nt
synonymous adj idem dēclārāns
synopsis n summārium nt
syringe n clystēr m
system n ratiō f, fōrmula f; (PHILOS) disciplīna f
systematic adj ōrdinātus, cōnstāns
systematically adv ratiōne, ōrdine
systematize vt in ōrdinem redigere

Tt

tabernacle *n* tabernāculum *nt*
table *n* mēnsa *f*; (*inscribed*) tabula *f*; (*list*) index *m*;
at ~ inter cēnam; **turn the tables on** pār parī
referre
tablet *n* tabula *f*, tabella *f*
taboo *n* rēligiō *f*
tabulate *vt* in ōrdinem redigere
tacit *adj* tacitus
tacitly *adv* tacitē
taciturn *adj* taciturnus
taciturnity *n* taciturnitās *f*
tack *n* clāvulus *m*; (*of sail*) pēs *m* ♦ *vt*: ~ **on** adsuere
♦ *vi* (*ship*) reciprocārī, nāvem flectere
tackle *n* armāmenta *ntpl* ♦ *vt* adgredī
tact *n* iūdicium *nt*, commūnis sēnsus *m*,
hūmānitās *f*
tactful *adj* prūdēns, hūmānus
tactfully *adv* prūdenter, hūmāniter
tactician *n* reī mīlitāris perītus *m*
tactics *n* rēs mīlitāris *f*, bellī ratiō *f*
tactless *adj* ineptus
tactlessly *adv* ineptē
tadpole *n* rānunculus *m*
tag *n* appendicula *f*
tail *n* cauda *f*; **turn** ~ terga vertere
tailor *n* vestītor *m*
taint *n* lābēs *f*, vitium *nt* ♦ *vt* inquināre,
contāmināre, īnficere
take *vt* capere, sūmere; (*auspices*) habēre;
(*disease*) contrahere; (*experience*) ferre; (*fire*)
concipere; (*meaning*) accipere, interpretārī; (*in
the act*) dēprehendere; (*person*) dūcere; ~ **after**
similem esse (*dat, gen*); ~ **across** trānsportāre;
~ **arms** arma sūmere; ~ **away** dēmere, auferre,
adimere, abdūcere; ~ **back** recipere; ~ **by
storm** expugnāre; ~ **care that** curāre ut/ne
(*subj*); ~ **down** dētrahere; (*in writing*) exscrībere;
~ **for** habēre prō; ~ **hold of** prehendere; ~ **in**
(*as guest*) recipere; (*information*) percipere,
comprehendere; (*with deceit*) dēcipere; ~ **in
hand** incipere, suscipere; ~ **off** dēmere;
(*clothes*) exuere; ~ **on** suscipere; ~ **out** eximere,
extrahere; (*from store*) prōmere; ~ **over** excipere;
~ **place** fierī, accidere; ~ **prisoner** capere;
~ **refuge in** cōnfugere ad (*acc*); ~ **the field** in
aciem dēscendere; ~ **to** sē dēdere (*dat*), amāre;
~ **to oneself** suscipere; ~ **up** sūmere, tollere;
(*task*) incipere, adgredī ad; (*in turn*) excipere;
(*room*) occupāre; ~ **upon oneself** recipere, sibī
sūmere
taking *adj* grātus ♦ *n* (MIL) expugnātiō *f*
tale *n* fābula *f*, fābella *f*

talent *n* (*money*) talentum *nt*; (*ability*) ingenium
nt, indolēs *f*
talented *adj* ingeniōsus
talk *n* sermō *m*; (*with another*) colloquium *nt*;
common ~ fāma *f*; **be the** ~ **of the town** in
ōre omnium esse ♦ *vi* loquī; (*to one*) colloquī
cum; ~ **down to** ad intellectum audientis
dēscendere; ~ **over** cōnferre, disserere dē
talkative *adj* loquāx
talkativeness *n* loquācitās *f*
tall *adj* prōcērus, grandis
tallness *n* prōcēritās *f*
tallow *n* sēbum *nt*
tally *n* tessera *f* ♦ *vi* congruere
talon *n* unguis *m*
tamarisk *n* myrīca *f*
tambourine *n* tympanum *nt*
tame *vt* domāre, mānsuēfacere ♦ *adj*
mānsuētus; (*character*) ignāvus; (*language*)
īnsulsus, frīgidus
tamely *adv* ignāvē, lentē
tameness *n* mānsuētūdō *f*; (*fig*) lentitūdō *f*
tamer *n* domitor *m*
tamper *vi*: ~ **with** (*person*) sollicitāre; (*writing*)
interpolāre
tan *vt* imbuere
tang *n* sapor *m*
tangible *adj* tāctilis
tangle *n* nōdus *m* ♦ *vt* implicāre
tank *n* lacus *m*
tanned *adj* (*by sun*) adūstus
tanner *n* coriārius *m*
tantalize *vt* lūdere
tantamount *adj* pār, īdem
tantrum *n* īra *f*
tap *n* epitonium *nt*; (*touch*) plāga *f* ♦ *vt* (*cask*)
relinere; (*hit*) ferīre
tape *n* taenia *f*
taper *n* cēreus *m* ♦ *vi* fastīgārī
tapestry *n* aulaea *ntpl*
tar *n* pix *f*
tardily *adv* tardē, lentē
tardiness *n* tarditās *f*, segnitia *f*
tardy *adj* tardus, lentus
tare *n* lolium *nt*
targe *n* parma *f*
target *n* scopus *m*
tariff *n* portōrium *nt*
tarn *n* lacus *m*
tarnish *vt* īnfuscāre, inquināre ♦ *vi* īnfuscārī
tarry *vi* morārī, commorārī, cunctārī
tart *adj* acidus, asper ♦ *n* scrīblīta *f*

tartly *adv* acerbē
tartness *n* asperitās *f*
task *n* pēnsum *nt*, opus *nt*, negōtium *nt*; **take to
~** obiūrgāre
taskmaster *n* dominus *m*
tassel *n* fimbriae *fpl*
taste *n* (*sense*) gustātus *m*; (*flavour*) sapor *m*;
(*artistic*) iūdicium *nt*, ēlegantia *f*; (*for rhetoric*)
aurēs *fpl*; **of ~** doctus; **in good ~** ēlegāns ♦ *vt*
gustāre, dēgustāre ♦ *vi* sapere; **~ of** resipere
tasteful *adj* ēlegāns
tastefully *adv* ēleganter
tastefulness *n* ēlegantia *f*
tasteless *adj* īnsulsus, inēlegāns
tastelessly *adv* īnsulsē, inēleganter
tastelessness *n* īnsulsitās *f*
taster *n* praegustātor *m*
tasty *adj* dulcis
tattered *adj* pannōsus
tatters *n* pannī *mpl*
tattoo *vt* compungere
taunt *n* convīcium *nt*, probrum *nt* ♦ *vt*
exprobrāre, obicere (*dat of pers, acc of charge*)
taunting *adj* contumēliōsus
tauntingly *adv* contumēliōsē
taut *adj* intentus; **draw ~** addūcere
tavern *n* taberna *f*, hospitium *nt*
tawdry *adj* vīlis
tawny *adj* fulvus
tax *n* vectīgal *nt*, tribūtum *nt*; **a 5 per cent tax**
vīcēsima *f*; **free from tax** immūnis ♦ *vt* vectīgal
impōnere (*dat*); (*strength*) contendere; **tax with**
(*charge*) obicere (*acc & dat*), īnsimulāre
taxable *adj* vectīgālis
taxation *n* vectīgālia *ntpl*
tax collector *n* exāctor *m*
tax farmer *n* pūblicānus *m*
taxpayer *n* assiduus *m*
teach *vt* docēre, ērudīre, īnstituere; (*thoroughly*)
ēdocēre; (*passive*) discere; **~ your grandmother**
sūs Minervam
teachable *adj* docilis
teacher *n* magister *m*, magistra *f*, doctor *m*;
(PHILOS) praeceptor *m*; (*of literature*) grammaticus
m; (*of rhetoric*) rhētor *m*
teaching *n* doctrīna *f*, disciplīna *f*
team *n* (*animals*) iugum *nt*
tear *n* lacrima *f*; **shed tears** lacrimās effundere
♦ *vt* scindere; **~ down** revellere; **~ in pieces**
dīlaniāre, discerpere, lacerāre; **~ off** abscindere,
dēripere; **~ open** rescindere; **~ out** ēvellere; **~ up**
convellere
tearful *adj* flēbilis
tease *vt* lūdere, inrītāre
teat *n* mamma *f*
technical *adj* (*term*) proprius
technique *n* ars *f*
tedious *adj* longus, lentus, odiōsus
tediously *adv* molestē
tedium *n* taedium *nt*, molestia *f*
teem *vi* abundāre
teeming *adj* fēcundus, refertus
teens *n*: **in one's ~** adulescentulus
teethe *vi* dentīre
tell *vt* (*story*) nārrāre; (*person*) dīcere (*dat*);
(*number*) ēnumerāre; (*inform*) certiōrem facere;

(*difference*) intellegere; (*order*) iubēre (+*acc and
infin*), imperāre (+ *'ut'* +*subj or* + *'ne'* +*subj*); **~ the
truth** vera dīcere; **~ lies** mentior ♦ *vi* valēre;
~ the difference between discernere; **I cannot
~** nesciō
telling *adj* validus
temerity *n* temeritās *f*
temper *n* animus *m*, ingenium *nt*; (*bad*) īra
f, īrācundia *f*; (*of metal*) temperātiō *f* ♦ *vt*
temperāre; (*fig*) moderārī (*dat*)
temperament *n* animī habitus *m*, animus *m*
temperamental *adj* incōnstāns
temperance *n* temperantia *f*, continentia *f*
temperate *adj* temperātus, moderātus, sobrius
temperately *adv* moderātē
temperature *n* calor *m*, frīgus *nt*; **mild
~** temperiēs *f*
tempest *n* tempestās *f*, procella *f*
tempestuous *adj* procellōsus
temple *n* templum *nt*, aedēs *f*; (*head*) tempus *nt*
temporal *adj* hūmānus, profānus
temporarily *adv* ad tempus
temporary *adj* brevis
temporize *vi* temporis causā facere, tergiversārī
tempt *vt* sollicitāre, pellicere, invītāre
temptation *n* illecebra *f*
tempter *n* impulsor *m*
ten *num* decem; **ten each** dēnī; **ten times**
deciēns
tenable *adj* inexpugnābilis, stabilis, certus
tenacious *adj* tenāx, firmus
tenaciously *adv* tenāciter
tenacity *n* tenācitās *f*
tenant *n* inquilīnus *m*, habitātor *m*; (*on land*)
colōnus *m*
tenantry *n* colōnī *mpl*
tend *vi* spectāre, pertinēre ♦ *vt* cūrāre, colere
tendency *n* inclīnātiō *f*, voluntās *f*
tender *adj* tener, mollis ♦ *vt* dēferre, offerre
tenderhearted *adj* misericors
tenderly *adv* indulgenter
tenderness *n* indulgentia *f*, mollitia *f*
tendon *n* nervus *m*
tendril *n* clāviculus *m*
tenement *n* habitātiō *f*; **block of tenements**
īnsula *f*
tenet *n* dogma *nt*, dēcrētum *nt*
tennis court *n* sphaeristērium *nt*
tenor *n* (*course*) tenor *m*; (*purport*) sententia *f*
tense *adj* intentus ♦ *n* tempus *nt*
tension *n* intentiō *f*
tent *n* tabernāculum *nt*; (*general's*) praetōrium *nt*
tentacle *n* bracchium *nt*
tentatively *adv* experiendō
tenterhooks *n*: **on ~** animī suspēnsus
tenth *adj* decimus; **for the ~ time** decimum;
men of the ~ legion decumānī *mpl*
tenuous *adj* rārus
tenure *n* possessiō *f*
tepid *adj* tepidus; **be ~** tepēre
tergiversation *n* tergiversātiō *f*
term *n* (*limit*) terminus *m*; (*period*) spatium *nt*;
(*word*) verbum *nt* ♦ *vt* appellāre, nuncupāre
terminate *vt* termināre, fīnīre ♦ *vi* dēsinere;
(*words*) cadere
termination *n* fīnis *m*, terminus *m*

terminology *n* vocābula *ntpl*
terms *npl* condiciō *f*, lēx *f*; **propose**
  ~ condiciōnem ferre; **be on good ~ in grātiā**
  esse; **we come to ~ inter nōs convenit**
terrain *n* ager *m*
terrestrial *adj* terrestris
terrible *adj* terribilis, horribilis, horrendus
terribly *adv* horrendum in modum
terrific *adj* formīdolōsus; vehemēns
terrify *vt* terrēre, perterrēre, exterrēre
terrifying *adj* formīdolōsus
territory *n* ager *m*, fīnēs *mpl*
terror *n* terror *m*, formīdō *f*, pavor *m*; **object of**
  ~ terror *m*; **be a ~ to** terrōrī esse *(dat)*
terrorize *vt* metum inicere *(dat)*
terse *adj* pressus, brevis
tersely *adv* pressē
terseness *n* brevitās *f*
tessellated *adj* tessellātus
test *n* experīmentum *nt*, probātiō *f*; *(standard)*
  obrussa *f*; **put to the ~** experīrī, perīclitārī;
  stand the ~ spectārī ♦ *vt* experīrī, probāre,
  spectāre
testament *n* testāmentum *nt*
testamentary *adj* testāmentārius
testator *n* testātor *m*
testify *vt* testificārī
testifying *n* testificātiō *f*
testily *adv* stomachōsē
testimonial *n* laudātiō *f*
testimony *n* testimōnium *nt*
testy *adj* difficilis, stomachōsus
tether *n* retināculum *nt*, vinculum *nt* ♦ *vt*
  religāre
tetrarch *n* tetrarchēs *m*
tetrarchy *n* tetrarchia *f*
text *n* verba *ntpl*
textbook *n* ars *f*
textile *adj* textilis
textual *adj* verbōrum
texture *n* textus *m*
than *conj* quam *(abl)*; **other ~** alius ac
thank *vt* grātiās agere *(dat)*; ~ **you** bene facis; **no,**
  ~ **you** benīgnē
thankful *adj* grātus
thankfully *adv* grātē
thankfulness *n* grātia *f*
thankless *adj* ingrātus
thanklessly *adv* ingrātē
thanks *n* grātiae *fpl*, grātēs *fpl*; **return ~** grātiās
  agere, grātēs persolvere; ~ **to you** operā tuā,
  beneficiō tuō; **it is ~ to sb that … not** per
  aliquem stat quominus *(subj)*
thanksgiving *n* grātulātiō *f*; *(public)* supplicātiō *f*
that *pron (demonstrative)* ille; *(relat)* quī ♦ *conj*
  (statement) acc & infin; *(command, purpose, result)* ut;
  (fearing) nē; *(emotion)* quod; **oh ~** utinam
thatch *n* culmus *m*, strāmenta *ntpl* ♦ *vt* tegere,
  integere
thaw *vt* dissolvere ♦ *vi* liquēscere, tabēscere
the *art not expressed; (emphatic)* ille; *(with compar)*
  quō … eō
theatre *n* theātrum *nt*
theatrical *adj* scēnicus
theft *n* fūrtum *nt*
their *adj* eōrum; *(ref to subject)* suus

theme *n* māteria *f*, argūmentum *nt*
themselves *pron* ipsī; *(reflexive)* sē
then *adv (time)* tum, tunc; *(succession)* deinde,
  tum, posteā; *(consequence)* igitur, ergō; **now and**
  ~ interdum; **only ~** tum dēmum
thence *adv* inde
thenceforth *adv* inde, posteā, ex eō tempore
theologian *n* theologus *m*
theology *n* theologia *f*
theorem *n* prōpositum *nt*
theoretical *adj* contemplātīvus
theory *n* ratiō *f*; ~ **and practice** ratiō atque ūsus
there *adv* ibī, illīc; *(thither)* eō, illūc; **from** ~ inde,
  illinc; **here and** ~ passim; ~ **is** est; *(interj)* ecce
thereabout, thereabouts *adv* circā, circiter,
  prope
thereafter *adv* deinde, posteā
thereby *adv* eā rē, hōc factō
therefore *adv* itaque, igitur, ergō, idcircō
therein *adv* inibī, in eō
thereof *adv* ēius, ēius reī
thereon *adv* īnsuper, in eō
thereupon *adv* deinde, statim, inde, quo facto
therewith *adv* cum eō
thesis *n* prōpositum *nt*
thews *n* nervī *mpl*
they *pron* iī, hī, illī
thick *adj* dēnsus; *(air)* crassus
thicken *vt* dēnsāre ♦ *vi* concrēscere
thickening *n* concrētiō *f*
thicket *n* dūmētum *nt*
thickheaded *adj* stupidus, hebes
thickly *adv* dēnsē; ~ **populated** frequēns
thickness *n* crassitūdō *f*
thickset *adj* brevis atque obēsus
thick-skinned *adj*: **be ~** callēre; **become**
  ~ occallēscere
thief *n* fūr *m*
thieve *vt* fūrārī, surripere
thievery *n* fūrtum *nt*
thievish *adj* fūrāx
thigh *n* femur *nt*
thin *adj* exīlis, gracilis, tenuis; *(attendance)*
  īnfrequēns ♦ *vt* attenuāre, extenuāre; ~ **out**
  rārefacere; ~ **down** dīluere
thine *adj* tuus
thing *n* rēs *f*; **as things are** nunc, cum haec ita
  sint
think *vi* cōgitāre; *(opinion)* putāre, existimāre,
  arbitrārī, rērī, crēdere; **as I ~** meā sententiā;
  ~ **about** cōgitāre dē; ~ **highly of** māgnī
  aestimāre; ~ **nothing of** nihilī facere; ~ **out**
  excōgitāre; ~ **over** reputāre, in mente agitāre
thinker *n* philosophus *m*
thinking *adj* sapiēns ♦ *n* cōgitātiō *f*; ~ **that** ratus,
  arbitratus
thinly *adv* exīliter, tenuiter; rārē
thinness *n* exīlitās *f*, gracilitās *f*; *(person)* maciēs
  f; *(number)* exiguitās *f*, īnfrequentia *f*; *(air)*
  tenuitās *f*
thin-skinned *adj* inrītābilis
third *adj* tertius; **for the ~ time** tertium ♦ *n* tertia
  pars *f*, triēns *m*; **two thirds** duae partēs, bēs *m*
thirdly *adv* tertiō
thirst *n* sitis *f* ♦ *vi* sitīre; ~ **for** sitīre
thirstily *adv* sitienter

thirsty *adj* sitiēns
thirteen *num* tredecim; ~ **each** ternī dēnī;
~ **times** terdeciēns
thirteenth *adj* tertius decimus
thirtieth *adj* trīcēsimus
thirty *num* trīgintā; ~ **each** trīcēnī; ~ **times**
trīciēns
this *pron* hīc
thistle *n* carduus *m*
thither *adv* eō, illūc
thole *n* scalmus *nt*
thong *n* lōrum *nt*, habēna *f*
thorn *n* spīna *f*, sentis *m*
thorny *adj* spīnōsus
thorough *adj* absolūtus, germānus; (*work*)
accūrātus
thoroughbred *adj* generōsus
thoroughfare *n* via *f*
thoroughly *adv* penitus, omnīnō, funditus
thoroughness *n* cūra *f*, dīligentia *f*
thou *pron* tū
though *conj* etsī, etiamsī, quamvīs (*subj*),
quamquam (*+indic*)
thought *n* (*faculty*) cōgitātiō *f*, mēns *f*, animus *m*;
(*an idea*) cōgitātum *nt*, nōtiō *f*; (*design*) cōnsilium
nt, prōpositum *nt*; (*expressed*) sententia *f*; (*heed*)
cautiō *f*, prōvidentia *f*; (RHET) inventiō *f*; **second
thoughts** posteriōrēs cōgitātiōnēs
thoughtful *adj* cōgitābundus; prōvidus
thoughtfully *adv* prōvidē
thoughtless *adj* incōnsīderātus, incōnsultus,
imprōvidus, immemor
thoughtlessly *adv* temerē, incōnsultē
thoughtlessness *n* incōnsīderantia *f*,
imprūdentia *f*
thousand *num* mīlle; **thousands** (*pl*) mīlia (*ntpl*
+gen); ~ **each** mīllēnī; ~ **times** mīlliēns; **three
~ tria** mīlia
thousandth *adj* mīllēsimus
thraldom *n* servitūs *f*
thrall *n* servus *m*
thrash *vt* verberāre
thrashing *n* verbera *ntpl*
thread *n* fīlum *nt*; **hang by a ~** (*fig*) fīlō pendēre
♦ *vt*: ~ **one's way** sē īnsinuāre
threadbare *adj* trītus, obsolētus
threat *n* minae *fpl*, minātiō *f*
threaten *vt* minārī (*dat of pers*), dēnūntiāre ♦ *vi*
imminēre, impendēre
threatening *adj* mināx, imminēns
threateningly *adv* mināciter
three *num* trēs; ~ **each** ternī; ~ **times** ter; ~ **days**
trīduum *nt*; ~ **years** triennium *nt*; ~ **quarters**
trēs partēs *fpl*, dōdrāns *m*
three-cornered *adj* triangulus, triquetrus
threefold *adj* triplex
three hundred *num* trecentī; **three hundred
each** trecēnī; **three hundred times** trecentiēn
three hundredth *adj* trecentēsimus
three-legged *adj* tripēs
three-quarters *n* dōdrāns *m*, trēs partēs *fpl*
thresh *vt* terere, exterere
threshing floor *n* ārea *f*
threshold *n* līmen *nt*
thrice *adv* ter
thrift *n* frūgālitās *f*, parsimōnia *f*

thriftily *adv* frūgāliter
thrifty *adj* parcus, frūgī
thrill *n* horror *m* ♦ *vt* percellere, percutere ♦ *vi*
trepidāre
thrilling *adj* mīrābilis
thrive *vi* vigēre, valēre, crēscere
thriving *adj* valēns, vegetus; (*crops*) laetus
throat *n* faucēs *fpl*, guttur *nt*; **cut the ~ of**
iugulāre
throaty *adj* gravis, raucus
throb *vi* palpitāre, micāre ♦ *n* pulsus *m*
throe *n* dolor *m*; **be in the throes of** labōrāre ex
throne *n* solium *nt*; (*power*) rēgnum *nt*
throng *n* multitūdō *f*, frequentia *f* ♦ *vt* celebrāre;
~ **round** stīpāre, circumfundī (*dat*)
throttle *vt* strangulāre
through *prep* per (*acc*); (*cause*) propter (*acc*),
abl ♦ *adv*: ~ **and ~** penitus; **carry ~** exsequī,
peragere; **go ~** trānsīre; **run ~** percurrere; **be
~ with** perfūnctum esse (*abl*)
throughout *adv* penitus, omnīnō ♦ *prep* per (*acc*)
throw *n* iactus *m*, coniectus *m* ♦ *vt* iacere,
conicere; ~ **about** iactāre; ~ **across** trāicere;
~ **away** abicere; (*something precious*) prōicere;
~ **back** rēicere; ~ **down** dēturbāre, dēicere;
~ **into** inicere; ~ **into confusion** perturbāre;
~ **off** excutere, exsolvere; ~ **open** patefacere;
~ **out** ēicere, prōicere; ~ **over** inicere; (*fig*)
dēstituere; ~ **overboard** iactūram facere
(*gen*); ~ **to** (*danger*) obicere; ~ **up** ēicere; (*building*)
exstruere; ~ **a bridge over** pontem inicere (*dat*),
pontem faciendum cūrāre in (*abl*); ~ **light on**
(*fig*) lūmen adhibēre (*dat*); ~ **a rider** equitem
excutere
throwing *n* coniectiō *f*, iactus *m*
thrum *n* līcium *nt*
thrush *n* turdus *m*
thrust *vt* trūdere, pellere, impingere; ~ **at** petere;
~ **away** dētrūdere; ~ **forward** prōtrūdere;
~ **home** dēfīgere; ~ **into** īnfigere, impingere;
~ **out** extrūdere
thud *n* gravis sonitus *m*
thug *n* percussor *m*, sīcārius *m*
thumb *n* pollex *m*; **have under one's ~** in
potestāte suā habēre
thump *n* plāga *f* ♦ *vt* tundere, pulsāre
thunder *n* tonitrus *m* ♦ *vi* tonāre, intonāre; **it
thunders** tonat
thunderbolt *n* fulmen *nt*
thunderer *n* tonāns *m*
thunderstruck *adj* attonitus
thus *adv* (*referring back*) sīc; (*referring forward*) ita;
~ **far** hāctenus
thwack *vt* verberāre
thwart *vt* obstāre (*dat*), officere (*dat*), remorārī,
frustrārī ♦ *n* (*boat's*) trānstrum *nt*
thy *adj* tuus
thyme *n* thymum *nt*; (*wild*) serpyllum *nt*
tiara *n* diadēma *nt*
ticket *n* tessera *f*
tickle *vt* tītillāre
tickling *n* tītillātiō *f*
ticklish *adj* lūbricus
tidal *adj*: ~ **waters** aestuārium *nt*
tide *n* aestus *m*; (*time*) tempus *nt*; **ebb ~** aestūs
recessus *m*; **flood ~** aestūs accessus *m*; **turn of**

the ~ commūtātiō aestūs; **the ~ will turn** (fig)
circumagētur hīc orbis
tidily adv concinnē, mundē
tidiness n concinnitās f, munditia f
tidings n nūntius m
tidy adj concinnus, mundus
tie n (bond) vinculum nt, cōpula f; (kin)
necessitūdō f ♦ vt ligāre; (knot) nectere; **tie
fast** dēvincīre, cōnstringere; **tie on** illigāre;
tie to adligāre; **tie together** colligāre; **tie up**
adligāre; (wound) obligāre
tier n ōrdō m
tiff n dissēnsiō f
tiger n tigris usu f
tight adj strictus, astrictus, intentus; (close)
artus; **draw ~** intendere, addūcere
tighten vt adstringere, contendere
tightly adv artē, angustē
tightrope n extentus fūnis; **~ walker** n
fūnambulus m
tigress n tigris f
tile n tegula f, imbrex f, later nt
till conj dum, dōnec ♦ prep usque ad (acc), in (acc);
not ~ dēmum ♦ n arca f ♦ vt colere
tillage n cultus m
tiller n (AGR) cultor m; (ship) clāvus m,
gubernāculum nt
tilt vt inclīnāre
tilth n cultus m, arvum nt
timber n (for building) māteria f; (firewood) lignum
nt
timbrel n tympanum nt
time n tempus nt; (lifetime) aetās f; (interval)
intervallum nt, spatium nt; (of day) hōra f;
(leisure) ōtium nt; (rhythm) numerus m; **another
~** aliās; **at times** aliquandō, interdum; **at all
times** semper; **at any ~** umquam; **at one ~ ...
at another** aliās ... aliās; **at that ~** tunc, id
temporis; **at the right ~** ad tempus, mātūrē,
tempestīvē; **at the same ~** simul; tamen;
at the wrong ~ intempestīvē; **beating
~ percussiō** f; **convenient ~** opportūnitās f;
for a ~ aliquantisper, parumper; **for a long
~** diū; **for some ~** aliquamdiū; **for the ~ being**
ad tempus; **from ~ to ~** interdum, identidem;
have a good ~ geniō indulgēre; **have ~ for**
vacāre (dat); **in ~** ad tempus, tempore; **in a
short ~** brevī; **in good ~** tempestīvus; **in the
~ of** apud (acc); **keep ~** (marching) gradum
cōnferre; (music) modulārī; **many times** saepe,
saepenumerō; **pass ~, spend ~** tempus sūmere,
dēgere; **several times** aliquotiēns; **some
~ aliquandō; waste ~** tempus terere; **what is
the time?** quota hōra est?; **~ expired** ēmeritus
time-honoured adj antīquus
timeliness n opportūnitās f
timely adj opportūnus, tempestīvus, mātūrus
timid adj timidus
timidity n timiditās f
timidly adv timidē
timorous adj timidus
timorously adv timidē
tin n stannum nt, plumbum album nt ♦ adj
stanneus
tincture n color m, sapor m ♦ vt īnficere
tinder n fōmes m

tinge vt imbuere, īnficere, tingere
tingle vi horrēre
tingling n horror m
tinkle vi tinnīre ♦ n tinnītus m
tinsel n bractea f; (fig) speciēs f, fūcus m
tint n color m ♦ vt colōrāre
tiny adj minūtus, pusillus, perexiguus
tip n apex m, cacūmen nt, extrēmum nt; **the tip
of** prīmus, extrēmus ♦ vt praefīgere; **tip over**
invertere
tipple vi pōtāre
tippler n pōtor m, ēbrius m
tipsy adj tēmulentus
tiptoes n: **on ~** suspēnsō gradū
tirade n obiūrgātiō f, dēclāmātiō f
tire vt fatīgāre; **~ out** dēfatīgāre ♦ vi dēfetīscī,
fatīgārī; **I ~ of** mē taedet (gen); **it tires** taedet (+
acc of person, gen of thing)
tired adj (dē)fessus, lassus; **~ out** dēfessus; **I am
~ of** mē taedet
tiresome adj molestus, difficilis
tiring adj labōriōsus, operōsus
tiro n tīrō m, rudis m
tissue n textus m
tit n: **give tit for tat** pār parī respondēre
Titan n Tītān m
titanic adj immānis
titbit n cuppēdium nt
tithe n decuma f
tithe gatherer n decumānus m
titillate vt titillāre
titillation n titillātiō f
title n (book) īnscrīptiō f, index m; (inscription)
titulus m; (person) nōmen nt, appellātiō f; (claim)
iūs nt, vindiciae fpl; **assert one's ~ to** vindicāre;
give a ~ to īnscrībere
titled adj nōbilis
title deed n auctōritās f
titter n rīsus m ♦ vi rīdēre
tittle-tattle n sermunculus m
titular adj nōmine
to prep ad (acc), in (acc); (attitude) ergā (acc); (giving)
dat; (towns, small islands, domus, rūs) acc ♦ conj
(purpose) ut ♦ adv: **come to** animum recipere; **to
and fro** hūc illūc
toad n būfō m
toady n adsentātor m, parasītus m ♦ vt adsentārī
(dat)
toadyism n adsentātiō f
toast n: **drink a ~** propīnāre ♦ vt torrēre; (drink)
propīnāre (dat)
today adv hodiē; **today's** hodiernus
toe n digitus m; **big toe** pollex m
toga n toga f
together adv ūnā, simul; **bring ~** cōgere,
congerere; **come ~** convenīre, congregārī; **put
~ cōnferre, compōnere
toil n labor m; (snare) rēte nt ♦ vi labōrāre; **~ at**
ēlabōrāre in (abl)
toilet n (lady's) cultus m
toilsome adj labōriōsus, operōsus
toil-worn adj labōre cōnfectus
token n īnsigne nt, signum nt, indicium nt
tolerable adj tolerābilis, patibilis; (quality)
mediocris; (size) modicus
tolerably adv satis, mediocriter

tolerance n patientia f, tolerantia f
tolerant adj indulgēns, tolerāns
tolerantly adv indulgenter
tolerate vt tolerāre, ferre, indulgēre (dat)
toleration n patientia f; (freedom) lībertās f
toll n vectīgal nt; (harbour) portōrium nt
toll collector n exāctor m; portitor m
tomb n sepulcrum nt
tombstone n lapis m
tome n liber m
tomorrow adv crās; **tomorrow's** crāstinus;
   the day after ~ perendiē; **put off till ~** in
   crāstinum differre
tone n sonus m, vōx f; (painting) color m
tongs n forceps m/f
tongue n lingua f; (shoe) ligula f; **on the tip of**
   one's ~ in prīmōribus labrīs
tongue-tied adj ēlinguis, īnfāns
tonnage n amphorae fpl
tonsils n tōnsillae fpl
tonsure n rāsūra f
too adv (also) etiam, īnsuper, quoque; (excess)
   nimis ♦ compar adj: **too far** extrā modum; **too**
   much nimium; **too long** nimium diū; **too**
   great to māior quam quī (subj); **too late** sērius;
   too little parum (gen)
tool n īnstrūmentum nt; (AGR) ferrāmentum nt;
   (person) minister m
tooth n dēns m; **~ and nail** tōtō corpore atque
   omnibus ungulīs; **cast in one's teeth**
   exprobrāre, obicere; **cut teeth** dentīre; **in the**
   teeth of obviam (dat), adversus (acc); **with the**
   teeth mordicus
toothache n dentium dolor m
toothed adj dentātus
toothless adj ēdentulus
toothpick n dentiscalpium nt
toothsome adj suāvis, dulcis
top n vertex m, fastīgium nt; (tree) cacūmen nt;
   (toy) turbō m; **from top to toe** ab īmīs unguibus
   usque ad verticem summum; **the top of**
   summus ♦ vt exsuperāre; **top up** supplēre ♦ adj
   superior, summus
tope vi pōtāre
toper n pōtor m
topiary adj topiārius ♦ n topiārium opus nt
topic n rēs f; (RHET) locus m; **~ of conversation**
   sermō m
topical adj hodiernus
topmost adj summus
topography n dēscrīptiō f
topple vi titubāre; **~ over** prōlābī
topsail n dolō m
topsyturvy adv praeposterē; **turn ~** sūrsum
   deōrsum versāre, permiscēre
tor n mōns m
torch n fax f, lampas f
torment n cruciātus m; (mind) angor m ♦ vt
   cruciāre; (mind) discruciāre, excruciāre, angere
tormentor n tortor m
tornado n turbō m
torpid adj torpēns; **be ~** torpēre; **grow**
   ~ obtorpēscere
torpor n torpor m, inertia f
torrent n torrēns m
torrid adj torridus

torsion n tortus m
torso n truncus m
tortoise n testūdō f
tortoiseshell n testūdō f
tortuous adj flexuōsus
torture n cruciātus m, supplicium nt;
   instrument of ~ tormentum nt ♦ vt torquēre,
   cruciāre, excruciāre
torturer n tortor m, carnifex m
toss n iactus m ♦ vt iactāre, excutere; **~ about**
   agitāre; **be tossed** (at sea) fluitāre
total adj tōtus, ūniversus ♦ n summa f
totality n ūniversitās f
totally adv omnīnō, plānē
totter vi lābāre, titubāre; **make ~** labefactāre
tottering n titubātiō f
touch n tāctus m; **a ~ of** aliquantulum (gen);
   finishing ~ manus extrēma f ♦ vt tangere,
   attingere; (feelings) movēre, tangere ♦ vi inter sē
   contingere; **~ at** nāvem appellere ad; **~ on** (topic)
   attingere, perstringere; **~ up** expolīre
touch-and-go adj anceps ♦ n discrīmen nt
touching adj (place) contiguus; (emotion)
   flexanimus ♦ prep quod attinet ad (acc)
touchstone n (fig) obrussa f
touchy adj inrītābilis, stomachōsus
tough adj dūrus
toughen vt dūrāre
toughness n dūritia f
tour n iter nt; (abroad) peregrīnātiō f
tourist n viātor m, peregrīnātor m
tournament n certāmen nt
tow n stuppa f; **of tow** stuppeus ♦ vt adnexum
   trahere, remulcō trahere
toward, towards prep ad (acc), versus (after noun,
   acc); (feelings) in (acc), ergā (acc); (time) sub (acc)
towel n mantēle nt
tower n turris f ♦ vi ēminēre
towered adj turrītus
town n urbs f, oppidum nt; **country**
   ~ mūnicipium nt ♦ adj urbānus
town councillor n decuriō m
townsman n oppidānus m
townspeople npl oppidānī mpl
towrope n remulcum nt
toy n crepundia ntpl ♦ vi lūdere
trace n vestīgium nt, indicium nt ♦ vt
   investīgāre; (draw) dēscrībere; **~ out** dēsignāre
track n (mark) vestīgium nt; (path) callis m,
   sēmita f; (of wheel) orbita f; (of ship) cursus m ♦ vt
   investīgāre, indāgāre
trackless adj invius
tract n (country) tractus m, regiō f; (book) libellus m
tractable adj tractābilis, facilis, docilis
trade n mercātūra f, mercātus m; (a business) ars
   f, quaestus m; **freedom of ~** commercium nt
   ♦ vi mercātūrās facere, negōtiārī; **~ in** vēndere,
   vēnditāre
trader n mercātor m, negōtiātor m
tradesman n opifex m
tradition n fāma f, mōs māiōrum m, memoria f
traditional adj ā māiōribus trāditus, patrius
traditionally adv mōre māiōrum
traduce vt calumniārī, obtrectāre (dat)
traducer n calumniātor m, obtrectātor m

traffic n commercium nt; (on road) vehicula ntpl
  ♦ vi mercātūrās facere; ~ **in** vēndere, vēnditāre
tragedian n (author) tragoedus m; (actor) āctor
  tragicus m
tragedy n tragoedia f; (fig) calamitās f, malum nt
tragic adj tragicus; (fig) tristis
tragically adv tragicē; male
tragicomedy n tragicocōmoedia f
trail n vestīgia ntpl ♦ vt trahere ♦ vi trahī
train n (line) agmen nt, ōrdō m; (of dress) īnstita f;
  (army) impedīmenta ntpl; (followers) comitēs mpl,
  satellitēs mpl, cohors f ♦ vt īnstituere, īnstruere,
  docēre, adsuēfacere; exercēre; (weapon) dīrigere
trainer n (sport) lanista m, aliptēs m
training n disciplīna f, īnstitūtiō f; (practice)
  exercitātiō f
trait n līneāmentum nt
traitor n prōditor m
traitorous adj perfidus, perfidiōsus
traitorously adv perfidiōsē
trammel vt impedīre
tramp n (man) planus m; (of feet) pulsus m ♦ vi
  gradī
trample vi: ~ **on** obterere, prōterere, prōculcāre
trance n stupor m; (prophetic) furor m
tranquil adj tranquillus, placidus, quiētus,
  sēdātus
tranquility n tranquillitās f, quiēs f, pāx f
tranquillize vt pācāre, sēdāre
tranquilly adv tranquillē, placidē, tranquillō
  animō
transact vt agere, gerere, trānsigere
transaction n rēs f, negōtium nt
transactor n āctor m
transalpine adj trānsalpīnus
transcend vt superāre, excēdere
transcendence n praestantia f
transcendent adj eximius, ēgregius, excellēns
transcendental adj dīvīnus
transcendentally adv eximiē, ēgregiē, ūnicē
transcribe vt dēscrībere, trānscrībere
transcriber n librārius m
transcript n exemplar nt, exemplum nt
transfer n trānslātiō f; (of property) aliēnātiō
  f ♦ vt trānsferre; (troops) trādūcere; (property)
  abaliēnāre; (duty) dēlēgāre
transference n trānslātiō f
transfigure vt trānsfōrmāre
transfix vt trānsfigere, trāicere, trānsfodere;
  (mind) obstupefacere; **be transfixed** stupēre,
  stupēscere
transform vt commūtāre, vertere
transformation n commūtātiō f
transgress vt violāre, perfringere ♦ vi
  dēlinquere
transgression n dēlictum nt
transgressor n violātor m
transience n brevitās f
transient adj fluxus, cadūcus, brevis
transit n trānsitus m
transition n mūtātiō f; (speech) trānsitus m
transitory adj brevis, fluxus
translate vt vertere, reddere; ~ **into Latin** Latīnē
  reddere
translation n: **a Latin ~ of Homer** Latīnē
  redditus Homērus

translator n interpres m
translucent adj perlūcidus
transmarine adj trānsmarīnus
transmission n missiō f
transmit vt mittere; (legacy) trādere, prōdere
transmutable adj mūtābilis
transmutation n mūtātiō f
transmute vt mūtāre, commūtāre
transom n trabs f
transparency n perlūcida nātūra f
transparent adj perlūcidus; (fig) perspicuus
transparently adv perspicuē
transpire vi (get known) ēmānāre, dīvulgārī;
  (happen) ēvenīre
transplant vt trānsferre
transport n vectūra f; (ship) nāvis onerāria
  f; (emotion) ēlātiō f, summa laetitia f ♦ vt
  trānsportāre, trānsvehere, trānsmittere; **be
  transported** (fig) efferrī, gestīre
transportation n vectūra f
transpose vt invertere; (words) trāicere
transposition n (words) trāiectiō f
transverse adj trānsversus, oblīquus
transversely adv in trānsversum, oblīquē
trap n laqueus m; (fig) īnsidiae fpl ♦ vt dēcipere,
  excipere; (fig) inlaqueāre
trappings n ōrnāmenta ntpl, īnsignia ntpl;
  (horse's) phalerae fpl
trash n nūgae fpl
trashy adj vīlis
Trasimene n Trasimēnus m
travail n labor m, sūdor m; (woman's) puerperium
  nt ♦ vi labōrāre, sūdāre; parturīre
travel n itinera ntpl; (foreign) peregrīnātiō f ♦ vi
  iter facere; (abroad) peregrīnārī; ~ **through**
  peragrāre; ~ **to** contendere ad, in (acc),
  proficīscī in (acc)
traveller n viātor m; (abroad) peregrīnātor m
traverse vt peragrāre, lūstrāre; ~ **a great
  distance** multa mīlia passuum iter facere
travesty n perversa imitātiō f ♦ vt perversē
  imitārī
tray n ferculum nt
treacherous adj perfidus, perfidiōsus; (ground)
  lūbricus
treacherously adv perfidiōsē
treachery n perfidia f
tread vi incēdere, ingredī; ~ **on** īnsistere (dat) ♦ n
  gradus m, incessus m
treadle n (loom) īnsilia ntpl
treadmill n pistrīnum nt
treason n māiestās f, perduelliō f; **be charged
  with** ~ māiestātis accūsārī; **be guilty of high
  ~ against** māiestātem minuere, laedere (gen)
treasonable adj perfidus, perfidiōsus
treasure n gāza f, thēsaurus m; (person) dēliciae
  fpl ♦ vt māximī aestimāre, dīligere, fovēre; ~ **up**
  condere, congerere
treasure house n thēsaurus m
treasurer n aerārī praefectus m; (royal) dioecētēs
  m
treasury n aerārium nt; (emperor's) fiscus m
treat n convīvium nt; dēlectātiō f ♦ vt (in any way)
  ūtī (abl), habēre, tractāre, accipere; (patient)
  cūrāre; (topic) tractāre; (with hospitality) invītāre;

~ **with** agere cum; ~ **as a friend** amīcī locō habēre

treatise n liber m

treatment n tractātiō f; (MED) cūrātiō f

treaty n foedus nt; **make a** ~ foedus ferīre

treble adj triplus; (voice) acūtus ♦ n acūtus sonus m ♦ vt triplicāre

tree n arbor f

trek vi migrāre ♦ n migrātiō f

trellis n cancellī mpl

tremble vi tremere, horrēre

trembling n tremor m, horror m ♦ adj tremulus

tremendous adj immānis, ingēns, vastus

tremendously adv immāne quantum

tremor n tremor m

tremulous adj tremulus

trench n fossa f

trenchant adj ācer

trenchantly adv ācriter

trend n inclīnātiō f ♦ vi vergere

trepidation n trepidātiō f

trespass n dēlictum nt ♦ vi dēlinquere; ~ **on** (property) invādere in (acc); (patience, time, etc) abūtī (abl)

trespasser n quī iniussū dominī ingreditur

tress n crīnis m

trial n (essay) experientia f; (test) probātiō f; (LAW) iūdicium nt, quaestiō f; (trouble) labor m, aerumna f; **make** ~ **of** experīrī, perīculum facere (gen); **be brought to** ~ in iūdicium venīre; **put on** ~ in iūdicium vocāre; **hold a** ~ **on** quaestiōnem habēre dē (abl)

triangle n triangulum nt

triangular adj triangulus, triquetrus

tribe n tribus m; gēns f; (barbarian) nātiō f

tribulation n aerumna f

tribunal n iūdicium nt

tribune n tribūnus m; (platform) rōstra ntpl

tribuneship, tribunate n tribūnātus m

tribunician adj tribūnicius

tributary adj vectīgālis ♦ n: **be a** ~ **of** (river) īnfluere in (acc)

tribute n tribūtum nt, vectīgal nt; (verbal) laudātiō f; **pay a** ~ **to** laudāre

trice n: **in a** ~ mōmentō temporis

trick n dolus m, fallācia f, fraus f, īnsidiae fpl, ars f; (conjurer's) praestīgiae fpl; (habit) mōs m ♦ vt fallere, dēcipere, ēlūdere; (with words) verba dare (dat); ~ **out** ōrnāre, distinguere

trickery n dolus m, fraus f, fallāciae fpl

trickle n guttae fpl ♦ vi mānāre, dēstillāre

trickster n fraudātor m, veterātor m

tricky adj lūbricus, difficilis

trident n tridēns m, fuscina f

tried adj probātus, spectātus

triennial adj trietēricus

triennially adv quartō quōque annō

trifle n nūgae fpl, paululum nt ♦ vi lūdere, nūgārī; ~ **with** lūdere

trifling adj levis, exiguus

triflingly adv leviter

trig adj lepidus, concinnus

trigger n manulea f

trim adj nitidus, concinnus ♦ vt putāre, tondēre; (lamp) oleum īnstillāre (dat) ♦ vi temporibus servīre

trimly adv concinnē

trimness n nitor, munditia f

trinket n crepundia ntpl

trip n iter nt ♦ vt supplantāre ♦ vi lābī, titubāre; ~ **along** currere; ~ **over** incurrere in (acc)

tripartite adj tripartītus

tripe n omāsum nt

triple adj triplex, triplus ♦ vt triplicāre

triply adv trifāriam

tripod n tripus m

trireme n trirēmis f

trite adj trītus

triumph n triumphus m; (victory) victōria f ♦ vi triumphāre; vincere; ~ **over** dēvincere

triumphal adj triumphālis

triumphant adj victor; laetus

triumvir n triumvir m

triumvirate n triumvirātus m

trivial adj levis, tenuis

triviality n nūgae fpl

trochaic adj trochaicus

trochee n trochaeus m

Trojan n Trōiānus m

troop n grex f, caterva f; (cavalry) turma f ♦ vi cōnfluere, congregārī

trooper n eques m

troops npl cōpiae fpl

trope n figūra f, trānslātiō f

trophy n tropaeum nt; **set up a** ~ tropaeum pōnere

tropic n sōlstitiālis orbis m; **tropics** pl loca fervida ntpl

tropical adj tropicus

trot vi tolūtim īre

troth n fidēs f

trouble n incommodum nt, malum nt, molestia f, labor m; (effort) opera f, negōtium nt; (disturbance) turba f, tumultus m; **take the** ~ **to** operam dare ut; **be worth the** ~ operae pretium esse ♦ vt (disturb) turbāre; (make uneasy) sollicitāre, exagitāre; (annoy) incommodāre, molestiam exhibēre (dat); ~ **oneself about** cūrāre, respicere; **be troubled with** labōrāre ex

troubler n turbātor m

troublesome adj molestus, incommodus, difficilis

troublesomeness n molestia f

troublous adj turbidus, turbulentus

trough n alveus m

trounce vt castīgāre

troupe n grex f, caterva f

trousered adj brācātus

trousers n brācae fpl

trow vi opīnārī

truant adj tardus ♦ n cessātor m; **play** ~ cessāre, nōn compārēre

truce n indutiae fpl

truck n carrus m; **have no** ~ **with** nihil commercī habēre cum

truckle vi adsentārī

truculence n ferōcia f, asperitās f

truculent adj truculentus, ferōx

truculently adv ferōciter

trudge vi rēpere, pedibus incēdere

true adj vērus; (genuine) germānus, vērus; (loyal) fīdus, fidēlis; (exact) rēctus, iūstus

truism n verbum trītum nt
truly adv rēvērā, profectō, vērē
trumpery n nūgae fpl ◆ adj vīlis
trumpet n tuba f, būcina f
trumpeter n būcinātor m, tubicen m
trump up vt ēmentīrī, cōnfingere
truncate vt praecīdere
truncheon n fustis m, scīpiō m
trundle vt volvere
trunk n truncus m; (elephant's) manus f; (box)
    cista f
truss n fascia f ◆ vt colligāre
trust n fidēs f, fīdūcia f; **breach of** ~ mala fidēs;
    held in ~ fīdūciārius; **put** ~ **in** fidem habēre
    (dat) ◆ vt confīdere (dat), crēdere (dat); (entrust)
    committere, concrēdere
trustee n tūtor m
trusteeship n tūtēla f
trustful adj crēdulus, fīdēns
trustfully adv fīdenter
trustily adv fidēliter
trustiness n fidēs f, fidēlitās f
trusting adj fīdēns
trustingly adv fīdenter
trustworthily adv fidēliter
trustworthiness n fidēs f, integritās f
trustworthy adj fīdus, certus; (witness) locuplēs;
    (authority) certus, bonus
trusty adj fīdus, fidēlis
truth n vēritās f, vērum nt; **in** ~ rē vērā
truthful adj vērāx
truthfully adv vērē
truthfulness n fidēs f
try vt (attempt) cōnārī; (test) experīrī, temptāre;
    (harass) exercēre; (judge) iūdicāre, cognōscere;
    try for petere, quaerere
trying adj molestus
tub n alveus m, cūpa f
tubby adj obēsus
tube n fistula f
tufa n tōfus m
tuft n crista f
tug vt trahere, tractāre
tuition n īnstitūtiō f
tumble vi concidere, corruere, prōlābī ◆ n cāsus
    m
tumbledown adj ruīnōsus
tumbler n pōculum nt
tumid adj tumidus, īnflātus
tumour n tūber nt
tumult n tumultus m, turba f; (fig) perturbātiō f
tumultuous adj tumultuōsus, turbidus
tumultuously adv tumultuōsē
tumulus n tumulus m
tun n dolium nt
tuna n thunnus m
tune n modī mpl, carmen nt; **keep in**
    ~ concentum servāre; **out of** ~ absonus,
    dissonus; (strings) incontentus ◆ vt (strings)
    intendere
tuneful adj canōrus
tunefully adv numerōsē
tunic n tunica f; **wearing a** ~ tunicātus
tunnel n cunīculus m
turban n mitra f, mitella f
turbid adj turbidus

turbot n rhombus m
turbulence n tumultus m
turbulent adj turbulentus, turbidus
turbulently adv turbulentē, turbidē
turf n caespes m
turgid adj turgidus, īnflātus
turgidity n (RHET) ampullae fpl
turgidly adv īnflātē
turmoil n turba f, tumultus m; (mind)
    perturbātiō f
turn n (motion) conversiō f; (bend) flexus m,
    ānfrāctus m; (change) commūtātiō f, vicissitūdō
    f; (walk) spatium nt; (of mind) adfectus m; (of
    language) sententia f, cōnfōrmātiō f; ~ **of**
    events mutātiō rērum f; **bad** ~ iniūria f; **good**
    ~ beneficium nt; ~ **of the scale** mōmentum nt;
    take a ~ **for the worse** in pēiōrem partem vertī;
    in turns invicem, vicissim, alternī; **in one's**
    ~ locō ōrdine ◆ vt vertere, convertere, flectere;
    (change) vertere, mūtāre; (direct) intendere,
    dīrigere; (translate) vertere, reddere; (on a lathe)
    tornāre; ~ **the edge of** retundere; ~ **the head**
    mentem exturbāre; ~ **the laugh against** rīsum
    convertere in (acc); ~ **the scale** (fig) mōmentum
    habēre; ~ **the stomach** nauseam facere; ~ **to**
    account ūtī (abl), in rem suam convertere ◆ vi
    versārī, circumagī; (change) vertere, mūtārī;
    (crisis) pendēre; (direction) convertī; (scale)
    prōpendēre; ~ **king's/queen's evidence**
    indicium profitērī; ~ **against** vt aliēnāre ab
    ◆ vi dēscīscere ab; ~ **around** (se) circumvertere;
    ~ **aside** vt dēflectere, dēclīnāre ◆ vi dēvertere,
    sē dēclīnāre; ~ **away** vt āvertere, dēpellere ◆ vi
    āversārī, discēdere; ~ **back** vi revertī; ~ **down** vt
    invertere; (proposal) rēicere; ~ **into** vi vertere in
    (acc), mūtārī in (acc); ~ **out** vt ēicere, expellere
    ◆ vi cadere, ēvenīre, ēvādere; ~ **outside in**
    excutere; ~ **over** vt ēvertere; (book) ēvolvere; (in
    mind) volūtāre, agitāre; ~ **round** vt circumagere
    ◆ vi convertī; ~ **up** vt retorquēre; (earth) versāre;
    (nose) corrūgāre ◆ vi adesse, intervenire;
    ~ **upside down** invertere
turncoat n trānsfuga m
turning n flexus m, ānfrāctus m
turning point n discrīmen nt, mēta f
turnip n rāpum nt
turpitude n turpitūdō f
turquoise n callais f ◆ adj callainus
turret n turris f
turreted adj turrītus
turtle n testūdō f; **turn** ~ invertī
turtle dove n turtur m
tusk n dēns m
tussle n luctātiō f ◆ vi luctārī
tutelage n tūtēla f
tutelary adj praeses
tutor n praeceptor m, magister m ◆ vt docēre,
    praecipere (dat)
tutorship n tūtēla f
twaddle n nūgae fpl
twang n sonus m ◆ vi increpāre
tweak vi vellicāre
tweezers n forceps m/f, volsella f
twelfth adj duodecimus ◆ n duodecima pars
    f, ūncia f; **eleven twelfths** deūnx m; **five**

twelfths quīncūnx *m*; **seven twelfths** septūnx *m*

twelve *num* duodecim; ~ **each** duodēnī; ~ **times** duodeciēns

twelvemonth *n* annus *m*

twentieth *adj* vīcēsimus ♦ *n* vīcēsima pars *f*; (*tax*) vīcēsima *f*

twenty *num* vīgintī; ~ **each** vīcēnī; ~ **times** vīciēns

twice *adv* bis; ~ **as much** duplus, bis tantō; ~ **a day** bis diē, bis in diē

twig *n* virga *f*, rāmulus *m*

twilight *n* (*morning*) dīlūculum *nt*; (*evening*) crepusculum *nt*

twin *adj* geminus ♦ *n* geminus *m*, gemina *f*

twine *n* resticula *f* ♦ *vt* nectere, implicāre, contexere ♦ *vi* sē implicāre; ~ **round** complectī

twinge *n* dolor *m*

twinkle *vi* micāre

twirl *vt* intorquēre, contorquēre ♦ *vi* circumagī

twist *vt* torquēre, intorquēre ♦ *vi* torquērī

twit *vt* obicere (*dat*)

twitch *vt* vellicāre ♦ *vi* micāre

twitter *vi* pīpilāre

two *num* duo; **two each** bīnī; **two days** biduum *nt*; **two years** biennium *nt*; **two years old** bīmus; **two by two** bīnī; **two feet long** bipedālis; **in two parts** bifāriam, bipartītō

two-coloured *adj* bicolor

two-edged *adj* anceps

twofold *adj* duplex, anceps

two-footed *adj* bipēs

two-headed *adj* biceps

two-horned *adj* bicornis

two hundred *num* ducentī; **two hundred each** ducēnī; **two hundred times** ducentiēns

two hundredth *adj* ducentēsimus

two-oared *adj* birēmis

two-pronged *adj* bidēns, bifurcus

two-way *adj* bivius

type *n* (*pattern*) exemplar *nt*; (*kind*) genus *nt*

typhoon *n* turbō *m*

typical *adj* proprius, solitus

typically *adv* dē mōre, ut mōs est

typify *vt* exprimere

tyrannical *adj* superbus, crūdēlis

tyrannically *adv* superbē, crūdēliter

tyrannize *vi* dominārī, rēgnāre

tyrannous *adj see* **tyrannical**

tyrannously *adv see* **tyrannically**

tyranny *n* dominātiō *f*, rēgnum *nt*

tyrant *n* rēx *m*, crūdēlis dominus *m*; (*Greek*) tyrannus *m*

tyro *n* tīrō *m*, rudis *m*

Uu

ubiquitous *adj* omnibus locīs praesēns
ubiquity *n* ūniversa praesentia *f*
udder *n* über *nt*
ugliness *n* foedītās *f*, dēförmitās *f*, turpitūdō *f*
ugly *adj* foedus, dēförmis, turpis
ulcer *n* ulcus *nt*, vomica *f*
ulcerate *vi* ulcerārī
ulcerous *adj* ulcerōsus
ulterior *adj* ulterior
ultimate *adj* ultimus, extrēmus
ultimately *adv* tandem, ad ultimum
umbrage *n* offēnsiō *f*; **take ~ at** indignē ferre, patī
umbrageous *adj* umbrōsus
umbrella *n* umbella *f*
umpire *n* arbiter *m*, disceptātor *m*
unabashed *adj* intrepidus, impudēns
unabated *adj* integer
unable *adj* impotēns; **be ~** nōn posse, nequīre
unacceptable *adj* ingrātus
unaccompanied *adj* sōlus
unaccomplished *adj* īnfectus, imperfectus;
  (*person*) indoctus
unaccountable *adj* inexplicābilis
unaccountably *adv* sine causā, repentē
unaccustomed *adj* īnsuētus, īnsolitus
unacquainted *adj* ignārus (*gen*), imperītus (*gen*)
unadorned *adj* inōrnātus, incōmptus; (*speech*)
  nūdus, ēnucleātus
unadulterated *adj* sincērus, integer
unadvisedly *adv* imprūdenter, incōnsultē
unaffected *adj* simplex, candidus
unaffectedly *adv* simpliciter
unaided *adj* sine auxiliō, nūdus
unalienable *adj* proprius
unalloyed *adj* pūrus
unalterable *adj* immūtābilis
unaltered *adj* immūtātus
unambiguous *adj* apertus, certus
unambitious *adj* humilis, modestus
unanimity *n* cōnsēnsiō *f*, ūnanimitās *f*
unanimous *adj* concors, ūnanimus; **be ~** idem
  omnēs sentīre
unanimously *adv* ūnā vōce, omnium cōnsēnsū
unanswerable *adj* necessārius
unanswerably *adv* sine contrōversiā
unappreciative *adj* ingrātus
unapproachable *adj* inaccessus; (*person*) difficilis
unarmed *adj* inermis
unasked *adj* ultrō, suā sponte
unassailable *adj* inexpugnābilis
unassailed *adj* intāctus, incolumis

unassuming *adj* modestus, dēmissus; **~ manners**
  modestia *f*
unassumingly *adv* modestē
unattached *adj* līber
unattempted *adj* intentātus; **leave**
  ~ praetermittere
unattended *adj* sōlus, sine comitibus
unattractive *adj* invenustus
unauthentic *adj* incertō auctōre
unavailing *adj* inūtilis, inānis
unavenged *adj* inultus
unavoidable *adj* necessārius
unavoidably *adv* necessāriō
unaware *adj* īnscius, ignārus
unawares *adv* inopīnātō, dē imprōvīsō; incautus
unbalanced *adj* turbātus
unbar *vt* reserāre
unbearable *adj* intolerābilis, intolerandus
unbearably *adv* intoleranter
unbeaten *adj* invictus
unbecoming *adj* indecōrus, inhonestus; **it is**
  ~ dēdecet
unbeknown *adj* ignōtus
unbelief *n* diffidentia *f*
unbelievable *adj* incrēdibilis
unbelievably *adv* incrēdibiliter
unbelieving *adj* incrēdulus
unbend *vt* remittere, laxāre ♦ *vi* animum
  remittere, aliquid dē sevēritāte remittere
unbending *adj* inexōrābilis, sevērus
unbiassed *adj* integer, incorruptus, aequus
unbidden *adj* ultrō, sponte
unbind *vt* solvere, resolvere
unblemished *adj* pūrus, integer
unblushing *adj* impudēns
unblushingly *adv* impudenter
unbolt *vt* reserāre
unborn *adj* nōndum nātus
unbosom *vt* patefacere, effundere
unbound *adj* solūtus
unbounded *adj* īnfinītus, immēnsus
unbridled *adj* īnfrēnātus; (*fig*) effrēnātus,
  indomitus, impotēns
unbroken *adj* integer; (*animal*) intractātus;
  (*friendship*) inviolātus; (*series*) perpetuus,
  continuus
unburden *vt* exonerāre; **~ oneself of** aperīre,
  patefacere
unburied *adj* inhumātus, īnsepultus
unbusinesslike *adj* iners
uncalled-for *adj* supervacāneus
uncanny *adj* mīrus, mōnstruōsus

uncared-for *adj* neglectus
unceasing *adj* perpetuus, adsiduus
unceasingly *adv* perpetuō, adsiduē
unceremonious *adj* agrestis, inurbānus
unceremoniously *adv* inurbānē
uncertain *adj* incertus, dubius, anceps; **be**
~ dubitāre, pendēre
uncertainly *adv* incertē, dubitanter
uncertainty *n* incertum *nt*; (*state*) dubitātiō *f*
unchangeable *adj* immūtābilis; (*person*) cōnstāns
unchanged *adj* immūtātus, īdem; **remain**
~ permanēre
uncharitable *adj* inhūmānus, malignus
uncharitableness *n* inhūmānitās *f*
uncharitably *adv* inhūmānē, malignē
unchaste *adj* impudīcus, libīdinōsus
unchastely *adv* impudīcē
unchastity *n* incestus *m*, libīdō *f*
unchecked *adj* līber, indomitus
uncivil *adj* inurbānus, importūnus, inhūmānus
uncivilized *adj* barbarus, incultus, ferus
uncivilly *adv* inurbānē
uncle *n* (*paternal*) patruus *m*; (*maternal*) avunculus
m
unclean *adj* immundus; (*fig*) impūrus, obscēnus
uncleanly *adv* impūrē
uncleanness *n* sordēs *fpl*; (*fig*) impūritās *f*,
obscēnitās *f*
unclose *vt* aperīre
unclothe *vt* nūdāre, vestem dētrahere (*dat*)
unclothed *adj* nūdus
unclouded *adj* serēnus
uncoil *vt* explicāre, ēvolvere
uncomely *adj* dēfōrmis, turpis
uncomfortable *adj* incommodus, molestus
uncomfortably *adv* incommodē
uncommitted *adj* vacuus
uncommon *adj* rārus, īnsolitus, inūsitātus;
(*eminent*) ēgregius, singulāris, eximius
uncommonly *adv* rārō; ēgregiē, ūnicē
uncommonness *n* īnsolentia *f*
uncommunicative *adj* tēctus, taciturnus
uncomplaining *adj* patiēns
uncompleted *adj* imperfectus
uncompromising *adj* dūrus, rigidus
unconcern *n* sēcūritās *f*
unconcerned *adj* sēcūrus, ōtiōsus
unconcernedly *adv* lentē
uncondemned *adj* indemnātus
unconditional *adj* absolūtus
unconditionally *adv* nullā condiciōne
uncongenial *adj* ingrātus
unconnected *adj* sēparātus, disiūnctus; (*style*)
dissolūtus
unconquerable *adj* invictus
unconquered *adj* invictus
unconscionable *adj* improbus
unconscionably *adv* improbē
unconscious *adj*: ~ **of** īnscius (*gen*), ignārus (*gen*);
become ~ sōpīrī, animō linquī
unconsciousness *n* sopor *m*
unconsecrated *adj* profānus
unconsidered *adj* neglectus
unconstitutional *adj* illicitus
unconstitutionally *adv* contrā lēgēs, contrā rem
pūblicam

uncontaminated *adj* pūrus, incorruptus, integer
uncontrollable *adj* impotēns, effrēnātus
uncontrollably *adv* effrēnātē
uncontrolled *adj* līber, solūtus
unconventional *adj* īnsolitus, solūtus
unconvicted *adj* indemnātus
unconvincing *adj* incrēdibilis, nōn vērī similis
uncooked *adj* crūdus
uncorrupted *adj* incorruptus, integer
uncouple *vt* disiungere
uncouth *adj* horridus, agrestis, inurbānus
uncouthly *adv* inurbānē
uncouthness *n* inhūmānitās *f*, rūsticitās *f*
uncover *vt* dētegere, aperīre, nūdāre
uncritical *adj* indoctus, crēdulus
uncultivated *adj* incultus; (*fig*) agrestis, rūsticus,
impolītus
uncultured *adj* agrestis, rudis
uncut *adj* intōnsus
undamaged *adj* integer, inviolātus
undaunted *adj* intrepidus, fortis
undecayed *adj* incorruptus
undeceive *vt* errōrem tollere (*dat*), errōrem
ēripere (*dat*)
undecided *adj* dubius, anceps; (*case*) integer
undecked *adj* (*ship*) apertus
undefended *adj* indēfēnsus, nūdus
undefiled *adj* integer, incontāminātus
undemonstrative *adj* taciturnus
undeniable *adj* certus
undeniably *adv* sine dubiō
undependable *adj* inconstāns, mōbilis
under *adv* īnfrā, subter ♦ *prep* sub (*abl*), īnfrā (*acc*);
(*number*) intrā (*acc*); (*motion*) sub (*acc*); ~ **arms**
in armīs; ~ **colour** (*pretext of*) speciē (*gen*), per
speciem (*gen*); ~ **my leadership** mē duce; ~ **the
circumstances** cum haec ita sint; **labour**
~ labōrāre ex; ~ **the eyes of** in cōnspectū (*gen*);
~ **the leadership of** *abl* + duce
underage *adj* impūbēs
undercurrent *n*: **an** ~ **of** lātens
underestimate *vt* minōris aestimāre
undergarment *n* subūcula *f*
undergo *vt* subīre, patī, ferre
underground *adj* subterrāneus ♦ *adv* sub terrā
undergrowth *n* virgulta *ntpl*
underhand *adj* clandestīnus, fūrtīvus ♦ *adv* clam,
fūrtim
underline *vt* subscrībere
underling *n* minister *m*, satelles *m/f*
undermine *vt* subruere; (*fig*) labefacere,
labefactāre
undermost *adj* īnfimus
underneath *adv* īnfrā ♦ *prep* sub (*abl*), īnfrā (*acc*);
(*motion*) sub (*acc*)
underprop *vt* fulcīre
underrate *vt* obtrectāre, extenuāre, minōris
aestimāre
understand *vt* intellegere, comprehendere; (*be
told*) accipere, comperīre; (*in a sense*) interpretārī;
~ **Latin** Latīnē scīre
understandable *adj* crēdibilis
understanding *adj* sapiēns, perītus ♦ *n*
intellegentia *f*; (*faculty*) mēns *f*, intellectus *m*;
(*agreement*) cōnsēnsus *m*; (*condition*) condiciō *f*

undertake *vt* suscipere, sūmere, adīre ad; (*business*) condūcere; (*case*) agere, dēfendere; (*promise*) recipere, spondēre
undertaker *n* dissignātor *m*
undertaking *n* inceptum *nt*, inceptiō *f*
undervalue *vt* minōris aestimāre
underwood *n* virgulta *ntpl*
underworld *n* īnferī *mpl*
undeserved *adj* immeritus, iniūstus
undeservedly *adv* immeritō, indignē
undeserving *adj* indignus
undesigned *adj* fortuïtus
undesignedly *adv* fortuïtō, temerē
undesirable *adj* odiōsus, ingrātus
undeterred *adj* immōtus
undeveloped *adj* immātūrus
undeviating *adj* dīrēctus
undigested *adj* crūdus
undignified *adj* levis, inhonestus
undiminished *adj* integer
undiscernible *adj* invīsus, obscūrus
undisciplined *adj* lascīvus, immoderātus; (*MIL.*) inexercitātus
undiscovered *adj* ignōtus
undisguised *adj* apertus
undisguisedly *adv* palam, apertē
undismayed *adj* impavidus, intrepidus
undisputed *adj* certus
undistinguished *adj* ignōbilis, inglōrius
undisturbed *adj* tranquillus, placidus
undo *vt* (*knot*) expedīre, resolvere; (*sewing*) dissuere; (*fig*) īnfectum reddere
undoing *n* ruīna *f*
undone *adj* infectus; (*ruined*) perditus; **be ~** perīre, disperīre; **hopelessly ~** dēperditus
undoubted *adj* certus
undoubtedly *adv* sine dubiō, plānē
undress *vt* exuere, vestem dētrahere (*dat*)
undressed *adj* nūdus
undue *adj* nimius, immoderātus, inīquus
undulate *vi* fluctuāre
undulation *n* spīra *f*
unduly *adv* nimis, plūs aequō
undutiful *adj* impius
undutifully *adv* impiē
undutifulness *n* impietās *f*
undying *adj* immortālis, aeternus
unearth *vt* ēruere, dētegere
unearthly *adj* mōnstruōsus, dīvīnus, hūmānō māior
uneasily *adv* aegrē
uneasiness *n* sollicitūdō *f*, perturbātiō *f*
uneasy *adj* sollicitus, anxius, inquiētus
uneducated *adj* illitterātus, indoctus, rudis; **be ~** litterās nescīre
unemployed *adj* ōtiōsus
unemployment *n* cessātiō *f*
unencumbered *adj* expedītus, līber
unending *adj* perpetuus, sempiternus
unendowed *adj* indōtātus
unendurable *adj* intolerandus, intolerābilis
unenjoyable *adj* iniūcundus, molestus
unenlightened *adj* rudis, inērudītus
unenterprising *adj* iners
unenviable *adj* nōn invidendus
unequal *adj* impār, dispār

unequalled *adj* ūnicus, singulāris
unequally *adv* inaequāliter, inīquē
unequivocal *adj* apertus, plānus
unerring *adj* certus
unerringly *adv* certē
unessential *adj* adventīcius, supervacāneus
uneven *adj* impār; (*surface*) asper, inīquus, inaequābilis
unevenly *adv* inīquē, inaequāliter
unevenness *n* inīquitās *f*, asperitās *f*
unexamined *adj* (*case*) incognitus
unexampled *adj* inaudītus, ūnicus, singulāris
unexceptionable *adj* ēmendātus; (*authority*) certissimus
unexpected *adj* imprōvīsus, inopīnātus, īnsperātus
unexpectedly *adv* dē imprōvīsō, ex īnspērātō, inopīnātō, necopīnātō
unexplored *adj* inexplōrātus
unfading *adj* perennis, vīvus
unfailing *adj* perennis, certus, perpetuus
unfailingly *adv* semper
unfair *adj* inīquus, iniūstus
unfairly *adv* inīquē, iniūstē
unfairness *n* inīquitās *f*, iniūstitia *f*
unfaithful *adj* īnfidēlis, īnfīdus, perfidus
unfaithfully *adv* īnfidēliter
unfaithfulness *n* īnfidēlitās *f*
unfamiliar *adj* novus, ignōtus, īnsolēns; (*sight*) invīsitātus
unfamiliarity *n* īnsolentia *f*
unfashionable *adj* obsolētus
unfasten *vt* solvere, refīgere
unfathomable *adj* īnfīnītus, profundus
unfavourable *adj* inīquus, adversus, importūnus
unfavourably *adv* inīquē, male; **be ~ disposed** āversō animō esse
unfed *adj* iēiūnus
unfeeling *adj* dūrus, crūdēlis, ferreus
unfeelingly *adv* crūdēliter
unfeigned *adj* sincērus, vērus, simplex
unfeignedly *adv* sincērē, vērē
unfilial *adj* impius
unfinished *adj* infectus, imperfectus
unfit *adj* inūtilis, incommodus, aliēnus
unfix *vt* refīgere
unflinching *adj* impavidus, firmus
unfold *vt* explicāre, ēvolvere; (*story*) expōnere, ēnārrāre
unfolding *n* explicātiō *f*
unforeseen *adj* imprōvīsus
unforgettable *adj* memorābilis
unforgiving *adj* implācābilis
unformed *adj* īnfōrmis
unfortified *adj* immūnītus, nūdus
unfortunate *adj* īnfēlīx, īnfortūnātus
unfortunately *adv* īnfēlīciter, male; **~ you did not come** male accidit quod nōn vēnistī
unfounded *adj* inānis, vānus
unfrequented *adj* dēsertus
unfriendliness *n* inimīcitia *f*
unfriendly *adj* inimīcus, malevolus; **in an ~ manner** inimīcē
unfruitful *adj* sterilis; (*fig*) inānis, vānus
unfruitfulness *n* sterilitās *f*
unfulfilled *adj* īnfectus, inritus

unfurl vt explicāre, pandere
unfurnished adj nūdus
ungainly adj agrestis, rūsticus
ungallant adj inurbānus, parum cōmis
ungenerous adj illīberālis; ~ **conduct** illīberālitās f
ungentlemanly adj illīberālis
ungirt adj discinctus
ungodliness n impietās f
ungodly adj impius
ungovernable adj impotēns, indomitus
ungovernableness n impotentia f
ungraceful adj inconcinnus, inēlegāns
ungracefully adv inēleganter
ungracious adj inhūmānus, petulāns, importūnus
ungraciously adv acerbē
ungrammatical adj barbarus; **be ~** soloecismum facere
ungrateful adj ingrātus
ungrudging adj largus, nōn invītus
ungrudgingly adv sine invidiā
unguarded adj intūtus; (word) incautus, incōnsultus
unguardedly adv temerē, incōnsultē
unguent n unguentum nt
unhallowed adj profānus, impius
unhand vt mittere
unhandy adj inhabilis
unhappily adv īnfēlīciter, miserē
unhappiness n miseria f, tristitia f, maestitia f
unhappy adj īnfēlix, miser, tristis
unharmed adj incolumis, integer, salvus
unharness vt disiungere
unhealthiness n valētūdō f; (climate) gravitās f
unhealthy adj invalidus, aeger; (climate) gravis, pestilens
unheard adj inaudītus; (LAW) indictā causā
unheard-of adj inaudītus
unheeded adj neglectus
unheeding adj immemor, sēcūrus
unhelpful adj difficilis, invītus
unhesitating adj audāx, prōmptus
unhesitatingly adv sine dubitātiōne
unhewn adj rudis
unhindered adj expedītus
unhinged adj mente captus
unhistorical adj fictus, commentīcius
unholiness n impietās f
unholy adj impius
unhonoured adj inhonōrātus
unhoped-for adj īnspērātus
unhorse vt excutere, equō dēicere
unhurt adj integer, incolumis
unicorn n monocerōs m
uniform adj aequābilis, aequālis ♦ n īnsignia ntpl; (MIL) sagum nt; **in ~** sagātus; **put on ~** saga sūmere
uniformity n aequābilitās f, cōnstantia f
uniformly adv aequābiliter, ūnō tenōre
unify vt coniungere
unimaginative adj hebes, stolidus
unimpaired adj integer, incolumis, illībātus
unimpeachable adj (character) integer; (style) ēmendātus
unimportant adj levis, nullīus mōmentī

uninformed adj indoctus, ignārus
uninhabitable adj inhabitābilis
uninhabited adj dēsertus
uninitiated adj profānus; (fig) rudis
uninjured adj integer, incolumis
unintelligent adj īnsipiēns, tardus, excors
unintelligible adj obscūrus
unintelligibly adv obscūrē
unintentionally adv imprūdēns, temerē
uninteresting adj frīgidus, āridus
uninterrupted adj continuus, perpetuus
uninterruptedly adv continenter, sine ullā intermissiōne
uninvited adj invocātus; ~ **guest** umbra f
uninviting adj iniūcundus, invenustus
union n coniūnctiō f; (social) cōnsociātiō f, societās f; (POL) foederātae cīvitātēs fpl; (agreement) concordia f, cōnsēnsus m; (marriage) coniugium nt
unique adj ūnicus, ēgregius, singulāris
unison n concentus m; (fig) concordia f, cōnsēnsus m
unit n ūniō f
unite vt coniungere, cōnsociāre, cōpulāre ♦ vi coīre; cōnsentīre, cōnspīrāre; (rivers) cōnfluere
unity n (concord) concordia f, cōnsēnsus m
universal adj ūniversus, commūnis
universally adv ūniversus, omnis; (place) ubīque
universe n mundus m, rērum nātūra f
university n acadēmia f
unjust adj iniūstus, inīquus
unjustifiable adj indignus, inexcūsābilis
unjustly adv iniūstē, iniūriā
unkempt adj horridus
unkind adj inhūmānus, inīquus
unkindly adv inhūmānē, asperē
unkindness n inhūmānitās f
unknowingly adv imprūdēns, īnscius
unknown adj ignōtus, incognitus; (fame) obscūrus
unlawful adj vetitus, iniūriōsus
unlawfully adv iniūriōsē, iniūriā
unlearn vt dēdiscere
unlearned adj indoctus, inērudītus
unless conj nisī
unlettered adj illitterātus
unlike adj dissimilis (+ gen or dat), dispār
unlikely adj nōn vērīsimilis
unlimited adj īnfīnītus, immēnsus
unload vt exonerāre, deonerāre; (from ship) expōnere
unlock vt reserāre, reclūdere
unlooked-for adj īnspērātus, inexpectātus
unloose vt solvere, exsolvere
unlovely adj invenustus
unluckily adv īnfēlīciter
unlucky adj īnfēlīx, īnfortūnātus; (day) āter
unmake vt īnfectum reddere
unman vt mollīre, frangere, dēbilitāre
unmanageable adj inhabilis
unmanly adj mollis, ēnervātus, muliebris
unmanneriness n importūnitās f, inhūmānitās f
unmannerly adj importūnus, inhūmānus
unmarried adj (man) caelebs; (woman) vidua
unmask vt nūdāre, dētegere
unmatched adj ūnicus, singulāris

unmeaning *adj* inānis
unmeasured *adj* īnfīnītus, immoderātus
unmeet *adj* parum idōneus
unmelodious *adj* absonus, absurdus
unmentionable *adj* īnfandus
unmentioned *adj* indictus; **leave ~** ōmittere
unmerciful *adj* immisericors, inclēmēns
unmercifully *adv* inclēmenter
unmerited *adj* immeritus, indignus
unmindful *adj* immemor
unmistakable *adj* certus, manifestus
unmistakably *adv* sine dubiō, certē
unmitigated *adj* merus
unmixed *adj* pūrus
unmolested *adj* intāctus
unmoor *vt* solvere
unmoved *adj* immōtus
unmusical *adj* absonus, absurdus
unmutilated *adj* integer
unnatural *adj* (*event*) mōnstruōsus; (*feelings*)
impius, inhūmānus; (*style*) arcessītus, pūtidus
unnaturally *adv* contrā nātūram; impiē,
inhūmānē; pūtidē
unnavigable *adj* innāvigābilis
unnecessarily *adv* nimis
unnecessary *adj* inūtilis, supervacāneus
unnerve *vt* dēbilitāre, frangere
unnoticed *adj:* **be ~** latēre, fallere
unnumbered *adj* innumerus
unobjectionable *adj* honestus, culpae expers
unobservant *adj* tardus
unobserved *adj:* **be ~** latēre, fallere
unobstructed *adj* apertus, pūrus
unobtrusive *adj* verēcundus; **be ~** fallere
unobtrusiveness *n* verēcundia *f*
unoccupied *adj* vacuus, ōtiōsus
unoffending *adj* innocēns
unofficial *adj* prīvātus
unorthodox *adj* abnōrmis
unostentatious *adj* modestus, verēcundus
unostentatiously *adv* nullā iactātiōne
unpaid *adj* (*services*) grātuītus; (*money*) dēbitus
unpalatable *adj* amārus; (*fig*) iniūcundus,
īnsuāvis
unparalleled *adj* ūnicus, inaudītus
unpardonable *adj* inexcūsābilis
unpatriotic *adj* impius
unpitying *adj* immisericors, ferreus
unpleasant *adj* iniūcundus, ingrātus, īnsuāvis,
gravis, molestus
unpleasantly *adv* iniūcundē, ingrātē, graviter
unpleasantness *n* iniūcunditās *f*, molestia *f*
unpleasing *adj* ingrātus, invenustus
unploughed *adj* inarātus
unpoetical *adj* pedester
unpolished *adj* impolītus; (*person*) incultus,
agrestis, inurbānus; (*style*) inconditus, rudis
unpopular *adj* invidiōsus, invīsus
unpopularity *n* invidia *f*, odium *nt*
unpractised *adj* inexercitātus, imperītus
unprecedented *adj* īnsolēns, novus, inaudītus
unprejudiced *adj* integer, aequus
unpremeditated *adj* repentīnus, subitus
unprepared *adj* imparātus
unprepossessing *adj* invenustus, illepidus
unpretentious *adj* modestus, verēcundus

unprincipled *adj* improbus, levis, prāvus
unproductive *adj* infēcundus, sterilis
unprofitable *adj* inūtilis, vānus
unprofitably *adv* frustrā, ab rē
unpropitious *adj* īnfēlīx, adversus
unpropitiously *adv* malīs ōminibus
unprotected *adj* indēfēnsus, intūtus, nūdus
unprovoked *adj* ultrō (*adv*)
unpunished *adj* impūnītus ♦ *adv* impūne
unqualified *adj* nōn idōneus; (*unrestricted*)
absolūtus
unquestionable *adj* certus
unquestionably *adv* facile, certē
unquestioning *adj* crēdulus
unravel *vt* retexere; (*fig*) ēnōdāre, explicāre
unready *adj* imparātus
unreal *adj* falsus, vānus
unreality *n* vānitās *f*
unreasonable *adj* inīquus, importūnus
unreasonableness *n* inīquitās *f*
unreasonably *adv* inīquē
unreasoning *adj* stolidus, temerārius
unreclaimed *adj* (*land*) incultus
unrefined *adj* impolītus, inurbānus, rudis
unregistered *adj* incēnsus
unrelated *adj* aliēnus
unrelenting *adj* implācābilis, inexōrābilis
unreliable *adj* incertus, levis
unreliably *adv* leviter
unrelieved *adj* perpetuus, adsiduus
unremitting *adj* adsiduus
unrequited *adj* inultus, inānis
unreservedly *adv* apertē, sine ullā exceptiōne
unresponsive *adj* hebes
unrest *n* inquiēs *f*, sollicitūdō *f*
unrestrained *adj* līber, impotēns, effrēnātus,
immoderātus
unrestricted *adj* līber, absolūtus
unrevenged *adj* inultus
unrewarded *adj* inhonōrātus
unrewarding *adj* ingrātus, vānus
unrighteous *adj* iniūstus, impius
unrighteously *adv* iniūstē, impiē
unrighteousness *n* impietās *f*
unripe *adj* immātūrus, crūdus
unrivalled *adj* ēgregius, singulāris, ūnicus
unroll *vt* ēvolvere, explicāre
unromantic *adj* pedester
unruffled *adj* immōtus, tranquillus
unruliness *n* licentia *f*, impotentia *f*
unruly *adj* effrēnātus, impotēns, immoderātus
unsafe *adj* perīculōsus, dubius; (*structure*)
īnstābilis
unsaid *adj* indictus
unsatisfactorily *adv* nōn ex sententiā, male
unsatisfactory *adj* parum idōneus, malus
unsatisfied *adj* parum contentus
unsavoury *adj* īnsuāvis, taeter
unscathed *adj* incolumis, integer
unschooled *adj* indoctus, inērudītus
unscrupulous *adj* improbus, impudēns
unscrupulously *adv* improbē, impudenter
unscrupulousness *n* improbitās *f*, impudentia *f*
unseal *vt* resignāre, solvere
unseasonable *adj* intempestīvus, importūnus
unseasonableness *n* incommoditās *f*

unseasonably *adv* intempestīvē, importūnē
unseasoned *adj (food)* nōn condītus; *(wood)* viridis
unseat *vt (rider)* excutere
unseaworthy *adj* īnfirmus
unseeing *adj* caecus
unseemly *adj* indecōrus
unseen *adj* invīsus; *(ever before)* invīsitātus
unselfish *adj* innocēns, probus, līberālis
unselfishly *adv* līberāliter
unselfishness *n* innocentia *f*, līberālitās *f*
unserviceable *adj* inūtilis
unsettle *vt* ad incertum revocāre, turbāre, sollicitāre
unsettled *adj* incertus, dubius; *(mind)* sollicitus, suspēnsus; *(times)* turbidus
unsew *vt* dissuere
unshackle *vt* expedīre, solvere
unshaken *adj* immōtus, firmus, stabilis
unshapely *adj* dēfōrmis
unshaven *adj* intōnsus
unsheathe *vt* dēstringere, stringere
unshod *adj* nūdis pedibus
unshorn *adj* intōnsus
unsightliness *n* dēfōrmitās *f*, turpitūdō *f*
unsightly *adj* foedus, dēfōrmis
unskilful *adj* indoctus, īnscītus, incallidus
unskilfully *adv* indoctē, īnscītē, incallidē
unskilfulness *n* īnscītia *f*, imperītia *f*
unskilled *adj* imperītus, indoctus; ~ **in** imperitus *(gen)*
unslaked *adj (lime)* vīvus; *(thirst)* inexplētus
unsociable *adj* īnsociābilis, difficilis
unsoiled *adj* integer, pūrus
unsolicited *adj* voluntārius ♦ *adv* ultrō
unsophisticated *adj* simplex, ingenuus
unsound *adj* īnfirmus; *(mind)* īnsānus; *(opinion)* falsus, perversus
unsoundness *n* īnfirmitās *f*; īnsānitās *f*; prāvitās *f*
unsparing *adj* inclēmēns, immisericors; *(lavish)* prōdigus
unsparingly *adv* inclēmenter; prōdigē
unspeakable *adj* īnfandus, incrēdibilis
unspeakably *adv* incrēdibiliter
unspoilt *adj* integer
unspoken *adj* indictus, tacitus
unspotted *adj* integer, pūrus
unstable *adj* īnstabilis; *(fig)* incōnstāns, levis
unstained *adj* pūrus, incorruptus, integer
unstatesmanlike *adj* illīberālis
unsteadily *adv* incōnstanter; **walk** ~ titubāre
unsteadiness *n (fig)* incōnstantia *f*
unsteady *adj* īnstabilis; *(fig)* incōnstāns
unstitch *vt* dissuere
unstring *vt* retendere
unstudied *adj* simplex
unsubdued *adj* invictus
unsubstantial *adj* levis, inānis
unsuccessful *adj* īnfēlīx; *(effort)* inritus; **be** ~ offendere; **I am** ~ mihī nōn succēdit
unsuccessfully *adv* īnfēlīciter, rē īnfectā
unsuitable *adj* incommodus, aliēnus, importūnus; **it is** ~ dēdecet
unsuitableness *n* incommoditās *f*
unsuitably *adv* incommodē, ineptē
unsuited *adj* parum idōneus

unsullied *adj* pūrus, incorruptus
unsure *adj* incertus, dubius
unsurpassable *adj* inexsuperābilis
unsurpassed *adj* ūnicus, singulāris
unsuspected *adj* latēns, nōn suspectus; **be** ~ latēre, in suspiciōnem nōn venīre
unsuspecting *adj* imprōvidus, imprūdēns
unsuspicious *adj* nōn suspicāx, crēdulus
unswerving *adj* cōnstāns
unsworn *adj* iniūrātus
unsymmetrical *adj* inaequālis
untainted *adj* incorruptus, integer
untamable *adj* indomitus
untamed *adj* indomitus, ferus
untaught *adj* indoctus, rudis
unteach *vt* dēdocēre
unteachable *adj* indocilis
untenable *adj* inānis, īnfirmus
unthankful *adj* ingrātus
unthankfully *adv* ingrātē
unthankfulness *n* ingrātus animus *m*
unthinkable *adj* incrēdibilis
unthinking *adj* incōnsīderātus, imprōvidus
unthriftily *adv* prōdigē
unthrifty *adj* prōdigus, profūsus
untidily *adv* neglegenter
untidiness *n* neglegentia *f*
untidy *adj* neglegēns, inconcinnus, squālidus
untie *vt* solvere
until *conj* dum, dōnec ♦ *prep* usque ad *(acc)*, in *(acc)*; ~ **now** adhūc
untilled *adj* incultus
untimely *adj* intempestīvus, immātūrus, importūnus
untiring *adj* impiger; *(effort)* adsiduus
unto *prep* ad *(acc)*, in *(acc)*
untold *adj* innumerus
untouched *adj* intāctus, integer
untoward *adj* adversus, malus
untrained *adj* inexercitātus, imperītus, rudis
untried *adj* intemptātus, inexpertus; *(trial)* incognitus
untrodden *adj* āvius
untroubled *adj* tranquillus, placidus, quiētus; *(mind)* sēcūrus
untrue *adj* falsus, fictus; *(disloyal)* īnfīdus, īnfidēlis
untrustworthy *adj* īnfīdus, mōbilis
untruth *n* mendācium *nt*, falsum *nt*
untruthful *adj* mendāx, falsus
untruthfully *adv* falsō, falsē
untuneful *adj* absonus
unturned *adj*: **leave no stone** ~ nihil intemptātum relinquere, omnia experīrī
untutored *adj* indoctus, incultus
unused *adj (person)* īnsuētus, īnsolitus; *(thing)* integer
unusual *adj* īnsolitus, inūsitātus, īnsolēns, novus
unusually *adv* īnsolenter, praeter cōnsuētūdinem
unusualness *n* īnsolentia *f*, novitās *f*
unutterable *adj* īnfandus, inēnārrābilis
unvarnished *adj (fig)* simplex, nūdus
unveil *vt (fig)* aperīre, patefacere
unversed *adj* ignārus *(gen)*, imperītus *(gen)*
unwanted *adj* supervacāneus
unwarily *adv* imprūdenter, incautē, incōnsultē

unwariness *n* imprūdentia *f*
unwarlike *adj* imbellis
unwarrantable *adj* inīquus, iniūstus
unwarrantably *adv* iniūriā
unwary *adj* imprūdēns, incautus, incōnsultus
unwavering *adj* stabilis, immōtus
unwearied, unwearying *adj* indēfessus, adsiduus
unweave *vt* retexere
unwedded *adj* (*man*) caelebs; (*woman*) vidua
unwelcome *adj* ingrātus
unwell *adj* aeger, aegrōtus
unwept *adj* indēflētus
unwholesome *adj* pestilēns, gravis
unwieldy *adj* inhabilis
unwilling *adj* invītus; **be ~** nolle
unwillingly *adv* invītus
unwind *vt* ēvolvere, retexere
unwise *adj* stultus, īnsipiēns, imprūdēns
unwisely *adv* īnsipienter, imprūdenter
unwittingly *adv* imprūdēns, īnsciēns
unwonted *adj* īnsolitus, inūsitātus
unworthily *adv* indignē
unworthiness *n* indignitās *f*
unworthy *adj* indignus (*abl*)
unwounded *adj* intāctus, integer
unwrap *vt* ēvolvere, explicāre
unwritten *adj* nōn scrīptus; **~ law** mōs *m*
unwrought *adj* īnfectus, rudis
unyielding *adj* dūrus, firmus, inexōrābilis
unyoke *vt* disiungere
up *adv* sūrsum; **up and down** sūrsum deōrsum; **up to** usque ad (*acc*), tenus (*abl, after noun*); **bring up** subvehere; (*child*) ēducāre; **climb up** ēscendere; **come up to** aequāre; **lift up** ērigere, sublevāre; **from childhood up** ā puerō; **it is all up with** āctum est dē; **well up in** gnārus (*gen*), perītus (*gen*); **what is he up to?** quid struit? ♦ *prep* (*motion*) in (*acc*) ♦ *n*: **ups and downs** (*fig*) vicissitūdinēs *fpl*
upbraid *vt* exprobrāre (*dat of pers, acc of charge*); obicere (*dat and acc*), increpāre, castīgāre
upbringing *n* ēducātiō *f*
upheaval *n* ēversiō *f*
upheave *vt* ēvertere
uphill *adj* acclīvis ♦ *adv* adversō colle, in adversum collem
uphold *vt* sustinēre, tuērī, servāre
upholstery *n* supellex *f*
upkeep *n* impēnsa *f*
upland *adj* montānus
uplift *vt* extollere, sublevāre
upon *prep* in (*abl*), super (*abl*); (*motion*) in (*acc*), super (*acc*); (*dependence*) ex (*abl*); **~ this** quō factō
upper *adj* superior; **gain the ~ hand** superāre, vincere
uppermost *adj* suprēmus, summus
uppish *adj* superbus
upright *adj* rēctus, ērēctus; (*character*) integer, probus, honestus
uprightly *adv* rēctē; integrē
uprightness *n* integritās *f*
upriver *adj, adv* adversō flūmine
uproar *n* tumultus *m*; clāmor *m*

uproarious *adj* tumultuōsus
uproariously *adv* tumultuōsē
uproot *vt* ērādīcāre, exstirpāre, ēruere
upset *vt* ēvertere, invertere, subvertere; **~ the apple cart** plaustrum percellere ♦ *adj* (*fig*) perturbātus
upshot *n* ēventus *m*
upside-down *adv*: **turn ~** ēvertere, invertere; (*fig*) miscēre
upstart *n* novus homō *m* ♦ *adj* repentīnus
upstream *adj, adv* adversō flūmine
upward, upwards *adv* sūrsum; **upward(s) of** (*number*) amplius
urban *adj* urbānus, oppidānus
urbane *adj* urbānus, cōmis
urbanely *adv* urbānē, cōmiter
urbanity *n* urbānitās *f*
urchin *n* (*boy*) puerulus *m*; (*animal*) echīnus *m*
urge *vt* urgēre, impellere; (*speech*) hortārī, incitāre; (*advice*) suādēre; (*request*) sollicitāre; **~ on** incitāre ♦ *n* impulsus *m*; dēsīderium *nt*
urgency *n* necessitās *f*
urgent *adj* praesēns, gravis; **be ~** īnstāre
urgently *adv* graviter
urn *n* urna *f*
usage *n* mōs *m*, īnstitūtum *nt*, ūsus *m*
use *n* ūsus *m*; (*custom*) mōs *m*, cōnsuētūdō *f*; **be of use** ūsuī esse, prōdesse, condūcere; **out of use** desuētus; **go out of use** exolēscere; **in common use** ūsitātus; **it's no use** nīl agis, nīl agimus ♦ *vt* ūtī (*abl*); (*improperly*) abūtī; (*for a purpose*) adhibēre; (*word*) ūsurpāre; **use up** cōnsūmere, exhaurīre; **used to** adsuētus (*dat*); solēre (*inf*); **I used to do** faciebam
useful *adj* ūtilis; **be ~** ūsuī esse
usefully *adv* ūtiliter
usefulness *n* ūtilitās *f*
useless *adj* inūtilis; (*thing*) inānis, inritus; **be ~** nihil valēre
uselessly *adv* inūtiliter, frustrā
uselessness *n* inānitās *f*
usher *n* (*court*) apparitor *m*; (*theatre*) dēsignātor *m* ♦ *vt*: **~ in** indūcere, intrōdūcere
usual *adj* ūsitātus, solitus; **as ~** ut adsolet, ut fert cōnsuētūdō, ex cōnsuētūdine; **out of the ~** īnsolitus, extrā ōrdinem
usually *adv* ferē, plērumque; **he ~ comes** venīre solet
usufruct *n* ūsus et fructus *m*
usurer *n* faenerātor *m*
usurp *vt* occupāre, invādere in (*acc*), ūsurpāre
usurpation *n* occupātiō *f*
usury *n* faenerātiō *f*, ūsūra *f*; **practise ~** faenerārī
utensil *n* īnstrūmentum *nt*, vās *nt*
utility *n* ūtilitās *f*, commodum *nt*
utilize *vt* ūtī (*abl*); (*for a purpose*) adhibēre
utmost *adj* extrēmus, summus; **at the ~** summum; **do one's ~** omnibus vīribus contendere
utter *adj* tōtus, extrēmus, summus ♦ *vt* ēmittere, ēdere, ēloquī, prōnūntiāre
utterance *n* dictum *nt*; (*process*) prōnūntiātiō *f*
utterly *adv* funditus, omnīnō, penitus
uttermost *adj* extrēmus, ultimus

Vv

vacancy n ināānitās f; (office) vacuitās f; **there is a**
~ locus vacat; **elect to fill a** ~ sufficere
vacant adj inānis, vacuus; **be** ~ vacāre
vacate vt vacuum facere
vacation n fēriae fpl
vacillate vi vacillāre, dubitāre
vacillation n dubitātiō f
vacuity n inānitās f
vacuous adj vacuus
vacuum n ināne nt
vagabond n grassātor m ♦ adj vagus
vagary n libīdō f
vagrancy n errātiō f
vagrant n grassātor m, vagus m
vague adj incertus, dubius
vaguely adv incertē
vain n vānus, inānis, inritus; (person) glōriōsus; **in**
~ frustrā
vainglorious adj glōriōsus
vainglory n glōria f, iactantia f
vainly adv frustrā, nēquīquam
vale n vallis f
valet n cubiculārius m
valiant adj fortis, ācer
valiantly adv fortiter, ācriter
valid adj ratus; (argument) gravis, firmus
validity n vīs f, auctōritās f
valley n vallis f
valorous adj fortis
valour n virtūs f
valuable adj pretiōsus
valuation n aestimātiō f
value n pretium nt; (fig) vīs f, honor m ♦ vt
aestimāre; (esteem) dīligere; ~ **highly** māgnī
aestimāre; ~ **little** parvī aestimāre, parvī facere
valueless adj vīlis, minimī pretī
valuer n aestimātor m
van n (in battle) prīma aciēs f; (on march) prīmum
agmen nt
vanguard n prīmum agmen nt
vanish vi diffugere, ēvānēscere, dīlābī
vanity n (unreality) vānitās f; (conceit) glōria f
vanquish vt vincere, superāre, dēvincere
vanquisher n victor m
vantage n (ground) locus superior m
vapid adj vapidus, īnsulsus
vapidly adv īnsulsē
vaporous adj nebulōsus
vapour n vapor m, nebula f; (from earth) exhālātiō f
variable adj varius, mūtābilis
variableness n mūtābilitās f, incōnstantia f
variance n discordia f, dissēnsiō f, discrepantia f;
at ~ discors; **be at** ~ dissidēre, inter sē discrepāre;
set at ~ aliēnāre

variant adj varius
variation n varietās f, vicissitūdō f
variegate vt variāre
variegated adj varius
variety n varietās f; (number) multitūdō f; (kind)
genus nt; **a** ~ **of** dīversī
various adj varius, dīversus
variously adv variē
varlet n verberō m
varnish n pigmentum nt; (fig) fūcus m
varnished adj (fig) fūcātus
vary vt variāre, mūtāre; (decorate) distinguere ♦ vi
mūtārī
vase n vās nt
vassal n ambāctus m; (fig) cliēns m
vast adj vastus, immānis, ingēns, immēnsus
vastly adv valdē
vastness n māgnitūdō f, immēnsitās f
vat n cūpa f
vault n (ARCH) fornix f; (jump) saltus m ♦ vi salīre
vaulted adj fornicātus
vaunt vt iactāre, ostentāre ♦ vi sē iactāre, glōriārī
vaunting n ostentātiō f, glōria f ♦ adj glōriōsus
veal n vitulīna f
vedette n excursor m
veer vi sē vertere, flectī
vegetable n holus nt
vehemence n vīs f, violentia f; (passion) ārdor m,
impetus m
vehement adj vehemēns, violentus, ācer
vehemently adv vehementer, ācriter
vehicle n vehiculum nt
Veii n Veiī, Vēiōrum mpl
veil n rīca f; (bridal) flammeum nt; (fig)
integumentum nt ♦ vt vēlāre, tegere
vein n vēna f
vellum n membrāna f
velocity n celeritās f, vēlōcitās f
venal adj vēnālis
vend vt vēndere
vendetta n simultās f
vendor n caupō m
veneer n (fig) speciēs f, fūcus m
venerable adj gravis, augustus
venerate vt colere, venerārī
veneration n venerātiō f, cultus m
venerator n cultor m
vengeance n ultiō f, poena f; **take** ~ **on** ulcīscī,
vindicāre in (acc); **take** ~ **for** ulcīscī, vindicāre
vengeful adj ultor
venial adj ignōscendus
venison n dāma f, ferīna f
venom n venēnum nt; (fig) vīrus nt
venomous adj venēnātus

vent n spīrāculum nt; (outlet) exitus m; **give ~ to** profundere, ēmittere ♦ vt ēmittere; (feelings on) profundere in (acc), ērumpere in (acc)
ventilate vt perflāre; (opinion) in medium prōferre, vulgāre
ventilation n perflāre
venture n perīculum nt; (gamble) ālea f; **at a ~ temerē** ♦ vi audēre ♦ vt perīclitārī, in āleam dare
venturesome adj audāx, temerārius
venturesomeness n audācia f, temeritās f
veracious adj vērāx, vēridicus
veracity n vēritās f, fidēs f
verb n verbum nt
verbally adv per colloquia; (translate) ad verbum, verbum prō verbo
verbatim adv ad verbum, totidem verbīs
verbiage n verba ntpl
verbose adj verbōsus
verbosity n loquendī prōfluentia f
verdant adj viridis
verdict n sententia f, iūdicium nt; **deliver a ~ sententiam prōnūntiāre; give a ~ in favour of** causam adiūdicāre (dat)
verdigris n aerūgō f
verdure n viriditās f
verge n ōra f; **the ~ of extrēmus; on the ~ of** (fig) prope (acc) ♦ vi vergere
verification n cōnfirmātiō f
verify vt cōnfirmāre, comprobāre
verily adv profectō, certē
verisimilitude n vērī similitūdō f
veritable adj vērus
veritably adv vērē
verity n vēritās f
vermilion n sandīx f
vermin n bestiolae fpl
vernacular adj patrius ♦ n patrius sermō m
vernal adj vērnus
versatile adj versūtus, varius
versatility n versātile ingenium nt
verse n (line) versus m; (poetry) versus mpl, carmina ntpl
versed adj īnstructus, perītus, exercitātus
versification n ars versūs faciendī
versify vt versū inclūdere ♦ vi versūs facere
version n (of story) fōrma f; **give a Latin ~ of** Latīnē reddere
vertex n vertex m, fastīgium nt
vertical adj rēctus, dīrēctus
vertically adv ad līneam, rēctā līneā, ad perpendiculum
vertigo n vertīgō f
vervain n verbēna f
verve n ācrimōnia f
very adj ipse ♦ adv admodum, valdē, vehementer ♦ superl: **at that ~ moment** tum māximē; **not ~ nōn ita**
vessel n (receptacle) vās nt; (ship) nāvigium nt
vest n subūcula f ♦ vt: **~ power in** imperium dēferre (dat); **vested interests** nummī locātī mpl
vestal adj vestālis ♦ n virgō vestālis f
vestibule n vestibulum nt
vestige n vestīgium nt, indicium nt
vestment n vestīmentum nt
vesture n vestis f
vetch n vicia f

veteran adj veterānus ♦ n (MIL) veterānus m; (fig) veterātor m
veto n interdictum nt; (tribune's) intercessiō f ♦ vt interdīcere (dat); (tribune) intercēdere (dat)
vex vt vexāre, sollicitāre, stomachum movēre (dat); **be vexed** aegrē ferre, stomachārī
vexation n (caused) molestia f; (felt) dolor m, stomachus m
vexatious adj odiōsus, molestus
vexatiously adv molestē
vexed adj īrātus; (question) anceps
via prep per (acc)
viaduct n pōns m
viands n cibus m
vibrate vi vībrāre, tremere
vibration n tremor m
vicarious adj vicārius
vice n (general) prāvitās f, perditī mōrēs mpl; (particular) vitium nt, flāgitium nt; (clamp) fībula f
viceroy n prōcūrātor m
vicinity n vīcīnia f, vīcīnitās f
vicious adj prāvus, vitiōsus, flāgitiōsus; (temper) contumāx
viciously adv flāgitiōsē; contumāciter
vicissitude n vicissitūdō f; **vicissitudes** pl vicēs fpl
victim n victima f, hostia f; (fig) piāculum nt; (exploited) praeda f; **be the ~ of labōrāre ex; fall a ~ to morī** (abl); (trickery) circumvenīrī (abl)
victimize vt nocēre (dat), circumvenīre
victor n victor m
victorious adj victor m, victrīx f; **be ~ vincere**
victory n victōria f; **win a ~ victōriam reportāre; win a ~ over vincere, superāre**
victory message n laureātae litterae fpl
victory parade n triumphus m
victual vt rem frūmentāriam suppeditāre (dat)
victualler n caupō m; (MIL) frūmentārius m
victuals n cibus m; (MIL) frūmentum nt, commeātus m
vie vi certāre, contendere; **vie with aemulārī**
view n cōnspectus m; (from far) prōspectus m; (from high) dēspectus m; (opinion) sententia f; **exposed to ~ in mediō; entertain a ~ sentīre; in ~ of propter** (acc); **in my ~ meā sententiā, meō iūdiciō; end in ~ prōpositum nt; have in ~ spectāre; point of ~ iūdicium nt; with a ~ to eō cōnsiliō ut ♦ vt īnspicere, spectāre, intuērī**
vigil n pervigilium nt; **keep a ~ vigilāre**
vigilance n vigilantia f, dīligentia f
vigilant adj vigilāns, dīligēns
vigilantly adv vigilanter, dīligenter
vigorous adj ācer, vegetus, integer; (style) nervōsus
vigorously adv ācriter, strēnuē
vigour n vīs f, nervī mpl, integritās f
vile adj turpis, impūrus, abiectus
vilely adv turpiter, impūrē
vileness n turpitūdō f, impūritās f
vilification n obtrectātiō f, calumnia f
vilify vt obtrectāre, calumniārī, maledīcere (dat)
villa n vīlla f
village n pāgus m, vīcus m; **in every ~ pāgātim**
villager n pāgānus m, vīcānus m
villain n furcifer m, scelerātus m
villainous adj scelestus, scelerātus, nēquam
villainously adv scelestē
villainy n scelus nt, nēquitia f

vindicate vt (*right*) vindicāre; (*action*) pūrgāre; (*belief*) arguere; (*person*) dēfendere, prōpugnāre prō (*abl*)
vindication n dēfēnsiō f, pūrgātiō f
vindicator n dēfēnsor m, prōpugnātor m
vindictive adj ultor, ulcīscendī cupidus
vine n vītis f; **wild** ~ labrusca f
vinedresser n vīnitor m
vinegar n acētum nt
vineyard n vīnea f, vīnētum nt
vintage n vindēmia f
vintner n vīnārius m
violate vt violāre
violation n violātiō f
violator n violātor m
violence n violentia f, vīs f, iniūria f; **do** ~ **to** violāre; **offer** ~ **to** vim īnferre (*dat*)
violent adj violentus, vehemēns; (*passion*) ācer, impotēns; ~ **death** nex f
violently adv vehementer, per vim
violet n viola f
viper n vīpera f
viperous adj (*fig*) malignus
virgin n virgō f ♦ adj virginālis
virginity n virginitās f
virile adj virīlis
virility n virtūs f
virtually adv rē vērā, ferē
virtue n virtūs f, honestum nt; (*woman's*) pudīcitia f; (*power*) vis f, potestās f; **by** ~ **of** ex (*abl*)
virtuous adj honestus, probus, integer
virtuously adv honestē
virulence n vīs f, vīrus nt
virulent adj acerbus
virus n vīrus nt
visage n ōs n, faciēs f
vis-à-vis prep exadversus (*acc*)
viscosity n lentor m
viscous adj lentus, tenāx
visible adj ēvidēns, cōnspicuus, manifestus; **be** ~ appārēre
visibly adv manifestō
vision n (*sense*) vīsus m; (*power*) aspectus m; (*apparition*) vīsum nt, vīsiō f; (*whim*) somnium nt
visionary adj vānus ♦ n somniāns m
visit n adventus m; (*formal*) salūtātiō f; (*long*) commorātiō f; **pay a** ~ **to** invīsere ♦ vt vīsere; ~ **occasionally** intervīsere; **go to** ~ invīsere
visitation n (*to inspect*) recēnsiō f; (*to punish*) animadversiō f
visitor n hospes m, hospita f; (*formal*) salūtātor m
visor n buccula f
vista n prōspectus m
visual adj oculōrum
visualize vt animō cernere, ante oculōs pōnere
visually adv oculīs
vital adj (*of life*) vītālis; (*essential*) necessārius, māximī mōmentī
vitality n vīs f; (*style*) sanguis m
vitally adv praecipuē, imprīmīs
vitals n viscera ntpl
vitiate vt corrumpere, vitiāre
vitreous adj vitreus
vitrify vt in vitrum excoquere
vituperate vt vituperāre, obiūrgāre
vituperation n vituperātiō f, maledicta ntpl

vituperative adj maledicus
vivacious adj alacer, vegetus, hilaris
vivaciously adv hilare
vivacity n alacritās f, hilaritās f
vivid adj vīvidus, ācer
vividly adv ācriter
vivify vt animāre
vixen n vulpēs f
vocabulary n verbōrum cōpia f
vocal adj; ~ **music** vōcis cantus m
vocation n officium nt, mūnus nt
vociferate vt, vi vōciferārī, clāmāre
vociferation n vōciferātiō f, clāmor m
vociferous adj vōciferāns
vociferously adv māgnīs clāmōribus
vogue n mōs m; **be in** ~ flōrēre, in honōre esse
voice n vōx f ♦ vt exprimere, ēloquī
void adj inānis, vacuus; ~ **of** expers (*gen*); **null and** ~ inritus ♦ n ināne nt ♦ vt ēvomere, ēmittere
volatile adj levis, mōbilis
volatility n levitās f
volition n voluntās f
volley n imber m
volubility n volūbilitās f
voluble adj volūbilis
volume n (*book*) liber m; (*mass*) mōlēs f; (*of sound*) māgnitūdō f
voluminous adj cōpiōsus
voluntarily adv ultrō, suā sponte
voluntary adj voluntārius; (*unpaid*) grātuītus
volunteer n (MIL) ēvocātus m ♦ vt ultrō offerre ♦ vi (MIL) nōmen dare
voluptuary n dēlicātus m, homō voluptārius m
voluptuous adj voluptārius, mollis, dēlicātus, luxuriōsus
voluptuously adv molliter, dēlicātē, luxuriōsē
voluptuousness n luxuria f, libīdō f
vomit vt vomere, ēvomere; ~ **up** ēvomere
voracious adj vorāx, edāx
voraciously adv avidē
voracity n edācitās f, gula f
vortex n vertex m, turbō m
votary n cultor m
vote n suffrāgium nt; (*opinion*) sententia f; **take a** ~ (*senate*) discessiōnem facere ♦ vi (*election*) suffrāgium ferre; (*judge*) sententiam ferre; (*senator*) cēnsēre; ~ **against** (*bill*) antīquāre; ~ **for** (*candidate*) suffrāgārī (*dat*); (*senator's motion*) discēdere in sententiam (*gen*) ♦ vt (*senate*) dēcernere
voter n suffrāgātor m
votive adj vōtīvus
vouch vi spondēre; ~ **for** praestāre, testificārī
voucher n (*person*) auctor m; (*document*) auctōritās f
vouchsafe vt concēdere
vow n vōtum nt; (*promise*) fidēs f ♦ vt vovēre; (*promise*) spondēre
vowel n vōcālis f
voyage n nāvigātiō f, cursus m ♦ vi nāvigāre
vulgar adj (*common*) vulgāris; (*low*) plēbēius, sordidus, īnsulsus
vulgarity n sordēs fpl, īnsulsitās f
vulgarly adv vulgō; īnsulsē
vulnerable adj nūdus; (*fig*) obnoxius; **be** ~ vulnerārī posse
vulture n vultur m; (*fig*) vulturius m

Ww

wad *n* massa *f*

wade *vi* per vada īre; **~ across** vadō trānsīre

waft *vt* ferre, vehere

wag *n* facētus homō *m*, ioculātor *m* ♦ *vt* movēre, mōtāre, agitāre ♦ *vi* movērī, agitārī

wage *n* mercēs *f*; (*pl*) mercēs *f*, manupretium *nt*; (*fig*) pretium *nt*, praemium *nt* ♦ *vt* gerere; **~ war on** bellum īnferre (*dat*)/gerere

wager *n* spōnsiō *f* ♦ *vi* spōnsiōnem facere ♦ *vt* dēpōnere, oppōnere

waggery *n* facētiae *fpl*

waggish *adj* facētus, rīdiculus

waggle *vt* agitāre, mōtāre

wagon *n* plaustrum *nt*, carrus *m*

waif *n* inops *m/f*

wail *n* ēiulātus *m* ♦ *vi* ēiulāre, dēplōrāre, lāmentārī

wailing *n* plōrātus *m*, lāmentātiō *f*

waist *n* medium corpus *nt*; **hold by the ~** medium tenēre

wait *n*: **have a long ~** diū exspectāre; **lie in ~** īnsidiārī ♦ *vi* manēre, opperīrī, exspectāre; **~ for** exspectāre; **~ upon** (*accompany*) adsectārī, dēdūcere; (*serve*) famulārī (*dat*); (*visit*) salūtāre

waiter *n* famulus *m*, minister *m*

waive *vt* dēpōnere, remittere

wake *vt* excitāre, suscitāre ♦ *vi* expergīscī ♦ *n* vestīgia *ntpl*; **in the ~** pōne, ā tergō; **follow in the ~ of** vestīgiīs īnstāre (*gen*)

wakeful *adj* vigil

wakefulness *n* vigilantia *f*

waken *vt* excitāre ♦ *vi* expergīscī

walk *n* (*act*) ambulātiō *f*, deambulātiō *f*; (*gait*) incessus *m*; (*place*) ambulātiō *f*, xystus *m*; **~ of life** status *m*; **go for a ~** spatiārī, deambulāre ♦ *vi* ambulāre, īre, gradī; (*with dignity*) incēdere; **~ about** inambulāre; **~ out** ēgredī

wall *n* mūrus *m*; (*indoors*) pariēs *m*; (*afield*) māceria *f*; **walls** *pl* (*of town*) moenia *ntpl* ♦ *vt* mūnīre, saepīre; **~ up** inaedificāre

wallet *n* pēra *f*

wallow *vi* volūtārī

walnut *n* iūglāns *f*

wan *adj* pallidus

wand *n* virga *f*

wander *vi* errāre, vagārī; (*in mind*) ālūcinārī; **~ over** pervagārī

wanderer *n* errō *m*, vagus *m*

wandering *adj* errābundus, vagus ♦ *n* errātiō *f*, error *m*

wane *vi* dēcrēscere, senēscere

want *n* inopia *f*, indigentia *f*, egestās *f*, pēnūria *f*; (*craving*) dēsīderium *nt*; **in ~** inops; **be in ~** egēre ♦ *vt* (*lack*) carēre (*abl*), egēre (*abl*), indigēre (*abl*); (*miss*) dēsīderāre; (*wish*) velle

wanting *adj* (*missing*) absēns; (*defective*) vitiōsus, parum idōneus; **be ~** deesse, dēficere ♦ *prep* sine (*abl*)

wanton *adj* lascīvus, libīdinōsus ♦ *vi* lascīvīre

wantonly *adv* lascīvē, libīdinōsē

war *n* bellum *nt*; **regular war** iūstum bellum; **fortunes of war** fortūna bellī; **outbreak of war** exortum bellum; **be at war with** bellum gerere cum; **declare war** bellum indīcere; **discontinue war** bellum dēpōnere; **end war** (*by agreement*) compōnere; (*by victory*) cōnficere; **enter war** bellum suscipere; **give the command of a war** bellum mandāre; **make war** bellum īnferre; **prolong a war** bellum trahere; **provoke war** bellum movēre; **wage war** bellum gerere; **wage war on** bellum īnferre (*dat*) ♦ *vi* bellāre

warble *vi* canere, cantāre

warbling *adj* garrulus, canōrus ♦ *n* cantus *m*

war cry *n* clāmor *m*

ward *n* custōdia *f*; (*person*) pupillus *m*, pupilla *f*; (*of town*) regiō *f* ♦ *vt*: **~ off** arcēre, dēfendere, prōpulsāre

warden *n* praefectus *m*

warder *n* custōs *m*

wardrobe *n* vestiārium *nt*

wardship *n* tūtēla *f*

warehouse *n* apothēca *f*

wares *n* merx *f*, mercēs *fpl*

warfare *n* bellum *nt*

warily *adv* prōvidenter, cautē

wariness *n* circumspectiō *f*, cautiō *f*

warlike *adj* ferōx, bellicōsus

warm *adj* calidus; (*fig*) ācer, studiōsus; **be ~** calēre; **become ~** calefierī, incalēscere; **keep ~** fovēre; **~ baths** thermae *fpl* ♦ *vt* calefacere, tepefacere, fovēre ♦ *vi* calefierī

warmly *adv* (*fig*) ferventer, studiōsē

warmth *n* calor *m*

warn *vt* monēre, admonēre

warning *n* (*act*) monitiō *f*; (*particular*) monitum *nt*; (*lesson*) documentum *nt*, exemplum *nt*

warp *n* stāmina *ntpl* ♦ *vt* dēprāvāre, īnflectere

warped *adj* (*fig*) prāvus

warrant *n* auctōritās *f* ♦ *vt* praestāre

warranty *n* cautiō *f*

warrior *n* bellātor *m*, bellātrīx *f*, mīles *m*

warship *n* nāvis longa *f*

wart n verrūca f
wary adj prōvidus, cautus, prūdēns
wash vt lavāre; (of rivers, sea) adluere; ~ **away**
dīluere; ~ **clean** abluere; ~ **out** (fig) ēluere ♦ vi
lavārī
washbasin n aquālis m
washing n lavātiō f
wasp n vespa f
waspish adj acerbus, stomachōsus
waste n dētrīmentum nt, intertrīmentum nt;
(extravagance) effūsiō f; (of time) iactūra f; (land)
sōlitūdō f, vastitās f ♦ adj dēsertus, vastus; **lay**
~ vastāre, populārī ♦ vt cōnsūmere, perdere,
dissipāre; (time) terere, absūmere; (with disease)
absūmere ♦ vi: ~ **away** tābēscere, intābēscere
wasteful adj prōdigus, profūsus; (destructive)
damnōsus, perniciōsus
wastefully adv prōdigē
wasting n tābēs f
wastrel n nebulō m
watch n (being awake) vigilia f; (sentry) statiō
f, excubiae fpl; **keep** ~ excubāre; **keep** ~ **on**,
keep ~ **over** custōdīre, invigilāre (dat); **set**
~ vigiliās dispōnere; **at the third** ~ ad tertiam
būcinam ♦ vt (guard) custōdīre; (observe) intuērī,
observāre, spectāre ad (acc); ~ **for** observāre,
exspectāre; (enemy) īnsidiārī (dat); ~ **closely**
adservāre
watcher n custōs m
watchful adj vigilāns
watchfully adv vigilanter
watchfulness n vigilantia f
watchman n custōs m, vigil m
watchtower n specula f
watchword n tessera f, signum nt
water n aqua f; **deep** ~ gurges m; **fresh** ~ aqua
dulcis; **high** ~ māximus aestus; **running**
~ aqua prōfluēns; **still** ~ stagnum nt; **fetch**
~ aquārī; **fetching** ~ aquātiō f; **cold** ~ frīgida f;
hot ~ calida f; **troubled waters** (fig) turbidae
rēs ♦ vt (land) inrigāre; (animal) adaquāre
water carrier n aquātor m; (Zodiac) Aquārius m
water clock n clepsydra f
waterfall n cataracta f
watering n aquātiō f; ~ **place** n (spa) aquae fpl
water pipe n fistula f
watershed n aquārum dīvortium nt
water snake n hydrus m
water spout n prēstēr m
watery adj aquōsus, ūmidus
wattle n crātēs f
wave n unda f, fluctus m ♦ vt agitāre, iactāre ♦ vi
fluctuāre
waver vi dubitāre, fluctuārī, nūtāre, vacillāre,
labāre, inclīnāre
wavering adj dubius, incōnstāns ♦ n dubitātiō
f, fluctuātiō f
wavy adj undātus; (hair) crispus
wax n cēra f ♦ vt cērāre ♦ vi crēscere
waxen adj cēreus
waxy adj cērōsus
way n via f; (route) iter nt; (method) modus m,
ratiō f; (habit) mōs m; (ship's) impetus m; **all**
the way from usque ad, ab; **by**
the way (parenthesis) etenim; **get in the way**
of intervenīre (dat), impedīre; **get under way**

nāvem solvere; **give way** (structure) labāre; (MIL)
cēdere; **give way to** indulgēre (dat); **go out of**
one's way to do ultrō facere; **have one's way**
imperāre; **in a way** quōdam modō; **in this**
way ad hunc modum; **it is not my way to** nōn
meum est (inf); **lose one's way** deerrāre; **make**
way dē viā dēcēdere; **make way for** cēdere (dat);
make one's way into sē īnsinuāre in (acc); **on**
the way inter viam, in itinere; **out of the way**
āvius, dēvius; (fig) reconditus; **pave the way for**
praeparāre; **put out of the way** tollere; **right of**
way iter; **stand in the way of** obstāre (dat); **that**
way illāc; **this way** hāc; **ways and means** opēs
fpl, reditūs mpl
wayfarer n viātor m
waylay vt īnsidiārī (dat)
wayward adj protervus, incōnstāns, levis
waywardness n libīdō f, levitās f
we pron nōs
weak adj dēbilis, īnfirmus, imbēcillus; (health)
invalidus; (argument) levis, tenuis; (senses) hebes
weaken vt dēbilitāre, īnfirmāre; (resistance)
frangere, labefactāre ♦ vi imminuī, labāre
weakling n imbēcillus m
weakly adj invalidus, aeger ♦ adv īnfirmē
weak-minded adj mollis
weakness n dēbilitās f, īnfirmitās f; (of argument)
levitās f; (of mind) mollitia f, imbēcillitās f; (flaw)
vitium nt; **have a** ~ **for** dēlectārī (abl)
weal n salūs f, rēs f; (mark of blow) vībex f; **the**
common ~ rēs pūblica f
wealth n dīvitiae fpl, opēs fpl; **a** ~ **of** cōpia f,
abundantia f
wealthy adj dīves, opulentus, locuplēs, beātus;
make ~ locuplētāre, dītāre; **very** ~ praedīves
wean vt lacte dēpellere; (fig) dēdocēre
weapon n tēlum nt
wear n (dress) habitus m; ~ **and tear**
intertrīmentum nt ♦ vt gerere, gestāre; (rub)
terere, conterere; ~ **out** cōnficere ♦ vi dūrāre;
~ **off** minuī
wearily adv cum lassitūdine, languidē
weariness n fatīgātiō f, lassitūdō f; (of) taedium
nt
wearisome adj molestus, operōsus, labōriōsus
weary adj lassus, fessus, dēfessus, fatīgātus ♦ vt
fatīgāre; **I am** ~ **of** mē taedet (gen)
weasel n mustēla f
weather n tempestās f, caelum nt; **fine**
~ serēnitās f ♦ vt superāre
weather-beaten adj tempestāte dūrātus
weave vt texere
weaver n textor m, textrix f
web n (on loom) tēla f; (spider's) arāneum nt
wed vt (a wife) dūcere; (a husband) nūbere (dat)
wedding n nūptiae fpl
wedge n cuneus m ♦ vt cuneāre
wedlock n mātrimōnium nt
weed n inūtilis herba f ♦ vt runcāre
weedy adj exīlis
week n hebdomas f
ween vt arbitrārī, putāre
weep vi flēre, lacrimārī; ~ **for** dēflēre, dēplōrāre
weeping n flētus m, lacrimae fpl
weevil n curculiō m
weft n subtēmen nt; (web) tēla f

weigh *vt* pendere, exāmināre; *(anchor)* tollere; *(thought)* ponderāre; ~ **down** dēgravāre, opprimere; ~ **out** expendere ♦ *vi* pendere

weight *n* pondus *nt*; *(influence)* auctōritās *f*, mōmentum *nt*; *(burden)* onus *nt*; **have great** ~ *(fig)* multum valēre; **he is worth his** ~ **in gold** aurō contrā cōnstat

weightily *adv* graviter

weightiness *n* gravitās *f*

weighty *adj* gravis

weir *n* mōlēs *f*

weird *adj* mōnstruōsus ♦ *n* fātum *nt*

welcome *adj* grātus, exspectātus, acceptus ♦ *n* salūtātiō *f* ♦ *vt* excipere, salvēre iubēre ♦ *interj* salvē, salvēte

welfare *n* salūs *f*

well *n* puteus *m*; *(spring)* fōns *m* ♦ *vi* scatēre ♦ *adj* salvus, sānus, valēns; **be** ~ valēre ♦ *adv* bene, probē; *(transition)* age ♦ *interj (concession)* estō; *(surprise)* heia; ~ **and good** estō; ~ **begun is half done** dīmidium factī quī coepit habet; ~ **done!** probē!; ~ **met** opportūnē venis; ~ **on in years** aetāte prōvectus; **all is** ~ bene habet; **as** ~ etiam; **as** ~ **as** cum ... tum, et ... et; **let** ~ **alone** quiēta nōn movēre; **take** ~ in bonam partem accipere; **wish** ~ favēre *(dat)*; **you may** ~ **say** iūre dīcis; **you might as** ~ **say** illud potius dīcās

well-advised *adj* prudēns

well-behaved *adj* modestus

wellbeing *n* salūs *f*

well-bred *adj* generōsus, līberālis

well-disposed *adj* benevolus, amīcus

well-informed *adj* ērudītus

well-judged *adj* ēlegāns

well-knit *adj* dēnsus

well-known *adj* nōtus, nōbilis; *(saying)* trītus

well-nigh *adv* paene

well-off *adj* beātus, fortūnātus; **you are** ~ bene est tibī

well-read *adj* litterātus

well-timed *adj* opportūnus

well-to-do *adj* beātus, dīves

well-tried *adj* probātus

well-turned *adj* rotundus

well-versed *adj* perītus, expertus

well-wisher *n* amīcus *m*, benevolēns *m*

well-worn *adj* trītus

welter *n* turba *f* ♦ *vi* miscērī, turbārī; *(wallow)* volūtārī

wench *n* muliercula *f*

wend *vt*: ~ **one's way** īre, sē ferre

west *n* occidēns *m*, sōlis occāsus *m* ♦ *adj* occidentālis

westerly, western *adj* occidentālis

westwards *adv* ad occidentem

west wind *n* Favōnius *m*

wet *adj* ūmidus, madidus; **be wet** madēre; **wet weather** pluvia *f* ♦ *vt* madefacere

wether *n* vervēx *m*

wet nurse *n* nūtrīx *f*

whack *n* ictus *m*, plāga *f* ♦ *vt* pulsāre, verberāre

whale *n* bālaena *f*

wharf *n* crepīdō *f*

what *pron (interrog)* quid; *(adj)* quī; *(relat)* id quod, ea quae; ~ **kind of?** quālis

whatever, whatsoever *pron* quidquid, quodcumque; *(adj)* quīcumque

wheat *n* trīticum *nt*

wheaten *adj* trīticeus

wheedle *vt* blandīrī, pellicere

wheedling *adj* blandus ♦ *n* blanditiae *fpl*

wheel *n* rota *f* ♦ *vt* flectere, circumagere ♦ *vi* sē flectere, circumagī

wheelbarrow *n* pabō *m*

wheeze *vi* anhēlāre

whelm *vt* obruere

whelp *n* catulus *m*

when *adv (interrog)* quandō, quō tempore ♦ *conj (time)* cum *(subj)*, ubī *(+ indic)*

whence *adv* unde

whenever *conj* quotiēns, utcumque, quandocumque, cum *(+ perf indic/pluperf indic)*; *(as soon as)* simul āc

where *adv* ubī; *(to)* quō; ~ ... **from** unde; ~ **to** quo *(interrog and relat)*

whereabouts *n* locus *m*; **your** ~ quō in locō sīs

whereas *conj* quōniam; *(contrast)* not expressed

whereby *adv* quō pāctō, quō

wherefore *adv (interrog)* quārē, cūr; *(relat)* quamobrem, quāpropter

wherein *adv* in quō, in quā

whereof *adv* cūius, cūius reī

whereon *adv* in quō, in quā

whereupon *adv* quō factō

wherever *conj* ubiubī, quācumque

wherewith *adv* quī, cum quō

wherry *n* linter *f*

whet *vt* acuere; *(fig)* exacuere

whether *conj (interrog)* utrum; *(single question)* num; *(condition)* sīve, seu; ~ ... **or** utrum ... an *(in indir question)*; *(in cond clauses)* seu (sive) ... seu (sive); ~ ... **not** utrum ... necne *(in indir question)*

whetstone *n* cōs *f*

whey *n* serum *nt*

which *pron (interrog)* quis; *(of two)* uter; *(relat)* quī ♦ *adj* quī; *(of two)* uter

whichever *pron* quisquis, quīcumque; *(of two)* utercumque

whiff *n* odor *m*

while *n* spatium *nt*, tempus *nt*; **for a** ~ parumper; **a little** ~ paulisper; **a long** ~ diū; **it is worth** ~ expedit, operae pretium est; **once in a** ~ interdum ♦ *conj (during the time that)* dum *(+ pres indic)*; *(all the time that)* dum *(+ imperf indic)* ♦ *vt*: ~ **away** dēgere, fallere

whilst *conj* dum

whim *n* libīdō *f*, arbitrium *nt*

whimper *n* vāgītus *m* ♦ *vi* vāgīre

whimsical *adj* facētus, īnsolēns

whimsically *adv* facētē

whimsy *n* dēliciae *fpl*, facētiae *fpl*

whine *n* quīritātiō *f* ♦ *vi* quīritāre

whinny *n* hinnītus *m* ♦ *vi* hinnīre

whip *n* flagellum *nt*, flagrum *nt* ♦ *vt* flagellāre, verberāre

whirl *n* turbō *m* ♦ *vt* intorquēre, contorquēre ♦ *vi* contorquērī

whirlpool *n* vertex *m*, vōragō *f*

whirlwind *n* turbō *m*

whisper n susurrus m ◆ vt, vi susurrāre, īnsusurrāre; ~ **to** ad aurem admonēre, in aurem dīcere

whistle n (instrument) fistula f; (sound) sībilus m ◆ vi sībilāre

white adj albus; (shining) candidus; (complexion) pallidus; (hair) cānus; **turn** ~ exalbēscere ◆ n album nt; (egg) albūmen nt

white-hot adj: **to be** ~ excandēscere

whiten vt dealbāre ◆ vi albēscere

whiteness n candor m

whitewash n albārium nt ◆ vt dealbāre

whither adv quō; **whithersoever** quōcumque

whitish adj albulus

whizz n strīdor m ◆ vi strīdere, increpāre

who pron quis; (relat) quī

whoever pron quisquis, quīcumque

whole adj tōtus, cūnctus; (unhurt) integer, incolumis; (healthy) sānus ◆ n tōtum nt, summa f, ūniversitās f; **on the** ~ plērumque

wholehearted adj studiōsissimus

wholeheartedly adv ex animō

wholesale adj māgnus, cōpiōsus; ~ **business** negōtiātiō f; ~ **dealer** mercātor m, negōtiātor m

wholesome adj salūtāris, salūbris

wholesomeness n salūbritās f

wholly adv omnīnō, tōtus

whoop n ululātus m ◆ vi ululāre

whose pron cūius

why adv cūr, quārē, quamobrem, qua de causa

wick n mergulus m

wicked adj improbus, scelestus; (to gods, kin, country) impius

wickedly adv improbē, scelestē, impiē

wickedness n improbitās f, scelus nt, impietās f

wicker adj vīmineus ◆ n vīmen nt

wide adj lātus, amplus; **be** ~ **of** aberrāre ab ◆ adv lātē; **far and** ~ longē lātēque

widely adv lātē; (among people) vulgō

widen vt laxāre, dilātāre

widespread adj effūsus, vulgātus

widow n vidua f

widowed adj viduus, orbus

widower n viduus m

widowhood n viduitās f

width n lātitūdō f, amplitūdō f

wield vt tractāre, gestāre, ūtī (abl)

wife n uxor f

wifely adj uxōrius

wig n capillāmentum nt

wild adj ferus, indomitus, saevus; (plant) agrestis; (land) incultus; (temper) furibundus, impotens, āmēns; (shot) temerārius; ~ **state** feritās f

wild beast n fera f

wilderness n sōlitūdō f, loca dēserta ntpl

wildly adv saevē

wildness n feritās f

wile n dolus m, ars f, fraus f

wilful adj pervicāx, contumāx; (action) cōnsultus

wilfully adv contumāciter; cōnsultō

wilfulness n pervicācia f, libīdō f

wilily adv astūtē, vafrē

wiliness n astūtia f

will n (faculty) voluntās f, animus m; (intent) cōnsilium nt; (decision) arbitrium nt; (of gods) nūtus m; (document) testāmentum nt; ~ **and pleasure** libīdō f; **against one's** ~ invītus; **at** ~ ad libīdinem suam; **good** ~ studium nt; **ill** ~ invidia f; **with a** ~ summō studiō; **without making a** ~ intestātus, intestātō ◆ vt (future) velle; (legacy) lēgāre; **as you** ~ ut libet

willing adj libēns, parātus; **be** ~ velle; **not be** ~ nōlle

willingly adv libenter

willingness n voluntās f

willow n salix f ◆ adj salignus

willowy adj gracilis

wilt vi flaccēscere

wily adj astūtus, vafer, callidus

wimple n mitra f

win vt ferre, obtinēre, adipisci; (after effort) auferre; (victory) reportāre; (fame) cōnsequī, adsequī; (friends) sibī conciliāre; **win the day** vincere; **win over** dēlēnīre, conciliāre ◆ vi vincere

wince vi resilīre

winch n māchina f, sucula f

wind[1] n ventus m; (north) aquilō m; (south) auster m; (east) eurus m; (west) favōnius m; **I get** ~ **of** subolet mihī; **run before the** ~ vento sē dare; **take the** ~ **out of (someone's) sails** ad inritum redigere; **there is something in the** ~ nescioquid olet; **which way the** ~ **blows** quōmodo sē rēs habeat

wind[2] vt torquēre; ~ **round** intorquēre ◆ vi flectī, sinuāre; ~ **up** (speech) perōrāre

windbag n verbōsus m

winded adj anhēlāns

windfall n repentīnum bonum nt

winding adj flexuōsus, tortuōsus ◆ n flexiō f, flexus m; **windings** pl (speech) ambāgēs fpl

windlass n māchina f, sucula f

window n fenestra f

windpipe n aspera artēria f

windward adj ad ventum conversus ◆ adv: **to** ~ ventum versus

windy adj ventōsus

wine n vīnum nt; (new) mustum nt; (undiluted) merum nt

winebibber n vīnōsus m

wine cellar n apothēca f

wine merchant n vīnārius m

wine press n prēlum nt

wing n āla f; (MIL) cornū nt, āla f; (of bird) penna f; **take** ~ ēvolāre; **take under one's** ~ patrōnus fierī (gen), clientem habēre, in custōdiam recipere

winged adj ālātus, pennātus, volucer

wink n nictus m ◆ vi nictāre; ~ **at** cōnīvēre (dat)

winner n victor m

winning adj blandus, iūcundus

winningly adv blandē, iūcundē

winning post n mēta f

winnings n lucra ntpl

winnow vt ventilāre; (fig) excutere

winnowing-fan n vannus f

winsome adj blandus, suāvis

winter n hiems f; (mid) brūma f ◆ adj hiemālis, hībernus ◆ vi hībernāre

winter quarters n hīberna ntpl

wintry adj hiemālis, hībernus

wipe vt dētergēre; ~ **away** abstergēre; ~ **dry** siccāre; ~ **off** dētergēre; ~ **out** dēlēre; ~ **the nose** ēmungere
wire n fīlum aēneum nt
wiry adj nervōsus
wisdom n sapientia f; (in action) prūdentia f; (in judgment) cōnsilium nt
wise adj sapiēns, prūdēns
wisely adv sapienter, prūdenter
wish n optātum nt, vōtum nt; (for something missing) dēsīderium nt; **wishes** pl (greeting) salūs f ♦ vt optāre, cupere, velle; ~ **for** exoptāre, expetere, dēsīderāre; ~ **good-day** salvēre iubēre; **as you** ~ ut libet; **I** ~ **I could** utinam possim
wishful adj cupidus
wishing n optātiō f
wisp n manipulus m
wistful adj dēsīderī plenus
wistfully adv cum dēsīderiō
wistfulness n dēsīderium nt
wit n (humour) facētiae fpl, salēs mpl; (intellect) argūtiae fpl, ingenium nt; **caustic wit** dicācitās f; **be at one's wits' end** valdē haerēre; **be out of one's wits** dēlīrāre; **have one's wits about one** prūdens esse; **to wit** nempe, dīcō
witch n sāga f, strīga f
witchcraft n veneficium nt, magicae artēs fpl
with prep (person) cum (abl); (thing) abl; (in company) apud (acc); (fight) cum (abl), contrā (acc); **be angry** ~ īrāscī (dat); **begin** ~ incipere ab; **rest** ~ **esse** penes (acc); **end** ~ dēsinere in (acc); **what do you want** ~ **me?** quid mē vis?
withdraw vt dēdūcere, dētrahere; (fig) āvocāre; (words) retractāre ♦ vi discēdere, abscēdere, sē recipere, sē subdūcere
withdrawal n (MIL) receptus m
wither vt torrēre ♦ vi dēflōrēscere
withered adj marcidus
withhold vt abstinēre, retinēre, supprimere
within adv intus, intrā; (motion) intrō ♦ prep intrā (acc), in (abl)
without adv extrā, forīs; **from** ~ extrīnsecus; **be** ~ vacāre (abl), carēre (abl) ♦ prep sine (abl), expers (gen); **I admire** ~ **fearing** ita laudō ut nōn timeam; ~ **breaking the law** salvīs lēgibus; **you cannot see** ~ **admiring** vidēre nōn potes quīn laudēs; **you cannot appreciate** ~ **seeing for yourself** aestimāre nōn potes nisi ipse vīderis; ~ **doubt** sine dubiō; ~ **the order of** iniūssū (gen); ~ **striking a blow** rē integrā
withstand vt resistere (dat), obsistere (dat); (attack) ferre, sustinēre
withy n vīmen nt
witless adj excors, ineptus, stultus
witness n (person) testis m/f; (to a document) obsignātor m; (spectator) arbiter m; (evidence) testimōnium nt; **call as** ~ antestārī; **bear** ~ testificārī; **call to** ~ testārī ♦ vt testificārī; (see) vidēre, intuērī
witnessing n testificātiō f
witticism n dictum nt; **witticisms** pl facētiae fpl
wittily adv facētē, salsē
wittingly adv sciēns
witty adj facētus, argūtus, salsus; (caustic) dicāx
wizard n magus m, veneficus m

wizardry n magicae artēs fpl
wizened adj marcidus
woad n vitrum nt
wobble vi titubāre; (structure) labāre
woe n luctus m, dolor m, aerumna f; **woes** pl mala ntpl, calamitātēs fpl; **woe to** vae (dat)
woeful adj tristis, maestus, aerumnōsus
woefully adv triste, miserē
wolf n lupus m, lupa f; **wolf's** lupīnus
woman n fēmina f, mulier f; **old** ~ anus f; **married** ~ mātrōna f; **woman's** muliebris
womanish adj muliebris, effēminātus
womanly adj muliebris
womb n uterus m
wonder n admīrātiō f; (of a thing) admīrābilitās f; (thing) mīrāculum nt, mīrum nt, portentum nt ♦ vi mīrārī; ~ **at** mīrārī, dēmīrārī
wonderful adj mīrus, mīrābilis, admīrābilis; ~ **to relate** mīrābile dictu
wonderfully adv mīrē, mīrābiliter, mīrum quantum
wonderfulness n admīrābilitās f
wondering adj mīrābundus
wonderment n admīrātiō f
wondrous adj mīrus, mīrābilis
wont n mōs m, cōnsuētūdō f
wonted adj solitus
woo vt petere
wood n silva f, nemus nt; (material) lignum nt; **gather** ~ lignārī; **touch wood!** absit verbō invidia ♦ adj ligneus
woodcutter n lignātor m
wooded adj silvestris, saltuōsus
wooden adj ligneus
woodland n silvae fpl ♦ adj silvestris
woodman n lignātor m
wood nymph n dryas f
woodpecker n pīcus m
wood pigeon n palumbēs m/f
woodwork n tigna ntpl
woodworker n faber tignārius m
woody adj silvestris, silvōsus
wooer n procus m
woof n subtēmen nt
wool n lāna f
woollen adj lāneus
woolly adj lānātus
word n verbum nt; (spoken) vōx f; (message) nūntius m; (promise) fidēs f; (term) vocābulum nt; ~ **for** ~ ad verbum, verbum ē verbō; **a** ~ **with you!** paucīs tē volō!; **break one's** ~ fidem fallere; **bring back** ~ renūntiāre; **by** ~ **of mouth** ōre; **fair words** blanditiae fpl; **give one's** ~ fidem dare; **have a** ~ **with** colloquī cum; **have words with** iūrgāre cum; **have a good** ~ **for** laudāre; **in a** ~ ūnō verbō, dēnique; **keep one's** ~ fidem praestāre; **of few words** taciturnus; **take at one's** ~ crēdere (dat)
wording n verba ntpl
wordy adj verbōsus
work n (energy) labor m, opera f; (task) opus nt; (thing done) opus nt; (book) liber m; (trouble) negōtium nt; **works** (MIL) opera ntpl; (mechanism) māchinātiō f; (place) officīna f ♦ vt (men) exercēre; (metal) fabricārī; (soil) subigere; (results) efficere; ~ **at** ēlabōrāre; ~ **in** admiscēre;

189

~ **off** exhaurīre; ~ **out** ēlabōrāre; ~ **up** (*emotion*) efferre; ~ **one's way up** prōficere ♦ *vi* gerī
workaday *adj* cottīdiānus
workhouse *n* ergastulum *nt*
working *n* (*mechanism*) māchinātiō *f*; (*soil*) cultus *m*
workman *n* (*unskilled*) operārius *m*; (*skilled*) opifex *m*, faber *m*; **workmen** operae *fpl*
workmanship *n* ars *f*, artificium *nt*
workshop *n* fabrica *f*, officīna *f*
world *n* (*universe*) mundus *m*; (*earth*) orbis terrārum *m*; (*nature*) rērum nātūra *f*; (*mankind*) hominēs *mpl*; (*masses*) vulgus *nt*; **of the** ~ mundānus; **man of the** ~ homō urbānus *m*; **best in the** ~ rērum optimus, omnium optimus; **where in the** ~ ubī gentium
worldliness *n* quaestūs studium *nt*
worldly *adj* quaestuī dēditus
worm *n* vermis *m* ♦ *vi*: ~ **one's way** sē īnsinuāre
worm-eaten *adj* vermiculōsus
wormwood *n* absinthium *nt*
worn *adj* trītus
worried *adj* sollicitus, anxius
worry *n* cūra *f*, sollicitūdō *f* ♦ *vi* sollicitārī ♦ *vt* vexāre, sollicitāre; (*of dogs*) lacerāre
worse *adj* pēior, dēterior; **grow** ~ ingravēscere; **make matters** ~ rem exasperāre ♦ *adv* pēius, dēterius
worsen *vi* ingravēscere, dēteriōr fierī
worship *n* venerātiō *f*, deōrum cultus *m*; (*rite*) sacra *ntpl*, rēs dīvīnae *fpl* ♦ *vt* adōrāre, venerārī, colere
worst *adj* pessimus, dēterrimus; ~ **enemy** inimīcissimus *m*; **endure the** ~ ultima patī ♦ *vt* vincere
worsted *n* lāna *f*
worth *n* (*value*) pretium *nt*; (*moral*) dignitās *f*, frūgālitās *f*, virtūs *f*; (*prestige*) auctōritās *f* ♦ *adj* dignus; **for all one's** ~ prō virīlī parte; **how much is it worth?** quanti vēnit?; **it is** ~ **a lot** multum valet; **it is** ~ **doing** operae pretium est
worthily *adv* dignē, meritō
worthiness *n* dignitās *f*
worthless *adj* (*person*) nēquam; (*thing*) vīlis, inānis
worthlessness *n* levitās *f*, nēquitia *f*; vīlitās *f*
worthy *adj* dignus; (*person*) frūgī, honestus; ~ **of** dignus (*abl*)
wound *n* vulnus *nt* ♦ *vt* vulnerāre; (*feelings*) offendere
wounded *adj* saucius
wrangle *n* iūrgium *nt*, rixa *f* ♦ *vi* iūrgāre, rixārī, altercārī
wrap *vt* involvere, obvolvere; ~ **round** intorquēre; ~ **up** involvere
wrapper *n* involucrum *nt*

wrapping *n* integumentum *nt*
wrath *n* īra *f*, īrācundia *f*
wrathful *adj* īrātus
wrathfully *adv* īrācundē
wreak *vt*: ~ **vengeance on** saevīre in (*acc*), ulcīscī
wreath *n* corōna *f*, sertum *nt*
wreathe *vt* (*garland*) torquēre; (*object*) corōnāre
wreck *n* naufragium *nt* ♦ *vt* frangere; (*fig*) perdere; **be wrecked** naufragium facere
wreckage *n* fragmenta *ntpl*
wrecked *adj* (*person*) naufragus; (*ship*) frāctus
wrecker *n* perditor *m*
wren *n* rēgulus *m*
wrench *vt* intorquēre, extorquēre; ~ **away** ēripere; ~ **open** effringere
wrest *vt* extorquēre
wrestle *vi* luctārī
wrestler *n* luctātor *m*, athlēta *m*
wrestling *n* luctātiō *f*
wretch *n* scelerātus *m*, nēquam homō *m*; **poor** ~ miser homō *m*
wretched *adj* īnfēlīx, miser; (*pitiful*) flēbilis
wretchedly *adv* miserē
wretchedness *n* miseria *f*; maestitia *f*
wriggle *vi* sē torquēre
wriggling *adj* sinuōsus
wright *n* faber *m*
wring *vt* torquēre; ~ **from** extorquēre
wrinkle *n* rūga *f* ♦ *vt* corrūgāre
wrinkled *adj* rūgōsus
wrist *n* prīma palmae pars *f*
writ *n* (*legal*) auctōritās *f*
write *vt* scrībere; (*book*) cōnscrībere; ~ **off** indūcere; ~ **on** īnscrībere (*dat*); ~ **out** exscrībere, dēscrībere; ~ **out in full** perscrībere
writer *n* (*lit*) scrīptor *m*, auctor *m*; (*clerk*) scrība *m*
writhe *vi* torquērī
writing *n* (*act*) scrīptiō *f*; (*result*) scrīptum *nt*
wrong *adj* falsus, perversus, prāvus; (*unjust*) iniūstus, inīquus; **be** ~, **go** ~ errāre ♦ *n* iniūria *f*, culpa *f*, noxa *f*, malum *nt*; **do** ~ peccāre, dēlinquere; **right and** ~ (*moral*) honesta ac turpia *ntpl* ♦ *vt* laedere, nocēre (*dat*); (*by deceit*) fraudāre
wrongdoer *n* maleficus *m*, scelerātus *m*
wrongdoing *n* scelus *nt*
wrongful *adj* iniūstus, iniūriosus, inīquus
wrongfully *adv* iniūriā, iniūstē, inīquē
wrong-headed *adj* perversus
wrong-headedness *n* perversitās *f*
wrongly *adv* falsō, dēprāvātē, male, perperam
wroth *adj* īrātus
wrought *adj* factus
wry *adj* dētortus; **make a wry face** ōs dūcere
wryness *n* prāvitās *f*

Yy

yacht *n* phasēlus *m*
yard *n* (*court*) ārea *f*; (*measure*) trēs pedēs
yardarm *n* antenna *f*
yarn *n* fīlum *nt*; (*story*) fābula *f*
yawn *n* hiātus *m* ♦ *vi* hiāre, ōscitāre; (*chasm*) dehiscere
ye *pron* vōs
yean *vt* parere
year *n* annus *m*; **every** ~ quotannīs; **for a** ~ **in** annum; **half** ~ sēmēstre spatium *nt*; **this year's** hōrnus; **twice a** ~ bis annō; **two years** biennium *nt*; **three years** triennium *nt*; **four years** quadriennium *nt*; **five years** quinquennium *nt*
yearly *adj* annuus, anniversārius ♦ *adv* quotannīs
yearn *vi*: ~ **for** dēsīderāre, exoptāre
yearning *n* dēsīderium *nt*
yeast *n* fermentum *nt*
yell *n* clāmor *m*; (*of pain*) ēiulātiō *f* ♦ *vi* clāmāre, eiulāre
yellow *adj* flāvus; (*pale*) gilvus; (*deep*) fulvus; (*gold*) luteus; (*saffron*) croceus
yelp *n* gannītus *m* ♦ *vi* gannīre
yeoman *n* colōnus *m*
yes *adv* ita vērō (est), māximē; (*correcting*) immo
yesterday *adv* herī ♦ *n* hesternus diēs *m*; **yesterday's** hesternus; **the day before** ~ nudius tertius

yet *adv* (*contrast*) tamen, nihilōminus, attamen; (*time*) adhūc, etiam; (*with compar*) etiam; **and yet** atquī, quamquam; **as yet** adhūc; **not yet** nōndum
yew *n* taxus *f*
yield *n* fructus *m* ♦ *vt* (*crops*) ferre, efferre; (*pleasure*) adferre; (*concession*) dare, concēdere; (*surrender*) dēdere ♦ *vi* cēdere; (*surrender*) sē dēdere, sē trādere; ~ **to the wishes of** mōrem gerere (*dat*), obsequī (*dat*)
yielding *adj* (*person*) facilis, obsequēns; (*thing*) mollis ♦ *n* cessio *f*; dēditiō *f*
yoke *n* iugum *nt* ♦ *vt* iungere, coniungere
yokel *n* agrestis *m*
yolk *n* vitellus *m*
yonder *adv* illīc ♦ *adj* ille, iste
yore *n*: **of** ~ quondam, ōlim
you *pron* tū, vōs
young *adj* iuvenis, adulēscēns; (*child*) parvus; **younger** iūnior, nātū minor; **youngest** nātū minimus ♦ *n* fētus *m*, pullus *m*, catulus *m*
young man *n* iuvenis *m*; adulēscēns *m*
youngster *n* puer *m*
your *adj* tuus, vester
yourself *pron* ipse
youth *n* (*age*) iuventūs *f*, adulescentia *f*; (*person*) iuvenis *m*, adulēscēns *m*; (*collective*) iuventūs *f*
youthful *adj* iuvenīlis, puerīlis
youthfully *adv* iuvenīliter

Zz

zeal n studium nt, ārdor m
zealot n studiōsus m, fautor m
zealous adj studiōsus, ārdēns
zealously adv studiōsē, ārdenter
zenith n vertex m
zephyr n Favōnius m
zero n nihil nt

zest n (taste) sapor m; (fig) gustātus m, impetus m
zigzag n ānfrāctus m ♦ adj tortuōsus
zither n cithara f
zodiac n signifer orbis m
zone n cingulus m

GRAMMAR AND VERB TABLES

INTRODUCTION

This book is designed to help pupils and students of Latin to understand the grammar of the language. For beginners, the book provides an introduction to and explanation of the basic forms. More advanced students will find it an invaluable guide for reference and revision.

All parts of speech (nouns, pronouns, adjectives etc) are treated separately and clearly explained for the benefit of learners. Differences in usages are illustrated by extensive examples from many Latin authors. American students and teachers, please note: this book is designed for use by students around the world, many of whom use British case ordering (Nom, Voc, Acc, Gen, Dat, Abl).

A special section on word order in Latin, one of the greatest problems for students and pupils, has been included to guide the learner through both simple and compound sentences.

For ease of reference, all necessary structures, such as Indirect Statement, Conditional Sentences etc, have been listed under Contents. Each is then explained, for both English and Latin usage, to show the learner how to recognize the structure and translate it into English. Further examples of all structures are provided, for practice.

Handy, practical hints are given in the section on Translation Guidelines, to highlight the more common problems that confront students, and to assist in translation.

The final part of the grammar section lists the many "false friends" or confusable words that often lead students and pupils astray when translating from Latin. This section is of particular importance for examination candidates.

Tables of regular verbs provide information on verb formation and usage, while unique verbs are given in full with their meanings. A special feature of the grammar is a list of the 400 most common verbs, both regular and irregular. Irregular parts of verbs are highlighted and the conjugation number of each listed, so that by referring to the table indicated by this number, any part of the verb may be deduced.

Contents

Abbreviations used

abl	ablative	**nt, neut**	neuter
acc	accusative	**nom**	nominative
adv	adverb	**pl**	plural
conj	conjunction	**plup**	pluperfect
dat	dative	**prep**	preposition
dep	deponent	**pron**	pronoun
f, fem	feminine	**sing**	singular
gen	genitive	**voc**	vocative
indic	indicative		
intrans	intransitive		
m, masc	masculine		

Nouns

A noun is the name of a person, thing or quality.

Gender

- In Latin, as in English, the gender of nouns, representing persons or living creatures, is decided by meaning. Nouns denoting male people and animals are masculine

vir	a man
Gaius	Gaius
cervus	stag

- Nouns denoting female people and animals are feminine

femina	a woman
Cornelia	Cornelia
cerva	doe/hind

- However, the gender of things or qualities in Latin is decided by the ending of the noun.

anulus (ring) *masc*
sapientia (wisdom) *fem*
barba (beard) *fem*
gaudium (joy) *nt*

Number

- Nouns may be singular, denoting one, or plural, denoting two or more. This is shown by change of ending

SINGULAR	*PLURAL*
ter**ra** (land)	ter**rae**
mod**us** (way)	mod**i**
op**us** (work)	oper**a**

Cases

- There are six cases in Latin, expressing the relationship of the noun to the other words in the sentence.

Nominative
the subject of the verb: **Caesar** died

Vocative
addressing someone/thing: Welcome, **Alexander**

Accusative
the object of the verb: The cat ate **the mouse**

Genitive
belonging to someone/thing: The home **of my friend**

Dative
the indirect object of the verb: I gave the book **to my son**

Ablative
says by, with or from whom/what: This was agreed **by the Senate**

Declensions

- Latin nouns are divided into five groups or declensions by the ending of their stems. Each declension has six cases, both singular and plural, denoted by different endings. The endings of the genitive singular case help to distinguish the different declensions.

	STEMS	GENITIVE SINGULAR
1st Declension	**-a**	**-ae**
2nd Declension	**-ŏ** or **u**	**-ī**
3rd Declension	**-i, u, consonant**	**-is**
4th Declension	**-ŭ**	**-ŭs**
5th Declension	**-ē**	**-ēi**

First Declension

- All nouns end in **-a** in the nominative case and all are feminine except when the noun indicates a male, *eg* **poēta** (a poet), **agricola** (a farmer), etc.

	SINGULAR		PLURAL	
Nom	femin**a**	*the woman*	femin**ae**	*women*
Voc	femin**a**	*o woman*	femin**ae**	*o women*
Acc	femin**am**	*the woman*	femin**ās**	*women*
Gen	femin**ae**	*of the woman*	femin**ārum**	*of the women*
Dat	femin**ae**	*to/for the woman*	femin**īs**	*to/for the women*
Abl	femin**ā**	*by/with/from the woman*	femin**īs**	*by/with/from the women*

- Note that **dea** (goddess) and **filia** (daughter), have their dative and ablative plurals **deābus** and **filiābus**

Second Declension

- Nouns of the second declension end in **-us**, or a few in **-er** or **-r**. All are masculine. Those few which end in **-um** are neuter.

	SINGULAR		PLURAL	
Nom	serv**us**	*slave*	serv**ī**	*slaves*
Voc	serv**e**		serv**ī**	
Acc	serv**um**		serv**ōs**	
Gen	serv**ī**		serv**ōrum**	
Dat	serv**ō**		serv**īs**	
Abl	serv**o**		serv**īs**	

	SINGULAR		PLURAL	
Nom	pu**er**	*boy*	puer**ī**	*boys*
Voc	pu**er**		puer**ī**	
Acc	puer**um**		puer**ōs**	
Gen	puer**ī**		puer**ōrum**	
Dat	puer**ō**		puet**īs**	
Abl	puer**ō**		puer**īs**	

5

NOUNS

Second Declension (continued)

	SINGULAR		PLURAL	
Nom	bellum	war	bella	wars
Voc	bellum		bella	
Acc	bellum		bella	
Gen	bellī		bellōrum	
Dat	bellō		bellīs	
Abl	bellō		bellīs	

- Note that proper names ending in -**ius** have vocative in -**ī, o Vergīlī** – o Virgil!

- **deus** (god), has an alternative vocative **deus**, and plural forms **di** in nominative and **dis** in dative and ablative.

Third Declension

- This is the largest group of nouns and may be divided into two broad categories, stems ending in a consonant and those ending in -**i**. All genders in this declension must be learnt.

Consonant Stems

- ending in -**l**

   consul, -is *m* (consul)

	SINGULAR	PLURAL
Nom	cōnsul	cōnsulēs
Voc	cōnsul	cōnsulēs
Acc	cōnsulem	cōnsulēs
Gen	cōnsulis	cōnsulum
Dat	cōnsulī	cōnsulibus
Abl	cōnsule	cōnsulibus

- ending in -**n**

   legio, -onis *f* (legion)

	SINGULAR	PLURAL
Nom	legiō	legionēs
Voc	legiō	legionēs
Acc	legiōnem	legionēs
Gen	legiōnis	legionum
Dat	legionī	legiōnibus
Abl	legione	legiōnibus

   flumen, -inis *nt* (river)

	SINGULAR	PLURAL
Nom	flumen	flumina
Voc	flumen	flumina
Acc	flumen	flumina
Gen	fluminis	fluminum
Dat	fluminī	fluminibus
Abl	flumine	fluminibus

- Note that the genitive plural of these nouns ends in -**um**.

- Stems ending in **-i**

  civis, -is *m/f* (citizen)

	SINGULAR	PLURAL
Nom	civis	civēs
Voc	civis	civēs
Acc	civem	civēs
Gen	civis	civium
Dat	civī	civibus
Abl	cive	civibus

- Note that these nouns have genitive plural in **-ium**.

Neuter Nouns

  mare, -is *nt* (sea)

SINGULAR		PLURAL
Nom	mare	maria
Voc	mare	maria
Acc	mare	maria
Gen	maris	marium
Dat	mari	maribus
Abl	marī	maribus

  animal, -is *nt* (animal)

SINGULAR		PLURAL
Nom	animal	animālia
Voc	animal	animālia
Acc	animal	animālia
Gen	animālis	animālium
Dat	animālī	animālibus
Abl	animālī	animālibus

- Note that the ablative singular of these neuter nouns ends in **-ī**.
- Nominative, vocative and accusative singular endings of neuter nouns are identical.
- Nominative, vocative and accusative plural endings of neuter nouns in **all** declensions end in **-ā**.

Monosyllabic Consonant Stems

- The following have their genitive plural in **-ium**:

arx, arcis f (citadel)	- arcium (of citadels)
gēns, gentis f (race)	- gentium (of races)
mōns, montis m (mountain)	- montium (of mountains)
nox, noctis f (night)	- noctium (of nights)
pōns, pontis m (bridge)	- pontium (of bndges)
urbs, urbis f (city)	- urbium (of cities)

Fourth Declension

- Nouns in this declension end in **-us** in the nominative singular and are mainly masculine. A few end in **-u** and are neuter.

exercitus, -ūs *m* (army)

	SINGULAR	PLURAL
Nom	exercit**us**	exercit**ūs**
Voc	exercit**us**	exercit**ūs**
Acc	exercit**um**	exercit**ūs**
Gen	exercit**ūs**	exercit**uum**
Dat	exercit**uī**	exercit**ibus**
Abl	exercit**ū**	exercit**ibus**

genū, -ūs *nt* (knee)

	SINGULAR	PLURAL
Nom	gen**ū**	gen**ua**
Voc	gen**ū**	gen**ua**
Acc	gen**ū**	gen**ua**
Gen	gen**ūs**	gen**uum**
Dat	gen**ū**	gen**ibus**
Abl	gen**ū**	gen**ibus**

- Note that a few common nouns are feminine, *eg* **domus** (house), **manus** (hand), **Idus** (Ides or 15th of the month).

- The form **domī** (at home) is an old form called locative, **domō** (from home) *abl sing*, **domōs** *acc pl* and **domōrum** *gen pl* are also used besides the fourth declension forms of **domus** (house).

Fifth Declension

- There are only a few nouns in this declension. All end in **-ēs** in the nominative case. Most are feminine, but **diēs** (day) and **meridiēs** (midday) are masculine.

diēs, diēī *m* (day)

	SINGULAR	PLURAL
Nom	di**ēs**	di**ēs**
Voc	di**ēs**	di**ēs**
Acc	di**em**	di**ēs**
Gen	di**ēī**	di**ērum**
Dat	di**ēī**	di**ēbus**
Abl	di**ē**	di**ēbus**

Cases

Use Of Cases

Nominative Case

The nominative case is used where:

- the noun is the **subject** of the verb (→**1**)
- the noun is a **complement** (→**2**)
- the noun is **in apposition** to the subject (→**3**)

Accusative Case

The accusative case is used:

- for the **direct object** of the verb (→**4**)
- with verbs of teaching and asking which take accusative of person and thing (→**5**)
- Verbs of naming, making *etc* take two accusatives for the same person or thing (→**6**)
- in exclamations (→**7**)
- to show extent of space (→**8**)
- to show extent of time (→**9**)
- to show motion to a place or country usually with a preposition (→**10**)
- to show motion towards, without a preposition, before names of towns and small islands (→**11**)

    Note also: **domum** (home), **rus** (to the country), **foras** (outside)

- for an object with similar meaning to the verb (*cognate*) (→**12**)

Examples

1 **Sextus** ridet
Sextus laughs

2 Romulus **rex** factus est
Romulus was made king

3 Marcus Annius, **eques Romanus**,
hoc dicit Marcus Annius, a Roman
businessman, says this

4 canis **baculum** petit
the dog fetches the stick

5 **puerum litteras** docebo
I shall teach the boy literature

6 **Ancum Martium regem** populus
creavit
The people made Ancus Martius
king

7 o **tempora**, o **mores**
what times, what conduct!

8 murus decem **pedes** altus est
the wall is 10 foot high

9 Troia decem **annos** obsessa est
Troy was under siege for 10 years

10 **ad Hispaniam** effugerunt
they escaped to Spain

11 **Athenas** legati missi sunt
Ambassadors were sent to Athens

12 **vitam** bonam **vixit**
he lived a good life

NOUNS

Dative Case

- Indirect object (*ie* to or for whom an action is performed) (→**1**)

- used with verbs of obeying (**parēre**), resisting (**resistere**), pleasing (**placēre**), ordering (**imperāre**) etc (→**2**)

- verb compounds (beginning **ad-**, **ob-**, **prae-**, **sub-**) denoting helping or hindering take dative (→**3**)

    adesse – come to help
    subvenire – help

- indicates possession (→**4**)

- is used with adjectives meaning "like" (**similis**), "fit" (**aptus**), "near" (**proximus**) (→**5**)

- indicates a purpose (known as *predicative dative*) (→**6**)

- shows the agent of gerund/gerundive (→**7**)

Examples

1 pecuniam **domino** dedit
he gave the money to his master

2 maria terraque **Deo** parent
land and sea obey God

3 Pompeius **hostibus** obstitit
Pompey opposed the enemy

4 Poppaea amica est **Marciae**
Poppaea is Marcia's friend

5 feles **tigris similis** est
the cat is like a tiger

6 nemo mihi **auxilio** est
there is no-one to help me

7 omnia errant agenda **nobis**
everything had to be done by us

Genitive Case

- Indicates possession (→**1**)

- Denotes part of a whole (→**2**)

- Indicates a quality, always with an adjective (→**3**)

- Is used as a predicate, where a person represents a quality (→**4**)

- Is used with superlatives (→**5**)

- Precedes **causa** and **gratia** (for the sake of) (→**6**)

- Is used after certain adjectives (→**7**)

    sciens (knowing)
    inscius (ignorant of)
    cupidus (desiring)
    particeps (sharing) *etc*

- Is used with verbs of remembering (**memini**) and forgetting (**obliviscor**) (→**8**)

- Follows verbs of accusing, convicting *etc* (→**9**)

- Represents value or worth (→**10**)

Examples

1 domus **regis**
the king's house

uxor **Augusti**
the wife of Augustus

2 quid **novi**
what news?

plus **cibi**
more food

3 magnae **auctoritatis** es
your reputation is great

4 **stulti est** hoc facere
it is the mark of a fool to do this

5 Indus est **omnium fluminum** maximum
the Indus is the greatest of all rivers

6 tu me **amoris causa** servavisti
you saved me for love's sake

7 Verres, **cupidus pecuniae**, ex hereditate praedatus est

Verres, greedy for money, robbed the estate

8 **mortis** memento
remember death

9 ante **actarum rerum** Antonius accusatus est
Antony was accused of previous offences

10 frumentum **minimi** vendidit
he sold com at the lowest price

flocci non facio
I don't care at all

Nouns

Ablative Case

- Indicates place, usually with the preposition "in" (→**1**)

    Note, however: **totā Asiā** – throughout Asia
    terrā marīque – by land and sea

- Indicates motion from, or down from a place, usually with prepositions **ex**, **de**, **a(b)** (→**2**)

- Note prepositions are omitted before names of towns, small islands and **domo** (from home), **rure** (from the country), **foris** (from outside) (→**3**)

- Represents time when or within which something happens (→**4**)

- Indicates origin, sometimes with prepositions **in**, **ex**, **a(b)** (→**5**)

- Is used to show material from which something is made (→**6**)

- Indicates manner (how something is done), usually with **cum** when there is no adjective, and without **cum** when there is an adjective (→**7**)

- Is used with verbs of depriving, filling, needing and with **opus est** (→**8**)

- Is used with deponent verbs **otur** (use), **abutor** (abuse), **fungor** (accomplish), **potior** (gain possession of) (→**9**)

- States cause (→**10**)

- To form **ablative absolute**, where a noun in the ablative is combined with a participle or another noun or adjective in the same case, to form an idea independent of the rest of the sentence. This is equivalent to an adverbial clause (→**11**)

Examples

1 Milo in **urbe** mansit
Milo remained in the city

2 **de equo** cecidit
He fell down from his horse

praedam **ex urbe ornatissima** sustulit
He stole booty from the rich city

3 **domo** cucurrerunt servi
The slaves ran from the house

4 **hac nocte** Agricola obiit
Agricola died on this night

decem annis Lacedaimonii non haec confecerunt
The Spartans did not complete this task within 10 years

5 Romulus et Remus, **Marte nati**
Romulus and Remus, sons of Mars

flumina **in Caucaso monte** orta
Rivers rising in the Caucasus mountains

6 statua **ex auro** facta est
The statue was made of gold

7 mulieres **cum virtute** vixerunt
The women lived virtuously

summa celeritate Poeni regressi sunt
The Carthaginians retreated at top speed

8 aliquem vita
to deprive someone of life

privare opus est mihi **divitiis**
I need wealth

9 **vi** et **armis** usus est
He used force of arms

10 leo **fame** decessit
The lion died of hunger

11 **exigua parte aestatis reliqua**, Caesar in Britanniam proficisci contendit
Although only a little of the summer remained, Caesar hurried to set out for Britain

Adjectives

An adjective adds a quality to the noun. It usually follows the noun but sometimes comes before it for emphasis. The adjective agrees with its noun in number, case and gender.

Gender

vir bonus (*masc*)	a good man
fēmina pulchra (*fem*)	a beautiful woman
bellum longum (*neut*)	a long war

Number

virī bonī (*pl*)	good men
fēminae pulchrae (*pl*)	beautiful women
bella longa (*pl*)	long wars

Case

virō bonō (*dat sing*)	for a good man
fēminās pulchrās (*acc pl*)	beautiful women
bellī longī (*gen sing*)	of a long war

- Adjectives are declined like nouns and usually arranged in two groups:
    1. those with endings of the first and second declensions
    2. those with endings of the third declension

First and Second Declensions
bonus, bona, bonum (good)

SINGULAR

	Masc	Fem	Neut
Nom	bonus	bona	bonum
Voc	bone	bona	bonum
Acc	bonum	bonam	bonum
Gen	bonī	bonae	bonī
Dat	bonō	bonae	bonō
Abl	bonō	bonā	bonō

PLURAL

	Masc	Fem	Neut
Nom	bonī	bonae	bona
Voc	bonī	bonae	bona
Acc	bonōs	bonas	bona
Gen	bonōrum	bonārum	bonōrum
Dat	bonīs	bonīs	bonīs
Abl	bonīs	bonīs	bonīs

First and Second Declensions (continued)
miser, misera, miserum (unhappy)

SINGULAR

	Masc	Fem	Neut
Nom	mis**er**	miser**a**	miser**um**
Voc	mis**er**	miser**a**	miser**um**
Acc	miser**um**	miser**am**	miser**um**
Gen	miser**ī**	miser**ae**	miser**ī**
Dat	miser**ō**	miser**ae**	miser**ō**
Abl	miser**ō**	miser**ā**	miser**ō**

PLURAL

	Masc	Fem	Neut
Nom	miser**ī**	miser**ae**	miser**a**
Voc	miser**ī**	miser**ae**	miser**a**
Acc	miser**ōs**	miser**ās**	miser**a**
Gen	miser**ōrum**	miser**ārum**	miser**ōrum**
Dat	miser**īs**	miser**īs**	miser**īs**
Abl	miser**īs**	miser**īs**	miser**īs**

- **liber** (free) and **tener** (tender) are declined like **miser**

pulcher, pulchra, pulchrum (beautiful)

SINGULAR

	Masc	Fem	Neut
Nom	pulch**er**	pulchr**a**	pulchr**um**
Voc	pulch**er**	pulchr**a**	pulchr**um**
Acc	pulchr**um**	pulchr**am**	pulchr**um**
Gen	pulchr**ī**	pulchr**ae**	pulchr**ī**
Dat	pulchr**ō**	pulchr**ae**	pulchr**ō**
Abl	pulchr**ō**	pulchr**ā**	pulchr**ō**

PLURAL

	Masc	Fem	Neut
Nom	pulchr**ī**	pulchr**ae**	pulchr**a**
Voc	pulchr**ī**	pulchr**ae**	pulchr**a**
Acc	pulchr**ōs**	pulchr**ās**	pulchr**a**
Gen	pulchr**ōrum**	pulchr**ārum**	pulchr**ōrum**
Dat	pulchr**īs**	pulchr**īs**	pulchr**īs**
Abl	pulchr**īs**	pulchr**īs**	pulchr**īs**

- **aeger** (sick), **crēber** (frequent), **integer** (whole), **niger** (black), **piger** (slow) and **sacer** (sacred) are declined like **pulcher**

- The following group of adjectives form their genitive singular in **-ius** and dative singular in **-i**:

alius, -a, -ud	another
alter, altera, alterum	one of two
neuter, neutra, neutrum	neither
nūllus, -a, -um	none
sōlus, -a, -um	alone
tōtus, -a, -um	whole
ūllus, -a, -um	any
ūnus, -a, -um	one
uter, utra, utrum	which of two?

sōlus (alone)

SINGULAR

	Masc	Fem	Neut
Nom	sōl**us**	sōl**a**	sōl**um**
Acc	sōl**um**	sōl**am**	sōl**um**
Gen	sōl**ius**	sōl**ius**	sōl**ius**
Dat	sōl**ī**	sōl**ī**	sōl**ī**
Abl	sōl**ō**	sōl**ā**	sōl**ō**

PLURAL

	Masc	Fem	Neut
Nom	sōl**ī**	sōl**ae**	sōl**a**
Acc	sōl**ōs**	sōl**as**	sōl**a**
Gen	sōl**ōrum**	sōl**arum**	sōl**ōrum**
Dat	sōl**īs**	sōl**īs**	sōl**īs**
Abl	sōi**īs**	sōl**īs**	sōl**īs**

Third Declension

Adjectives of the third declension, like nouns, may be divided into two broad types, those with consonant stems and those with vowel stems in -**i**.

Consonant Stems

These have **one** ending in nominative singular.

prūdēns (wise)

	SINGULAR		
	Masc	*Fem*	*Neut*
Nom	prūd**ēns**	prūd**ēns**	prūd**ēns**
Voc	prūd**ēns**	prūd**ēns**	prūd**ēns**
Acc	prūd**entem**	prūd**entem**	prūd**ēns**
Gen	prūd**entis**	prūd**entis**	prūd**entis**
Dat	prūd**entī**	prūd**entī**	prūd**entī**
Abl	prūd**entī**	prūd**entī**	prūd**entī**

	PLURAL		
	Masc	*Fem*	*Neut*
Nom	prūd**entēs**	prūd**entēs**	prūd**entia**
Voc	prūd**entēs**	prūd**entēs**	prūd**entia**
Acc	prūd**entēs**	prūd**entēs**	prūd**entia**
Gen	prūd**entium**	prūd**entium**	prūd**entium**
Dat	prūd**entibus**	prūd**entibus**	prūd**entibus**
Abl	prūd**entibus**	prūd**entibus**	prūd**entibus**

- **dīligēns** (careful), **innocēns** (innocent), **potēns** (powerful), **frequēns** (frequent), **ingēns** (huge) are declined like **prūdēns**

amāns (loving)

	SINGULAR		
	Masc	*Fem*	*Neut*
Nom	am**āns**	am**āns**	am**āns**
Voc	am**āns**	am**āns**	am**āns**
Acc	am**antem**	am**antem**	am**āns**
Gen	am**antis**	am**antis**	am**antis**
Dat	am**antī**	am**antī**	am**antī**
Abl	am**ante**	am**ante**	am**ante**

	PLURAL		
	Masc	*Fem*	*Neut*
Nom	am**antēs**	am**antēs**	am**antia**
Voc	am**antēs**	am**antēs**	am**antia**
Acc	am**antēs**	am**antēs**	am**antia**
Gen	am**antium**	am**antium**	am**antium**
Dat	am**antibus**	am**antibus**	am**antibus**
Abl	am**antibus**	am**antibus**	am**antibus**

- All present participles are declined like **amans**, although present participles of the other conjugations end in -**ēns**

- When participles are used as adjectives -**ī** is used instead of -**e** in ablative singular case

felix (lucky)

SINGULAR

	Masc	Fem	Neut
Nom	fēlix	fēlix	fēlix
Voc	fēlix	fēlix	fēlix
Acc	felicem	felicem	fēlix
Gen	felicis	felicis	felicis
Dat	felicī	felicī	felicī
Abl	felicī	felicī	felicī

PLURAL

	Masc	Fem	Neut
Nom	fēlicēs	fēlicēs	fēlicia
Voc	fēlicēs	fēlicēs	fēlicia
Acc	fēlicēs	fēlicēs	fēlicia
Gen	fēlicium	fēlicium	fēlicium
Dat	fēlicibus	fēlicibus	fēlicibus
Abl	fēlicibus	fēlicibus	fēlicibus

- **audāx** (bold) and **ferōx** (fierce) are declined like **fēlix**

- Note that all the above adjectives have the same case endings in all genders except for the neuter accusative singular and the neuter nominative, vocative and accusative plural.

Vowel Stems

The following adjectives have **two** endings in nominative singular, one for masculine and feminine, one for neuter.

fortis, forte (brave)

SINGULAR

	Masc	Fem	Neut
Nom	fortis	fortis	forte
Voc	fortis	fortis	forte
Acc	fortem	fortem	forte
Gen	fortis	fortis	fortis
Dat	fortī	fortī	fortī
Abl	fortī	fortī	fortī

PLURAL

	Masc	Fem	Neut
Nom	fortēs	fortēs	fortia
Voc	fortēs	fortēs	fortia
Acc	fortēs	fortēs	fortia
Gen	fortium	fortium	fortium
Dat	fortibus	fortibus	fortibus
Abl	fortibus	fortibus	fortibus

- **brevis** (short), **facilis** (easy), **gravis** (heavy), **levis** (light), **omnis** (all), **tristis** (sad), **turpis** (disgraceful), **talis** (of such a kind), and **qualis** (of which kind), are declined like **fortis**.

Third Declension (continued)

The following adjectives have **three** endings in nominative singular.
  ācer, ācris, ācre (sharp)

SINGULAR

	Masc	*Fem*	*Neut*
Nom	ācer	ācris	ācre
Voc	ācer	ācris	ācre
Acc	ācrem	ācrem	ācre
Gen	ācris	ācris	ācris
Dat	ācrī	ācrī	ācrī
Abl	ācrī	ācrī	ācrī

PLURAL

	Masc	*Fem*	*Neut*
Nom	ācrēs	ācrēs	ācria
Voc	ācrēs	ācrēs	ācria
Acc	ācrēs	ācrēs	ācria
Gen	ācrium	ācrium	ācrium
Dat	ācribus	ācribus	ācribus
Abl	ācribus	ācribus	ācribus

- **alacer** (lively), **equester** (of cavalry), and **volucer** (winged), are declined like **acer**, and **celer** (swift), declines similarly, but keeps -**e**- throughout (*eg* **celer, celeris, celere**)

Use of Adjectives

There are two ways of using adjectives.

- They can be used **attributively**, where the adjective in English comes before the noun: the new car

- An attributive adjective in Latin usually follows its noun but may sometimes come before it with a change of meaning (→**1**)

- They can be used **predicatively**, where the adjective comes after the verb: the car is new (→**2**)

- If an adjective describes two nouns, it agrees in gender with the nearer (→**3**)

- When an adjective describes two subjects of different sex it is often masculine plural (→**4**)

- When an adjective describes two subjects representing things without life it is often neuter plural (→**5**)

Examples

1 res **parvae**
small things

in parvis rebus
in unimportant matters

civis **Romanus** sum
I am a Roman citizen

2 Servi erant **fideles**
The slaves were faithful

3 Antonius, vir consilii **magni** et prudentiae
Antony, a man of great wisdom and prudence

4 frater et soror sunt **timidi**
Brother and sister are frightened

5 Calor et ventus per artus **praesentia** erant
Warmth and wind were present in the limbs

Comparative and Superlative

Adjectives also have comparative forms *eg* I am **luckier** than you, and superlative forms *eg* the **noblest** Roman of them all.

Formation

- The comparative is formed by adding -**ior** (*masc* and *fem*) and -**ius** (*neut*) to the consonant stem of the adjective and the superlative by adding -**issimus, -a, -um** to the stem:

POSITIVE	**altus**	high
	audāx	bold
	brevis	short
	prūdēns	wise

COMPARATIVE	**altior**	higher
	audācior	bolder
	brevior	shorter
	prūdentior	wiser

SUPERLATIVE	**altissimus**	highest
	audācissimus	boldest
	brevissimus	shortest
	prūdentissimus	wisest

- If the adjective ends in -**er** (*in masc nom sing*) add -**rimus** to form the superlative.

POSITIVE	**ācer**	sharp
	celer	swift
	miser	unhappy
	pulcher	beautiful

COMPARATIVE	**ācrior**	sharper
	celerior	swifter
	miserior	more unhappy
	pulchrior	more beautiful

SUPERLATIVE	**ācerrimus**	sharpest
	celerrimus	swiftest
	miserrimus	most unhappy
	pulcherrimus	most beautiful

Comparative and Superlative (continued)

• Six adjectives ending in -**ilis** (*in masc nom sing*) add -**limus** to the stem to form the superlative.

POSITIVE	facilis	easy
	difficilis	difficult
	similis	like
	dissimilis	unlike
	gracilis	slight
	humilis	low
COMPARATIVE	facilior	easier
	difficilior	more difficult
	similior	more like
	dissimilior	more unlike
	gracilior	more slight
	humilior	lower
SUPERLATIVE	facillimus	easiest
	difficillimus	most difficult
	simillimus	most like
	dissimillimus	most unlike
	gracillimus	most slight
	humillimus	lowest

Irregular comparison

• Some adjectives have irregular comparative and superlative forms:

POSITIVE	bonus	good
	malus	bad
	parvus	small
	magnus	big
	multus	much
	multī	many
COMPARATIVE	melior	better
	pēior	worse
	minor	smaller
	māior	bigger
	plūs	more
	plūrēs	more
SUPERLATIVE	optimus	best
	pessimus	worst
	minimus	smallest, least
	māximus	biggest
	plūrimus	most
	plūrimī	most

- Note that all adjectives ending in **-us** preceded by a vowel (except those ending in **-quus**) form comparative and superlative thus:

idōneus	suitable
magis idōneus	more suitable
māxime idōneus	most suitable
but	
antīquus	old
antīquior	older
antīquissimus	oldest

- Note the following comparatives and superlatives where there is no positive form:

exterior	outer	**extrēmus**	furthest
inferior	lower	**infīmus** *or* **īmus**	lowest
superior	upper, higher	**suprēmus** *or* **summus**	highest
posterior	later	**postrēmus**	latest

Declension of Comparative and Superlative

- All comparatives decline like adjectives of the third declension.

	SINGULAR		PLURAL	
	Masc/Fem	*Neut*	*Masc/Fem*	*Neut*
Nom	**altior**	**altius**	**altiōrēs**	**altiōra**
Voc	**altior**	**altius**	**altiōrēs**	**altiōra**
Acc	**altiōrem**	**altius**	**altiōrēs**	**altiōra**
Gen	**altiōris**	**altiōris**	**altiōrum**	**altiōrum**
Dat	**altiōrī**	**altiōrī**	**altiōribus**	**altiōribus**
Abl	**altiōre**	**altiōre**	**altiōribus**	**altiōribus**

- Note ablative singular in **-e**.

- All superlatives decline like adjectives of first and second declensions (*eg* **bonus, bona, bonum**).

Comparative and Superlative (continued)

Use

- The comparative is often followed by **quam** (than), or the thing or person compared is given in the ablative case (→**1**)

- Sometimes the comparative can be translated by "rather" or "quite" (→**2**)

- The comparative is often strengthened by "**multo**" (→**3**)

- Sometimes the superlative can be translated by "very", or even as a positive adjective in English (→**4**)

- "**quam**" with the superlative means "as ... as possible" (→**5**)

Examples

1 Marcus est **altior quam soror**
Marcus est **altior sorore**
Marcus is taller than his sister

2 Gallus erat **fortior**
the Gaul was rather brave

3 **multo carior**
much dearer

4 **vir sapientissimus**
a very wise man

integerrima vita
of virtuous life

5 **quam paucissimi**
as few people as possible

Adverbs

An adverb modifies a verb, adjective, another adverb or a noun. It answers questions such as "how?", "when?", "why?", "where?", "to what extent?".

Formation

Some are formed from nouns *eg* **furtim** (stealthily) or pronouns **aliās** (at other times) but most are formed from adjectives.

- Accusative singular neuter of adjectives of extent:

multum	much	**nimium**	too much
paulum	a little	**aliquantum**	somewhat
prīmum	first	**cēterum**	for the rest

- Adjectives in -us and -**er** change to -**e**:

altē	highly	**miserē**	wretchedly

- Ablative forms of these adjectives in -**o** or -**a**:

certē *or* **certō**	certainly	**verē**	in truth
dextrā	on the right	**verō**	certainly

- Adjectives of the third declension add -**ter**/-**iter**:

audacter	boldly	**celeriter**	quickly	**prudenter**	wisely

Position

- An adverb comes before the verb, adjective, adverb or noun that it modifies (→**1**)

- However adverbs of time often come at the beginning of the sentence (→**2**)

Examples

1 **vehementer** errabas, Verres
you were making a big mistake, Verres

nimium libera respublica
too free a state

bis consul
twice consul

2 **cras mane** putat se venturum esse
He thinks he will come tomorrow morning

saepe hoc mecum cogitavi
I often thought this over by myself

ADVERBS

Common Adverbs

- **Manner** – "how?"

ita	thus	**crudeliter**	cruelly
sīc	thus	**iustē**	justly
aliter	otherwise	**liberē**	freely
fortē	by chance	**repentē**	suddenly
magnoperē	greatly		

- **Time** – "when?"

iam, nunc	now	**(n)umquam**	(n)ever
simul	at the same time	**iterum**	again
anteā	before	**saepe**	often
posteā	afterwards	**hodiē**	today
cōtīdiē	every day	**herī**	yesterday
diū	for a long time	**crās**	tomorrow
mox	soon	**postrīdiē**	next day
interim or **-ea**	meanwhile	**statim**	immediately
tum	then		

- **Place** – "where?"

ubi?	where?	**unde**?	where from	**quō**?	where to?
ibi	there	**inde**	from there	**eō**	to there
hīc	here	**hinc**	from here	**hūc**	to here
usquam	anywhere	**nusquam**	nowhere		

- **Others**

etiam	also	**fortasse**	perhaps
quoque	also	**consultō**	on purpose
quidem	indeed	**scīlicet**	no doubt

Comparison of Adverbs

The comparative form of the adverb is the nominative singular neuter of the comparative adjective. The superlative of the adverb is formed by changing -**us** of the superlative adjective to -**e**.

POSITIVE	COMPARITIVE	SUPERLATIVE
altē	**altius**	**altissimē**
highly	more highly	most highly
audacter	**audacius**	**audacissimē**
boldly	more boldy	most boldy
bene	**melius**	**optimē**
well	better	best
breviter	**brevius**	**brevissimē**
briefly	more briefly	most briefly
diū	**diūtius**	**diūtissimē**
for a long time	longer	longest
facile	**facilius**	**facillimē**
easily	more easily	most easily
magnoperē	**magis**	**maximē**
greatly	more	most
male	**peius**	**pessimē**
badly	worse	worst
miserē	**miseries**	**miserrimē**
wretchedly	more wretchedly	most wretchedly
multum	**plūs**	**plūrimum**
much	more	most
paulum	**minus**	**minimē**
a little	less	least
prope	**propius**	**proxime**
near	nearer	nearest
saepe	**saepius**	**saepissimē**
often	more often	most often

Notes on use of the comparative adjective may be applied also to the comparative adverb (see comparative adjective section).

Examples

rem totam brevius cognoscite
Find out about the whole matter more briefly

magis consilio quam virtute vicit
He won more because of his strategy than his courage

legiones diutius sine consule fuerunt
The legions were too long without a consul

multo plus
much more

optime
very well

mihi placebat Pomponius maxime vel minime
I liked Pomponius the most or disliked him the least

optimus quisque id optime facit
All the best people do it best

quam celerrime
as quickly as possible

Pronouns

Personal Pronouns

The pronouns **ego** (I), **nos** (we), **tu** (you, *sing*), **vos** (you, *pl*) decline as follows:

		SINGULAR		
Nom	**ego**	I	**tū**	you
Acc	**mē**	me	**tē**	you
Gen	**meī**	of me	**tuī**	of you
Dat	**mihi**	to/for me	**tibi**	to/for you
Abl	**mē**	by/with/from me	**tē**	by/with/from you

		PLURAL		
Nom	**nōs**	we	**vōs**	you
Acc	**nōs**	us	**vōs**	you
Gen	**nostrum**	of us	**vestrum**	of you
Dat	**nōbis**	to/for us	**vobis**	to/for you
Abl	**nōbis**	by/with/from us	**vōbis**	by/with/from you

Possessive

meus, -a, -um	my	**tuus, -a, -um**	your
noster, -ra, -rum	our	**vester, -ra, -rum**	your

- **nostri** and **vestri** are alternative forms of genitive plural.

- Possessives are sometimes used instead of the genitive of personal pronouns:

  odium tuum
  hatred of you

- For the third person pronoun, he/she/it, Latin uses **is, ea, id**:

	Masc		SINGULAR Fem		Neut	
Nom	**is**	he	**ea**	she	**id**	it
Acc	**eum**	him	**eam**	her	**id**	it
Gen	**ēius**	of him	**ēius**	of her	**ēius**	of it
Dat	**eī**	to him	**eī**	to her	**eī**	to it
Abl	**eō**	by him	**ea**	by her	**eo**	by it

		PLURAL				
Nom	**eī**	they	**eae**	they	**ea**	they
Acc	**eōs**	them	**eās**	them	**ea**	them
Gen	**eōrum**	of them	**eārum**	of them	**eōrum**	of them
Dat	**eīs**	to them	**eīs**	to them	**eīs**	to them
Abl	**eīs**	by them	**eīs**	by them	**eīs**	by them

Use

- Pronouns as subjects (I, you) are not usually used in Latin. The person of the verb is indicated by the ending (*eg* **misimus** – we sent), **ego**, **nos** *etc* are used only for emphasis:

  ego vulgus odi, **tū** amas
  I hate crowds, you love them

- The genitive forms **nostrum** and **vestrum** are used partitively:

  multi **nostrum**   many of us   pauci **vestrum**   a few of you

Reflexive Pronouns

Acc	mē	myself	tē	yourself
Gen	meī		tuī	
Dat	mihi		tibi	
Abl	mē		tē	

Acc	nōs	ourselves	vōs	yourselves
Gen	nostrum		vestrum	
Dat	nōbis		vōbis	
Abl	nōbis		vōbis	

• These are identical in form to personal pronouns.

Acc	sē	himself/herself/itself/themselves
Gen	suī	
Dat	sibi	
Abl	sē	

• Reflexive pronouns are used to refer to the subject of the sentence:

quisque **se** amat
everybody loves themselves
me lavo
I wash myself

Determinative Pronouns

- **is** – he/that, **ea** – she, **id** – it: as above
- **idem** (the same)

		SINGULAR	
	Masc	*Fem*	*Neut*
Nom	**īdem**	**eadem**	**idem**
Acc	**eundem**	**eandem**	**idem**
Gen	**ēiusdem**	**eīusdem**	**eīusdem**
Dat	**eīdem**	**eīdem**	**eīdem**
Abl	**eōdem**	**eadem**	**eōdem**

		PLURAL	
Nom	**eīdem**	**eaedem**	**eadem**
Acc	**eōsdem**	**eāsdem**	**eadem**
Gen	**eōrundem**	**eārundem**	**eōrundem**
Dat	**eīsdem**	**eīsdem**	**eīsdem**
Abl	**eīsdem**	**eīsdem**	**eīsdem**

- **ipse** (himself/herself/itself/themselves)

		SINGULAR	
	Masc	*Fem*	*Neut*
Nom	**ipse**	**ipsa**	**ipsum**
Acc	**ipsum**	**ipsam**	**ipsum**
Gen	**ipsīus**	**ipsīus**	**ipsīus**
Dat	**ipsī**	**ipsī**	**ipsī**
Abl	**ipsō**	**ipsā**	**ipsō**

		PLURAL	
Nom	**ipsī**	**ipsae**	**ipsa**
Acc	**ipsos**	**ipsās**	**ipsa**
Gen	**ipsōrum**	**ipsārum**	**ipsōrum**
Dat	**ipsīs**	**ipsīs**	**ipsīs**
Abl	**ipsīs**	**ipsīs**	**ipsīs**

Demonstrative Pronouns

- **hic** (this/these)

SINGULAR

	Masc	*Fem*	*Neut*
Nom	**hīc**	**haec**	**hoc**
Acc	**hunc**	**hanc**	**hoc**
Gen	**hūius**	**hūius**	**hūius**
Dat	**huīc**	**huīc**	**huīc**
Abl	**hōc**	**hāc**	**hōc**

PLURAL

Nom	**hī**	**hae**	**haec**
Acc	**hōs**	**hās**	**haec**
Gen	**hōrum**	**hārum**	**hōrum**
Dat	**hīs**	**hic**	**hīs**
Abl	**hīs**	**hīs**	**hīs**

- **ille** (that/those)

SINGULAR

	Masc	*Fem*	*Neut*
Nom	**ille**	**illa**	**illud**
Acc	**ilium**	**illam**	**illud**
Gen	**illīus**	**illīus**	**illīus**
Dat	**illī**	**illī**	**illī**
Abl	**illō**	**iliā**	**illō**

PLURAL

Nom	**illī**	**iilae**	**illa**
Acc	**illōs**	**illās**	**illa**
Gen	**illōrum**	**illārum**	**illōrum**
Dat	**illīs**	**illīs**	**illīs**
Abl	**illīs**	**illīs**	**illīs**

- Note that **īdem**, **hīc**, **ille** and all their parts may be adjectives as well as pronouns

Examples

1 **eadem** femina
the same woman

hic puer
this boy

tu autem **eadem** ages?
Are you going to do the same things?

2 patria est carior quam **nos ipsi**
Our native land is dearer than ourselves

3 **hac** remota, quomodo **ilium** aestimemus?
When she is removed, how are we to judge him?

4 **nos** oportet opus conficere
We must complete the task

5 accusatores dicunt **te ipsam** testem **eius** criminis esse
The prosecutors claim that you yourself are the witness of that crime

6 sed **haec** omitto; ad **illa** quae **me** magis moverunt respondeo
But I pass over these matters; I reply to those which have affected me more deeply

7 pax **vobis**cum
Peace be with you!

8 puella intravit; **ea mihi** litteras dedit
The girl came in; she gave me a letter

Relative Pronouns

SINGULAR

	Masc		Fem		Neut	
Nom	**quī**	who	**quae**	who	**quod**	which/that
Acc	**quem**	whom	**quam**	whom	**quod**	which/that
Gen	**cūius**	whose	**cūius**	whose	**cūius**	of which
Dat	**cuī**	to whom	**cuī**	to whom	**cuī**	to which
Abl	**quō**	by whom	**quā**	by whom	**quō**	by which

PLURAL

	Masc		Fem		Neut	
Nom	**quī**	who	**quae**	who	**quae**	which
Acc	**quōs**	whom	**quās**	whom	**quae**	which
Gen	**quōrum**	whose	**quārum**	whose	**quōrum**	of which
Dat	**quibus**	to whom	**quibus**	to whom	**quibus**	to which
Abl	**quibus**	by whom	**quibus**	by whom	**quibus**	by which

- A relative pronoun attaches a subordinate clause to a word preceding it (its antecedent). It agrees with this word in number and gender but takes its case from its own clause (→**1**)

- **quidam, quaedam, quoddam** (a certain, somebody)
  quīcumque, quaecumoue, quodcumque (whoever/ whatever), decline in the same way as the relative above (→**2**)

Examples

❶ iuvenis cuius librum Sextus legit laetus erat
The young man, whose book Sextus read, was happy

Fortunata, quae erat uxor Trimalchionis, saltare coeperat
Fortunata, who was Trimalchio's wife, had begun to dance

tum duo crotaiia protulit quae Fortunatae consideranda dedit
Then she brought out a pair of earrings which she gave to Fortunata to look at

❷ quidam ex legatis
a certain ambassador

tu, quicumque es
you, whoever you are

Interrogative Pronouns

SINGULAR

	Masc		Fem		Neut	
Nom	**quis**	who?	**quis/quae**	who?	**quid**	what?
Acc	**quem**	whom?	**quam**	whom?	**quid**	what?
Gen	**cūius**	whose?	**cūius**	whose?	**cūius**	of what?
Dat	**cuī**	to whom?	**cuī**	to whom?	**cuī**	to what?
Abl	**quō**	by whom?	**quā**	by whom?	**quō**	by what?

PLURAL

	Masc		Fem		Neut	
Nom	**quī**	who?	**quae**	who?	**quae**	what?
Acc	**quōs**	whom?	**quās**	whom?	**quae**	what?
Gen	**quōrum**	whose?	**quārum**	whose?	**quōrum**	of what?
Dat	**quibus**	to whom?	**quibus**	to whom?	**quibus**	to what?
Abl	**quibus**	by whom?	**quibus**	by whom?	**quibus**	by what?

- The interrogative pronoun is used to ask questions and usually is the first word in the sentence (→1)

- **quisquis, quisquis, quidquid** (whoever, whatever)
  quisque, quisque, quidque (each)
  quisquam, quisquam, quicquam (anyone, anything)
  aliquis, aliquis, aliquid (someone, something)
  These pronouns decline in the same way as **quis** above (→2)

Examples

1 **quae fuit enim causa quamobrem isti mulieri venenum dare vellet Caelius?**
What was the reason why Caelius wanted to give that woman poison?

quid agam, iudices?
What am I to do, men of the jury?

quos ad cenam invitavisti?
Whom did you invite for dinner?

quorum agros Galli incenderunt?
Whose fields did the Gauls bum?

2 **quisque** is est
whoever he is

si **quemquam** video
if I see anyone

liber **alicuius**
someone's book

Prepositions

A preposition expresses the relationship of one word to another. Each Latin preposition governs a noun or pronoun in the accusative or ablative case. Some prepositions govern both cases. Some may also be used as adverbs eg **prope** (near).

Position

- Prepositions generally come before the noun, or an adjective or equivalent qualifying the noun *eg*

ad villam	to the house
ad Ciceronis villam	to Cicero's house

- **cum** follows a personal pronoun *eg*

mēcum	with me

Prepositions governing the Accusative

On the following pages you will find some of the most frequent uses of prepositions in Latin. In the list below, the broad meaning is given on the left, with examples of usage following. Prepositions are given in alphabetical order.

ad to/towards (*a place or person*)	**oculos ad caelum sustulit** he raised his eyes to heaven
at, in the direction of, with regard to	**ad Capuam profectus sum** I set out in the direction of Capua **ad portas** at the gates **ad duo milia occisi** about 2000 were killed **nil ad me attinet** it means nothing to me
adversum (-us) opposite	**sedans adversus te** sitting opposite you
towards	**adversus Italiam** towards (ie facing) Italy
against	**adversum flumen** against the stream
ante before (*of place and time*), used with ordinal number in dates	**ante meridiem** before midday **ante limen** before the doorway **ante diem quintum Kalendas Ianuarias** 28th December (*ie* 5th before Kalends of January)

apud	
at/near (usually with persons)	**Crassus apud eum sedet**
	Crassus is sitting near him
in the writing of	**apud Platonem**
	in Plato's writings
before (*authorities*)	**apud pontifices**
	before the high priests

circum (circa)	
around, about (of place, people)	**circum forum**
	around the forum
	circum Hectorem
	around Hector
	circa montes
	around the mountains
	circa decem milia Gallorum
	about ten thousand Gauls

contra	
against	**contra hostes**
	against the enemy
	contra ventos
	against the wind
opposite	**contra Britanniam**
	facing Britain

extra	
outside of	**extra muros**
	outside the walls
beyond (*of place and time*)	**extra iocum**
	beyond a joke

inter	
between	**inter oppositos exercitus**
	between the opposing armies
	amans inter se
	loving each other
among	**inter saucios**
	among the wounded
	inter manus
	within reach
during	**inter hos annos**
	during these years

intra	
within (*of place and time*)	**intra parietes**
	within the walls
	intra quattuor annos
	within four years

ob	
on account of	**quam ob rem**
	therefore
	ob stultitiam
	on account of your foolishness

Prepositions governing the Accusative (continued)

per
through

per noctem
through the night

by means of

per vos
by means of you

per aetatem periit
he died of old age

per deos iuro
I swear by the gods

post
after (*of time and place*)

post urbem conditam
after the foundation of the city

post tergum
behind your back

praeter
beyond

praeter naturam
beyond nature

besides

praeter se tres alios adduxit
he brought three others besides himself

except for

praeter paucos
except for a few

prope
near

prope me habitavit
he lived near me

propter
on account of

propter metum mortis
on account of fear of death

secundum
along (*of place*)

secundum flumen
along the river

immediately after (*time*)

secundum quietem
on waking from sleep

according to

secundum naturam
according to nature

trans
across

vexillum trans vallum traicere
to take the standard across the rampart

trans Rhenum
across the Rhine

ultra
beyond (*of time, degree etc*)

ultra vires
beyond one's power

Prepositions governing the Ablative

Those which are spatial represent the idea of rest in a place or motion from a place.

a(b)

from (*of place, people, direction, time*)   **ab area hostes deiecti sunt**
the enemy were driven from the citadel
a nobis abesse
to be distant from us
a dextrā
from the right
a tertiā horā
from the third hour

by (*agent*)   **ab amicis desertus**
abandoned by friends

cum

with   **vade mecum**
go with me!
cum curā loqui
to speak with care
cum Augusto coniurare
to conspire with Augustus
summa cum laude
with distinction

dē

down from   **dē caelō demittere**
to send down from heaven

away from   **de tricliniō extra**
to go away from the dining room

about   **cogitare de hāc rē**
to think about this matter
dē industriā
on purpose

during *or* at (*of time*)   **dē nocte**
at night, during the night

ē(x)

out of (*from*)   **ē carcere effugerunt**
they escaped from prison
ex equis desilire
to jump from their horses
quidam ex Hispania
someone from Spain
statua ex argentō facta
a statue made of silver

immediately after   **ex consulatu**
immediately after his consulship

from   **ex hōc diē**
from that day
ex aequō
equally

Prepositions governing the Ablative (continued)

pro

for/on behalf of   **pro se quisque**
each one for himself/ herself
pro patriā morī
to die for one's country

according to   **pro viribus agere**
to act according to one's ability

in front of   **pro rostris**
in front of the rostrum

sine

without   **sine spē**
without hope
sine pecuniā
without money

Prepositions governing Accusative and Ablative

in
with accusative

into	**in hanc urbem venire** to come into the city
till	**in primam lucem dormivit** he slept till dawn
against	**in rem publicam aggredi** to attack the state

with ablative

in	**puella in illā domō laetē vivebat** the girl lived happily in that house
on	**in capite coronam gerebat** he wore a crown on his head
	in animo habere to intend (to have in one's mind)
within (of time)	**in omni aetate** within every age
in (of condition)	**in parte facilis, in parte difficilis** easy in parts, difficult in others

sub
with accusative

beneath	**sub iugum mittere** to send beneath the yoke (*ie* into slavery)
below (*with verb of motion*)	**sub ipsum murum** just below the wall
before (*of time*)	**sub vesperum** just before nightfall

with ablative

under (*of place and power*)	**sub montibus constituere** to station under the mountains
	sub Nerone under the power of Nero

super
with accusative

over, above (*of place*), in addition	**super capita hostium** over the heads of the enemy
	alii, super alios, advenerunt they arrived one after the other

with ablative

concerning/about	**super his rebus scribam** I shall write about these matters

Numerals

Cardinal and Ordinal Numbers

		CARDINAL	ORDINAL
1	I	ūnus, -a, -um	prīmus, -a, -um
2	II	duo, -ae, -o	secundus, -a, -um
3	III	trēs, tria	tertius, -a, -um
4	IV	quattuor	quartus, -a, -um
5	V	quīnque	quīntus, -a, -um
6	VI	sex	sextus, -a, -um
7	VII	septem	septimus, -a, -um
8	VIII	octō	octāvus, -a, -um
9	IX	novem	nōnus, -a, -um
10	X	decem	decimus, -a, -um
11	XI	ūndecim	ūndecimus, -a, -um
12	XII	duodecim	duodecimus, -a, -um
13	XIII	tredecim	tertius decimus, -a, -um
14	XIV	quattuordecim	quartus decimus, -a, -um
15	XV	quīndecim	quintus decimus, -a, -um
16	XVI	sēdecim	sextus decimus, -a, -um
17	XVII	septendecim	septimus decimus, -a, -um
18	XVIII	duodēvigintī	duodēvicēsimus, -a, -um
19	XIX	ūndevigmtī	undēvicēsimus, -a, -um
20	XX	vigintī	vicēsimus, -a, -um
21	XXI	vigintī ūnus	vicēsimus prīmus
30	XXX	trīginta	trīcēsimus
40	XL	quadrāgintā	quadrāgēsimus
50	L	quīnquāgintā	quīnquāgēsimus
60	LX	sexāgintā	sexāgēsimus
70	LXX	septuāgintā	septuāgēsimus
80	LXXX	octōgintā	octōgēsimus
90	XC	nōnagintā	nōnāgēsimus
100	C	centum	centēsimus
200	CC	ducentī, -ae, -a	ducentēsimus
300	CCC	trecentī, -ae, -a	trecentēsimus
400	CCCC	quadringentī -ae, -a,	quadringentēsimus
500	D (IƆ)	quīngentī, -ae, -a	quīngentesimus
600	DC	sescentī, -ae,	sescentesimus
700	DCC	septingentī, -ae, -a	septingentēsimus
800	DCCC	octingentī, -ae, –a	octingentēsimus
900	DCCCC	nōngentī, -ae, -a	nōngentēsimus
1000	M (CIƆ)	mīlle	mīllēsimus
2000	MM	duo mīlia	bis mīllesimus
1,000,000		deciēs centēna (centum)	mīlia

- Fractions are expressed as follows:

  dimidia pars 1/2
  tertia pars 1/3
  quārta pars 1/4

- Ordinal numbers (→**1**) decline like 1st and 2nd declension adjectives

- Cardinal numbers (→**2**) do not decline except for **ūnus, duo, trēs** and hundreds (**ducenti** etc)

- **unus** declines as 1st and 2nd declension adjectives except that the genitive singular ends in **-ius** and the dative in **–i**

- **duo** (two) declines as follows:

	Masc	*Fem*	*Neut*
Nom	**duo**	**duae**	**duo**
Acc	**duōs**	**duas**	**duo**
Gen	**duōrum**	**duārum**	**duōrum**
Dat	**duōbus**	**duābus**	**duōbus**
Abl	**duōbus**	**duābus**	**duōbus**

   ambō, -ae, -a (both) declines in the same way

- **trēs** (three) declines as follows:

	Masc	*Fem*	*Neut*
Nom	**trēs**	**trēs**	**tria**
Acc	**trēs**	**trēs**	**tria**
Gen	**trium**	**trium**	**trium**
Dat	**tribus**	**tribus**	**tribus**
Abl	**tribus**	**tribus**	**tribus**

- Genitive of hundreds, *eg* **trecentī** ends -**um** (→**3**)

- **mīlia** (thousands) declines as follows:

Nom	**mīlia**
Acc	**mīlia**
Gen	**mīlium**
Dat	**mīlibus**
Abl	**mīlibus**

- **mīlle** (thousand) does not decline.

Examples

1 coquus **secundam** mensam paraverat
The cook had prepared the second course

legionis **nonae** milites magnam partem hostium interfecerunt
Soldiers of the ninth legion killed a large number of the enemy

2 decem **milia** passuum exercitus progressus est
The army advanced 10 miles

Cerberus, qui **tria** capita habebat, in antro recubuit
Cerberus, who had three heads, crouched in the cave

stellae **novem** orbes confecerunt
The stars completed nine orbits

duodeviginti onerariae naves huc accedebant
Eighteen cargo ships were approaching

Caesar **trecentos** milites trans Padanum traiecit
Caesar transported three hundred soldiers across the River Po

da mi basia **mille**
Give me a thousand kisses

3 trecentum militum
of three hundred soldiers

4 duo milia passuum (*gen*)
2000 paces *or* 2 miles

Distributive Numerals

These are used when repetition is involved as when multiplying (→**1**)

1	**singulī, -ae, -a**	*one each*
2	**bīnī, -ae, -a**	*two each*
3	**ternī (trinī)**	
4	**quaternī**	
5	**quīnī**	
6	**sēnī**	
7	**septēnī**	
8	**octonī**	
9	**novēnī**	
10	**dēnī**	

Numeral Adverbs

1	**semel**	*once*
2	**bis**	*twice*
3	**ter**	
4	**quater**	
5	**quīnquiēs**	
6	**sexiēs**	
7	**septiēs**	
8	**octiēs**	
9	**noviēs**	
10	**deciēs**	

(→**2**)

Examples

1 **bini** gladiatores
(*describing* pairs *of gladiators*)

bina castra
two camps

quaternos denarios in **singulas** vini amphoras
4 denarii each for a bottle of wine

2 non plus quam **semel**
not more than once

decies centena milia sestertium or **decies** sestertium
1,000,000 sesterces

ter quattuor
twelve (*three times four*)

Dates

- Events of the year were usually recorded by using the names of the consuls holding office that year (→**1**)

- From the late republic the date of the foundation of Rome was established – 753 BC – and time was calculated from this date (→**2**)

- The four seasons were: (→**3**)

ver, veris (*nt*)	spring
aestās, -atis (*f*)	summer
autumnus, -i (*m*)	autumn
hiems, -is (*f*)	winter

- The months were reformed by Julius Caesar (7 of 31 days, 4 of 30, 1 of 28, and an extra day each leap year). Each month (**mensis, -is,** *m*) was identified by the following adjectives:

Iānuārius	January
Februārius	February
Martius	March
Āprīlis	April
Māius	May
Iūnius	June
Iulīus (Quintīlis)	July
Augustus (Sextīlis)	August
September	September
Octōber	October
November	November
December	December

- Three important days each month were:

Kalendae, -arum (*fpl*)	Kalends or 1st
Nonae, -arum (*fpl*)	Nones or 5th/7th
Idus, -uum (*fpl*)	Ides or 13th/15th

Examples

1 **Nerone iterum L. Pisone consulibus**
pauca memoria digna evenerunt
Few incidents worth recording took
place during the year when Nero
and Lucius Piso were consuls (AD 57)

Lentulo Gaetulico C. Calvisio consulibus decreta sunt triumphi
insignia Poppaeo Sabino
A triumph was voted to Poppaeus
Sabinus during the consulship of
Lentulus Gaetulicius and Gaius
Calvisius

2 **ab urbe condita**
since the foundation of Rome

ante urbem conditam
before the foundation of the city

post urbem conditam
after the foundation of the city

3 ineunte **aestate**
in the beginning of summer

media **aestate**
midsummer

iam **hieme confecta**
when winter was already over

vere ineunte Antonius Tarentum navigavit
At the beginning of spring, Antony
sailed to Tarentum

Dates (continued)

- In March, July, October and May, Nones fall on the 7th and Ides on the 15th day (5th and 13th in all other months).

- To refer to these dates, the ablative is used (→**1**)

- To refer to the day before these dates, use **pridiē** (→**2**)

- All other days were reckoned by counting (inclusively) the days before the next main date, "ante diem" + accusative of ordinal numbers and the next main date were used:
  9th of February is 5 days before the 13th of February (counting inclusively). 28th April is 4 days before 1st May (→**3**)

- An easy way to work out such dates is to add one to Nones and Ides and subtract the Latin number. Add two to the number of days in the month before the Kalends, again subtracting the given Latin number. You will then have the date in English.

- The day was divided into twelve hours **horae, -arum** (*fpl*). The hours of darkness into four watches of three hours each, **vīgiliae, -arum** (*fpl*), from 6–9 pm, 9–12 pm, 12–3 am, 3–6 am

- Other ways of expressing time:

primā luce	at dawn
solo orto	at sunrise
solis occasu	at sunset
media nocte	at midnight
noctu, nocte	at night
mane	in the morning
meridie	at midday
sub vesperum	towards evening
vespere	in the evening (→**4**)

Examples

❶ Kalendīs Martiis
on the 1st of March

Idibus Decembribus
on the 13th of December

Idibus Martiis Caesar a Bruto interfectus est
Caesar was killed by Brutus on the 15th of March

❷ pridie Nonas Ianuarias (Non. Ian.)
4th January

❸ ante diem quintum Idus Februarias
9th February

ante diem quartum Kalendas Maias
28th April

❹ prima hora
at the first hour (6–7 am)

tertia vigilia
during the third watch (midnight–3 am)

tertia fere vigilia navem solvit
He set sail after midnight (during the third watch)

ipse hora circiter quarta diei cum primis navibus Britanniam attigit
He himself reached Britain with the first ships around 10 o'clock in the morning

vespere vinum optimum convivae bibunt
In the evening, the guests drink vintage wine

Sentence Structure

Simple Sentences

Word order in English is stricter than in Latin. The usual English order – subject+verb+object – differentiates the meaning of sentences such as, "The cat caught the mouse" and "The mouse caught the cat". Latin order is more flexible since the endings of words clearly show their function, whatever their position in the sentence.

Compare the following:

feles murem cepit	the cat caught the mouse
murem cepit feles	it was the cat that caught the mouse

The sentences are identical in meaning, although the emphasis is different. This difference in word order often makes it difficult for English translators to unravel long Latin sentences. However there are certain principles to help:

- The normal *grammatical* word order in Latin is:
  Subject first, Predicate after (by Predicate understand "verb")

- Expressions qualifying the subject (*ie* adjectives) must be near the subject

- Expression qualifying the predicate (*eg* objects, adverbs, prepositional phrases) must be near the verb

Thus the usual word order of a simple sentence is:
(Connecting Word)
Subject
(Adjective)
Object
Adverbs *or* prepositional phrases
Predicate (verb) (→**1**)

Examples

❶ at **hostes** magnam virtutem in extrema spe salutis **praestiterunt**
But the enemy showed great courage, finally hoping to save themselves

Ariovistus ad postulata Caesaris pauca **respondit**
Ariovistus briefly replied to Caesar's demands

iste **Hannibal** sic hanc Tertiam **dilexit**
Thus that Hannibal loved this Tertia

Simple Sentences (continued)

- Another principle is *emphasis*, where the words are in an unusual order, *eg* subject last, predicate first (→**1**)

- Questions usually begin with interrogatives (→**2**)

- Adjectives may precede or follow nouns. Check agreement of endings (→**3**)

- Genitives usually follow the governing word (→**4**)

- Words in apposition usually follow one another, although "rex" often comes first (→**5**)

- Adverbs usually come before their verb, adjective or adverb (→**6**)

- Prepositions usually come before their nouns (→**7**) but note, magna **cum** cura (with great care).

- Finally, watch out for the omission of words, particularly parts of **esse** (to be) (→**8**)

Examples

1 horum adventu **redintegratur | seditio** (subject last)
On their arrival trouble broke out once more

confecerunt me | infirmitates meorum (verb first)
I have been upset by the illnesses of my slaves

2 **quid** hoc loco potes dicere, homo amentissime?
What can you say at this point, you madman?

quis clarior in Graecia Themistocle?
Who (is) more famous in Greece than Themistocles?

3 **bello magno** rictus
conquered in a great war

magna domus
a large house

4 multi **nostrum**
many of us

filius **Augusti**
Augustus' son

5 Cicero, **consul**
Cicero, the consul

rex Tarquinius
King Tarquinius

6 **vix** cuiquam persuadebatur
hardly anyone could be persuaded

multo carius
much dearer

7 **in** villam
into the house

sub monte
under the mountain

8 **pudor inde et miseratio et patris Agrippae, Augusti avi memoria (est)**
A feeling of pity and shame came over them and they remembered her father Agrippa and her grandfather Augustus

Compound Sentences

A compound sentence is one with a main clause and one or more subordinate clauses. In Latin this is called a **period**, where the most important idea is kept to the end.

- conservate parenti filium, parentem filio, (1) ne aut senectutem iam prope desperatam contempsisse aut adulescentiam plenam spei | maximae non modo non aluisse vos verum etiam perculisse atque adflixisse videamini (2). (Cic. – Pro Caelio 32.80)

    1. Main clause
    save a son for his father, a father for his son.
    2. Negative purpose clause
    lest you appear either to have cast aside an old man near despair or that you have failed to sustain a young man full of the highest hopes, but have even struck him down and ruined him.

    Note that this sentence builds towards a climax at the end. The most important verbs here are **perculisse** and **adflixisse** rather than **videamini** (you may seem). Notice also the rhythm of the last two words. Repetition of similar phrases is common – **parenti filium, parentem filio**. This sentence is a good illustration of an orator's style.

- Historical style is much simpler, often a subordinate clause followed by a main clause:

    cum equites nostri funditoribus sagittariisque flumen transgressi essent (1), cum equitatu proelium commiserunt (2)

    1. Subordinate adverbial clause of time
    when our cavalry had crossed the river with slingers and archers
    2. Main clause
    they joined battle with the cavalry

- Participle phrase followed by the **main clause** and **subordinate** clause:

    nec patrum cognitionibus satiatus iudiciis (1), adsidebat in cornu tribunalis (2), ne praetorem curuli depelleret (Tac Ann I 75)

    1. Participle phrase
    nor was he (the emperor) satisfied with taking part in Senate trials
    2. Main clause
    he used to sit in the ordinary lawcourts
    3. Subordinate clause of purpose
    in case he pushed the praetor from his curule chair

Many other combinations of clauses are possible. It is important to relate the sentence to its context and to the passage as a whole as Latin sentences are linked logically. It is often helpful when translating a long sentence to pick out subjects and verbs in order to recognize the structure of the clauses and grasp the overall meaning of the sentence.

Direct Statement

The basic patterns involved in direct statement have been illustrated under **Simple Sentences** (*see* p 43).

Direct Questions

In Latin a direct question can be expressed as follows by:

- an interrogative pronoun (→**1**)

   quis? (who?), **quid**? (what?), **cur**? (why?)

- adding -**ne** to the first word, where no definite answer is indicated (→**2**)

- **nonne**, when the expected answer is YES (→**3**)

- **num**, when the expected answer is NO (→**4**)

- **utrum ... an(non)**
  -ne ... an(non)
  ... an(non)
  in double questions (→**5**)   } (whether) ... or (not)

Examples

1 **quis** est
Who is it?

quid dicit?
What is he saying?

cur lacrimas?
Why are you crying?

2 times**ne** Verrem?
Are you scared of Verres?

3 **nonne** cladem audivisti?
Surely you heard of the defeat?
or You heard of the defeat, didn't you?

4 **num** heri venisti?
Surely you didn't come yesterday?
or You didn't come yesterday, did you?

5 utrum has condiciones accepistis **annon**?
Have you accepted these conditions or not?

Direct Command

- A direct command in Latin is expressed in the second person by the imperative if positive, by **nolī(te)** with the present infinitive if negative (→**1**)

- A direct command in the first or third persons is expressed by the present subjunctive, with **nē** if negative (→**2**)

Wishes

- Wishes are expressed in Latin by **utinam** with the subjunctive, **utinam nē** when negative (→**3**)

- **vellem** may also be used with imperfect or pluperfect subjunctive to express wishes (→**4**)

Examples

1 **venite** mecum
come with me

noli me tangere
don't touch me

2 **vivamus** atque **amemus**
let us live and let us love

ne **fiat** lux
let there not be light

3 **utinam** frater redeat
I wish my brother would return (*future*)

utinam ne vere scriberem
I wish I were not writing the truth (*present*)

utinam brevi moratus esses
I wish you had stayed a little (*past*)

4 **vellem** me ad cenam **invitavisses**
I wish you had invited me to dinner

Indirect Statement

"You are making a mistake" is a *direct statement*. "I think that you are making a mistake" is an *indirect statement*.

- The indirect statement is the object clause of "I think". In indirect statement in Latin, the subject of the clause (*eg* te) goes into the accusative case, the verb is an infinitive (*errare*):

    Puto **te errare**
    I think that you are making a mistake

- This pattern is used after verbs of saying, thinking, perceiving, knowing (→**1**)

Examples

❶

audire	hear	**negare**	say … not
cognoscere	discover	**nescire**	not to know
credere	believe	**putare**	think
dicere	say	**scire**	know
intellegere	understand	**sentire**	perceive
meminisse	remember	**videre**	see
narrare	tell		

Translation

- The *present infinitive* refers to actions happening at the same time and may be translated – is, are, was, were.

- The *perfect infinitive* refers to prior action and may be translated – has, have, had.

- The *future infinitive* refers to future action and may be translated – will, would.

putamus	**te errāre**	We think	that you are making a mistake
	te errāvisse		that you have made a mistake
	te errātūrum esse		that you will make a mistake

putabamus	**te errāre**	We thought	that you were making a mistake
	te errāvisse		that you had made a mistake
	te errātūrum esse		that you would make a mistake

- Notice that when the main verb is *past tense*, translate the present infinitive – "was, were", the past infinitive – "had", the future infinitive – "would".

- The reflexive pronoun **sē** is used to refer to the subject of the main verb (→**1**)

- Translate **negō** – I say that... not (→**2**)

- Verbs of promising, hoping, threatening or swearing (*eg* **promitto, pollicēor, spērō, minor, iuro**) are followed by an accusative and mture infinitive (→**3**)

Examples

1 senex dixit **se** thesaurum invenisse
The old man said that he had found treasure

2 **negavit** servum domum venturum esse
He said that the slave would not come home

3 **promisi me festinaturum esse**
I promised that I would hurry

sperabat se hoc confecturum esse
He hoped that he could complete this
or He hoped to complete this

Further Examples

creditores existimabant **eum** totam pecuniam **perdidisse**
His creditors thought that he had lost all his money

memini **simulacra** deorum de caelo **percussa esse**
I remember that the gods' statues were struck down from the heavens

vidistine **Catonem** in bibliotheca **sedere**?
Did you see Cato sitting in the library?

iuro **me** pro patria fortiter **pugnaturum esse**
I swear that I shall fight bravely for my country

iam ego credo **vos** verum **dixisse**
I now believe that you spoke the truth

negavit **nihil** umquam pulchrius statua **fuisse**
He said that nothing had ever been more beautiful than that statue

Indirect Question

"Where did he come from?" is a *direct question*. "I asked where he had come from" is an *indirect question*. Latin uses the same interrogative words (**quis** – who, **quid** – what *etc*) and the verb in indirect questions is always subjunctive

> rogavi **unde venisset**
> I asked where he had come from

- Latin uses six different forms of the subjunctive in this construction in a precise sequence depending on the main verb (→**1**)

Examples

1 rogo   **unde veniat**   I ask   where he comes from   (*present*)
           unde venerit   where he has come from   (*perfect*)
           unde venturus sit   where he will come from   (*future*)

   rogavi   **unde veniret**   I asked   where he was coming from   (*imperfect*)
           unde venisset   where he had come from   (*pluperfect*)
           unde venturus esset   where he would come from   (*future perfect*)

Translation

Translation of tenses in indirect question is *easy*, because English uses the same tenses as Latin, as can be seen on page 50.

- The reflexive pronoun **se** is used to refer to the subject of the main verb (→**1**)
- **utrum … an** (if … or), **utrum … necne** (whether … or not) are also used in indirect questions (→**2**)
- **num** is used to mean "if" in indirect questions (→**3**)

Examples

1 **rogavit quando se visuri essemus**
He asked when we would see him

2 **roga utrum iverit an manserit**
Ask whether he went or stayed

roga utrum manserit necne
Ask whether he stayed or not

rogavit utrum Scylla infestior esset Chaiybdis necne
He asked whether Charybdis was more dangerous than Scylla or not

3 **nescio num venturi sint**
I don't know if they will come

Further Examples

nescimus quid facturi simus
We don't know what we shall do

mirum est quanta sit Roma
It is amazing how big Rome is

or The size of Rome is amazing

exploratores cognoverunt quanti essent Poeni
Scouts discovered what the numbers of the Carthaginians were

incredibile est quomodo talia facere potuerit
It is incredible how he was able to do such things

nemo audivit quid rex constituisset
No one heard what the king had decided
or No one heard the king's decision

Indirect Command

"Come here" is a *direct command*. "I ordered you to come here" is an *indirect command*. Indirect commands in Latin are expressed by **ut** (when positive) or **nē** (when negative) and have their verbs in the subjunctive (→**1**)

- Latin uses two tenses of the subjunctive, present or imperfect, in this construction. It uses the present subjunctive if the main verb is present or future tense and imperfect subjunctive if the main verb is in the past tense. (→**2**)

Translation

- The English translation of the indirect command is the same, whichever tense is used in Latin – the infinitive (eg to come)

- The reflexive **se** is used to refer to the subject of the main verb (→**3**)

- Common verbs introducing indirect command are:

hortor	encourage
moneo	warn
oro	beg
persuadeo	persuade
rogo	ask

- Only **iubeo** (to order), **veto** (to tell... not), are usually used with the infinitive in Latin (→**4**)

Examples

1 tibi imperavi **ut venīrēs**
I ordered you to come

tibi imperavi **ne venires**
I forbade you to come

milites oravit **ne** in castris diutius **manerent**
He begged his soldiers not to stay in camp any longer

hoc rogo, mi Tiro, **ne temere naviges**
I beg you, my dear Tiro, not to sail carelessly

2 tibi **impero ut venias** (*present*)
I order you to come

tibi **imperavi ut venires** (*imperfect*)
I ordered you to come

deos precor **ut** nobis **parcant**
I beg the gods to spare us

amicos roga **ut veniant**, operamque **dent**, et messim hanc nobis **adiuvent**
Ask your friends to come and lend a hand and help us with this harvest

3 nos oravit ut **sibi** cibum daremus
He begged us to give him food

4 iubeo eos **navigare**
I order them to sail

veto eos **navigare**
I tell them not to sail

mater me **vetuit** in murum **ascendere**
Mother forbade me to climb on the wall

Antonius eos **iussit** adventum **suum exspectare**
Antony told them to await his arrival

Purpose or Final Clauses

There are two ways of expressing purpose in English:

> I am hurrying to the city to see the games
> *or* I am hurrying to the city so that I may see the games

- In Latin **ut** is used with the present or imperfect subjunctive, to express purpose. The present subjunctive is used if the main verb is in the present or future tense and the imperfect subjunctive if the main verb is in the past tense (→**1**)

- Negative purpose clauses are introduced by **ne** which can be translated "so that... not", "in case", "to avoid", "lest" *etc* (→**2**)

- If there is a comparative adjective or adverb in the Latin sentence **quō** is used instead of **ut** (→**3**)

- The relative **qui, quae, quod** may be used instead of **ut**, if it refers to an object in the main clause (→**4**)

- After negative **ne**, **quis** is used instead of **aliquis** to mean "anyone"

- Note that **se** is used to refer to the subject of the main verb (→**5**)

- **ad** is used with the gerundive to express purpose (→**6**)

- The supine **-um** is used after verbs of motion to express purpose (→**7**)

Examples

1 ad urbem festino **ut** ludos **videam**
I am hurrying to the city to see the games

ad urbem festinavi **ut** ludos **viderem**
I hurried to the city to see the games

filium multo cum fletu complexus, pepulit **ut abiret**
Embracing his son tearfully, he drove him to leave

2 Tiberius hoc recusavit **ne** Germanicus imperium **haberet**
Tiberius refused this lest Germanicus had power

pontem resciderunt **ne** hostes flumen **transirent**
They broke down the bridge in case the enemy crossed the river

3 puellae cantabant **quo** laetiores essent **hospites**
The girls sang to make their guests happier

4 rex sex milites delegit **qui** ad Graeciam **proficiscerentur**
The king chose six soldiers to set off for Greece

5 in silvis se abdidit **ne quis se** videret
He hid in the woods lest anyone should see him

sed **ut** venenum manifesto comprehendi **posset**, constitui locum iussit, **ut** eo **mitteret** amicos, **qui laterent**, cum venisset Licinius, venenumque traderet, comprehenderent
But *so that the poison could be seized openly*, he ordered that a place be appointed, *to send friends there, to hide*. When Licinius came to hand over the poison they could arrest him.

6 Verres ad Siciliam venit **ad urbes diripiendas**
Verres came to Sicily to plunder its cities

7 veniunt **spectatum**
They come to see

Result or Consecutive Clauses

> The road is so long that I am tired
> It was so hot that we could not work

In both these sentences, a result or consequence is expressed in English by using words such as

> **so ... that** (positive)
> **so that ... not** (negative)

- In Latin the following words are frequently used in the main clause

adeo	to such an extent
ita	thus, so
talis	of such a kind
tam	so
tantus	so great
tot	so many

- In the result clause, **ut** (so that) and **ut ... non** (so that ... not) are used with the present or imperfect subjunctive. Present subjunctive is used where the main verb is in the present and the imperfect subjunctive is used where the main verb is past (→**1**)

Note that **eum** is used to refer to "him" instead of **se** when referring to the subject of the main clause as in the first example (→**1**)

Examples

1 Gallus **tam** ferox est **ut** omnes Romani eum **timeant**
The Gaul is so fierce that all the Romans are scared of him

tanta erat tempestas **ut** nautae navem **non solverent**
So great was the storm that the sailors could not set sail

nemo est **adeo** stultus **ut non** discere **possit**
No one is so stupid that he can't learn

tot sententiae erant **ut nemo consentiret**
There were so many opinions that no one could agree

tales nos esse putamus **ut** ab omnibus **laudemur**
We think that we are the sort of people to be praised by everyone

Verbs of Fearing

In Latin, verbs of fearing (**timeo, metuo, paveo, vereor**) are followed by **nē**, **nē non** or **ut** with the present and perfect, imperfect and pluperfect subjunctive according to sequence of tenses:

- The present subjunctive represents present and future tenses in English

> I am afraid he is coming
> I am afraid he will come

- The perfect subjunctive represents the past tense in English

> I am afraid that he has come

- When the verb of fearing is in the past tense, imperfect and pluperfect subjunctive are used in Latin instead (→**1**)

- **nē** is used if the fear is expressed in a positive sentence (ie I am afraid he will come), **nē non, ut** is used if the fear is expressed negatively (ie I am afraid that he won't come) (→**2**)

- As in English, the infinitive can follow a verb of fearing, provided that the subjects of both are the same (→**3**)

Examples

❶ **veritus sum ne veniret**
I was afraid he was coming

veritus sum ne venisset
I was afraid that he had come

❷ **vereor ne amicus veniat**
I am afraid lest my friend comes
or lest my friend will come

vereor ne amicus non veniat
I am afraid that my friend won't come

vereor ut amicus venerit
I am afraid that my friend has not come

verebar ne amicus non venisset
I was afraid that my friend had not come

metuo ne virtutis maiorum nostrum obliviscamur
I am afraid that we shall forget the courage of our ancestors

paves ne ducas tu illam
You are afraid to marry her

Verres, **veritus ne** servi bellum in Sicilia **facerent**, multos in vincula coniecit
Verres, fearing that slaves might revolt in Sicily, threw many into prison

Romani **verebantur ne** fortiter **non pugnavissent**
The Romans were afraid that they had not fought bravely

❸ **timeo abire**
I am afraid to go away

mulier timebat manere sola
The woman was scared to remain alone

Conditional Sentences

Compare the following two sentences in English:

(a) If I tell you a lie, you will be angry
(b) If I were to tell you a lie, you would be angry

The first is a *logical statement of fact*, stating what *will* happen, the second is a *hypothesis*, stating what *would happen*.

For the first type of sentence, Latin uses the indicative mood in both main and conditional clauses. For the second type, Latin uses the subjunctive mood in both main and conditional clauses.

Translate type (a) as follows:

si hoc **dicis**, sapiens **es**
if you say this, you are wise

si hoc **dicebas**, sapiens **eras**
if you were saying this, you were wise

si hoc **dixisti**, erravisti
if you said this, then you made a mistake

si hoc **dixeris**, errabis
if you say this, you will make a mistake

Notice that the same tenses in English are used as in Latin except in the last sentence. Latin is more precise – *you will have said this*, before you make a mistake, therefore Latin uses the *future perfect* tense.

- Consider also the following sentence:

si me **amabis**, mecum **manebis**
If you love me, you will stay with me

Latin uses the *future* tense in both clauses, English uses the *present* tense in the "if" clause. Both actions, "loving" and "remaining" *logically* refer to the *future*.

Translate type (b) as follows:

(*present*)
si hoc **dicas**, **erres**
if you were to say this, you would be making a mistake

(*imperfect*)
si hoc **diceres**, **errares**
if you said (or were saying) that, you would be making a mistake

(*pluperfect*)
si hoc **dixisses**, **erravisses**
if you had said that, you would have made a mistake

Notice that both tenses of the subjunctive are the same in the above examples. Sometimes an imperfect may be used in one clause and the pluperfect in the other:

si pudorem **haberes**, Roma **abiisses**
if you had any sense of shame, you would have left Rome

Negative Conditional Sentences

- **nisi** (unless) is the negative of **si** (if) (→**1**)

- **si non** (if not), is less common and negates one word, or is used when the same verb is repeated (→**2**)

Examples

1 **nisi** id statim **feceris**, ego te **tradam** magistratui
Unless you do this immediately, I shall hand you over to the magistrate

nisi utilem **crederem**, non pacem **peterem**
Unless I thought it useful, I would not be seeking peace

2 **si** me **adiuveris**, laeta **ero**; **si** me **non adiuveris**, tristis **ero**
If you help me, I shall be happy; if you don't help me, I shall be sad

si navigatio **non morabitur**, mox te **videbo**
If my sailing is not delayed, I shall see you soon

Further Examples

(b) quis illum sceleratum fuisse **putavisset, si tacuisset?**
Who would have thought he was a rascal, if he had kept quiet?

(b) multi **agerent** et **pugnarent si** rei publicae **videretur**
Many would act and fight, if the state decided

(a) **gaudemus si** liberi in horto **ludunt**
We are happy if the children play in the garden

(b) **si quis** in caelum **ascendisset**, pulchritudinem siderum **conspexisset**
If anyone had gone up to heaven, he would have seen the beauty of the stars

Concessive Clauses

In English, Concessive clauses usually begin with "although":

> Although he is rich, he is not happy
> I shall succeed although it is difficult

- **quamquam** (although) is followed by the indicative (→**1**)

  Note that **tamen** (however) is often used in the main clause in concessive sentences

- **quamvis** (although) is always followed by the subjunctive (→**2**)

- **cum** in the sense "although" is always followed by the subjunctive (→**3**)

- **etsi** (although) takes the indicative or subjunctive according to the same rules as **si** (*see* p 56). The indicative is more common (→**4**)

Examples

1 medici **quamquam intellegunt**, numquam **tamen** aegris de morbo dicunt
Although doctors know, they never tell their patients about their illness

quamquam Aeneas dicere volebat, Dido solo fixos oculos aversa tenebat
Although Aeneas wished to speak, Dido turned away and kept her eyes fixed on the ground

2 **quamvis** frater **esset** molestus, Marcus eum amavit
Although his brother was a nuisance, Marcus loved him

feminae, **quamvis** in periculo **essent**, tamen liberos servaverunt
Although the women were in danger, yet they saved their children

3 **cum non didicissem** geometrias, litteras sciebam
Although I had not learnt geometry, I knew my letters

non poterant, **cum vellent**, Lucium liberare
They were not able, although they wished, to free Lucius

4 **etsi** servus **est**, certe persona est
Although he is a slave, he is a person

etsi victoriam non reportavissetis, tamen vos contentos esse oportebat
Although you had not won a victory, yet you should have been content

etsi domi **esset filius iuvenis**, agros ipse colebat
Although he had a young son at home, he cultivated the fields by himself

Causal Clauses

Clauses which begin with the words "because" or "since" and give a reason for something are often called causal clauses in English.

- Causal clauses have their verbs in the indicative when the *actual* cause is stated. They are introduced by **quod**, **quia** (because), and **quoniam** (since) (→**1**)

- **quod** is used with the subjunctive when the cause is only *suggested* (→**2**)

- **non quod** (+ *subj*) ... **sed quia** (+ *indic*) not because ... but because ..., is used when the first reason is discarded. The true reason is expressed in the indicative (→**3**)

- **cum** (since, as) is always followed by the subjunctive (→**4**)

- **qui** with the subjunctive can be used to mean "since" (→**5**)

Examples

❶ non iratus sum **quod** in me **fuisti** asperior
I am not angry because you were too harsh towards me

in crypta Neapolitana vecti, timebamus **quia** longior et obscurior carcere **erat**
Travelling in the Naples tunnel, we were afraid because it was longer and darker than a prison

quoniam ita tu **vis**, ego Puteolos tecum proficiscar
Since you wish this, I shall set off with you to Pozzuoli

❷ templa spoliare non poterant **quod** religione **impedirentur**
They could not plunder the temples because (they said) they were prevented by religious feelings

❸ mater semper maxime laboravit **non quod** necessarium **esset sed quia** honestum esse **videbatur**
Mother always worked very hard, not because it was necessary but because it seemed proper

❹ quae **cum** ita **sint**, Catilina, egredere ex urbe!
Since this is so, Catilina, leave the city!

Caesar, **cum** in continente hiemare **constituisset**, ad Galliam rediit
Since Caesar had decided to spend the winter on the mainland, he returned to Gaul

❺ sapiens erat **qui** studiis totos annos **dedisset**
He was wise since he had devoted all his years to study

Temporal Clauses

Clauses denoting time are introduced by conjunctions, *eg* **ubi** (when) followed by verbs in the indicative. Some conjunctions, *eg* **cum** (when) may also take the subjunctive. (→**1**)

Conjunctions followed by the indicative:

ut	when, as
ubi	when

cum primum	
ubi primum	} as soon as
ut primum	

simul ac	} as soon as
simul atque	

quotiens	as often as, whenever
quamdiu	as long as, while
ex quo (tempore)	ever since

postquam	} after (**post** or **postea** may be separated from **quam**)
posteaquam	

Examples

❶ **ut** valetudo Germanici Romae **nuntiata est**, magna ira erat
When Germanicus' state of health was announced in Rome, there was great anger

ubi primum classis visa est, **complentur** non modo portus sed moenia ac tecta
As soon as the fleet was seen, not only the harbour but the walls and rooftops were filled (with people)

quod **ubi cognitum est** hostibus, universi nonam legionem nocte aggressi sunt
When this was discovered by the enemy, all of them attacked the ninth legion at night

quotiens proficiscor, pluit
Every time I set out, it rains

manebat **quamdiu poterat**
He stayed as long as he could

Septimus annus est, milites, **ex quo** Britanniam **vicistis**
It is seven years, soldiers, since you conquered Britain

postquam vallum **intravit**, portas stationibus **confirmavit**
After entering the fortification, he strengthened the gates with guards

post tertium diem **quam redierat**, mortuus est
He died three days after his return

Conjunctions which take the indicative or subjunctive:

cum

- **when** with indicative and often **tum** in the main clause (→**1**)

- **whenever** with the following pattern of tenses in the indicative: (→**2**)
    + **perfect** followed by **present** tense
    + **future perfect** followed by **future** tense
    + **pluperfect** followed by **imperfect** tense

- **when, as** with the imperfect or pluperfect subjunctive narrative (→**3**)

dum

- **while** with indicative

    the present tense is used when **dum** means "during the time that" (→**4**)

- Note that where the same tense (here, the future) is used in both clauses, **dum** means "all the time that". Latin uses future **vivam** more accurately than English "live" (→**5**)

Examples

1 cum tu Romae **eras, tum** ego domi eram
When you were in Rome, I was then at home

2 cum **surrexerat, cadebat**
Whenever he got up, he fell down

cum domum **veni**, amicum **visito**
Whenever I come home, I visit my friend

3 Socrates, **cum** triginta tyranni **essent**, non exibat
Socrates didn't go out when there were 30 tyrants

cum id Caesari **nuntiatum esset** ab urbe profectus est
When that message had been given to Caesar, he set out from the city

4 dum haec **geruntur** sex milia hominum ad Rhenum contenderunt
While this was going on, 6000 men marched to the Rhine

5 dum **vivam**, laeta ero
While I live, I shall be happy

Temporal Clauses (continued)

Conjunctions which take the indicative or subjunctive (continued)

dum, donec

- **until** with subjunctive, often with the sense of purpose or suspense (→**1**)

antequam, priusquam

- **before** with indicative (→**2**)

- **ante** and **prius** may be separated from **quam** especially in negative sentences (→**3**)

- **before** with subjunctive, usually with a sense of purpose or limit (→**4**)

Examples

❶ multa Antonio concessit **dum** interfectores patris **ulcisceretur**
He made many concessions to Antony until he could avenge his father's killers

Haterius in periculo erat **donec** Augustam auxilium **oraret**
Haterius was in danger until he begged for Augusta's help

❷ **antequam finiam**, hoc dicam
Before I finish, I shall say this

priusquam gallus **cantabit**, ter me negabis
Before the cock crows, you will deny me three times

❸ neque **prius** fugere destiterunt **quam** ad castra **pervenerunt**
They didn't stop running away before reaching their camp

❹ consul Romam festinavit **antequam** Hannibal eo **perveniret**
The consul hurried to Rome before Hannibal could reach it

ita cassita nidum migravit **priusquam** agricola frumentum **meteret**
And so the lark abandoned her nest before the fanner could reap the corn

Comparative Clauses

- These are adverbial clauses which express likeness, agreement (or the opposite) with what is stated in the main clause (→**1**)

- When the comparative clause states a fact (as above) the verb is in the **indicative**. The commonest words of comparison are (→**2**)

    ut (as), **sicut** (just as), **aliter ac, aliter ut** (different from), **idem ac, idem atque, qui etc** (the same as)

- When the comparative clause is purely **imaginary**, the verb is **subjunctive**. The commonest words used with this type of clause are (→**3**)

    velut(si), quasi, tamquam (si) (as if)

Examples

❶ eadem dixi ac prius dixeram
I said the same as I had said before

❷ ego ita ero, ut me esse oportet
I shall be as I should be

sicut lupus agnos rapit, ita mater liberos servat
just as the wolf snatches the lamb, so the mother saves her children

haud aliter se gerebat ac solebat
He behaved as he usually did
or He behaved no differently from usual

idem abierunt qui venerant
The same men vanished as came

❸ velutsi haec res nihil ad se pertinuisset, tacebat
He remained silent, as if this thing had nothing to do with him

hic flammae Aetnae minantur quasi ad caelum sublatae sint
Here Aetna's flames threaten, as if raised to the heavens

Cleopatram salutaverunt tamquam si esset regina
They greeted Cleopatra as if she were queen

Relative Clauses

- Relative clauses are more common in Latin than in English. They are introduced by the following:

qui, quae, quod	which, who, that
ubi	where, in which
unde	from where, from which

- These relatives come at the beginning of the clause but after prepositions.

- The relative agrees with a word which precedes it – its *antecedent* – in gender and number, but takes its case from its own clause (→**1**)

    qui is masculine plural agreeing with antecedent **Romani**, nominative because it is the subject of **incenderunt**

- **quā** is feminine singular agreeing with **regio**, ablative after preposition in (→**2**)

- **quos** is masculine plural agreeing with **servos**, accusative because it is the object of **iudicavit** (→**3**)

- The relative **quod** refers to a sentence, and **id** is omitted (**id quod** – that which). This is often used in parenthesis, and not attached grammatically to the rest of the sentence.

    After **cuius** (of, concerning which) the noun **laudationis** is repeated (→**4**)

- The relative sometimes agrees with the following word, especially with the verb **esse** (→**5**)

Examples

1 hi sunt Romani **qui** libros incenderunt
These are the Romans who burnt the books

2 haec est regio **in qua** ego sum natus
This is the region in which I was born

3 servos **quos** ipse iudicavit, eos sua sponte liberavit
He willingly freed those slaves whom he himself had judged

4 deinde, **quod** alio loco antea dixi, quae est ista tandem laudatio, **cuius laudationis** legati et principes et publice tibi navem aedificatam, et privatim se ipsos abs te spoliatos esse dixerunt? (**Cicero**, Verres V 58)
Well then, as I said earlier elsewhere, what does that praise consist of, namely that publicly the ambassadors and chief citizens said a ship had been built for you, but privately that they themselves had been robbed by you?

5 iusta gloria **qui** fructus virtutis est, bello quaeritur
True glory, which is the reward of courage, is looked for in war

Use of Subjunctive in Relative Clauses

- The subjunctive is used in relative clauses dependent on infinitives or subjunctives (→**1**)

- When **qui** is used with the subjunctive, it may express cause (→**2**)

  quippe is sometimes used with **qui** in this sense

- When **qui** *etc* is used with the present or imperfect subjunctive, it may express purpose (→**3**)

- **qui** with the subjunctive is used with the following (→**4**)

dignus est **qui**	he is worthy of
idoneus est **qui**	he is fit to
sunt **qui**	there are people who
nemo est **qui**	there is no one who

- At the beginning of a sentence, any part of **qui, quae, quod** may be used as a connective (instead of the demonstrative) with the previous sentence. Translate it in English by "this" or "that" (→**5**)

Examples

1 quis sit **cui** vita talis **placeat**?
Who is there that likes such a life?

2 multa de mea sententia questus est Caesar (**quippe**) **qui** Ravennae Crassum ante **vidisset**
Caesar complained a lot about my decision since he had seen Crassus at Ravenna previously

3 legatos misit **qui** pacem **peterent**
He sent ambassadors to ask for peace

4 **sunt qui** dicere **timeant**
There are some who are afraid to speak

nemo **idoneus** aderat **qui responderet**
There was nobody there capable of replying

5 **quod** cum **audivisset**, soror lacrimas fudit
When she heard this, my sister shed tears

quae cum ita **sint**, Vatinium defendant
Since this is so, I shall defend Vatinius

Negatives

There are several ways of forming a negative in Latin.

non

- This is the common negative in the indicative and usually stands before the verb, although it may be put in front of any word for emphasis (→**1**)
- Two negatives in the same sentence make an affirmative (→**2**)

haud

- This makes a single word negative, usually an adjective or an adverb (→**3**)
- It is also used in expressions such as **haud scio an** (I don't know whether), and **haud dubito** (I don't doubt) (→**4**)
- **haudquaquam** means not at all (→**5**)

Examples

❶ ante horam tertiam noctis de foro **non discedit**
He didn't leave the forum before nine o'clock at night

Ambarri Caesarem certiorem faciunt se, vastatis agris, **non facile** vim hostium ab oppidis prohibere
The Ambarri informed Caesar that it was **not easy** for them, since their territory was destroyed, to keep the enemy force away from their towns

Caesar **non exspectandum** sibi statuit dum Helvetii pervenirent
Caesar decided **not to wait** till the Swiss arrived

❷ **non** possum **non facere**
I must do

non sumus **ignari**
We are well aware

❸ **haud** magnus
not great

haud procul
not far away

❹ **haud scio an** ire mihi liceat
I don't know whether I am allowed to go

❺ homo bonus, **haudquaquam** eloquens
A good man but not at all a good speaker

ne

- This is the negative of the imperative and subjunctive. It is also used in many subordinate clauses where the verb is in the subjunctive (→**1**)

- **Wishes** (→**2**)

- **Purpose** (→**3**)

- **Indirect command** (→**4**)

- **Fearing** (→**5**)

Examples

1 ne diutius **vivamus**
Let us **not live** any longer

2 utinam **ne** id **accidisset**
I wish that it **had not happened**

3 agnus celeriter fugit ne lupi se **caperent**
The lamb ran away quickly **in case** the wolves caught it

4 pater mihi imperavit **ne abirem**
Father told me **not to go away**

5 cives metuebant **ne** Tiberius libertatem sibi **non redderet**
The citizens were afraid that Tiberius **would not give** them **back** their freedom

veritus sum **ne** id quod accidit **adveniret**
I was afraid that what did in fact happen **might take place**

Negatives (continued)

Other Negatives

- neque ... neque   neither ... nor (→**1**)

- neque ... quisquam   neither anyone *or* and no one
  neque ... quidquam   neither anything *or* and nothing
  neque ... umquam   neither ever *or* and never
  nemo ... umquam   no one ever *or* never anyone
  nihil ... umquam   nothing ever *or* never anything (→**2**)

- Notice the following combinations:

nonnulli	some	*but*	nulli ... non	all
nonnihil	somewhat	*but*	nihil ... non	everything (→**3**)

- non solum ... sed etiam   not only ... but also
  non solum ... sed quoque   not only ... but also (→**4**)

- Roman authors repeat negatives for effect (→**5**)

Examples

1 neque illo adit **quisquam neque** eis ipsis **quidquam** praeter oram maritimam
notum est
Neither did anyone approach that place, nor did they themselves know anything
except the coast

2 neque post id tempus **umquam** summis nobiscum copiis hostes contenderunt
And after that the enemy never engaged in battle with us at full strength

ego **nihil umquam** feci solus
I never did anything alone

3 nonnulli amici
some friends

nulli amici non venerunt
all my friends came

4 Herennius Pontius, iam gravis annis, **non solum** militaribus **sed quoque**
civilibus muneribus abscesserat
Herennius Pontius, now old, had withdrawn not only from military but also
from civic duties

5 nihil audio quod audisse, **nihil** dico quod dixisse paeniteat; **nemo** apud me
quemquam sinistris sermonibus carpit, **neminem** ipse reprehendo, **nisi**
tamen me cum parum commode scribo; **nulla** spe, **nullo** timore solicitor, **nullis**
rumoribus inquietor; mecum tantum et cum libellis loquor (**Pliny** Ep 1, 9)
I hear nothing that I would regret having heard, I say nothing that I would
regret having said; at home nobody nags me with vicious remarks, I don't blame
anyone except myself when I write badly; no hope or fear worries me, no idle talk
disturbs me; I speak only to myself and to my books

Translation Guidelines

Translating from Latin into English can be both a challenge and a pleasure. The word order of both languages is different: word order shows the relationship of words in English, in Latin it is shown by word endings. Sentences are generally shorter in English, structures simpler. Latin sentences often contain more subordinate clauses, sometimes embedded in other clauses, and often build up to form a long periodic sentence. Subject matter is two thousand years distant in time, although many ideas are still familiar to us today. The following guidelines are suggested to help in translation.

Guidelines

- *Establish the context* of the passage to be translated. Read the introduction in English carefully, find out *who* or *what* is being discussed, *when* and *where* the action took place.

- *Read through the whole passage* fairly quickly to gain some general understanding of the passage, however incomplete.

- *Focus on each sentence*, either taking each word as it comes, or establishing subject/verb/object according to your normal approach. Many find it helpful to pick out the verbs and work out the structure of the clauses. Watch for agreement of adjectives with nouns and how prepositional phrases fit in.

- *Watch conjunctions* **et**, **sed** *etc* and connectives such as **tamen** (however), and **igitur** (therefore). These help explain the logic of the passage as a whole.

- *Note punctuation*. It can be helpful in isolating clauses within the sentences, or marking off an ablative absolute.

- *Be open-minded*. Does **cum**, for example, mean "when", "since", or "although"? Don't decide till the whole sentence is worked out.

- *Use dictionaries carefully*. Check words of similar spelling, check endings. Once you have found the right Latin word, check all of its meanings before deciding on the correct translation.

- *Watch out for features of style eg* use of two adjectives with same meaning *etc*.

- Finally, *check your translation*. Does the narrative or logic of the passage seem consistent? Does your English sound natural? Does it represent the tone or style of the Latin passage? At this stage, fill in any blanks or make corrections.

Translation Problems

Finding the subject

- Look for a noun with a nominative ending. Check with verb ending for agreement. If there is no nominative, the subject will be indicated by the verb ending. Remember that, in Latin, the subject is continued from the previous sentence unless there is clear indication otherwise (→**1**)

Adjective agreement

- Check which adjective agrees with which noun in number, case and gender. Remember that it may be separated from its noun.

    a   b   b   a
    te **flagrantis atrox hora Caniculae** nescit tangere
    The blazing Dog Star's fierce daytime heat can't touch you

Passive

- Often it is better to turn a Latin passive verb into an active verb in English (→**2**)

Tense

- English is not so precise as Latin in its use of tenses. Use the tense that seems most natural in English, for example, English past tense for historic present in Latin, or English present tense for Latin future perfect in a conditional clause (→**3**)

Examples

❶ **consules** et armare plebem et inermem pati **timebant**. **sedabant** tumultum, sedando interdum **movebant**.
The consuls were afraid both to arm the people and to leave them unarmed. **They quelled** the riot, but sometimes, in quelling it, **they stirred it up again.**

❷ hoc a tu **demonstrari** et **probari** volo
I wish you to demonstrate and prove this
or I wish this to be demonstrated and proved by you

❸ hoc faciam si **potuero** (*future perfect*)
I shall do this if I can (*present*)

Ablative absolute

> **hostibus victis** can be translated:
>
> when the enemy had been beaten
> after beating the enemy
> they beat the enemy and ...
> although the enemy were beaten

Choose the version that makes most sense within the context of the passage.

Omission of esse

- Parts of **esse** (to be) are often omitted and have to be supplied in English (→**1**)

Omission of small words (ut, id, eo, hic *etc*)

- Check that you do not omit to translate these words – they are often very important (→**2**)

Neuter plurals

- **omnia** (everything) and **multa** (many things) are often mistranslated.

Impersonal passives

- It is worthwhile learning these (→**3**)

Examples

1 sed Germanicus quanto (**erat**) summae spei propior, tanto impensius pro Tiberio niti
But the nearer Germanicus **was** to succeeding, the more strenuously he exerted himself on behalf of Tiberius

2
eo	to there (*adv*), by, with or from him (*abl of pronoun*)
id ... quod	that which
hic	this (*pron*), here (*adv*)
fit ... ut	it happens ... that

3
allatum est	it was announced
cognitum est	it was discovered
pugnatum est	a battle was fought
traditum est	it was recorded
visum est	it seemed

Translation Problems (continued)

Similarity of English/Latin Words

A higher percentage of English words are derived from Latin than from any other source. This can be helpful when trying to deduce the meaning of a Latin word, *eg* **portus** (port). But **porta** (gate) may cause confusion. The following examples taken from actual examination scripts provide a cautionary note. The correct translation follows in brackets:

Examples

prima luce nuntius hic **Ameriam** venit
At dawn the messenger came to America
(*At dawn the messenger came to Ameria*)

sex et quinquaginta **milia passuum** in cisio pervolavit
56 thousand flew past in a chariot
(*He quickly travelled fifty-six miles in a chariot*)

ut mori **mallet**
He would rather be killed by a mallet
(*To prefer to die*)

legati **crediderunt**
The embassy got credit
(*The ambassadors believed*)

False Friends/Confusables

ad (+ *acc*)	to, towards	**constituō**	I decide
ab (+ *abl*)	from, by, with	**consist**	I stop
adeo	to such an extent	**crīmen**	charge
adeō	I approach	**scelus**	crime
aestās	summer	**cum** (*prep*)	with
aestus	heat, tide	**cum** (*conj*)	when, since, although
aetas	age	**dominus**	master
aura	breeze	**domus**	house
aures (*pl*)	ears	**equitēs** (*pl*)	horsemen
aurum	gold	**equus**	horse
avis	bird	**fama**	fame, report
avus	grandfather	**fames**	hunger
cadō	I fall	**forte**	by chance
caedō	I cut, kill	**fortis**	brave (not strong)
cēdō	I go, yield	**fugāre**	to put to flight
campus	plain	**fugere**	to flee, escape
castra (*pl*)	camp	**hōra**	hour
cēterum	but	**hōrum** (*gen pl*)	of these
cēterī (*pl*)	the rest	**iaceō**	I lie
coepī	I began	**iaciō**	I throw
coēgi	I forced		

imperātor	general (*not* emperor)	**quīdam**	a certain (person)
imperātus	ordered (*past participle*)	**quīdem**	indeed
inveniō	I find (*not* come in)	**reddō, -ere**	I give back
invītō	I invite	**redeō, -īre**	I go back
invītus	unwilling	**serviō, -īre**	I serve
iter, -ineris	journey	**servō, -āre**	I save
iterum	again	**sōl, -is**	sun
lātus, -a, -um	broad	**soleō, -ēre**	I am accustomed
lātus, -a, -um	brought	**solitus sum**	
lātus, -eris	side	**solum, -i**	soil
līber, -ri	book	**sōlus, -a, -um**	alone
līber, -a, -um	free	**tamen**	however
līberī, -orum (*pl*)	children	**tandem**	at last
libertus, -i	freedman	**ut(ī)**	in order that, as, when
magister, -ri	master	**uti** (*dep*)	to use
magistratus	magistrate	**vallis, -is**	valley
malus, -a, -um	bad	**vallum, -i**	wall, rampart
malum, -i	apple	**victor**	winner
mālo, mā[[le	I prefer	**victus** (*past part*)	beaten
manus, - ūs	hand, band	**vinctus** (*past part*)	bound
mānēs, -ium	spirits of dead	**vīs**	force
miser, -a, -um	unhappy	**vīres, -ium**	strength
mīseram	I had sent (*plup of* mitto)	**vir, -ī**	man
morior, -ī	I die	**virga, -ae**	stick
moror, ārī	I delay	**virgo, -inis**	girl
nauta	sailor	**vīta, -ae**	life
nāvis	ship	**vītō, -āre**	I avoid
nēmō	no one		
nimium	too much		
occāsio	opportunity		
occāsus (solis)	setting (of sun)		
occidere	to fall, set		
occīdere	to kill		
opem	help		
opera, -ae	work		
opus, -eris	task		
opus est	it is necessary		
ōra, -ae	coast		
ōrō, -āre	I pray, beg		
ōs, ōris	face		
ōs, ōssis	bone		
parcō, -ere	I spare		
pareō, -ere	I obey		
pario, -ere	I give birth to		
parō, -are	I prepare		
passus, -us	a pace		
passus, -a, -um	suffered (*past participle of* **patior**)		
porta, -ae	gate		
portus, -us	port		
portō, -are	I carry		
quaerō, -ere	I seek		
queror, -ī	I complain		

73

Conjugations

There are four patterns of regular Latin verbs called conjugations. Each can be identified by the ending of the **present infinitive**:

- First conjugation verbs end in **-āre** (*eg* am**āre** – to love)
- Second conjugation verbs end in **-ēre** (*eg* hab**ēre** – to have)
- Third conjugation verbs end in **-ere** (*eg* mitt**ere** – to send)
- Fourth conjugation verbs end in **-īre** (*eg* aud**īre** – to hear)

Each regular verb has three **stems**:

- A **present stem** which is found by cutting off **-re** from the present infinitive (*eg* am**ā**re, hab**ē**re, mitt**e**re, aud**ī**re).

- A **perfect stem** which is formed by adding **-v** to the present stem in the first and fourth conjugations (*eg* amav**ī**, audīv**ī**), and by adding **-u** to the present stem in the second conjugation (*eg* habu**ī**).

  In the third conjugation there are several possible endings (*eg* scrips**ī**, dīx**ī**).

  Some short verbs lengthen the stem vowel (*eg* lēg**ī**), others double the first consonant and vowel (*eg* cucurr**ī**).

- A **supine stem** which is formed by cutting off **-um** from the supine forms (*eg* amāt**um**, habit**um**, miss**um**, audīt**um**).

Tenses

These forms of the verb show when an action takes place, in the present, in the past or in the future.

In Latin there are six tenses:

<table>
<tr><td>1</td><td>Present</td><td rowspan="3">} formed from the present stem</td></tr>
<tr><td>2</td><td>Imperfect</td></tr>
<tr><td>3</td><td>Future</td></tr>
</table>

<table>
<tr><td>4</td><td>Perfect</td><td rowspan="3">} formed from the perfect stem</td></tr>
<tr><td>5</td><td>Pluperfect</td></tr>
<tr><td>6</td><td>Future Perfect</td></tr>
</table>

Tenses Formed from the Present Stem

The following endings are added to the stem:

	PRESENT	IMPERFECT	FUTURE	
			Conj 1 and 2	Conj 3 and 4
sing				
1st person	-ō	-bam	-bō	-am
2nd person	-s	-bas	-bis	-ēs
3rd person	-t	-bat	-bit	-et
pl				
1st person	-mus	-bāmus	-bimus	-ēmus
2nd person	-tis	-bātis	-bitis	-ētis
3rd person	-nt	-bant	-bunt	-ent

Note that the above endings show the number and person of the subject of the verb. Subject pronouns are therefore not normally necessary in Latin.

Conjugations

1	2	3	4
INFINITIVE			
amare	habēre	mittere	audīre
PRESENT STEM			
ama-	habē-	mitte-	audī-
PRESENT			
amō	habeo	mittō	audiō
amās	habēs	mittis	audīs
amat	habet	mittit	audit
amāmus	habēmus	mittimus	audīmus
amātis	habētis	mittitis	audītis
amant	habent	mittunt	audiunt
IMPERFECT			
amābam	habēbam	mittēbam	audiēbam
amābās	habēbās	mittēbās	audiēbās
amābat	habēbat	mittēbat	audiēbat
amābāmus	habēbāmus	mittēbāmus	audiēbamus
amābātis	habēbātis	mittēbātis	audiēbātis
amābant	habēbant	mittēbant	audiēbant
FUTURE			
amābō	habēbō	mittam	audiam
amābis	habēbis	mittēs	audiēs
amābit	habēbit	mittet	audiet
amābimus	habēbimus	mittēmus	audiēmus
amābitis	habēbitis	mittētis	audiētis
amābunt	habēbunt	mittent	audient

Tenses (continued)

Use:

The Present

In Latin, the present tense expresses what is going on now and can be translated into English in two ways (*eg* **laborat** – he works, he is working)

- The present is often used in Latin instead of a past tense to make the action more exciting (→**1**)
- Sometimes the Latin present tense is used to describe an action begun in the past and still continuing (→**2**)

The Imperfect

- Describes what went on or continued for a time (→**3**)
- Denotes an action repeated in the past (→**4**)
- Is used when an action is intended or interrupted (→**5**)
- Is sometimes translated "had" when used with **iam** (→**6**)

The Future

- Is used in Latin as in English to denote what will or is going to be or to happen (→**7**)
- Is occasionally used as a command (→**8**)
- After "**si**" (if) in conditional sentences, it is sometimes translated as present tense in English (→**9**)

Examples

1 **prima luce Caesar Gallos oppugnat**
Caesar attacked the Gauls at dawn

2 **Alexander iam tres annos regit**
Alexander has been ruling for three years now

3 **pluebat** – it was raining

4 **fortiter pugnabant**
They used to fight bravely
or They kept fighting bravely

5 **Romam intrabam**
I was about to enter Rome

6 **multos iam dies villam habitabat**
He had already lived in the house for many days

7 **hoc faciemus**
We shall do this
or We are going to do this

erit gloria
There will be glory

8 **non me vocabis**
Don't call me

9 **si id credes, errabis**
If you believe this, you will be making a mistake

Tenses Formed from the Perfect Stem

To the appropriate perfect stem add the following endings:

	PERFECT	PLUPERFECT	FUTURE PERFECT
sing			
1st person	-ī	-eram	-erō
2nd person	-istī	-erās	-eris
3rd person	-it	-erat	-erit
pl			
1st person	-imus	-erāmus	-erimus
2nd person	-istis	-erātis	-eritis
3rd person	-ērunt	-erant	-erint

Conjugations

1	2	3	4
PERFECT STEM			
amāv-	habu-	mīs-	audīv-
PERFECT			
amāvī	habuī	mīsī	audīvī
amāvistī	habuistī	mīsistī	audīvistī
amāvit	habuit	mīsit	audīvit
amāvimus	habuimus	mīsimus	audīvimus
amāvistis	habuistis	mīsistis	audīvistis
amāvērunt	habuērunt	mīserunt	audīvērunt
PLUPERFECT			
amāveram	habueram	mīseram	audīveram
amāverās	habuerās	mīserās	audīverās
amāverat	habuerat	mīserat	audīverat
amāverāmus	habuerāmus	mīserāmus	audīverāmus
amāverātis	habuerātis	mīserātis	audīverātis
amāverant	habuerant	mīserant	audīverant
FUTURE PERFECT			
amāverō	habuerō	mīserō	audīverō
amāveris	habueris	mīseris	audīveris
amāverit	habuerit	mīserit	audīverit
amāverimus	habuerimus	mīserimus	audīverimus
amāveritis	habueritis	mīseritis	audīveritis
amāverint	habuerint	mīserint	audīverint

Tenses (continued)

Use:

The Perfect

- In Latin, the perfect tense is equivalent to the simple past tense (*eg* **vīdī** – I saw) and the perfect tense (*eg* **vīdī** – I have seen) in English.

- It states past action particularly in narrative (→**1**)

- Expresses an action completed in the past which still has effect in the present (→**2**)

The Pluperfect

- Denotes an action completed in the past before another past action (→**3**)

The Future Perfect

- Denotes completing something in the future (→**4**)

- Is often used with **volō, possum, nolō** *etc* (→**5**)

- Denotes an action which precedes another action in the future, often in a subordinate clause (→**6**)

Examples

1 **veni, vidi, vici**
I came, I saw, I conquered

2 **spem in fide alicuius habuerunt**
They place their hope in someone's good faith

3 **Mithridates urbem Asiae clarissimam obsederat quam L. Lucullus virtute liberavit**
Mithridates had besieged the most famous city in Asia that Lucius Lucullus freed by his courage

4 **id fecero**
I shall have done it

5 **si potuero, faciam**
If I can, I shall do it

6 **qui prior venerit, prior discedet**
First to come will be first to go

The Passive

Verbs may be active or passive. In **active** forms of the verb, the subject carries out the action (*eg* Brutus **killed** Caesar). In **passive** forms of the verb, the subject receives the action (*eg* Caesar **was killed** by Brutus).

Conjugations

To form the passive tenses of regular verbs, substitute the following endings for those of the present, imperfect and future active tenses (conjugated on page 75):

- In the present 1st person sing the ending is **-or**.
- In the imperfect, the endings are added to **-ba**.
- In the future (conjugations 1 and 2), the endings are added to **-bo** (1st person sing), **-be** (2nd person sing), and **-bi** for other persons. In conjugations 3 and 4, the 1st person sing ending is **-ar**.

sing		*pl*	
1st person	**-r**	1st person	**-mur**
2nd person	**-ris**	2nd person	**-minī**
3rd person	**-tur**	3rd person	**-ntur**

Conjugations

1	2	3	4
PRESENT PASSIVE			
amor	habeor	mittor	audior
amāris	habēris	mitteris	audīris
amatur	habētur	mittitur	audītur
amāmur	habēmur	mittimur	audīmur
amāminī	habēminī	mittiminī	audīminī
amāntur	habēntur	mittuntur	audīuntur
IMPERFECT PASSIVE			
amābar	habēbar	mittēbar	audiēbar
amābaris	habēbāris	mittēbāris	audiēbāris
amābatur	habēbātur	mittēbātur	audiēbātur
amābamur	habēbāmur	mittēbāmur	audiēbāmur
amābaminī	habēbāminī	mittēbāminī	audiēbāminī
amābantur	habēbantur	mittēbantur	audiēbantur
FUTURE PASSIVE			
amābor	habēbor	mittar	audiar
amāberis	habēberis	mittēris	audiēris
amābitur	habēbitur	mittētur	audiētur
amābimur	habēbimur	mittēmur	audiēmur
amābiminī	habēbiminī	mittēminī	audiēmini
amābuntur	habēbuntur	mittentur	audientur

The Passive (continued)

Translation

Present Passive

1. I am loved   we are loved
   you (*sing*) are loved   you (*pl*) are loved
   he/she/it is loved   they are loved
2. I am held *etc*
3. I am sent *etc*
4. I am heard *etc*

Imperfect Passive

1. I was loved   we were loved
   you (*sing*) were loved   you (*pl*) were loved
   he/she/it was loved   they were loved
2. I was held *etc*
3. I was sent *etc*
4. I was heard *etc*

Future Passive

1. I shall be loved   we shall be loved
   you (*sing*) will be loved   you (*pl*) will be loved
   he/she/it will be loved   they will be loved
2. I shall be held *etc*
3. I shall be sent *etc*
4. I shall be heard *etc*

- "going to be" may also be used to translate the future.

Perfect, Pluperfect and Future Perfect Passive

These tenses consist of the past participle (formed from the supine stem) and tenses of the verb **sum** (to be). The past participle endings agree in number and gender with the subject of the verb.

Conjugations

1	2	3	4	
PERFECT PASSIVE				
amātus	habitus	missus	audītus	**sum**
-a, -um	-a, -um	-a, -um	-a, -um	**es**
				est
amātī	habitī	missī	audītī	**sumus**
-ae, -a	-ae, -a	-ae, -a	-ae, -a	**estis**
				sunt
PLUPERFECT PASSIVE				
amātus	habitus	missus	audītus	**eram**
				erās
				erat
amātī	habitī	missī	audītī	**erāmus**
				erātis
				erant
FUTURE PERFECT PASSIVE				
amātus	habitus	missus	audītus	**erō**
				eris
				erit
amātī	habitī	missī	audītī	**erimus**
				eritis
				erunt

The Passive (continued)

Translation

Perfect Passive

1	I have been loved	we have been loved
	you (*sing*) have been loved	you (*pl*) have been loved
	he/she/it has been loved	they have been loved
2	I have been held *or* I was held *etc*	
3	I have been sent *or* I was sent *etc*	
4	I have been heard *or* I was heard *etc*	

Pluperfect Passive

1	I had been loved	we had been loved
	you (*sing*) had been loved	you (*pl*) had been loved
	he/she/it had been loved	they had been loved
2	I had been held *etc*	
3	I had been sent *etc*	
4	I had been heard *etc*	

Future Perfect Passive

1	I shall have been loved	we shall have been loved
	you (*sing*) will have been loved	you (*pl*) will have been loved
	he/she/it will have been loved	they will have been loved
2	I shall have been held *etc*	
3	I shall have been sent *etc*	
4	I shall have been heard *etc*	

Examples

1 **milites a populo occisi sunt**
The soldiers were killed by the people

2 **populus milites occidit**
The people killed the soldiers

- Note that the subject of the passive verb in (**1**) becomes the object of the active verb in (**2**).

- Often in English it is better to translate the meaning actively as in (**2**).

- The **agent** of the action is translated by **a**(**b**) with the ablative case as in **a populo** (**1**) – by the people.

- The **thing** causing the action is translated by the ablative case alone

  saxo percussus erat
  He had been struck by a rock

The Subjunctive

So far all verbs described have belonged to the indicative mood, which states facts. The subjunctive mood represents ideas, possibilities or necessities and is often translated by auxiliary verbs such as **may**, **might**, **could**, **would**, **should** or **must**. There are four tenses active and passive – present, imperfect, perfect and pluperfect.

Formation of Active

The present subjunctive active is formed from the present stem, the imperfect from the infinitive. To these add the endings

-m, -s, -t, -mus, -tis, -nt.

- Note that in first conjugation present the preceding vowel is **-e**, and in all others **-a**.
- The present subjunctive active is sometimes translated by using "**may**" (→1)
- The imperfect subjunctive active is sometimes translated by using "**might**" (→2)

Conjugations

1	2	3	4

PRESENT SUBJUNCTIVE ACTIVE

1	2	3	4
amem	habeam	mittam	audiam
amēs	habeās	mittās	audiās
amet	habeat	mittat	audiat
amēmus	habeāmus	mittāmus	audiāmus
amētis	habeātis	mittātis	audiātis
ament	habeant	mittant	audient

IMPERFECT SUBJUNCTIVE ACTIVE

1	2	3	4
amārem	habērem	mitterem	audīrem
amāres	haberēs	mitterēs	audīrēs
amāret	habēret	mitteret	audīret
amārēmus	habērēmus	mitterēmus	audīrēmus
amārētis	habērētis	mitterētis	audīrētis
amārent	habērent	mitterent	audīrent

Examples

1 **amem** – I may love

mittas – you (*sing*) may send

habeat – he may have

audiant – they may hear

2 **mitteretis** – you (*pl*) might send

haberem – I might have

amaret – she might love

audirent – they might hear

The Subjunctive (continued)

Formation of Passive

The passive of the present and imperfect subjunctive is easily formed by substituting the normal passive endings (**-r, -ris, -tur, -mur, -mini, -ntur**) for the active ones.

Conjugations

1	2	3	4
PRESENT SUBJUNCTIVE PASSIVE			
amer	habear	mittar	audiar
amēris	habeāris	mittāris	audiāris
amētur	habeātur	mittātur	audiātur
amēmur	habeāmur	mittāmur	audiāmur
amēminī	habeāminī	mittāminī	audiāminī
amentur	habeantur	mittantur	audiantur
IMPERFECT SUBJUNCTIVE PASSIVE			
amārer	habērer	mitterer	audīrer
amārēris	habērēris	mitterēris	audīrēris
amārētur	habērētur	mitterētur	audīrētur
amārēmur	habērēmur	mitterēmur	audīrēmur
amārēminī	habērēminī	mitterēminī	audīrēminī
amārentur	habērentur	mitterentur	audīrentur

- The present subjunctive passive is sometimes translated by using **"may be"** (→**1**)

- The imperfect subjunctive passive is sometimes translated by using **"might be"** (→**2**)

Examples

1 **habeamur** – we may be held

amer – I may be loved

mittamini – you (*pl*) may be sent

audiantur – they may be heard

2 **audiremini** – you (*pl*) might be heard

amaretur – he might be loved

haberentur – they might be held

mitterer – I might be sent

Perfect and Pluperfect Subjunctive Active

Both perfect and pluperfect subjunctive active are formed from the perfect stem as follows:

Conjugations

1	2	3	4
PERFECT SUBJUNCTIVE ACTIVE			
amāverim	habuerim	mīserim	audīverim
amāveris	habueris	mīseris	audīveris
amāverit	habuerit	mīserit	audīverit
amāverimus	habuerimus	mīserimus	audīverimus
amāveritis	habueritis	mīseritis	audīveritis
amāverint	habuerint	mīserint	audīverint
PLUPERFECT SUBJUNCTIVE ACTIVE			
amāvissem	habuissem	mīsissem	audīvissem
amāvissēs	habuissēs	mīsissēs	audīvissēs
amāvisset	habuisset	mīsisset	audīvisset
amāvissēmus	habuissēmus	mīsissēmus	audīvissēmus
amāvissētis	habuissētis	mīsissētis	audīvissētis
amāvissent	habuissent	mīsissent	audīvissent

- The Perfect subjunctive active is sometimes translated by using **"may have"** with the past participle in English (→**1**)

- The Pluperfect subjunctive active is sometimes translated by using **"might have"** with the past participle in English (→**2**)

Examples

1 miserit – he may have sent

   habuerint – they may have had

   audiveris – you (*sing*) may have heard

   amaveritis – you (*pl*) may have loved

2 amavissemus – we might have loved

   habuisset – he might have had

   audivissent – they might have heard

   misissem – I might have sent

The Subjunctive (continued)

Perfect and Pluperfect Subjunctive Passive

Both perfect and pluperfect subjunctive passive are formed from the supine stem and the present and imperfect subjunctive of **sum** respectively:

Conjugation

1		2		3		4	
PERFECT SUBJUNCTIVE PASSIVE							
amatus	**sim**	habitus	**sim**	missus	**sim**	audītus	**sim**
	sīs		**sīs**		**sīs**		**sīs**
	sit		**sit**		**sit**		**sit**
pl							
amatī	**sīmus**	habitī	**sīmus**	missī	**sīmus**	audītī	**sīmus**
	sītis		**sītis**		**sītis**		**sītis**
	sint		**sint**		**sint**		**sint**
PLUPERFECT SUBJUNCTIVE PASSIVE							
amatus	**essem**	habitus	**essem**	missus	**essem**	audītus	**essem**
	essēs		**essēs**		**essēs**		**essēs**
	esset		**esset**		**esset**		**esset**
pl							
amatī	**essēmus**	habitī	**essēmus**	missī	**essēmus**	audītī	**essēmus**
	essētis		**essētis**		**essētis**		**essētis**
	essent		**essent**		**essent**		**essent**

- The perfect subjunctive passive is sometimes translated by using **"may have been"** with the past participle in English (→**1**)

- The pluperfect subjunctive passive is sometimes translated by using **"might have been"** with the past participle in English (→**2**)

Examples

1 **habitus sis** – you (*sing*) may have been held
   missi simus – we may nave been sent
   auditus sim – I may have been heard
   amati sint – they may have been loved

2 **amati essemus** – we might have been loved
   habiti essent – they might have been held
   missus esses – you (*sing*) might have been sent
   auditus essem – I might have been heard

The Imperative

This is the mood of command. It has two forms, 2nd person *sing* and *pl*, active (→**1**) and passive (→**2**).

Conjugations

	1	2	3	4
IMPERATIVE ACTIVE				
sing	amā	habē	mitte	audī
pl	amāte	habēte	mittite	audīte
IMPERATIVE PASSIVE				
sing	amāre	habēre	mittere	audīre
pl	amāmini	habēmini	mittīmini	audīminī

Examples

1 **pecuniam mittite, o cives**
Citizens, send money! (active)

spem habe
Have hope! (active)

2 **in curia audimini**
Be heard in the senate! (passive)

ab omnibus semper amare, Romule
Always be loved by everyone, Romulus (passive)

The Infinitive

The infinitive was originally a noun and can be used in this way in Latin (*eg* **amare** – to love or loving). There are three types, present, future and perfect, both active and passive, formed as follows:

Active

	1	**2**
PRESENT	amā**re**	habē**re**
FUTURE	amāt**ūrus esse**	habit**ūrus esse**
PERFECT	amā**visse**	habu**isse**

	3	**4**
PRESENT	mitte**re**	audī**re**
FUTURE	miss**ūrus esse**	audīt**ūrus esse**
PERFECT	mīs**isse**	audī**visse**

Translation

to love	to have
to be going to love	to be going to have
to have loved	to have had
to send	to hear
to be going to send	to be going to hear
to have sent	to have heard

Passive

	1	**2**
PRESENT	amā**rī**	habē**rī**
FUTURE	amā**tum īrī**	habi**tum īrī**
PERFECT	amā**tus esse**	habi**tus esse**

	3	**4**
PRESENT	mitt**ī**	audī**rī**
FUTURE	miss**um īrī**	audī**tum īrī**
PERFECT	miss**us esse**	audī**tus esse**

Translation

to be loved	to be had
to be going to be loved	to be going to be had
to have been loved	to have been had
to be sent	to be heard
to be going to be sent	to be going to be heard
to have been sent	to have been heard

- In the future active **-urus, -a, -um** and in the perfect passive **-us, -a, -um** agree in number and gender with the noun or pronoun in indirect speech.

Uses of the Infinitive

- It can be used as a neuter noun

- As the subject of the sentence (→**1**)

- With certain nouns such as **fas** (right), **nefas** (wrong) (→**2**)

- As the object of the following verbs: (→**3**)

volō	I wish	**cupiō**	I desire
nolō	I do not wish	**sinō**	I allow
possum	I am able to, can	**cogō**	I force
sciō	I know (how)	**audeō**	I dare
nesciō	I do not know	**conor**	I try
debeō	I ought	**desinō**	I stop
soleō	I am accustomed	**dubitō**	I hesitate
incipiō	I begin	**coepi**	I begin

- It can be used to describe a rapid series of events instead of using the perfect tense (→**4**)

Examples

1 **errare est humanum**
To err is human

2 **nefas est templa destruere**
It is wrong to destroy temples

3 **volo domum redire**
I wish to return home

desine mortuos commemorare
Stop remembering the dead

Romam exstinctam esse cupit
He wishes Rome blotted out

4 **ille non tollere oculos, non remittere stilum, tum fragor adventare et intra limen audiri**
He did not raise his eyes nor put down his pen, then the noise came closer and could be heard inside the door.

Participles

There are three participles (or verbal adjectives) in Latin: the present active, the perfect passive and the future active.

The Present Participle

This is formed from the present stem by adding **-ns** and lengthening the previous vowel. The genitive ending is **-ntis**.

Conjugations

1	2	3	4
am**ā**ns	hab**ē**ns	mitt**ē**ns	audi**ē**ns
loving	having	sending	hearing

- Note that these decline like group 3 adjectives ending in **-ns** with ablative singular, in **-i** when used as an adjective and in **-e** when used as a verb. They agree in number, case and gender with nouns or pronouns in the sentence.

Use

- It denotes an action going on at the same time as the main verb (→**1**)

- It can be used as a noun (→**2**)

Examples

❶ pro patria pugnantes iuvenes mortui sunt
The young men died *while fighting* for their country

Romulo regnante, Roma urbs parva erat
While Romulus was ruling, Rome was a small city

❷ lacrimae adstantium
the tears of *people standing by*

The Perfect Participle

This is formed from the supine stem by adding the endings **-us**, **-a**, **-um**. It declines like first and second declension adjectives (see pages 13–15)

Conjugation

1	2	3	4
amā**tus**	habi**tus**	mis**sus**	audī**tus**
(having	(having	(having	having
been) loved	been) held	been) sent	been) heard

Use

• It denotes an action that is completed before that of the main verb (→**1**)

• English is less precise in the use of tenses and frequently uses a present to translate a Latin past participle.

The Future Participle

This is formed by adding **-urus**, **-a**, **-um** to the supine stem. It declines like first and second declension adjectives.

Conjugations

1	2	3	4
amā**tūrus**	habi**tūrus**	mis**sūrus**	audī**tūrus**
going to love	going to have	going to send	going to hear

Use

• It denotes an action that is going to take place (→**2**)

• The forms **futurus** (going to be) and **venturus** (going to come) are often used as adjectives.

Examples

1 **equites Romani auditi ad senatum adducti sunt**
The Roman businessmen *were heard* and then were brought before the Senate

castra capta incendimus
We *captured* the camp and burnt it
or *Capturing* the camp, we burnt it

2 **nos morituri te salutamus**
We who are about to die salute you

Gerunds and Gerundives

The **gerund** is a **verbal noun** and is active.

The **gerundive** is a **verbal adjective** and is passive.

The gerund is formed by adding -**ndum** to the present stem. It declines like a neuter noun -**ndum**, -**ndi**, -**ndo**, -**ndo**.

The gerundive declines like first and second declension adjectives -**us**, -**a**, -**um**.

Conjugations

1	2	3	4
GERUND			
ama**ndum**	habe**ndum**	mitte**ndum**	audie**ndum**
loving	having	sending	hearing
GERUNDIVE			
ama**ndus**	habe**ndus**	mitte**ndus**	audie**ndus**
requiring	requiring	requiring	requiring
to be loved	to be held	to be sent	to be heard

Use of Gerund and Gerundive

- The gerund is often used with the accusative case to express **purpose** (→**1**)

- If the verb has a direct object, the gerundive is used instead (→**2**)

- The gerund is used in the genitive case with nouns and adjectives (→**3**) such as
  ars (art), **spes** (hope), **cupidus** (eager), **peritus** (skilled)

- Both the gerund and the gerundive can be used in the genitive with **causa** to
  express **purpose** (→**4**)

- The gerundive can be used to imply **obligation** and the person is expressed by the
  dative case (→**5**)

- If the verb cannot take a direct object, the impersonal form is used (→**6**)

- Both the gerund and the gerundive can be used in the ablative case (→**7**)

Examples

1 **venit ad regnandum**
He came to rule

2 **venit ad pacem petendam**
He came to make peace

3 **spes videndi**
Hope of seeing

peritus equitandi
Skilled in riding

4 **dicendi causa**
to speak

pacis petendae causa
For the sake of making peace

5 **poenae nobis timendae sunt**
Punishment must be feared by us
or We must fear punishment

6 **mihi parendum est**
You must obey me

7 **docendo discimus**
We learn by teaching

me puniendo effugit
By punishing me he escaped

Impersonal Verbs

Impersonal verbs are used in the third person singular only

- To describe the weather (→**1**)

- To express feeling. The person affected appears in the accusative case and the cause in the genitive case (→**2**)

- To express permission or pleasure. The person affected appears in the dative case. The verb is often followed by a present infinitive (→**3**)

- To express happening, following *etc*. These are followed by **ut** with the subjunctive mood (→**4**)

fit ut	it happens that
accidit ut	it happens that
sequitur ut	it follows that

- Certain intransitive verbs are used impersonally in the passive (→**5**)

- Verbs of saying, believing *etc* are used impersonally in the perfect passive tense (→**6**)

- The verbs **interest** (it is of importance) and **refert** (it is of concern) are followed usually by **meā, tuā, nostrā, vestrā** (→**7**)

- Sometimes **interest** is followed by genitive of the person (→**8**)

- The following verbs are followed by a present infinitive. The person involved appears in the accusative case (→**9**)

me decet	it is fitting for me
me oportet	I must/ought

Examples

1 **pluit** **fulgurat**
it is raining there is lightning

tonat **ningit**
there is it is snowing
thunder

2 **me miseret** **me miseret**
I am sorry for **sociorum**
I am sorry for my
me paenitet comrades
I repent of

3 **mihi licet** **nobis placet**
I am it is pleasing to us
allowed to *or* we like

tibi videtur
it seems good to you
or you decide

4 **fit ut** **fit ut fallar**
it happens it happens that I am
that mistaken

accidit ut
it happens that

5 **pugnatum est in mari**
the battle was fought at sea

vivitur in oculis omnium
life is lived in the sight of everyone

6 **nuntiatum est**
it has been announced

**mihi dictum est Germanos
transiisse Rhenum**
I was told that the Germans had
crossed the Rhine

7 **nihil mea refert**
it is of no interest to me

8 **Caesaris interest**
it is important to Caesar

9 **nos morari oportuit**
we ought to have waited

Deponent Verbs

Deponent verbs are passive in form but active in meaning. They also have present and future participles and future infinitives which are active. The perfect participle is also active in meaning. Otherwise the conjugation is similar to that of regular verbs.

First Conjugation

cōnārī (to try)

INDICATIVE		SUBJUNCTIVE	
PRESENT			
cōnor	I try *etc*	cōner	I may try *etc*
cōnāris		cōnēris	
cōnātur		cōnētur	
cōnāmur		cōnēmur	
cōnāminī		cōnēminī	
cōnāntur		cōnentur	
IMPERFECT			
cōnābar	I was trying *etc*	cōnārer	I might try *etc*
cōnābāris		cōnārēris	
cōnābātur		cōnārētur	
cōnābāmur		cōnārēmur	
cōnābāminī		cōnārēminī	
conabantur		cōnārentur	
FUTURE			
cōnābor	I shall try *etc*		
cōnāberis			
cōnābitur			
cōnābimur			
cōnābiminī			
cōnābuntur			

PERFECT

conātus	**sum**	I tried	conātus	**sim**	I may have tried
-a, -um	**es**	you tried *etc*	-a, -um	**sis**	you may have tried *etc*

PLUPERFECT

conātus	**eram**	I had tried	conātus	**essem**	I might have tried
-a, -um	**eras**	you had tried *etc*	-a, -um	**esses**	you might have tried *etc*

FUTURE PERFECT

conātus	**ero**	I shall have tried
-a, -um	**eris**	you will have tried *etc*

IMPERATIVE

conāre	*sing*	try
conāminī	*pl*	try

INFINITIVES

Present	conārī	to try
Future	conāturus esse	to be going to try
Perfect	conātus esse	to have tried

PARTICIPLES

Present	conāns	trying
Future	conāturus	going to try
Perfect	conātus	having tried

GERUND	conāndum	trying

GERUNDIVE	conāndus	requiring to be tried

Deponent Verbs (continued)

Second, Third, Fourth Conjugations

These are conjugated like the passive form of verbs of the corresponding conjugations. A summary is provided as follows:

Second Conjugation

verērī (to fear, be afraid)

INDICATIVE

Present	ver**eor**	I am afraid
Imperfect	verē**bar**	I was afraid
Future	verē**bor**	I shall be afraid
Perfect	veritus **sum**	I was afraid
Pluperfect	veritus **eram**	I had been afraid
Future Perfect	veritus **erō**	I shall have been afraid

SUBJUNCTIVE

Present	verē**ar**	I may be afraid
Imperfect	verē**rer**	I might be afraid
Perfect	veritus **sim**	I may have been afraid
Pluperfect	veritus **essem**	I might have been afraid

IMPERATIVE

Singular	verē**re**	be afraid
Plural	verē**minī**	be afraid

INFINITIVES

Present	verē**rī**	to be afraid
Future	veritū**rus esse**	to be going to be afraid
Perfect	veritus **esse**	to have been afraid

PARTICIPLES

Present	verē**ns**	fearing, being afraid
Future	veritū**rus**	going to fear or be afraid
Perfect	veri**tus**	having feared or been afraid (active)

GERUND	vere**ndum**	fearing
GERUNDIVE	vere**ndus**	requiring to be feared

Third Conjugation

sequī (to follow)

INDICATIVE

Present	sequ**or**	I follow
Imperfect	sequeba**r**	I was following
Future	sequa**r**	I shall follow
Perfect	secūtu**s sum**	I followed
Pluperfect	secūtu**s eram**	I had followed
Future Perfect	secūtu**s erō**	I shall have followed

SUBJUNCTIVE

Present	sequa**r**	I may follow
Imperfect	sequere**r**	I might follow
Perfect	secūtu**s sim**	I may have followed
Pluperfect	secūtu**s essem**	I might have followed

IMPERATIVE

Singular	sequ**ere**	follow
Plural	sequ**iminī**	follow

INFINITIVES

Present	sequ**ī**	to follow
Future	secūt**ūrus esse**	to be going to follow
Perfect	secūtu**s esse**	to have followed

PARTICIPLES

Present	sequ**ēns**	following
Future	secūt**ūrus**	going to follow
Perfect	secūt**us**	having followed

GERUND	sequ**endum**	following
GERUNDIVE	sequ**endus**	requiring to be followed

Deponent Verbs (continued)

Fourth Conjugation

mentīrī (to lie)

INDICATIVE
Present	mentior	I lie
Imperfect	mentiēbar	I was lying
Future	mentiar	I shall lie
Perfect	mentītus sum	I lied
Pluperfect	mentītus eram	I had lied
Future Perfect	mentītus erō	I shall have lied

SUBJUNCTIVE
Present	mentiar	I may lie
Imperfect	mentīrer	I might lie
Perfect	mentītus sim	I may have lied
Pluperfect	mentītus essem	I might have lied

IMPERATIVE
Singular	mentīre	lie
Plural	mentiminī	lie

INFINITIVES
Present	mentīrī	to lie
Future	mentitūrus esse	to be going to lie
Perfect	mentitus esse	to have lied

PARTICIPLES
Present	mentiēns	lying
Future	mentīturus	going to lie
Perfect	mentītus	having lied

GERUND	mentiendum	lying

GERUNDIVE	mentiendus	requiring to be lied to

Semi-deponent Verbs

A few verbs are passive in form and active in meaning in only the perfect tenses. All other tenses are active in form and meaning. These are:

audēre	to dare
gaudēre	to be glad
solēre	to be accustomed
confidere	to trust

INDICATIVE		
Present	aud**eō**	I dare
Imperfect	aud**ēbam**	I was daring
Future	aud**ēbo**	I shall dare

SUBJUNCTIVE		
Present	aud**eam**	I may dare
Imperfect	aud**ērem**	I might dare

IMPERATIVE		
Singular	aud**ē**	dare
Plural	aud**ētē**	dare

INFINITIVE		
Present	aud**ēre**	to dare

PRES PARTICIPLE	aud**ēns**	daring

GERUND	aud**endum**	daring

GERUNDIVE	aud**endus**	requiring to be dared

All other parts are **passive** in form:

INDICATIVE		
Perfect	aus**us sum**	I dared
Pluperfect	aus**us eram**	I had dared
Future Perfect	aus**us erō**	I shall have dared

SUBJUNCTIVE		
Perfect	aus**us sim**	I may have dared
Pluperfect	aus**us essem**	I might have dared

PARTICIPLES		
Perfect	aus**us**	having dared
Future	aus**ūrus**	going to dare

INFINITIVES		
Perfect	aus**us esse**	to have dared
Future	aus**ūrus esse**	to be going to dare

Unique Verbs

The following verbs are different from the conjugations described so far:

esse (to be)

Indicative

PRESENT

sum	I am
es	you (*sing*) are
est	he/she/it is
sumus	we are
estis	you (*pl*) are
sunt	they are

IMPERFECT

eram	I was
eras	you (*sing*) were
erat	he/she/it was
erāmus	we were
erātis	you (*pl*) were
erant	they were

FUTURE

erō	I shall be
eris	you (*sing*) will be
erit	he/she/it will be
erimus	we shall be
eritis	you (*pl*) will be
erunt	they will be

Subjunctive

PRESENT

sim	I may be
sīs	you (*sing*) may be
sit	he/she/it may be
sīmus	we may be
sītīs	you (*pl*) may be
sint	they may be

IMPERFECT

essem	I might be
essēs	you (*sing*) might be
esset	he/she/it might be
essēmus	we might be
essētis	you (*pl*) might be
essent	they might be

Indicative

PERFECT

fuī	I have been, was
fuistī	you (*sing*) have been/were
fuit	he/she/it has been/was
fuimus	we have been/were
fuistis	you (*pl*) have been/were
fuērunt	they have been/were

PLUPERFECT

fueram	I had been
fuerās	you (*sing*) had been
fuerat	he/she/it had been
fuerāmus	we had been
fuerātis	you (*pl*) had been
fuerant	they had been

FUTURE PERFECT

fuerō	I shall have been
fuerīs	you (*sing*) will have been
fuerit	he/she/it will have been
fuerīmus	we shall have been
fuerītis	you (*pl*) will have been
fuerint	they will have been

Subjunctive

PERFECT

fuerim	I may have been
fuerīs	you (*sing*) may have been
fuerit	he/she/it may have been
fuerīmus	we may have been
fuerītis	you (*pl*) may have been
fuerint	they may have been

PLUPERFECT

fuissem	I might have been
fuissēs	you (*sing*) might have been
fuisset	he/she/it might have been
fuissēmus	we might have been
fuissētis	you (*pl*) might have been
fuissent	they might nave been

Imperative

Singular	**es**	be
Plural	**este**	be

Infinitives

Present	**esse**	to be
Future	{ **futurus esse** / **fore** }	to be going to be
Perfect	**fuisse**	to have been

Participle

futūrus	going to be

• Compounds of **esse** are listed in the principal parts on pages 113-121.

Unique Verbs (continued)

posse (to be able)

- This verb is formed from **pot-** and **-esse**. Note that **t** becomes **s** before another **s**.

Indicative

PRESENT

possum	I am able
potes	you (*sing*) are able
potest	he/she/it is able
possumus	we are able
potestis	you (*pl*) are able
possunt	they are able

IMPERFECT

poteram	I was able *etc*
poterās	
poterat	
poterāmus	
poterātis	
poterant	

FUTURE

poterō	I shall be able *etc*
poteris	
poterit	
poterimus	
poteritis	
poterunt	

Subjunctive

PRESENT

possim	I may be able *etc*
possis	
possit	
possīmus	
possītis	
possint	

IMPERFECT

possem	I might be able *etc*
possēs	
posset	
possēmus	
possētis	
possent	

Indicative

    PERFECT

    potuī   I have been able *etc*
    potuistī
    potuit
    potuimus
    potuistis
    potuĕrunt

    PLUPERFECT

    potueram   I had been able *etc*
    potuerās
    potuerat
    potuerāmus
    potuerātis
    potuerant

    FUTURE PERFECT

    potuerŏ   I shall have been able *etc*
    potueris
    potuerit
    potuerimus
    potueritis
    potuerint

Subjunctive

    PERFECT

    potuerim   I may have been able *etc*
    potueris
    potuerit
    potuerimus
    potueritis
    potuerint

    PLUPERFECT

    potuissem   I might have been able *etc*
    potuissēs
    potuisset
    potuissēmus
    potuissētis
    potuissent

Infinitives

    posse   to be able
    potuisse   to have been able

Unique Verbs (continued)

ferre (to bear)

Active

Indicative

PRESENT		
ferō	I bear *etc*	
fers		
fert		
ferimus		
fertis		
ferunt		
IMPERFECT		
ferēbam	I was bearing	
FUTURE		
feram	I shall bear	
PERFECT		
tulī	I bore	
PLUPERFECT		
tuleram	I had borne	
FUTURE PERFECT		
tulerō	I shall have borne	

Subjunctive

PRESENT		
feram	I may bear *etc*	
ferās		
ferat		
ferāmus		
ferātis		
ferant		
IMPERFECT		
ferrem	I might bear	
PERFECT		
tulerim	I may have borne	
PLUPERFECT		
tulissem	I might have borne	

Infinitives

Present	**ferre**	to bear
Future	**lātūrus esse**	to be going to bear
Perfect	**tulisse**	to have borne

Imperatives

Singular	**fer**	bear
Plural	**ferte**	bear

Supine   **lātum**

Passive

Indicative

PRESENT		
feror	I am borne *etc*	
ferris		
fertur		
ferimur		
feriminī		
feruntur		
IMPERFECT		
ferēbar	I was being borne	
FUTURE		
ferar	I shall be borne	
PERFECT		
lātus sum	I was borne	
PLUPERFECT		
lātus eram	I had been borne	
FUTURE PERFECT		
lātus erŏ	I shall have been borne	

Subjunctive

PRESENT		
ferar	I may be borne *etc*	
ferāris		
ferātur		
ferāmur		
feramīnī		
ferantur		
IMPERFECT		
ferrer	I might be borne	
PERFECT		
lātus sim	I may have been borne	
PLUPERFECT		
lātus essem	I might have been borne	

Infinitives

Present	**ferri**	to be borne
Future	**lātum īrī**	to be going to be borne
Perfect	**lātus esse**	to have been borne

Imperatives

Singular	**ferre**	be borne
Plural	**feriminī**	be borne

Participles

Present	**ferēns**	bearing
Future	**lātūrus**	going to bear
Perfect	**lātus**	having been borne/carried

Gerund	**ferendum**	bearing
Gerundive	**ferendus**	requiring to be borne

Unique Verbs (continued)

fieri (to become, be made)

- This verb is the passive form of **facere** – to make.

Indicative

PRESENT	
fīō	I become
fīs	you (*sing*) become
fit	he/she/it becomes
(fimus)	
(fitis)	
funt	
IMPERFECT	
fiēbam	I was becoming
FUTURE	
fīam	I shall become
PERFECT	
factus sum	I became
PLUPERFECT	
factus eram	I had become
FUTURE PERFECT	
factus erō	I shall have become

Subjunctive

PRESENT	
fīam	I may become *etc*
fīās	
fīat	
fīāmus	
fīātis	
fīant	
IMPERFECT	
fierem	I might become
PERFECT	
factus sim	I may have become
PLUPERFECT	
factus essem	I might have become

Infinitives

Present	**fierī**	to become
Future	**factum īrī**	to be going to become
Perfect	**factus esse**	to have become

Participle

Perfect	**factus**	having become

Gerundive	**faciendus**	becoming

ire (to go)

- The stem is **i-**. Before a, o, u, it changes to **e-**.

Indicative

PRESENT
eo — I go *etc*
īs
īt
īmus
ītis
eunt

IMPERFECT
ībam — I was going

FUTURE
ībō — I shall go

PERFECT
īvī or **iī** — I went/have gone

PLUPERFECT
īveram — I had gone

FUTURE PERFECT
īverō — I shall have gone

Subjunctive

PRESENT
eam — I may go *etc*
eās
eat
eāmus
eātis
eant

IMPERFECT
īrem — I might go

PERFECT
īverim — I may have gone

PLUPERFECT
īvissem — I might have gone

Infinitives
Present	**īre**	to go
Future	**ītūrus esse**	to be going to go
Perfect	**īvisse** or **īsse**	to have gone

Imperative
Singular	**ī**	go
Plural	**īte**	go

Participles
Present	**iēns** (*gen* **euntis**)	going
Future	**itūrus**	going to go

Gerund
eundum — going

Unique Verbs (continued)

velle (to wish)

Indicative

PRESENT
volō	I wish/am willing *etc*
vīs	
vult	
volumus	
vultis	
volunt	

IMPERFECT
volēbam	I was wishing
volēbās	
volēbat	
volēbāmus	
volēbātis	
volēbant	

FUTURE
volam	I shall wish

PERFECT
voluī	I wished/have wished

PLUPERFECT
volueram	I had wished

FUTURE PERFECT
voluerō	I shall have wished

Subjunctive

PRESENT
velim	I may wish
velīs	
velit	
velīmus	
velītis	
velint	

IMPERFECT
vellem	I might wish
vellēs	
vellet	
vellēmus	
vellētis	
vellent	

PERFECT
voluerim	I may have wished

PLUPERFECT
voluissem	I might have wished

Infinitives
Present	**velle**	to wish
Perfect	**voluisse**	to have wished

Participle   **volēns, -entis**   wishing

nōlle (not to wish, to be unwilling)

- This verb was originally **nōn volo**.

Indicative

	PRESENT	
	nolō	I do not wish *etc*
	nōn vis	
	nōn vult	
	nōlumus	
	nōn vultis	
	nōlunt	
	IMPERFECT	
	nōlēbam	I was not wishing
	nōlēbas	
	nōlēbat	
	nōlēbāmus	
	nōlēbātis	
	nōlēbant	
	FUTURE	
	nōlam	I shall not wish
	PERFECT	
	nōlui	I have not wished
	PLUPERFECT	
	nōlueram	I had not wished
	FUTURE PERFECT	
	nōluerō	I shall not have wished

Subjunctive

	PRESENT	
	nōlim	I may not wish
	nōlīs	
	nōlit	
	nōlīmus	
	nōlītis	
	nōlint	
	IMPERFECT	
	nōllem	I might not wish
	nōllēs	
	nōllet	
	nōllēmus	
	nōllētis	
	nōllent	
	PERFECT	
	nōluerim	I may not have wished
	PLUPERFECT	
	nōluissem	I might not have wished

Infinitives

Present	**nōlle**	not to wish
Perfect	**nōluisse**	not to have wished

Participle	**nōlens, -entis**	not wishing

Unique Verbs (continued)

malle (to prefer)

• This verb is formed from **ma volō** or **magis volō** (I wish more).

Indicative

PRESENT
mālō	I prefer
māvīs	
māvult	
mālumus	
māvultis	
mālunt	

IMPERFECT
mālēbam	I was preferring
mālēbās	
mālēbat	
malebamus	
mālēbātis	
mālēbant	

FUTURE
mālam	I shall prefer

PERFECT
mālui	I preferred

PLUPERFECT
mālueram	I had preferred

FUTURE PERFECT
māluerō	I shall have preferred

Subjunctive

PRESENT
mālim	I may prefer
mālīs	
mālit	
mālīmus	
mālītis	
mālint	

IMPERFECT
māllem	I might prefer
māllēs	
māllet	
māllēmus	
māllētis	
māllent	

PERFECT
māluerim	I may have preferred

PLUPERFECT
māluissem	I might have preferred

Infinitives

Present	**mālle**	to prefer
Perfect	**māluisse**	to have preferred

Defective Verbs

The following verbs have only a few forms which are used. These are shown below.

inquam (I say)

PRESENT
inquam
inquis
inquit
īnquimus
inquitis
inquiunt

This verb is mainly used in the third person singular

inquiēbat	he said
inquiet	he will say
inquit	he said

avēre	to hail, say "hello"
salvēre	to hail
valēre	to say goodbye

- These verbs are found mainly in infinitives as above or imperatives:

avē, salve	hello (sing)
avēte, salvēte	hello (pl)
valē (sing), **valēte** (pl)	goodbye

- Four verbs, **ōdī, meminī, coepī, nōvī** are found only in the perfect stem but are translated as follows:

ōdī	I hate	**meminī**	I remember
ōderam	I hated	**memineram**	I remembered
ōderō	I shall hate	**meminerō**	I shall remember
odisse	to hate	**meminisse**	to remember

coepī	I begin	**nōvī**	I know
coeperam	I began	**nōveram**	I knew
coeperō	I shall begin	**nōverō**	I shall know
coepisse	to begin	**nōvisse**	to know

Likewise subjunctive:

| **ōderim** | I may hate | **meminerim** | I may remember |
| **ōdissem** | I might hate | **meminissem** | I might remember |

| **coeperim** | I may begin | **nōverim** | I may know |
| **coepissem** | I might begin | **nōvissem** | I might know |

Principal Parts of Common Verbs

Latin verbs are most usefully listed under four principal parts, from which all other tenses *etc* may be formed or recognized

	1ST PERSON PRESENT ACTIVE	PRESENT INFINITIVE	1ST PERSON PERFECT ACTIVE	SUPINE
1st Conjugation	amō	amāre	amāvī	amātum
2nd Conjugation	habeō	habēre	habuī	habitum
3rd Conjugation	mittō	mittere	mīsī	missum
4th Conjugation	audiō	audīre	audīvī	audītum

400 of the most common verbs in Latin are listed below.

Included are the following:

- 120 regular verbs. Their conjugations are indicated by numbers 1–4. All parts of these verbs can be deduced from the model conjugations on pp 74–92.

- Nearly 300 verbs which are irregular in parts (highlighted in bold), mainly in the perfect and supine. Again their conjugation is indicated by the number of the group to which they belong. Regular parts of these verbs and person endings *etc* may be deduced from the models of conjugations 1–4. Many compound verbs are included (*eg* afficio from ad-facio).

- Eight unique verbs and their compounds. These are marked bold throughout and a page reference is given *in italics* for these.

- Defective verbs which are shown in full in the main text. Again a page reference *in italics* is provided

		Conj *Page*			Conj *Page*
abdō, abdere, **abdidī**, **abditum**	hide	**3**	adiuvō, adiuvāre, **adiūvī**, **adiūtum**	help	**1**
abeō, abīre, abiī, abitum	go away		administrō, administrāre, administrāvī, administrātum	administer	**1**
abicio, abicere, **abiēcī**, **abiectum**	throw away	**3**			
absum, abesse, afuī	be away		adsum, adesse, adfuī	be present	
accēdō, accēdere, **accessī**, **accessum**	approach	**3**	adveniō, advenīre, **advēnī**, **adventum**	reach	**4**
accidō, accidere, **accidī**	happen	**3**	aedificō, aedificāre, aedificāvī, aedificātum	build	**1**
accipio, accipere, **accēpī**, **acceptum**	receive	**3**			
accūsō, accūsāre, accūsāvī, accūsātum	accuse	**1**	**afferō, afferre, attulī, allātum**	bring to	
addō, addere, **addidī**, **additum**	add	**3**	afficiō, afficere, **affēcī**, **affectum**	affect	**3**
adeō, adīre, adiī, aditum	approach		aggredior, aggredī, **aggressus sum**	attack	**3**
adimō, adimere, **adēmī**, **ademptum**	take away	**3**	agnōscō, agnōscere, **agnōvī**, **agnitum**	recognize	**3**
			agō, agere, **ēgī**, **āctum**	do/drive	**3**

		Conj Page			Conj Page
alō, alere, **aluī, altum**	feed	3	cadō, cadere, **cecidī, cāsum**	fall	3
ambulō, ambulāre, ambulāvī, ambulātum	walk	1	caedō, caedere, **cecīdī, caesum**	cut/kill	3
āmittō, āmittere, **āmīsī, āmissum**	lose	3	canō, canere, **cecinī, cantum**	sing	3
amō, āmare, amāvī, amātum	love	1	capiō, capere, **cēpī, captum**	take	3
animadvertō, animadvertere, **animadvertī, animadversum**	notice	3	careō, carere	lack	2
aperiō, aperīre, **aperuī, apertum**	open	4	carpō, carpere, **carpsī, carptum**	pick	3
appāreō, appārēre, appāruī, apparitum	appear	2	caveō, cavēre, **cāvī, cautum**	beware	2
appellō, appellāre, appellāvī, appellātum	call	1	cedō, cedere, **cessī, cessum**	go/give way	3
appropinquō, appropinquāre, appropinquāvī, appropinquātum	approach	1	cēlō, cēlāre, cēlāvī, cēlātum	hide	1
arbitror, arbitrārī, arbitrātus sum	think	1	cernō, cernere, **crēvi, crētum**	perceive	3
arcessō, arcessere, **arcessīvī, arcessītum**	send for	3	cieō, ciēre, **cīvī, citum**	rouse	2
ārdeō, ārdēre, **ārsī, ārsum**	burn	2	cingō, cingere, **cinxī, cinctum**	surround	3
armō, armāre, armāvī, armātum	arm	1	circumdō, circumdāre, **circumdēdī, circumdātum**	place round	1
ascendō, ascendere, **ascendī, ascēnsum**	climb up	3	clāmo, clamāre, clamāvī, clamātum	shout	1
aspiciō, aspicere, **aspexī, aspectum**	look at	3	claudō, claudere, **clausī, clausum**	close	3
attingō, attingere, **attigī, attactum**	touch	3	**coepī, coeptus**	begin	111
audeō, audēre, **ausus sum**	dare	2	cōgitō, cōgitāre, cōgitāvī, cōgitātum	think	1
audiō, audīre, audīvī, audītum	hear	4	cognoscō, cōgnōscere, **cōgnōvī, cōgnītum**	find out	3
auferō, auferre, abstutī, ablātum	take away		cogō, cōgere, **coēgī, coāctum**	collect/ compel	3
augeō, augēre, **auxī, auctum**	increase	2	colō, colere, **coluī, cultum**	look after/ worship	3
			collocō, collocāre, collocāvī, collocātum	place	1
bibō, bibere, **bibī**	drink	3	commoveō, commovēre, **commōvī, commōtum**	upset	2

	Conj
	Page

Verb	Meaning	Conj
comparō, comparāre, **comparāvī, comparātum**	get ready	1
comperiō, comperīre, **comperī, compertum**	discover	4
compleō, complēre, **complēvī, complētum**	fill	2
comprehendō, comprehendere, **comprehendī, comprehēnsum**	grasp	3
concurrō, concurrere, **concurrī, concursum**	run together	3
condō, condere, **condidī, conditum**	found	3
conficiō, conficere, **confēcī, confectum**	finish	3
confīdō, confīdere, **confīsus sum**	trust	3
confīrmō, confīrmare, **confīrmāvī, confīrmatūm**	strengthen	1
confiteor, confitērī, **confēssus sum**	confess	2
congredior, congredī, **congressus sum**	meet	3
coniciō, conicere, **coniēcī, coniectum**	throw	3
coniungō, coniungere, **coniūnxi, coniūnctum**	join	3
coniūrō, coniūrāre, **coniūrāvī, coniūrātum**	conspire	1
conor, conārī, **conātus sum**	try	1
consentiō, consentire, **consēnsī, consēnsum**	agree	4
consistō, consistere, **constitī, constitum**	stop	3
conspiciō, conspicere, **conspexī, conspectum**	catch sight of	3
constō, constāre, **constitī**	agree	1
constituō, constituere, **constituī, constitūtum**	decide	3

Verb	Meaning	Conj
construō, construere, **constrūxī, constructum**	construct	3
consulo, consulere, **consului, consultum**	consult	3
consūmō, consūmere, **consūmpsī, consūmptum**	use up	3
contemnō, contemnere, **contempsī, contemptum**	despise	3
contendō, contendere, contendī, contentum	strive/hurry	3
contingō, contingere, **contigī, contactum**	touch	3
conveniō, convenīre, **convēni, conventum**	meet	4
corripio, corripere, **corripuī, correptum**	seize	3
crēdo, crēdere, **crēdidī, crēditum**	believe	3
crescō, crescere, **crēvī, crētum**	grow	3
culpō, culpāre, culpāvī, culpātum	blame	1
cunctor, cunctārī, cunctātus sum	delay	1
cupiō, cupere, **cupīvī, cupītum**	desire	3
cūrō, cūrare, cūravī, curātum	look after	1
currō, currere, **cucurrī, cursum**	run	3
custōdio, custōdīre, custōdīvī, custōdītum	guard	4
damnō, damnāre, damnāvī, damnātum	condemn	1
debeō, dēbēre, dēbuī, dēbitum	have to/owe	2
dēdō, dēdere, **dēdidī, dēditum**	hand over/ yield	3
dēducō, dēdūcere, **dēdūxī, dēdūctum**	bring/escort	3
dēfendō, dēfendere, **dēfendi, dēfensum**	defend	3

	Conj Page
dēficiō, dēficere, **dēfēcī**, **dēfectum**	revolt/fail 3
deiciō, dēicere, **dēiēcī**, **dēiectum**	throw down 3
dēlēctō, dēlēctāre, dēlectāvī, dēlectatum	delight 1
dēleō, dēlere, **dēlēvī**, **dēlētum**	destroy 2
dēligō, dēligere, **dēlēgī**, **dēlēctum**	choose 3
dēmōnstrō, dēmōnstrāre, dēmōnstrāvī, dēmōnstrātum	show 1
dēpōnō, dēpōnere, **dēposuī**, **dēpositum**	lay down 3
dēscendō, dēscendere, **dēscendī**, **dēscensum**	go down 3
dēsero, dēsere, **dēseruī**, **dēsertum**	desert 3
dēsiderō, dēsiderāre, dēsideravī, dēsiderātum	long for 1
dēsiliō, dēsilire, **dēsiluī**, **dēsultum**	jump down 3
dēsino, dēsinere, **dēsiī**, **dēsitum**	stop/leave off 3
dēsistō, dēsistere, **dēstitī**	stop/leave off 3
dēspērō, dēspērare, dēspērāvī, dēspērātum	despair 1
dēstruō, dēstruere, **dēstrūxī**, **dēstructum**	destroy 3
dīcō, dīcere, **dīxī**, **dictum**	tell/say 3
dīligō, dīligere, **dīlexī**, **dīlēctum**	love 3
dīmittō, dīmittere, **dīmīsī**, **dīmissum**	send away 3
discēdō, discēdere, **discessī**, **discessum**	go away 3
discō, discere, **didicī**	learn 3
dīvidō, dīvidere, **dīvīsī**, **dīvīsum**	divide 3
dō, dāre, **dedī**, **datum**	give 1

	Conj Page
doceō, docēre, docuī, doctum	teach 2
doleō, dolēre, doluī, dolitum	grieve 2
dormiō, dormīre, dormīvī, dormītum	sleep 4
dubitō, dubitāre, dubitāvī, dubitātum	doubt 1
dūcō, dūcere, **dūxī**, **ductum**	lead 3
ēdō, ēdere, **ēdī**, **ēsum**	eat 3
efficiō, efficere, **effēcī**, **effectum**	complete 3
effugiō, effugere, **effūgī**	escape 3
ēgredior, ēgredī, **egressus sum**	go out 3
ēmō, ēmere, **ēmī**, **ēmptum**	buy 3
eō, īre, **īvī**, **itum**	go 107
errō, errāre, errāvī, errātum	wander/ be wrong 1
ērumpō, ērumpere, **ērūpī**, **ēruptum**	burst out 3
excitō, excitāre, excitāvī, excitātum	arouse 1
exeō, exīre, exiī, exitum	go out
exerceō, exercēre, exercuī, exercitum	exercise/ train 2
exīstimō, exīstimāre, exīstimāvī, exīstimātūm	think 1
expellō, expellere, **expulī**, **expulsum**	drive out 3
experior, experīrī, **expertus sum**	try/test 4
exspectō, exspectāre, exspectāvī, exspectātum	wait for 1
exuō, exuere, **exuī**, **exūtum**	take off 3
faciō, facere, **fēcī**, **factum**	do/make 3

		Conj Page
fallō, fallere, **fefellī**, falsum	deceive	3
faveō, favēre, **fāvī**, fautum	favour	2
ferō, ferre, tulī, lātum	bring/bear	104
festīnō, festīnāre, festīnāvī, festīnātum	hurry	1
fīgō, fīgere, **fīxī, fīxum**	fix	3
fingō, fingere, **finxī**, fictum	invent	3
fiō, fierī, factus sum	become/ happen	106
flectō, flectere, **flexī**, flexum	bend	3
fleō, flēre, **flēvī, flētum**	weep	2
fluō, fluere, **flūxī**, flūxum	flow	3
frangō, frangere, **frēgī**, frāctum	break	3
fruor, fruī, **frūctus** or **fruitus sum**	enjoy	3
fugiō, fugere, **fūgī**, fugitum	flee/escape	3
fugō, fugāre, fūgāvī, fugātum	put to flight	1
fundō, fundere, **fūdī**, fūsum	pour	3
fungor, fungī, **fūnctus sum**	perform	3
gaudeō, gaudēre, **gāvīsus sum**	be glad	2
gemō, gemere, **gemuī**, gemitum	groan	3
gerō, gerere, **gessī**, gestum	carry on/ wear	3
gignō, gignere, **genuī**, genitum	produce	3
habeō, habēre, habuī, habitum	have/keep	2
habitō, habitāre, habitāvī, habitātum	live (in)	1
haereō, haerēre, **haesī**, haesum	stick	2

		Conj Page
hauriō, haurīre, **hausī**, haustum	drain away	4
horreō, horrēre, horruī	stand on end	2
hortor, hortārī, hortātus sum	encourage	1
iaceō, iacēre, iacuī	lie down	2
iaciō, iacere, **iēcī**, iactum	throw	3
ignōscō, īgnoscere, **īgnōvī, īgnōtum**	forgive	3
immineō, imminēre	threaten	2
impediō, impedīre, impedīvī, impedītum	hinder	4
impellō, impellere, **impulī, impulsum**	drive on	3
imperō, imperāre, imperāvī, imperātum	order	1
incendō, incendere, **incendī, incēnsum**	burn	3
incipiō, incipere, **coepī, coeptum**	begin	3
incitō, incitāre, incitāvī, incitātum	drive on	1
inclūdō, inclūdere, **inclūsī, inclūsum**	include	3
incolō, incolere, **incoluī**	live (in)	3
īnferō, īnferre, intulī, illātum	bring against	
ingredior, ingredī, **ingressus sum**	enter	3
īnstituō, īnstituere, **īnstituī, īnstitūtum**	set up	3
īnstruō, īnstruere, **īnstrūxī, īnstrūctum**	set/draw up	3
intellegō, intellegere, **intellēxī, intellēctum**	realize	3
interficiō, interficere, **interfēcī, interfectum**	kill	3
intersum, interesse	be among/ be important (*impers*)	
intrō, intrāre, intrāvī, intrātum	enter	1

		Conj *Page*
invenio, invenīre, **invēnī, inventum**	come upon/find	4
invitō, invitāre, invitāvī, invitātum	invite	1
irrumpō, irrumpere, **irrūpī, irruptum**	rush into	3
iubeo, iubēre, **iussī, iussum**	order	2
iūdicō, iūdicāre, iūdicāvī, iūdicātum	judge	1
iungō, iungere, **iūnxī, iūnctum**	join	3
iūrō, iūrāre, iūrāvī, iūrātum	swear	1
iuvō, iuvāre, **iūvī, iūtum**	help	1
lābor, lābī, **lāpsus sum**	slip	3
labōrō, labōrāre, labōrāvī, labōrātum	work	1
lacessō, lacessere, **lacessīvī, lacessītum**	harass	3
lacrimō, lacrimāre, lacrimāvī, lacrimātum	weep	1
laedō, laedere, **laesī, laesum**	hurt	3
lateō, latēre, latuī	lie hidden	2
laudō, laudāre, laudāvī, laudātum	praise	1
lavō, lavāre, **lāvī,** lautum/lavātum/**lōtum**	wash	1
legō, legere, **lēgī, lēctum**	read/choose	3
levō, levāre, levāvī, levātum	lighten	1
līberō, līberāre, līberāvī, līberātum	free	1
licet, licēre, licuit	it is allowed	2
locō, locāre, locāvī, locātum	place	1
loquor, loquī, **locūtus sum**	speak	3
lūdō, lūdere, **lūsī, lūsum**	play	3

		Conj *Page*
lustrō, lustrāre, lustrāvī, lustrātum	purify/scan	1
mālo, mālle, māluī	prefer	*110*
mandō, mandāre, mandāvī, mandātum	command/trust	1
maneō, manēre, **mānsī, mānsum**	remain/stay	2
meminī, meminisse	remember	*111*
mentior, mentīrī, mentītus sum	tell lies	4
metūō, metuere, **metuī**	fear	3
minor, minārī, minātus sum	threaten	1
minuō, minuere, **minuī, minūtum**	lessen	3
miror, mirārī, mirātus sum	wonder (at)	1
misceō, miscēre, **miscui, mixtum**	mix	2
misereor, miserērī, miseritus sum miseret, miserēre, miseruit (*eg* me miseret tui – I am sorry for you)	pity	2
mittō, mittere, **mīsī, missum**	send	3
mōlior, mōlīrī, mōlītus sum	strive/toil	4
moneō, monēre, monuī, monitum	advise/warn	2
morior, morī, **mortuus sum**	die	3
moror, morārī, morātus sum	delay/loiter	1
moveō, movēre, **mōvī, mōtum**	move	2
mūnio, mūnīre, mūnīvī/mūniī, mūnītum	fortify	4
mūtō, mūtāre, mūtāvī, mūtātum	change	1
nancīscor, nancīscī, **na(n)ctus sum**	obtain	3

VERBS: PRINCIPAL PARTS

		Conj Page
nārrō, nārrāre, nārrāvī, nārrātum	tell	1
nāscor, nāscī, **nātus sum**	be born	3
nāvigō, nāvigāre, nāvigāvī, nāvigātum	sail	1
necō, necāre, necāvī, necātum	kill	1
negō, negāre, negāvī, negātum	refuse/deny	1
neglegō, neglegere, **neglēxī, neglēctum**	neglect	3
nesciō, nescīre, nescīvī or iī, nescītum	not to know	4
noceō, nocēre, nocuī, nocitum	harm	2
nōlō, nōlle, nōluī	not to wish/ be unwilling	109
nōscō, nōscere, **nōvī, nōtum** (in perfect tenses translate as "know")	get to know	3
nūntiō, nūntiāre, nūntiāvī, nūntiātum	announce	1
obeō, obīre, obīvī or iī, obitum	die	
obiciō, obicere, **obiēcī, obiectum**	throw to/ oppose	3
oblīvīscor, oblīvīscī, **oblītus sum**	forget	3
obsideō, obsidēre, **obsēdī, obsessum**	besiege	2
obtineō, obtinēre, obtinuī, **obtentum**	hold/obtain	2
occidō, occidere, **occidī, occāsum**	fall	3
occīdō, occīdere, **occīdī, occīsum**	kill	3
occupō, occupāre, occupāvī, occupātum	seize	1
occurrō, occurrere, **occurrī, occursum**	meet	3
ōdī, ōdisse	hate	111
offerō, offerre, obtulī, oblātum	present	

		Conj Page
oportet, oportēre, oportuit	be proper/ ought	2
opprimō, opprimere, **oppressī, oppressum**	crush	3
oppugnō, oppugnāre, oppugnāvī, oppugnātum	attack	1
optō, optāre, optāvī, optātum	wish	1
orior, orīrī, **ortus sum**	arise	4
orō, orāre, orāvī, orātum	beg/plead	1
ornō, ornāre, ornāvī, ornātum	decorate/ equip	1
ostendō, ostendere, **ostendī, ostentum**	show	3
pācō, pācāre, pācāvī, pācātum	pacify	1
paenitet, paenitēre, paenituit	repent of	2
pandō, pandere, **pandī, passum**	spread out	3
parcō, parcere, **pepercī, parsum**	spare	3
pareō, parēre, paruī	obey	2
pariō, parere, **peperī, partum**	give birth to	3
parō, parāre, parāvī, parātum	prepare	1
pāscō, pāscere, **pāvī, pāstum**	feed	3
patefaciō, patefacere, **patefēcī, patefactum**	open	3
pateō, patēre, patuī	be open	2
patior, patī, **passus sum**	suffer/allow	3
paveō, pavēre, **pavī**	fear	2
pellō, pellere, **pepulī, pulsum**	drive	3
pendeō, pendēre, **pependī** (intrans)	hang	2
pendō, pendēre, **pependī, pēnsum**	weigh/pay	3

118

		Conj Page			Conj Page
perdō, perdere, **perdidī, perditum**	lose/destroy	3	prōcēdō, prōcēdere, **prōcessī, prōcessum**	advance	3
pereo, perīre, periī, peritum	perish		prōdō, prōdere, **prōdidī, prōditum**	betray	3
perficiō, perficere, **perfecī, perfectum**	complete	3	proficīscor, proficīscī, **profectus sum**	set out	3
pergō, pergere, **perrēxī, perrēctum**	proceed	3	prōgredior, prōgredī, **progressus sum**	advance	3
permittō, permittere, **permīsī, permissum**	allow	3	prohibeō, prohibēre, prohibuī, prohibitum	prevent	2
persuadeō, persuadēre, **persuasī, persuasum**	persuade	2	prōmittō, prōmittere, **prōmīsī, prōmissum**	promise	3
pertineō, pertinēre, pertinuī, **pertentum**	concern	2	prōvideō, prōvidere, **prōvīdī, prōvisum**	take precautions	2
perturbō, pertūrbāre, perturbāvī, perturbātum	confuse	1	pugnō, pugnāre, pugnāvī, pugnātum	fight	1
perveniō, pervenīre, **pervēnī, perventum**	arrive at	4	pūniō, pūnīre, pūnīvī or iī, pūnītum	punish	4
petō, petere, **petīvī, petītum**	seek/ask	3	putō, putāre, putāvī, putātum	think	1
placeō, placēre, placuī, placitum	please	2	quaerō, quaerere, **quaesīvī, quaesītum**	ask/seek	3
placet, placēre, placuit	it seems good	2	queror, querī, **questus sum**	complain	3
polliceor, pollicērī, **pollicitus sum**	promise	2	quiēscō, quiēscere, **quiēvī, quiētum**	keep quiet	3
pōnō, pōnere, **posuī, positum**	place/put	3			
portō, portāre, portāvī, portātum	carry	1	rapiō, rapere, **rapuī, raptum**	snatch/seize	3
poscō, poscere, **poposcī**	ask for/ demand	3	recipiō, recipere, **recēpī, receptum**	receive/ recover	3
possum, posse, potui	to be able	102	recūsō, recūsāre, recūsāvī, recūsātum	refuse	1
postulō, postulāre, postulāvī, postulātum	demand	1	reddō, reddere, **reddidī, redditum**	give back/ return	3
potior, potīrī, potitus sum	gain possession of	4	**redeō, redīre, rediī, reditum**	come back/ return	
praebeō, praebēre, praebuī, praebitum	show	2	redūcō, redūcere, **redūxī, reductum**	bring back	3
praeficiō, praeficere, **praefēcī, praefēctum**	put in command of	3	regō, regere, **rēxī, rēctum**	rule	3
praestō, praestāre, **praestitī, praestatum**	stand out	1	regredior, regredī, **regressus sum**	retreat	3
premō, premere, **pressī, pressum**	press	3	relinquō, relinquere, **relīquī, relictum**	leave	3

119

		Conj Page
remittō, remittere, **remīsī**, **remissum**	send back	3
reor, rērī, **ratus sum**	think	2
repellō, repellere, **reppulī**, **repulsum**	drive back	3
reperiō, reperīre, **repperī**, **repertum**	find	4
resistō, resistere, **restitī**	resist	3
respiciō, respicere, **respexī**, **respectum**	look back	3
respondeō, respondēre, **respondī**, **respōnsum**	answer	2
restō, restāre, **restitī**	remain	1
restituō, restituere, **restituī**, **restitūtum**	restore	3
retineō, retinēre, **retinuī**, **retentum**	hold back	2
rideō, ridēre, **rīsī**, **rīsum**	laugh	2
rogō, rogāre, rogāvī, rogātum	ask	1
rumpō, rumpere, **rūpī**, **ruptum**	burst	3
ruō, ruere, **ruī**, **rutum** (**ruitūrus** – fut part)	rush/fall	3
sciō, scīre, **scīvī/iī**, **scītum**	know	4
scrībō, scrībere, **scrīpsī**, **scrīptum**	write	3
sēcernō, sēcernere, **secrēvī**, **sēcrētum**	set apart	3
secō, secāre, **secuī**, **sectum**	cut	1
sedeō, sedēre, **sēdī**, **sessum**	sit	2
sentiō, sentīre, **sēnsī**, **sēnsum**	feel/perceive	4
sepeliō, sepelīre, sepelīvī, **sepultum**	bury	4
sequor, sequī, **secūtus sum**	follow	3
serō, serere, **sēvī**, **satum**	sow	3

		Conj Page
serviō, servīre, servīvī, servītum	serve/ be a slave	4
servō, servāre, servāvī, servātum	save	1
simulō, simulāre, simulāvī, simulātum	pretend	1
sinō, sinere, **sīvī**, **situm**	allow	3
sistō, sistere, **stitī**, **statum**	set up	3
soleō, solere, **solitus sum**	be used to	2
sollicitō, sollicitāre, sollicitāvī, sollicitātum	worry	1
solvō, solvere, **solvī**, **solūtum**	loosen	3
sonō, sonāre, **sonuī**, **sonitum**	sound	1
spargō, spargere, **sparsī**, **sparsum**	scatter/ sprinkle	3
spectō, spectāre, spectāvī, spectātum	look at	1
spērō, spērāre, spērāvī, spērātum	hope	1
spoliō, spoliāre, spoliāvī, spoliātum	rob/plunder	1
statuō, statuere, **statuī**, **statūtum**	set up	3
sternō, sternere, **strāvī**, **strātum**	cover/ overthrow	3
stō, stāre, **steti**, **stātum**	stand	1
struō, struere, **strūxī**, **strūctum**	build	3
studeō, studēre, studuī	study	2
suādeō, suādēre, **suāsī**, **suāsum**	advise	2
subeō, subīre, subīī, subitum	undergo	
succēdō, succēdēre, **successī**, **successum**	go up/relieve	3
succurro, succurrere, succurri, succursum	help	3
sum, esse, **fuī**, **futūrus**		100
sūmō, sūmere, **sūmpsī**, **sūmptum**	take	3

	Conj Page			Conj Page
superō, superare, superāvī, superātum	overcome	1	ulcīscor, ulcīscī, **ultus sum**	punish/ avenge	**3**
supersum, superesse, superfuī	survive		urgeō, urgēre, **ursī**	press/urge	2
surgō, surgēre, **surrēxī, surrēctum**	rise/get up	3	urō, urere, **ussī, ustum**	burn	3
suscipiō, suscipere, **suscēpī, susceptum**	undertake	3	ūtor, ūtī, **ūsus sum**	use	3
suspicor, suspicārī, suspicātus sum	suspect	1	valeō, valēre, valuī, valitum	be strong	2
sustineō, sustinēre, sustinuī, **sustentum**	sustain	2	vastō, vastāre, vastāvī, vastātūm	destroy	1
			vehō, vehere, **vēxī, vectum**	carry	3
taceō, tacēre, tacuī, tacitum	be silent	2	vendō, vendere, **vendidī, venditum**	sell	3
taedet, taedēre, taeduit, **taesum est**	be tired of	2	veniō, venīre, **vēnī, ventum**	come	4
tangō, tangere, **tetigī, tactum**	touch	3	vereor, verērī, veritus sum	fear	2
tegō, tegere, **tēxī, tectum**	cover	3	vertō, vertere, **vertī, versum**	turn	3
tendō, tendere, tetendī, tentum or **tēnsum**	stretch	3	vescor, vescī	feed on	3
teneō, tenēre, tenuī, **tentum**	hold	2	vetō, vetāre, **vetuī, vetitum**	forbid	1
terreō, terrēre, terruī, territum	terrify	2	videō, vidēre, **vīdī, vīsum**	see	2
timeō, timēre, timuī	fear	2	vigilō, vigilāre, vigilāvī, vigilātum	stay awake	1
tollō, tollere, **sustulī, sublātum**	raise/remove	3	vinciō, vincīre, **vinxī, vinctum**	bind	4
tonō, tonāre, **tonuī**	thunder	1	vincō, vincere, **vīcī, victum**	defeat/ conquer	3
torqueō, torquēre, **torsī, tortum**	twist	2	vitō, vitāre, vitāvī, vitātum	avoid	1
trādō, trādere, **trādidī, trāditum**	hand over	3	vivō, vivere, **vīxī, victum**	live	3
trahō, trahere, **trāxī, tractum**	drag	3	vocō, vocāre, vocāvī, vocātum	call/invite	1
traicio, traicere, **traiecī, traiectum**	take across	3	**volō, velle, voluī**	wish/want	108
trānseō, trānsīre, trānsīī, trānsitum	cross over		volvō, volvere, **volvī, volūtum**	roll	3
tueor, tuērī, tuitus sum	look at	2	voveō, vovēre, **vōvī, vōtum**	vow	2

GRAMMAR AND VERB TABLES INDEX

The following index lists comprehensively both grammatical terms and key words in English and Latin.

Grammar and Verb Tables Index